StarOffice™ 6.0
Office Suite *Companion*

SOLVEIG HAUGLAND | **FLOYD JONES**

Sun Microsystems Press
A Prentice Hall Title

The publisher offers discounts on this book when ordered in bulk quantities. For more
information, contact: Corporate Sales Department, Phone: 800-382-3419; Fax: 201-236-7141;
E-mail: corpsales@prenhall.com; or write: Prentice Hall PTR, Corp. Sales Dept.,
One Lake Street, Upper Saddle River, NJ 07458.

Editorial/production supervisor: *Nicholas Radhuber*
Acquisitions editor: *Gregory G. Doench*
Editorial assistant: *Brandt Kenna*
Manufacturing manager: *Alexis R. Heydt-Long*
Cover design director: *Jerry Votta*
Cover designer: *Talar Boorujy*
Marketing manager: *Debby vanDijk*

Sun Microsystems Press:
Publisher: *Michael Alread*

10 9 8 7 6 5 4 3 2

ISBN: 0-13-038473-9

Sun Microsystems Press
A Prentice Hall Title

This book is dedicated to mom and dad, who always told me I could do whatever I wanted, and more.

– SH

To Lila. I kept my promise. Let's go to Estes Park this weekend.

– FJ

Table of Contents

Part V: Impress 633

Preface

Note – See *Top Ten Reasons to Use StarOffice or OpenOffice.org* on page 5.

It used to be that the saying "You get what you pay for" ranked up there with such indisputable truths as, "What goes up must come down," "Water is wet," and "I had to restart Windows today." But since StarOffice is a miniscule $75 at the time we write this book, "you get what you pay for" is not only disputable, but just plain false. Plus OpenOffice.org beats that—it's free.

Sun Microsystems' StarOffice is a full-featured, remarkably good office suite that matches Microsoft Word program for program, and goes a giant step further with a great graphics program. StarOffice's applications for working with documents, spreadsheets, slide presentations, web sites, graphics, and databases make StarOffice or OpenOffice.org the best office suite choice, hands down.

Create a Web site start-to-finish (along with graphics, animations, and image maps). Open your old WordStar files from college and your WordPerfect files from your first job. Scrape your jaw on the ground when you see how small the file sizes are.

What goes up must come down. Water is wet. StarOffice 6.0 and OpenOffice.org are spectacular (the reviewers on Amazon think so too), and have a bunch of enhancements over StarOffice 5.2. We spent time in a few of Sun's usability sessions, between 5.2 and 6.0, and we're satisfied and impressed that Sun incorporated a lot of crucial feedback.

(And yes, I really *did* have to restart Windows today.)

Microsoft Office Compatibility

StarOffice is particularly strong in its ability to open Microsoft Office file formats and save the documents back as Microsoft Office files. It even boasts an AutoPilot that automatically converts entire directories of Word, Excel, and PowerPoint documents and their templates to StarOffice formats.

What It Runs On

StarOffice runs on Windows, Linux, Lindows, and Solaris. The OpenOffice.org group is working on versions for Mac OSX, FreeBSD, and other platforms.

About This Book

This is a book that lets you find what you need quickly and get it done. This isn't a book for "dummies", with epic-length procedures for cutting and pasting. On the other hand, we don't include extensive details on those sexy technical issues like mime types and LDAP

We wrote the book that we would want: all the important stuff, but nothing too basic or technically impractical for the intermediate user (and with a little humor along the way). We also talked to hundreds of new StarOffice and OpenOffice.org users, so we were able to document what people really need to do.

Reading Is Fundamental

If you're like most intermediate users, you already know enough to be dangerous, which means you'll probably just dive in and try to do things in StarOffice without any help. Sometimes that strategy works, other times it doesn't. If it doesn't, read the relevant sections in this book.

For instance, one of the most frequently asked questions is "How do I print spreadsheet headings on every page?" The answer has been in this book all along. Go read *Repeating Spreadsheet Headings (Rows or Columns) on Each Page* on page 628.

We also indexed the living daylights out of this book, so use the Index, too, particularly a little entry we like to call "troubleshooting".

What Now?

You can get more info on StarOffice and OpenOffice.org in Chapter Chapter 1, *Introduction to StarOffice 6.0 and OpenOffice 1.0*, on page 3. You'll find the top ten reasons to use StarOffice and OpenOffice.org, essentials about each program, the new features, and tips for you Microsoft Office users on switching over.

Download and install StarOffice or OpenOffice.org if you haven't already. See Chapter Chapter 2, *Installation*, on page 19 for more information.

Go through Chapter Chapter 5, *Setup and Tips*, on page 97. It gives you an overview of the StarOffice work environment and shows you lots of useful things that will help you no matter which StarOffice applications you're using.

Use the tutorials. We've included something for those of you who like to plunge in quickly and get your hands dirty, without reading all the procedures ahead of time. At the beginning of most major parts of the book, there's a section called *Quick Start* that contains a *Guided Tour*. The guided tour leads you through specific steps that will help you get to know a lot of the features for each product, including features you probably won't come across while just exploring, as well as few tips that will make using StarOffice and OpenOffice.org a breeze.

Don't panic!

Acknowledgements

We'd like to thank the friends who donated their time to reading and commenting on drafts of the book, in return for nothing but a t-shirt and chance at fame through appearing in the examples: Caron Newman, Carlene Bratach, Paul Bratach, Barry Fish, Takane Aizeki, Scott Hudson, Bryan Basham, Arnaud Insinger, Patrick Born, Steve "Shewi" Osvold, and Dan "Born in the spring of increased gyration" Batten. May the road rise up to meet you, may your hard drives fragment slowly, and your applications be robust and user friendly.

Thanks to Simon "Dread Pirate" Roberts for his generosity, his technical expertise, his easy-mounting Linux machine, and that he not only helped a whole bunch on the first go-around but came at it full force for the update.

Thanks to Greg Anderson, goat-roper extraordinaire, who Knows All.

Thanks to Erwin Tenhumberg, whose proactive and extraordinary assistance during the update made it possible for Solveig to retain nearly all her hair.

Thanks to Rob Reiner, for being such a darned fine film maker, and to Peter van der Linden, for proving that computer books can be good reading.

Thanks to Patti Guerrieri, Eileen Clark, the team of tireless production and proofing eyes at Prentice Hall, and the technical reviewers, who cranked out the invaluable proofs and technical changes to us as fast as we could type them in.

Thanks to all the folks at OpenOffice.org, who produce and answer questions on such great software.

Thanks to Floyd for daydreaming during that staff meeting and coming up with the idea for writing this book in the first place, and to Greg Doench and Rachel Borden, for shepherding us through the book-writing process. And thanks to SolBean for taking it by the horns and hanging on till the buzzer.

Also big thanks to Dave Landers, Deb Scott, Jari Paukku, Dave Nelson, Bryan Gambrel, Leila Chucri, Sarah Bate, Jimbo Rose, the SES team, eBeth Duran, Mark Leiker, Michael Bohn, John Will, Jeff "Big Daddy" Chacon, Anthony "Duke" Reynoso, the McCulloughs (for all the babysitting and marital intervention), and of course, Ma and Pa. Thanks to Larissa Carroll for being flexible.

And to everyone else we forgot and owe money to.

StarOffice™ 6.0

Getting Started

Introduction to StarOffice 6.0 and OpenOffice.org 1.0

IN THIS CHAPTER

One-Minute Guide

StarOffice and OpenOffice.org are your free tickets to ride the Microsoft Office train without actually going anywhere near the station. StarOffice and OpenOffice.org open all the Microsoft Office formats—Word, Excel, and PowerPoint. And you can save any file in any of those formats, too. You can create a new Microsoft text document, spreadsheet, or set of slides without ever using Microsoft.

Goes beyond Microsoft Office In addition, StarOffice and OpenOffice.org open over 200 other formats. Your old AmiPro and Interleaf and WordPerfect files, GIFs and SVG and PNG graphics—just about anything. Not only do you get the ability to open and edit all the files Microsoft does, but you get a whole lot more.

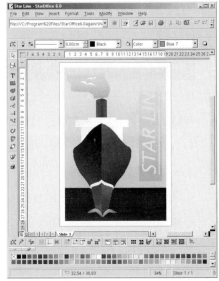

StarOffice and OpenOffice.org StarOffice and OpenOffice.org are two very similar versions of the same software. Sun took StarOffice, gave the source code to the OpenOffice.org community, and then kept developing StarOffice themselves. So you've got StarOffice, backed and developed by Sun Microsytems, and OpenOffice.org, backed and developed by the OpenOffice.org open source community. StarOffice gives support and training; OpenOffice.org has a lot of documentation and FAQs on its site, too.

The features are pretty similar, so you can use this book with either one. Whenever there are significant differences, we'll point them out.

What each one costs StarOffice is $75, OpenOffice.org is free.

Going from Microsoft Office to StarOffice or OpenOffice.org StarOffice and OpenOffice.org are somewhat similar to Microsoft Office. If you're an MS Office user, you'll still have to do some learning, but you'll have lots of "Oh, this is the same" moments. Plus, with StarOffice and OpenOffice.org you've got a great drawing/image editing program, Draw, which goes way beyond the minor tools you get in Microsoft Office. Draw is an excellent program, simpler for some than Adobe products, but with lots of power and features.

Get started Just hit Chapter Chapter 2, *Installation*, on page 19, or to learn more, read "StarOffice Essentials" on page 7 or "OpenOffice.org Essentials" on page 8. To see what's changed, see "What's New in StarOffice and OpenOffice" on page 11.

Top Ten Reasons to Use StarOffice or OpenOffice.org

Here are the ten best reasons to switch from whatever you're on now to StarOffice or OpenOffice.org.

1   StarOffice: $75. OpenOffice.org: Free. Microsoft Office: Rather more; up to $450.

Not being a slave to whatever Microsoft wants to do with pricing, distribution, licensing, and world domination in general: Priceless.

2   Government agencies publish forms in Word and Excel format. Universities require that students submit papers in Word format. Elementary schools publish their school lunch menus in Word format, for heaven's sake.

Who's going to pay $450 to read a lunch menu? Just get StarOffice or OpenOffice.org. Even if you don't need most of the features, it means you can read everything in the closed Microsoft world without living in it.

3   Whatever annoyances you heard about regarding StarOffice 5.2, forget it. 6.0 rules. Really. (We spent about 1200 total hours writing the StarOffice 5.2 Companion. Believe us, we know 6.0 is better.) Check out the reviews of StarOffice 6.0 on Amazon. Reviewers are saying "Thank you, Sun, for such a great product." We haven't seen that on the Microsoft Office site.

4   Writer (the Word equivalent) is better than Word. It doesn't have more features, since Word has been suffering from terminal feature bloat since about 1996. Writer has what you need, plus better long document handling features. Hate Word master documents? Use Writer: the master document feature is more like FrameMaker's book feature. (Writer can't match FrameMaker, but FrameMaker is a different type of program.)

5   This just in: It's official. Bill Gates has enough money. Do you? If you and your children in elementary school, your children at college, your small business, medium business, enterprise, educational institution, church, synagogue, library, government agency, law firm, sports league, volunteer organization, or Summons Service'n'Ice Cream Parlor have all the money you need, great. But if not, you need the money more than Bill does. Save it and go with StarOffice or OpenOffice.org.

6   It's the best drawing program you've never used. It's got 3D stuff you've probably not come across in Word's drawing feature, Visio-like connector tools for architectural and electrical diagrams, cool auto-measuring lines that display the measurement of any object in the drawing (1-1 or to scale). And fancy text manipulation through FontWorks. Plus raster editing (like editing out the red eyes or your ex in your birthday photos) in all the applications. You can happily waste days playing with Draw. Go to *Guided Tour of Draw: Vector and Raster Graphics* on page 755 to get guided through some of these features.

7   No muss, no fuss data sources for mail merge (sending form letters to the 1204 people in your contacts database), etc. All you need is your customer list in a text file. The rest is incredibly slick and easy. Just open that text file in Calc (the spreadsheet program) and it automatically creates a nice neat spreadsheet for you. Then use that spreadsheet to do mail merges, create a form, or anything else you want. Forget Access—the StarOffice and OpenOffice.org data source are generally all you need. We've included a tutorial to prove how easy it is; see page 871.

8   UNIX users, get jiggy. No offense, but Applix and the other desktop publishing applications lacked a certain something. Anyone who's not an enthusiastic LaTeK user is breathing a huge sigh of relief. Plus UNIX folks can now stay off of Windows 24-7, since if you had to go on the road to give a presentation before, you pretty much had to go Windows and PowerPoint.

9   StarOffice 6.0 files might be the smallest files you ever create. StarOffice 6.0 files aren't in a binary format anymore (like pretty much all the other desktop applications). They're XML. Which means that it's not a Special Secret Formula that no one else can figure out, so other applications can open and deal with that format. It also means that you can write and write, and import all sorts of graphics, and your file sizes will still be miniscule. We wrote some 6.0 Writer documents that approached 80 pages and were still under 100k. Impress, Draw, and Calc all make really small files too. The days of your memory or hard disk groaning under the load of your work files are over.

10   It's a great principle. Open standards. XML. Nobody has a stranglehold on anyone else. Nobody in Redmond controls anything you do. This is the way software should be. And is.

StarOffice Essentials

StarOffice is a full-featured office suite that you can use to create text documents and Web pages, spreadsheets, slide presentations, and drawings and images. Its three main distinguishing characteristics are that it handles (opens and creates) Microsoft Office formats, as well as nearly 200 other formats; its price is microscopic compared to Microsoft Office; and it runs on Linux, Lindows, and Solaris as well as Microsoft Windows. And for anyone who's experienced Microsoft's licensing fees and regulations, StarOffice and OpenOffice.org are a breath of fresh air on that front too.

Note – Most of what's true about StarOffice is applicable to OpenOffice.org, too. For specifics about OpenOffice.org platforms, see *OpenOffice.org Essentials* on page 8.

Applications and Features

There are four main applications:

- Writer/Web for producing text documents and Web pages

- Calc for spreadsheets

- Impress for slide presentations

- Draw for drawings (vector graphics) and image editing (raster graphics)

Built into some or all of the applications are the following great features and add-ons:

- AutoPilots to guide you through creating new documents and importing data

- Charts and equations

- Data source connection capabilities for easy mail merges and access to your existing databases

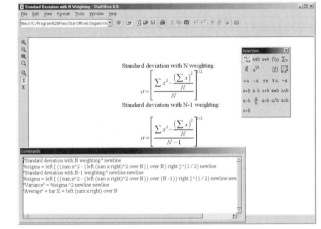

- XML file formats for easy opening by other applications, plus extremely small file sizes

- Easy, high-quality conversion to and from Microsoft Office and other files

- HTML hotlinks from text or buttons

- A huge gallery of clip art you can use in your documents, modify, and add to

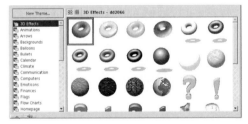

- Animation in presentations, plus animated GIFs

- Available in many languages, plus Asian language support

Licensing and Pricing

StarOffice is, in general, $75. You can use it yourself but you can't, of course, make copies for anyone else. Schools and educational institutions can receive StarOffice 6.0 office suite for the cost of media and shipping. For more details, go to Sun's StarOffice Education Web site. You can order StarOffice from www.sun.com/staroffice, Amazon, or buy it from retailers like Best Buy and CompUSA.

OpenOffice.org Essentials

Note – OpenOffice.org is the name of the program—it can't be referred to as OpenOffice because a Korean software package already has that name.

OpenOffice.org 1.0.1 is the current release at the time this book was written. OpenOffice.org is pretty much the same as StarOffice; OpenOffice.org 1.0 corresponds roughly to StarOffice 6.0. OpenOffice.org and StarOffice started from the same piece of code. Since then, Sun has been working on StarOffice, and an organization of open source programmers, has been working on OpenOffice.org. So there are some differences between them, but they're basically the same program.

You can copy, distribute, or otherwise use OpenOffice absolutely for free. StarOffice has some restrictions, is not free anymore, and StarOffice 5.2 (free for download) is no longer available.

Reasons to Use OpenOffice.org

So when was the last time you sent a Microsoft Word feature request to Bill Gates and got him to put it in? Here's what happened when Rob Pegoraro from the Washington Post submitted a feature request, reprinted by permission.

"I reported that a complaint I'd filed at the OpenOffice.org Web site about its word processor's inadequate word-count feature had gotten a real, live response....Several e-mails and a month later, a few programmers had cooked up a macro that allowed OpenOffice's word processor to count words in a selected block of text, not just the whole document."

...I was happy to add this tool to my copy of OpenOffice, which has since become my day-to-day word processor, much to my surprise. I know there are real differences between this and Microsoft Office, and OpenOffice sometimes has its own moments of clunkiness ...overall, I don't feel like I'm missing much by not using The Software That Everybody Else Runs."

Learning About Newly Developed Features

Sign up for the `allfeatures@openoffice.org` mailing list, through `www.openoffice.org`.

Differences Between StarOffice and OpenOffice.org

StarOffice 6.0 is a commercial product aimed at organizations and consumers while OpenOffice.org 1.0 is aimed at users of free software, independent developers and the open source community.

By and large, it's pretty much the same product. Figure 1-1 on page 10 shows the same document in StarOffice and in OpenOffice.org.

The source code available at OpenOffice.org does not consist of all of the StarOffice code. Usually, the reason for this is that Sun pays to license third party code to include in

StarOffice that which it does not have permission to make available in OpenOffice.org. Items in StarOffice but not in OpenOffice.org include:

- Certain fonts
- The database component (Adabas D)
- Some templates (but see `www.ooextras.org`)
- The clip art gallery isn't as big
- Some sorting functionality (Asian versions)
- Certain file filters, including WordPerfect (but they're working on it)

You'll also see occasional differences in the layout of windows, such as where a certain checkbox option appears, but usually not differences in the options available in a window.

All development on platforms beyond Solaris, Linux, and Windows is being done by OpenOffice.org.

You can find out about features on `allfeatures@openoffice.org`; to sign up for this or other mailing lists, go to `http://www.openoffice.org/mail_list.html`.

Spreadsheet in **StarOffice**. All formats are available for both, in the Formats list for the date format. The same formats for other types, such as currency, are not available in both.

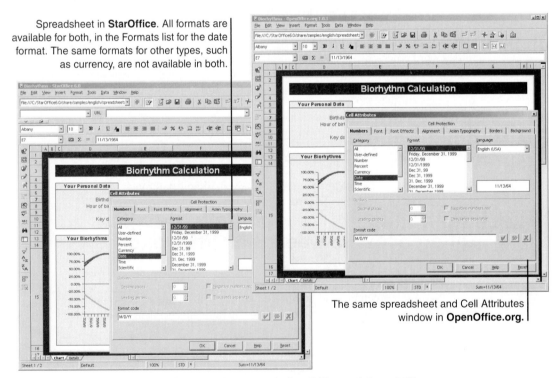

The same spreadsheet and Cell Attributes window in **OpenOffice.org**.

Figure 1-1   The same document in StarOffice and OpenOffice.org

OpenOffice.org on Other Platforms

Porting projects—switching OpenOffice.org over to work with other platforms—have been going on for a while. The one receiving the most attention at the time this book was written is the Mac OSX porting project. In May 2002 OpenOffice.org released a pre-alpha "Developer Build" for OpenOffice.org on Mac OSX., targeted at developers familiar with developing for the Mac OS X platform.At that time, the download was available at http://porting.openoffice.org/mac/ooo-osx_downloads.html

Other projects include Power PC and FreeBSD. For more information, go to http://porting.openoffice.org/

No release date for porting projects has been announced as of August 2002.

OpenOffice.org Extras

All the templates, etc. in StarOffice don't come with OpenOffice.org. However, Travis Bauer's Web site, www.ooextras.org, has what might be called a plethora of templates and other "extras."

Writing Macros

The StarOffice and OpenOffice.org API is available through www.openoffice.org. Contact that site for information about developing applications that integrate with either application, or about joining an OpenOffice.org project.

The following have information about how the project began, and submitting code:

http://www.openoffice.org/about.html

http://www.openoffice.org/contributing.html

What's New in StarOffice and OpenOffice

StarOffice 6.0 and OpenOffice.org 1.0 are fairly different from StarOffice 5.2. Key differences are that the unified desktop is gone, Schedule Mail and StarBase are gone, and the focus groups they did on usability were taking good notes. There's more detail on those and other changes in the following sections.

Compatibility and Migration

StarOffice 5.2, StarOffice 6.0, and OpenOffice.org all play nicely together—you don't need to uninstall any of them. Just be sure to uninstall StarOffice 6.0 BETA before you do any 6.0 GA installation.

You can open 5.2 files in StarOffice 6.0 or OpenOffice.org 1.0, plus save new files back to 5.2. There's an AutoPilot for mass import from 5.2.

Migration is pretty good; it doesn't do everything but does take care of customization and mail. See Chapter 3, *Migrating From StarOffice 5.2*, on page 47.

Removed Applications and Features

The new StarOffice 6.0 and OpenOffice.org are leaner and trimmer than the somewhat overburdened 5.2 release. This section gives you a quick overview of what's out, and how to compensate for a few of the removals.

What's Gone or Really Different

They took out:

- The whole integrated desktop thing, including Explorer and Beamer and some associated features.

- FTP through Explorer.

- Image as a separate application, though most of the features are still present. Just click on the raster image once or twice in any of the other applications and the image editing toolbar and menus will appear.

- Mail, though you can export your mail and address book, and connect to an existing address book like Netscape or Outlook.

- Schedule, including Palm Pilot.

- Creating databases (though you can still connect to a variety of databases through ODBC, JDBC, etc.). See *Removal of Database Creation Ability, Except Adabas* on page 12. Adabas is still included in StarOffice, but not OpenOffice.org.

- Support for creating frames in Web.

- The Pack feature for presentations. It was removed because the files are so small they don't need packing. The Impress Player standalone program was also removed.

Removal of Database Creation Ability, Except Adabas

Instead of creating and maintaining a proprietary StarOffice database format (.sdb), StarOffice Base 6.0 works with common database connection standards like JDBC and databases like dBase. You can still create an Adabas database from StarOffice.

You can still create database tables, queries and forms, though this varies a bit depending on the underlying method of data storage.

New Application-Wide Features

Here's a somewhat detailed list of what's new. Not a lot is new that will affect how you use the specific features—it's more a case of structure and underpinnings that changed to make the whole experience better.

XML file format Remember creating Impress and Writer files that were over 2 MB before you even got going? That's over. You can create a Writer file that's a couple kilobytes per page. Formatting'll kick it up, but it's still really impressive. You'll have to really work hard to get even a 1 MB file.

SVG and EPS Think Illustrator is the only application for creating cool vector graphics that scale well? Think again. EPS rendering and reading is better, and you can export drawings to SVG, Scalable Vector Graphics, an XML-based format.

Font stuff There are new "metrically compatible" TrueType Microsoft Windows core fonts. Font substitution is better. You can set up font substitution with a new improved algorithm that makes the matching better, including across platforms.

Asian font support It's got Unicode support, Ruby text, and double-byte character support. The Asian version of StarOffice, by the way, is *StarSuite*. Supported fonts are:

- Japanese: HG Mincho Light J
- Chinese Simplified: MSung Light SC
- Chinese Traditional: MSung Light
- Korean: HY MyeongJo Light K

Image editing features in all applications Click on any GIF or other raster object and the editing toolbar, formerly only in Image, appears.

Gallery The Gallery of pictures and sounds from 5.2 was moved from the Explorer/ Beamer area to Tools > Gallery. It's got a whole lot more in it now. You can add to the existing themes, which you couldn't before, and make your own new themes of images and sounds.

OpenOffice.org The Gallery feature is present in OpenOffice.org but smaller.

Password encryption The XML-based file format also supports password encryption for text documents and spreadsheets. Passwords are stored as encrypted hash values. When saving files to the old binary format, passwords arn't encrypted. However, when you load a document from a former version, the password will be encrypted again.

Standard address book support You don't have your old 5.2 address book but you can connect to the one you use for mail, or other address books. The AutoPilot steps you through connecting to your address book.

Improved HTML export You can define the text encoding for the HTML export choosing from a variety of character sets, including Unicode, using the new Character Set dialog box in the HTML Compatibility dialog box.

MathML equation support Supports exports and imports of the W3 XML format.

Enhanced cut and paste The Paste button on the Function bar has a drop-down menu where you choose whether you want to paste in the text or object's original format or in a special format. They're the same options you get when you choose Edit > Paste Special.

Better undo/redo You can undo a lot farther back than before; set up the number of undo steps by choosing Tools > Options > *program* > General.

Writer and Web

Better labels You can modify existing label brands and types and save them as your own label format; includes the latest Avery label specifications.

Section protection enhanced You can assign different passwords to individual sections. In previous StarOffice version, you could only use one password for all sections. Choose Insert > Section > Format > Section > Protect Record.

Password protection for recording editing changes The Records feature is typically used to make changes visible when two or more people collaborate on one document. Choose Edit > Changes > Protect Records.

Improved numbering Restart the numbering of lines with every new page. Choose Tools > Line Numbering.

Negative indents You can set negative (left or right) indents to paragraphs and tables, and specify the first line indent independently from the left indent of a paragraph. Choose Format > Paragraph > Indents & Spacing.

For tables you can also set negative values for the alignment from left. This lets you align tables independently of the page setup margins.

Hyphenation Define the minimal number of characters for hyphenation by choosing Tools > Options > Language Settings > Writing Aids.

Vertical text Want to write something down the side of your page? You got it. There are now vertical versions of the three Draw text creation tools, available in Writer through the Show Drawing Tools menu.

Calc

ROMAN and ARABIC functions Convert a value between 0 and 3999 to a Roman style, or convert a text that represents a Roman number into a value (between 0 and 3999).

Additional new functions The new functions are:

- MIRR: Calculate the modified internal rate of return for a series of cash flows with interest rates for investments and reinvestments.
- CELL: Provide information about content, formatting or location of a specific cell.

- ISPMT: Calculate the interest of a credit or investment with constant redemption rates.

- Analysis Addin: Provide new analysis functionality and improved Excel import.

Import HTML tables into spreadsheets Insert data from external sources (like linked areas or WebQueries). Choose Insert > External Data.

Sort options Specify language- and locale-dependent sort options. The default sort option depends on the system language setting and locale. Choose Data > Sort > Options.

Matrix arrays Improved complex scientific calculations. The number of elements that can be used in a matrix array, has been increased. In former versions this number was limited to 16384 elements per matrix, the new limit is 512k elements.

New print options *Suppress output of empty pages*: If this option is active, pages that don't contain cell contents or drawing objects are not printed. Cell attributes (like borders or background color) are an exception and don't count as content. *Print only selected sheets:* If this option is active, choosing All in the print dialog prints only selected sheets.

Improved calculation time and use less memory The maximum string length in formulas has been increased from 255 bytes to 64KB.

Improved operations Perform multiple operations with greater flexibility. This feature now extends to formulas that contain references to other formulas. A multiple operation is no longer restricted to act only on the formula selected in the dialog box. Instead, cell addresses that are indirectly referred to are replaced in every formula encountered during the calculation of a multiple operation.

Improved percentage calculations The percent sign operator is recognized in formulas and the result is displayed formatted as a percent value if appropriate. The percent sign operator divides the preceding subexpression by 100. This helps with Excel conversion.

Improved recognition of English date formats This is in addition to the default formats set by the system language, when importing a text file into Calc. This enables you to import formats such as 12-Mar-01 independent of the format used by system language. Choose File > Open > Text filter.

Improved Import and export of 16-bit Unicode text files Choose File > Open or File > Save As. and select the Text CSV format.

Improved display of line breaks Solve the problem of having different line breaks appear on print and on screen when you select the line break alignment option for cells. Using this option shows line breaks as they appear in print on-screen.

Hyphenate text in cells This option is when used with the Line Break wrap option.

Database Access and Data Source Creation

You can't create new databases anymore, except with Adabas. You can create *data sources*, just StarOffice hookups to a stored source of data, that connect to something as simple as an address book, a spreadsheet, or a text file. So yes, you can create new *data sources*, plus you can connect via JDBC, etc. to industry standard databases like Oracle. See Chapter 35, *Creating and Modifying Data Sources*, on page 869.

Connect to data sources instead of making them Instead of creating and maintaining a proprietary StarOffice database format (.sdb), StarOffice Base 6.0 only works with data sources. StarOffice Base 6.0 can connect and administer a wide variety of data sources and provide data access to all StarOffice components. Choose Tools > Data Sources and name new data sources, and use them in your documents. Build connections to existing data sources, specify (Calc or Microsoft Excel) spreadsheet documents as data sources, design and edit database tables, define new queries or edit existing ones, and create links to remote data sources.

Administration You can also copy tables and queries between data sources, and copy a query as a table.

Import your StarOffice 5.2 (or earlier) databases The Database Import AutoPilot will store your existing StarOffice queries, forms, and reports in the new DataAccess.xml configuration file. Form documents will be stored as regular documents.

Assign a database table to a combo or list box Pick up data through a field.

New form events *Before reloading*: Called before a reload on the form is executed. *Before unloading:* Called before the form is unloaded. Previously, these events could only be used with a scripting language. Form Functions (on the Main toolbar) > Form Properties > Events.

Edit table indexes This component has been completely rewritten. A new Index Design button on the Table Design toolbar gives you one-click access to Indexes dialog box. Right-click a table in the Data Sources browser and select Edit Table from the context.

UTF-8 character suite support This support does not extend to ADO data sources (which don't have a character set), and dBase data sources.

Draw, Impress, and Image-Editing Features

Rotate meta files Used to be, you couldn't rotate metafiles, just bitmaps. Now you can.

Maximum size for cacheing Set an upper limit (in KB) for the total graphics cache size as well as cache a single graphic object. If the size of one object exceeds this predefined size, the graphics output is not cached, which means that the graphic is directly rendered on-screen every time you move or access the graphic. Choose Tools > Options > StarOffice > General.

Vertical text Want to write something down the side of your page? You got it. There are now vertical versions of the three Draw text creation tools, available in Writer as well through the Show Drawing Tools menu.

Printing options for graphics and gradients The new options include the following; to get to them, choose Tools > Options > StarOffice > Print.

- Reduced Transparency: Treat all transparent objects as non-transparent.

- No transparency: Always reduces transparency completely.

- Reduce gradients: Decreases the number of gradient steps to the real number set when the gradient was defined.

- Reduce bitmaps: Prints transparent bitmaps at the maximum resolution (in dpi). Convert colors to grayscale renders output in grayscale.

EPS and SVG export Create both formats by exporting from Draw.

Switching From Microsoft Office

Are you a dissatisfied Microsoft Office user? Come on in, the software's fine.

Ten good reasons If you haven't, read *Top Ten Reasons to Use StarOffice or OpenOffice.org* on page 5.

Take it out for a spin Dip your toe in the pool. Download OpenOffice.org and see how you like it. Note: OOo has no WordPerfect import filter at this time, though we're working on it. Then see if you want to just keeping using it happily, or if you want to buy StarOffice.

Try converting files
Once you've dipped your toe in the pool, try a test import. We're pretty sure it'll go really well. Just open a Microsoft Office file by simply choosing File > Open and choosing the right format in the format dropdown list.

You can also do a mass import using the AutoPilot, shown at right. It's no-risk experimentation since it leaves your Microsoft documents intact, just creating converted copies.

Spend some time with the tutorials Get to know StarOffice or OpenOffice.org.

- Chapter 5, *Setup and Tips*, on page 97
- *Guided Tour of Writer* on page 170
- *Guided Tour of Web* on page 448
- *Guided Tour of Calc* on page 504
- *Guided Tour of Impress* on page 638
- *Guided Tour of Draw: Vector and Raster Graphics* on page 755
- *Tutorial: Creating a Data Source* on page 871

Installation

IN THIS CHAPTER

Quick Start

If you've got the software on CD and you're just installing on your own machine, stick the CD in the drive. The installation program should start automatically; if it doesn't, just navigate to *platform*/office60 and double-click the setup.exe file. (For OpenOffice.org or for StarOffice purchased via download, the directory structure might be different.) Follow the directions on screen.

Migration Notes

For full migration information, see Chapter 3, *Migrating From StarOffice 5.2*, on page 47.

*   If you've been using StarOffice 6.0 beta, you **must** remove it before installing. See "Removing StarOffice 6.0 Beta Software Before Migrating" on page 48.
*   If you've been using StarOffice, you **must** be on StarOffice 5.2, not a prior version.
*   If you've been using StarOffice 5.2 Mail as your mail program, you **must** select the option labeled Migrate your personal data from StarOffice 5.2. See "Migrating Your StarOffice 5.2 Mail to Another Mail Program" on page 51 for more information.

General Note

The standard installation doesn't install all the text filters. If you plan to convert FrameMaker, Interleaf, or other files, use the Custom Install. Or do Standard, then go back and reinstall additional components (see "Installing Additional Components" on page 35).

Preparing to Install

This section covers information that's helpful to know before you install.

Getting StarOffice or OpenOffice Software and Books

StarOffice 5.2 was free to download; with this 6.0 release, different methods for obtaining the software are in place. OpenOffice.org, the open source version of StarOffice, is free to download.

Obtaining a StarOffice CD You can buy the packaged CD from Amazon, and buy the software as a packaged product or download from Sun Microsystems.

*   http://www.amazon.com

- `http://www.sun.com/staroffice` (or, at at the time of writing, `http://wwws.sun.com/software/star/staroffice/6.0/get/index.html`)

Sun now charges $75 for StarOffice 6.0, for standard use. Enterprise pricing at the time of writing was as follows:

StarOffice 6.0 Office Suite (U.S. Only). The enterprise software offering consists of:

- Right to use (RTU) license. $50.00/user (150 users) down to $ 25.00/user (10,000 users)

- Media kits - binary CDs. $25.00 - five CD sets

Downloading or Ordering OpenOffice   You can download the OpenOffice (officially, "OpenOffice.org") software for free.

OpenOffice's Web site is `http://www.openoffice.org` (at the time of writing, downloads were at `http://www.openoffice.org/dev_docs/source/1.0.0/index.html`)

You can obtain additional documentation and other resources from `http://www.lastturtle.com`.

If you're using Lindows, the operating system from `www.lindows.com` and sold preinstalled through Walmart, get OpenOffice.org or Starffice as noted above or through the ClicknGo feature. The ClicknGo icon is circled in Figure 2-1.

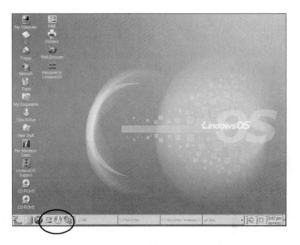

Figure 2-1   Downloading OpenOffice.org on Lindows through ClicknGo

The Lindows download system automatically configures StarOffice or OpenOffice.org when you use ClicknGo; it all happens in the background so that the application is ready to go.

Note – Lindows is a combination of the easy interface of a Windows system, and the great architecture of Linux. They've got some pretty dandy deals with preinstalled systems; if you're looking at how to get the best deal for your money, it's definitely worth a trip to lindows.com, walmart.com, or just walking into Walmart.

Obtaining StarOffice Companion books and tutorials Copies of "StarOffice 6.0 Companion" and related resources are available not only through bookstores and online resources such as Amazon.com, but also at `http://www.lastturtle.com.`.

Additional Product Installation Information

See the Installation Guide that comes with OpenOffice.org and the User's Guide included with StarOffice.

StarOffice and OpenOffice.org System Requirements

Basically, you just need to be running Windows, Linux, or Solaris, with 128 MB RAM or more. The following information provides more detail and was correct as of publication date of this book. For the latest StarOffice information, see the StarOffice Web site, `http://www.sun.com/staroffice`.

Patches are available at `http://sunsolve.sun.com`; click on the Patches link.

64 MB is listed; this is a minimum. You'll be happier with at least 128 MB RAM.

Windows

- Microsoft Windows 95, 98, ME, NT, 2000, or XP Pentium compatible PC
- 64 MB RAM
- 250 MB available hard disk space
- 800x600 or higher-resolution graphic device with 256 colors

Solaris

- Solaris 7 Operating Environment (SPARC Platform Edition) or higher (Solaris 8 recommended)
- 128 MB RAM
- 250 MB available hard disk space
- X Server with 800x600 or higher-resolution graphic device with 256 colors

Patches are required for Solaris 7 and Solaris 8. Patches are available at `http://sunsolve.sun.com`; click on the Patches link.

The required patches for Solaris 7 are: 106327-08, 106300-09 (64 bit only) or higher. The required patches for Solaris 8 are: 108434-01, 108435-01 (64 bit only) or higher.

Linux

- Linux Kernel version 2.2.13 or higher, `glibc` 2.1.2 or higher
- Pentium compatible PC
- 64 MB RAM
- 250 MB available hard disk space X Server with 800x600 or higher-resolution graphic device with 256 colors

Note – If you encounter installation problems, the `glibc` version might be the problem. For instance, RedHat Linux 6.0 comes with `glibc` 2.1 which is not currently (as of summer 2002) supported for StarOffice 6.0. Check `http://sunsolve.sun.com/staroffice` and search on `linux` for solutions; there is a non-verified workaround for using `glibc` 2.1 on that site.

Lindows

Lindows is a newly announced operating system, from www.lindows.com and sold preinstalled on computers through Walmart. Refer to the Lindows ClicknGo download system to determine the OpenOffice.org or StarOffice system requirements for Lindows. We recommend that you have at least 128 MB of RAM and 250 MB available hard disk space free for StarOffice or OpenOffice.org.

What Gets Installed

To see what your options are before you commit to installation, start the installer and choose the Custom Installation. (See Figure 2-8 on page 28.) As you review it, you'll see that the standard installation doesn't install many of the text filters. If you plan to convert FrameMaker, Interleaf, or other files, use the Custom Install. Or do Standard, then go back and reinstall additional components (see *Installing Additional Components* on page 35).

Operating System-Specific Notes

Be sure to read these notes before you start the install.

Windows The program sometimes does not run when there are mutations or other special characters in the login-name/user-name or in the system directories. When you have these characters (ASCII > 127, e.g. ä, ü, é, etc.) in your login-name/user-name, StarOffice won't function. A patch is available for this problem at the following site. Just follow the StarOffice Patches link once you access the site.

`http://supportforum.sun.com`

Solaris Before installing StarOffice 5.2 under Solaris you must install a Sun Microsystems operating system patch. StarOffice won't work without this patch. Refer to the INDEX.TXT file on the CD or in the downloaded software for more information.

Linux Review the following notes:

- You **must** mount your CD-ROM drive with Execute rights to be able to run the setup script from the CD. If you don't, a message stating "Permission denied" will appear.

  Mount it with the command:

  ```
  mount -o exec /dev/cdrom /cdrom
  ```

  or add in the file /etc/fstab "exec" for the CD.

- If you run the client installation of the multiuser installation with ./setup, the installation can freeze. This can happen with a normal user or root. To solve this, get the latest XFree86 at http://ftp.xfree86.org/pub/XFree86/. Be sure to follow the installation instructions and system prerequisites stated on the site.

Lindows See the support site at www.lindows.com for support notes.

The current latest Lindows version (SPX) had problems with OpenOffice, but installs downloaded on or after June 15th 2002 are corrected.

UNIX in general For OpenOffice.org, you can do a non-graphical installation with the ./install command. See the installation guide included with OpenOffice.org.

Installing StarOffice or OpenOffice.org

Most people should just use the single-user installation process, next.

If you're installing the program for an organization and you want some files, like templates, on the network, use *Installation: Multi-User* on page 32. The information in this section is organized as follows:

Installation: Single-User

Note – If you want to install the program, single-user, on several computers, you can do a variation on the multi-user install and save yourself some time. Run the server install (*Installing on the Server* on page 33). Then run the client install on each computer (*Install-*

ing on Each Client on page 34), but select the Local installation option, not the smaller client installation.

The installation is pretty straightforward—just stick the CD in the drive and go, with a few questions here and there.

Screen shots from the StarOffice installation are shown, but the process is the same, or very similar, for OpenOffice.org.

StarOffice

1   Be sure you've read the operating system-specific notes on page 20 and that you have at least 250 MB of free space where you'll be installing.

2   In a Linux or Solaris environment, be sure you're logged in as the user who will be running the program.

3   If you're installing from CD, insert the CD in your CD-ROM drive. The installation program will start automatically. If it doesn't, navigate to *platform*/office60 and double-click the setup.exe file. (For OpenOffice.org or for StarOffice purchased via download, the directory structure might be different.)

4   The window in Figure 2-2 will appear. Click Next.

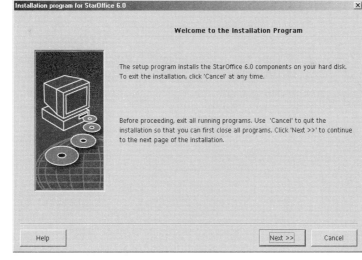

Figure 2-2   Introductory window of installation

5   The window in Figure 2-3 will appear. It contains operating system-specific information about the installation (your window might look different). Read the displayed information carefully, then click Next.

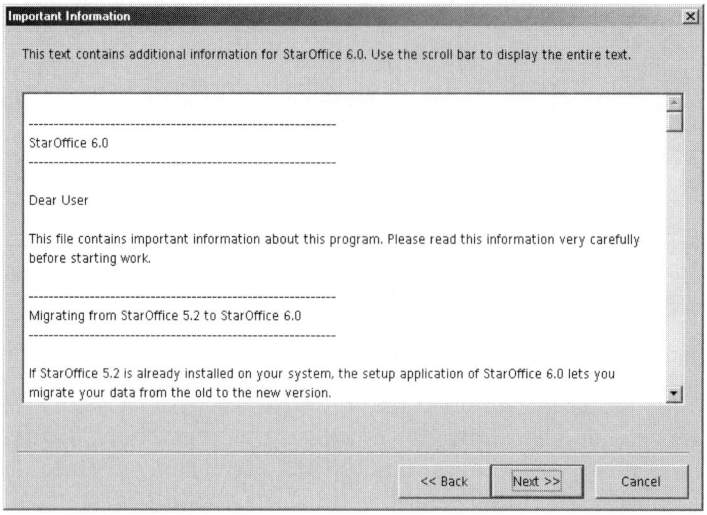

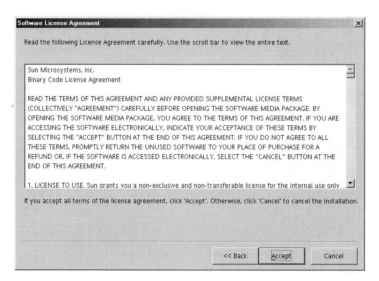

Figure 2-3   Installation information

6   The window in Figure 2-4 will appear, displaying the license agreement. Review it and, if you agree to the terms, click Accept.

Figure 2-4   License agreement

7   If you currently have the program installed, the window in Figure 2-5 will appear.

Note – If you've been using StarOffice 5.2 Mail as your mail program, you **must** select **Import personal data** to get any of that data into 6.0 or OpenOffice.org 1.0. See *Migrating Your StarOffice 5.2 Mail to Another Mail Program* on page 51.

Mark this option unless you have a good reason not to. You need to mark it to transfer any 5.2 mail files to another program, and it'll save setup time with the Internet Setup Wizard.

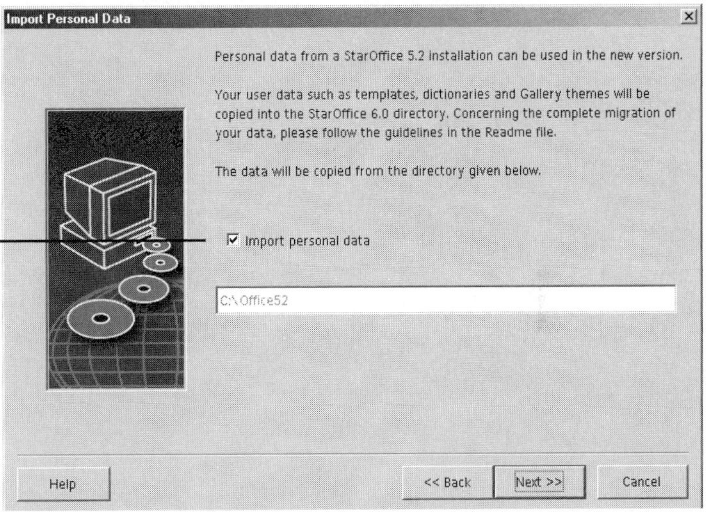

Figure 2-5   Specifying existing user data location

Select the Import personal data option and enter the path to your old directory; it's a good idea to do it to avoid a lot of repeated setup. For more information see page 49.

8   If you don't choose to import, the personal data window in Figure 2-6 will appear. You can enter it now, or do it later on (choose Tools > Options > *program*).

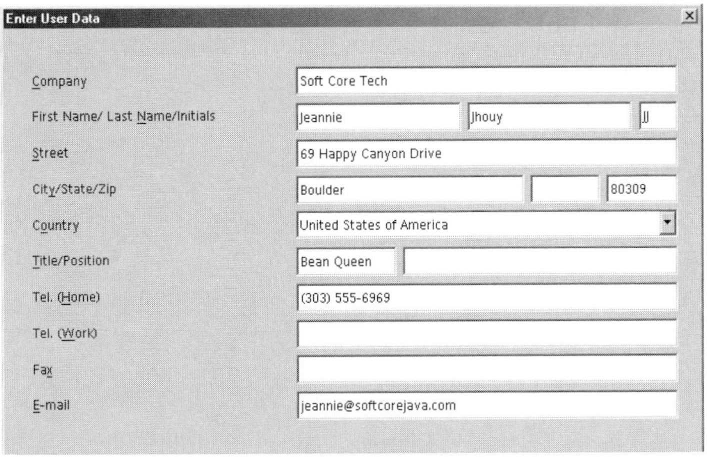

Figure 2-6   Personal information window

9   The installation type window shown in Figure 2-7 will appear, then take step A or B.

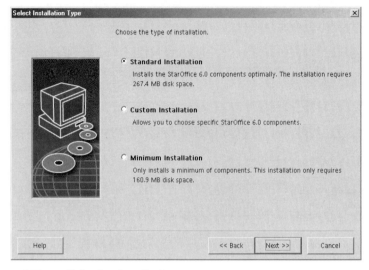

Figure 2-7   Selecting installation type

a)   In Figure 2-7, pick Standard, or Custom if you want a little more control.
(Minimal isn't a good idea since you don't know what it's leaving out.)

b)   If you chose Custom Installation, the window in Figure 2-8 will appear. Expand
the options and double-click any item that you don't want to install. Click Next.

Double-click an item to reverse it from installed to not installed or vice versa. Any item that won't be installed will appear white. Any group containing items that won't be installed will be light blue.

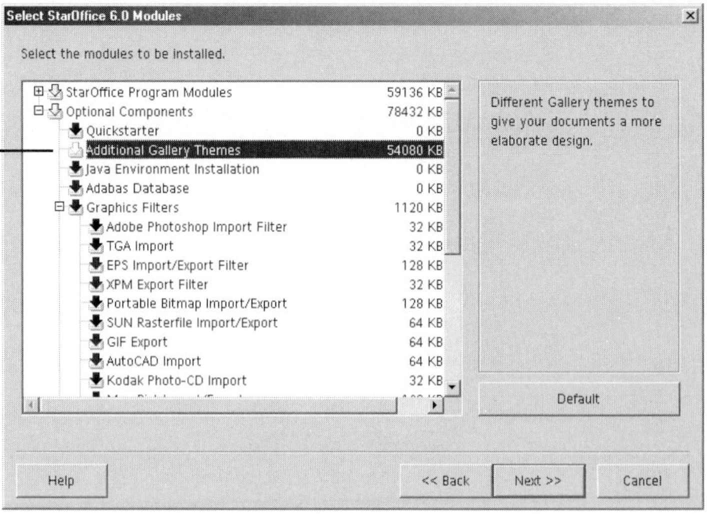

Figure 2-8   Selecting components to install for the Custom Installation

10 The window in Figure 2-9 will appear. Enter the directory and click Next.

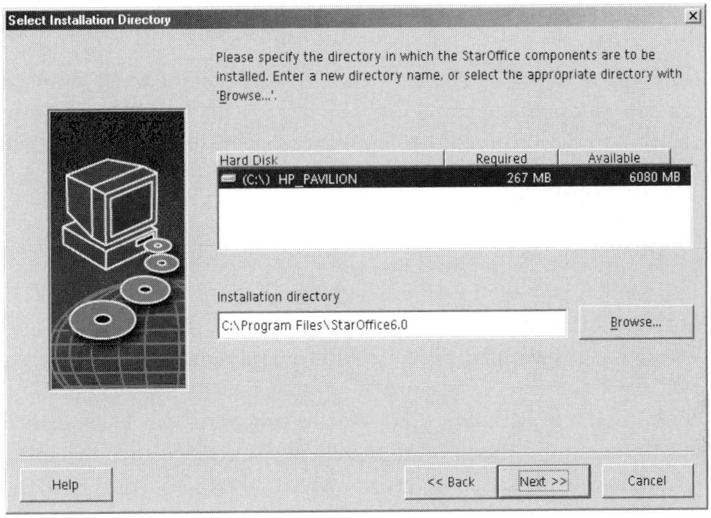

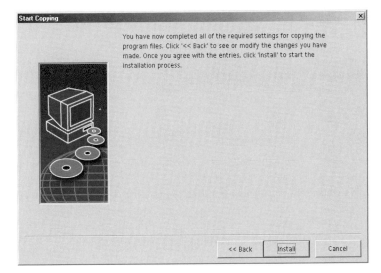

Figure 2-9   Selecting installation location

11 If you selected Custom Installation, a window will appear that allows you to specify the components you want. Expand the Program Modules item and select any additional items.

12 The window in Figure 2-10 will appear. Click Install to begin copying files.

Figure 2-10   End of installation options

13 The window in Figure 2-11 will appear. If you mark any of these file types, when you double-click them or right-click on them in Explorer and choose Open, they will be opened in StarOffice or OpenOffice.org automatically.

Note – If you're wondering whether to leave them marked or not, unmark them; you can use your operating system tools later to associate them if you want. Check these carefully; if you're already used to opening and editing HTML files in Netscape or Dreamweaver, for instance, be sure to deselect HTML before continuing.

Click Next.

14 The window in Figure 2-12 will appear. The program needs Java software in order to run some of its features, and provides the JRE 1.3.1 (Java Runtime Environment). The JRE is installed because the API (the rules and underlying programs that the StarOffice and OpenOffice.org programmers use) is written partly in Java. If you don't install the JRE, then you won't be able to run any enhancements or add-ons that other programmers write. And in general, StarOffice and OpenOffice.org have been known to run a little more nervously without its JRE. Just install it.

In StarOffice 5.2, StarOffice automatically associated itself only with .html files. In this release, marking this option will make the program your default editor for .html, .htm, and .shtml files.

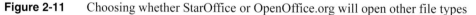

Setup Program for StarOffice 6.0

Select the file types that are to be opened with StarOffice 6.0.
StarOffice 6.0 will automatically open the following file types:

File types

☑ Microsoft Word Documents

☑ Microsoft Excel Spreadsheets

☑ Microsoft PowerPoint Presentations

Default HTML editor

☑ StarOffice 6.0 Writer/Web

Help   OK   Cancel

Figure 2-11   Choosing whether StarOffice or OpenOffice.org will open other file types

You definitely want the 1.3.1 JRE Other JRE or JDK sources might be listed in the window; however, it's best to install the one provided. Click Install. In Solaris and Linux the install will run with no further prompting; in Windows, a few windows will appear that will guide you through the installation process.

When the install is complete, select the Java 1.3.1 that is added to the list in the window and click OK.

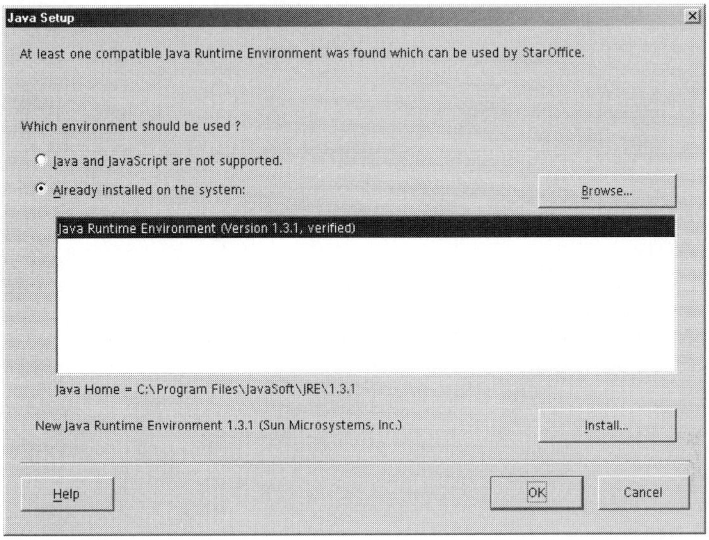

Figure 2-12   Java setup

15 The installation process will continue for quite a while; a progress bar will show how much of the process is complete and approximately how much time is left.

The installation program sits for quite a while on the last item, Registration of the components. Even though it looks like it's done, it's not until you get the window in Figure 2-13.

16 A window will appear, either stating that you've alread got the Adabas database, or that you can now install it. If you think you might want to do database development with Adabas, go ahead and install it; just follow the installation wizard instructions. If you're saying "What's Adabas?" then you probably don't need to install it. You can install it later if necessary. See *Installing Adabas for Use With StarOffice* on page 36.

17 The window in Figure 2-13 will appear, stating that the installation is complete. Click Complete as instructed.

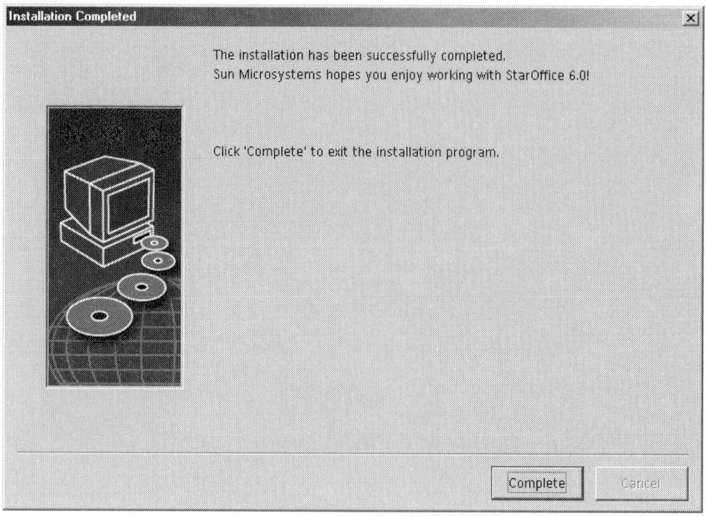

Figure 2-13   Installation complete

Installation: Multi-User

You'll be installing the program on the server, then running a setup file that gets installed on the server, to install the program on clients.

- The **files installed on the server** include program and help files, including the `setup` file used to run the client install, and a `share` directory containing shared resources such as templates, and configuration settings for items like printers.

- The **files installed on the client** include program and help files, including the `soffice` file used to start the program on the client, and a `user` directory containing files created by the user on that client (includes modified templates, client-specific configurations, etc.).

- An options window in the program determines where the program looks by default for your files. See "Viewing Where Data Is Stored" on page 39 for more information.

The information in this section is organized as follows:

- *Installing on the Server* on page 33

- *Making the Installed Files Available to Clients and General Troubleshooting* on page 33

- *Installing on Each Client* on page 34

Installing on the Server

Complete the server installation in a directory with sufficient disk space (see *StarOffice and OpenOffice.org System Requirements* on page 22) and to which all users have read/write access.

Note – You don't get prompted to install Adabas for the network installation. To install it and learn more, see *Installing Adabas for Use With StarOffice* on page 36.

---

1   Be sure you've read the operating system-specific notes on page 20.

2   If you've got a previous version of the program installed, first check for the following files on your system:

   •   .sversionrc in the Solaris or Linux home directory

   •   .sversion.ini in the Windows directory

   Open the files; they contain the path and version number of the program if it is currently installed. If the version number is 6.0, you need to uninstall the program first (see *Removing StarOffice or OpenOffice.org* on page 44). For more information about these files, see *Installing the Same Version Multiple Times on the Same Computer* on page 38.

3   Insert the CD in the server's CD-ROM drive. In Solaris and Linux, you'll probably need to mount the CD-ROM, typically with a command like mount /mnt/cdrom

4   In a Linux or Solaris environment, be sure you're logged in as the user who will be running the program.

5   In a terminal window, navigate to the directory on the CD for your operating system. Type the appropriate command and press Enter:
    ./setup -net (Linux or Solaris) or ./setup.exe -net (Windows)

6   Continue through the installation, which from this point on is the same as the single-user installation starting on page 24. When you get the option for Standard, Custom, or Minimal Installation, select Custom and select all items for installation. Click to open the Writer module and double-click it to make all items, including the import filters, turn blue.

Making the Installed Files Available to Clients and General Troubleshooting

You need to make sure the location where you installed the program on the server is accessible to client machines via the network.

You'll probably have to fuss with the directory permissions. All client machines will need read and execute permissions so that you can run the setup file on the server to do the client installation, and so that users can get at the files they need (including templates, icons, etc.).

Check the access permissions on all the directories where you installed the program. The program directory and all subdirectories need to have read and execute permission for any users accessing the program (group and other, for example, in Solaris). If they don't, use the appropriate procedures for your operating system to set the permissions.

Note – In Solaris, and on most Linux computers, you can run the following command to assign read and execute rights to group and other for all directories within the stated directory. As with all operations that affect permissions, this should be completed only by an experienced system administrator.

```
find office60 -type d -exec chmod go+r {} \;
```

This means, starting with the office60 directory (or the name of your OpenOffice.org installation directory) and continuing through all subdirectories, apply read and execute permissions for group and other.

Depending on how your system is set up, users might not automatically have read, write, and execute permissions on their temporary directory, and that they can copy files into that directory. Check those permissions, as well, before beginning the client install.

Finally, take a look at the files in the share directory on the server. Any modifications or new files users make are generally saved in their own user folder, and aren't available to other users. If you want users to be able to create new or modified versions of those files, such as templates, and share them on the server, set the permissions appropriately and let users know where to save their new templates or other files. However, note that with this approach, users can permanently change shared resources if they modify the original instead of making a copy.

You might encounter problems in Windows if you install the program in the root directory and the number of files in the root directory exceeds 256. Solaris and Linux installations might fail if the home directory on the server isn't available.

Installing on Each Client

Note – If you run the client installation of the multiuser installation with ./setup, the installation can freeze. This can happen with a normal user or root. To solve this, get the latest XFree86 at http://ftp.xfree86.org/pub/XFree86/. Be sure to follow the installation instructions and system prerequisites stated on the site.

Complete this procedure **on each client computer**, or have each user complete it.

1   In a Linux or Solaris environment, log into the client computer as the user who will be running the program there.

1   On the client computer, navigate to the newly installed `office/program` directory **on the server where you installed the program**. (You don't need the CD for the client installation.)

2   Double-click the `setup` file or `setup.exe` file (not the `soffice` file, which just runs the program), or run either of the following commands:
    `./setup` or `./setup.exe`

Note – If you have problems accessing the file, be sure that the correct access rights are set on the server computer for the client user, especially if you let the program create the installation directory.

---

3   A welcome window will appear. Click Next. Continue through the installation. The only difference from the installation you've already seen is that, instead of Standard Custom or Minimal installations, you will be offered the options of Standard Workstation Installation.

Select **Standard Workstation Installation**, unless you want all the files to be local. (That is, you're just trying to get the program onto a bunch of single-user machines fast, without using the CD.)

4   Continue until the installation completes.

Installing Additional Components

If you didn't install everything you needed to, just run the install again and pick Custom Installation.

1   Insert the CD-ROM in the drive, if you're using the CD.

2   Start the installation the same way you did before, with the `setup` or `setup.exe` file.

3   In the Installation Program window, select the Modify installation option. Click Next.

4   In the Select Modules window, make the icon dark blue next to everything you want installed.

Note – It's a good idea to just install everything. Double-click on the Program Modules and Optional Components items until the icons for both are colored.

---

5   Click Complete. Continue the installation.

Installing Adabas for Use With StarOffice

OpenOffice.org

Adabas isn't included in Openoffice.org.

You're prompted to install Adabas database as part of the regular installation, at the end. This only happens with the single user installation, not the network installation.

To install Adabas now, locate the *operatingsystem*/adabas directory on the installation CD, or in your expanded download, and run the adabas setup application.

Limitations

Adabas is a database from Software AG provided with StarOffice. It isn't the standard version; there's a five-user limit as well as a hundred-user limit. Contact Software AG or www.adabas.com if you want more.

Adabas directory names can have a maximum of 40 characters and a minimum of 10 characters. If you do the math, that means you're got only 15-30 left over for the Adabas directory name. Keep the DBROOT directory as short as you possibly can.

The name of the Adabas database you create is limited to a quaintly old-fashioned 8 characters.

UNIX Installation

Solaris You'll need the following kernel parameters. Change to root and add these lines to the /etc/system file., then restart the computer.

```
set msgsys:msginfo_msgmni = 10
set shmsys:shminfo_shmmax = 300000000
set shmsys:shminfo_shmmni = 100
set shmsys:shminfo_shmseg = 100
set semsys:seminfo_semmni = 100
set semsys:seminfo_semmns = 100
set semsys:seminfo_semmap = 100
```

UNIX Install the database as root for multi-user systems and as the appropriate user for single-user systems.

1   Close all shells that you might have running. Log out, then log in as the appropriate user.

2   Start the setup application in the CD or installation download directory *operatingsystem*/adabas and follow the dialogs. Follow the installation wizard through as directed onscreen.

3   Once the installation is complete, check your environment variables.

    Check the environment variables using the command echo $DBROOT. The variables need to point to where you installed Adabas.

```
DBROOT -> <Adabas_directory>
DBWORK -> <Adabas_directory>/sql
DBCONFIG -> <Adabas_directory>/sql
LD_LIBRARY_PATH -> <Adabas_directory>/lib
PATH -> <Adabas_directory>/bin:<Adabas_directory>/pgm
```

If the environment variables aren't as shown, check the .profile file. It should have these lines for Adabas installations that were installed in the export/adabas directory.

```
# by Sun Microsystems setup
set DBROOT=/export/adabas
set DBWORK=$DBROOT/adabas/sql
set DBCONFIG=$DBROOT/adabas/sql
set PATH=$DBROOT/bin:$DBROOT/pgm:$PATH
set LD_LIBRARY_PATH=$DBROOT/lib:$LD_LIBRARY_PATH
export DBROOT DBWORK DBCONFIG PATH LD_LIBRARY_PATH
```

Windows Installation

Install the Adabas on the same computer as StarOffice.

Note – Don't use any blank spaces in the directory path where you install Adabas. So installing it in C:\Program Files is out.

1   Run adabas.exe in the windows/adabas directory on the StarOffice CD or in the downloaded installation directory.

2   Follow the setup wizard through to completion.

3   When installation is done, open a DOS window and use the echo command; you're going to be checking whether some variable values got set correctly during installation.

Type this in your DOS window: c:>echo %DBROOT and you should get something like this back: c:\Db\Adabas (or wherever you installed Adabas).

Type this: c:>echo %DBWORK and you should get this back: C:\Db\Adabas\sql

Type this: c:>echo %DBCONFIG and you should get this back: C:\Db\Adabas\sql

If you don't get the correct, or any, directories back for these commands, add the following lines to your autoexec.bat file.

In the following lines, *fullpathtoAdabas* is a variable; replace it with your actual Adabas directory such as C:\db\Adabas.

```
set DBROOT=fullpathtoAdabas
set DBWORK=%DBROOT%\sql
set DBCONFIG=%DBROOT%\sql
set path=%path%;%DBROOT%\bin;%DBROOT%\pgm
```

Installing or Reinstalling the JRE

1 Go to the installed `program` directory and run the file `j2re-1_3_1_02*` or `j2re-1_3_1_02-win-i.exe`. Follow the onscreen installation wizard.

2 In the same directory, run `jvmsetup` or `jvmsetup.exe`; in the window that opens, select the right JRE and click OK.

Installing the Same Version Multiple Times on the Same Computer

If you install the program, then attempt to do another installation of the same version on the same computer, you'll get a whiny error message saying no, sorry, it's already installed, as shown in Figure 2-14.

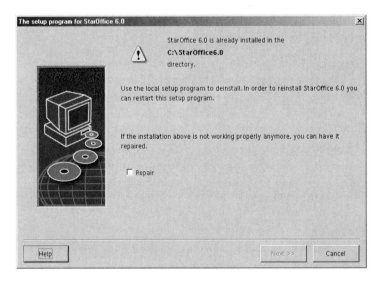

Figure 2-14   What you see if you start the installation with the program already installed

The message states that you must remove it first (for instructions see page 44) if you want to reinstall.

The install program knows that you've already got an installed version of 6.0 because of the following registry-type file that tracks where and how the program is installed:

- `.sversionrc` in the UNIX home directory

- `.sversion.ini` in the `Windows\Application Data` directory

The contents look something like Table 2-1:

Table 2-1   `sversionrc` and `sversion.ini` files for StarOffice

Windows	UNIX
[Versions]	[Versions]
;StarOffice 5.1a=C:\Office51a	;StarOffice 5.1a=/home/solveigh/Office51a
StarOffice 5.2=C:\Office52	StarOffice 5.1=/home/solveigh/Office
OpenOffice.org 641=file:///C:/ openoffice	StarOffice 5.2=/home/solveigh/office52
StarOffice 6.0=file:///C:/ Program%20Files/StarOffice6.0	StarOffice 6.0=/home/solveigh/staroffice60

You can run the 6.0 install without uninstalling your current 6.0 installation if you comment out—put a semicolon in front of—the current installation location of StarOffice. For example, if you had the file shown previously on your system, and you wanted to also install StarOffice 6.0 just at C:\staroffice, you'd add a semicolon in front of the line for the current 6.0 installation:

```
[Versions]
;StarOffice 5.1a=C:\Office51a
StarOffice 5.2=C:\Office52
OpenOffice.org 641=file:///C:/openoffice
;StarOffice 6.0=file:///C:/Program%20Files/StarOffice6.0
```

Keep in mind that this will almost certainly mess up the program icons that the installation adds to your task bar or Start menu. When you start StarOffice, be sure to do so by typing `./soffice` in a terminal window, in the appropriate `office60` directory.

Note – Make a backup of any files you edit.

Viewing Where Data Is Stored

You can use a couple different sources to see where your data ended up, and where the program is looking for it.

In addition, the Paths window within the program's general options is very useful, in order to see where each client installation looks for files. Choose Tools > Options > StarOffice or OpenOffice.org > Paths; the window in Figure 2-15 will appear. Scroll through the list to see where each type of file is stored.

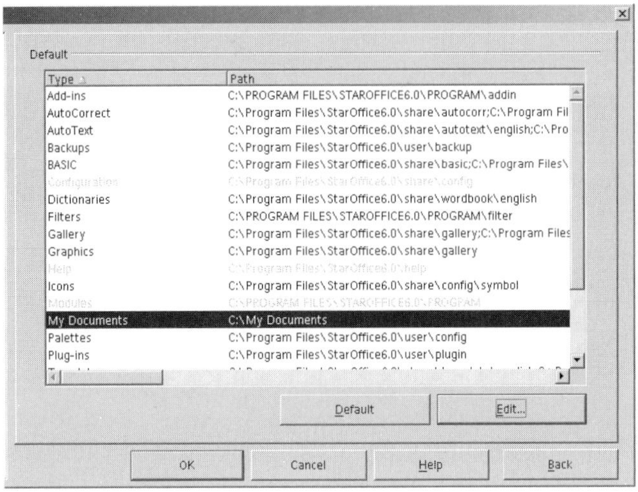

Figure 2-15   File paths window

If both the server and client are listed, it means that files of that type such as templates that are provided by StarOffice are stored on the server, but new or modified files of that type are stored locally.

Note – Refer to *Specifying the Default Directory You Save to and Open Files In* on page 136 if you want to change where the client looks for files. Be sure that, if you change from the client to the server, the files on the server have permissions that allow the client to access them. In addition, all files might not be installed on the client, so exercise caution when switching from server to client.

Troubleshooting

This section covers commonly experienced installation problems, as well as what to try and where to get help in general. See also *Making the Installed Files Available to Clients and General Troubleshooting* on page 33.

Most Commonly Experienced Issues

StarOffice or OpenOffice.org already installed If you got any error messages about already having the program installed, check for the following files on your system:

- .sversionrc in the Solaris or Linux home directory

- .sversion.ini in the Windows\Application Data directory

Open the files; they contain the path and version number of program if it is currently installed. You can either uninstall that version, or do some sneaky editing to fool the program into thinking it's gone. See *Installing the Same Version Multiple Times on the Same Computer* on page 38.

UNIX client installation freezing   If you run the client installation of the multiuser installation with `./setup`, the installation can freeze. This can happen with a normal user or root. To solve this, get the latest XFree86 at `http://ftp.xfree86.org/pub/XFree86` Be sure to follow the installation instructions and system prerequisites stated on the site.

General installation or startup problems   Depending on how your system is set up, you might not have the correct permissions to the directory where you're trying to install. Make sure you can read, write, and execute in the program directory and in your system temporary directory.

Trouble starting or running the program on client   If you have any problems starting a client, with messages such as "Cannot determine current directory" or "Cannot initialize gallery," check the file access rights on the server. All clients must be able to read and execute in all directories within the installed program directory on the server.

The program not starting, or claiming it's still running   In UNIX, killing the program doesn't always bring down the underlying process, just the interface. When you try to start it again, the operating system thinks the program is still running, so nothing happens. If you kill the program, use a command like `ps -ef` to list processes, then kill any that correspond to the `soffice.bin` file or the server installation of the program.

The following Solaris command searches for all processes containing `soffice`:

```
ps -ef | grep soffice
```

It also might have started and you just can't see it. The program occasionally likes to hang out up at the very top of your screen, sometimes. If you see a horizontal line that looks like the bottom of a window, drag it down. If it won't move, hold down the Alt key, then drag it.

Cannot find file *filename*   Start the program in a terminal window. Navigate to the program directory on your computer (not the server computer) and type `./soffice`

Command not found   Search for the .sversionrc file in your home directory or sversion.ini in Windows (locations vary) and do one of the following options:

*   Open the file and remove the line `StarOffice 6.0 = file:///some_path`
*   Move the file or rename it

Installer cannot run in this mode   The JRE that comes with the program wasn't installed or is damaged. Reinstall it and reselect it; see *Installing or Reinstalling the JRE* on page 38.

Installation failed message   The program was running while you installed. Shut it down, restarting your machine if necessary, and run the installation again. Also check the quick launch icon, the butterfly icon in the lower right corner of your task bar. Right click it and select Close.

Linux installation problems   This is a broad category; however the following are solutions to the installation failing, and not being able to start an installed version of the program.

- Make sure that the `/var/tmp` directory has enough free space.

- Check the `SAL_DO_NOT_USE_INVERT50` variable and make sure it's set to `true`.

- Install a new S3 Savage graphics driver from `http://www.probo.com/timr/savage40.html`

Missing java.ini   Make sure you're installing only the client version, if you're on a networked installation of the program. If that doesn't work, reinstall and reselect the 1.3.1 JRE. See *Installing or Reinstalling the JRE* on page 38.

*.dll not found   Make sure that no other tasks except `explorer` and `systray` are running. Press Ctrl. + Alt +Delete to get the task manager and end all other tasks.

Installed the wrong language   Uninstall the program and reinstall with the new language setting.

Other Things to Try

Try all the basics:

- Make sure the JRE 1.3.1 that comes with the program is installed and selected. See *Installing or Reinstalling the JRE* on page 38.

- Check the .sversionrc or `sversion.ini` and either delete or comment out (with a semicolon) the line indicating the 6.0 install, or just rename the file.

- Make sure the program isn't running. Shut it down, restarting your machine if necessary. Also check the quick launch icon, the butterfly icon in the lower right corner of your task bar. Right click it and select Close.

- If you installed the StarOffice 6.0 Beta, uninstall it.

- Run the repair option.

- On UNIX, and possibly in Windows, nothing remotely related to the program, whether your GhostScript application or the program itself or your data sources, should be installed in a directory with a space in it. So if you're having problems, make sure nothing you're using is in C:\Program Files, for instance.

Good Online Information Sources

Note – If you're having problems, always check *Troubleshooting* on page 40.

There's a mass of help and troubleshooting information out there; here are the sources that are worth checking.

- Check the OpenOffice.org help lists and FAQs. If you're trying to find out something particularly hairy, this is your best bet:
  - `http://www.openoffice.org/faq.html`
  - `http://documentation.openoffice.org/user_faq/index.html`
  - `http://documentation.openoffice.org/HOW_TO/index.html`
  - `http://documentation.openoffice.org/setup_guide/index.html`
  - `http://dba.openoffice.org/FAQ`.
  - Join the `users@openoffice.org` or `allfeatures@openoffice.org` mailing list, at `http://www.openoffice.org/mail_list.html`. `allfeatures` is the mailing list for new features.
- The site `http://openoffice.swiki.net` contains FAQs as well as Portuguese and French translations.
- Check Sun's FAQs. Much of the information in those FAQs is here too, but specific "What if it's a month ending with a K and I'm running a JavaStation desktop" problems aren't in this book.
  - `http://wwws.sun.com/software/star/staroffice/6.0/techfaq.html`
  - `http://wwws.sun.com/software/star/staroffice/6.0/migrationfaq.html`
  - `http://wwws.sun.com/software/star/staroffice/6.0/faq.html`
- Check Sun's StarOffice help sites.
  - `http://sunsolve.sun.com/staroffice/` (The new StarOffice Support Portal for registered users with search capabiltiies)
  - `http://supportforum.sun.com/staroffice/` (free)
- An independent StarOffice group has the site `http://www.staroffice.com`. StarDesk deals with questions and there are User, Developer, and International forums.
- Also check the Web site of StarOffice guru Werner Roth: `http://www.wernerroth.de/en/staroffice`
- Database information for ODBC and UNIX can be found at `http://unixodbc.org`. See `http://www.unixodbc.org/doc/OOoMySQL.pdf` in particular.
- Macro-specific sites are listed in *Finding Macros and Macro Information* on page 964.

Repairing Damaged Installations

If you suddenly start having problems with particular applications, or if the program just won't start, the files might be damaged. StarOffice and OpenOffice.org both have a built-in "file repair kit" that can help.

1   In Linux or Solaris, click the program icon on your taskbar and choose Setup. In Windows, choose Start > Programs > *programname* > Setup.

   You also can locate the installed program's \program directory and double-click the setup or setup.exe file.

2   Select the Repair option.

3   Click Complete to run the installation.

Removing StarOffice or OpenOffice.org

To remove the program, follow these steps.

Multi-User Uninstall

For clients, complete the single-user uninstall. For the server, delete the installed program's main directory from the server computer.

Single-User Uninstall

1   Click the program icon on your taskbar and choose Setup, or locate the setup or setup.exe file in your installed \program directory. (In Windows, you can choose Start > Programs > *program_name* > Setup.)

2   Select Deinstallation and click Next.

3   Select Delete all files if you want to delete configuration files and files you've created, in addition to the program files. Click Complete.

Getting Started

Once you've run the actual installation, just start up the program. All the things you might want to do at this point are listed here:

*   *Startup: Single-User* on page 45
*   *Startup: Multi-User* on page 45
*   *Registration for StarOffice* on page 45
*   *Removing StarOffice or OpenOffice.org* on page 44
*   *Help With StarOffice and OpenOffice.org* on page 46

If you're all done with installation and the program is working great, go to these sections of the book:

- Chapter 5, *Setup and Tips*, on page 97 has some extremely useful tips that will make using the program easier.
- *Creating UNIX Printers* on page 60 if you're on Linux or Solaris
- To get started learning about the program, go to the *Quick Start* section for the applicatoin you want to learn.

Startup: Single-User

A program item will be added to your desktop; choose StarOffice 6.0 or OpenOffice.org to start. You also can locate the executable file (`setup` or `setup.exe`) in the directory where you installed, and double-click it. (The program item won't appear until you restart the computer.)

Note – You'll probably be prompted to register if you're using StarOffice. See *Registration for StarOffice* on page 45.

Startup: Multi-User

You don't need to start anything on the server. Start the program on each client, either with the program item added to the desktop or running the `setup` or `setup.exe` file in the **client's** installation directory.

Note – You'll probably be prompted to register if you're using StarOffice. See *Registration for StarOffice* on page 45.

Registration for StarOffice

When you start StarOffice, you can register at that time, or ask to be prompted to later. Registering isn't required, but as a registered user, you will receive technical support if problems with your software arise. You will also always receive the latest information and news pertaining to StarOffice. Furthermore, only registered StarOffice users have access to the knowledge database on the Sun Web site.

In a multi-user system, it's a good idea for every user to register who wants to individually get this information.

Your registration as a StarOffice user can only be completed online. To register as a StarOffice user you have the following two options:

- Choose Help > Registration. You will automatically be sent to a Web site containing a registration form.

- After you start StarOffice, a dialog appears where you will be asked if you want to register as a StarOffice user. In this dialog, select the Register now option. You will automatically be sent to the registration form.

Once you register, you will receive a user name and password from us which you can use at any time to change your registration data. Sun Microsystems will only store your submitted data for internal purposes and will not forward it to third parties.

Help With StarOffice and OpenOffice.org

With this book, you've got a good foundation of information on the way the program is supposed to work, as well as many of the ways it doesn't work, and what to do about it. In addition, the Help in the latest version is considerably improved.

Hit *Troubleshooting* on page 40, of course.

Check the index of this book, period; a lot of settings that will solve your problems are buried in very small checkboxes on the back tab of a window you've never seen before. But it's indexed.

If you encounter problems you can't immediately find the solutions to, check the **troubleshooting** entry in the index of this book. We tried to get everything that's a bit unusual into that entry. For example, the Permission Denied error on Linux is indexed under **troubleshooting**.

And then just go to *Good Online Information Sources* on page 42.

Migrating From StarOffice 5.2

Quick Migration Overview

Before you begin, don't worry about uninstalling StarOffice 5.2. 5.2 and 6.0 and OpenOffice.org all coexist happily together.

However, uninstall StarOffice 6.0 Beta before you do anything else.

The migration from StarOffice 5.2 is generally pretty simple:

- You need to be on StarOffice 5.2, not a prior version.

- StarOffice 5.2 and 6.0, and OpenOffice.org 1.0 all co-exist peacefully on the same machine. So you don't need to uninstall 5.2, though you do need to upgrade to 5.2 if you're on 5.1, and you need to uninstall the StarOffice 6.0 Beta if you've got it.

- When you install StarOffice 6.0 and OpenOffice.org 1.0, you get to choose to import personal data like your name (which shows up in notes and other places), so that's taken care of automatically.

- The StarOffice document converter (File > AutoPilot > Document Converter) will convert all your 5.2 documents to 6.0 at once.

This section covers specifics on how to deal with details of your migration that might not go smoothly such as UNIX printers, or migrating StarOffice 5.2 features that don't exist anymore, like Mail.

Removing StarOffice 6.0 Beta Software Before Migrating

You must remove the 6.0 Beta release of StarOffice before you install 6.0 GA or migrate.

UNIX To invoke the setup for the deleting the software, open a terminal window.

Type cd, then press Return. Type ls and press Return. This will list the files and directories in your Home directory. Find the directory you installed StarOffice 6.0 beta in. This is typically staroffice6.0 or StarOffice6. Change to this StarOffice directory by typing:

```
cd office60beta_directory
```

Press Return, then type:

```
 ./setup
```

This calls the Staroffice setup program. Select the Remove option and choose to Delete all files.

If this does not work, edit the ~/sversionrc file and remove this line:

```
StarOffice 6.0=file:///office60beta_path
```

Save the file.

Type `rm -rf /office60beta_path` in a terminal window to delete the StarOffice 6.0 installation directory.

Windows Right click on the StarOffice Quickstarter in your taskbar (A butterfly in the lower right corner) and select Exit Quickstarter. Now choose Start > Programs > StarOffice 6.0 Beta > Setup. Remove the program and choose to delete all files.

Note – Although the Delete all files option states that it will delete all user-created documents, it—well, it doesn't. Not checking this option leaves behind a lot of junk files in the directory, including files that will make the final installation crash when initiating the presentation module for the first time.

Migrating 5.2 Personal Data and Setup Options

When you install, you are prompted to migrate personal data. You probably want to mark this option. The data migrated to 6.0 includes:

- Text document, spreadsheet, presentation, drawing and user preferences. This includes files for colors and hatches like .sob and .soh files.
- Any user settings for user information: AutoCorrection, Autotext, backup preferences, backup directory, Internet (Proxy) settings, gallery, plugins, templates, wordbooks, your standard work (data) folder (copied to your home directory for Solaris users and the My Documents folder for Windows users), and user dictionaries.
- To keep your customized menu, keyboard, statusbar and toolbar configurations, locate the .cfg file (`office52/user/config/soffice.cfg`). Load it into the current release of the program by choosing Tools > Configuration > Load.

The following user preferences and data are ***not*** migrated automatically and should be updated manually: math symbols, paths settings, module settings in the Tools > Options windows, bookmarks, Calc addins, and basic macros.

It does not migrate email data or preferences; see *Migrating Your StarOffice 5.2 Mail to Another Mail Program* on page 51.

Migrating Mail, Address Book, and Newsgroups

None of the proprietary mail, address book, or newsgroups for 5.2 are supported. However, there are migration measures to cover a lot of the issues.

Exporting Locally Saved News

The current release of the software does not provide a newsreader. For any locally saved news articles in StarOffice software version 5.2, select the news group in Explorer and right click it, then choose File > Export. It will be exported to an ASCII file.

Migrating Your StarOffice 5.2 Address Book

The current release doesn't support the 5.2 address book, but supports any address books on your system in standard formats such as Netscape.

1   Export your address data from StarOffice 5.2 software to an alternative application, such as Netscape or Mozilla.

To get the address book into a spreadsheet, just drag it to a new blank spreadsheet as shown in Figure 3-1.

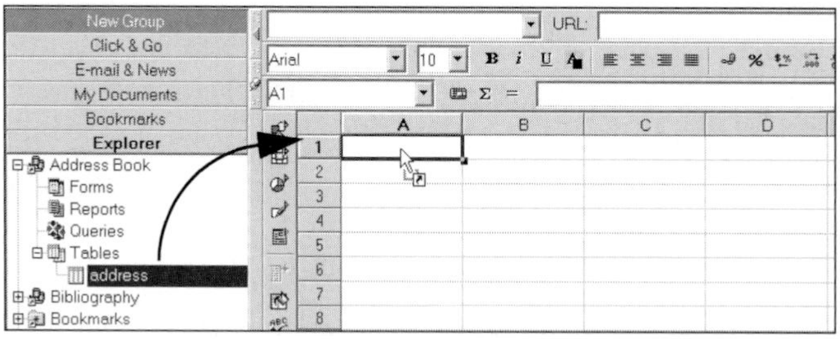

Figure 3-1   Drag address book from Explorer to new empty spreadsheet in work area

It will appear in the spreadsheet (see Figure 3-2). Then save it to text or another format.

To export to CVF, in Explorer select the Explorer slider, expand Address book, expand Tables, right-click address, and choose Export to Vcard.

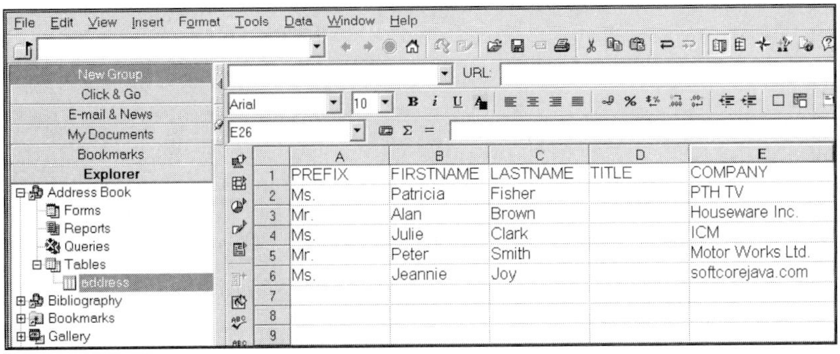

Figure 3-2   Address book opens in new empty spreadsheet

2   Using the current release Address Data Source AutoPilot, you can access your
Address Book data directly from StarOffice software. In the current release of the
software, choose File > AutoPilot > Address Data Source (see Figure 3-3).

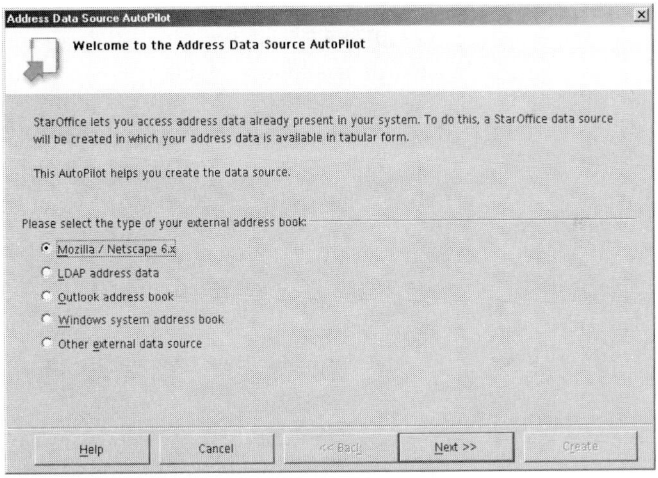

Figure 3-3   Address book opens in new empty spreadsheet

Migrating Your StarOffice 5.2 Mail to Another Mail Program

IMAP mail can be read when configured to do so by another mail program, so no
conversion is necessary.

StarOffice 6.0 and OpenOffice.org 1.0 don't include the 5.2 Mail program. You'll need to
use Netscape, Outlook Express, or another compatible mail program to import your
StarOffice mail files.

Note – Don't uninstall the old StarOffice 5.x version before you have successfully completed migrating your email.

Exporting Mail to ASCII

Select the inbox, outbox, or any other folder in the Email and News slider of Explorer and right click it. Choose File > Export. It will be exported to an ASCII file.

Exporting to .dbx for Use By Another Mail Program

1   Install the current software. During installation, be sure to select the option labeled Import personal data.

   This option transfers your personal data from your StarOffice 5.2 directory to your new current release directory. It then adds and installs a new Autopilot to the StarOffice 5.2 directory to export your mail boxes.

2   Start StarOffice 5.2. You'll see the new Autopilot E-Mail Converter when you choose File > AutoPilot.

3   Enter the appropriate StarOffice 5.2 mail directory and destination directory, as shown in Figure 3-4. See the notes following this figure for mail program-specific notes.

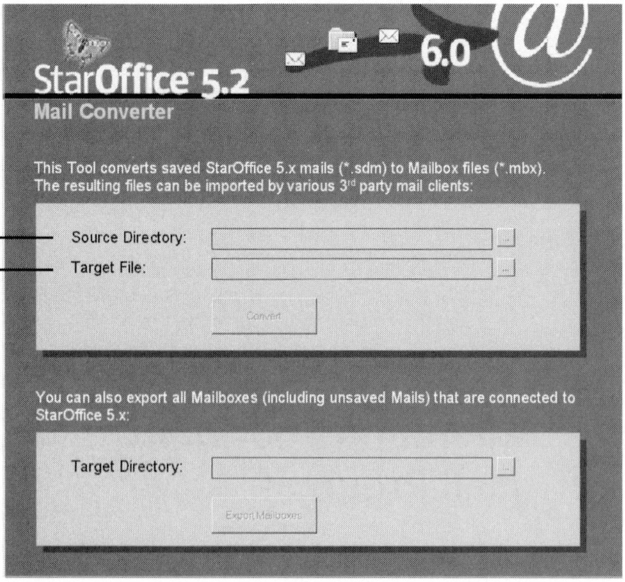

The Autopilot creates a file with the extension .mbx for each mail account. Enter the directory for your 5.2 mail stored in .sdm files.

You can export it to any directory now and copy the file when you're done, or enter the mail directory of your mail program if you know it now.

Figure 3-4   StarOffice 5.2 mail converter AutoPilot

Note – Your POP3 and IMAP mail account will be converted, but note that only the **locally saved email** will be converted. IMAP typically stores the mail on the mail server. For such mail accounts it is better to create a new IMAP mail in your Netscape manually.

Netscape 4.xx mail directory The directory is shown when you choose Edit > Preferences > Mail & Newsgroups > Mail Servers > Local Mail Directory.

Netscape 6.1 and newer, Mozilla 0.94 and higher Use the Email and Discussion Preferences dialog box to determine where your Local Folders directory is. Export the 5.2 mail to that directory.

Outlook Express Export the mailbox file (*.mbx file) to the Local Folders directory of the mail client.

4   Click Convert then make the appropriate change below.

Netscape Remove the extensions of all .mbx files.

Outlook Express Rename the extension of the previous exported .mbx file to *.dbx; for example, rename `mymail.mbx` as `mymails.dbx`.

5   Repeat the previous steps for any other .sdm files you need to convert.

6   Convert any other mail files associated with StarOffice by entering a target directory for them in the bottom Target Director field of the AutoPilot window. Click export mailboxes.

7   Start your email program; you will see the StarOffice mail in the inbox.

Exporting StarOffice Schedule Data

The current release of the software does not include a Schedule application or server. Export your tasks and appointments to an alternative schedule application and server. For Sun's new iCal calendar server geared for enterprises. The Schedule export supports vCalendar, XML-iCalendar and iCalendar formats.

To export your Schedule data, open a task or event view in StarOffice 5.2 and choose File > Export (see Figure 3-5).

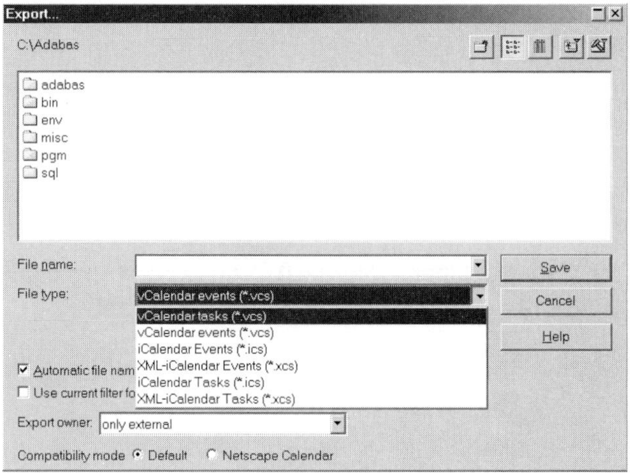

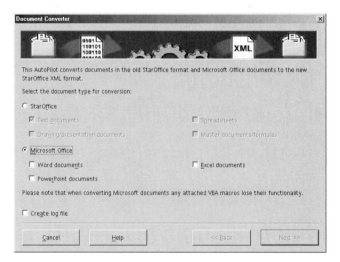

Figure 3-5   Exporting Schedule data

Converting 5.2 Files to 6.0 Files and Reading 5.2 Files

To convert all files at once, in the current release of the software choose File > AutoPilot > Document Converter.

Figure 3-6   Batch converter

However, if you just open a 5.2 file in 6.0, it will be converted without problems.

Backward/forward compatibility 5.2 files can be read in 6.0, but 6.0 files cannot be read in 5.2. However, you can save any 6.0 file to 5.2 format by just choosing File > Save As in the current release of the software.

Default save format If you want the default file format to be 5.2 when you're using 6.0, choose Tools > Options > Load/Save > General, and set the default file formats to 5.2 in the Standard File Format area.

Conversion for graphics and other objects When converting StarOffice 5.x files to the current release either manually or using the AutoPilot, all StarOffice software objects embedded as an OLE object, such as charts or graphics, are automatically converted to the new release's XML format.

Converting UNIX 5.2 Printers

Use the StarOffice 6.0 printer administration tool `spadmin` in the current release's installed directory.

1   After installing the current release of the software, start the `spadmin` application.

2   Click the New Printer button at the bottom of the window that appears.

Select the option titled Import Printers From a StarOffice Installation. ——

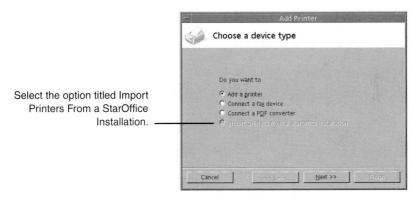

Figure 3-7   Main window of New Printer Device AutoPilot

3   In the window that apears, select the last option in the option list, then click Next.

4   The tool will convert all 5.2 printers, then display them.

Macros

By and large, no 5.1 or previous macros are converted or supported in the current release. Macros from StarOffice 5.2 macros should work and require only limited changes. For more information see *Appendix: Macros* on page 963.

Migrating Data and Databases

The migration issues with databases and 6.0 aren't all that extensive. Here are a couple tips and the "what's new" information.

Changes in This Release

Instead of creating and maintaining a proprietary StarOffice database format (.sdb), the current release of the software works with numerous widely distributed data sources. You can connect and administer a wide variety of data sources and provide data access to all office suite software components.

- StarBase is no longer available.
- The report engine and the AutoPilots to create tables, forms, queries and reports are no longer available.
- The Data Source window lets you connect to data sources, not create them. You can connect to any existing data source via ODBC/JDBC driver that usually comes with the database itself. See *Creating a Data Source Based on Text Files* on page 881.
- This is with the exception of Adabase databases, which you can still create. Going beyond simple creation, i.e., administering them through Adabas tools, is beyond the scope of this book

Converting Databases

The database engine (AdabasD) provided with StarOffice 5.2 software is the same in 6.0, so there is no need to update your database engine when installing StarOffice 6.0 software. The only difference is that in 5.2, queries and forms are stored in a separate (.sdb) file. When migrating to 6.0, these (.sbd) files can be imported to 6.0 using the StarOffice 5.2 Database Import AutoPilot from the File, AutoPilot menu. The data itself (as stored in the database (.dbf) is in no way affected). The AutoPilot automatically converts your queries and forms to 6.0, allowing you to easily access your data. See *Migrating a StarOffice 5.2 Database and Creating a Data Source* on page 905.

Adabas Documentation

Developing for Adabas is outside the scope of this book. We recommend that you go to the Adabas Web site and check out their technical documentation.

```
http://www.softwareag.com/adabas/
```

```
http://www.softwareag.com/adabas/technical/description.htm
```

Printer Setup and Printing

Creating UNIX Printers

Use the information in this section for printer and fax setup in Linux and Solaris operating environments. For printing procedures and additional information, see the subsequent sections in this chapter.

Note – This section applies only to UNIX users. Windows users should simply use their standard operating system printer setup windows, then continue to *Setup and Printing for All Operating Systems* on page 79.

How to Print Right Now

StarOffice and OpenOffice.org automatically install the "Generic Printer" and it usually works right away. If you haven't tested printing yet, just print a Writer document to your Generic Printer (choose File > Print) and see what happens. If it prints and makes you happy, and that's all you need, ignore the rest of this chapter. If it doesn't work, see *Setting Up a New Printer With an Existing or Imported Driver* on page 61 or set up a new printer following the directions in *Setting Up a New Printer With an Existing or Imported Driver* on page 61.

Converting StarOffice 5.2 UNIX Printers

Use the printer administration tool `spadmin` to take all your 5.2 printers and bring them into 6.0. It's in the directory of your new installation.

Once you've finished, use the other procedures in this section to double-check the properties for your converted printers. The setup windows and names of options have changed dramatically from 5.2. It's all for the better, much simpler and easier, but it's a good idea to check nonetheless.

1   After installing StarOffice 6.0 or OpenOffice.org 1.0, start the `spadmin` application.

2   Click the New Printer button at the bottom of the window that appears.

3   In the window that apears, select the last option in the option list, then click Next.

4   The tool will convert all 5.2 printers, then display them. See Figure 4-1.

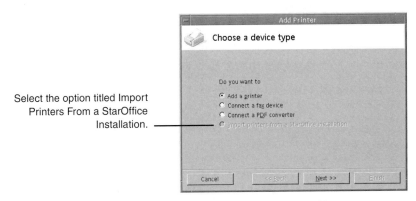

Select the option titled Import Printers From a StarOffice Installation.

Figure 4-1 Main window of New Printer Device AutoPilot

Setting Up a New Printer With an Existing or Imported Driver

The program automatically sets itself up with a Generic Printer that prints to your computer's default printer. You should be fine to print using that printer; if you aren't, follow these steps to specify the right printer.

Note – Whatever you do, don't delete the Generic Printer. You'll need it in order to just open, much less print, files that were created with older versions of StarOffice, or otherwise just think that they need a Generic Printer in order to just exist on your system. This doesn't make much sense, but it's true nonetheless. In addition, the Generic Printer is what's used to print to a file (PostScript).

---

1 Start the spadmin tool in the StarOffice 6.0 or OpenOffice.org 1.0 directory. The window in Figure 4-2 will appear.

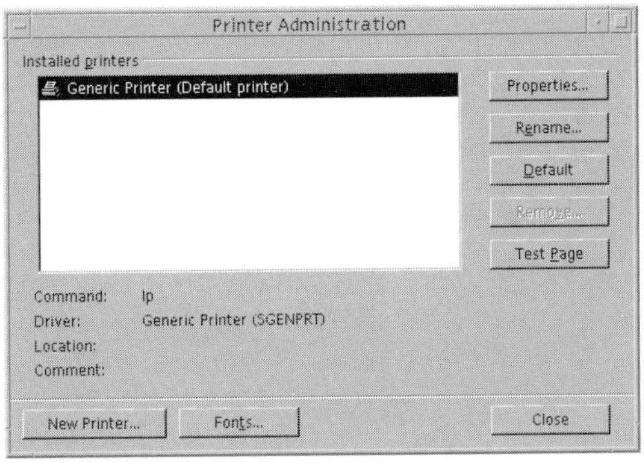

Figure 4-2 Main printer administration window

2 Click New Printer.

3 The window in Figure 4-3 will appear. Keep Add a printer selected and click Next.

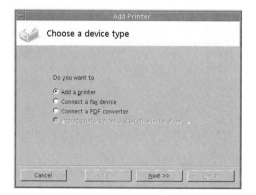

Figure 4-3   Choosing to create a new printer

4 The window in Figure 4-4 will appear. Select the appropriate driver and click Next. If the driver you want isn't there, click Import and locate the directory where the driver is, then select it again when it appears in Figure 4-4. Click Next.

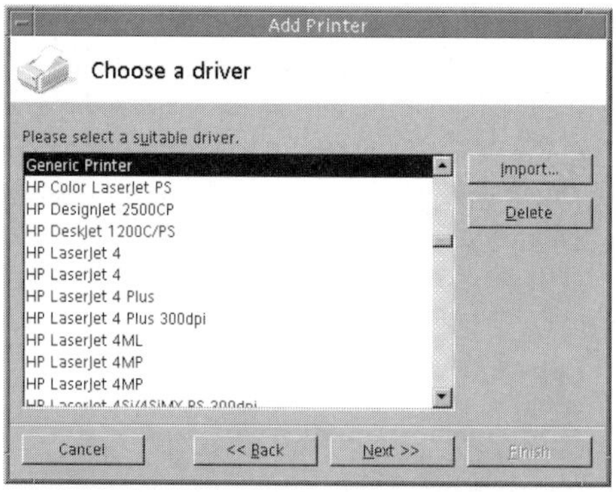

Figure 4-4   Selecting or importing a printer driver

5 The window in Figure 4-5 will appear. Select the appropriate command line for the printer you want to print to and click Next.

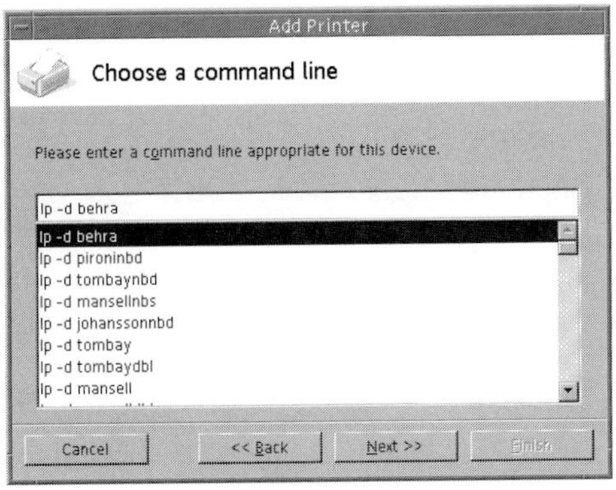

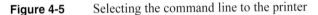

Figure 4-5   Selecting the command line to the printer

6   The window in Figure 4-6 will appear. Name the new printer and click Next.

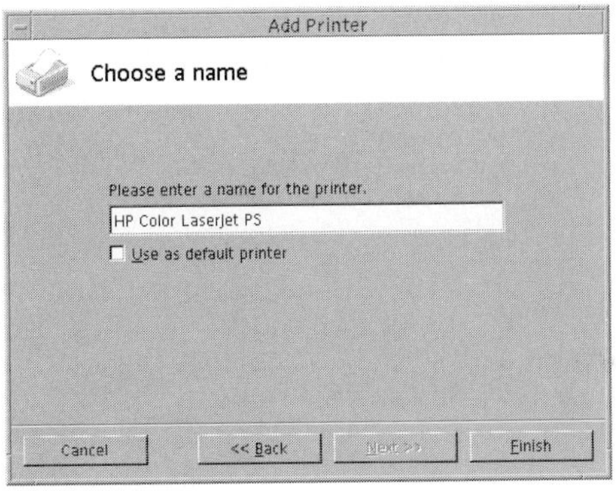

Figure 4-6   Name the printer

Setting Up a Duplex Printer or Making a Duplex Printer Print Single-Sided

If a printer can print duplex, it's almost certainly already set up to print duplex. This procedure points out the settings that control duplex printing, how to turn it off, and how to modify it to "tumble" or print duplex flip flopped from the usual way.

Be careful of the Create Single Print Jobs option in the Form Letter or Print Options window, for any application, when you print to a duplex printer. If this option is selected, each new print job will begin on a new page even if you are using a duplex printer. If this field is not checked then the first page of the second copy might be printed on the reverse side of the last page of the first copy, especially if there is an odd page number.

1   Start the `spadmin` tool in the StarOffice 6.0 or OpenOffice.org 1.0 directory. The window in Figure 4-7 will appear.

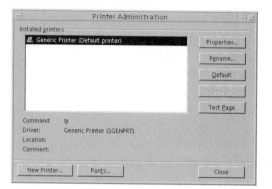

Figure 4-7   Main printer administration window

2   Select the printer you want to configure and click Properties. The window in Figure 4-8 will appear.

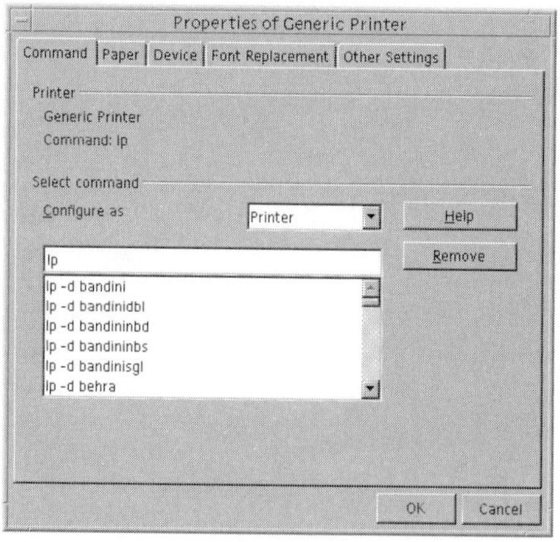

Figure 4-8   Printer properties

3   Select the Paper tab and click the Duplex dropdown list to see the duplex options (see Figure 4-9).

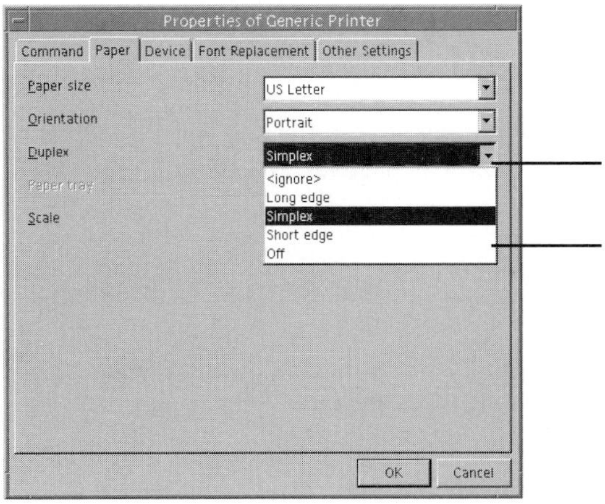

All options might not be available with all printers: Ignore and Simplex are usually available for all duplex-capable printers, however.

Ignore means use the default printer settings and ignore the program settings. Simplex and Long Edge are standard duplex (flips the image over the long edge), Short Edge flips the image over the short edge, similar to Duplex Tumble, and None means no duplex printing.

Figure 4-9   Selecting a queue (the duplex-enabled printer)

Figure 4-10 shows the differences between the two types.

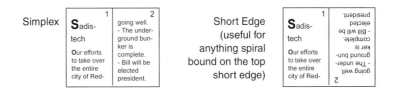

Figure 4-10   Difference between Simplex/Long Edge and Short Edge

The None option turns off duplexing so that each page is printed on a different sheet of paper. The Ignore option prints the page the same was as DuplexNoTumble (standard duplex printing).

4   Click OK to close the window and save changes.

Note – To turn the duplex feature on and off on the fly in Solaris and UNIX, choose File > Print and select the printer. Click the Properties button and in the Printer Properties window, click the Paper tab. From the Duplex list, select the option you want.

Setting Up General Printer Options

The Configure button lets you open the Printer Properties window, where you can set options like duplex printing, input trays, paper size and orientation, device information, and margins. (For duplex printing, see *Setting Up a Duplex Printer or Making a Duplex Printer Print Single-Sided* on page 63.) You don't have to enter information in this window; default values are set up for each window, and document-specific windows let you specify much of the same information. Those windows generally override anything you set here.

Note – For detailed information on how portrait and landscape printing really works, see *Specifying Portrait or Landscape Orientation* on page 86, as well as the printing procedure for each application.

1   Start the `spadmin` tool in the StarOffice 6.0 or OpenOffice.org 1.0 directory. The window in Figure 4-7 will appear.

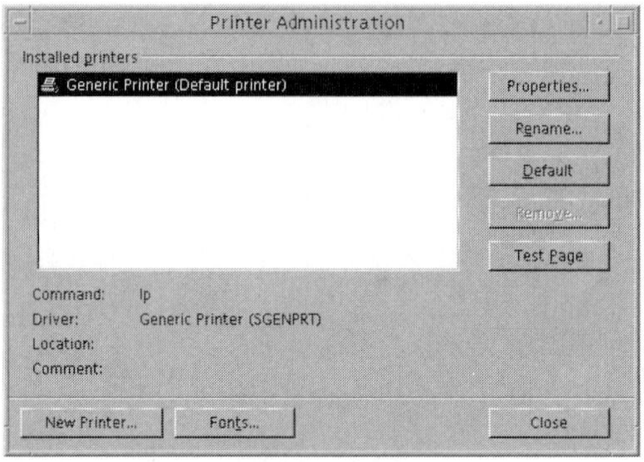

Figure 4-11   Main printer administration window

2   Select the printer you want to configure and click Properties.

3   Enter the appropriate information in the Paper, Device, and Additional settings tabs of the Printer properties window (Figure 4-12 through Figure 4-14).

Note – If you're using the generic printer driver, to support older PostScript printers select Level 1 under PostScript. Otherwise select Level 2. If your printer can only issue black and white output, set Grayscale under Color; otherwise set Color. If conversion under Grayscale leads to poor results, you can always set Color under Color and leave the conversion to the printer or PostScript emulator.

4   When you've finished, click OK.

Select the paper size you want as the default.

Select the page orientation you want as the default. (Document-specific page settings generally override whatever you set here.)

All options aren't available for all printers; make the appropriate selection here.

If you want to print using a scale other than 100%, enter the scale here.

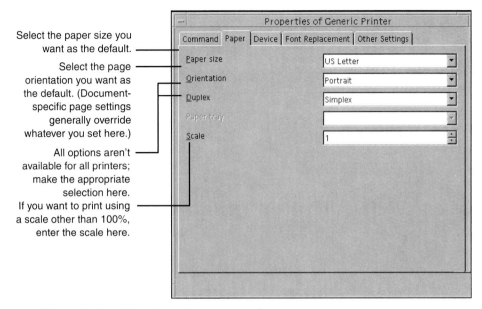

Figure 4-12   Entering printer paper options

Enter the margins you want for the printer. Document-specific margins override these settings.

Click Default to enter default margins for all four fields (shown).

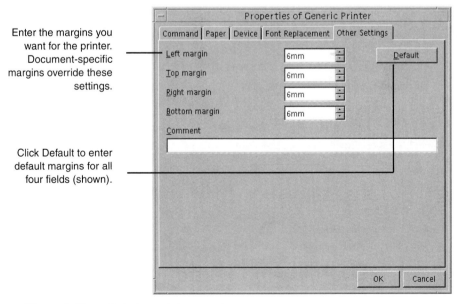

Figure 4-13   Entering printer margins

Select an item; the
corresponding options
are listed in the Current
value list.
Select a new value for
the item if necessary.

Select the type of color or
grayscale you want to
print with (that the printer
supports).

Enter the color depth you
want to use (that the
printer supports).

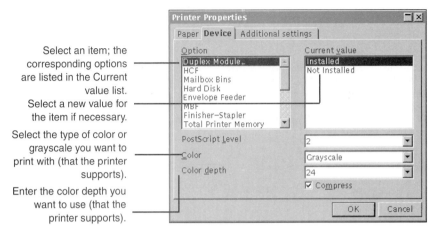

Figure 4-14   Entering printer device options

Changing the Displayed Name of a Printer

1   Open the Printer Setup window.

2   Select the printer, such as Generic Printer, in the Installed printers list.

3   Click Rename.

4   Enter a new name in the Install window and click OK.

Making a Printer Your Default Printer

Your default printer is the one a document is printed to when you click the Print File
Directly icon in the function bar.

1   Open the Printer Setup window.

2   Select the printer you want and click the Default Printer button.

Note – You can't remove a printer if it's your default printer.

Removing a Printer

If you don't want a printer in the list of available printers anymore, follow these steps.

1   Open the Printer Setup window.

2   If the printer is your default printer, select a different printer in the list and click
Default Printer. You can't remove your default printer.

3   Select the printer you want to remove and click Remove. Click Yes when prompted.

Setting Up Faxing Capabilities

You can fax documents directly from the program you're using, if you have a fax modem and have installed a fax driver. To fax, see *Faxing* on page 84.

1   Start the `spadmin` tool in the StarOffice 6.0 or OpenOffice.org 1.0 directory. The window in Figure 4-15 will appear.

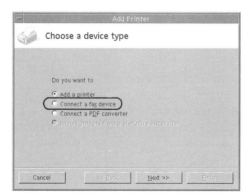

Figure 4-15   Main printer administration window

2   Click New Printer. The window in Figure 4-16 will appear. Choose to create a new fax connection and click Next.

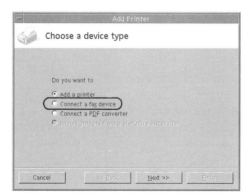

Figure 4-16   Choose to connect a fax device

3   The window in Figure 4-17 will appear. Select the default driver, or another driver. The windows you see next will depend on what you choose here.

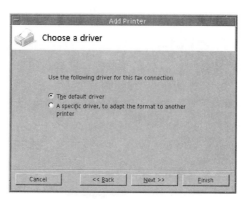

Figure 4-17   Choose the default driver or new driver

4   If you chose the default driver The window in Figure 4-18 will appear. The path you enter is entirely dependent on your system's fax capabilities. When you've entered it in the top field, click Next. Skip to step 6.

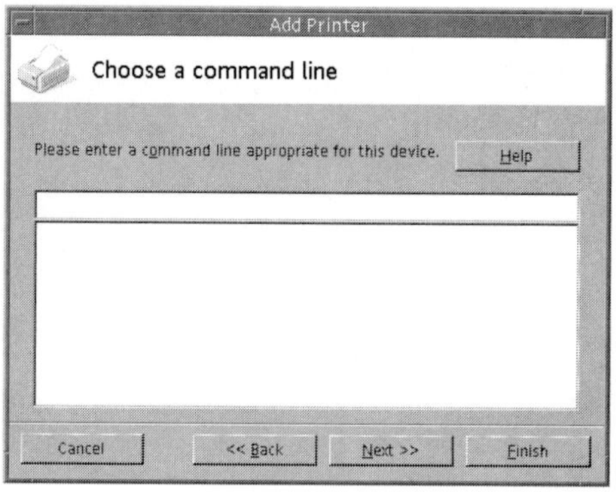

Figure 4-18   Enter a fax path window

5   If you chose to use another driver The window in Figure 4-19 will appear. Select the driver to use for the fax. If the right driver isn't there, click Import and point to the directory where the driver is located, then select it when it appears in Figure 4-19.

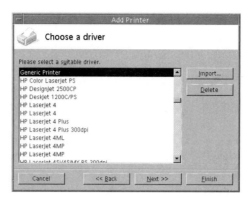

Figure 4-19   Choose a fax driver window

Click Next. The window in Figure 4-20 will appear. Enter the path and click Next, then continue to step 6.

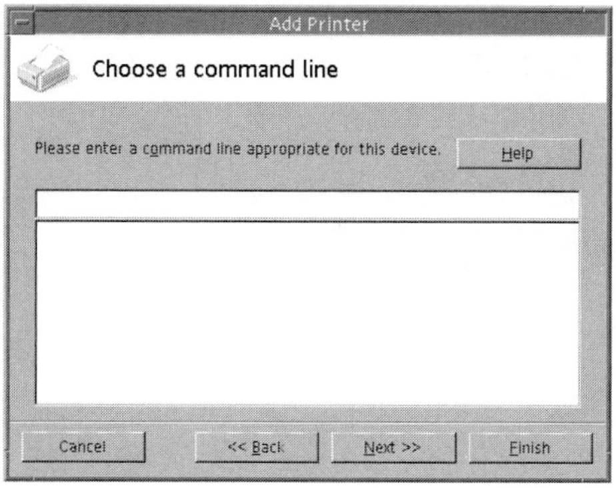

Figure 4-20   Enter a fax path window

6   Once you've specified the fax driver, either by using the default or selecting a specific one, the Choose a Name window will appear as shown in Figure 4-21. Name the fax and click Finish. The fax will be available in printer dropdown lists and in the main `spadmin` window.

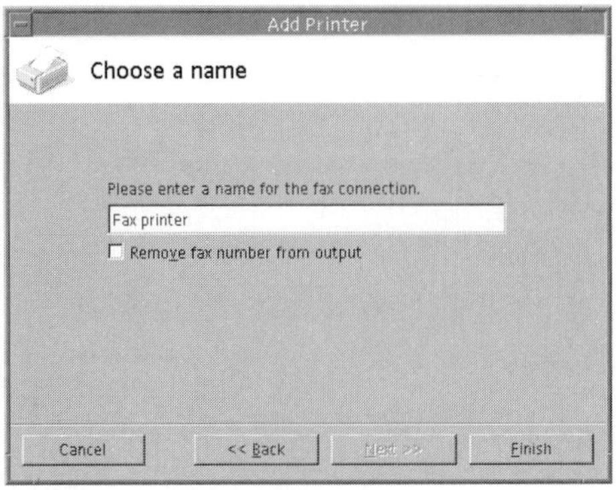

Figure 4-21   Name the fax connection

Setting Up Printing to PDF

You can print directly to PDF *if* you have GhostScript or a similar capability on your system. If you don't, skip this procedure and just print to PostScript (see *Considerations for Printing to PostScript or PDF* on page 81), and use Adobe Distiller to create a PDF from the PostScript file.

Note – On UNIX, and possibly in Windows, nothing remotely related to the program, whether your GhostScript application or the program itself or your data sources, should be installed in a directory with a space in it. So if you're having problems, make sure nothing you're using is in C:\Program Files, for instance.

---

1   Start the spadmin tool in the StarOffice 6.0 directory; see Figure 4-22.

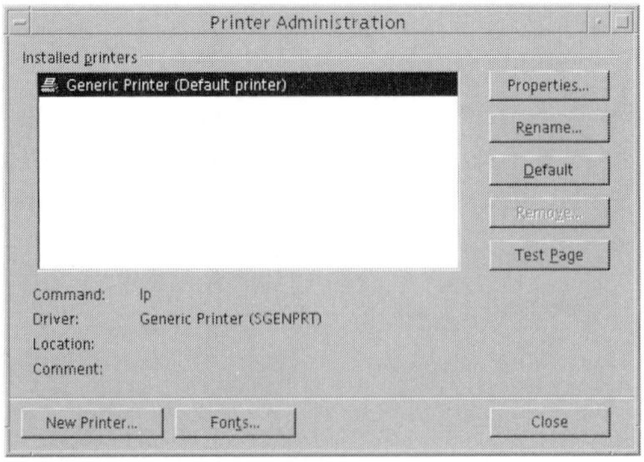

Figure 4-22   Main printer administration window

2   Click New Printer. The window in Figure 4-23 will appear.

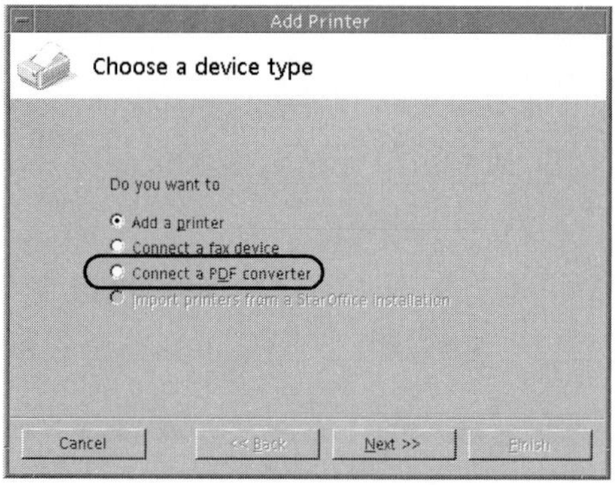

Figure 4-23 Add Printer window — Choose a device type, with "Connect a PDF converter" circled

Figure 4-23   Choose to connect a PDF converter

3   The window in Figure 4-24 will appear. Choose the default, Distiller, or another driver. The windows you see next will depend on what you choose here. Click Next.

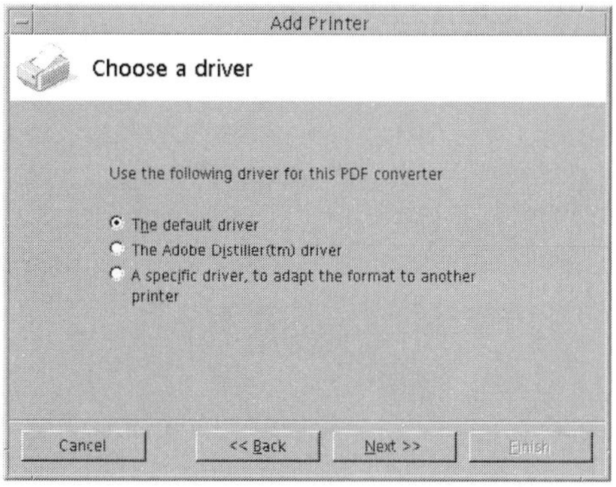

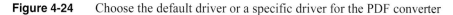

Figure 4-24 Add Printer window — Choose a driver for the PDF converter

Figure 4-24   Choose the default driver or a specific driver for the PDF converter

4   If you chose the default driver or Distiller The window in Figure 4-25 will appear. The path you enter is entirely dependent on your system's PDF capabilities. When you've entered it in the top field, click Next. Skip to step 6.

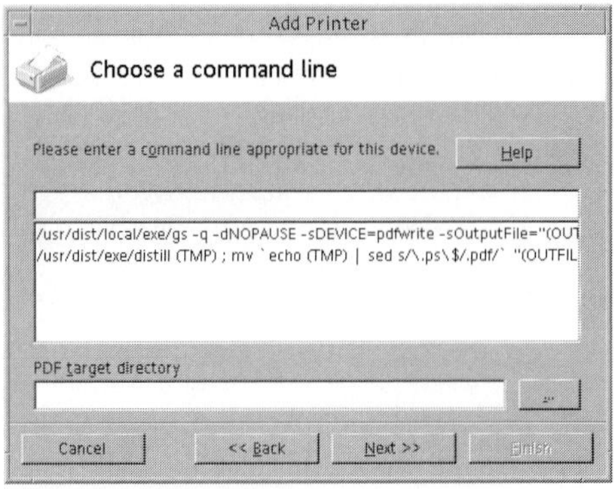

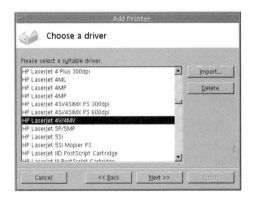

Figure 4-25   Enter a PDF converter path window

5   If you chose another driver The window in Figure 4-26 will appear. Select the driver and click Next.

Figure 4-26   Enter a PDF converter path window

In Figure 4-27, enter the path to the PDF writer and click Next. Continue to step 6.

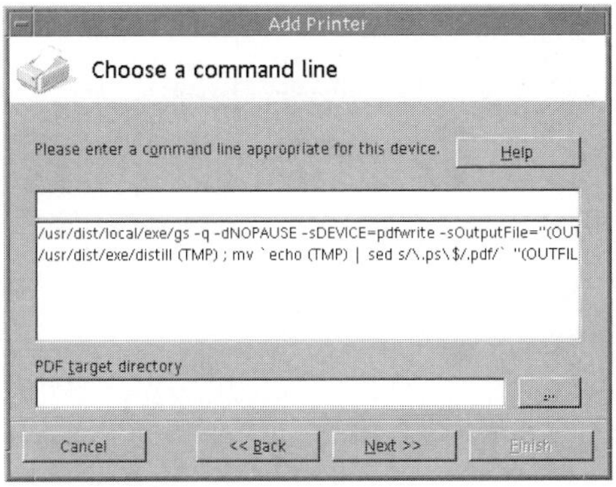

Figure 4-27   Enter a PDF converter path window

6   Once you've specified a driver by either means, the window in Figure 4-28 will appear. Name the PDF writer and click Finish. The PDF writer will be available in printer dropdown lists and in the main spadmin window.

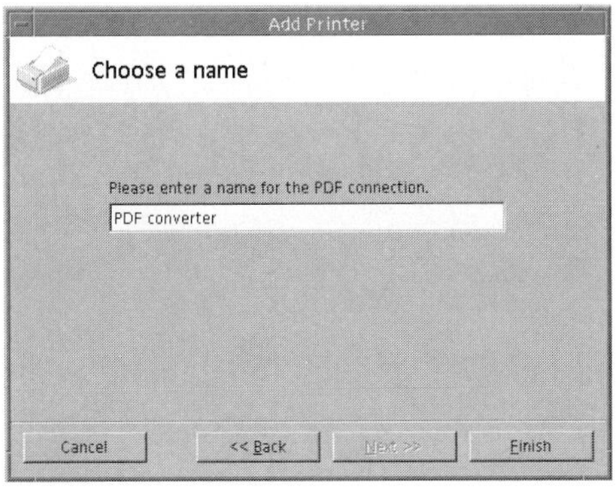

Figure 4-28   Name the PDF converter

Adding Fonts

Note – StarOffice 6.0 works best with the PC truetype fonts.

1   Start the spadmin tool in the StarOffice 6.0 or OpenOffice.org 1.0 directory; the tool is shown in Figure 4-29.

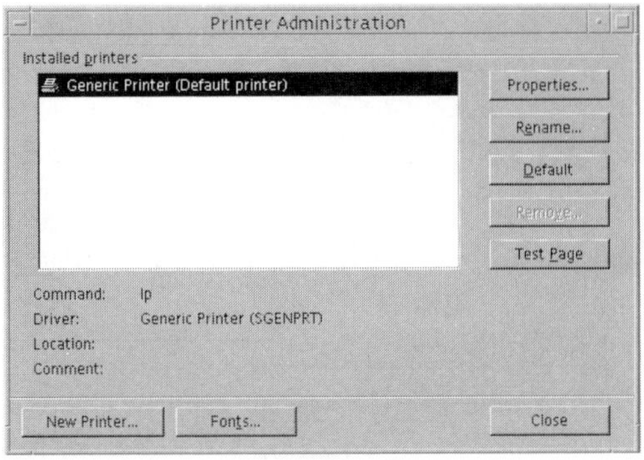

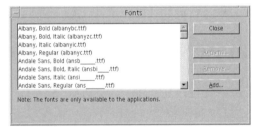

Figure 4-29   Main printer and font administration window

2   Click the Fonts button; the Fonts window (Figure 4-30) will appear.

Figure 4-30   Fonts display and adding window

3   Click Add and chose the location of the fonts.

Setting Up Per-Printer Font Substitution

See also the font substitution instructions in *Setting up Program-Wide Font Substitution* on page 78. Any setting you create in this procedure overrides a conflicting setting in the Options window.

1   Start the spadmin tool in the StarOffice 6.0 or OpenOffice.org 1.0 directory; the tool is shown in Figure 4-31.

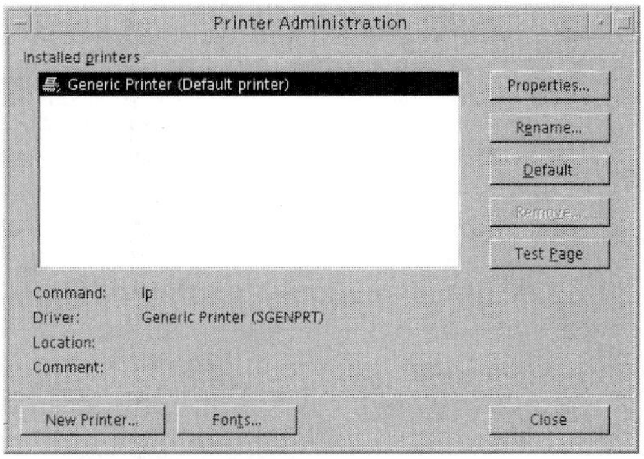

Figure 4-31   Main printer and font administration window

2   Click the Properties button and select the Font Replacement tab; the window in Figure 4-32 will appear.

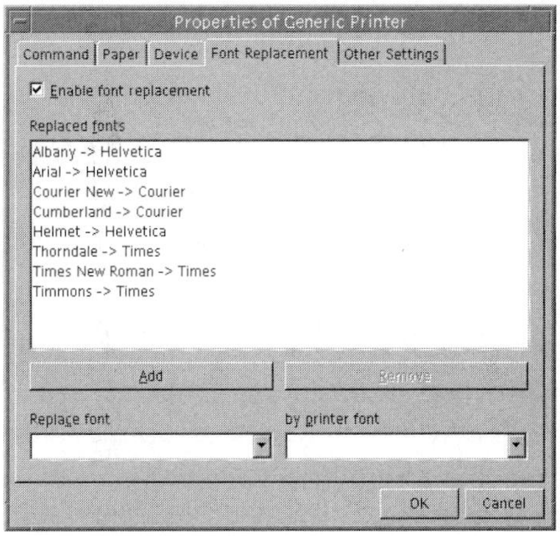

Figure 4-32   Font substitution

3   Select a font from the left dropdown list, and the font you want the printer to use from the right dropdown list, as shown in Figure 4-33. Then click Add.

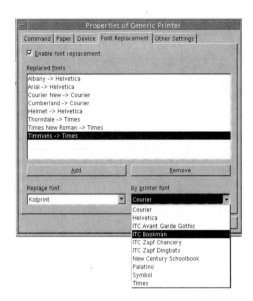

Figure 4-33   Entering a font substituion

Setting up Program-Wide Font Substitution

Note – This procedure is overridden by settings in *Setting Up Per-Printer Font Substitution* on page 76. However, this procedure applies to all applications and all printers; the UNIX setup can be done per printer.

The font substitution appears to let you substitute one font for another onscreen and have it print normally; or have the substitution take place all the time (onscreen and printing). However, the way it works is that you can either substitute some of the fonts all of the time, or none of the fonts none of the time (i.e., the Screen only setting doesn't work).

1   Choose Tools > Options > StarOffice > Font Replacement or Tools > Options > OpenOffice.org > Font Replacement.

2   Select the appropriate original font and the font to substitute, as shown in Figure 4-34.

3   Click the green check mark.

4   Select the Apply Replacement table checkbox.

5   Select the Always checkbox next to the newly added substitution.

6   Click OK.

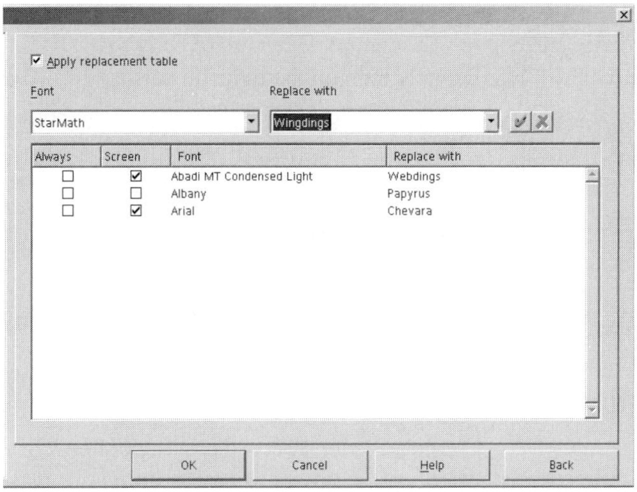

Figure 4-34   Setting up font substitutions

Removing Font Replacement

Use this procedure to delete a font replacement.

1   Select Tools > Options > *program* > Font Replacement.

2   In the list of replacements, select the replacement you want to remove and click the red X button.

3   Click OK.

If you want to leave font substitution information intact but disabled, deselect the Apply replacement table option and click OK.

Setup and Printing for All Operating Systems

Before you begin, add any printers you want, configure them, and set printer options. If you're using UNIX, follow the directions in the previous section, *Creating UNIX Printers* on page 60. If you're using Windows, refer to your operating system documentation.

Standard Printing

As with most things in this office suite, there's a quick way and a more controlled way; we've covered them both.

Quick Printing

You can print one copy of your entire document directly to the default printer by clicking the Print File Directly icon on the function bar.

To specify your default printer, see *Making a Printer Your Default Printer* on page 68.

Printing Using the Print Window

1 Choose File > Print.

2 In the Print window (Figure 4-35), enter the appropriate options.

3 Click Properties if you need to set or verify printer-specific options. These options are covered in *Setting Up General Printer Options* on page 65.

4 Click Options to enter application-specific printing options. See the printing information for the application you're using for more information.

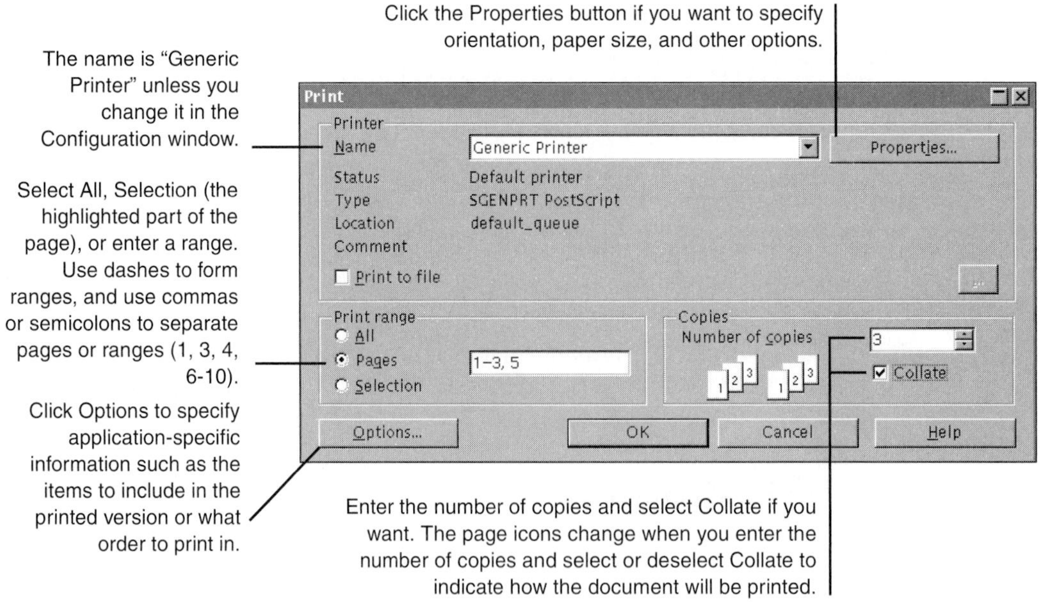

Click the Properties button if you want to specify orientation, paper size, and other options.

The name is "Generic Printer" unless you change it in the Configuration window.

Select All, Selection (the highlighted part of the page), or enter a range. Use dashes to form ranges, and use commas or semicolons to separate pages or ranges (1, 3, 4, 6-10).

Click Options to specify application-specific information such as the items to include in the printed version or what order to print in.

Enter the number of copies and select Collate if you want. The page icons change when you enter the number of copies and select or deselect Collate to indicate how the document will be printed.

Figure 4-35 Specifying options using the Print window

5 Select what to print: All (the entire document), Range (a range of slides or pages), or Selection (the currently selected text or graphics). Use dashes to form ranges, and use commas or semicolons to separate pages or ranges (1, 3, 4, 6-10).

> **Note –** The program defaults to Selection, rather than All or Range, if anything in the document is selected. Check this each time you print.

6   Enter the number of copies and, if it's two or more, choose whether to collate.

7   Click OK to print. A message will appear, stating the name of the printer that the document is being printed to.

If you have problems printing, check to be sure the margins and orientation are set correctly, especially in Draw and Impress. (Choose Format > Page and select the Page tab.) In addition, make sure you've selected the right paper format, such as Letter. See Figure 4-36.

Make a selection here appropriate for the country where you're located (User format can cause problems; select a different format for best results.)

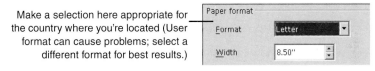

Figure 4-36   Selecting the right paper format

Printing to PostScript and PDF

Considerations for Printing to PostScript or PDF

You can print to either of the following:

- PostScript – Many Solaris and Linux users can read PostScript files; a common file-reading application is GhostScript.

- Adobe's Acrobat PDF – A very widely used, portable file format with low storage size requirements. In order to turn PostScript files into PDF files, you need the Adobe Acrobat product.

Solaris tip If you're on a network in Solaris, you can use the following command to see if Distiller is available: `which distill` If you have Distiller, you can create PDFs from PostScript files by typing `distill filename.ps`.

Just get a printer driver You don't need an actual PostScript printer to print to a PostScript file. You just need the printer driver installed on your system. There's a lot of good information on PostScript print drivers on the Adobe Web site: `http://www.adobe.com`.

Windows printer driver If you're using Windows, you can install the HP LaserJet 4V/4MV PostScript printer and set the Print to File option for it. (See your Windows documentation if you need help installing printers.) This is a good print driver for producing PostScript files. If your PostScript files end up in grayscale and you want to print in color or display the document electronically with color (as in a PDF file), go to

`http://www.adobe.com`. The windows version is at `http://www.adobe.com/`
`support/downloads/product.jsp?product=pdrv&platform=win`

No directory name spaces On UNIX, and sometimes in Windows, nothing remotely
related to the program, whether your GhostScript application or the program itself or your
data sources, should be installed in a directory with a space in it. So if you're having
problems, make sure nothing you're using is in `C:\Program Files`, for instance.

Printing to a PostScript File in Any Operating System

Follow these steps to print a PostScript file. Once you've created it, refer to the
documentation from Adobe or use the appropriate program to create a PDF file.

1   Install the PostScript printer driver according to the installation instructions that were
    included with it. (In Solaris and Linux, all printers are PostScript.)

2   Choose File > Print to print the document.

3   Select the PostScript printer in your list of printers, and select the Print to file option,
    as shown in Figure 4-37.

To print to a file, select
the Print to file option and
enter the path and the file
name, **with a .ps**
extension.

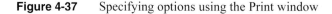

Figure 4-37   Specifying options using the Print window

4   When you select the Print to file option, a window is displayed to let you name and
    select the path for the PostScript file that will be printed. When you name the file, be
    sure to give it a `.ps` file extension. The default might be .prn; if so change it to .ps.

5   Click OK to print.

    A message will appear, stating the name of the printer that the document is being
    printed to. This is fine; the document will still be printed to a file.

Note – If you have problems printing to a file, switch printers and try again.

Printing to a PDF File in UNIX

This depends on what software you have on your system.

- You can simply print to the PDF device you set up in *Setting Up Printing to PDF* on page 72.
- If you have Adobe Distiller, print to a PostScript file then turn it into a PDF using Distiller, or print directly to PDF using the Adobe PDF driver.

Printing to PDF in Windows

Typically, print to a PostScript file, then use the appropriate program to print to PDF, or print directly to PDF using the Adobe PDF driver.

Printing Mail Merges and Other Documents Based on Data Sources

To print a document containing data from a data source, such as a holiday newsletter mail merge, you can't just choose File > Print. Instead, choose File > Form Letter, specify the data source you're using and where to print it, then click OK. See *Printing* on page 399 for more information.

Note – Printing envelopes doesn't work on Windows. Just use labels. See *Creating Simple Labels or Business Cards by Choosing File > New* on page 370.

Printing From the Command Line

Open a terminal window and specify the application (Writer, Calc, etc.) and the file name. Make sure they match type; for instance, printing a Draw file and specifying Calc won't work.

UNIX

1   In a terminal window, move to the installed program's `program` directory.

    If it's not on your local machine, enter the full path to the network's `program` directory, such as

    `/usr/distr/shared/staroffice6.0/program`

2   Enter the following command:

    `module -print fullpath_tofile.fileextension`

    So for a Writer document, the command would be this locally:

    `swriter -print customerlist.sxw`

And this if you are using the client installation of a multiuser system:

```
/usr/distr/shared/staroffice6.0/program/swriter -print customerlist.sxw
```

The module names are `swriter`, `simpress`, `scalc`, and `sdraw`.

3 Files will be printed to the default printer for your installation.

Windows

Figure 4-38 shows how the Run window should look to print a StarOffice Writer document. The steps provide more detail.

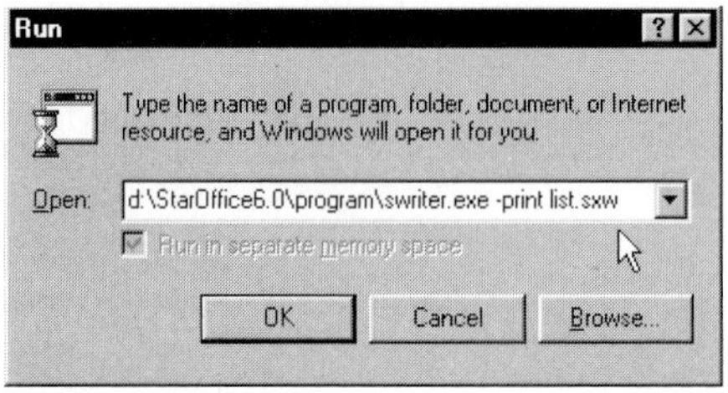

Figure 4-38   Printing a Writer document from Run window

1 Open a terminal window or choose Start > Run. Type the full path, locally or on the network, to the `soffice.exe` file, such as `C:\StarOffice6.0\program`

2 After that path, type the following command:

module -print *fullpathtofile.fileextension*

So for a StarOffice Writer document, the command would be like this locally:

```
C:\StarOffice6.0\swriter.exe -print customerlist.sxw
```

And like this if you are using the client installation of a multiuser system:

```
H:\sharedfiles\staroffice6.0\program\swriter.exe -print customerlist.sxw
```

The module names are `swriter.exe`, `simpress.exe`, `scalc.exe`, and `sdraw.exe`.

3 Files will be printed to the default printer for your installation.

Faxing

If you have a fax modem connected to your computer, you can fax your current document directly from your computer. To set up faxing in Solaris or Linux, see *Setting Up Faxing Capabilities* on page 69; in Windows, use the tools provided with your operating system.

Creating a Cover Letter Using Autopilot or a Template

You can use Autopilot and the program's templates to create a Writer fax cover sheet for one recipient or many. See *Creating Documents From a Fax Template* on page 392 and *Creating a Fax Using the Fax AutoPilot* on page 385.

Faxing Any Document

Faxing one document that doesn't contain data source fields Typically, you should be able to just choose File > Print and select the fax driver in the Name list. Refer to the documentation included with your fax modem for more information. Some fax software, however, requires you to enter the phone number; refer to your fax software documentation for more information.

Faxing documents containing data source fields See *Printing* on page 399.

Program-Wide Print Setup Options

The settings you make for a printer generally trump anything else if they conflict. However, this isn't usually the case. You'll want to take a look at the print options under the Tools menu, as well.

1   Start the program by choosing Start > Programs > *program* > *document_type* or by double-clicking the StarOffice6 or OpenOffice.org icon in your installed program directory.

2   Choose Tools > Options > Print and enter the appropriate options. These are covered in the printing chapter for the application you're using.

Substituting One Font for Another

Note – UNIX users, see also *Setting Up Per-Printer Font Substitution* on page 76. This procedure applies to all applications and all printers; the UNIX setup can be done per printer. It also overrides any conflicting substitutions you've set up here.

The font substitution appears to let you substitute one font for another onscreen and have it print normally; or have the substitution take place all the time (onscreen and printing). However, the way it works is that you can either substitute some of the fonts all of the time, or none of the fonts none of the time (i.e. the Screen only setting doesn't work).

1   Choose Tools > Options > *program* > Font Replacement.

2   Select the appropriate original font and the font to substitute, as shown in Figure 4-39.

3   Click the green check mark.

4   Select the Apply Replacement table checkbox.

5   Select the Always checkbox next to the newly added substitution.

6   Click OK.

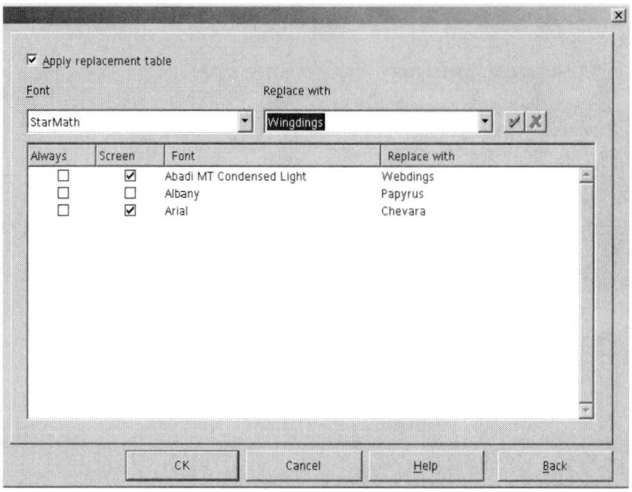

Figure 4-39   Setting up font substitutions

Page Layout Setup Options

This section covers everything to do with what happens inside the page margins. If you're having problems getting printing to happen how you want, the answer is probably in one of the following sections.

Specifying Portrait or Landscape Orientation

There are a lot of places you can set page orientation (portrait or landscape). It can get a little confusing, so we've provided Table 4-1 to show you (all in one place) where you can go to set document and printer margins.

Table 4-1   Orientation-setting windows

Window	Navigation	Book section/Notes
Print Options (for Page Preview mode) These settings are used only if you print using the Print icon in the Page Preview window.	In Calc, Writer, and Web with Print Layout on, choose File > Page Preview. Click the Print options page view icon.	Calc: Chapter 24, *Printing in Calc*, on page 625 Writer and Web: *Printing Multiple Pages With Page Preview* on page 432

Table 4-1   Orientation-setting windows

Window	Navigation	Book section/Notes
Page Style Overrides any setting in the Printer Properties window.	In Writer, Web, Draw, Calc, and Impress, choose Format > Page.	Calc: Chapter 24, *Printing in Calc*, on page 625 Writer and Web: Figure 7-37 on page 228 Draw: *Page Setup* on page 759 Impress: *Specifying Landscape or Portrait Orientation* on page 747
Printer Properties Is overridden by anything in the Format > Page window.	In Linux and Solaris, open the Printer Installation window (double-click the Printer Setup icon), then click Configure. On all platforms, choose File > Printer Setup, select a printer and click Properties. Select the Paper tab.	*Setting Up General Printer Options* on page 65
Page Setup Determines page size, orientation, paper	All; choose Format > Page	When you switch between orientations, the paper setup can change.In general it should be either letter or A4.

Setting Margins

You can set the margins for each printer in Printer Setup (Figure 4-13 on page 67). However, most of the same windows that let you set orientation let you set margins, as well (for most applications, choose Format > Page and click the Page tab). Those settings generally override anything in the Printer Setup window.

The margin information for printers sets the maximum possible area for printing; margin information for documents can set margins within those bounds, but not outside. Keep track of the margin options for both, when you print.

If you're using headers and footers, keep in mind that those need to be within the printer margins, as well.

Note – In Draw and Impress, the margin settings occasionally go crazy and provide defaults for new documents that just aren't usable. Be sure to check margins in all documents, but in Draw and Impress in particular, if you're having problems getting the results you want.

Fitting Multiple Pages Onto One Sheet

The program provides brochure printing, handout printing, and page preview features. Use the following cross-references to find the information you need.

Table 4-2   Printing multiple pages on one sheet

Feature	Application	Navigation	Book Section	Comments
Switch to multiple columns*	Web, Writer	Format > Page, click the Columns tab.	*Setting Up Multicolumn Pages* on page 230.	*While not strictly speaking a two-page-per-sheet feature, this is a good way of taking an existing document and making it fit onto a page differently.
Brochure printing	Web, Writer, Impress, Draw	File > Print > Options	*Printing Brochures* on page 90	A bit cantankerous, and squishes the text smaller. In general, use Landscape orientation.
Handouts (similar to Page Preview)	Impress (Draw files are easily adaptable to Impress files)	Click the Handout icon on the right side of the work area	*Creating Slide Handouts* on page 729	Very dependable and customizable.
Page Preview (similar to Handouts)	Calc, Writer, Web	Calc: File > Page Preview Writer: File > Page Preview Web: File > Page Preview when Print Layout is activated	Calc: Figure 24-6 on page 632 Writer and Web: *Printing Multiple Pages With Page Preview* on page 432	Similar to brochure printing: squishes the text size, and whatever you do, choose Landscape layout. Just not all that good a feature.
Tile	Draw, Impress	File > Print > Options or Tools > Options > Drawing/ Presentation > Print	See *Printing Options Setup* on page 846.	Be sure that your page size is smaller than the page size of the paper you'll print on, or it'll only fit once and no tiling will occur.

Fitting a Document Onto One Page

The program provides different ways for you to "scrunch" data that overflows one page so that it will print using only one sheet of paper.

Table 4-3   Information for fitting a document onto one page

Feature	Application	Navigation	Book Section
Page Setup	Calc	Calc: Format > Page > Sheet	Chapter 24, *Printing in Calc*, on page 625
Fit to size	Draw, Impress	File > Print > Options	Draw: *Printing Options Setup* on page 846 Impress: *Setting Printing Options* on page 747
Scale	Printer setup	File > Print, click Properties	*Setting Up General Printer Options* on page 65

Note – In Draw or Impress, you'll be prompted if a slide won't fit onto the page. See *Selecting an Option in the Print Warning Window* on page 96.

Printing Left or Right Pages, or in Reversed Order

If your printer prints pages backwards, instead of starting at 1, you can print from Web and Writer in reversed order.

You can also print only the left, or only the right, pages from Writer.

1   Choose Tools > Options > *application* > Print, or by choosing File > Print > Options.

> **Note –** If you use the first navigation option, all subsequent documents will have the settings you apply in step 2. If you use the second navigation method, the settings will apply only to the document you're currently working with.

2   Select the Left pages, Right pages (Writer only), or Reversed options.

Specifying Print Settings for Bitmaps, Transparency, and Color/Grayscale

Ironically, it can take more time and memory to print transparent graphics than regular ones. (To make a graphic transparent, select it in Draw and choose Format > Area > Transparency, or select a bitmap in any application and when the raster toolbar appears, go to the far right and adjust the transparency in the Transparency field.)

You can also set options that make graphics grayscale, and other features shown in Figure 4-40. Choose Tools > Options > Print and make the appropriate selections.

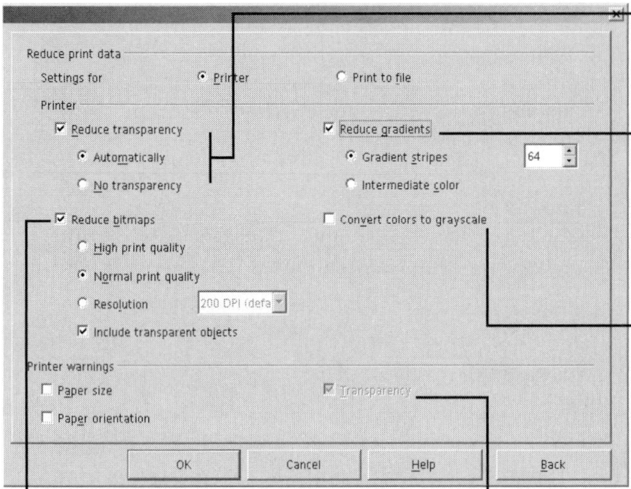

Select **Reduce Transparency** so your machine and printer don't have to deal with the extra work involved in printing a semi transparent object.

Automatically—Object is printed only if object covers more than a quarter of the page

No transparency—Object just isn't printed.

If you're using gradients, you can reduce how granular the printing is by selecting Reduce Gradients.

Gradient Stripes—The maximum number of stripes to print between the beginning and end color.

Intermediate Color—Only one intermediate color, rather than many stripes, is printed between beginning and end color.

Select **Convert Colors to Grayscale** to print all colored objects only in grayscale.

Transparency ensures that you're tipped off when you print that there are transparent objects in the document. The message lets you ignore the transparent objects, or go ahed and print them, which takes longer if you haven't reduced transparent printing time using the options in this window.

Select this option to print bitmaps with reduced quality.
High—300 DPI; **Normal**—200 DPI.
Resolution—Specify a resolution in the corresponding field. You can only specify a lower resolution than your printer can handle.
Include transparent objects—If marked the settings under Reduce Bitmaps apply to transparent objects, too.

Figure 4-40   Selecting graphics print options

Printing Brochures

In Impress, Draw, Web, and Writer, you can print a a document so that it can be made into a brochure. When the pages of the printed brochure are folded in half and stapled, there are two slides on each side of each page, and they're in the correct order for a brochure. Two pages are printed on each sheet of paper. (You'll need to change the paper size in Page Setup to fit the document onto letter-size paper; see the procedure for tips on setting margins.)

How Brochure Printing Works

Here's how brochure printing works for an eight-page brochure, if you're not using a duplex printer.

- Select Brochure and print Right or Front only to a single-sided printer – The program prints pages 8, 1, 6, and 3, in that order, on two sheets of paper.

- Select Brochure and print Left or Back only to a single-sided printer – The program prints pages 2, 7, 4, and 5, in that order, on two sheets of paper.

- Select Brochure and print both front and back to a tumbled duplex printer – The program prints 8, 1, 2, 7, 6, 3, 4, and 5, on two sheets of paper.

Figure 4-41 shows what the output would look like for a portrait document printed in Draw or Impress.

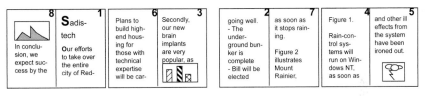

Figure 4-41   Brochure output for a portrait document in Draw or Impress

Figure 4-42 shows what the output would look like for a landscape document.

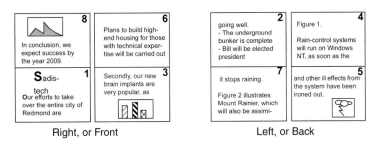

Figure 4-42   Brochure output for a landscape document

Figure 4-43 shows what happens in Writer and Web for landscape or portrait orientation.

The fun thing about printing brochures is that it works two or three different ways, among four applications. Both applications print the pages in the same order, as shown in Figure 4-41 and Figure 4-42, but the page dimensions are different. The brochure is one-fourth the size of the original document. the program shrinks the font and page dimensions so that you only print on half of a letter-sized piece of paper, as shown at right, but doesn't turn the page 90 degrees, as it should.

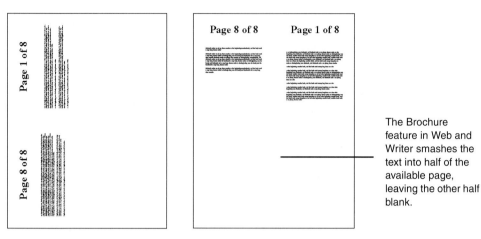

Page 1 of 8
Page 8 of 8
Page 8 of 8
Page 1 of 8
The Brochure feature in Web and Writer smashes the text into half of the available page, leaving the other half blank.

Figure 4-43 Brochure output in Web and Writer, landscape and portrait

Before You Begin

Note on brochures in Web You're better off having a duplex-capable printer, or else you're printing two copies of every brochure. See *Setting Up a Duplex Printer or Making a Duplex Printer Print Single-Sided* on page 63 for more information.

Setup for Draw and Impress You'll need to modify the page size, then adjust the content as necessary to fit within the smaller page size.

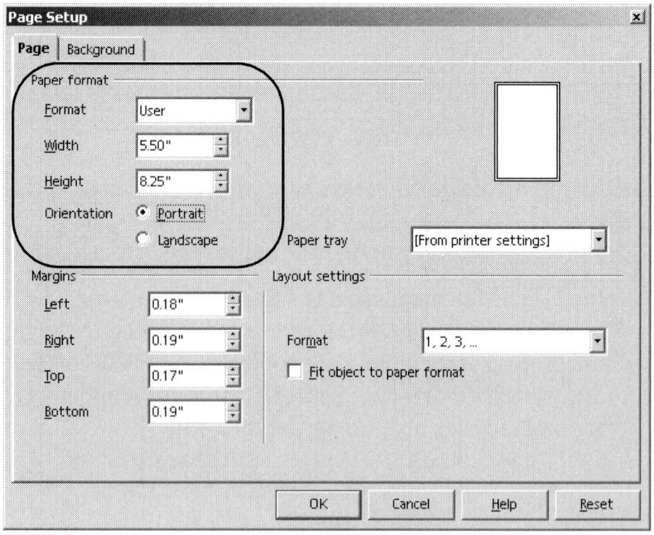

For a **portrait** document, width should be half the long side of the paper you're printing to. For **landscape**, width should be the same as the short side.
For a **portrait** document, height should be the same as the short side of the paper you're printing to. For **landscape**, height should be half the long side.
Page Setup
Page
Background
Paper format
Format
User
Width
5.50"
Height
8.25"
Orientation
Portrait
Landscape
Paper tray
[From printer settings]
Margins
Left
0.18"
Right
0.19"
Top
0.17"
Bottom
0.19"
Layout settings
Format
1, 2, 3, ...
Fit object to paper format
OK
Cancel
Help
Reset

Figure 4-44 Draw and Impress: Page setup for a brochure

If you print without changing the margins, you'll end up with only 2/3 of the contents of the odd pages. Choose Format > Page and select the Page tab. From the Paper format list, select User paper size and enter dimensions in the Width and Height fields below it. Figure 4-44 illustrates the settings for a portrait document printed on letter-size paper.

Printing the Brochure on a Duplex Printer

1   Choose File > Print.

2   Be sure your document margins and size are set up correctly, according to the setup instructions earlier in this section.

3   Be sure your duplex printer is set up correctly, according to Table 4-4. See *Setting Up a Duplex Printer or Making a Duplex Printer Print Single-Sided* on page 63 for more information.

Table 4-4   Duplex printing settings

Application	Orientation	Duplex setting
Writer, Web	Portrait	Simplex
	Landscape	Short Side
Draw and Impress	Portrait	Landscape
	Landscape	Landscape

4   In the Print window, click the Properties button. In the printer setup window, set the orientation to landscape or portrait, and select the correct paper size.

Note – It usually doesn't matter what you put in this window, but it does for brochures. The orientation and paper size must match what you specified in the page setup window for the document.

---

5   In the Print window, click Options.

6   Select the Brochure option and, if you're using Writer, Draw, or Impress, select the Front (or Right) option.

7   Click OK, then click OK again to print.

Printing the Brochure on a Single-Sided Printer

1   Choose File > Print.

2   Be sure your document margins and size are set up correctly, according to the setup instructions earlier in this section.

3   In the Print window, click the Properties button. In the printer setup window, set the orientation to landscape or portrait, and select the correct paper size.

> **Note** – It usually doesn't matter what you put in this window, but it does for bro-chures. The orientation and paper size must match what you specified in the page setup window for the document.

4   In the Print window, click Options.

5   Select the Brochure option and, if you're using Writer, Draw, or Impress, select the Front (or Right) option.

6   Click OK, then click OK again to print.

7   Put the printed pages into the printer, correct side up, and choose File > Print again.

> **Note** – If your printer prints cover sheets for every print job, add an extra sheet of paper on **top** of the sheets, or turn off cover sheets.

8   Click Properties again and make sure that the orientation and paper size are still correct.

9   Click Options again. In the Printer Options window, select Brochure again.

- If you're using Web, select Reversed
- If you're using Writer, Draw, or Impress, select Left (or Back)

10   Click OK, then click OK again to print.

11   If you're using Web, you now have two copies of the brochure. The odd sheets of paper (not pages) go together, and the even sheets of paper go together.

Commercial Print Setup

If you're sending out pages for printing, you'll want to check the colors, as well as potentially set up the document for a DocuTech.

Setting Up Pages for DocuTech 135 Signature Printing

If you're producing bound documents through a print shop, and the print shop has a Xerox DocuTech 135 printing machine, here's a trick that can ultimately save paper, give you a standard book size, and potentially reduce the time it takes to print and bind documents.

Using this trick only if it's acceptable that your bound documents be 7 inches wide by 8.5 inches tall (legal-size paper turned landscape and either cut in half or folded).

This trick also involves printing the document to a PostScript file. See *Considerations for Printing to PostScript or PDF* on page 81.

If you really want to impress the folks at the print shop, make your total page count divisible by 4.

1   Create left and right page styles using the **Letter 8.5 x 11 in** page format with **Portrait** orientation (Page Style window, Page tab).

2   Set the left and right page margins to the settings shown in Figure 4-45.

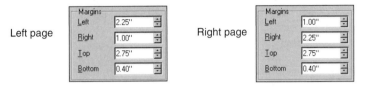

Left page   Right page

Figure 4-45   Setting left/right page margins for DocuTech signature printing

3   Print the document to a PostScript file using your PostScript printer driver.

4   Give the file to the print shop, and tell them you want it printed in one of the following ways:

•   Signature using legal-size paper; saddle-stitch binding. (This means folded in half and bound on the fold. Only use this if your document is less than 100 pages.)

•   Signature using legal-size paper; two-up binding (cut in half). (For spiral binding or perfect binding.)

Setting Up Colors for Commercial Printing

If you'll be printing high-quality color copies of a document, you should probably switch color models from RGB (red-green-blue, the model used by your monitor) to CMYK (cyan-magenta-yellow-black, the model used by commercial printers). Both palettes are included in the program, though RGB is the default. Here's how to switch to CMYK.

1   Choose Format > Area.

2   In the Area window, click the Colors tab.

3   Click Open.

4   Select CMYK from the Color sample list.

5   Click the Load Color List icon.

6   In the `config` folder, select the `cmyk.soc` file and click Open.

7   Assign CMYK colors to the document.

Uncommonly Used Setup Options

The program provides you with some of the most amazing options. We like the first one best. But hey, at least you can control the features.

Determining Whether Printing a Document Means Your Document Has Changed and Needs Saving

Ever bring up a document, touch *nothing* in it, print it, and get prompted to save it when you close it? Well, you can turn that off if you want. Choose Tools > Options > *program* > General and unmark the option titled Printing Sets Document Modified Status.

Managing Print Warnings

If your document doesn't match some of the restrictions or parameters for printing, the occasional warning will appear.

Setting Up Paper Size and Orientation Notifications

You can choose whether an error message should pop up when your document settings and printer settings don't match. You can have a warning for neither, one or both. The warning window is covered in *Selecting an Option in the Print Warning Window*.

The warning window also appears if you don't have these options marked, when the paper size and orientation match but the image is just too big for the output—for example, if you've drawn a rectangle that goes outside any of the page margins you've set for the document. But it doesn't hurt to have this additional level of protection; it can save you some frustration while you're finding out why your document isn't printing correctly.

1   Choose Tools > Options > General > Print.

2   Select the Paper size and/or Paper orientation options, then click OK.

  • Paper size (legal versus standard, for example) – If the current printer does not have the required paper size for the document, an error message will appear.

  • Paper orientation (landscape versus portrait) – If the printer cannot print using the orientation you've specified for the document, an error message will appear.

Selecting an Option in the Print Warning Window

If you set up the notification described in *Setting Up Paper Size and Orientation Notifications*, or if a slide won't fit the page setup options you've specified, the window in Figure 4-46 will appear when necessary.

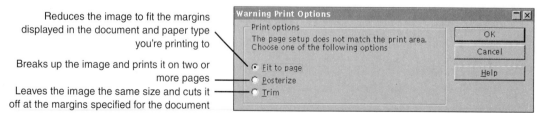

Reduces the image to fit the margins displayed in the document and paper type you're printing to

Breaks up the image and prints it on two or more pages

Leaves the image the same size and cuts it off at the margins specified for the document

Figure 4-46   Print Options warning window

Setup and Tips

Setting Up StarOffice and OpenOffice.org

Perhaps more than other applications, StarOffice and OpenOffice.org behavior is governed to a large extent by the setup options. These are found primarily under Tools > Options, as well as Tools > AutoCorrect/AutoFormat, and Tools > Configure, and various other nooks and crannies throughout the product.

Through knowing those nooks and crannies, you can control a huge amount of StarOffice behavior when you know where to look. And this is where to look.

So spend 15 minutes with this chapter. If not setting everything up then getting to know what's in here so you can tweak settings later if necessary. Be sure to check *Turning Off Annoying Features* on page 131 and *Controlling How StarOffice Changes Text and Does AutoCompletion* on page 124.

You don't need to understand every single feature to be proficient. However, if you know the stuff we cover in this chapter, you'll be a lot happier—and you'll be the one answering your friends' StarOffice or OpenOffice.org questions.

Note – Some of the program's options have different names than you might expect. For example, in order to "wrap" text in a spreadsheet cell, you need to select an option called "Line Break." In order to make the options clearer, we refer to them by their more conventional names. Instead of the four different terms that the program uses to describe the background of a presentation, for example, we just say "background," then direct you to the option with the non-traditional name.

OpenOffice.org

Some of the setup options' navigation in this chapter is listed as Tools > Options > StarOffice. If you're using OpenOffice.org, it's Tools > Options > OpenOffice.org instead. Most of the time, we just say "Tools > Options > *program* and you get to pick according to what you're using.

Note – This chapter covers setup options for features you can use throughout the program. For application-specific features, check the setup information for the application.

Getting Help

This section describes some of the more useful ways of finding help using the program.

Finding What You Need in this Book

One of the best things about StarOffice is that many of its features are shared. For example, you can insert spreadsheets and other objects like graphics in Writer, Impress, and other programs; drawing tools are available in Draw, Impress, Writer, and so on.

This means you have hundreds of features at your fingertips. However, it also means you might not be sure where to look for information on the topic. We generally cover major features like inserting objects in only one or two places. We use a lot of cross-references, but we don't cross-reference everything.

If you're looking for information on a feature in the chapter for your program and you can't find it, don't assume it's not in the book. It's probably just in another section, primarily here in this chapter. First and foremost we recommend you use the index.

Help and Help Agent

Help Agent is the context-sensitive online help system. Wherever you are in StarOffice (the context), Help Agent displays help for that specific context. *Turning Off the Help Agent* on page 132 shows you how to turn off Help Agent if it becomes annoying (because it pops up constantly).

But Help Agent can be useful—when you display it on your own terms—when you need it. Launch Help Agent by choosing Help > Help Agent. And of course by pressing F1 for regular help.

In general, the Help is pretty good. Use it; it'll help.

Controlling Tooltips

Tooltips are the pop-up labels that display when the mouse pointer hovers over a button or menu item. Tooltips are an excellent way to discover features and capabilities without having to consult a manual or the help system.

Basic tooltips display by default. You can also show more detailed (extended) tips, or turn tips off altogether. Just choose Help > Tips or Help > Extended Tips to toggle whether they're on or off.

Help Online for StarOffice and OpenOffice.org

See *Good Online Information Sources* on page 42.

Using the Navigator to Move Within and Between Documents

The Navigator (press F5) is your friend. It lets you identify and jump to elements in the current and other documents.It's not just for Writer; you can define and use styles for spreadsheets, slides, drawings, and Web pages too. For more information see *Managing and Moving Around in Files Using Navigator* on page 306.

Setting Up and Managing the Menus and Interface

Knowing where the controls are is the first step; setting up shortcuts is a big step toward ease and efficiency, as well.

Finding and Using All the Toolbars

The program does a good job of giving you a lot of icons, displayed all the time, so you can just click and get on with your work. Make sure they're all displayed; choose View > Toolbars > and be sure all are marked. They're shown in Figure 5-1. You also have the Stylist (press F12), which is a great quick way to format.

The **menu bar**. To make sure you can see all the menu options, currently available or not, see *Disappearing Icons and Menu Items*.

Load URL field displays current document, local or online.

The **URL** field displays the currently selected link in the page (highlighted at the bottom of the screen). Field at its left displays name of link.

The **function bar**. It controls top-level stuff like whether a document is editable, and quick printing.

The **hyperlink bar**. Lets you open an Internet document on your machine, search using a search engine, and add Hyperlinks.

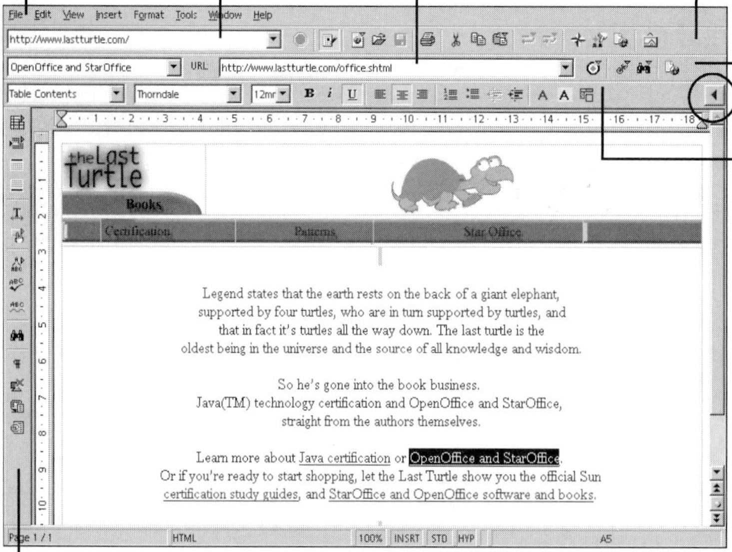

The **object bar** has the basics: Text formatting plus directly applicable features, specific to the application, like cell formatting for spreadsheets or text highlighting for text documents.

Note: This toolbar switches to the table or formula bar; click the arrow at the far right, circled, to toggle back and forth.

The **main toolbar**. These are sometimes duplicates of what you get under the menus, and tend to be things like inserting fields or aligning objects. Long-click each tool to get its corresponding tearoff menu. Click a tool to use it once; double-click a tool to use it as long as you want.

Figure 5-1   The toolbars and menu bar (Writer shown)

The **formula bar**, below, is available only in Calc. Use it to quickly insert cell contents and formulas.

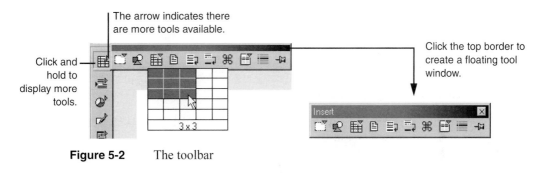

Seeing All the Things You Can Do With a Toolbar Icon

Toolbar icons, shown in Figure 5-2, are more than they seem. If a toolbar icon has a green arrow, that means there are more options for you to select by clicking and holding the left mouse button down on the icon.

The toolbar icons with green arrows can display different icons on the main toolbar. For example, the Insert button on the toolbar displays the Insert Table icon if a table was the last thing you inserted.

Figure 5-2   The toolbar

Note – When you use the drawing tools, you can double-click the icons to repeat drawings without clicking the icon multiple times. For example, if you want to draw more than one rectangle, double-click the rectangle icon and draw one rectangle after another. To stop drawing rectangles, click in an open area of the workspace.

You can also add and remove toolbar icons by right-clicking the toolbar, choosing Visible Buttons, and selecting or deselecting tools.

Disappearing Icons and Menu Items

If you're looking for a menu item or icon that was there a second ago, and now it's nowhere to be found, it's probably just in hiding. If you can't find it using any of these procedures, then:

- Select text or graphics in the document; some items don't show up until you've specified what you're going to apply the effect to

- You don't have the right component in your document; for instance, if you are trying to choose Edit > Links, you might not have any links. (That is, all your graphics are copied in, not linked to.)

- To see all the menu items that might ever appear, choose Tools > Configure and select the Menu tab.

Making the Right Set of Formatting Icons Appear on the Object Bar

The object bar is context sensitive, which means it shows the tools you can use depending on the task you're trying to perform. For example, as Figure 5-3 illustrates, if the cursor is in a paragraph, the object bar displays tools for basic text and paragraph formatting. If your cursor is in a table, it shows tools for working with tables.

However, when you're in a table and want to format text, you can replace the table object bar with the text formatting object bar by clicking the arrow at the far right of the object bar, as shown in Figure 5-3.

Object bar when the cursor is in a paragraph

Object bar when the cursor is in a table   Click this button to switch back to the
                                                            object bar for paragraph/text formatting.

Figure 5-3   The context-sensitive object bar

Finding Hidden Icons on the Right End of the Toolbar

If your monitor is small, if you've resized the program, or if the display settings in your operating system make it so you can't see all available icons in the function bar, option bar, or toolbar, a small set of arrows is displayed to let you view these icons (Figure 5-4).

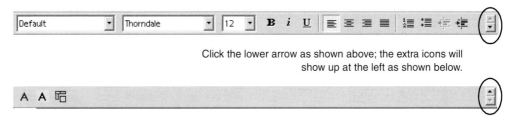

Click the lower arrow as shown above; the extra icons will
show up at the left as shown below.

Figure 5-4   Viewing hidden icons

Showing Inactive Menu Items

A certain software design tendency has been in vogue recently that has caused confusion
and frustration among many users (which isn't good, because frustration leads to anger,
anger leads to hate, and hate leads to endless episodes).

We're speaking of the practice of hiding inactive menu items. The way it works is that
when you're not allowed to perform a certain action at a given point, the menu item you
would use to perform the action is hidden rather than turned gray.

This practice causes confusion, because if you expect to be able to do something but don't
see the menu item for it, you may assume that the software is broken or was installed
incorrectly. On the other hand, if you see the menu item grayed out, you'll probably
assume, correctly, that you must not be able to use that feature for some reason.

Fortunately, the program resolves this dilemma nicely and lets you change inactive menu
items from hidden (the default) to gray, saving you from a lot of frustration.

1   Choose Tools > Options > *program* > View.

2   Select the Inactive Menu Items option.

3   Click OK.

Viewing inactive menu items is also useful for seeing
features that are available in the program. If the menu items are hidden, you may never
know that certain features exist.

Showing All the Icons on the Toolbars

If you like to format using the toolbars, use this procedure to make sure all icons are
showing on all the toolbars. By default, the program only shows the icons it thinks you
need the most.

1   Choose View > Toolbars and make sure all toolbars are showing.

2   Right-click on any toolbar and choose Visible Buttons. Select any icon you want
     displayed that doesn't have a checkmark next to it. Figure 5-4 shows the Visible
     Buttons menus for the object bar and function bar.

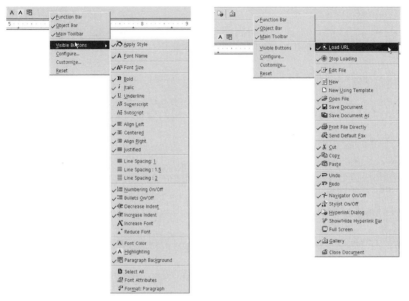

Figure 5-5   Showing icons on the toolbars (object bar and function bar respectively)

Customizing Menus

The program lets you manipulate its menu bar by creating, changing, and reorganizing
menu items.

You won't necessarily be considered a nerd for using this functionality, but it is getting
into advanced user territory. Most users aren't likely to use or need this functionality, so
we won't go into detailed procedures for customizing your menus. Instead, the
information presented here is meant merely to help guide you if you are feeling
adventuresome and want to change a menu or two.

Each application has its own set of menus. If you want to modify menus for a specific
application, make sure the application is active when you begin.

1   Choose Tools > Configure.

2   Select the Menu tab (see Figure 5-6).

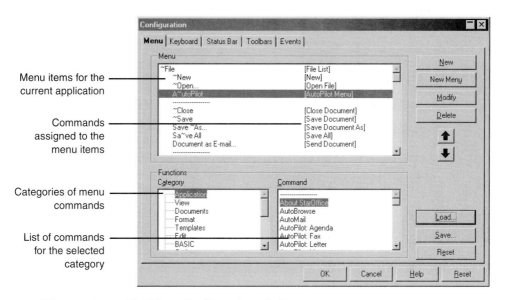

Menu items for the current application

Commands assigned to the menu items

Categories of menu commands

List of commands for the selected category

Figure 5-6   The Menu Configuration window

Menus are stored in configuration (.cfg) files. By default they're in the Office60\user\config folder. When you create, modify, and save menus, you're making changes to a .cfg file.

Table 5-1 describes elements of this window. It's provided to help guide you through making menu changes.

Table 5-1   Elements of the Menu Configuration window

Field/Button	Description
Menu	Displays the contents of the entire menu bar for the active application.
~ (the tilde symbol)	In the names of menu items, the tilde (~) precedes a letter that will be underlined as a menu keyboard shortcut.
---------------------	The separator line, available in the Command field, draws a physical line between menu items. Use this to separate logical groups of commands (such as cut, copy, and paste).
Category	This field is how the program organizes commands. The list provides general categories that house commands, which appear in the Command field when you select a category.
Command	This field displays the commands, or actions, that you can assign to menu items. If you don't see the command you want to use, select a different category in the Category field.

Table 5-1   Elements of the Menu Configuration window

Field/Button	Description
New button	Inserts a new item below the selected menu item.
New Menu button	Inserts a new menu item below the selected menu item. New menus display inside of existing menus and have fly-out submenus. To rename the new menu item, right-click it.
Modify button	Replaces the selected menu item with the selected command.
Delete button	Deletes the selected menu item. You can't delete top-level menu items, such as File and Edit.
↑ ↓	Moves the selected menu item up or down in the list.
Load button	Lets you select another configuration file to edit and/or load as the program configuration, which includes settings for menus, keyboard shortcuts, the status bar, toolbars, and events.
Save button	Lets you save the active configuration file.
Reset button	Resets the menu to that of the previously saved .cfg file. Any unsaved changes are lost.

Assigning Shortcut Keys to Menu Items

The program lets you assign actions to keyboard keys, or combinations of keys. A number of these shortcut keys are set up by default, such as the F9 key to recalculate Calc spreadsheets or the F11 key to launch the Stylist.

Each application has its own set of shortcut keys. For example, in Writer, the F12 key turns numbering on and off; in Calc, the F12 key lets you define a cell group.

You can also assign shortcut keys to run any macros you create. For example, if you create a macro that inserts the text "Java™" (or any other product name with a trademark or registration mark), you can assign that macro to a shortcut key that automatically inserts that text when you press the key.

If you want to modify shortcut keys for a specific application, make sure the application is active when you begin. This procedure is the same for assigning a new shortcut as it is for replacing an existing shortcut.

1   Choose Tools > Configure.

2   Select the Keyboard tab (see Figure 5-7).

3   In the Keyboard list, select the key or key combination you want to use.

4   In the Category list, select the category containing the command you want to assign.

Any macros you've created will be stored in one of the macro categories.

The commands for the category you select are displayed in the Command list.

5   Select the command you want to assign to the keyboard shortcut.

6   Click the Assign button.

The name of the command is inserted next to the shortcut in the Keyboard list.

7   Click OK.

For more guidance on this window, see Table 5-2.

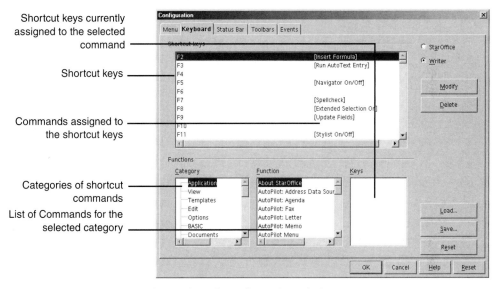

Figure 5-7   The Keyboard Configuration window

Note – Even if you don't want to assign or modify shortcut keys, the Keyboard tab is a great reference for viewing the shortcuts you can use.

Keyboard shortcuts are stored in configuration (`.cfg`) files. By default they're in the `Office60\user\config` folder. When you assign, modify, and save shortcut key settings, you're making changes to a `.cfg` file.

Table 5-2 describes elements of the Keyboard Configuration window. It's provided to help guide you through making shortcut key changes.

Table 5-2   Elements of the Keyboard Configuration window

Field/Button	Description
Keyboard	Lists all available keys and key combinations and the respective commands assigned to them.
Category	This field is how the program organizes commands. The list provides general categories that contain commands, which appear in the Command list when you select a category.
Command	Lists the commands, or actions, that you can assign to keys. If you don't see the command you want to use, select a different category in the Category field.
Keys	Displays the key or key combination assigned to the selected command. If this field is empty, no key or key combination is assigned to the command.
Delete button	Deletes the command assigned to the selected shortcut key.
Load button	Lets you select another configuration file to edit and/or load as the program configuration, which includes settings for menus, keyboard shortcuts, the status bar, toolbars, and events.
Save button	Lets you save the active configuration file.
Reset button	Resets the keyboard shortcuts to their previously saved settings. Any unsaved changes are lost.

Specifying Button Size and GUI Style

This is where you get to set various noncrucial display options, like where the mouse shows up and whether your system looks like a Mac.

Choose Tools > Options > *program* > View and make the appropriate entries.

Note – The option on the right in Figure 5-9 *could* useful for those of you who are doing visual scripting and need to pick the top tab, or the third tab. Or maybe it's just something some loud guy in a focus group reallllly wanted.

You can make StarOffice look like a Mac, XWindows, or OS/2.

Mark these options to make StarOffice open up just like you left it, whenever you close it and restart.

Keep this marked so that you can always get to menu options no matter how small the selection area or how far left or right you are.

Figure 5-9 explains how Single line tab headings work.

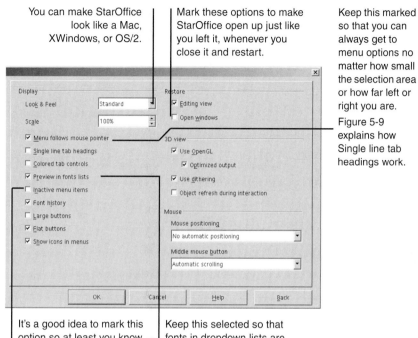

It's a good idea to mark this option so at least you know what you can't do, rather than hunting all over for it.

Keep this selected so that fonts in dropdown lists are shown in their font: Arioso is displayed in Arioso font, etc.

Figure 5-8   Setting general display options

Leave Single Line Tab Headings unmarked, and tabs in windows like the paragraph style definition window look normal.

Mark Single Line Tab Headings, and you get, well, single-line tab headings in your windows. And you have to click that big black arrow to see all of them.

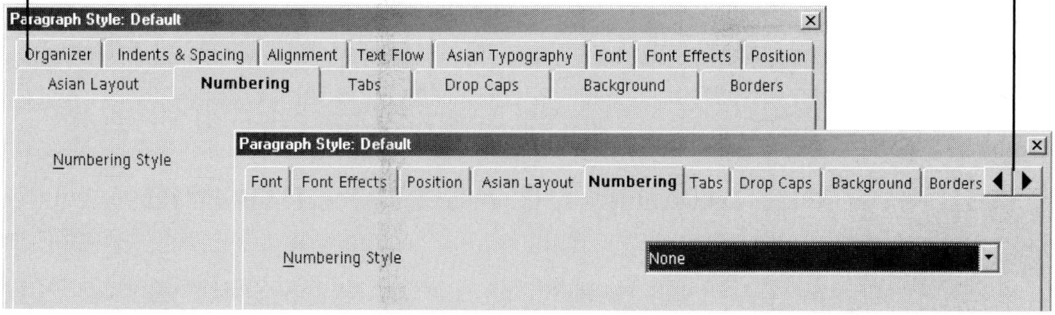

Figure 5-9   Specifying how tabs look in windows with multiple tabs, effect of Single Line Tab Headings option

Making Everything Onscreen Bigger

It's great to be able to fit lots of stuff onscreen but useless if you can't see it well. For instance, on Windows 2000 the icons for using layers and backgrounds in Impress might as well be teeny tiny Rorshach tests.

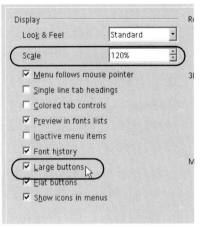

To make everything bigger and readable, choose Tools > Options > *program* > View. In the Scale field, select something like 120% and see how that works for you. Also select the Large Buttons option if you want.

Right-Clicking: Just Do It

Get right-click happy. Some of the best shortcuts and most efficient ways of doing things happen through right-click menus.

You can click the right mouse button just about anywhere in the program to bring up a context-sensitive menu. Sometimes a right-click is the only way to access some features, like *Update*, which refreshes the Explorer window.

Lefties If you've configured your left mouse button to act as the right mouse button, left-click to bring up context menus.

Note – If you use the online help, the term "context menu" means the right-click menu.

Setting Up Font Substitution

See *Adding Fonts* on page 75, *Setting Up Per-Printer Font Substitution* on page 76, *Setting up Program-Wide Font Substitution* on page 78, and to enlarge fonts, see *Making Everything Onscreen Bigger* on page 110.

Enabling and Setting Up Asian Fonts and Formatting

One of the big new features is Asian language support. To enable it and use it, just follow these steps.

Note – You need to enable Asian Language Support to have the three new vertical text tools from Draw, available in Draw, Impress, and Writer.

1   Choose Tools > Options > Language Settings > Languages. Select the Enabled option at the bottom of the window in Figure 5-10.

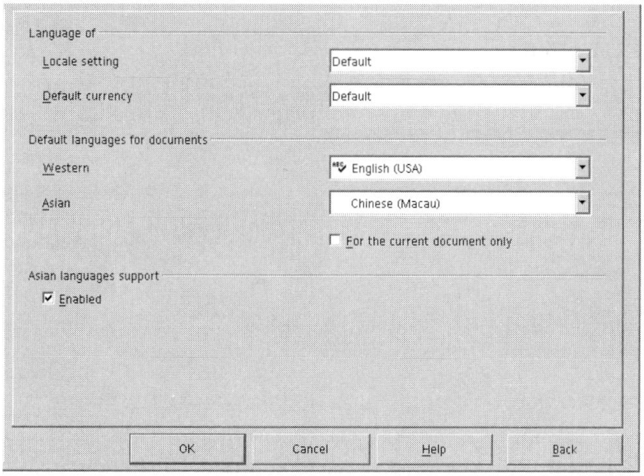

Figure 5-10   Enabling Asian language support

2   To specify default fonts for new documents, choose Tools > Options > StarOffice > Basic Fonts (Asian Language). Select the appropriate options in Figure 5-11.

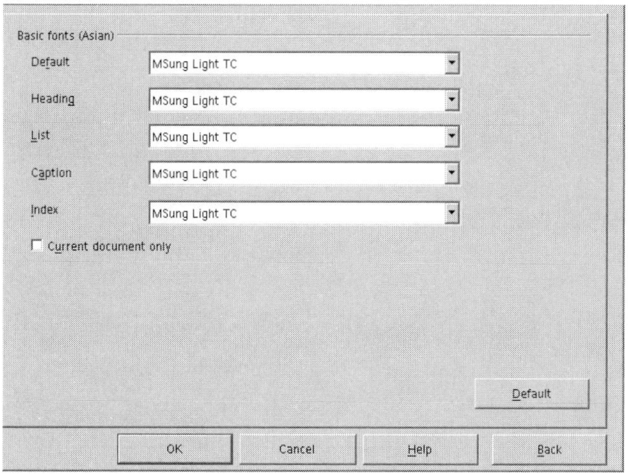

Figure 5-11   Basic default options for Asian languages

3   Choose Tools > Options > Language Settings > Writing Aids. Select the appropriate options in Figure 5-12.

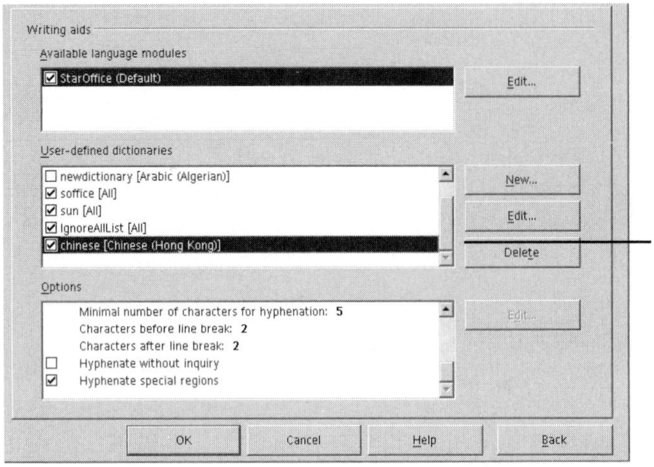

The figure shows a "Writing aids" dialog with the following elements:

Writing aids

Available language modules
- ☑ StarOffice (Default)   Edit...

User-defined dictionaries
- ☐ newdictionary [Arabic (Algerian)]   New...
- ☑ soffice [All]
- ☑ sun [All]   Edit...
- ☑ IgnoreAllList [All]
- ☑ chinese [Chinese (Hong Kong)]   Delete

Options
- Minimal number of characters for hyphenation: 5   Edit...
- Characters before line break: 2
- Characters after line break: 2
- ☐ Hyphenate without inquiry
- ☑ Hyphenate special regions

OK   Cancel   Help   Back

(callout:) Select or add any options you need for Asian languages, including adding dictionaries.

Figure 5-12   Selecting writing aids options

4   Choose Tools > Options > Language Settings > Searching in Japanese. Select the appropriate options in Figure 5-13.

Note – To see this option, Asian Language Support must be enabled; see Figure 5-10.

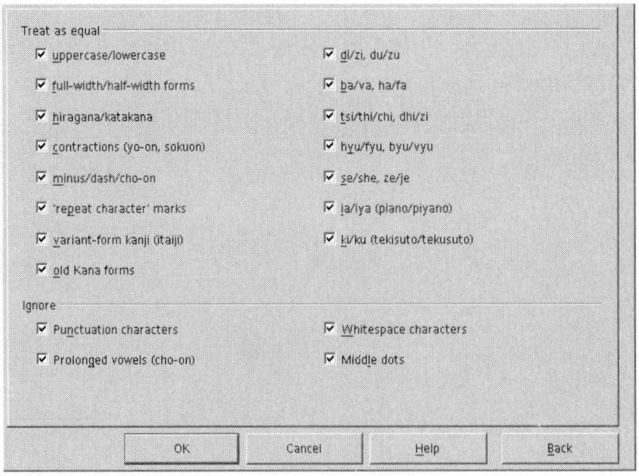

The figure shows a dialog with these options:

Treat as equal
- ☑ uppercase/lowercase   ☑ di/zi, du/zu
- ☑ full-width/half-width forms   ☑ ba/va, ha/fa
- ☑ hiragana/katakana   ☑ tsi/thi/chi, dhi/zi
- ☑ contractions (yo-on, sokuon) ☑ hyu/fyu, byu/vyu
- ☑ minus/dash/cho-on   ☑ se/she, ze/je
- ☑ 'repeat character' marks   ☑ ia/iya (piano/piyano)
- ☑ variant-form kanji (itaiji) ☑ ki/ku (tekisuto/tekusuto)
- ☑ old Kana forms

Ignore
- ☑ Punctuation characters   ☑ Whitespace characters
- ☑ Prolonged vowels (cho-on)   ☑ Middle dots

OK   Cancel   Help   Back

Figure 5-13   Selecting Japanese search options

5   Choose Tools > Options > Language Settings > Asian Layout. Select the appropriate options in Figure 5-14.

Note – To see this option, Asian Language Support must be enabled; see Figure 5-10.

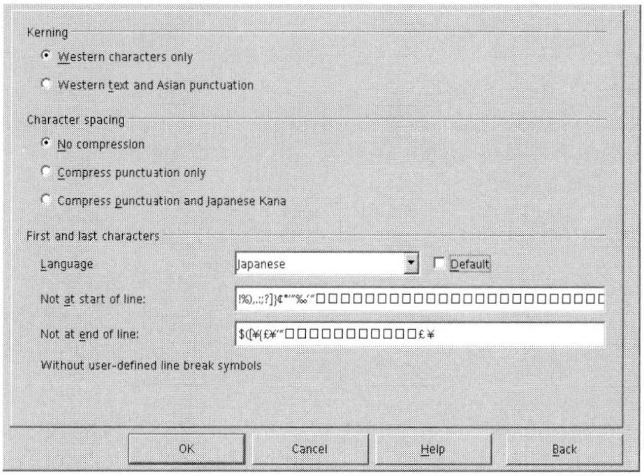

Figure 5-14   Selecting writing aids options

Once you've done the basic setup, go ahead and use the formatting in your documents. The following illustrations show some of the windows where it's available.

1   To set formatting for Asian languages, choose Format > Character > Asian. Layout. Select the appropriate options in Figure 5-15.

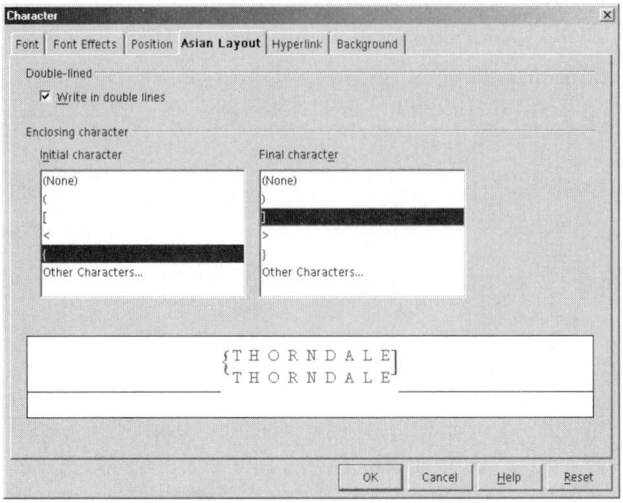

Figure 5-15   Asian language layout setup

2   Choose Format > Character > Font; select the appropriate options in Figure 5-16.

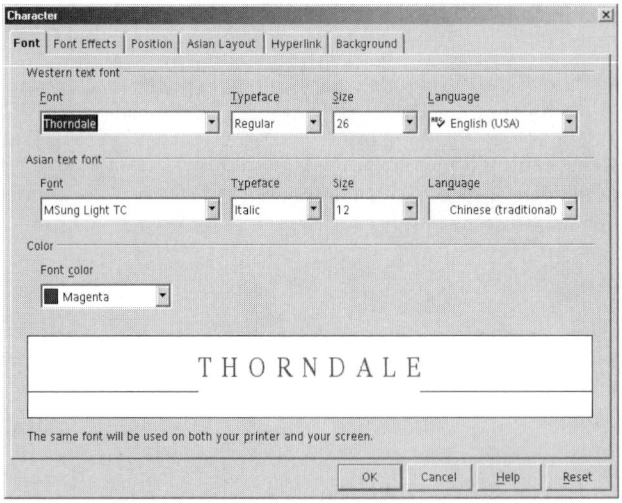

Figure 5-16   Select Asian font and size

3   Choose Format > Paragraph and select the Asian Typography tab. Select the appropriate options in Figure 5-18.

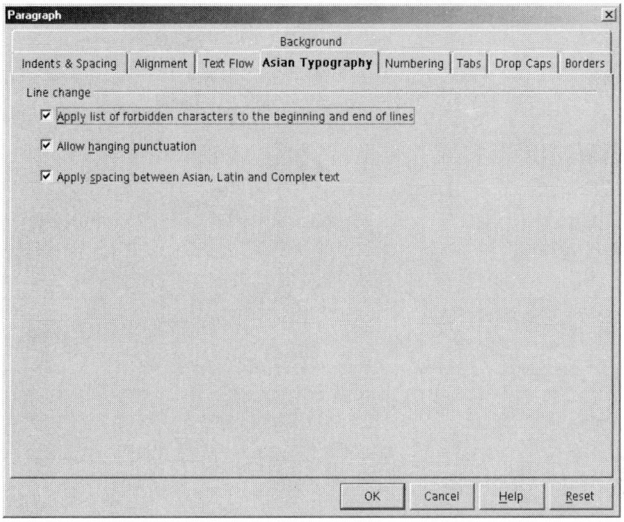

Figure 5-17   Select Asian Typography paragraph formatting

4   Choose Format > Ruby to specify Ruby text (explanations corresponding to Asian characters). Select the appropriate options in Figure 5-18.

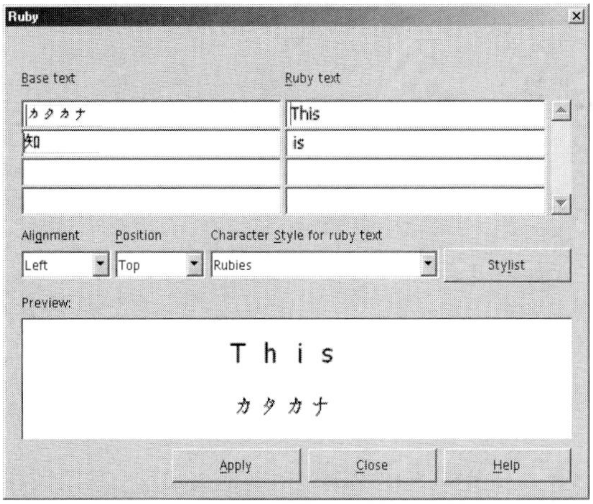

Figure 5-18   Select Ruby text options

5   Choose Format > Styles > Catalog > New or Modify; the Asian Layout and Asian Topography tabs let you specify style characteristics (Figure 5-19).

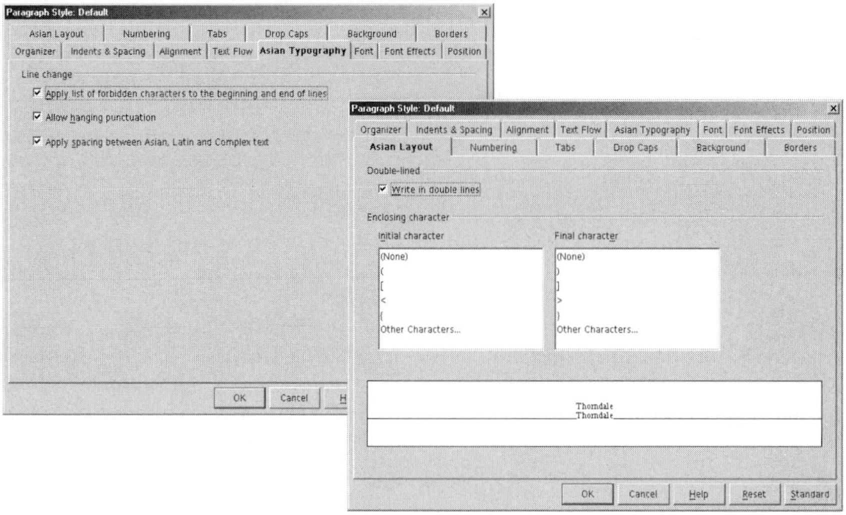

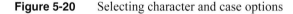

Figure 5-19   Specify Asian settings in styles

6   Choose Format > Character/Case to choose how case is evaluated in Asian fonts
(Figure 5-20).

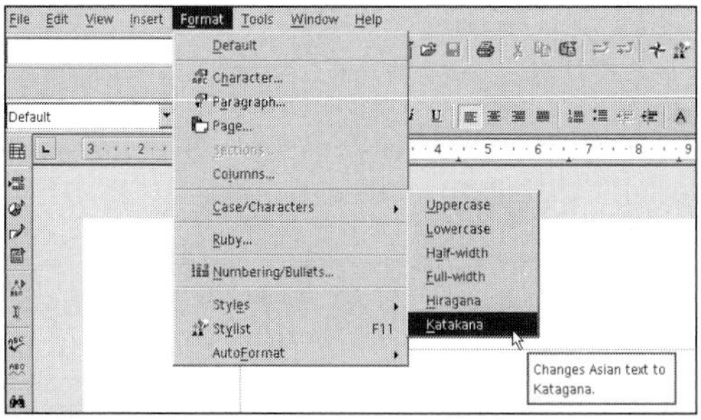

Figure 5-20   Selecting character and case options

Specifying Zoom and Measurement Unit

This section covers the things that control the document's appearance.

Specifying the Unit of Measurement

You need to do this per application. Choose Tools > Options > *application* > General and
select the measurement unit you want.

Setting Default Zoom View for Documents

When you create a new document, the blank starting page (whether it's a text document, a spreadsheet, or a slideshow presentation), opens in a standard zoom view, or scale. If you want new document pages to appear larger or smaller in the work area, change the default scaling percentage.

1   Select Tools > Options > General > View.

2   In the View window, change the percentage in the Scaling field.

3   Click OK.

Using and Setting Up Graphics and Colors

While many of the following settings are of use in Draw particularly, they affect any document containing graphics or colors.

Inserting Graphics and Objects in StarOffice Documents

You can insert any raster file, such as a GIF or JPG, into a StarOffice document. You can also insert any standard file, a new spreadsheet, a plug-in, and more. For more detail, refer to Chapter 8, *Adding Objects and Links to Documents*, on page 265.

1   Click the location in the document where you want to insert the picture.

2   Click on the Insert or Insert Object icon on the main toolbar (shown above). The selections vary by application. You can also choose Insert > Graphics or Insert > Object. Then just make the appropriate selection for what you want to insert.

Viewing Images and Sounds in the Gallery

With a full installation, StarOffice includes a library (called the Gallery) of stock art, sounds, and animated GIF files. A Gallery folder near the top of the Explorer group provides a way to view thumbnail sketches in Beamer. The Gallery is composed of links to source files.

1   Choose Tools> Gallery.

2   The Gallery appears, with the categories (themes) on the left side, as shown in Figure 5-21.

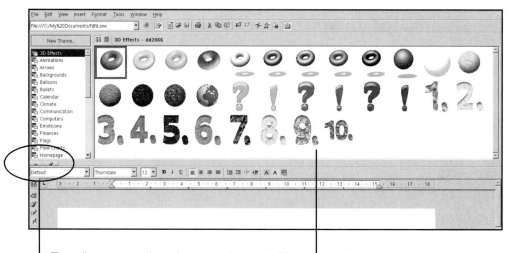

The gallery appears above the current document. If it seems to be on but you can't see it, click the arrow here and it should appear. Click the thumbtack if your document is disappearing under the Gallery.

To add an item to your document, just select it and drag it into the document.

Figure 5-21   Viewing the gallery

3   Select the right theme, then drag a graphic into your document.

Adding Gallery Items to Your Own Themes and Creating Themes

You can add your own pictures, sounds, and animations to themes you've created, and you can mix all types of files, such as pictures, sounds, and animated GIFs, in a single theme. You can't rearrange items by dragging them between galleries, and you can't add items to existing themes.

This procedure covers how to create or open your own theme, and add items to it.

1   Display the Gallery by choosing Tools > Gallery. If the Gallery is already checkmarked, look for the small arrow at the left side of the work area and click it (see Figure 5-21).

2   Create or open a theme.

•   If you need to create a new theme, click the New Theme button.

•   If you've got an existing theme to add items to, select it in the left side of the Gallery and right-click it, then select Properties.

The window for creating themes and adding items to existing themes, is shown in Figure 5-22. It's called Properties of New Theme or Properties of *theme_name*.

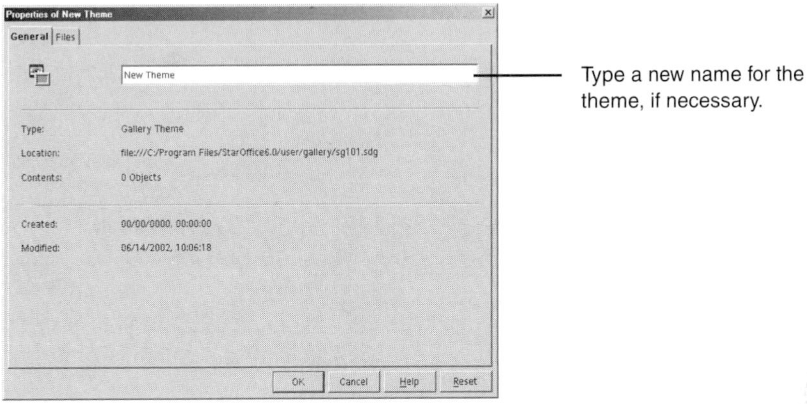

Type a new name for the theme, if necessary.

Figure 5-22   Theme and items window

3   Click the Files tab. Select the type of files you'll be looking for, or just leave the selection as All. The window is shown in Figure 5-23.

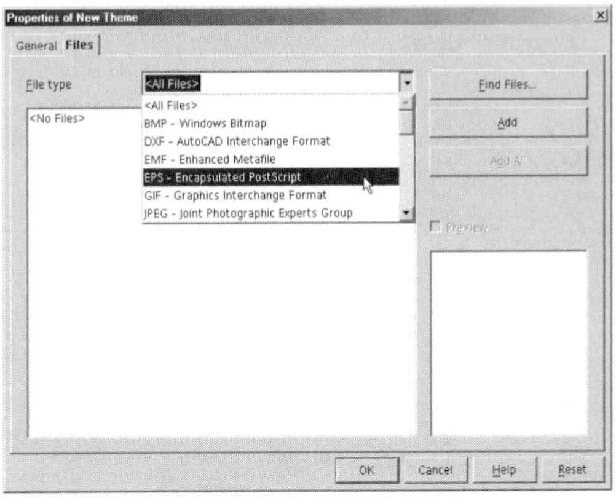

Figure 5-23   Specifying file type to look for

4   Click the Find Files button and navigate to the directory containing the files (Figure 5-24), then click OK. You can only get to the directory in this step; you'll select the files in the next step.

Figure 5-24   Navigate to the directory where the files are

5   The graphics in that directory will appear (Figure 5-25); if you specified a particular file type, only files of that type will be listed. To see thumbnails of the files, select Preview, then select any file to view it.

Figure 5-25   Previewing files from the directory you selected

6   To add a file, select it and click Add. To add them all, click Add All. The files will be added by reference, not copied, to the Gallery.

7   Click OK to save changes and close the window. You can select the new theme now in the Gallery and see the file or files you added (Figure 5-26).

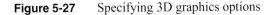

Figure 5-26   Previewing files from the directory you selected

Setting 3D Display Options

Note – Be sure to check the graphics printing options in *Specifying Print Settings for Bitmaps, Transparency, and Color/Grayscale* on page 89. These affect how transparent graphics and gradients are managed during printing, among other things.

Choose Tools > Options > *program* > View.

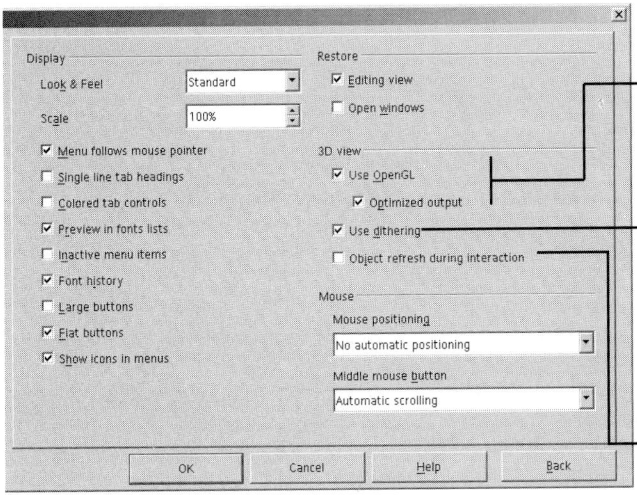

To use OpenGL, or not use OpenGL: that is the question. It looks pretty much the same onscreen and printed both ways.

Select Use dithering to improve onscreen display if your monitor doesn't support enough colors. You lose linear resolution in favor of color resolution; just pick whatever makes your screen look best.

Usually, you only see the frame, kind of a box around the object, being rotated when you're rotating, then when you stop you see the object in the new position. Selecting this option lets you see the object throughout the whole rotation. However, this will inhale memory so use it with caution.

Figure 5-27   Specifying 3D graphics options

Managing the Amount of Memory Used on Graphics

Note – Be sure to check the graphics printing options in *Specifying Print Settings for Bitmaps, Transparency, and Color/Grayscale* on page 89. These affect how transparent graphics and gradients are managed during printing, among other things.

Ever have your machine slow to a crawl with really big graphics in a document? You can limit the amount of memory that StarOffice will allocate to caching graphics. Once you go over this limit, it dumps the graphics from memory when you don't need it and loads the whole graphic again when you display it again. If you're happy now, don't mess with this; if you've having problems, change the settings and see what suits you.

Choose Tools > Options > StarOffice > Memory and look at the Graphics Cache section.

Note – The Remove From Memory setting doesn't really affect the document containing the graphics but will affect objects, graphics and other non-text information not currently displayed on the screen. The default is listed as 00:10, 0 hours and 10 minutes. Adjust so it's comfortable for your usage.

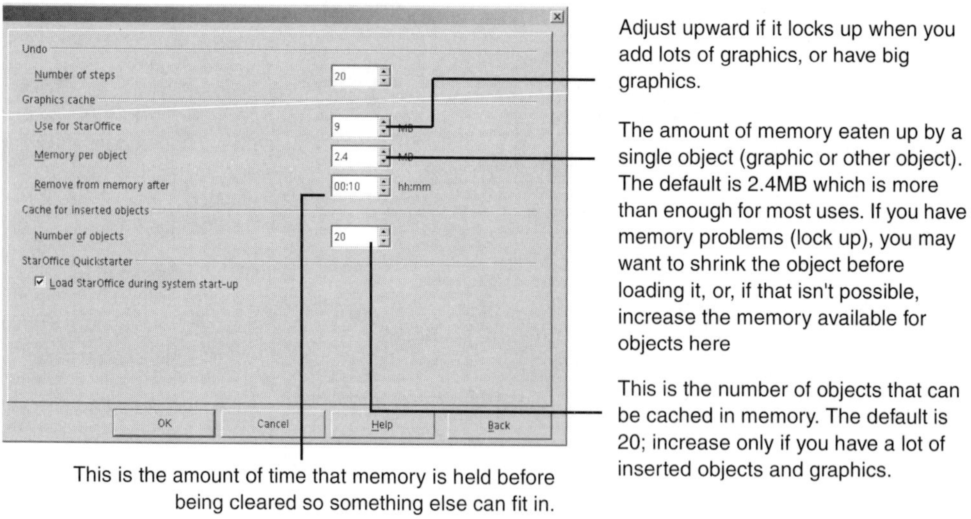
Undo
Number of steps
20
Graphics cache
Use for StarOffice
9
Memory per object
2.4
Remove from memory after
00:10
hh:mm
Cache for inserted objects
Number of objects
20
StarOffice Quickstarter
Load StarOffice during system start-up
OK
Cancel
Help
Back
Adjust upward if it locks up when you add lots of graphics, or have big graphics.
The amount of memory eaten up by a single object (graphic or other object). The default is 2.4MB which is more than enough for most uses. If you have memory problems (lock up), you may want to shrink the object before loading it, or, if that isn't possible, increase the memory available for objects here
This is the number of objects that can be cached in memory. The default is 20; increase only if you have a lot of inserted objects and graphics.
This is the amount of time that memory is held before being cleared so something else can fit in.

Figure 5-28 Graphics cache settings

Changing the Default Color for New Objects or Creating a New Color

Blue7 is an attractive color, but if you more often want to create a rectangle or page background in another color, select something else. Choose Tools > Options > StarOffice Colors and select a different color.

If you have a specific color, just generally or a specific RGB or CMYK combination that you'd like available in all applications, you can create that too.

1 Select RGB or CMYK.

2 Specify the color:

  • Enter the right numbers in the color fields

  • Click Edit to see the full spectrum of possibilities.and click on the color you want, as shown in Figure 5-29, and click OK.

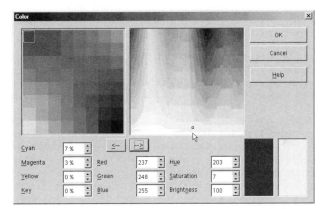

Figure 5-29   Selecting a new color in the Color window

  • In the main color options window, type a new name in the Name field and click Add. The new color and name will appear as shown in Figure 5-30.

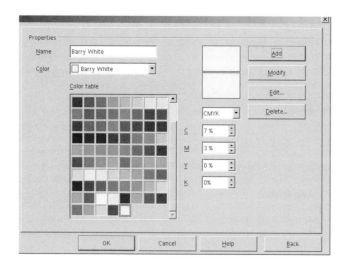

Figure 5-30   Selecting a new color in the Color window

The new color will show up in other applications in
color dropdown lists.

Controlling How StarOffice Changes Text and Does AutoCompletion

As you type in StarOffice, a lot of interesting—and unexpected—things can happen. For
example, words are capitalized automatically, spelling is changed, words are completed,
fractions are reformatted, and Internet URLs turn into hyperlinks. Any of these automatic
changes can be helpful or annoying, depending on what you want to happen. The good
thing is that you can control exactly how StarOffice makes automatic changes.

The place to control these changes is in the AutoCorrect window. With a document open,
choose Tools > AutoCorrect. With a text or HTML document open, the menu option is
called AutoCorrect/AutoFormat.

Correcting and Formatting as You Type

If you make consistent typos such as "teh" instead of "the," or if you want to create an
automatic copyright symbol "©" by typing "(C)", you can have StarOffice apply those
changes automatically as you type.

1   With a document of some type open, choose Tools > AutoCorrect. (With a text or HTML document open, the menu item is AutoCorrect/AutoFormat.)

2   In the AutoCorrect window, select the Replace tab, which displays the current text replacement settings, as shown in Figure 5-31.

3   In the Replace field, type the typo or character you want to replace with something else.

4   In the With field, type the replacement word or character.

5   Click the New button.

6   When you're finished creating replacements, click OK.

To enter a special character, such as a © symbol, close the AutoCorrect window, insert the special character in a document (Insert > Special Character), copy it, open the AutoCorrect window, and paste the character into the Replace or With fields.

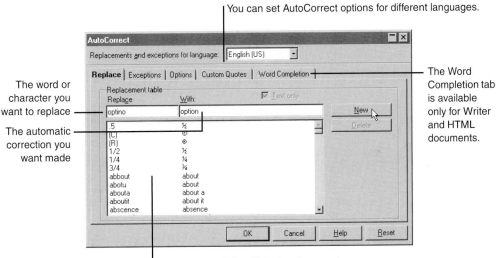

You can set AutoCorrect options for different languages.

The word or character you want to replace

The automatic correction you want made

The Word Completion tab is available only for Writer and HTML documents.

There's a predefined list of replacements.

Figure 5-31   The AutoCorrect window

To delete a replacement, select it in the list and click the Delete button. If you use spreadsheets, you should delete the line that replaces .5 with 1/2.

Controlling Capitalization

By default, the program tries to capitalize the first letter after a period and a space. For example, if you use "attn." as shorthand for "attention," the program capitalizes the first letter of the next word in the sentence.

The program also changes words that begin with two capital letters by changing the second capital to lowercase. This feature is designed for fast typists who sometimes don't let go of the Shift key quickly enough before typing the second letter of a word. But there may be certain words that you do want to begin with two capital letters. For example, if you type the name of a software company called "MSmonopoly," the program changes the second letter to lowercase to make "Msmonopoly." (Since this rule applies only to words that begin with two capitals, the program won't change words that begin with three or more capitals, such as "MSMonopoly," because it assumes since you haven't let go of the Shift key by the third letter, you intentionally want capital letters.)

To stop this behavior altogether, see Activating and Deactivating Automatic Changes, next. However, if you want the program to make the changes automatically in some cases but not in others, use this procedure to add exceptions to those rules. The program comes with a default set of predefined exceptions to prevent automatic first-letter capitalizations.

1   With a document of some type open, choose Tools > AutoCorrect. (With a text or HTML document open, the menu item is AutoCorrect/AutoFormat.)

2   In the AutoCorrect window, select the Exceptions tab.

3   Type an exception you want to add in either the Abbreviations or Words with TWo INitial CApitals fields, and click New to add it to the list, as shown in Figure 5-32.

4   When you're finished, click OK.

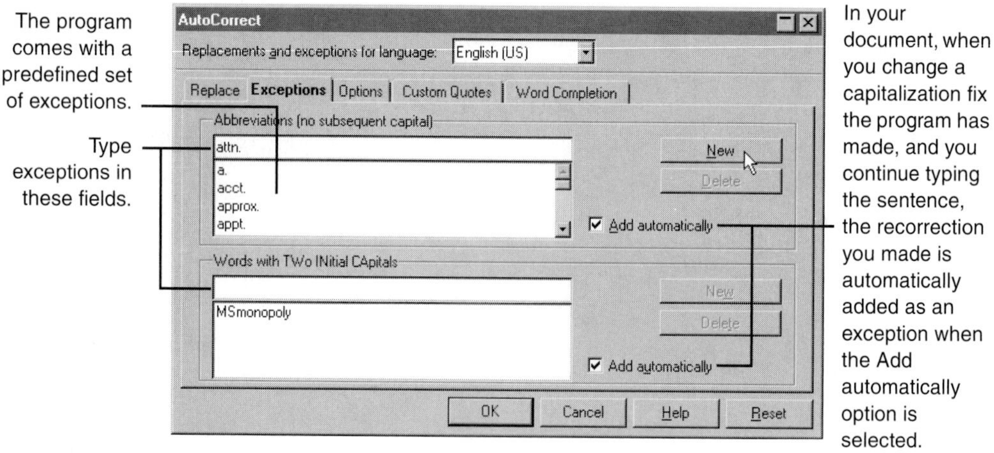

The program comes with a predefined set of exceptions. —

Type exceptions in these fields.

In your document, when you change a capitalization fix the program has made, and you continue typing the sentence, the recorrection you made is automatically added as an exception when the Add automatically option is selected.

Figure 5-32   Controlling automatic capitalization by creating exceptions

To delete an exception, select it in the list and click the Delete button.

Activating and Deactivating Automatic Changes

This procedure shows you how to activate and deactivate the specific types of automatic text changes the program makes.

1   With a document of some type open, choose Tools > AutoCorrect. (With a text or HTML document open, the menu item is AutoCorrect/AutoFormat.)

2   In the AutoCorrect window, select the Options tab.

3   Select or deselect the types of automatic corrections you want the program to make.

     See Table 5-3 for descriptions of the options.

4   When you're finished, click OK.

The program gives you clues about the functionality of some options by the way it names them. For example, TWo INitial CApitals illustrates the types of words that feature will change automatically; and the Automatic *bold* and _underline_ option shows you the characters you need to type on the keyboard to automatically bold or underline words.

An option is activated if there's an "x" in its check box.

Table 5-3   Options for automatic text changes

Option	Description
Use replacement table	Uses the replacements listed in the Replace tab of the AutoCorrect window.
Correct TWo INitial CApitals	This is a great feature for fast typists. It automatically sets a second letter from capital to lowercase when you don't let go of the Shift key quickly enough after typing a first capital letter. You can set exceptions to this rule in the Exceptions tab of the AutoCorrect window.
Capitalize first letter of every sentence	After you type a period and a space, this feature automatically changes the next letter to a capital if you type it lowercase. You can set exceptions to this rule in the Exceptions tab of the AutoCorrect window.
Automatic *bold* and _underline_	Automatically turns a word bold if you type an asterisk before and after the word, and underlines a word if you type an underscore character before and after the word.
URL recognition	If you type a group of characters that the program thinks is a link to a Web site (a URL), such as `http://www.sun.com`, this feature automatically converts the group of characters into a hyperlink. Instead of turning this feature off, you can remove URL hyperlinking in your document on a case-by-case basis by pressing Ctrl+Z to undo the automatic hyperlink after it happens, or by dragging through the hyperlink to select it and choosing Format > Default.
Replace 1st... with 1st...	If you type 1st, 2nd, 3rd, 4th, etc., this option automatically makes the letters after the number superscript, such as 1st, 2nd, 3rd, 4th.

Table 5-3   Options for automatic text changes

Option	Description
Replace 1/2... with $\frac{1}{2}$...	When you type a fraction (two numbers separated by a forward slash), this feature changes the fraction to a special character. Only fractions that have corresponding special characters for the current font are converted. Most standard fonts have only three special characters for the fractions 1/4, 1/2, and 3/4.
Replace dashes	When you type a dash with a space on either side of it, this option converts the dash from a hyphen to a longer en dash.
Ignore double spaces	This option lets you type only a single space between characters.
Apply Numbering > Symbol:	This option works only when you use the "Standard," "Text body," or "Text body indent" paragraph styles. If you type a number followed by a period, a space (or tab), and some text, then press Enter, this option autonumbers the paragraph as if you clicked the numbering icon in the object bar. If you type a hyphen followed by a space (or tab) and some text, then press Enter, the hyphen is converted to a long dash bullet character. If you type a + or a * character followed by a space (or tab) and some text, the paragraph becomes bulleted as if you clicked the bullets icon in the object bar. You can change the bullet character used for the + or * symbol by selecting the name of this option in the AutoCorrect window and clicking the Edit button.
Apply border	With this option, typing certain characters in succession and pressing Enter automatically creates a border line under the paragraph. The following character combinations illustrate the respective types of borders they create. – – – becomes _____ === becomes _____ *** becomes _____ ~~~ becomes _____ ### becomes _____ You can modify the border by clicking in the paragraph just above the line, choosing Format > Paragraph, and changing the setting on the Borders tab. To remove a border added with this option, click in the paragraph just above the line and choose Format > Default.

Table 5-3   Options for automatic text changes

Option	Description
Create table	With this option activated, you can create a table from the keyboard by typing a '+' to signify column borders, typing successive '-' characters to signify column widths, and pressing Enter at the end of the line. For example, typing +-----------------------+----------------------------+------------+ and pressing Enter creates a three-column table.
Apply styles	This option is for applying heading formats automatically, and works only when you use the "Standard" paragraph style. When you begin a paragraph with a capital letter and don't end the sentence with a period, pressing Enter twice at the end of the line automatically changes the line to the Heading 1 paragraph style. The extra paragraph below the heading is removed. If you press the Tab key twice before typing the heading text, pressing the Enter key twice at the end of the line automatically changes the line to the Heading 2 paragraph style. Three tabs creates a Heading 3, and so on.
Remove blank paragraphs	With this option activated, choose Format > AutoFormat > Apply (or Apply and Edit Changes) to remove all blank paragraphs from your document. If you're using the direct cursor, this option is indispensable.
Replace custom styles	With this option activated, choose Format > AutoFormat > Apply (or Apply and Edit Changes) to convert any custom styles applied in your document to their equivalent default styles in the program.
Replace bullets with:	This option works only on paragraphs using the "Standard" paragraph style. The paragraphs must begin with a '*', '+', or '-', be followed by a space (or tab) and some text. With this option activated, choose Format > AutoFormat > Apply (or Apply and Edit Changes) to convert these paragraphs into bulleted paragraphs with a bullet character of your choice. To change the bullet character used, select the name of this option in the AutoCorrect window and click the Edit button.
Replace "standard" quotes with „custom" quotes	With this option activated, choose Format > AutoFormat > Apply (or Apply and Edit Changes) to convert single and double quote marks to the quote characters that are set in the Custom Quotes tab of the AutoCorrect window.
Combine single line paragraphs if length greater than %	This option works only on paragraphs using the "Standard" paragraph style. With this option activated, choose Format > AutoFormat > Apply (or Apply and Edit Changes) to combine adjacent, single-line paragraphs into a single paragraph. The single-line paragraphs must be at least as wide (with relation to the total page width) as the percentage set for this option. To change the percentage on this option, select the option name in the AutoCorrect window and click the Edit button. If you activate this option while you have existing text in the document, none of the existing text is affected. Only the text you type after you activate the option is affected.

Managing AutoCompletion

As you type in a text or HTML document, the program tries to guess what you're typing and inserts the rest of the words automatically. Sometimes it's what you want—sometimes it's bizarre and frightening.

If you want to take the time to change the way the program completes words by default, you can actually make this feature productive for you by limiting the words you want the program to complete. For example, if in your business correspondence you use words that are tricky to spell or you're typing product names with trademark or copyright symbols over and over, you can limit Word Completion to those words.

See Figure 5-33 for tips on making Word Completion an asset rather than an annoyance.

Word completion works only on single words. If you want to insert more than one word automatically into a document, see *Creating and Inserting AutoText* on page 180.

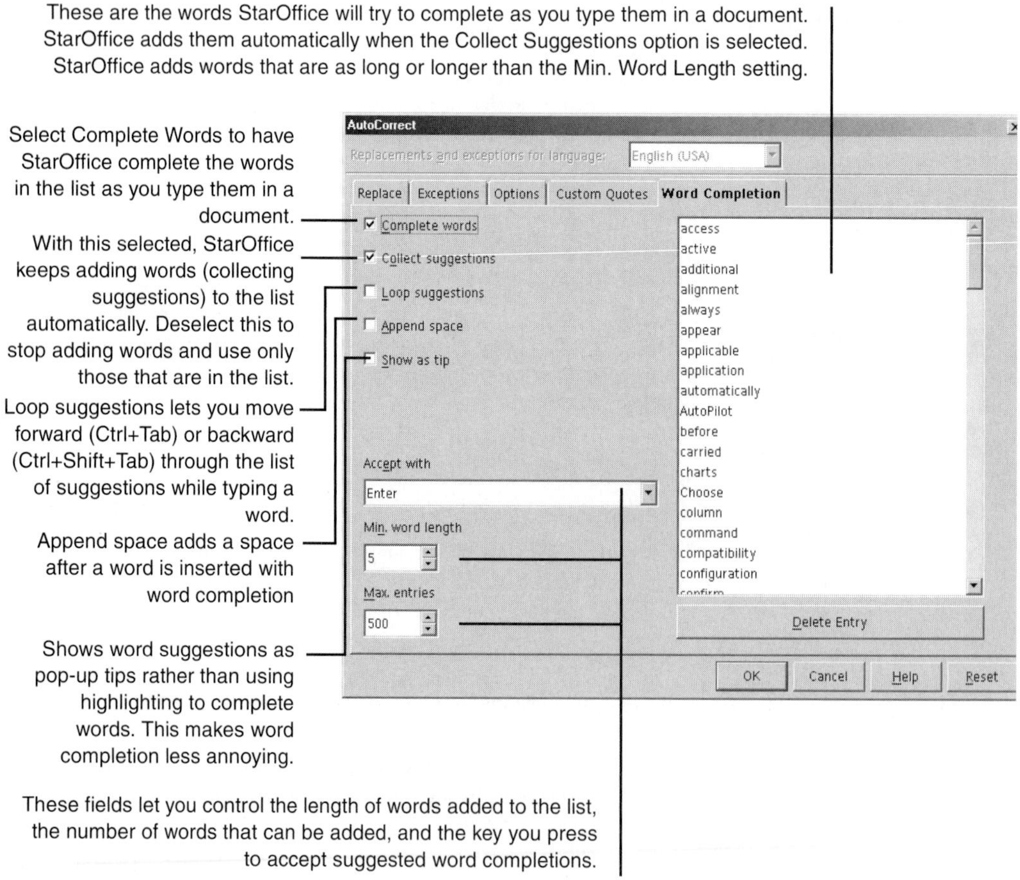
These are the words StarOffice will try to complete as you type them in a document. StarOffice adds them automatically when the Collect Suggestions option is selected. StarOffice adds words that are as long or longer than the Min. Word Length setting.
Select Complete Words to have StarOffice complete the words in the list as you type them in a document.
With this selected, StarOffice keeps adding words (collecting suggestions) to the list automatically. Deselect this to stop adding words and use only those that are in the list.
Loop suggestions lets you move forward (Ctrl+Tab) or backward (Ctrl+Shift+Tab) through the list of suggestions while typing a word.
Append space adds a space after a word is inserted with word completion
Shows word suggestions as pop-up tips rather than using highlighting to complete words. This makes word completion less annoying.
These fields let you control the length of words added to the list, the number of words that can be added, and the key you press to accept suggested word completions.
AutoCorrect
Replacements and exceptions for language:
English (USA)
Replace
Exceptions
Options
Custom Quotes
Word Completion
Complete words
Collect suggestions
Loop suggestions
Append space
Show as tip
Accept with
Enter
Min. word length
5
Max. entries
500
access
active
additional
alignment
always
appear
applicable
application
automatically
AutoPilot
before
carried
charts
Choose
column
command
compatibility
configuration
Delete Entry
OK
Cancel
Help
Reset

Figure 5-33 Setting Word Completion to be useful instead of annoying

Configuring What Key to Press to Accept AutoSuggestion

If you set up the program to do word completion as in Figure 5-33, you might not have noticed you can specify what key to press when you're typing along and want to accept the word suggested.

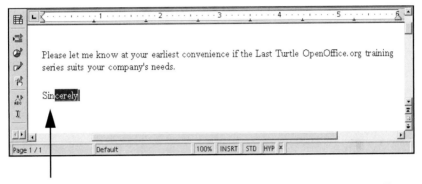

You typed Sin and the program suggests that the word you want is Sincerely. To accept the highlighted text (cerely) and move to the end of the word, press Enter (the default key) or specify a different word in the AutoCorrect/AutoFormat window.

Figure 5-34   Selecting the key to press to accept the suggested word

If you're happy with Enter as the key to press, you don't need to do anything. To change it, choose Tools > AutoCorrect/AutoFormat. You'll see the graphic at right. Accept with list in the window. Select the key you want to press to accept the suggested word.

To turn this feature off:

1   With a text or HTML document open, select Tools > AutoCorrect/AutoFormat.

2   Select the Word Completion tab.

3   Deselect the Complete Words option and click OK.

Turning Off Annoying Features

If you weren't charmed or impressed by the features in the section on managing the automatic features, here's how to just turn them off.

Note – Because some features have a Schroedinger-like capability of being annoying or not depending on how you look at them, see also the following, not included in this section: *Selecting the Open and Save Dialog Boxes to Use* on page 134, *Configuring What Key to Press to Accept AutoSuggestion* on page 131, *Good Online Information Sources* on page 42, *Repairing Damaged Installations* on page 44, *Disappearing Icons and Menu Items* on page 101, *Setting Up Security* on page 149, *Using Automatic Spellcheck* on page 190, *Disassociating StarOffice and OpenOffice.org From HTML and Microsoft Files* on page 156, and *Automatically Saving at a Specified Interval* on page 155.

Turning Off the Help Agent

The program offers its own context-sensitive help system called the Help Agent (which is actually a useful feature, but it can be distracting if it pops up constantly). In theory it's similar to the Microsoft Office Assistant (the paper clip). By default, just about every time you start to perform a new task, the Help Agent icon pops up in the lower right corner. Click on it to get information specific to the task you're trying to perform (assuming you close the window each time it launches).

The program lets you turn off the Help Agent for all topics.

1   Choose Tools > Options > *program* > General.

2   In the Help Agent section of the window, deselect the Activate option (see Figure 5-35).

3   If you just want to restrict the amount of time the Agent spends displayed, change the number of seconds.

4   Click OK. You can reset Help Agent to its default behavior by selecting the Reset to default start settings option and clicking OK.

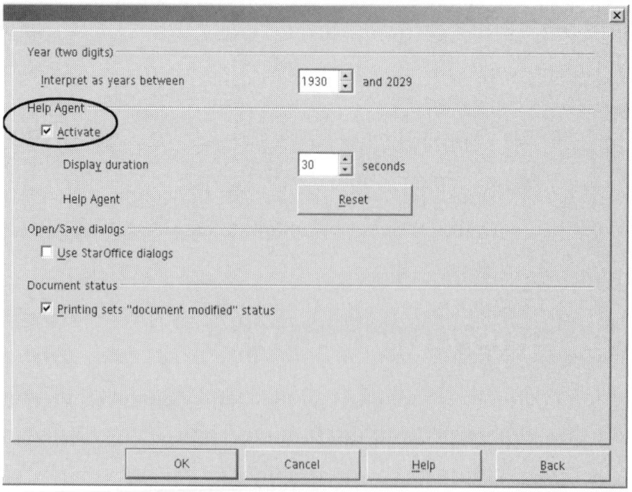

Figure 5-35   Turning off the Help Agent

Preventing and Removing Automatic Hyperlinking of URLs

We've all been there. You put in a URL like www.mymoneymakingscheme.com, and now it's all underlined and hyperlinked and every time you select it, it opens the Web site.

How do you make it normal text again? Just follow these steps.

1   Turn off URL recognition. Choose Tools > AutoCorrect/ AutoFormat, then click the Options tab. Deselect both URL Recognition options.

Replace	Exceptions	**Options**	Custom Quotes	Word Completion

[M]	[T]	
☐	☐	Use replacement table
☐	☐	Correct TWo INitial CApitals
☐	☐	Capitalize first letter of every sentence
☐	☐	Automatic *bold* and _underline_
☐	☐	URL Recognition

For the best in technical training, come to http://www.lastturtle.com

2   Click *next to* the misbehaving hyperlinked URL.

3   Hold down the Shift key and press the appropriate left or right arrow key to highlight the URL.

4   Then choose Format > Default.

Dealing With That Series of # Symbols Turning Into a Double Line

A series of # symbols is a keyboard short cut to creating a solid line below a paragraph in a text document. To switch it back to # symbols, select the line and choose Format -> Default.

Turning Off Auto Completion as You Type

As you type in a text or HTML document, the program tries to guess what you're typing and inserts the rest of the words automatically. Most of the time the words it completes aren't the words you really want. To turn this feature off:

1   With a text or HTML document open, select Tools > AutoCorrect/AutoFormat.

2   Select the Word Completion tab.

3   Deselect the Complete Words option and click OK.

To use it and configure the key to press to accept the suggestion, see *Managing AutoCompletion* on page 130 and *Configuring What Key to Press to Accept AutoSuggestion* on page 131.

Turning Off Everything Automatic

This should get pretty much everything off that's going on without your permission.

1   See *Using Automatic Spellcheck* on page 190.

2   See *Automatically Saving at a Specified Interval* on page 155 and turn it off.

3   See *Using Automatic File Extensions* on page 158 and don't do it.

4   See *Disassociating StarOffice and OpenOffice.org From HTML and Microsoft Files* on page 156.

5   Choose Tools > Options > Text Document > Table and Tools > Options > Text Document > Table. Deselect the Number Recognition option in each window.

6   Choose Format > AutoFormat and *unmark* everything that shows up until you don't see checkmarks next to any of the options.

7   Use the program for a while. If it's still doing automatic stuff, complete the next step.

8   Choose Tools > AutoCorrect/AutoFormat (this varies somewhat among applications.) Click on every tab and turn off everything.

   • On the Replace tab, delete anything that's still driving you crazy; you can click Reset at the bottom of the window to restore everything deleted if you need to later.

   • On the Exceptions tab, unmark the AutoInclude options.

   • On the Options tab, deselect everything.

   • On the Word Completion tab, deselect Complete Words.

Working With Directories

This section provides useful tips for working with documents.

Selecting the Open and Save Dialog Boxes to Use

You can use the gussied-up StarOffice or OpenOffice.org dialog boxes, or your own standard system type. Figure 5-36 shows the differences for Windows.

If you like whatever you've got right now, skip this procedure. If you want to switch, choose Tools > Options > *program* > General and deselect Use StarOffice dialogs or Use OpenOffice.org dialogs (see Figure 5-37).

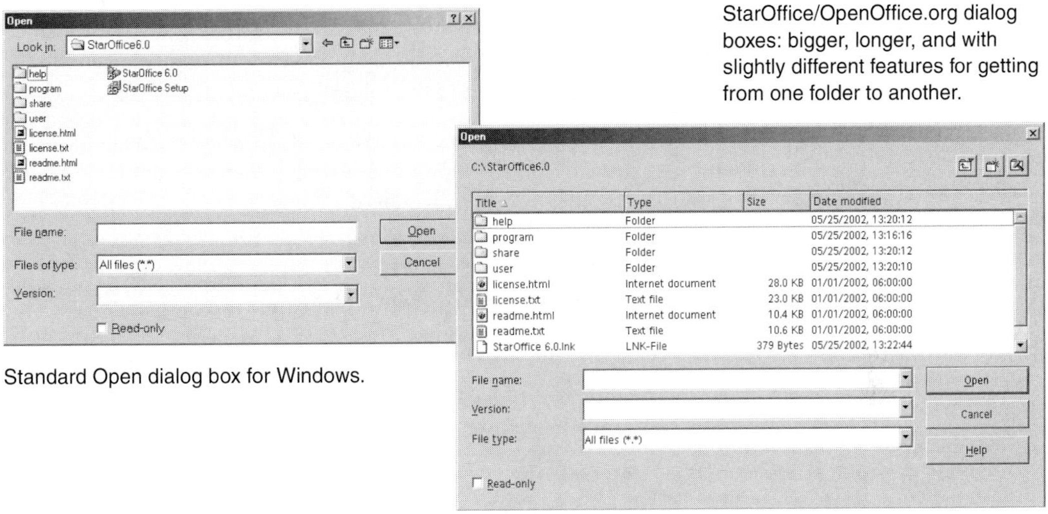

StarOffice/OpenOffice.org dialog boxes: bigger, longer, and with slightly different features for getting from one folder to another.

Standard Open dialog box for Windows.

Figure 5-36   Standard and OpenOffice.org/StarOffice style Open (same for Save) dialog boxes

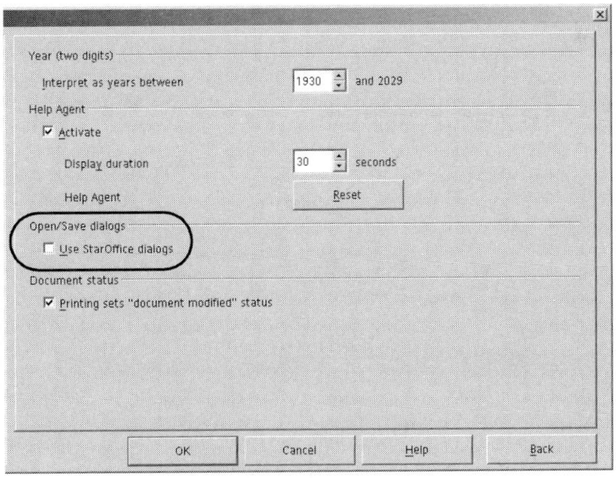

Figure 5-37   Switching dialog box type

Specifying the Default Directory You Save to and Open Files In

When you save, open, or insert a file, the program opens the Save As, Open, and Insert windows with a default folder selected. The program uses two different default folders: one for opening and saving files and one for inserting graphics. You can change either of these default folders to make it easier to get to the folders you commonly use.

You'll find this feature extremely useful, especially if you spend a lot of time working in a specific directory. For example, if you're going to be inserting a lot of graphics from a specific folder, it's a hassle to click through a bunch of folders in the Insert window to reach the folder you want. By resetting the graphics path to the folder you want, the Insert window opens to that folder automatically. And if it doesn't, you can just click the Default Directory button in the Insert window to show your folder.

1   Choose Tools > Options > *program* > Paths (see Figure 5-38).

2   In the list of paths, select the Graphics folder to change its default, or select the My Documents folder to change its default.

3   Click Edit.

4   In the Select Path window, navigate to the folder you want to use as your work folder and click Select.

5   Click OK.

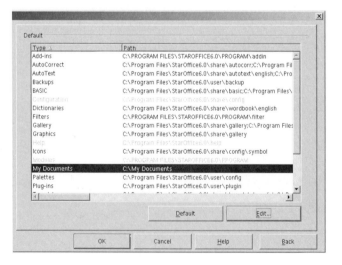

Figure 5-38   Changing default paths

Another benefit of changing the My Documents path is when you're working on a network. In the Explorer window, under the Explorer group, the Workplace item sometimes lists everyone's home directory, showing you more folders than you normally want to see—especially if all you want to see is your home directory. By changing My Documents to your home directory, you can view only your home directory by clicking the My Documents slider in the Explorer window.

In the Paths window (Figure 5-38) you can change other system paths. Many are the program's system-level paths and should be left alone. You may want to change others at some point, such as the Download path. Download is the default folder for storing files downloaded from the Internet. If the program crashes and you lose your work, check the path to the Backup copies to see where a possible backup copy may exist.

Note – If you want to revert back to the default path for an item, select it in the Paths window and click the Default button.

Changing File Paths in Dialog Boxes

In any dialog box or window that lets you navigate through your system folders (for example, the Save As window), you don't have to navigate solely by clicking the Up One Level and Default Directory buttons, or by double-clicking folders. You can also enter the path you want directly in the File name field and press Enter (see Figure 5-39).

Solaris Note – In Solaris, you can type the tilde symbol (~) in the File name field and press Enter to reach your home directory.

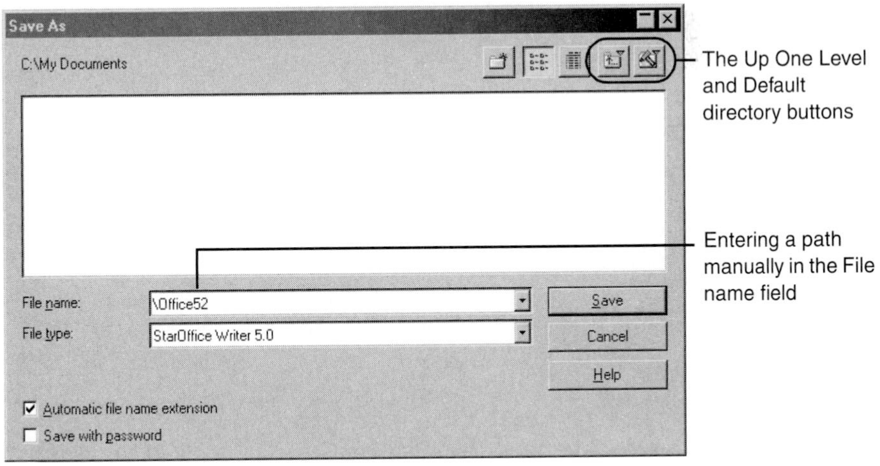

Figure 5-39   Navigating by typing a path directly in the File name field

Setting Up and Using Internet Features

With the removal of the Web browsing feature (kind of) and Mail, there isn't much left in the program that uses Internet settings. The features left include browsing by just typing a full HTTP URL in the Load URL field, and sending a document as an email. (Choose File > Send > Document as Email.) This ability also applies to mail merges; you can do a mail merge to paper, to email, or to files. The settings in this section help your merges to email work, too.

If you're converting from 5.2, you probably don't need to enter much, if anything. If Internet features aren't working the way you want, make the appropriate changes using the procedures in this section.

Setting Up Proxy Information for Internet Access

Why proxy options? Because you can complete the rather superfluous *Bringing Up a Web Page* on page 442 and *Using Web's Search Connection* on page 442. You can probably skip this.

Use the window shown in Figure 5-40 to define the settings for the proxy server. Default settings for your current proxies are often read from your system and set up automatically, so you might not need to change anything.

Proxies The proxy server can be manually or automatically set up to access the Internet over an interconnected network. A proxy is a computer in the network acting as a kind of clipboard for data transfer. Whenever you access the Internet from a company network and request a Web page that has already been read by a colleague, the proxy will be able to display it much more quickly as long as it's still in memory. All that needs to be checked in this case is that the page stored in the proxy is the latest version. If this is the case, the page won't have to be downloaded from the much slower Internet but can be loaded directly from the proxy.

Figuring out your proxy names and ports Ask your system administrator or Internet service provider for the proxies and ports to enter. You can also check your browser for the proxies and ports you use. In Netscape, choose Edit > Preferences > Advanced > Proxies. In Internet Explorer, choose Tools > Internet Options > Connections. Depending on the provider, it may or may not be necessary to always use a proxy. For example, no proxy is required for AOL or CompuServe.

Server names Always enter server names without the protocol prefix (`http`, `ftp`, etc.). For example, enter `starnews.stardivision` rather than `http://starnews.stardivision`.

Select Manual if you use a proxy; select None If you want to set up a connection directly on your computer to an Internet provider that doesn't use a proxy.

Enter the proxy and port, if any, for URLs starting with http:// No proxy is required for AOL or CompuServe.

Enter the name of the FTP proxy to use for FTP connections, and port.

Enter the name of the SOCKS proxy and port.

List the servers that don't need proxy servers, such as servers requested in your local network. Examples include www.sun.*

Select Automatic to automatically adopts the DNS from the system settings (recommended). This lets you, for example, when going into the Internet, automatically use the name server suggested by the provider.

If you want to specify a DNS server select Manual and in the text box enter the IP address of the DNS server to be used in the normal notation for IP addresses.

Figure 5-40   Proxy options

Proxies and ports Ask your system administrator or ISP for the port for each proxy. The maximum value is 65535. If you enter a higher number, the value will be set at 0 and an error message will appear.

DNS Server You can use the setup window to set the name of the DNS (Domain Name System). The DNS name server is there to translate the full name of the host that you enter as URL, such as www.lastturtle.com, into its 32-bit IP address. The 32-bit numbers of IP addresses are shown in a simplified way as four decimal numbers separated by dots. Each decimal number is a number from 0 to 255, and represents the first, second, third and final 8 bits of the entire 32 bits.

Setting Up the Ability to Search the Web

The only reason to complete this section is so that you can then use the rather superfluous *Using Web's Search Connection* on page 442. You can probably skip this; we're documenting it out of an overdeveloped sense of duty.

Note – Sometimes you don't get the hyperlink bar, which contains features like the Search (the Web) icon and the link-creating URL fields. That is, you might have the hyperlink bar, but it's entirely blank. This can be corrected, sometimes, by reinstalling. If you don't have the hyperlink bar, though, don't worry about it. The Search feature is extraneous at best, and the Hyperlink Dialog icon is relocated to the topmost bar of your work area. (Oddly enough, even distributions without the Search icon still have the Search Setup feature.)

The program lets you use any of several popular search engines to search the Internet straight from the program, without having to go to a particular search engine site. See *Using Web's Search Connection* on page 442 for information on how to search and selecting the search engine to use.

Several search engines are already set up for you; you probably don't need to change these settings unless you need to do some tweaking, or want to add a search engine to the list.

1 Choose Tools > Options > Internet > Search (Figure 5-41).

2 Enter the appropriate information with the information in the window as well as the guidelines following the illustration.

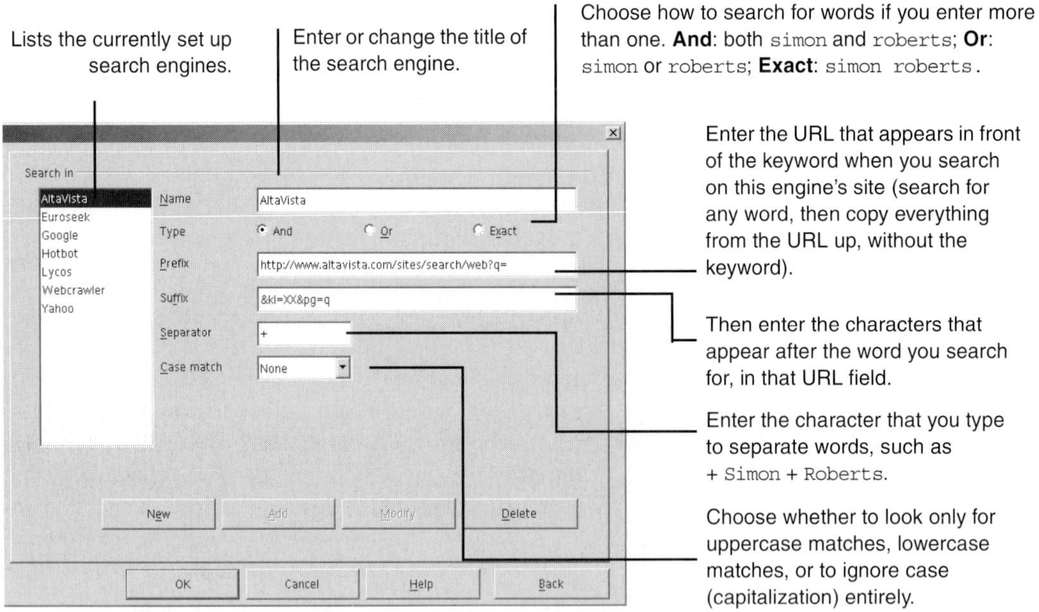
Lists the currently set up search engines.
Enter or change the title of the search engine.
Choose how to search for words if you enter more than one. **And**: both `simon` and `roberts`; **Or**: `simon` or `roberts`; **Exact**: `simon roberts`.
Enter the URL that appears in front of the keyword when you search on this engine's site (search for any word, then copy everything from the URL up, without the keyword).
Then enter the characters that appear after the word you search for, in that URL field.
Enter the character that you type to separate words, such as + `Simon` + `Roberts`.
Choose whether to look only for uppercase matches, lowercase matches, or to ignore case (capitalization) entirely.
Search in
AltaVista
Euroseek
Google
Hotbot
Lycos
Webcrawler
Yahoo
Name
AltaVista
Type
And
Or
Exact
Prefix
http://www.altavista.com/sites/search/web?q=
Suffix
&kl=XX&pg=q
Separator
+
Case match
None
New
Add
Modify
Delete
OK
Cancel
Help
Back

Figure 5-41 Search options

Here are some guidelines for figuring out what the prefix (the codes the engine puts in front of what you're searching for), suffix (the code after the keyword), and the separator (what goes between multiple keywords) are for each new search engine.

1 Activate the search engine and perform a search with at least two words.

2   Copy the URL from the URL field in the Function bar and paste it into a blank document.

3   Change the conditions for the search in the search engine, if it offers you the choice.

4   Again, copy the contents of the URL field.

5   Compare the URLs with the sample URLs that you can copy from the fields of this dialog. You should then be able to recognize the prefix, suffix, and separator for various conditions.

Specifying Whether Paths to Objects Are Absolute or Relative

What this applies to   This applies to objects and graphics you've inserted in documents via a link. That is, the graphics are still in their original location but a reference to them is in the document. If you've inserted the graphic without marking the Link option, this doesn't matter. This is demonstrated in Figure 5-42.

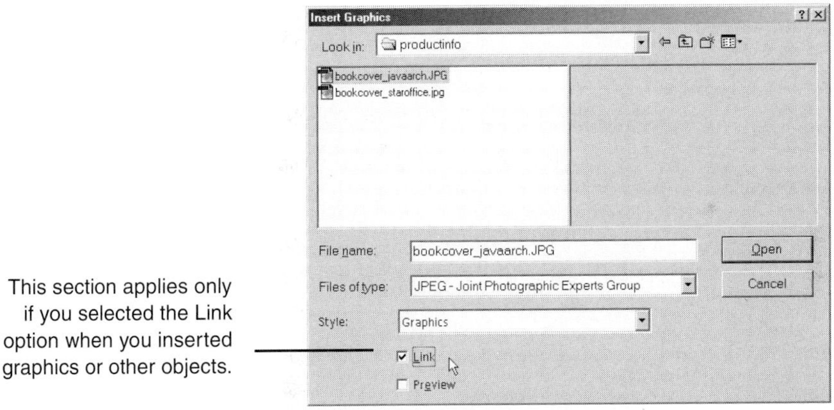

This section applies only if you selected the Link option when you inserted graphics or other objects.

Figure 5-42   Option controlling whether graphics are linked to or inserted directly

Let's say you've got these directories and files, as shown in Figure 5-43.

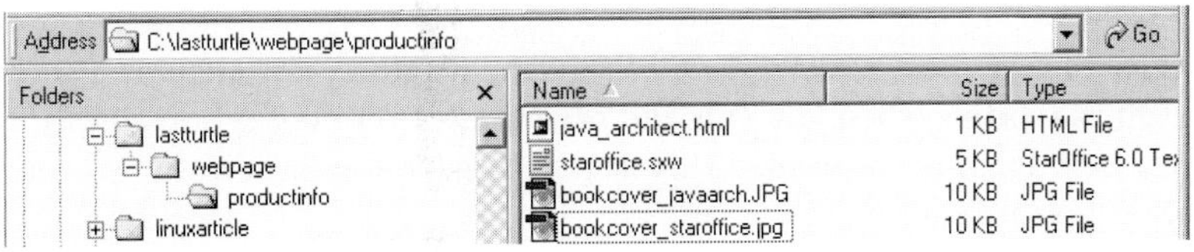

Figure 5-43   Example files and locations

The deal with relative and absolute paths In general, you want to leave them relative, the default value. The rest of this section is about why.

If you have relative paths from the text and HTML documents, then your pathnames are saved as just `bookcover_javaarch.jpg` and `bookcover_staroffice.jpg`. If they're absolute, then the actual code in the files is
`C:\lastturtle\webpage\productinfo\bookcover_javaarch.jpg` and
`C:\lastturtle\webpage\productinfo\bookcover_staroffice.jpg`.

Both are fine for now, but if you upload the text and HTML files to a `bin\cart\products` directory on your Web server, it won't work, even if the graphics are still in the same directory. Likewise, if you send the documents and graphics to other people working on the Last Turtle Web site, and they put the files in different directories or on their D drive, the links will get screwed up.

*   Relative paths are more convenient if the files you link to are part of the same set of subfolders and unlikely to change location.

*   Relative paths are possible only if the source document and the link are located on the same drive.

Choose Tools > Options > Load/Save > General. In the Save URLs relative to section of the window, select or deselect the Relative to file system and Relative to Internet options. The window is shown in Figure 5-44.

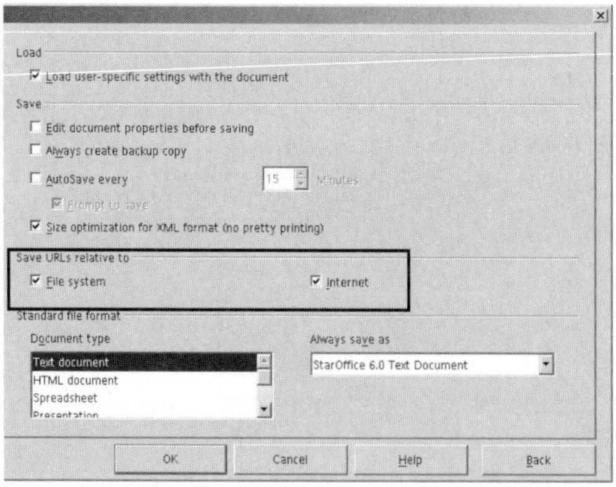

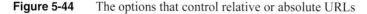

Figure 5-44   The options that control relative or absolute URLs

If you change your options from relative to absolute, this changes URLs previously saved as relative when you edit and save files containing relative links. It's system-wide, not document-specific. This works the same way in reverse; whatever's set is how the document behaves.

If you plan to put a page online as part of your Web site, unless you really know what you're doing, make sure that both options are set to Relative and you save the documents, before you put the pages online.

Note – Tool tips, the Graphics window, and the Edit Links window (choose Edit > Links), always display the absolute path, even if only the relative path is saved. In HTML files, you can choose View > HTML Source to see what's actually saved in the link's HTML code.

Setting Up How the Program Reads and Exports HTML Files

If you ever save or export your documents to HTML, or if you just plain create HTML documents, take a look at the settings in Tools > Options > Load/Save > HTML Compatibility, shown in Figure 5-45.

See also *Making an HTML Version of a Document* on page 144 to see what happens when you save a document as the Web/Writer fake HTML format.

The size that text appears in an HTML document is often defined by specifying just Size 1, etc., rather than a specific font size. The reading application, StarOffice or your browser, chooses how big Size 1 should be. If you want to change how StarOffice reads HTML files like this, enter different font sizes in these fields.

Mark this to import as notes anything that StarOffice doesn't recognize as a normal HTML tag.

Mark this to ignore any font settings in the document and just use StarOffice font sizes and settings from your style settings.

Select a browser or format here if you have a strong preference about what standards to use when you choose File > Export Source or when you save a document as HTML.

Select this to display a warning that macros will not be usable.

If you want to use a different character set, select it here.

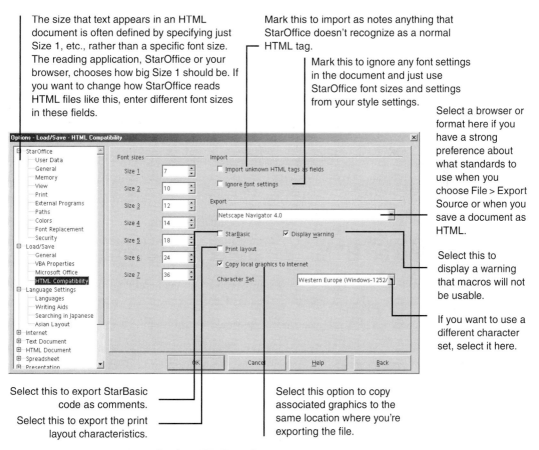

Select this to export StarBasic code as comments.

Select this to export the print layout characteristics.

Select this option to copy associated graphics to the same location where you're exporting the file.

Figure 5-45   Setting HTML options

Selecting the Program for the Send as Email Feature

Choose Tools > Options > *program* > External Programs. Leave the default as is unless you've got a really good reason to change it.

Sending a Document as Email

1   Make sure your email program is running and that you're connected to the Internet.

2   Open the program and the document you want to send as an email.

3   Choose File > Send > Document as Email, or File > Document as Email.

4   Your specified email program will appear, showing you a new empty email with the document attached, as shown in Figure 5-46.

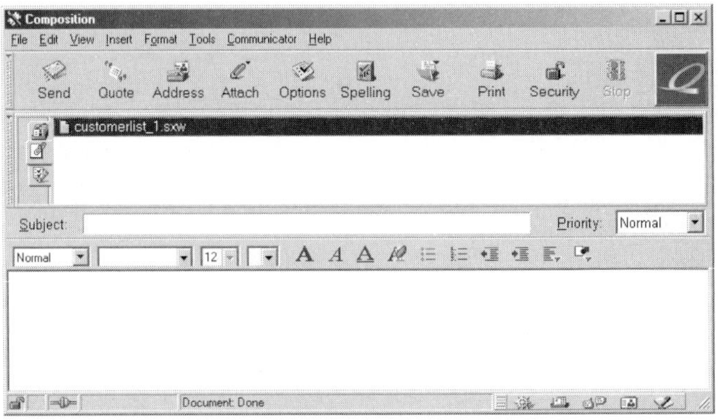

Figure 5-46   Sending a document as an email

Making an HTML Version of a Document

This varies from application to application. However, in general you can choose File > Save As, or File > Export, and select the HTML format.

You can also, in HTML, choose View > Source, then choose File > Export Source.

For information on what the HTML itself is like, see *What StarOffice and OpenOffice.org HTML Is Like* on page 454.

Note that when you Save As in Writer, you only get the Web (Writer) option, which is not in fact actual HTML. Not even if you make sure you add an HTML file extension. One main tipoff is that the View > Source option is not available. They often look the same way when viewed in a browser, but not always.

Setting Undos and Number of Recent Documents You Can Open

Click on File to see the old documents you've opened, then just select one to open it up again. Click on Undo to undo actions. These procedures tell you how to configure the number of each available:

Specifying Number of Possible Undos

Undoing past actions is everyone's fantasy; the program lets you do it up to a hundred times. The default is 20; to change it, choose Tools > Options > *program* > Memory and enter the appropriate number (100 is the max) in the Number of Steps field.

Showing More than Four Recent Documents in the File List

The program keeps track of the four files you opened and closed most recently. This is a great feature but a little limited. If you want to increase the number to keep track of, follow the steps in this procedure. It's simply a matter of modifying the Common.xml file that stores a list of your most recently opened files; you just have to put in a line that says "Keep track of 9 files, OK" (or whatever number you want). There doesn't seem to be a limit but don't go nuts; we'd recommend that you keep it under 20.

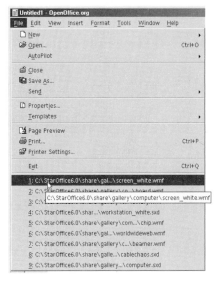

⚠ Make a full backup or two of the Common.xml file before you go anywhere near these files. The location is specified in step 2.

1 Start TextPad (www.textpad.com) or another text editor that handles XML files well. Don't use Notepad.

2 Open the following file, for StarOffice or OpenOffice.org. An example for both is shown in Figure 5-47.

```
~/staroffice6.0/user/config/registry/instance/org/openoffice/Office/common.xml

~/openoffice/user/config/registry/instance/org/openoffice/Office/common.xml
```

Figure 5-47   Paths to common.xml file

> **3**   Look for the `<History>` tag; the entries are alphabetical. You'll see something like the code shown in Figure 5-48.

```
<History>
  <List cfg:element-type="HistoryType">
    <HistoryType state="replaced" cfg:name="h0">
      <Filter cfg:type="string">StarOffice XML (Writer)</Filter>
      <Password cfg:type="string"/>
      <Title cfg:type="string">file:///C:/docs/newdocs/karenstory.sxw</Title>
      <URL cfg:type="string">file:///C:/docs/newdocs/karenstory.sxw</URL>
    </HistoryType>
```

> *and so on, with a lot more <HistoryType> entries...*

```
  </List>
  <PickList cfg:element-type="HistoryType">
    <HistoryType state="replaced" cfg:name="h0">
      <Filter cfg:type="string">StarOffice XML (Writer)</Filter>
      <Password cfg:type="string"/>
      <Title cfg:type="string">file:///C:/docs/newdocs/karenstory.sxw</Title>
      <URL cfg:type="string">file:///C:/docs/newdocs/karenstory.sxw</URL>
    </HistoryType>
```

> *and so on, with three more <HistoryType> entries; these are the files displayed as your four most recent files under the File menu...*

```
  </PickList>
</History>
```

Figure 5-48   Truncated contents of the entire <History> tag in the Common.xml file

> **4**   Replace the contents of the entire `<History>` tag, i.e., `<History>` through `</History>` inclusive, with the text shown in Figure 5-48. The example changes StarOffice to display 9 recently opened files; enter whatever number you want. (However, be sensible and keep it at double digits; we figure under 20 is a good idea.)

```
<History>
  <PickListSize cfg:type="int">9</PickListSize>
</History>
```

Figure 5-49   Replacement text for the <History> tag

Note – It does seem a little drastic to replace all those pages of entries. We understand if you're hesitant; we were too. However, it works beautifully. And remember that you've got the backup copy of Common.xml to go back to if anything's goofed up.

Fun With XML

This section is for anyone with the tiniest inner geek or curiosity about how your files are constructed.

Getting to Know Your Files' Inner XML

The reason StarOffice and OpenOffice.org files are so small is that they're stored in XML, not binary format. You can also just unzip any file to see the XML files that make it up. Each regular document file has separate XML files that make it up, such as one containing the content, one containing the formatting, and so on.

When you use a ZIP program to unzip a document, you'll get the following files.

- The plain text content `content.xml`. You can view this file with a standard text editor.

   `content.xml` is stored without indents so it's not that easy to read, but takes up less space. You can make it more readable by choosing Tools > Options > Load/Save > General and *deselecting* the Size Optimization for XML Format option.

- `meta.xml` contains the information about the document displayed under File > Properties.

   If you save a document with security, only `meta.xml` is not secured.

- `settings.xml` contains further information like printer settings and data sources.

- `styles.xml` contains the styles defined for the document.

- The `meta-inf/manifest.xml` file describes the structure of the XML file.

Information about graphics is contained in additional subdirectories.

The DTD (document type descriptor) files are at `office\share\dtd`. You can get more information about the DTD and associated licenses at `www.openoffice.org`.

Doing Incredibly Dangerous Things With XML Configuration Files

We're not going to show you how to shoot yourself in the foot, but we'll tell you where the gun is if you really want to know.

The following directories, for StarOffice and OpenOffice.org, are chock full of configuration files. Some of them contain settings you specify in the Tools > Options windows; some you can't get to except through editing the files directly.

Make a full backup or two before you go anywhere near these files.

As noted in *Showing More than Four Recent Documents in the File List* on page 145, editing the Common.xml file lets you open a near infinite number of old documents by selecting them from the file menu. However, you really should know your way around XML to even think about touching these files.

Figure 5-50 shows the directories; Figure 5-48 shows examples of the `Writer.xml` and `DataAccess.xml` files.

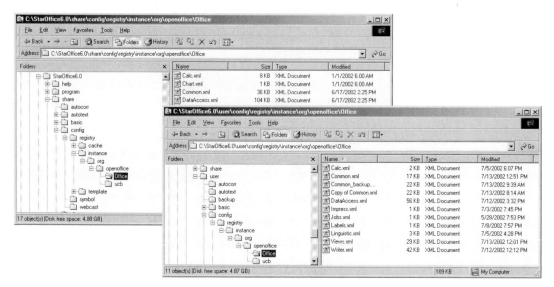

Figure 5-50   Locations of XML configuration files

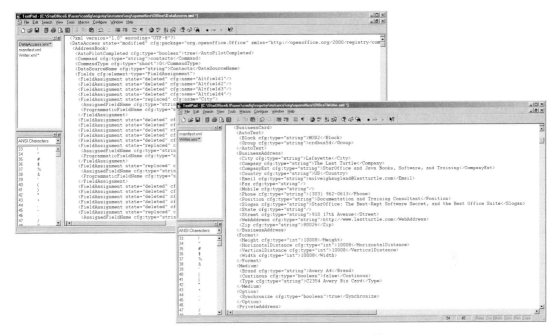

Figure 5-51   The `DataAccess.xml` and `Writer.xml` files

As you can see, files like `Writer.xml` contain some relatively innocuous information like business card data; if you just change your address here, not much bad will happen (probably). If you start messing around with field definitions, that's a little more serious. Also keep in mind that any data stored here might also be stored elsewhere and conflicts could cause uncalled for whackiness in your documents.

Setting Up Security

The program has a lot of options that make you feel safe about opening potentially macro-ridden documents.

Password-Protecting Documents

See *Password-Protecting Documents* on page 158, and *Protecting or Hiding Text Using a Section* on page 416.

Setting Java Options

Choose Tools > Options > *program* > Security. Mark options in Figure 5-53.

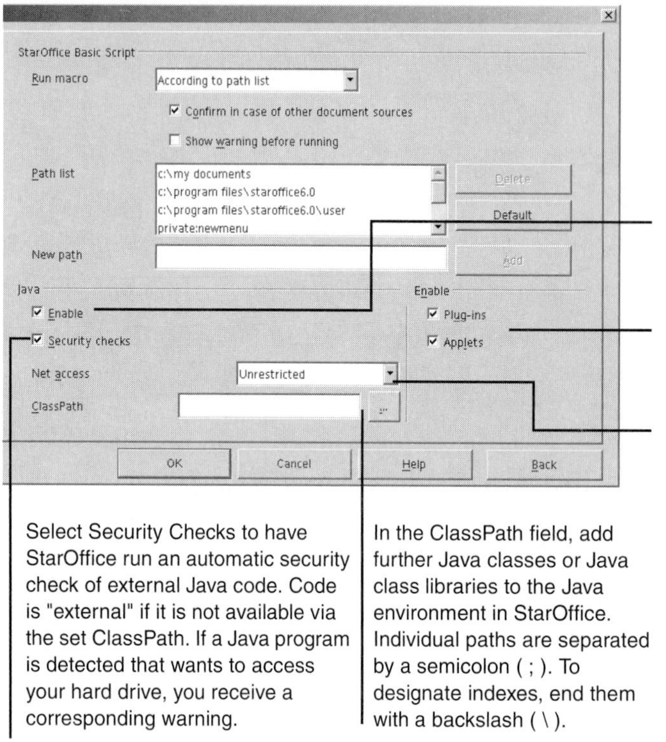
StarOffice Basic Script
Run macro
According to path list
Confirm in case of other document sources
Show warning before running
Path list
c:\my documents
c:\program files\staroffice6.0
c:\program files\staroffice6.0\user
private:newmenu
Delete
Default
New path
Add
Java
Enable
Security checks
Net access
Unrestricted
ClassPath
Enable
Plug-ins
Applets
OK
Cancel
Help
Back
Keep Enable marked unless you have a good reason not to; StarOffice has a few Java programs that need to run. Mark Security checks if you want StarOffice to keep an eye on what Java runs.
If you need to disable plugins and applets in StarOffice documents, unmark these options.
Use the Net Access options to control the access that Java applications on your network have to your StarOffice documents. You can allow unrestricted access, restrict this to the current host (your computer), or by choosing None completely prohibit it.
Select Security Checks to have StarOffice run an automatic security check of external Java code. Code is "external" if it is not available via the set ClassPath. If a Java program is detected that wants to access your hard drive, you receive a corresponding warning.
In the ClassPath field, add further Java classes or Java class libraries to the Java environment in StarOffice. Individual paths are separated by a semicolon (;). To designate indexes, end them with a backslash (\ ).

Figure 5-52 Specifying Java options

Notes on the Security Checks option for Java programs When the Security Checks option is deselected, applets can read and write on all drives. Since JavaScript can access the entire Java environment via the LiveConnect interface, this is also possible for JavaScript when the check is deactivated.

Java classes that are started via the ClassPath, are not subject to any security checks, unlike the Java classes that, for example, are started via an <APPLET> tag in an HTML page.

You can deselect the security checks under either of the following conditions:

- If you know precisely what the applet, Java application, or JavaScript will execute,
- If you are logged on as a Guest under Windows NT / 2000 or UNIX and you are therefore prevented by the operating system from reading and corrupting security-related data.

Controlling Microsoft Documents Containing OLE Objects and Basic Macro Code

Choose Tools > Options > Load/Save and look at the VBA Properties and Microsoft Office windows, shown in Figure 5-53.

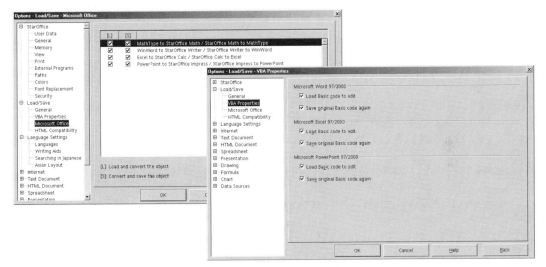

Figure 5-53   Setting OLE and Basic options

Specifying StarBasic Macro Options

To just turn everything off Choose Tools > Options > *program* > Security and turn off macros.

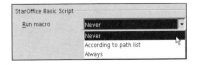

If you'll be handling StarOffice 5.2 or other documents that have StarBasic macros in them, you can determine how and when to run them. The trouble with this of course is that StarOffice still needs some StarBasic scripts to run. Unless you really need to change something, you can leave the defaults as is.

1   Choose Tools > Options > *program* > Security and use Figure 5-54 and the subsequent notes to select the right options.

- The Microsoft Office settings let you specify whether to load and convert OLE Objects in Microsoft files when you open them in the program. Go ahead and leave all these marked unless you have specific reasons for wanting to leave the OLE objects as is.

- The VBA Properties window covers what happens when you open files containing Microsoft's Basic macro code. Unless you absolutely never and never will interchange documents with a Microsoft user, leave all of these checked. Leaving them checked disables the macro code, which is a darned good thing. Select any of the options and press F1 to read more about them in the Help.

The Run Macro list lets you specify how and when to run macros: Always just means always; Never means never; and According to Path List restricts running to only paths in the Path List field below.

If you selected According to Path List in the Run Macro list, Confirm In Case is available. It means that if a macro is in a document that you open from a source not named in the Path List field, you will be prompted to run it or not before the macro is run. If this option is not selected, the macro will be run without any notification.

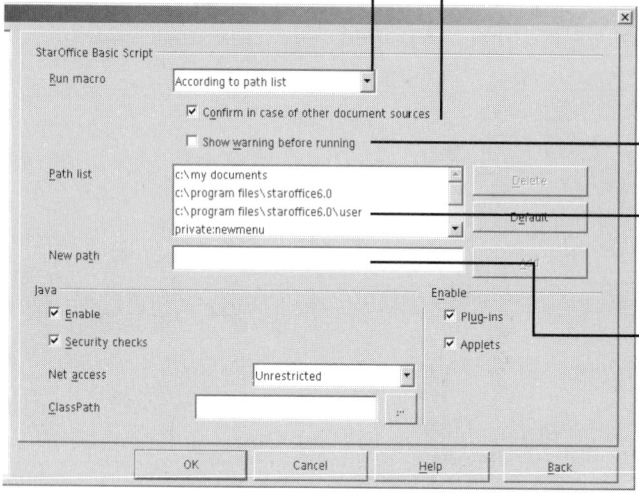

Selecting the Show Warning option means that a warning will appear whenever a macro is about to be run, regardless of the source. This also applies when a document containing formulas with macro calls is loaded.

If you selected According to Path List, this lists the locations where documents must exist for their macros to be run.

To add a path to the Path List, enter it in the New Path field and click Add.

Figure 5-54   Setting StarBasic Options

2   Choose Tools > Options > Browser > HTML and consider whether you need to select the StarBasic option. It must be selected for the program to consider the StarOffice Basic instructions when exporting in HTML format. You must activate this option before you create the StarOffice Basic Script, since otherwise it will not be inserted.

StarOffice Basic and HTML   StarOffice Basic scripts have to be in the header of the HTML document. After you add the macro to the document, it will appear in the source text of the HTML document (in the header) with the following syntax (a "Hello World" example macro is used):

```
<HEAD>
(any additional content)
<SCRIPT LANGUAGE="STARBASIC">
<!--
' $LIBRARY: library_name
' $MODULE: module_name
Sub test
msgbox "Hello World"
End Sub
```

```
// -->
</SCRIPT>
</HEAD>
```

Note – If you restrict the list of trustworthy URLs or choose **Run Macro > Never**, you may receive an error message about missing access rights when you try to run a script, e.g. when you attempt to run an AutoPilot or to load a template. If you want to be careful but not too careful, select According to Path List from the Run Macro list, then put the path to your program's directory, such as `C:\StarOffice6.0`, in the Path List.

You can restore the standard for safe URLs if you have made changes by clicking **Default**.

Setting Up and Viewing Document Characteristics

This section provides useful tips for working with StarOffice documents.

Naming a Document

The name of the document you're working with is displayed in the upper left corner. It's the filename unless you specify a document name.

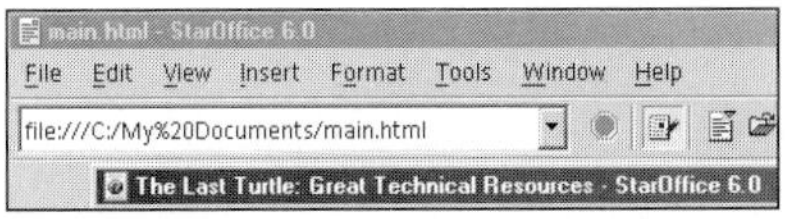

To specify the document name, choose File > Properties and click the Description tab. Enter a name and any other information, then click OK. The window is in Figure 5-55.

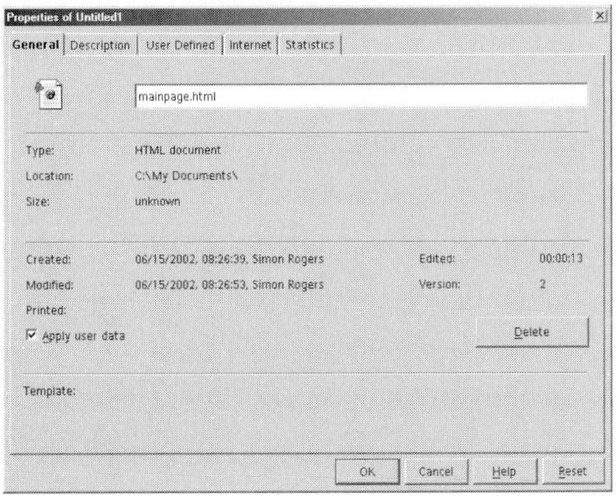

Figure 5-55   Viewing wordcount and other document statistics

Click OK to make the new document name will show up in the document title bar.

Finding the Number of Words or Characters in a Document

Choose File > Properties and click the Statistics tab. Click Update to be sure you're seeing the latest information; the window is shown in Figure 5-56.

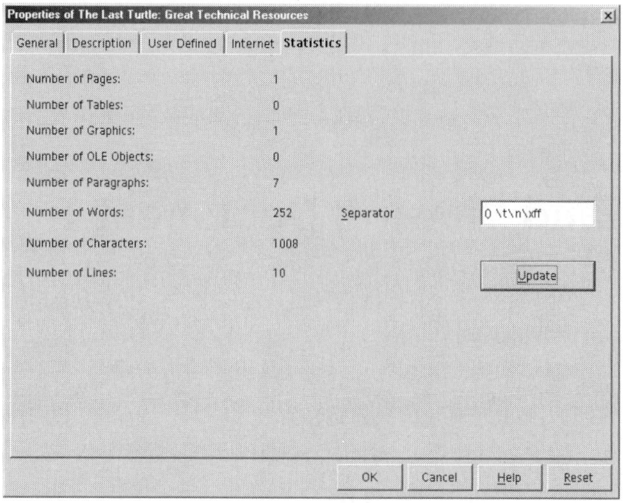

Figure 5-56   Viewing wordcount and other document statistics

To count the number of words in a paragraph or other text selection. use OpenOffice.org; this feature was in development while this book was written. Alternatively, copy the text selection to a new document, then choose File > Properties.

Setting Options That Control Document Properties

Choose Tools > Options > Load/Save > General. Specify the appropriate options as shown in Figure 5-57.

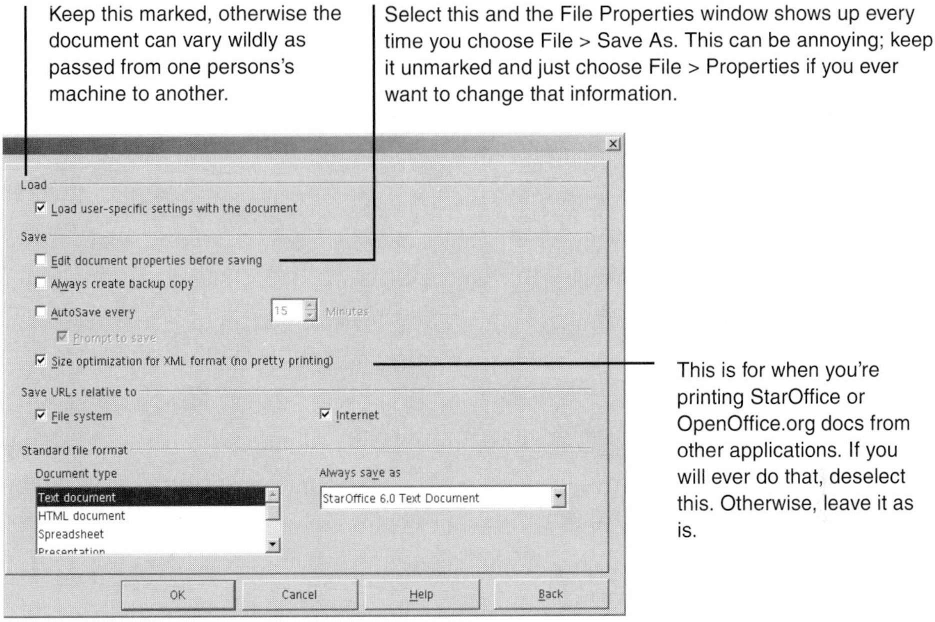

Keep this marked, otherwise the
document can vary wildly as
passed from one persons's
machine to another.

Select this and the File Properties window shows up every
time you choose File > Save As. This can be annoying; keep
it unmarked and just choose File > Properties if you ever
want to change that information.

This is for when you're
printing StarOffice or
OpenOffice.org docs from
other applications. If you
will ever do that, deselect
this. Otherwise, leave it as
is.

Figure 5-57   Options that control what happens when the document is passed around

Getting Your Name and Initials to Show Up in Notes and Document Properties

Choose Tools > Options > *program* > User Data. Enter your information, then click OK.
The information enter here shows up when you choose File > Properties in a document
you've created, and your initials are used to identify you when you enter notes (Insert >
Note) in Writer and Web.

Automatically Saving at a Specified Interval

Note – To turn off this feature, deselect Always Create Backup Copy and AutoSave
Every.

1   Choose Tools > Options > Load/Save > General. See Figure 5-58.

2   Be sure Always Create Backup Copy and Autosave Every are selected.

3   Select Prompt to Save if you want a message to pop up before saving.

4   Enter the number of minutes between every save in the Minutes field.

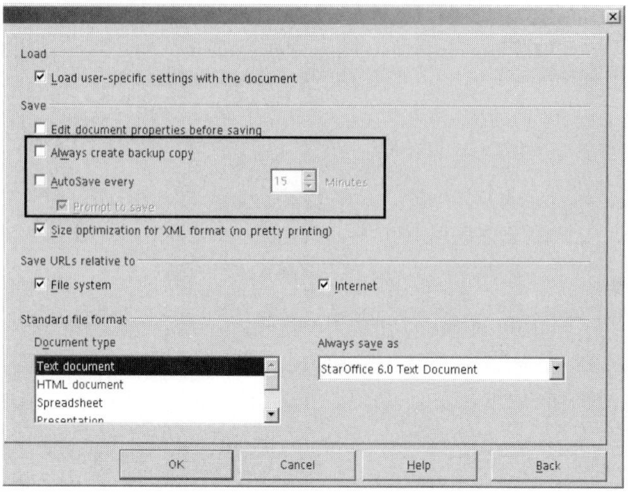

Figure 5-58 Options to mark to save automatically

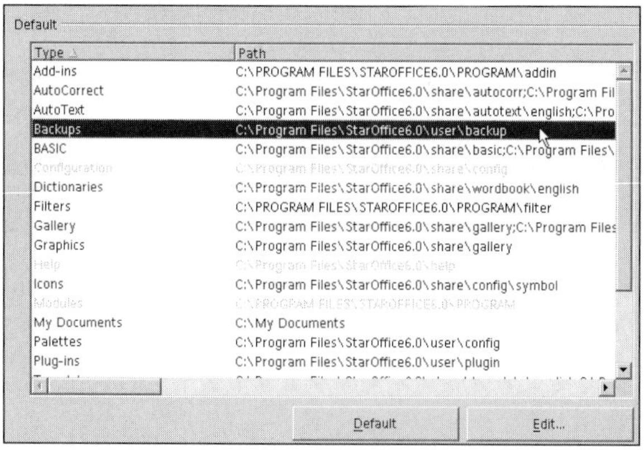

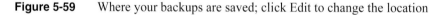

Figure 5-59 Where your backups are saved; click Edit to change the location

5 Choose Tools > Options > *program* > Paths. The window is shown in Figure 5-59. If
you want to change where the backups are saved to, select the Backups line and click
edit, then enter the new path. Click OK.

Disassociating StarOffice and OpenOffice.org From HTML and Microsoft Files

If you weren't paying extremely close attention when you installed, you probably left the
default setting on, the one that automatically opens HTML (and HTM and SHTML) files

in the program. The same defaults were applied to Microsoft Word, Excel, and PowerPoint files. If StarOffice or OpenOffice.org isn't your preferred editor for any of these types, you can disassociate it from those files quite easily.

Windows

Do either of the following:

- Use your operating system tools (View > Folder Options in some versions) to change the application associated with your HTM, HTML, and SHTML files, and Microsoft files.
- Choose Start > Run and in the Open field, type a path like the following, entering the correct path to your Microsoft Office directory, where `program.exe` represents the appropriate program file for the program that you need to register (word.exe, excel.exe, powerpnt.exe).

```
C:\Program Files\Microsoft Office\Office\program.exe /regserver
```

Solaris CDE

1 Locate the `~/.dt/types/StarOffice60.dt` file.

2 Always take appropriate cautions when editing system configuration files; back up this file before you continue.

3 Remove the HTML data below from the `StarOffice60.dt` file, then log out of your computer and log in again. (You have to restart your operating system; it's not enough to restart the program.)

```
DATA_ATTRIBUTES StarOffice_HTML
{
    ACTIONS Open
    ICON Html
}

DATA_CRITERIA StarOffice_HTMLA
{
    DATA_ATTRIBUTES_NAME StarOffice_HTML
    MODE !d
    NAME_PATTERN *.html
}

ACTION Open
{
    ARG_TYPE StarOffice_HTML
    TYPE MAP
    MAP_ACTION StarOffice
```

}

4   If completing this section doesn't work, look for any other .dt files, such as
Old-StarOffice60.dt, and rename them with .old after the .dt. For example,
rename Old-StarOffice60.dt to Old-StarOffice60.dt.old.

Using Automatic File Extensions

When you save a document, you can have the program add the file extension
automatically. You should use this feature most of the time, especially if you can't
remember the StarOffice and OpenOffice.org extensions. Incorrect file extensions you
type manually can make it difficult to track down files later.

In the Save As window, select the Automatic file name extension option before clicking
Save (see Figure 5-60). The program adds the extension automatically.

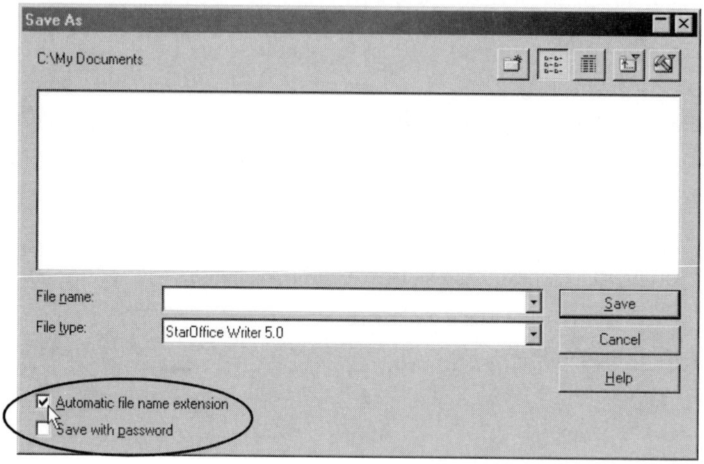

Figure 5-60   Adding file extensions automatically

Password-Protecting Documents

You can assign passwords to documents to keep unauthorized people from opening them.
When you password-protect a document, you're prompted to enter the password when
opening it.

1   In the Save As window, select the Save with password option.

2   When you click Save, the Enter Password window is displayed, as shown in
Figure 5-61.

3   Type in a password, type the password again in the Confirm field, and click OK.

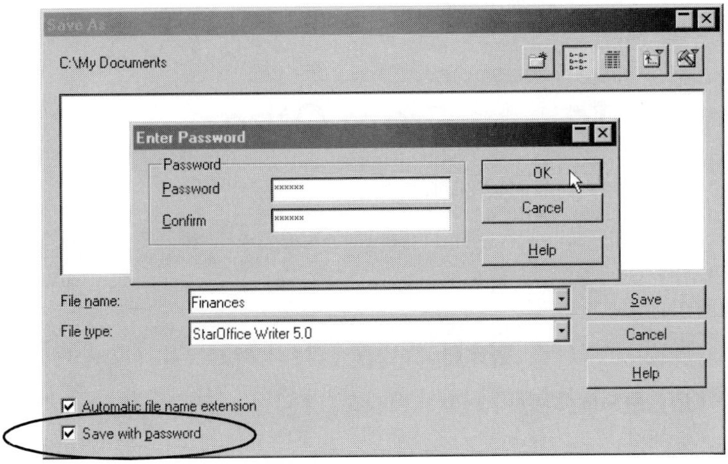

Figure 5-61   Password-protecting a document

Note – If you forget the password, you're out of luck. You can't open or print the document without it. You may want to write down document passwords somewhere, or store them in a text file in an obscure folder on your system.

To turn password protection off for a document, open the document, choose File > Save As, and deselect the Save with password option.

Opening Corrupt Documents

Once in a while (but not too often) a file will become corrupt, resulting in a couple of possible things happening when you try to open the corrupt file: a message telling you the file is corrupt, or the program crashing.

Use this procedure to open a corrupt file, which will recover most if not all of the data.

1   Choose File > Open.

2   In the Open window, select the corrupt file.

3   Press Ctrl+Alt+L.

4   Click OK in the message box that appears.

5   Click the Open button to open the file.

6   Choose File > Save As, and give the file a new name.

You can then open the new file normally.

You might also want to try repairing the program in general. See *Repairing Damaged Installations* on page 44.

Converting To and From Other Applications

You can make StarOffice and OpenOffice.org into Microsoft and vice versa, as outlined in the following procedures.

Specifying Settings for Opening Other Word Processing Documents

Formatting definitions are not always the same in all word processing programs. Define here for example, if you want your Writer documents to be compatible with the MS Word application. The settings defined in this are only valid for the current document and can only be defined separately for each document. These checkboxes are therefore, only active if a text document has been opened.

1   Choose Tools > Options > Text Document > General, as shown in Figure 5-62.

2   Add spacing between paragraphs and tables in the current document. In Writer paragraph spacing is defined differently than in Microsoft Word documents.

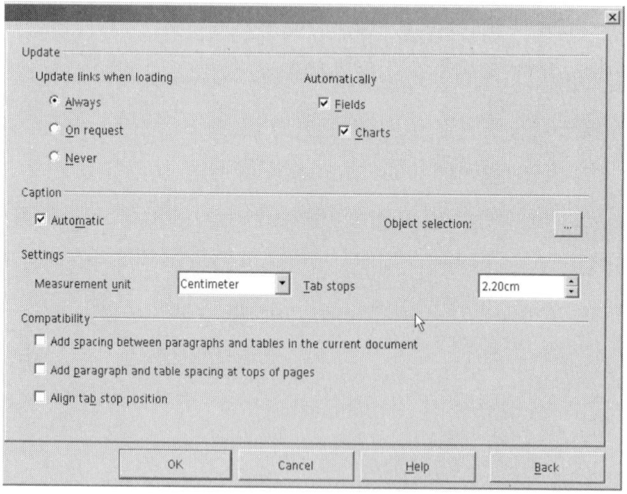

Figure 5-62   Specifying How to Interpret Other Text Documents

If between two paragraphs you have defined spacing above and below each paragraph, the spacing is added in MS Word documents while Writer uses only the larger of the two spaces.

If the spacing between paragraphs and between tables are to be added in Writer, then mark the field.

3   Add paragraph and table spacing to start of pages – If this box is checked, the paragraph spacing to the top will also be effective at the beginning of a page or column if the paragraph is positioned on the first page of the document. The same applies for a page break.

If you import a Microsoft Word document, the spaces are automatically added during the conversion.

4   Aligning tab positions – If this field is marked, centered and right-aligned paragraphs containing tabs are formatted as a whole in the center or aligned to the right. If this field is not marked, only the text to the right of the last tab, for example, is aligned to the right, while the text to the left remains where it is.

Converting Microsoft Office and StarOffice 5.2 Documents

Note – You can't import password protected MS Office files. Microsoft does not specify how they protect their files, so converting or reading the files isn't possible. Any protected MS files you attempt to import just aren't imported.

The easiest way to convert a single Microsoft Word, Excel, or PowerPoint document to a StarOffice or OpenOffice.org format is simply to open it and save it as a Writer, Calc, or Impress document. You can even get tricky and, for example, open a Word 95 document in Writer and save it as a Word 97 document.

While the program can also open documents created in many other applications, it has an automated tool called the AutoPilot for converting Microsoft Word, Excel, and PowerPoint documents and templates to StarOffice and OpenOffice.org documents and templates. One of the most powerful AutoPilot features is that it can convert entire folders of Microsoft Office documents and templates to StarOffice/OpenOffice.org documents and templates in one shot.

The batch converter leaves your Microsoft documents intact, creating converted copies.

Note – After converting Microsoft Office documents,

Considerations.doc	260 KB Microsoft Word Doc...	8/7/2002 6:33 PM
Considerations.sxw	49 KB OpenOffice.org 1.0...	8/7/2002 6:35 PM

you'll see one of the many delights of switching from Microsoft—plummeting file sizes.

1   Select File > AutoPilot > Document Converter. Figure 5-63 appears.

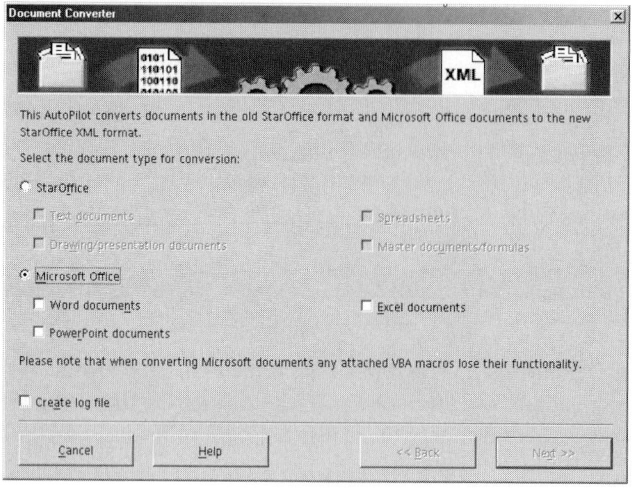

Figure 5-63   Document Converter, first window

2   Select Microsoft files to convert, then the types of Microsoft files, as shown in Figure 5-64. Click Next.

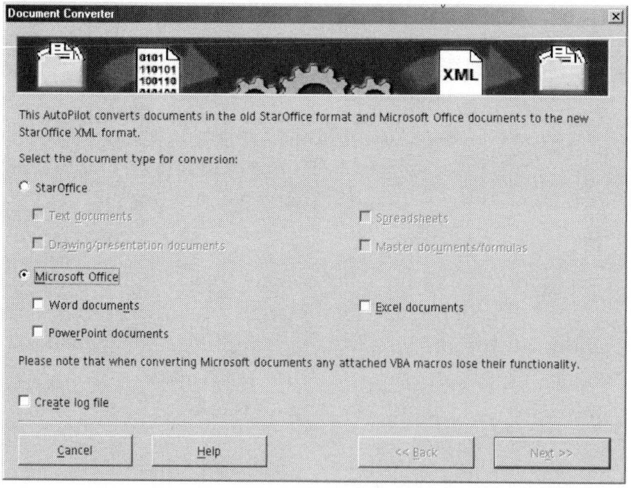

Figure 5-64   Document Converter, second window

3   Choose to convert templates, documents, or both, then specify the source and destination directories, as shown in Figure 5-65. Click Next.

Note – You'll get an additional window like the one in Figure 5-65 for every type of document you chose to convert in Figure 5-64. If you're converting Word, Power-Point, and Excel files, you'll get two more windows prompting you for conversion settings.

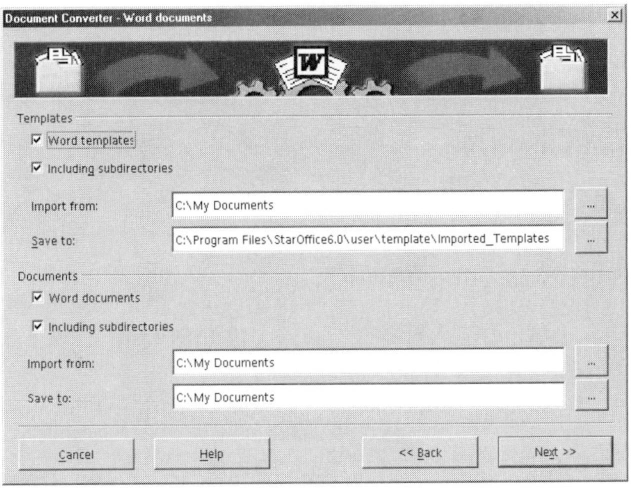

Figure 5-65   Document Converter, third window

4   A confirmation window like the one shown in Figure 5-66 will appear.

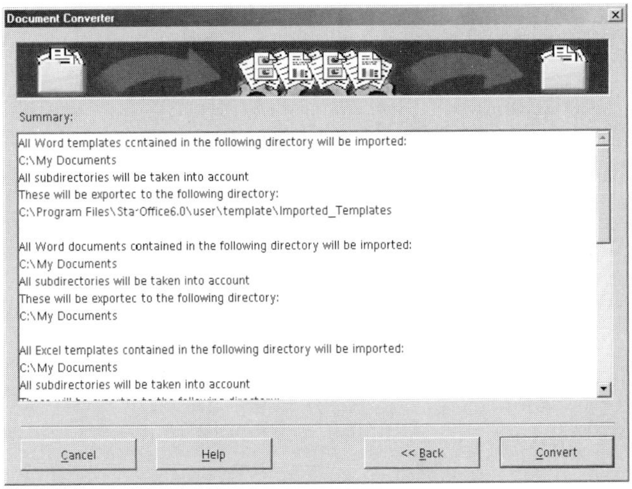

Figure 5-66   Final window of the Microsoft Office Import AutoPilot

5   Click Convert to convert the files. Messages will appear in the Document Converter window, monitoring the conversion process. Click Finished when the process is done to close the window.

Automatically Saving in StarOffice 5.2 or Microsoft Office Formats

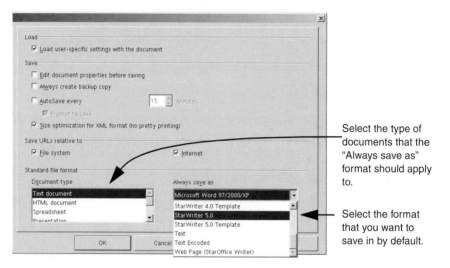

Figure 5-67   Setting default save format for each type of document

If you work with others who need documents in StarOffice 5.2 or Microsoft Office formats, you can always just choose File > Save As and save in that format. However, if you do this a lot, it's easier to make the default format the one you need anyway.

Choose Tools > Options > Load/Save > General, as shown in Figure 5-67.

Printing Setup and Printing

See the printing setup options in *Program-Wide Print Setup Options* on page 85.

Writer

Getting Started With Writer

Quick Start

This section contains the following information to help you get started quickly:

- A checklist that points you to common tasks for quick reference
- Feature overview
- Multiple ways of starting Writer
- An overview of the Writer work area
- A guided tour

See Chapter 5, *Setup and Tips*, on page 97 for general tips that can make working with the program a lot easier.

Quick Start Checklist

If you need to create a document quickly, the following sections should be particularly helpful:

- Starting a document based on a template – *Creating a Writer Document From a Template* on page 176
- Adding headers and footers – *Inserting Headers and Footers* on page 282
- Adding page numbers – *Regular Ol' Page Numbering* on page 314
- Formatting paragraphs – *Quick Paragraph Formatting* on page 206
- Adding graphics – *Inserting an Existing Graphic* on page 268, *Inserting a Gallery Image* on page 269, and *Tips for Adjusting Inserted Objects* on page 298
- Printing and creating PDF files – Chapter 12, *Printing in Writer*, on page 429

Writer Features

Writer is every bit as powerful as any word processing application on the market, and in many ways it's superior. Following are some of the features that set Writer apart:

Document Filters Writer has a huge number of filters for opening documents created in other formats. Its filter for Microsoft Word is particularly good.

Graphics Support You can insert graphics of just about every conceivable format, including Adobe Photoshop PSD.

Conversion From Microsoft The AutoPilot (wizard) lets you convert Microsoft Office documents (even entire directories of them) with a few clicks.

Book Creation Writer offers superior features for creating multi-file books.

Table Features You can perform calculations in Writer tables, and create charts to illustrate the table data. Charts update dynamically when table contents change. Another indispensable table feature is repeatable table headings: type it once, and when a table breaks to a new page the heading appears on the next page automatically.

Text Selection Writer lets you select nonconsecutive blocks of text.

Version Control You can store versions of a Writer document as it moves through a lifecycle, letting you revert back to an earlier version if necessary. Writer also offers a full set of editing aids that display changes made to a document.

With the conditional sections feature, you can select any parts of your document and assign conditional names to those parts. You can then hide or password-protect those conditional sections, letting you show and hide sections to create different versions of the same document. (See *Using Sections to Create Multiple Versions of the Same Document* on page 411 for practical ways to use this feature.) Sections also support content reuse, letting you insert links to sections in other documents, and those sections are updated automatically when the source sections change.

Mail Merge When you're creating a mail merge, you can drag database fields from a database and drop them into a Writer document.

Table of Contents Hyperlinking For easy troubleshooting of tables of contents, or to let readers jump to sections in a document automatically, Writer lets you set up hyperlinks in table of contents entries.

Starting Writer

You can start Writer by choosing File > New > Text Document.

Help With Writer

In addition to the Help topics mentioned in *Getting Help* on page 98, see *Good Online Information Sources* on page 42.

The Writer Work Area

Use tooltips to get to know Writer. There are tooltips for almost all fields and icons. Just position your mouse over anything you want to know the name of. You can turn tooltips on and off by choosing Help > Tips.

Clicking the Help button in a window or pressing F1 is the quickest way to get help for that window. If only general help appears, click in a field in the window.

Figure 6-1 shows the major components of the Writer environment

The **function bar** displays the path of the open file and lets you access global functions.

The **object bar** lets you apply formatting to selected text.

The **ruler** lets you view page dimensions and set tab stops. Right-click the ruler to change the unit of measurement shown on the ruler.

The **toolbar** lets you access commonly used word processing features.

In addition to showing global program commands, the **menu bar** shows commands specific to the active application.

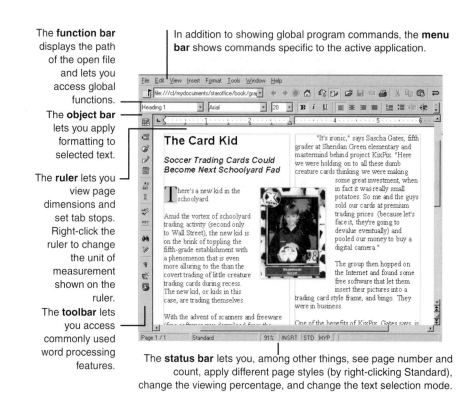

The **status bar** lets you, among other things, see page number and count, apply different page styles (by right-clicking Standard), change the viewing percentage, and change the text selection mode.

Figure 6-1   The Writer work area

Guided Tour of Writer

Use this tutorial to give you a brief introduction to the Writer environment.

1   Launch Writer.

2   Type the following in the document: Gift Ideas for the Boss

3   Press the F11 key to display the Stylist.

4   In the Stylist, make sure the Paragraph Styles icon is selected to display the paragraph styles.

5   Right-click the zoom percentage box in the status bar and select a percentage that displays the document in a comfortable size for you.

6 Click in the text you typed. In the Stylist, double-click Heading 1. The text you typed changes.

7 Press the End key to jump to the end of the line, and press Enter.

8 Type the following four paragraphs (pressing Enter at the end of each):

```
Following are the top three gift ideas for the boss:

New crystal ball

Replacement case of spearmint Euphoria Gum

Machiavelli's Essential New Age Guide to Dealing With Smart
Aleck Minions
```

9 Select the last three paragraphs by dragging through them.

10 In the object bar, click the bullets icon. If you don't see the icon, use Figure 6-2 for guidance.

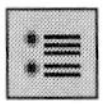

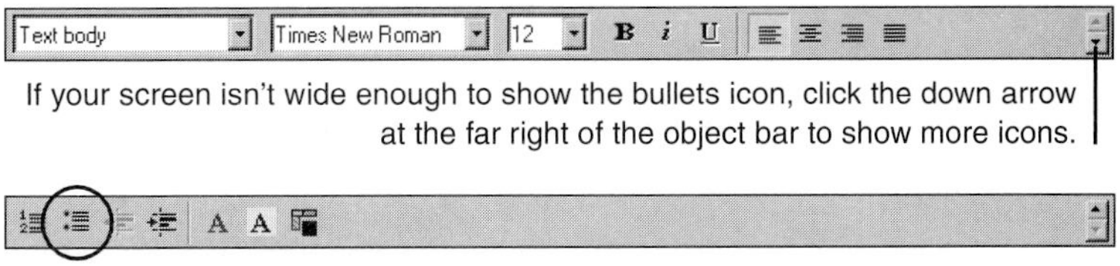

If your screen isn't wide enough to show the bullets icon, click the down arrow at the far right of the object bar to show more icons.

Figure 6-2   Showing more icons

The last three sentences become a bulleted list.

11 With the bulleted paragraphs still highlighted, click the Increase Indent icon in the object bar. The list indents to the right.

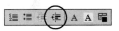

12 Click in the `Gift Ideas for the Boss` heading paragraph, and select Format > Paragraph.

13 In the Paragraph window (Figure 6-3 on page 172), on the Indents & Spacing tab, change the Bottom spacing to .25 (don't forget the decimal point in front).

14 Click OK. The space increases between the heading paragraph and the first body paragraph.

15 Select the entire heading paragraph and select Format > Character.

16 In the Character window, on the Font tab, change the color to Red.

17 Click OK. The paragraph font color changes to Red.

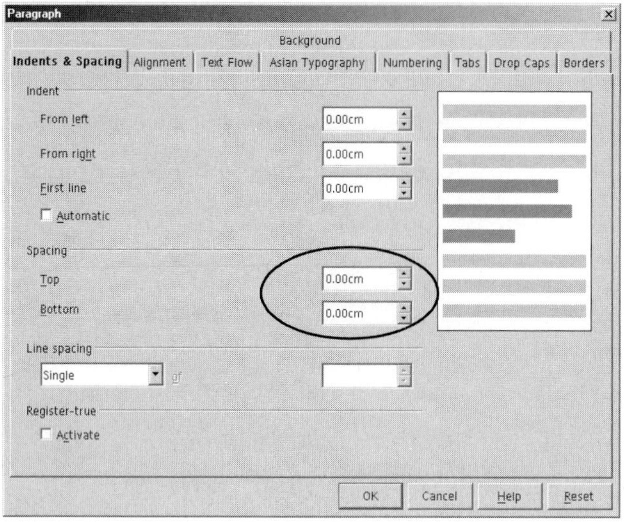

Figure 6-3   The Paragraph window

18 Click at the end of the last bulleted paragraph and press Enter. Another bullet is
       displayed.

19 Click the Bullets icon to end the bulleted list, or just press Enter again.

In the next steps you'll insert a table. You may need to adjust your zoom percentage to see
more of the page.

20 In the toolbar click and hold down the
       Insert icon. Another set of icons is
       displayed.

21 Move the pointer to the table icon. A small
       table picture is displayed below the icon. Move the pointer into the table picture so
       that two columns and four rows are selected (Figure 6-4), and release the mouse
       button.

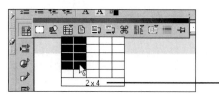

Column x Row dimensions

Figure 6-4   Inserting a two-column, four-row table

A two-column, four-row table is inserted into the document.

22 In the two heading row cells, type the following: `GiftPrice`

Notice the table headings have their own paragraph format.

23 Type the gift names in the remaining cells of the Gift column, and type their prices in the Price cells. (After you enter the last price, click below the table.)

```
Crystal Ball            $45
Euphoria Gum            $18
Machiavelli's Guide     $120
```

Because you added dollar signs, the program adds .00 to the end of the numbers.

In the final steps you'll insert a header that includes the date and page number.

24 Select Insert > Header > Standard. A header text box is displayed.

25 In the main toolbar, click and hold down the Insert Fields icon, and select Date. The current date is displayed in the header.

26 Press the Tab key twice.

27 Click and hold down the Insert Fields icon again, and select Page Numbers. The page number is displayed in the right side of the header.

Post-Tutorial Tip

When you applied the Heading 1 paragraph style to your heading earlier in the exercise, the heading took on automatic format properties (font, font size, font color, and spacing between the heading and the first body paragraph). Let's say that after you made these changes to the heading (increasing the space between paragraphs and changing the font color to red), you wanted all your Heading 1 paragraphs to have the new formats. Simply highlight the entire paragraph, then click and drag it onto the Heading 1 item in the Stylist, as shown in Figure 6-5.

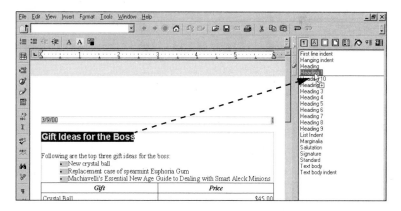

Figure 6-5   Updating a style by dragging and dropping

Writer Setup Options

There are hundreds of setup options—probably more than you will ever need to control. Choose Tools > Options > Text document to view the Writer options.

We don't go through each window of options one by one, for the following reasons:

- The important settings are covered in procedures throughout the book.
- Many are self-explanatory.
- The default settings for these options are *generally* well chosen.

However, the options aren't in an obvious place in any of the menu bars or object bars— you need to choose Tools > Options > Text document—so we've pointed them out here to make sure you're aware of them. It's also helpful to know what types of functions these options do control, so if you want to know that before you start using this program, open the options now to get an idea of their scope before continuing.

The options are default values used for each new Writer document.

Keyboard Shortcuts

Table 6-1 lists some of the more useful keyboard shortcuts that can save you time while working with Writer documents.

Table 6-1   Useful Writer keyboard shortcuts

Pressing this...	Does this
F5	Opens/Closes Navigator window (whether it's docked or undocked).
F11	Opens/Closes the Stylist window (whether it's docked or undocked).
Home	Moves the cursor to the beginning of the line.
End	Moves the cursor to the end of the line.
Ctrl+Home	Jumps to the beginning of the document.
Ctrl+End	Jumps to the end of the document.
F9	Updates fields (such as cross-references, dates, and page numbers).
Ctrl+Enter	Creates a manual page break.
F12	Applies numbering to selected paragraphs. Also removes numbering.
Shift+F12	Applies bullets to selected paragraphs. Also removes bullets.
Shift+Enter	Creates a soft return. In a paragraph, a soft return drops the cursor to the next line (properly indented in a bulleted or numbered list) without creating a new paragraph.

Table 6-1   Useful Writer keyboard shortcuts

Pressing this...	Does this
Ctrl+b	Applies/Removes bold formatting in selected text.
Ctrl+i	Applies/Removes italic formatting in selected text.
Ctrl+u	Applies/Removes underlining in selected text.
Ctrl+z	Undo. Reverses the previous change you made.
Ctrl+Space	Creates a nonbreaking space to keep items together on the same line.
Ctrl+a	Selects all contents of the document.

Creating a New Document

You can create a new Writer document in a number of ways: from scratch, with the AutoPilot, or based on a template.

Creating a Document From Scratch

Choose File > New > Text Document.

Using AutoPilot to Create a Document

The AutoPilot is a powerful tool that guides you through the creation of four types of Writer documents: a letter, a fax, an agenda, or a memo. AutoPilot formats your document based on the elements you choose to include in the document (such as a logo, subject line, date, agenda topics, and owners, etc.). The AutoPilot for the letter and fax even let you set up mail merge fields from a database. (For more information on mail merges, see Chapter 10, *Mail Merges, Business Cards, and More*, on page 351.)

AutoPilot also lets you save the document as a template.

The best way to see how AutoPilot creates documents is to experiment with it. If you're not sure what a specific option is in an AutoPilot window, select the option and see how it appears in the document after you click the Create button.

1   Choose File > AutoPilot > (Letter, Fax, Agenda, or Memo).

2   Follow the instructions and explanations in AutoPilot (Figure 6-6). You don't have to go through every window; you can click the Create button at any time.

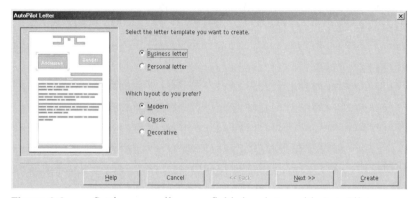

Figure 6-6   Setting up mail merge fields in a letter with AutoPilot

For more information on hooking up to a data source using an AutoPilot, see *Creating Mail Merge Letters and Faxes With Data Sources Using AutoPilots* on page 380.

Creating a Writer Document From a Template

Note – All the templates, etc. in StarOffice don't come with OpenOffice.org. However, Travis Bauer's excellent Web site, www.ooextras.org, has what might be called a plethora of templates and other "extras." Additionally, some Microsoft Word templates, if you have that application lying around, work quite well when converted from Word just by being opened or by using the conversion AutoPilot. See *Automatically Saving in StarOffice 5.2 or Microsoft Office Formats* on page 164.

You can create new documents from templates. For more information on templates, see *Using Templates* on page 256.

1   Choose File > New > Templates and Documents.

2   In the New window (see Figure 6-7), select a template category from the Categories list. Categories correspond to template folders within the Office60 folder.

3   Select the template you want in the Templates list.

     If you want to preview the template and see a description of it, click the More button and select the Preview option.

4   Click OK. A new Writer document opens with the template formatting and styles.

When you save the document, it saves as a Writer document (not as a template) by default.

When you create a document from a template using this procedure, you can look at the document properties (File > Properties, General tab) to see the name of the template the document is based on.

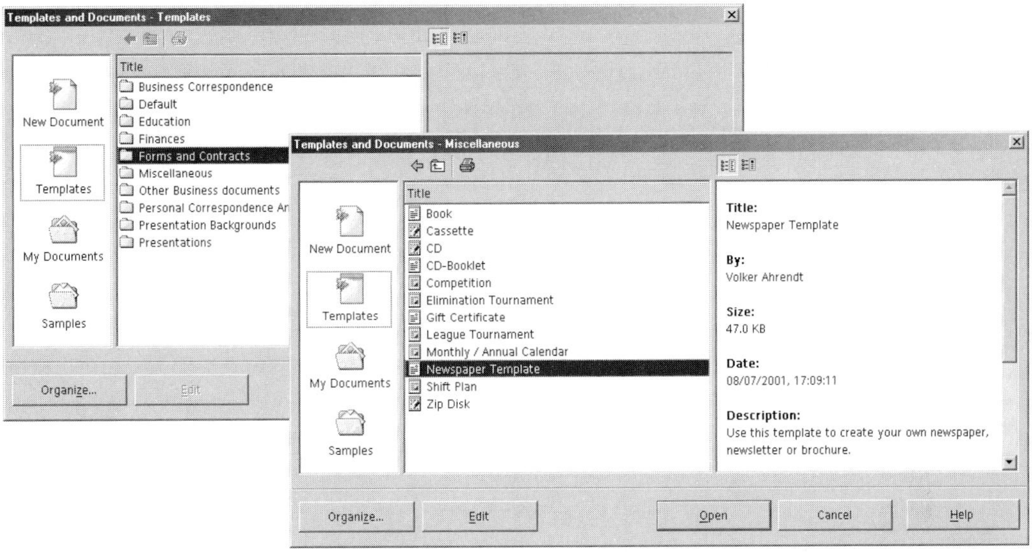

Figure 6-7   Creating a new document from a template

If your template is located in a folder other than one of the program's template folders (`office\share\template\`*`language`*`\`*`template_folder`* or `office\user\template\`*`template_folder`*), you won't be able to select the template in the New window. You have to move the template to one of the template folders so you can select it in the New window.

Note – If you don't want to use any of the existing templates, use the AutoPilot to create a specific type of document. See *Using AutoPilot to Create a Document* on page 175.

Changing Default Fonts and the Default Template

When you create a new Writer document from scratch (see page 175), Writer uses its Standard template for the new, blank document. The Standard, or default, template has its own paragraph formatting styles defined. For example, standard body text is set to a certain font, as are headings, bulleted and numbered lists, figure captions you insert, and text in indexes you generate.

To change the default fonts or template, see *Changing Default Fonts and the Default Template* on page 177.

Working With Non-Writer Documents

One of StarOffice's and OpenOffice.org's greatest strengths is its ability to open documents that were created in other word processing applications—in fact, in a multitude of other applications. In particular, the programs are good at opening and converting documents that were created in Microsoft Office.

If you want to view the file types you can convert, choose File > Open. In the Open window, click the File type field and scroll through the list of formats.

In addition to opening documents of other formats into Writer, you can also insert them into existing Writer documents, where they take on the Writer format automatically. See *Inserting Other Documents* on page 297.

To see which kinds of document formats Writer can save to, make sure Writer is active and choose File > Save As. Click the File type field and scroll through the list of formats.

Opening an Existing Document

Just choose File > Open and navigate to the document.

Getting All the Filters for Importing Other Documents

The standard install doesn't give you all the filters for other documents like FrameMaker. If you're having problems importing documents, do the custom installation and select all text document filters. See *Installing Additional Components* on page 35.

OpenOffice.org, at the time this book went to press, didn't include a filter for WordPerfect.

Turning Writer Documents Into HTML

See *Making an HTML Version of a Document* on page 144. The resulting HTML has a lot of <class> tags; it's not clean HTML.

Sending a Document as Email

See *Sending a Document as Email* on page 144.

Controlling Measurement and Ruler Display

The following sections provide tips to help you get the most out of Writer.

Displaying a Vertical Ruler

By default, Writer displays a horizontal ruler in documents. You can also turn on a vertical ruler. This is particularly useful for lining up objects in a document such as graphics.

1   Choose Tools > Options > Text document > Layout.

2   Select the Vertical ruler option.

3   Click OK.

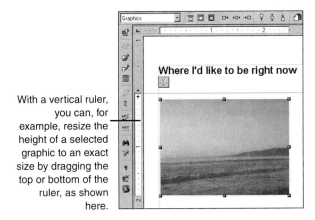

With a vertical ruler, you can, for example, resize the height of a selected graphic to an exact size by dragging the top or bottom of the ruler, as shown here.

Figure 6-8   Displaying a vertical ruler

Changing the Unit of Measurement

You can change the unit of measurement shown on the ruler by right-clicking the ruler. However, this doesn't change the unit of measurement shown in formatting and other windows throughout Writer. To change the overall Writer unit of measurement:

1   Choose Tools > Options > Text Document > General.

2   Change the unit of measurement in the Meas. units field, and Click OK.

Creating and Inserting AutoText

If there's a set of boilerplate text you use frequently that you don't want to retype every time you use it, such as an email signature, trademarked term, or company letterhead heading, create an AutoText entry for it in Writer. This is also used when you create business cards from the program's templates or use other business correspondence templates. When you do this, you can insert it quickly—either with a keyboard shortcut or by selecting it from a list of AutoText items.

AutoText entries can be formatted and can include graphics, tables, and fields.

Creating AutoText Entries

1   In a Writer document, create the text you want to turn into AutoText. Apply formatting and include graphics if desired.

2   Select the text and elements you want to include.

3   Click the AutoText tool in the main toolbar to display the AutoText window.

4   Type a Name and Shortcut for the new AutoText.

5   Select the category (below the Name field) in which you want to store the new AutoText (see Figure 6-9).

    Categories are simply containers for organizing AutoText items. If you want to create your own categories for storing AutoText items, see *Adding New AutoText Categories* on page 182.

6   Click and hold down the AutoText button, and select New, as shown at right.

7   The new AutoText name is displayed in its category. Click the + symbol to the left of the category you added it to, to see the name.

8   Click Close, or click Insert if you want to add it to your document. This is a good idea, just to test the AutoText. Also click on the AutoText icon in the main toolbar and see that the new item shows up, in the category you added it to.

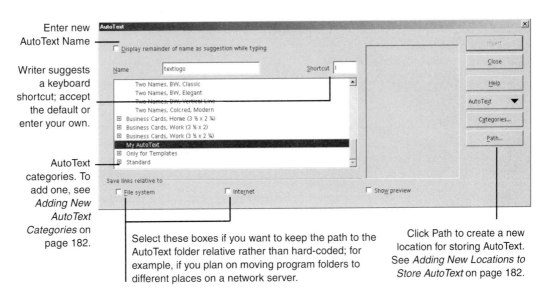

Enter new AutoText Name ⎯

Writer suggests a keyboard shortcut; accept the default or enter your own.

AutoText categories. To add one, see *Adding New AutoText Categories* on page 182.

Select these boxes if you want to keep the path to the AutoText folder relative rather than hard-coded; for example, if you plan on moving program folders to different places on a network server.

Click Path to create a new location for storing AutoText. See *Adding New Locations to Store AutoText* on page 182.

Figure 6-9   The AutoText window

The Path button If you want to use other paths than the default AutoText path, you must add the new paths either by clicking the Path button in the AutoText dialog or by modifying the AutoText option by choosing Tools > Options > *program* > Paths. See *Adding New Locations to Store AutoText* on page 182.

The entries AutoCorrect, AutoText, Basic, Templates and Gallery in that Paths window may indicate more than one path. In a network environment, for example, the {netinstall} directory contains several files. They are accessible to all users, but cannot normally be changed, since users have read-only access. For that reason, AutoText modules defined by the users themselves are automatically placed in the directory below {userinstall}, to which he also has write-access.

Editing Existing AutoText Items

1   With Writer active, click the AutoText tool in the toolbar.

2   Select the name of the AutoText you want to edit.

3   Click the AutoText button and select Edit. The AutoText window closes and the AutoText opens in a new Writer document.

4   Make edits to the AutoText in Writer.

5   Select the edited AutoText.

6   Click the AutoText tool in the toolbar.

7   In the AutoText window, select the name of the AutoText you edited.

8   Click the AutoText button and select Replace.

9   Click Close.

Adding New Locations to Store AutoText

If you want to store AutoText in a location other than the default locations, you need to explicitly add it using this procedure.

1   With Writer active, click the AutoText tool in the toolbar.

2   In the AutoText window (see Figure 6-9), click the Path button.

3   The Select Paths window will appear (see Figure 6-10). Enter the new location and click OK.

Click Add to bring up
the paths dialog.

Click OK when you've
finished adding paths.

Figure 6-10   Adding a new AutoText location

Adding New AutoText Categories

The AutoText categories are simply storage containers for organizing AutoText. Writer comes with three predefined categories: signature, standard, and template. You can add your own categories for storing AutoText you create.

You might want to add a new location for the AutoText category before you begin; you can't add it on the fly. If you do, see *Adding New Locations to Store AutoText* on page 182.

1   With Writer active, click the AutoText tool in the toolbar.

2   In the AutoText window (see Figure 6-11), click the Categories button.

3   In the Categories window, type the name of the category you want to add.

4   Click New.

5   Click OK.

Type the name of the new category and click New. ⟶

Path where the category will be stored. If the path you want isn't here, see *Adding New Locations to Store AutoText* on page 182.

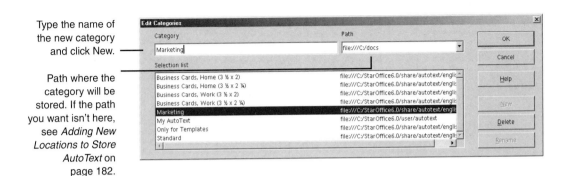

Figure 6-11   Adding a category

Moving AutoText to Different Categories

To move AutoText items from one category to another, drag the AutoText item you want to move into the new category, as shown in Figure 6-12.

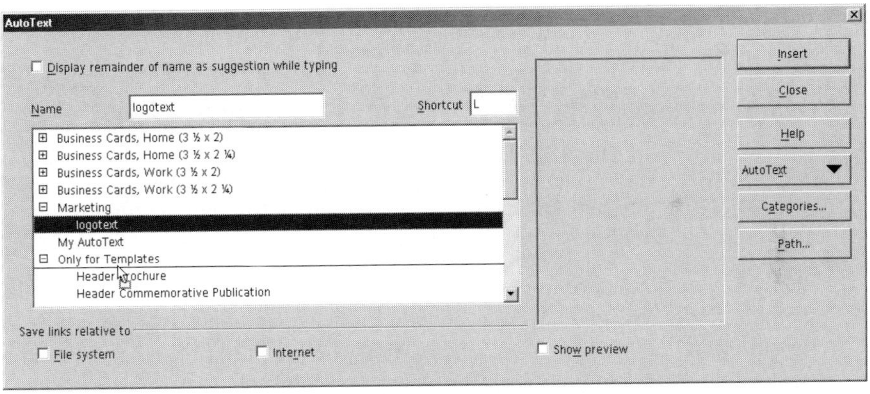

Figure 6-12   Dragging AutoText into another category

Inserting AutoText Entries in Your Document

See the previous procedures for information on creating, editing, and organizing AutoText.

1   In your open document, click where you want to insert the AutoText.

2   Click and hold the AutoText tool in the toolbar, choose the category of the AutoText, and select the AutoText name, as shown in Figure 6-13.

If you know the shortcut for the AutoText you want to insert, you can also type it (for example, "SL") and press the F3 key.

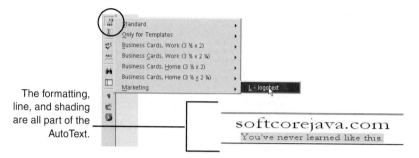

The formatting, line, and shading are all part of the AutoText.

Figure 6-13   AutoText inserted from the toolbar

Note – To use and edit the information in the Fields window, see *Creating and Inserting Predefined Information Using Fields* on page 284.

Selecting Text

This section covers tips and tricks about how to grab what you want and do stuff to it.

About the Direct Cursor Feature: Just Say No

The direct cursor feature, which we don't recommend you use, lets you click in any blank area of a page to insert empty paragraphs and tabs up to the point where you click. Activate direct cursor by clicking its tool on the toolbar.

The reason we don't recommend using it is because creating spacing by inserting a bunch of empty paragraphs and tabs runs counter to good paragraph style control. (See *Power Formatting With Styles* on page 241.) Also, if you forget to turn the feature off, you could accidentally add paragraphs and tabs where you didn't really want to, and you'd have to take another step to undo it.

But if you do use direct cursor, make sure to use it with nonprinting characters turned on (also on the toolbar) so you can see the results.

You can set specific options for the behavior of direct cursor by choosing Tools > Options > Text document > Formatting Aids.

Selecting Nonconsecutive Blocks of Text

Writer lets you select nonconsecutive blocks of text for cutting, copying, deleting, and formatting.

1   In the status bar, click the box that says STD until it reads ADD, as shown in Figure 6-14. Choosing ADD changes the text selection mode.

Note – We found that it seems to work without changing the text selection mode, but wanted to make sure we included both methods.

---

2   Select nonconsecutive blocks of text.

After you perform an action on nonconsecutive text selections, such as deleting, cutting, or pasting, selection mode returns to STD automatically.

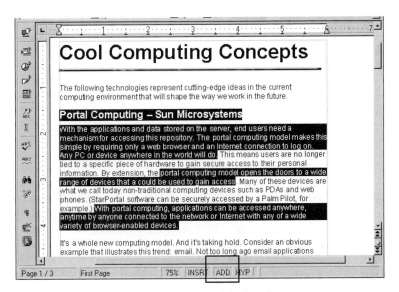

Figure 6-14   Selecting nonconsecutive blocks of text

Quotation Marks, ™ Symbols, Inline Text, and Word Counts

This section covers how to get those necessary, non-standard characters into your documents.

Word Count Setup and Procedures

Doing a Word or Character Count of a Document or Paragraph

Choose File > Properties and click the Statistics tab. The number of words, characters, paragraphs, and other items in the document are displayed.

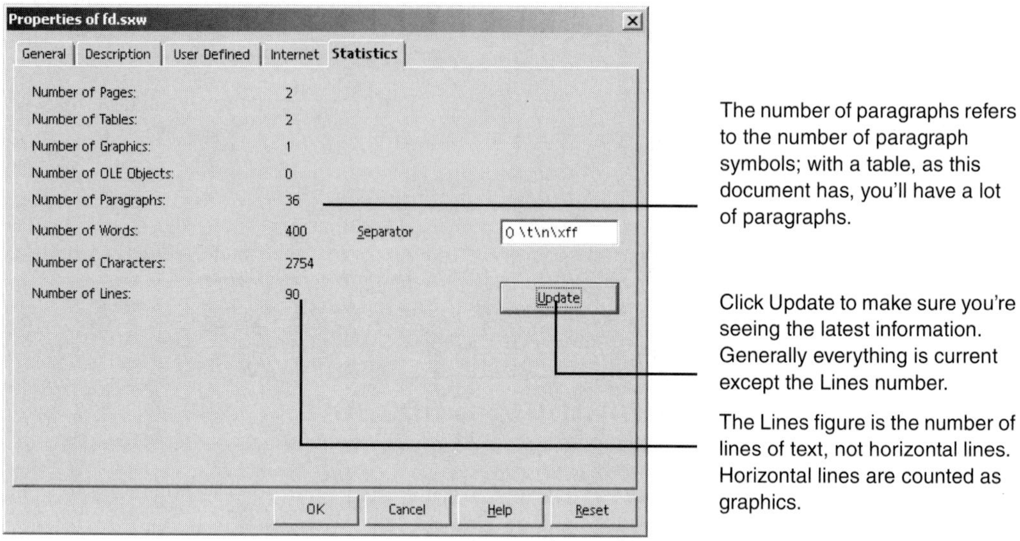

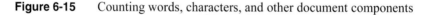

Properties of fd.sxw
General
Description
User Defined
Internet
Statistics
Number of Pages: 2
Number of Tables: 2
Number of Graphics: 1
Number of OLE Objects: 0
Number of Paragraphs: 36
Number of Words: 400
Separator
0 \t\n\xff
Number of Characters: 2754
Number of Lines: 90
Update
OK
Cancel
Help
Reset
The number of paragraphs refers to the number of paragraph symbols; with a table, as this document has, you'll have a lot of paragraphs.
Click Update to make sure you're seeing the latest information. Generally everything is current except the Lines number.
The Lines figure is the number of lines of text, not horizontal lines. Horizontal lines are counted as graphics.

Figure 6-15 Counting words, characters, and other document components

To count a subset of your document, you'll need to copy and paste the paragraph or other subset into a different document, and choose File > Properties again. Or check `http://www.ooextras.org` for OpenOffice.org's macro that does the count.

Specifying Characters That Affect Counts

Choose File > Properties and click the Statistics tab. The window is shown in Figure 6-16.

Properties of The Last Turtle: Great Technical Resources
General
Description
User Defined
Internet
Statistics
Number of Pages: 1
Number of Tables: 0
Number of Graphics: 1
Number of OLE Objects: 0
Number of Paragraphs: 7
Number of Words: 252
Separator
0 \t\n\xff
Number of Characters: 1008
Number of Lines: 10
Update
OK
Cancel
Help
Reset

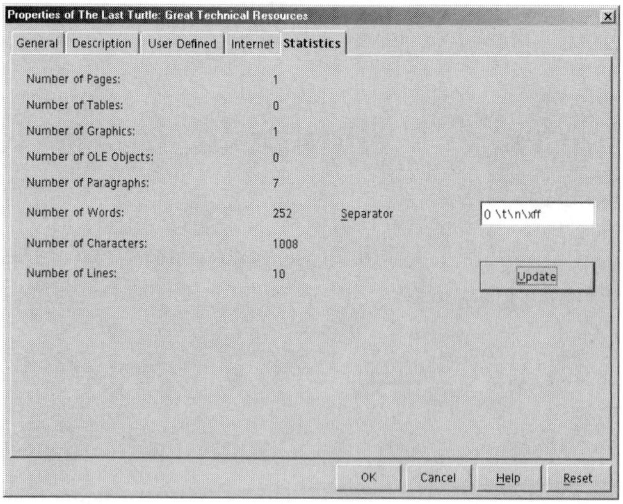

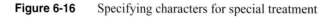

Figure 6-16 Specifying characters for special treatment

- If you want words containing slashes, dashes, and so on to be counted as separate words, enter the relevant character in the Separator field. This ensures that combined words such as Smith/Owens or Smith&Owens are counted as two words.

- You can also enter special characters and non-printable characters so that any ASCII hexadecimal code in your document will be read correctly.

- Special characters such as \n (line feed) and \t (tab) are also supported.

Setting Up Quotation Marks

The most common use of this feature is to control the type of quotation marks used in a document. More specifically, use this feature to switch back and forth between using straight quotes and curly quotes (called "smart quotes" in other applications).

This feature also lets you substitute single and double quotes with any other characters you want.

1   With a document of some type open, choose Tools > AutoCorrect. (With a text or HTML document open, the menu item is AutoCorrect/AutoFormat.)

2   In the AutoCorrect window, select the Custom Quotes tab.

3   Set the options for using quotes. Use Figure 6-17 for guidance.

4   Click OK.

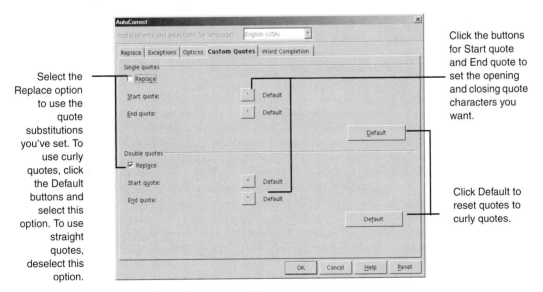

Select the Replace option to use the quote substitutions you've set. To use curly quotes, click the Default buttons and select this option. To use straight quotes, deselect this option.

Click the buttons for Start quote and End quote to set the opening and closing quote characters you want.

Click Default to reset quotes to curly quotes.

Figure 6-17   Setting quote options

Inserting the ™ Symbol, Accents Marks, and Hundreds of Other Special Characters

Not only does the program have the new Asian language support, it has special characters enough to satisfy any appetite or document needs. Plus the usual basics like ™ and ®.

1   Choose Insert > Special Character. The window is shown in Figure 6-18.

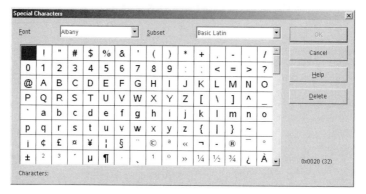

Figure 6-18   The Special Characters window

2   Select the font if you want to specify the formatting, but you can change it once you put it in the document, The font matters only for things like WingDings, where the characters really do change based on the font.

3   Either select a subset, or just scroll through. The item you select in the Subset field just moves you to the beginning of that set in the scrolling window; it doesn't show you a whole different set of characters.

Note – If you commonly use a word with a special character, such as a product name with a trademark symbol, you can set up an AutoText entry for it. See *Creating Auto-Text Entries* on page 180.

---

4   Select one or more characters to insert. If you click on ®, then on ™, before clicking Insert, both will be inserted in the document. Which is only a benefit, not a drawback, since of course you can delete anything you don't want. The window is shown in Figure 6-19.

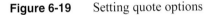

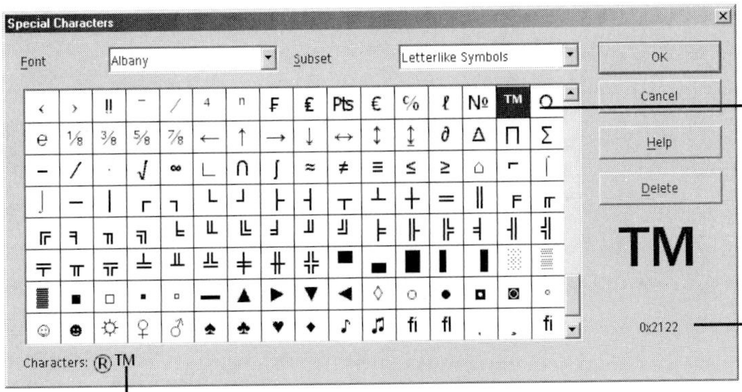
Special Characters
Font
Albany
Subset
Letterlike Symbols
OK
Cancel
Help
Delete
TM
0x2122
Characters: ®TM
Click on every character you want, in the order you want them. When you're done, click OK to insert the characters.
The hexadecimal equivalent is shown here; see also *Specifying Characters That Affect Counts* on page 186.
Every character you have selected is displayed here; they will all be inserted when you click OK.

Figure 6-19 Setting quote options

5 Click OK; the characters will appear in your document.

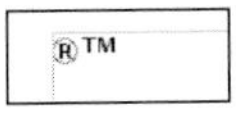
®TM

Adding In-Line Explanatory Text for a Word or Phrase

Ruby text allows you to add explanatory text next to complex Asian characters. Choose Format > Ruby and enter the base text (the Asian characters) and the corresponding explanatory text. This is also useful if you anticipate an audience whose native language is not the document's language, or if your document contains many technical terms that your audience will appreciate reminders of their meanings.

To insert text, follow these steps.

1 Chose Format > Ruby. The window is shown in Figure 6-20.

2 Enter the complex text in the first field in the left column, and the explanatory text in the right column. Beneath the columns, specify how to format the explanatory text.

3 Click OK. The phrase and explanation will be inserted in the document.

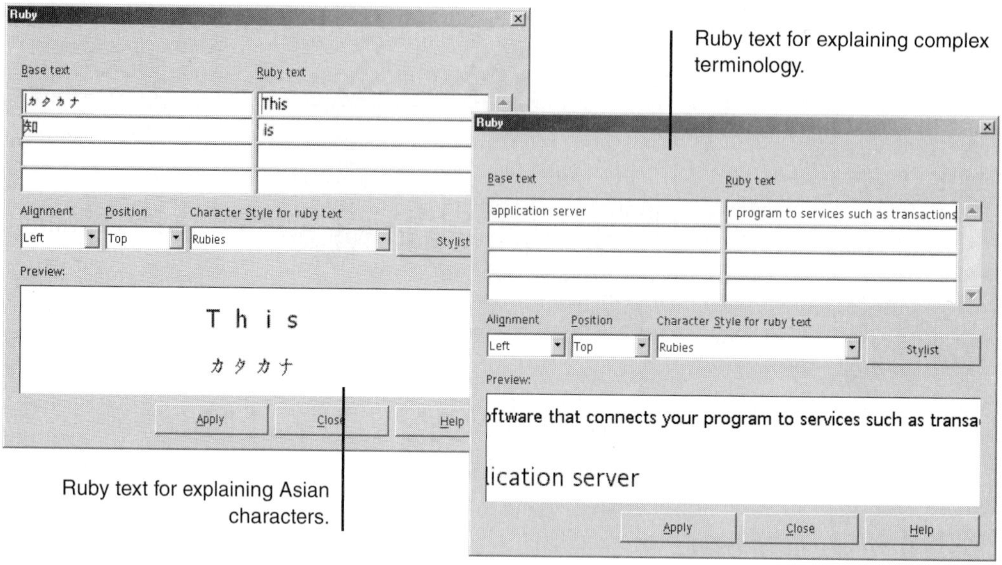

Ruby text for explaining complex terminology.

Ruby text for explaining Asian characters.

Figure 6-20   Setting up explanatory Ruby text

Click Apply; the text and explanation will appear in your text, as shown in Figure 6-21. The formatting of the Ruby text depends on your formatting selections.

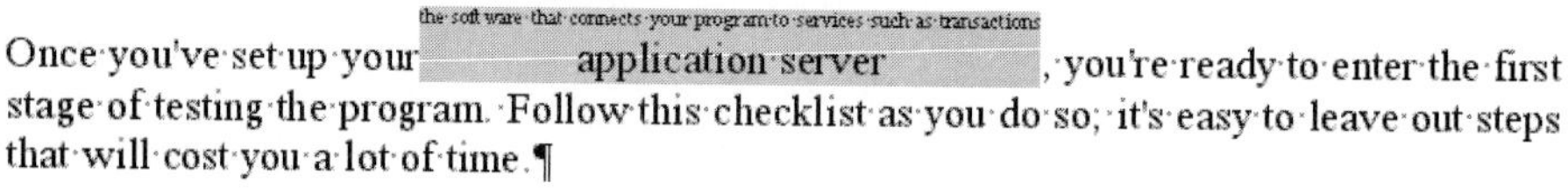

Once you've set up your application server, you're ready to enter the first stage of testing the program. Follow this checklist as you do so; it's easy to leave out steps that will cost you a lot of time.¶

Figure 6-21   Ruby text, used here to add inline text explanation of technical term

Spellchecking and Hyphenation

Not only do you get to just run normal spellcheck, there's all sorts of extra stuff to tweak.

Using Automatic Spellcheck

The automatic spell checking feature places a squiggly line under misspelled words.

- Choose Tools > Options > Language Settings > Writing Aids. Under Options, select AutoCheck. Click OK.

- Choose Tools > Spellcheck > AutoSpellcheck and select it so that there's a checkmark next to the option.

- Or turn automatic spell check on and off while working in a document by clicking the AutoSpellcheck button on the toolbar.

Spellchecking

1   If you want to only spellcheck a portion of the document, select it.

> Ever since that terrible day when I changed my hair colour to puce, my life has been a shambles.

2   Choose Tools > Spellcheck > Check or press F7; the spellcheck window will appear as shown in Figure 6-19.

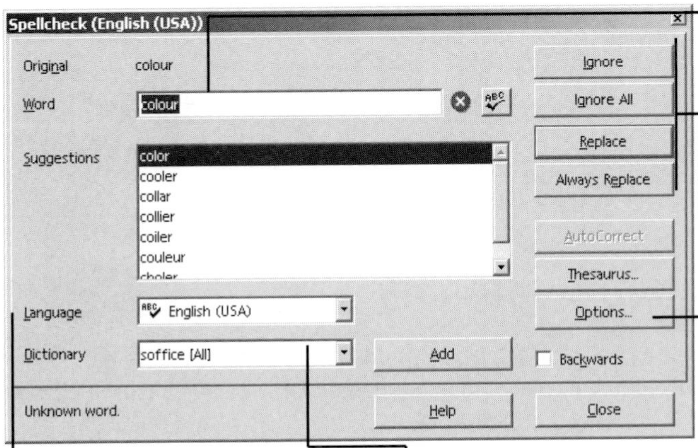

American English is selected as the language in the Language list, so the British spelling of colour was caught as a misspelling and the American spelling color is offered as a correction.

Click the appropriate button depending on whether you want to ignore this word, or replace it with a selection from Suggestions.

Clicking Options opens the same window available from Tools > Options > Language Settings > Writing Aids, where you can choose whether to ignore capitals, what dictionaries to use, etc. See Figure 6-23 on page 192 for more information.

Selecting a different language here has no effect; it reverts back the minute you do anything else in the window.

To add the found word to a dictionary, select it in the Dictionary list and click Add.

Figure 6-22   Spellchecking

Customizing Spell Check

Whether you use spell check manually (Tools > Spellcheck > Check) or automatically (by clicking the AutoSpellcheck icon in the toolbar to underline misspelled words), you can set the rules for spell check.

1   Choose Tools > Options > Language Settings > Writing Aids.

2   Select the options you want, as shown in Figure 6-23.

3   Click OK.

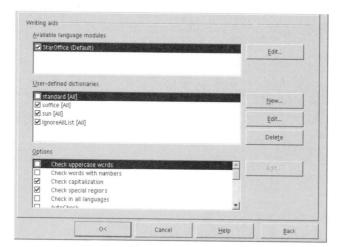

Figure 6-23   Setting Spelling and Language options, Writing Aids window

Note – You must select a language for spellchecking.

Adding a Custom Dictionary

The program performs spell check against a system dictionary (or more than one dictionary if you installed support for more than one language). It also checks spelling against custom dictionaries. the program lets you add and modify custom dictionaries.

The main reason to use a custom dictionary is to speed the spell check process. If you're going to use terms in your documents that a spell check would normally catch (such as product names, unique spellings of common words, and so on), you can add these words to a custom dictionary so that spell check will recognize them.

1   Choose Tools > Options > Language Settings > Writing Aids.

2   In the User-Defined Dictionaries area, click the New button.

3   In the New Dictionary window, type the name of the dictionary, select the applicable language, and click OK.

4   In the Options window, select the new dictionary and click the Edit button.

5   In the Edit Custom Dictionary window (Figure 6-25), add the dictionary terms you want. When you're finished, click Close.

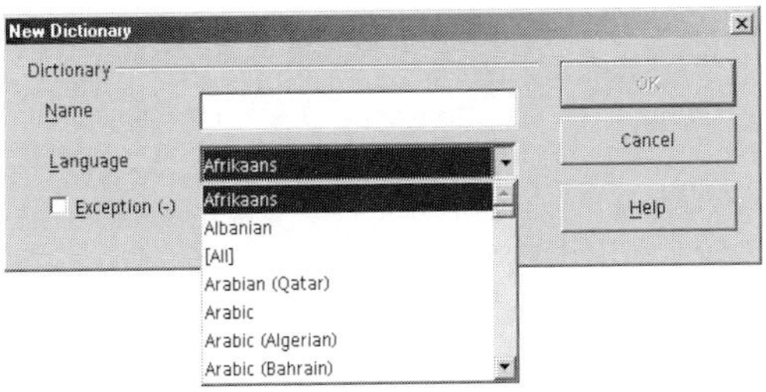

Figure 6-24   Creating a new dictionary

6   To use the custom dictionary in spell checks, click the box next to it in the custom
     dictionaries list to put an 'x' next to it.

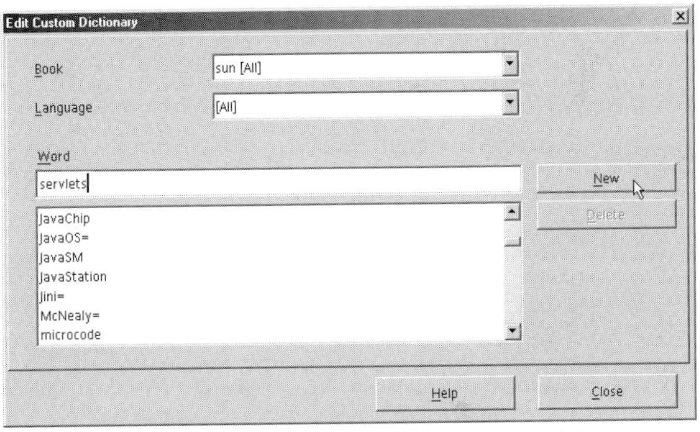

Figure 6-25   Adding terms to a dictionary

Spellcheck Troubleshooting

Sometimes the program will hang or crash during a spellcheck, or it might ignore a few
blaatently mispilled werds. Here are a couple solutions or workarounds.

Check the Dictionaries

- Check that the spellcheck dictionaries are actually in

  `office/share/wordbook/`*language*

  not in `/opt`, `/user`, or another directory. The dictionary files have .dic extensions.

  If they're not in that location, move them there.

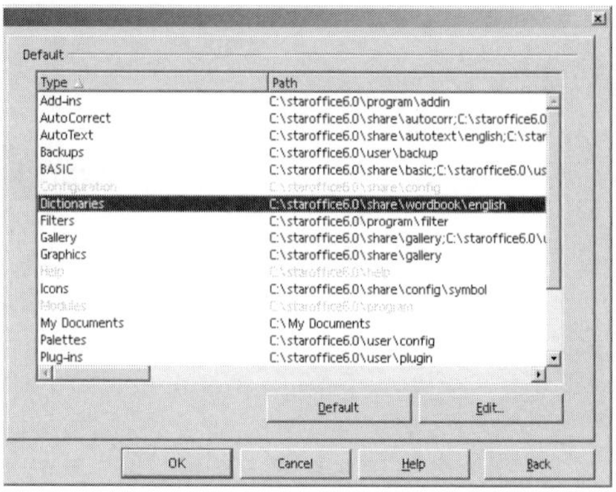

- If that doesn't work, change the location where the program looks for spellcheck dictionaries.

    - Choose Tools > Options > *program* > Load/Save and select the Dictionaries option.

    - Click Edit and specify where the dictionaries actually are.

    - If that still doesn't work, restart the program and try again.

Select the Right Language

1   Select all the documents in the document then choose Format > Characters.

2   In the Font tab and the Language list, check for the right language. See Figure 6-26.

3   If it's something like Estonian (and you don't write in Estonian), select the right language and click OK. If nothing is selected, select the right language and click OK.

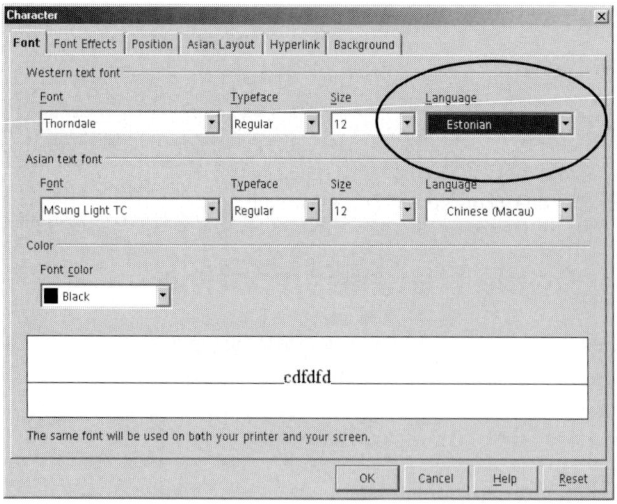

Figure 6-26   Selecting the right language to prevent problems while spellchecking

Use AutoSpellcheck

If your document crashes during spellcheck anyway, especially at the end of the document when it's about to head back up to the top of the document, just don't use normal spellcheck. Use AutoSpellcheck (see *Using Automatic Spellcheck* on page 190).

Setting Hyphenation Rules

The program's Language options let you set default global hyphenation rules for documents. The settings are only default, which means they can be overridden by modifying individual paragraph formats in text, HTML, and presentation documents.

Once hyphenation has occurred throughout a text, HTML, or presentation document, you can change the hyphenation of individual occurrences by choosing Tools > Hyphenation and moving among hyphenated words.

1   Choose Tools > Options > Language Settings > Language.

2   In the Hyphenation rules section of the Options window, set the rules you want. Specify minimum number for hyphenation, hyphenate without inquiry, or hyphenate special regions. See Figure 6-27.

To better control automatic hyphenation, set the minimum number of characters allowed before or after a hyphen.

If this field is marked, you will never be asked for a manual hyphenation. If the field is not marked, when a word is not recognized you will be presented with a dialog for entering hyphens.

Special regions are areas outside the regular text flow, such as headers and footers.

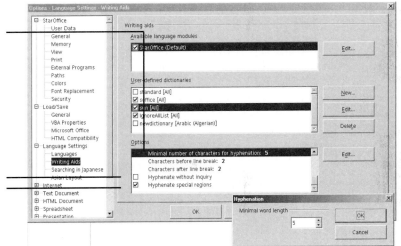

Figure 6-27   Setting default hyphenation rules

3   Click OK.

Useful Tips

Here's another section of solutions to odd but everyday issues.

Getting Rid of Empty Pages

1   Choose View > Nonprinting Characters so that there's a check mark next to the menu option.

2   You should be able to see the extra paragraph returns or other items that are creating the extra page. Delete the characters.

If that doesn't take care of it choose View > Online Layout. Scroll through the document and make sure no extra pages are showing. Choose View > Online Layout again to turn it off; your extra pages should be gone.

Another possible cause is that every table automatically has a nondeletable paragraph return after it. So make the page margins bigger, make your table a little bit smaller, or otherwise mess around with the table so it's just a bit smaller and doesn't make that extra page after it.

Adding Content Before a Section or Table

Press Alt + Return twice to insert a paragraph return in front of a section (see *Using Sections to Create Multiple Versions of the Same Document* on page 411). This also works with indexes and tables since they're both types of sections.

Also you can delete the table or index (select all except the final carriage return and right-click, then choose Delete). Then when you generate it again, don't select the Protected Against Manual Changes option.

Freezing Text So It Can't Be Modified

Use a section. (You can learn more about sections in *Using Sections to Create Multiple Versions of the Same Document* on page 411.)

Sections are specific named areas of your document— just select it and choose Insert > Section, and you've got a section. Then you get to set options like whether it's protected from editing. See at right.

One of the things you can do to a section is protect it from editing. See *Protecting or Hiding Text Using a Section* on page 416 to create a protected section.

7

Formatting Documents

Asian Language Setup and Use

One of the big new features is Asian language support.

- Asian language support is available throughout the program so is covered in *Enabling and Setting Up Asian Fonts and Formatting* on page 110, and *Enabling and Setting Up Asian Fonts and Formatting* on page 110.

- Asian language formatting is also covered in *Using the Character Formatting Window* on page 200 and *Using the Paragraph Format Window* on page 208.

- To use Ruby text to add explanations of complex terms or for any extra in-line text, see *Adding In-Line Explanatory Text for a Word or Phrase* on page 189.

Quick Character Formatting

For simple, quick-and-dirty character formatting such as changing font and font size, and applying bold, italic, and underline, use the object bar (Figure 7-1). For more advanced character formatting options, see *Using the Character Formatting Window* on page 200.

This section shows you quick character formatting tricks, especially those you might not be familiar with.

Using the Object Bar

Using the object bar to do character formatting is fairly straightforward (see Figure 7-1). You can change font, font size, and apply or remove bold, italic, and underline formatting.

If the cursor is in a table, the object bar changes. See *Disappearing Icons and Menu Items* on page 101. (Use the arrow that will be displayed at the far right of the object bar if you want to switch from the table object bar to the text formatting object bar.)

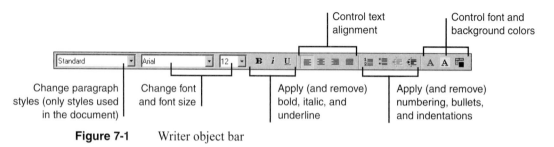

Figure 7-1   Writer object bar

Note – You can also select the text you want to format and right-click to choose different formatting options.

Quick Font and Character Background Color

There are two other object bar tools for character formatting you might not be as familiar with, as shown in Figure 7-2: font color and highlighting. The colors are from the program's standard color palette, as well as any colors you've created and added to the palette.

Click and hold down to select font color, or click to apply the color you selected last.

Click and hold down to select background highlighting, or click to apply the color you selected last.

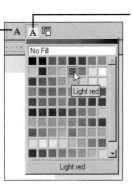

Figure 7-2   Setting font and background colors

Using the Format Stylist "Format Painter" Tool

If you've used Microsoft Word, you know its Format Painter tool, which lets you copy all the formatting characteristics from one item and apply it to another. Writer has the same thing, called Fill Format.

It works a little differently from Word; it copies only something in the Stylist. On the other hand, it keeps working; you don't have to keep copying again and again.

1   Choose Format > Stylist to display the Stylist, and you'll see the paint-can-looking icon at the right side. Click it so the icon is slightly lighter and recessed.

2   Switch to the right style category containing the style you want to apply to text. (At this point you might realize you need to set up a new style. If so, right-click in the Stylist and choose New and create the style.) Once you've got the style selected, go to the next step.

The rain in Spain falls mainly on the plains.

3   Move the pointer over the text or object you want to apply the style to and click; the style will be applied to whatever you click on.

The rain in Spain falls mainly on the plains.

4   Click the formatting icon again when you're done, to turn off the formatting.

Using the Character Formatting Window

This section describes the more advanced character formatting options of the Character format window.

1 Select the text you want to format.

2 Choose Format > Character. The Character window is displayed.

3 Apply the character formats you want and click OK.

When selecting text to apply character formatting, be aware of selecting spaces at the beginning or end of the selection, because the spaces get formatted, too. For example, if you're applying a fixed-width font (such as `courier`) to some selected text and you've selected the space after the text, the space will become fixed-width and may make the spacing seem too big. To avoid this, select a word by double-clicking it. To select more than one word, double-click the first word and drag through the other words you want to select.

Figure 7-3 through Figure 7-5 describe character formatting options on each of the tabs in the Character window. For Asian formatting specific tabs, see Figure 7-11 – Figure 7-12.

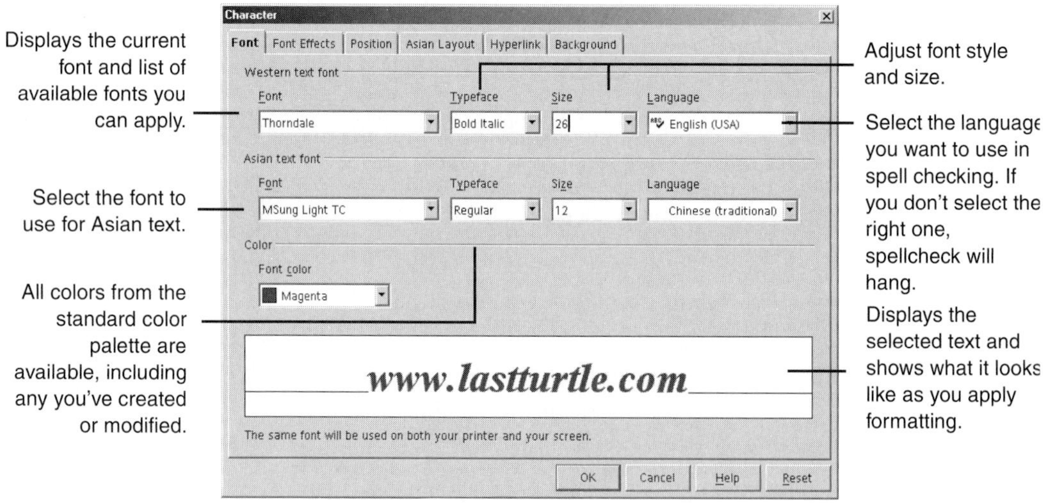

Displays the current font and list of available fonts you can apply.
Select the font to use for Asian text.
All colors from the standard color palette are available, including any you've created or modified.
Adjust font style and size.
Select the language you want to use in spell checking. If you don't select the right one, spellcheck will hang.
Displays the selected text and shows what it looks like as you apply formatting.
Character
Font
Font Effects
Position
Asian Layout
Hyperlink
Background
Western text font
Font
Typeface
Size
Language
Thorndale
Bold Italic
26
English (USA)
Asian text font
Font
Typeface
Size
Language
MSung Light TC
Regular
12
Chinese (traditional)
Color
Font color
Magenta
www.lastturtle.com
The same font will be used on both your printer and your screen.
OK
Cancel
Help
Reset

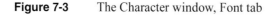

Figure 7-3 The Character window, Font tab

Select the underlining style you want, if any.

Select the strikethrough style you want, if any.

Select the style for an additional emphasis mark, then specify in the Position list where the mark sould appear. This window shows a dotted emphasis mark

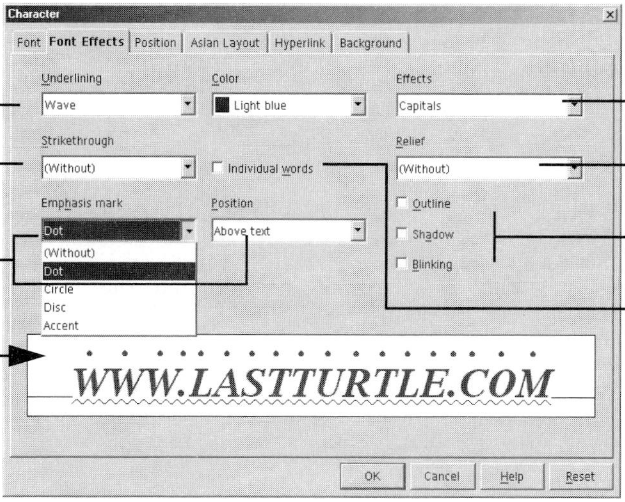

Select from capitals first letter caps, and other effects.

The Relief options like Emboss don't have much of an effect.

Select additional effects.

Select Individual Words if you don't want underlines, emphasis marks, or strikethroughs continued through spaces.

Figure 7-4   The Character window, Font Effects tab

Use the Position options to specify Superscript or Subscript, then either enter the change in height and size manually or just select Automatic.

Make the *font* wider by entering a value over 100 in the Scale Width field; narrow it by entering a smaller value.

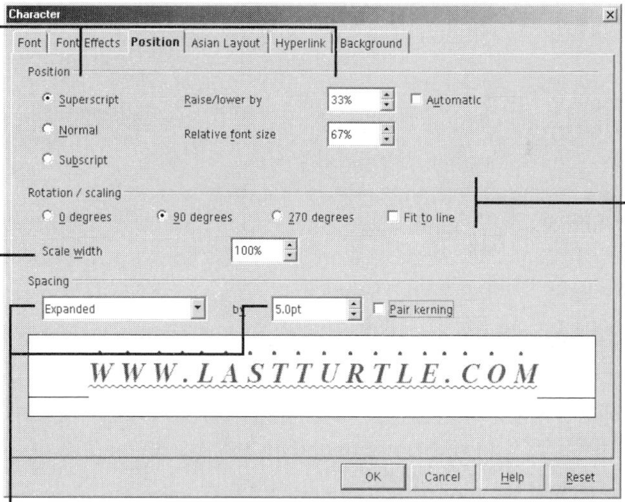

You can make the text vertical in the Rotation/ Scaling section, typing from bottom to top (90) or top to bottom (270).

Select Fit to Line to squish or expand the selected text into the height set under Format > Paragraph > Indents & Spacing. See page 202.

Expand or contract the *spacing between the letters* by specifying Expanded or Condensed and specifying the number of points.

Figure 7-5   The Character window, Position tab

Note – Pair kerning puts characters closer together to improve text appearance.

Making Horizontal Text Fit Within the Line Spacing Height (Using the Fit to Line Option)

What the feature does The Fit to Line option from Figure 7-5 fits the vertical text into the height of the line as shown in Figure 7-6.

The words "one" and "two" are part of the text flow, but formatting was applied so that they are vertical.

In addition, the Fit to Line formatting was applied to control how wide (how high) they are. Fit to Line means that no matter how much space the word would normally take up, whether it's "one" or "pneumo-authoritative,:" it will only be as wide (high) as the amount of space allotted to the rest of the normal text.

As you can see at right, the words "one" and "two" are as wide (high) as the amount of space allotted to each line of the normal horizontal text.

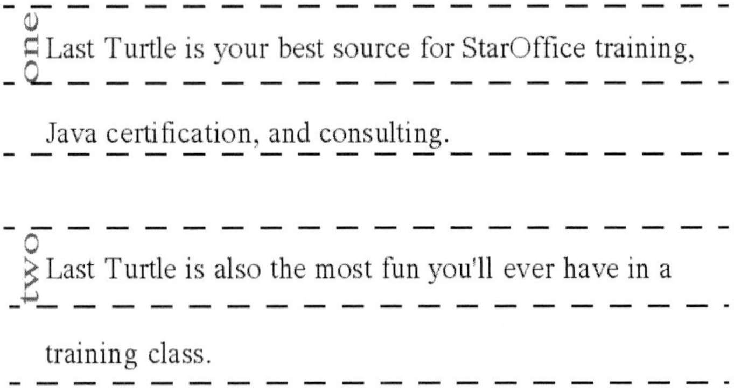

one Last Turtle is your best source for StarOffice training,

Java certification, and consulting.

two Last Turtle is also the most fun you'll ever have in a

training class.

Figure 7-6   How the Fit to Line option works

The height of the line, or *leading*, is controlled by the setting in the Paragraph window. Choose Format > Paragraph and select the Indents & Spacing tab. It's Single by default, i.e., equivalent, more or less, to the font size or a little bit bigger. Unless you want a really squished vertical word, or unless your vertical text is a lot smaller, you want the leading to be bigger than single spacing.

Rules for making it work To make the Fit to Line feature work, you *must* follow these rules:

• Under Format > Paragraph > Alignment, select only Top, Middle, or Bottom in the Alignment list. This is not optional.

• Do it right the first time. (You never knew vertical leading formatting could be so unforgiving.) If you set the vertical line spacing, then twist the text and make it vertical and fit it to the line at that time, that's great. But then changing the vertical line spacing to something different won't update how squished or expanded the vertical text is. You'll have to select the text, choose Format > Default, and start all over again.

Applying the Fit to Line feature Follow these steps.

1   Choose Format > Paragraph and select the Indents & Spacing tab. Under the Line Spacing heading, set the correct line spacing.

2   Select the text you want to be vertical and run into the horizontal text.

3   Choose Format > Character and click the Position tab.

4   Select the appropriate horizontal setting, 90 degrees or 270 degrees, then select Fit to
Line. See Figure 7-7 to see the settings to apply; see Figure 7-8 for an example of
how it works.

Specify how you want the text
rotated, 90 degrees or 270
degrees.

Select Fit to Line.

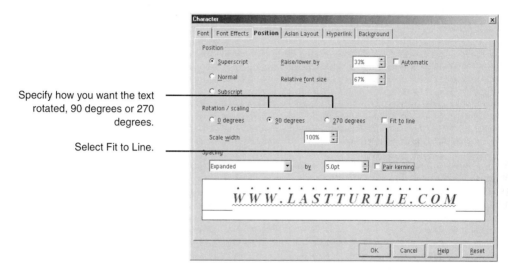

Figure 7-7   Setting horizontal and Fit to Line options

The regular
text was
indented to
improve the
appearance of
the text;
normally it
would wrap to
the far left
margin.

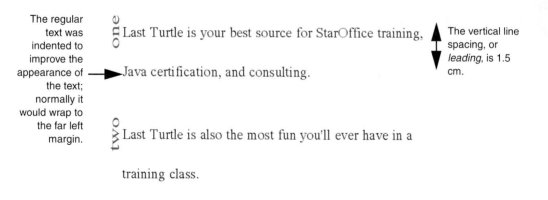

Last Turtle is your best source for StarOffice training,

The vertical line
spacing, or
leading, is 1.5
cm.

Java certification, and consulting.

Last Turtle is also the most fun you'll ever have in a

training class.

If the first letter or letters of the vertical text are cut off in your document, you
need to select the correct alignment as noted in the list of rules previously.

Figure 7-8   How Fit to Line works

Related advanced formatting features This feature is *kind of* like the feature that lets
you make a few letters bigger than all the others, but keeping the text horizontal. Kind of

like those big letters at the beginning of old manuscripts. See Figure 7-22 on page 213. See also *Adding Vertical and Diagonal Text to Documents* on page 238.

Putting Two Characters Together (Pair Kerning)

Pair kerning also supports non-English characters (ligatures) such as æ. Your printer driver must support ligatures to display and print them correctly.

Changing Text Width With Scale Width and Spacing Options

Figure 7-9 shows the differences between scale width (changing the font width) and spacing (changing the width of the spaces between text).

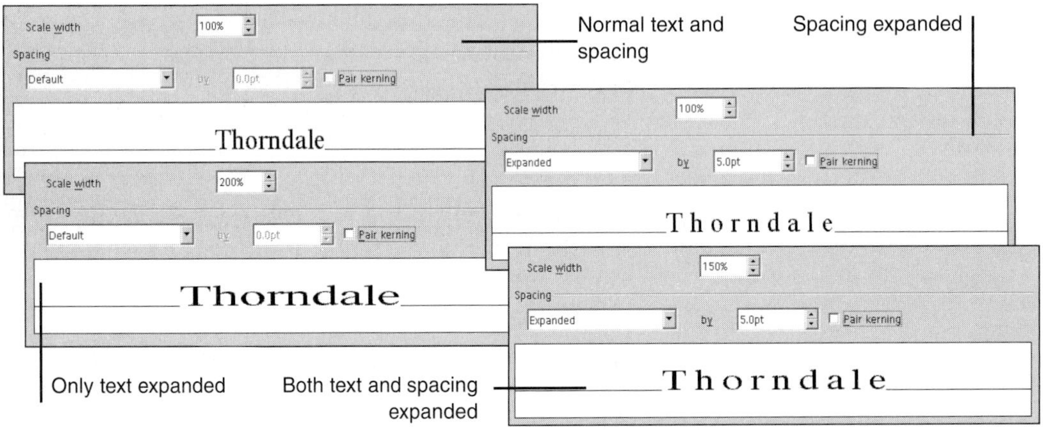

Figure 7-9   Expanding text, spacing, neither, or both

Figure 7-10 shows the background tab for characters.

You can select a background color for the selected text from the standard color palette, or from colors you've created yourself (shown). To remove a background color, select No Fill.

Name of selected color.

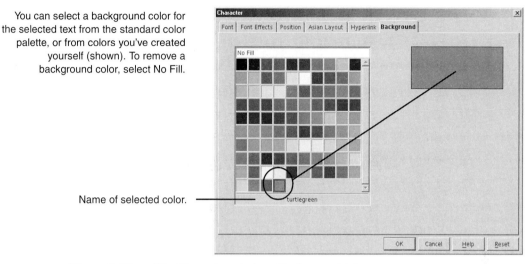

Figure 7-10   The Character window, Background tab

Asian Character Formatting

Ensure that you've set up Asian text formatting correctly using the information in *Enabling and Setting Up Asian Fonts and Formatting* on page 110. Then make the appropriate selections in the Font and Asian Layout tabs of the Character window, shown in Figure 7-11 and Figure 7-12. Asian Language Support must be enabled; see Figure 5-10 on page 111.

If you select Write in Double Lines, text is formatted in two lines as shown in the preview area below.

If you want the text set off at the beginning and end, select the beginning and end characters here.

When you select Other Characters, the Special Characters window opens and allows you to select a character there.

Displays the effect of the options you've selected.

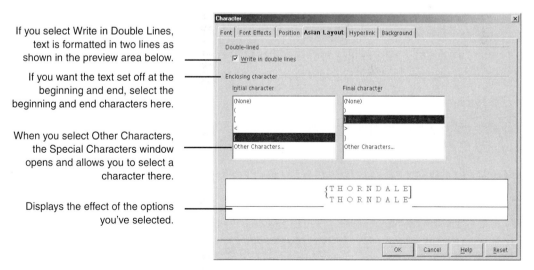

Figure 7-11   Specifying how Asian text should be laid out

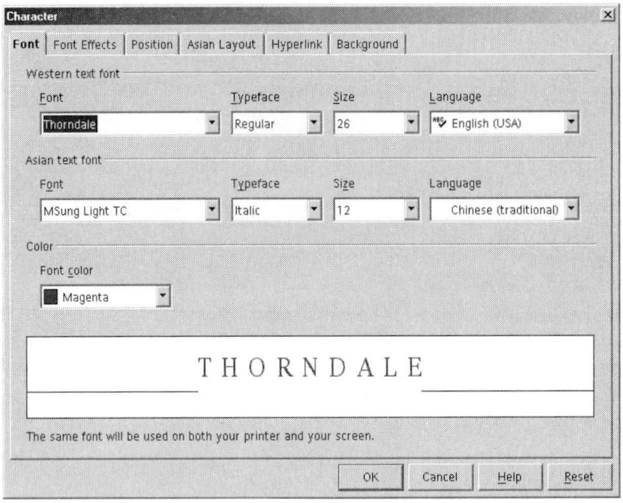

Figure 7-12   Specifying what font and language to use for Asian text

Quick Paragraph Formatting

Unlike character formatting where the text you want to format must be highlighted, paragraph formatting only requires that the cursor be somewhere in the paragraph you want to format.

For quick paragraph formatting such as justification, numbering, bulleting, indenting, setting tabs, and applying a background color, use the object bar and ruler. For more advanced paragraph formatting options, see *Using the Paragraph Format Window* on page 208.

Using the object bar and ruler for paragraph formatting is fairly straightforward. Following are a few quick paragraph formatting tricks you might not be aware of.

Quick Indenting

If you want to tweak paragraph indentations for one or more paragraphs without going into the Paragraph window, change them on the ruler.

1   Select the paragraph(s) you want to indent.

2   On the horizontal ruler, click and drag the bottom triangle to set the left indent.

     The bottom triangle moves the top triangle as well.

3   Click and drag the top triangle to set the indent for the first line, as in Figure 7-13.

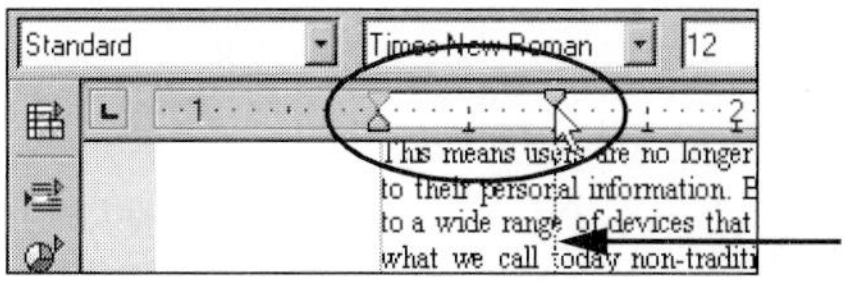

As you drag the triangle, a dotted line runs through the text to help you line up the indentation.

Figure 7-13   Setting the indent from the ruler

Quick Tab Setting

You can insert and move tab settings on the horizontal ruler for one or more paragraphs.

1   Select the paragraph(s) for which you want to insert or adjust the tab settings.

2   Click the tab button to the left of the ruler repeatedly to select the type of tab you want to insert (left, right, decimal, or centered).

3   Click the place on the ruler where you want the tab to be, as shown in Figure 7-14.

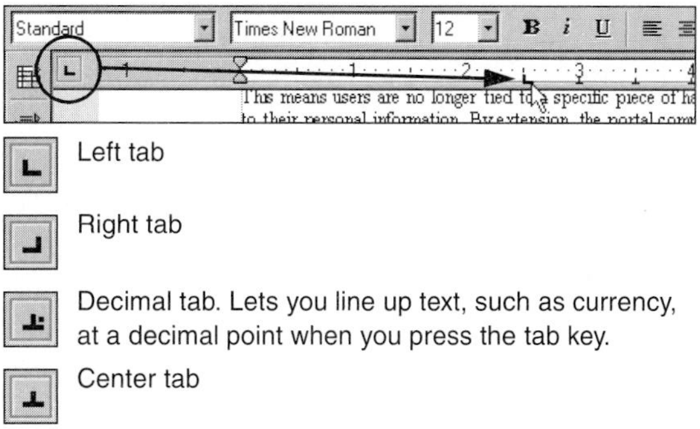

Click the tab icon repeatedly until you see the kind of tab you want to insert, then click on the ruler to place the tab.

Left tab

Right tab

Decimal tab. Lets you line up text, such as currency, at a decimal point when you press the tab key.

Center tab

Figure 7-14   Setting tabs on the ruler

To adjust a tab setting, drag the tab marker along the ruler. To remove a tab setting, drag it off the ruler.

For areas on the ruler where you haven't inserted a custom tab stop, Writer uses its default tab settings, which are defined in Tools > Options > Text document > Layout, in the Tab stops area of the window.

Setting Paragraph Background Color

You can set paragraph background color from the object bar. The colors are from the program's standard color palette, as shown in Figure 7-15.

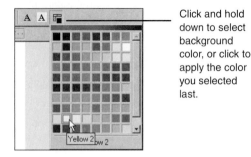

Click and hold
down to select
background
color, or click to
apply the color
you selected
last.

Figure 7-15   Setting background color for a paragraph from the object bar

Using the Paragraph Format Window

This section describes the more advanced paragraph formatting options of the Paragraph format window.

Note – The Paragraph format window doesn't let you change the font for a paragraph. To change a paragraph font style manually, you must select the entire paragraph and use character formatting (see *Using the Character Formatting Window* on page 200). Changing font attributes this way differs from using styles, because the paragraph style definition includes font settings—which is yet another reason why using styles is a good idea. See *Why You Should Use Styles* on page 242 and *Standard Paragraph Styles* on page 245.

Basic Paragraph Formatting

You can also access many of the following manual paragraph formatting options with right-click menus.

1   Click in the paragraph you want to format.

2   Right-click and choose Paragraph. The Paragraph window is displayed.

3   Apply the paragraph formats you want and click OK. See Figure 7-16.

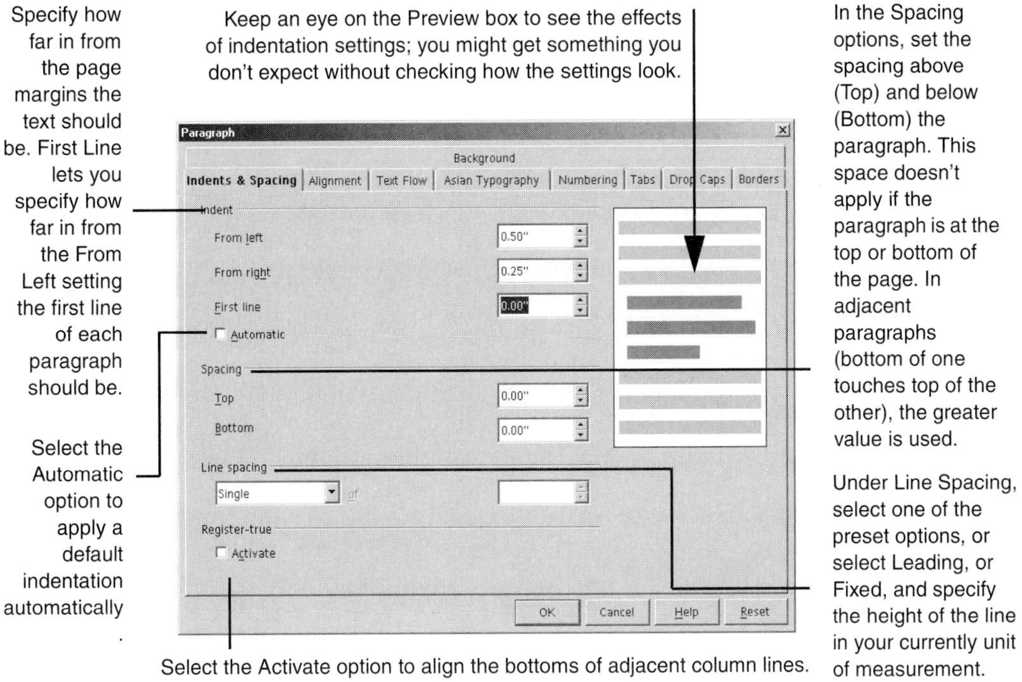

Specify how far in from the page margins the text should be. First Line lets you specify how far in from the From Left setting the first line of each paragraph should be.

Keep an eye on the Preview box to see the effects of indentation settings; you might get something you don't expect without checking how the settings look.

In the Spacing options, set the spacing above (Top) and below (Bottom) the paragraph. This space doesn't apply if the paragraph is at the top or bottom of the page. In adjacent paragraphs (bottom of one touches top of the other), the greater value is used.

Select the Automatic option to apply a default indentation automatically

Under Line Spacing, select one of the preset options, or select Leading, or Fixed, and specify the height of the line in your currently unit of measurement.

Select the Activate option to align the bottoms of adjacent column lines.

Figure 7-16   The Paragraph window, Indents & Spacing tab

Note – To specify vertical alignment within the line spacing, see Figure 7-18.

Creating a Hanging Indent

See Figure 7-16 and make the appropriate entries in the fields under the Indent heading. You'll see the effect in the preview area. For instance, a .25 inch hanging style, you would enter .25 in the From Left field. Then enter -.25 in the First Line field.

You can also choose Format > Stylist and select the Hanging Indent style.

Controlling Vertical Text Alignment

The Alignment tab in Figure 7-18 on page 210 is where you select the default settings for the vertical alignment of text characters in the text line. You can select Automatic, Baseline, Top, Middle, and Bottom. This has an effect only if your line spacing from the Indents & Spacing tab is larger then the font size. Figure 7-17 demonstrates the differences among the options.

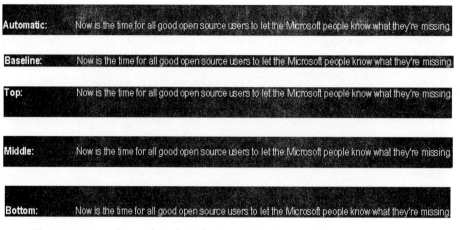

Figure 7-17   Examples of vertical text alignment options

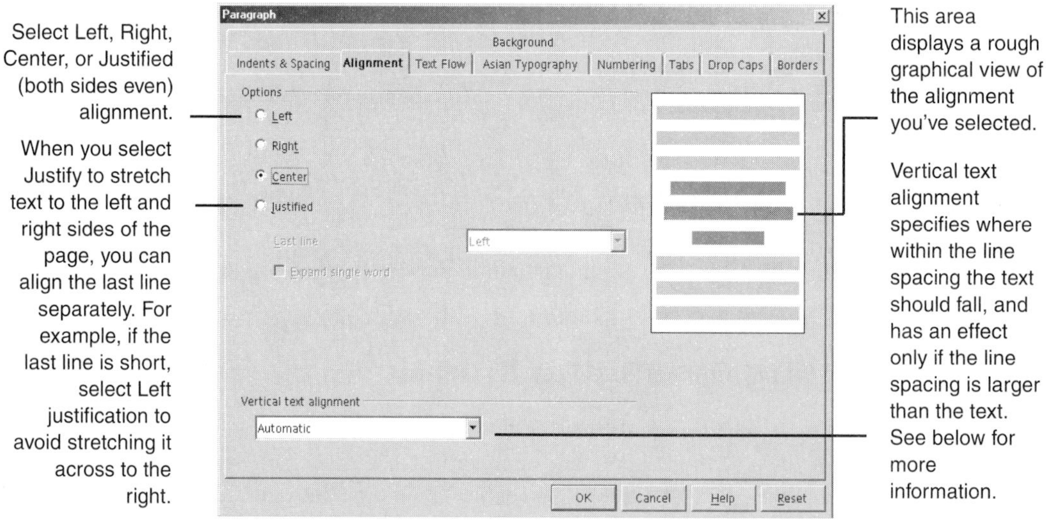

Select Left, Right, Center, or Justified (both sides even) alignment.

When you select Justify to stretch text to the left and right sides of the page, you can align the last line separately. For example, if the last line is short, select Left justification to avoid stretching it across to the right.

This area displays a rough graphical view of the alignment you've selected.

Vertical text alignment specifies where within the line spacing the text should fall, and has an effect only if the line spacing is larger than the text. See below for more information.

Figure 7-18   The Paragraph window, Alignment tab

Controlling Text Flow, Page Breaks, and Hyphenation

Figure 7-19 provides detail on how to specify text flow.

The With Page Style option is quite useful, since it lets you specifying whether a specific page template or page number is to be used after a page break. For more information on switching page styles, see *Applying and Switching Page Styles* on page 253.

Under Options, select the Break option to select either a Page or Column break for the selected paragraph. Select Before to move the paragraph to the next page or column; select After to move the next paragraph to the next page or column.

When you select the Page and Before options to move a paragraph to a new page, you can select the With page style option and apply a page style for the new page (choose from the list of currently defined page styles).

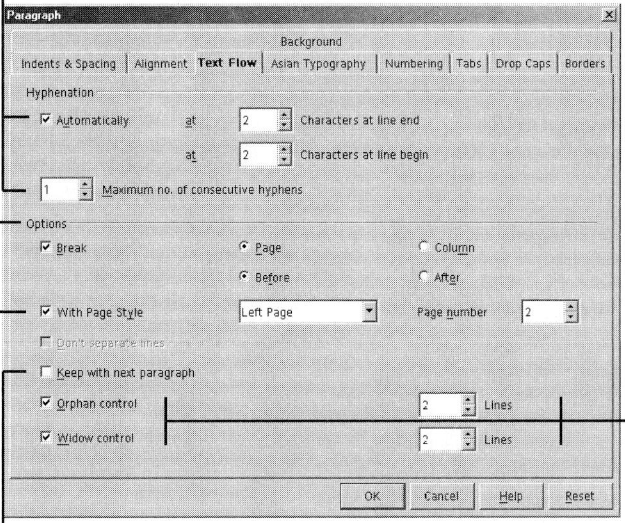

Select the Automatically option to hyphenate end-of-line words. You can prevent Writer from getting too hyphenation happy by controlling the number of characters that must be present at the end and beginning of a line, and by limiting the number of consecutive lines that can be hyphenated.

You can set the minimum number of paragraph lines that must appear on the previous page (orphan) or following page (widow) when a paragraph crosses pages. Selecting the orphan or widow options deactivates the Don't separate lines option, and vice versa.

The Keep with next paragraph option lets you, for example, keep a heading with the text that follows it if a page break occurs.

Figure 7-19   The Paragraph window, Text Flow tab

Setting Up Numbering

The Numbering tab in Figure 7-20 provides detail on how to do numbering.

You can apply currently defined numbering/bulleting styles to the selected paragraph(s). You either have to know what the numbering styles look like, or you have to apply the styles to find out. When you define your own styles, you'll know what they look like (see the tip on page 243).

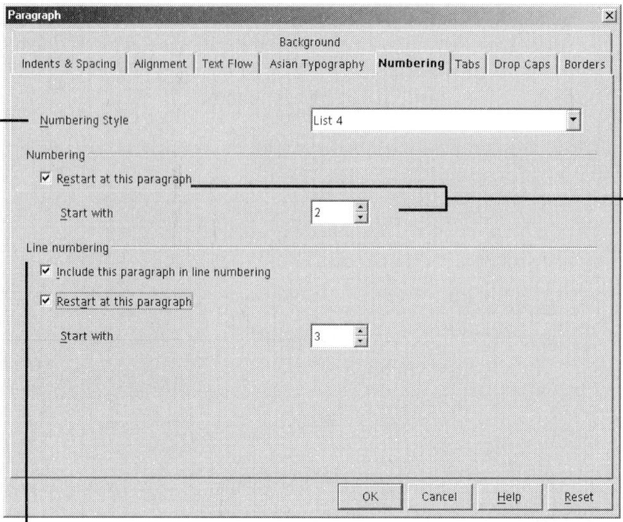

If you have a list of numbered paragraphs and you want to restart the numbering of the selected paragraph, select the Restart at this paragraph option and set the number you want the paragraph to start with.

If you're using line numbering in the margins of a document, you can use the Line Numbering options to control if and how the selected paragraph is numbered. (This is mainly for editing purposes. See *Numbering Lines* on page 422.)

Figure 7-20   The Paragraph window, Numbering tab

Setting Up Paragraph Tabs

The Tabs tab in Figure 7-21 provides detail on how to specify the tab stops.

Enter the new tab Position (measured from the page margins, not from the edge of the entire page), and select the Type. The Type lines up tabbed paragraphs to the decimal character you specify (for example, for currency amounts).

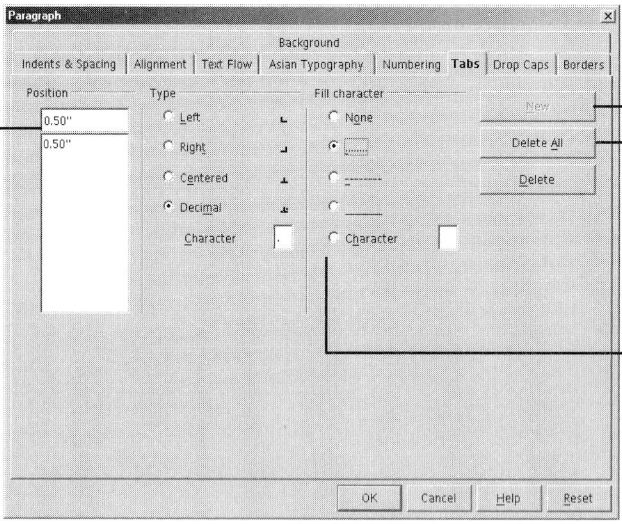

Click New to add the tab you entered.

Click Delete All to remove all tabs. The paragraph then uses the default tab stops set up in Tools > Options > Text document > Layout.

Set any Fill characters that will appear between the point where you press tab, and the tab position.

Figure 7-21   The Paragraph window, Tabs tab

Use the Fill Characters option for a table of contents to create the dotted line from a TOC entry to its corresponding page number.

Formatting the First Letters of a Paragraph

The Drop Caps tab in Figure 7-22 shows how to do this.

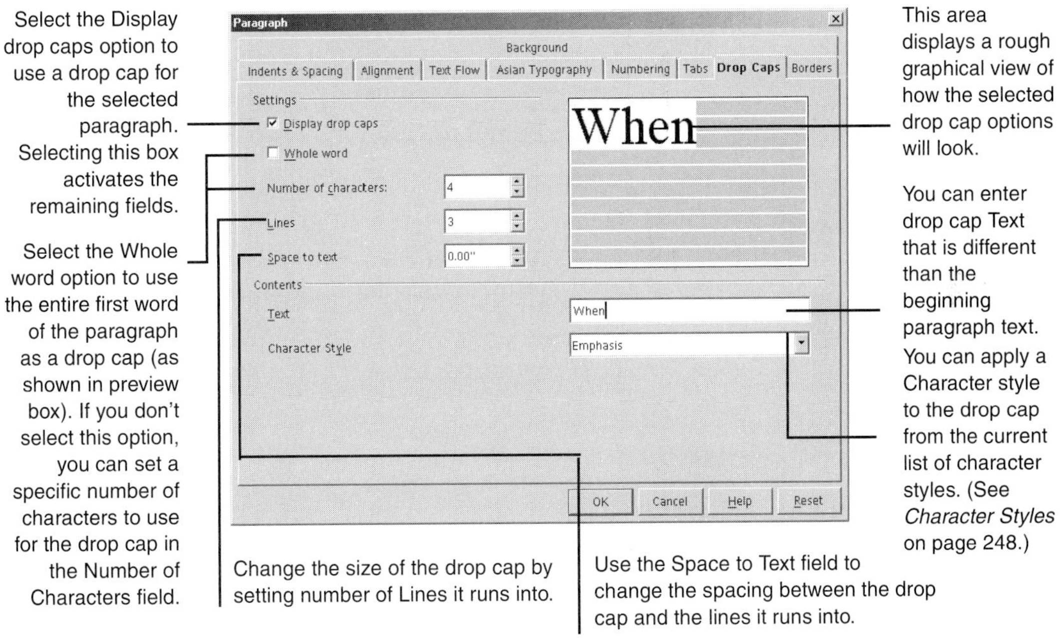
Select the Display drop caps option to use a drop cap for the selected paragraph. Selecting this box activates the remaining fields.
Select the Whole word option to use the entire first word of the paragraph as a drop cap (as shown in preview box). If you don't select this option, you can set a specific number of characters to use for the drop cap in the Number of Characters field.
Change the size of the drop cap by setting number of Lines it runs into.
Use the Space to Text field to change the spacing between the drop cap and the lines it runs into.
This area displays a rough graphical view of how the selected drop cap options will look.
You can enter drop cap Text that is different than the beginning paragraph text.
You can apply a Character style to the drop cap from the current list of character styles. (See Character Styles on page 248.)
Paragraph
Background
Indents & Spacing
Alignment
Text Flow
Asian Typography
Numbering
Tabs
Drop Caps
Borders
Settings
Display drop caps
Whole word
Number of characters:
4
Lines
3
Space to text
0.00"
When
Contents
Text
When
Character Style
Emphasis
OK
Cancel
Help
Reset

Figure 7-22 The Paragraph window, Drop Caps tab

Paragraph Colors, Graphics, and Borders

Use the window in Figure 7-23 to specify the borders, if any, around the paragraph.

Use the window in Figure 7-24 to select a graphic to use in the background of your document, so that the standard text flows over it. Position it using the selections in the Type area of the Paragraph window.

The following tips pertain to using text borders and backgrounds.

Putting a box around text To put two paragraphs within a box, such as a heading and a paragraph, add a soft return (Shift+Enter) between the paragraphs and format the heading and body text manually.

Click one of the Line Arrangements boxes to apply that border style. Click the empty first box to clear all line (not shadow) settings.

Select a Line and line color for the border.

Specify how far away from the paragraph the outer edge of the shadow should be.

The gray box in the Frame area represents the entire paragraph. You can add or remove lines relative to the paragraph by clicking above, below, or to either side of, the gray box. Click Spacing to set the spacing between the lines and the text.

Make a selection from the Color list to change the shadow color from gray to another color.

If you make a change in one box that you want in all boxes, select Synchronize.

Click a Shadow Style Position box to apply that shadow angle to the line. Click the first Position box to clear shadow settings.

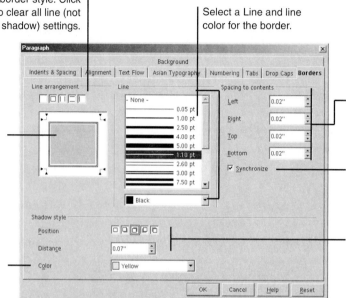

Figure 7-23   The Paragraph window, Borders tab

In the As field, select whether you want Color or a Graphic for the paragraph background. Selecting a color is straightforward, so this window shows options for using a graphic.

Clicking Browse brings up the Search graphic window for selecting the graphic you want to use. In the Search graphic window, select the Link option to activate the Link field in this window. To keep the size of your document smaller, use the Link option for graphics.

If the graphic is smaller than the paragraph area, use the Type options to position the graphic relative to the paragraph. If you select Position, click a circle to position the graphic behind the paragraph.

Select Preview to see the graphic in the preview area.

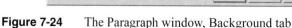

Figure 7-24   The Paragraph window, Background tab

Using background colors and graphics Using a dark or detailed graphic or color can wash out text. However, using a dark graphic or color with white font can produce nice results.

Since a graphic, if it's large, can fill the entire dimensions of a paragraph, the text runs into the edges of the graphic. A background color behaves the same way. If you want to create space between the text and the edges of the graphic or color, try using a text frame inside the paragraph. See *Inserting Frames and Floating Frames* on page 291.

Numbering, Bullets, and Outlining

Get ready to nummmmber.

Using Basic Numbering, Bullets, and Outlining

This section describes how to format quickly with numbers, bullets, and outlining. It also shows you how to customize your numbering, bulleting, and outlining so that you have more control over the number and bullet formats at different levels of indentation.

Quick Numbering and Bulleting

Select the text to number or bullet and click the appropriate icon on the object bar.

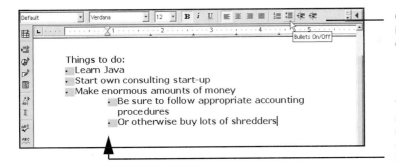

Click the indent or promote icons to change the bulleting or number level.

To turn off the gray boxes around the bullets or numbers, choose View > Field Shadings so that the check mark is no longer next to Field Shadings.

Figure 7-25   Quick bulleting or numbering

Standard Numbering and Bulleting

If you want to use more interesting numbers or bullets, use this procedure. The quickest way to apply numbering and bulleting is to set up numbering and bulleting styles, especially if you're going to use the same kinds again and again. See *Power Formatting With Styles* on page 241.

1   Highlight the paragraphs you want to bullet, or position the cursor where you want to begin a new list.

2 Choose Format > Numbering/Bullets.

3 In the Numbering/Bullets window (Figure 7-26), select the numbering or bullets you want to use in the Bullets, Numbering style, or Graphics tabs. (It's a good idea not to select the Link option. See the note in Figure 7-26.)

4 Click OK.

If you select the Link graphics option and send the file to someone, they won't be able to see the bullets if they don't have the bullet graphics to link to or if the path to the graphics is different than it is on your system.

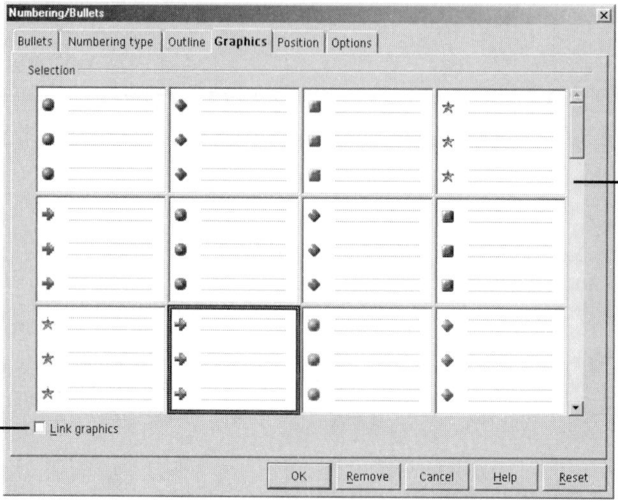

Scroll down in the Graphics tab to see more bullet styles. These styles are from the Bullets gallery.

Figure 7-26 Predefined bullet styles in the Graphics tab

If you're starting a new bulleted or numbered list, type the text at the first list item and press Enter. The new paragraph takes on the number or bullet format. If you press Enter at a numbered or bulleted paragraph that doesn't have text with it, the bullet or number is removed from the paragraph.

To restart numbering, see Figure 7-19 on page 211.

Quick Outlining

This procedure shows you how to create a basic outline format based on a predefined set of outlining styles.

1 Position the cursor where you want to begin outlining.

2 Choose Format > Numbering/Bullets.

3 In the Outline tab, select the style of outlining you want to use, as shown in Figure 7-27.

4 Click OK. The window closes and the first-level number appears in the text.

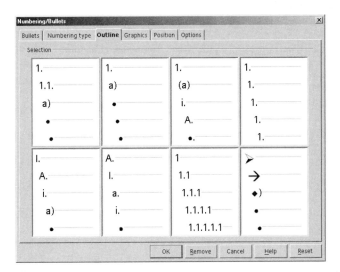

Figure 7-27   Predefined outline styles

As you press Enter at the end of a line, you stay at the same numbering level and the numbering increments. To move in a level, press the Tab key. To move out a level, press Shift+Tab.

Customizing Numbering, Bullets, and Outlining

There are many aspects to customizing numbering, bulleting, and outlining. Besides changing font and characters, perhaps the most important reason for customization is setting up different tiers, or indented levels, as Figure 7-28 shows.

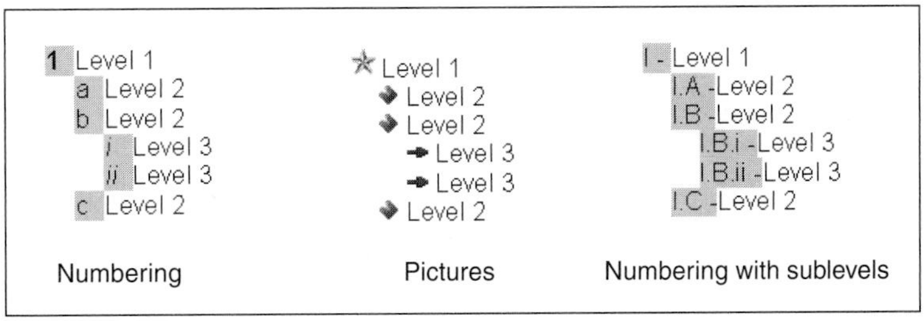

Figure 7-28   Numbering/Bullet levels

1   Position the cursor where you want to begin numbering or bullets, or highlight the text you want to number or bullet.

2   Choose Format > Numbering/Bullets. The Numbering/Bullets window is displayed.

3   Select the Customize tab.

4   In the Level box, select a level number. Levels correspond to the level of indentation. The higher the level number, the greater the indentation.

5   In the Numbering field, select the type of numbering or bullet you want the level to be.

6   Set any appropriate options for the level (such as Before, After, or Character Style). See Figure 7-29 and Figure 7-30 for more information.

7   Set up any other levels you want to customize.

8   When you're finished, click OK.

9   Begin using your custom numbering/bulleting (see page 221).

Writer uses default position and spacing for each level. If you want to fine-tune the position and spacing of the levels, see *Fine-Tuning the Position and Spacing of Levels* on page 220.

Numbering means "Numbers or Bullets?" not attributes of just numbering.The format area displays different options depending on the numbering you choose.

Select a character style for the numbered or bulleted list, and a character to use instead of a bullet.
Note: These options vary; see Figure 7-30.

When you select a level number, every option you set in the Format area of the window applies to that level. If you select the 1-10 level item, the options you set apply to all 10 possible levels.

The Preview area displays a rough graphical view of the options you apply to the different levels.

Caution: If you select the Consecutive numbering option, numbering is consecutive from level to level. That is, numbering won't restart at each

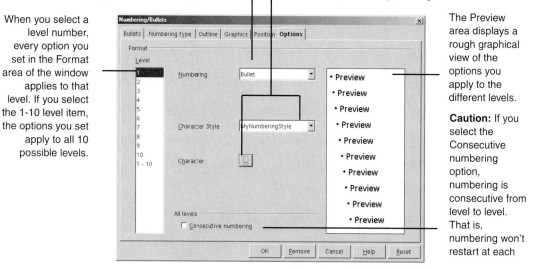

Figure 7-29   The Numbering/Bullets window, Options tab

The Format area of the Numbering/Bullets window displays different options depending on your selection in the Numbering field. The pictures in Figure 7-30 illustrate these different options.

When you select a numbering format

Type any characters that will appear before the number, such as Figure, or after the number, such as a period or colon. See also *Inserting Captions* on page 300.

Select the character style you want to use for the numbers. See *Character Styles* on page 248. This lets you use a different font for the numbering and the body text.

Set the amount of higher-level numbering you want to include in the level's numbering; for example, "Section 1.2.1" includes numbering for two levels higher.

Select the number you want the level to start at.

When you select Graphics

You can change the width and height of the bullet. Select the Keep ratio option to have the height adjust automatically when you adjust the width, and vice versa.

Click Select and choose your own file or a bullet picture from the Gallery.

Select the orientation of the picture in relation to the baseline or the text.

When you select Bullet

Select the character style you want to use for the numbers. See *Character Styles* on page 248.

Click to select a bullet from the Special Characters.

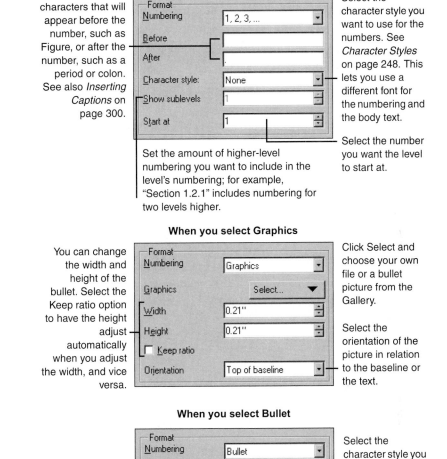

Figure 7-30   Format options for different Numbering selections

You can also mix numbers and bullets when setting your levels.

Fine-Tuning the Position and Spacing of Levels

You can change the default position and spacing Writer uses for numbers and bullets.

1. Click in the numbered or bulleted paragraph you want to change.
2. Choose Format > Numbering/Bullets.
3. In the Numbering/Bullets window, select the Position tab.
4. Select a level in the Level box, and adjust its settings. Select and adjust all levels you want to change.
5. When you're finished, click OK. Figure 7-31 describes the options in the Position tab.

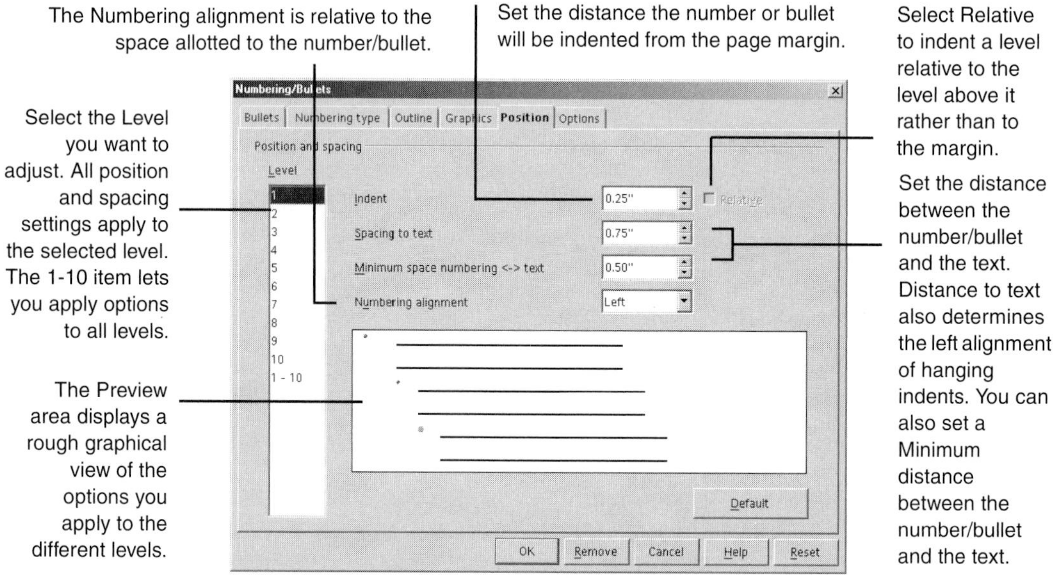

The Numbering alignment is relative to the space allotted to the number/bullet.
Set the distance the number or bullet will be indented from the page margin.
Select Relative to indent a level relative to the level above it rather than to the margin.
Select the Level you want to adjust. All position and spacing settings apply to the selected level. The 1-10 item lets you apply options to all levels.
Set the distance between the number/bullet and the text. Distance to text also determines the left alignment of hanging indents. You can also set a Minimum distance between the number/bullet and the text.
The Preview area displays a rough graphical view of the options you apply to the different levels.
Numbering/Bullets
Bullets
Numbering type
Outline
Graphics
Position
Options
Position and spacing
Level
Indent
0.25"
Relative
Spacing to text
0.75"
Minimum space numbering <-> text
0.50"
Numbering alignment
Left
1 2 3 4 5 6 7 8 9 10 1 - 10
Default
OK
Remove
Cancel
Help
Reset

Figure 7-31 The Numbering/Bullets window, Position tab

Saving Numbering/Bullet Customizations

The customization only applies to the paragraphs that use it. For example, if you create and use a customized numbering hierarchy in one place in a document, you can't click the numbering button in the object bar and continue using the customized numbering system at another point in the document. You'd either have to copy the first line of the customized numbering style and paste it elsewhere in the document, or recreate the numbering system in the Numbering/Bullets window for a different part of the document. To save your customization, create a new numbering style. See *Creating a Numbering Style* on page 250.

Cross-Referencing Paragraph Numbering

If you want to cross-reference the autogenerated numbers/text of a paragraph, such as "Figure 5-1" in a caption paragraph style, you need to number those paragraph formats in a different way. See *Outline Numbering* on page 308.

Changing Indent Levels With the Tab Key

As you press Enter at the end of a numbered or bulleted paragraph, you stay at the same numbering level. To move in a level, press the Tab key. To move up a level, press Shift+Tab. If you're using numbering, the numbering increments according to the level.

Outline Numbering

See *Outline Numbering* on page 308.

User-Definable Number Formatting for Cells and Fields

See *Number Formatting in Cells* on page 280.

Formatting Footnotes

These footnote settings apply to footnotes you insert by choosing Insert > Footnote.

Choose Format > Page and click the Footnotes/Endnotes tab. Use Figure 7-40 for guidance.

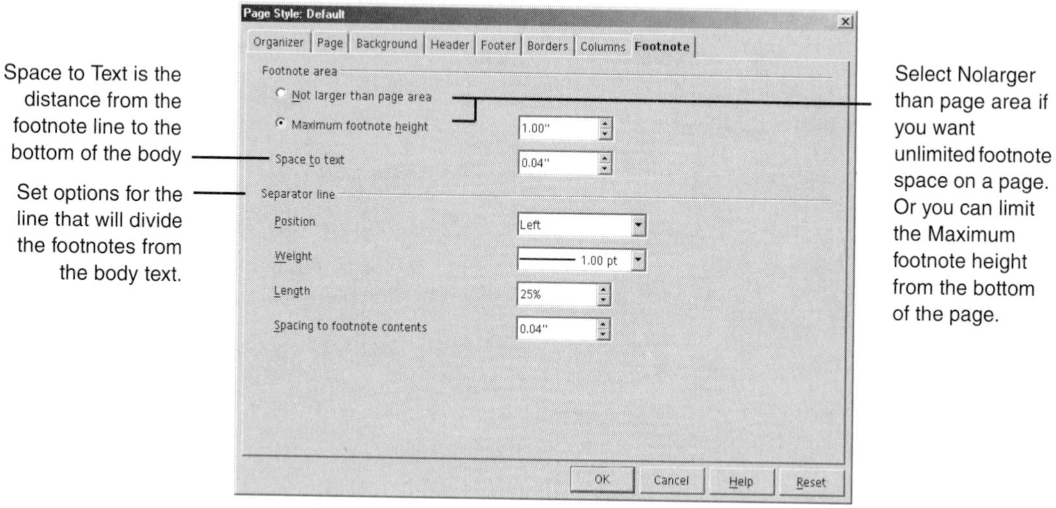
Space to Text is the distance from the footnote line to the bottom of the body
Set options for the line that will divide the footnotes from the body text.
Page Style: Default
Organizer
Page
Background
Header
Footer
Borders
Columns
Footnote
Footnote area
Not larger than page area
Maximum footnote height
1.00"
Space to text
0.04"
Separator line
Position
Left
Weight
1.00 pt
Length
25%
Spacing to footnote contents
0.04"
OK
Cancel
Help
Reset
Select Nolarger than page area if you want unlimited footnote space on a page. Or you can limit the Maximum footnote height from the bottom of the page.

Figure 7-32 The Page Style window, Footnote tab

Using Headers and Footers in Basic Documents

Headers and footers, the text areas that appear at the top and bottom of a page, contain information that runs from page to page, such as page number, date, the title of the current page heading, copyright information, and notes about confidential and proprietary information.

Usually when you enter information into headers and footers, the information repeats automatically as new pages are created. If you are using alternating left and right pages, each can have its own headers and footers, so that all right-page headers and footers are the same, as are all left-page headers and footers.

Note – To use more complex headers and footers in books and longer documents, see *Headers and Footers in Books* on page 313.

Setting Up Headers and Footers, Consistent or Different on Each Page

Header and footer setup is part of the window you get from choosing Format > Page.

1 Choose Format > Page.

2 Click the Header tab, make the appropriate entries, then click the Footer tab. Use Figure 7-33 and Figure 7-34 for guidance. Figure 7-34 shows example headers and explains the window settings further.

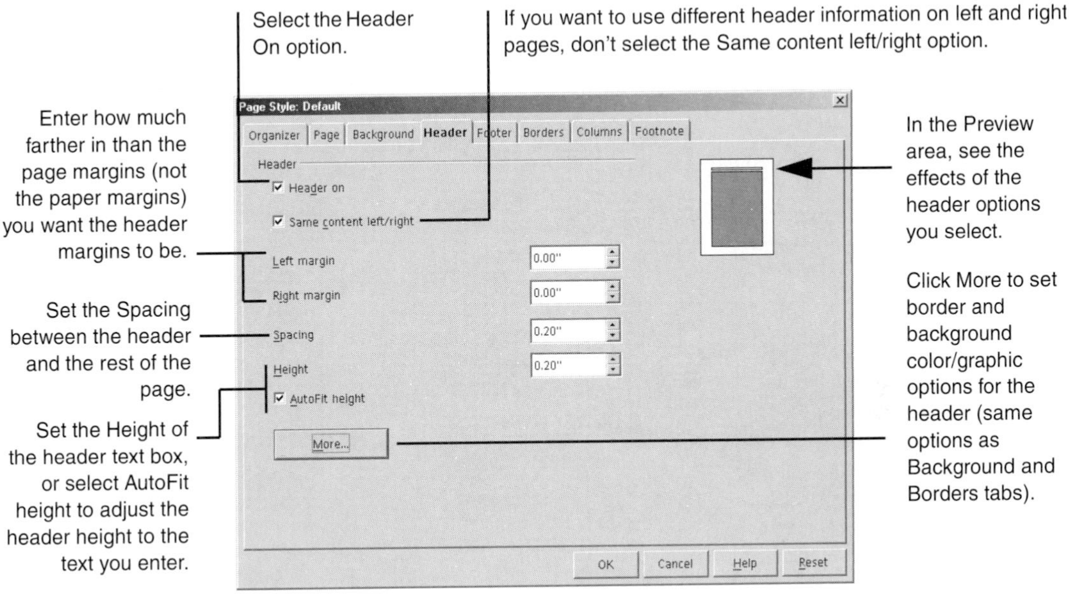
Select the Header On option.
If you want to use different header information on left and right pages, don't select the Same content left/right option.
Enter how much farther in than the page margins (not the paper margins) you want the header margins to be.
Set the Spacing between the header and the rest of the page.
Set the Height of the header text box, or select AutoFit height to adjust the header height to the text you enter.
In the Preview area, see the effects of the header options you select.
Click More to set border and background color/graphic options for the header (same options as Background and Borders tabs).
Page Style: Default
Organizer
Page
Background
Header
Footer
Borders
Columns
Footnote
Header
Header on
Same content left/right
Left margin
0.00"
Right margin
0.00"
Spacing
0.20"
Height
0.20"
AutoFit height
More...
OK
Cancel
Help
Reset

Figure 7-33 The Page Style window, Header tab

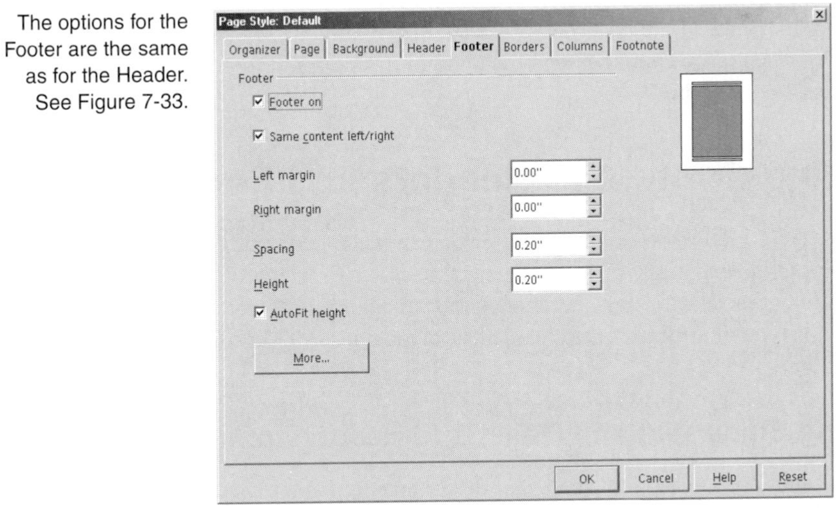
The options for the Footer are the same as for the Header. See Figure 7-33.
Page Style: Default
Organizer
Page
Background
Header
Footer
Borders
Columns
Footnote
Footer
Footer on
Same content left/right
Left margin
0.00"
Right margin
0.00"
Spacing
0.20"
Height
0.20"
AutoFit height
More...
OK
Cancel
Help
Reset

Figure 7-34 The Page Style window, Footer tab

Figure 7-34 shows example headers and explains the window settings further.

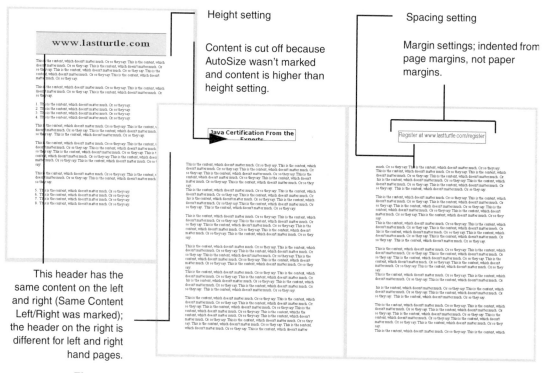

Height setting

Content is cut off because AutoSize wasn't marked and content is higher than height setting.

Spacing setting

Margin settings; indented from page margins, not paper margins.

This header has the same content on the left and right (Same Content Left/Right was marked); the header on the right is different for left and right hand pages.

Figure 7-35   Example headers

Header and footer margins   When you insert headers and footers, they don't run beyond the margin settings of the document. Instead, they automatically adjust the main text area of the document. You cannot extend the width of headers and footers beyond the document's page width.

Adding Content to Headers and Footers

Since headers and footers are text boxes, you can include anything in a header or footer that you can include in the main document. Most often you'll probably want to include such information as date, page number, author, filename, and section headings. Instead of typing this type of information in manually, you can insert fields that contain this information.

Adding Static Text and Objects to Headers and Footers

Headers and footers can take whatever you throw at'em—in general, just consider them normal document area.

Inserting Fields Such as Date and Page In Headers and Footers

Note – You can also use AutoText to insert predefined data. See *Creating and Inserting AutoText* on page 180.

Fields contain information such as page numbers, dates, and section headings that are generated automatically by Writer. For more information on fields, see *Creating and Inserting Predefined Fields for Headers and Footers*.

1   Click in the exact spot in the header or footer where you want to insert a field.

2   In the toolbar, click and hold down the Insert Fields tool, and choose the field you want to insert. (You can also choose Insert > Fields.)

If you don't see the field you want, choose Other, and select the field you want to use in the Fields window. For definitions of the fields in this window, see the online help.

Creating and Inserting Predefined Fields for Headers and Footers

Fields are bits of information, such as page numbers, dates, document headings, cross-references, index markers, database fields, and a host of other information that Writer generates or that you can insert. For example, you can insert a field into a document that shows the date that the document was last modified, or you can insert page numbering to show the current page number along with the total page count, as shown in Figure 7-36.

You can insert fields into any part of a document where you can enter text, and the field text takes on the properties of the paragraph style it's inserted into. You can also apply character formats to fields.

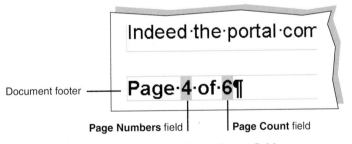

Indeed·the·portal·com

Document footer ——— **Page·4·of·6¶**

Page Numbers field   **Page Count** field

Figure 7-36   Page Numbers and Page Count fields

Page Numbering on page 314 shows specific uses of fields in long documents and books.

Changing the Date Format for the Date Field

When you choose Insert > Fields > Date, it's always inserted in MM/DD/YY format. We don't know how to change this default format, but you can do either of the following:

*   You can change the format each time by double-clicking the field and selecting a different format in the Edit Fields window.

*   Select the inserted date field after you've correctly formatted it, then select it and create a new AutoText entry. See *Creating and Inserting AutoText* on page 180.

Turning Off the Gray Background

Any time you insert a field or any other element that's generated by Writer, it is displayed with a nonprinting gray background by default. If you don't want to see the gray background on-screen, choose View > Field Shadings.

However, we recommend leaving field shading on, because it helps you distinguish between what you enter as text and what is generated by Writer.

Advanced Use of "Other" Fields

Additional fields, based on conditions and other more complex functions, are used in data source connections, conditional formatting, and other purposes. You don't need to know about them now just for basic headers and footers; when you want to learn more, see the section in the data sources chapter titled *Setting Up Stored Data in Fields and AutoText* on page 855.

Formatting Headers and Footers

Writer provides the following default header and footer paragraph styles: Header, Header left, Header right, Footer, Footer left, and Footer right. The left and right styles are used when your document is set up to alternate between left and right pages. You can format headers and footers manually, or you can change any of their styles. If you need help with formatting, see Chapter 7, *Formatting Documents*, on page 197.

Removing Headers and Footers

You can remove headers and footers on the fly by choosing Insert > Header (or Insert > Footer) and selecting the page style that has a check mark next to it. You can also turn headers and footers off within each page style (see *Creating Page Styles* on page 251).

Using Different Headers and Footers Within a Document

Every time you want new content for the header or footer, just make a new page style—page styles control what header and footer are used.

1   First, make sure you've read *Setting Up Headers and Footers, Consistent or Different on Each Page* on page 222.

2   Then see *Creating Page Styles* on page 251 to name and create the style itself such as `goodfooter` and `badfooter`.

3   To apply your page styles, see *Applying and Switching Page Styles* on page 253. This section tells you how to switch from one style to another, including restarting page numbers.

4   Put the appropriate content in the headers and footers. If you want the content to change, use different variables or text in the headers and footers of each new page style.

Page Layout

Note – It's a good idea to also take a look at *Page Layout Setup Options* on page 86.

Pretty much everything you need to control for one document's page layout is available through choosing Format > Page.

•   For page layout regarding books, including more complex page numbering, see Chapter 9, *Books and Longer Documents*, on page 305.

•   For powerful page layout capabilities using frames, see *Using Frames for Advanced Page Layout* on page 233.

•   For information about headers and footers, see *Setting Up Headers and Footers, Consistent or Different on Each Page* on page 222.

Basic Page Formatting: Margins and More

1   Open the document you want to format.

2   Choose Format > Page.

3   Make the appropriate selections in the windows shown in Figure 7-37.

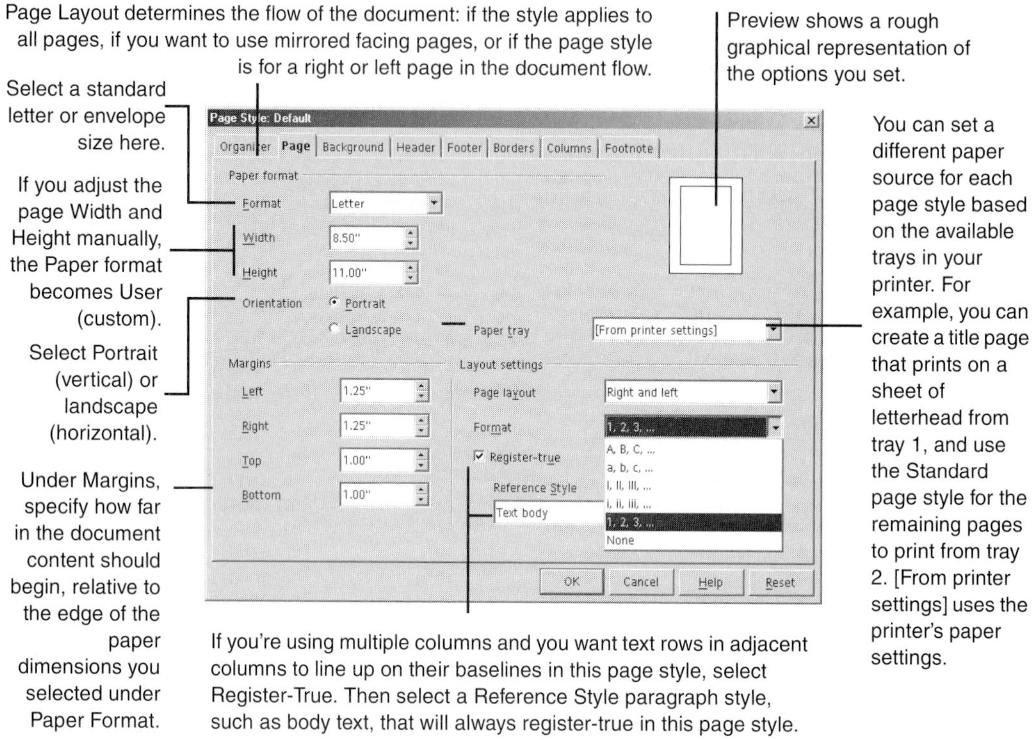
Page Layout determines the flow of the document: if the style applies to all pages, if you want to use mirrored facing pages, or if the page style is for a right or left page in the document flow.
Preview shows a rough graphical representation of the options you set.
Select a standard letter or envelope size here.
If you adjust the page Width and Height manually, the Paper format becomes User (custom).
Select Portrait (vertical) or landscape (horizontal).
Under Margins, specify how far in the document content should begin, relative to the edge of the paper dimensions you selected under Paper Format.
You can set a different paper source for each page style based on the available trays in your printer. For example, you can create a title page that prints on a sheet of letterhead from tray 1, and use the Standard page style for the remaining pages to print from tray 2. [From printer settings] uses the printer's paper settings.
If you're using multiple columns and you want text rows in adjacent columns to line up on their baselines in this page style, select Register-True. Then select a Reference Style paragraph style, such as body text, that will always register-true in this page style.
Page Style: Default
Organizer
Page
Background
Header
Footer
Borders
Columns
Footnote
Paper format
Format
Letter
Width
8.50"
Height
11.00"
Orientation
Portrait
Landscape
Paper tray
[From printer settings]
Margins
Left
1.25"
Right
1.25"
Top
1.00"
Bottom
1.00"
Layout settings
Page layout
Right and left
Format
1, 2, 3, ...
A, B, C, ...
a, b, c, ...
I, II, III, ...
i, ii, iii, ...
1, 2, 3, ...
None
Register-true
Reference Style
Text body
OK
Cancel
Help
Reset

Figure 7-37 The Page Style window, Page tab

Page Backgrounds and Borders

Jazz up the page a bit with a variety of borders, and backgrounds of colors—standard or colors you've created—or graphics.

Note – The background is printed only within the page margins, not to the edge of the paper.

---

1 Choose Format > Page.

2 Click the Borders tab and make selections there. Use Figure 7-38 for guidance.

3 Click the Background tab and make selections there. Use Figure 7-39 for guidance.

See Figure 7-24 to put a graphic in the background of one paragraph.

Click one of the predefined Line Arrangements to apply that border style. Click the empty first box to clear all line (not shadow) settings.

Select a line style and line color for the border.

Specify how far the lines should be from the text in the page. If you make an entry in one field that you want in all fields, click Synchronize.

The gray box in the Frame area represents the entire page. You can add or remove lines relative to the page by clicking above, below, or to either side of the gray box.

Click a Shadow Style Position box to select a shadow angle. Click the first box for no shadow. In the Distance field, specify how far the shadow should be from the page text.

You can choose a shadow color from the standard color palette.

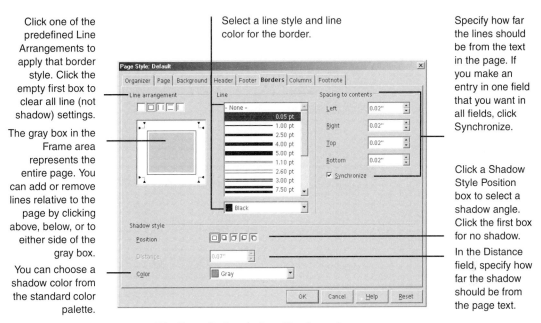

Figure 7-38   The Page Style window, Borders tab

The following tips pertain to using text borders and backgrounds.

Putting a box around text   To put two paragraphs within a box, such as a heading and a paragraph, add a soft return (Shift+Enter) between the paragraphs and format the heading and body text manually.

Using background colors and graphics   Using a dark or detailed graphic or color can wash out text. However, using a dark graphic or color with white font can produce nice results.

Since a graphic, if it's large, can fill the entire dimensions of a paragraph, the text runs into the edges of the graphic. A background color behaves the same way. If you want to create space between the text and the edges of the graphic or color, try using a text frame inside the paragraph. See *Inserting Frames and Floating Frames* on page 291.

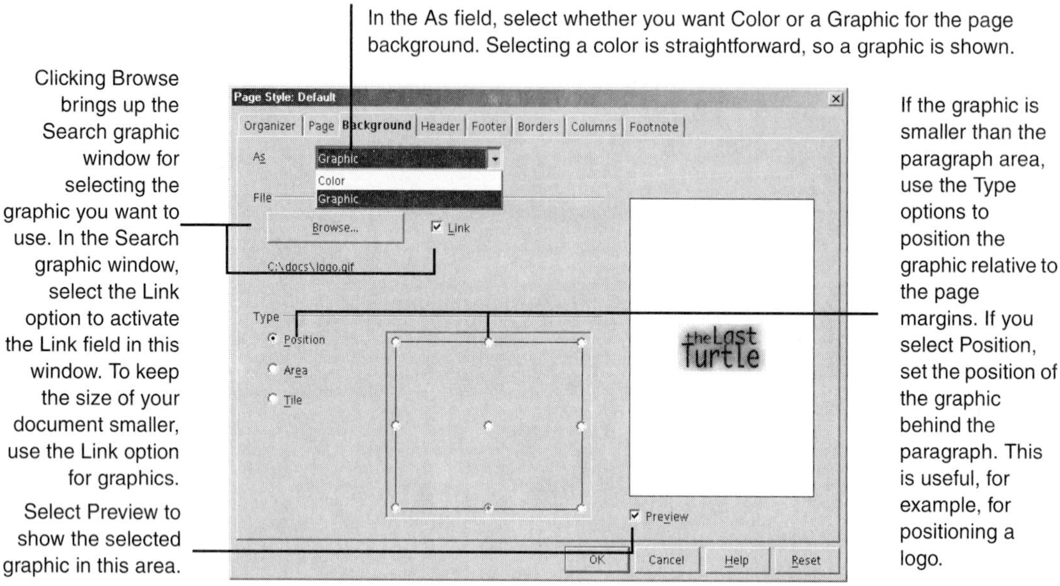
In the As field, select whether you want Color or a Graphic for the page background. Selecting a color is straightforward, so a graphic is shown.
Clicking Browse brings up the Search graphic window for selecting the graphic you want to use. In the Search graphic window, select the Link option to activate the Link field in this window. To keep the size of your document smaller, use the Link option for graphics.
Select Preview to show the selected graphic in this area.
If the graphic is smaller than the paragraph area, use the Type options to position the graphic relative to the page margins. If you select Position, set the position of the graphic behind the paragraph. This is useful, for example, for positioning a logo.
Page Style: Default
Organizer
Page
Background
Header
Footer
Borders
Columns
Footnote
As
Graphic
Color
Graphic
File
Browse...
Link
C:\docs\logo.gif
Type
Position
Area
Tile
theLast
Turtle
Preview
OK
Cancel
Help
Reset

Figure 7-39 The Page Style window, Background tab

Setting Up Multicolumn Pages

The column layout feature works really well. Also note that the same multicolumn features are present within a frame—which in turn could be positioned across one or more of your columns. Applies to sections, too. The number of columns is very nearly dizzying.

Note – You can set up a single paragraph, text box, or frame in a multicolumn format, as well.

Standard Column Formatting

1 Choose Format > Page.

2 Click the Columns tab and make the appropriate selections, then click the Borders tab and make selections there. Use Figure 7-40 for guidance.

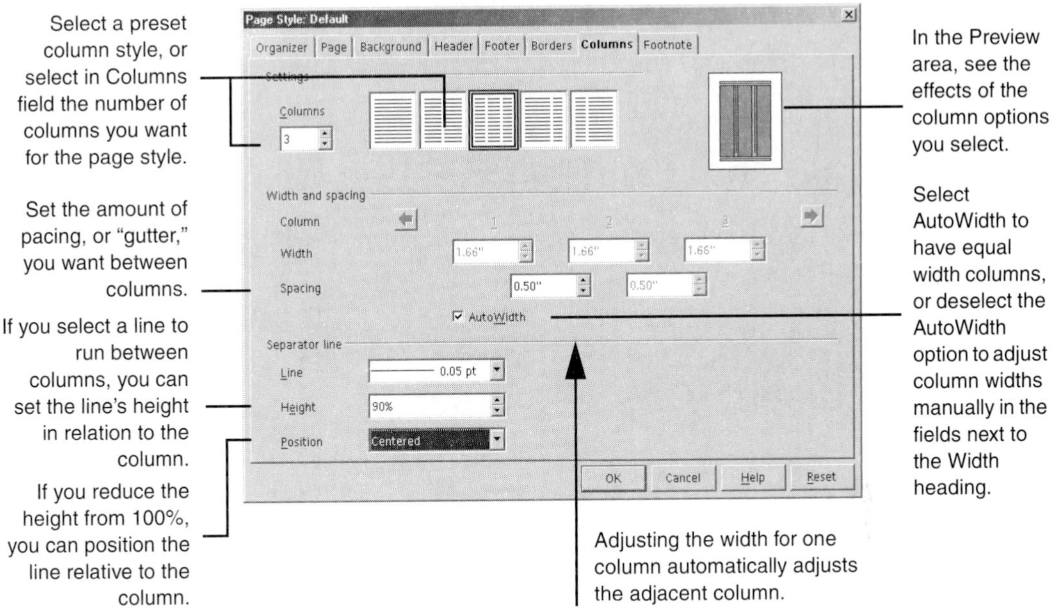
Select a preset column style, or select in Columns field the number of columns you want for the page style.
Set the amount of pacing, or "gutter," you want between columns.
If you select a line to run between columns, you can set the line's height in relation to the column.
If you reduce the height from 100%, you can position the line relative to the column.
In the Preview area, see the effects of the column options you select.
Select AutoWidth to have equal width columns, or deselect the AutoWidth option to adjust column widths manually in the fields next to the Width heading.
Adjusting the width for one column automatically adjusts the adjacent column.
Page Style: Default
Organizer
Page
Background
Header
Footer
Borders
Columns
Footnote
Columns
Width and spacing
Column
Width
Spacing
AutoWidth
Separator line
Line
0.05 pt
Height
90%
Position
Centered
OK
Cancel
Help
Reset

Figure 7-40 The Page Style window, Columns tab

Quickly Changing Columns Within a Paragraph

Note – When you create a column this way, the columns become a *section*. If you ever want to use Writer's document comparison tools, be aware that the comparison tool doesn't currently recognize, and therefore can't compare, text in sections.

You can also start with a blank multiple-column area by selecting an empty paragraph and setting columns as described in this procedure.

You can change the number of columns for a selected block of text.

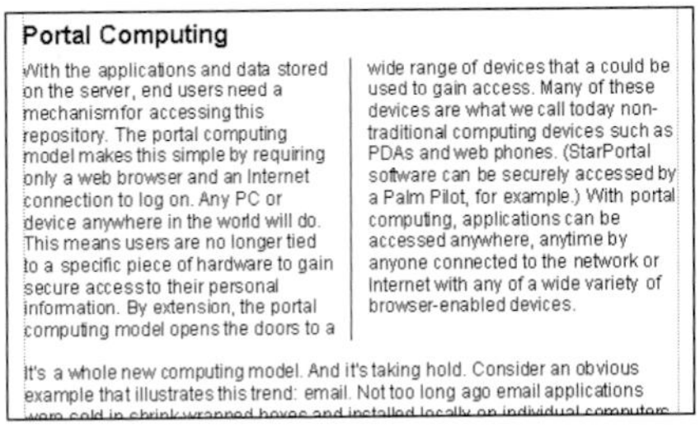
Portal Computing

With the applications and data stored on the server, end users need a mechanism for accessing this repository. The portal computing model makes this simple by requiring only a web browser and an Internet connection to log on. Any PC or device anywhere in the world will do. This means users are no longer tied to a specific piece of hardware to gain secure access to their personal information. By extension, the portal computing model opens the doors to a wide range of devices that a could be used to gain access. Many of these devices are what we call today non-traditional computing devices such as PDAs and web phones. (StarPortal software can be securely accessed by a Palm Pilot, for example.) With portal computing, applications can be accessed anywhere, anytime by anyone connected to the network or Internet with any of a wide variety of browser-enabled devices.

It's a whole new computing model. And it's taking hold. Consider an obvious example that illustrates this trend: email. Not too long ago email applications

1 Select the text you want.

2 Choose Format > Columns.

3 In the Columns window, set the options you want. See Figure 7-40.

4 Click OK.

Specifying Page Orientation

In general, just choose Format > Page, click the Page tab, and select Portrait or Landscape. This applies to all pages that use the current page style.

Things That Control Orientation

To see how to control orientation throughout the program, see *Page Layout Setup Options* on page 86.

Setting Up a Landscape Page in a Portrait Document (Or Vice Versa)

Create a page style with landscape orientation, then just apply it wherever you need that orientation. The following steps provide the detail.

Step 1: Creating the Landscape Page Style

1   Open the Stylist by choosing Format > Stylist.

2   In the Stylist window, click on the Page Styles icon.

3   The Default style should already be highlighted. Right-click on it and choose New.

4   In the window that appears, name the style. Click the Page tab and select Landscape.

5   Make any other selections you want for the page style

6   Click OK to save the style and close the window.

Step 2: Switching Orientations

Switching orientations is easier than you'd think. Do this procedure to switch from your document's standard page style to the one you just created, then use it again to switch back to the normal page style.

1   Put your cursor in your document where you want the orientation to change.

2   Choose Insert > Manual Break.

3   In the window that appears, select Page Break. In the style list, select the style you want to begin. If you're at the point in the document where landscape ends and portrait begins, for instance, just select Standard or whatever page layout you use for portrait orientation.

Using Frames for Advanced Page Layout

Writer isn't Quark or Pagemaker, but it does offer you frames to give you a good start.

Frames, or text frames, give you the ability to insert— anywhere— one or more columns of text

> **Great Java Resources**
>
> If you're tired of boring training and lackluster books, get ready for a change.
>
> Want to learn Java the fun way? Just go to www.softcorejava.com and get started. Read the Java Stories, or learn with games.
>
> For certification study guides, also head to www.lastturtle.com, to get books straight from the exam authors.

and objects. You can insert anything, even another frame. You can connect one frame to another, in order to easily start a story on page 1, then direct the reader to page 42 to continue reading it.

Floating frames hold an entire, open file inside of a frame, whether it's a graphic, a slide presentation, a web page, or a spreadsheet. When you insert a floating frame, you can work with that file within Writer as if you were working with the file itself. Menus, the toolbar, and the object bar all change to let you work with the file in the floating frame.

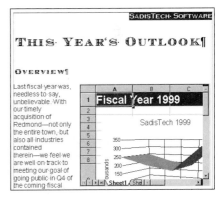

Combining the two with the other object-insertion features in this chapter lets you put just about anything just about anywhere in your document. Insert a text frame inside a table or vice versa; create a floating frame, then put a multi-column text frame, a graphic, and a spreadsheet inside the text frame.

Inserting a Quick Text Frame

1   In the toolbar at the left side of the work area, click and hold down the Insert tool at the top of the toolbar (not the Insert Object tool).

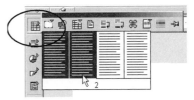

2   While holding down your mouse, move the mouse to the first tool and click on it. Move your mouse down and over to select the number of columns you want to insert.

3   Release the mouse; it will change from a standard mouse pointer to cross hairs.

4   Click in the document and draw the text box in the location where you want to anchor it.

You can apply more precise formatting to the text by selecting it, right-clicking, and choosing Frame.

Inserting a Text Frame With More Control

Use this procedure if you want more up-front control over the properties of the text box you want to insert.

1   Click where you want to insert the text box.

2   Choose Insert > Frame (not Floating Frame).

3   In the Frame window, set the options you want. Except for the Columns tab, which is fairly straightforward, the options are described in *Tips for Adjusting Inserted Objects* on page 298.

Inserting a Floating Frame Linked to an Existing Graphic, Document, or Object

A floating frame is much more than a text box. It can contain an entire file of any type that the program can open.

1   Click where you want to insert the floating frame.

2   In the toolbar, click and hold down the Insert Object tool, and click the Insert Floating Frame tool.

3   In the Frame Properties window, click the ⬚ button to select the file.

4   Set the remaining properties for the window. Use Figure 7-41 for guidance. Figure 7-42 shows an example of a floating frame.

5   Click OK.

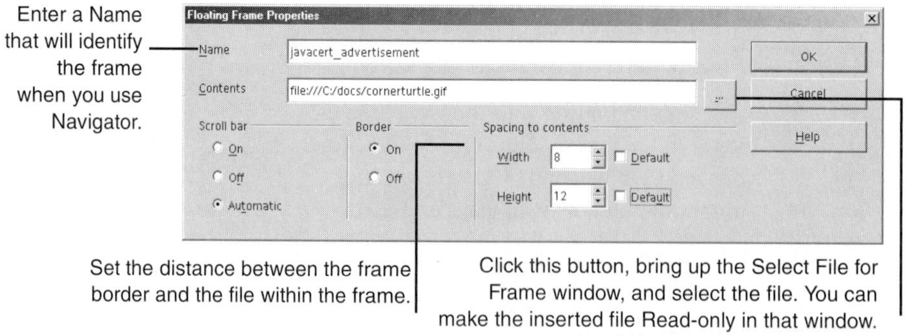

Enter a Name that will identify the frame when you use Navigator.

Set the distance between the frame border and the file within the frame.

Click this button, bring up the Select File for Frame window, and select the file. You can make the inserted file Read-only in that window.

Figure 7-41   Inserting a floating frame

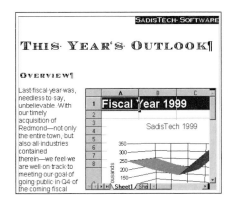

The contents of a floating frame can be edited inside Writer as if you were editing the file in its native application: Calc, Draw, etc. You can also save the file inside the floating frame. In this example, a spreadsheet file is in the floating frame.

Figure 7-42   Example of a floating frame

Selecting or Typing in a Text Frame or Frame

Frames are just slightly tricky to get into, but only if you don't know how.

To type or insert objects in a text frame Click outside the frame in the document. Then single-click inside a column in the text frame.

To select the frame itself in order to format it, move the mouse to the frame border until the mouse turns to crosshairs, then single click on the border.

> **Great Java Resources**
> If you're tired of boring training and lackluster books, get ready for a change.
>
> Want to learn Java the fun way? Just go to www.softcorejava.com and get started. Read the Java Stories, or learn with games.
>
> For certification study guides, also head to www.lastturtle.com, to get books straight from the exam authors.

Then right-click and select Frame, or double-click, to bring up the Frame formatting window.

Creating Text Flow Between Separate Frames

You get a great deal of power over your text flow and page layout using linked text frames. You can link frames to each other even when they are on different pages of a document. The text will automatically flow from one to the other.

1   Create the frames you want to link. (Frames, not floating frames.) The second frame *must* be completely empty; that means not even a caption.

2   In order to create a link, click the edge of the frame you want to link (typically the first of two). Eight handles will appear around the edges, as shown in Figure 7-43.

Figure 7-43   Selecting a frame to be linked

3   Click the Link Frames icon on the object bar, also shown in Figure 7-43. The mouse pointer will change to the icon shown at right.

4   Move the mouse pointer to inside the second text frame. When the icon changes and an outline appears around the frame, click in the frame. This is shown in Figure 7-44.

Figure 7-44   Linking to the second frame

5   A line will appear between the two linked frames, as shown in Figure 7-45.

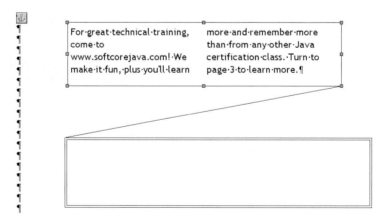

Figure 7-45   The linked frames

6   You can move the second frame anywhere in the document, and enter text in the frame and format it. Keep adding frames if you want; just make sure each new one is totally blank until it's linked. See Figure 7-46.

For·great·technical·training, come·to www.softcorejava.com!·We make·it·fun,·plus·you'll·learn

more·and·remember·more than·from·any·other·Java certification·class.·Turn·to page·3·to·learn·more.¶

Technical·Training That·Works¶

When·was·the·last·time you·had·a·good·time·at training,·and·remembered what·you'd·learned·the

next·day?·With softcorejava.com,·you'll·be shocked·at·how·much·fun you'll·have,·and·the knowledge·is·yours·for·life. What·makes·it·so·fun?¶

•   Active·participation¶

•   You·create·your·own knowledge·¶

•   You·don't·sit·and·listen to·a·droning·instructor for·hours·at·a·time¶

•   Softcorejava.com's

unique·Java·stories make·the·concepts come·alive¶

Certification·You·Can Count·On¶

Want·to·make·sure·your

$150·is·well·spent?·Come to·a·softcorejavacom seminar.¶

Figure 7-46   Three linked frames, which can be anywhere within a document (separate pages)

Unlinking Frames

To unlink the frames, **select the first frame** and click the Unlink icon on the toolbar. If more than two frames are linked, clicking the Unlink icon will unlink the last frame in the chain. You can only unlink in a "last in, first out" approach, not one particular link.

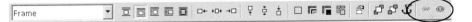

If it isn't displayed, show it by showing visible buttons for the object bar. See *Showing All the Icons on the Toolbars* on page 103.

When a linked frame is selected, any existing links are indicated by a connecting line.

Notes on Frames

Linking is only possible from one frame to the next. That means that a frame that is already linked to a frame cannot be linked to another frame which follows. Therefore, the link icon cannot be activated if a frame already has a next link. Also, two frames can only be unlinked with the Unlink Frames icon from the first frame.

Frames can't be linked if any of the following are true:

•   The target is not empty. An (automatically) captioned frame is not empty and can therefore not be the target of a link.

•   The target already has a previous link.

- Source and target are in different sections, i.e., one frame is in a header and the other frame is in a footer.
- The source already has a next link.
- Source and target are the same.
- Closed chains of frames, or chains from the inside out or from the outside in are also not permissible. The latter is the case if you inserted a frame into another frame and want to link them with each other.

Adjusting the Main Content in a Document Containing Frames

Presumably your document also contains normal text and objects that's not in the frames. In order to format where that content shows up in relationship to the inserted frames, see *Tips for Adjusting Inserted Objects* on page 298.

Controlling Page Flow in a Document With Inserted Objects

See *Tips for Adjusting Inserted Objects* on page 298.

Adding Vertical and Diagonal Text to Documents

You can create vertical text in two ways: making the standard text vertical using page layout options, or using the Draw tools available in Writer to create separate text frames that are vertical. See Figure 7-47 on page 239 for an example of making standard text vertical.

- Make your normal text vertical. Choose Format > Character and click the Position tab. See Figure 7-5 on page 201 for more detail.
- Use the vertical text Draw tool. See *Inserting Frames and Floating Frames* on page 291.
- To have text to goes diagonally across the page, just create a text frame. Select it, right-click and choose Position and Size, click the Rotation tab, and rotate the frame 90 degrees. Close the window. Then right-click again and choose the kind of Wrap you want. See Figure 7-48 on page 239.

Specify 90 degrees for text as shown, or 270 degrees for text that goes from top to bottom.

If you want the text to be exactly as high as the vertical line spacing, or leading, for the rest of the text in your document, select the Fit to Line option in the Character window's Position tab.

The displayed text is inside a frame, so that the main body of the document can be included and horizontal, next to it.

To turn off the nonprinting shading, choose View > Field Shadings.

This section of text was created with the vertical text tool (circled) and given a yellow background. Just rotate the text frame 180 degrees to have the text flow from bottom to top.

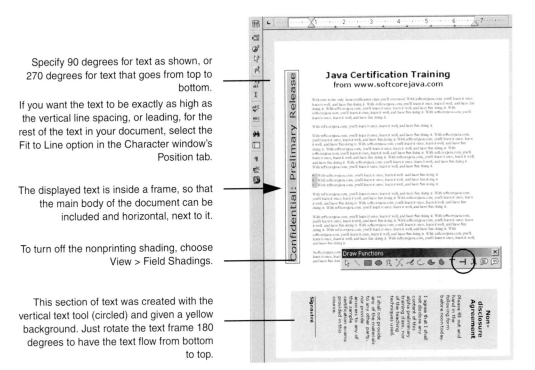

Figure 7-47   Vertical text using the Character window's Position tab and the Draw functions' vertical text tool

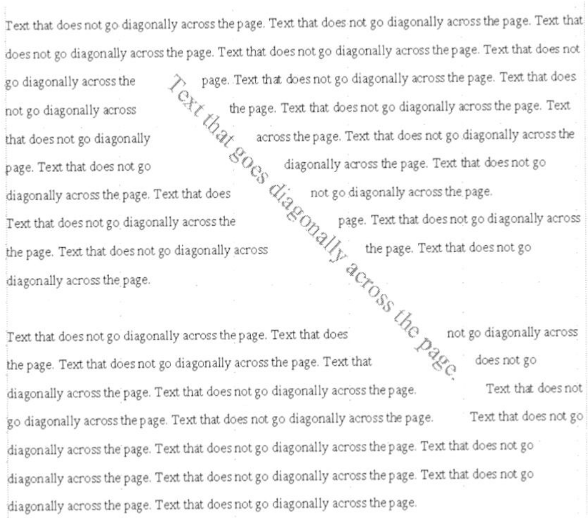

Figure 7-48   Diagonal text frame

Example: Creating a Complex Page Layout

Before you begin, you can get information about sections from *Using Sections to Create Multiple Versions of the Same Document* on page 411, *Tables* on page 271, and generally inserting objects in Chapter 8, *Adding Objects and Links to Documents*, on page 265.

See Figure 7-50 for this example. Keep in mind that you can format each page differently using the Page Styles window (Format > Page), using different layouts and different headers and footers in each page, or at whatever intervals you choose.

These are two separate frames: one one-column, one two-column. **2-column** is displayed in the style field above.

The graphic is inserted, anchored to the page, and the Wrap option is Parallel. (Choose Insert > Graphics > From File to insert a graphic. In the Graphics window, select the Type tab and under Anchor select Page, then select the Wrap tab, and select Parallel.)

Frames are linked so text flows from one frame to another automatically.

Basic page layout is a 3-column page layout created by choosing Format > Page > Column and selecting 3 columns.

This is continued on page 3.

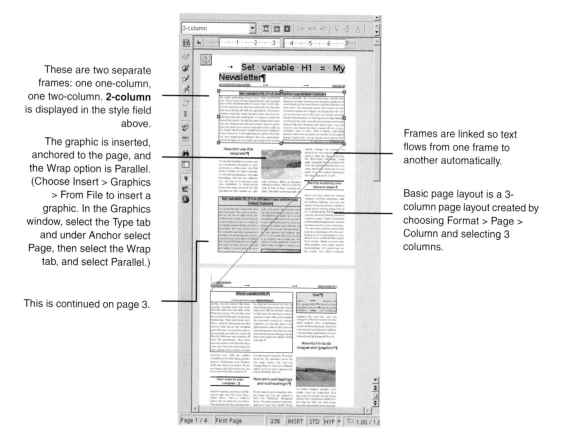

Figure 7-49   Template incorporating several complex page layout features

Throw in vertical or diagonal text (*Adding Vertical and Diagonal Text to Documents* on page 238) in the page or within a frame or column, plus background graphics for a page or paragraph, and you've got a whole lot of tools to make the document whatever you want.

For an example, choose File > New > Templates and Documents. Select the Miscellaneous category, then open the Newsletter Template. Then when prompted in the formatting dialog box, accept the default settings and click OK. Figure 7-50 shows the template.

OpenOffice.org users might not have this template. It contains frames, floating frames, linked frames, and a three-column layout set up though the Page Layout window's Column tab.

All the templates, etc. in StarOffice don't come with OpenOffice.org. However, Travis Bauer's excellent Web site, www.ooextras.org, has what might be called a plethora of templates and other "extras."

In addition to the elements used here, you can add floating frames, name sections in order to create multiple versions of a document or set aside the section for special formatting, use tables in the layout or within frames, and insert charts and other objects, alone or within frames or floating frames.

Power Formatting With Styles

In the previous sections we talked about formatting characters and paragraphs manually, which is how most people format: selecting text and either clicking quick-formatting tools on the object bar and ruler or choosing a Format menu item to set specific formatting options.

There are legitimate reasons to use only manual formatting (such as quick formatting of short documents whose styles you don't plan to reuse). However, to get the most out of Writer and to work more quickly with more consistency, use styles and templates.

About Writer Styles

Note – The styles for normal page contents, bibliographies, etc. are paragraph styles. If you've used Microsoft Word or other programs, you might be used to them as page styles.

Paragraphs, text, pages, and other elements have certain characteristics: for example, a heading (like the one just above this paragraph) that is 16-pt. bold Helvetica with a 3/4-inch left indent. A style is simply a name given to this set of characteristics, such as *Heading 2*.

Figure 7-50 illustrates the five types of styles in Writer. You've already created and formatted everything here; this Styles section just tells you how to create predefined groups of the attributes that are easy to apply, and transfer to different documents and templates.

Paragraph Styles determine such things as font, paragraph spacing, indents, borders, bullets, numbering, and following paragraphs.

Character Styles determine font style for selected text within a paragraph.

Numbering Styles determine number/ bullet characters and spacing.

Page Styles determine such things as margins, columns, headers, and footers.

Frame Styles determine such things as frame size, position, and wrapping. This example shows an anchored text frame that contains a paragraph style.

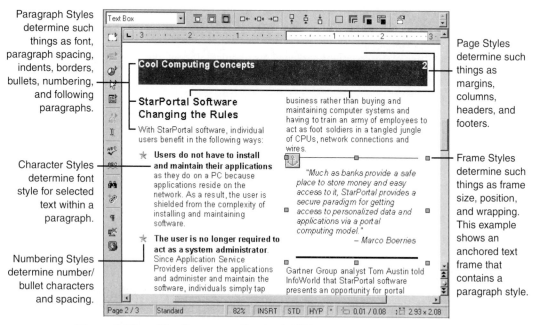

Figure 7-50   The five types of styles in Writer

Why You Should Use Styles

Following are the reasons why you should use styles. Any one of these reasons alone justifies using them.

Instant Formatting With a double-click you can transform a plain text paragraph into one with a different font, font size, font color, indentation, spacing, alignment, and background color. All paragraphs that are given that style are identical.

Automation When you end a paragraph and press Enter, the next paragraph can become another style automatically. For example, pressing enter at the end of a heading can put you directly into a body paragraph style. Also, when you modify a style, all paragraphs with that style are updated automatically. Automation is good! It doesn't mean "cookie-cutter"; it means you work more quickly, efficiently, and consistently.

Maintaining consistency Using styles ensures your documents will maintain a consistent style.

Running headers and footers If you want the main headings in your document to appear automatically in the header or footer of the document, your main headings need to be styles.

Table of contents generation Writer uses heading styles to generate tables of contents automatically. Using styles for figure and table captions also lets you build lists of figures and tables.

How Styles Work in Writer

The Stylist should be your closest companion in Writer. To show it (and hide it), press the F11 key.

Behind the scenes, styles also use styles in Writer. For example, if a paragraph style uses numbering or bullets, you'll select the numbering style to use within the paragraph style. Also, in numbering styles, you can assign a character style to use for the numbering or bullet characters.

Styles apply only to the document in which you create them. To make styles in one document available to other documents, see *Loading Styles From Another Document* on page 258.

About the Stylist

The Stylist, shown at right, is the control center for viewing, applying, adding, modifying, and deleting styles. Table 7-1 provides more detail about the categories.

The Style Catalog You can also create, modify, and delete styles using the Style Catalog (Format > Styles > Catalog).

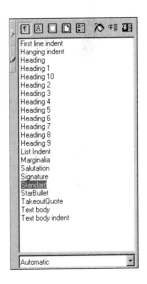

Tips for Using Styles

With the Stylist docked, make sure you have tooltips turned on (Help > Tips) to help you select the style type you want. When the mouse pointer hovers over a style type button, its name is displayed. (If the Stylist is a floating window, the name of the selected style category is displayed in the window's title bar.)

Writer comes with a predefined set of styles: paragraph, character, numbering, page, and frame. These defaults are designed to get you going, but ultimately you'll want to modify the defaults or create your own styles. If you find you're not using a lot of the default styles (especially the paragraph and character styles), and since you can't delete them, stay in the Custom Styles category of the Stylist. This will help you more quickly find the styles you do want to use, which also makes using styles less intimidating, because you're not swimming in a sea of unfamiliar styles names you had no part in creating. And since it's good practice not to go too overboard creating a multitude of possible styles (you should only create the ones you'll really use), the Custom Styles category should give you plenty of room to store all the styles you need.

You don't have to have all your styles perfect before you start using them. You'll want to make adjustments to them as you work. The great thing about styles is that you can change them when you want, and all of the paragraphs that use them are updated automatically.

Table 7-1 describes style categories, in the drop-down list at the bottom of the Stylist.

Table 7-1   Writer Stylist categories

Category	Description
All	Shows all defined styles for each style type.
Applied Styles	Shows all the styles you've used in your document so far. Since these applied styles are also displayed in the object bar, take advantage of this by selecting a different category in the Stylist. This lets you see styles for two categories at once.
Custom Styles	Shows the styles you've created beyond the default styles provided by Writer. The styles you create remain in this category even if you assign them to a different category.
Hierarchical	Displays styles in a hierarchical tree view. If a style has a plus sign next to it (+), click the plus sign to view the styles that were created based on that style.
The following categories apply only to paragraph styles	
Automatic	Allows the category to change based on where the cursor is located in the document. For example, if the cursor is in a body paragraph, the Text Styles category is shown. If the cursor is moved to within a header, the Special Styles category is shown.
Text Styles	Shows styles that are related to heading and body text.
Chapter Styles	Shows styles that are related to chapter-level text, such as titles and subtitles.
List Styles	Shows an ungodly and confusing amount of hanging indent paragraph styles without bullets. Use this category only if you want to get dizzy. Instead, create your own numbered and bulleted list paragraph styles and store them in a category other than this one.
Index Styles	Shows styles that are related to indexes and tables of contents.
Special Styles	Shows styles that are used in special regions such as headers, footers, and tables.
HTML Styles	Shows styles that are used in HTML documents. Use this category when you're working in Writer/Web.
Conditional Styles	Shows the paragraph styles that have conditions. For example, a paragraph style that behaves differently in a table than it does in regular body text.

Standard Paragraph Styles

This section describes how to create paragraph styles.

- For information on applying styles, see page 253
- For modifying styles, see page 254
- For deleting styles, see page 255
- For changing the category of styles, see page 255

Creating a paragraph style is fairly easy. In fact, if you know how to format paragraphs manually (see *Using the Paragraph Format Window* on page 208), you know 90 percent of creating a paragraph style.

1   In the Stylist, click the Paragraph Styles button.

2   Select the category in which you want to put the new style.

3   If you want to create a new style based on an existing style, select the style you want to base it on before you right-click.

4   Right-click in the Stylist and select New. The Paragraph Style window is displayed.

5   Set the formatting options for the paragraph. (See the field descriptions in *Using the Character Formatting Window* on page 200 and *Using the Paragraph Format Window* on page 208 for more information.)

6   In the Organizer tab, type a name for the style.

Use a name that will help you remember what the style either looks like or is used for.

7   Set the options in the Condition tab, if applicable. (See Figure 7-51 on page 246.)

8   Click OK.

Figure 7-51 shows paragraph style options on the Organizer tab.

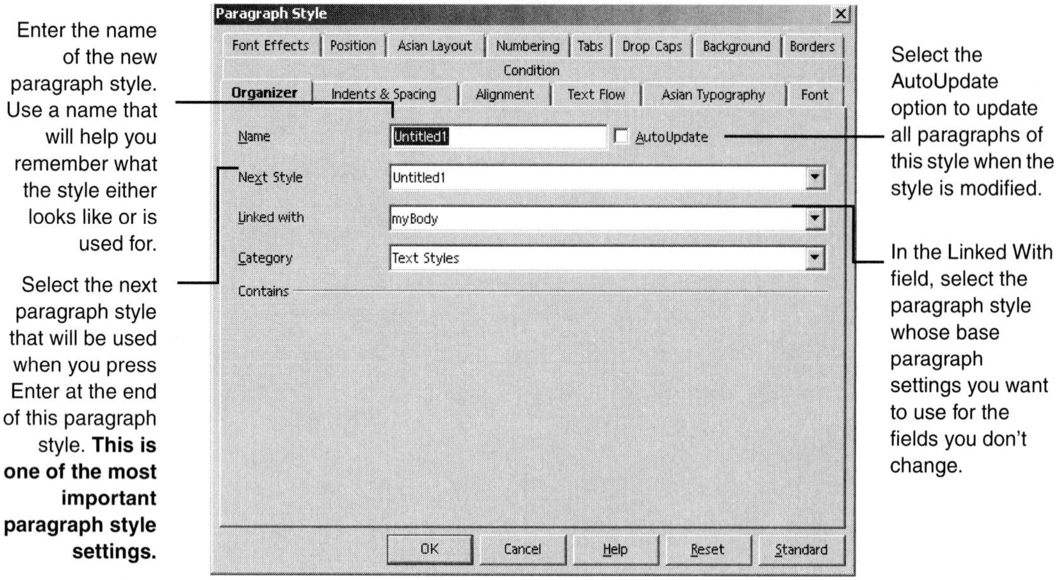

Enter the name of the new paragraph style. Use a name that will help you remember what the style either looks like or is used for.

Select the next paragraph style that will be used when you press Enter at the end of this paragraph style. **This is one of the most important paragraph style settings.**

Select the AutoUpdate option to update all paragraphs of this style when the style is modified.

In the Linked With field, select the paragraph style whose base paragraph settings you want to use for the fields you don't change.

Figure 7-51   The Paragraph Style window, Organizer tab

Conditional Paragraph Styles

Figure 7-51 shows paragraph style options on the Condition tab.

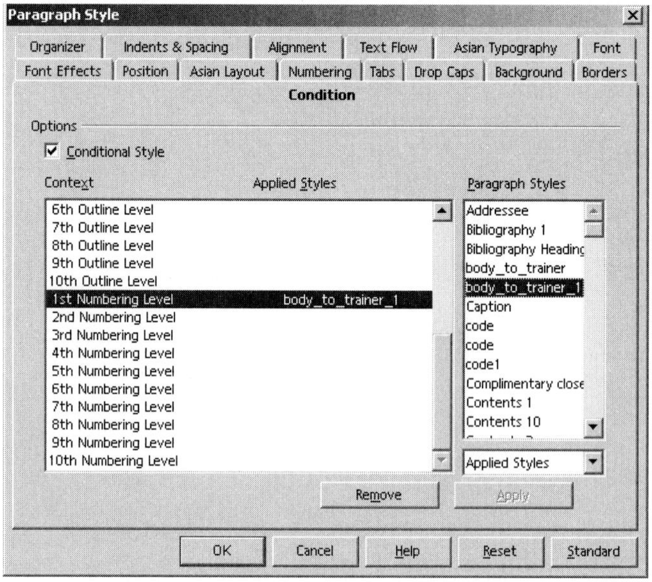

Figure 7-52   The Paragraph Style window, Condition tab

About conditional paragraphs StarOffice lets you can create different conditions for how a paragraph style is used. For example, you can have the Text Body paragraph style take on different characteristics when it's used in different places (under different conditions): in headers, body text, tables, and so on. There's no compelling reason why you'd want to use this feature over creating separate paragraph formats. There is, however a compelling reason *not* to use this feature: it can be a maintenance nightmare. As the following section on Using Conditions shows, this feature adds an unnecessary layer of complexity when you're simply trying to modify a paragraph style.

Using conditions When you want to modify a paragraph style, look first to see if it has a Condition tab with condition settings. Here's why: Because conditional paragraphs can take on different paragraph style characteristics when they're used in different contexts, modifying them can get confusing.

For example, suppose a body text paragraph is a 10 pt. regular (not bold) font in a body paragraph, and it has a conditional setting that makes it appear as a 12 pt. italic font in a text box. If you want to change the text box font, you may be thrown by the fact that the font definition for a text body paragraph doesn't match what is shown in the text box. You might then be tempted to make a wholesale change to the text body font to see if that fixes the seeming font disparity. If you do that, the font for all text body paragraphs change, but the text in the text box remains the same because the condition remains the same.

Table 7-2   Extended descriptions of categories in the Condition tab

Name	Meaning
Automatic	Displays Styles appropriate to the current context.
All Styles	Displays all Styles of the active Style category.
Applied Styles	Displays the Styles (of selected category) applied in the current document. These can also be selected from the Object bar.
Custom Styles	Displays all user-defined Styles of the selected Style category.
Character Styles	Displays appropriate Styles for text.
Chapter Styles	Displays appropriate Styles for chapters.
List Styles	Displays appropriate Numbering Styles for lists.
Index Styles	Displays appropriate Styles for indexes.
Special Region Styles	Displays appropriate Styles for special regions (e.g., headers, footnotes, tables, captions).
HTML Styles	Displays a list of Styles for HTML documents.
Conditional Styles	Displays the user-defined Conditional Styles.
Hierarchical	Displays the Styles in the selected Style category in a hierarchical list. To display the Styles in sublevels, click on the plus sign next to the name of the Style.

Creating a Paragraph Style Using Drag and Drop

You can also create a style by drag and drop. This method doesn't let you set Organizer or Condition tab options.

1   In your document, format the paragraph manually (see *Using the Paragraph Format Window* on page 208 and *Using the Character Formatting Window* on page 200).

2   In the Stylist, click the Paragraph Styles button and select a paragraph style category to which you want to add the style.

3   In the document, select the paragraph you want to add, click and hold on the selection, and drag the pointer into the Stylist, as shown in Figure 7-53.

    Make sure you don't drag onto the name of an existing style, because you will overwrite the style.

4   In the Create Style window, type a name for the style and click OK.

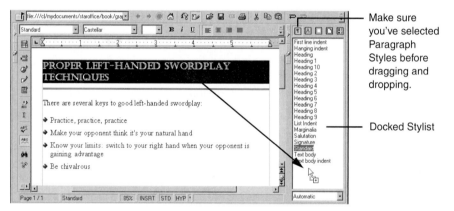

Figure 7-53   Creating a paragraph style using drag and drop

Cross-referencing paragraphs that have numbering If you want to cross-reference the autogenerated numbers/text of a paragraph, such as "Figure 5-1" in a caption paragraph style, you need to number those paragraph formats in a different way. See *Outline Numbering* on page 308.

Character Styles

This section describes how to create character styles. For information on applying styles, see page 253; for modifying styles, see page 254; for deleting styles, see page 255; for changing the category of styles, see page 255.

Creating a Character Style

Creating a character style is fairly easy. In fact, if you know how to format characters manually (see *Using the Character Formatting Window* on page 200), you know 90 percent of creating a character style.

1   In the Stylist, click the Character Styles button.

2   At the bottom of the Stylist, select the category in which you want to put the new style.

3   If you want to create a new style based on an existing style, select the style you want to base it on before you right-click. For more information on this, see Figure 7-54.

4   Right-click in the Stylist and select New. The Character Style window is displayed.

5   Set the formatting options for the character style.

See the field descriptions in *Using the Character Formatting Window* on page 200 for more information.

6   In the Organizer tab, type a name for the style.

Use a name that will help you remember what the style either looks like or is used for.

7   Click OK.

The character style doesn't include hyperlink properties, which are offered in the Character window (Format > Character). You must set hyperlink properties on a case-by-base basis. See Figure 8-1 on page 266 for details.

Figure 7-54 shows the options in the Organizer tab.

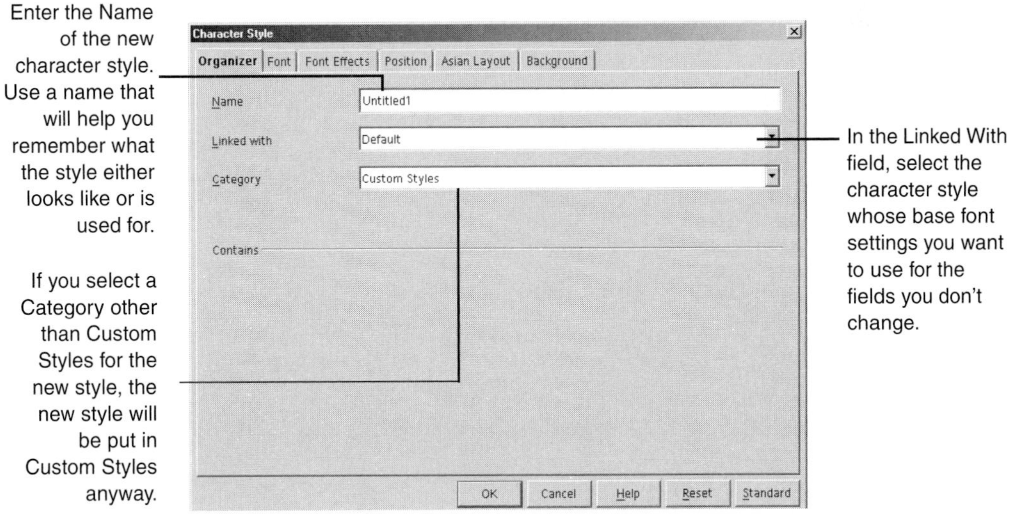

Enter the Name of the new character style. Use a name that will help you remember what the style either looks like or is used for.

If you select a Category other than Custom Styles for the new style, the new style will be put in Custom Styles anyway.

In the Linked With field, select the character style whose base font settings you want to use for the fields you don't change.

Figure 7-54   The Character Style window, Organizer tab

Creating a Character Style Using Drag and Drop

You can also create a style by drag and drop. This method doesn't let you set Organizer tab options.

1   Format the characters manually (see *Using the Character Formatting Window* on page 200).

2   In the Stylist, click the Character Styles button and select a character style category to which you want to add the style.

3   In the document, select the text you want to add, click and hold on it, and drag the pointer into the Stylist.

Make sure you don't drag onto the name of an existing style, because you will overwrite the style.

4   In the Create Style window, type a name for the style and click OK.

Numbering and Bullet Styles

You can save custom numbering or bulleted lists by creating styles for them. Numbering Styles (which can include bullet styles) let you quickly apply custom numbering to any part of your document.

This section describes how to create numbering styles.

For information on applying styles, see page 253; for modifying styles, see page 254; for deleting styles, see page 255; for changing the category of styles, see page 255.

Creating a Numbering Style

Creating a numbering style is fairly easy. In fact, if you know how to format with numbers and bullets manually (see *Using Basic Numbering, Bullets, and Outlining* on page 215), you know 90 percent of creating a numbering style.

1   In the Stylist, click the Numbering Styles button.

2   Right-click in the Stylist and select New. The Numbering Style window is displayed.

3   Set the numbering options for the numbering style.

4   In the Organizer tab, type a name for the style.

Use a name that will help you remember what the style either looks like or is used for.

5   Click OK.

Note – You can also use a numbering style as part of a paragraph style, so that when you apply a paragraph style in the document, the numbering or bullets appear automatically. See *Creating Page Styles* on page 251

Creating a Numbering Style Using Drag and Drop

You can also create a numbering style by drag and drop.

1   Format the numbering/bullets manually (see *Using Basic Numbering, Bullets, and Outlining* on page 215 and *Customizing Numbering, Bullets, and Outlining* on page 217).

2   In the Stylist, click the Numbering Styles button.

3   In the document, select the first line of the custom numbering you want to add, click and hold on it, and drag the pointer into the Stylist.

You don't have to select the number/bullet in that paragraph; just the text.

Make sure you don't drag onto the name of an existing style, because you will overwrite the style.

4   In the Create Style window, type a name for the style and click OK.

Creating Page Styles

Page styles control such elements as margins, headers, footers, columns, and which page styles follow each other.

Note – Page styles are the key to using different headers and footers in your document, since headers and footers are controlled by the page style in use.

For information on applying styles, see page 253; for modifying styles, see page 254; for deleting styles, see page 255; for changing the category of styles, see page 255.

1   In the Stylist, click the Page Styles button.

2   Select the category in which you want to put the new style.

3   Right-click in the Stylist and select New. The Page Style window is displayed.

4   Set the options you want for the page.

If you need help setting options, refer to the following figures.

5   Click OK.

Figure 7-55 shows page style options on each of the tabs in the Page Style window. The other windows are explained in *Page Layout* on page 227.

Enter the name of
the new page style.

Select the next
page style that will
always follow this
page style.

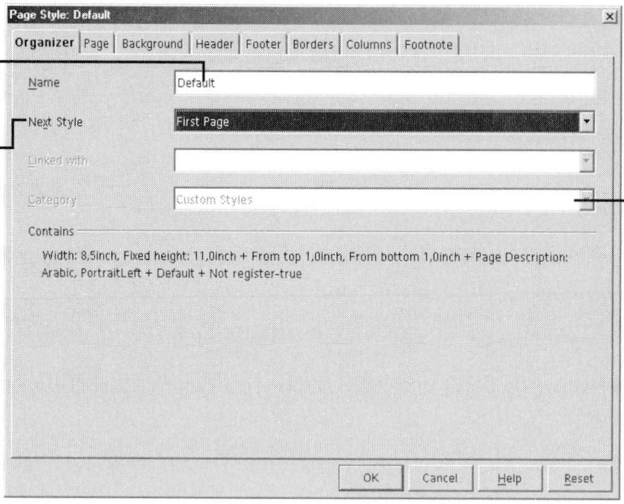

If you select a
category other
than Custom
Styles for the new
style, the new
style will be put in
Custom Styles
anyway.

Figure 7-55   The Page Style window, Organizer tab

About the Next Style Field As you create custom styles, you may need to wait to set this field until all the page styles you want to use are created.

About the Page Layout Field If your document seems to skip pages in the page numbering or starts documents at page zero, try setting the Page Layout field (in the Page tab) to All.Frame Styles

Frames are boxes you insert into a document to hold paragraphs and graphics around which you want to wrap the body text of your document. Frame styles let you use a consistent format for frames you commonly use. Frame styles control such attributes as frame size, position, wrapping, borders, backgrounds, and number of columns. You can even assign macros to run when the frame is selected.

For information on applying styles, see page 253; for modifying styles, see page 254; for deleting styles, see page 255; for changing the category of styles, see page 255.

Creating Frame Styles

To learn about frames, see *Using Frames for Advanced Page Layout* on page 233.

1   In the Stylist, click the Frame Styles button.

2   Select the category in which you want to put the new style.

3   Right-click in the Stylist and select New. The Frame Style window is displayed.

4   Set the options you want for the frame, and click OK.

Creating a frame style is similar to setting frame properties when you insert one in a document. See *Tips for Adjusting Inserted Objects* on page 298.

Applying Styles

1   Select the paragraph, character, page, or frame to which you want to apply a style.

2   In the Stylist, select the type of style you want to apply, select a category, and double-click the name of the style you want to use.

Applying Paragraph Styles

As you apply styles in the document, the object bar displays styles you've applied so far. You can then apply styles from the object bar as well.

Applying Character Styles

You get more control over selecting words by double-clicking them. For example, you don't have to take time pinpointing the cursor to avoid selecting spaces before or after a word.

To select a series of words, double-click the first word, and as you drag through the remaining words you want to select, each word is selected in full. Again, this lets you drag quickly without having to avoid selecting the space after the last word.

You can also select nonsequential words by double-clicking. See *Selecting Nonconsecutive Blocks of Text* on page 184.

Applying Frame Styles

To apply a frame style, you must first insert a frame. See *Inserting Frames and Floating Frames* on page 291.

After you insert a frame, the frame styles appear in the Stylist. Double-click a frame style to apply it to the frame you inserted.

Removing Numbers and Bullets

Remove numbering or bulleting in a paragraph by clicking in the numbered or bulleted paragraph (or highlighting multiple paragraphs) and clicking the Numbering or Bullets icons in the object bar.

Applying and Switching Page Styles

In a page style, the Next style field on the Organizer tab forces a page to be followed by a specific page: for example, a left page is followed by a right page and vice versa. So if you apply a page style to a page by double-clicking the page style in the Stylist, all subsequent pages will follow the Next style rules begun by the page style you've applied.

You can break the flow of page styles by creating a manual break. For example, you can break a left/right page flow at the end of a section by manually inserting a blank page with no headers or footers. Here's how:

1 Click in the exact place in the document where you want to create a break.

If you're breaking at a heading, click at the very beginning of the heading.

2 Choose Insert > Manual Break.

3 Select Page Break, and in the Style field, select the page style you want to use for the new page.

4 If you want the page to restart at a page number other than what is used in the regular page flow, select the Change page number option and set the page number the new page will begin with.

For a practical example of changing page numbering, see *Chapter-Page Numbering* on page 316.

5 Click OK.

You can also use this technique to switch between portrait and landscape page styles.

Modifying Styles

1 In the Stylist, select the style type containing the style you want to modify.

2 Select the category the style belongs to.

3 Right-click the style and select Modify.

If you're modifying a paragraph style, check to see if the paragraph style has a Condition tab with conditional settings.

4 Change settings for the style. If you need formatting guidance, see the previous formatting sections.

5 Click OK.

6 If a style doesn't update automatically in the document, select the name of the style in the Stylist and click the Update Style button at the top of the Stylist.

About updating paragraphs If you try to update a paragraph but the paragraph font doesn't change, you may have applied a character style to the paragraph that is overriding the paragraph style. To fix this, select the entire paragraph and choose Format > Default. This removes the character style override and lets the paragraph use its own style.

Modifying Styles Using Drag and Drop

You can also modify paragraph, character, and numbering styles by drag and drop:

1   Format the paragraph, characters, or numbering manually (with the object bar or from the Format menu).

2   In the Stylist, select the type of style you're modifying and select the category the style belongs to.

3   In the document, select the modified paragraph, characters, or numbering; click and hold on it; and drag the pointer into the Stylist and onto the name of the style you want to modify.

The character style doesn't include hyperlink properties, which are offered in the Character window (Format > Character). You must set hyperlink properties on a case-by-base basis. See Figure 8-1 on page 266 for details.

Deleting Styles

Default styles cannot be deleted. This procedure applies to custom styles you've created.

Before you delete a style, select it in the Stylist, right-click it, select Modify, and select the Organizer tab. Look at the style selected in the Based on field (if applicable). When you delete the style, if it was used in the document, the parts of the document that were assigned that style become the style shown in the Based on field.

1   In the Stylist, select the style you want to delete.

2   Right-click it, and select Delete.

3   Click Yes in the confirmation window.

Changing Style Categories

You can reorganize the styles you create by moving them into different categories. However, you can't change the categories of default Writer styles.

1   In the Stylist, select the style whose category you want to change.

2   Right-click it, and select Modify.

3   Select the Organizer tab.

4   In the Category field, select the new category you want to use.

5   Click OK.

All styles you create are custom, and therefore put in the Custom Styles category. Changing a style from the custom category to another category simply puts your custom style in an additional category.

Using Templates

Up to this point in the chapter we've progressed from manually setting specific formatting characteristics to grouping those characteristics into specific styles. Styles are containers for characteristics. This section takes the progression a step further by talking about templates, which are containers for styles.

A template is a document that was created with specific styles that can be used as a model for creating a specific type of document. For example, the program installs with templates to help you create resumes, memos, fax cover sheets, budgets, calendars, newsletters, HTML documents, envelopes, and a bevy of other types of documents.

Templates are even more than containers for styles. They can also contain predefined text, graphics, pagination, work environment settings (toolbars, keyboard shortcuts, etc.), and other elements that will always be used in a new document of that type.

OpenOffice.org

All the templates, etc. in StarOffice don't come with OpenOffice.org. However, Travis Bauer's excellent Web site, `www.ooextras.org`, has what might be called a plethora of templates and other "extras."

Creating a Document From a Template

See *Creating a Writer Document From a Template* on page 176.

If you want to just use the styles from a template, see *Loading Styles From Another Document* on page 258.

Switching to a Different Template

You can't change to a different template once you've created a document. However, you can bring styles in from another template or document. See *Loading Styles From Another Document* on page 258.

About the Standard Template

When you start a new Writer document, Writer bases the new document on a template called Standard, which has a standard set of styles and some behind-the-scenes functionality. If you don't like the default style settings provided by the Standard template (for example, if you want to use a different font size for the Text body or heading styles), you can have Writer use another template for new documents.

If all you want to do is start new documents with different font faces than those provided by the Standard template, there's an easy way to change the default standard fonts. See *Changing Default Fonts and the Default Template* on page 177.

Changing Default Fonts in the Standard Template

These changes apply to Writer's Standard template only.

1   Select Tools > Options > Text document > Basic Fonts.

2   Change fonts for the respective types of paragraphs (see Figure 7-56).

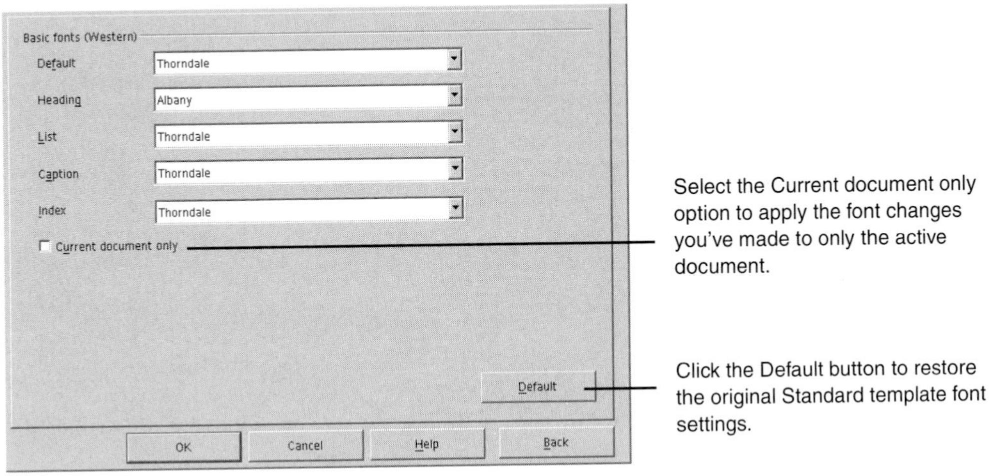

Select the Current document only option to apply the font changes you've made to only the active document.

Click the Default button to restore the original Standard template font settings.

Figure 7-56   Changing the default fonts used by Writer's Standard template

Modifying the Standard Template

The Standard template is used as the basis for every document you create by choosing File > New > Text Document. If you find you always have to change the formatting of your new documents to suit your requirements, it is time to use a separate template, known as the **default template**.

1   Create or open a document that contains your favorite Styles and formatting.

2   Delete the text of the document if you want, so that only the Styles and other settings remain.

3   Save the document as template by choosing File > Templates > Save. Save it in the Default location. The main directory for the displayed directories is `office\user\template`.

4   Choose File > Templates> Organize.

5   In the list at the left, double-click Default. The name of the default template you just saved will appear under it. Select the name.

6   Right-click the name and choose Set as Default Template. Close the window. This template will now be used as the default template when you choose File > New > Text document.

Switching Back to the Standard Template for New Documents

If you switched from the Standard template to another template for creating new documents (see previous procedure), use this procedure to switch back to the Standard template.

1   Choose File > Templates > Organize.

2   Right-click in either of the list boxes or open the submenu of the Commands button.

3   Choose Reset Default Template. This command opens a submenu in which you see every document type for which you have selected a default template. Select the document type you want to assign the default settings to.

The Standard template will now be used whenever you start a new Writer document.

Loading Styles From Another Document

If you want a document to use styles from another document or a template, you can load all styles or individual styles.

This procedure isn't the same as using a template to create a document. See *Creating a Writer Document From a Template* on page 176.

Loading All Styles

1   Start a new document or open the document into which you want to load different styles.

2   Choose Format > Styles > Load.

3   In the File type field, select whether you want to load styles from a Writer document (files ending in .swx) or a Writer template (files ending in .vor).

4   At the bottom of the window, select the types of styles you want to load, as shown in Figure 7-57.

Select the Overwrite option to replace the style definitions for styles with the same name. If you don't select Overwrite, style settings with the same name won't be overwritten in the open document.

If you're loading styles from a template, you can also click the Templates button at the bottom of the window to select a template.

If you don't see the styles update automatically in the Stylist, click one of the other style buttons in the Stylist, then click the button of the styles you want to see.

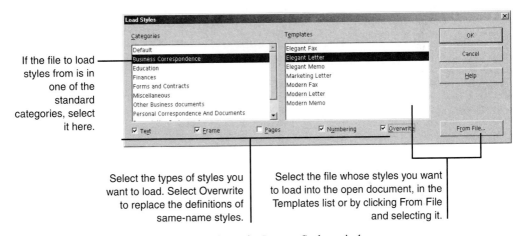

If the file to load styles from is in one of the standard categories, select it here.

Select the types of styles you want to load. Select Overwrite to replace the definitions of same-name styles.

Select the file whose styles you want to load into the open document, in the Templates list or by clicking From File and selecting it.

Figure 7-57   Loading styles from the Import Styles window

Loading Individual Styles

If you want to load individual styles from one document into another (rather than loading all styles), use the template Organizer.

1   With Writer active, choose File > Templates > Organize.

You can also choose Format > Styles > Catalog, and click the Organizer button.

2   In the Document Templates window (Figure 7-58), below each list box, select whether you want to view Document Templates or Documents.

One list box will be used to copy styles from a document into the document listed in the other list box.

3   In one list box, double-click the file whose styles you want to use, then double-click the Styles icon below it. The styles used in the document are displayed.

4   In the other list box, double-click the name and the Styles icon of the document into which you want to load the styles.

5   Drag the style(s) you want to use from one document to the other. Use Figure 7-58 for guidance on using the Template Management window.

Drag individual styles from one document into another document or template. Different styles have different icons.

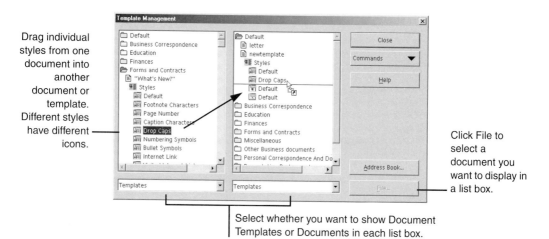

Click File to select a document you want to display in a list box.

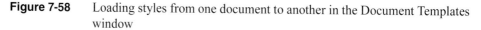

Select whether you want to show Document Templates or Documents in each list box.

Figure 7-58   Loading styles from one document to another in the Document Templates window

Creating a Template

Creating a template isn't much more than formatting a document, adding boilerplate content to it if you want, and saving it in template format.

If all you want to use a template for is to automatically insert boilerplate stuff like a company logo and address for a letterhead, you can also use the AutoText feature. See *Creating and Inserting AutoText* on page 180.

1   Create a document, adding any styles, formatting, graphics, tables, and any other content you want to use for a template.

2   Choose File > Templates > Save.

3   In the Document Templates window, enter new name for template.

4   Select a template category in which you want to store the template. (To create your own template category, see *Creating a Template Category* on page 262.)

5   Click OK. The template is ready to use.

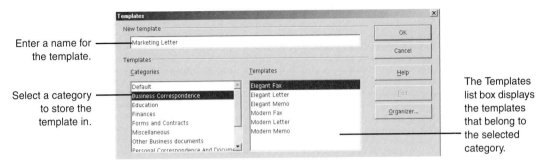

Enter a name for the template.

Select a category to store the template in.

The Templates list box displays the templates that belong to the selected category.

Figure 7-59   Creating a new template in the Document Templates window

Editing Templates

If you edit one of the default templates, you might notice that it uses a handful of automated fields. For help on fields, see Chapter 9, *Headers, Footers, and Fields*, on page 281.

1   With Writer active, choose File > Templates > Organize.

2   In the Document Templates window, select Document Templates in the field at the bottom of the window.

3   Double-click the folder containing the template you want to edit.

4   Select the template you want to edit.

5   Click the Commands button and choose Edit.

6   Modify and save the template.

If you want to edit a template that isn't stored in a template folder, you can edit it by choosing File > Templates > Edit and double-clicking the template you want.

Importing and Exporting Templates in the Organizer

Importing and exporting templates is simply a way of moving template files into and out of the template folders.

This procedure shows you how to import and export templates using the Organizer. You can also import and export templates in the Explorer window by moving them into and out of the subfolders of the template folder.

Importing a Template to a Category

1   With Writer active, choose File > Templates > Organize.

2   In the Document Templates window, choose Document Templates in the field at the bottom of the window.

3   Select the template folder into which you want to import the template.

4   Click the Commands button and choose Import Template.

5   Locate and double-click the template you want to import.

Exporting a Template to a Different Category

1   With Writer active, choose File > Templates > Organize.

2   In the Document Templates window, select Document Templates in the field at the bottom of the window.

3   Double-click the category containing the template you want to export.

4   Select the template you want to export.

5   Click the Commands button and choose Export Template.

6   In the Save As window, navigate to the folder to which you want to export the template.

7   Click Save.

Importing Microsoft Office Templates

See *Converting Microsoft Office and StarOffice 5.2 Documents* on page 161.

Organizing Templates

In addition to letting you edit, import, and export templates, and share styles between documents, the Document Templates Organizer lets you create template categories.

Creating a Template Category

This procedure shows you how to create a template category using the Organizer. You can also create a category by adding a new subfolder to the template folder in the Explorer window.

1   With Writer active, choose File > Templates > Organize.You can also choose Format > Styles > Catalog, and click the Organizer button.

2   Select Document Templates in the field at the bottom of the window.

3   Select any of the template folders.

4   Click the Commands button and choose New.

5   A new *Untitled* folder is displayed with the name highlighted. Type the name of the new template category.

Moving Templates to Different Categories

This procedure shows you how to move templates to different categories using the Organizer. You can also move templates to different categories in the Explorer window by moving them around between the subfolders of the template folder.

1   With Writer active, choose File > Templates > Organize.

You can also choose Format > Styles > Catalog, and click the Organizer button.

2   Select Document Templates in the field at the bottom of the window.

3   Double-click the folder containing the template you want to move.

4   Hold down the Shift key and drag the template you want to move into another category folder.

If you don't hold down the Shift key while you drag, you copy the template rather than move it.

Deleting Templates and Template Categories

1   With Writer active, choose File > Templates > Organize.

You can also choose Format > Styles > Catalog, and click the Organizer button.

2   Select Document Templates in the field at the bottom of the window.

3   Select the category folder or template you want to delete.

4   Click the Commands button and choose Delete.

5   Click Yes in the confirmation window.

Editing Values of Fields in Business Correspondence Templates

See *Setting Up Fixed Data for Business Cards or Labels* on page 360 and *Creating and Inserting Predefined Information Using Fields* on page 284.

Adding Objects and Links to Documents

Graphics Setup

Before you go too far into inserting graphics, make sure you at least know the setup options you can control for graphics, gradients, etc. They affect how the program handles memory set aside to display graphics, and printing issues.

*   *Managing the Amount of Memory Used on Graphics* on page 122
*   *Specifying Print Settings for Bitmaps, Transparency, and Color/Grayscale* on page 89

Hyperlinking Text to a File or URL

You can link text to such things as an Internet address, an email address, a macro, a network file, or, heaven forbid, a hard-coded path to a file on your hard drive. (If you set up a hyperlink that points to a file on your computer's hard drive, others won't be able to get to the file when they click the hyperlink.)

The actual result to the text is that it changes to show that it's a hyperlink, similar to how linked words appear on a Web page.

If you link to a file, especially if the file isn't in a standard format like HTML or PDF, the person clicking the link must have the software installed to open the file. If you're working on a stand-alone computer but you plan on uploading the current file to a network, you can manually enter a relative path to a file on the network (for example, /net/sounds/cartman.wav), so that when you upload the file, the link will work.

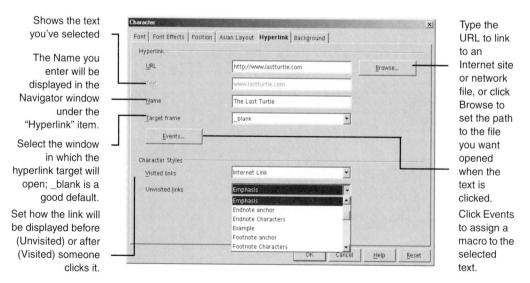

Shows the text you've selected

The Name you enter will be displayed in the Navigator window under the "Hyperlink" item.

Select the window in which the hyperlink target will open; _blank is a good default.

Set how the link will be displayed before (Unvisited) or after (Visited) someone clicks it.

Type the URL to link to an Internet site or network file, or click Browse to set the path to the file you want opened when the text is clicked.

Click Events to assign a macro to the selected text.

Figure 8-1   The Character window, Hyperlink tab

Drawing in Writer

You can use Writer's vector drawing tools to add line drawings to your documents. (New in this release is vertical text, shown in the illustration at right.)

Drawing Basic Shapes

This procedure covers the basics of drawing; for full coverage of how to get the most from drawings, see the coverage of Draw and the image editing features, starting with *Creating and Opening Draw Files* on page 758.

1   Click and hold down the Show Draw Functions button on the toolbar to display the drawing tools you can use.

2   Click the dark border at the top of the icons that you see to get the separate tearoff menu.

3   Click the icon of the shape you want to draw. The pointer turns into cross hairs, and the object bar displays Draw options.

Note – To use a tool once, just click the icon once. To use it until you're ready to switch to something else, in order to draw multiple objects of that type, double-click the icon.

---

4   Draw the object where you want it to display in the document, as shown in Figure 8-2.

5   With the drawing selected, set the color and line options you want.

6   If you want to add text inside the object, just double-click in the object and start typing. To control how the resulting text wraps, click outside the object in the document. Then click on the object border, right-click and choose Text. Select or deselect the options under Text.

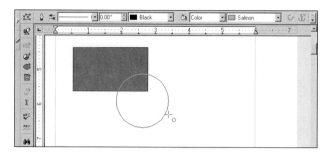

Figure 8-2   Inserting drawings in documents

Inserting Text Frames Containing Vertical Text

1   Make sure vertical text is enabled.
Choose Tools > Options > Language
Settings > Languages and in the
Asian Language Support section,
select the Enabled option.

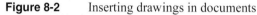

2   Click and hold down the Show Draw
Functions button and select the
vertical text tool.

3   Draw a text frame and type in the frame. If you just draw the frame and then don't
type, the frame will disappear.

Inserting Graphics

You can insert raster graphics (pixels) and vector graphics (line drawings) into Writer
documents. For more information on raster and vector graphics, see Chapter 29, *Creating
Drawings*, on page 751, and Chapter 31, *Editing Images*, on page 831.

For information on adjusting inserted graphics within the flow of a text document, such as
anchoring, moving, and wrapping text around, see *Tips for Adjusting Inserted Objects* on
page 298.

Inserting an Existing Graphic

You can insert any raster file, such as a GIF or JPG, into a Writer document.

1   Click the location in the document where you want to insert the picture.

2   Click and hold the Insert tool on the toolbar, and click the Insert Graphics tool.

You can also choose Insert > Graphics > From File.

3   Select the file you want, then click Open.

4   Select the Preview option if you want to see the graphic before you insert it.

5   Select the Link option, as shown in Figure 8-3, if you want to be connected to the original file. The picture in the document will be updated when the picture file is updated. It also helps keep your document file size down. However, changing the location of the inserted file will break the link.

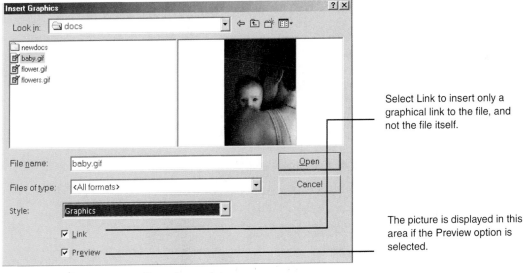

Figure 8-3   Inserting a picture

Note – If you select Link and the file is on a Web page or you haven't sent out the graphics to everyone you sent the spreadsheet too, you'll have problems. See *Think Hard Before Linking to Inserted Objects* on page 702.

Inserting a Gallery Image

You can drag and drop images from the Gallery into a Writer document. Just choose Tools > Gallery; if it doesn't appear, click the small triangle at the upper left corner of the work area. Drag any object in the gallery into your document. See *Using and Setting Up Graphics and Colors* on page 117 for more detail.

Inserting a Graphical Horizontal Line

1　Click where you want to insert the graphical horizontal line.

2　Choose Insert > Horizontal line.

3　Select the line you want to use, and click OK.

Inserting a Graphic From Another Application

See *Inserting an Object Created in Any Application* on page 292.

Editing Graphics

For information on editing the content of raster graphics, just click in the image to see the formatting toolbar appear. For more information, see Chapter 31, *Editing Images*, on page 831.

Cropping and Resizing Inserted Pictures

After you insert a picture, you can crop it directly in Writer without having to modify the picture in the source.

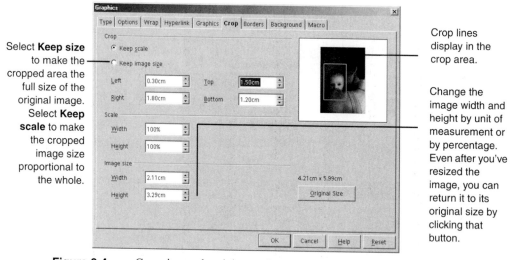

Figure 8-4　Cropping and resizing an image

Note – To crop more easily and creatively, see *Cropping an Image in Any Shape* on page 835.

1   Double-click the image.

2   In the Graphics window, click the Crop tab.

3   Set the crop and resize options you want. See Figure 8-4 for guidance.

4   Click OK.

Tables

Writer gives you a lot of flexibility for inserting tables and formatting tables. Perhaps the most powerful table feature is the ability to perform basic calculations in cells, and to create charts based on table contents.

Note – For information on creating charts, see *Charts* on page 284. To quickly insert data from a data source as a table, see *Formatting Data Source Data as a Writer Table* on page 395.

Inserting a Quick Table

This method of inserting a table gives you only a basic table with a single-line border around all cells. If you want to insert a table with more formatting, see the next procedure.

1   Click the location in the document where you want to insert the table.

2   Click and hold the Insert tool on the toolbar.

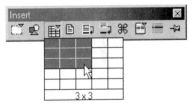

3   Click the Insert Table tool. A small grid is displayed below the Insert Table tool.

4   Move the pointer through the grid and select the number of rows and columns you want the table to be. The grid expands as you move the pointer into its borders, and the table dimensions display at the bottom of the grid.

The row count includes a table header row and borders by default. If you want to change these and other defaults, choose Tools > Options > Text document > Insert, or Tools > Options > Text document > Table.

Inserting and Formatting a Table

You can also insert tables while controlling its appearance.

1   Choose Insert > Table.

2 In the Insert Table window, enter a table name. The table name is used to identify the table when Navigator is used.

3 Set the number of columns and rows, and set the header options. To apply preset formatting to the table, click the AutoFormat button.

4 In the AutoFormat window, click the More button.

5 Set the elements you want to AutoFormat. Figure 8-5 and Figure 8-6 describe options in the Insert Table and AutoFormat windows.

Type a name for the table that will identify it when you use Navigator.

If you select the Header option, the number or rows you set includes a header row.

If you select an AutoFormat, the Border option is moot.

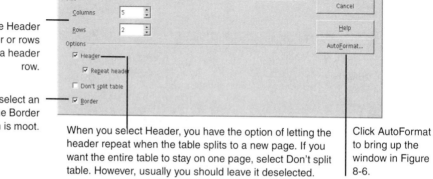

When you select Header, you have the option of letting the header repeat when the table splits to a new page. If you want the entire table to stay on one page, select Don't split table. However, usually you should leave it deselected.

Click AutoFormat to bring up the window in Figure 8-6.

Figure 8-5 Inserting a table

When you select a Format, it is displayed in the Preview area.

Select the Formatting options you want. See the effects of selecting and deselecting options in the Preview area.

Click the More button at right to see these fields.

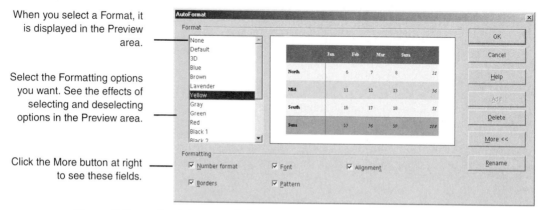

Figure 8-6 Applying a predefined AutoFormat

Note – If your table runs to the bottom of the page and disappears, deselect the Don't Split option. If that doesn't work, try deselecting the Repeat Header option as well.

Making the Table Heading Repeat

See Figure 8-5 and be sure the Header and Repeat Header options are marked.

Joining Two Tables

1 You must put the tables right next to each other as shown below.

For the·best·in·technical·training,·come·to·http://www.lastturtle.com¶

¶

¶	¶	¶	¶	¶
¶	¶	¶	¶	¶
¶	¶	¶	¶	¶
¶	¶	¶	¶	¶

¶

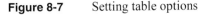

2 Put the cursor in a cell in one of the fields. Right-click and choose Merge Tables.

Setting Up How Tables Are Created By Default

Before you begin, complete table setup options. If you're having problems with tables, it's probably because of a setting that's doing stuff you don't expect. See Figure 8-7.

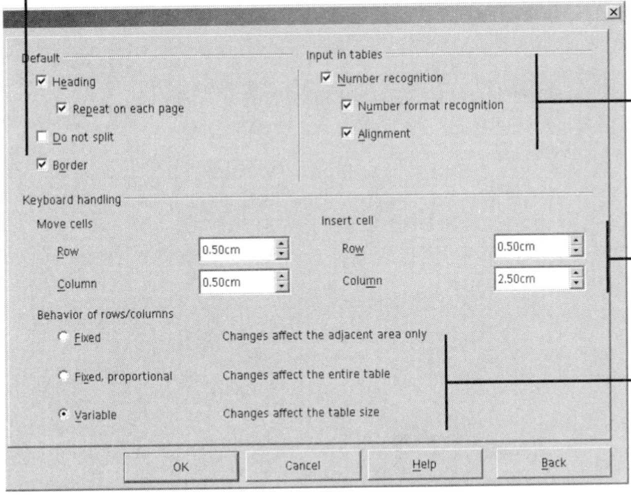

Select these options to have a row designated for a table heading, and if you want to then repeat that on each page, and choose whether to have a border.
Default
Heading
Repeat on each page
Do not split
Border
Input in tables
Number recognition
Number format recognition
Alignment
Keyboard handling
Move cells
Row
0.50cm
Column
0.50cm
Insert cell
Row
0.50cm
Column
2.50cm
Behavior of rows/columns
Fixed
Changes affect the adjacent area only
Fixed, proportional
Changes affect the entire table
Variable
Changes affect the table size
OK
Cancel
Help
Back
These options enable automatic formatting and alignment; if automatic formatting bugs you, turn it off.
These control the default distance that rows and columns move when you move them on the keyboard by pressing ALT and an arrow key, or when you insert new rows and columns using the icons on the table-contextual object bar or the right-click context menu.
Choose how changes to rows and columns should affect the rows and columns surrounding them.

Figure 8-7 Setting table options

Creating Nested Tables

You've got a table, but how do you put a table inside another table? If you put the cursor inside a table cell and choose Insert > Table, the table window pops up but on the Background tab. The ability to insert another table is grayed out. So you can fool the program into thinking you're not in a table by inserting a frame in that cell, then putting the nested table inside that frame.

1   Choose Tools > Options > Load/Save > HTML Compatibility.

2   Be sure Netscape 4.x is selected as the export format. Click OK.

3   In an HTML document, choose Insert > Table and make the first table the way you want it. This is the top table; you'll create the table inside it in the following steps.

4   Click inside the cell where you want to add the nested table.

5   Choose Insert > Frame. The frame will appear in the cell as shown in Figure 8-8.

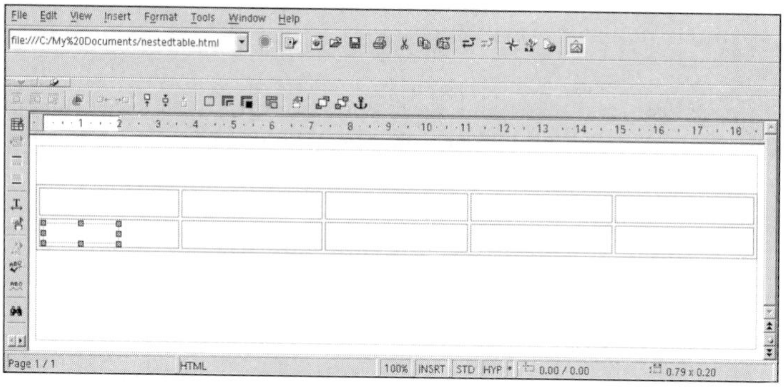

Figure 8-8   Inserting a frame in a table to hold the nested table

6   Click in the frame as shown at right.

7   Choose Insert > Table and create the inner table as shown in Figure 8-8.

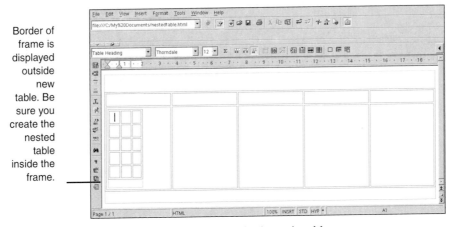

Border of frame is displayed outside new table. Be sure you create the nested table inside the frame.

Figure 8-9   Inserting the nested table in the main table

8   Format the tables as you want them.as shown in Figure 8-8.

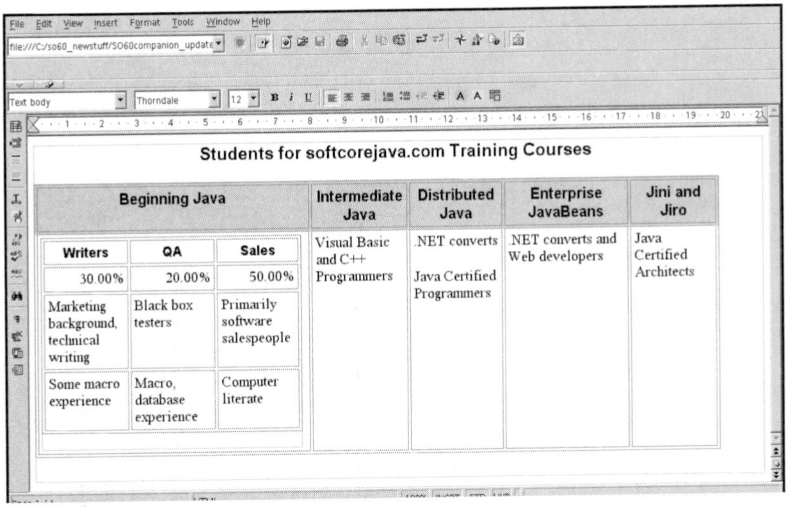

Figure 8-10   Formatting main and nested table

Using the Table Formatting and Modifying Tools on the Object Bar

When you click inside a table, the object bar changes to show the table formatting tools in Figure 8-11.

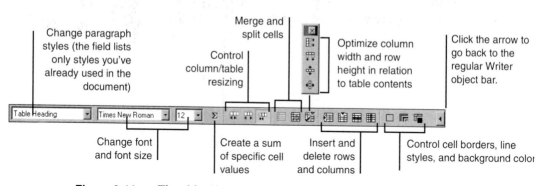

Figure 8-11   The object bar when the cursor is in a table

To switch back to the text formatting tools in the object bar, click the large left-pointing arrow at the right side of the object bar.

If you simply want to apply (or remove) bold, italicize, or underline table text formatting, use the following keyboard shortcuts instead of switching to the text formatting object bar.

Bold – Ctrl+B

Italic – Ctrl+I

Underline – Ctrl+U

You can use these shortcuts in combination with each other to make selected text ***bold italic***, for example.

Repeating One or More Heading Rows

The first row of a table is always the header row, whether or not you apply some kind of a table heading paragraph format to it. To make the header row repeat when the table breaks to a new page:

1   Click in the table, right-click, and choose Table.

2   In the Text Flow tab, select the Repeat heading option.

3   Click OK.

If you want more than one heading row to repeat, select the cells in the heading and choose Format > Cell > Split. Then, in the Split Cells window, set the number of rows you want the heading row to be, select the Horizontally option, and click OK.

Controlling How Tables Break Over Pages

There are three windows with options that determine how tables break when they hit a page break. The Do Not Split or Don't Split Table selection, if marked, means that Writer tries to keep your table on one page. With a 3-page table, this can cause problems. You probably want it unmarked everywhere.

1   Choose Format > Table and click the Text Flow tab (Figure 8-15 on page 279).

2   Choose Tools > Options > Text Document > Table (Figure 8-7 on page 273). This window controls how tables are inserted by default.

3   When you're inserting a table via Insert > Table, you'll see the top window in Figure 8-5 on page 272.

General Table Formatting

Use this procedure for more overall table formatting, such as changing table width, alignment, space above and below the table in the document, determining whether the table breaks to a new column or page or whether the heading repeats, and tweaking table borders and background.

You need to have a table created before any of the menu choices will be available.

For quick border and background color formatting, use the object bar.

1   Click in the table. If you want to change specific cell borders or background, select the cells you want to modify.

2   Right-click and choose Table.

You can also choose Format > Table.

3   Make modifications to the table in the Table Format window.

Use Figure 8-12 through Figure 8-16 for guidance.

The Name field is used to identify the table when you use Navigator. Use a name that will make it easy for you to tell what's in the table later just by the name.

Adjust the **total width** of the table. This width relates to the information on the Columns tab. *If the table width is less than the page width, you won't be able to manually widen the table.* Select **Relative** to make the table width a percentage of the page width.

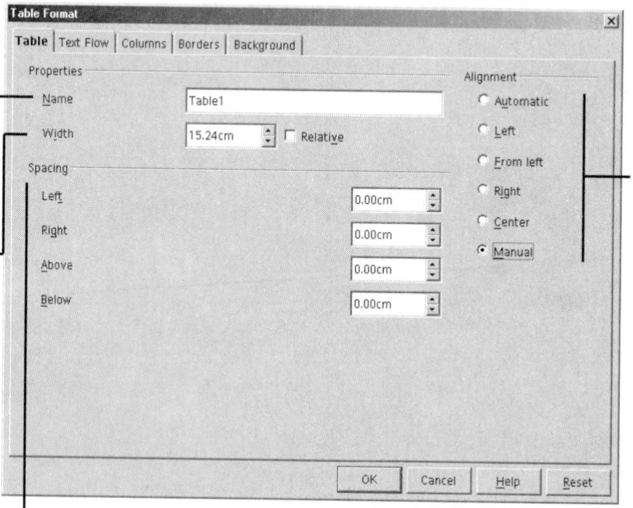

Table Format

Table | Text Flow | Columns | Borders | Background

Properties
Name   Table1
Width   15.24cm   ☐ Relative

Spacing
Left   0.00cm
Right   0.00cm
Above   0.00cm
Below   0.00cm

Alignment
○ Automatic
○ Left
○ From left
○ Right
○ Center
● Manual

OK   Cancel   Help   Reset

If you select **Automatic**, the table will fill document width (controlled by page margin settings). Select **Left** to align table at left but control where table ends on the rights; vice versa for **Right**. Select **From Left** and specify distance of table from left margin, the right side will end at the right page margin. Select **Center** to center the table and specify distance from right and left margins. Select **Manual** to control right and left margins.

If the Left or Right option is dimmed, it means the table will be aligned at the left or right page margin, respectively. Otherwise enter the distance the table should be from the left page margin, right page margin, from the text immediately above it (the **Above** option), and from the text immediately following the table (the **Below** option).

Figure 8-12   The Table Format window, Table tab

When you select the Page and Before options to move a table to a new page, select the With page style option and apply a page style for the new page (choose from the list of current page styles).

Select Don't split table to keep the entire table on a page; select Repeat heading to have the table heading repeat if the table splits to another page.

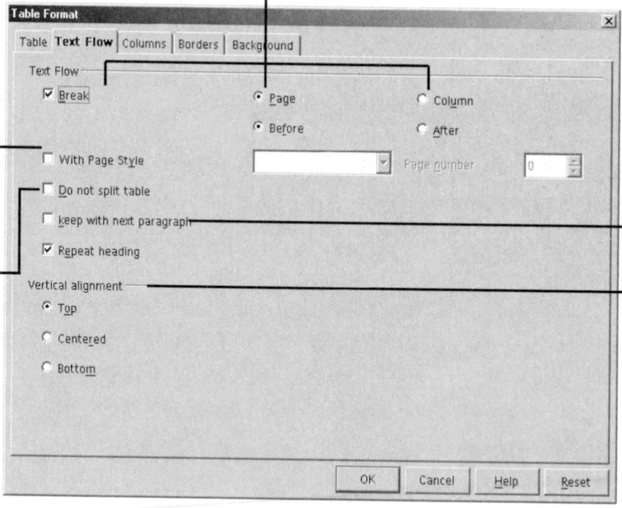

Select Break ito break to a new column or page. Select Before to move the table to the next page or column; select After to move the next body text to the next page or column.

Table Format

Table | **Text Flow** | Columns | Borders | Background

Text Flow
☑ Break   ○ Page   ○ Column
                 ● Before   ○ After
☐ With Page Style   Page number   0
☐ Do not split table
☐ keep with next paragraph
☑ Repeat heading

Vertical alignment
● Top
○ Centered
○ Bottom

OK   Cancel   Help   Reset

The Keep with next paragraph option lets you, for example, keep the table with the table caption that follows it if a page break occurs.

Set the Vertical alignment for cell text with relation to the top and bottom of the cell.

Figure 8-13   The Table Format window, Text Flow tab

Select **Adapt table width** to have the existing table expand proportionately by the **Remaining Space** amount. Remaining space is the amount of space the table can expand to the Width field in the Table tab.

If you select the Adjust columns proportionally option, adjusting the **Column** width of one column automatically adjusts the width of the other columns. Width adjustment stops when the **Remaining space** is zero.

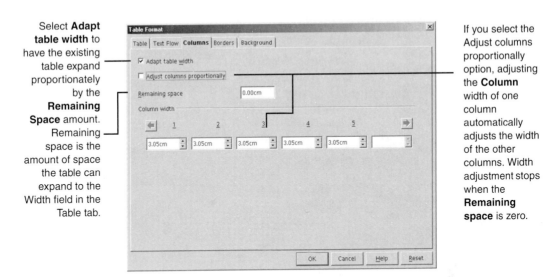

Figure 8-14   The Table Format window, Columns tab

Setting cell borders is similar to setting paragraph borders. If you need help, see Figure 7-23 on page 214.

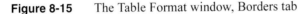

Figure 8-15   The Table Format window, Borders tab

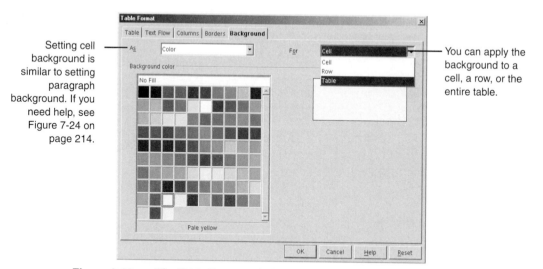

Setting cell background is similar to setting paragraph background. If you need help, see Figure 7-24 on page 214.

You can apply the background to a cell, a row, or the entire table.

Figure 8-16   The Table Format window, Background tab

Protecting Cell Contents

You can keep the contents of certain cells from being edited directly by protecting them, effectively making them read-only.

1   Select the cells you want to protect.

2   Right-click, and choose Cell > Protect.

To make a cell writable again, select it, right-click, and choose Cell > Unprotect.

Number Formatting in Cells

You can assign different number formats to specific cells, so that when you type in a value or perform a calculation, the value automatically becomes a dollar amount, a percentage, a date, or whichever format you've chosen.

Changing Number Formatting

You can also change number-formatted cells back to regular text format using this procedure.

1   Select the cell(s) you want to format.

2   Right-click and choose Number Format. You can also choose Format > Number Format.

3   Select a numbering format category and set options for it.

Use Figure 8-17 for guidance.

4 Click OK.

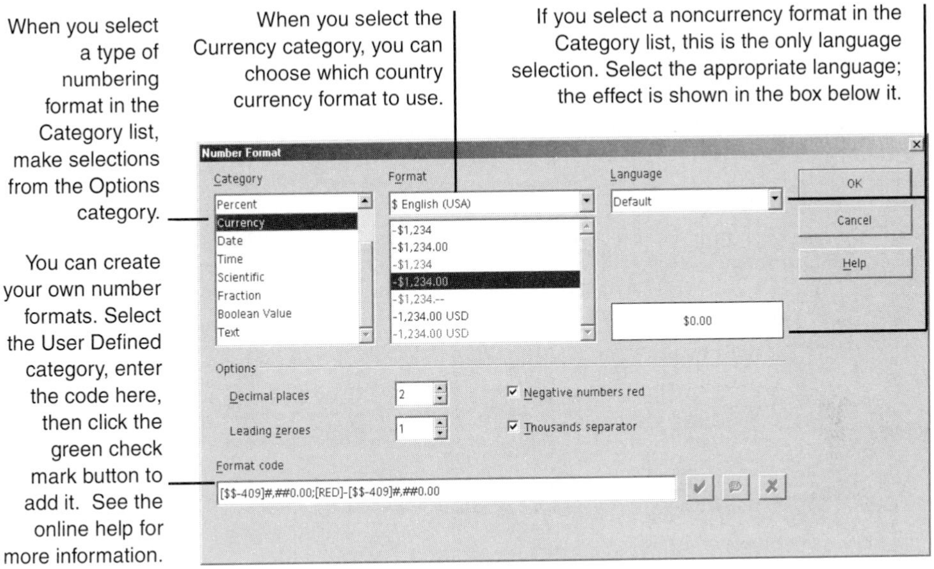
When you select a type of numbering format in the Category list, make selections from the Options category.
You can create your own number formats. Select the User Defined category, enter the code here, then click the green check mark button to add it. See the online help for more information.
When you select the Currency category, you can choose which country currency format to use.
If you select a noncurrency format in the Category list, this is the only language selection. Select the appropriate language; the effect is shown in the box below it.
Number Format
Category
Percent
Currency
Date
Time
Scientific
Fraction
Boolean Value
Text
Format
$ English (USA)
-$1,234
-$1,234.00
-$1,234
-$1,234.00
-$1,234.--
-1,234.00 USD
-1,234.00 USD
Language
Default
$0.00
OK
Cancel
Help
Options
Decimal places
2
Leading zeroes
1
Negative numbers red
Thousands separator
Format code
[$$-409]#,##0.00;[RED]-[$$-409]#,##0.00

Figure 8-17 Setting number format options

Creating Your Own Number Formats

There's a huge list of formats in the number format window in Figure 8-17. However, if you need to make your own, you can do that too.

The number format codes can consist of up to three sections separated by a semicolon (;).

- If the code has two sections, the first represents positive values and zero, and the second negative values.
- If a code has three sections, the first is for positive values, the second for negative values and the third for zero.
- You can also define conditions yourself, in this case you can make the first section of hits dependent on the first condition, the second section dependent on the second condition and the third section will only be run if the first two conditions do not apply.

See the Help for information on doing this; it's got lots of great information and examples.

Tweaking Tables Once You've Created Them

Who inserts a table just the way they want it? Here's how to quickly change what's there, or insert or delete rows and columns.

Changing Column Widths Using the Table Formatting Bar

Position the mouse pointer on top of a table cell border. When the pointer changes to a double arrow, click and drag to the new width.

Making Column Widths Equal Using the Table Formatting Bar

1　Select the columns you want to make equal widths.

2　In the object bar (which now shows table tools), click and hold down the Optimize button, then click the Space Columns Equally button.

You can change the default column width used when you insert a table. Choose Tools > Options > Text document > Table, and make the change in the Insert area of the Options window.

For more precise control over column and table width, see *General Table Formatting* on page 277.

Insertin'and Rows

You can insert rows and columns into a table after you've already created it.

1　Click in a row or column next to where you want to make the insertion.

The new rows or columns you insert will share the same formatting as the selected row or column.

2　Right-click, and choose Row > Insert, or Column > Insert. (There are also Insert Row and Insert Column buttons on the object bar.)

3　In the Insert window, set the number of rows or columns you want to insert, and designate whether you want to insert them before or after the selected area in the table.

4　Click OK.

To adjust the default column widths when columns are inserted, choose Tools > Options > Text document > Table, and make the adjustment in the Insert section of the Options window.

Deleting Columns, Rows, and Entire Tables

1　Select the first cell(s) in the row(s) or column(s) you want to delete.

2　Right-click the selection and choose Row > Delete, or Column > Delete.

There are also Delete Row and Delete Column buttons on the object bar.

Be careful when you delete columns and rows. If you select a column for deletion, but you right-click and choose Row > Delete, all selected rows are deleted rather than the column. That means if you select an entire column, you will delete the entire table by right-clicking and choosing Rows > Delete.

Changing Row Height

You can change the space between cell text and top and bottom of the cell by changing the row height. Increasing the row height also lets you to see the effects of the vertical alignment of the cell contents.

1 Select the rows you want to change.

2 Right-click and choose Row > Height. You can also choose Format > Row > Height.

3 In the Row Height window, set the new size.

4 Select the Fit to size option if you want the row height to adjust automatically with the amount and size of text entered.

Changing Vertical Alignment

When you increase the space above and below cell text by increasing the row height, you can vertically align the text to display at the top, middle, or bottom of the cell. To do this, select the cells you want to align, right-click, and choose Cell > (Top, Center, or Bottom).

Gift Idea	Price
New Crystal Ball	$45.00
Case of euphoria gum	$18.00
Machiavelli's New Age Guide	$120.00

Top aligned — (New Crystal Ball)
Center aligned — (Case of euphoria gum)
Bottom aligned — (Machiavelli's New Age Guide)

Figure 8-18   Vertical alignments

Merging and Splitting Cells

You can merge multiple cells so that they become a single cell, and you can split a single cell into multiple cells.

1 Select the cells you want to merge or split.

2 Click the Merge or Split button on the object bar, or right-click and choose Cell > (Merge or Split).

Quickly Making a Chart From the Data in Your Table

Select the table and choose Insert > Object Chart. The AutoPilot will guide you through and you'll have a chart based on your table data before you know what's happened to you.

See page 594 for more information.

Charts

The Chart tool lets you create charts based on information in Writer tables. You can use a wizard to help you set options for the chart.

Creating and Modifying Charts

The process for creating and modifying charts in Writer is the same as it is for creating them in Calc. See *Charts* on page 594.

Automatically Updating Charts

Follow this procedure to update charts automatically when the tables they were based on change.

1   Choose Tools > Options > Text document > General.

2   Under Automatically, select the Charts option.

3   Click OK.

Manually Updating Charts

You can set Writer to update charts manually when the contents of tables change. A good reason to do this is if you're making frequent changes to tables and you don't want charts to update until you're finished making changes. Constant chart updates take up memory and processing power and potentially slow down the table editing process.

1   Choose Tools > Options > Text document > Other.

2   Deselect the Update charts automatically option.

3   Click OK.

4   When you change the contents of a table, click somewhere in the table and press the F9 key.

Spreadsheets

When you insert a Calc spreadsheet into Writer, you literally insert a spreadsheet. Whether you copy part of a spreadsheet and paste it into Writer or insert the entire spreadsheet through OLE (Object Linking and Embedding), you can double-click the spreadsheet and edit it as if you're working in Calc.

The inserted spreadsheet is standalone, has no links to the original spreadsheet, and cannot be saved as a separate spreadsheet file.

For information on adjusting inserted spreadsheets within the flow of a text document, such as anchoring, moving, and wrapping text around, see *Tips for Adjusting Inserted Objects* on page 298.

Inserting a New Empty Spreadsheet

1   Choose Insert > Object > OLE Object.

2   In the Insert OLE Object window, keep Create New selected and select Spreadsheet.

3   Click OK.

4   Increase or decrease the number of displayed columns by dragging the resize handles or by dragging the columns to increase or decrease column size.

5   Click in the cells to make the Calc object bar appear; enter and format data as you would normally.

6   When you click outside the object, the rows and columns will disappear and only the data will be displayed. Double-click the object to get the formatting ability back.

Inserting Part of an Existing Spreadsheet

1   With both Writer and the desired Calc spreadsheet open, select the cells in the spreadsheet you want to insert in Writer.

2   Press Ctrl+C or choose Edit > Copy to copy.

3   Switch to your Writer document, and click where you want to insert the spreadsheet.

4   Choose Edit > Paste Special.

5   In the Paste Special window, select Calc Spreadsheet and click OK.

The spreadsheet is displayed in the Writer document as an object with green resize handles, as shown in Figure 8-19. You can edit the spreadsheet in Writer after you insert it. See *Editing Inserted Existing Calc Spreadsheets* on page 287.

You can also use this procedure to insert spreadsheets from other spreadsheet applications. In the Paste Special window, select the appropriate spreadsheet type.

Figure 8-19   Inserting part of a Calc spreadsheet

If your Calc and Writer documents are displayed side by side, you can also select cells in a spreadsheet and click and drag them into the Writer document.

Inserting a Whole Existing Spreadsheet

In addition to inserting part of a Calc spreadsheet into Writer, you can insert an entire spreadsheet. This usually works best if you're inserting into a landscape page. This is a hit-and-miss procedure, though, because if your spreadsheet is wider than the Writer page, or if it has more rows than can fit on a page, the results won't be good. Instead, consider converting a spreadsheet to a Writer table. See *Converting a Spreadsheet to a Writer Table* on page 288.

To insert a whole spreadsheet:

1   Click in Writer where you want to insert the spreadsheet.

2   In the toolbar, click and hold down the Insert Objects tool, and click the Insert OLE Object tool.

3   In the Insert OLE Object window (Figure 8-20), select the Create from file option.

4   Click the Search button, and double-click the spreadsheet you want to insert.

5   Click OK.

You can also insert a blank spreadsheet by selecting the Create new option in the Insert OLE Object window.

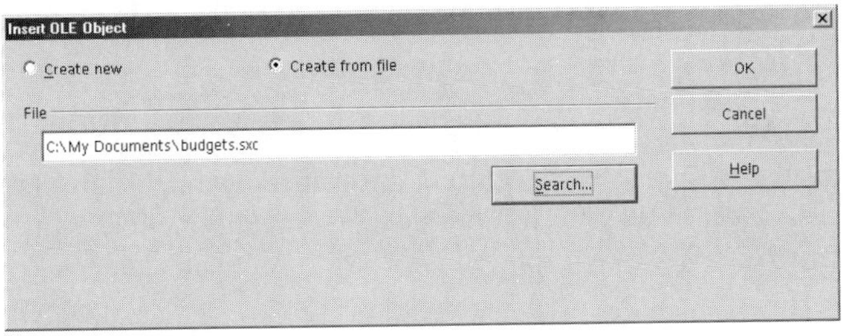

Figure 8-20 Inserting a whole Calc spreadsheet

Editing Inserted Existing Calc Spreadsheets

If you inserted only selected cells from a Calc spreadsheet, only this data—not any other data in the original spreadsheet—is brought into Writer.

1 In Writer, double-click the Calc spreadsheet object.

The object's resize handles turn black, and the spreadsheet becomes an editable Calc spreadsheet, with spreadsheet tabs, scroll bars, menus, tools, a formula bar, and the Calc object bar (see Figure 8-21).

2 Make changes to the spreadsheet (this doesn't change the original spreadsheet).

3 Click outside of the spreadsheet to get out of edit mode.

The cells that were displayed in the spreadsheet window when you got out of edit mode now display. To change the cells that are displayed, double-click to get back into edit mode, and use the scrollbars to view the correct cells.

When you edit an inserted Calc spreadsheet, you have all the controls available when you're working in Calc itself, such as inserting graphics, shown here.

Editing the object doesn't affect the original spreadsheet.

Figure 8-21 Editing an inserted Calc spreadsheet

Updating Automatically as the Spreadsheet Changes

This feature works in Windows only. You can insert a Calc spreadsheet into Writer so that when you edit the spreadsheet file itself, the changes automatically appear in the spreadsheet object in Writer. The drawback to using this method is that the spreadsheet object pasted into Writer is displayed as a basic, unformatted table.

1   In Calc, select the cells you want to insert into Writer.

2   Press Ctrl+C or choose Edit > Copy to copy.

3   Switch to your Writer document, and click where you want to insert the spreadsheet.

4   Choose Edit > Paste Special.

5   In the Paste Special window, select DDE link, and click OK.

   DDE stands for Dynamic Data Exchange.

Deleting a DDE Linked Spreadsheet

If you use the previous procedure to insert a Calc spreadsheet into Writer, you can't delete the table by simply selecting its cells and deleting rows or columns. You have to click in the paragraph above or below the table, drag through it so that the whole thing is selected, and press Delete.

Converting a Spreadsheet to a Writer Table

If you want to put the contents of a spreadsheet in a Writer document, but the spreadsheet is too big to fit on the Writer pages, use this procedure to convert the spreadsheet to a Writer table that will span multiple pages.

1   Select the contents of the spreadsheet.

2   In Writer, click where you want to insert the table, and choose Edit > Paste Special.

3   In the Paste Special window, select the Unformatted text option, and click OK.

   The text of the spreadsheet is pasted into the Writer document.

4   Select the text that was just pasted into Writer, and choose Tools > Text <-> Table.

5   In the Convert Text to Table window, select the Tabs option, as shown in Figure 8-22.

6   Select any other options or formatting you want.

7   Click OK.

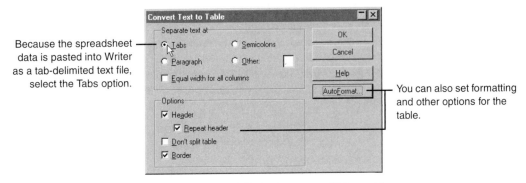

Convert Text to Table
Separate text at
Tabs
Semicolons
Paragraph
Other:
Equal width for all columns
OK
Cancel
Help
AutoFormat...
Options
Header
Repeat header
Don't split table
Border
Because the spreadsheet data is pasted into Writer as a tab-delimited text file, select the Tabs option.
You can also set formatting and other options for the table.

Figure 8-22 Converting tab-delimited text to a Writer table

Doing Spreadsheet Calculations in Writer Tables and Text

You don't even need to switch over to Calc to get complex calculations into your document; just insert them in Writer.

Making Calculations in Writer Table Cells

One of the most impressive features of Writer tables is the ability to perform calculations in cells like the ones you can create in a spreadsheet application.

Inserting a Sum Quickly

1 Click in the cell you want to contain the solution to the formula, as in Figure 8-23

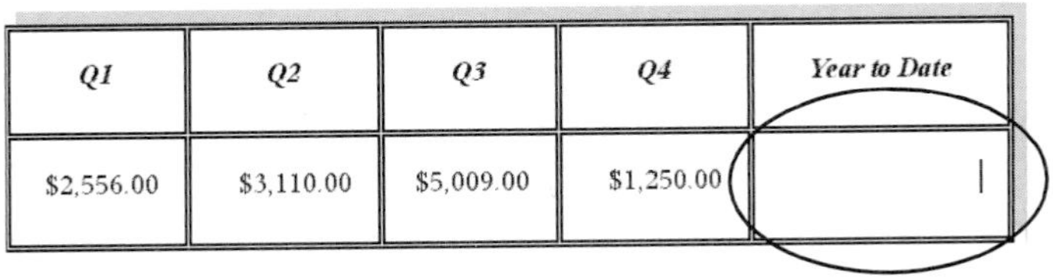

Q1
Q2
Q3
Q4
Year to Date
$2,556.00
$3,110.00
$5,009.00
$1,250.00

Figure 8-23 Where you want the sum to appear

2 Click the sum icon in the object bar, as shown at right.

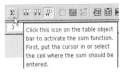

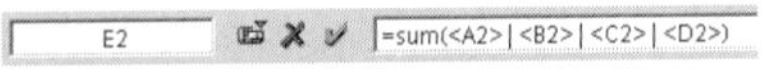

Click this icon on the table object bar to activate the sum function. First, put the cursor in or select the cell where the sum should be entered.

3 The default formula that the program thinks you want will appear in the function bar.

E2
=sum(<A2>|<B2>|<C2>|<D2>)

4   Click the green arrow; the sum will appear in the table as shown in Figure 8-24.

Q1	Q2	Q3	Q4	Year to Date
$2,556.00	$3,110.00	$5,009.00	$1,250.00	$11,925.00

Figure 8-24   The automatic sum inserted in the cell

Inserting a Formula

1   Click in the cell you want to contain the solution to the formula.

2   Press the F2 key to display the formula box (just above the object bar).

3   Enter a formula. Be sure to begin the formula with an equals sign, and click cells to include a reference to their contents in the formula. If you need help with structuring your formula and using cell references, see Chapter 20, *Calculating and Manipulating Data*, on page 563.

    You can also click and hold down the Formula button in the formula bar for help inserting certain formula elements.

4   Click the Apply button or press Enter to calculate the formula.

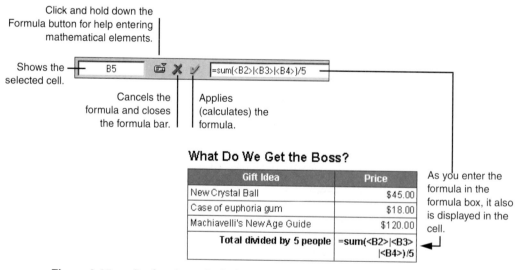

Figure 8-25   Performing calculations in Writer tables

When you change numbers in the cells that were referenced in the formula, the calculated amount changes. If for some reason it doesn't change, click in the calculated cell and press the F9 key.

If you want to include more sophisticated tables in your Writer docs, you can insert parts of or entire Calc spreadsheets. See *Spreadsheets* on page 285.

The syntax for cell references is different in a Writer table than it is in a Calc spreadsheet. In a Writer table, cell references must be opened and closed by the less-than and greater-than symbols. For example, a reference to cell B4 would need to be entered as <B4>. If you're building a formula, and you click a cell to add it to the formula, this syntax is used automatically.

Also, as shown in Figure 8-25, you can use a pipe symbol "|" instead of a plus symbol "+". You can't do that in Calc.

Making Calculations in Body Text

You can also make one-time calculations outside of cells in the body text of your document, though this isn't particularly useful if any of the numbers in your formula changes, because the calculated amount won't adjust automatically.

1   Enter the formula in your text followed by an equals sign. For example:

   `(45+15+120)/5=`

2   Copy the formula.

3   Press F2, and paste the formula into the formula box.

4   Press Enter. The solution to the formula is displayed in the text as a field.

Inserting Frames and Floating Frames

Writer isn't Quark or Pagemaker, but it does offer you frames to give you a good start.

Frames, or text frames, give you the ability to insert— anywhere— one or more columns of text

Great Java Resources

If you're tired of boring training and lackluster books, get ready for a change.

Want to learn Java the fun way? Just go to www.softcorejava.com and get started. Read the Java Stories, or learn with games.

For certification study guides, also head to www.lastturtle.com, to get books straight from the exam authors.

and objects. You can insert anything, even another frame. Choose Insert > Frame .

Floating frames hold an entire, open file inside of a frame, whether it's a graphic, a slide presentation, a Web page, or a spreadsheet. When you insert a floating frame, the program lets you work with that file within Writer as if you were working with the file in its native application. Menus, the toolbar, and the object bar all change to let you work with the file in the floating frame. Choose Insert > Floating Frame.

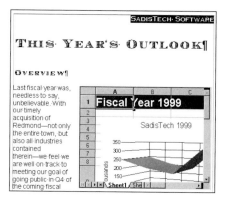

In order to format where that content shows up in relationship to the inserted frames, see *Tips for Adjusting Inserted Objects* on page 298.

We've covered the procedures for frames and floating frames in the page layout section; see *Using Frames for Advanced Page Layout* on page 233.

Inserting an Object Created in Any Application

Feel like inserting a new Illustrator graphic into your Writer document? If you have Illustrator, that is. For Illustrator or scores of other formats, just insert the object and create it in the native application. This section also covers how to insert an empty StarOffice or OpenOffice.org file.

Inserting an Existing Object Created in an External Program

1   Choose Insert > Object > OLE Object.

2   Keep the Create New item selected, then Further Objects at the bottom of the Object Type field.

3   The Insert Object will appear. Select Create From File.

4   A browse field will appear. Click Browse and select the file.

5   Click OK.

Inserting a New Object Created in an External Program

1   Choose Insert > Object > OLE Object.

2   Keep the Create New item selected, then Further Objects at the bottom of the Object Type field.

3   The Insert Object will appear. Keep Create New selected.

4   The lists displays scores of formats like Acrobat, Photoshop, Bitmap Image, Illustrator document, and even Yahoo!WebCam Viewer. Select a format that you can create on your computer (if you don't have Illustrator, selecting Illustrator won't do any good).

5   Click OK.

6   The application that you operating system associates with that type of file will open. Create the image or document you want and close the window. The object will appear in your document.

Inserting an Icon That Opens an Inserted Object

Complete *Inserting a New Object Created in an External Program* on page 293 or *Inserting an Existing Object Created in an External Program* on page 292. In the Insert Object window, select the Display as Icon option.

Once you've inserted the object, you can double-click the icon to open the inserted object.

Inserting a New Empty StarOffice or OpenOffice.org Object

1   Choose Insert > Object > OLE Object.

2   Keep the Create New item selected, then select the correct application in the list below. Click OK.

3   Click in the object to create it; the application-specific object bar will appear with the object and you can edit it if you want.

Mathematical Formulas

A tool called Math lets you insert and build formulas in a document.

Note – StarOffice 6.0 and OpenOffice.org support import and exports for MathML files, the standardized W3 XML file format for equation exchange.

For information on adjusting inserted formulas within the flow of a text document, such as anchoring, moving, and wrapping text around, see *Tips for Adjusting Inserted Objects* on page 298.

Inserting and Building Formulas

When you insert a formula, you have to build it using Math's formula notation language. Math makes entering the formula notation easier with formula tools that insert notation automatically. Use the formula tools to help you learn the formula language.

1 Click where you want to insert the formula.

2 In the toolbar, click and hold down the Insert Objects tool, and click the Insert Formula tool.

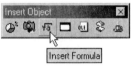

3 Enter the formula in the Commands window (Figure 8-26). To use the formula tools, choose View > Selection, or right-click in the Commands window. As you build the formula, it is displayed inside the document.

4 When you're finished, press the Esc key to close the Commands window.

In the Selection window, click categories at the top to display different elements underneath. As you choose elements, they're inserted into the formula.

Figure 8-26 Inserting a formula

Changing the Formula Format

You can change the font, spacing, and alignment of formulas you create.

Changing Font Face

You can change the font face for individual elements of a formula.

1   With the formula Commands window active, select Format > Fonts.

2   In the Font Types window, click the Modify button to select a different font for a specific element of the formula.

3   Click OK.

As you assign a different font to a formula element, that font becomes available for selection in the field next to the element.

Changing Font Size

You can change overall font size for the entire formula, and you can adjust the relative font sizes of parts of the formula.

1   With the formula Commands window active, select Format > Font Size.

2   In the Font Sizes window, changing the Base size changes the font for the entire formula.

3   Adjust the relative percentage sizes of parts of the formula.

4   Click OK.

Changing Spacing Between Formula Elements

1   With the formula Commands window active, select Format > Spacing.

2   In the Spacing window, click the Category button and choose the item you want to adjust.

3   As you make adjustments in the left side of the window, a preview area displays the effects of your changes.

4   Click OK.

To return to the spacing defaults, click the Default button in the Spacing window.

Changing Alignment of Formula Elements

You can set the elements in a formula to be aligned left, center, or right relative to the width of the formula box in your document.

1   With the formula Commands window active, select Format > Alignment.

2   Select Left, Centered, or Right, and click OK.

Inserting Special Characters in Formulas

You can insert special characters into your formula.

1   In the Commands window, click in the formula where you want to insert a special character.

2   Choose Tools > Symbols > Catalog, or click the Symbols tool on the toolbar.

3   In the Symbols window, select the symbol you want, and click Insert.

4   Click Close.

Creating and Importing Formula Files

You can create standalone formula files in Math, then import them into a Writer document.

Creating a Formula File

1   Choose File > New > Formula. The Math environment is displayed.

2   Create a formula in the Commands window.

3   Choose File > Save As. In the Save As window, the File type should say Math 5.0.

4   Name the file, set the path to the folder you want, and click Save.

Importing a Formula File Into Writer

1   Insert a formula in Writer. See *Inserting and Building Formulas* on page 294.

2   With the Commands window active, choose Tools > Import Formula.

3   Select the formula file, and click Insert.

Documents

Note – To insert documents into frames for advanced page layout capability, see *Using Frames for Advanced Page Layout* on page 233.

Writer lets you insert, or import, entire text documents into the flow of a Writer document. The documents you insert can be in a wide range of non-Writer formats. You can also insert parts of other Writer documents.

The inserted document uses the page formatting of the document you insert it into; but if you insert another Writer document, it brings all of its styles with it.

Inserting Other Documents

1   In Writer, click where you want to insert the document.

2   On the toolbar, click and hold down the Insert tool, then click the Document tool.

3   At the bottom of the Insert window, select the File type of the document you want to insert, then find and select the document.

4   Click Insert. The document is brought into Writer.

Inserting Parts of Writer Documents

See *Linking to a Section in Another Document* on page 418.

Scanning Images Into Documents

Typically when you scan an image, especially if it's just one picture, the scanner includes all the empty space around the image as part of the scan. This can make a scanned object take up a lot of space when you scan it into Writer. But Writer lets you crop pictures, which is perfect for handling scanned images.

If you want to save images you scan, we recommend scanning them into Image and saving them. You can then insert them into Writer. (Or you can scan them into Writer, then copy and paste them into Image.)

For information on adjusting scanned images within the flow of a text document, such as anchoring, moving, and wrapping text around, see *Tips for Adjusting Inserted Objects* on page 298.

1   Make sure your scanner and software are properly installed and configured, and that the scanner is turned on and plugged into the computer.

2   In Writer, click where you want to insert the scanned image.

3   Choose Insert > Graphics > Scan > Request. Use the scanner software that launches to scan the image. After the scan, you may need to close the scanner software. The scanned image is displayed in Writer.

To crop the image, see *Cropping and Resizing Inserted Pictures* on page 270.

Tips for Adjusting Inserted Objects

When you insert an object, you can change how it is displayed and affects the flow of the document. For example, you can change its size and position, determine how text wraps around it or how much space there is between the object and the body text, anchor it to a paragraph or in the middle of a sentence as a character, set hyperlink properties, and apply borders and backgrounds.

You can access these controls by selecting and right-clicking an object to see menu options, or by double-clicking it to change settings in a window. These tips don't apply to tables.

The following are some of the more useful tips for adjusting inserted objects.

Anchoring an Object

Objects are anchored to keep them at an exact point in a document. As the document changes, the object moves or remains in place as the document changes, depending on the anchoring options you set. When you select an object, an anchor icon is displayed, showing you where the object is anchored.

You can move this anchor by dragging it to a different place in the document, which also moves the object.

In the toolbar, click the Nonprinting Characters tool to show paragraph symbols and help you more accurately anchor an object.

Moving Objects

You can move objects in a document just by clicking and dragging them.

Creating Space Around Objects

Here's how to increase or decrease the space between an object and the body text:

1   Click the object. For some objects, like floating frames, you may need to position the cursor over the object until the cursor changes to cross hairs with arrows before you click.

2   Choose Format > Object. (If the object is a graphic, choose Format > Graphics.) You can also double-click the object.

3   In the window that is displayed, select the Wrap tab.

4   In the Spacing area of the window, adjust the top, bottom, left, and right spacing as desired.

5   Click OK.

Manually Resizing Objects

If you want to manually resize an object by clicking it and dragging its resize handles, you can maintain their exact proportions as you resize by holding down the Shift key while you drag from a corner resize handle.

Adding Controls and Buttons

See Chapter 36, *Creating and Using Forms, Controls, and Events*, on page 925.

Lining Up Objects on a Grid

You can exercise more control over your alignment of objects in a document by using a grid to line things up, as Figure 8-27 on page 299 illustrates.

To set grid options for your documents:

1   Choose Tools > Options > Text document > Grid.

2   In the Options window, set the grid options, as described in Figure 8-28 on page 300.

3   Click OK.

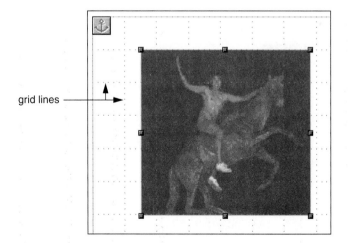

Figure 8-27   Using a grid to align objects

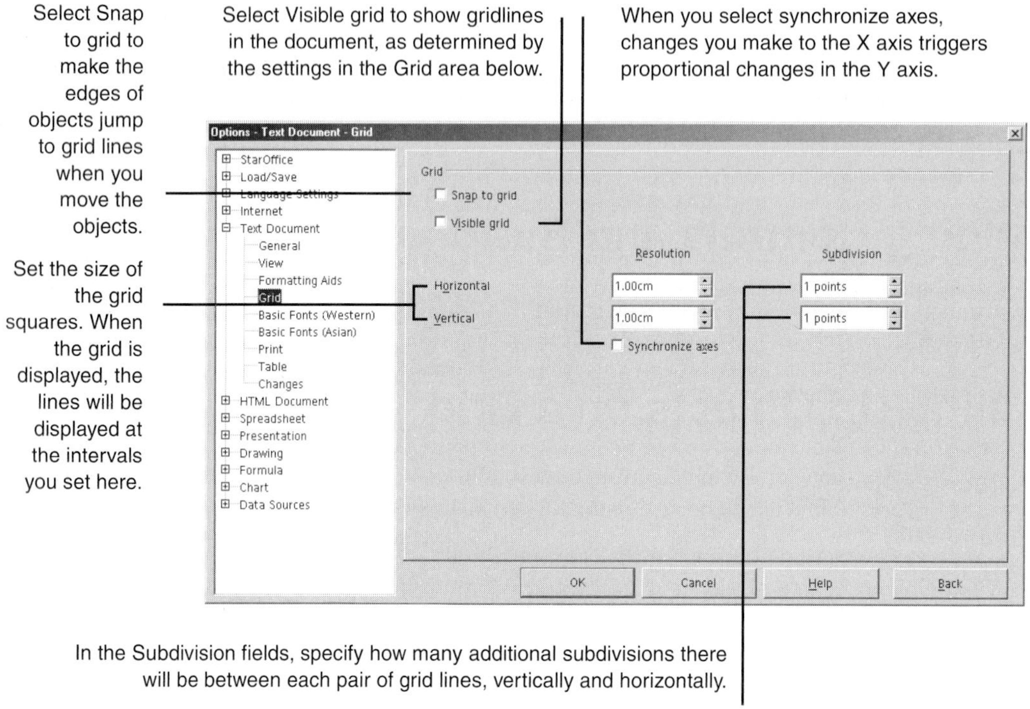

Select Snap to grid to make the edges of objects jump to grid lines when you move the objects.
Select Visible grid to show gridlines in the document, as determined by the settings in the Grid area below.
When you select synchronize axes, changes you make to the X axis triggers proportional changes in the Y axis.
Set the size of the grid squares. When the grid is displayed, the lines will be displayed at the intervals you set here.
Options - Text Document - Grid
StarOffice
Load/Save
Language Settings
Internet
Text Document
General
View
Formatting Aids
Grid
Basic Fonts (Western)
Basic Fonts (Asian)
Print
Table
Changes
HTML Document
Spreadsheet
Presentation
Drawing
Formula
Chart
Data Sources
Grid
Snap to grid
Visible grid
Resolution
Subdivision
Horizontal
Vertical
1.00cm
1.00cm
1 points
1 points
Synchronize axes
OK
Cancel
Help
Back
In the Subdivision fields, specify how many additional subdivisions there will be between each pair of grid lines, vertically and horizontally.

Figure 8-28 Setting grid options

Inserting Captions

Use the following procedure to insert captions for illustrations, drawings, tables, and any other objects you insert.

There are a couple of ways you can insert captions: using Writer's caption tool, or creating your own autonumbered paragraph formats. There are benefits and drawbacks to each:

Using Writer's Caption Tool The benefit is that you can insert captions automatically whenever you insert an object in Writer. One drawback is that the caption is inserted directly above or below the object, and you have to manually change the spacing between each object and its caption. Another drawback is that you can edit the caption title directly. It's not created as an non-editable field.

Using AutoNumbered Paragraph Formats One benefit is that you can't edit the caption title or number. It's all one non-editable field. Another benefit is that it's easier to control the spacing between the paragraph format and the object. The drawback is that you have to manually apply the paragraph format to get the caption title and number. It's not inserted automatically when you insert an element like a graphic.

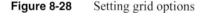

With either method you can generate a list of figures, tables, or lists of any other elements.

Inserting Captions Automatically with the Caption Tool

You can have Writer insert captions automatically when you insert objects into Writer.

1   Choose Tools > Options > Text document > General.

2   Select the Automatic option, and click the ellipses button.

3   In the Caption window, select the box next to each object for which you want to generate an automatic caption, and set the caption options for each, as shown in Figure 8-29.

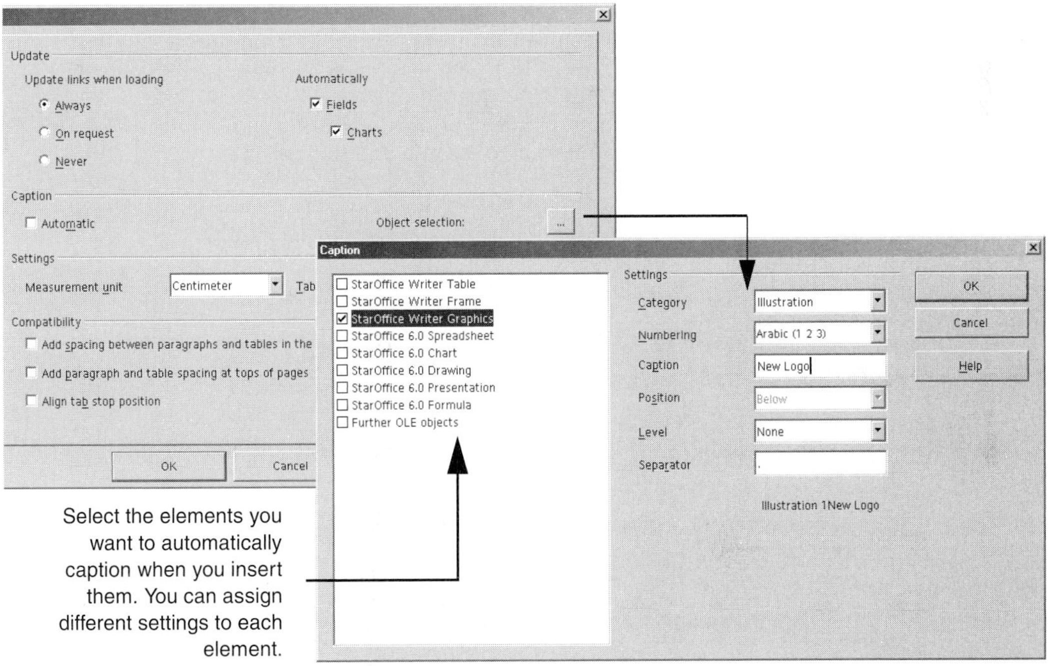

Select the elements you want to automatically caption when you insert them. You can assign different settings to each element.

Figure 8-29   Setting automatic caption options

4   Click OK in the Caption window.

5   Click OK in the Options window.

If you want to use chapter-number numbering for the captions (such as "Illustration 3-5"), make sure you've defined a top-level paragraph, such as Heading 1, as the level 1 outline number with an auto-generated chapter number. See *Outline*

Numbering on page 308. Also, in the Caption window (Figure 8-29), set the Level field to None. For some reason this creates the number format correctly.

Each type of caption has a corresponding paragraph style that you can modify. But in the paragraph format for each type of caption (Graphic, Illustration, and so on), be sure **not** to assign a numbering style on the Numbering tab. That will mess up your automatic caption numbering.

To stop automatic captioning, simply deselect the Automatic option in the Options window.

Inserting Captions Manually with the Caption Tool

If you don't want to insert captions automatically you can insert them manually.

1   If you want to use chapter-number numbering for the captions (such as "Illustration 3-5"), make sure you've defined a chapter paragraph that uses an auto-generated chapter number. See *Outline Numbering* on page 308.

2   Select the inserted object you want to insert a caption for.

3   Choose Insert > Caption.

4   Set options for the caption in the Caption window. See Figure 8-30.

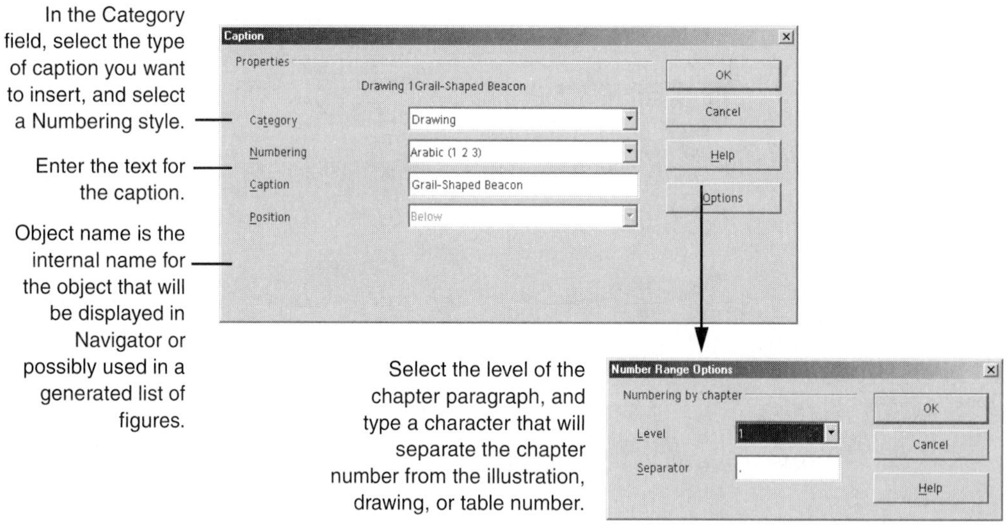

In the Category field, select the type of caption you want to insert, and select a Numbering style.

Enter the text for the caption.

Object name is the internal name for the object that will be displayed in Navigator or possibly used in a generated list of figures.

Select the level of the chapter paragraph, and type a character that will separate the chapter number from the illustration, drawing, or table number.

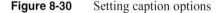

Figure 8-30   Setting caption options

5   If you want to use chapter-number caption numbering, click the Options button, set the options you want, and click OK. See Figure 8-30.

6   Click OK in the Caption window.

Each type of caption has a corresponding paragraph style that you can modify.

Caption Numbering with Paragraph Formats

You can create a numbered paragraph style specifically designed for captions (figure, table, or whatever kind of caption you want to create). For example, if you insert a picture into your document, you can apply the caption paragraph format you created below the picture, and it will automatically insert **Figure #:** as the paragraph numbering, letting you type the caption after it.

For example, use the Before and After fields (shown in Figure 8-31) to get the following numbering (which, as you can see, also includes letters):

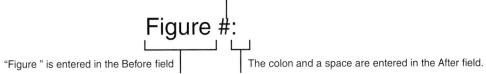

The # stands for the automatic number Writer generates, based on the number definition of that type of paragraph style. So if this is the third instance of the FigureCaption paragraph, the # would be 3.

Figure #:

"Figure " is entered in the Before field   The colon and a space are entered in the After field.

Figure 8-31   Example of setting up caption numbering

Captions without a chapter number This procedure deals with paragraph and numbering styles. It's for straight caption numbering without including a chapter number. For more information, see page 245 and page 250.

1   Create a *numbering* style and name it; for example, "FigureCaption." See Figure 8-31 for an example of setting up the numbering style for figures.

2   Create a *paragraph* style called, for example, "FigureCaption."

3   In the numbering properties for the paragraph style, select the "FigureCaption" numbering style. Then, whenever you apply the FigureCaption paragraph style, the numbering appears like this automatically.

Create a different kind of paragraph and numbering format for each type of caption you want to use, such as tables, illustrations, and so on.

Captions using a chapter number This procedure shows you how to create a paragraph style that includes a chapter number in the caption number, such as "Figure 4-2."

This procedure involves using outline numbering. For more information, see page 308.

1   Create a *paragraph* style called, for example, "FigureCaption." Do **not** assign a numbering style on the Numbering tab of the paragraph style.

2 After you create the paragraph style, choose Tools > Outline Numbering.

3 In the Outline Numbering window (Figure 8-32), select Level 1, make sure the paragraph style is the chapter-level style (such as Heading 1) that will be the first style used in the document, and make sure it's set up to generate a chapter number (in the Number field).

4 Select any other level in the Outline Numbering window, and assign your caption paragraph to it. If you skip a level or more from Level 1, assign a numbering style to each level between Level 1 and the level of your caption.

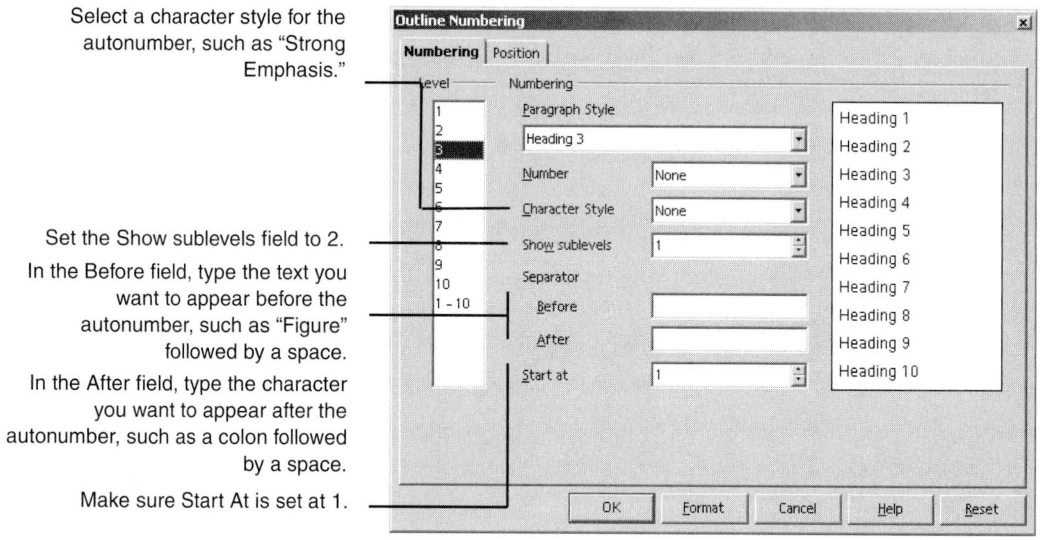

Select a character style for the autonumber, such as "Strong Emphasis."

Set the Show sublevels field to 2.

In the Before field, type the text you want to appear before the autonumber, such as "Figure" followed by a space.

In the After field, type the character you want to appear after the autonumber, such as a colon followed by a space.

Make sure Start At is set at 1.

Figure 8-32 Setting up caption numbering to include the chapter number

Books and Longer Documents

Overview

Writer's master document feature is a lot closer to FrameMaker than to Word. We like it a lot, and think you'll be pleasantly surprised.

If you're creating long documents, you're likely to want to use elements like cross-references, running heads, tables of contents, indexes, and other lists, like lists of figures. Writer has some decent tools for doing all this. If your long documents are getting a little too long and difficult to manage, Writer has a master document feature that lets you group multiple files into a single book, where you can create a single table of contents, an index (and other lists), create cross-references between book files, and use continuous page numbering. In this chapter, the terms *book* and *master document* are synonymous.

Creating a master document means you'll need to stretch your mental muscles and apply your existing knowledge of Writer styles (see *Power Formatting With Styles* on page 241) and headers and footers (see *Using Headers and Footers* on page 282). This knowledge is particularly useful when it comes to troubleshooting your master documents.

This chapter shows you first how to create and maintain a master document, then how to perform tasks that are common to long documents and books.

Note – When working with long documents, you might want to keep file size to a minimum. In that case, when you insert graphics, select the Link option. This puts an image of a graphic in the document without inserting the entire graphic file. The drawback to this is that Writer always has to know where those graphic files are. So when you send or move the files, you must also send or set new links to the graphics files.

Managing and Moving Around in Files Using Navigator

Navigator is a tool used throughout the program. In Writer, Navigator serves three main purposes:

- Navigator holds and lets you maintain files in a master document (as described in the Creating Books (Master Documents) section starting on page 319).

- Navigator lets you locate and jump to different parts of your document quickly.

- Navigator lets you drag and drop hyperlinked references from one part of a document into another part, or from one document to another.

Launching Navigator

When you create a master document, Navigator launches automatically in master document mode. Otherwise, press the **F5** key to open and close the Navigator window, or choose Edit > Navigator.

Master document navigator When a master document is open, you can switch between the master document Navigator and the regular Navigator by clicking the Toggle button, as shown in Figure 9-1.

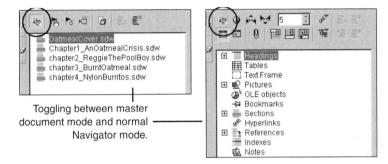

Toggling between master document mode and normal Navigator mode.

Figure 9-1   Navigator in master document view and regular view

Navigating

If you're in normal Navigator mode, the Navigator window displays all the parts of your document: Headings, tables, pictures, bookmarks, and so on, as shown in Figure 9-2. These different parts are displayed in a hierarchical tree view that lets you expand and contract groups of things. You can also customize the way Navigator displays its contents.

Navigator also offers a variety of ways you can jump to different parts of your document.

If you just want to jump from item type to item type (for example, from heading to heading), click the Navigation button at the bottom of the vertical scroll bar, and select the type of item you want to jump to. Then click the up and down arrow buttons above and below the Navigation button to jump to the previous or next instances of the item.

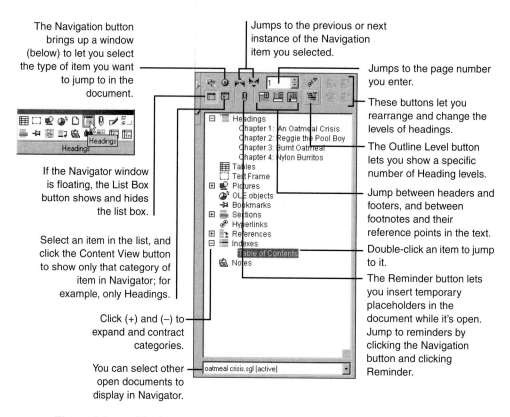

The Navigation button brings up a window (below) to let you select the type of item you want to jump to in the document.

If the Navigator window is floating, the List Box button shows and hides the list box.

Select an item in the list, and click the Content View button to show only that category of item in Navigator; for example, only Headings.

Click (+) and (−) to expand and contract categories.

You can select other open documents to display in Navigator.

Jumps to the previous or next instance of the Navigation item you selected.

Jumps to the page number you enter.

These buttons let you rearrange and change the levels of headings.

The Outline Level button lets you show a specific number of Heading levels.

Jump between headers and footers, and between footnotes and their reference points in the text.

Double-click an item to jump to it.

The Reminder button lets you insert temporary placeholders in the document while it's open. Jump to reminders by clicking the Navigation button and clicking Reminder.

Figure 9-2   Navigator

Outline Numbering

This section tells you how to do outline numbering in the following sections:

Understanding Outline Numbering

This feature is one of the most confusing and non-intuitive in the entire program; and if it didn't play such an important part in how other features work, you'd be wise to ignore it altogether.

However, outline numbering is essential if you want to:

- Cross-reference paragraph numbers

  Even if you set up numbering in a paragraph style, if you don't use outline numbering, you can't cross-reference the generated number or generated text, such as "Chapter 1", "Figure 2-7", or a number such as "1.1.2" preceding an outlined item.

- Number graphics, tables, and other inserted elements, using the chapter number and the number of the element in the document, such as "Figure 5-1"
- Set up running headings in document headers and footers

Automatic numbering for paragraphs isn't a new concept we're just presenting in this book. In fact, *Quick Paragraph Formatting* on page 206 talks about just that. Outline numbering is different than paragraph numbering, because Writer depends on outline numbering to enable the features in the previous list.

Limitations of outline numbering Before we show you how to set up outline numbering, we need to note a few limitations.

- Only one paragraph style can be used as *the* chapter paragraph, even though you'll see 10 paragraph style levels in the Outline Numbering window.
- Of the paragraph styles listed **in the Outline Numbering window**, Writer uses the first of those paragraph styles it encounters in the document or book as the chapter-level heading.

  For example, if you want to use a Heading 2 as a running head in the header or footer of a document or book, but a Heading 1 appears before a Heading 2 as the first paragraph style in the document, Writer sees the Heading 1 as the chapter paragraph and you can't use the Heading 2 for running heads.

  To fix this problem you'd have to unassign Heading 1 from the list of paragraph styles in the Outline Numbering window so that it's not one of the paragraphs assigned to use outline numbering.

- If you want to use a page numbering format that uses chapter-page (such as 3-1, where 3 is the chapter number), or if you want to number inserted objects like graphics using a numbering format such as "Figure 2-7", you must assign a number format (in the Outline Numbering window) to the level that will serve as the chapter number. But because only one paragraph style can be the chapter paragraph, you can only set up a running head that displays the contents of the chapter-numbered paragraph. Make sure the paragraph style you want to use for the outline numbering is set as the Level 1 paragraph style in the Outline Numbering window.

Simplicity is a virtue But the aforementioned limitations, it turns out, are good for a couple of reasons: one, they discourage using chapter-page numbering (such as 3-5 for chapter 3, page 5), which makes it difficult for readers to find page numbers; and two, you're forced to keep your headers and footers simple (yet helpful) by using only one running head.

Figure 9-3 shows different outline autonumbering styles for the chapter paragraph.

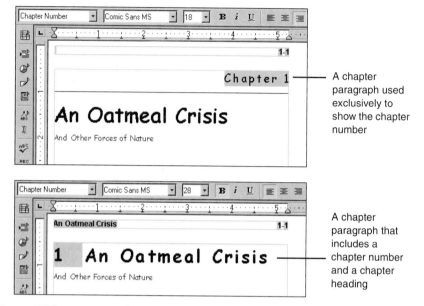

Notice the headers in each example. The second example has a running head, which is the text of the chapter title. But in the first example, because the chapter number includes only an auto-generated number, there's no title text to display as a running head.

Figure 9-3   Different automatic outline numbering styles for a chapter paragraph

Setting Up Outline Numbering

It may be helpful to review *Understanding Outline Numbering* on page 308 before using this procedure.

1   Decide which heading level you want to use as your chapter number.

2   Choose Tools > Outline Numbering.

3   In the Outline Numbering window, select Level 1.

4   In the Paragraph style field, select the paragraph style you want to use for the chapter.

  The paragraph style you select doesn't have to be set up with a chapter autonumber. This can simply be the paragraph style you want to use in running heads.

5   If the paragraph style you select as the Level 1 style isn't the style of the first paragraph in the document or book, unassign from the Outline Numbering window any styles that appear before the Level 1 style in the document.

  To do this, select the levels for the styles you want to remove, and in the Paragraph styles field, select None.

6   If you want the paragraph style to include an automatic chapter number, select a Number format and set appropriate numbering options. See Figure 9-4.

7   Click the Position tab (also Figure 9-4), and set any applicable options, especially if you want to indent the chapter paragraph style or set the amount of spacing between the chapter number and the chapter text.

Position changes to the outline numbering style override (but don't replace) the indents and spacing of the paragraph style itself.

8   Click OK.

The Show sublevels field is extremely important when you want to use hierarchical outline numbering or figure/table numbering that includes the chapter number. For example, assign the Graphic and Table styles to whichever outline levels you want, and set the sublevel of each to a value of 2. That means the Figure/Table paragraph numbering will pick up the level 1 chapter number and generate its own number, such as "Figure 1-5".

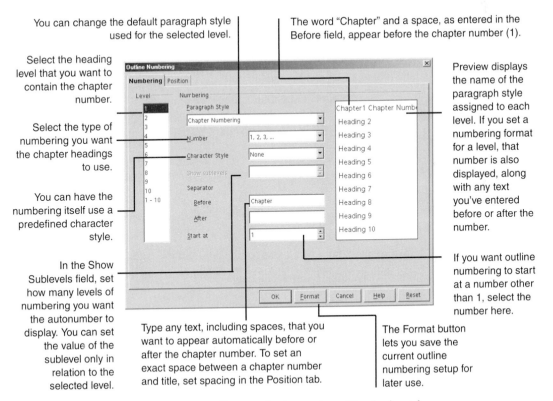

You can change the default paragraph style used for the selected level.

The word "Chapter" and a space, as entered in the Before field, appear before the chapter number (1).

Select the heading level that you want to contain the chapter number.

Select the type of numbering you want the chapter headings to use.

You can have the numbering itself use a predefined character style.

In the Show Sublevels field, set how many levels of numbering you want the autonumber to display. You can set the value of the sublevel only in relation to the selected level.

Preview displays the name of the paragraph style assigned to each level. If you set a numbering format for a level, that number is also displayed, along with any text you've entered before or after the number.

If you want outline numbering to start at a number other than 1, select the number here.

Type any text, including spaces, that you want to appear automatically before or after the chapter number. To set an exact space between a chapter number and title, set spacing in the Position tab.

The Format button lets you save the current outline numbering setup for later use.

Figure 9-4   Setting outline numbering options: Numbering tab

The Show Sublevels field In the Show Sublevels field, set how many levels of numbering you want the autonumber to display. For example, a sublevel number of 3 will include 3 autonumbers for a paragraph: the numbering of the level 1 and 2 paragraphs (incremented), and the numbering of its own paragraph. You can set the value of the sublevel only in relation to the selected level.

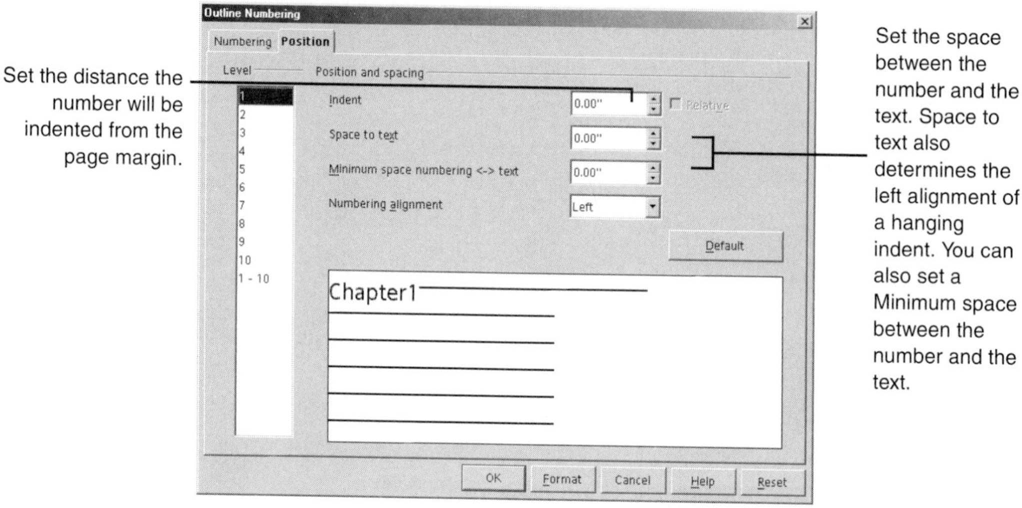

Set the distance the number will be indented from the page margin.
Set the space between the number and the text. Space to text also determines the left alignment of a hanging indent. You can also set a Minimum space between the number and the text.
Outline Numbering
Numbering
Position
Level
Position and spacing
Indent
Space to text
Minimum space numbering <-> text
Numbering alignment
0.00"
Left
Relative
Default
Chapter1
OK
Format
Cancel
Help
Reset

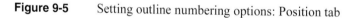

Figure 9-5 Setting outline numbering options: Position tab

Saving Different Outline Numbering Versions

The program lets you save different versions of outline numbering that you can switch between. If you want to save the current combination of outline settings to revert back to later:

1 In the Outline Numbering window, click the Format button, and choose Save As, as shown in Figure 9-6.

2 In the Save As window, type a name for the configuration, and click OK.

The saved format is available to all documents.

To select a saved outline numbering versions later, click the Format button, choose the format, and click OK to apply it to the document.

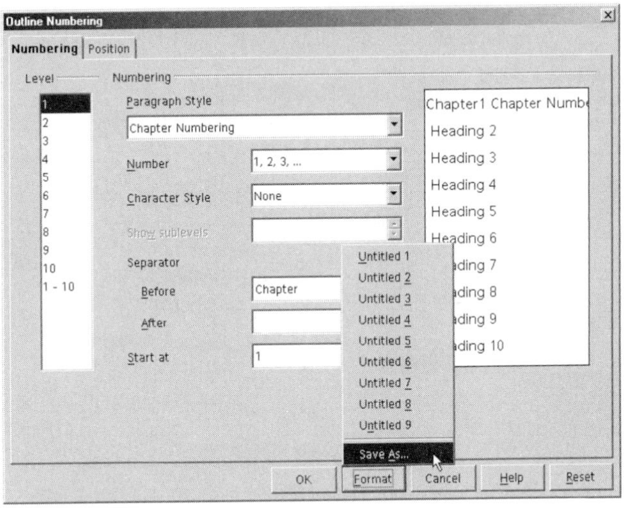

Figure 9-6   Saving an Outline Numbering configuration

Headers and Footers in Books

Headers and footers are essential for longer documents and books. At the very least they hold page numbers. But the more reader-friendly approach is to also include such information as the name of the publication and the current main heading in the document (a running head), as shown in Figure 9-7. In fact, the headers of this book show those very things.

For more information on headers and footers and the types of information you can insert in them, see *Using Headers and Footers in Basic Documents* on page 222.

Figure 7-33 on page 223 and Figure 7-34 on page 223 show how to set up headers and footers for the page styles you'll use in your books and longer documents. Those settings merely ensure that the header and/or footer text boxes will be displayed on your pages. This section shows you how to put the stuff you want in those headers and footers.

To get the most flexibility with headers and footers, use alternating left/right page styles (see *Applying and Switching Page Styles* on page 253 and the Next style field in Figure 7-55 on page 252). That way you can have separate headers and footers that contain different information. For example, you could display the page number and name of the book on all left pages, and show the page number and the name of the current main heading (a running head) on all right pages. Another possibility is putting the name of the publication on the left and right footers, and putting the running head and page number in the left and right headers.

Header with a
running head
and page
number

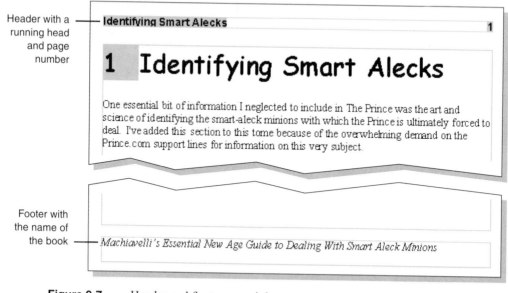

Identifying Smart Alecks   1

1 Identifying Smart Alecks

One essential bit of information I neglected to include in The Prince was the art and
science of identifying the smart-aleck minions with which the Prince is ultimately forced to
deal. I've added this section to this tome because of the overwhelming demand on the
Prince.com support lines for information on this very subject.

Footer with
the name of
the book

Machiavelli's Essential New Age Guide to Dealing With Smart Aleck Minions

Figure 9-7   Header and footer on a right page

Page Numbering

This section shows you a few common page numbering techniques that should cover 95
percent of your page numbering needs: regular ol' page numbering, transitioning from one
numbering style to another (for example, lowercase Roman numerals to regular Arabic
numbers), and using a chapter-page numbering style, such as 3-1.

Regular Ol' Page Numbering

Simplicity is a beautiful thing. Here's how to insert regular page numbers in your headers
and footers.

1   Click in the header or footer where you want to insert the page number.

2   In the toolbar, click and hold down the Insert Fields tool, and choose Page Numbers.

3   If you're using alternating headers and footers in a document (as determined in the
     page style), insert the page number on the alternate page(s).

     Use alternating headers and footers, for example, in left and right page styles, if you
     want the page number to be on the far left and far right sides of your pages.

If you want to use a *page # of #* format, insert Page Number and Page Count fields in the
header or footer, as shown in Figure 9-2 on page 284.

Transitioning to a Different Numbering Style

This procedure shows you how to transition from one numbering scheme, such as lowercase Roman numerals for front matter (title page, table of contents, preface), to another numbering scheme where the body of the document starts.

Note – This isn't a quick procedure. Some work with page styles is involved. If you need help with page styles, see *Creating Page Styles* on page 251.

For troubleshooting purposes, you should also be aware of the general effects of applying page styles to a document. See *Applying and Switching Page Styles* on page 253.

1   Create different page styles for the sections that will use different page numbering.

    For example, create alternating PrefaceLeft and PrefaceRight page styles that use a lowercase Roman numeral numbering scheme for a Preface section (as shown in Figure 9-8), and create Left and Right page styles for the main part of the document or book that use a regular Arabic numbering scheme.

Figure 9-8   Setting a numbering scheme for a page style

2   Apply the beginning page styles to the document.

    For example, apply a Title page style to the first page of the document, which is followed by alternating PrefaceLeft and PrefaceRight page styles.

3   Click at the beginning of the heading you want to begin the main body section, at which you will restart numbering.

4   Choose Insert > Manual Break.

5   In the Insert Break window, select Page break.

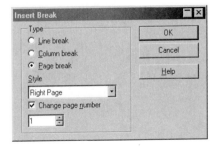

6   In the Style field, choose the page style you want to begin the main body of the document.

7   Select the Change page number option.

    The number 1 appears by default. If you want the main body to start with a number other than 1, change the value.

8   Click OK.

The flow of alternating PrefaceRight and PrefaceLeft pages is overridden, and the new flow of alternating Right and Left page styles begins with its new numbering scheme.

Chapter-Page Numbering

This procedure shows you how to set up page numbering that shows the chapter number and restarts the page number when a new chapter starts. For example, the first page of Chapter 3 would be numbered 3-1.

This style is easier on the author, because changes in one chapter don't throw off the page numbering for the rest of the document; but it's baaaaaaad for the reader who's trying to find pages in the document. (It's your conscience.) We present this section because, unfortunately, this page numbering style is still widely used.

If you want to use this procedure, you have to be okay with the fact that each chapter heading (the Heading 1 style, for example) will start on a new page and have an automatically generated chapter number. You also have to be okay with the fact that the only type of running head you'll be able to use is the chapter-level heading. For more information on that, see Using Running Heads next.

1   Make sure you've set up outline numbering in the document so that a paragraph style uses an automatically generated chapter number.

See *Setting Up Outline Numbering* on page 310.

2   Position the cursor in the header or footer where you want to insert page numbering.

3   Press Ctrl+F2 to display the Fields window.

4   On the Document tab, in the Type list, select Chapter.

5   In the Format list, select Chapter number without separator, as shown in Figure 9-9.

This option inserts only the automatically generated chapter number without any Before or After text. If you want to show Before or After text in the page numbering, such as "Chapter," select Chapter number in the Format list.

6   Click Insert. Keep the Fields window open.

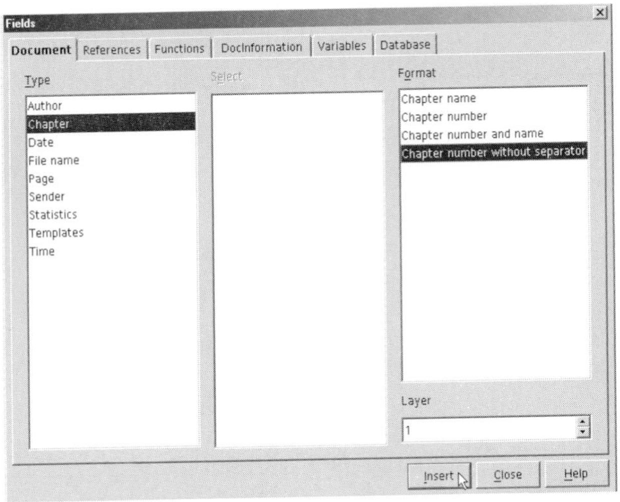

Figure 9-9   Inserting the "chapter" number

7 In the header or footer, insert a separator character after the chapter number you just inserted.

8 In the Fields window, select the Type called Page, select Page Numbers in the Select list, and select a page number style in the Format list.

9 Click Insert.

You can close the Fields window.

10 If you're using more than one set of headers and footers in the document, copy and paste the page numbering to all pertinent headers or footers.

11 Edit the paragraph that is set as the chapter paragraph. For example, if you're using Heading 1 as your chapter paragraph, select the Heading 1 paragraph style in the Stylist, right-click, and choose Modify.

12 In the Paragraph Style window, click the Text Flow tab, and set the options shown in Figure 9-10.

13 Click OK.

Select Break, Page, and Before. ——

Select With page style and select a page style the paragraph will start on.

Change the page number to 1.

Figure 9-10   Restarting page numbering

With this type of page numbering set up, when Writer sees a Heading 1 (or whichever is the chapter heading), it puts the heading at the top of a new page and restarts the page numbering, as shown in Figure 9-11.

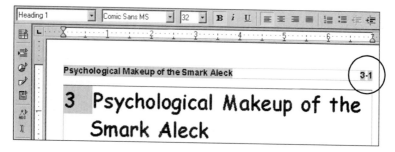

Figure 9-11   Chapter-page numbering

Using Running Heads

Running heads show the current text of a certain paragraph, like a heading. For example, you can have the contents of the current Heading 1 display on each page. Each new instance of a Heading 1 changes the running head text starting at that point until another Heading 1 appears in the document. This very book uses running heads in the header: chapters on the left pages, and Heading 1 titles on the right pages.

1   Set up outline numbering so that the paragraph style you want to use for the running head is selected as Level 1 in the Outline Numbering window.

    See *Outline Numbering* on page 308.

2   Click in the header or footer where you want to insert the numbering.

3   Press Ctrl+F2 to bring up the Fields window.

4   On the Document tab, in the Type list, select Chapter.

5   In the Format list, select Chapter name.

6   Click Insert.

7   If you're using more than one set of headers and footers in the document, copy and paste the running head to all pertinent headers or footers.

Creating Books (Master Documents)

A master document looks just like any other Writer document. The difference is that a master document is made up of separate Writer files, as shown in Figure 9-12.

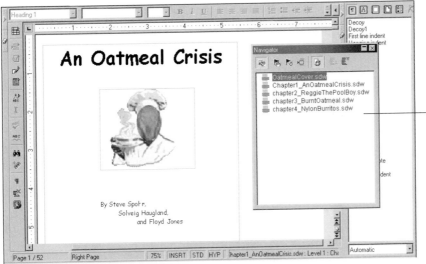

A master document looks just like a regular Writer document in the work area. But when you open the Navigator window (F5), you see a list of all the individual files that compose the master document, and you get a set of tools (icons) for working with master documents.

Figure 9-12   A master document

When you create a master document, all the files you include are displayed in a single read-only document (meaning you can't edit it directly), as if all of your files were really a single file. The read-only document is composed of links to the individual documents. The master document lets you rearrange the order of files, lets you add a master table of contents and index, and allows cross-referencing between its files.

Note – We like the master document a whole lot better than the master file feature in Word. The master document hasn't reached FrameMaker's book file, but it's way beyond Word's master file.

Master Document Principles

There are a few principles involved with master documents that will help you plan, work with, and troubleshoot master documents.

- When you add a file to a master document, the master document automatically imports the styles for that file. However, any additions or changes to styles in the master document itself do not affect the source file styles.

  What does this mean? You can create separate styles, such as page styles, to be used for only the master document. However, if you change or add a style to a master document, and you want that change or addition in the source file as well, you have to make the change in both places.

- Often when you work with master documents you'll do a lot of fine-tuning. For example, you may decide to use different fonts or page layouts along the way. Master documents have their own styles that are separate from the styles of the individual documents it contains. So you can fine-tune a master document by modifying its own styles.

  You can then load the styles from the master document into its source documents if you want to update their styles to match the master document. See *Loading Styles From Another Document* on page 258.

  If you want to keep master document styles different than the styles of the source documents, you can use and maintain different templates for each.

- A Writer file can be used in multiple master documents.

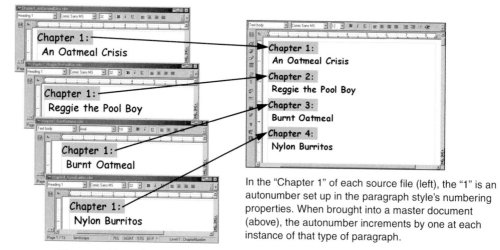

In the "Chapter 1" of each source file (left), the "1" is an autonumber set up in the paragraph style's numbering properties. When brought into a master document (above), the autonumber increments by one at each instance of that type of paragraph.

Figure 9-13   Autonumbers increment in a master document

- When put in a master document, source files behave exactly the way you've set them up. For example, if page numbering in your source files is set up to be continuous, page numbering will increment between files in the master document. So if Chapter 1 ends at page 56, Chapter 2 will start numbering at 57 in the master document—unless the page numbering in the Chapter 2 source file is set to restart page numbering.

Any paragraphs styles with autonumber properties are also incremented in a master document. For example, if you have a "Chapter Number" paragraph style with a numbering format that automatically displays "Chapter #" (where # is an autonumber), outline numbering will be consecutive in the master document (Chapter 1, Chapter 2, and so on), as shown in Figure 9-13.

Creating a Master Document

You can create a master document from an existing file, or you can create one from scratch. The only minor advantage to creating a master document from an existing file is that the file is added to the master document automatically, saving you a step.

Creating a Master Document From Scratch

1   Choose File > New > Master document.

     A blank document appears, along with the Navigator window in master document view. Navigator shows an item called Text.

2   Add the files you want to include in the master document. In the Navigator window, click and hold down the Insert button, and choose File.

3   In the Insert window, find and double-click the first file you want to add.

4   Add the rest of the files the same way.

     As you add files, their contents display in the document.

5   Delete the Text item. Select it, right-click, and choose delete.

6   After you add the files, you can rearrange them in the master document by selecting one and clicking the Move Up or Move Down button in Navigator.

7   If you want to use all the styles from your documents, load them into the master document. If you need help doing this, see *Loading Styles From Another Document* on page 258.

8   Save the master document.

The Insert button in the docked Navigator window

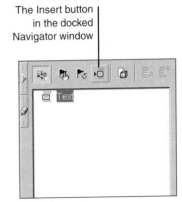

Select a file and click the Move Up or Move Down button.

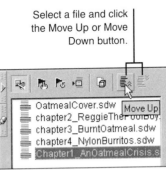

Creating a Master Document From an Existing File

1   With a Writer document open that you want to include in the master document, choose File > Send > Create Master Document.

2   In the Name and Path window, navigate to the location where you want to store the master document file, type in a file name, and click Save.

A blank Writer master document is displayed in the work area, and Navigator opens in master document mode. Navigator displays a new file named after the source file, with a number appended to the end of the name.

3   Follow the steps in the previous procedure for adding and rearranging files in the master document.

4   Delete the blank document that Writer used to start the master document. Select the file in Navigator, right-click, and choose Delete.

Master Document Headers and Footers

While you can't edit the body of the master document, you can edit the headers and footers. This lets you create the custom headers and footers you may need for the master document. Headers and footers are associated with page styles, so changing page styles also changes the headers and footers used.

Using Page Styles in a Master Document

You can create your own styles for a master document to use a different layout for the book than what is used in the source files. the program also comes with a couple of book templates you can borrow page styles from. For more information on templates, see *Using Templates* on page 256.

If you want to change a page style for a given page, click in the header or footer and apply the page style (you can't click in the body of the master document, because it's read-only). This tip also comes with a warning, because the page style you apply uses its own header and footer settings, as well as its own Next Style for the page style that will follow it. This could cause a chain reaction that requires you to modify a lot of page styles to get the flow you want.

Editing Master Document Source Files

In order to change the content of the master document, you must edit the source files that make up the master document. Edit source files by double-clicking them in the master document Navigator window. You can also open them the way you normally open files.

You have to save the changes you make in the source files for the master document to pick up the changes.

Updating the Master Document

There are different aspects to updating a master document. The main aspect has to do with updating the links to the content of the files so that the most current content is displayed in the master document. The other aspect of updating master documents is updating styles if you change styles in the source files.

The master document has to be updated when its files change. Updating a master document refreshes the links to the source files, displays the files in their current state, and updates generated information (like page numbering, the table of contents, and the index).

Updating Links Automatically

When you open a master document you previously saved, Writer asks you if you want to update all links. Writer is asking you if you want to update the master document to reflect the current state of all its document files. You can set the automatic link update options in Tools > Options > Text document > Other, in the Update Links area. If you select Always, when you open the master document, Writer updates the links to the files without prompting you.

If you select On request, Writer prompts you to update the links whenever you open the master document. If you select Never, Writer opens the master document without updating the links, and you need to update them manually.

Updating Links Manually

With the master document open, you can manually update individual pieces of the master document, or you can update the whole thing. Select a master document file in Navigator, click and hold down the Update button in Navigator, and select one of the following options:

*   Selection – Updates the selected item, whether it's a file or a section of the table of contents.

*   Indexes – Updates all generated lists (table of contents, index, list of figures, etc.).

*   Links – Updates all files without updating indexes.

*   All – Updates all files and indexes.

Updating Styles

If you edit styles in your source documents, you'll need to reload them into the master document, and vice versa. For information on updating styles in master documents, see *Master Document Principles* on page 319.

Cross-Referencing

Cross-referencing information is essential to long documents. You want to be able to tell readers where related material is located in the document, and you want to be able to use heading titles and page numbers. While setting up cross-referencing is a little clunky in Writer, it works.

You can only set cross-references in a single document. You can't cross-reference between files in a master document

The basic principle behind cross-referencing in Writer is that you have to set a cross-reference marker that can be pointed at, or referenced. When you want to insert a cross-reference to an item, you have to locate its marker and insert a reference to it.

Set the Reference Marker

Note – For more information about reference fields, see Table 9-1 on page 285.

1   Select the exact text in a document you want to reference.

2   Press Ctrl+F2 (or choose Insert > Fields > Other) to bring up the Fields window.

3   Click the References tab.

4   In the Type list, select Set Reference.

5   Type a name for the reference in the Name field. Make it a name you can recognize later.

6   Click Insert. The name you typed is displayed in the Selection list. This is the marker name you'll point to later to reference the item.

You can leave the Fields window open while you perform the next steps.

Create a Cross-Reference to the Marker

1   Click in the document where you want to insert a cross-reference. (Enter any necessary text, such as *See* and *on page*, in front of where you want to insert the cross-reference.)

2   In the Fields window, click the References tab.

3   In the Type list, select Insert Reference.

4   In the Selection list, select the reference you want to insert.

5   In the Formats list, select Reference to insert the name of the reference, or select Page to insert the page number to the reference. (You have to insert each separately.)

6   Click Insert.

Adding a Hyperlink Cross-Reference

In a long document (not a master document), you can create a cross-reference as a hyperlink, so that when you click on it you jump to that part of the document.

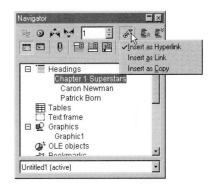

1   Open Navigator (press the F5 key).

2   In the Navigator window, click and hold down the Drag Mode button, and select Insert as Hyperlink.

3   At the bottom of the Navigator window, make sure the active document is selected in the drop-down list.

4   In the list of items, expand (click the "+" next to) the item, such as Headings, containing the item you want to insert into the document as a hyperlink.

5   Drag the item from the Navigator window into the document where you want it to appear.

People reading the document online must open the document in StarOffice or OpenOffice.org for the hyperlinks to work.

Creating a Table of Contents

You can insert a table of contents into a single long document or into a master document. There are different procedures for each.

Quick, impulsive TOC insertion If you just want to quickly insert a TOC (table of contents) now without fuss, just choose Insert > Indexes and Tables > Indexes and Tables. Make sure Table of Contents is selected twice in the lists, and that Entire Document is selected in the third list, then click OK.

Note – In Writer, a table of contents is a type of "index." Index is the all-encompassing term for tables of contents, indexes, lists of figures, and so on. Debate the terminology all you want, but just know that any type of list with associated page numbers is created through a menu item called "Indexes" off the Insert menu.

Setting Up What's Included in the TOC

Make sure you've got the basics—headings—plus anything else that should show up.

Standard Headings: The Key to TOCs

A table of contents is easiest to create if you've used styles for headings rather than just selecting plain text and manually making it big and bold. See *Power Formatting With Styles* on page 241 for more information on styles.

Make sure you've used paragraph styles for the headings in your document, such as Heading 1 or any that you've created. Heading styles are the basis of tables of contents; as long as you've used them, you're going to end up with *something* in your TOC.

Marking Special Table of Contents Entries

There may be instances where you want to include certain parts of a document in a table of contents. For example, say you're creating a table of contents that contains entries for Heading 1 and Heading 2 items only, but there's a single item at the Heading 4 level that is an extremely important section, and you want to include it in the table of contents as well. You can mark that item as a special entry for inclusion in the table of contents.

1   In your document, select the text you want to include in the table of contents.

    In a master document, you need to select the text in the source file.

2   Choose Insert > Indexes and Tables > Entry.

3   In the Insert Index Entry window (Figure 9-14), select Table of Contents in the Index field.

    The text you selected in the document shows up in the Entry field automatically.

4   In the Level field, set the level of the item as it will appear in the table of contents.

5   Click Insert.

6   The Insert Index Entry stays open for you to select and insert more text in the document.

7   When you're finished inserting special table of contents entries, click Close.

When you generate the table of contents, be sure that in the Insert Index window, on the Index tab, you select the Index marks option. If you don't, your special table of contents entries won't be included in the index.

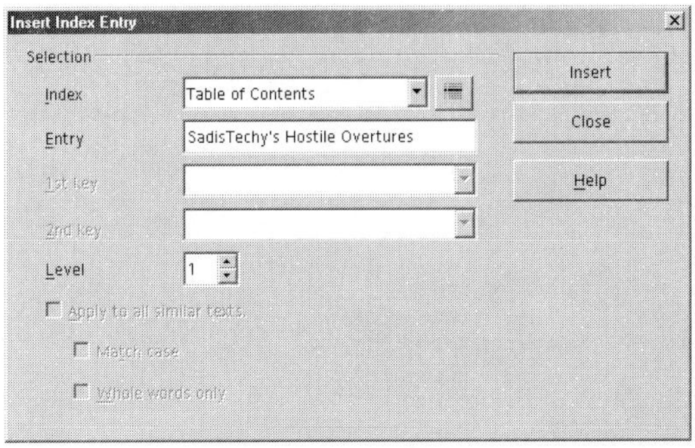

Figure 9-14   Marking special entries for inclusion in a table of contents

Inserting a Table of Contents

Select the appropriate procedure depending whether you're working in a single standard document, or in a master document.

Inserting a Table of Contents Into a Standard Document

Use this procedure for inserting a table of contents into a single document rather than a master document. The procedure for inserting a table of contents into a master document follows this one.

Make sure you've used paragraph styles for the headings in your document, such as Heading 1 or any that you've created.

Also mark any text you want to include in the table of contents (see *Marking Special Table of Contents Entries* on page 326).

1   Click in the document where you want to insert the table of contents.

2   Choose Insert > Indexes and Tables > Indexes and Tables.

In the Insert Index/Table window, set the options you want. The import sections are to select Table of Contents in both lists and, typically, to select Entire Document in the middle of the window.

3   When you're finished, click OK.

To have more control over how it's generated, see *Advanced Setup for Tables of Contents* on page 329.

To format the paragraph styles in the table of contents, see *Formatting and Editing a Table of Contents* on page 332.

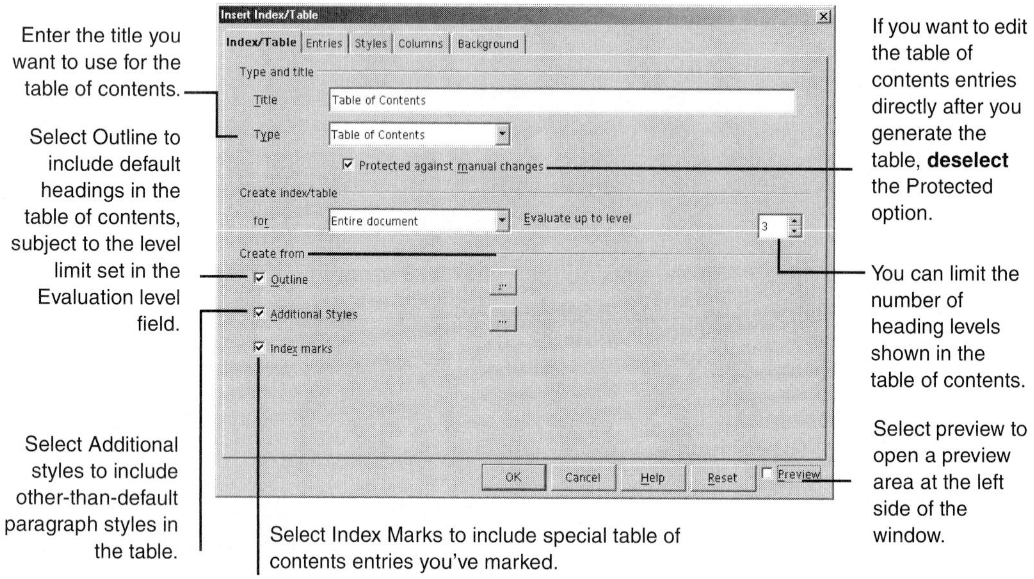

Enter the title you want to use for the table of contents.

Select Outline to include default headings in the table of contents, subject to the level limit set in the Evaluation level field.

Select Additional styles to include other-than-default paragraph styles in the table.

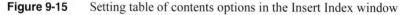

If you want to edit the table of contents entries directly after you generate the table, **deselect** the Protected option.

You can limit the number of heading levels shown in the table of contents.

Select preview to open a preview area at the left side of the window.

Select Index Marks to include special table of contents entries you've marked.

Figure 9-15   Setting table of contents options in the Insert Index window

---

Note – Select Additional styles to include other-than-default paragraph styles in the table. Then click the ellipsis points button to set the additional styles; the Assign Styles window, shown in Figure 9-17, will appear.

Inserting a Table of Contents Into a Master Document

1   With the master document open, make sure Navigator is open (press the F5 key), and toggle to the master document view.

2   In the Navigator window, select the file you want to put the table of contents before.

3   In Navigator, click and hold down the Insert button, and choose Table of Contents.

4   Set the options for the table of contents. If you need help setting options, see *Inserting a Table of Contents* on page 327.

5   Click OK.

As in a single document, all parts of a table of contents have their own paragraph formats that you can modify. Click in a line of the table of contents, and the name of the style is highlighted in the Stylist under paragraph styles, as shown in Figure 9-20 on page 333.

To have more control over how it's generated, see *Advanced Setup for Tables of Contents* on page 329.

To format the paragraph styles in the table of contents, see *Formatting and Editing a Table of Contents* on page 332.

Advanced Setup for Tables of Contents

If you want to go beyond the quick TOC, here are some controls you can apply to what's in it, and how it looks.

Previewing the TOC

When you insert indexes and tables of contents, select the Preview option in the lower right corner of the Index tab, in the Insert Index/Table window. You'll see how the TOC or index will look with the current settings. An example is shown at right.

Understanding the Table of Contents Formatting Codes

If you're the acronym type, think of it as SOCML (StarOffice's Complex Markup Language). When you select a table of contents level in the Entries tab (shown at right; see also Figure 9-17 on page 331), you can customize the way that level in the table of contents is displayed. Do this by working with the table of contents codes. Here's what each of the codes means.

- <E#> – If the paragraph level (for example, Heading 1) uses outline numbering, this tag inserts the full chapter number definition, whether it's *1*, *Chapter 1*, or whatever.

  See *Outline Numbering* on page 308.

- <E> – Inserts the text of the heading.

- <T> – Inserts a tab with leader dots. The tab distance and leader dots are defined in the paragraph styles used for table of contents entries, such as Contents 1, Contents 2, and so on.

- <#> – Inserts the page number.

- <LS> and <LE> – Opening and closing tags that enclose the part of the table of contents entry you want to hyperlink to its respective section of the document.

Specifying Advanced Setup Options

Choose Insert > Indexes and Tables > Indexes and Tables. Then use the Assign Styles window in Figure 9-16. (In the Index/Table tab, click the browse icon (...) next to Additional Styles to get to the Assign Styles window.) Then use the Entries tab in Figure 9-17 to set additional options, if necessary.

Figure 9-18 explains the codes and how to set them up, and Figure 9-19 shows how to select the styles for the TOC.

Select a paragraph style you want to include in the table of contents, and click the arrows at the bottom of the window to assign the style to a table of contents level (based on the numbers at the top of the window). Click OK when you're finished.

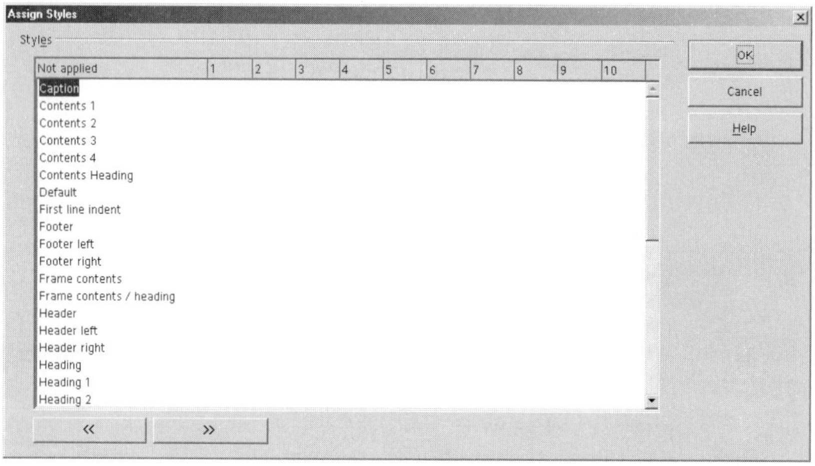

Figure 9-16   Setting table of contents options in the Assign Styles window

To delete part of the structure section at the top, click on it and press Delete.

To add a chapter number, spot for entry text, tab stop, page number, or hyperlink, click in the part of the Structure area where you want it, and click the corresponding button.

Select a table of contents heading level you want to define.

In the boxes in the Structure area, enter the codes and text that define the selected level of your table of contents; they are explained in more detail in Figure 9-16. See also *Understanding the Table of Contents Formatting Codes* on page 329.

You can type codes in manually or click the buttons in this row to insert codes. (If a button is grayed, its code has already been used.)

Insert hyperlink codes (LS=LinkStart and LE=LinkEnd) before and after the part of the table of contents line you want to hyperlink.

Figure 9-17   Defining what's in each level of a table of contents

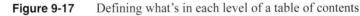

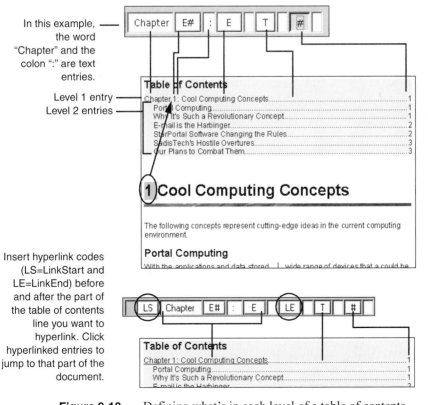

In this example, the word "Chapter" and the colon ":" are text entries.

Level 1 entry

Level 2 entries

Insert hyperlink codes (LS=LinkStart and LE=LinkEnd) before and after the part of the table of contents line you want to hyperlink. Click hyperlinked entries to jump to that part of the document.

The tab and page number codes (T and #) are outside of the hyperlink codes and are therefore not hyperlinked.

Figure 9-18   Defining what's in each level of a table of contents

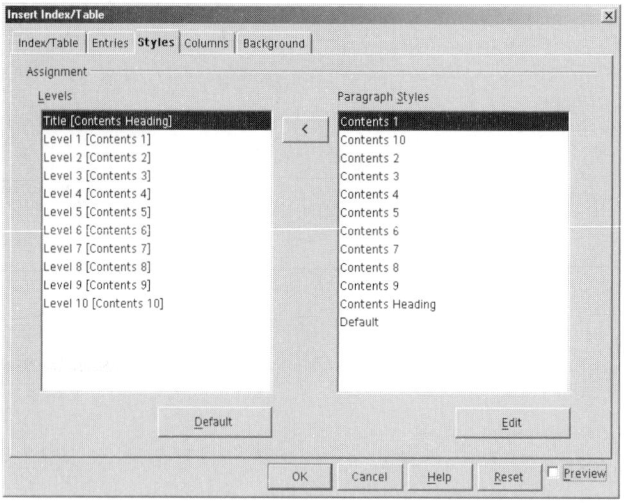

Figure 9-19   Selecting the styles you want to be able to use in the table of contents

Formatting and Editing a Table of Contents

A table of contents is typically a big block of read-only text that you can't edit directly (though you can change this effect in the first tab of the Insert Index window, shown in Figure 9-16 on page 330). Best practices are to regenerate the table of contents to change the text inside of it; because if you change just the table of contents entry, the heading used to generate it is still incorrect, and if you regenerate the table of contents for some reason, the incorrect heading will reappear.

In terms of formatting, you can change the formatting of the table of contents entries without regenerating the table of contents.

Basic Table of Contents Formatting

Each level in a table of contents has its own paragraph style. For example, level 1 headings by default are associated with the "Contents 1" paragraph style, which uses plain ol' vanilla formatting. To change the formatting of table of contents levels, modify their associated paragraph formats.

You can tell which paragraph style is associated with a level by clicking in a line of the table of contents. The paragraph style used for it will be highlighted in the Stylist, as shown in Figure 9-20.

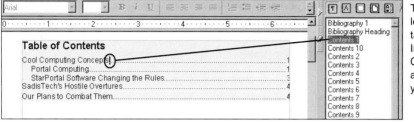

The cursor is in a level 1 entry in the table of contents. In the Stylist, Contents 1 is the associated style you must modify.

Figure 9-20   Identifying styles used for table of contents levels

For more information on modifying paragraph styles, see *Standard Paragraph Styles* on page 245.

Advanced Table of Contents Formatting

Instead of using and modifying the default paragraph table of contents styles, you can assign other paragraph styles to table of contents entries. Using this procedure you can also change the number of columns used for the table of contents, and you can add background color or graphics to the table of contents.

1   Click in the table of contents, right-click, and choose Edit Index.

2   In the Insert Index window, select the Styles tab. See Figure 9-21.

   The Levels list displays the table of contents title and the 10 possible table of contents levels, with the paragraph styles that are assigned to those levels (in parentheses).

   The Paragraph styles list displays all the paragraph styles defined in the document.

3   In the Levels list, select the item you want to assign a different paragraph format to.

4   In the Paragraph styles list, select the paragraph style you want to assign to the selected level.

   You can't assign Writer's default Heading # styles to levels, but you can assign them to the table of contents title.

5   Click the Assign button.

6   Set column options in the Columns tab, and set background color or graphic options in the Background tab.

   These settings are similar to those used in defining page styles. If you need more information, see Figure 7-40 on page 231 for column information and Figure 7-39 on page 230 for background information.

7   Click OK.

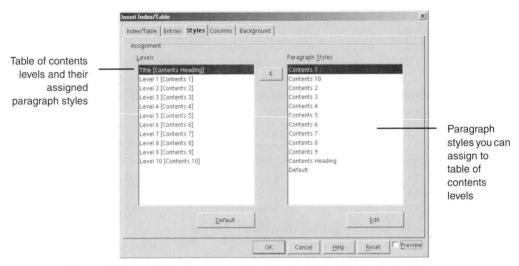

Table of contents levels and their assigned paragraph styles

Paragraph styles you can assign to table of contents levels

Figure 9-21 Assigning paragraph styles to table of contents levels

Fixing Page Flow After You Insert a Table of Contents or Adding New Content Before the Table of Contents

When you insert a table of contents above the content of your document, you may need to paginate your document so that the table of contents is by itself on one (or more) pages, and the body of your document starts on a new page. Figure 9-17 on page 331 shows a table of contents that is sitting right above the body of the document.

In a master document, you must use this procedure on the individual source files.

1. Click at the beginning of the body of the document and press Ctrl+Enter to break the body to a new page.

2. If you're using left and right page styles, and the table of contents ends on a right page, you may also need to click at the end of the table of contents and create a page break so that an empty left page is created.

   This lets you start the body of the document on a right page. See *Applying and Switching Page Styles* on page 253.

3. After you change pagination, update the table of contents (next).

Editing a Table of Contents

Editing a table of contents involves tasks like including or excluding certain types of paragraph styles that are displayed, altering the way entries are displayed, associating levels with other-than-default paragraph formats, and making other fundamental changes to a table of contents.

If your basic table of contents setup is just as you want it, and you've simply added new content to your document, you only need to update the table of contents, not edit it. See Updating or Deleting a Table of Contents, next.

To edit a table of contents:

1   Click in the table of contents.

2   Right-click, and choose Edit Index.

3   In the Insert Index window, make the changes you want. If you need help, see Figure 9-16, Figure 9-17, and Figure 9-21.

4   Click OK.

Updating or Deleting a Table of Contents

If your page count changes, or you just don't want to have a TOC anymore, follow the steps in one of these procedures.

Updating a Table of Contents

If the contents or page count of a document changes after a table of contents has been generated, update the table of contents using this procedure.

However, if you need to make more fundamental changes to the table of contents structure, you need to edit the table of contents. See the previous procedure.

1   Click in the table of contents.

2   Right-click and choose Update Index.

Removing a Table of Contents

You can't remove a table of contents by selecting it and deleting it. To remove a table of contents, click in it, right-click, and choose Remove Index.

Creating an Index

There are professional indexers in the world. Their work can dramatically increase the quality of a book. Conversely, a poor index can cause a lot of reader frustration. So assuming you do not aspire to be a professional indexer, we'll leave you with perhaps the most useful advice a professional indexer is likely to give you to create a decent index: pretend you're a reader.

Stepping into the reader's shoes helps you anticipate what information the reader will want to find in the index. If a section in your document or book contains important information on creating a file, which words might the target reader look for in the index to get to that information? "Creating a file" is an obvious choice. But might they also look under the word "File"? What about "Generating"? "Adding"? "Starting"? Or what about "Document" in addition to "File"? Or even more specifically, "Text document" or "Spreadsheet"? The index terms you use may not even appear in the text of a document or book.

The index entries you insert are up to you. But looking at your index from a reader's perspective helps ensure that the index will be more useful than it otherwise would be.

Marking Index Entries

For Writer to generate an index with related page numbers, you must mark the items you want to index right where they appear in the document.

1   Select the text you want to use as the index entry. You can also just click inside the word you want to index.

2   Choose Insert > Indexes and Tables > Entry.

3   In the Insert Index Entry window, select Alphabetical Index in the Index field.

4   Set the remaining options for the entry. Use Figure 9-22 for guidance.

5   Click Insert.

The Insert Index Entry window stays open for you to mark other index entries in the document.

When you insert an index entry, the selected word gets a gray background (if View > Field Shadings is activated).

Select Alphabetical Index in the Index field. | The text you select in the document appears in the Entry field.

Enter any **1st**- or **2nd**-level entries you want the **Entry** to be under. All 1st and 2nd entries are stored in their list boxes to let you select them later. This ensures naming consistency and reduces the need to troubleshoot later, which can be a painful process.

If you select Main entry, Writer generates the index entry with a different paragraph style than it uses for other entries, letting you format it differently if you want.

The entry in this example produces this hierarchy:

Insert Index Entry

Selection
Index: Alphabetical Index
Entry: Redmond, taking over
1st key: main strategy
2nd key: chips, implanting in neck
☐ Main entry
☐ Apply to all similar texts
☐ Match case
☐ Whole words only

Insert | Close | Help

Alphabetical Index

Sun Microsystems
    portal computing   1

If you select Apply to all similar texts, all instances of the Entry text in the document are marked as index entries. You can also determine that similar text entries must match the case of the current entry.

Figure 9-22   Making index entries

Note – You can also prevent partial words from being marked by selecting the Whole Words Only.

Inserting an Index Into a Single Document

Previewing TOCs and indexes When you insert indexes and tables of contents, select the Preview option in the lower right corner of the Index tab, in the Insert Index/Table window. You'll see how the TOC or index will look with the current settings. The preview window is shown at right.

Use this procedure for inserting a table of contents into a single document rather than a master document. The procedure for inserting a table of contents into a master document follows this one.

You don't have to insert all your index entries before you generate an index. You can go back and make additional entries, then update the index.

1   Click in the document where you want to insert the index.

2   Choose Insert > Indexes and Tables > Indexes and Tables.

3   In the Insert Index window, select Alphabetical Index in the Type field.

4   Set the options in the Index tab. Use Figure 9-23 for guidance.

5   Set options in the remaining tabs. If you need guidance, *Inserting a Table of Contents* on page 327 contains similar information.

6   Click OK.

All parts of an index have their own paragraph formats you can modify. Click in a line of the index, and the name of the style is highlighted in the Stylist under paragraph styles.

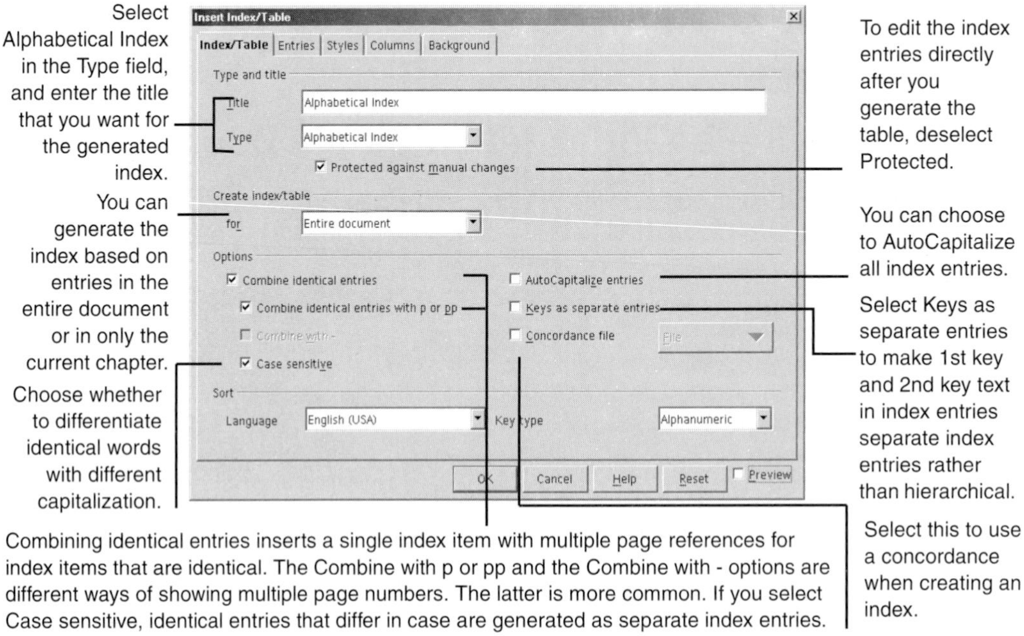

Select Alphabetical Index in the Type field, and enter the title that you want for the generated index.

You can generate the index based on entries in the entire document or in only the current chapter.

Choose whether to differentiate identical words with different capitalization.

Insert Index/Table

Index/Table | Entries | Styles | Columns | Background

Type and title

Title: Alphabetical Index

Type: Alphabetical Index

☑ Protected against manual changes

Create index/table

for: Entire document

Options

☑ Combine identical entries
☑ Combine identical entries with p or pp
☐ Combine with –
☑ Case sensitive

☐ AutoCapitalize entries
☐ Keys as separate entries
☐ Concordance file   File

Sort

Language: English (USA)   Key type   Alphanumeric

OK | Cancel | Help | Reset | ☐ Preview

To edit the index entries directly after you generate the table, deselect Protected.

You can choose to AutoCapitalize all index entries.

Select Keys as separate entries to make 1st key and 2nd key text in index entries separate index entries rather than hierarchical.

Select this to use a concordance when creating an index.

Combining identical entries inserts a single index item with multiple page references for index items that are identical. The Combine with p or pp and the Combine with - options are different ways of showing multiple page numbers. The latter is more common. If you select Case sensitive, identical entries that differ in case are generated as separate index entries.

Figure 9-23   Setting index options in the Insert Index window

Using a Concordance to Help Create an Index

If you're creating an alphabetical index as shown in Figure 9-23, you can use a concordance, an extra file with guidance for how to create the index.

What It Is

It's a way of setting up ahead of time how you're going to index anyway. Let's say that you're indexing a cookbook that has grown out of your fabulous collection of brownie recipes.

Every time you come across a particular bread recipe, then, you probably want to index it:

```
bread:sourdough
bread:banana
```

and so on.

And since people have different opinions about whether banana bread is really cake or bread, you'll probably want a few things to show up in both, as well as just making lots of cake entries:

```
cake:banana bread
cake:eating it too
```

It's also nice to be able to set up a bunch of phrases to be indexed under one phrase. Let's say that you know everyone west of the Mississippi talks about apple crisp, which is right and proper. and that's the term you use in the cookbook. You also talk about hot dishes, though you know that folks east of the Mississippi are going to be looking for recipes on apple cobbler and casseroles. You can use the concordance to set up a mapping between cobbler and crisp, and also a mapping between hotdish and casserole.

How It Works

We created a small recipe book and a concordance for its index. Figure 9-24 shows the words that were in your recipe book and mentioned in the concordance for indexing.

Words in book
```
banana bread
sourdough bread
chocolate cake
apple crisp
hot dish
```

Words not in book
```
apple cobbler
casserole
```

Figure 9-24   Words in the example recipe book that were picked up by the concordance, and words not in book that were also indexed

Figure 9-25 shows the concordance and the generated index, and how the concordance affects the index.

The actions taken based on the concordance include:

- The term `hot dish` was found and turned into `casserole`, and made into a subentry of `hot dishes`. It was also listed simply as `hot dish` for people who don't know what a `casserole` is.

Note – If you're expanding your index, it would also make a lot of sense to simply set up the concordance to find hot dish in

Search term	Alternative ...	1st key	2nd key	Comment	Match case	Word only
hot dish		hot dish			No	No
hot dish		casserole			No	No

the book and index it as `casserole` and as `hot dish` as main entries, not subentries.

- The term `banana bread` was found and subindexed under `dessert breads`.

- The term `apple crisp` was found and indexed as `apple cobbler`. The term `apple crisp` was also subindexed as `apple crisp`, under `coffee cakes`.

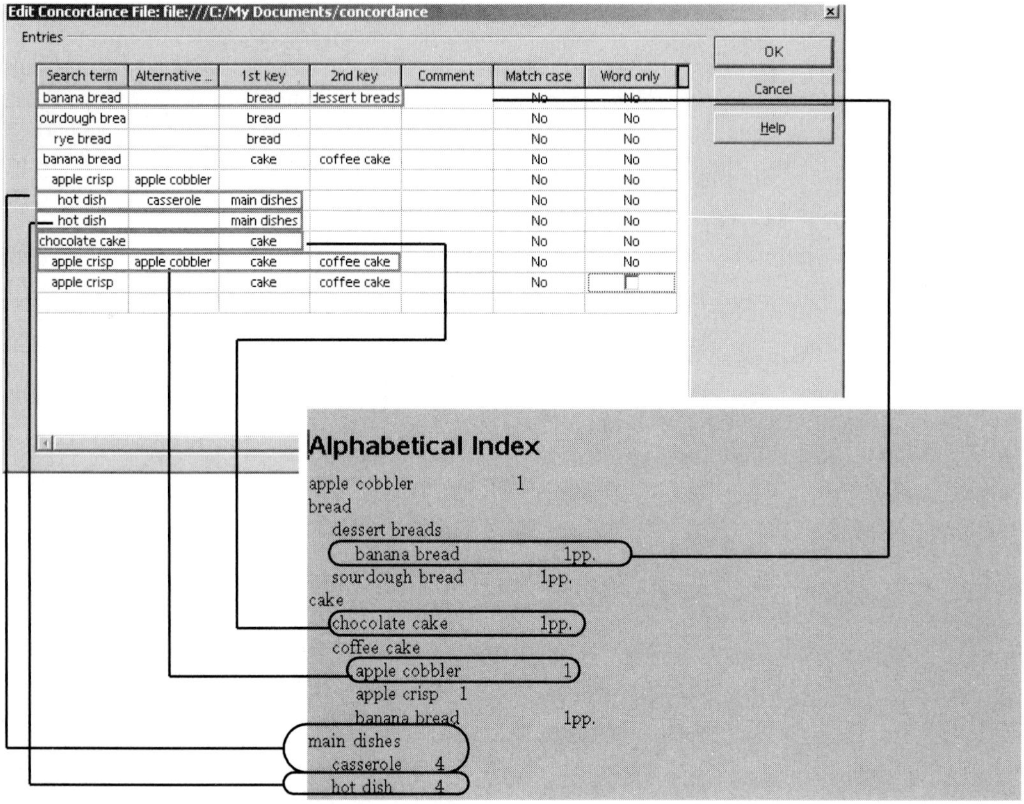

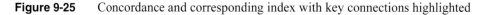

Figure 9-25   Concordance and corresponding index with key connections highlighted

Terminology

If you want to create one in this procedure, you'll need to know the following terms.

- Search term – The text you're looking for in the document and want to enter a related index entry for.

- Alternative entry – The text you want to put in the index itself.

- Key1 and Key2 – The first and second level entries, like bread:sourdough.

- Match case – The system will consider identical words with different case as different words. If Bread is a search term, the concordance will ignore bread.

- Word only – The search term should be found only when on its own. If you select Word only, bread will be found but breading won't.

Selecting or Creating a Concordance

1   To use a concordance, select Concordance and from the dropdown list in Figure 9-23 and select Open or Edit.

If you select Open, a window will prompt you to select an `.sdi` concordance file.

If you select Edit, you'll be prompted to enter a filename. Then the Edit Concordance File window will appear, shown in Figure 9-26.

2   Make the appropriate entries, then click OK.

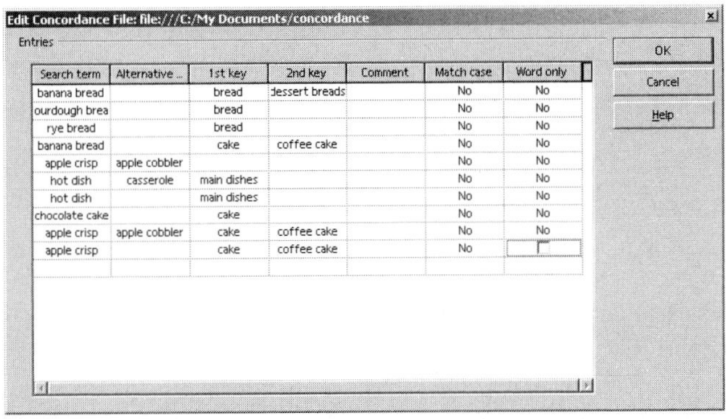

Figure 9-26   Creating a concordance file for generating an index

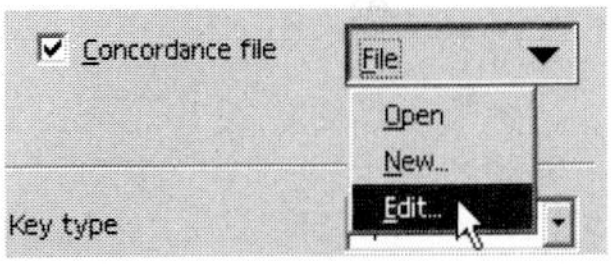

To edit it later, select Edit from the concordance dropdown list in the Index and Tables window.

To stop using it, deselect the Concordance option.

Inserting an Index Into a Master Document

1   With the master document open, make sure Navigator is open (press the F5 key), and toggle to the master document view in Navigator.

2   In the Navigator window, select the last file of the master document.

3   In Navigator, click and hold down the Insert button, and choose Index.

4   Set the options for the Index. See the previous section if you need help setting options.

5   Click OK.

6   If you want to move the index to a different place in the master document, select the index item in the Navigator (master document view), and click one of the Move buttons to position the index where you want.

All parts of an index have their own paragraph formats that you can modify. Click in a line of the table of contents, and the name of the style is highlighted in the Stylist under paragraph styles.

Formatting and Editing an Index

The principles and procedure for formatting and editing an index are the same as that for formatting and editing a table of contents. See *Formatting and Editing a Table of Contents* on page 332.

Updating or Deleting an Index

The procedure is the same as that for updating a table of contents. See *Updating or Deleting a Table of Contents* on page 335.

Note – With indexes but not tables of contents, you have to be careful what you select. You can't select the final carriage return of the generated index or you won't see the Remove Index option. The figure at right shows the correct way to select an index in order to delete it; the dark area shows what should be selected; note the final line is partly light, showing it's not selected.

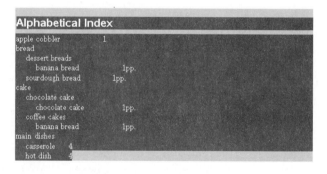

Tips for Troubleshooting Indexes

Indexes never end up perfect the first time. In order to fix an index, you really should fix the index entries rather than editing the index itself, then update the index. Unfortunately, there's no streamlined way to jump from an index item to the index marker in the document to fix it. You have to hunt and peck through the document(s), which can be really time-consuming. Use the following tips to help with the troubleshooting process.

• Choose View > Field Shadings. This shows the gray background of index entries.

- To locate index entries in a document, use the Navigation tool. (Click the little dot button at the bottom of the vertical scroll bar, click Index entry, and use the up and down arrows above and below the button to jump to the previous or next entry.) If you 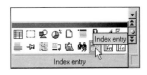 click the lower arrow to move to the next entry, the cursor is in the perfect position to use the next tip.

- You can click in an index entry and choose Edit > Index Entry to bring up the Edit Index Entry window (Figure 9-27), which lets you change, delete, and move to previous and next index entries.

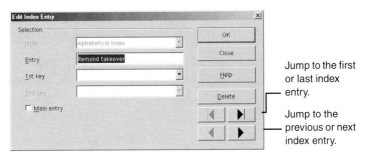

Jump to the first or last index entry.

Jump to the previous or next index entry.

Figure 9-27   Troubleshooting an index

Creating Lists of Figures and Other Lists

If you've used captions in your document for figures, tables, and other elements (see *Inserting Captions* on page 300), you can create lists of these elements.

Inserting a List Into a Single Document

1   Click where you want to insert the list.

2   Choose Insert > Indexes and Tables > Indexes and Tables.

3   In the Insert Index/Table window, select the Type of list you want to generate.

-   If you used your own paragraph styles for captioning, select User-Defined.

-   If you used Writer's caption tool to enter captions, select Illustration Index or Index of Tables.

4   Enter a Title for the list.

5   Set options in the Index tab. Use Figure 9-28 for guidance.

6   Set options in the remaining tabs. If you need guidance, the information in *Inserting a Table of Contents* on page 327 contains similar information.

7   Click OK.

To generate a list based on caption paragraph styles you've created, select User-Defined in the Type Field, select the Styles option (only), click the ellipsis button, and set the paragraph style you want to generate the list with.

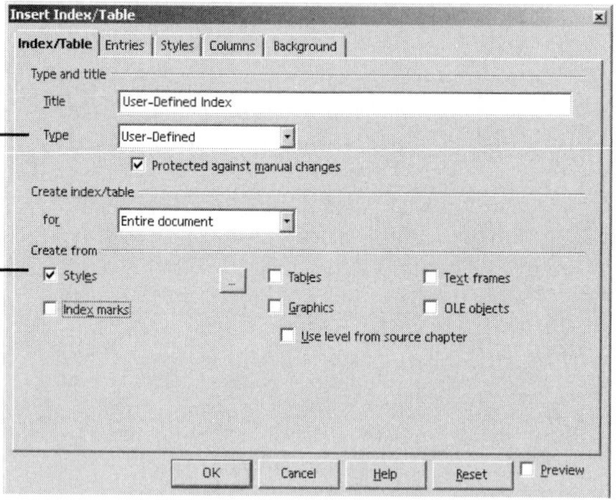

Figure 9-28   Setting options for index-type lists

Select a paragraph style you want to include in the list, and click the arrows at the bottom of the window to assign the style to level 1 (based on the numbers at the top of the window). Click OK when you're finished.

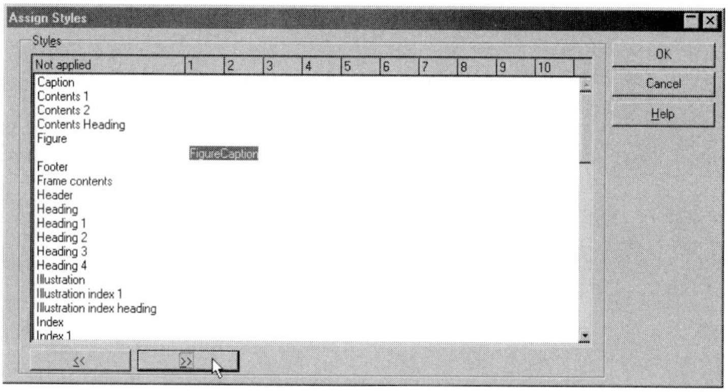

Figure 9-29   Selecting paragraph styles

The list title and items have their own paragraph styles you can modify, just like tables of contents and indexes.

You can also generate lists of objects you've inserted in a document. In the Insert Index window, select the type called Table of Objects, and select the types of objects you want to list (such as Chart, Calc, and so on).

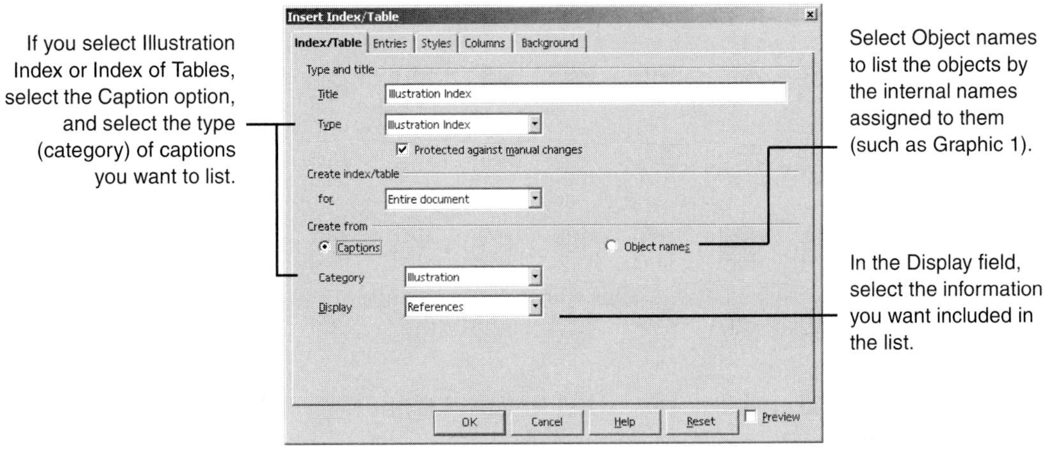

If you select Illustration Index or Index of Tables, select the Caption option, and select the type (category) of captions you want to list.

Select Object names to list the objects by the internal names assigned to them (such as Graphic 1).

In the Display field, select the information you want included in the list.

Figure 9-30   Setting options for Illustration Index or Index of Tables

Inserting a List in a Master Document

You can insert one or more lists in a master document.

1   With the master document open, make sure Navigator is open (press the F5 key), and toggle to the master document view in Navigator.

2   In the Navigator window, select the last file of the master document.

3   In Navigator, click and hold down the Insert button, and choose User-Defined Index.

4   In the Type field, select the type of caption list you want to create.

5   Set the options for the list. See the previous section if you need help setting options.

6   Click OK.

7   Select the list item in the Navigator (master document view), and click the Move Up or Move Down buttons to move the list to the desired location in the master document.

All parts of a list have their own paragraph formats that you can modify. Click in a line of the table of contents, and the name of the style is highlighted in the Stylist under paragraph styles.

Formatting and Editing Lists

The principles and procedures for formatting and editing lists are the same as those for formatting and editing a table of contents. See *Formatting and Editing a Table of Contents* on page 332.

Updating Lists

The procedure for updating lists is the same as that for updating a table of contents. See *Updating or Deleting a Table of Contents* on page 335.

Bibliographies

Writer lets you store bibliography information for different publications you'll reference in your documents. Once bibliography information is stored, you can insert bibliography references in your document, then generate a formatted bibliography at the end of a document.

Because the program uses the default bibliography database table, called *biblio*, to generate bibliographies, use only this table to store bibliography information in a database. The only alternative to store bibliography information in a database is to store it inside individual documents.

Entering and Editing Bibliography Information

To view the bibliography and edit the content document, choose View > Data Sources and make the changes, then click the Save icon above the records.

For additional details and procedures on data sources, see Chapter 35, *Creating and Modifying Data Sources*, on page 869.

Storing Bibliography Information in an Individual Document

Bibliography entries stored in a document are *not* stored in the included bibliography database. There isn't a compelling reason to store bibliography information this way. Storing it in the bibliography database ensures that all documents have access to the information. However, if for some reason your bibliography database becomes inaccessible or corrupted, use this procedure as a workaround.

1   Click in the document where you want to insert a bibliography reference.

2   Choose Insert > Indexes and Tables > Bibliography Entry.

3   In the Insert Bibliography Entry window, select the From document content option.

4   Click New.

5   In the Define Bibliography Entry window, enter bibliography information. See Figure 9-31.

      The Short name you enter will be used in bibliography drop-down lists.

6   Click OK.

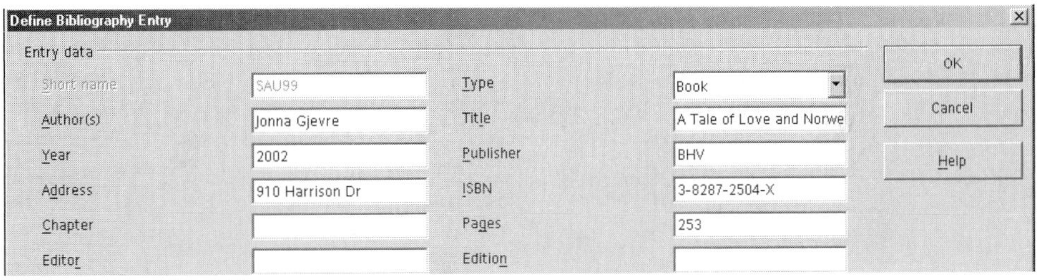

Figure 9-31   A portion of the Define Bibliography Entry window

Inserting Bibliography References in a Document

You can insert references to bibliography items that are stored either in the bibliography database or within a document itself.

See *Entering and Editing Bibliography Information* on page 346.

1   Click in the document where you want to insert a bibliography reference.

2   Choose Insert > Indexes > Bibliography Entry.

3   In the Insert Bibliography Entry window, select whether you want to insert a bibliography reference from the bibliography database or from the document content.

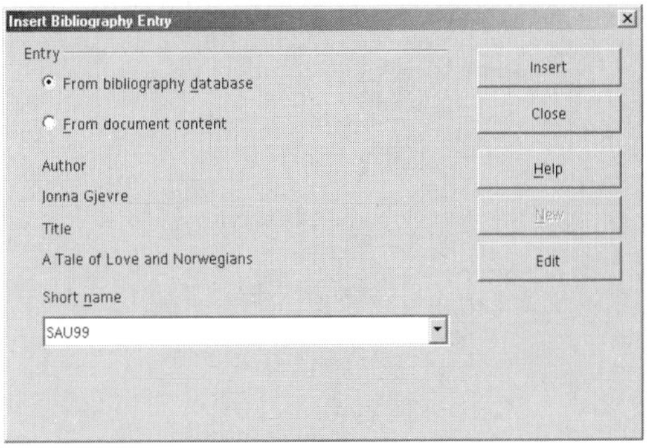

If you select the From document content option, you have to have already created and inserted the bibliography reference using the procedure in *Storing Bibliography*

Information in an Individual Document on page 346 in order to see any items in the drop-down list.

4   In the Short name field, select the bibliography entry you want to insert.

5   Click Insert.

Writer inserts a bracketed reference containing the bibliography item's short name. You can change this reference to show an endnote number rather than the short name. To do this, when you generate the bibliography, be sure in the Insert Index window, on the Index tab, to select the Number entries field.

Generating a Bibliography

You can generate a bibliography for a single document or a master document.

Inserting a Bibliography Into a Single Document

1   Make sure you've inserted bibliography references in the document. See *Inserting Bibliography References in a Document* on page 347.

2   Click in the document where you want to insert the bibliography.

3   Choose Insert > Indexes and Tables > Indexes and Tables.

4   In the Insert Index window, select Bibliography in the Type field.

5   Enter a Title for the bibliography.

6   Select the Number entries option if you want to change all the bibliography references in the document to numbers, as shown in Figure 9-32.

These numbers will correspond with numbered bibliography entries in the generated list.

7   Set options in the remaining tabs. If you need guidance, the information in *Inserting a Table of Contents* on page 327 contains similar information.

8   Click OK.

Figure 9-32   A bibliography reference and a generated bibliography

Inserting a Bibliography Into a Master Document

1   With the master document open, make sure Navigator is open (press the F5 key), and toggle to the master document view in Navigator.

2   In the Navigator window, select the last file of the master document.

3   In Navigator, click and hold down the Insert button, and choose User-Defined Index.

4   In the Type field, select Bibliography.

5   Select the Number entries option if you want to change all the bibliography references in the document to numbers.

    These numbers will correspond with numbered bibliography entries in the generated list.

6   Set options in the remaining tabs. If you need guidance, the information in *Inserting a Table of Contents* on page 327 contains similar information.

7   Click OK.

8   Select the bibliography item in the Navigator (master document view), and click the Move Up or Move Down buttons to move the bibliography to the desired location in the master document.

All parts of a list have their own paragraph formats that you can modify. Click in a line of the table of contents; the style name is highlighted in the Stylist under paragraph styles.

Formatting and Editing Bibliographies

The principles and procedures for formatting and editing bibliographies are the same as those for formatting and editing a table of contents. See page 332

Updating Bibliographies

The procedure for updating a bibliography is the same as that for updating a table of contents. See *Updating or Deleting a Table of Contents* on page 335.

Spacing Before a Section, Index, or Table

Press Alt + Return twice to insert a paragraph return in front of a section (see *Using Sections to Create Multiple Versions of the Same Document* on page 411). This also works with indexes and tables since they're both types of sections. Also, you can delete the table or index (select all except the final carriage return and right-click, then choose Delete). Then when you generate it again, don't select the Protected Against Manual Changes option.

Mail Merges, Business Cards, and More

Getting Started With Business Documents

Letters to everyone on your customer list, business cards with cool graphics in the background, labels, faxes. They're not terribly complicated, you just need to know a little bit before you start.

1   Read *The Basic Steps for Creating and Printing Mail Merges and Business Cards* on page 352.

2   Take a look at *A Little Background on Mail Merges* on page 353.

3   And if you want some more background on where the information is coming from, see *All the Ways You Can Create Stored Data and Bring It Into Documents* on page 354.

The Basic Steps for Creating and Printing Mail Merges and Business Cards

Just as there are two kinds of people in this world (those who are satisfied with vanilla, and those who know that rocky road is the only way to go), there are two kinds of documents you can print in this chapter:

*   Mail merge documents, like a holiday newsletter to all the relatives you really hate, or labels for everyone you need to ship your highly popular grail-shaped beacon to.

*   Fixed data documents: business cards for yourself or any one other person, or return address labels likewise for only one person.

Mail merge documents   Documents based on lots of different data: one letter, saying "Please buy our grail shaped beacons `yournamehere`," addressed to *many* people. The people's names are sucked out of the source of the data, or *data source*.

Steps for making mail merge documents:

1   **Set up the data.** This is all covered in *Setting Up Data to Use in Mail Merge Documents and Business Cards* on page 355.

2   **Create the document you want to print and suck the data into it.** There are lots of ways to do this; it all depends on what you want to do, and how much formatting and work you want to do.

    *   Check out *Creating Mail Merge Letters and Faxes With Data Sources Using AutoPilots* on page 380

    *   *Creating Your Own Mail Merge Documents From Data Sources* on page 393

    *   Or *Dragging a Data Source Field Into a Document* on page 396 and *Doing Additional Formatting to Your Own Data Source-Based Documents* on page 398.

3   **Print**. It's not your ordinary File > Print, so follow the instructions in *Printing* on page 399.

Fixed data documents Documents based on just one set of data: one label or business card document, saying "Rob van der Womplet can be reached at rob@womplet.com and would really like you to hire him to do some Web graphics," containing the information of *one* person. The name is sucked out of fixed data because, you know, why print business cards for a lot of other people? If you did, however, print labels based on your customer list, then they'd automatically be mail merge documents, what with being based on the addresses of *many different people*.

Steps for making mail merge documents:

1   **Set up the data.** This is all covered in *Setting Up Fixed Data for Business Cards or Labels* on page 360.

2   **Create the document you want to print and suck the data into it.** There are lots of ways to do this. Check out *Creating Business Cards and Labels Using Fixed Data* on page 366 and *Envelopes* on page 376.

3   **Print**. Just File > Print like usual.

A Little Background on Mail Merges

A Spoon Full of Mail Merge

A *mail merge* involves inserting the names of data source fields into your document. For example, in the heading of a letter, the inserted data source fields would look something like Figure 10-1:

```
<PREFIX> <FIRSTNAME> <LASTNAME>
<TITLE>
<COMPANY>
<ADDRESS>
<CITY>, <STATEPROV>   <POSTALCODE>

Dear <FIRSTNAME> <LASTNAME>,
```

Figure 10-1   Example of fields in a mail merge letter

These fields form a link to your *data source*, pull the information out of it, and put it into your document. In Writer, you can drag and drop these fields from your data source into your document, or get them into a new document based on a template, using an AutoPilot that walks you through the process.

A single group of information in a data source is called a *record*. A record can include a lot of information, such as a person's first name, last name, address, phone number, email address, spouse's name, children's names, and whether or not you've already sent them a Christmas card.

If you do a mail merge using a one-page letter, all the relevant information in a single record is inserted onto the page. A new page is created for each record used in the database.

You can send mail merges directly to your printer, email them, or you can send them to files, where you can open them and print them out later.

Mail Merge Printing is a Two-Step Process

Any data source printing is a two-phase process:

- First, you use a procedure in this section to create a document, from an AutoPilot, template, or from scratch, containing records from a particular data source. You specify the formatting of the document in general, as well as the data source and the fields to use.

- Then you need to follow the directions in the next main section, *Printing* on page 399, to essentially say "Yes, I really do want to print from that data source," specify a few printing options like filtering, and print.

It's kind of annoying because you'd think you'd be able to just print after the first step, but on the other hand, it gives you more flexibility because it gives you a chance to switch data sources (which works as long as the same field names are in the new data source), mess around with the printing options, etc.

All the Ways You Can Create Stored Data and Bring It Into Documents

When you do mailings, business cards, labels, etc., you have two things: a document, and the data that you pull into the document. There are a bunch of different data sources you can use, and different ways to get that data into your document. Table 10-1 shows you want the options are and where we cover them.

Once you've skimmed the table, go ahead and complete the procedures in this chapter you need to use.

Table 10-1   Topics related to stored data and using it

Tasks you want to do	Where you do it	Where to go in this book
Setting up predefined data: signatures, business cards, etc.	AutoText icon in main toolbar	*Creating AutoText Entries* on page 864
Using those predefined bits of data	AutoText icon in main toolbar	*Inserting AutoText Entries in Your Document* on page 868
Setting up predefined bits of data like page numbers, conditional fields, etc.	Insert > Fields > Other, or double-click a field to edit it or create a new one	*Editing Fields* on page 863
Using those bits of data	Insert > Fields > Other	*Inserting Fields* on page 857
Setting up databases and data sources	Tools > Data Sources	Chapter 35, *Creating and Modifying Data Sources,* on page 869
Taking predefined bits of data and/or fields from data sources, and doing mail merges	File > AutoPilot > Letter or other selections, or View > Data Source	This chapter.
Creating a form for viewing data source information, containing fields, buttons, etc., using the AutoPilot	File > AutoPilot > Form	*Forms, What Are They Good For?* on page 926
Creating your own form for viewing data source information	Form Functions icon on the main toolbar	*Creating a Form Using AutoPilot* on page 932
Making fields in forms run a macro when you complete a task in a form	Form Functions icon, right-click. Choose Control or Form	*Macro Basics* on page 965
Bring a data source into a spreadsheet using the Data Pilot	Data > Data Pilot	*Using the Data Pilot to Make a Spreadsheet With Automatic Totals* on page 520

Setting Up Data to Use in Mail Merge Documents and Business Cards

Want mail merges? Go straight to *Setting Up Data for Your Mail Merge Documents.* Want business cards or labels with information about just you, or just one other person? Go to *Setting Up Fixed Data for Business Cards or Labels.*

For extra tips, read these sections:

* *Switching to a Different Data Source for a Mail Merge Document*
* *Advanced Information Management With the Fields Window*

Setting Up Data for Your Mail Merge Documents

You have to do these two procedures:

- Set up at least one data source; see Chapter 35, *Creating and Modifying Data Sources*, on page 869.

- Tell the program which data source to use for templates, in *Specifying the Data Source to Use With Templates* on page 356.

The rest is nice to know but not vital.

Specifying the Data Source to Use With Templates

This procedure is different from the AutoPilot that simply lets you create a data source from an address book (*Setting Up Any Address Book as a Data Source* on page 902).

To use templates, see *Creating Mail Merges From Data Sources Using Templates* on page 389.

OpenOffice.org

All the templates, etc. in StarOffice don't come with OpenOffice.org. However, Travis Bauer's excellent Web site, www.ooextras.org, has what might be called a plethora of templates and other "extras."

The program needs to know what data to use in templates You need to specify which single data source and table you want to use for templates in its Business Correspondence and Personal Correspondence categories. The templates have a bunch of fields like Name and Address, all of them crying out for you to specify where it should suck Name and Address data from.

Every time you open a template, you'll get the window at right. To use your data source, select the Several Recipients option. To just use the template for one copy, select One Recipient.

Use of This Template
Addressee
○ One recipient
● Several recipients (address database)
OK
Cancel

You can't specify it when you open the template; you need to set it up ahead of time.

Usually it's an address book, but it can be any data source you want.

What the program does when you open a template   It all depends on whether it knows what to do.

- If you specified a data source before you open a template, then the program's happy and uses that data. (It gives you the choice to just ignore data sources if you only want to use the template for one recipient.)

- If you don't specify a data source, the program will just throw up its hands in defeat and put a bunch of "placeholder" fields in the templates instead of fields that correspond to data. You get to delete them and type the right data over them, or just delete them. This isn't disastrous; you just need to know, that's what happens if the program can't get at any real data.

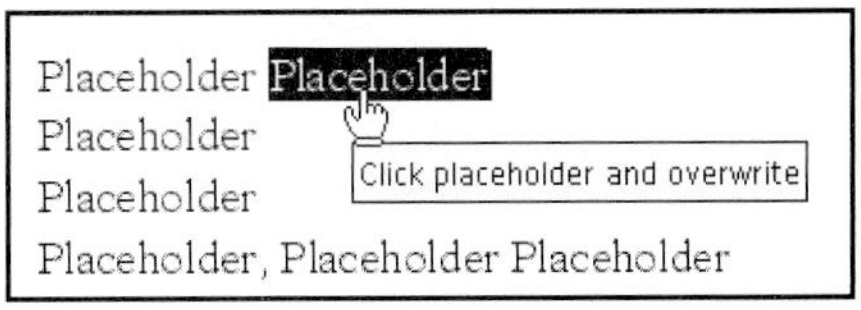

The placeholders also appear anytime there's a field in the template, such as Third Alternate Fax Number, that you don't have in your data source or didn't set up in the following procedure to map to something in your data source.

Selecting the data source to use   Just follow these steps; it's pretty simple.

1   Be sure that the address book or books you want to use is set up as a data source. See *Setting Up Any Address Book as a Data Source* on page 902.

2   Choose File > Templates > Address Book Source.

3   The window in Figure 10-2 will appear. Enter the appropriate options, then click OK.

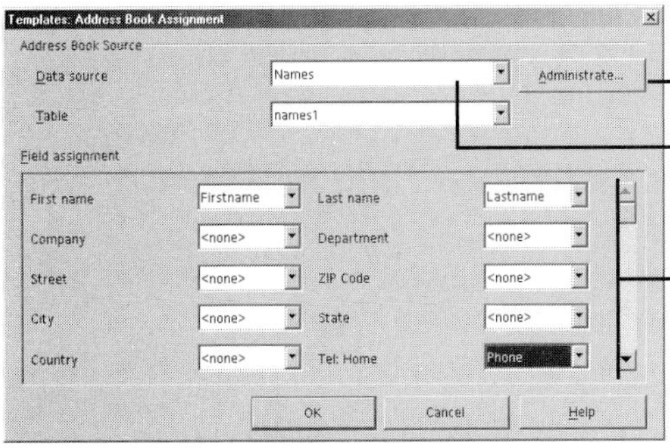

Click Administrate if you want to make some changes to the selected data source; it opens the Data Source window.

Select the data source and the table to use. You should just have one table for the address book.

Program templates use many address book fields. When it opens a template, the program will look in your address book for a value called First Name, Company, etc.—the labels at left. If it can't find something in your address book that seems similar, it will create an empty "Placeholder" field in the template. Here's where you can tell the program that First Name to it is Firstname in your address book, that Tel: Work to it is Work Phone in your address book, and so on.

Figure 10-2   Selecting the data source to use as a business correspondence default address book

Note – You might end up with empty spaces or lines if your data source isn't all that the program thinks it should be. See *Fixing Problems With Empty Fields* on page 404 to fix this.

Use Queries or Tables as the Source of Data

Queries and tables are treated the same way; if you find it useful to use your "just the first and last names in the addressbook table of everyone in Colorado" query instead of the whole addressbook table, use that query instead of the table. See *Exporting Data Sources to Another Format* on page 922 for more information.

Only One Data Source Table Can Be Used Per Document

Unfortunately, you can't print a document with more than one table without getting extra-techy with queries. (See Chapter 35, *Creating and Modifying Data Sources*, on page 869.)

How to Send Letters to Everyone in Your Writer Document

Got a Writer file full of names and addresses that you want to do a mail merge with? No problem. Just set it up as a data source.

1   Save the Writer file as plain text. (Choose File > Save As and in the format dropdown list of the Save As window, select Text.)

2   Give it a name like `myfileofaddresses.txt`. Put it in a directory where it's the only text file, or where it cohabits with other text files that you want grouped in the same data source.

3   Set up that text file as a data source. See *Creating a Data Source Based on Text Files* on page 881.

Then just follow the steps you've already seen outlined in *The Basic Steps for Creating and Printing Mail Merges and Business Cards* on page 352.

How to Send Letters to Everyone in Your Calc or Excel Spreadsheet

This is even easier. No preliminary steps; just see *Creating a Data Source for a Spreadsheet* on page 884. Then just follow the steps you've already seen outlined in Setting up Data Sources for Mail Merge Documents

Editing the "Fixed" Data Values in Business Document Templates

When you create a mail merge document from an AutoPilot or template, you'll often see something like the fields at right. These values are drawn from all over the program, including user properties, so how you edit them varies. Sometimes you can't edit them, but most of the time you can get to them by double-clicking, or selecting them and clicking Edit, as described in this procedure.

Sender (fixed)

Sender (fixed), Sender (fixed) Sender (fixed)
Tel.: Sender (fixed), Fax: Sender (fixed)

Date (fixed)

• Choose Tools > Options > *program* > User Data and enter the values there.

- Double-click the field in the document; the Edit Fields window will appear. Select the field and click Edit or double-click it. If it's editable, an editing window will appear.

Restricting the Data Source Information to Use in a Document, Using Queries and Filters

You might not always want to just base a document on all the records, with all the fields, in a table. See the following for instructions.

Limiting the Information in a Document Using Queries

Queries are subsets of a table, such as "give me the first name and last name of everyone in my address book in Colorado." (Expressed in SQL or using the query design window; see *Exporting Data Sources to Another Format* on page 922 for more information.) You get to limit the number of fields the program uses, as well as the number of records.

You save that query, with a name like "colorado_names", and you can use that instead of a table as the source of the data the program sucks into your document.

Limiting the Information in a Document Using Filters

With filters, you can include and/or exclude specific records. Choose View > Data Sources and in the data source area, click the Default Filter icon in the object bar to bring up the Filter window. In the Filter window, set the filtering conditions.

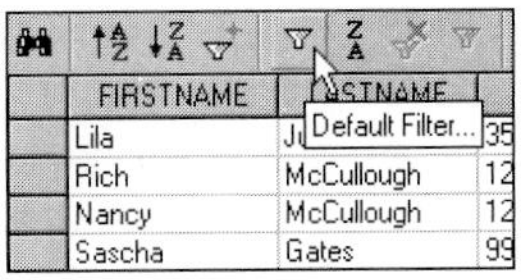

Use Figure 10-3 for guidance.

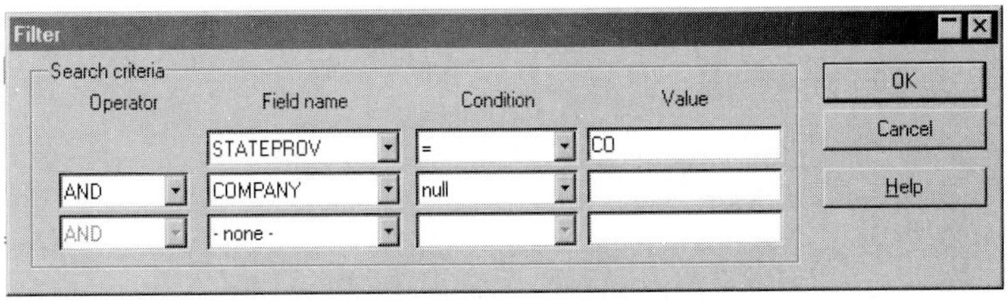

This filter setting will produce the following results: the record will be included in the merge if its STATEPROV value equals CO; and it will be included if the COMPANY field is empty (null). All other records will be excluded.

Figure 10-3   Basic record filtering

Setting Up Fixed Data for Business Cards or Labels

Read the next section, *The Three Sets of Fixed Data Variables Used for Business Cards*. Then decide what kind of data to set up, at least at first, based on the instructions in that section.

The adventurous can also check out *Creating Your Own AutoText for Business Cards and Correspondence* on page 361, *Editing Field Values in Business Card AutoText* on page 361, and *Advanced Information Management With the Fields Window* on page 365.

The Three Sets of Fixed Data Variables Used for Business Cards

There's fixed data for business cards all over the place; three different kinds of fixed data, in fact three different sources. We think this is kind of odd, and wanted to point it out to avoid confusion. It's particularly odd and potentially confusing since sometimes you see exactly the same business card layout choices, but with different data than you get in another window.

- **Values in the Business Cards window (best for structured if lengthy business card creation and lots of card design choices)** – To edit the values for the Business Card window business cards, see *Creating a Sheet of Business Cards From a Template* on page 366. To create business cards, see the same procedure.

- **Predefined AutoText entries (best for quick business card creation with one design choice)** – To edit the values for the standard business card AutoText entries, see *Editing Field Values in Business Card AutoText* on page 361. To use the entries in general, see *Inserting AutoText Entries in Your Document* on page 183. To create business cards based on the data, see *Creating Business Cards From the Business Card Template* on page 373.

- **Just plain label information (best for plain, quick cards based on data you might have already filled in)** – To edit the values for labels or business cards created by choosing File > New > Labels and selecting the Address option in the Labels tab, choose Tools > Options > *program* > User Data. You might have already entered this data. To create business cards or labels this way, see *Creating Simple Labels or Business Cards by Choosing File > New* on page 370.

Creating Your Own AutoText for Business Cards and Correspondence

If there's a set of boilerplate text you use frequently that you don't want to retype every time you use it, such as an email signature, trademarked term, or company letterhead heading, create an AutoText entry for it in Writer. This is also used when you create business cards from the templates or use other business correspondence templates. When you do this, you can insert it quickly—either with a keyboard shortcut or by selecting it from a list of AutoText items.

AutoText entries can be formatted and can include graphics, tables, and fields.

For more information about AutoText generally, see *Creating and Inserting AutoText* on page 864.

Editing Field Values in Business Card AutoText

Note – These are not the same values used for creating a sheet of business cards by choosing File > New > Business Cards. For more information, see *The Three Sets of Fixed Data Variables Used for Business Cards* on page 360.

If you plan to use any of the business card AutoText or business correspondence templates, it's a good idea to edit the fields now that will show up in those templates. There's a lot of preformatted AutoText in business card format that's very convenient to use; just insert it by clicking on the AutoText icon in the main toolbar. However, since it's all business cards for someone named `Frederick Fexample`, you'll probably want to update the information.

Take a look at the business cards Before you begin, get a sense of the business cards you'll be able to use. With Writer active, click the AutoText tool in the main toolbar. In the AutoText window (see Figure 10-4), expand the Business Cards categories. You'll need to edit the values for Personal cards and Business cards. Most of the designs simply reuse a basic set of information; however, there's a lot of information: personal and business names and addresses, slogans, and so on.

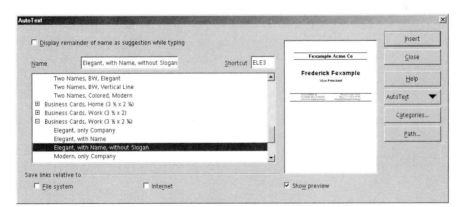

Figure 10-4   Business Card categories

Decoding the system We have to admit, we spent some time struggling over how exactly this whole fields/AutoText thing works. You double-click on one thing, you get A; you double-click on it again and you get B. So expect to be confused. But stick to these steps, and you'll be able to change the values for standard fields used in templates and AutoText.

Here's the basics. There are a lot of fields to edit when you choose Insert > Fields > Other. Mostly, you can ignore them. Click on the Variables tab. Now you're closer to seeing the only things you need to worry about right now. How it works is laid out in Figure 10-5.

Now that you know how it works, here's the procedure.

1 Choose Insert > Fields > Other.

2 Select the Variables tab, then select the User Fields type in the left column of the window.

3 Select the first item in the Select list. Its name and value will appear at the bottom of the window. Change the value to one appropriate for your business cards and click the green check mark.

4 Repeat the previous step for each item in the Selection list.

5 Click Close.

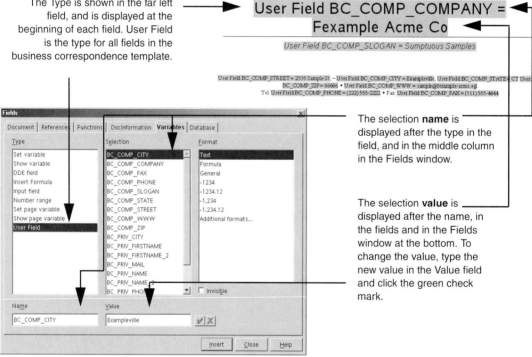

The Type is shown in the far left field, and is displayed at the beginning of each field. User Field is the type for all fields in the business correspondence template.

The selection **name** is displayed after the type in the field, and in the middle column in the Fields window.

The selection **value** is displayed after the name, in the fields and in the Fields window at the bottom. To change the value, type the new value in the Value field and click the green check mark.

Figure 10-5   How the fields you insert with business card AutoText relate to the fields in the Fields window

Switching to a Different Data Source for a Mail Merge Document

Imagine you've created the world's greatest holiday newsletter, and you've set it up as a mail merge to print a copy for everyone on your usual list. But you've just met a bunch of great people through your winter Ultimate Frisbee hot tub league and now you want to send the newsletter to everyone in the Ultimate online registration dBase database. What do you do? Just use the same newsletter document, but switch data sources.

Using the Exchange Database Window

Both databases must show matching field names and field types, so that after the exchange, the fields for inserting field names still display meaningful results.

1   Open the document.

2   Choose Edit > Exchange Database.

3   Select the new data source and table in Figure 10-6 and click OK. Be sure to select the new database and table also in the Form Letter window when you print the document.

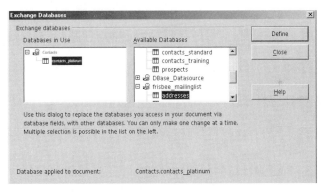

Figure 10-6   Exchanging databases

Selecting a Different Data Source in the Form Letter Window

You can easily switch from one data source to another just by selecting a different data source and table when you're in the Form Letter window, ready to print. (Choose File > Form Letter; see *Printing* on page 399.) However, the field names must be exactly the same or a lot of data won't get printed.

Manually Switching Data Source or Fields

You can switch from one table to another easily as long as it has exactly the same field names. See *Printing* on page 399. If not, use this procedure.

1   Open a template.

2   Double-click the field you want to change. The Edit Fields: Database window will appear, displaying the data source and field you double-clicked. This is shown in Figure 10-7.

3   In the Database Selection list, scroll to the data source, table, and field that you want to use instead, and double-click it.

4   Repeat until you've changed all the fields. (You can click the right-facing arrow to go to the next field in the document.) All fields must be in the same table.

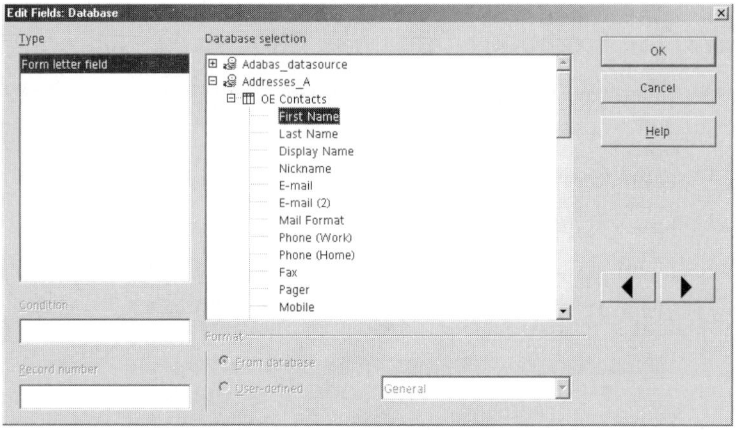

Figure 10-7   Changing to a different data source, table, and field

Advanced Information Management With the Fields Window

Press Ctrl + F2, or double-click a field in a template you create in this chapter, and you'll see the Fields window. Its contents and tabs vary depending on what's going on in the document you've got open. You can manage data for mail merges or fixed-data documents using this window. To learn more about using and defining these fields, see *Creating and Inserting Predefined Information Using Fields* on page 284. To learn the syntax for conditional fields, see the extensive online help.

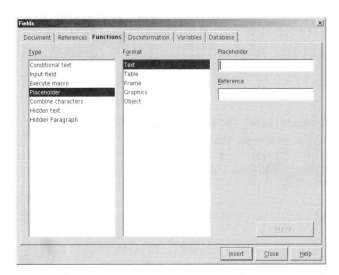

Figure 10-8   The fields window, controlling static and function-based field content

The fields window gives you a great deal of control over how fields data prints. You can define the static text for variables like the ones used in business cards, or set up conditional printing terms like the ones covered in *Fixing Problems With Empty Fields* on page 404.

Creating Business Cards and Labels Using Fixed Data

The standard way to create a sheet of business cards is with the provided templates. To provide maximum convenience and simplicity, we've provided additional alternate ways to create business cards.

Note – Before you begin, review *The Three Sets of Fixed Data Variables Used for Business Cards* on page 360.

Creating a Sheet of Business Cards From a Template

There are about three times as many business card layouts as you could ever possibly need. Here's how to select a design, format and printing options, and fill out the information that'll show up in your business cards.

Create Business Cards Using the Existing User Data and a Labels Template

If you just choose File > New > Labels, you can create business cards by selecting the Address data option in the Labels tab. Otherwise you'll need to enter a bunch of new information, personal and business versions, in the next procedure. The labels you get that way are plainer, though; this procedure provides templates of design with graphics, etc. See *Creating Simple Labels or Business Cards by Choosing File > New* on page 370 for more detail on how to do it that way.

Creating Business Cards and Entering New Data

Note – The personal and business information that will appear on the cards is stored in *officedirectory*\user\config\registry\instance\org\openoffice\ Office\Writer.xml. See *Fun With XML* on page 147 for more information about these files.

1   Choose File > New > Business Cards.

2   The Business Cards window will appear. Figure 10-9 through Figure 10-14 explain what to enter in the fields for each tab.

3   Click New Document; the business card document will appear. An example is shown in Figure 10-9.

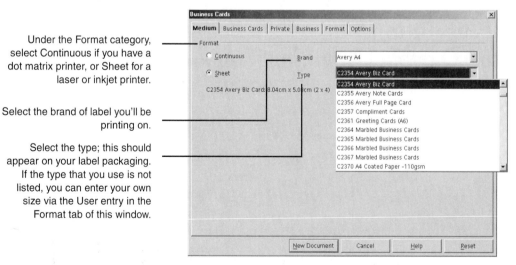

Under the Format category, select Continuous if you have a dot matrix printer, or Sheet for a laser or inkjet printer.

Select the brand of label you'll be printing on.

Select the type; this should appear on your label packaging. If the type that you use is not listed, you can enter your own size via the User entry in the Format tab of this window.

Figure 10-9   Selecting the layout and paper you'll be printing on

Select the card design you want to use. The design will be displayed in the preview area at right.

Select the category of the business card you want to use. If you created or moved business cards you want to use to your own category, that category will be listed here.

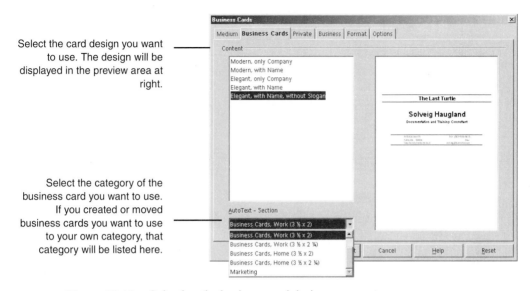

Figure 10-10   Selecting the business card design you want

Enter all the information you think you might want on private business cards. It's a good idea to enter it all anyway; it's easier to delete it later than fill it in, and you might like one of the private card designs better than any of the business designs.

Note that the Zip, City, Country and State aren't where you'd expect.

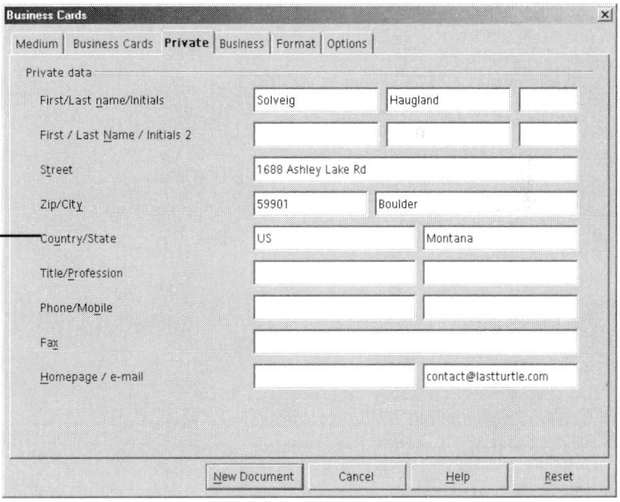

Figure 10-11   Entering information to display in private (home/personal) card designs

Enter all the information you think you might want on business cards.

Note that the Zip, City, Country and State aren't where you'd expect.

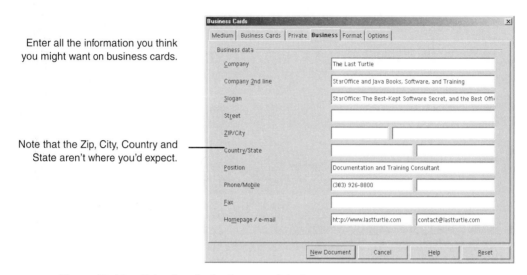

Figure 10-12 Selecting the business card design you want

If you didn't find the dimensions and layout you needed in the Medium tab's Type list, create it here. If you found the type you needed, just ignore this window.

If you create your own layout here, be sure to test it thoroughly on scratch paper before you print on business card paper.

Click Save to save this design; the Save Label Format window will appear where you can select a category and name it. You'll be able to select it again later in the Medium tab.

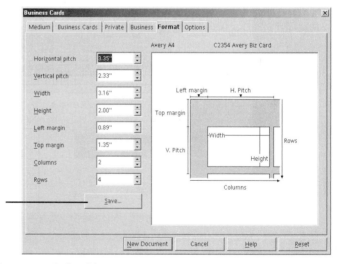

Figure 10-13 Specifying a user-defined layout

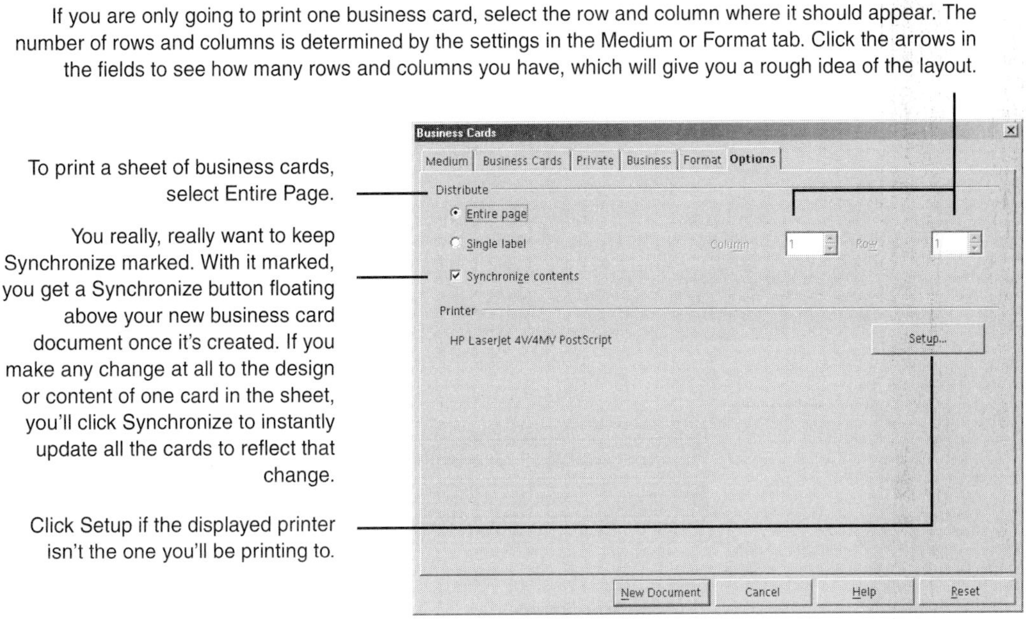

If you are only going to print one business card, select the row and column where it should appear. The number of rows and columns is determined by the settings in the Medium or Format tab. Click the arrows in the fields to see how many rows and columns you have, which will give you a rough idea of the layout.
To print a sheet of business cards, select Entire Page.
You really, really want to keep Synchronize marked. With it marked, you get a Synchronize button floating above your new business card document once it's created. If you make any change at all to the design or content of one card in the sheet, you'll click Synchronize to instantly update all the cards to reflect that change.
Click Setup if the displayed printer isn't the one you'll be printing to.
Business Cards
Medium
Business Cards
Private
Business
Format
Options
Distribute
Entire page
Single label
Column
Row
Synchronize contents
Printer
HP LaserJet 4V/4MV PostScript
Setup...
New Document
Cancel
Help
Reset

Figure 10-14 Selecting whether to print one card or a whole sheet

If you make any changes, click this button to update all instances of the card in the document.
Synchronize Labels

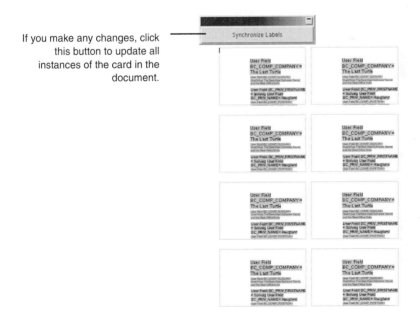

Figure 10-15 An example of the business card created using the Business Cards window

If you keep getting just one label in your new document rather than multiples, check the rows and columns settings in the Format tab of the Business Cards window.

| Columns | 2 |
| Rows | 4 |

Note – If all this all seems unnecessarily complicated, it's simpler if you follow the steps in *Creating Simple Labels or Business Cards by Choosing File > New* on page 370 or *Creating Business Cards From the Business Card Template* on page 373 for more information.

Creating Simple Labels or Business Cards by Choosing File > New

See also *Creating Labels for a Mail Merge From the Business Card Template* on page 373, and *Envelopes* on page 376. They're two other ways to create documents addressed to records in a data source. The first procedure lets you select from some fancy predefined templates; this procedure doesn't give you any additional layout options besides data source or address data, and the option to specify the size of the label or card.

You can print labels for other people, or using your own data from Tools > Options > *program* > User Data, using this procedure.

1   Choose File > New > Labels. The Labels window will appear.

2   Make the appropriate entries in each of the three tabs, then click New Document. Use Figure 10-16 to Figure 10-18 for guidance. Figure 10-19 shows a finished example.

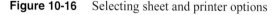

Select Address to just use your own data that you entered under Tools > Options > *program* > User Data. It'll erase anything you've already specified from the data source.

To print a label for each record in a data source (or just a few), select the data source and table, then insert the appropriate fields. Click in the Label Text area and press Return every time you want a line break.

Select Continuous for dot matrix or Sheet for inkjet and laserjet printers.

Select the Brand and Type for the labels you'll be printing on; it should appear on the label packaging. If what you want isn't displayed, you can create your own format in the Format tab.

Figure 10-16   Selecting sheet and printer options

Note – As you insert the fields, afterwards in the new document, be sure you space the fields appropriately and put in the appropriate carriage returns. Otherwise you'll end up with: `RuthieBoughten666AspenLaneBerthoudCO80022`

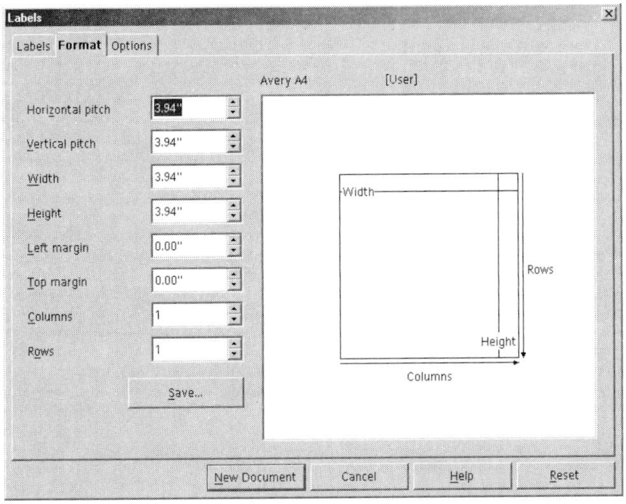

If you didn't find the layout you wanted in the Brand and Type selection of the Labels tab, set up the layout here.

Figure 10-17   Selecting sheet and printer options

If you are only going to print one business card, select the row and column where it should appear. The number of rows and columns is determined by the settings in the Medium or Format tab. Click the arrows in the fields to see how many rows and columns you have, which will give you a rough idea of the layout.

To print a sheet of business cards, select Entire Page.

You really, really want to keep Synchronize marked. With it marked, you get a Synchronize button floating above your new business card document once it's created. If you make any change at all to the design or content of one card in the sheet, you'll click Synchronize to instantly update all the cards to reflect that change.

Click Setup if the displayed printer isn't the one you'll be printing to.

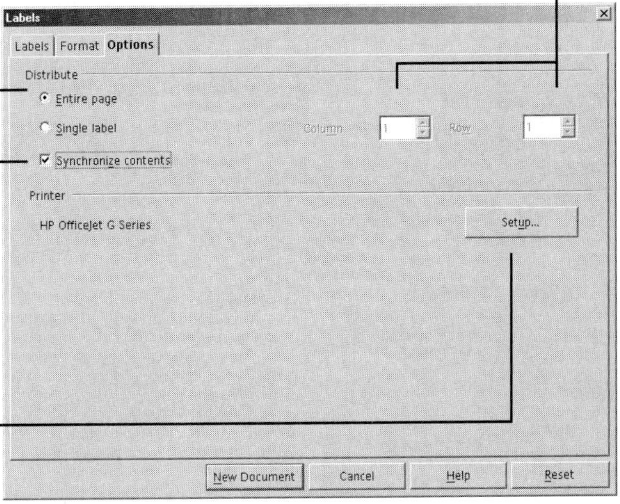

Figure 10-18   Selecting sheet and printer options

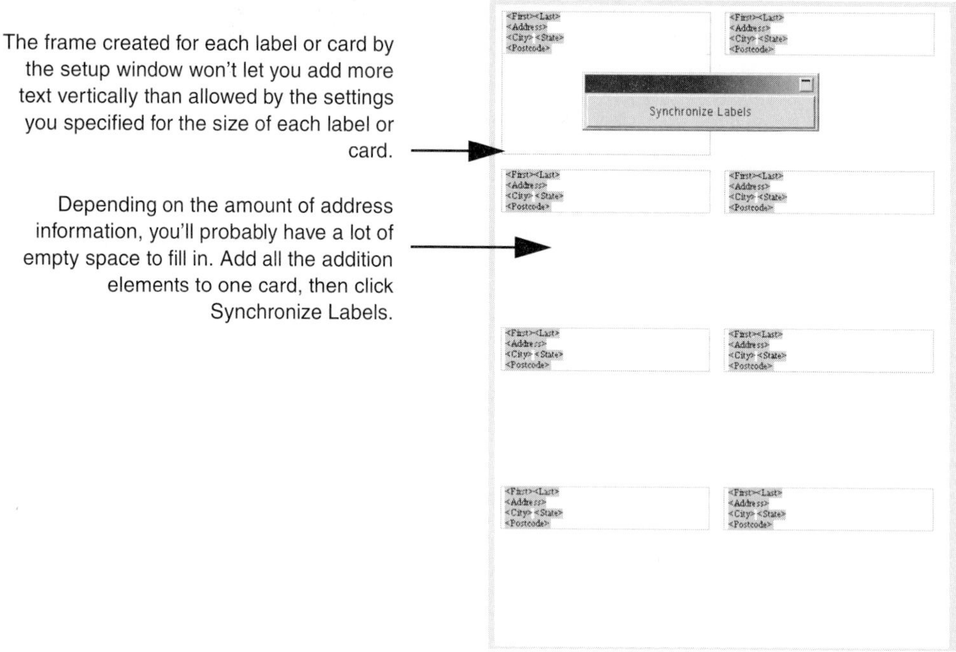
The frame created for each label or card by the setup window won't let you add more text vertically than allowed by the settings you specified for the size of each label or card.
Depending on the amount of address information, you'll probably have a lot of empty space to fill in. Add all the addition elements to one card, then click Synchronize Labels.
Synchronize Labels
<First><Last>
<Address>
<City> <State>
<Postcode>

Figure 10-19 Labels created using the Labels window

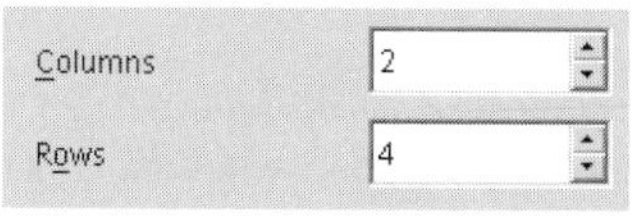
Columns
2
Rows
4

If you keep getting just one label in your new document rather than multiples, check the rows and columns settings in the Format tab of the Labels window.

To print the labels, if you used a data source, see *Printing* on page 399. Otherwise just choose File > Print.

Creating Business Cards From the Business Card Template

Figure 10-45 shows the business card template. Creating business cards is similar to creating a letter; see *Creating Documents From a Letter Template* on page 390. Be sure you've set up the data that the template uses; double-click each field to define it, or choose Tools > Options > *program* > User Data.

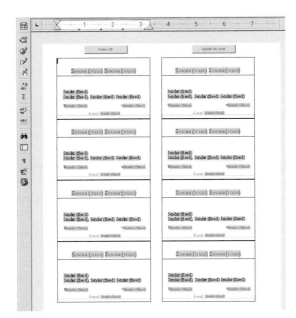

Figure 10-20   Example of the Business Card template

Creating Labels for a Mail Merge From the Business Card Template

Just use the procedure for creating business cards, to get the right formatting. Use the template or the AutoPilot; see *Creating a Sheet of Business Cards From a Template* on page 366 or *Creating Business Cards From the Business Card Template* on page 373. Then drag the right information into that preformatted structure, following the directions in *Dragging a Data Source Field Into a Document* on page 396.

Note – Be sure to use the same data source as the data source for the letters that the envelopes go with.

Editing AutoText Business Card Design and Content

If you like the business cards, mostly, then just tweak them to get them how you want them. Follow the steps in *Editing Existing AutoText Items* on page 181.

Creating Your Own Business Cards Without Variables

While having variable fields for your name, address, etc. allows you flexibility, it also adds a level of complexity. It's also hard to tell exactly how much space the text will take up when the field names are displayed. Here's a way to make it simple, so you don't even need to do the extra data source-related printing step at the end of this procedure.

Creating a Single Business Card

Note – Be sure you've set up your business data following the instructions in *Creating Your Own AutoText for Business Cards and Correspondence* on page 361.

Type up your business information in a 2 x 3 1/2 (or other appropriate dimension) format. Use a frame (Insert > Frame) to keep the text in the right dimensions, if you like.

Instead, you can insert any of the Business Card AutoText entries (see *Inserting AutoText Entries in Your Document* on page 183) to use as a model. Then just select the text and type your own plain text over it. Your text should retain the character and paragraph formatting.

Then just make it into an AutoText entry. See *Creating AutoText Entries* on page 180.

Creating a Sheet of Business Cards Without Variables

1   Choose File > New > Business Cards.

2   In the Business Cards window, click the Medium, Business Cards, Format, and Options tabs, and make the selections you want. (See *Creating a Sheet of Business Cards From a Template* on page 366 for more detail.) The Business Cards tab is shown in Figure 10-2.

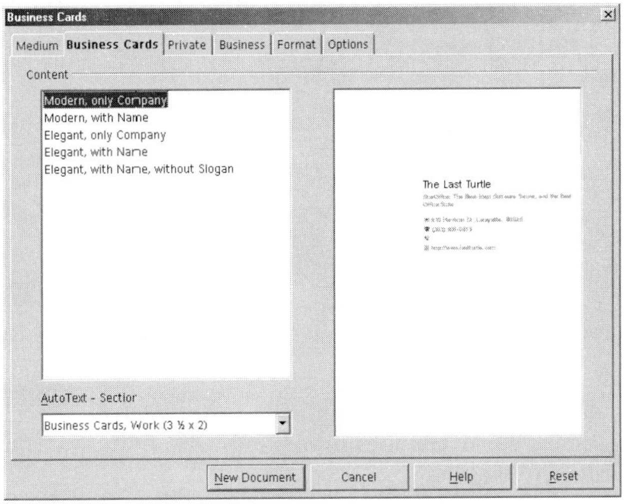

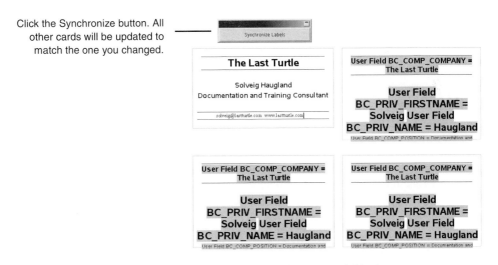

Figure 10-21   Selecting the business card design you want

3   As with the procedure for creating a single business card, now simply type your own text over the fields. This is shown in Figure 10-2.

Click the Synchronize button. All other cards will be updated to match the one you changed.

Figure 10-22   Redesigning the card and entering nonvariable data

4   Click the Synchronize button. All other cards will be updated to match the one you changed.

5   Save the document as a Writer document, or as a template if you want to use it as a template.

Quickly Inserting a Single Existing Business Card Using AutoText

The quickest way to get one or more business cards is to just insert one of the predefined AutoTexts. Click the AutoText icon on the main toolbar and navigate to the right category, then select the business card you want.

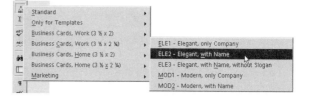

The business card data will be inserted in the document. To create multiple copies, just copy and paste it, or else use one of the business card templates.

To edit the values of the fields, see *Editing Field Values in Business Card AutoText* on page 361.

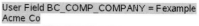

Note – Remember that this data is different than the data you would get from using the next procedure, *Creating a Sheet of Business Cards From a Template* on page 366.

To print what you've created, see *Printing* on page 399.

Envelopes

One word: don't. The envelope template is badly set up and doesn't connect to a data source. It's adequate if you just want to print one envelope with data that you type in, but there's no benefit in doing that rather than making you own and choosing the envelope layout in Format > Page. You're much better off creating your own envelope template or document. See *Using the Envelope Template* on page 376.

However, to make matters worse, on Windows the envelope printing doesn't work. You'll shred a lot of envelopes proving this, so take our word for it. Print labels instead. See *Creating Labels for a Mail Merge From the Business Card Template* on page 373.

If you feel strongly about printing envelopes using the existing template, we sincerely wish you luck, and are now backing out of the room.

Using the Envelope Template

1   Choose File > New > Templates and Documents.

2   Open the Personal Correspondence and Documents category.

3   Select the Envelope template and click Open.

4   Select One Recipient or Several Recipients in the dialog box that appears; however note that since the envelope template doesn't in reality support using data sources, and the fields you get only look like they're going to print from your data source, it hardly matters what you pick here.

5   The appropriate fields from your assigned data source should appear in the document. If necessary, double-click any of them to edit them, or delete them and type the correct information. An example is shown in Figure 10-23.

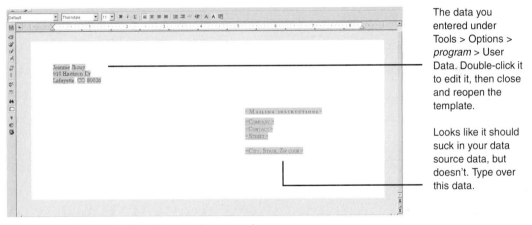

The data you entered under Tools > Options > *program* > User Data. Double-click it to edit it, then close and reopen the template.

Looks like it should suck in your data source data, but doesn't. Type over this data.

Figure 10-23   The envelope template

6   If you need to do any modification of the envelope size, choose Format > Page and select a different envelope size in the dropdown list shown in Figure 10-24.

7   Print a test page on a standard sheet of paper. The data is printed on the left side of the paper, as you'll see on the test page. Use that test page to determine how to insert the envelope.

8   Print the envelope. It doesn't matter whether you choose portrait or landscape in the Print Options window; the envelope always prints with the return address in the lower left part of the printable area.

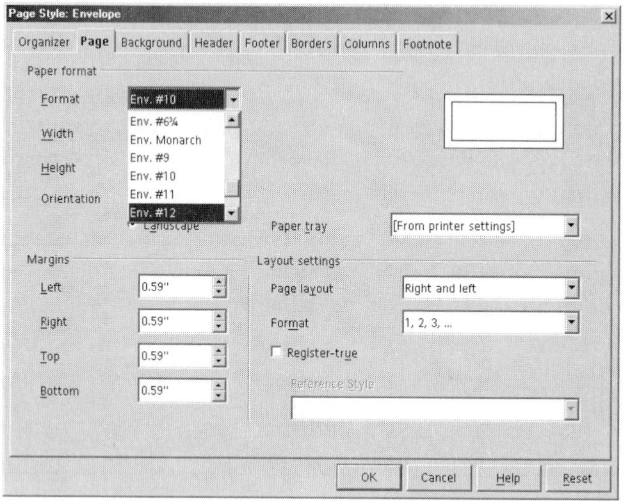

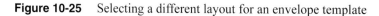

Figure 10-24 Selecting a different layout for an envelope template

Creating Your Own Envelope Template

Note – If you want to print envelopes for a mail merge, you must not save the envelope document in this procedure until after you've dragged the database fields into the document. We don't know why it works that way.

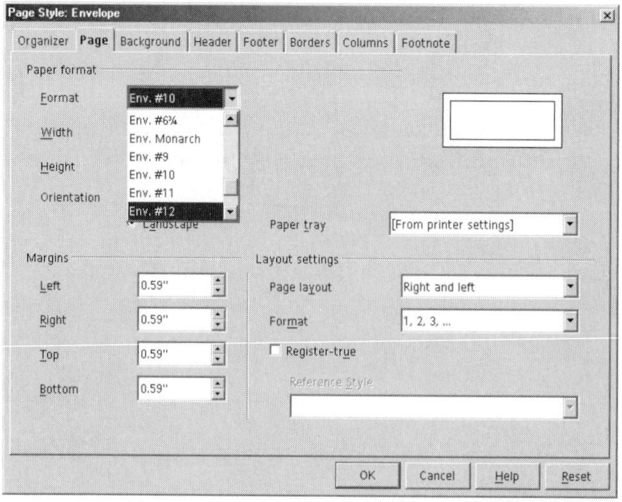

Figure 10-25 Selecting a different layout for an envelope template

1   Create a new empty text document. Don't save it. Choose Format > Page and select the envelope dimension you want as shown in Figure 10-25 on page 378. Consult the online help for advice on picking one.

2   Select the landscape layout. This affects only how you see it onscreen, not how it prints. This just makes it possible to use normal text input for the addresses instead of using the sideways text tool.

3   In the same menu, select Manual Feed.

4   Type your return address in the upper left corner.

5   Enter the address information for the recipient(s).

    •   For just one recipient, just type the information.

    •   For multiple recipients for a mail merge, choose View > Data Sources. Select the data source and table, and drag the appropriate fields in and format them, as shown in Figure 10-26. See *Dragging a Data Source Field Into a Document* on page 396 for more detail.

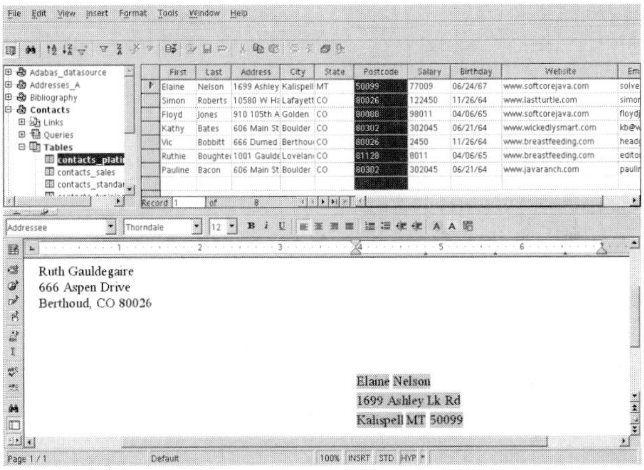

Figure 10-26   Dragging data source fields into an envelope template

6   Print a test page on a standard sheet of paper to see how the document prints: what side up, left or right, whether it's the right size, etc.

7   Insert the envelope correctly in the paper tray.

8   Print the envelope(s).

    •   To print a letter to just one recipient whose address you've already typed in, simply choose File > Print.

    •   To print a mail merge to several recipients, choose File > Form Letter. Follow the instructions in *Printing or Emailing Mail Merge Documents* on page 400.

> **Note –** It doesn't matter whether you choose portrait or landscape in the Print Options window; the envelope always prints with the return address in the lower left part of the printable area.

Creating Mail Merge Letters and Faxes With Data Sources Using AutoPilots

Use these procedures to create and print any letter, fax, agenda, or memo with different data in every copy. Examples include personally addressed letters to everyone on your customer list and envelopes to match; labels for everyone on your holiday gift list.

Choose File > AutoPilot; you'll see that you can make a letter, fax, agenda, or memo.

Use AutoPilots for just formatting The AutoPilots let you specify a lot about a document—formatting, what elements to put in, and what data source to use, if any. You can click Create in any window; you don't have to stay on for the whole ride if all you want is the basic document for an Elegant Fax, for instance.

Use AutoPilots as an easy way to hook up to a data source While hooking up to a data source is pretty easy in general, it's definitely simple in the AutoPilots. It's a great way to create a letter individually addressed to each of your customers.

Creating a Letter Using the Letter AutoPilot

1   Choose File > AutoPilot > Letter. The window in Figure 10-27 will appear.

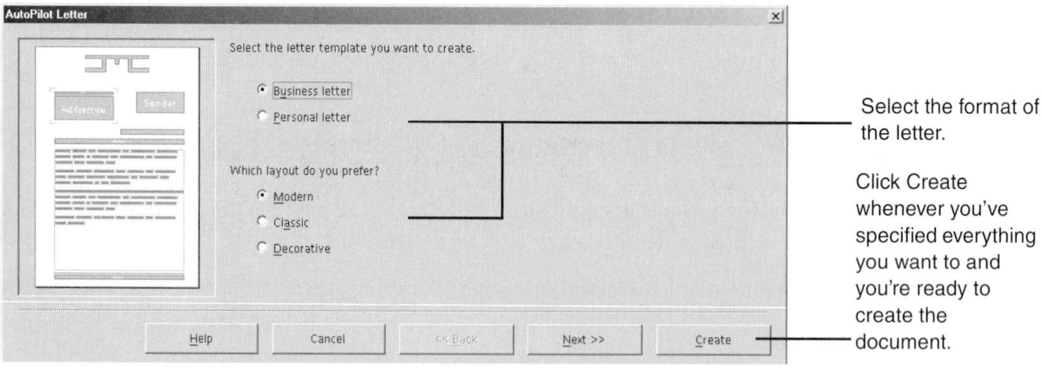

Figure 10-27   Selecting a letter type and layout

2   Click next; the window in Figure 10-28 will appear. Select a logo if any, specify whether it's text or graphics, and set the location and size.

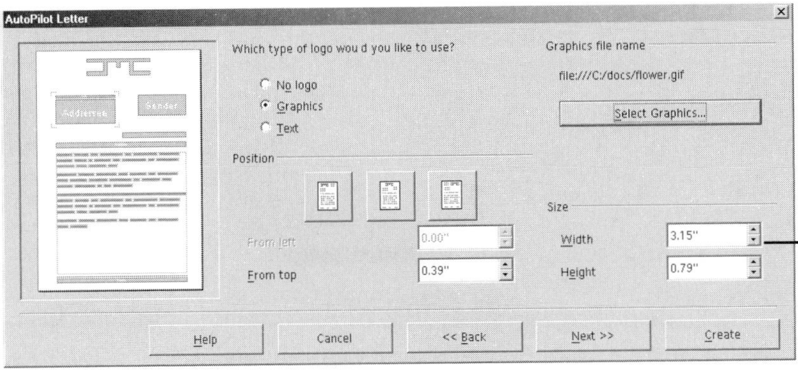

The default measurement isn't adjusted automatically for any graphic you insert. If you use a graphic, it will almost certainly be skewed in the created document. However, it's easy to adjust it in the finished document so this entry doesn't matter.

Figure 10-28   Specifying information about your logo

3   Click next; the window in Figure 10-29 will appear. Enter the sender address if it isn't displayed automatically from data by choosing Tools > Options > *program* > User Data.

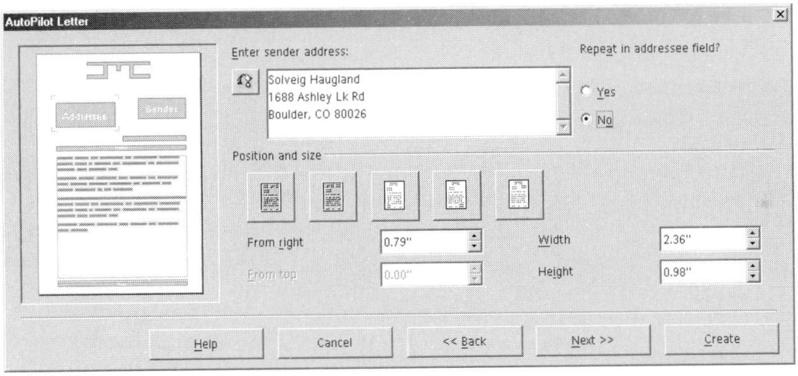

Specify where your address should appear.

Figure 10-29   Entering your address and positioning it

4   Click next; the window in Figure 10-30 will appear. If you want to create a mail merge with a different letter addressed to each person in a list, select the data source, table, and fields.

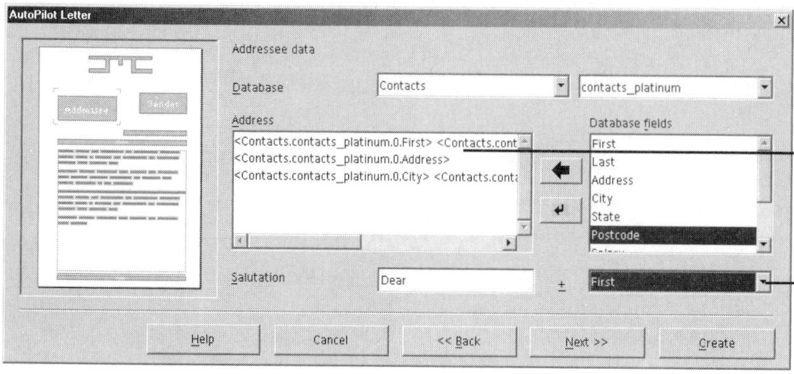

Click in the Address column and press Enter, in order to make line breaks. Also enter the correct spacing between fields. Otherwise all the fields you insert will be on the same line. You can fix this in the generated document, as well.

Specify a salutation, if any.

Figure 10-30   Specifying the data source and table containing information about the people you're sending the letter to

5   Click Next; the window in Figure 10-31 will appear. Enter the dates, page numbers, subjects, etc. that you want included. You can delete some or all of them later if necessary.

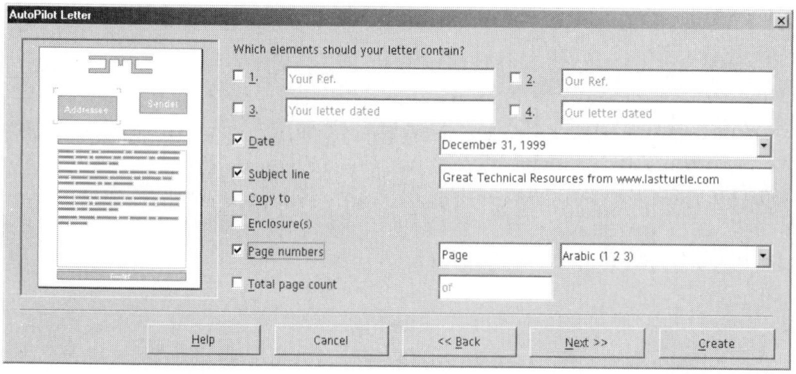

Select and type extra elements to include, such as references and subject lines, and specify how page numbering if any should be formatted.

Figure 10-31   Setting up page numbering, subject lines and dates, and references

6   Click Next; the window in Figure 10-32 will appear. Specify position and content for the footer, if any.

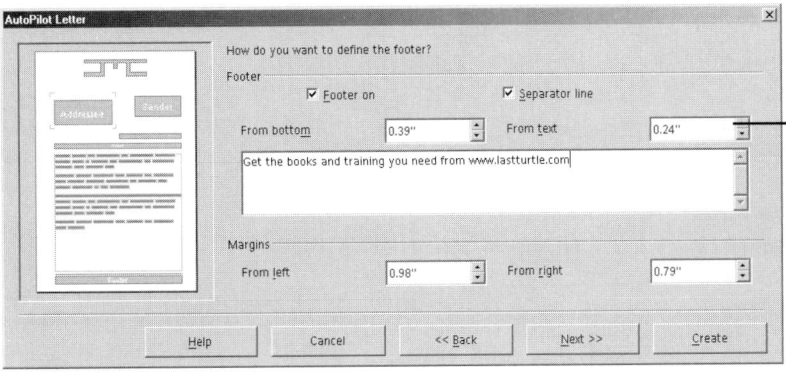

Selecting this option inserts a line above the footer; see the bottom of Figure 10-36 on page 385 for an example.

Figure 10-32   Setting up the footer

7   Click Next; the window in Figure 10-33 will appear. Specify how the second and subsequent pages should be laid out.

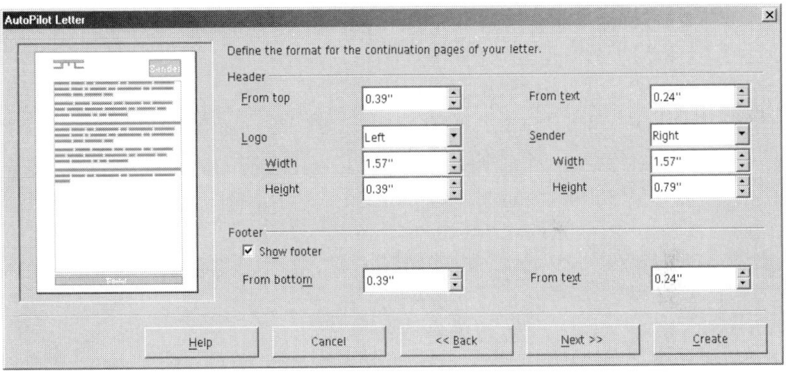

Figure 10-33   Setting up the header

8   Click Next; the window in Figure 10-34 will appear. Enter information about how the template you're creating will be named and saved, and how documents generated from it will be named and saved. The template is the document generated by the AutoPilot; the document is a saved instance of the template, or a file generated by the File > Form Letter printing process.

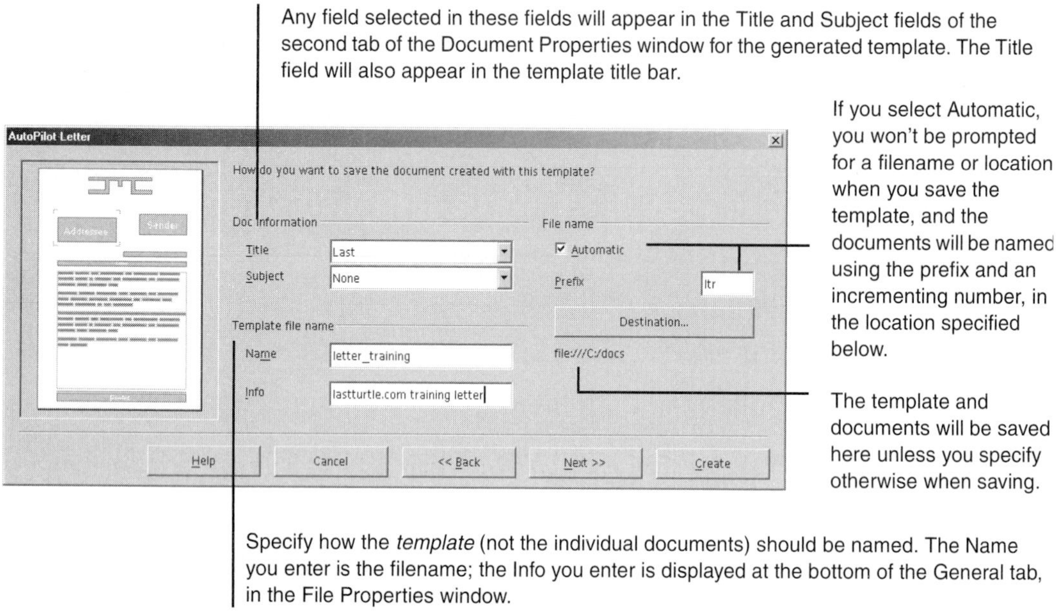
Any field selected in these fields will appear in the Title and Subject fields of the second tab of the Document Properties window for the generated template. The Title field will also appear in the template title bar.
If you select Automatic, you won't be prompted for a filename or location when you save the template, and the documents will be named using the prefix and an incrementing number, in the location specified below.
The template and documents will be saved here unless you specify otherwise when saving.
Specify how the *template* (not the individual documents) should be named. The Name you enter is the filename; the Info you enter is displayed at the bottom of the General tab, in the File Properties window.
AutoPilot Letter
How do you want to save the document created with this template?
Doc information
Title
Last
Subject
None
File name
Automatic
Prefix
ltr
Destination...
file:///C:/docs
Template file name
Name
letter_training
Info
lastturtle.com training letter
Help
Cancel
<< Back
Next >>
Create

Figure 10-34 Specifying save options

9 Click Next; the window in Figure 10-35 will appear. Specify the miscellaneous details it asks for, then click Create.

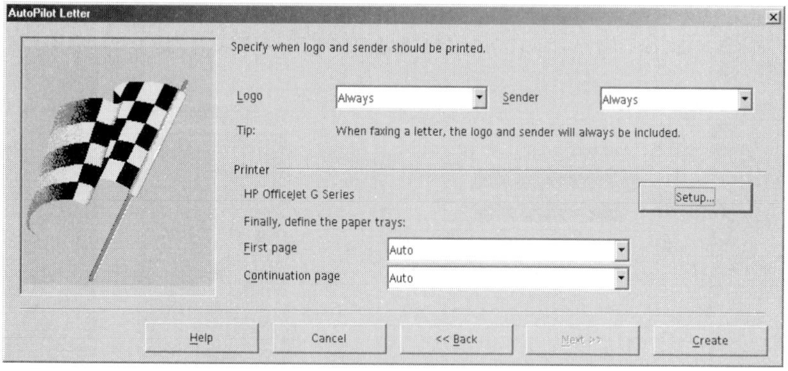
AutoPilot Letter
Specify when logo and sender should be printed.
Logo
Always
Sender
Always
Tip:
When faxing a letter, the logo and sender will always be included.
Printer
HP OfficeJet G Series
Setup...
Finally, define the paper trays:
First page
Auto
Continuation page
Auto
Help
Cancel
<< Back
Next >>
Create

Figure 10-35 Specifying finishing details

10 The template will be created and opened; an example is shown in Figure 10-36.

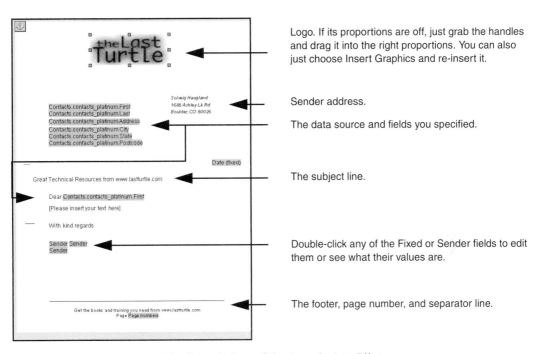

Figure 10-36   The first window of the Agenda AutoPilot

To print what you've created, if you used data source fields, see *Printing* on page 399.

Creating a Fax Using the Fax AutoPilot

Note – To set up faxing, see *Creating UNIX Printers* on page 60. See also *Creating Documents From a Fax Template* on page 392.

Choose File > AutoPilot > Fax. Enter the appropriate options; use Figure 10-37 through Figure 10-44 for guidance.

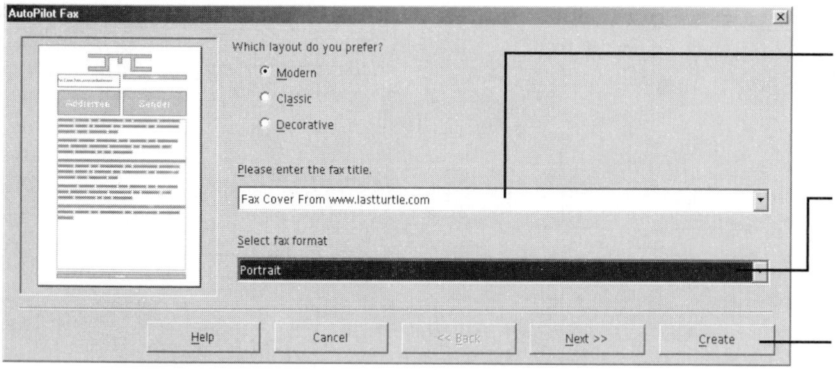
AutoPilot Fax
Which layout do you prefer?
Modern
Classic
Decorative
Please enter the fax title.
Fax Cover From www.lastturtle.com
Select fax format
Portrait
Help
Cancel
<< Back
Next >>
Create
Select or type the text for the title displayed at the top left of the fax.
Specify the fax format/orientation.
Click Create whenever you're ready to create the document.

Figure 10-37 Selecting a letter type and layout

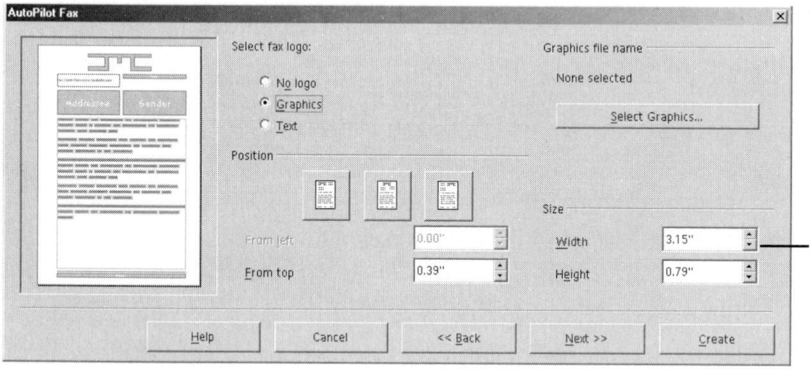
AutoPilot Fax
Select fax logo:
No logo
Graphics
Text
Position
From left
0.00"
From top
0.39"
Graphics file name
None selected
Select Graphics...
Size
Width
3.15"
Height
0.79"
Help
Cancel
<< Back
Next >>
Create
The default measurement isn't adjusted automatically for any graphic you insert. If you use a graphic, it will almost certainly be skewed in the created document. However, it's easy to adjust it in the finished document so this entry doesn't matter much.

Figure 10-38 Selecting a logo and logo location

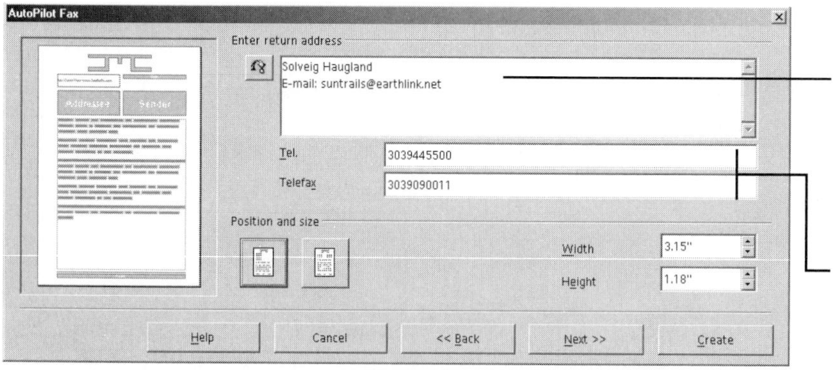
AutoPilot Fax
Enter return address
Solveig Haugland
E-mail: suntrails@earthlink.net
Tel.
3039445500
Telefax
3039090011
Position and size
Width
3.15"
Height
1.18"
Help
Cancel
<< Back
Next >>
Create
The information entered under Tools > Options > *program* > User Data is displayed here; edit it or add to it. It will appear on the fax at the top.
Enter your own Phone and Fax information so the faxed person can

Figure 10-39 Specifying your contact information

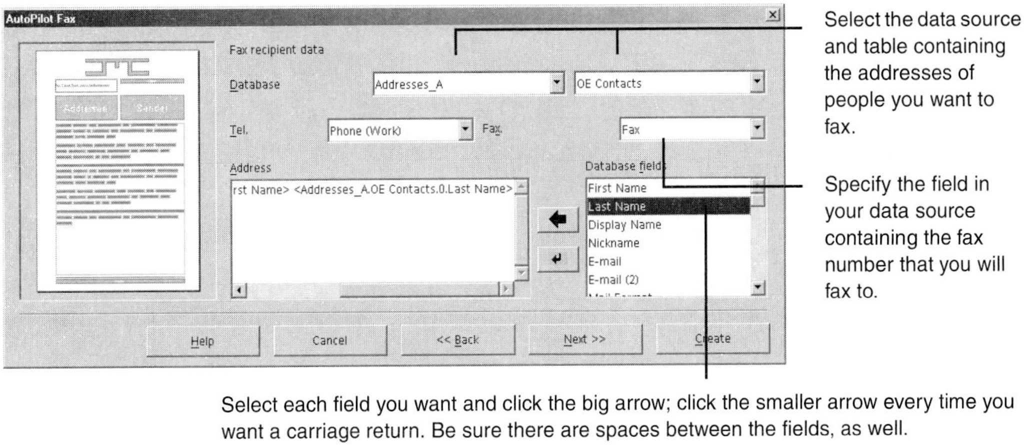

AutoPilot Fax
Fax recipient data
Database
Addresses_A
OE Contacts
Tel.
Phone (Work)
Fax
Fax
Address
rst Name> <Addresses_A.OE Contacts.0.Last Name>
Database fields
First Name
Last Name
Display Name
Nickname
E-mail
E-mail (2)
Help
Cancel
<< Back
Next >>
Create
Select the data source and table containing the addresses of people you want to fax.
Specify the field in your data source containing the fax number that you will fax to.
Select each field you want and click the big arrow; click the smaller arrow every time you want a carriage return. Be sure there are spaces between the fields, as well.

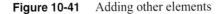

Figure 10-40 Specifying who to fax to

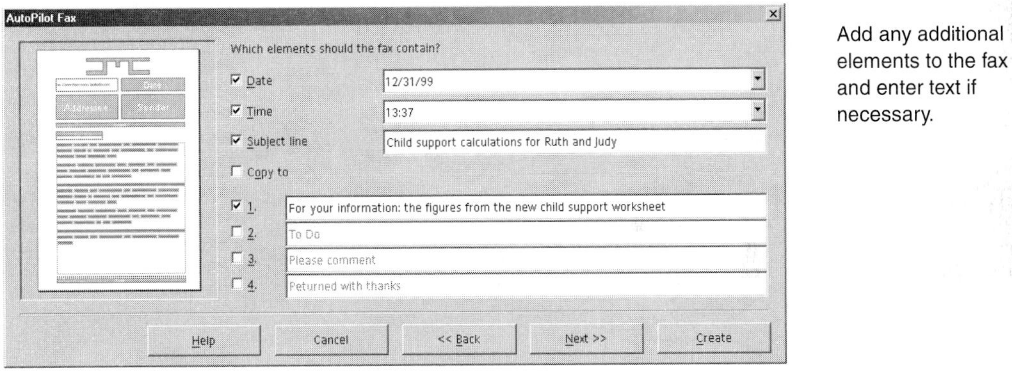

AutoPilot Fax
Which elements should the fax contain?
Date
12/31/99
Time
13:37
Subject line
Child support calculations for Ruth and Judy
Copy to
1.
For your information: the figures from the new child support worksheet
2.
To Do
3.
Please comment
4.
Returned with thanks
Help
Cancel
<< Back
Next >>
Create
Add any additional elements to the fax and enter text if necessary.

Figure 10-41 Adding other elements

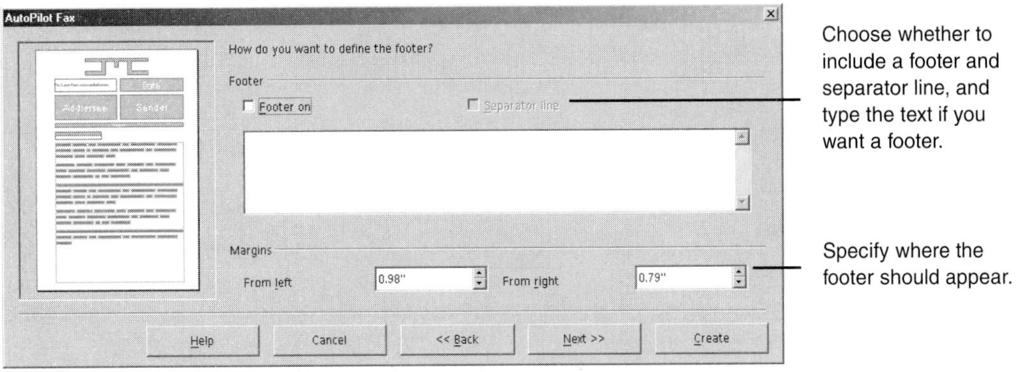

AutoPilot Fax
How do you want to define the footer?
Footer
Footer on
Separator line
Margins
From left
0.98"
From right
0.79"
Help
Cancel
<< Back
Next >>
Create
Choose whether to include a footer and separator line, and type the text if you want a footer.
Specify where the footer should appear.

Figure 10-42 Setting up a footer

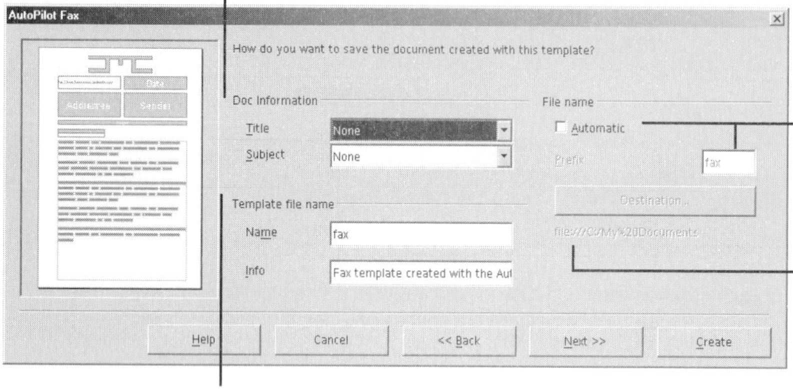
Any field selected in these fields will appear in the Title and Subject fields of the second tab of the Document Properties window for the generated template. The Title field will also appear in the template title bar.
If you select Automatic, you won't be prompted for a filename or location when you save the template, and the documents will be named using the prefix and an incrementing number, in the location specified below.
The template and documents will be saved here unless you specify otherwise when saving.
Specify how the *template* (not the individual documents) should be named. The Name you enter is the filename; the Info you enter is displayed at the bottom of the General tab, in the File Properties window.
AutoPilot Fax
How do you want to save the document created with this template?
Doc Information
Title
None
Subject
None
File name
Automatic
Prefix
fax
Destination...
Template file name
Name
fax
Info
Fax template created with the Aut
Help
Cancel
<< Back
Next >>
Create

Figure 10-43 Specifying save options

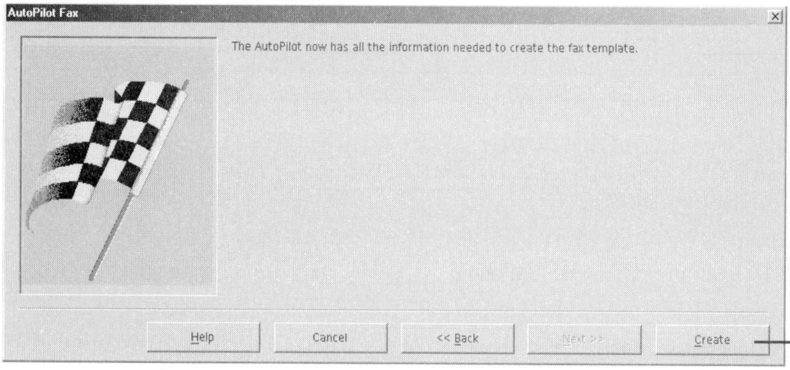
AutoPilot Fax
The AutoPilot now has all the information needed to create the fax template.
Help
Cancel
<< Back
Next >>
Create
You're done; click Create.

Figure 10-44 The process is done; click Create.

To fax what you've created, if you used data source fields, see *Printing* on page 399.

Creating an Agenda or Memo Using an AutoPilot

The agenda and memo are simple and don't involve reliance on data. Just choose File > AutoPilot > Agenda or File > AutoPilot > Memo and the AutoPilot will walk you through. The first window is shown in Figure 10-45.

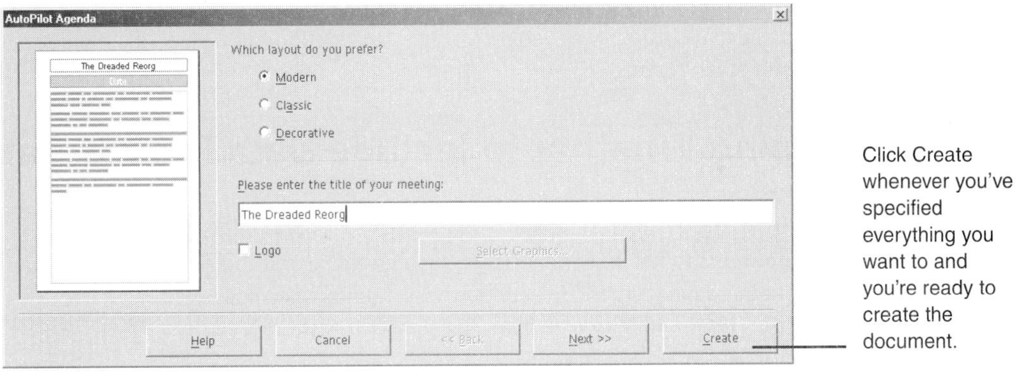

Click Create whenever you've specified everything you want to and you're ready to create the document.

Figure 10-45   The first window of the Agenda AutoPilot

Creating Mail Merges From Data Sources Using Templates

Choose File > New > Templates and Documents. The templates in the Business Correspondence and Personal Correspondence and Documents are suitable for business cards or mail merges. Both categories are shown in Figure 10-46.

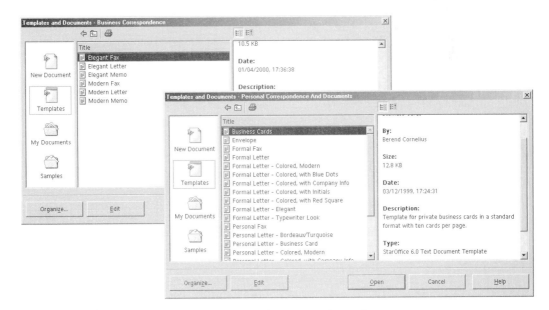

Figure 10-46   Business or personal correspondence documents

All the templates, etc. in StarOffice don't come with OpenOffice.org. However, Travis Bauer's excellent Web site, `www.ooextras.org`, has what might be called a plethora of templates and other "extras."

Choosing Whether to Include Data From a Data Source

The program wants to fill in its data fields, such as Name and Zip code, with information from one of your data sources. Be sure you've set up the data source already; see *Specifying the Data Source to Use With Templates* on page 356.

Before you use any template where you want to create a separate copy for each record in a data source, check that the right data source is set up. You can't change to a different source (not easily, at least) once you've opened the template.

Every time you open a template, you'll get the window at right. To use your data source, select the Several Recipients option. To just use the template for one copy, select One Recipient.

Creating Documents From a Letter Template

Figure 10-47 shows examples of two of the letter templates. To use one of the templates, follow these steps.

Note – The process is very simple, really—the following steps just provide more detail about it all. Choose File > New > Templates and Documents, open a category and template, and select One Recipient or Several Recipients when prompted. That's all.

---

1   Check that you're using the right data source for templates by choose File > Templates > Address Book Source. Switch to another one if necessary. See *Specifying the Data Source to Use With Templates* on page 356 for more information.

2   Choose File > New > Templates and Documents.

3   In the Templates and Documents category, be sure Templates is selected in the column at left.

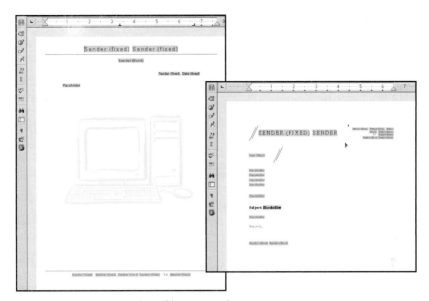

Figure 10-47   Examples of letter templates

4 Double-click a category, typically Business Correspondence or Personal Correspondence and Templates. (See Figure 10-46.) The templates in that category will appear. Select one to see more information about it in the right-hand display area.

5 To create a new untitled document based on the selected template, click Open. The document will appear.

Note – To edit the template itself, click Edit, then make the changes and save under the same name.

---

6 The Use of This Template window at right will appear. To use your data source, select the Several Recipients option. To just use the template for one copy, select One Recipient.

7 If you selected Several Recipients, the fields in the document that the program can find fields for will change to indicate the data source and field name. The data source will appear above the document, splitting the screen. An example is shown in Figure 10-48.

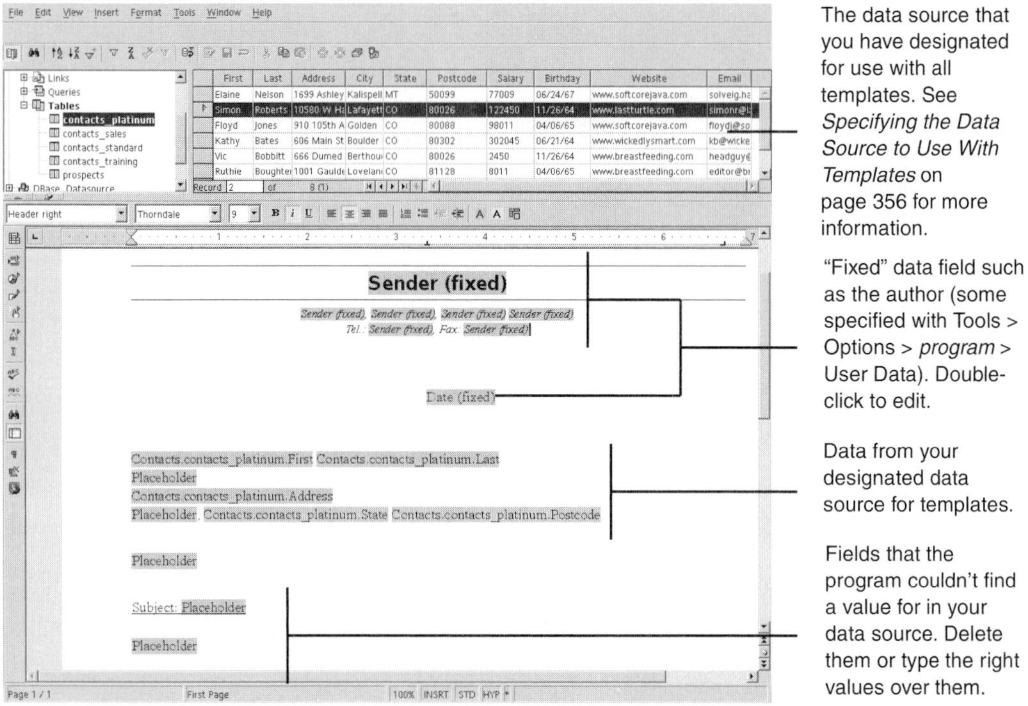

The data source that you have designated for use with all templates. See *Specifying the Data Source to Use With Templates* on page 356 for more information.

"Fixed" data field such as the author (some specified with Tools > Options > *program* > User Data). Double-click to edit.

Data from your designated data source for templates.

Fields that the program couldn't find a value for in your data source. Delete them or type the right values over them.

Figure 10-48   Document created from a template, with its corresponding data source

8   To view the values of the fields rather than the field names, choose View > Fields to remove the check mark next to Fields.

9   To change the format or value of any of the Fixed fields, double-click it and change it in the Edit Fields window that appears.

If any Placeholder fields are displayed, it means the program couldn't find fields in your designated data source for the information that's supposed to be displayed. Delete the fields or type over them with the right data. You can also drag in fields from a data source; see *Dragging a Data Source Field Into a Document* on page 396.

Creating Documents From a Fax Template

An example of a fax template is shown in Figure 10-49.

Creating a fax from a fax template is similar to creating a letter; see *Creating Documents From a Letter Template* on page 390.

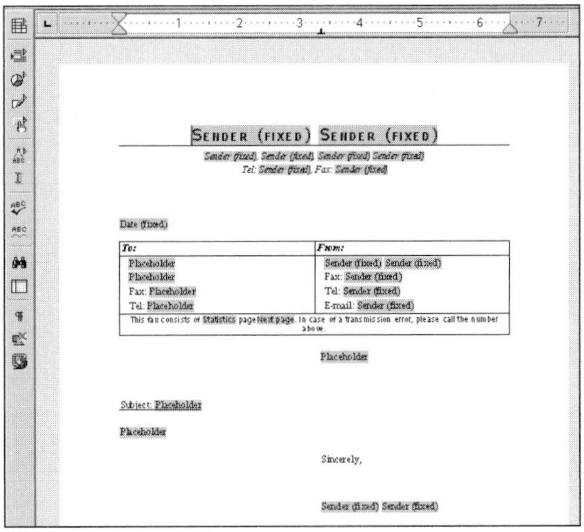

Figure 10-49   Example of a fax template

Creating Your Own Mail Merge Documents From Data Sources

This section simply covers how to "roll your own" if the AutoPilot or template approach doesn't suit your needs. It shows you how to get information from your data sources quickly and simply into documents you create yourself. (For more information, see Chapter 35, *Creating and Modifying Data Sources*, on page 869).

Inserting Data Source Data as Fields or Plain Text

If all you want to do is get some information from data sources into a regular ol' Writer document, here's how. (You can use the dragging approach in spreadsheets, too.)

You can insert the data as fields or plain text. The advantage of inserting as fields is that the data is still defined as X field from Y table from Z data source. You can change data sources later as long as the name of the field is the same. Figure 10-50 shows an example of both.

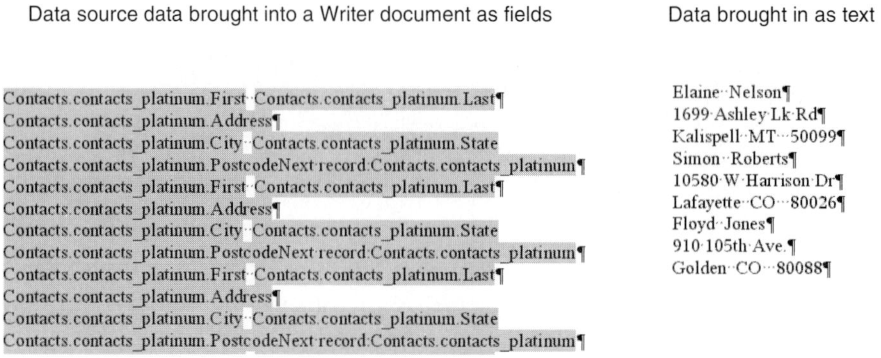
Data source data brought into a Writer document as fields
Data brought in as text
Contacts.contacts_platinum.First Contacts.contacts_platinum.Last¶
Contacts.contacts_platinum.Address¶
Contacts.contacts_platinum.City Contacts.contacts_platinum.State
Contacts.contacts_platinum.PostcodeNext record:Contacts.contacts_platinum¶
Contacts.contacts_platinum.First Contacts.contacts_platinum.Last¶
Contacts.contacts_platinum.Address¶
Contacts.contacts_platinum.City Contacts.contacts_platinum.State
Contacts.contacts_platinum.PostcodeNext record:Contacts.contacts_platinum¶
Contacts.contacts_platinum.First Contacts.contacts_platinum.Last¶
Contacts.contacts_platinum.Address¶
Contacts.contacts_platinum.City Contacts.contacts_platinum.State
Contacts.contacts_platinum.PostcodeNext record:Contacts.contacts_platinum¶
Elaine Nelson¶
1699 Ashley Lk Rd¶
Kalispell MT 50099¶
Simon Roberts¶
10580 W Harrison Dr¶
Lafayette CO 80026¶
Floyd Jones¶
910 105th Ave.¶
Golden CO 80088¶

Figure 10-50 Data source brought in as fields and as text

1 Open a new Writer document.

2 Choose View > Data Sources.

3 Expand the data source viewing list at the left and navigate to the data source and table you want to get data from, as shown in Figure 10-51.

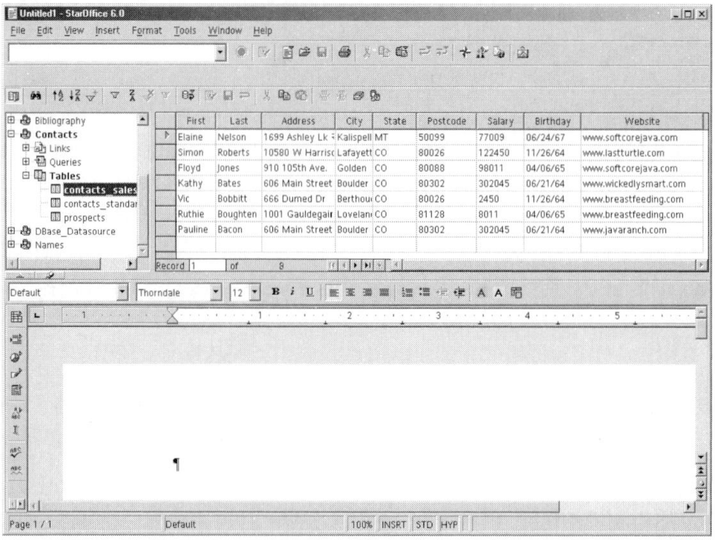
Untitled1 - StarOffice 6.0
File Edit View Insert Format Tools Window Help
Bibliography
Contacts
Links
Queries
Tables
contacts_sales
contacts_standar
prospects
DBase_Datasource
Names
First Last Address City State Postcode Salary Birthday Website
Record 1 of 8
Default
Thorndale
Page 1 / 1
Default
100% INSRT STD HYP

Figure 10-51 Viewing data source fields

4 Click the empty rectangle at the upper left corner as shown in Figure 10-52.

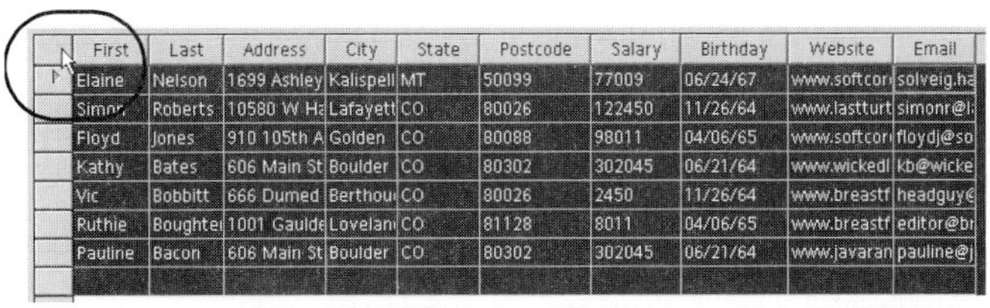

Figure 10-52   Selecting the data in the data source viewer to drag to the document

5   Drag the table into the document. The window in Figure 10-53 will appear. Make the appropriate entries and click OK.

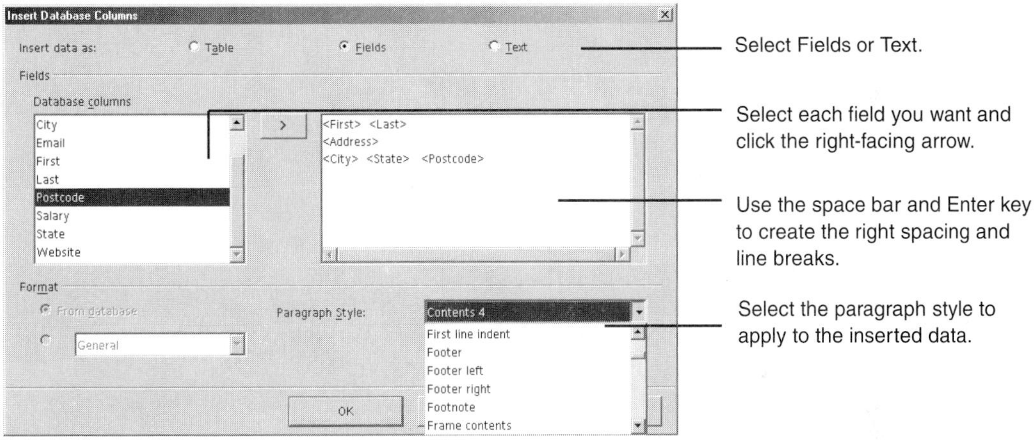

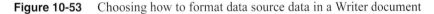

Figure 10-53   Choosing how to format data source data in a Writer document

To print what you've created, see *Printing* on page 399.

Formatting Data Source Data as a Writer Table

If all you want to do is get some information from data sources into a regular ol' Writer document, here's how. (You can use the dragging approach in spreadsheets, too.) Choose View > Data Sources.

1   Open a new Writer document.

2   Choose View > Data Sources.

3   Expand the data source viewing list at the left and navigate to the data source and table you want to get data from.

4   Click the empty rectangle at the upper left corner and drag it into the document.

5 The window in Figure 10-54 will appear. Make the appropriate entries and click OK.

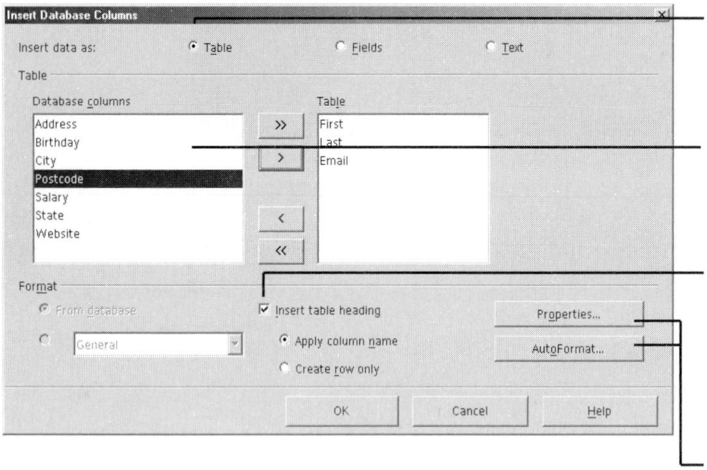
Insert Database Columns
Insert data as:
Table
Fields
Text
Table
Database columns
Address
Birthday
City
Postcode
Salary
State
Website
Table
First
Last
Email
Format
From database
General
Insert table heading
Apply column name
Create row only
Properties...
AutoFormat...
OK
Cancel
Help
Select Table.
Select each field you want and click the right-facing arrow. It's usually not a good idea to just insert all with the double arrow because they will be created in the table in the order they're listed here: alphabetically.
Choose whether to insert a table heading row. Apply Column Name creates a heading row based on the column headings listed in the Database Columns list; Create Row Only creates a blank heading row.
Click Properties or AutoFormat to apply formatting to the table you'll insert.

Figure 10-54 Specifying the structure of the table to insert

Figure 10-55 shows an inserted table; the AutoFormat button was used to apply the blue table format theme.

You can print it directly without an extra step since the data is plain text, not fields.

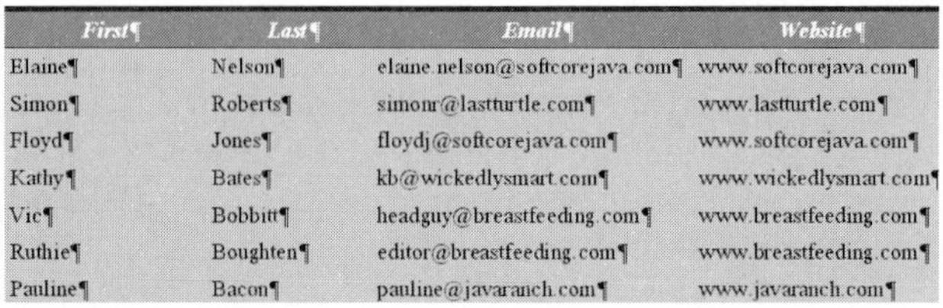

First¶	Last¶	Email¶	Website¶
Elaine¶	Nelson¶	elaine.nelson@softcorejava.com¶	www.softcorejava.com¶
Simon¶	Roberts¶	simonr@lastturtle.com¶	www.lastturtle.com¶
Floyd¶	Jones¶	floydj@softcorejava.com¶	www.softcorejava.com¶
Kathy¶	Bates¶	kb@wickedlysmart.com¶	www.wickedlysmart.com¶
Vic¶	Bobbitt¶	headguy@breastfeeding.com¶	www.breastfeeding.com¶
Ruthie¶	Boughten¶	editor@breastfeeding.com¶	www.breastfeeding.com¶
Pauline¶	Bacon¶	pauline@javaranch.com¶	www.javaranch.com¶

Figure 10-55 A field created from inserting a data source

Dragging a Data Source Field Into a Document

Note – Don't save the document before you do this. For whatever reason, it has to be done in a new empty document.

1 Open a new Writer document and don't save it.

2 Choose View > Data Sources.

3   Expand the data source viewing list at the left and navigate to the data source and table you want to get data from, as shown in Figure 10-56.

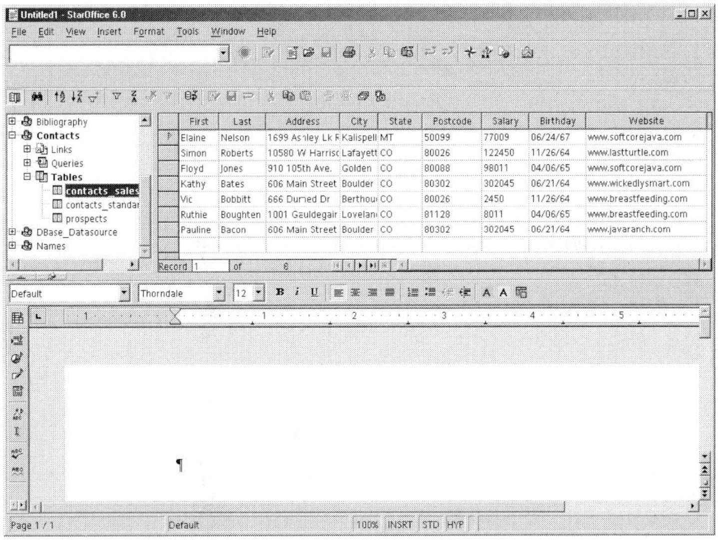

Figure 10-56   Viewing data source fields

4   Select the first field you want to appear in the document, such as the first name, by clicking on the heading such as First and dragging the heading into the document (see Figure 10-57).

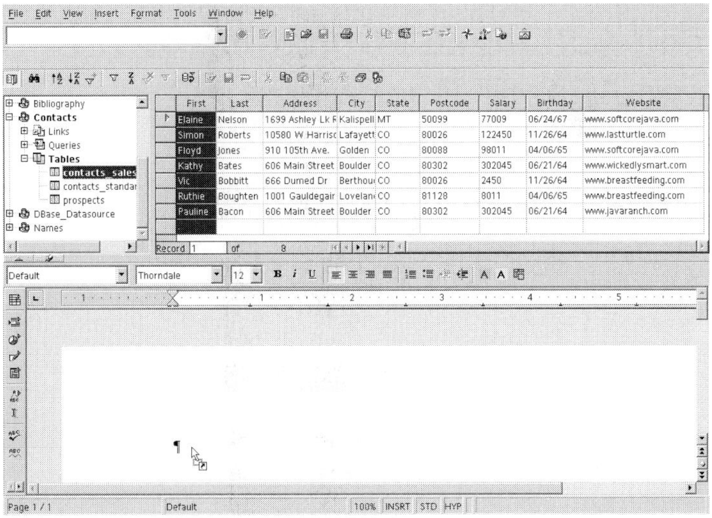

Figure 10-57   Dragging database fields into a document for mail merge

5   The field will appear in the document as shown in Figure 10-58.

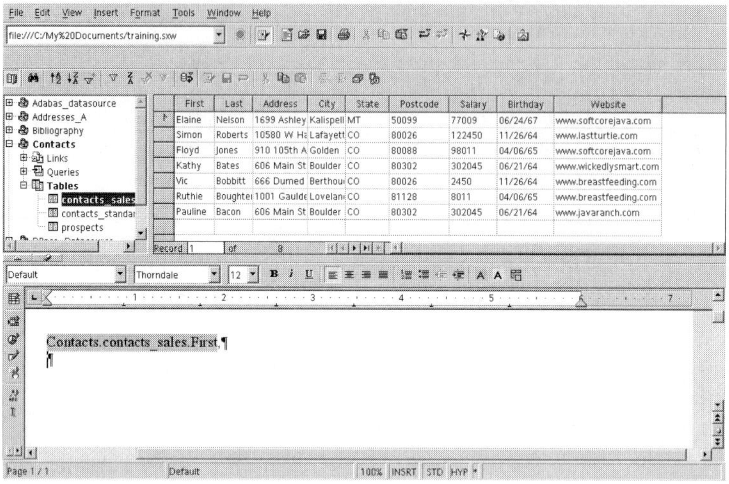

Figure 10-58   Result of dragging a data source field into your own document

6   Drag in any additional fields. Make sure you put the correct spacing in between the fields, and the correct line breaks. Otherwise you'll end up with something like this in your document:

ElaineNelson626AspenLaneBerthoudCO80022

To print what you've created, see *Printing* on page 399.

Doing Additional Formatting to Your Own Data Source-Based Documents

Once you've dragged a field or a table into a document, you can add text and AutoText to create your own mail merge document or other type of document, as shown in Figure 10-59. Add standard fields by choosing Insert > Fields. To add AutoText, see *Creating and Inserting AutoText* on page 864.

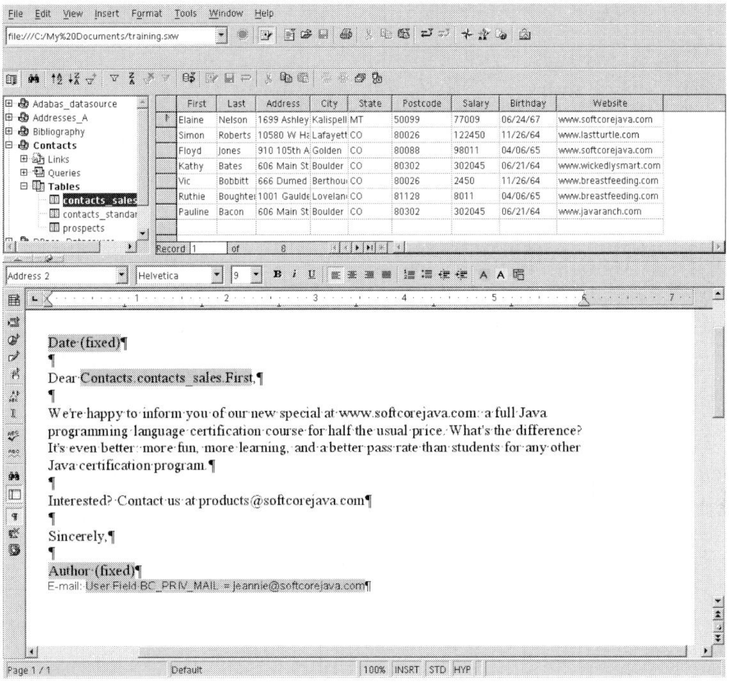

Figure 10-59   Finishing a document containing data source data

To print the document, see *Printing* on page 399.

Printing

You've set up your documents at this point, from scratch or from templates.

Business document people, just choose File > Print.

Mail merge people: until you bring up the Form Letter window and tell the program, "Yes, I really do want to print using this data," you get only blanks or the field names when you print.

Printing Any Document Based on Fixed Data

Just choose File > Print; you're using fixed data so the program can handle printing it normally. See Chapter 12, *Printing in Writer*, on page 429.

To print labels or business cards containing different data on every cards, see *Printing* on page 399.

Printing or Emailing Mail Merge Documents

1   Open the document you want to print.

2   Choose File > Form Letter. The window in Figure 10-60 will appear. If you want to change data sources or tables, do so now, and enter any filtering or other printing options. The following subsections demonstrate how to print to a printer, how to email, or print to files.

Printing to a Printer

Figure 10-60 shows the options for printing to a printer.

1   Specify the appropriate options in this window, then click OK.

2   The print window will then appear; enter any options in that window and click Print. Note that in the Print window, you enter the number of pages in the document to print, not the number of records. Typically you'll want to choose to print All pages, not a range of pages.

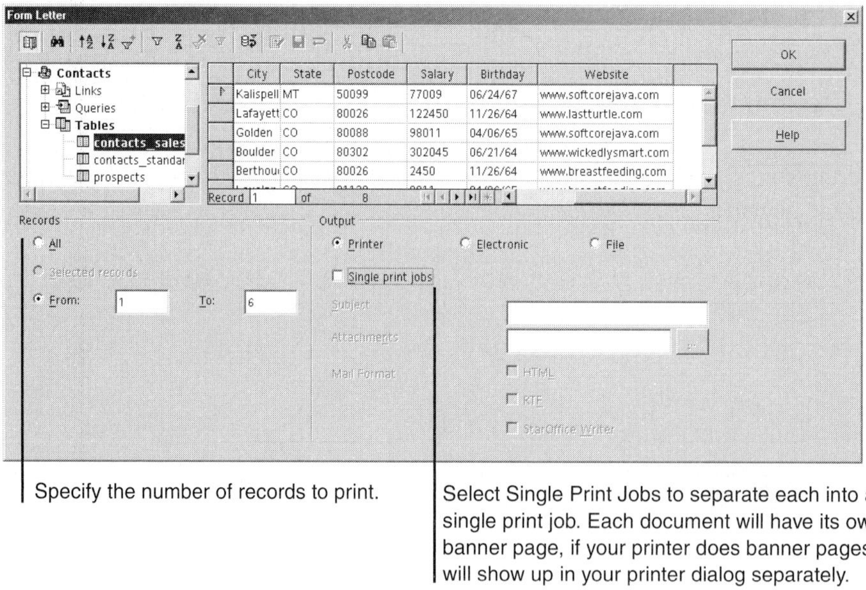

Specify the number of records to print.

Select Single Print Jobs to separate each into a single print job. Each document will have its own banner page, if your printer does banner pages, and will show up in your printer dialog separately.

Figure 10-60   Printing a document containing data source data to a printer

Be careful of the Create Single Print Jobs option in the Form Letter or Print Options window, for any application, when you print to a duplex printer. If this option is selected, each new print job will begin on a new page even if you are using a duplex printer. If this field is not checked then the first page of the second copy might be printed on the reverse side of the last page of the first copy, especially if there is an odd page number.

Emailing Recipients

Figure 10-61 shows the options for emailing recipients. Be sure your email program is already up and running, and that you're completely logged into it, before you click OK in this window.

Be careful about sending a document that has graphics in it. If you inserted the graphics using the Link option, your recipients won't be able to see the graphics if the link points to a location that only you can access, like your own hard drive or a folder on the network that only you have access to. It's a good idea to email PDFs if your document has any inserted objects.

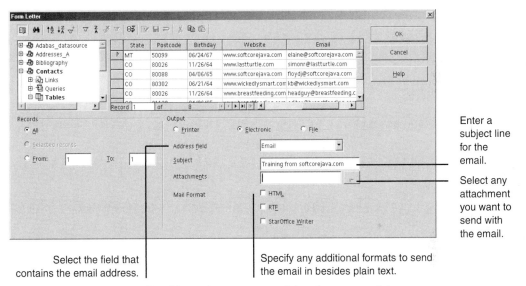

Figure 10-61   Emailing a document containing data source data

Printing to Writer Files

Figure 10-62 shows the options for printing to a printer, emailing the letter, or printing to a Writer file.

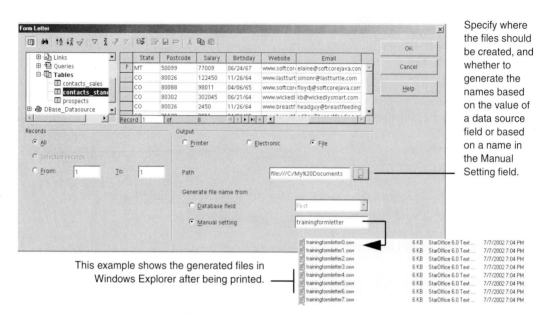

Specify where the files should be created, and whether to generate the names based on the value of a data source field or based on a name in the Manual Setting field.

This example shows the generated files in Windows Explorer after being printed.

Figure 10-62 Printing a document containing data source data to a file

Faxing

Be sure that your fax device is set up; see *Setting Up Faxing Capabilities* on page 69. Also make sure that your data source for templates was set up correctly and that the program knows which field in your data source should be used as the fax field. See *Specifying the Data Source to Use With Templates* on page 356.

Then follow the procedure for letters; see *Printing or Emailing Mail Merge Documents* on page 400.

Pick Printer as the output method and then, in the Print window, select your fax device, as shown in Selecting a fax device.

Faxing to one recipient Be sure that your fax device is set up. Then just choose File > Print and in the Print window, select your fax device, as shown in Figure 10-63. Your fax software will take you from there, prompting you to enter the fax number.

This is covered in *Setting Up Faxing Capabilities* on page 69 and *Faxing* on page 84.

Figure 10-63   Selecting a fax device

Printing and Layout Tips

Showing Data Instead of Field Names

When you create just about any document in this chapter, the name of the field, such as CONTACTS_FIRSTNAME, will be displayed instead of the data itself. Since the data source and name are hardly ever the same length as the data itself, this makes it hard to judge how much space the data will take up, whether the printed version will look good or wrap hideously, etc.

Select Fields to remove the check mark and show data instead of field names.

In order to see the data instead of the field names, choose View > Fields to remove the check mark next to Fields.

Spacing Between Data Source Fields

Often you'll be presented with a window like this that lets you insert the fields you want to appear in the document. Or you'll be able to simply drag the fields from the data source viewer. In either case, make sure you space the fields appropriately

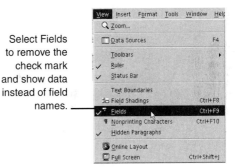

and put in the appropriate carriage returns, preferably in the insertion window or if necessary later in the created document. Otherwise you'll end up with:

```
ElaineNelson626AspenLaneBerthoudCO80022
```

Fixing Empty Fields and Lines

With mail merge documents or business cards, you might end up with empty spaces or lines if your data source doesn't have all the fields in the template, or if there isn't data for all the fields. See *Fixing Problems With Empty Fields* on page 404 to fix this.

Printing Envelopes Doesn't Work Well on Windows

Just use labels. See *Creating Simple Labels or Business Cards by Choosing File > New* on page 370.

Fixing Problems With Empty Fields

If some records in the database don't have certain fields filled in, those empty fields will create extra spaces and blank lines in the mail merge. Use the following merge fields as an example.

```
<PREFIX> <FIRSTNAME> <LASTNAME>
<COMPANY>
<ADDRESS>
<CITY>, <STATE> <POSTALCODE>
```

If a record doesn't have a Mr., Ms., Dr., or whatever in the Prefix field, the merge will show an empty space before the first name. Also, if the record doesn't have any company information entered, there will be an empty paragraph between the name and the address.

Here's how to make the merge remove the empty space and the blank line. (You can use the techniques in these procedures to tighten up other parts of mail merges.)

Fixing the Empty Space Problem

This procedure shows you how to fix empty space on a line caused by empty fields. A prime example of this issue is when a database record doesn't have a prefix (Mr., Ms., Dr.) for one of your contacts. So we use a <PREFIX> field as an example in this procedure.

Note – For more information about conditions, see *Condition Syntax* on page 864.

---

1   Don't put a space between the Prefix and the First name fields, so that it looks like this: <PREFIX><FIRSTNAME>

2   In the document, click between the two fields, and press Ctrl+F2 to bring up the Fields window.

3   Click the Functions tab.

4   In the Type list, select Hidden Text.

5   In the Condition field, type PREFIX. (Or whatever the name of the field is that's turning up empty in your documents.)

6   In the Text field, press the space bar to enter a space.

7   Click Insert.

The condition you just entered means that if a PREFIX exists in a record, it will be printed with a space after it. If there's no prefix in the record, the line will begin with the first name.

Fixing the Empty Line Problem

This procedure shows you how to fix empty lines caused by empty fields. A prime example of this is when a database record doesn't have company information for one of your contacts, so we use a <COMPANY> field as an example.

1   Click in front of the <COMPANY> field.

2   Press Ctrl+F2 to bring up the Fields window.

3   Click the Functions tab.

4   In the Type list, select Hidden Paragraph.

5   In the Condition field, enter COMPANY EQ "" (which translated means, "if COMPANY equals nothing").

6   Click Insert.

The condition you just entered means that if there's nothing in the company field, create a hidden paragraph. That brings the address information just beneath the name information in the mail merge.

Sorting and Searching the Data Source

You can sort the data to print in a different order, and search for a particular record. See *Sorting* on page 921 and *Filtering* on page 921.

chapter

11

Creating and Controlling Different Document Versions

IN THIS CHAPTER

The Two Ways of Controlling Versions of Documents

There are two different aspects to keeping track of different versions of a document.

- The most common aspect is keeping track of incremental changes in a document so that, if necessary, you can revert back to a previously saved version of the document. This is covered in *Document Version Control With Editing and Version Tools* on page 408.

- The second aspect has to do with maintaining two or more distinct versions of a document. This is covered in *Using Sections to Create Multiple Versions of the Same Document* on page 411.

  One document contains all versions, but different parts of the document can be turned on or off, depending on the audience the document is aimed at. For example, a software company could have a marketing document on a certain software product that contains not only generic information about the product, but also information that is specific to three software platforms. Using conditional text, you can print three different versions of the document, each targeted to a specific software platform audience.

  Using another example, you can create a single classroom instruction guide, but print one with instructor notes and one without.

  In this chapter we'll refer to this second aspect of version control as using *sections*.

- Two additional tools, editing tools and notes, help you add comments to a document with greater and lesser degrees of sophistication respectively. These are covered in *Using the Automated Editing Tools* on page 422 and *Using Notes* on page 427.

Document Version Control With Editing and Version Tools

There truly is no substitute for a good version control software product, where you can check content into and out of a database that controls the process with strict rules and security. Just short of that, however, Writer lets you save incremental versions of a document.

As you work on a document, you can save snapshots of it as it develops. Versioning lets you view prior versions of a document, make visual comparisons between the current version and prior versions, accept or reject those changes, or revert back to a prior version.

Saving Versions of a Document

You must save a document before you can create versions for it. That is, if you start a new document, you can't create versions until you save the document.

To create a version:

1   With the document open, choose File > Versions.

2   In the Versions window (Figure 11-1), click the Save New Version button.

3   In the Insert Version Comment window, type a description of the version, and click OK.

The version is added to list with a time and date stamp, your name (as taken from Tools > Options > *program* > User Data), and the version description.

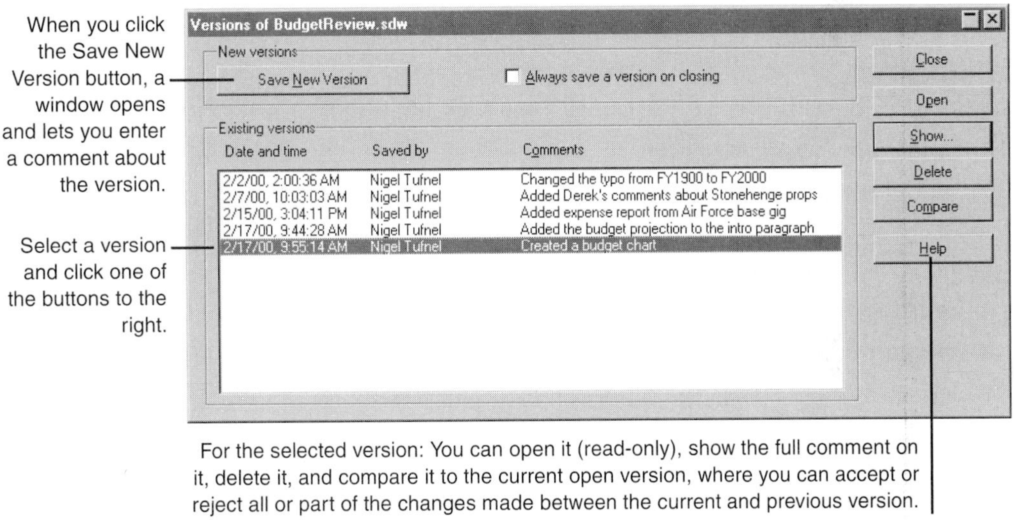

When you click the Save New Version button, a window opens and lets you enter a comment about the version.

Select a version and click one of the buttons to the right.

For the selected version: You can open it (read-only), show the full comment on it, delete it, and compare it to the current open version, where you can accept or reject all or part of the changes made between the current and previous version.

Figure 11-1   Maintaining versions of a document

To delete a version (you're not prompted to confirm a deletion), select it in the list and click the Delete button.

Opening Versions

You can open a version in read-only mode to view it. While you can't edit previous versions of a document, you can compare the working version with a previous version, which lets you reject any changes made between the two versions. See *Comparing Versions of a Document* on page 410.

In order to open a prior version of a document, a prior version has to have been created. See *Saving Versions of a Document* on page 409.

To open a prior version:

1   With the source document open, choose File > Versions.

2   In the Versions window (Figure 11-1), select the version you want to view, and click the Open button.

You can also open read-only versions of a document from the Open window (File > Open) by selecting the version you want from the Versions field.

Comparing Versions of a Document

This procedure shows you how to compare different versions of the same document, which is different than comparing two separate documents (see *Comparing Separate Documents* on page 422).

When you compare versions, the program automatically turns on change marks (Edit > Changes > Show). You can change the way these change marks look in Tools > Options > Text document > Changes.

Note – The program doesn't currently support comparing content that's in special regions, such as headers, footers, footnotes, frames, fields, and sections. And since manually inserted columns are tagged as sections, content in columns can't be compared. Yes, this is a drag. If you want to use columns *and* compare documents to prior versions, consider making your page styles multi-column instead.

To compare different versions of a document:

1   With the source document open, choose File > Versions.

2   In the Versions window (Figure 11-1 on page 409), select the version you want to compare to the open document.

3   Click the Compare button.

The Accept or Reject Changes window appears, and the document shows change marks that differentiate the two versions. You can accept and reject changes (see *Accepting or Rejecting Changes* on page 425), or close the Accept or Reject Changes window and view the changes in the document itself.

The change marks that are displayed are in relation to the current version. For example, if you compared the current version to Version 3, the change marks show how Version 3 differs from the current version.

To see what the change marks mean, go to Tools > Options > Text document > Changes.

To get the Accept or Reject Changes window back, choose Edit > Changes > Accept or Reject.

Reverting to Prior Versions of a Document

Sometimes people just need to start over. If you create many versions of a document, then decide that you want to go back and use one of the older versions, either to replace the current version or as the starting point for a new document, use this procedure.

1   With the document open, choose File > Versions.

2   In the Versions window (Figure 11-1 on page 409), select the version you want to revert back to.

3   Click the Compare button.

4   In the Accept or Reject Changes window, click the Reject All button.

    This rejects all the changes made up to the current version.

5   Close the Accept or Reject Changes window.

6   Either save the document as the current document (**which overwrites the current version**), or choose File > Save As to save the document as another document.

Using Sections to Create Multiple Versions of the Same Document

Note – If you want to visually compare documents with Writer's change tools, know that the program doesn't currently support comparing content that's in special regions, such as headers, footers, footnotes, frames, fields, and sections. So if you use sections, you won't be able to compare the content inside sections.

Sections, in their simplest form, are blocks of text that you name. They show up in your documents with borders around them, as shown in Figure 11-2.

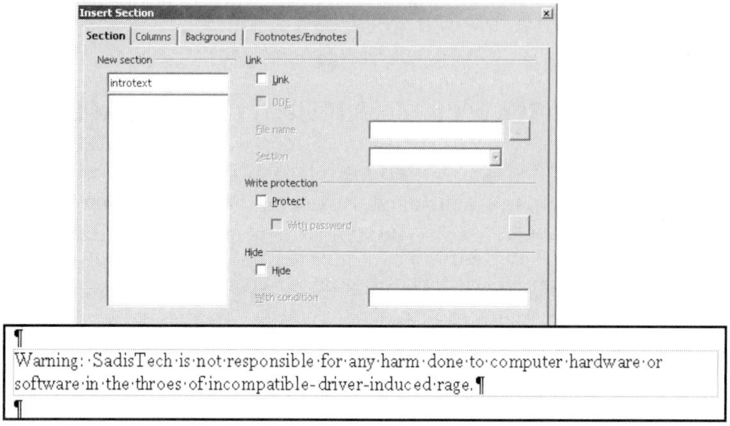

Figure 11-2   Section and section setup window

However, you have the following options that let you control:

- Whether the sections can be deleted
- Hiding and showing the sections
- Hiding and showing the sections based on a condition
- Basing the section on the content of another document, or on a section in another document

This opens up huge possibilities, including the following scenarios:

Single-source documentation Sections let you create truly object-oriented technical or training documentation without a lot of cutting and pasting. Let's say you're doing training documentation on the widget, the womplet, and the wicket, as well as a big reference manual on it.

- In the training documentation you present the information on each bit by bit to not overwhelm the students.
- So on page 2 of the training documentation you insert a section linked to the Intro section of the `widget.sxw` document, the `womplet.sxw` document, and the `wicket.sxw` document, all of which are already in your completed reference document.
- On page 26 you insert a section linked to the *Why You Care About Widgets* section of the `widget.sxw` document. And so on.

Note – Keep in mind that you can convert any Writer document to Word, and use the Word document with products such as RoboHelp.

One document for multiple audiences If you're in HR and you're putting together information for the whole company on the impending reorg, you're probably going to want to put in information for managers or directors that the regular people don't get to see. Put all the sensitive information in sections, and hide or show it when you create the final versions, in Writer or PDF, to email to the rest of the company. Or if you're putting together a proposal to sell products for your small business, you probably want to target the Girl Scouts differently than Nike. Sections let you put all the text in one document, then just hide all the Nike stuff when you create the version for the Girl Scouts.

Legal documents If you create a lot of legal contracts, you can create small, reusable sections, each of which can be inserted into a new contract document, and linked so that when the individual sections change, they're updated in the long contract document automatically.

Note – Many legal offices use templates based on WordPerfect, circa version 5.5. StarOffice reads WordPerfect documents, which you can then just use in StarOffice format, or convert to Word format to send to people requiring that format.

This part of the chapter shows you how to create a section, then hide it, and show it again.

Creating and Formatting Basic Sections

Note – To use the more advanced features, links and conditional hiding, see *Linking to a Section in Another Document* on page 418 or *Hiding a Section With or Without a Condition* on page 417.

1   Select the text you want to make a section. You don't have to select the last paragraph return in order to include the whole line in the section; if you select as shown in Figure 11-3, both full lines will be included in the section.

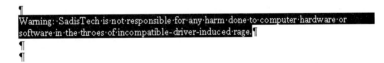

Figure 11-3   How to select text you want to make into a section

2   Choose Insert > Section.

3   In the Insert Section window (Figure 11-4), type a meaningful name for the section in the New Section box.

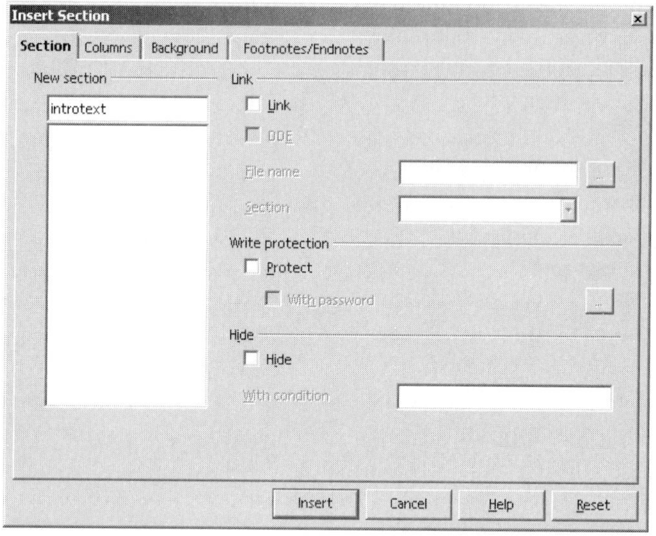

Figure 11-4   Creating a basic section

4   Click the Columns tab if you want the section to have more than one column, and make the appropriate entries; the window is shown in Figure 11-5. For more information on columns, see Figure 7-40 on page 231.

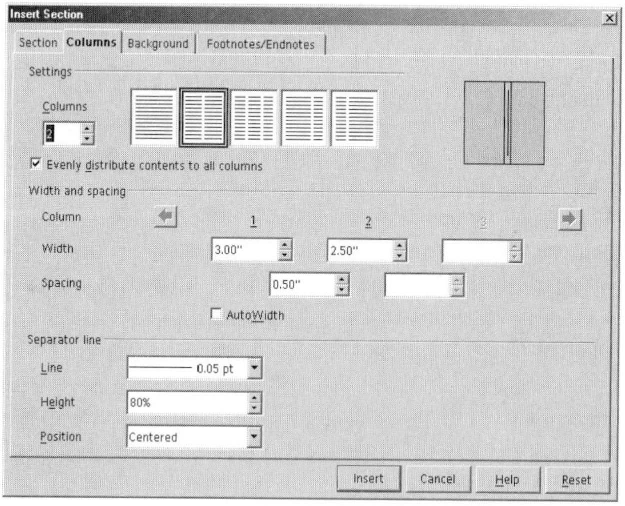

Figure 11-5   Specifying column setup for the section

5   Click the Background tab if you want the section to have a colored or graphical background and make the appropriate entries; the window is shown in Figure 11-6. For more information on backgrounds, see Figure 7-39 on page 230.

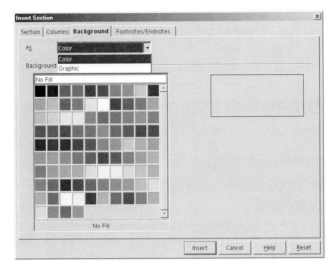

Figure 11-6   Selecting a background for the section

6   Click the Footnotes/Endnotes tab and specify how you want footnotes and endnotes to be managed for the section; the window is shown in Figure 11-7. For more information on footnotes, see Figure 7-32 on page 222.

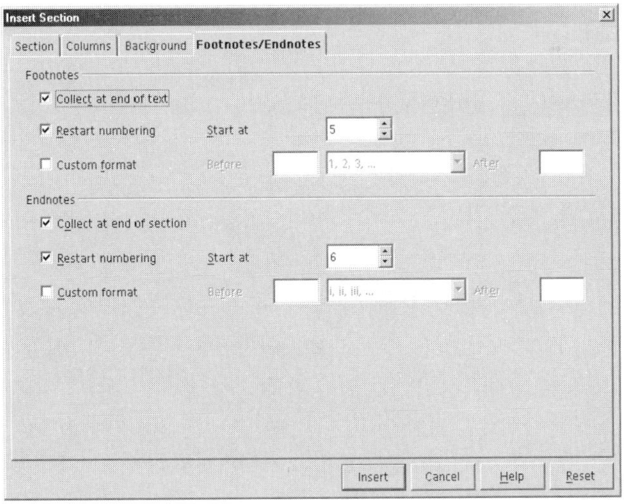

Figure 11-7   Determining how footnotes and endnotes for the section should be managed.

7   Click Insert.
The text you
designated as
a section will
appear in the document.

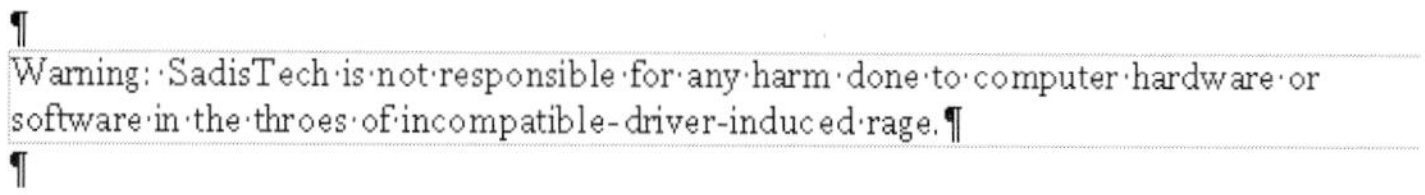

¶
Warning: ·SadisTech·is·not·responsible·for·any·harm·done·to·computer·hardware·or
software·in·the·throes·of·incompatible-·driver-induced·rage.¶
¶

Protecting or Hiding Text Using a Section

1   Select the text you want to make a section.

2   Choose Insert > Section.

3   In the Insert Section window (Figure 11-8), type a meaningful name for the section in
the New Section box.

4   Select the Protected option to make the section read-only and enter a password if you
want. (It's a good idea to do so; it gives you more flexibility later on for editing.)

5   Select the Hidden option to hide the section in the document.

Note – If you hide the section, it'll be hard to find again. There's no hidden section
character or other flag for you to use to track it down. You might want to insert icons,
horizontal lines, use a frame, or some other breadcrumb system to make sure you can
find it again.

6   Click Insert.

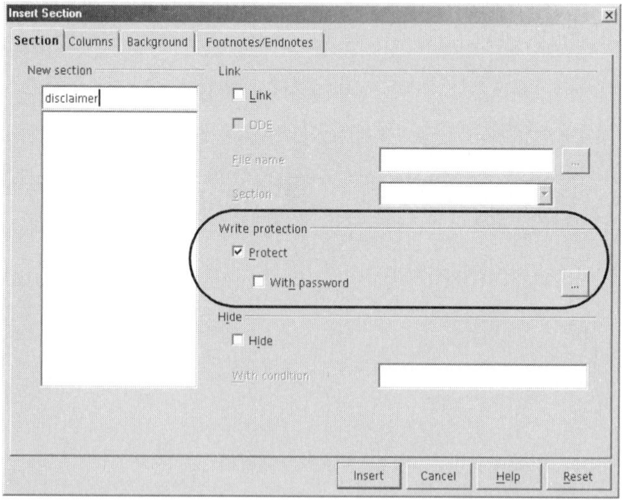

Figure 11-8   Creating a protected section

When someone attempts to edit a protected section that has no password, the message at right will appear.

Anyone with the rights to change the section with a password should select the section, choose Edit > Sections, and make the appropriate changes. They'll be prompted to enter a password, as shown in Figure 11-9.

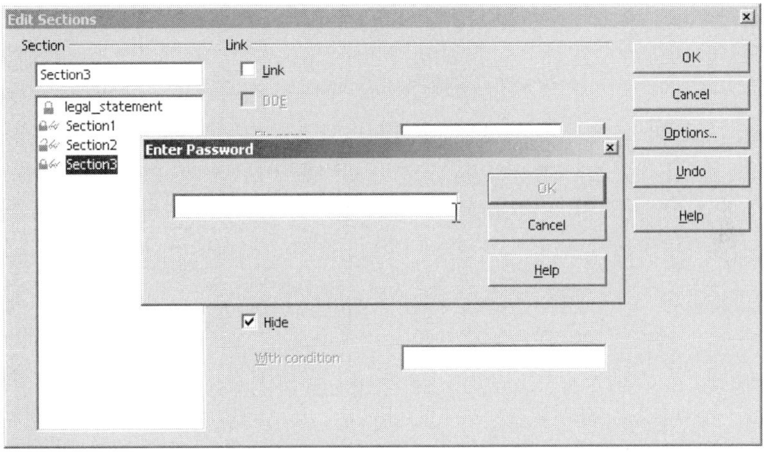

Figure 11-9   Being prompted to enter a password, in order to change a password-protected section

Hiding a Section With or Without a Condition

1   Select the text you want to make a section.

2   Choose Insert > Section.

3   In the Insert Section window (Figure 11-10), type a meaningful name for the section in the New Section box.

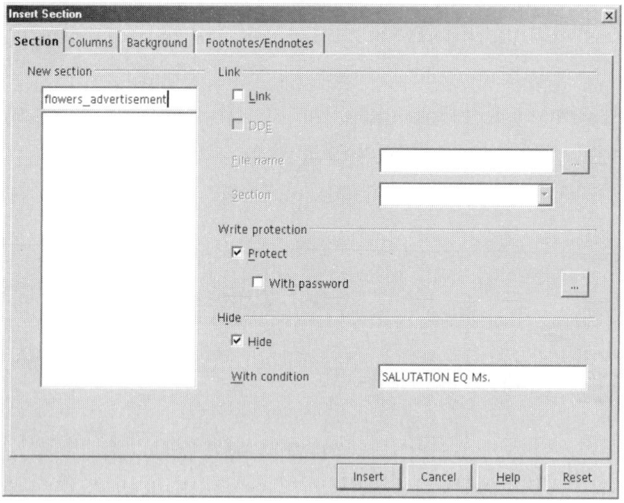

Figure 11-10   Creating a conditional section

4   Select the Hide option and enter the condition.

Enter the condition under which the section is to be hidden. If the condition is TRUE, the section will be hidden. Conditions are logical expressions, such as "SALUTATION EQ Mr.". Using the mail merge form letter function, for example, if you have defined a database field "Salutation", containing either "Mr.", "Ms." or "Sir or Madam", you can specify that a section only be printed if the salutation is "Mr.".

As another example, you can define the field variable "x" and set the value to 1. Then specify the condition for hiding the field: "x eq 1". The defined section will only be displayed if the field variable "x" is assigned a different value.

5   Click Insert.

More Information

More on condition syntax To learn the syntax for condition writing, see the online help.

More on creating fields to base conditions on See *Creating and Inserting Predefined Information Using Fields* on page 284, as well as the online help.

Linking to a Section in Another Document

You can insert a section from another document as a link, which means when the section in the source document changes, all the other documents that link to it get updated, as well. An example is shown in Figure 11-11.

The source document must have sections defined in order for this procedure to work.

1   Position the cursor where you want to insert the section, and choose Insert > Section.

2   In the Insert Section window, select the Link option.

3   Click the Browse button.

4   In the Insert window, select the document containing the sections you want to link to, and click Insert. The document is added to the File name field. The window is shown in Figure 11-12.

5   In the Section field, select the section in the source document, if any, that you want to link to.

6   In the New section field, name the section as you want it to be labeled in the current document.

7   Click OK.

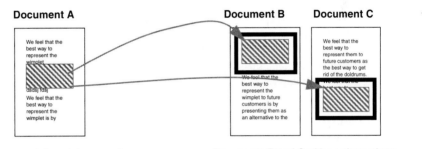

Document A contains a section.

Documents B and C with sections whose contents are links to the section in document A.

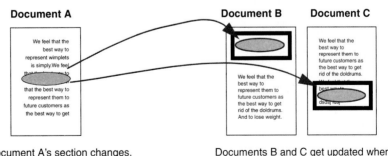

Document A's section changes.

Documents B and C get updated whenever the linked section in document A changes.

Figure 11-11   Linking a section to a section in another document

---

Note – Refer to *Creating and Formatting Basic Sections* on page 413 for details on setting values in the Columns, Background, and Footnotes and Endnotes tabs.

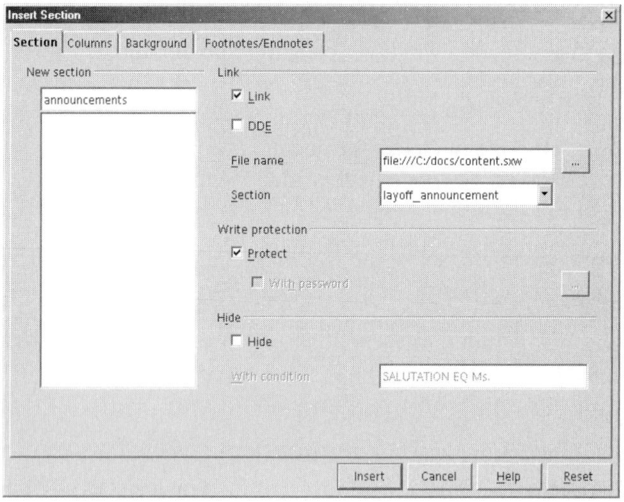

Figure 11-12 Creating a section based on a link to a section in another document

You can also insert a link as a DDE link. For more information, select the DDE option and click the Help button.

If a document uses links, make sure you update it in case the source files have changed. Update the links by choosing Tools > Update > Links. You can also determine how links are updated in the Options window by choosing Tools > Options > Text document > Other. If you choose the Always option in this window, links are updated automatically when you open the document. If you choose the On request option, you're prompted to update links every time you open the document. If you choose the Never option, links are not updated when you open the document. You must update them manually using Tools > Update > Links.

If you want to see where the source of a link is, choose Format > Sections, and in the Edit Sections window, select the section that is the link to view its details.

Modifying and Deleting Sections

There's always a second chance with sections.

Just Deleting a Section

If you delete a section that is a link, like the one in Document A from Figure 11-11, the text remains in the linking document (Documents B and C). However, the link to the source document is broken.

1   First choose View > Nonprinting Characters so all the carriage return paragraph markers and other symbols appear.

2 Select the section contents and paste them elsewhere if you just want to delete the fact that it's in a section, not the content itself.

3 Select the paragraph marker immediately before the section, and all paragraph markers in the section; this is shown below in Figure 11-13. You have to select it like this or only any remaining text will be deleted (and sometimes not even that). However, as you also have probably noticed, you don't have to select the last carriage return in the section (though it does you no harm if you do).

Warning: SadisTech is not responsible for any harm done to computer hardware or software in the throes of incompatible-driver-induced rage.

Figure 11-13 How to select a section for deletion

4 Press Delete.

Modifying a Section's Behavior

After you create sections, you can go back and change their behavior.

1 Choose Format > Sections.

2 In the Edit Sections window, select the section you want, as shown in Figure 11-14.

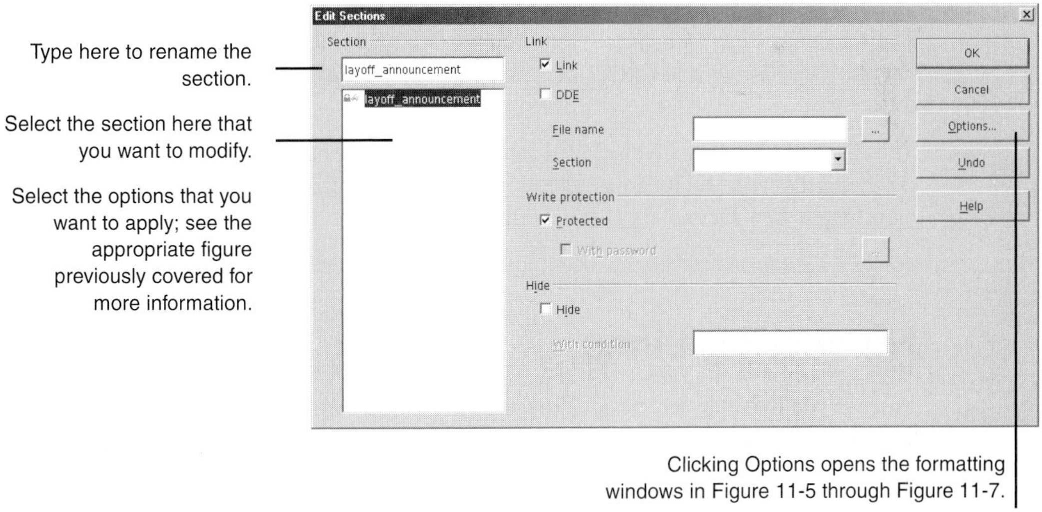

Type here to rename the section.
Select the section here that you want to modify.
Select the options that you want to apply; see the appropriate figure previously covered for more information.
Edit Sections
Section
layoff_announcement
layoff_announcement
Link
Link
DDE
File name
Section
Write protection
Protected
With password
Hide
Hide
With condition
OK
Cancel
Options...
Undo
Help
Clicking Options opens the formatting windows in Figure 11-5 through Figure 11-7.

Figure 11-14 Changing section options

3 Select the options for the section. To rename the section, just type a new name in the top field of the Section area.

4 Click OK.

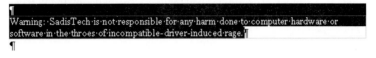

Using the Automated Editing Tools

Writer offers a number of tools to let you compare documents and show the effects of changes made to documents.

Comparing Separate Documents

This procedure shows you how to compare two separate documents, which is different than comparing different versions of the same document (see *Comparing Versions of a Document* on page 410).

Note – You can't compare content that's in special regions, such as headers, footers, footnotes, frames, fields, and sections. And since manually inserted columns are tagged as sections, content in columns can't be compared. Yes, this is a drag. If you want to use columns *and* compare documents, consider making your page styles multi-column instead.

To compare two separate documents:

1   Open the document you want to use as the basis for the comparison.

2   Choose Edit > Compare Document.

3   In the Insert window, select the document you want to compare to the open document, and click Insert.

The Accept or Reject Changes window appears. You can either use it to accept or reject changes (see *Accepting or Rejecting Changes* on page 425) or close it to view the visual differences.

The change marks that are displayed are in relation to the starting document. For example, if you started with Document A, then selected Document B to compare it to, the change marks show how Document B differs from Document A.

To see what the change marks mean, go to Tools > Options > Text document > Changes.

Numbering Lines

You can add line numbers beside lines in Writer. Line numbers are good references for quickly referencing locations in a document; like delivering an edit over the phone.

1   Choose Tools > Line Numbering. Figure 11-15 will appear.

Set the line numbering style and the relative position of the numbering to the body of the document.

Set the interval of lines to be numbered. If you set it to 1, every line will be numbered. If you set it at 5, every fifth line will be numbered.

If you set an Interval greater than 1, you can enter separator Text vertically between numbers.

Specify what and how you want to count.

Example of line numbering as it's set in the window above

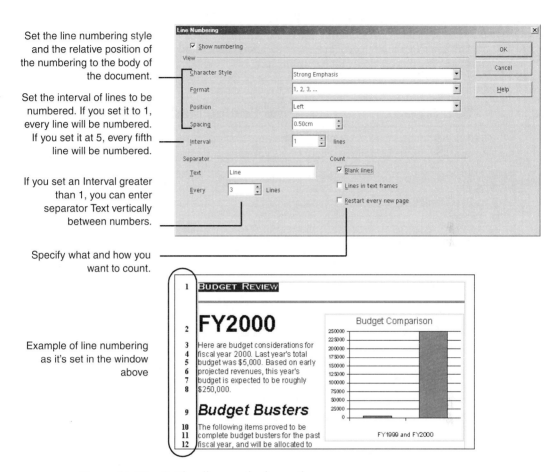

Figure 11-15   Setting line numbering options

2   In the Line Numbering window, select the Show numbering option, and customize any of the options for displaying line numbering.

3   Click OK.

To remove line numbering, deselect the Show numbering option.

You can further control line numbering through paragraph styles, which let you restart line numbering at specific paragraph styles or let you not include paragraph styles in line numbering. See Figure 7-20 on page 212.

Using Change Bars and Other Editing Marks

You can show the effects of changes to a document in many different ways, such as displaying change bars in the margins next to text and automatically formatting text in different ways when it is deleted, inserted, or if the text attributes simply change.

Setting Up Change Bars and Editing Marks

1   Set up the options for change bars and edits. Choose Tools > Options > Text document > Changes.

2   Set the options you want. Use Figure 11-16 for guidance.

3   Click OK.

The editing marks don't show up in your document right away. You must complete the next procedure to show them.

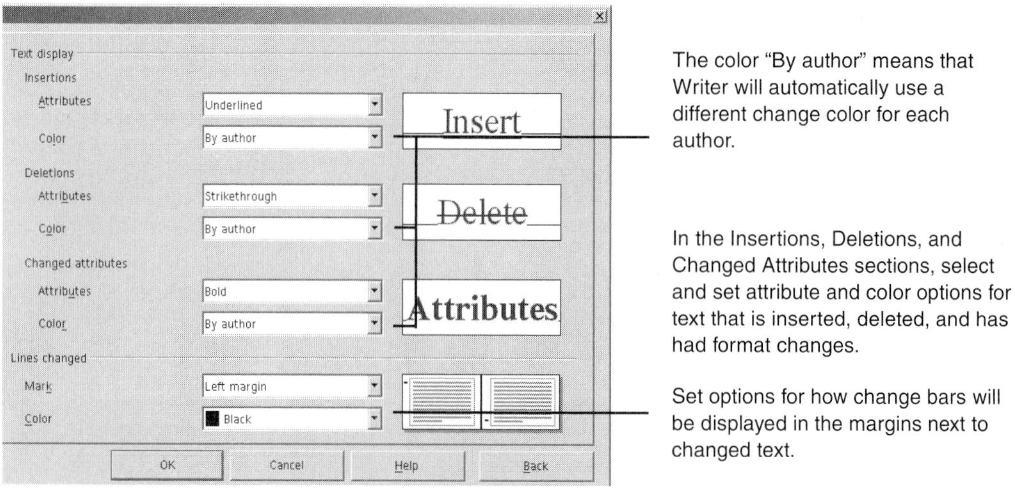

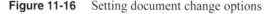

The color "By author" means that Writer will automatically use a different change color for each author.

In the Insertions, Deletions, and Changed Attributes sections, select and set attribute and color options for text that is inserted, deleted, and has had format changes.

Set options for how change bars will be displayed in the margins next to changed text.

Figure 11-16   Setting document change options

You can't assign change formats to specific authors. The program randomly assigns different colors and styles when a different author edits the content.

Showing Change Bars and Editing Marks

1   Choose Edit > Changes > Record to keep track of the changes.

2   Choose Edit > Changes > Show to display the changes made.

You can turn off the Show option at any time, and as long as the Record option is selected, changes will be tracked. But if you turn off the Record option, changes to the document will no longer be recorded.

Accepting or Rejecting Changes

Writer gives you the opportunity to accept or reject changes made to a document. When you accept a change, the content becomes a normal part of the current document. When you reject a change, the change returns to its previous state in the document.

In order to accept or reject changes, Writer needs to know that changes have occurred, which means that the Record feature needs to be activated while you work with documents (Edit > Changes > Record).

To accept or reject changes:

1 Choose Edit > Changes > Accept or Reject.

2 In the Accept or Reject Changes window (Figure 11-17), you can select one or more items in the list to accept or reject.

   You can modify the list of changes by clicking the Filter tab (Figure 11-18) and setting the criteria for which changes will be shown in the List tab.

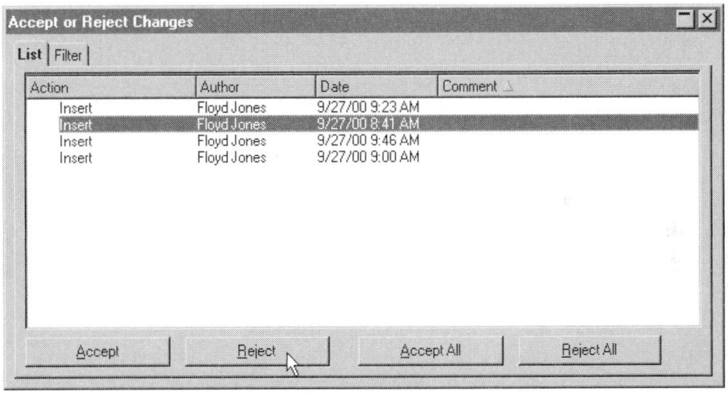
Accept or Reject Changes
List
Filter
Action
Author
Date
Comment
Insert
Floyd Jones
9/27/00 9:23 AM
Insert
Floyd Jones
9/27/00 8:41 AM
Insert
Floyd Jones
9/27/00 9:46 AM
Insert
Floyd Jones
9/27/00 9:00 AM
Accept
Reject
Accept All
Reject All

Figure 11-17 Accepting and rejecting changes

3 In the List tab, click the appropriate button at the bottom of the window.

   Whether you accept or reject changes, the items you accept or reject are removed from the Accept or Reject Changes window.

4 Close the window when you're finished.

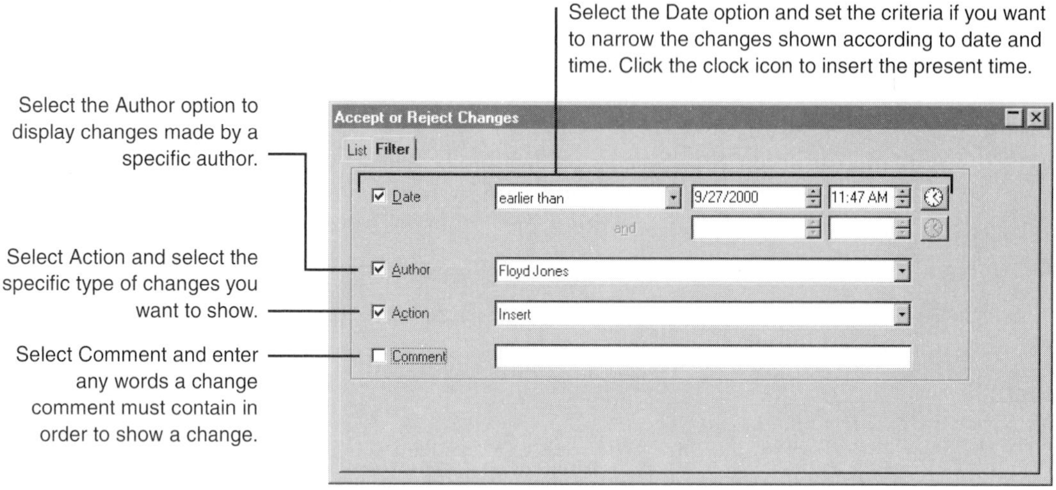

Select the Date option and set the criteria if you want to narrow the changes shown according to date and time. Click the clock icon to insert the present time.
Select the Author option to display changes made by a specific author.
Select Action and select the specific type of changes you want to show.
Select Comment and enter any words a change comment must contain in order to show a change.
Accept or Reject Changes
List
Filter
Date
earlier than
9/27/2000
11:47 AM
and
Author
Floyd Jones
Action
Insert
Comment

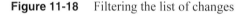

Figure 11-18 Filtering the list of changes

Note – Rejecting changes is a great way to perform a selective undo. When you use undo, in order to undo something five steps back, you have to undo the previous four steps as well. With the accept/reject feature, you can pinpoint the exact action you want to undo (reject). While each change is given a generic description, you can pinpoint the change you want to reject like this: With the Accept or Reject Changes window open, select the change, and the change is highlighted in the document. Then click the Reject button.

Protecting Your Document When You Send It to Other People to Edit

It's all very well to send around your document to other people to get feedback. (Well, you have to pretend that you like to do it.) However, what if someone decides to rewrite part of your original document without recording it as a change? See Figure 11-19.

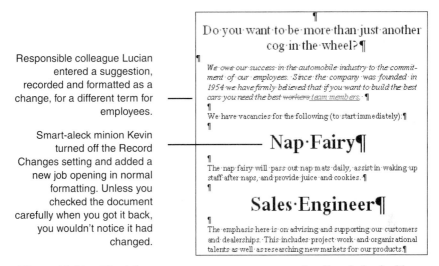

Responsible colleague Lucian entered a suggestion, recorded and formatted as a change, for a different term for employees.

Smart-aleck minion Kevin turned off the Record Changes setting and added a new job opening in normal formatting. Unless you checked the document carefully when you got it back, you wouldn't notice it had changed.

Figure 11-19   The job announcement you sent around, callously hacked by a co-worker

You can make sure that any input is recorded as a change, with nice red fonts and underlining, by turning on the Protect Changes features. Once it's on, you specify the password people have to enter in order to turn it off (and you don't tell anyone). Now you've ensured that everything anyone types in your document shows up as an edit, and no one can change the original text.

1   Get your document the way you want it.

2   Choose Edit > Changes > Protect Records.

3   In the Enter Password window that appears, enter the password, then enter it again to verify it.

4   Send out your document and chuckle madly.

Once you get the document back, you can stop new text being formatted as an edit by choosing Edit > Changes > Protect Records again so that the check mark next to Protect Records disappears. You'll be prompted to enter the same password you entered in step 3.

Using Notes

Notes are a way to insert comments in a document, with a flag that shows that a note is there, but without showing the text itself. Notes are a great way for authors and reviewers to communicate with one another.

Inserting Notes

1   Click in the document where you want to insert a note.

2   Choose Insert > Note.

3   In the Insert Note window (Figure 11-20), enter the appropriate information.

4   Click OK. The note will be indicated with a yellow rectangle at the point in the text where you inserted the note.

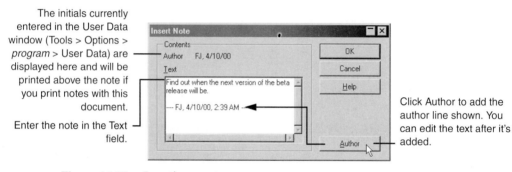

The initials currently entered in the User Data window (Tools > Options > *program* > User Data) are displayed here and will be printed above the note if you print notes with this document.

Enter the note in the Text field.

Click Author to add the author line shown. You can edit the text after it's added.

Figure 11-20   Inserting a note

Viewing and Editing Notes

1   Double-click the yellow note indicator.

2   The Edit Note window is like the Insert Note window, except that you can browse from note to note using the arrows.

3   You can change the note, or add your own comments below the current note. If you're adding to a current note, your initials from the Tools > Options > *program* > User Data window will replace the ones currently identifying the note.

Printing Notes

The Print Options window lets you choose whether to print notes, and where. See *Writer Printing Options* on page 431 for more information.

Showing and Hiding Note Indicators

To show or hide note indicators, choose Tools > Options > Text document > Contents and select or deselect the Notes option.

Printing in Writer

Printing Procedures

Most of the procedures you need are in Chapter 4, *Printer Setup and Printing*, on page 59. In particular, see:

- *Creating UNIX Printers* on page 60
- *Standard Printing* on page 79
- *Setting Up Printing to PDF* on page 72
- *Printing to PostScript and PDF* on page 81
- *Printing Brochures* on page 90
- *Printing From the Command Line* on page 83
- *Specifying Portrait or Landscape Orientation* on page 86
- And in the Mail Merge chapter, *Printing* on page 399

The rest of the procedures here cover Writer-specific printing or procedures that aren't worth sending you to the other side of the book for.

Basic Printing

Follow these steps if you want to specify particular options, or use the Print File Directly icon on the program toolbar, which uses the options and printer last selected. See also *Standard Printing* on page 79.

1   Choose File > Print.

2   Select a printer, or select the Print to file option and enter a file name. To print to a PostScript file, enter a name with a .ps extension.

3   Click Options and select the appropriate print options (see Figure 12-1), then click OK.

4   Select what to print: All (the entire document), Pages (a range of pages), or Selection (the currently selected text or objects). Use dashes to form ranges, and use commas or semicolons to separate pages or ranges (1, 3, 4, 6-10).

> **Note –** The program often defaults to Selection, rather than All, as the range of pages to print. Check this each time you print.

5   Enter the number of copies and, if it's two or more, choose whether to collate.

6   Click Print.

Writer Printing Options

The printing options you set using this procedure apply to all Writer documents you work with.

1   Choose Tools > Options > Text document > Print. You can also choose File > Print and go into the print options to see the window in Figure 12-1.

2   Select what you want to print.

Single print jobs and duplex printers   Be careful of the Create Single Print Jobs option in the Form Letter or Print Options window, for any application, when you print to a duplex printer. If this option is selected, each new print job will begin on a new page even if you are using a duplex printer. If this field is not checked then the first page of the second copy might be printed on the reverse side of the last page of the first copy, especially if there is an odd page number.

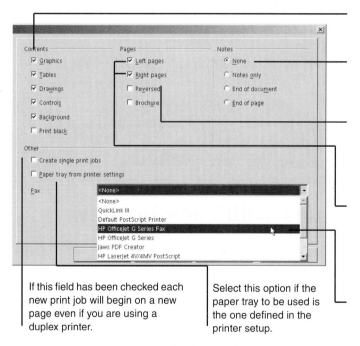

Choose whether to include graphic objects, notes, handouts, and an outline of the presentation.

Determine whether and how to print notes that were inserted using Insert > Note.

Select Reversed to reverse the order of the page printing to last page first, especially if your printer prints with pages facing up. Select Brochure to enable the brochure printing options. See page 90 for more information.

Select Left pages and Right pages to print those pages. The only reason you'd deselect one is if you wanted to print double-sided: printing all left pages, for example, lets you flip them over and print the right pages on the back.

To fax, select the fax device you want. See *Setting Up Faxing Capabilities* or page 69.

If this field has been checked each new print job will begin on a new page even if you are using a duplex printer.

Select this option if the paper tray to be used is the one defined in the printer setup.

Figure 12-1   Selecting printing options

Printing Notes

The Print Options window lets you choose whether to print notes in the page. See *Using Notes* on page 427.

The author line is printed only if added by note inserter. ──

Author and date of last change are printed here. ──

```
Page: 1 Line: 2 Author: SH 3/18/02
I've never seen this feature before. Are you
hallucinating?
----SH, 3/18/00, 1:17 PM----
The Incan monkey god himself told me about it.
----FJ, 3/19/00, 4:17 AM----

Page: 1 Line: 13 Author: FJ 3/19/02
Check this before sending in final files.
----SH, 3/18/00, 2:24 PM----
This works. I tested it myself, you meddling fishwife.
----FJ, 3/19/00, 4:17 AM----
```

Figure 12-2   How notes are printed

You can choose one of the following note printing options; examples are shown in Figure 12-2.

- None – Notes aren't printed.

- Notes only – Only the notes are printed, not the page content.

- End of document – The notes are printed on one or more separate sheets of paper, at the end of the document.

- End of page – The notes for each page are printed on one or more separate sheets of paper, after each page on which there are notes.

If the yellow note flag is showing when you print, it won't show on the printed copy.

Printing Multiple Pages With Page Preview

You can squeeze several pages of a document onto a single sheet of paper for compressed printing. In addition to these approaches, use your operating system's printing tools.

1   With a Writer document open, choose File > Page Preview. See Figure 12-3.

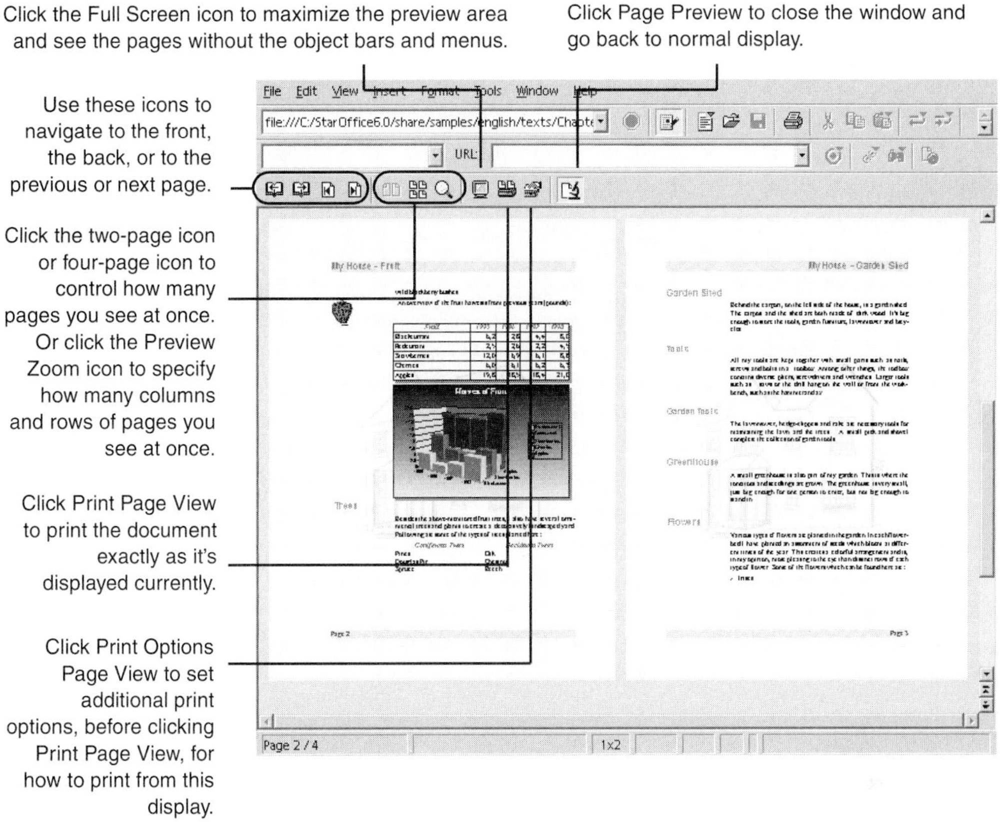
Click the Full Screen icon to maximize the preview area and see the pages without the object bars and menus.
Click Page Preview to close the window and go back to normal display.
Use these icons to navigate to the front, the back, or to the previous or next page.
Click the two-page icon or four-page icon to control how many pages you see at once. Or click the Preview Zoom icon to specify how many columns and rows of pages you see at once.
Click Print Page View to print the document exactly as it's displayed currently.
Click Print Options Page View to set additional print options, before clicking Print Page View, for how to print from this display.
File Edit View Insert Format Tools Window Help
Page 2 / 4
1x2

Figure 12-3 Page Preview window

2 In the Page Preview object bar, click the Print Options Page View icon.

3 In the Print Options window, set the options you want. Use Figure 12-1 for guidance.

4 Click OK. In the Page Preview object bar, click the Print Page View icon to print the document according to the options you set for compressed printing. The Print Options window is shown in Figure 12-4.

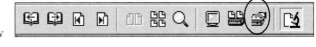

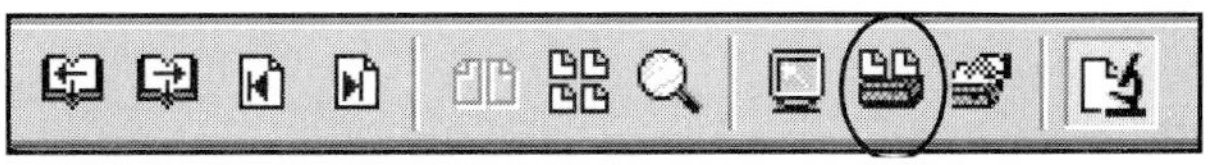

The rows and columns you set represent the number of pages that will print on a single sheet. ────

You can set extra spacing ──── around the edge of the printed sheet.

You can increase the ──── horizontal spacing between columns and the vertical spacing between rows.

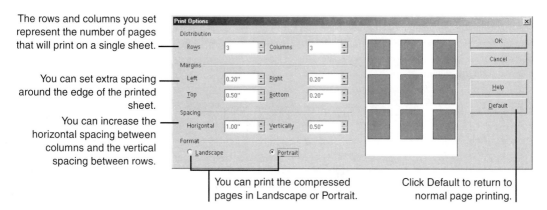

You can print the compressed pages in Landscape or Portrait.

Click Default to return to normal page printing.

Figure 12-4   Print Options window for printing from Page Preview

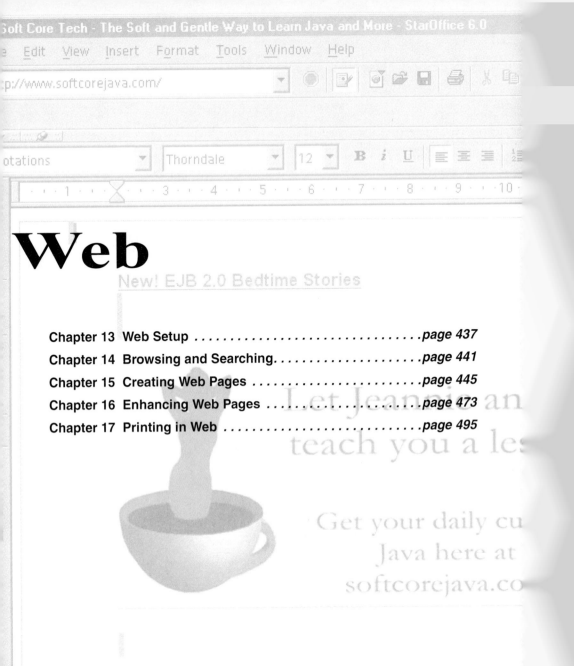

Web

New! EJB 2.0 Bedtime Stories

Let Jeannie an

teach you a le

Get your daily cu

Java here at

softcorejava.co

Please come in.

chapter

13

Web Setup

Program-Wide HTML and Internet Setup Options

Make sure you've already read and done the tasks in *Setting Up and Using Internet Features* on page 138, which is Internet stuff that applies to all of StarOffice and OpenOffice.org. See *Setting Up and Using Internet Features* on page 138.

Controlling What Application Opens Documents

If you weren't paying extremely close attention when you installed the program, you probably left the default setting on, the one that automatically opens HTML (and HTM and SHTML) files in StarOffice or OpenOffice.org. The same defaults were applied to Microsoft Word, Excel, and PowerPoint files. You can back out this association quite easily. See *Disassociating StarOffice and OpenOffice.org From HTML and Microsoft Files* on page 156.

HTML Document Options

This section covers setup options under Tools > Setup > HTML Document. For print options, see *Web Printing Options* on page 497.

If you want to use *Bringing Up a Web Page* on page 442 or *Using Web's Search Connection* on page 442, both of which you can do very satisfactorily in your own browser, ignore all setup options. They're off in Chapter 5, *Setup and Tips*, on page 97, since you can use the features in any application. If you really want to do either of those procedures, go to *Setting Up Proxy Information for Internet Access* on page 138 and *Setting Up the Ability to Search the Web* on page 139.

HTML Import and Export Options

These options are set under Tools > Options > Load/Save > HTML Compatibility. See *Setting Up How the Program Reads and Exports HTML Files* on page 143.

Specifying the Default Page Background

Choose Tools > Options > HTML Document > Background. Select a color to have all new HTML documents have that color background by default, or select No Fill.

Specifying the Color For HTML Source Code

Choose Tools > Options > HTML Document > Source. Select the colors you want.

View Options

Choose Tools > Options > HTML Document > View. The window in Figure 13-1 lets you pick what parts of each HTML page are shown by default.

Note – You can choose to hide graphics here by deselecting the Graphics and objects option. You can load graphics on a page by page basis by right-clicking and choosing Load Graphics.

Guides are light lines around the objects that let you see them better onscreen. Guides while moving shows exactly where objects will end up. Simple handles are smaller than large handles; large handles are 3D.

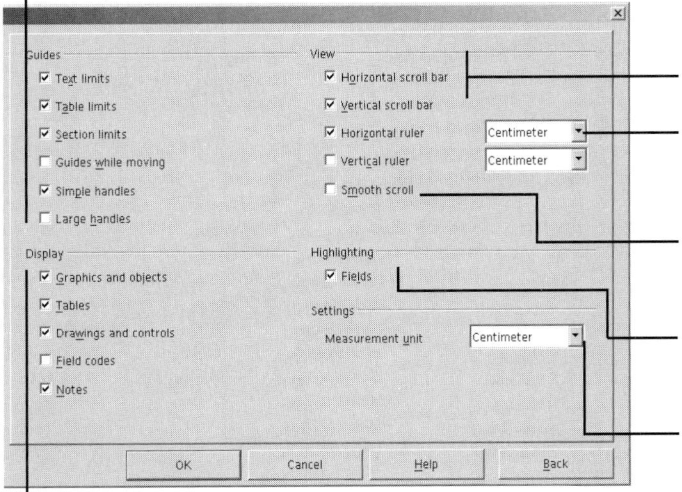

Mark everything unless you specifically don't want to see one of these.

Ignore the unit of measurement fields; whatever you select in Measurement Unit below overrides these settings once you click OK.

Smooth scroll doesn't seem to affect scrolling.

Select Fields if you want to show gray highlighting with fields you insert by choosing Insert > Fields.

Choose the unit of measurement to be used for the grid and rulers.

Choose what to show. Selecting Field codes displays inserted fields' name and type as well as contents in pages. Fields are things like date and page number that you insert by choosing Insert > Fields. This is for display only; the Print options window that you can access once you choose File > Print lets you choose whether to print items like fields and notes.

Figure 13-1   Contents display options in Web grid setup window

Grid Options

You can set the dimensions for a grid, which you can display, and snap objects to. (Snapping to the grid means objects you create, insert, or move will be aligned with the closest gridpoint.) Use the Grid window, shown in Figure 13-2.

The grid, when displayed, is a set of very faint dots, one at each point where the X and Y grid axes intersect. If you selected Visible grid and it doesn't seem to be visible, take a closer look at the work area—it's just that the dots are light and far apart. You can't darken the grid display, but you can increase the number of dots by increasing the number of points in the Subdivision fields. This adds more dots to each line.

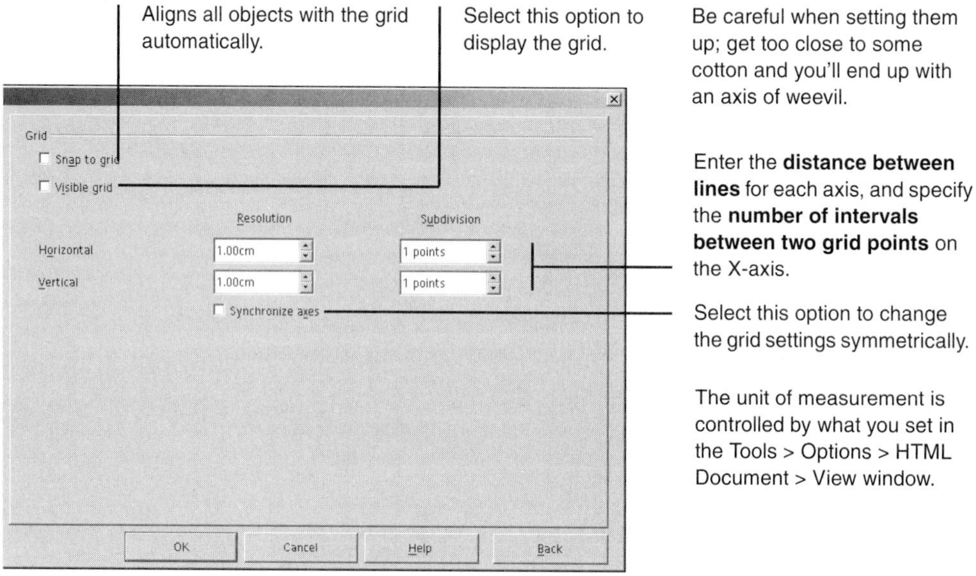

Figure 13-2   Setting standard grid options

Displaying the Hyperlink Bar

Note – Sometimes you don't get the hyperlink bar, which contains features like the Search (the Web) icon and the link-creating URL fields. Reinstalling sometimes makes it appear.

The hyperlink bar, which contains the icons you can use to browse and search, sometimes isn't displayed by default. Choose View > Toolbars > Hyperlink Bar to display it.

Figure 13-3   Hyperlink bar

Browsing and Searching

IN THIS CHAPTER

Bringing Up a Web Page

Note – You probably don't need to read anything in this chapter, unless you have a deep and intimate love for the StarOffice or OpenOffice.org browser. And if you do we *don't* want to know about it.

You've probably already noticed the Load URL field at the top of the object and function bars. This is a leftover from StarOffice 5.2. You can still kind of browse with it—type the full URL in the Load URL field (Figure 14-1). Press Enter. (If the field isn't displayed, choose View > Toolbars > Hyperlink Bar.)

If you get errors, check the setup options described in *Web Setup* on page 437, particularly proxies.

Type the URL in the Load URL field and press Enter.

The page is brought up in edit mode.If you click on any of the links, the target of the link will be launched in your standard browser.

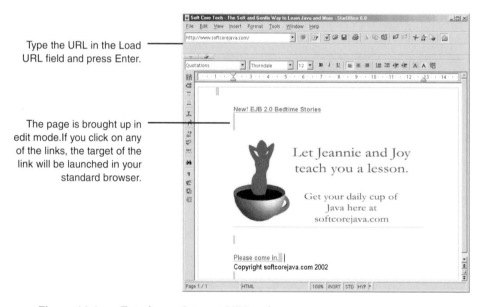

Figure 14-1   Entering an Internet URL to browse

Using Web's Search Connection

You can search the Internet from StarOffice or OpenOffice.org.

Note – We're still not sure why StarOffice 6.0, in purging other less than vital features, kept the search feature. It's kind of nice, perhaps, to be able to search directly from StarOffice. But it's not that hard to just go to Netscape and search there.

1   Complete *Setting Up the Ability to Search the Web* on page 139.

2   Type what you want to search for in the document, or select it if it's already there. For
    instance, type +java +fun + softcorejava.com and select the text.

3   Click the Find icon in the hyperlink bar and select the search engine you want to use,
    as shown in Figure 14-2.

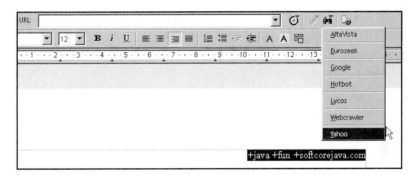

Figure 14-2   Choosing a search engine to use to search for the selected terms

---

Note – Some distributions of StarOffice and OpenOffice.org don't have the hyperlink
bar, which contains features like the Search (the Web) icon and the link-creating URL
fields. That is, you might have the hyperlink bar, but it's entirely blank. If this is the
case, reinstall, and if it still doesn't appear, don't worry about it.

---

4   The search engine you selected will be loaded and displayed with your matches in the
    browser, as shown in Figure 14-3.

Figure 14-3   Choosing a search engine to use to search for the selected terms

The browser used is the one associated in your operating system with the URL:HTTP
function.

Using FTP and Netscape to Upload Files

You should be able to just type the FTP target you want into the Load URL field and press enter. It works for HTTP. We couldn't get it to work for FTP. (Former 5.2 users, you might get weird messages with StarOffice looking for your soffice.exe. Disassociate StarOffice from any actions that start with URL, such as URL:HTTP. In Windows, this is usually under Folder Options.)

However, there are bunches of free FTP programs, such as CuteFTP. You can also just use Netscape.

1   In a regular browser, type the URL in the browser field.
`ftp://`*`userID`*`:`*`password`*`@`*`site`*. For example,
`ftp://joy:hotbeans@softcorejava.com`

2   The site will come up, as shown in Figure 14-4.

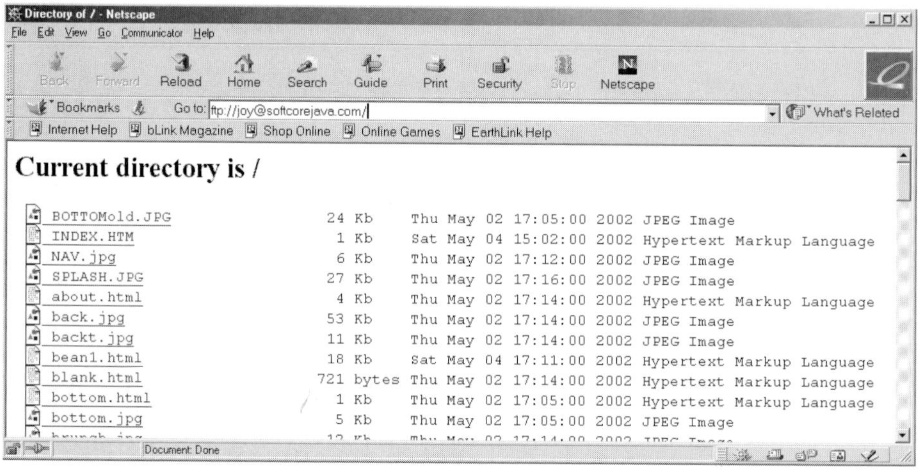

Figure 14-4   Using Netscape's FTP feature

3   To upload a file, choose File > Upload.

Creating Web Pages

Quick Start

This section contains the following information to help you get started:

- A checklist for quickly making a Web page
- Feature overview
- How to get going making Web pages
- A five-minute tutorial

Note – Writer and Web are fairly similar: many features, such as styles and templates, are nearly identical. See *Writer* on page 165 if you can't find the information you need in the chapters for Web.

See *Setup and Tips* on page 97 for general tips that can make life with the program easier.

Quick Start Checklist

If you have to make a Web page tonight for a presentation tomorrow morning at 8:00, these are the sections that will probably do you the most good right now:

- Create a file – *Creating a New HTML Document Based on a Template* on page 450
- Add graphics – *Adding and Formatting Graphics* on page 468
- Print it – *Printing in Web* on page 495

Web Features

Web features include, but aren't limited to:

Powerful file-creation features The Impress AutoPilot provides templates and samples that let you quickly and easily pick attributes like formatting and backgrounds.

Text formatting Full Writer text entry and formatting.

On-the-fly editable HTML source While some WYSIWYG editors don't let you edit the source code, Web lets you view it, edit it, and save it all in the same window. Web also comes with modifiable color coding that makes HTML more readable.

Insert hyperlinks in any document You can link to FTP sites, Web sites, other local documents, even to a command that creates a new document.

Insert graphics, spreadsheets, etc You can insert a variety of files, as well as files such as spreadsheets and graphs, and include any graphics by inserting graphics or using Draw's graphics tools. All Draw tools are available in Impress.

Animated GIFs and marquees Create all sorts of goings-on in your Web pages. Animated GIFs are actually an Impress feature but are used more commonly in Web pages.

Active content You can add applets, scripts, plugins, and hyperlinks to macros.

Forms and fields You can add a variety of buttons, dropdown lists, and so on, linking them to a site or to a database.

Starting Web

Choose File > New > HTML Document, or File > AutoPilot > Web Page.

The Web Work Area

The Web editor work area is shown in Figure 15-1.

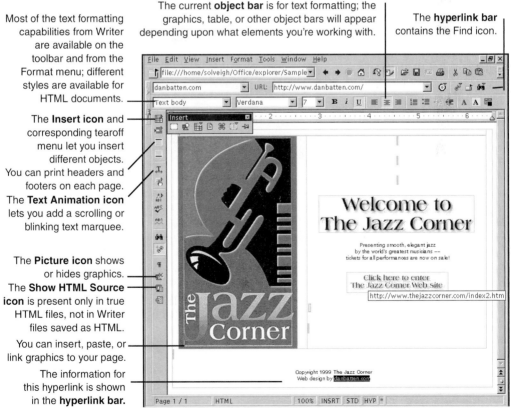

Most of the text formatting capabilities from Writer are available on the toolbar and from the Format menu; different styles are available for HTML documents.

The current **object bar** is for text formatting; the graphics, table, or other object bars will appear depending upon what elements you're working with.

The **hyperlink bar** contains the Find icon.

The **Insert icon** and corresponding tearoff menu let you insert different objects. You can print headers and footers on each page.

The **Text Animation icon** lets you add a scrolling or blinking text marquee.

The **Picture icon** shows or hides graphics.

The **Show HTML Source icon** is present only in true HTML files, not in Writer files saved as HTML.

You can insert, paste, or link graphics to your page.

The information for this hyperlink is shown in the **hyperlink bar.**

Figure 15-1   Web editor work area

Help With Web

In addition to the Help topics mentioned in *Getting Help* on page 98, see *Good Online Information Sources* on page 42.

Guided Tour of Web

This should take about ten to fifteen minutes.

1   Choose File > Autopilot > Web Page. Walk through the windows, selecting a style you like and creating the page.

2   Save the file, then close the document.

3   Choose File > New > HTML Document.

4   Choose Tools > Gallery. If the Gallery option is already marked, look at the small arrow at the left side of the work area and click it.

5   Scroll through the graphics and pick one you like; the rest of the tutorial will make more sense if you go to the Pictures category and select forest1.jpg.

6   Select the graphic. Right click and choose Graphics; the Graphics window will appear.

7   Reduce the size of the graphic approximately by half, but keep the same proportions. Then choose how you want the text to wrap (in the Wrap tab), and name the graphic (in the Options tab).

8   Click OK to close the Graphics window.

9   Above the graphic, type the following heading: The Three Terrors of the Fireswamp

10 Click in the text and assign it the Heading 1 style, in the Apply Style list at the left side of the object bar. (If the object bar isn't displayed, choose View > Toolbars > Object Bar.)

11 Click the Text Animation icon on the toolbar.

12 Draw a rectangle across the bottom of the page and **without clicking anywhere else** type Flame spurts, lightning sand, and ROUSes

13 Click elsewhere on the page; the text will start rolling by. Select the text and use the object bar to make it 36 points high. (This is slightly tricky—double-click in the text then drag the mouse carefully to select the text.)

14 Right-click on the text and choose Character. In the Character window, select Magenta and click OK.

15 Right-click the text frame and choose Text. In the Text window, select the Text Animation tab. In the Effects list, select Scroll Back and Forth, and click the right-pointing arrow. Click OK.

16 Below the animated text marquee, type the following: `Additional Information`

17 Select the text you just typed and click the **Hyperlink Dialog** icon (not the Hyperlink icon) in the hyperlink bar.

18 In the Hyperlink window, type the following URL in the Target field, then click Apply, and click Close:

`http://us.imdb.com/Title?0093779`

19 Save the file.

20 Click the hyperlink to the Web site. Notice that it opens the Web site but closes the file you were working on. Close the Web site and reopen the file.

21 This time, hold down the Ctrl key while clicking the hyperlink. The Web site will come up in its own window this time.

22 Save this document and note its location.

23 Choose File > Save As under a different name in the same directory. Change the Heading 1 text to blue and save the file again.

Creating New HTML Files

The program has extensive setup options that let you pick default values for any new HTML files you create or open. Before you begin, see *HTML Document Options* on page 438 and *Specifying Whether Paths to Objects Are Absolute or Relative* on page 141.

Note – If you want your documents to be read by a browser other than Web, be sure to test your HTML documents in that browser before you distribute them. Web text formatting, especially multiple levels of bulleting, doesn't always translate well. In addition, if you edit the document with another HTML editor, the odds increase that the formatting you originally applied will be changed when you view the file again, in Web or another browser.

Creating a New Blank HTML Document

Choose File > New > HTML Document.

This creates a blank document with the usual styles, including Heading 1 through Heading 6, List Contents, and Horizontal Line.

It also has, by default, a header containing the full path to the file, date, time, and document title. To change either, see *Using Headers and Footers* on page 472.

Creating a New HTML Document Based on a Template

The program provides two distinct sets of templates you can use for HTML documents:

*   One in the /share/template/*language*/ folder (this is on the server, in a multi-user system), which you've probably seen before.

*   A different set that you can access only through AutoPilot

The template folder doesn't have many templates suitable for Web pages; you'll probably be able to find what you want more easily by using AutoPilot.

To create templates, see *Creating and Modifying Styles and Templates* on page 456.

Using AutoPilot

1   Choose File > AutoPilot > Web Page.

2   In the AutoPilot Web Page window (Figure 15-2), select the template you want in the left-hand column. It will be displayed behind the window in the work area.

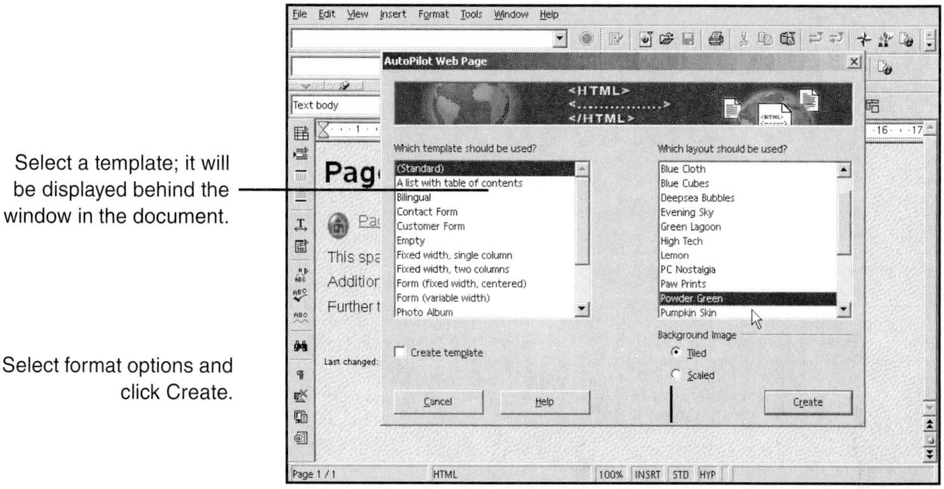

Select a template; it will be displayed behind the window in the document.

Select format options and click Create.

Figure 15-2   Selecting a template on which to base a Web page

3   Select the style you want in the right-hand column.

4   Click Create.

Using the File > New > Templates and Documents

This lets you base a document on one of the predefined Writer templates, or any template you've created.

1   Choose File > New > Templates and Documents.

2   In the New window, select the category and template.

     None of the categories scream "Web," but you can use anything you see listed (Figure 15-3) that was created for Writer.

3   Choose File > Save As and save the document as an HTML document.

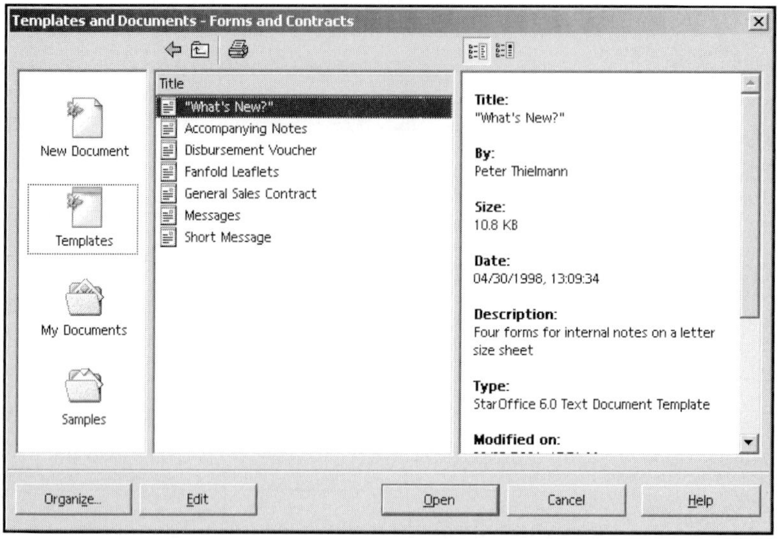

Figure 15-3   Creating a new file from a template

OpenOffice.org doesn't have the same collection of templates as StarOffice. To get some
OpenOffice.org templates, see www.ooextras.org.

Checking What Template Your Document Is Based On

If your document is acting weird and you want to make sure you created it based on the
right template, choose File > Properties and click the General tab. The template used by
the document is displayed at the bottom of the window.

Changing Defaults for New Documents

You can change the default font (not the font size) for Standard, Heading, List, Caption,
and Index styles. Choose Tools > Options > Text Document > Default Font. Select the
defaults you want. Don't select the Current heading only option if you want this to apply
to all subsequent documents.

To change the attributes of styles that appear in each new document you create, or to add
styles, see *Styles* on page 458.

Extensive file and template information is also included in Writer, since Writer and Web
have very similar functions. See *Creating and Modifying Styles and Templates* on
page 456, and *Styles* on page 458.

Changing Existing Documents to HTML

You can get virtually anything you create or import into HTML format.

Exporting Presentations and Drawings

You can easily convert Impress and Draw documents to HTML. See *Creating an HTML Version of Your Presentation* on page 735 for more information.

Saving Files in HTML Format

You also can choose File > Save As to save in an HTML format. Calc, for instance, has the HTML (Calc) format.

Publishing HTML Files With Embedded Documents

You can insert a spreadsheet, Writer document, or other file in an HTML document, and post the HTML document on the Web.

Opening any Text File in HTML

Select the file in Beamer and choose Open With, then select HTML or HTML (Writer).

The program will give you an error message sometimes, though not consistently, when you do this. If it happens, just sigh and open the file, then use Save As to pick the format you want.

Saving a Writer File in HTML

You can easily convert Writer files, or any file you can open in Writer, to HTML. (If you need to get a document into Writer, the best way is to save it in .RTF format, then choose File > Open in StarOffice or OpenOffice.org.)

1   Open the Writer document.

2   Choose File > Save As.

3   Select the HTML (Writer) format and enter a new name if you want. Click Save.

Note – The document icon in the task bar will change to the HTML icon, but you won't see the HTML-specific toolbars and menu commands until you close the file and reopen it. It doesn't work to choose File and then select the name of the file, to reopen it—you have to close it, then choose File > Open to open it as a true HTML file.

Opening an HTML Document

Before you start opening files, it's a good idea to set options for opening Web pages created using other browsers. See *HTML Document Options* on page 438.

Choose File > Open to open another HTML file.

What StarOffice and OpenOffice.org HTML Is Like

To see the source, choose View > Source in a Web document.

When you Save As HTML in Writer, you only get the Web (Writer) option, which is not in fact actual HTML. Not even if you make sure you add an HTML file extension. One main tipoff is that the View > Source option is not available. They often look the same way when viewed in a browser, but not always.

The HTML is created, in Writer and again even if you paste the same content into a new HTML page, very lazily with lots of <style> tags. If you like your HTML clean, don't rely on the program. However, it's a decent place to start, especially if you have a lot of tables to make. The tables come out relatively well.

Figure 15-4 through Figure 15-6 show the HTML output for a sample file:

- Figure 15-4 shows the document in Netscape.

Technical Training Resources

Go to the following URLs for great StarOffice and Java information and training:

http://www.softcorejava.com

http://www.lastturtle.com

http://www.javaranch.com

Figure 15-4   Document viewed in Netscape

- Figure 15-5 shows the HTML for a new HTML page in the program with the same content *typed* in, not pasted (this is normal HTML the way it was intended).

```
<P>Go to the following URLs for great StarOffice and Java information and
training:</P>
<P><A HREF="http://www.softcorejava.com/">http://www.softcorejava.com</A><P>
<P><A HREF="http://www.lastturtle.com/">http://www.lastturtle.com</A></P>
<P><A HREF="http://www.javaranch.com/">http://www.javaranch.com</A></P>
<P><BR><BR>
</P>
</BODY>
</HTML>
```

Figure 15-5   The HTML for a new HTML page in StarOffice with the same content *typed* in, not pasted

- Figure 15-6 shows the HTML source of a Writer page saved as Web (Writer), viewed in Netscape, and the same content *copied and pasted* into a new Web page in Writer:

```
<P STYLE="margin-bottom: 0cm"><BR></P>
<P STYLE="margin-right: 5.52cm; margin-bottom: 0cm">Go to the following URLs for
great StarOffice and Java information and training:</P>
<P STYLE="margin-right: 5.52cm; margin-bottom: 0cm"><BR> </P>
<P STYLE="margin-right: 5.52cm; margin-bottom: 0cm"><A HREF="http://
www.softcorejava.com/">http://www.softcorejava.com</A></P>
<P STYLE="margin-right: 5.52cm; margin-bottom: 0cm"><A HREF="http://
www.lastturtle.com/">http://www.lastturtle.com</A></P>
<P STYLE="margin-right: 5.52cm; margin-bottom: 0cm"><A HREF="http://
www.javaranch.com/">http://www.javaranch.com</A></P>
<P STYLE="margin-right: 5.52cm; margin-bottom: 0cm"><BR> </P>
```

Figure 15-6   The HTML source of a Writer page saved as Web (Writer), viewed in Netscape, and the same content copied and pasted into a new Web page in Writer

Exporting the HTML Source Code

Choose View > HTML Source, then choose File > Export Source.

The HTML you get is dependent on HTML compatibility setup options; see *Setting Up How the Program Reads and Exports HTML Files* on page 143.

What to Do If You Can't Edit a File

If you click the Reload icon, use the forward or backward arrows, or go to a Web page and

then return to the document, you might find the toolbar gone and the file uneditable. This is just the program's default behavior; click the Edit File icon again and you'll be back to edit mode.

Creating and Modifying Styles and Templates

Templates are predesigned files with styles, sometimes text, and other elements that reduce the amount of work you need to do every time you create a new document. Styles are pre-set groups of formatting characteristics that you can apply to text or graphics. Styles and templates go hand-in-hand for a number of reasons:

- They're both really good ways to cut down on the time it takes to do your work
- Templates are the primary way your styles are organized and stored

Since Writer and Web are so similar, you can learn how to use styles and templates in Web by just going to the sections of the Writer documentation where it's covered:

- *Power Formatting With Styles* on page 241
- *Using Templates* on page 256

This section covers a few things that are specific to Web, or are so common that we didn't want to send you chasing cross-country across the book for them.

Templates

Writer contains extensive information on templates, most of which is applicable to HTML as well as Writer files.

Using AutoPilot to Create an HTML Template

There are two ways to create a new document based on a template: AutoPilot (see page 450), or just choosing File > New > From Template. Using the steps in the following procedure makes a template that's available for either approach.

1   Choose File > AutoPilot > Web Page.

2   In the AutoPilot Web Page window, select the document structure in the left column and design options in the right column.

3   Select the Create template option and click Create.

4   In the Document Templates window (Figure 15-7), make entries and click OK.

Enter the name (document name, not filename) of the new template here.

Use the Organizer to rearrange templates, or click Edit (the dimmed button) to edit the template now.

Select a template category.

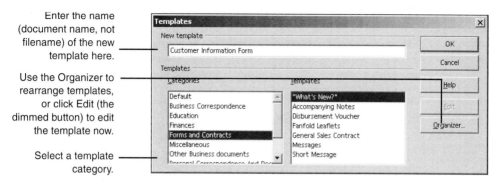

Figure 15-7   Creating a new template using AutoPilot and Document Templates windows

You never actually get to specify the filename of the template. However, it's not important.

Creating a Standard HTML Template

You can base a document on this type of template only by choosing File > New > From Template; they don't show up in the list of templates in AutoPilot.

1   Create an HTML document with the fonts, graphics, and other formatting that you want to base other documents on.

> **Note –** It doesn't work to create the styles in a Writer document, or find a document containing those styles and open it in Writer, and then save as HTML. The styles disappear. You need to create the styles in the actual HTML document.

2   Choose File > Save As.

3   In the Save As window, select Writer/Web Template as the file type

4   Save the file in the appropriate subfolder of `share/template/language` (in a multi-user environment, these files are on the server computer), or in your `user/template` folder.

Modifying Any HTML Template

1   Open the template you want to modify, in `share/template/language` (in a multi-user environment, these files are on the server computer), or in your `user/template` folder.

2   Make the changes.

3   Save the file, making sure that the file format remains StarWriter/Web Template.

Styles

This section covers a couple tips on Web and styles. For full coverage of the ins and outs of styles, see *Power Formatting With Styles* on page 241.

To get styles from one document to another, follow the instructions the Writer documentation for *Loading All Styles* on page 258 and *Loading Individual Styles* on page 259.

You can also just create a new template that has the styles you want, and use that template as the basis for all new documents. Create an HTML file, create the styles, then save as an HTML/Writer template. For more information, see *Creating a New HTML Document Based on a Template* on page 450.

Note – When you're looking for the style in Stylist, select All Styles in the dropdown list at the bottom.

Using Sections

You can use *sections* to partition off parts of an HTML page to be treated differently from others: a different background, number of columns, protected from editing, etc. They're the same in Web as Writer; see *Modifying and Deleting Sections* on page 420.

Creating Tables

You have a fair amount of control over tables in Web, including whether the table dimensions are absolute or relative, lots of formatting options, and other options.

Setting Up How Tables Are Created By Default

Before you begin, complete table setup options first. If you're having problems with tables, it's probably because of a setting that's doing stuff you don't expect. Refer to Figure 15-8; open the window by choosing Tools > Options > HTML Document > Table.

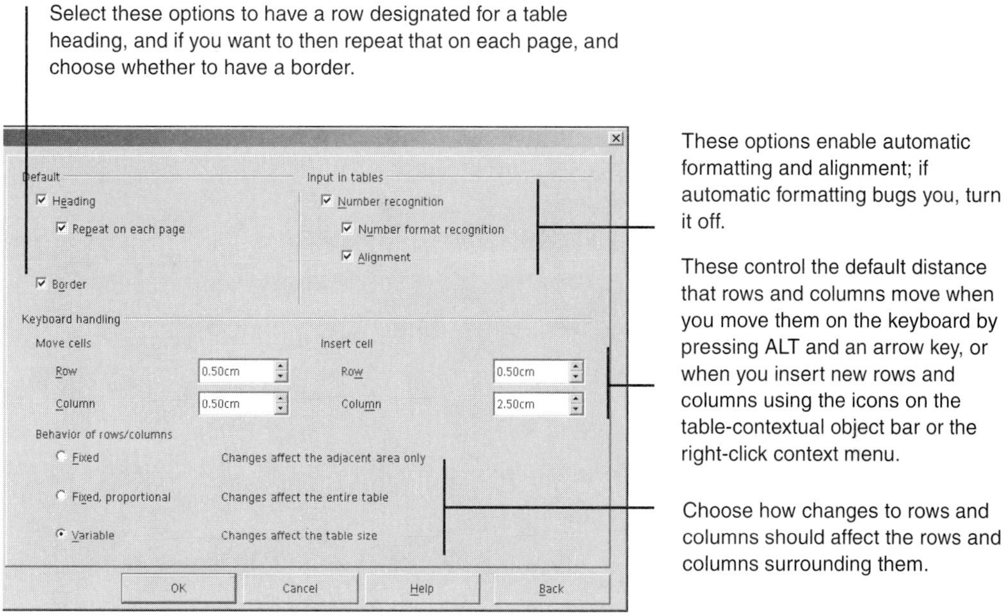

Select these options to have a row designated for a table heading, and if you want to then repeat that on each page, and choose whether to have a border.
Default
Heading
Repeat on each page
Border
Input in tables
Number recognition
Number format recognition
Alignment
Keyboard handling
Move cells
Row
0.50cm
Column
0.50cm
Insert cell
Row
0.50cm
Column
2.50cm
Behavior of rows/columns
Fixed
Changes affect the adjacent area only
Fixed, proportional
Changes affect the entire table
Variable
Changes affect the table size
OK
Cancel
Help
Back
These options enable automatic formatting and alignment; if automatic formatting bugs you, turn it off.
These control the default distance that rows and columns move when you move them on the keyboard by pressing ALT and an arrow key, or when you insert new rows and columns using the icons on the table-contextual object bar or the right-click context menu.
Choose how changes to rows and columns should affect the rows and columns surrounding them.

Figure 15-8 Setting table options

Quickstart: Using the Table Formatting Icons in the Toolbar

The table feature in Web is similar to Writer's, though not identical. When you select or insert a table (choose Insert > Table), the table object bar appears (Figure 15-9).

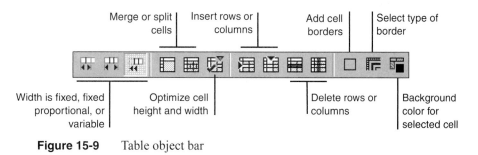

Merge or split cells
Insert rows or columns
Add cell borders
Select type of border
Width is fixed, fixed proportional, or variable
Optimize cell height and width
Delete rows or columns
Background color for selected cell

Figure 15-9 Table object bar

Note – If you don't see the table object bar, choose View > Toolbars and mark Object Bar. If it still doesn't appear, click the arrow at the far right of the object bar.

Inserting a New Table

To insert a new blank or preformatted table, follow these steps.

1   Choose Insert > Table.

2   If you want to make a relatively basic table, make the appropriate entries in this window (Figure 15-10) and click OK. You're done.

The table name is displayed only in Navigator, not in HTML source or in the Web page.

Select Header to include a row that prints the table title, and select Repeat header to print it at the top of every page.

Choose whether there should be a border around each cell in the table.

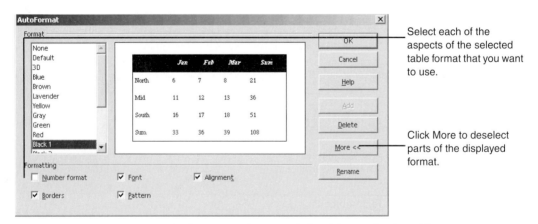

Click AutoFormat to choose from predefined table formats.

Figure 15-10   Creating a table

3   To take advantage of the program's predefined formats, click AutoFormat and select one of the formats in the AutoFormat window (Figure 15-11), then click OK.

Select each of the aspects of the selected table format that you want to use.

Click More to deselect parts of the displayed format.

Figure 15-11   Selecting or creating a predefined format for the table

Modifying Table Dimensions

Once you've got the table, here's how to tweak it using menus and the table object bar.

Column/Row Dimensions

Select the cell, column, or row you want, and right-click. Choose Row, Column, or Cell to get options for modifying the width, etc.

You also can click anywhere in the table and see the vertical bars marking each column. Drag them to change column width.

The table generally wants to keep its full width and won't let you modify it via changing column width. You'll need to change the overall table dimensions.

Table Dimensions

1   To change overall table width, right-click and choose Table.

2   In the Table window's Table tab, select any alignment except Automatic.

> **Note –** This is important; in order to make the table width relative to the page, for example, the Relative option in the Table tab needs to be enabled. It's grayed out, however, when Automatic alignment is selected, and Automatic is the default when the program creates a table.

3   To enter an absolute width, enter a measurement in the Width field; to make the width a proportion of the displayed page, select Relative and enter a percentage.

Formatting Text in a Table

When you insert a table, the text object bar disappears and the table object bar replaces it. To  get at the text formatting object bar when you're in a table, use the arrow at the far right side of the object bar. (If you can't see it, enlarge the window or click the small down arrow at the right side of the object bar.)

Just click the arrow circled in the above figure to switch from one object bar to the other.

Once in a while, you'll click in a table and the table object bar won't appear. Again, just click the arrow to get the table object bar.

Creating Nested Tables

You've got a table, but how do you put a table inside another table? If you put the cursor inside a table cell and choose Insert > Table, the table window pops up but on the Background tab. The ability to insert another table is grayed out. So you can fool the program into thinking you're not in a table by inserting a frame in that cell, then putting the nested table inside that frame.

1   Choose Tools > Options > Load/Save > HTML Compatibility.

2   Be sure Netscape 4.x is selected as the export format. Click OK.

3   In an HTML document, choose Insert > Table and make the first table the way you want it. This is the top table; you'll create the table inside it in the following steps.

4   Click inside the cell where you want to add the nested table.

5   Choose Insert > Frame. The frame will appear in the cell as shown in Figure 15-12.

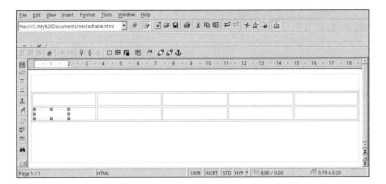

Figure 15-12   Inserting a frame in a table to hold the nested table

6   Click in the frame.

7   Choose Insert > Table and create the inner table as shown in Figure 15-13.

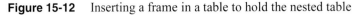

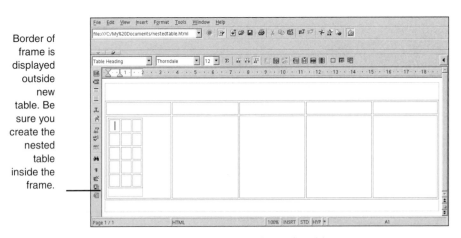

Border of frame is displayed outside new table. Be sure you create the nested table inside the frame.

Figure 15-13   Inserting the nested table in the main table

8   Format the tables as you want them, as shown in Figure 15-14.

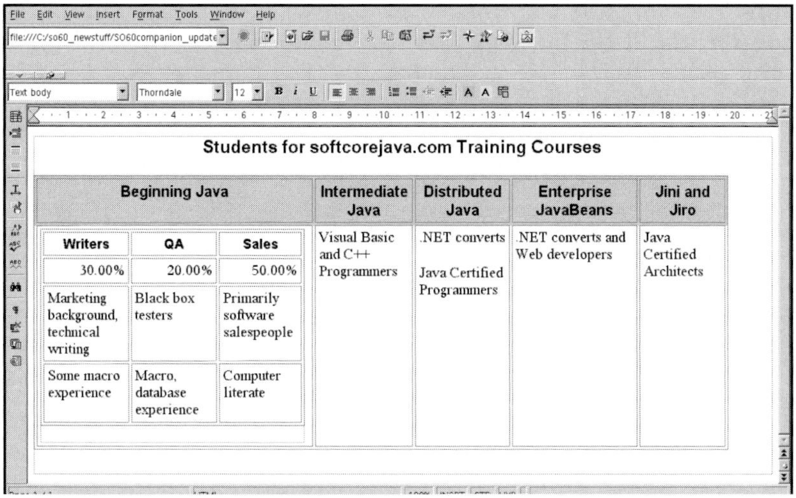

Figure 15-14   Formatting main and nested table

The HTML source that's created looks like Figure 15-15 below.

```
<TABLE WIDTH=935 BORDER=1 CELLPADDING=5 CELLSPACING=4>
    <COL WIDTH=360>
    <COL WIDTH=120>
    <COL WIDTH=115>
    <COL WIDTH=159>
    <COL WIDTH=105>
    <THEAD>
        <TR VALIGN=TOP>
            <TH WIDTH=360 BGCOLOR="#cccccc">
                <P><FONT FACE="Arial, sans-serif">Beginning Java</FONT></P>
            </TH>
            <TH WIDTH=120 BGCOLOR="#cccccc">
                <P><FONT FACE="Arial, sans-serif">Intermediate Java</FONT></P>
            </TH>
            <TH WIDTH=115 BGCOLOR="#cccccc">
                <P><FONT FACE="Arial, sans-serif">Distributed Java</FONT></P>
            </TH>
            <TH WIDTH=159 BGCOLOR="#cccccc">
                <P><FONT FACE="Arial, sans-serif">Enterprise JavaBeans</FONT></P>
            </TH>
            <TH WIDTH=105 BGCOLOR="#cccccc">
                <P><FONT FACE="Arial, sans-serif">Jini and Jiro</FONT></P>
            </TH>
        </TR>
    </THEAD>
    <TBODY>
        <TR VALIGN=TOP>
            <TD WIDTH=360>
```

```
                    <P><IMG SRC="nestedtable_html_8bcd267.gif" NAME="Frame1" ALT="Frame1"
        ALIGN=BOTTOM></P>
                </TD>
                <TD WIDTH=120>
                    <P>Visual Basic and C++ Programmers</P>
                </TD>
                <TD WIDTH=115>
                    <P>.NET converts</P>
                    <P>Java Certified Programmers</P>
                </TD>
                <TD WIDTH=159>
                    <P>.NET converts and Web developers</P>
                </TD>
                <TD WIDTH=105>
                    <P>Java Certified Architects</P>
                </TD>
            </TR>
        </TBODY>
    </TABLE>
    <P><BR><BR>
    </P>
    </BODY>
</HTML>
```

Figure 15-15 HTML source created from nested tables

Inserting Notes

Notes are a way to insert comments in an HTML document, using a flag that shows that a note is there, but without showing the text itself. Note indicators are shown in HTML editors when you're in edit mode, but not when the page is being viewed. The icon at the right shows both the Netscape and the note indicators.

The insert note feature is essentially a way to add the following HTML text:

```
<!--notetext-->
```

or

```
<!--notetext

----author_and_date_information-->
```

The program provides you with a window for inserting, and one for editing, which makes it a little simpler.

Notes can be read by other browsers, and vice versa.

Showing and Hiding Note Indicators

To show or hide note indicators, choose Tools > Options > HTML Document > Contents and select or deselect the Notes option. This applies to the indicator for scripts, as well.

Inserting Notes

1   Choose Insert > Note.

2   In the Insert Note window (Figure 15-16), enter the appropriate information.

The information currently entered in the Initials field of the User Data window (Tools > Options > General > User Data) are displayed here and printed above the note.

Enter the note in the Text field.

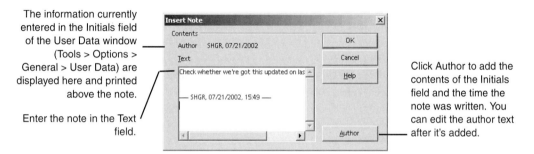

Click Author to add the contents of the Initials field and the time the note was written. You can edit the author text after it's added.

Figure 15-16   Inserting a note

3   Click OK. The note will be indicated with a yellow rectangle at the point in the text where you inserted the note. This yellow note flag is visible only when you're in edit mode, as with most Web page editors.

Note – The indicator is visible only if you selected the Display notes option in the Tools > Options > HTML Document > Contents window.

Editing Notes

1   Double-click the yellow note indicator, just barely visible under the W in the illustration at right.

2   The Edit Note window is like the Insert Note window, except that you can browse from note to note using the arrows.

3   You can change the note, or add your own comments below the current note. If you're adding to a current note, your initials from the general user options window will replace the ones currently identifying the note.

Printing Notes

The Print Options window lets you choose whether to print notes, and where. See page 497 for more information, and an illustration of how notes are printed.

Note – Printing isn't all that it could be; the notes are printed only after each page, or at the end of the entire document. You can't print them right where they appear in the document, and the yellow note indicator isn't printed, either. However, the printed note does cite the line and page where the note appears.

Viewing and Editing HTML Source

Before you begin, complete the HTML Document setup, particularly in the window on page 439, which lets you determine the colors for different types of tags in the HTML source. Choose Tools > Options > Load/Save > HTML Compatibility.

You can edit the HTML source directly in Web; you don't need to open the HTML file in a text editor. Just choose View > HTML source, click the Edit File icon in the function bar, and make your changes. Then deselect the HTML source in the View menu and save changes.

To get the HTML source into a separate file, you can copy and paste, or choose File > Export source.

The file must be saved in order to view the source; if nothing shows up, check to be sure you've saved the file at least once already. Also be sure that the icon in the titlebar is a Netscape-like icon; it might be a "Writer/Web" document, which ain't HTML.

Adding and Formatting Text

Most of the text-formatting capabilities in Web are the same as in Writer. See *Formatting Documents* on page 197 for more information. This section describes the few features specific to HTML documents.

Before you begin, make sure you're in edit mode (click the Edit File icon).

Note – The text formatting icons should be displayed on the object bar whenever you're inserting or formatting text. If table-related icons or other non-text icons are displayed instead, click the arrow at the far right of the object bar. (If the object bar itself isn't displayed, choose View > Toolbars > Object Bar.)

Figure 15-17 points out the primary HTML text formatting capabilities.

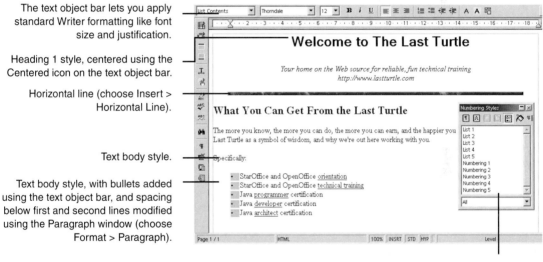

The text object bar lets you apply standard Writer formatting like font size and justification.

Heading 1 style, centered using the Centered icon on the text object bar.

Horizontal line (choose Insert > Horizontal Line).

Text body style.

Text body style, with bullets added using the text object bar, and spacing below first and second lines modified using the Paragraph window (choose Format > Paragraph).

Standard HTML styles are available by default; you can modify and create them using the same features as in Writer.

Figure 15-17   Basic HTML-specific text formatting features

You can promote and demote headings to quickly reorganize your document, using Navigator. (Press F5 to display it.) See *Using the Paragraph Format Window* on page 208 for more information.

If you want your documents to be read by a browser other than Web, be sure to test your HTML documents in that browser before you distribute them. Web text formatting, especially multiple levels of bulleting, doesn't always translate well. In addition, if you edit the document with another HTML editor, the odds increase that the formatting you originally applied will be changed when you view the file again, in Web or another browser.

Adding and Formatting Graphics

Adding graphics can enliven your Web pages, and slow them to a crawl when people try to view them on the Internet. How you use them is up to you; when creating pages, do refer to information sources on design and on how to maximize visual interest while minimizing load time.

Graphics are pretty much the same throughout the program; they're already covered in the StarWriter documentation in *Inserting Graphics* on page 268. This section covers graphics information specific to Web, or that's common enough to put here, too.

Adding a Graphic

You can add graphics three ways:

- Insert one using Insert > Graphic.
- Insert one by inserting a text-based file containing graphics: choose Insert > File.
- Paste in a graphic from another document like Draw, using standard operating-system commands.

Inserting

Choose Insert > Graphics and navigate to the graphic you want. The resulting HTML source will look something like this:

```
<IMG SRC="file:///home/solveigh/graphics/beans.gif"
NAME="Graphic2">
```

Practice good HTML practices and change the link to a relative one; if the document and image will be in the same directory, just change it to the following, and change the name if you want as well.

```
<IMG SRC="beans.gif"
NAME="Graphic2">
```

Note – You can click the Properties button in the Insert Graphics window if you want to set properties like wrapping, the graphic name, etc. Information about using the Graphics window and the graphics object bar is included in *Inserting Graphics* on page 268.

Pasting and Inserting via Another File

Choose Insert > File and select the file, containing graphics, to insert.

All graphics in the inserted file will be saved with the document. The HTML source will look something like this:

```
<IMG SRC="sv302303.jpg" NAME="Graphic1" >
```

The name of the graphic is generated automatically, and the file is saved as a JPG.

Note – Each time you save the document, the graphic will be saved again under a different automatically generated name. If you save five times. for example, you'll have five JPG graphics in the folder with your HTML document, with various automatically generated names. This can add up, so use pasting or insertion via another document judiciously.

Changing Links to Graphics or Other Documents in a Document

If you moved one or more graphics or OLE objects (such as spreadsheets or drawings) to a different location, you can update the links in your document using the Edit Links window in Figure 15-18. You can also use this window to just check where your graphics are coming from.

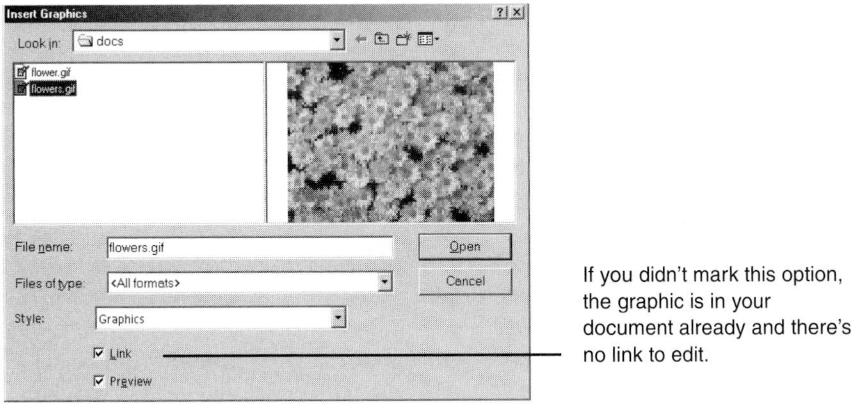

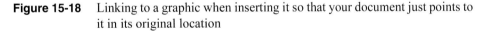

If you didn't mark this option, the graphic is in your document already and there's no link to edit.

Figure 15-18   Linking to a graphic when inserting it so that your document just points to it in its original location

Note – This window is to modify linked objects, not objects that you just inserted. If the Links option in the Edit menu is grayed out or not displayed, it means that all the objects in your document were copied there and there are no links to modify. Figure 15-18 shows the Link option that had to be marked when you inserted objects, in order to have links to edit using this procedure.

1   Choose Edit > Links; all non-text links will be displayed in the Edit Links window.

2   Select any link or links to change and click Modify.

•   If you selected only one link, the Link graphics window will appear; select the correct path to the graphic.

- If you selected two or more links, the Select Directory window will open. Select the folder where you want the selected links to point.

3   The new location or locations for the selected link is displayed in the Edit Links window. **You're not done yet. Click Update.** The window is shown in Figure 15-19. Click Close when you're done.

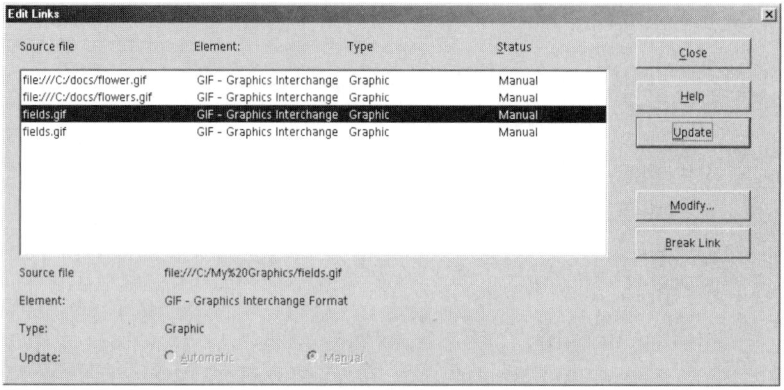

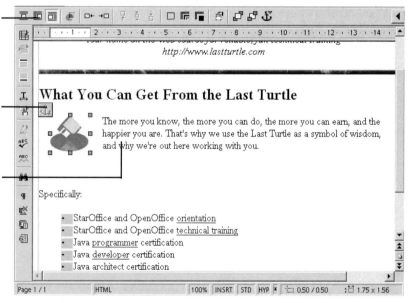

Figure 15-19   Viewing and editing links in a document

Setting Graphics Properties

Graphics positioning and formatting object bar appears when you select an object.

Graphic is anchored to, or associated with, the page, a paragraph, or a character. You also can anchor it as a character.

Text wraps around graphics based on your settings in the Graphics window (right-click the graphic and choose Graphics).

You can resize objects using the same window, and set borders using the object bar.

Figure 15-20   Inserting and formatting graphics

Once you've added the graphic, you can use the graphics properties tools to edit it as necessary. Properties are illustrated in Figure 15-20 on page 470.

Information about using the Graphics window (right-click the object and choose Graphics) and the graphics object bar is included in *Inserting Graphics* on page 268.

Inserting a Horizontal Line

You can use the Horizontal line style for a simple line, or choose Insert > Horizontal Line to select a graphical line (Figure 15-21).

Select Plain for the basic line that's used with the Horizontal line style, or select one from the list.

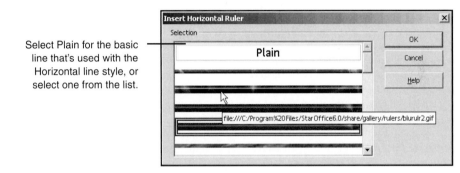

Figure 15-21   Inserting a graphical horizontal line

You can resize the inserted graphical line, but not reposition it.

Page Formatting

The program provides a number of document-wide properties and setup options. See also the Writer sections *Page Layout* on page 227, *Using Frames for Advanced Page Layout* on page 233, and *Example: Creating a Complex Page Layout* on page 240.

Page Setup

Choose Format > Page to view page setup windows for HTML documents; use the Page, Header, and Footer tabs. The windows are the as in Writer; see *Creating Page Styles* on page 251.

Seeing How the Document Will Look Printed

Generally, an HTML document displayed in StarOffice or OpenOffice.org just fills up all the available space and wraps when it needs to, regardless of the settings you've entered in the Page tab of the Page styles window (choose Format > Page).

To see how the document will look when printed, with the page and margin settings you've applied, click the Print Layout On/Off icon on the toolbar.

For information on using Page Preview, which lets you print multiple pages on one sheet of paper and other options, see *Fitting Multiple Pages Onto One Sheet* on page 88.

Using Headers and Footers

You can use the Insert menu or the Insert Header and Insert Footer icons to reserve an area to print information on each page, such as page numbers, file name, and so on. This can be particularly useful with Web pages because they aren't divided into pages online, and it can be difficult to keep track of page order, the document name, and so on if you're distributing printed copies.

Headers and footers function similarly in Writer and Web. See *Headers, Footers, and Fields* on page 281 for more information.

Seeing Headers and Footers

Headers and footers are visible in the document only when Print Layout is activated using the Print Layout On/Off icon on the toolbar.

Adding to Headers and Footers

Use the header and footer in combination with the Insert Fields icon, which lets you insert fields containing page numbers, dates, etc.

Removing and Modifying Headers and Footers

To edit the information in the headers and footers, be sure you're in Print Layout view (see previous section); the headers and footers will be displayed. To remove a row in the header or footer, just delete it as you would a table row (select it, then click the Delete Row icon in the object bar).

You also can delete the header or footer through the Page Format window. Just choose Format > Page and click the Header and Footer tabs. Deselect the Header on and Footer on options.

Setting and Viewing Document Properties

See *Setting Up and Viewing Document Characteristics* on page 153.

Enhancing Web Pages

Adding Hyperlinks to Documents

One of the program's most powerful features is the ability to insert a link to any file or site, into any of its document. With the document open in edit mode, or in other modes such as delivering a presentation, you can click the link to go to the file or site.

You can insert links not only in HTML documents but in Writer, Calc, Impress, and any other documents where the hyperlink bar is available.

To **unlink** items, see *Unlinking* on page 482.

This section covers the following topics:

- How the Hyperlink Toolbar Icons Work
- Setting Relative or Absolute URL Save Options
- Linking to a File, Web Site, FTP Site, Telnet, or Event
- Linking to Targets
- Linking to a New Email or News Document
- Linking to a New Empty File

How the Hyperlink Toolbar Icons Work

The three different URL fields, and all sorts of Link and Hyperlink icons, make it a little hard to figure out what kinds of links you can do with each of the parts of the work area. Figure 16-1 points out the key differences among the link-related features, for inserting hyperlinked text and buttons (inserting graphics that you can hyperlink is covered later in this section).

The Load URL field controls what's displayed right now: the file you're editing, the Web site you're viewing, and so on.

Clicking the Hyperlink Dialog icon opens the Hyperlink window, allowing you to specify what the selected text should link to.

Links you create using the Hyperlink Dialog window have automatic tooltips showing the URL.

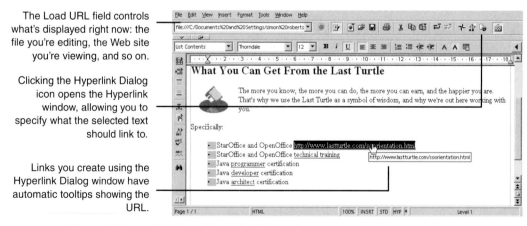

Figure 16-1   Getting to know the link tools

Setting Relative or Absolute URL Save Options

The Save options window contains two fields that control how URLs are saved: relative to the file system or Internet, or absolute. See *Specifying Whether Paths to Objects Are Absolute or Relative* on page 141 to specify how you want URLs saved.

Note – Tool tips always display the absolute path, even if only the relative path is saved. In HTML files, you can choose View > HTML Source to see what's really in the link.

Linking to a File, Web Site, FTP Site, Telnet, or Event

The Hyperlink window lets you create links not only to Web sites and files, but to items such as new email or news documents and scripts. It also lets you set up names for the links, so you can reference those links in scripts. This procedure provides an overview; more advanced features such as linking to a macro are covered in other sections in this and other Web chapters.

An *event* is a function such as clicking, passing the mouse over an object, and so on.

1   Open any document.

2   Position the cursor in the document where you want the link to appear.

3   Click the Hyperlink Dialog icon.

4   On the left side of the window
    (see Figure 16-2), leave Internet selected, or select Document.

    Enter as many links as you want, then click Close.

Note – To change the link later, you can't select it and click the Hyperlink Dialog icon again. You need to select it and choose Edit > Hyperlink.

Enter the site or file that the hyperlink should be directed to.

You can click this to open your browser and find a link, but generally it's not worth the effort. Just use your browser directly.

Click Target if you're linking to a document with targets, then select the target from a list.

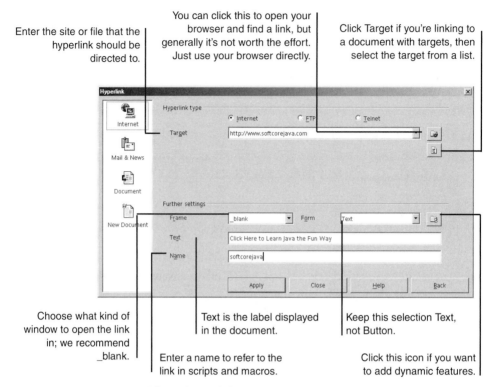

Choose what kind of window to open the link in; we recommend _blank.

Text is the label displayed in the document.

Keep this selection Text, not Button.

Enter a name to refer to the link in scripts and macros.

Click this icon if you want to add dynamic features.

Figure 16-2   Adding a hyperlink:

Linking to Targets

Targets are points within your document that you can specifically link to; for example, you might want to set up a short table of contents at the beginning of the document, and link each line to a particular heading within the document. You can also link to specific objects (these vary depending on the application you're using). This is particularly useful for going to a specific paragraph within a long document.

Linking to a Heading or Object Within a Document

This works with Web, Writer, and Calc documents, but not Impress, Draw, or Image. In Calc you can link to other sheets, and to range names and database ranges.

Note – The heading-linking feature is extremely inconsistent; if you find that clicking on your hyperlink takes you absolutely nowhere, you'll need to do it in the HTML. So don't beat your head against this feature too long. We've covered that in the next procedure, *Linking to a Target Within a Document* on page 478.

1   Open the document.

2   If you're linking to a heading, be sure that one of the styles in heading1 through heading5 is applied. (Choose Format > Stylist.)

3   Select the text that you want hotlinked, so that users clicking on that text will go to a graphic, table, heading, or other element of a document.

4   Click the Hyperlink Dialog icon to display the Hyperlink window (Figure 16-3).

5   In the region on the left side of the window, select Document.

6   If the target item is in a different document, click the Open file icon next to the Path field and select the file.

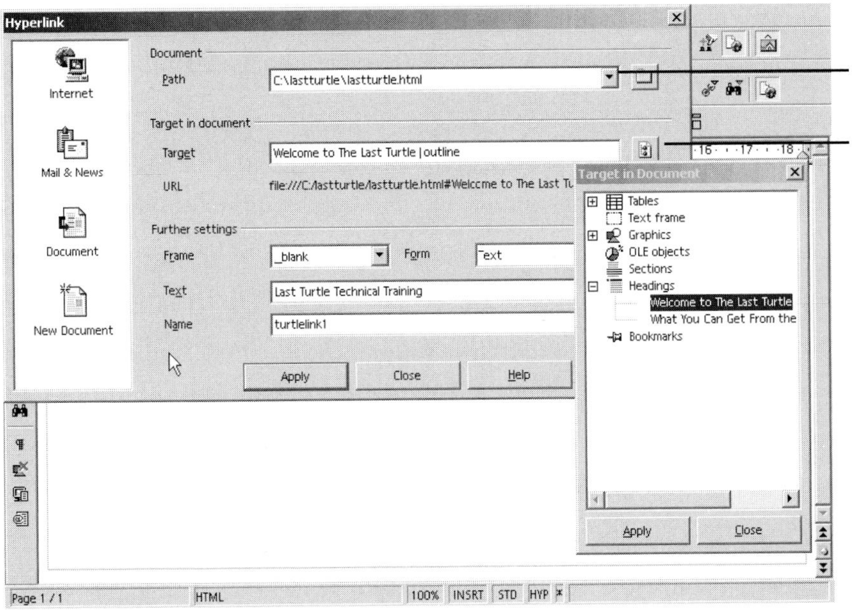

If the item to link to is in another document, specify that document here.

Use this icon to open the Navigator (shown as Target in Document here) and select the object to link to.

Clicking the Target icon opens a version of the navigator, listing all items within your document. Select an item, such as a graphic, and click Apply.

Figure 16-3   Linking to a graphic target or other file target

7   Click the Target in document icon by the Target field to open the navigator, then select the item you want to link to.

8   Click Apply, then Close. In the Hyperlink window, click Apply and Close also.

Note – To name graphics and tables so you can tell which one to select in Navigator, right-click and choose Graphics or Table. Enter a name in the Graphics or Table tab.

Linking to a Target Within a Document

The Hyperlink window doesn't let you link to any text that doesn't have a heading style in the range Heading 1 through Heading 5 applied to it. It also frequently falls flat when you try to link to headings. We've provided instructions on how to do it the old-fashioned way in HTML. (HTML novices, this is extremely easy.)

Creating the Target, Using HTML

1 Open the document containing the items you want to be able to jump to, such as headings within a long document, graphics, or other elements. An example is shown in Figure 16-4.

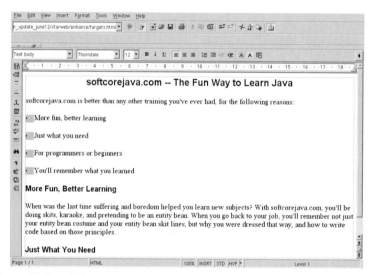

Figure 16-4 File you want to add targets to

2 Plan what you want name the targets: for example, the headings in Figure 16-4 might be morefun, justneed, progbeg, and remember. Just make sure they're all unique.

3 Click the Show HTML Source icon on the toolbar (the last tool) or choose View > HTML Source.

4 Locate the first heading and type the following in front of the heading text:

```
<A NAME="target_name"></A
```

For example, the line for the heading "More Fun, Better Learning" might look like this:

```
<H2><A NAME="morefun"></A>More Fun, Better Learning</H2>
```

5   Repeat the previous step for all elements in the document that you want to be able to jump to.

6   Save the file first, then switch off the HTML source, returning to normal view.

Linking to the Target You Created Using HTML

1   If you want to link from a different document, open it, or just keep the same document open.

2   Choose View > Source.

3   Go to the HTML for the text you want to link *from*. For example, you might have a table of contents at the beginning of the document:

- More fun, better learning
- Just what you need
- For programmers or beginners
- You'll remember what you learned

Go to the text for the first bullet:

```
<UL>
    <LI><P>More fun, better learning</P>
    <LI><P>Just what you need</P>
    <LI><P>For programmers or beginners</P>
    <LI><P>You'll remember what you learned</P>
</UL>
<P><FONT FACE="Arial, sans-serif"><A NAME="morefun"></A><B>More Fun, Better
    Learning</B></FONT></P>
```

4   Add the name of the target as shown in bold in the following example, to everything you want to click on and go to a target.

```
<UL>
    <LI><P><A HREF="morefun">More fun, better learning</A></P>
    <LI><P><A HREF="justneed">Just what you need</A></P>
    <LI><P><A HREF="progbeg">For programmers or beginners</A></P>
    <LI><P><A HREF="remember">You'll remember what you learned</A></P>
</UL>
<P><FONT FACE="Arial, sans-serif"><A NAME="morefun"></A><B>More Fun, Better
    Learning</B></FONT></P>
```

Linking to a New Email or News Document

The Hyperlink window lets you create links not only to Web sites and files, but to items such as new email or news documents and scripts. It also lets you set up names for the links, so you can reference those links in scripts.

Note – More advanced features such as linking to a macro are covered later.

---

1   Open any document.

2   Position the cursor in the document where you want the link to appear.

3   Click the Hyperlink Dialog icon.

4   In the region on the left, select Mail & News (see Figure 16-5).

Enter as many links as you want, then click Close.

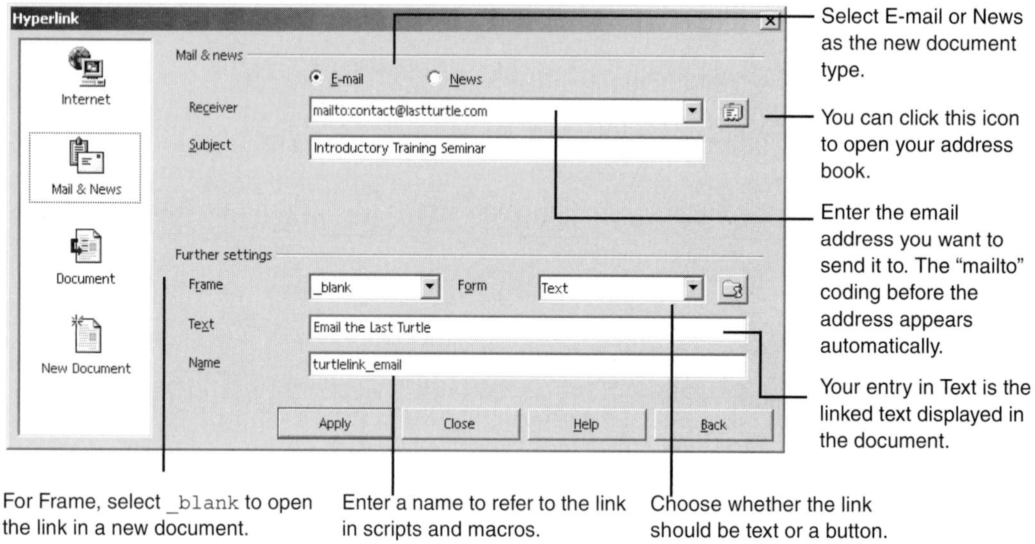

Figure 16-5   Linking to a new email document or news document

Linking to a New Empty File

This feature opens a new empty file of the type you specify when the hyperlink is clicked.

1   Open any document.

2   Position the cursor in the document where you want the link to appear.

3   Click the Hyperlink Dialog icon.

4   In the region on the left, select New Document (Figure 16-6).

Enter as many links as you want, then click Close.

The files are created based on the standard template for the application you select.

Enter the file name; it will be
created in your work folder if
you don't specify a path.

Select Edit now to open the
document when you create it,
or Edit later to only create it.

Select the type of
document to create.

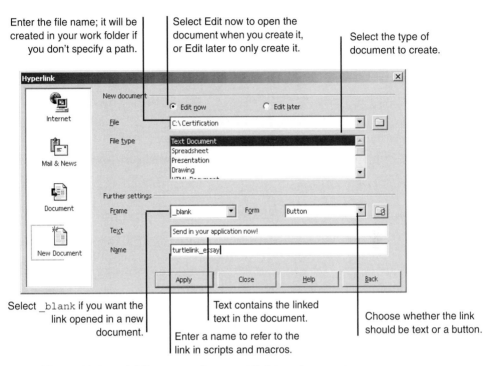

Select `_blank` if you want the
link opened in a new
document.

Text contains the linked
text in the document.

Enter a name to refer to the
link in scripts and macros.

Choose whether the link
should be text or a button.

Figure 16-6   Adding a new document link to a document

Adding Hyperlinks to Graphics

This procedure describes how to add a hyperlink to a graphic you've **already** inserted.

Note – This works only with graphics added using Insert > Graphic, not pasted graphics.

1   Select the graphic, then right-click it and choose Graphics.

2   In the Graphics window, click the Hyperlink tab.

3   Enter the hyperlink information, as shown in Figure 16-7.

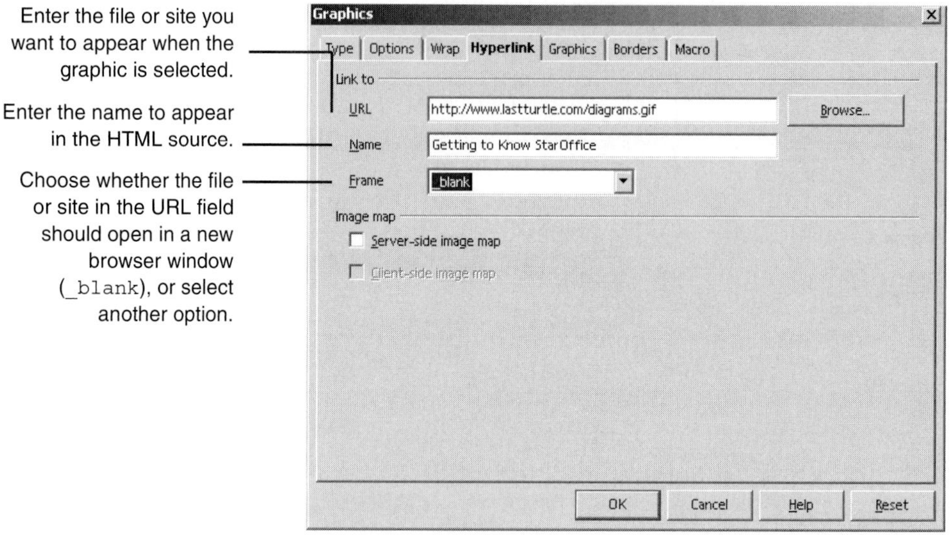

Enter the file or site you want to appear when the graphic is selected.

Enter the name to appear in the HTML source.

Choose whether the file or site in the URL field should open in a new browser window (_blank), or select another option.

Graphics

Type | Options | Wrap | **Hyperlink** | Graphics | Borders | Macro

Link to

URL: http://www.lastturtle.com/diagrams.gif   Browse...

Name: Getting to Know StarOffice

Frame: _blank

Image map

☐ Server-side image map

☐ Client-side image map

OK | Cancel | Help | Reset

Figure 16-7   Hyperlinking a graphic

Unlinking

To unlink a graphic, just open the Graphics window again (right-click and choose Graphics), then click the Graphics tab, delete the URL and click OK.

To unlink a text or button hyperlink, deleting the URL doesn't work. To unlink any text, button, or graphic, select and choose Format > Default.

Viewing and Editing Links in a Document

To change existing links, or see exactly what the link is, you have several options. You can edit the HTML source code, of course. The rest of the options are covered here.

Using the Hyperlink Window

Just select the item and open the Hyperlink window again (click the Hyperlink Dialog icon) to make changes.

Unlinking a Text Link

Select it and choose Format > Default.

Quickly Changing a Text or Button Link

Select a text or button link in the window, change the URL in the Internet URL field, then click the Hyperlink icon on the hyperlink toolbar or press Enter.

Editing an Individual Text Link

Select a link and choose Edit > Hyperlink.

Curiously, this works only for text links created using the Internet URLs or Hyperlink window, not for button links created using that window, or for any graphics links.

Inserting Spreadsheets and Other Objects

The program lets you insert the following into an HTML document:

*   Graphics: any existing raster (GIF, JPG, etc.) graphic.

*   Files: any existing document that can be converted to text, such as HTML or Writer. See *Inserting a Text-Based File* in this section.

*   OLE objects: new or existing spreadsheet, drawing, chart, image, formula, or presentation. See *Inserting Files and Objects* in this section.

Note – OLE objects aren't dynamically updated. If you change the original, the inserted object doesn't change, and vice versa. The advantage of using OLE objects is that they retain their original properties, and you can edit them in the HTML document.

---

*   Formulas and charts. See *Charts* on page 284 and *Mathematical Formulas* on page 293.

Inserting a Text-Based File

Note – The font size of the file might be a lot different when it's inserted.

---

1   Choose Insert > File and navigate to the file you want.

Insert > File can convert only text-based files. To insert other files, use one of the other Insert menu options.

2   Select the closest filter to convert with, if you're prompted to, and click OK.

The contents of the file will be inserted, with their original formatting in an editable format.

Inserting Files and Objects

A very useful feature you might have overlooked is inserting OLE objects—it's just a techy way of inserting another file, like a drawing or a spreadsheet, into your document. OLE stands for object linking and embedding; it means you can edit the file using its native editing capabilities, even when it's inserted in a different document. OLE objects include new or existing spreadsheets, drawings, charts, images, formulas, and presentations.

You can't move OLE objects to other applications via the clipboard or drag and drop in or out of the program.

Inserting an Existing Object

Editing OLE objects that exist as separate files varies, depending on which files are open.

- If you edit the inserted OLE object, the original never changes.

- If the original and the HTML file containing the inserted object are both open, changes you make in the original take effect only in the inserted object.

- If the HTML document is not open, the changes take place only in the original.

Once you've inserted the object, the next time you save the HTML document, the object will be saved and a .gif file, such as sv335337.gif, will be created in the same directory as the HTML file. A new .gif will be created each time you save the HTML file.

1   Choose Insert > Object > OLE Object.

2   In the Insert OLE Object, select Create from file and select the file you want.

3   The file will appear in the HTML document (see Figure 16-8).

4   If Navigator is active, a form of the Navigator will appear, allowing you to manage the object.

5   To edit the object in your HTML document, right-click it and choose Edit. See the notes at the beginning of this procedure on how editing is affected by which files are open.

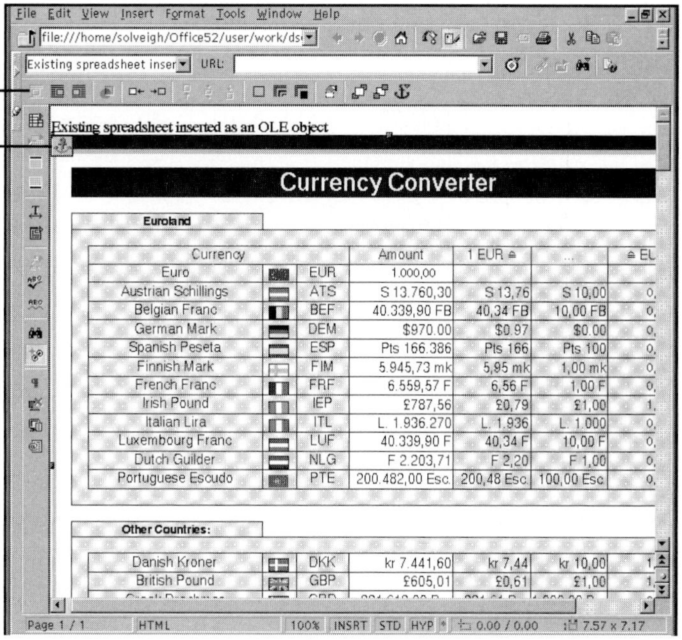

The object toolbar is displayed; right-click and choose Edit to display the toolbar for the type of file you inserted. ——

The anchor for the object is — displayed here.

Figure 16-8   Inserted object

Inserting a New Object

1   Choose Insert > Object > OLE Object.

2   In the Insert OLE Object window (Figure 16-9), select Create New, then select the type of object to insert.

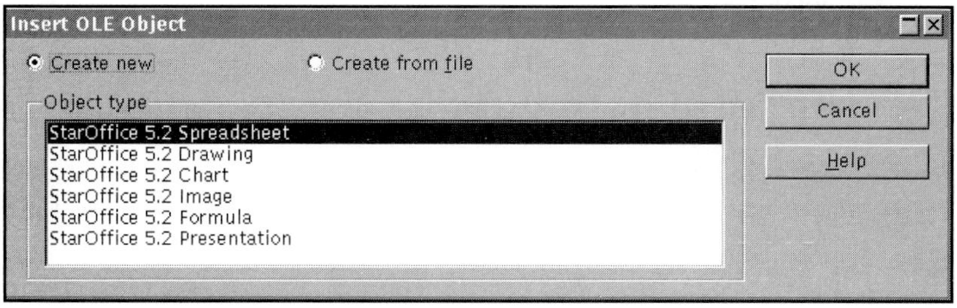

Figure 16-9   Inserting a new object

3   Click OK; the new object will appear.

4   If Navigator is active, a form of the Navigator will appear, allowing you to manage the object.

Click in the object to access the file type's object bar. Right-click to access the standard options (Figure 16-10).

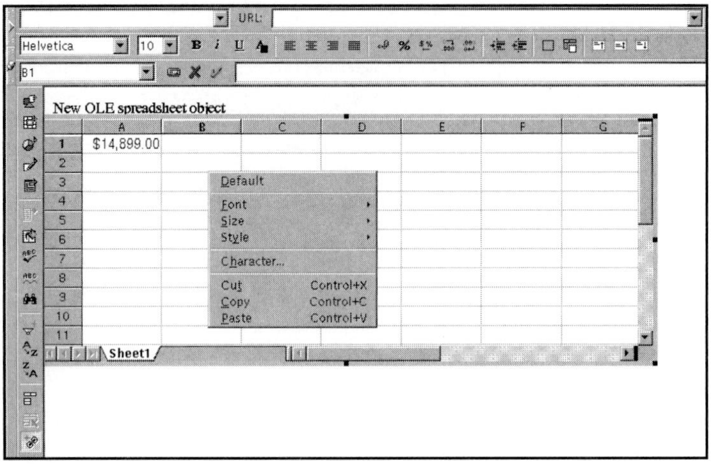

Figure 16-10   New OLE spreadsheet inserted into an HTML document

Using Animated GIFs and Animated Text

Scrolling or blinking text marquees and animated GIFs can create startling effects in your pages and presentations; however, use them with caution. You've probably seen animated graphics in Web pages, where they can be attention-grabbing and effective if used properly, and annoying and distracting if not.

In addition, note that marquees aren't supported in all browsers; Netscape 4.75 doesn't support them.

Creating a Text Marquee

The program provides its own way to insert a piece of text that scrolls across your Web page, such as "All Hipwaders 50% Off," or "Be Elf-Dander Free Today".

1   Click the Text animation icon in the toolbar.

2   Draw the rectangle where you want the text. If you want the text to scroll, draw the rectangle across the entire scrolling area (Figure 16-11).

Be sure to draw it in the correct place in the page; you can drag the borders later to resize it, but you can't move it.

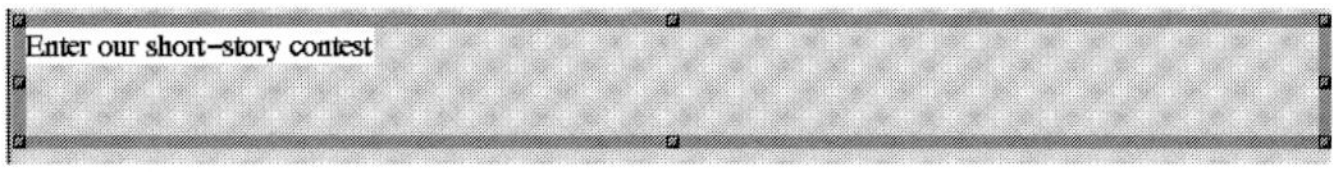

Figure 16-11   Creating a text marquee text box

3   Immediately type the text in the rectangle. (This is important; if you click outside the rectangle, it will disappear and you won't be able to reselect it.)

4   Select the text. Use the Character window or the text object bar to format the text.

5   Be sure the text isn't selected, then right-click on the text frame and choose Text. Click the Text Animation tab (Figure 16-12) and enter the appropriate information.

6   Click outside the frame; the text will run.

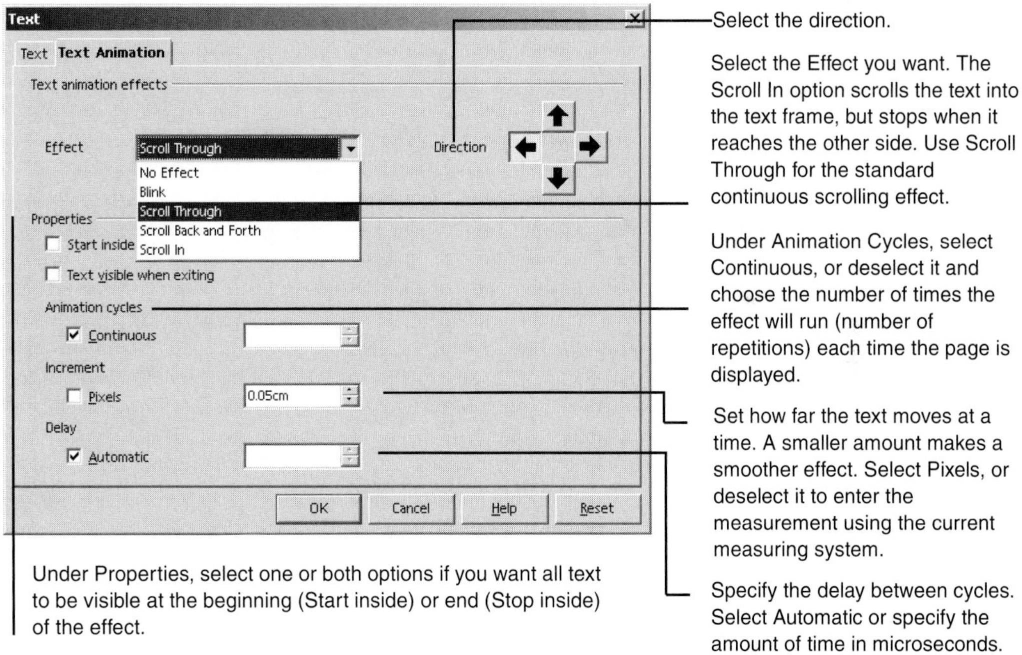

Select the direction.

Select the Effect you want. The Scroll In option scrolls the text into the text frame, but stops when it reaches the other side. Use Scroll Through for the standard continuous scrolling effect.

Under Animation Cycles, select Continuous, or deselect it and choose the number of times the effect will run (number of repetitions) each time the page is displayed.

Set how far the text moves at a time. A smaller amount makes a smoother effect. Select Pixels, or deselect it to enter the measurement using the current measuring system.

Under Properties, select one or both options if you want all text to be visible at the beginning (Start inside) or end (Stop inside) of the effect.

Specify the delay between cycles. Select Automatic or specify the amount of time in microseconds.

Figure 16-12   Setting text marquee options

Animated GIFs

If you've surfed the Web much, you've seen animated icons flashing information like "New!" or "Enter Our Spamku Contest!" with text, graphics, or both. You can add these to your Web pages using Impress, following the instructions in *Animated GIFs* on page 722.

Creating Image Maps

You can make a useful, impressive-looking Web page with an image map, a graphic that has multiple hyperlinks to different locations.

The Web page in Figure 16-13 is a good candidate for an image map; the blueprint of the house provides information as well as a good way to navigate through the site.

An image map of this graphic could link to a different site for each room in the house.

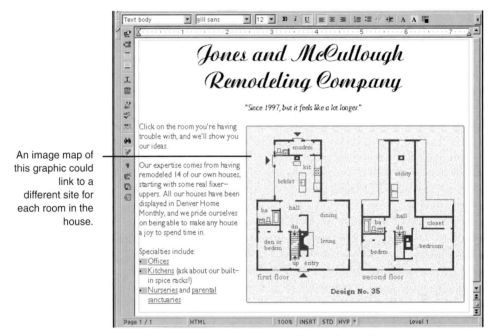

Figure 16-13   Web page with graphic that can be used as an image map

Image maps are remarkably straightforward to use. Follow these steps.

1   Add the graphic to your Web page.

2   Select the graphic; the graphic object bar will appear.

3   Click the Image Map icon.

4   The Image Map Editor window will appear (Figure 16-14).

5   Click one of the four shape tools, such as Rectangle, and draw on the graphic the outline of the first area you want to link.

6   Enter link information for the area. Click the green Apply arrow to save changes after you draw and enter information for each area.

Use these tools to
change the shape of the
area you draw. See
page 762 for more
information.

The text you enter here
will appear when the
mouse passes over the
area; if you don't enter
anything, the address
will be displayed.

Enter the site or file to
link to. To link to a
macro or script, click the
Macro icon and refer to
page 494.

Any area you've defined
is shown dimmed, with
green handles.

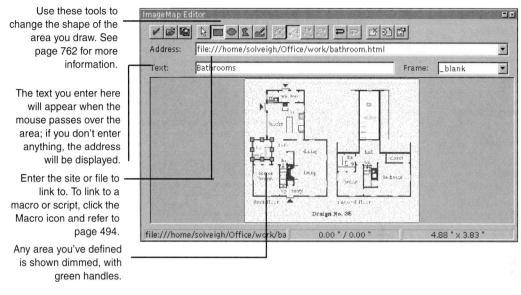

Figure 16-14   Drawing areas to link from in the image map

Adding Applets and Plugins

Applets are mini-programs, written in the Java programming language, that can run within
a browser. Plugins add functionality such as the ability to play certain sound formats.

Applets

It's up to you to either locate or write the applet itself. Once you have the file, though,
follow these steps to add it to any document.

1   Use the Insert Applet feature on the toolbar's Insert tearoff
menu, or choose Insert > Object > Applet.

2   The Insert Applet window will appear (Figure 16-15).
Enter the applet information and click OK.

Note – If you enter parameters, be sure that you enter them exactly right, especially
paths to files. The program won't do any checking for you, and will continue to
attempt to find the referenced file, slowing down your system. "Applet not initial-
ized" will appear in the status bar.

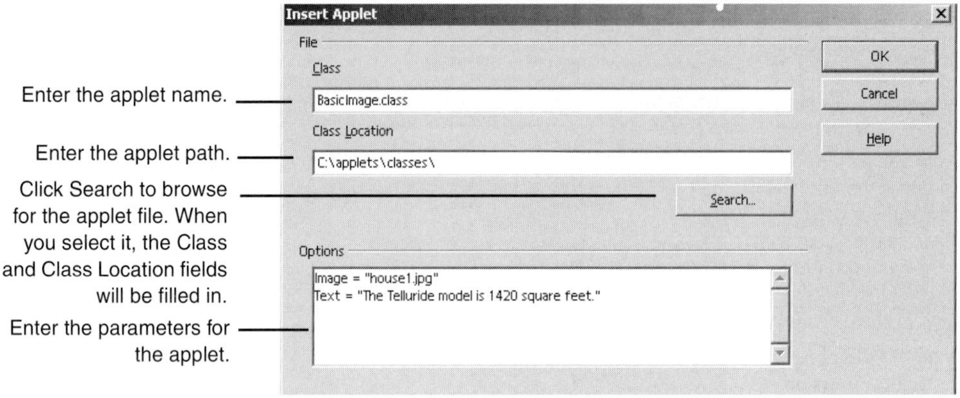

Enter the applet name. ——

Enter the applet path. ——

Click Search to browse
for the applet file. When
you select it, the Class
and Class Location fields
will be filled in. ——

Enter the parameters for ——
the applet.

Figure 16-15 Inserting an applet

Plugins

Plugins are browser extensions that offer additional functions. If you need to add one to a document, follow these steps.

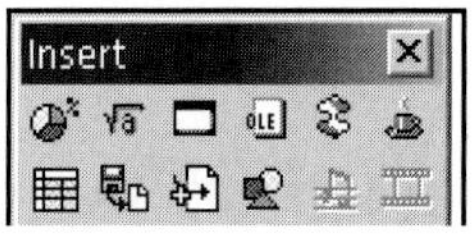

1 Use the Insert Plugin feature on the toolbar's Insert tearoff menu, or choose Insert > Object > Plugin.

2 The Insert Plugin window will appear (Figure 16-16). Enter the plugin information and click OK.

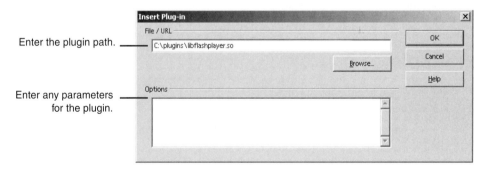

Enter the plugin path. ——

Enter any parameters ——
for the plugin.

Figure 16-16 Inserting a plugin

Using Macros, Scripts, and Events

Learning More Before You Begin

Ensure you've set the right setup option in *Specifying StarBasic Macro Options* on page 151.

This section covers basics of how to link to or insert scripts, macros, and events, just in the context of having them in your HTML page. These are advanced topics; to learn more about macros, see *Macro Basics* on page 965. To learn more about events, see Chapter 36, *Creating and Using Forms, Controls, and Events*, on page 925.

What You Can Do in This Section

This section covers how to add scripts to any document, whether by inserting them in a document so that they're run when the document is loaded, or associating them with a graphic or text link.

You can also link macros and JavaScript to text or button hyperlink events.

Finally, you can create controls, like a push button, and attach them to macros or events. *Events* are actions like moving the mouse over the hyperlink, clicking the mouse on the hyperlink, and moving the mouse away from the hyperlink.

Inserting Scripts in Documents

You can insert JavaScript in documents. The inserted script is indicated by a small green square.

To attach JavaScript to a control, such as a button; see *Macro and Events Basics* on page 951; to attach it to a hyperlink, see *Using Macros, Scripts, and Events* on page 491.

Showing and Hiding Script Indicators

To show or hide note indicators, choose Tools > Options > HTML Document > Contents and select or deselect the Notes option. This applies to the indicator for notes, as well.

Inserting a Script

1   Choose Insert > Script.

2   The Insert Script window will appear (Figure 16-17). Enter the plugin information and click OK.

Specify the type of script you're inserting.

Select the source for the script, then enter the URL or the script text.

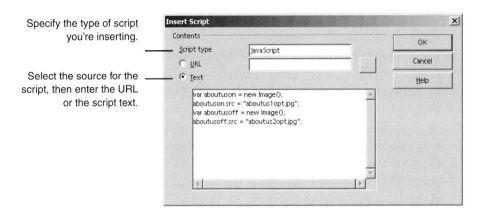

Figure 16-17   Inserting a script

Editing Scripts

1   Double-click the green script indicator.

2   The Edit Script window is like the Insert Script window, except that you can browse from script to script using the arrows.

Printing Scripts

The Print Options window lets you choose whether to print document scripts and notes, and where. See page 497 for more information.

Just Typing Macros in the HTML Source

StarOffice or OpenOffice.org macros have to be in the header of the HTML document. After you add the macro to the document, it will appear in the source text of the HTML document (in the header) with the following syntax (a "Hello World" example macro is used):

```
<HEAD>
(any additional content)
<SCRIPT LANGUAGE="STARBASIC">
<!--
' $LIBRARY: library_name
' $MODULE: module_name
Sub test
msgbox "Hello World"
End Sub
// -->
</SCRIPT>
</HEAD>
```

Inserting Hyperlinks to Macros and Scripts

You've already learned how to make text and graphics hyperlinks that will take you to a file or Web page. You can also make them run scripts, using the procedures in this section.

Linking Macros and Scripts to Text or a Button

1 Open any document.

2 Position the cursor in the document where you want the link to appear.

3 Choose Insert > Hyperlink or click the Hyperlink Dialog icon.

4 On the left side of the Hyperlink window, select any of the options: Internet, New Document, etc.

5 Set up the link for the appropriate type of link (see page 475 through page 480).

6 Click the Events icon.

7 In the Assign Macro window (Figure 16-18), select one of the events.

Note – If you add an existing macro, be sure the macro's library (the category it's listed within) is activated. Choose Tools > Macros, click the Organizer button, then click the Libraries tab and be sure the checkbox next to the library is checked.

Enter the appropriate information, then click OK.

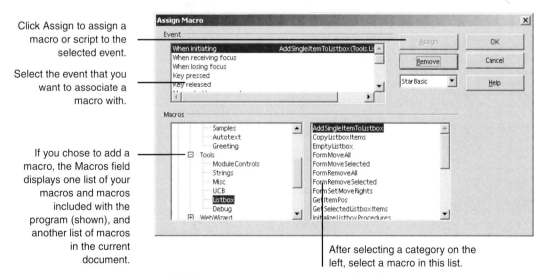

Click Assign to assign a macro or script to the selected event.

Select the event that you want to associate a macro with.

If you chose to add a macro, the Macros field displays one list of your macros and macros included with the program (shown), and another list of macros in the current document.

After selecting a category on the left, select a macro in this list.

Figure 16-18   Linking a button or text to a macro using the Assign Macro window

Linking Macros to Graphics

If you've added a graphic to a document, you can use the Graphics window to make it trigger an action.

1   Right-click the graphic and choose Graphics.

2   In the Graphics window, click the Macro tab (Figure 16-19).

3   Select an event that will trigger the macro.

    Enter the appropriate information, then click OK.

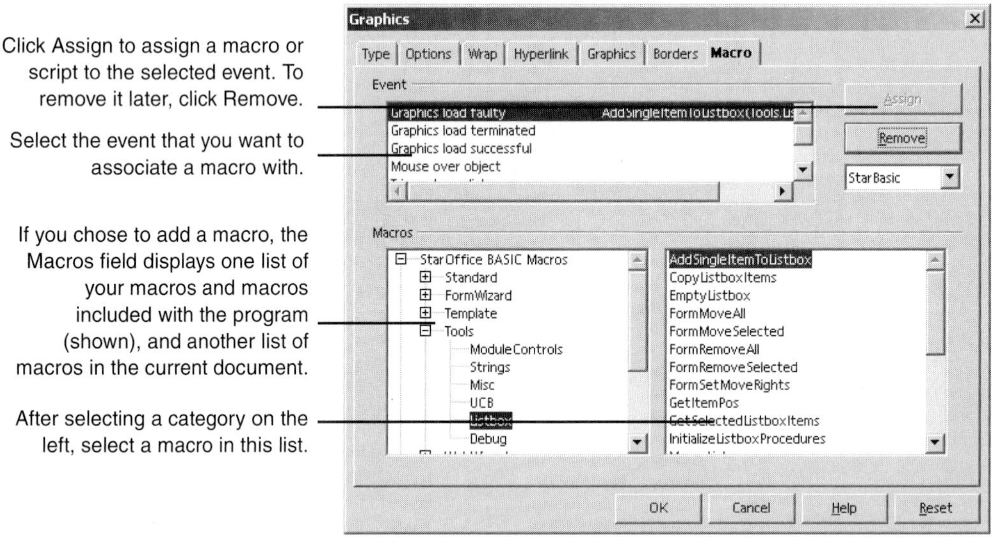

Click Assign to assign a macro or script to the selected event. To remove it later, click Remove.

Select the event that you want to associate a macro with.

If you chose to add a macro, the Macros field displays one list of your macros and macros included with the program (shown), and another list of macros in the current document.

After selecting a category on the left, select a macro in this list.

Figure 16-19   Linking a graphic to a macro using the Graphics window

Note – Most of the macro-insertion features in the program let you insert a macro from the Standard and other libraries, and from the document you're currently in, but not any other documents you've created. If you're having trouble finding the macro you want, it's probably in a separate document. You'll need to cut and paste it into a module in the Standard library, a new library, or create a module for it in your current document.

Printing in Web

Printing Procedures

Most of the procedures you need are in Chapter 4, *Printer Setup and Printing*, on page 59. In particular, see:

- *Creating UNIX Printers* on page 60
- *Standard Printing* on page 79
- *Setting Up Printing to PDF* on page 72
- *Printing to PostScript and PDF* on page 81
- *Printing Brochures* on page 90
- *Printing From the Command Line* on page 83
- *Specifying Portrait or Landscape Orientation* on page 86
- In the Writer printing chapter, *Printing Multiple Pages With Page Preview* on page 432
- In the Writer printing chapter, *Printing Notes* on page 431
- And in the Mail Merge chapter, *Printing* on page 399

The rest of the procedures here cover Web-specific printing or procedures that aren't worth sending you to the other side of the book for.

Basic Printing

Follow these steps if you want to specify particular options, or use the Print File Directly icon on the program toolbar, which uses the options and printer last selected. See also *Standard Printing* on page 79.

1 Choose File > Print.

2 Select a printer, or select the Print to file option and enter a file name. To print to a PostScript file, enter a name with a .ps extension.

3 Click Options and select the appropriate print options (see Figure 17-1). Click OK.

4 Select what to print: All (the entire document), Pages (a range of pages), or Selection (the currently selected text or objects). Use dashes to form ranges, and use commas or semicolons to separate pages or ranges (1, 3, 4, 6-10).

> **Note –** The program often defaults to Selection, rather than All, as the range of pages to print. Check this each time you print.

5 Enter the number of copies and, if it's two or more, choose whether to collate.

6 Click Print.

Web Printing Options

1   Choose Tools > Options > HTML Document > Print, or choose File > Print and click
     the Options button.

2   Select what you want to print.

It's a good idea to select the Create single print jobs option. If you don't select it, the first
page of the second copy might be printed on the back of the last page of the first copy.

If you select a printer in the Print window and a fax here, the printer will be used.

The Print Options window is shown in Figure 17-1.

Select the elements you want to print. Select Print black if you want
all text printed black, regardless of its onscreen color.

Choose to print in reversed order, or
to print as a brochure (see page 90).

Choose how to print notes (see
information on page 497).

Select the Create Single Print Jobs
option to start each additional copy of
the document on a new page, even if
you are using a duplex printer.

For printers with multiple trays, this
option specifies that the defined paper
source in the printer setup will be
used.

To fax the document, select the fax
machine here or in the main print
window. (See *Setting Up Faxing
Capabilities* on page 69.)

Figure 17-1   Selecting printing options

Single print jobs and duplex printers Be careful of the Create Single Print Jobs option
in the Form Letter or Print Options window, for any application, when you print to a
duplex printer. If this option is selected, each new print job will begin on a new page even
if you are using a duplex printer. If this field is not checked then the first page of the
second copy might be printed on the reverse side of the last page of the first copy,
especially if there is an odd page number.

Brochures The Brochure feature is implemented in an extremely clumsy way. If you'd
like to read more about it, however, see *Printing Brochures* on page 90.

Printing notes The Print Options window lets you choose whether to print notes in the
page. (To add notes to your documents, see *Inserting Notes* on page 465.) To print notes,
see *Printing Notes* on page 431.

Calc

Getting Started With Calc

Quick Start

This section contains the following information to help you get started quickly:

*   A checklist that points you to common tasks for quick reference
*   Feature overview
*   Multiple ways of starting Calc
*   An overview of the Calc work area
*   A five-minute tutorial

See Chapter 5, *Setup and Tips*, on page 97 for general tips that can make working with the program easier.

Quick Start Checklist

If you need to create a spreadsheet quickly, the following sections should be particularly helpful:

*   Starting a document based on a template – *Creating a Calc Document From a Template* on page 513
*   Adding and renaming sheets – *Adding Sheets to a Spreadsheet* on page 525
*   Formatting cells – *Quick Cell Formatting* on page 543
*   Adding charts – *Inserting Charts* on page 594 and *Modifying Charts* on page 596
*   Adding headers and footers – *Setting Up Headers and Footers* on page 553
*   Controlling printing, including repeating headings – *Repeating Spreadsheet Headings (Rows or Columns) on Each Page* on page 628

Calc Features

Calc is every bit as powerful as any spreadsheet application on the market, and in many ways it's superior. Following are some of the features that set Calc apart:

Document Filters Calc has a huge number of filters for opening documents created in other formats. Its filter for Microsoft Excel is particularly good.

Graphics Support You can insert graphics of just about every conceivable format, including Adobe Photoshop PSD.

Conversion from Microsoft The AutoPilot (wizard) lets you convert Microsoft Office documents (even entire directories of them) with a few clicks.

Version Control You can store versions of a Calc document as it moves through a lifecycle, letting you revert back to an earlier version if necessary. Calc also offers a full set of editing aids that display changes made to a document.

Sort Lists You can define lists of items, such as months, that sort in a particular order rather than alphabetically or numerically.

Conditional Formatting You can set cells to dynamically change formats based on the values in cells.

Seamless Compatibility With Databases You can drag a database table and drop it into Calc to open it in a spreadsheet, and you can turn a spreadsheet into a database by dragging it onto a database table in the Explorer window. Calc also lets you save spreadsheets as dBase database tables.

Cell Protection You can lock cells so the data can't be changed manually.

Controlling Valid Entries Calc lets you allow only specific values or ranges of values to be entered in a cell.

Scenarios You can store many sets of data within the same block of cells, letting you select from a list of scenarios you set up. For example, you can store interest rate information for many banks in the same cell, and switch between the banks from a drop-down list. If the cell is used in a formula, the results of the formula change when you select a different bank.

Goal Seek If you know the total you want a cell to contain, but you don't know one of the values needed in a formula to reach that total, this feature calculates the missing value.

Starting Calc

Choose File > New > Spreadsheet.

Help With Calc

In addition to the Help topics mentioned in *Getting Help* on page 98, see *Good Online Information Sources* on page 42.

The Calc Work Area

Use tooltips to get to know Calc. There are tooltips for almost all fields and icons. Just position your mouse over anything you want to know the name of. You can turn tooltips on and off by choosing Help > Tips.

Clicking the Help button in a window or pressing F1 is the quickest way to get help for that window. If only general help appears, click in a field in the window.

Figure 18-1 shows the major components of the Calc environment.

The function bar displays the path of the open file and lets you access global functions.

In addition to showing global commands, the menu bar shows commands specific to the active application.

The object bar lets you apply formatting to selected cells and text.

The formula bar lets you enter formulas, create a quick sum, launch the Function AutoPilot, and navigate to spreadsheet areas you've named

The toolbar lets you access commonly used spreadsheet features.

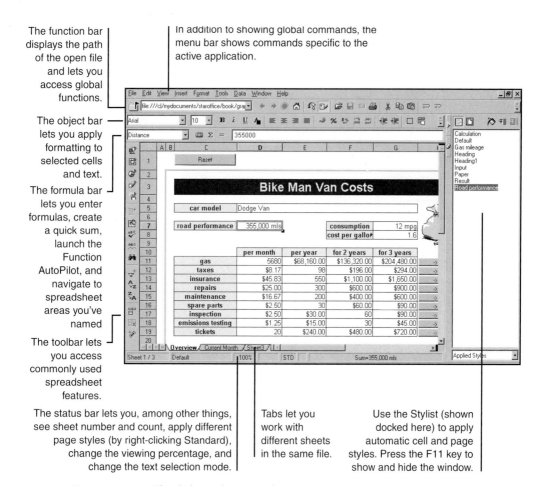

The status bar lets you, among other things, see sheet number and count, apply different page styles (by right-clicking Standard), change the viewing percentage, and change the text selection mode.

Tabs let you work with different sheets in the same file.

Use the Stylist (shown docked here) to apply automatic cell and page styles. Press the F11 key to show and hide the window.

Figure 18-1   The Calc work area

Guided Tour of Calc

Use this tutorial to give you a brief introduction to the Calc environment.

1   Launch Calc.

2   Click cell **A1**, type `Credit Card Calculator`, and press Enter. Cell A2 becomes selected.

	A	B	C
1	Credit Card Calculator		
2			
3			

3   Click cell **A1** again, and in the object bar, change the font size to 24.

You can also right-click the cell, choose Format Cells, and in the Cell Attributes window select the Font tab to change the font size.

4 Click the number 1 in the gray box of row 1. The entire row is selected.

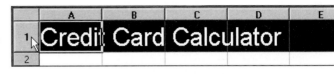

5 In the object bar, click the Background Color icon, and select a light background color for row 1.

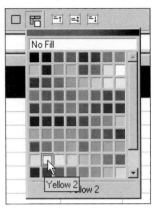

6 In this step you'll enter some row headings. Enter the following text in the corresponding cells, pressing Enter after each entry. (Click each cell to enter the text):

- **A4** – `APR

(Don't forget the single quote at the beginning. It allows you to use the acronym APR [annual percentage rate] in all capital letters so that Calc doesn't read it as the month April.)

- **B4** – Monthly Interest
- **C4** – Starting Balance
- **D4** – Monthly Payment

Notice that not all the text shows in the cells now, as shown in Figure 18-2. Normally you can resize the column widths, have the text wrap in the cells, or both. In this tutorial we'll have you wrap the text.

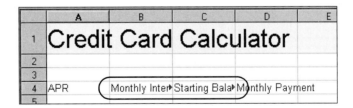

Figure 18-2   Text that is too wide for cells

7 Click and hold down the mouse button in cell A4, and drag across the row so that rows **A4 through D4** are selected.

8 Choose Format > Cells.

9 In the Cell Attributes window, click the Alignment tab.

10 Select the Line break option and click OK. The text in those cells wraps to show all the text, as shown in Figure 18-3.

Cell Attributes

Numbers | Font | Font Effects | **Alignment** | Asian Typography | Borders | Background | Cell Protection

Text alignment

Horizontal
Default

Indent
0pt

Vertical
Middle

Text direction

ABCD

Degrees
0

Reference edge

	A	B	C	D
1	Credit Card Calculator			
2				
3				
4	APR	Monthly Interest	Starting Balance	Monthly Payment
5				

Spacing to grid lines

Left 0.01"   Top 0.01"

Right 0.01"   Bottom 0.01"

Text flow

☑ Line break

☐ Hyphenation active

OK   Cancel   Help   Reset

Figure 18-3   Wrapping text in cells

11 Select cells **A4 through D4** again.

12 In the object bar, click the Bold icon to make the text bold, and click the centered text alignment icon to center the text in the cells.

13 With the cells still highlighted, in the object bar click and hold down the Borders icon, and select the border that shows a line beneath a cell.

14 Select cell **A5** and click the % icon on the object bar. This tells the cell to display a percentage (even though there's no confirmation when you click the icon). Enter the number `.18` (don't forget the decimal point). Press the Tab key.

15 In cell **B5**, click the % icon on the object bar. Now enter the following small formula in the cell, pressing the Tab key afterwards:

`=A5/12`

This formula means divide the contents of cell A5 by 12. What you're doing is figuring a monthly interest rate percentage by dividing the annual percentage rate by 12 months.

16 In cell **C5**, click the Currency icon. This tells the cell to display a dollar amount. Enter 7000. This beginning balance is the amount you have charged to your credit card (ouch!). Press the Tab key.

17 In cell **D5**, click the Currency icon and enter the number 250. This is the amount you're going to pay each month. Press Enter.

Figure 18-4 shows how your spreadsheet should look so far:

	A	B	C	D
1	Credit Card Calculator			
2				
3				
4	APR	Monthly Interest	Starting Balance	Monthly Payment
5	18.00%	1.50%	$7,000.00	$250.00
6				

Figure 18-4   This is how your spreadsheet should look at this point

18 In cells **A8 through D8**, enter the following text, then make the text bold and centered with a line under the cells (as you did starting in step 11), as shown in Figure 18-5.

7				
8	Payment #	Interest	Principal	Balance
9				

Figure 18-5   Formatting heading cells

19 In cell **A9**, under Payment #, type 1.

20 In cell **B9**, under Interest, click the currency icon on the object bar and enter the following formula, then press the Tab key:

`=$B$5*$C$5`

This formula multiplies the contents of cell B5 by the contents of cell C5 (multiplying the monthly interest rate by the credit card balance). The dollar signs ($) are absolute cell references, which we go into detail about on page 572.

21 In cell **C9**, under Principal, click the Currency icon and enter the following formula, then press the Tab key:

`=$D$5-B9`

This formula subtracts the amount of interest you're paying that month from your monthly payment, which gives you the amount of principal subtracted from your overall credit card balance.

22 In cell **D9**, under Balance, enter the following formula, then press the Tab key:

`=$C$5-C9`

This subtracts the Principal of the monthly payment from the Starting Balance credit card balance. Your spreadsheet should now look like Figure 18-6.

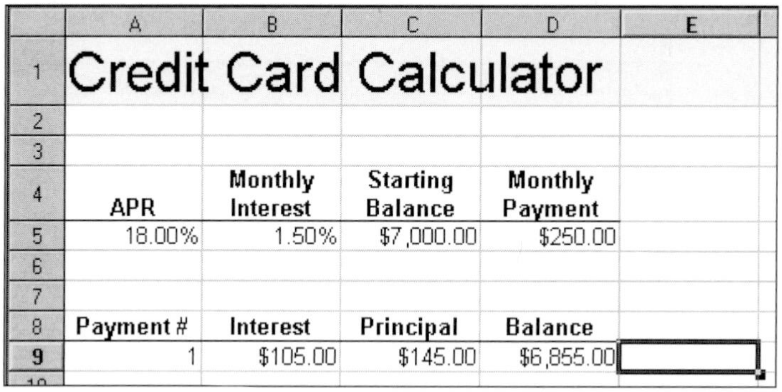

	A	B	C	D	E
1	Credit Card Calculator				
2					
3					
4	APR	Monthly Interest	Starting Balance	Monthly Payment	
5	18.00%	1.50%	$7,000.00	$250.00	
6					
7					
8	Payment #	Interest	Principal	Balance	
9	1	$105.00	$145.00	$6,855.00	

Figure 18-6   This is how your spreadsheet should look at this point

The next steps may seem a little redundant, but they set the stage for the really cool part of the tutorial.

23   In cell **A10**, the Payment # column, type the number 2.

24   Select cells **B10 through D10** and click the Currency icon.

25   In cell **B10**, in the Interest column, enter the following formula, followed by the Tab key:

=D9*$B$5

26   In cell **C10**, in the Principal column, enter the following formula followed by the Tab key:

=$D$5-B10

27   In cell **D10**, in the Balance column, enter the following formula followed by the Tab key:

=D9-C10

Your spreadsheet should now look like Figure 18-7.

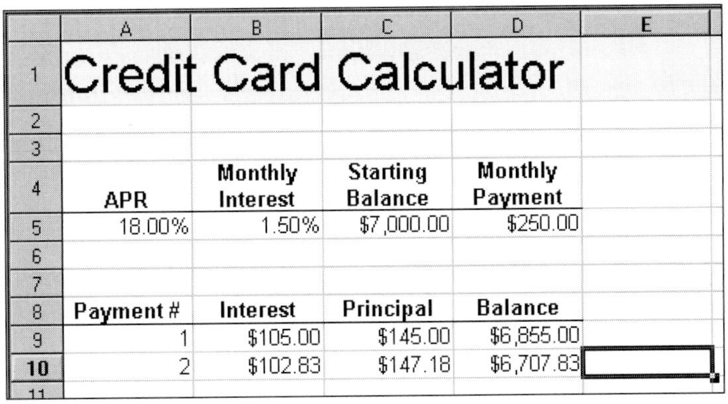

	A	B	C	D	E
1	Credit Card Calculator				
2					
3					
4	APR	Monthly Interest	Starting Balance	Monthly Payment	
5	18.00%	1.50%	$7,000.00	$250.00	
6					
7					
8	Payment #	Interest	Principal	Balance	
9	1	$105.00	$145.00	$6,855.00	
10	2	$102.83	$147.18	$6,707.83	
11					

Figure 18-7   This is how your spreadsheet should look at this point

Now comes the fun part. You're going to fill in data about successive payments automatically by clicking and dragging.

28 Select cells **A10 through D10**.

29 On the lower right corner of the selected area, there's a little black square (called the automatic fill handle). Move the mouse pointer on top of that little square. The pointer changes to cross hairs. Click and hold down the mouse button, drag down to row 19, and release the mouse button. The entire selected area fills in with data.

Figure 18-8 illustrates this.

If the new information is all exactly the same, press the F9 key to recalculate the spreadsheet.

If you hadn't used absolute and relative cell references in your formulas (discussed on page 572), you would have gotten some crazy results that didn't make sense financially when you filled down.

You can fill down even further the same way by selecting cells A19 through D19 and dragging down. You can drag down to where you can see how many payments it's going to take to pay off the credit card.

Figure 18-8   Dragging to fill down

Now let's do something depressing and calculate the total amount of interest you're going to pay based on the number of payments you've filled in.

30 In cell **E8**, create a column heading called Total Interest Paid, formatted the same way as the other column headings.

31 In cell **E9**, click the Currency icon and enter the following formula, followed by the Tab key:

=SUM(B9:B500)

This formula simply adds up all the amounts in the Interest column, from cells B9 to B500 (in case you ever fill down that far), as shown in Figure 18-9.

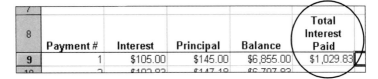

Figure 18-9   Calculating the total interest paid

32 Get out your scissors and cut up your credit card!

Post-Tutorial Tips

The beauty of spreadsheets is that, if they're set up somewhat correctly (that is, if you set cells up to calculate based on values in other cells, as you did in this exercise), you can change a value in one or two cells to update the values in the entire spreadsheet.

For example, if you change the APR percentage in the tutorial spreadsheet (don't forget to start with a decimal point), your entire spreadsheet updates to show what your payment information would be at a different annual interest rate. You can also see different payment scenarios by entering a different monthly payment amount.

Make sure you don't try to change spreadsheet information by typing inside cells that have formulas in them. That messes up the whole automated nature of the spreadsheet and can throw off lots of other cell amounts. You can tell if a cell has a formula in it by selecting the cell and looking in the formula bar.

Note – You can protect yourself *from* yourself by protecting certain cells you don't want changed, making it so you can't type anything in them. See *Protecting Cells From Modification* on page 604.

Calc Setup Options

Calc lets you control hundreds of options—probably more than you will ever need to control. Choose Tools > Options > Spreadsheet to view the Calc options.

We don't go through each window of options one by one, for the following reasons:

*   The important settings are covered in procedures throughout the book.

*   Many are self-explanatory.

*   The default settings for these options are generally well chosen.

However, the options aren't in an obvious place in any of the menu bars or object bars—you need to choose Tools > Options > Spreadsheet—so we've pointed them out here to make sure you're aware of them (see Figure 18-10). It's also helpful to know what types of functions these options do control, so if you want to know that before you start using this program, open the options now to get an idea of their scope before continuing.

The options are default values used for each new Calc spreadsheet.

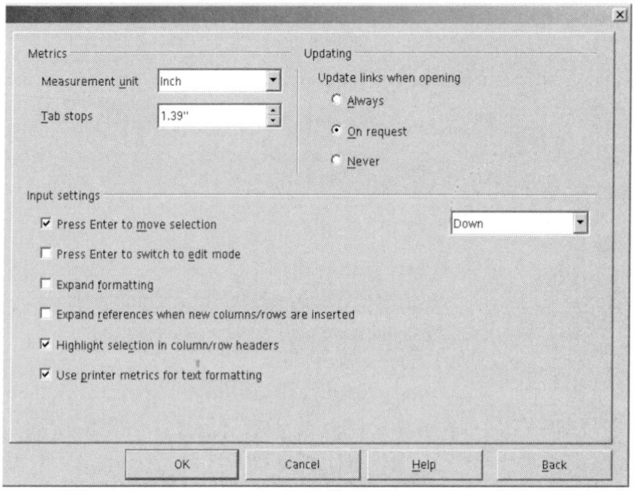

Figure 18-10　Location of Calc setup options, General Spreadsheet options

Keyboard Shortcuts

Table 18-1 lists some of the more useful keyboard shortcuts that can save you time while working with Calc spreadsheets.

Table 18-1　The more useful Calc keyboard shortcuts

Pressing this...	Does this
Backspace	Deletes the contents of a cell without bringing up the Delete Contents window.
F5	Opens/Closes Navigator window (whether it's docked or undocked).
F11	Opens/Closes the Stylist window (whether it's docked or undocked).
F9	Recalculates the spreadsheet if it's not set to recalculate automatically (Tools > Cell Contents > AutoCalculate).
Home	Moves to the first cell in a row.
End	Moves to the last cell in a row, corresponding to the last column in the spreadsheet that contains data.

Table 18-1 The more useful Calc keyboard shortcuts

Pressing this...	Does this
Shift+F4	Lets you apply absolute and relative cell references to selected cell address text. For example, if you have the text C4 highlighted in a formula, press Shift+F4 to toggle among different absolute/relative combinations, such as $C$4, C$4, and $C4. See *Relative and Absolute Cell References* on page 572.
Shift+F5	Trace dependents. Arrows point to the cells that depend on the selected cell (refer to it). This is a great spreadsheet troubleshooting tool.
Shift+F6	Trace precedents. Arrows point to the cells that the current cell refers to. This is a great spreadsheet troubleshooting tool.
Ctrl+Page Up	Move to previous sheet.
Ctrl+Page Down	Move to next sheet.
Ctrl+b	Applies/Removes bold formatting in selected text.
Ctrl+i	Applies/Removes italic formatting in selected text.
Ctrl+u	Applies/Removes underlining in selected text.
Ctrl+z	Undo. Reverses the last action made.
Ctrl+a	Selects all of the document.

Creating a New Document

You can create a new Calc document in a number of ways:

- From scratch
- Using a template
- Using an existing Calc document (by using File > Save As)

Creating a Document From Scratch

Choose File > New > Spreadsheet.

Creating a Calc Document From a Template

You can create new documents from templates. For more information on templates, see *Using Templates* on page 256.

1   Choose File > New > Templates and Documents.

2   In the New window, select a template category from the Categories list.

3   Select the spreadsheet template you want from the Templates list. See Figure 18-11.

   If you want to preview the template and see a description of it, click the More button and select the Preview option.

4   Click OK. A new Calc document opens with the template formatting and styles.

When you save the document, it saves as a Calc document (not as a template) by default.

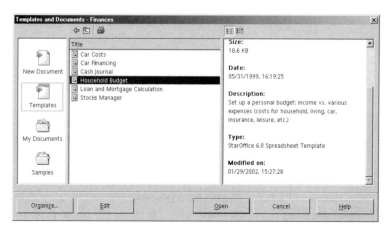

Figure 18-11   Creating a new document from a template

OpenOffice.org doesn't have the same templates as StarOffice. For OpenOffice.org templates and more, see www.ooextras.org.

If your template is located in a folder other than one of the template folders (office\share\template*language**template_folder* or office\user\template*template_folder*), you won't be able to select the template in the New window. Either move the template to one of the template folders so you can select it in the New window, or choose File > Open to open the template and create a new document.

Opening Another Document in Calc

You can open a variety of spreadsheets, text files, and other documents in Calc spreadsheet format.

Opening Any Spreadsheet

To open any spreadsheet, just choose File > Open and navigate to the file. To see what spreadsheets or other formats are supported, click the format dropdown list and browse a while.

Converting Microsoft Office Spreadsheets to Calc

See *Converting To and From Other Applications* on page 160.

Opening an HTML Table in Calc: Simple

Choose File > Open and be sure All is selected as the file type. Select the HTML file you want to open. Then switch to Text CSV as the file format in the Open dialog, and click OK.

See also *Saving a Spreadsheet in HTML Format* on page 523 and *Sending a Spreadsheet as Email* on page 524.

Inserting an HTML Table or WebQuery Using Insert External Data

Calc can automatically insert, formatted somewhat differently, an entire HTML page or Web Query, or just one or more selected tables from an HTML page. The page can be local or a URL on the Web.

1 Prepare the HTML file, if it's local. You might only be able to get Calc to recognize it if it's got an .shtml extension. It depends on what your system associates with HTML. An example is shown in Figure 18-12.

2 Open a new or existing spreadsheet.

3 Choose Insert > External Data. The window in Figure 18-13 will appear.

theLast Turtle
Training schedule for November 2002
Training schedule for December 2002
Students
Holidays
Teaching team conference

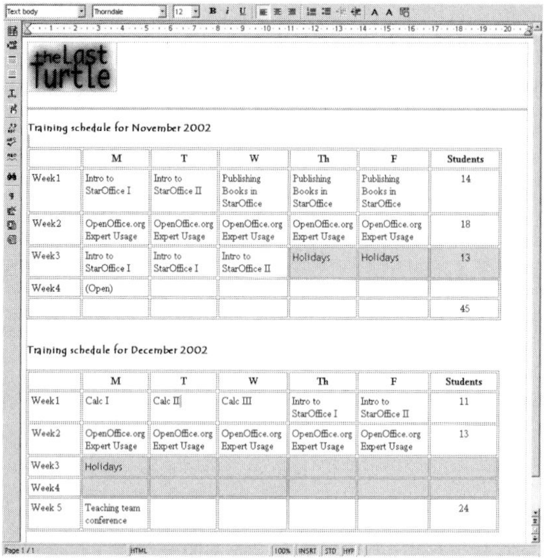

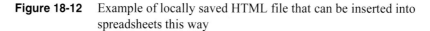

Figure 18-12 Example of locally saved HTML file that can be inserted into spreadsheets this way

4 Click the browse icon to select the HTML file or type the URL of the Web page. Use Figure 18-13 for guidance in making other selections, then click OK.

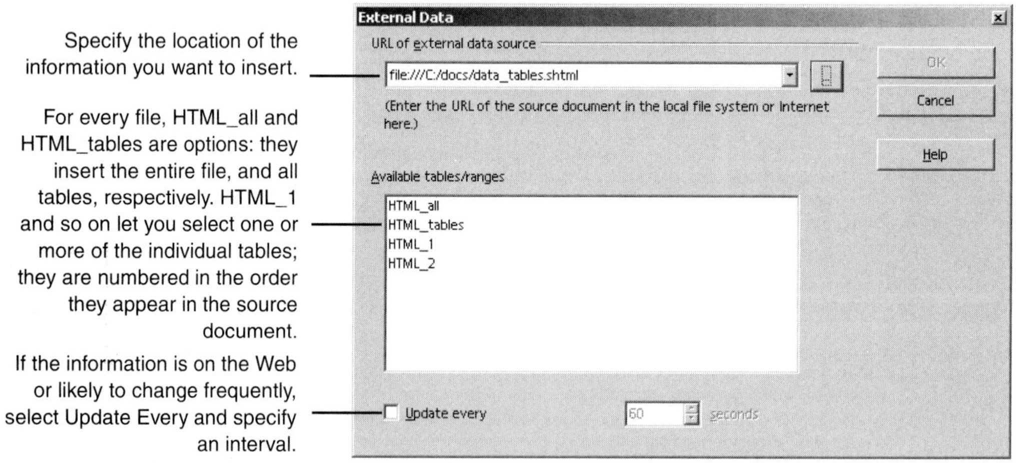

Specify the location of the information you want to insert.
For every file, HTML_all and HTML_tables are options: they insert the entire file, and all tables, respectively. HTML_1 and so on let you select one or more of the individual tables; they are numbered in the order they appear in the source document.
If the information is on the Web or likely to change frequently, select Update Every and specify an interval.
External Data
URL of external data source
file:///C:/docs/data_tables.shtml
(Enter the URL of the source document in the local file system or Internet here.)
Available tables/ranges
HTML_all
HTML_tables
HTML_1
HTML_2
Update every
60
seconds
OK
Cancel
Help

Figure 18-13 External Data window: selecting items to insert from file

5 Figure 18-13 shows the results of selecting the HTML_tables option.

	M	T	W	Th	F	Students
Week1	Intro to StarOf	Intro to StarOf	Publishing Boc	Publishing Boc	Publishing Boc	14
Week2	OpenOffice.or	OpenOffice.or	OpenOffice.or	OpenOffice.or	OpenOffice.or	18
Week3	Intro to StarOf	Intro to StarOf	Intro to StarOf	Holidays	Holidays	13
Week4	(Open)					
						45

	M	T	W	Th	F	Students
Week1	Calc I	Calc II	Calc III	Intro to StarOf	Intro to StarOf	11
Week2	OpenOffice.or	OpenOffice.or	OpenOffice.or	OpenOffice.or	OpenOffice.or	13
Week3	Holidays					
Week4						
Week 5	Teaching team	conference				24

Figure 18-14   Inserted HTML tables, HTML_tables option

6   If you need to make the text wrap in each cells, select all cells, right-click, and choose
Format Cells. Then click the Alignment tab, and select the Line Break option.

Importing a Text File or Spreadsheet

Make sure the text file you want to import is set up with *delimiters*. A delimiter is just a
technical term for some kind of character, such as a tab or a semicolon, that marks the
stopping and starting points of data that will be separated into different spreadsheet cells.

For example, the semicolons in the text line in Figure 18-15 allow Calc to import the data
into separate cells in a spreadsheet row:

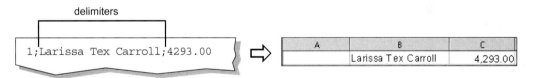

Figure 18-15   Text delimiter

Delimiters can be any character that your system supports. You can even use tab character
or a space as your delimiter. Text files can also be *fixed width*. That means your text file
doesn't necessarily use delimiters, but each "column" in your text file is a specific width
that Calc can translate into a spreadsheet column.

You can set up a data source that's a text file or a spreadsheet, so getting a text file into a
spreadsheet doesn't help you a great deal. However, once you've got the data in a
spreadsheet it's easier to create what the data source tool reads as different "tables"
(different sheets). It's also just easier to manipulate. Also, if you're having problems
opening a spreadsheet in Calc, you can get it in much more easily by using text file as the
intermediate format.

1   Get the source file into the right format.

- Get the spreadsheet into CSV text format. This depends on the spreadsheet.

- Evaluate what separates the fields in the text file. If it's spaces, that's fine as long as there aren't any spaces within each field. This is probably fine for files with numeric information. However, for an address book, where you might have a field like "910 Harrison Ave" with two spaces in it, you'll get three different columns. For that type of file, you'll probably have to go through the file and use a tab, semicolon, or other character to separate the fields. Figure 18-16 shows what happens when you import text files like that.

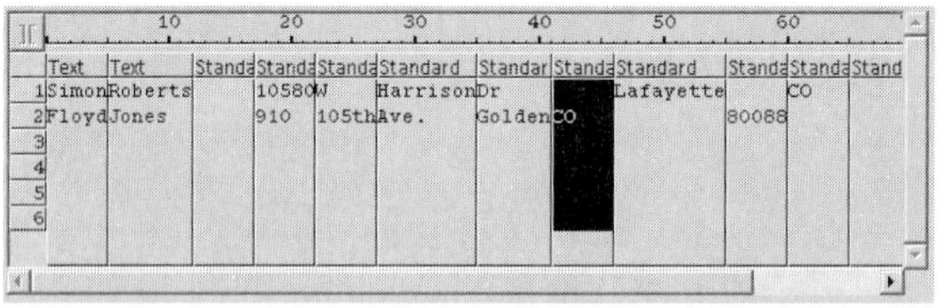

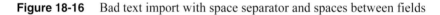

Figure 18-16   Bad text import with space separator and spaces between fields

2   Open a new empty Calc spreadsheet. **Choose File > Open and select Text CSV in the file format list. This is crucial; it won't work if you don't specify that format.** Text CSV is about 3/4 of the way down the list; just press T a few times to find it.

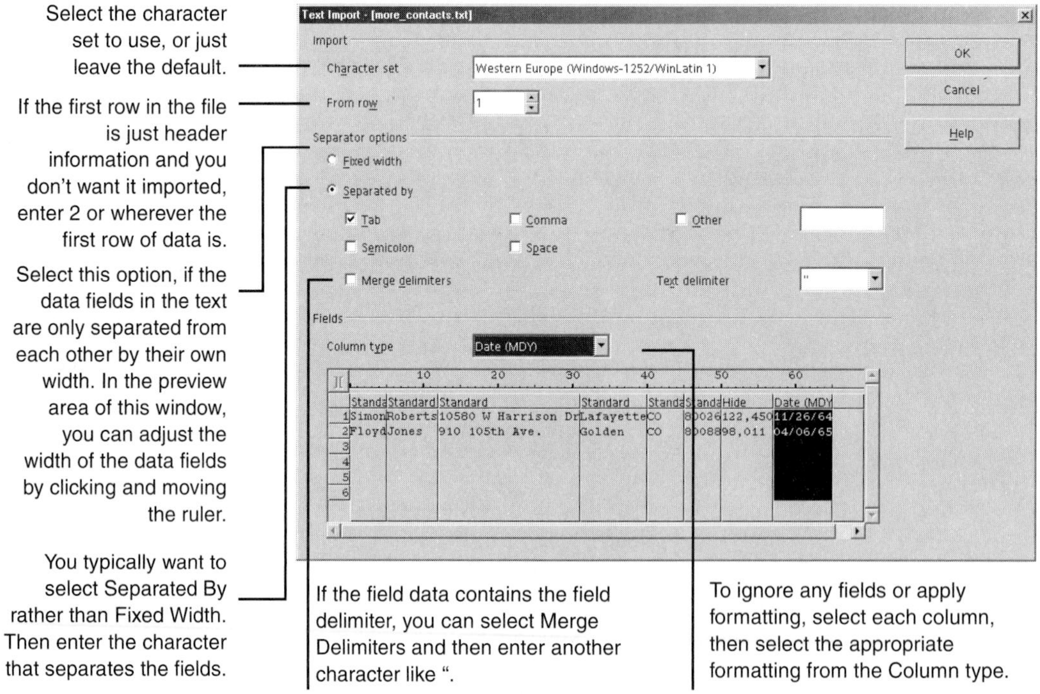

Select the character set to use, or just leave the default.

If the first row in the file is just header information and you don't want it imported, enter 2 or wherever the first row of data is.

Select this option, if the data fields in the text are only separated from each other by their own width. In the preview area of this window, you can adjust the width of the data fields by clicking and moving the ruler.

You typically want to select Separated By rather than Fixed Width. Then enter the character that separates the fields.

If the field data contains the field delimiter, you can select Merge Delimiters and then enter another character like ".

To ignore any fields or apply formatting, select each column, then select the appropriate formatting from the Column type.

Figure 18-17   Specifying how to import the text data

3   The Text Import window will appear. Select appropriate options; see Figure 18-17.

4   Click OK. The data will appear as you formatted it in an untitled Calc spreadsheet, as shown in Figure 18-18. Save the file as a Calc spreadsheet.

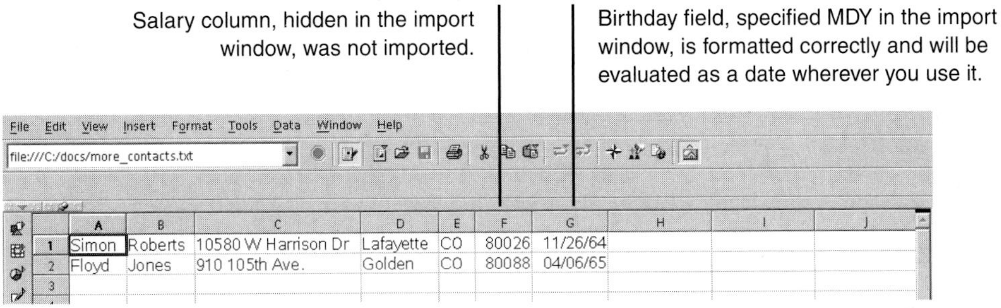

Salary column, hidden in the import window, was not imported.

Birthday field, specified MDY in the import window, is formatted correctly and will be evaluated as a date wherever you use it.

Figure 18-18   Imported data appears in Calc spreadsheet

Simple Procedures for Bringing Data Sources Into Spreadsheets

Don't let the title put you off—making a data source, as well as getting the data into your spreadsheets, is really easy.

A data source is any kind of stored data—a spreadsheet listing your favorite CDs and their serial numbers, a dBase database with your customer list, or a plain text file containing all the people who get your holiday newsletter. See Chapter 35, *Creating and Modifying Data Sources*, on page 869, if you haven't set up any data sources yet.

Note – For information on mail merges, putting data source data into letters or envelopes and printing a copy for each record in your data source, see Chapter 10, *Mail Merges, Business Cards, and More*, on page 351.

This section covers easy procedures for taking data from one of your data sources and putting it in a spreadsheet.

- Using the Data Pilot to Make a Spreadsheet With Automatic Totals describes the AutoPilot, which walks you through the process and lets you create new fields that automatically total data in the data source

- Dragging Data From a Data Source Into a Spreadsheet is a simpler method that just lets you pick the data you want and put it in a spreadsheet.

Using the Data Pilot to Make a Spreadsheet With Automatic Totals

This procedure lets you bring in any thing you've set up as a data source into a spreadsheet. The data source can be another spreadsheet, a database, or a text file. To define data sources, see *Creating Data Sources* on page 880.

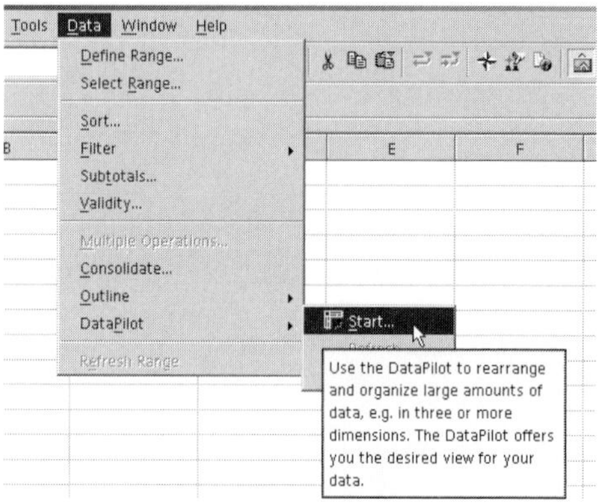

1   Start a new Calc spreadsheet.

2   Choose Data > Data Pilot as shown in Figure 18-24.

3   In the Select Source window in Figure 18-19, select Data Source Registered in StarOffice. Click OK.

Figure 18-19   Selecting type of data source

4   Make the appropriate selections in the Select Data Source window in Figure 18-20.

Database is the name you assigned to the data source; data source is the name of the tables from the data source definition window.

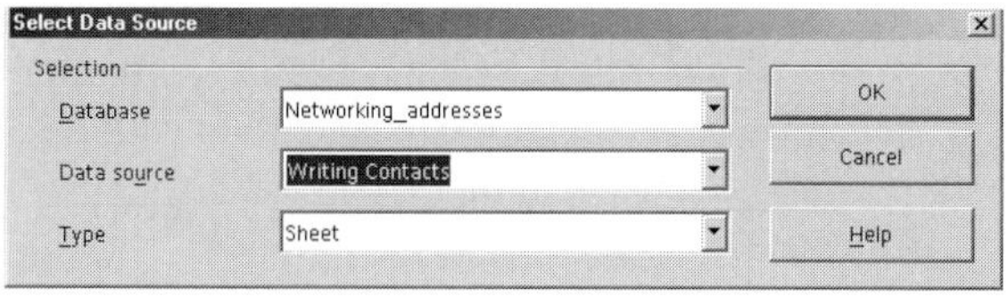

Figure 18-20   Selecting the data source and table

5   Make selections in the Select Data Source window in Figure 18-21, then click OK.

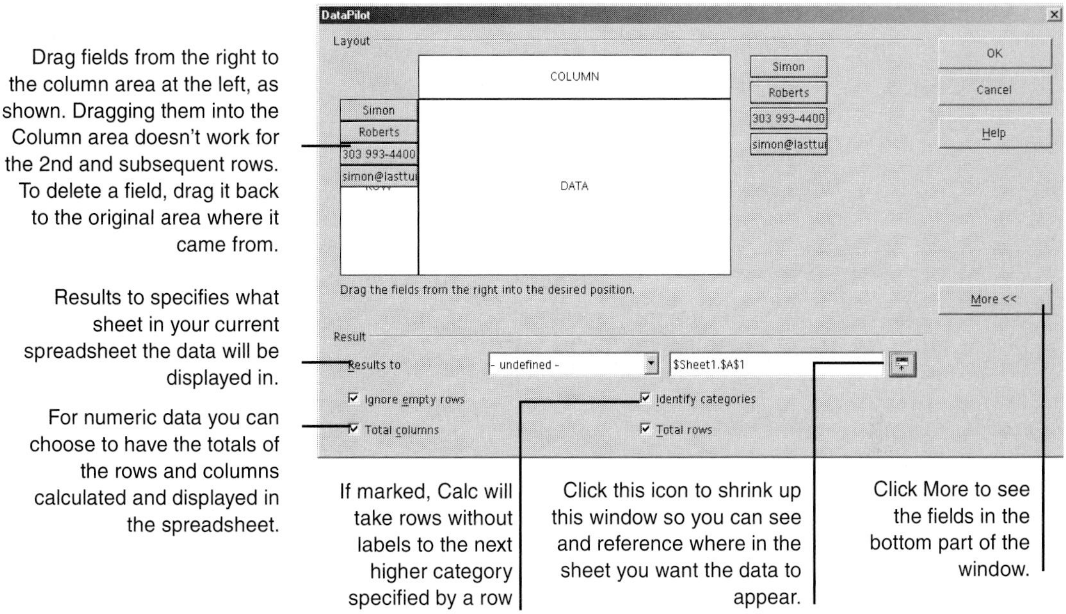

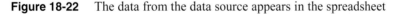

Drag fields from the right to the column area at the left, as shown. Dragging them into the Column area doesn't work for the 2nd and subsequent rows. To delete a field, drag it back to the original area where it came from.

Results to specifies what sheet in your current spreadsheet the data will be displayed in.

For numeric data you can choose to have the totals of the rows and columns calculated and displayed in the spreadsheet.

If marked, Calc will take rows without labels to the next higher category specified by a row

Click this icon to shrink up this window so you can see and reference where in the sheet you want the data to appear.

Click More to see the fields in the bottom part of the window.

Figure 18-21   Select how to import the data

6   The data from the data source appears in the spreadsheet, as shown in Figure 18-22.

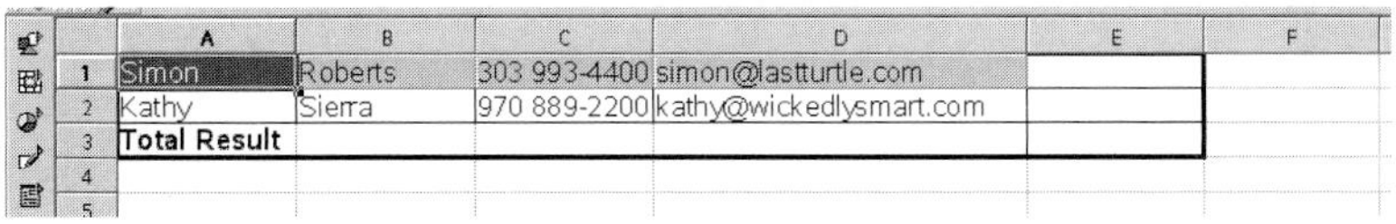

	A	B	C	D	E	F
1	Simon	Roberts	303 993-4400	simon@lastturtle.com		
2	Kathy	Sierra	970 889-2200	kathy@wickedlysmart.com		
3	Total Result					
4						
5						

Figure 18-22   The data from the data source appears in the spreadsheet

To refresh or delete the data in the spreadsheet, choose Data > Data Pilot and select Refresh or Delete.

Dragging Data From a Data Source Into a Spreadsheet

Note – You can paste a table into a presentation, but you're better off putting it in a spreadsheet or text document, then inserting that document. It's not very manageable and difficult to format.

These procedures tell you how to bring in anything you've set up as a data source into a spreadsheet. To define data sources, see *Creating Data Sources* on page 880.

1 Choose View > Data Sources.

2 In the data source viewing area that appears, select a data source from the area at the left, then select a table from that data source.

3 Select the upper left corner of the corresponding data area on the right side of the window, and drag it into the spreadsheet. This is illustrated in Figure 18-23.

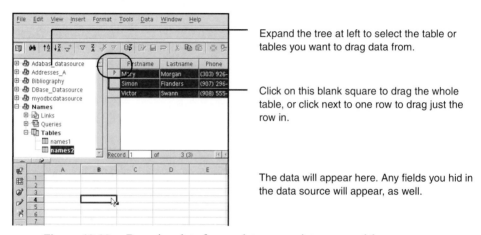

Figure 18-23 Dragging data from a data source into a spreadsheet

Exporting Calc Spreadsheets to Other Formats

Getting the data out of Calc into another format is easy, and you have a lot of options for what format to switch to.

Saving One or All Spreadsheets in 5.2 or Excel Format

Choose File > Save As and select the appropriate format from the format dropdown list. It's also a good idea to delete the previous file extension such as .sxc from the file name, and select Automatic File Extension in the dialog box. Then click OK.

See also *Automatically Saving in StarOffice 5.2 or Microsoft Office Formats* on page 164.

Saving a Calc Spreadsheet as a Text File

When you save a Calc spreadsheet as a delimited text file, only the active sheet in the spreadsheet is saved. To save more than one sheet as a text file, you must repeat this procedure for each sheet.

1. With the spreadsheet open, select the sheet containing the data you want to save as a text file.
2. Choose File > Save As.
3. In the File type list, select Text CSV.
4. Type a File name. If you mark the Automatic file name extension option, the program will automatically add a `.txt` extension.
5. Set the path to the folder in which you want to save the file.
6. Click Save.
7. Set the options you want in the Export of text files window. Use Figure 18-24.
8. Click OK.
9. If you get a subsequent warning saying that only the active sheet was saved, click OK.

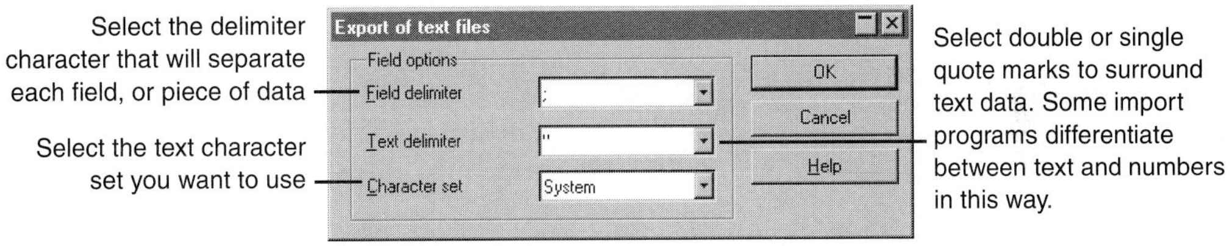
Select the delimiter character that will separate each field, or piece of data
Select the text character set you want to use
Export of text files
Field options
Field delimiter
Text delimiter
Character set
System
OK
Cancel
Help
Select double or single quote marks to surround text data. Some import programs differentiate between text and numbers in this way.

Figure 18-24 Setting options for exporting to a text file

If you want to open the text file, first close the spreadsheet file you used to create the text file. Otherwise the text file will open in read-only mode.

Saving a Spreadsheet in HTML Format

Choose File > Save as and select Web Page (Calc) in the format dropdown list. Delete the `.sxc` file extension and select Automatic File Extension.

Figure 18-25 and Figure 18-26 show an example of a Calc spreadsheet saved in HTML. The Save As feature exports all sheets to the same Web page and creates links at the top so you can easily click to each sheet.

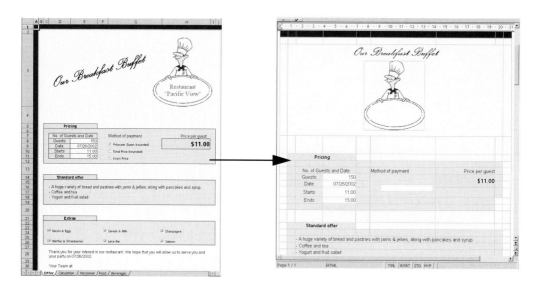

Figure 18-25   Original spreadsheet (first of five original sheets) and HTML version

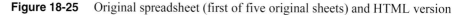

Figure 18-26   Original spreadsheet (second of five original sheets) and HTML version

Sending a Spreadsheet as Email

Instead of launching Mail, creating a new mail message, and attaching a Calc file to it, you can send an open Calc file as an email attachment or as the contents of an email message.

1   Be sure your mail program is up and running.

2   With the document you want to mail open, choose File > Send > Document as Email.

3   A new empty email will appear with the file as an attachment (Figure 18-27). Address the email, add content to the body if you want, then send the email as usual.

4   In the Send Mail window (see Figure 18-27), select whether you want the file sent as an attachment or as the contents of the email and click OK.

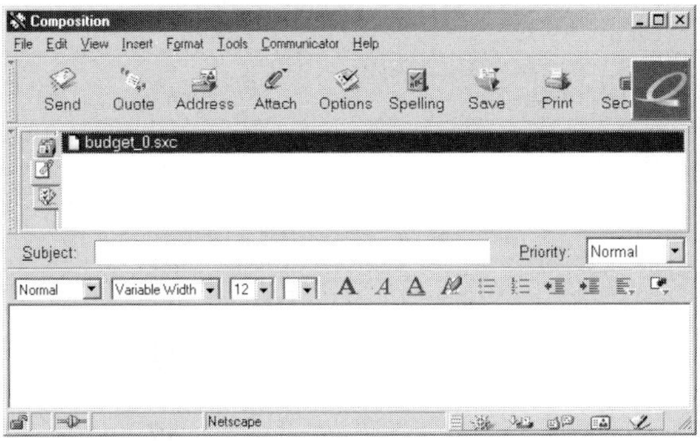

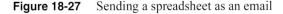

Figure 18-27   Sending a spreadsheet as an email

If the document is unsaved, the program displays the Save As window. Save the file.

Creating and Maintaining Sheets

A Calc file can contain multiple spreadsheets (called sheets), each of which has a tab at the bottom of the Calc window. This helps you keep different financial information separate in a single file. For example, you can set up a sheet for income information, a second sheet for expense information, and a third sheet that contains combined information about the first two sheets along with a chart. You switch between sheets by clicking their tabs.

When you start a new spreadsheet document, the file comes with three sheets by default, called Sheet1, Sheet2, and Sheet3. These are just a starting point to get you going.

This section shows you how to add, rename, reorder, and delete sheets, and resize the viewing area of the sheet tabs.

Adding Sheets to a Spreadsheet

1   Select the sheet tab you want to add sheets before or after.

2   Right-click the sheet tab, and choose Insert.

3   In the Insert Sheet window, set the insertion options. Use Figure 18-28 for guidance.

4   Click OK.

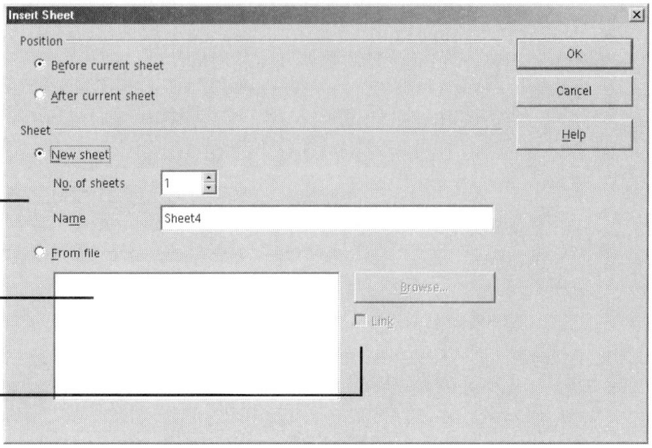

If you select only one sheet to insert, you can Name the tab for the new sheet. If you select more than one sheet to insert, Calc creates generic sheet names.

You can insert sheets from an existing Calc file. Select From file, click Browse, and select the file.

Select Link to insert the new sheet as a link to the source file. The sheet will update when the source file changes.

Figure 18-28   Adding a sheet

Updating Linked Sheets

If you add a sheet in Calc that is a link to a sheet in another spreadsheet file (see previous procedure), you can update the added sheet when the source file containing that sheet is modified. When you open the file containing the link, the program by default prompts you to update links. (You can change this default in Tools > Options > Spreadsheet > Other.)

You can also update the link as you're working by choosing Edit > Links, selecting the linked sheet in the Edit Links window, and clicking the Update button. Changes you make to the source file must be saved before changes are reflected in the linked sheet.

Note – If you don't see the Links item in the Edit menu, or if you don't see the linked sheet listed in the Edit Links window, the sheet was inserted as a copy rather than a link. Delete the sheet and re-insert it as a link. (See *Adding Sheets to a Spreadsheet* on page 525.)

Renaming Sheets

1   Select the sheet you want to rename.

2   Right-click the tab, and choose Rename.

3   Type the new name in the Rename Sheet window and click OK.

Reordering Sheets

1 Select the sheet you want to move.

2 Drag the tab to the new location in the row of tabs.

Deleting Sheets

Deleting a sheet deletes all the data on the sheet. You can't delete sheets that have been protected (see *Protecting Cells From Modification* on page 604).

1 Select the sheet you want to delete.

2 Right-click the tab, and choose Delete.

3 Click Yes in the confirmation window.

Resizing and Navigating in the Tab Area

As you add sheets and change sheet names, you may not be able to see all tabs at once. Use the tips in Figure 18-29 to navigate in the tab area of a spreadsheet document.

Figure 18-29   Navigating the tab area

Row Limit

There is a limit of 32,000 rows per spreadsheet. The explanation at `http://sc.openoffice.org/row-limit.html` keeps updated information.

Using Navigator to Move Within and Between Documents

Navigator is a tool used throughout the program. In Calc, Navigator serves two main purposes:

- Navigator lets you locate and jump to different parts of your document quickly

- Navigator lets you drag and drop hyperlinked references from one part of a document into another part, or from one document to another.

Launching Navigator

Press the F5 key to open and close the Navigator window, or choose Edit > Navigator.

Navigating and Inserting

The Navigator window, shown in Figure 18-30, displays all the parts of your document: sheets, named areas, inserted objects, and so on. These different parts are displayed in a hierarchical tree view that lets you expand and contract groups of things. You can also customize the way Navigator displays its contents.

Navigator also offers a variety of ways you can jump to different parts of your document.

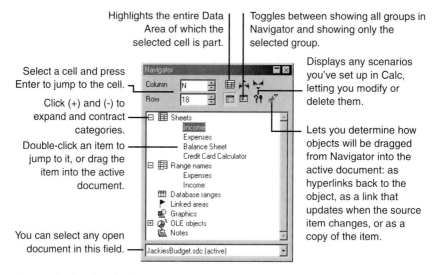

Figure 18-30   Navigator

Searching and Replacing

Choose Edit > Find and Replace, and make the appropriate entries; see Figure 18-31.

Click Attributes or Format to specify attributes like Blinking, or formatting like a font or color.

Enter what you want to search for, and what to replace it with if anything, in these fields.

Whole Words Only means that searching for **off** doesn't get found in **office**.

Backwards means search from bottom to top in the document.

Select Regular Expressions to use advanced syntax to look for patterns. See the online help for syntax, in the topic List of Regular Expressions.

Select Search for Styles and enter the name of the style to search for, in the Search For field.

Select Similarity Search and click the browse icon that activates. The window is shown in Figure 18-32.

Select Sounds Like to search for words you set up under Tools > Options > Languages > Searching in Japanese.

Figure 18-31   Find and Replace window

WildCard Search

Select the Regular Expressions option; see the online help for complete details. Use an asterisk for 0 to many occurrences of any character. Use a period for a wildcard character for one character. `office.` finds both `officer` and `offices`.

Similarity Search

Similarity Search lets you do fuzzier searching. If you want to find anything that's kind of like "office", you can look for "office" and find "official", "officious," and if you set it up loosely enough, "off." The window is shown in Figure 18-30.

Specify how many characters can be different between the word you're searching for and the words you want to find. If you're looking for offices and you enter 1 exchange character, you'll find officer but not official.

Specify how many characters longer the found words can be.

Specify how many characters shorter the found words can be.

Select Combine to make found words meet all the conditions.

Figure 18-32   Doing "fuzzy" searching with Similarity Search

Data Entry and Formatting

Entering Text and Numbers

You may see the title of this section and say, "Duh." Yes, you just use the keyboard for basic text and number entry in a spreadsheet. But there are a few issues and considerations to take into account while entering stuff into cells. Those issues and considerations are presented in the following sections.

Basic Entry

Be sure the Formula Bar is showing. (Choose View > Toolbars and make sure there's a checkmark next to Formula.) Then click in the cell where you want the data to appear, type in the data entry field, then press Enter or click the green checkmark icon.

Text That Is Wider Than Cells

By default, text you enter into a cell that is too wide for the cell just runs through the next cell(s)—unless you enter data into a cell that the text runs through, as shown in Figure 19-1.

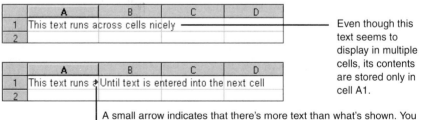

Even though this text seems to display in multiple cells, its contents are stored only in cell A1.

A small arrow indicates that there's more text than what's shown. You can either resize the column or wrap the text.

Figure 19-1   Default behavior of text that is wider than a cell

You can fix text that gets cut off by either resizing the column (see page 540) or by wrapping text inside the cell (next).

Wrapping Text in Cells

1   Select the cell(s) in which you want text to wrap.

2   Right-click the cell and choose Format Cells.

3   In the Cell Attributes window, select the Alignment tab.

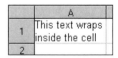

4   In the lower right section of the window, select the Line break option.

5   Click OK.

Use the object bar to control the alignment of wrapped text.

Numbers That Are Wider Than Cells

If you enter a number that is longer than the width of the cell (see Figure 19-2), pound characters (###) are displayed instead of the number when you press Enter. This can also happen when decimal places and symbols are added to a number automatically, as in a currency amount, or when you increase font size or apply bold formatting. To fix this, resize the column. (See *Resizing Columns* on page 540.) If you don't want to resize the column, you can try reducing the font size of the number.

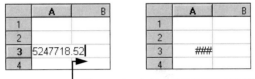

The number is too wide for the cell. When you press Enter, ### characters are displayed.

Figure 19-2   Numbers that are wider than cells

Keeping Text Exactly as You Typed It

Sometimes Calc will change the format of the text or number you enter in a cell. In particular, Calc removes the zeros you enter in front of numbers to the left of a decimal point, and it turns certain words you may enter in all capital letters to lowercase letters. For example, if you

With single quote	Without single quote
APR	Apr
01	1
JUNE	June

type 01 into a cell, Calc turns changes it to be just 1; or if you type in APR (for annual percentage rate), Calc thinks you mean the month April and changes it to Apr.

To make Calc display exactly what you type, begin the entry with a single quote mark, such as '01 or 'APR.

Entering Percentages

When you set cells to display numbers as percentages (by selecting the cells and clicking the % icon in the object bar, Calc multiplies numbers you enter in those cells by 100. So when you enter numbers you want to display as percentages, be sure to start with a decimal point.

For example, if you want a cell to display 9%, enter the number as .09.

By default, Calc adds two decimal places to percentages. So when you enter .15, Calc turns the number into 15.00%. To remove decimal places, select the cells, right-click them, choose Format Cells, and make the change on the Numbers tab. For more information on this and other cell formats, see *Quick Cell Formatting* on page 543.

Changing 1/2 to .5

The AutoCorrect feature automatically corrects common typos as you're typing and converts character combinations into special characters.

When you're working with Calc, you may not want certain items replaced as you're typing. For example, if you type .5, Calc changes it to the fraction 1/2 by default, which isn't good for spreadsheet entry. To change the way the program handles AutoCorrect:

1   Choose Tools > AutoCorrect.

2   Modify the AutoCorrect options in one of two ways:

- Select the Replace tab to modify or delete AutoCorrect entries.

- Select the Options tab to deselect the text replacement settings you don't want to use.

Editing Cell Contents

You can edit the contents of a cell in a number of ways:

- Select a cell and edit its content in the formula bar.

- Double-click a cell and edit its content directly in the cell.

    This is particularly useful when you're pasting text from a text document into a cell, because the paragraphs won't be put into separate cells.

- Select a cell and press Enter to edit its contents directly in the cell. To set this up, choose Tools > Options > Spreadsheet > Input, select the option next to Press Enter to switch to edit mode, and click OK.

Deleting Cell Contents

When you select a cell and press the **Delete** key, Calc brings up the Delete Contents window to let you select specific cell elements, such as text, numbers, formulas, and formatting. This is a tremendously useful feature if you want to delete some elements in a cell but not others.

However, if all you want to do is delete the contents without being prompted, select a cell and press the Backspace key.

Filling

You can enter data into cells automatically by using Calc's fill feature. There are two different ways to fill, depending on whether you want to fill the exact same data or increment data.

You can fill data in any direction: down, up, left, or right.

Filling Exactly the Same Data

Use this procedure to duplicate the contents of a cell down a column or across a row.

1   Click and hold down the left mouse button on the cell whose contents you want to fill.

2   Drag in the desired direction to highlight the cells you want to contain the data.

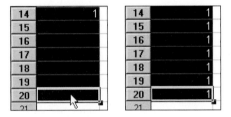

3   Choose Edit > Fill > *direction*, where *direction* is the direction you dragged to select the cells.

You can also fill the exact same data by holding down the Ctrl key and filling with the automatic fill handle (next procedure).

Filling to Increment Data

Use this procedure to automatically increment data as you fill down a column or across a row.

Automatic fill only increments data that Calc recognizes, for example, numbers, dates, and cell references. If Calc doesn't recognize data, automatic fill simply duplicates the data exactly.

1   Select the cell(s) whose contents you want to fill.

2   Move the mouse pointer on top of the automatic fill handle in the lower right of the selected cell. The mouse pointer changes shape.

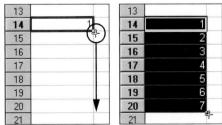

3   Click and hold down the left mouse button on the automatic fill handle, and drag in the desired direction of the fill, selecting all the cells you want to contain data.

When you use automatic fill on cells that contain cell references, you can get strange results if you don't use the correct combination of absolute and relative cell references. For information on this, see *Relative and Absolute Cell References* on page 572.

If you hold down the Ctrl key while you drag the automatic fill handle, the data will stay the same rather than increment.

AutoInputting Text

You can have Calc automatically fill in text as you're entering it. Using the AutoInput feature (Tools > Cell Contents > AutoInput), Calc matches the text you type in a cell against text entered in the same column. For example, if the name *Derek Smalls* is entered in a column, and you type the letter *D* in another cell in that column, Calc automatically fills in the rest of the word for you. So all you'd have to do is type *D* and press Enter to put another *Derek Smalls* in a cell.

However, if the name *Derek Smalls* is in a cell and the name *David St. Hubbins* is in another cell in that column (both start with *D*), Calc waits for the next unique letter before it tries to AutoInput the text.

Using and Creating Value Lists

Using Selection Lists

If you do a lot of repetitive text entry in spreadsheets, and you don't want to use AutoInput (previous section), you can use selection lists to select text you've entered previously.

1   Select the cell in which you want to enter text.

2   Right-click the cell, and choose Selection List.

    A list of all text entered in the column is displayed.

3   Choose the text you want to enter in the cell.

If you don't get a selection list, the column may contain data that's too varied.

Setting Up Sort Lists

Calc makes filling in cell information easy and automatic by using the automatic fill feature (see *Filling to Increment Data* on page 535). The idea is to type one piece of information in a cell, select the cell, and drag the little square in the lower right corner of the cell in any direction to fill in a consecutive list of items.

For example, say you want to track sales in your organization's five biggest cities, and you either want to list those cities in regional order (or you don't want to have to type each one in manually in every spreadsheet you create). Set up a sort list for those cities so that when you enter one city name, you can use automatic fill to enter the names of the remaining cities, as shown in Figure 19-3.

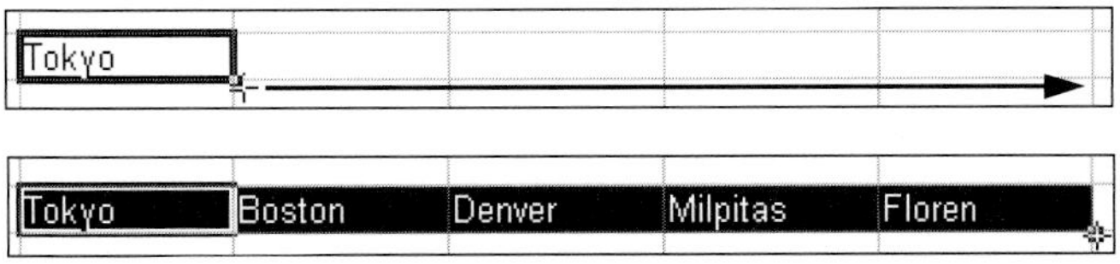

Figure 19-3   A sort list of cities

Adding a Sort List

1   Choose Tools > Options > Spreadsheet > Sort lists.

2   Click the New button.

3   In the Entries area, type the list of items in the order you want them, as shown in Figure 19-4.

Press Enter after each entry. You can also separate entries with a comma. If you use a comma to separate items, don't add a space after each comma.

4   When you're finished entering the list, click the Add button and click OK.

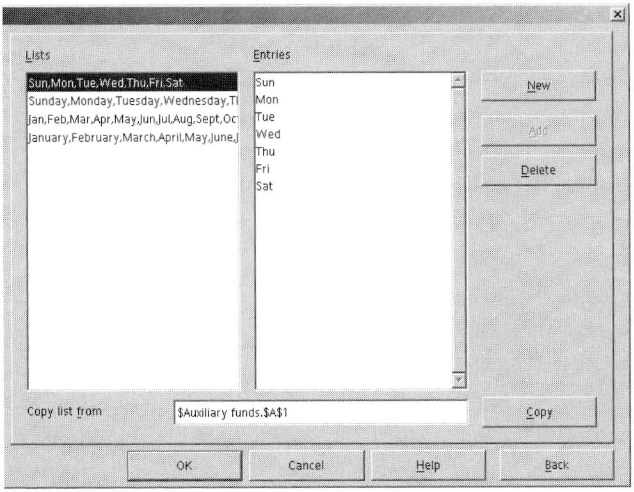

Figure 19-4   Adding a sort list

When you do an automatic fill for the sort list, dragging to the left or up fills in cells with the values that precede the one you entered.

Note – You can also enter a new sort list by selecting a range of cells in Calc, opening the Sort List options window, clicking the Copy button, and clicking OK (see Figure 19-5).

Copy list from	$Sheet1.$G$6:$K$6	Copy

Figure 19-5   Copying a sort list from the spreadsheet

You don't have to set up sort lists for numbering or dates. Calc knows how to handle those already.

Modifying a Sort List

1   Choose Tools > Options > Spreadsheet > Sort lists.

2   In the Lists box, select the list you want to edit. Its contents display in the entries box, as shown in Figure 19-6.

3   Edit the list by changing the text in the Entries list and pressing Enter after each item

4   Click the Modify button.

5   Click OK.

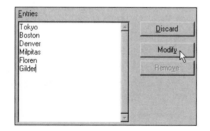

Figure 19-6   Modifying a sort list

Deleting a Sort List

1   Choose Tools > Options > Spreadsheet > Sort lists.

2   In the Lists box, select the list you want to remove.

3   Click the Remove button, click Yes in the confirmation window, and click OK.

Changing Enter Key Direction

By default, when a cell is highlighted and you press Enter in Calc, the cell selection jumps down. You can change the direction from jumping down to jumping right, left, or up.

1   Choose Tools > Options > Spreadsheet > Input.

2   Make sure the Press Enter to move selection option is selected, and change the direction in the drop-down list to the right.

3   Make sure the Press Enter to switch to edit mode option in the same window is deselected.

4   Click OK.

Working With Columns and Rows

This section contains basic shortcuts for selecting cells, and for resizing, selecting, hiding, inserting, and deleting rows and columns.

Selecting Entire Rows, Columns, and Spreadsheets

You can select entire rows and columns, or the entire spreadsheet (see Figure 19-7) to format, cut, copy, paste, or delete the contents of cells.

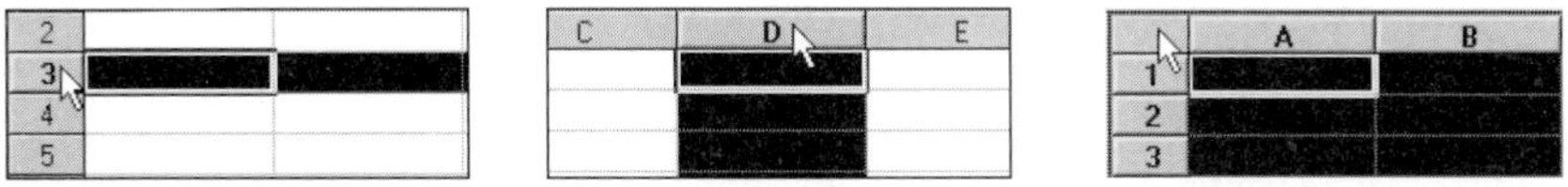

To select an entire row, click the gray box containing the row number.

To select an entire column, click the gray box containing the column letter.

To select the entire spreadsheet, click the empty gray box in the upper left of the spreadsheet.

Figure 19-7   Selecting an entire row, column, and spreadsheet

You can also press Ctrl+A to select all cells in a spreadsheet.

Selecting Non-Adjacent Cells

Calc lets you select cells that aren't right next to each other for formatting or deleting the contents of cells (see Figure 19-8). You can't copy, cut, or paste selected non-adjacent cells.

1 Shift+click the first cells you want to select.

2 Release the Shift key, hold down the Ctrl key, and click the cells you want to select.

While you're holding down the Ctrl key, you can also hold down the Shift key to select a range of cells.

	A	B	C	D
1	Credit Card Calculator			
2				
3				
4	APR	Monthly Interest	Starting Balance	Monthly Payment
5	18.00%	1.50%	$7,000.00	$250.00
6				
7				
8	Payment #	Interest	Principal	Balance
9	1	$105.00	$145.00	$6,855.00
10	2	$102.83	$147.18	$6,707.83
11	3	$100.62	$149.38	$6,558.44
12	4	$98.38	$151.62	$6,406.82

Figure 19-8   Selecting non-adjacent cells

Resizing Rows

1 Move the mouse pointer over the bottom border of the gray box containing the row number. The pointer changes shape.

2 Drag to the new size, or double-click the line below the row to set the row height to fit the row height to the tallest piece of data.

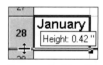

Drag or double-click.

If you drag to a new height, keep an eye on the tooltip while you're dragging. It displays the height of the row.

You can also control the height of rows more precisely by selecting the row(s), right-clicking, choosing Height, and entering an exact width.

Resizing Columns

1 Move the mouse pointer over the right border of the gray box containing the column letter. The pointer changes shape.

2 Drag to the new size, or double-click the line to the right of the column to set the column to fit the widest piece of data.

Drag or double-click.

If you drag to a new width, keep an eye on the tooltip while you're dragging. It displays the width of the column.

You can control the widths of columns more precisely by selecting the column(s), right-clicking, choosing Column Width, and entering an exact width. You can also resize multiple columns at the same time.

Hiding Rows and Columns

One of the main reasons to hide rows or columns is if they contain information that is used to aid in calculations, but that you don't want to display in the spreadsheet.

As an alternative to hiding rows and columns, consider putting different types of data on separate sheets. See *Break It Up* on page 590.

Hidden columns and rows don't print.

1   Select the entire row or column you want to hide. (See *Selecting Entire Rows, Columns, and Spreadsheets* on page 539.)

2   Right-click the gray box of the selected row or column and choose Hide.

Showing Hidden Rows and Columns

1   Select the entire rows or columns on both sides of the hidden row(s) or column(s).

2   Right-click the gray box of the selected row or column and choose Show.

Inserting Rows and Columns

When you insert columns or rows, Calc automatically adjusts all cell references in the spreadsheet so that your calculations don't get goofed up.

1   Select an entire row or column. (See *Selecting Entire Rows, Columns, and Spreadsheets* on page 539.)

    Rows are inserted above the selected row; columns are inserted to the left of the selected column.

2   Right-click the gray box of the selected row or column and choose Insert Rows or Insert Columns, depending on which is selected.

You can insert multiple rows or columns. The number of rows or columns inserted is exactly the number you selected.

Deleting Rows and Columns

When you delete columns or rows, Calc automatically adjusts all cell references in the spreadsheet so that your calculations don't get goofed up. However, any information contained in the deleted rows or columns is also deleted.

1   Select the entire rows or columns you want to delete. (See *Selecting Entire Rows, Columns, and Spreadsheets* on page 539.)

2   Right-click the gray box of the selected row(s) or column(s) and choose Delete Rows or Delete Columns, depending on which are selected.

Jazzing Up Spreadsheets With AutoFormat

The program comes with a set of predefined table formats that can help jazz up a spreadsheet for printing. You can apply those, or create your own and apply one.

Applying an AutoFormat

To apply one of these AutoFormats to a spreadsheet:

1   Select the area to which you want to apply an AutoFormat.

2   Choose Format > AutoFormat.

3   In the AutoFormat window, select the format and options you want. Use Figure 19-9 for guidance.

4   Click OK.

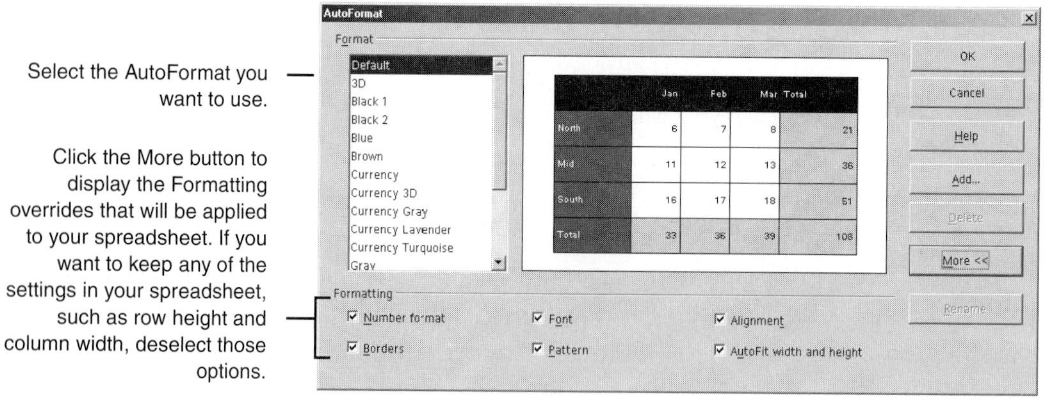

Select the AutoFormat you want to use.

Click the More button to display the Formatting overrides that will be applied to your spreadsheet. If you want to keep any of the settings in your spreadsheet, such as row height and column width, deselect those options.

Figure 19-9   Applying an AutoFormat to a spreadsheet

If you don't like the results of the AutoFormat, click the Undo icon in the function bar until your spreadsheet is back to where it was before you applied the AutoFormat. If you don't have enough undos to get back to your starting format, reformat the spreadsheet manually.

A more automated way to get back to a previous format is if you add the previous format as an AutoFormat that you can select in the AutoFormat list (next procedure).

Adding an AutoFormat

You can add your own spreadsheet formats to the list of the program's AutoFormats.

1   Format the spreadsheet the way you want it.

    You don't have to include data in the spreadsheet; just column, row, and cell formatting.

2   Select the formatted area, and choose Format > AutoFormat.

3   In the AutoFormat window, click the Add button.

4   In the Add AutoFormat window, type a name for the new format, and click OK.

    Your format is added to the list.

5   Click OK in the AutoFormat window.

You can delete or rename AutoFormats by selecting them in the AutoFormat window and clicking the Delete or Rename buttons.

Quick Cell Formatting

This section provides information for basic cell formatting techniques in Calc you perform manually by selecting cells and applying different attributes to them. Cell formats apply to cells and to the data contained within them.

If you work with spreadsheets a lot, and you reuse a lot of common elements and formatting such as headings, totals, borders, colors, and so on, we highly recommend using styles. See *Power Formatting With Styles and Templates* on page 558.

For simple, quick-and-dirty cell formatting such as changing font and font size, applying bold, italic, and underline, applying vertical and horizontal text alignment, applying background colors and borders to cells, and making cells display currency or percentage formats, use the object bar. For more advanced character formatting options, see *Applying Formatting and Security Using the Cell Attributes Window* on page 546.

Protected cells cannot be formatted. Format menu options are not available for cells that are protected. For more information, see *Protecting Cells From Modification* on page 604.

Conditional Formatting

Because conditional formatting is closely related to cell contents that change as a result of formulas, it is covered in the next chapter. See *Conditional Formatting* on page 582.

Quick Number Formats

You can apply basic currency and percentage formats to cells by selecting the cells and clicking either the Currency or Percent icons on the object bar. You can also remove currency or percent formatting by selecting the cells you want and clicking the Standard icon in the object bar.

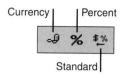

Quick Decimal Control

You can add decimals places to and remove them from selected cells by clicking the Add Decimal Place or Delete Decimal Place icons on the object bar.

Removing decimal places means that calculated or manually entered amounts that have decimals are rounded to the nearest decimal place. For example, if a cell is set to show a currency amount with no decimal places, and you enter the number 15.75, Calc displays $16.

Changing the Default Number of Decimal Places

By default, Calc includes two decimal places in number formats. You can change the default number of decimal places. Removing decimal places means that calculated or manually entered amounts that have decimals are rounded to the nearest decimal place. For example, if a cell is set to show a currency amount with no decimal places, and you enter the number 15.75, Calc displays $16.

1   Choose Tools > Options > Spreadsheet > Calculate.

2   Change the number in the Decimal places field and click OK.

Quick Font and Cell Background Color

You can change font and background colors from the object bar for selected cells.

1   Select the cells whose font or background color you want to change.

2   Click the Font Color or Background Color icons on the object bar, in Figure 19-10.

3   Select the color you want. The colors are from the standard color palette.

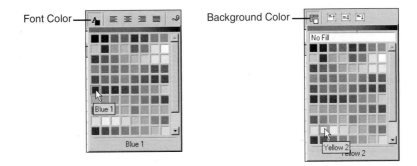

Figure 19-10   Setting font and cell background colors

Quick Cell Borders

Select the cells you want to apply a border to, click the Borders icon on the object bar, and select the type of border you want to apply.

For different types of lines, use the Borders tab in the Cell Attributes window. See *Applying Formatting and Security Using the Cell Attributes Window* on page 546.

Quick Vertical Alignment

If row heights are larger than the height of the data inside the row cells, you can change the vertical alignment of the cell data, as shown in Figure 19-11. Select the cells you want to vertically align and click one of the Align icons on the object bar.

Figure 19-11   Different vertical alignments

Hiding Zero Values

You can show only relevant spreadsheet data by hiding cell values that are zero.

1   Choose Tools > Options > Spreadsheet > Contents.

2   Deselect the Zero Values option and click OK.

Merging Cells

You can select multiple cells and make them, in appearance, as one cell. This is particularly useful, for example, when you want to apply background formatting to text that spans multiple cells. When the multiple cells are merged, you only have to set the background color for one cell. If you don't merge the cells, you'd have to set the background color for each cell the text spans.

1   Select the cells you want to merge.

2   Choose Format > Merge Cells > Define.

> If more than one of the cells contains data, a dialog box asks you how you want to handle the data, as shown in Figure 19-12.

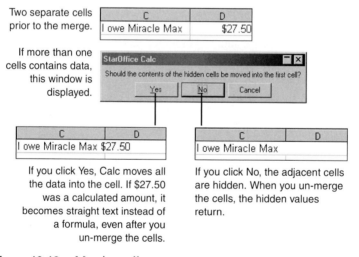

Figure 19-12   Merging cells

To un-merge cells, select the merged cell and choose Format > Merge Cells > Remove.

Instead of merging cells that contain text and numbers, which removes any formulas that generated the numbers (as shown in Figure 19-12), you can combine those cells in a different part of the spreadsheet through concatenation. Concatenation leaves the original data, including formulas, intact. See *Combining Cells* on page 584.

Applying Formatting and Security Using the Cell Attributes Window

This section describes the more advanced cell formatting options of the Cell Attributes window. To access the Cell Attributes window, select the cells you want to format, right-click a selected cell, and choose Format Cells. You can also choose Format > Cells in the menu bar.

Figure 19-13 through Figure 19-20 describe formatting options on each of the tabs in the Cell Attributes window.

When you select a data type, you can choose different Format options.

You can change the language for category types that use text such as month names.

When you select the Currency category, you can choose which country currency format to use.

Set values for numbers that can use decimals, leading zeros, negative values, or thousands separators,

You can create your own number formats. This is a detailed procedure with extensive syntax rules; see the online help for more information.

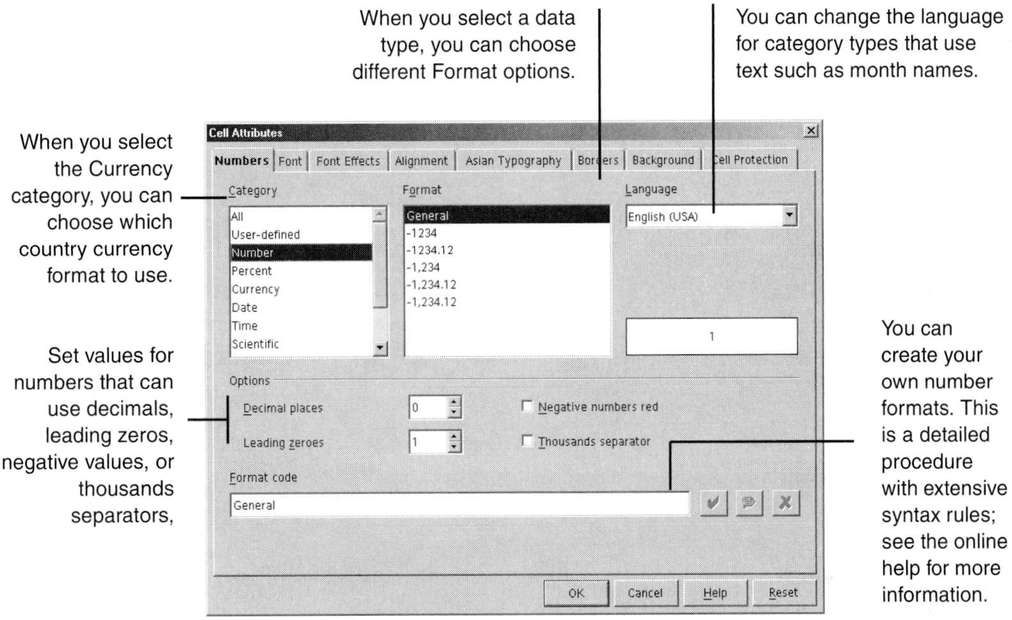

Figure 19-13   Cell Attributes window, Numbers tab

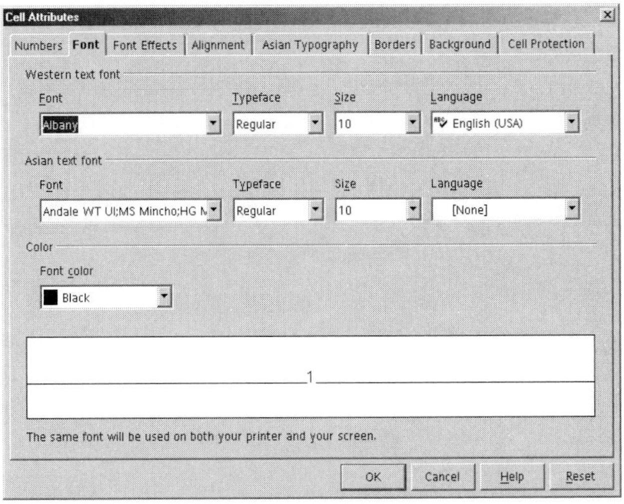

Figure 19-14   Cell Attributes window, Font tab

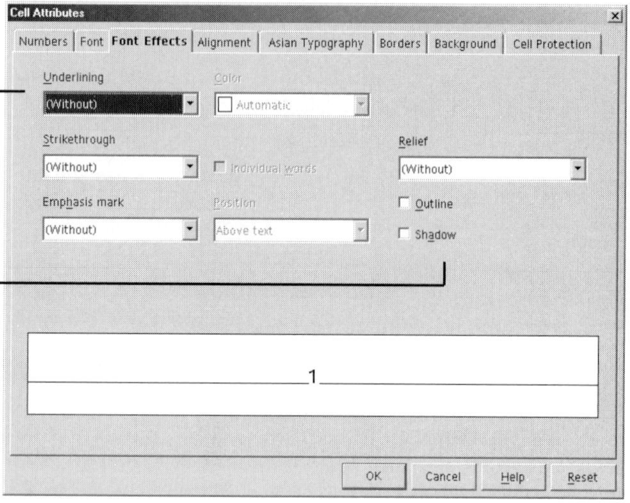

Select any options you want for underlining and the color for underlining, strikethrough, and emphasis.
From the Relief list, select Embossed or Engraved. If you don't want embossing or engraving, you can select Outline, Shadow, or both.
Cell Attributes
Numbers
Font
Font Effects
Alignment
Asian Typography
Borders
Background
Cell Protection
Underlining
(Without)
Color
Automatic
Strikethrough
(Without)
Individual words
Relief
(Without)
Emphasis mark
(Without)
Position
Above text
Outline
Shadow
OK
Cancel
Help
Reset

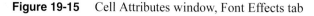

Figure 19-15 Cell Attributes window, Font Effects tab

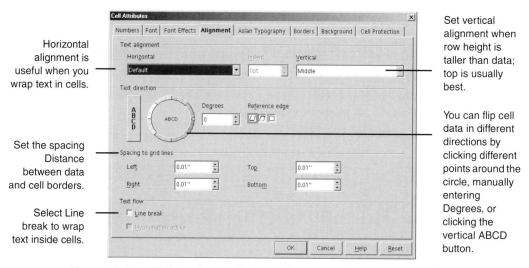

Horizontal alignment is useful when you wrap text in cells.
Set the spacing Distance between data and cell borders.
Select Line break to wrap text inside cells.
Set vertical alignment when row height is taller than data; top is usually best.
You can flip cell data in different directions by clicking different points around the circle, manually entering Degrees, or clicking the vertical ABCD button.
Cell Attributes
Numbers
Font
Font Effects
Alignment
Asian Typography
Borders
Background
Cell Protection
Text alignment
Horizontal
Default
Indent
0pt
Vertical
Middle
Text direction
ABCD
Degrees
0
Reference edge
Spacing to grid lines
Left
0.01"
Top
0.01"
Right
0.01"
Bottom
0.01"
Text flow
Line break
Hyphenation active
OK
Cancel
Help
Reset

Figure 19-16 Cell Attributes window, Alignment tab

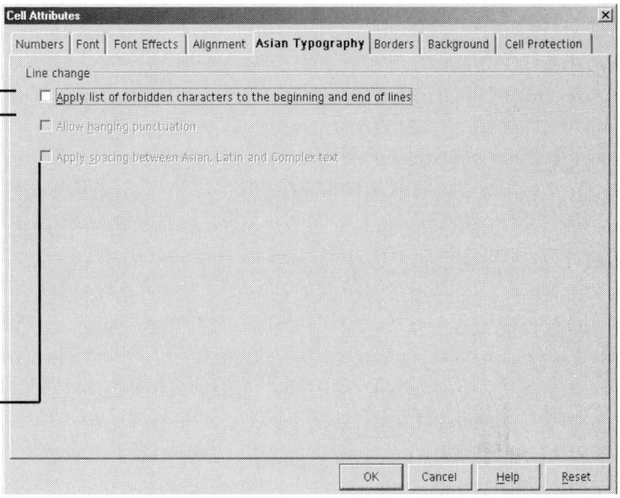
If you select this option, the characters not allowed at the beginning and end of the line are not broken. Enter the list via Tools > Options > Language Settings > Asian Layout.
If you select this option, the comma and period of the corresponding sentence characters will not be broken at the next line but—perhaps even over and beyond the right margin —come out in the same line.
If you select this option, a space is automatically inserted between Asian, Latin and complex texts.
Cell Attributes
Numbers
Font
Font Effects
Alignment
Asian Typography
Borders
Background
Cell Protection
Line change
Apply list of forbidden characters to the beginning and end of lines
Allow hanging punctuation
Apply spacing between Asian, Latin and Complex text
OK
Cancel
Help
Reset

Figure 19-17 Cell Attributes window, Font tab

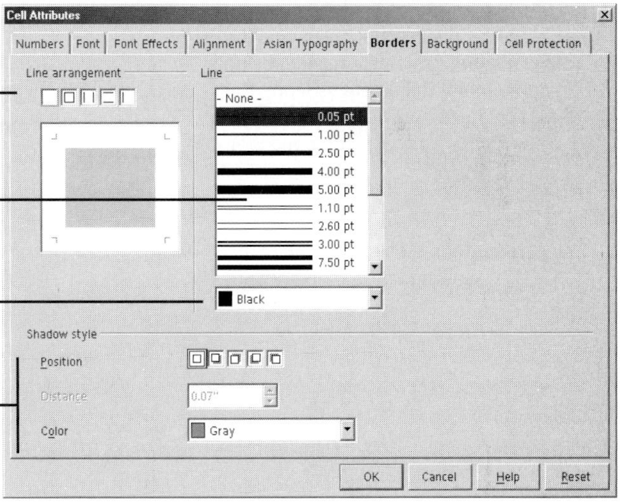
Click one of the Presets boxes to apply that border style. Click the empty first box to clear all line (not shadow)
Select the type of line you want for the specified preset line arrangement.
You can choose a border line Color from the standard color palette.
Select a shadow, if any, for the cell itself, the shadow angle, the distance of the shadow from the cell, and shadow color.
Cell Attributes
Numbers
Font
Font Effects
Alignment
Asian Typography
Borders
Background
Cell Protection
Line arrangement
Line
- None -
0.05 pt
1.00 pt
2.50 pt
4.00 pt
5.00 pt
1.10 pt
2.60 pt
3.00 pt
7.50 pt
Black
Shadow style
Position
Distance
0.07"
Color
Gray
OK
Cancel
Help
Reset

Figure 19-18 Cell Attributes window, Borders tab

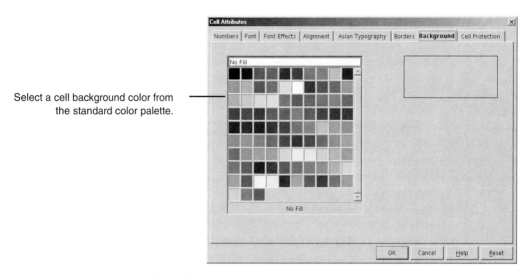

Select a cell background color from the standard color palette.

Figure 19-19 Cell Attributes window, Background tab

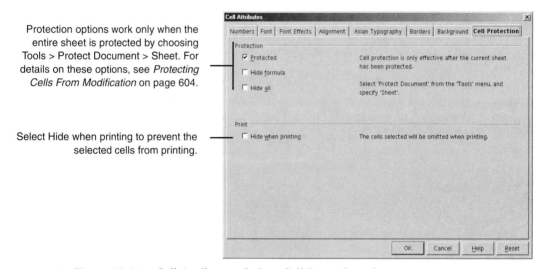

Protection options work only when the entire sheet is protected by choosing Tools > Protect Document > Sheet. For details on these options, see *Protecting Cells From Modification* on page 604.

Select Hide when printing to prevent the selected cells from printing.

Figure 19-20 Cell Attributes window, Cell Protection tab

Page Setup

You can control the look of the spreadsheet printout in a number of ways, as illustrated in the following procedures.

Setting Page and Sheet Options

Calc page styles control many aspects of how a printed spreadsheet looks. They also control other printing aspects such as the paper size used, page numbering style, and the direction Calc uses to create the flow of pages (top to bottom or left to right).

You'll set the majority of these options on the Page and Sheet tabs of the Page Styles window.

1 With the spreadsheet document open containing the sheets you want to set options for, choose Format > Page to display the Page Styles window.

  You can also get to this window from the Stylist (F11) by clicking the Page Styles icon, right-clicking the page style used for the sheet, and choosing Modify.

2 Set the appropriate options in the Page and Sheet tabs. Use Figure 19-21 through Figure 19-24 for guidance.

3 Click OK.

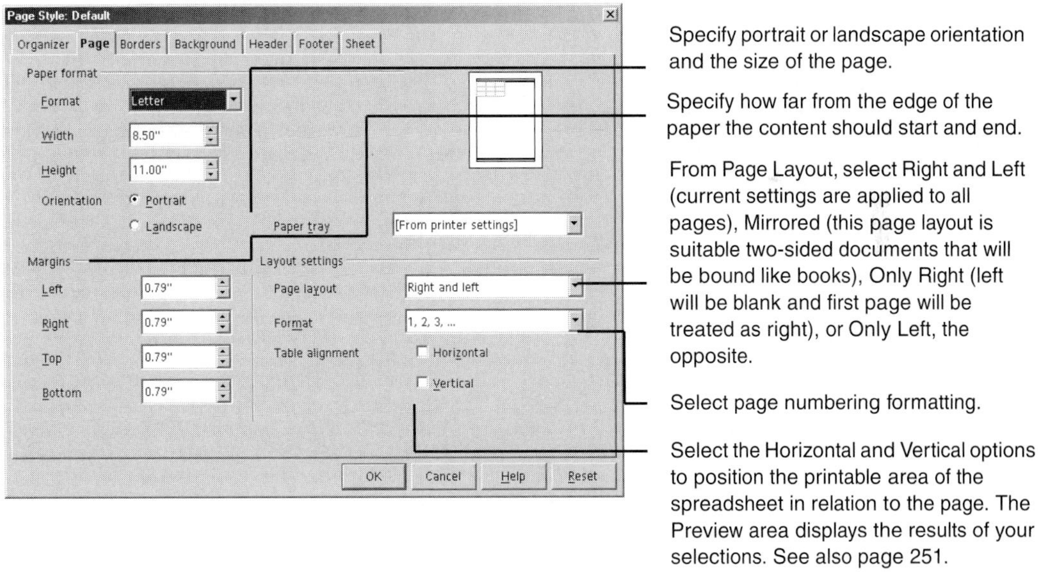

Page Style: Default
Organizer
Page
Borders
Background
Header
Footer
Sheet
Paper format
Format
Letter
Width
8.50"
Height
11.00"
Orientation
Portrait
Landscape
Paper tray
[From printer settings]
Margins
Left
0.79"
Right
0.79"
Top
0.79"
Bottom
0.79"
Layout settings
Page layout
Right and left
Format
1, 2, 3, ...
Table alignment
Horizontal
Vertical
OK
Cancel
Help
Reset
Specify portrait or landscape orientation and the size of the page.
Specify how far from the edge of the paper the content should start and end.
From Page Layout, select Right and Left (current settings are applied to all pages), Mirrored (this page layout is suitable two-sided documents that will be bound like books), Only Right (left will be blank and first page will be treated as right), or Only Left, the opposite.
Select page numbering formatting.
Select the Horizontal and Vertical options to position the printable area of the spreadsheet in relation to the page. The Preview area displays the results of your selections. See also page 251.

Figure 19-21 Setting Page and Sheet printing options: Page tab

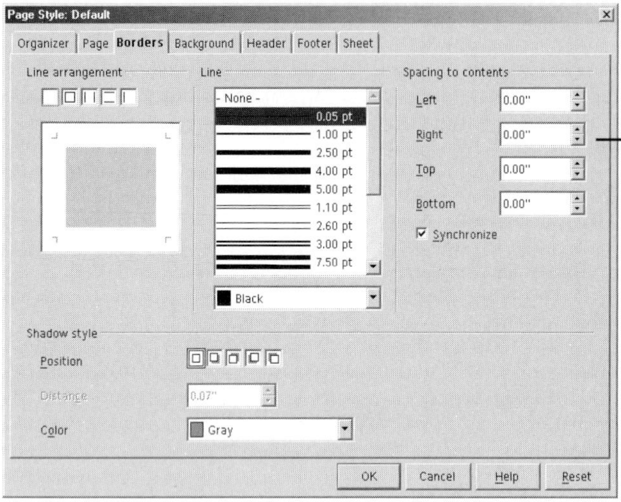

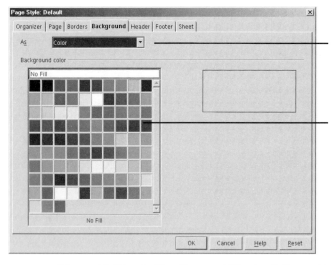

Specify how far from the edge of the paper the content should start and end.

In the rest of the window, specify the lines and shadows that you want around the page as a whole. You can't see the effects on the spreadsheet in normal view, though you can see the effects in grayscale by choosing File > Page Preview (not Page Break Preview).

Figure 19-22   Setting Page and Sheet printing options: Borders tab

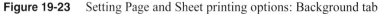

Select a color, or graphic background for the spreadsheet as a whole. If you select Graphic, the window will allow you to browse to the graphic file and to tile or simply display the graphic.

Select a background color or other type of fill for the spreadsheet as a whole. Select No Fill to remove a color.

Figure 19-23   Setting Page and Sheet printing options: Background tab

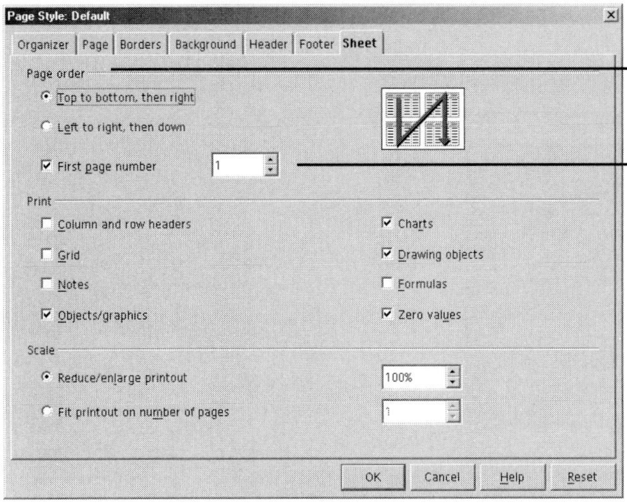

Select the direction Calc will use to create the page flow.

If you want page numbering to begin with a number other than 1, select the First page number option and select the alternative number.

Select the Print and Scale options later when you're ready to print. These are covered in *Selecting Spreadsheet Elements to Print* on page 630.

Figure 19-24 Setting Page and Sheet printing options: Sheet tab

Setting Up Headers and Footers

You can print spreadsheets with header and footer information that includes any text you type, the name of the spreadsheet file, the name of the sheet, page numbers, total page count, date, and time. You can also format the header and footer font.

Each page style has its own header and footer information.

1 With the spreadsheet document open containing the sheets you want to set header and footer information for, choose Format > Page to display the Page Styles window.

You can also get to this window from the Stylist (F11) by clicking the Page Styles icon, right-clicking the page style used for the sheet, and choosing Modify.

2 Set the appropriate options in the Header and Footer tabs. Use Figure 19-25 and Figure 19-26 for guidance.

3 Click OK.

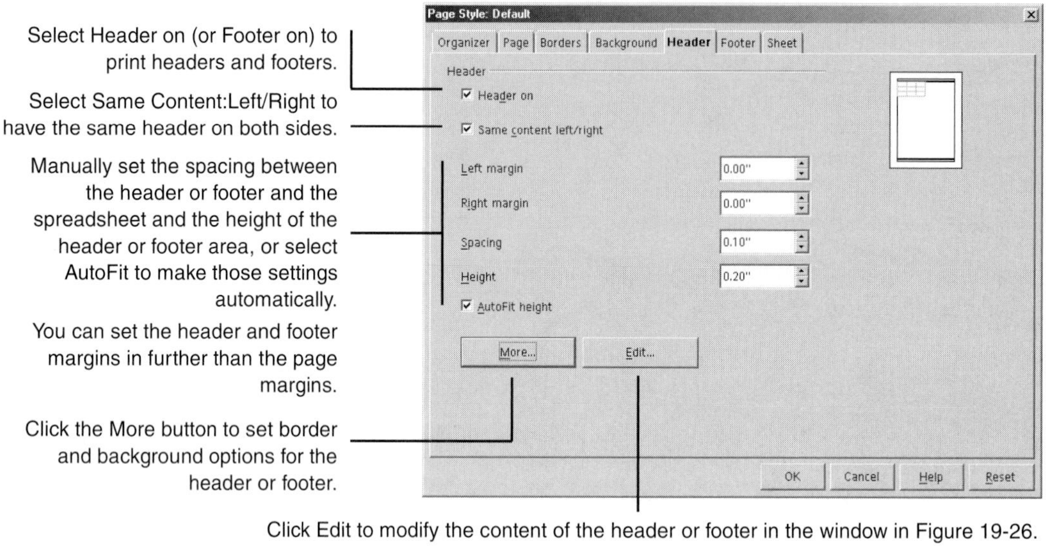

Select Header on (or Footer on) to print headers and footers.

Select Same Content:Left/Right to have the same header on both sides.

Manually set the spacing between the header or footer and the spreadsheet and the height of the header or footer area, or select AutoFit to make those settings automatically.

You can set the header and footer margins in further than the page margins.

Click the More button to set border and background options for the header or footer.

Page Style: Default

Organizer | Page | Borders | Background | **Header** | Footer | Sheet

Header
☑ Header on
☑ Same content left/right

Left margin   0.00"
Right margin   0.00"
Spacing   0.10"
Height   0.20"
☑ AutoFit height

[More...]   [Edit...]

[OK] [Cancel] [Help] [Reset]

Click Edit to modify the content of the header or footer in the window in Figure 19-26.

Figure 19-25   Setting up headers and footers: basics

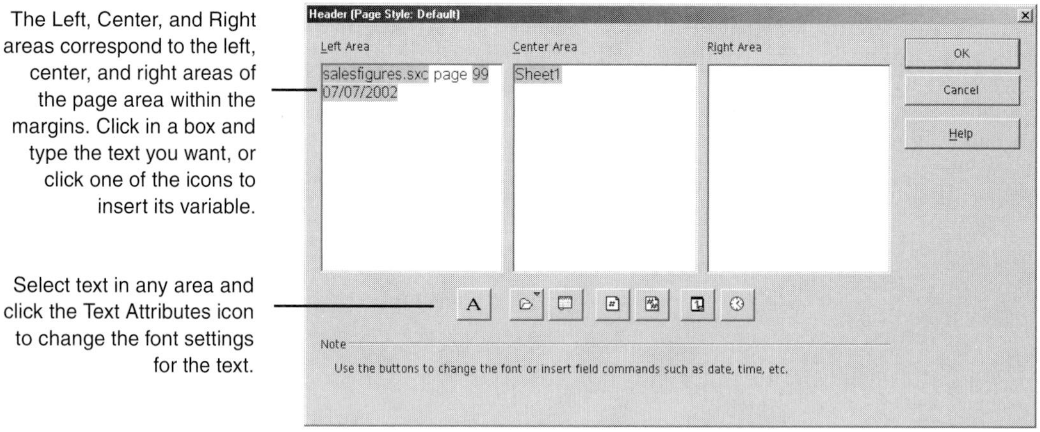

The Left, Center, and Right areas correspond to the left, center, and right areas of the page area within the margins. Click in a box and type the text you want, or click one of the icons to insert its variable.

Select text in any area and click the Text Attributes icon to change the font settings for the text.

Header [Page Style: Default]

Left Area   Center Area   Right Area

salesfigures.sxc page 99   Sheet1
07/07/2002

[OK]
[Cancel]
[Help]

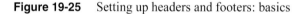 A 🖉 ▭ ▣ ▣ ▣ 🕐

Note
Use the buttons to change the font or insert field commands such as date, time, etc.

Figure 19-26   Setting up headers and footers: specifying content

You can also edit headers and footers for the active page style by choosing Edit > Headers & Footers.

If Calc won't let you insert page numbers in a header or footer, make sure you have a numbering style selected in the Page Style window on the Page tab. If numbering is set to None, you can't insert a page number in a header or footer.

Things That Affect Page Numbering

A whole bunch of things affect page numbering: the Format option for number formatting from Figure 19-21, the First Page Number option from Figure 19-24 for guidance, and the settings you specify for headers and footers formatting in Figure 19-26. In addition, the Page Layout selection you made in Figure 19-21 and the options under the Same Content Left/Right option in Figure 19-26 affect whether the numbering is the same on both sides. Header and footer settings override other settings.

Previewing Page Breaks

To give you an idea of how pages are going to break when you print your spreadsheet, and to show you the page flow direction Calc is going to create, turn on Calc's Page Break Preview feature by choosing View > Page Break Preview.

Calc reduces the viewing percentage of the spreadsheet, displays large nonprinting page number watermarks behind each page, and inserts nonprinting page break lines (see figure at right).

With Page Break Preview activated, you can still work in the spreadsheet, and you can increase the viewing percentage by right-clicking the viewing percentage box in the status bar and choosing the viewing percentage you want.

To increase the amount of spreadsheet that fits on a page, choose Format > Page, and in the Page Style window, select the Pages tab and decrease the margin settings. If after that you still need to fit more on a page, try resizing the columns. You can also go to the Page Style window, select the Sheet tab, and adjust the Scale settings. See Figure 19-21 on page 551 for details

Inserting Manual Row and Column Breaks

If while in Page Break Preview (previous procedure) or by using the print preview (File > Page Preview) you see the need to create manual page breaks to better control the print output of your spreadsheet, select the row or column you want to break on and choose Insert > Manual Break > (Row Break or Column Break).

To remove manual breaks, choose Edit > Remove Manual Break > (Row Break or Column Break).

Manual breaks may not always be the answer, however. Sometimes creating good page breaks may just be a matter of resizing rows or columns.

Controlling Spreadsheet Layout and Scrolling

As your spreadsheet grows, it's useful to controlling scrolling within it.

Creating Non-Scrolling Regions

If you have long rows or columns of data that extend well beyond the viewable area of the spreadsheet window, scrolling to the areas you want to see means you no longer see the column or row labels associated with the data you're viewing. For example, if you have a spreadsheet that has columns for different types of dollar amounts (interest paid, payment, and balance), and you scroll down to see data beyond the bottom border of the work area, you may not remember which column corresponds to which type of dollar amount because your column headings have scrolled up.

To fix this problem, you can make column or rows non-scrolling (see Figure 19-27).

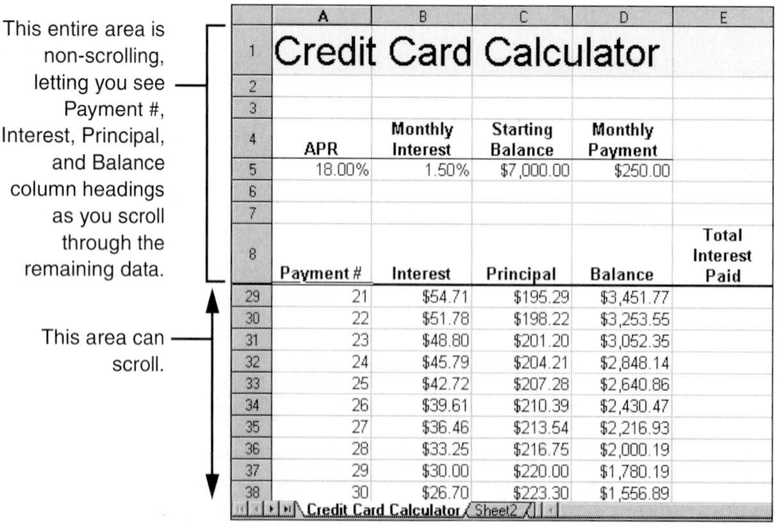

This entire area is non-scrolling, letting you see Payment #, Interest, Principal, and Balance column headings as you scroll through the remaining data.

This area can scroll.

Figure 19-27   Non-scrolling region

Horizontal Non-Scrolling Region

1   Select the row below the row you want to be in the non-scrolling region. All rows above the selection will be non-scrolling.

2   Choose Window > Freeze.

Vertical Non-Scrolling Region

1   Select the column to the right of the column you want to be in the non-scrolling region. All columns to the left of the selection will be non-scrolling.

2   Choose Window > Freeze.

Horizontal and Vertical Non-Scrolling Regions

1   Click the cell that is below the row and to the right of the column you want to make non-scrolling; for example, cell B2.

2   Choose Window > Freeze.

Turning Off Non-Scrolling Regions

Choose Window > Freeze.

Splitting a Window

If your spreadsheet is larger than the boundaries of your screen, and you're constantly scrolling to work with different parts of the spreadsheet, consider splitting it. Splitting lets you view and work with different sections of a spreadsheet simultaneously.

You can split the spreadsheet vertically, horizontally, or into fourths, depending on which cell is selected.

The split command won't work if cell A1 is selected.

Splitting vertically   Select any cell in row 1 (except cell A1) and choose Window > Split.

Splitting horizontally   Select any cell in column A (except cell A1) and choose Window > Split.

Splitting into fourths   Select any cell in the middle of the spreadsheet and choose Window > Split.

Resizing the split   You can resize the split areas by moving the cursor over the split line until it changes shape, then clicking and dragging the line to the new position, as shown in Figure 19-28.

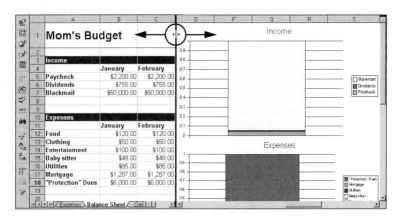

Figure 19-28   Resizing a split area

To unsplit the window, choose Window > Split.

Power Formatting With Styles and Templates

In the previous sections we talked about formatting cells manually, which is how most people format: selecting cells and either clicking quick-formatting tools on the object bar and ruler or choosing Format > Cells to set specific formatting options.

There are legitimate reasons to use only manual formatting (such as quick formatting of a short spreadsheet whose styles you don't plan to reuse). However, to get the most out of Calc and to work more quickly with more consistency, use styles and templates.

There are two types of styles in Calc: Cell Styles, which affect cells and their contents, and Page Styles, which affect pagination and print output.

Why You Should Use Styles

Using styles in Calc is a no-brainer, especially if you work with spreadsheets a lot.

Following are the reasons why you should use styles. Any one of these reasons alone justifies using them.

Instant Formatting With a double-click you can transform a plain cell into one with a different font, font size, font color, indentation, spacing, alignment, and background color. All cells that are given that style are identical.

Automation When you modify a style, all cells with that style are updated automatically. Automation is good! It doesn't mean "cookie-cutter"; it means you work more quickly, efficiently, and consistently.

Maintaining Consistency Using styles ensures your spreadsheets will maintain a consistent style.

Conditional Formatting You can set a cell to take on specific cell formats automatically when the contents of the cell reach a certain state, or condition (see *Conditional Formatting* on page 582).

Using the Stylist

If you use styles in Calc, the Stylist should be your closest companion. To show it (and hide it), press the F11 key.

Styles apply only to the spreadsheet in which you create them. To make styles in one document available to other documents, see *Loading Individual Styles* on page 259.

The Stylist, shown in Figure 19-29, is the control center for viewing, applying, adding, modifying, and deleting styles. The following picture and table describes the elements of the Stylist.

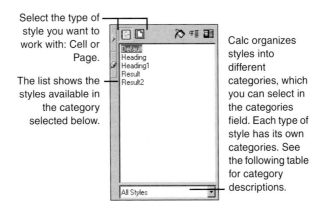

Select the type of style you want to work with: Cell or Page.

The list shows the styles available in the category selected below.

Calc organizes styles into different categories, which you can select in the categories field. Each type of style has its own categories. See the following table for category descriptions.

Figure 19-29   The Stylist

Table 19-1 describes style categories in the drop-down list at the bottom of the Stylist.

Table 19-1   Calc Stylist categories

Category	Description
All	Shows all defined styles for each style type.
Applied Styles	Shows all the styles you've used in your spreadsheet so far.

Table 19-1   Calc Stylist categories

Category	Description
Custom Styles	Shows the styles you've created beyond the default styles provided by Calc. The styles you create remain in this category even if you assign them to a different category.
Hierarchical	Displays styles in a hierarchical tree view. If a style has a plus sign next to it (+), click the plus sign to view the styles that were created based on that style.

The Style Catalog You can also create, modify, and delete styles using the Style Catalog (Format > Style Catalog).

Tips for Using Styles

With the Stylist docked, make sure you have tooltips turned on (Help > Tips) to help you select the style type you want. When the mouse pointer hovers over a style type icon, its name is displayed. (If the Stylist is a floating window, the name of the selected style category is displayed in the window's title bar.)

You don't have to have all your styles perfect before you start using them. You'll want to make adjustments to them as you work. The great thing about styles is that you can change them when you want, and all of the cells and pages that use them are updated automatically.

Cell Styles

Cell styles control all elements included in cell formatting.

This section describes how to create cell styles. For information on applying styles, see page 561; for modifying styles, see page 561; for deleting styles, see page 561.

Creating a Cell Style

Creating a cell style is fairly easy. In fact, if you know how to format text manually (see *Quick Cell Formatting* on page 543), you know 90 percent of creating a text style.

1   In the Stylist, click the Cell Styles icon.

2   Select the category in which you want to put the new style.

3   Right-click in the Stylist and select New. The Cell Style window is displayed.

   If you want to create a new style based on an existing style, select the style you want to base it on before you right-click.

4   Set the options you want for the cell style.

5   Click OK.

Page Styles

Page styles control such elements as margins, borders, background, headers, footers, and spreadsheet printing options.

Creating a Page Style

1   In the Stylist, click the Page Styles icon.

2   Select the category in which you want to put the new style.

3   Right-click in the Stylist and select New. The Page Style window is displayed. See Figure 19-21 through Figure 19-21 for more information.

4   Set the options you want for the page, and click OK.

    If you need help setting Page, Borders, and Background options, see the *Creating Page Styles* on page 251 section in Writer on page 251.

Applying Styles

1   Select the cell(s) or page to which you want to apply a style.

2   In the Stylist, select the type of style you want to apply (cell or page), select a category, and double-click the name of the style you want to use.

To return to a generic style, double-click the Default style.

Modifying Styles

1   In the Stylist, select the style type containing the style want to modify.

2   Select the category the style belongs to.

3   Right-click the style and select Modify.

4   Change settings for the style.

5   Click OK.

6   If a style doesn't update automatically in the document, select the name of the style in the Stylist and click the Update Style icon at the top of the Stylist.

Deleting Styles

You can't delete default styles. You can delete only custom, user-defined styles.

Before you delete a style, select it in the Stylist, right-click it, select Modify, and select the Organizer tab. Look at style selected in the Based on field (if applicable). When you delete the style, if it was used in the spreadsheet, the parts of the spreadsheet with that style become the style shown in the Based on field.

1   In the Stylist, select the style you want to delete.

2   Right-click it, and select Delete.

3   Click Yes in the confirmation window.

Templates

Calc uses the same template principles as other StarOffice and OpenOffice.org applications. For a full description of templates and procedures for previewing, creating, maintaining, and applying templates to documents, see the Writer section, *Using Templates* on page 256.

The only sub-section that doesn't apply to Calc is *Loading All Styles* on page 258.

Formatting Using Color Themes

Calc also comes with a predefined set of themes you can apply to your spreadsheets. Themes are like templates that contain only predefined styles.

You can't add themes to Calc, and you can't modify them. You can, however, modify their styles after you apply them to your spreadsheets.

1   Click the Choose Themes icon on the main toolbar.

2   In the Theme Selection window, select the theme you want to apply to the spreadsheet. Double-click it to preview it.

3   Click OK.

To remove the effects of a theme, click the Choose Themes icon in the toolbar and select the Standard theme.

Calculating and Manipulating Data

About Spreadsheet Calculations

Spreadsheet cells seem simple enough. You just type stuff in a little box, format it, and maybe even enter small formulas that add up numbers in a column. But when you understand what's possible inside of a single cell, a blank spreadsheet looks less like a blank white space with a bunch of lines and more like complex organism waiting to take shape.

A single cell, which can contain a large formula for making a complex calculation, can also be referenced by other cells, letting you nest formulas within formulas. Spreadsheets can get tricky, but they can also be fun to use. If you understand the basics of how to perform calculations in Calc, you can go a long way in creating and troubleshooting spreadsheets.

See also *Using the Data Pilot to Make a Spreadsheet With Automatic Totals* on page 520.

Formula Basics

This section describes the basic elements used in formulas and the rules Calc uses to calculate formulas.

Basic Operators

Table 20-1 shows the operators (symbols that enable calculations and other operations) you'll use frequently in formulas.

= The equals sign is the most important symbol in formulas. All formulas must begin with it. Without it, a formula is not a formula, but a text string.

Table 20-1　　Basic operators you'll use in formulas

Operator	Description	Example
=	Equals sign. All formulas must begin with this.	=2+2
^	Exponent. Raises the number to the left of the operator to the power of the number on the right.	=10^2 (same as 10^2)
*	Multiply	=5*5
/	Divide	=24/6
+	Add	=B5+12
-	Subtract	=C1-E17
<	Less than	=If(A4<45;"Buy more Sun stock";"Sell")

Table 20-1   Basic operators you'll use in formulas

Operator	Description	Example
>	Greater than	=If(A5>45;"Sell";"Buy more Sun stock")
<=	Less than or equal to	=If(F2<=.05;"Refinance";"Don't refinance")
>=	Greater than or equal to	=If(F3>=.24;"Call to lower interest rate";"Grin and bear it")
<>	Not equal to	=If(D3<>D4;"Debits do not equal credits";"Your books balance")
:	Range of cells. Includes all cells from the cell to the left of the colon to the cell to the right of the colon.	=sum(A1:A25) (Adds up all cells from A1 to A25)
;	Non-consecutive cells and separating formula parts. Let's you include non-consecutive cells in a calculation.	=sum(A1;A7;A25) (Adds up cells A1, A7, and A25) See also the IF() formulas above. Semi-colons are used where commas are used in other spreadsheet applications.
!	Intersection	=sum(A1:B3!B2:C7) (Calculates the sum of all cells in the intersection. In this example, the result is the sum of cells B2 and B3)

Order of Evaluation for Expressions

What's the answer to the following math problem?

=5+10*2-14/2+4

If you start the problem left-to-right, the answer is 12. Calc also calculates left-to-right, but it also follows algebraic ordering rules for the order it calculates: it multiplies and divides first, then adds and subtracts. With that in mind, let's simplify the problem by solving the multiplication and division parts first:

=5+20-7+4

Then handle the addition and subtraction, working left-to-right, and the answer is 22.

Exponents If you include exponents in your formulas (for example, 10^2, which is written as 10^2 in Calc), those are calculated before multiplication and division.

Using Parentheses to Control Calculation Order

You can exercise more control over the calculation order by using parentheses. This is also an algebra thing. Calc solves formulas within parentheses first (using algebraic ordering within the parentheses) before it solves the rest of the formula.

Using the previous formula as an example, Table 20-2 shows how using parentheses in different ways can produce different solutions.

Table 20-2   Using parentheses to control calculation order

Formula	Solution
=(5+10)*2-(14/2+4)	19
=5+(10*2-14)/2+4	12
=(5+10*2)-14/(2+4)	22.67
=5+10*(2-14/2)+4	-41

Inevitably as you use parentheses, you'll need to control calculation order further by nesting parentheses within parentheses. For example:

=(9*(10-7))/((8*3)-(7*3))+10^2

Calc solves formulas the inner parentheses first. The solution to this formula is 109 (10^2 is the same as 10^2, or 100).

Since most of your formulas will contain cell references (rather, *should* contain cell references), creating a calculation order with parentheses can get tricky, because you're constantly trying to see which cell references represent which numbers. For example, =(A7*(SUM(B5:B7)))/D2. There are a couple of tricks you can use to help visually map cell references to the numbers they reference:

- Even if you're not finished with your formula, press Enter to save the formula in its current state. Most likely you will get an error message in the cell, which is okay. Double-click the cell. Calc color codes the cell references in the formula and highlights the referenced cells in with corresponding colors. This helps you edit the formula.

- Use the trace precedents and dependents feature to have arrows point back and forth from the cell containing the formula to all the referenced cells. See *Tracing Precedents, Dependents, and Errors* on page 591.

Entering Formulas Manually

The previous section, Formula Basics, provides the basic information necessary for entering formulas. This section expands on that by highlighting tools that help automate formula entry, going into more detail on using cell references, and showing a couple of power user formula procedures.

Function Overview

Calc makes the formula entry process easier and more powerful by providing a library of functions. Functions are keywords like SUM, SQRT, and IF that let you perform specific tasks.

For example, the SUM function lets you add an entire range of cells. Without the SUM function you'd have to enter =B1+B2+B3+B4+B5 to add up the contents of those cells. With the SUM function, you can write the same formula as =SUM(B1:B5). Because functions are so useful, powerful, and essential in creating spreadsheets, Calc comes with a veritable boatload of them; functions that do everything from figuring sums and square roots, to letting you set up conditions within a cell that can make the cell display different values depending on whether the condition is true or false. (That's the IF function). There's even a function to help you figure out monthly payments on a loan (the PMT function).

The following sections highlight useful functions and tools.

Quick Sum

Calc lets you add up rows or columns with a mouse click.

1   Click the cell that you want to contain the sum of the row or column.

2   Click the Sum icon on the function bar.

     Calc automatically enters the sum function and the appropriate range of cells in the row or column, as shown in Figure 20-1.

3   Make sure the range of cells is correct, change the range if necessary, and press Enter.

Figure 20-1   Doing a quick sum

Changing the Range Selection for a Sum

You don't have to be directly in the row or column you want to add up. You can click any cell, click the Sum icon, and change the range of cells simply by dragging through the range of cells you want to include. You can also select non-adjacent cells and cell ranges by holding down the Ctrl key while you select.

Inserting Subtotals Automatically

If you have a column of numbers you plan on adding up, Calc has a tool to let you insert automatic subtotals after selected rows to generate a running balance. Figure 20-2 shows what subtotals look like.

This feature inserts rows for the generated subtotals. So if you have links set up to cells prior to inserting subtotals, references to those cells could be thrown off after you insert subtotals. For example, if a formula points to cell $A$5, the data in that cell could get bumped to a different cell address by the insertion of subtotals, making the formula point to the wrong cell. (See *Using Cell References* on page 571 for information that can help you avoid this problem.)

The moral of the story is that if you want to insert subtotals, be aware of the potential impacts of inserting extra rows.

	A	B	C
1	**Q1 Expenses**		
2			
3	1/1/00	New strings	$450
4	1/1/00	New amp that goes to 11	$5,300
5	1/1/00	New guitar (not for playing)	$5,400
6	2/17/00	Electronic pods	$25,000
7	2/17/00	Paternity suit	$230,000
8	3/5/00	Cover reprint (darker black)	$7,000
9	3/5/00	Fliers (for new lead guitarist)	$10,000
10	3/5/00	Hotel room repairs	$1,828

	A	B	C
1	**Q1 Expenses**		
2			
3	1/1/00	New strings	$450
4	1/1/00	New amp that goes to 11	$5,300
5	1/1/00	New guitar (not for playing)	$5,400
6	*1/1/00 Sum*		*$10,700*
7	2/17/00	Electronic pods	$25,000
8	2/17/00	Paternity suit	$230,000
9	*2/17/00 Sum*		*$255,000*
10	3/5/00	Cover reprint (darker black)	$7,000
11	3/5/00	Fliers (for new lead guitarist)	$10,000
12	3/5/00	Hotel room repairs	$1,828
13	*3/5/00 Sum*		*$18,828*
14	*Grand Total*		*$284,528*

Calc automatically adds outline tools and headings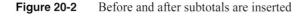

Figure 20-2   Before and after subtotals are inserted

1   Select the area of data for which you want to create subtotals.

2   Choose Data > Subtotals.

3   In the Subtotals window, set the options you want. Use Figure 20-3 for guidance.

   In the Subtotals window, you can add more layers to the data groupings (creating groups within groups) by entering the appropriate settings in the 2nd Group and 3rd Group tabs, as well. In the example in Figure 20-2, the data is grouped by date and the dollar amounts are subtotaled, as the settings in Figure 20-3 indicate.

4   Click OK.

Setting up subtotal options is a logical process. For example, you wouldn't want to subtotal a column containing names. The Subtotals tool will let you set any options you want. Just be aware that if the results look strange, you may have to go back and think through the setup process.

When you create subtotals, Calc also adds outline functionality, letting you expand and contract groups, as shown in Figure 20-2.

In the Group by field, select the column by which you want to group the data. Assign second and third groups if appropriate in the 2nd and 3rd tabs.

In the Calculate subtotals for list, select the column(s) for which you want to generate subtotals.

Select the type of calculation (function) you want to perform to generate subtotals.

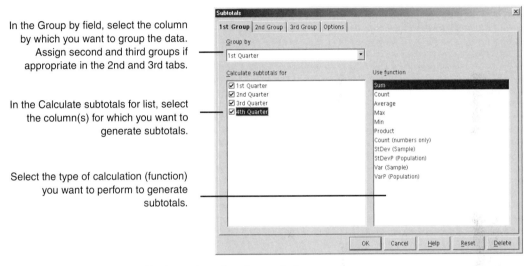

Figure 20-3   Setting subtotal options, tab 1

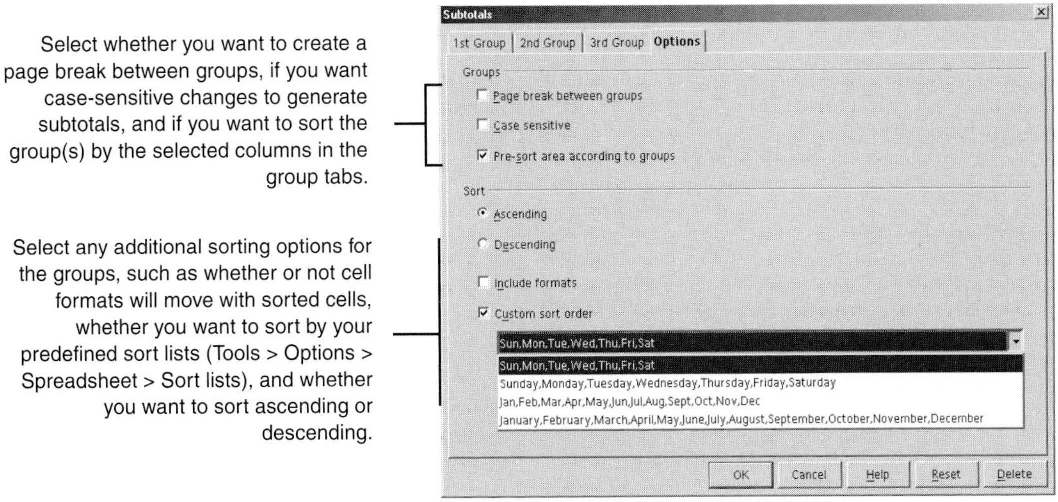

Select whether you want to create a page break between groups, if you want case-sensitive changes to generate subtotals, and if you want to sort the group(s) by the selected columns in the group tabs.

Select any additional sorting options for the groups, such as whether or not cell formats will move with sorted cells, whether you want to sort by your predefined sort lists (Tools > Options > Spreadsheet > Sort lists), and whether you want to sort ascending or descending.

Figure 20-4   Setting subtotal options, Options tab

Using the Function AutoPilot

Calc has a wizard called the Function AutoPilot that helps you build formulas. To use the
Function AutoPilot:

1   Click the cell that you want to contain
    the function.

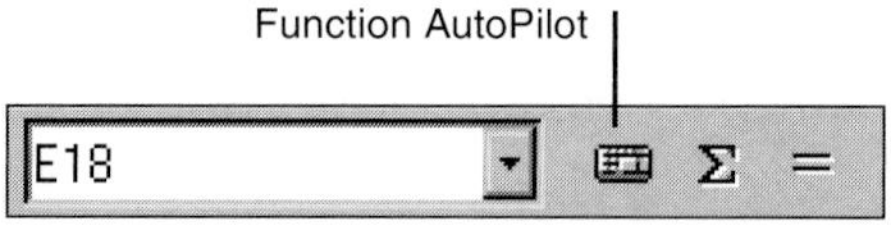

2   Click the Function AutoPilot icon on
    the function bar.

3   In the Function AutoPilot window (Figure 20-5), select a function. Click Next.

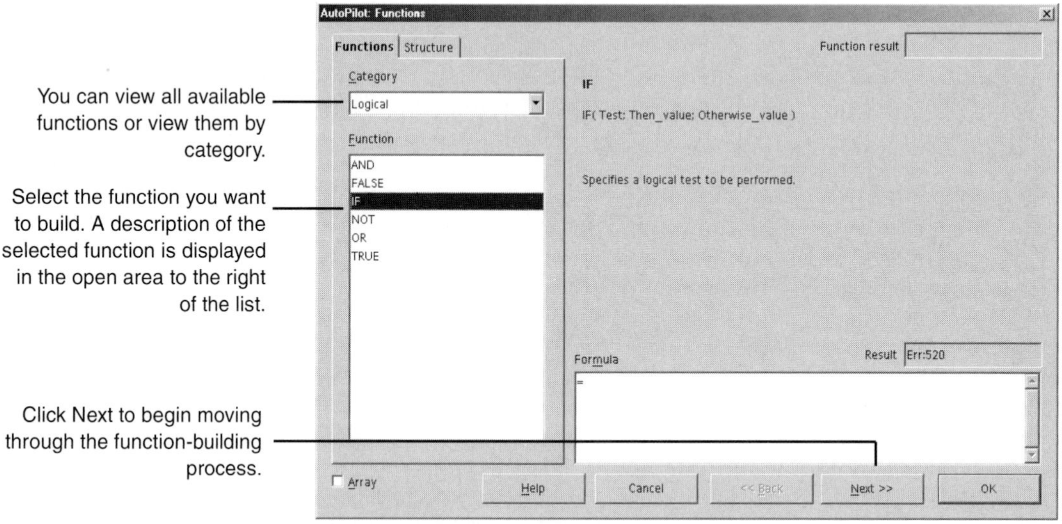

Figure 20-5   Using the Function AutoPilot to select functions

4   In the second Function AutoPilot window, build the formula; see Figure 20-6.

5   When you're finished building the formula, click OK.

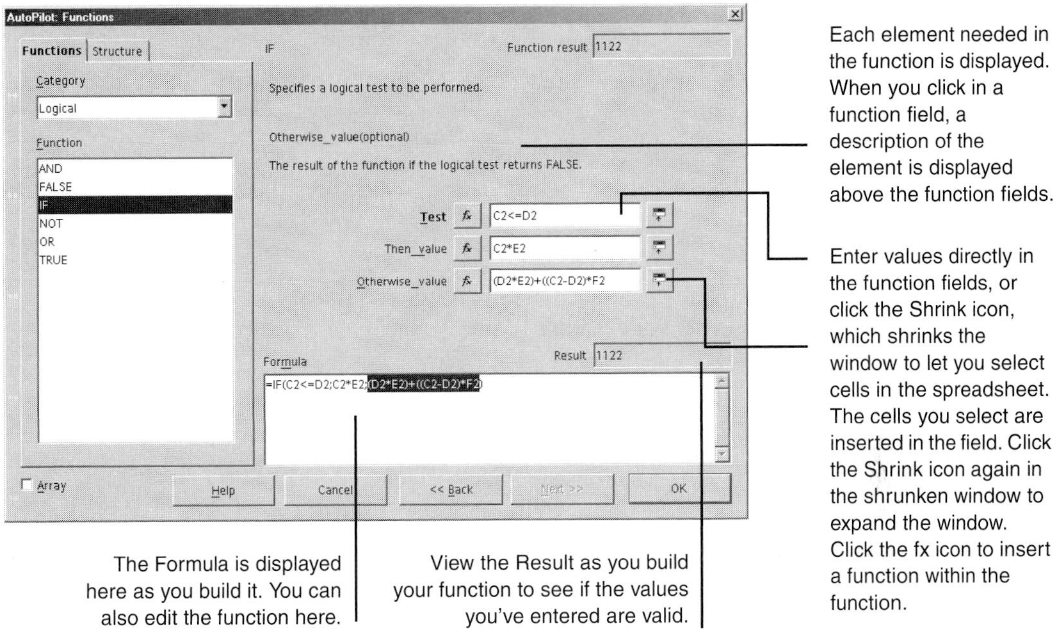
AutoPilot: Functions
Functions
Structure
Category
Logical
Function
AND
FALSE
IF
NOT
OR
TRUE
IF
Function result 1122
Specifies a logical test to be performed.
Otherwise_value(optional)
The result of the function if the logical test returns FALSE.
Test
C2<=D2
Then_value
C2*E2
Otherwise_value
(D2*E2)+((C2-D2)*F2
Formula
Result 1122
=IF(C2<=D2;C2*E2;(D2*E2)+((C2-D2)*F2)
Array
Help
Cancel
<< Back
Next >>
OK
Each element needed in the function is displayed. When you click in a function field, a description of the element is displayed above the function fields.
Enter values directly in the function fields, or click the Shrink icon, which shrinks the window to let you select cells in the spreadsheet. The cells you select are inserted in the field. Click the Shrink icon again in the shrunken window to expand the window. Click the fx icon to insert a function within the function.
The Formula is displayed here as you build it. You can also edit the function here.
View the Result as you build your function to see if the values you've entered are valid.

Figure 20-6 Using the Function AutoPilot to build functions

Using Cell References

Cell references are cell addresses, such as A1, B4, and C5, entered into formulas. Cell references are what make spreadsheets so flexible, because as the values within cells change, the cell references stay the same: cell B4 is cell B4, whether the value inside it is 2 or (5*(4^3))/7.

When you build formulas with cell references, the formulas not only stay smaller and more manageable, but they also stay the same even when the contents of cells change.

Following are tips for using cell references.

Click, Don't Type

You don't have to type cell references manually into a formula. As you're building a formula, you can click cells and cell ranges in a spreadsheet to enter those cells and ranges as cell references, as shown in Figure 20-7.

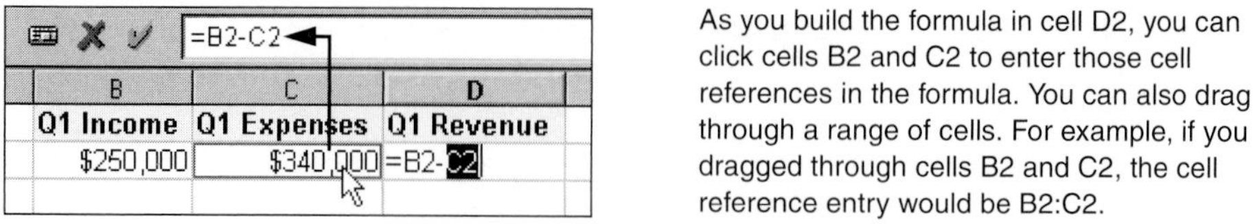

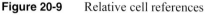

As you build the formula in cell D2, you can click cells B2 and C2 to enter those cell references in the formula. You can also drag through a range of cells. For example, if you dragged through cells B2 and C2, the cell reference entry would be B2:C2.

Figure 20-7   Clicking cells to include them as cell references in a formula

Relative and Absolute Cell References

Figure 20-8 shows a quick look at the physical makeup of relative and absolute cell references before we begin the discussion of them.

A1	$A$1	$A1
Relative reference	Absolute reference to the column and row	Absolute reference to the column and relative reference to the row.

Figure 20-8   Relative and absolute cell references

Relative cell references See Figure 20-9. When you select and cut or copy a group of cells that have a calculated value, then paste the cells into a new location, Calc changes the cell references in the formulas so that the calculated values remain intact.

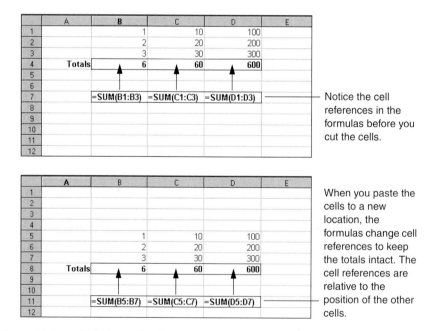

Notice the cell references in the formulas before you cut the cells.

When you paste the cells to a new location, the formulas change cell references to keep the totals intact. The cell references are relative to the position of the other cells.

Figure 20-9   Relative cell references

This is possible because the cell references in the formulas are **relative** to the rest of the cells. No matter where the group of cells moves, they keep the same relation to the other cells, as Figure 20-9 illustrates.

To see how relative cell references differ in looks from absolute cell references, see the section on absolute cell references, next.

Absolute cell references There may be times when using relative cell references doesn't work well; for example, when you're referencing cells whose locations will never change. These cells have an **absolute** position.

Absolute cell references come mainly into play when you're using Calc's automatic fill feature (see *Filling to Increment Data* on page 535), which increments values and cell references as you fill.

Sometimes you may not want cell references to increment. Using the Credit Card Calculator in the *Guided Tour of Calc* on page 504, there is a row of cells containing values that need to be referenced at all times, whose locations will never change, as shown in Figure 20-10.

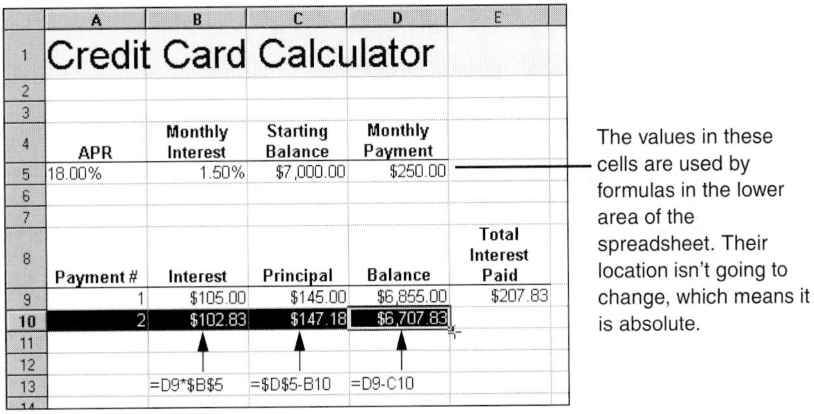

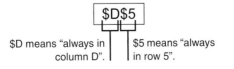

The values in these cells are used by formulas in the lower area of the spreadsheet. Their location isn't going to change, which means it is absolute.

Figure 20-10   Using absolute cell references

To set up references to cells that aren't going to change locations, put a dollar sign in front of the column letter and row number. For example, see Figure 20-11.

$$\$D\$5$$

$D means "always in column D". $5 means "always in row 5".

Figure 20-11   Example of absolute references

In Figure 20-10, if you didn't use absolute cell references in the formulas in row 10, and you tried to do an automatic fill, the references to the cells in row 5 would increment from, for example, D5 to D6, from D6 to D7, and so on, throwing off your calculations. When you enter the absolute cell reference to $D$5, the cell reference stays pointed at cell D5 even when you use automatic fill.

You don't have to put a dollar sign in from of the column *and* the row. You can use different combinations of absolute/relative cell references, depending on how you're going to use automatic fill. As a general rule:

- If you're going use automatic fill to fill across rows (left and right), put a dollar sign before column letters.

- If you're going to use automatic fill up and down in columns, put the dollar sign in front of row numbers.

- If you're referencing cells that will never change location, put a dollar sign in front of the column letter and row number.

Note – Calc has a keyboard shortcut for setting absolute cell references. In a formula, when you highlight a cell reference, press Shift+F4 repeatedly to set the absolute cell reference combination you want, as shown in Figure 20-12.

The absolute cell reference combination
changes each time you press Shift+F4.

Figure 20-12   Using Shift+F4 to set absolute cell references

Updating Calculations

As you change values and formulas in your spreadsheet, you want the contents of the entire spreadsheet to update accordingly. You can set up Calc to update the spreadsheet automatically as you make each change, or you can update the spreadsheet manually.

One reason you might want to update a spreadsheet manually is if it's large and has a lot of linked elements, like charts and linked content from other spreadsheets. If it takes a second or two for the linked elements to update each time you make a change in the spreadsheet, that can get frustrating. Manually updating the spreadsheet lets you make all your changes and then update all at once.

Updating Automatically

1 Update links to data in other sheets or Calc files (if applicable). See *Updating Linked Sheets* on page 526.

2 Choose Tools > Cell Contents.

3 If AutoCalculate doesn't have a check mark next to it, choose AutoCalculate. (A check mark means it's activated.)

Updating Manually (F9)

1 Update links to data in other sheets or Calc files (if applicable). See *Updating Linked Sheets* on page 526.

2 Choose Tools > Cell Contents.

3 If AutoCalculate has a check mark next to it, choose AutoCalculate to remove the check mark.

4 When you want to update the spreadsheet, press the F9 key.

Double-Checking Totals

Because calculations can get tricky, especially if you're using cell references in other sheets and other Calc files, it's good practice to double-check results.

Double-checking a total is simply a matter of calculating the total a different way, as Figure 20-13 illustrates.

	A	B	C	D	
1	**Balance Sheet**				
2					
3					
4	Period	Income	Expenses	Balance	This total was generated by adding cells D6 through D8.
5					
6	January	$167,700.00	$11,150.00	$156,550.00	
7	February	$57,850.00	$255,002.50	($197,152.50)	
8	March	$11,200.00	$18,827.56	($7,627.56)	This total was generated by totalling cells D6 through D8, then subtracting the total of cells C6 through C8.
9			Total	($48,230.06)	
10					
11			Double-check	($48,230.06)	
12					

Figure 20-13 Double-checking totals

You can also double-check totals in conjunction with conditional formatting to visually set off totals that don't match (see *Conditional Formatting* on page 582). You can also use the

IF function (next) to generate text if your totals don't match. For example, "Your totals don't match. You're in big trouble. Call your attorney."

IF Function

The IF ("if") function is one of the most useful functions. It's described here to not only help you use it, but to illustrate the possibilities that functions present.

The logic that Calc uses in the IF function is the same logic you use in language all the time. For example: "If you put that wagon wheel coffee table in the living room, I'm leaving; otherwise, I'll stay." In other words, if something is true, something specific will happen. Otherwise, something else will happen.

Here's how you would give Calc your wagon wheel coffee table (WWCT) ultimatum:

=IF(WWCT in living room;"I'll go";"Otherwise I'll stay")

(You really don't need to tell Calc this. Calc is not notorious for putting wagon wheel coffee tables in people's living rooms, unlike other spreadsheet programs.)

So let's get real. In your spreadsheets, you'll use the IF function when the value of a specific cell will fluctuate. For example, if you're keeping track of a budget, and you want a visual cue to tell you when the total amount you've actually spent is over your budget, you can have a cell display certain text to indicate when you're still within your budget and display different text when you're over budget, as shown in Figure 20-14.

	A	B	C	D	E
1	Item	Budget	Spent		
2					
3	Food	$100	$122		
4	Clothing	$50	$20		
5	Utilities	$80	$107		
6	Entertainment	$75	$60		
7	Total	$305	$309	You're over budget! Shame on you.	
8					
9					
10		=IF(C7<=B7;"You're within budget.";"You're over budget! Shame on you.")			

This is the IF function entered in cell D7. It says, if the amount in cell C7 is less than or equal to the amount in cell E7, display the text, "You're within budget."; otherwise, display the text, "You're over budget! Shame on you."

Figure 20-14   Using IF to berate oneself for going over budget

Notice that each section inside the IF function is separated by a semi-colon. This differs from Excel, which uses commas. Put text within double quotes.

A more complex use of the IF function involves using cell references as conditions, as the following example illustrates.

Let's say a salesperson makes 5 percent commission on sales up to $10,000, and 8 percent on the amount of sales over $10,000.

You could set up an IF function that calculates the total amount of commission, taking into account a higher percentage on sales over $10,000, as shown in Figure 20-15. The math in this kind of formula can get really tricky, so be sure you check your work.

The spreadsheet in Figure 20-15 is set up to allow flexibility. Instead of entering the numbers $10,000, 5%, and 8% directly into the formula, they are entered into cells. The formula then references those cells, which means you can change the values in the cells without changing the formula. For example, if the Target amount changed from $10,000 to $8,000, or if the commission percentages changed, you can change those values in the cells, and the commission amount is adjusted automatically.

You can also use the IF formula in conjunction with conditional formatting to have the cell contents display in different styles when conditions change. See *Conditional Formatting* on page 582.

Here's a logical representation of the formula.

=IF(TotalSales<=10000;TotalSales*.05;(10000*.05)+((TotalSales-10000)*.08)

      If this...   **do this...**   **otherwise do this**

Here's how the formula would actually look in Calc using cell references.

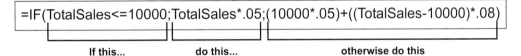

	A	B	C	D	E	F	G
1	Month	Sales	Total Sales	Target	Pre-$10,000	Post-$10,000	Commission
2	January	$4,000	$12,000	$10,000	5%	8%	$660
3	February	$5,000					
4	March	$3,000					
5							
6					=IF(C2<=D2;C2*E2;(D2*E2)+((C2-D2)*F2))		
7							

This is the formula in cell G2.

Figure 20-15   IF function used for calculating total commission earned

Sorting Data

You can change the order of data in a spreadsheet by sorting it; for example, to arrange a list of items and its corresponding data in alphabetical order.

1   Select *all* of the cells you want to sort, as shown in Figure 20-16.

2   Choose Data > Sort.

3   In the Sort window, set the sort options you want. Use Figure 20-17 for guidance.

4 Click OK.

Be sure to select *all* the cells you want included in the sort. Any cells that aren't selected aren't included in the sort, which could throw your data off quite a bit.

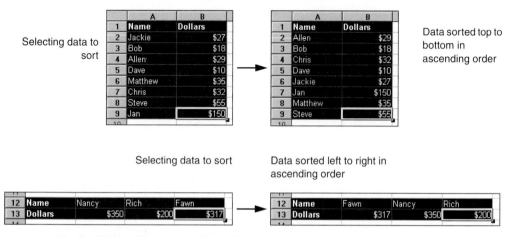

Figure 20-16 Examples of sorted data

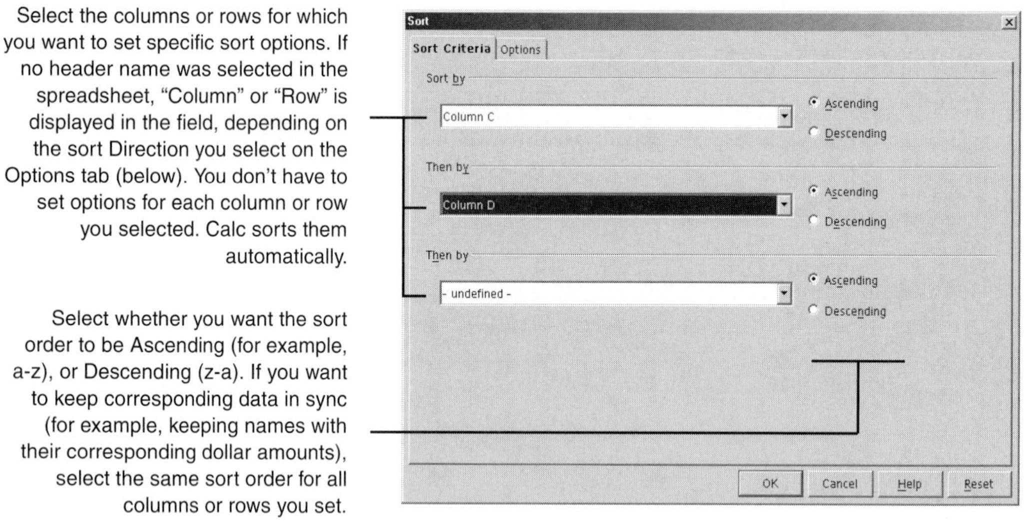

Select the columns or rows for which you want to set specific sort options. If no header name was selected in the spreadsheet, "Column" or "Row" is displayed in the field, depending on the sort Direction you select on the Options tab (below). You don't have to set options for each column or row you selected. Calc sorts them automatically.

Select whether you want the sort order to be Ascending (for example, a-z), or Descending (z-a). If you want to keep corresponding data in sync (for example, keeping names with their corresponding dollar amounts), select the same sort order for all columns or rows you set.

Figure 20-17 Sorting data, Sort Criteria tab

Note – You can also use sort buttons on the toolbar for quick sorting in ascending or descending order.

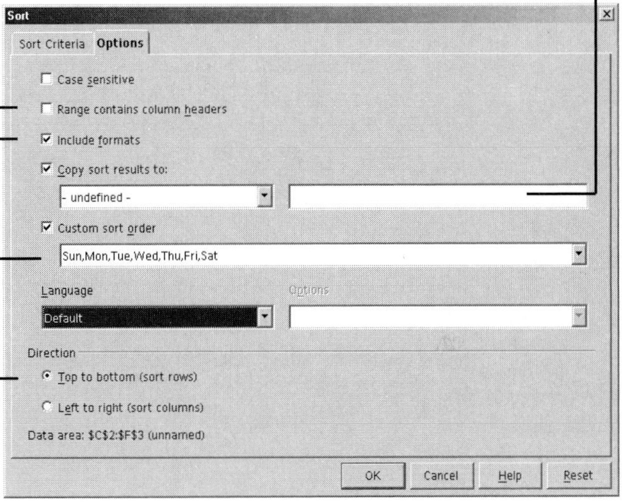
Select the Copy Sort Results To option to copy the sort results to either a named area in the spreadsheet (see page 613) or to a designated cell or range on the current sheet or on another sheet. Select a named area in the drop-down field, or enter a spreadsheet address in the field to the right of the drop-down list; for example, enter *Sheet1.A5* to send the results to Sheet1 beginning at cell A5.
If you selected column or row headers in the spreadsheet and you don't select the Range Contains Column Headers option, the headers are sorted.
Select Include formats to keep data with its corresponding cell format.
If the selected cells are defined as a sort list, you can select the Custom sort order option and select the custom order in which to sort the data.
If you want to sort the data vertically, select Top to bottom. If you want to sort horizontally, select Left to right.
Sort
Sort Criteria
Options
Case sensitive
Range contains column headers
Include formats
Copy sort results to:
- undefined -
Custom sort order
Sun,Mon,Tue,Wed,Thu,Fri,Sat
Language
Options
Default
Direction
Top to bottom (sort rows)
Left to right (sort columns)
Data area: $C$2:$F$3 (unnamed)
OK
Cancel
Help
Reset

Figure 20-18 Sorting data, Options tab

Filtering Data

While sorting rearranges spreadsheet data, Calc also lets you filter spreadsheet data to display only the data you want to see.

There are different complexity levels of filtering you can perform, represented in the following subsections. Advanced filtering isn't covered, because it involves working with spreadsheets as databases, which also isn't covered.

AutoFilter

AutoFilter is the quickest and easiest way to filter in Calc. It inserts a drop-down list button on one or more data columns that lets you select from a list of data that appears in the column(s). For example, if you have a spreadsheet that lists projects, deliverables, owners, due dates, and comments, you could set up an AutoFilter to let you select and view only the entries for one project, as illustrated in Figure 20-19.

The spreadsheet has three projects in the Project column: PDQ, XYZ, and IOU.

	A	B	C	D	E
1	Project	Deliverable	Owner	Date Due	Lame Excuses for Late Delivery
2	PDQ	Sabotage SadisTech's Web site	Darlene	1/17/00	Marketing set the deadline
3	XYZ	Put Broomfield campus on top of Flatirons for April Fool's joke	McNealy	4/1/00	My boss is a tyrant and hates me
4	IOU	Rewrite OO-666	Surupa	1/27/00	Ran out of Advil
5	IOU	Convert OO-666 to Kanji	Elizabeth	3/4/00	I thought you wanted it by MY due date
6	XYZ	Show up for work	Floyd	6/21/99	Too many beer lunches
7	PDQ	Convert War and Peace to XML	Solveig	12/25/99	The t-shirts weren't made, so I didn't think it was an official project yet
8	XYZ	Convert Broomfield campus to digital for move to top of Flatirons	Simon	3/30/00	Used the vi editor I developed myself
9	PDQ	Write "StarOffice Guide for Ultimate Frisbee Players"	Bryan	3/30/00	The restricted space of my cubicle stifles my creativity
10	IOU	Install rear view mirrors in all cubes	Jeannie	2/29/00	Had to clean poop off the carpet from when I brought my dog in
11	PDQ	Commission cubist portrait for next all-hands meeting	Hambly	5/7/00	The company's insulated coffee mugs leak, and I've spent a lot of time—and money—at the cleaners

When you set up an AutoFilter for the Project column, you can click the drop-down arrow to select a project name to display only those project items.

	A	B	C	D	E
1	Project	Deliverable	Owner	Date Due	Lame Excuses for Late Delivery
2	PDQ	Sabotage SadisTech's Web site	Darlene	1/17/00	Marketing set the deadline
7	PDQ	Convert War and Peace to XML	Solveig	12/25/99	The t-shirts weren't made, so I didn't think it was an official project yet
9	PDQ	Write "StarOffice Guide for Ultimate Frisbee Players"	Bryan	3/30/00	The restricted space of my cubicle stifles my creativity
11	PDQ	Commission cubist portrait for next all-hands meeting	Hambly	5/7/00	The company's insulated coffee mugs leak, and I've spent a lot of time—and money—at the cleaners

Figure 20-19   Using an AutoFilter

To use AutoFilter:

1   In your spreadsheet, select the columns you want to use AutoFilter on. (Select a column by clicking the column letter.)

   If you want to use AutoFilter on all columns, don't select any columns. Just perform the next step.

2   On the toolbar, click the AutoFilter icon.

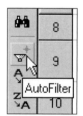

Run the filter by clicking the drop-down arrow in the column heading and choosing an item.

To view the entire spreadsheet after you select an AutoFilter item, click the drop-down arrow and choose All. If you choose Standard, the Standard Filter window is displayed to let you set up a standard filter. Choose Top 10 to display the highest 10 values only.

If AutoFilter is set up for more than one column, you can select one item with AutoFilter, then narrow the list further by selecting a second AutoFilter item. An AutoFilter drop-down arrow turns blue when you've selected an item in its column.

After you filter using AutoFilter, you can run the standard filtering tool to further pinpoint the data you want to see.

To stop using AutoFilter, click the AutoFilter icon on the toolbar. If for some reason your row numbers and column letters stop at the end of your spreadsheet data after you turn AutoFilter off, click the AutoFilter icon twice to turn to turn AutoFilter on and off again.

Standard Filtering

Calc's Standard filtering tool let you refine your filtering options further than you can with AutoFilter, letting you more pinpoint the exact data you want to view.

A main physical difference between AutoFilter and standard filtering is that AutoFilter provides a drop-down list of items to select from. Standard filtering simply applies the filtering options you've set and displays the relevant data.

1   Choose Data > Filter > Standard Filter.

2   In the Standard Filter window, set the filtering options you want. Use Figure 20-20 for guidance.

3   Click OK.

The spreadsheet displays only the items that meet the filtering criteria. To turn filtering off and return to the original spreadsheet, choose Data > Filter > Remove Filter.

The standard filter lets you select up to three filtering criteria. Select a column heading (Field name), a comparison operator (Condition), and the Value the Condition will measure against. Selecting AND means that condition must *also* be met.

If the spreadsheet uses column headings, select this option so you can select the heading names in the Field name list.

If you want to copy the filter results to another area or sheet instead of displaying the results in the active sheet, select the Copy option and either select the named area or click the Shrink icon to select the sheet/area you want to copy to.

Mark the No duplication option to combine duplicate rows into a single row.

Click the More button to expand and contract the Options area of the window.

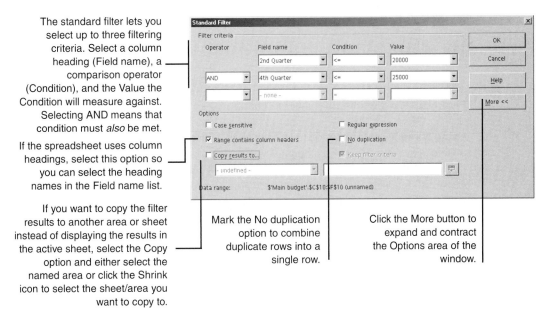

Figure 20-20   Setting standard filtering options

Conditional Formatting

You can set cells up to take on specific formatting characteristics automatically when certain conditions are met. For example, when the calculated value in a cell meets or exceeds a specific number, a plain cell with plain text can become a cell with large text, a colored background, and a thick border.

In order for this to work, you have to create the cell styles you want to use in conditional formatting. See *Cell Styles* on page 560.

1   Select the cell(s) to which you want to apply conditional formatting.

2   Choose Format > Conditional Formatting.

3   In the Conditional Formatting window, set up conditions and assign styles to them. Use Figure 20-21 for guidance.

4   Click OK.

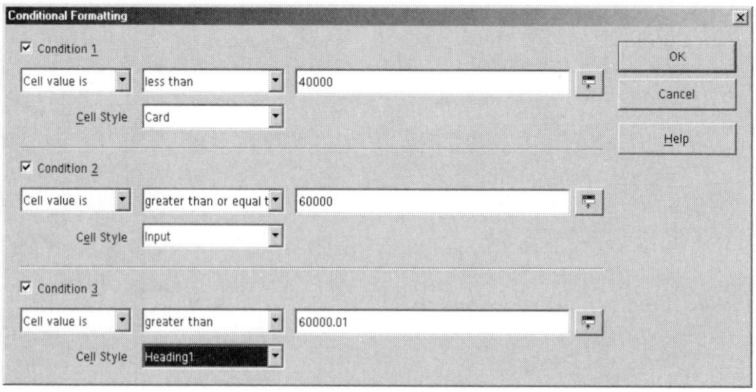

Figure 20-21   Setting conditional formatting

Using conditional formatting for text entries   Conditional formatting can also work for text you enter in cells. For example, if you're building a data sheet for a software product that lists different features by operating system (Solaris, Linux, and Monopoly), you can apply different cell background and font color automatically for of each operating system name you enter. Use Figure 20-22 for guidance.

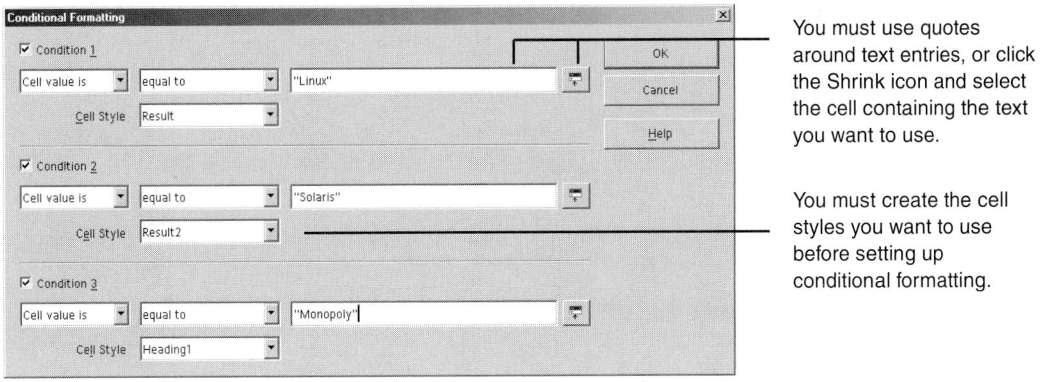

Figure 20-22   Conditional formatting on text entries

Controlling Content and Formatting When Pasting Data

Calc's Paste Special feature gives you a lot of flexibility with how you paste cell contents from your system's clipboard.

With a normal copy (or cut) and paste, the cells you copy and paste elsewhere in a spreadsheet simply replace the values in the target cells. With Paste Special, you can copy a group of cells that contain, for example, the number 2; and when you paste onto a group of target cells, Paste Special lets you add, subtract, multiply, or divide by the values you're pasting (in this case, the number 2).

Paste Special works just as well when you're pasting values generated by a formula. However, when you paste formula-generated values onto target cells, the target cell values don't update when the formulas that were pasted on them change.

1   Copy or cut the values you want to paste.

2   Select the target cells you want to manipulate.

3   Choose Edit > Paste Special.

4   In the Paste Special window, set the paste options. Use Figure 20-23 for guidance.

5   Click OK.

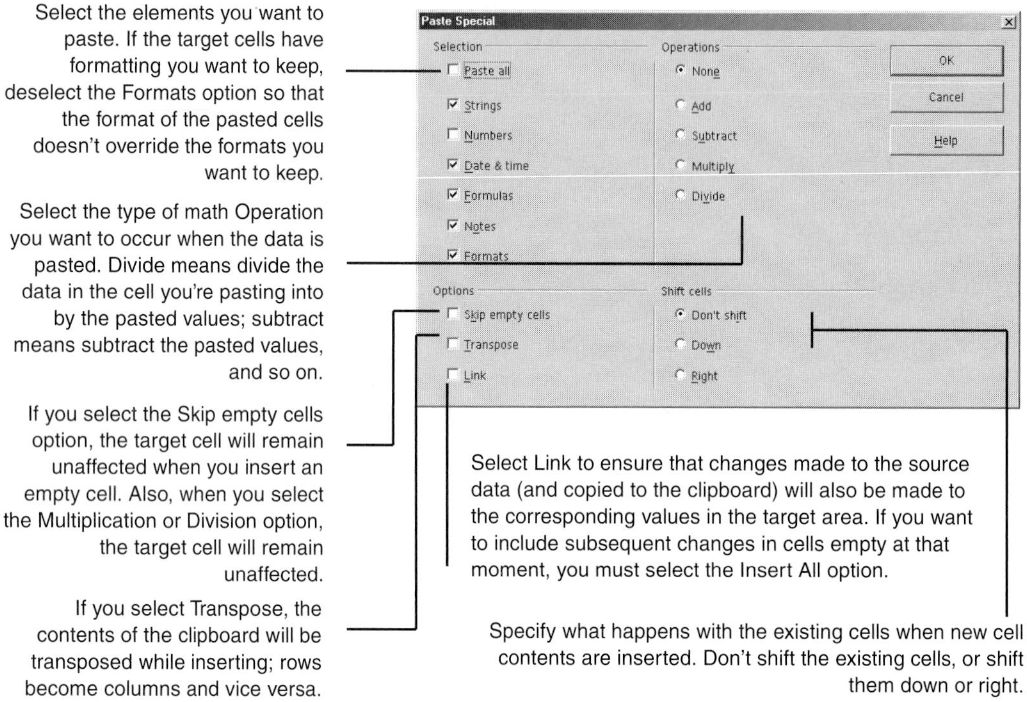
Select the elements you want to paste. If the target cells have formatting you want to keep, deselect the Formats option so that the format of the pasted cells doesn't override the formats you want to keep.
Select the type of math Operation you want to occur when the data is pasted. Divide means divide the data in the cell you're pasting into by the pasted values; subtract means subtract the pasted values, and so on.
If you select the Skip empty cells option, the target cell will remain unaffected when you insert an empty cell. Also, when you select the Multiplication or Division option, the target cell will remain unaffected.
If you select Transpose, the contents of the clipboard will be transposed while inserting; rows become columns and vice versa.
Paste Special
Selection
Paste all
Strings
Numbers
Date & time
Formulas
Notes
Formats
Operations
None
Add
Subtract
Multiply
Divide
OK
Cancel
Help
Options
Skip empty cells
Transpose
Link
Shift cells
Don't shift
Down
Right
Select Link to ensure that changes made to the source data (and copied to the clipboard) will also be made to the corresponding values in the target area. If you want to include subsequent changes in cells empty at that moment, you must select the Insert All option.
Specify what happens with the existing cells when new cell contents are inserted. Don't shift the existing cells, or shift them down or right.

Figure 20-23 Using Paste Special to manipulate data

Note – Unless the check box Skip empty cells is selected, empty cells will be taken into account. An empty cell in the source area will replace the contents of the corresponding cell in the target area if it is inserted without any operations. For the multiplication and division operations, an empty cell is converted to a cell with 0 as its content. This means that the result of the multiplication is always 0, and the division operation results in the error message #VALUE!.

With the Link option, you can also link sheets within the same spreadsheet. If the link extends to other documents, a DDE link is automatically created. A DDE link is inserted as a matrix formula and can only be modified as a whole.

Combining Cells

There may be times when you need to *concatenate*, or combine, text and calculated numbers in a single cell. You may also need to combine the contents of multiple text cells or multiple calculated amount cells into a single cell.

Figure 20-24 shows two concatenation examples.

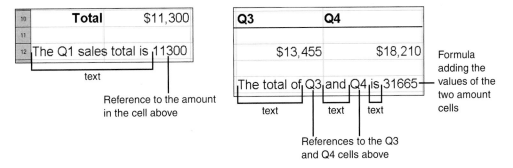

Figure 20-24   Concatenation examples

There are two ways to concatenate cells: a simple way that lets you combine text with a single cell reference or formula (used in the first example in Figure 20-24), and a more advanced way that lets you combine multiple text strings and cell references (used in the second example in Figure 20-24).

Simple Concatenation

When you want to combine text with a single cell reference or a formula (that can include multiple cell references), use the following syntax in a cell:

```
="The text you want to type "&C5
```

or

```
="The text you want to type "&sum(C2:C4)
```

After you type the ampersand (&) in the formula, you can click cells in the spreadsheet rather than typing them manually to insert them in the formula.

Notice this is written as a formula, which begins with the equals sign (=). Notice the space between the last letter of text and the quotation marks. You need to add that space if you want a space between the text and the amount.

Here is how the first example in Figure 20-24 is written:

```
="The Q1 sales total is "&B10
```

Advanced Concatenation

When you want to combine multiple amounts and text strings in a cell, use the following syntax in a cell. This involves using Calc's CONCATENATE function.

```
=CONCATENATE(cell/text/formula;cell/text/formula;...)
```

In this syntax example, cell/text/formula means you can use a cell reference, text, or a formula. Each item is separated by a semicolon (;). You can use as many items as you want.

Here's how the second example in Figure 20-24 is written:

```
=CONCATENATE("The total of";D4;" and ";E4;" is ";SUM(D6:E6))
```

Notice the spaces in the " and " and " is " items. These are necessary to separate the text from the amounts.

This syntax of using a semicolon (;) to separate items is an important difference between Excel and Calc. In Excel, you separate items with a comma (,).

In this example, there are five semicolons that separate six items. You could instead write the formula differently to combine text and numbers, reducing the number of items you need to separate from six to three:

```
=CONCATENATE("The total of "&D4;" and "&E4;" is "&SUM(D6:E6))
```

This technique is accomplished by putting an ampersand in front of a cell reference or formula when it's directly combined with text, as illustrated in the previous Simple Concatenation procedure.

Combining Sheets and Linking to Other Spreadsheets

Spreadsheets are versatile creatures. Oftentimes your spreadsheet use is limited only by your imagination. Use the following procedures as a mental primer to help expand your understanding of what's possible with Calc.

Combining Data From Many Sheets Into One Sheet

It's good practice to use multiple sheets to organize spreadsheets (see *Break It Up* on page 590).

The main idea behind this procedure is to build separate pieces of information on different sheets, then include bits of data from each of the separate sheets onto another sheet (which we'll call a master sheet in this procedure). A good example of this is a profit and loss (P&L) report, which combines data from separate income and expense sheets to create a report on a third sheet, as shown in Figure 20-25. The data from the income and expense sheets is pasted into the P&L sheet as links, so that when the data on those sheets changes, the data on the P&L sheet updates automatically.

1   In one of the sheets, select the cell(s) you want to reference.

You can select an individual cell or a range of cells that are adjacent. You can't copy a group of non-adjacent cells.

2   Choose Edit > Copy.

3   Switch to the master sheet, and click the cell(s) or inside of the formula you want to insert the reference into.

4   Choose Edit > Paste Special.

5   In the Paste Special window, select the Link option at the bottom of the window, and click OK.

The data is inserted as a reference to the sheet it was copied from.

6   Repeat these steps for all data in other sheets you want to reference.

As an alternative to using the Paste Special command, you can enter the reference manually using the following syntax:

=$SheetName.$A$1

(SheetName is the exact name that appears on the sheet's tab at the bottom of the Calc window.) Use that exact syntax (without the equals sign) when using that cell reference inside formulas.

Strictly speaking, this isn't a link by normal standards that is updated like a link (by choosing Edit > Links and clicking Update). It's a reference that is automatically or manually calculated (see *Updating Calculations* on page 574).

Note – Notice the use of the $ in the cell references. This signifies an absolute reference. For more information, see *Relative and Absolute Cell References* on page 572.

You can also insert entire sheets from other Calc files into a spreadsheet, by copy or by link. See *Adding Sheets to a Spreadsheet* on page 525.

About the Calc Consolidation Feature   Calc also has a feature called Consolidation (Data > Consolidate) that lets you combine and perform calculations on separate groups of data. The effect of creating links to data is identical to the more manual copy and paste special process in the previous procedure. However, Consolidate isn't an extremely intuitive tool, and you're likely to get more predictable results by using the previous copy/ paste special procedure for combining separate pieces of data in one sheet or area and setting up calculations manually.

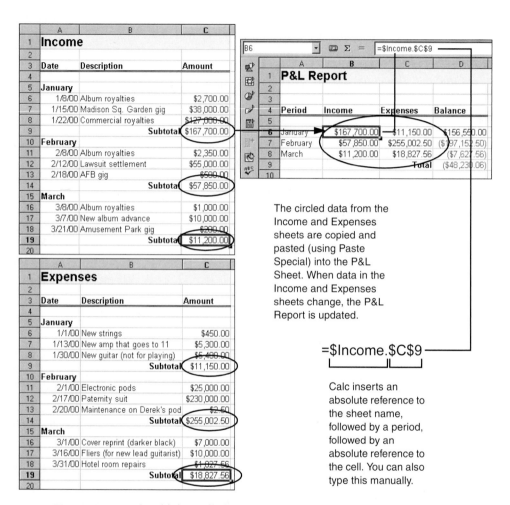

Figure 20-25   Combining cells in many sheets on a master sheet

Linking to Data in Other Calc Files

This procedure is the same in concept to the previous procedure, Combining Data From Many Sheets Into One Sheet, except that you link to cells in other Calc files.

1   Open the file(s) containing the cells you want to reference in the current spreadsheet.

2   Select the cell(s) in the other spreadsheet file you want to reference.

> You can select an individual cell or a range of cells that are adjacent. You can't copy a group of non-adjacent cells.

3   Choose Edit > Copy.

4   Switch to the working spreadsheet file, and click the cell(s) or inside of the formula you want to insert the reference into.

5   Choose Edit > Paste Special.

6   In the Paste Special window, select the Link option at the bottom of the window, and click OK.

Calc inserts the reference as a DDE link to the source file.

7   Repeat these steps for all the data in other spreadsheets you want to reference.

As an alternative to having other spreadsheet files open, you can enter the reference manually using the following syntax:

On Linux and Solaris

=DDE("soffice";"/home/docs/Filename.sdc";"'SheetName'.A1")

On Windows

=DDE("soffice";"C:\My Documents\Filename.sdc";"'SheetName'.A1")

The Windows example shows a path to a hard drive rather than to a network location.

/home/docs and C:\My Documents are the paths to the file. The filename is the exact filename. SheetName is the exact name on the sheet tab containing the data. A1 is the cell being referenced. The SheetName is enclosed in single quotes, and the SheetName and cell reference are enclosed together in double quotes.

Use that exact syntax (without the equals sign) when using that cell reference nested within formulas.

Using Form Controls to Enter Values

You can enter values in cells by creating drop-down lists to select different values. For more information, see *Drop-Down Lists, Buttons, and Other Controls* on page 601.

Tips for Using Spreadsheets

Using spreadsheets wisely has a lot to do with making spreadsheets as automated as possible, which ultimately makes it easier for you to maintain them. The following considerations explain this further.

Put Every Piece of Data in a Separate Cell

Put every piece of data in a separate cell as much possible. For example, if you want to divide a dollar amount by 12 to get a monthly dollar amount, consider putting 12 in a separate cell; so that instead of 30000/12, you get 30000/B5. That way, you can change 12 to 4 to show a quarterly amount, or to 6 to show a semi-annual amount.

When you put everything in cells, all your formulas can contain cell references, making them more dynamic (they update automatically when cell contents change). Automation also means you spend less time tinkering with numbers that are manually entered in formulas.

Break It Up

In the same way that it's good practice to put values in cells and reference them in formulas (rather than entering values in the formulas themselves), it's also good practice to divide your spreadsheets into logical parts, with each part on a separate sheet. For example, if you're maintaining income and expense information to create a balance sheet, a single sheet containing all that data could get pretty crowded. A better way would be to track income on one sheet, expenses on another sheet, and build the balance sheet report on a third sheet.

Putting different types of information on different sheets is essential to managing complexity and minimizes the amount of tinkering you have to do, such as hiding rows and columns.

For example, separate sheets are good for reusing data that you need on many sheets, such as interest rates, budget limits, dates, recurring dollar amounts (like mortgage payments), and so on. You can set up such information on a single sheet and reference it on all your other sheets.

At the very least, even if you're going to keep all your data on a single sheet, keep common data in a separate area for easy reference.

Troubleshooting Spreadsheets

Following are useful ways to troubleshoot and fix problems with spreadsheets.

Calculated Amounts Are Incorrect

There could be a few causes for calculated amounts that are incorrect.

- If your spreadsheet contains numbers that don't show decimal places, Calc rounds numbers to the nearest dollar, throwing off calculated amounts in the spreadsheet Simply add decimal places to cells. See *Quick Decimal Control* on page 544.

- If your spreadsheet contains links to data in other sheets or other Calc files, make sure you update the links to that data so that the most current data is shown. See *Updating Linked Sheets* on page 526.

- If you used automatic fill to enter spreadsheet data automatically, make sure your relative and absolute cell references are set correctly. See *Relative and Absolute Cell References* on page 572.

Showing Formulas in Cells

You can switch from displaying calculated amounts to displaying the actual formulas used to generate values. This helps you better see relationships among cells.

Choose Tools > Options > Spreadsheet > Contents, select the Formulas option, and click OK.

Tracing Precedents, Dependents, and Errors

You can have Calc display arrows to and from a selected cell, pointing to the other cells that the current cell references, called *precedents*, or the cells that reference the current cell, called *dependents*. Tracing precedents, dependents, and errors help troubleshoot calculated amounts by showing you exactly which cells are used in a calculation.

If a cell contains an error, Calc's error tracing can point to the cell(s) causing the error.

For more information, see *Pointing to Cell References and Errors* on page 616.

Value Highlighting

Use Calc's value highlighting feature to visually set off different types of elements in a spreadsheet to help you differentiate between calculated amounts, values entered manually, and text.

Choose View > Value Highlighting to turn value highlighting on and off. See *Value Highlighting* on page 617 for more information.

Value highlighting is a great troubleshooting tool to help you better see different spreadsheet elements, which you can use in conjunction with other troubleshooting tools like tracing precedents and dependents.

Printing Problems

See *Things that Control Spreadsheet Printing* on page 626. In addition, be sure you've followed the instructions in Chapter 4, *Printer Setup and Printing*, on page 59.

Adding Objects to Spreadsheets

Charts

The Chart feature wizard guides you through creating graphical charts that represent your spreadsheet data.

While you can create charts for data in non-adjacent cells, you'll get the best chart results if you use data in adjacent cells.

Basic Chart Example

Figure 21-1 shows a sample chart and the elements of each.

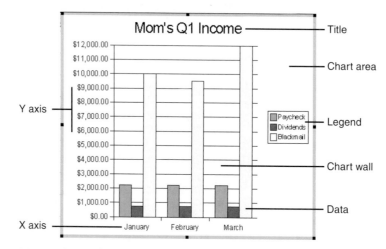

Figure 21-1   Parts of a sample 2-D bar chart

Inserting Charts

1   In the spreadsheet, select the cells you want to include in the chart.

2   In the toolbar, click and hold down the Insert Object icon, and click the Insert Chart icon. As you move the mouse pointer into the spreadsheet, the pointer changes to cross hairs.

3   In the spreadsheet, click and drag to create the area that the chart will fill.

The AutoFormat Chart wizard launches. While the wizard is mostly self-explanatory and guides you through the chart creation process, Figure 21-2 through Figure 21-4 provide some specific guidance.

You can create the chart at any point in the wizard by clicking the Create button. If you click Create in the first window, StarChart inserts a default chart.

In this data example, the selected cells include the column headings (months) and row headings (income categories).

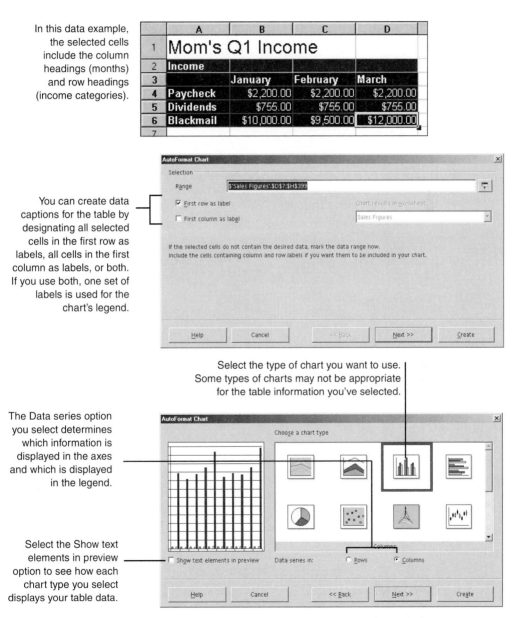

You can create data captions for the table by designating all selected cells in the first row as labels, all cells in the first column as labels, or both. If you use both, one set of labels is used for the chart's legend.

Select the type of chart you want to use. Some types of charts may not be appropriate for the table information you've selected.

The Data series option you select determines which information is displayed in the axes and which is displayed in the legend.

Select the Show text elements in preview option to see how each chart type you select displays your table data.

Figure 21-2   Selected data and the first two AutoFormat Chart windows

The third window lets you select a specific style of chart of the type you've selected. You can also add and remove grid lines in this window.

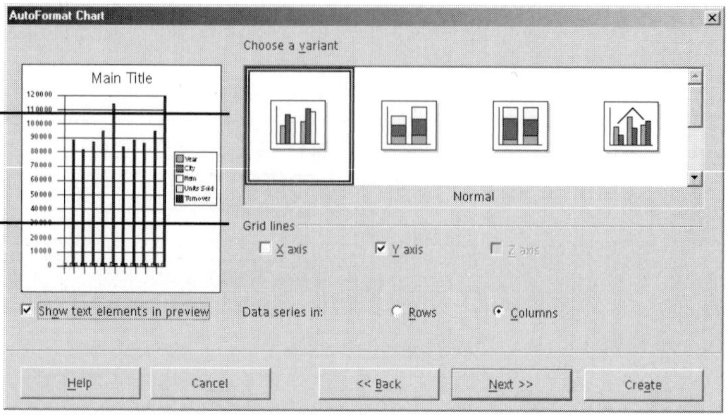

Figure 21-3   The second AutoFormat Chart window

In the last window, you can enter a chart title and any axis titles.

If you choose not to display a legend, you may be removing a piece of information that's critical to the chart. In this chart, the legend will show income categories.

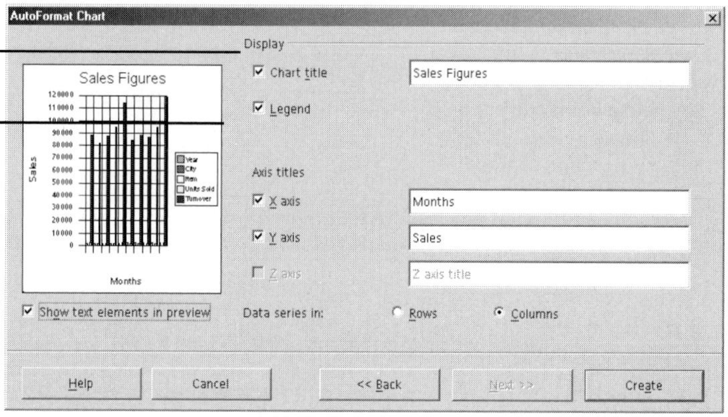

Figure 21-4   The third AutoFormat Chart window

If you have trouble getting your chart the way you want it, try different combinations of the First row as label and First column as label options in the first window, and the Data series in (Rows and Columns) in the last three windows.

Modifying Charts

Once you've created a chart, you can change it in lots of ways. A chart is composed of many different parts, each of which you can modify.

Modifying General Chart Attributes Using the Main Toolbar

Double-click the chart to make the tools in Figure 21-5 appear in the main toolbar at the left side of the work area. The tools are fairly self-explanatory.

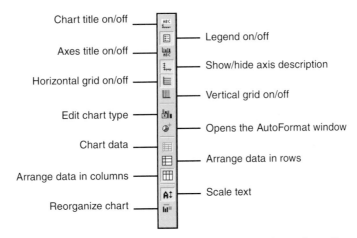

Chart title on/off

Legend on/off

Axes title on/off

Show/hide axis description

Horizontal grid on/off

Vertical grid on/off

Edit chart type

Opens the AutoFormat window

Chart data

Arrange data in rows

Arrange data in columns

Scale text

Reorganize chart

Figure 21-5   Chart modification tools, which appear on the main toolbar when you **double-click** an existing chart in the spreadsheet

Modifying Additional Formatting and Data Calculation Using the Chart Modification Window

Getting to this window is tricky, so be sure you follow the clicking instructions exactly.

1   Select the chart so that green handles appear around the outside of the chart.

2   Double-click the chart so that the green handles change to black.

3   Double-click in the inner chart area displaying the actual data (the pie or bar area, for instance). You must double-click on an area that represents data, such as a bar.

Make the appropriate selections. Most windows are self-explanatory; Table 21-1 describes the options in all tabs. Figure 21-6 on page 598 shows an example chart.

Table 21-1   Tabs in chart modification windows

Tab	Description
Borders	Lets you select a line or border style, color, width, and transparency for the selected chart object.
Area	Lets you select a color, gradient style, hatching pattern, or bitmap for the area of the selected object. You can also set more specific options for the selection you make.
Transparency	Lets you set transparency (color intensity) options for the option you selected in the Area tab. The higher the transparency, the lighter the color, hatching, or bitmap will be. You can also choose to set gradient transparency options that let you fade the color or bitmap from darker to lighter in different ways.
Characters	Lets you change font characteristics of the selected element.

Table 21-1   Tabs in chart modification windows

Tab	Description
Font Effects	Lets you apply additional formatting effects, such as outlining or strikethrough, to the select element.
Data Labels	Lets you add the value (as a number or percentage) and the heading label to the selected data. An example is shown in Figure 21-6.
Statistics	2D charts only. Lets you view statistical information in the chart, such as mean, variance, standard deviation, and margin of error.
Options	Lets you view a secondary Y axis and set the spacing between data in the chart.

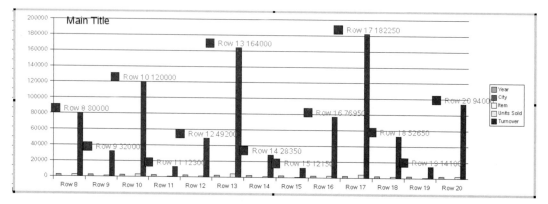

Figure 21-6   Applying data labels with all Data Labels options marked

Modifying the Data Range

Select the outer frame of the chart, not an element within the chart, right-click and choose Modify Data Range. Enter the range in the window in Figure 21-7, then click Create.

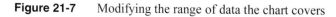

Figure 21-7   Modifying the range of data the chart covers

Adding and Changing Chart Organization and Formatting Details

After you generate a chart you can go back and change specific details about the chart, such as the title, axes labels, grid lines, and whether the data series is in rows or columns.

1   Make sure the chart is selected with black selection handles. (Select it, then double-click it so the green handles change to black.)

2   Right-click the chart, and choose AutoFormat.

3   The AutoFormat Chart wizard launches to let you modify the elements you want.

4   When you're finished, click Create.

Changing the Type of Chart

After you generate a chart, you can change the chart type. For example, if you generate a bar chart, you can change it to a pie chart.

1   Double-click the chart so the tools in Figure 21-5 on page 597 appear.

2   Click the Chart Type tool; the Chart Type window in Figure 21-8 will appear. Select the type you want.

3   Click OK.

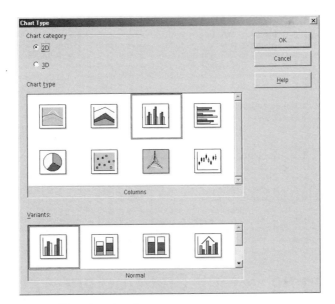

Figure 21-8   Changing the chart type

Changing a Chart's Background, Lines, and Transparency

When a chart is selected for editing, you can change the background of the chart area and chart wall.

1 Select the chart. Then double-click the chart; the green handles will change to black.

2 Right-click the chart, and choose Chart Area (or Chart Wall).

3 Modify the options for Line, Area, and Transparency. See Figure 21-1 on page 597 for more information.

If the chart is 3D, you can also change the chart floor (the base of the X axis).

Rotating 3D Charts

If you generate a 3D chart, you can rotate the chart to a different 3D angle.

Figure 21-9 shows how to rotate 3D charts.

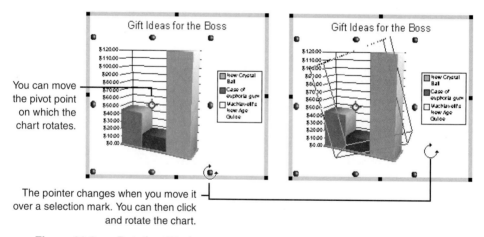

You can move the pivot point on which the chart rotates.

The pointer changes when you move it over a selection mark. You can then click and rotate the chart.

Figure 21-9 Rotating 3D charts

Updating Charts

Charts in Calc follow the same update rules as the spreadsheet. See *Updating Calculations* on page 574.

Changing Default Chart Colors

Calc uses a standard set of colors for data when it generates a chart. You can change the default colors used.

1   Choose Tools > Options > Chart > Default colors. See Figure 21-10.

2   Select the color of the data series you want to change, and click a new color in the color palette.

Repeat for each color you want to change.

3   Click OK.

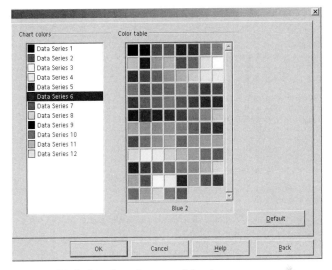

Figure 21-10   Default colors for spreadsheets

Drop-Down Lists, Buttons, and Other Controls

You can add controls to your spreadsheets, such as drop-down lists and buttons, that are attached to macros that were recorded or written in StarBasic or JavaScript. You're only limited by your imagination in how you can use controls in your spreadsheets.

This sections describes two possibilities for using controls in spreadsheets: adding a drop-down list that lets you select from a predefined list of values to populate a cell; and adding buttons that let you sort spreadsheet columns in ascending or descending order by clicking them.

Even though these sections give you the specific procedures for implementing these controls, the principles and mechanics are the same for setting up controls using other scenarios.

For full details, see Chapter 36, *Creating and Using Forms, Controls, and Events*, on page 925.

Graphics and Drawings

The procedures for adding graphics and drawings to spreadsheets are similar to those used in Writer. See *Inserting Graphics* on page 268.

Note – If you select Link and the file is on a Web page or you haven't sent out the graphics to everyone you sent the spreadsheet too, you'll have problems. See *Think Hard Before Linking to Inserted Objects* on page 702.

Mathematical Formulas

The procedures for adding formula objects to spreadsheets are similar to those used in Writer. See *Mathematical Formulas* on page 293.

Floating Frames

The procedures for adding floating frames to spreadsheets is similar to those used in Writer. See *Using Frames for Advanced Page Layout* on page 233.

Updating Links to Graphics and Objects

Whenever you add an object to a spreadsheet as a link, such as a graphic file you want to update in the spreadsheet when the file changes, determine how the link is updated.

Automatically Updating Links

To have Calc automatically update links to files in a spreadsheet, choose Tools > Options > Spreadsheet > Other. Then select the Always option.

If you select On request, Calc prompts you to update the links whenever you open the document. If you select Never, Calc opens the document without updating the links, and you need to update them manually.

Manually Updating Links

If you don't have Calc set up to update links automatically, Choose Edit > Links. This menu option is available only if you've inserted an object in the spreadsheet by link. In the Edit Links window, select the link you want to update, and click the Update button.

Useful Spreadsheet Tools

Protecting Cells From Modification

You can protect any and all cells in a spreadsheet from being modified in any way. When someone clicks a protected cell, the program displays a message saying that the cell can't be modified.

Cell protection is useful when you want to protect calculated amounts, protect cells containing formulas you painstakingly created, or to help guide data entry. In short, cell protection helps make your spreadsheets dummy-proof.

There are two aspects to the cell protection process, as illustrated in Figure 22-1. First, each cell has a "Protected" option you can select or deselect. Second, you must turn cell protection on from the Calc menu, which protects all cells that have their Protected option selected.

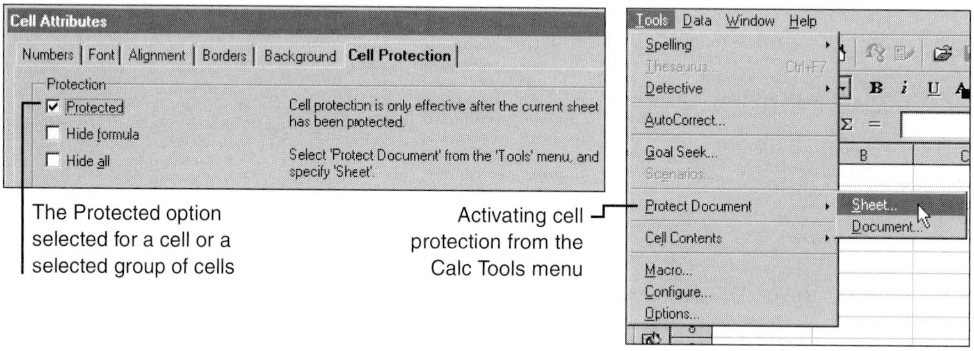

Figure 22-1   The two aspects of cell protection

By default, all cells in a spreadsheet have the Protected option selected. Because you may want to protect only a handful of cells, you may find it easier to turn cell protection off for all cells, then go back and select only the cells you want to protect. This procedure guides you through this process.

The procedure assumes that the cells you want to protect already contain the data you want in them and are formatted the way you want them.

1   Click the gray box above row 1 and left of column A to highlight the entire spreadsheet.

2   Right-click in the spreadsheet and choose Format Cells.

3   In the Cell Attributes window (Figure 22-1), select the Cell Protection tab and deselect the Protected option.

4   Click OK.

5   In the spreadsheet, select the cells you want to protect. See *Selecting Non-Adjacent Cells* on page 539.

6 Right-click one of the selected cells and choose Format Cells.

7 In the Cell Protection tab, select the Protected option.

8 Click OK.

9 Choose Tools > Protect Document > Sheet to protect the sheet. If you've set up cells for protection on multiple sheets, choose Tools > Protect Document > Document to protect all sheets.

10 In the Protect Sheet (or Protect Document) window that appears, you can set a password that applies to unprotecting the cells.

> If you don't want to require a password for unprotecting the cells, don't enter a password in this window. Just click OK.

If you forget your password for unprotecting sheets, you're out of luck. You have to live with the cell protection. You can't even delete a protected sheet. You can, however, copy a protected cell to and paste it into an unprotected cell, where it will become unprotected.

Protected cells can still change format with conditional formatting if the conditional formatting was applied before the cells were protected.

Controlling Valid Entries

You can help guide yourself and others through data entry in Calc by restricting cells to receive specific values and ranges of whole numbers, decimal values, dates, and times. You can also specify specific text lengths allowed in cells.

For example, you can have a cell reject decimal or negative entries by setting it up to receive only whole numbers. Or you can set up a cell to reject any text entries longer than 20 characters.

When you set up validity rules for cells, you can also create help text that will pop up when any of the cells is selected, telling the user what's allowed in the cell. You can also provide warnings when invalid entries are made, and allow invalid entries to be either accepted or rejected.

1 Select the cell(s) for which you want to set up validity rules.

> See *Selecting Non-Adjacent Cells* on page 539.

2 Choose Data > Validity.

3 Set the validity rules, help text, and error messages. Use Figure 22-2 through Figure 22-4 for guidance.

4 Click OK.

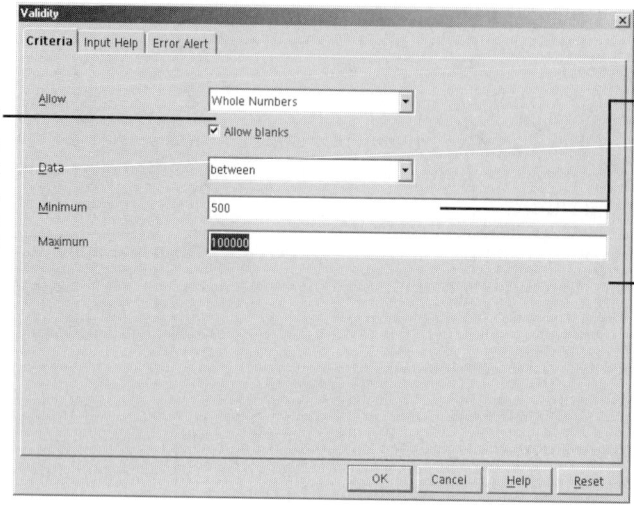

Validity
Criteria
Input Help
Error Alert
Allow
Whole Numbers
Allow blanks
Data
between
Minimum
500
Maximum
100000
OK
Cancel
Help
Reset
Select the type of data allowed in the cell(s). Select the Allow blanks option if you want to allow empty spaces in the cell(s).
Select the operator that will let you set the allowable values.
Enter the appropriate values and limits for the data type and operator you selected. Use appropriate formats. For text limits, enter numeric values.

Figure 22-2 Setting the values for valid entries

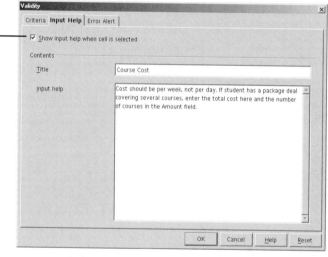

Validity
Criteria
Input Help
Error Alert
Show input help when cell is selected
Contents
Title
Course Cost
Input help
Cost should be per week, not per day. If student has a package deal covering several courses, enter the total cost here and the number of courses in the Amount field.
OK
Cancel
Help
Reset
Mark the Show input help option to display a popup help explanation when the cell is selected in the spreadsheet. Type the popup help Title and text. In the text, consider giving format hints, such as "MM/DD/YY" for a date entry.

Figure 22-3 Entering pop-up text to help users with entry

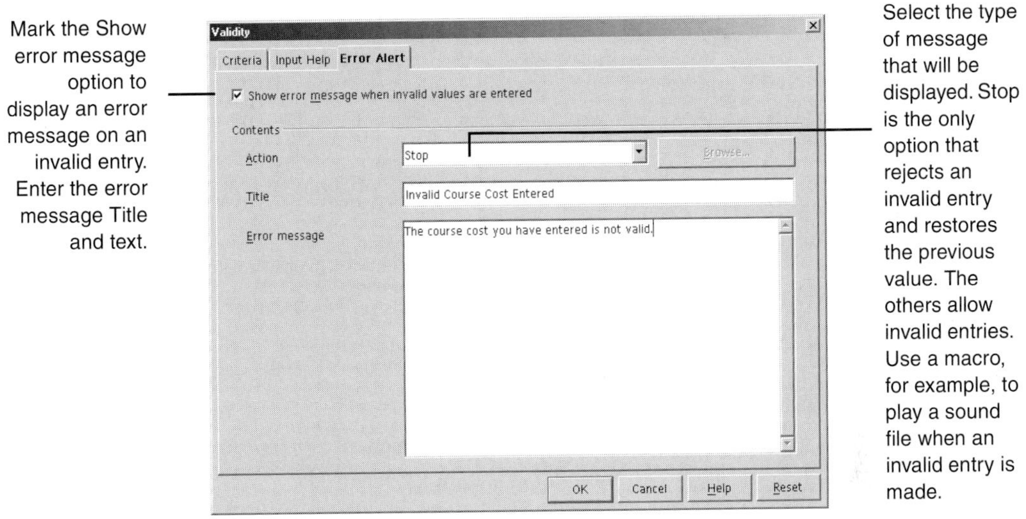

Mark the Show error message option to display an error message on an invalid entry. Enter the error message Title and text.
Validity
Criteria
Input Help
Error Alert
Show error message when invalid values are entered
Contents
Action
Stop
Browse...
Title
Invalid Course Cost Entered
Error message
The course cost you have entered is not valid.
OK
Cancel
Help
Reset
Select the type of message that will be displayed. Stop is the only option that rejects an invalid entry and restores the previous value. The others allow invalid entries. Use a macro, for example, to play a sound file when an invalid entry is made.

Figure 22-4 Typing the text that will appear on an invalid entry

Figure 22-5 shows the results of the settings in Figure 22-2 through Figure 22-4.

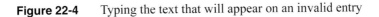

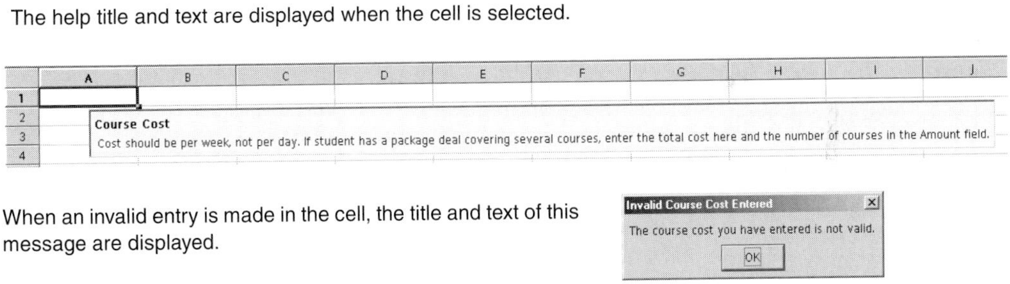

The help title and text are displayed when the cell is selected.
Course Cost
Cost should be per week, not per day. If student has a package deal covering several courses, enter the total cost here and the number of courses in the Amount field.
When an invalid entry is made in the cell, the title and text of this message are displayed.
Invalid Course Cost Entered
The course cost you have entered is not valid.
OK

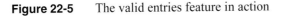

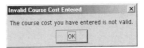

Figure 22-5 The valid entries feature in action

Using Scenarios

Calc's scenarios tool is one of the coolest features any spreadsheet application could provide. In its simplest form, it lets you create a drop-down list of values to select from for a given cell. In its fullest form, it lets you enclose a set group of cells whose contents change when you select a different item from the drop-down list.

For example, you could set up a scenarios list that lets you choose among different percentage rates for a cell. That cell, in turn, is used in formulas elsewhere in the spreadsheet; so when you select a different percentage rate from the drop-down list, the values in the spreadsheet adjust automatically.

In a more involved example, you could set up a scenarios list that lets you choose among names of different home equity lenders. As you select a different lender, you get different values for things like annual percentage rate, the percentage of equity you can borrow against, and the number of loan years. The cells containing these values, in turn, can be referenced in formulas elsewhere in your spreadsheet to calculate things like the total amount of money you can borrow from that lender, the total amount of interest you'll end up paying, and how much of your credit card debt you'll be able to pay off with the loan amount.

In the latter example, each home equity lender you set up would be a single scenario. A single drop-down list contains multiple scenarios.

Figure 22-6 shows three examples of scenarios.

One Variable

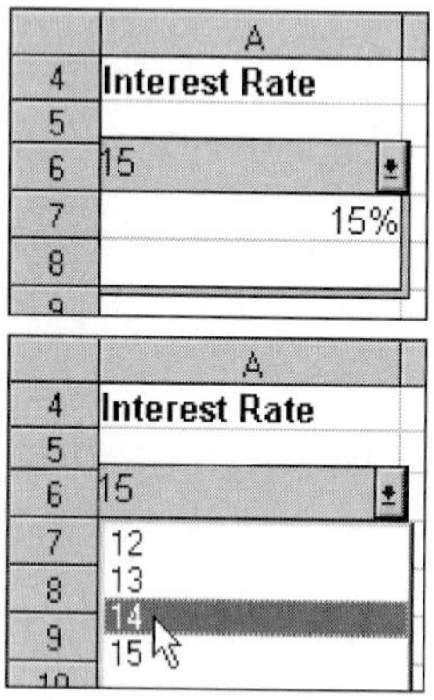

Two Variables

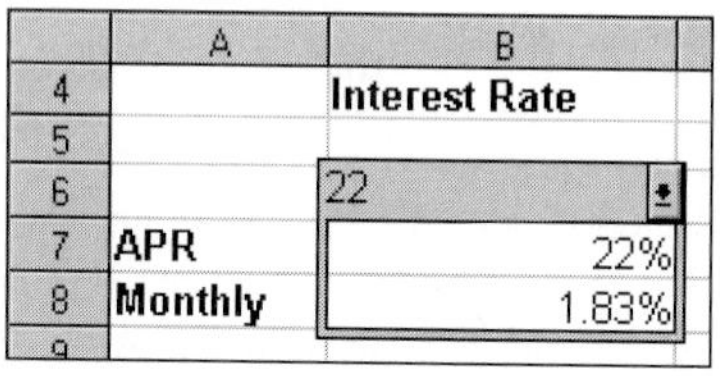

This set of scenarios includes predefined interest rates and an automatic monthly interest rate calculation. Cell B8 is a formula based on the value in cell B7. As you create new scenarios, you only need to change the percentage value and the formula stays the same (=$B$7/12).

Six Variables

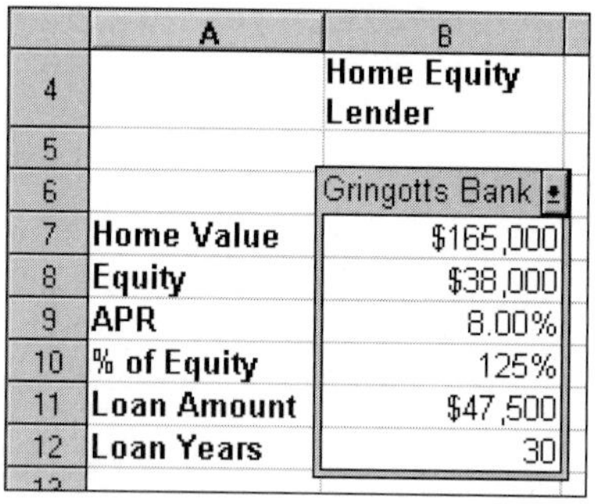

This set of scenarios lets you select from a list of home equity lenders, each with its own set of information, such as annual percentage rate, percentage of equity you can borrow against, and loan years. Cell B11 is calculated by multiplying cells B8 and B10.

In this simple set of scenarios, you can select from a list of percentage rates. The drop-down list is how you select different scenarios.

Figure 22-6   Examples of scenarios

Creating Scenarios

Before you jump in and start creating scenarios, set up your spreadsheet, and try to group your scenario variables in a single area of the spreadsheet. In particular, set up row or column labels next to the values that will be used in the scenarios.

1   Select the cells you want to include in your scenarios.

You must select at least two cells to create a scenario. If you only have one cell you want to create a drop-down list for, just leave the second cell blank.

You can select cells vertically and horizontally. All selected cells will be included in your scenarios. You can also select non-adjacent cells. Each non-adjacent cell will have its own drop-down list, but you can switch among scenarios from any of the non-adjacent drop-down lists to change all non-adjacent cell values.

2   Choose Tools > Scenarios.

3   In the Create Scenarios window, type a name for the scenario, add comments about the scenario, and mark the settings you want.

4   Click OK.

5   To add another scenario to the drop-down list, select all the cells in the scenarios area, choose Tools > Scenarios, create the new scenario, and click OK.

The name of the new scenario is displayed in the scenarios list title bar. Change all appropriate cell values in the scenario area of the spreadsheet to reflect the scenario you just added.

6   Rinse and repeat. (Sorry. Just a little clean humor.)

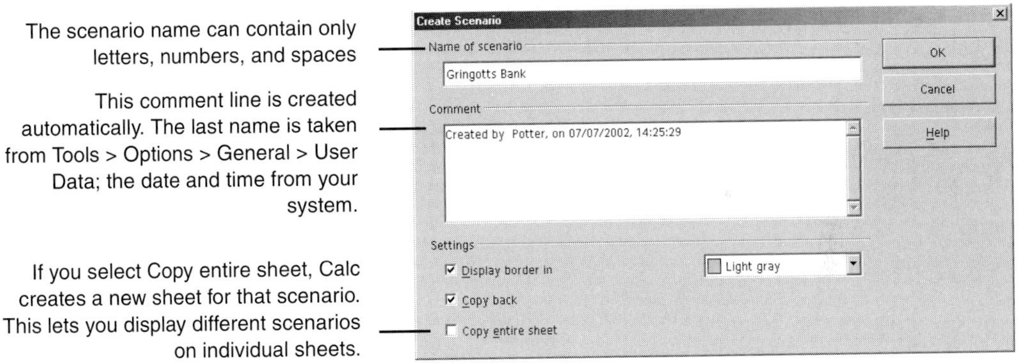

The scenario name can contain only letters, numbers, and spaces

This comment line is created automatically. The last name is taken from Tools > Options > General > User Data; the date and time from your system.

If you select Copy entire sheet, Calc creates a new sheet for that scenario. This lets you display different scenarios on individual sheets.

Figure 22-7   Creating a scenario

Scenarios are stored in individual sheets, not for the entire document. So you can have duplicate scenario names from sheet to sheet.

You can also apply conditional formatting to scenario cells to display different scenario values using different cell formats.

You cannot switch between scenarios if cell protection is turned on.

Modifying Scenarios

There are two different aspects of modifying scenarios: by modifying the values in each scenario, or by modifying the properties of each scenario (name, comments, or border color).

Changing Scenario Values

1   Select the sheet containing the scenario(s) you want to modify.

2   In the scenarios drop-down list, select the scenario containing the values you want to modify.

3   Change the scenario's values directly in the spreadsheet.

You might be tempted to apply cell protection to scenarios so they can't be easily changed. Resist that temptation, because with cell protection turned on you can't switch among scenarios.

Changing Scenario Properties

After you've created scenarios, you can rename them, modify their comments, and change the border colors of the scenarios area.

1   Select the sheet containing the scenario(s) you want to modify.

2   Press the F5 key to display Navigator.

3   In the Navigator window, click the Scenarios button to display the list of scenarios.

4   Right-click the name of the scenario you want to modify, and choose Properties.

5   In the Edit Scenarios window (Figure 22-7 on page 609), change the properties for the scenario.

6   Click OK.

Deleting Scenarios

When you delete a scenario, you also delete the spreadsheet values associated with it—unless the scenario you're deleting is the currently selected scenario in the spreadsheet. In that case, the values remain in the spreadsheet, but the scenario title bar says "(empty)". When you switch to another scenario, the data in the (empty) scenario is replaced by data for the newly selected scenario.

1   Select the sheet containing the scenario(s) you want to modify.

2   Press the F5 key to display Navigator.

3   In the Navigator window, click the Scenarios button to display the list of scenarios.

4   Right-click the name of the scenario you want to delete, and choose Delete.

5   Click Yes in the confirmation window.

Using Goal Seek

Sometimes you'll know the desired result of a problem before you know a crucial piece needed to reach that result. For example, say you hold 200 shares of stock that you bought at $52 a share. You've told yourself you're going to hold onto the stock until your earnings on it reach $100,000. You know what the end result should be ($100,000), but you don't know what price the stock needs to reach to make your earnings equal $100,000. One of the variables, in this case the desired stock price, is unknown.

Calc's goal seek feature is perfect for this type of unknown variable math problem.

The key to using goal seek is to set up all the variables in the spreadsheet (except for the unknown variable you're trying to solve), and enter the necessary formula in the cell that contains your desired goal. Figure 22-8 provides an example of how you'd set up a spreadsheet for using goal seek.

	A	B	C	D
1	Number of shares	Purchase Price	Sell Price	Total Value
2	200	$52		=($C$2-$B$2)*$A$2

You already know the number of shares you own and the price you purchased those shares at.

You're trying to figure out the sell price needed to reach $100,000.

You know the formula to reach your desired goal of $100,000: sell price minus purchase price times number of shares.

Figure 22-8 Preparing your spreadsheet for using goal seek

Goal seek works by looking at the formula that will be used to reach the desired goal, taking the desired goal value you enter to know what the result of the formula should be, and performing the behind-the-scenes math necessary to produce the unknown variable.

Following is the procedure for using goal seek once your spreadsheet is prepared.

1   Select the cell containing the formula that will result in your desired goal.

2   Choose Tools > Goal Seek.

3   Enter the necessary information in the Goal Seek window. Use Figure 22-9 for guidance.

4   Click OK.

5   If your formula is set up correctly and the necessary variables are set up in the spreadsheet to support the formula, goal seek tells you it was successful.

6   Click OK in the confirmation window.

Calc fills in the missing variable to make the formula cell equal the desired goal.

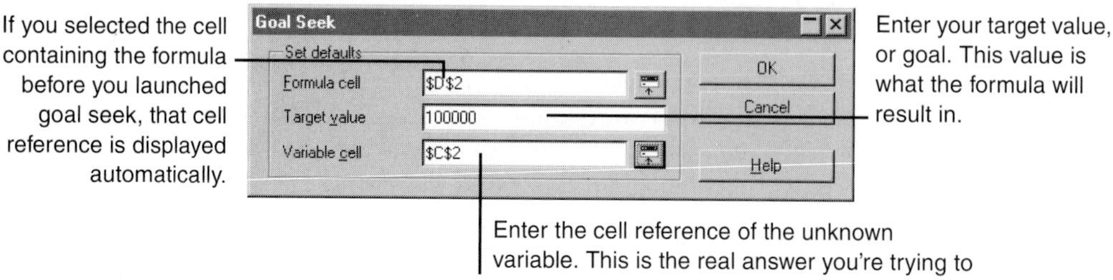

If you selected the cell containing the formula before you launched goal seek, that cell reference is displayed automatically.

Enter your target value, or goal. This value is what the formula will result in.

Goal Seek

Set defaults

Formula cell $D$2

Target value   100000

Variable cell $C$2

OK

Cancel

Help

Enter the cell reference of the unknown variable. This is the real answer you're trying to

Figure 22-9   Entering values in the Goal Seek window

If goal seek wasn't successful, the confirmation window tells you it was unsuccessful and asks if you want to insert the suggested value displayed. It doesn't matter if you accept this value or not, since you'll probably need to double-check your formula and the cells it references to make sure everything is set up correctly, then run goal seek again to insert the correct value for the variable.

Outlining

Calc's outline feature is simply a way to let you select the rows and columns you want to expand and contract. This feature is particularly useful when you've got a large spreadsheet that has multiple parts. For example, if a single sheet contains detailed income *and* expense information, you can group rows by month so you can expand and contract those rows. In addition, you could group the entire income area, making it easy to contract so you can get to the expense section more quickly.

1   Select the rows or columns you want to group.

2   Choose Data > Outline > Group.

If you grouped rows, the outline pane is displayed to the left of the spreadsheet, letting you expand and contract the groups.

If you grouped columns, the outline pane is displayed above the spreadsheet.

3   Create additional groups or subgroups.

Figure 22-10 illustrates how to expand and contract outline groups.

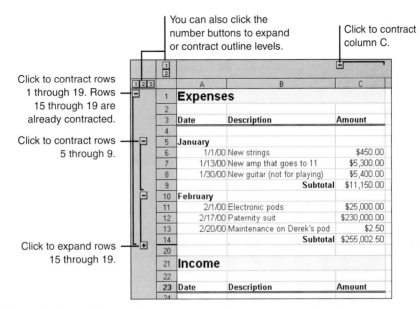

Figure 22-10   Using outline to expand and contract spreadsheet areas

To ungroup an area, select its rows or columns and choose Data > Outline > Ungroup.

You can't switch between showing a sheet in outline view and hiding outline view. If you no longer want to use outlining for a sheet, or if you want to recreate outlining from scratch, choose Data > Outline > Remove.

Naming Spreadsheet Areas

Calc lets you name sections of your spreadsheet to make those areas more meaningful. For example, you can select a column of first quarter sales numbers and name that area "Q1Sales".

This is a useful feature for a couple of reasons. When you name areas in Calc, you can jump to those areas quickly in the spreadsheet, either from the Navigator window or from the drop-down list in the formula bar, as shown in Figure 22-11. You can also include names in formulas rather than cell ranges, making formulas more meaningful. The following example illustrates this:

=SUM(B6:B9) can be written as =SUM(Q1Sales)

You can jump to named areas of a spreadsheet by selecting a name in the formula bar drop-down list (above), or by double-clicking the named area in the Navigator window (right).

Figure 22-11   Jumping to named areas of a spreadsheet

You can name ranges individually, or select multiple rows and columns and create multiple named areas automatically with one procedure.

Naming a Single Region

1   Select the region you want to name.

2   Choose Insert > Names > Define.

3   In the Define Names window, type the name of the named area in the top box, as shown in Figure 22-12.

4   Click OK.

If you want to name more than one region, you can keep the Define Names window open by clicking Add instead of OK in step 4. You can then enter another name, click the Shrink button to select a new region in the spreadsheet, click the Shrink button again, and click Add.

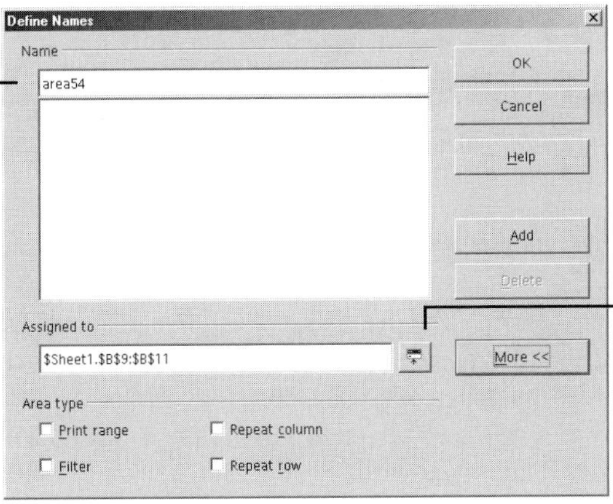
Type the name of the new named area
Click the Shrink button to select the area in the spreadsheet you want to name
Define Names
Name
area54
OK
Cancel
Help
Add
Delete
Assigned to
$Sheet1.$B$9:$B$11
More <<
Area type
Print range
Repeat column
Filter
Repeat row

Figure 22-12 Defining a named region

Naming Multiple Regions Automatically

You can select a big area of a spreadsheet that contains multiple regions you'd like to name, then use this procedure to create multiple named areas out of the big area. When you use this procedure, Calc creates names for regions based on column and/or row headings in the selected area. An example is shown in Figure 22-13, followed by steps.

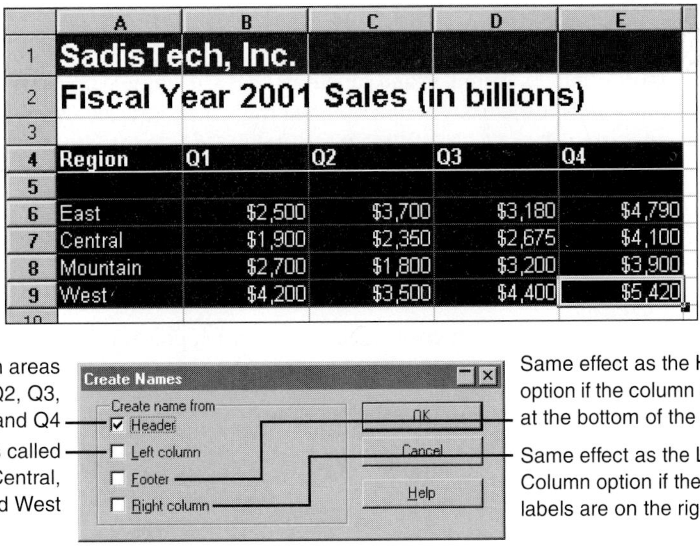
In the selected area, there are many possibilities for named regions. The descriptions in the Create Names window below show the different possible named areas that will be created when each option is selected.
SadisTech, Inc.
Fiscal Year 2001 Sales (in billions)
Region Q1 Q2 Q3 Q4
East $2,500 $3,700 $3,180 $4,790
Central $1,900 $2,350 $2,675 $4,100
Mountain $2,700 $1,800 $3,200 $3,900
West $4,200 $3,500 $4,400 $5,420
Will create 4 column areas called Region, Q1, Q2, Q3, and Q4
Will create 5 row areas called Region, East, Central, Mountain, and West
Create Names
Create name from
Header
Left column
Footer
Right column
OK
Cancel
Help
Same effect as the Header option if the column labels are at the bottom of the area
Same effect as the Left Column option if the row labels are on the right
You can also select multiple options to create more areas. In this example, if you selected Header and Left Column, 9 areas would be created.

Figure 22-13 Creating multiple named regions with one procedure

1   Select the area containing all the regions you want to name.

2   Choose Insert > Names > Create.

3   In the Create Names window, select the naming options you want. See Figure 22-13.

4   Click OK.

Deleting Area Names

You can delete the name assignments you've given to areas. Deleting names doesn't affect the data areas they were assigned to. However, if you delete the names of areas you've used in formulas (such as =sum(Q1)), the formulas will no longer work. Also, if you delete a name that was used to create a hyperlink to the area by dragging from Navigator, the hyperlink will no longer work.

1   Choose Insert > Names > Define.

2   In the Define Names window, select a name you want to delete, and click the Delete button.

3   Click Yes in the confirmation window.

4   Click OK.

Pointing to Cell References and Errors

Cells can sometimes contain references to a lot of other cells, especially when you use more complex formulas and functions. Also, a single cell can be referenced in a lot of other cells. Calc has a couple of great tools that draw arrows to or from a selected cell, pointing to the other cells that the current cell references, called *precedents*, or the cells that reference the current cell, called *dependents*.

Tracing precedents and dependents are great for troubleshooting, because they show you exactly which cells are used in a calculation, making it easier to spot incorrect cell references.

Calc also includes an error tracing tool, which points to the cells causing an error in a particular cell.

1   Select the cell you want to trace.

2   Choose Tools > Detective > (Trace Precedents, Trace Dependents, or Trace Error).

Arrows appear, pointing to the relevant references, as illustrated in Figure 22-14.

Credit Card Calculator			
APR	Monthly Interest	Starting Balance	Monthly Payment
18.00%	1.50%	$7,000	$250

Payment	Interest	Principal	Balance
Jan 15, 00	$105	$145	$6,855
Feb 15, 00	$103	$147	$6,708
Mar 15, 00	$101	$149	$6,558
Apr 15, 00	$98	$152	$6,407
May 15, 00	$96	$154	$6,253
Jun 15, 00	$94	$156	Err:511

Tracing precedents

Credit Card Calculator			
APR	Monthly Interest	Starting Balance	Monthly Payment
18.00%	1.50%	$7,000	$250

Payment	Interest	Principal	Balance
Jan 15, 00	$105	$145	$6,855
Feb 15, 00	$103	$147	$6,708
Mar 15, 00	$101	$149	$6,558
Apr 15, 00	$98	$152	$6,407
May 15, 00	$96	$154	$6,253
Jun 15, 00	$94	$156	Err:511

Tracing dependents

Credit Card Calculator			
APR	Monthly Interest	Starting Balance	Monthly Payment
18.00%	1.50%	$7,000	$250

Payment	Interest	Principal	Balance
Jan 15, 00	$105	$145	$6,855
Feb 15, 00	$103	$147	$6,708
Mar 15, 00	$101	$149	$6,558
Apr 15, 00	$98	$152	$6,407
May 15, 00	$96	$154	$6,253
Jun 15, 00	$94	$156	Err:511

Tracing an error

Figure 22-14   Tracing precedents, dependents, and errors

You can remove the arrows by choosing Tools > Detective, and selecting the relevant remove item. If you're going to use traces on a regular basis, consider assigning a shortcut key removing traces. See *Assigning Shortcut Keys to Menu Items* on page 106. Select the Options category, then select the Remove All Traces command.

Value Highlighting

Use Calc's value highlighting feature to visually set off different types of elements in a spreadsheet. Value highlighting assigns the following colors to different spreadsheet elements, which override all font colors while value highlighting is activated:

- **Black** – Text displays in black.
- **Blue** – Numbers entered manually and dates display in blue.
- **Green** – Calculated amounts, formulas, and other information display in green.

To use value highlighting, choose View > Value Highlighting. To use globally for all spreadsheet documents, choose Tools > Options > Spreadsheet > Contents, mark the Value Highlighting checkbox, and click OK.

Value highlighting is a great troubleshooting tool to help you better see different spreadsheet elements.

Conditional Formatting

See *Conditional Formatting* on page 582.

Version Control and Editing Tools

Keeping Incremental Versions of Documents

You can save different versions of a single document as the document goes through incremental changes.

The process of saving document versions is exactly as it is for saving versions of Writer documents. See *Document Version Control With Editing and Version Tools* on page 408.

Recording and Showing Changes

You can have Calc keep track of changes made to a spreadsheet and insert colored cell borders and row/column lines at the areas where additions, modifications, or deletions were made. Calc also tracks changes by the users making them. Calc identifies users by the settings in the Tools > Options > General > User Data window.

Calc also lets you accept or reject the changes made to the spreadsheet.

Setting Change Options

Before you begin recording and showing changes to a spreadsheet, set the color options Calc will use to mark changes.

1 Choose Tools > Options > Spreadsheet > Changes.

2 In the Changes window, set the color options you want for each type of modification.

3 Use Figure 23-1 for guidance; click OK when you're done.

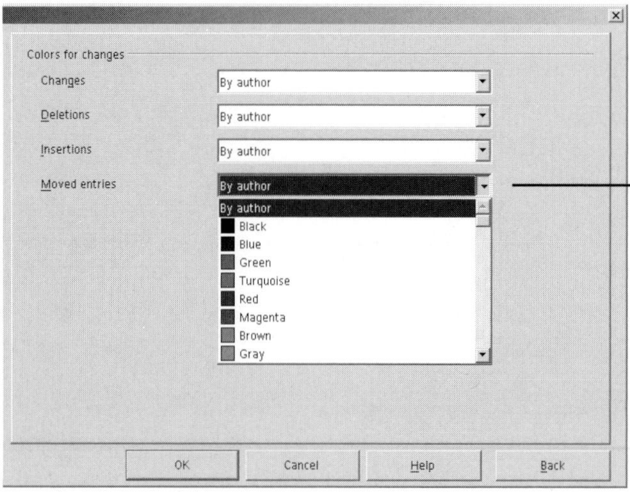

If you select By author, Calc uses a different color for each author making changes. If you select a color, that color will always be used regardless of the author.

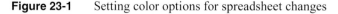

Figure 23-1 Setting color options for spreadsheet changes

Recording Changes

Once your color options are set for spreadsheet changes (previous procedure), use this procedure to begin recording changes.

Recording and showing changes are two different things. You can record changes without actually showing them in the spreadsheet, and you can switch back and forth between showing and hiding the changes being recorded.

1   Choose Edit > Changes > Record.

A check mark next to the Record item means Calc is recording changes.

2   Set the options for showing the changes (page 621).

Calc keeps track of deleted rows and columns, drawing a colored line across or down the borders at the points where the rows or columns were deleted.

To stop recording changes, choose Edit > Changes > Record to remove the check mark next to the Record item.

Adding Comments to Changes

When you change a spreadsheet cell, you can also add a comment to that change. This helps people understand why you made the change. This feature works only when changes are being recorded, as described in the previous procedure.

1   Choose Edit > Changes > Comments.

2   In the Comments window, enter your comment and click OK.

Change notes are displayed in the popup message of a changed cell (Figure 23-2).

You can also review all the comments attached to changes by clicking the arrow buttons in the Comments window.

Showing Changes

Calc gives you many options for viewing recorded spreadsheet changes. By default, when you turn recording on, Calc displays all changes made to cells by putting colored borders around modified cells and providing a popup note of the change when you select or move the mouse pointer over a modified cell. Figure 23-2 illustrates this.

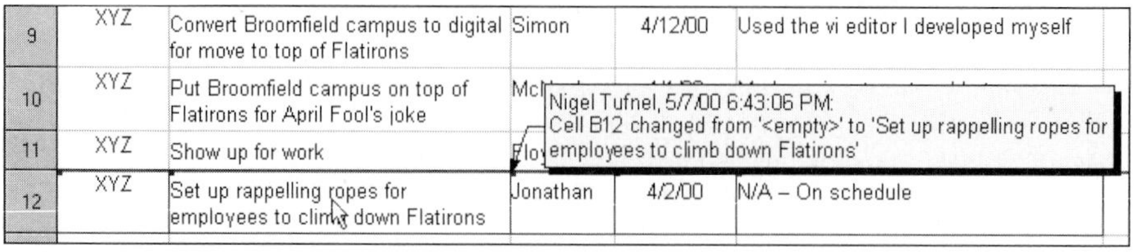

9	XYZ	Convert Broomfield campus to digital for move to top of Flatirons	Simon	4/12/00	Used the vi editor I developed myself
10	XYZ	Put Broomfield campus on top of Flatirons for April Fool's joke	McI		
11	XYZ	Show up for work	Flo		
12	XYZ	Set up rappelling ropes for employees to climb down Flatirons	Jonathan	4/2/00	N/A – On schedule

Nigel Tufnel, 5/7/00 6:43:06 PM:
Cell B12 changed from '<empty>' to 'Set up rappelling ropes for employees to climb down Flatirons'

Figure 23-2   Calc's default mode for showing changes

Calc lets you be more selective in which changed cells are shown, letting you view changes by a specific author, between specific dates and times, within a specific range of cells, with certain words in the comments, and by changes that have been accepted or rejected.

1   Choose Edit > Changes > Show.

2   In the Show window, set the show options you want. Use Figure 23-3 for guidance.

3   Click OK.

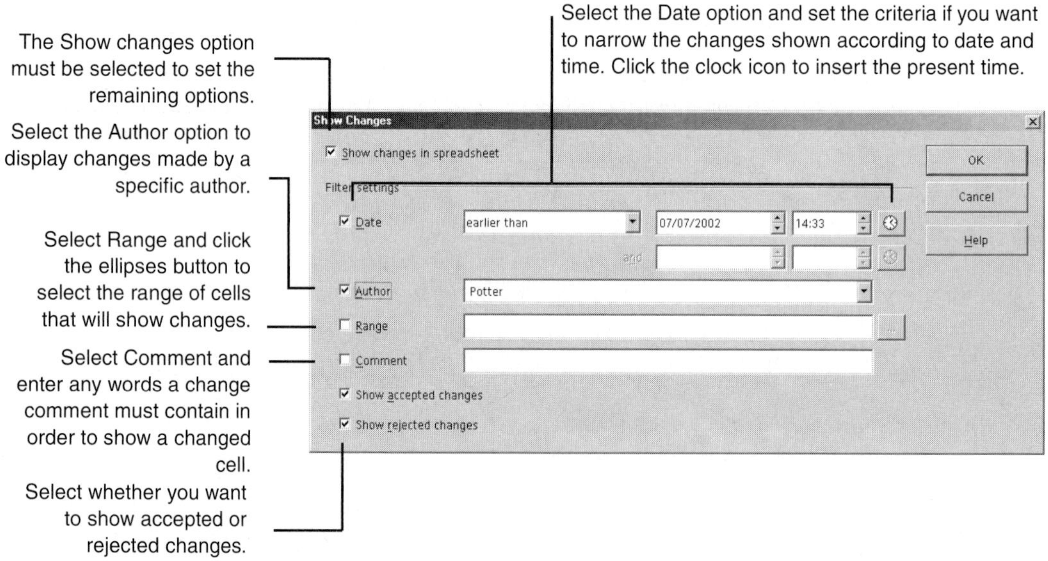

The Show changes option must be selected to set the remaining options.

Select the Author option to display changes made by a specific author.

Select Range and click the ellipses button to select the range of cells that will show changes.

Select Comment and enter any words a change comment must contain in order to show a changed cell.

Select whether you want to show accepted or rejected changes.

Select the Date option and set the criteria if you want to narrow the changes shown according to date and time. Click the clock icon to insert the present time.

Figure 23-3   Setting options for narrowing which changed cells are displayed

Calc's change indicators don't print.

If you want to continue recording changes but hide all the change indicators in the spreadsheet, deselect the Show changes in spreadsheet option.

Accepting or Rejecting Changes

Calc gives you the opportunity to accept or reject changes made to a spreadsheet. When you accept a change, the content becomes a normal part of the spreadsheet without change indicators. When you reject a change, the change returns to its previous state in the spreadsheet as items with change indicators.

In order to accept or reject changes, Calc needs to know that changes have occurred, which means that the Record feature needs to be activated while you work with spreadsheets (Edit > Changes > Record).

To accept or reject changes:

1   Choose Edit > Changes > Accept or Discard.

2   In the Accept or Reject window (Figure 23-4), you can select one or more items in the list to accept or reject.

   You can modify the list of changes by clicking the Filter tab and setting the criteria for which changes will be shown in the List tab. These criteria are the same as those shown in Figure 23-3.

3   Click the appropriate button at the bottom of the window.

   Whether you accept or reject changes, the items you accept or reject are removed from the Accept or Reject Changes window. When you accept changes, the change is kept in the document. When you reject changes, the change is reversed to its prior state.

4   Close the window when you're finished.

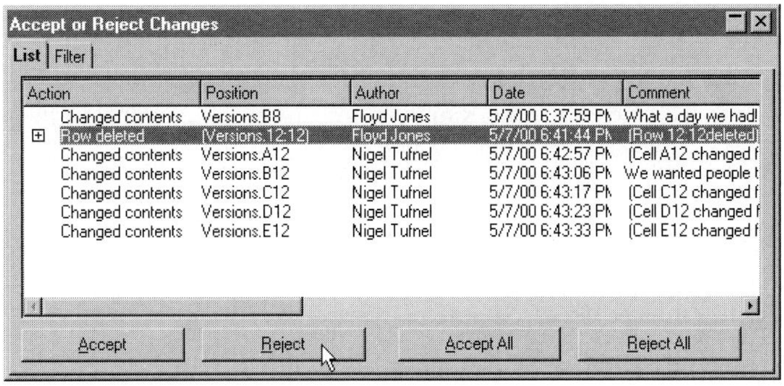

Figure 23-4   Accepting and rejecting changes

Using Notes

Calc lets you attach notes to individual cells. Notes are a great tool for elaborating on cell contents without putting all that extra information in cells, especially when the cell contains a formula. Notes are also good for suggesting that changes be made to cells.

1   Select the cell you want to attach a note to.

2   Choose Insert > Note.

A small popup box with a yellow background appears.

3   Type the text of the note in the popup box.

You can press Enter to break to a new line in the note box.

4   When you're finished, click outside the note box to insert the note.

A tiny red nonprinting square is displayed in the upper right corner of the cell to indicate that a note is attached to the cell.

To view the note, select or move the mouse pointer onto the cell. The note displays in a popup window, as shown in Figure 23-5.

Figure 23-5   Viewing a note

To modify a note, select the cell, right-click, choose Show Note, and change the note contents. To delete the note, simply delete the entire contents of the note.

Printing in Calc

Printing a Spreadsheet

Set the appropriate options using the appropriate options in this chapter, and by consulting the program-wide printing setup and procedures in Chapter 4, *Printer Setup and Printing*, on page 59.

Things that Control Spreadsheet Printing

There are many factors that determine what gets printed in a spreadsheet document and how it looks when it's printed. It's helpful to know some of these factors up front to give you a general idea of how to set up a spreadsheet for printing and where to look if you're having trouble controlling printing.

*   The Page Style window – See *Setting Page and Sheet Options* on page 551. You get to this window by choosing Format > Page with the spreadsheet open that you want to print. You can also get to this window from the Stylist, by right-clicking the page style used for the sheet and choosing Modify.

    The Page tab determines margins, paper size, orientation (portrait or landscape), page layout, page numbering style, and placement of the cells relative to the page (horizontally and vertically).

    The Sheet tab determines which spreadsheet elements are printed, direction that sheets are printed (top to bottom or left to right), the first number used for page numbering, scaling of the printed pages, and the maximum number of pages that will print.

    The Page Style window also lets you set page borders, background colors, and page headers and footers.

*   The Print Options window – See *Choosing What Sheets to Print* on page 627.

*   The Cell Attributes window, Cell Protection tab – See *Keeping Specific Cells From Printing* on page 631. You get to this window by selecting the cells you want, right-clicking, and choosing Format Cells. You can also get to it by choosing Format > Cells.

    In the Cell Protection tab of this window, there's an option to let you hide selected cells when printing. If this option is selected for cells, their contents will not print.

*   Print Ranges – See *Repeating Spreadsheet Headings (Rows or Columns) on Each Page* on page 628. If you define a specific range of cells to print by choosing Format > Print Ranges > (Define, Add, or Edit), only those cells will print. If you select the Edit item, you can also determine which row or column headings will repeat on each printed page.

*   Page breaks – Accept the default ones, set your own, or just change the column width to adjust where page breaks occur. Check the page size (see *Setting Page and Sheet*

Options on page 551), and preview and adjust page breaks (*Previewing Page Breaks* on page 555). Also take into account where your headers and footers, if any, are positioned (see *Setting Up Headers and Footers* on page 553).

- Your printer's properties – Most printers let you set properties such as orientation (portrait or landscape), print scaling, and the range of pages to print. Make sure these settings aren't conflicting with the print results you want. See Chapter 4, *Printer Setup and Printing*, on page 59.

Printing a Mail Merge From Data in a Spreadsheet

Let's say you've got a bunch of names in a spreadsheet and you want to send a letter to each of them, addressed personally to them, something like "Dearest *yournamehere*, please give me a job." It's easy to do.

1   Just set up the spreadsheet as a data source. See *Creating a Data Source for a Spreadsheet* on page 884.

2   Then make your document. Follow the instructions in one of the following: *Creating a Letter Using the Letter AutoPilot* on page 380, *Creating Documents From a Letter Template* on page 390, or *Dragging a Data Source Field Into a Document* on page 396 and *Doing Additional Formatting to Your Own Data Source-Based Documents* on page 398.

3   Then print that sucker using the specific printing instructions outlined in *Printing or Emailing Mail Merge Documents* on page 400.

Choosing What Sheets to Print

Be sure to also refer to *Program-Wide Print Setup Options* on page 85.

Choose Tools > Options > Spreadsheet > Print, or else File > Print and click Options. There are only two options:

- Suppress Output of Empty Pages – If this field is marked, empty pages where there are no cell contents and draw objects are printed. Cell attributes such as margins or background color are not cell contents. The empty pages are not counted during page numbering.

- Print Only Selected Sheets – Prints only selected sheets in the spreadsheet. To select a sheet for printing, click on the sheet name on the bottom margin of the workspace while keeping the Ctrl key pressed.

Repeating Spreadsheet Headings (Rows or Columns) on Each Page

If you have a single heading row or column for a particularly large amount of data, you can set up the heading to repeat on each new printed page. This procedure shows two ways, one where you select what you want to repeat, and one where you type it in.

Selecting the Row or Column Range to Repeat

1   Select the row(s) or column(s) to repeat as shown at right.

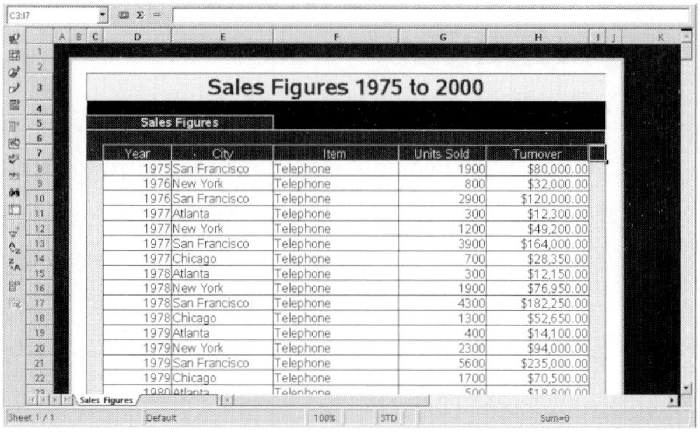

2   Choose Insert > Names Define. Enter the name of the area in the Name field and click Add.

    You must click Add, not just OK, or it won't work.

3   The name will be added to the list. Select it in the list and click More (see Figure 24-1). Select Repeat row or Repeat column. Click OK.

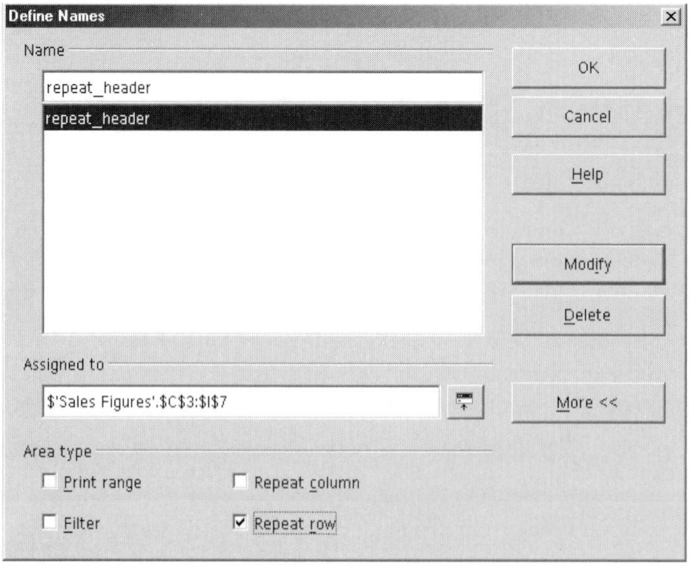

Figure 24-1   Specifying that rows or columns should be repeated

4   Repeat the previous steps if you have defined repeatable rows and also want to repeat columns, or vice versa.

5   Choose Format > Print Ranges > Edit. In the Rows to repeat list, select the name you assigned to the repeatable area. (see Figure 24-2). Do the same in the Columns to Repeat area if you're repeating columns, as well.

Figure 24-2   Selecting the name of the area to repeat

Entering the Row or Column Range to Repeat

1   Choose Format > Print Ranges > Edit.

2   In the Edit Print Areas window (Figure 24-3), enter the row or column references containing the headers you want to repeat.

3   Click OK.

You can designate more than one row or column as repeatable, shown in Figure 24-3.

In the Rows to repeat and Columns to repeat, notice the cell references are just row numbers or column letters, such as $1 and $A. In this example, rows 1 and 2 will be repeated ($1:$2). You can also fill in the cell references by clicking the Shrink icon and select cells in the row(s) or column(s) you want to repeat.

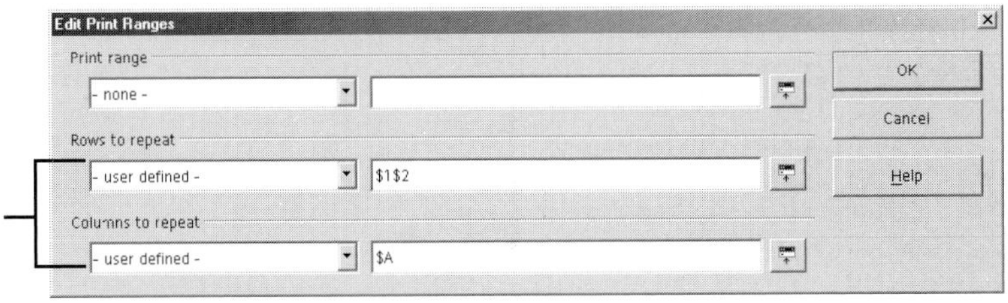

Figure 24-3   Setting up spreadsheet headers to repeat on printed pages

Setting a Print Range

By default, Calc prints all sheets containing data in a spreadsheet document. You can designate a specific group of cells as the only cells in the spreadsheet that will print. This feature is useful when you want to print an individual sheet or select parts of a spreadsheet rather than the whole document.

1 Select the cells you want to include in the print range.

2 Choose Format > Print Ranges > Define.

To add cells to the already defined print range, select the new cells and choose Format > Print Ranges > Add. You can also add cells to the print range by choosing Format > Print Ranges > Edit, and entering the cell references in the Print Area field.

To remove a print range so that the entire spreadsheet is available for printing, choose Format > Print Ranges > Remove.

Selecting Spreadsheet Elements to Print

The first place to determine what gets printed in a spreadsheet is in the Page Style window on the Sheet tab, where you can include or exclude such fundamental elements as charts, graphics, and drawings.

1 With the spreadsheet open that you want to print, choose Format > Page.

2 In the Sheet tab (Figure 24-4), select the elements you want to print, and deselect the elements you don't want to print. Then click OK.

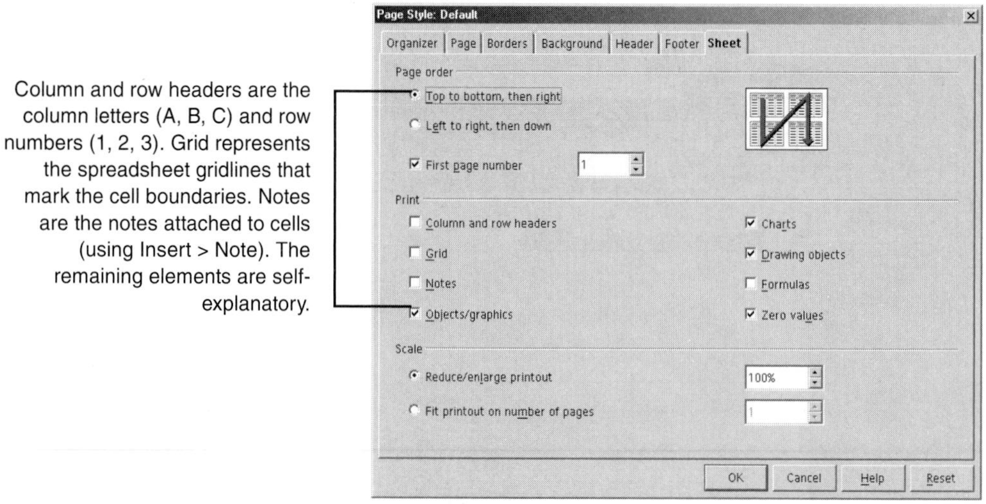
Column and row headers are the column letters (A, B, C) and row numbers (1, 2, 3). Grid represents the spreadsheet gridlines that mark the cell boundaries. Notes are the notes attached to cells (using Insert > Note). The remaining elements are self-explanatory.
Page Style: Default
Organizer
Page
Borders
Background
Header
Footer
Sheet
Page order
Top to bottom, then right
Left to right, then down
First page number
1
Print
Column and row headers
Grid
Notes
Objects/graphics
Charts
Drawing objects
Formulas
Zero values
Scale
Reduce/enlarge printout
100%
Fit printout on number of pages
1
OK
Cancel
Help
Reset

Figure 24-4 Selecting spreadsheet elements to print

Page Size and Numbering

Be sure the spreadsheet is set up correctly, according to the information in *Page Setup* on page 550, and *Power Formatting With Styles and Templates* on page 558.

Keeping Specific Cells From Printing

Calc lets you prevent the contents of certain cells from printing. This feature is useful if you want to print spreadsheets for general distribution, but you want to suppress sensitive information such as payroll or personnel information.

1   Select the cells containing the values you don't want to print.

2   Right-click one of the selected cells and choose Format Cells.

3   In the Cell Attributes window, select Cell Protection tab.

4   Select the Hide when printing option.

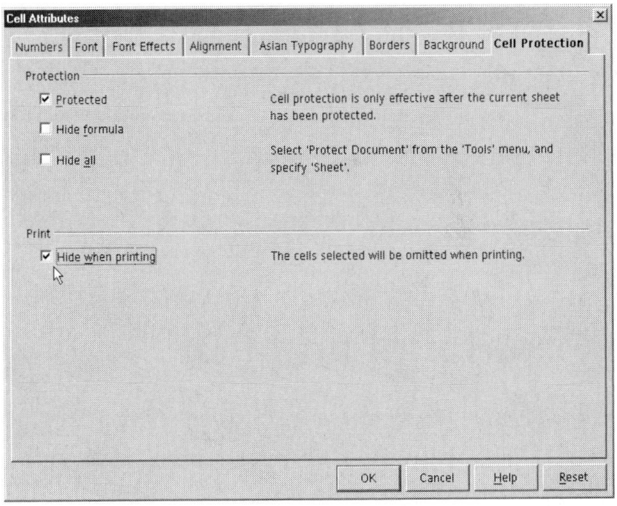

Figure 24-5   Preventing a cell from being printed

5   Click OK. You can also keep entire rows and columns from printing by hiding them. See *Hiding Rows and Columns* on page 541.

Reducing or Increasing the Number of Pages the Spreadsheet Prints On

With the spreadsheet document open containing the sheets you want to set options for, choose Format > Page to display the Page Styles window.

You can also get to this window from the Stylist (F11) by clicking the Page Styles icon, right-clicking the page style used for the sheet, and choosing Modify.

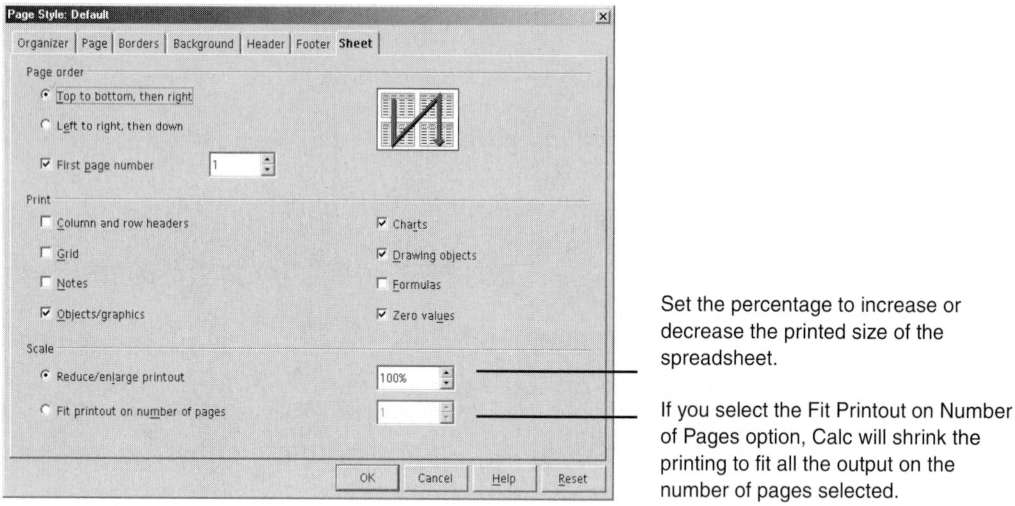

Set the percentage to increase or decrease the printed size of the spreadsheet.

If you select the Fit Printout on Number of Pages option, Calc will shrink the printing to fit all the output on the number of pages selected.

Figure 24-6   Setting Page and Sheet printing options: Sheet tab

Printing to PostScript and PDF

See *Setup and Printing for All Operating Systems* on page 79.

Printer and Font Setup

See Chapter 4, *Printer Setup and Printing*, on page 59.

Impress

Creating Presentations

Quick Start

This section contains the following information to help you get started quickly:

- A checklist for quickly making a presentation
- Feature overview
- A tutorial

See *Setup and Tips* on page 97 for general tips to make working with Impress easier.

Note – Many features are available throughout the program, but we don't cover them in every program's section. Check the index, or refer to *Setup and Tips* on page 97 or *Writer* on page 165 if you can't find the information you need in the chapters for Impress.

Quick Start Checklist

If you've got a presentation to deliver tomorrow at 8:00 AM, here's what to do:

- Create the presentation – *Using AutoPilot to Create a Presentation* on page 641
- Add content and insert objects – *Adding Text* on page 685 and *Adding Charts, Pictures, and Objects* on page 701
- Run it to preview it – *Delivering a Presentation* on page 732
- Print it – *Printing a Presentation* on page 748

Impress Features

Impress lets you create professional-looking presentations, or slide shows, for delivery at business meetings, sales conferences, and other events. Impress includes Draw's vector graphics features, as well as the usual capabilities of inserting charts and other items.

Note – To see examples of Impress capabilities, open some of the sample files in `sam-ples/language/presentations`.

Impress features include, but aren't limited to:

Powerful file-creation features The Impress AutoPilot lets you quickly and easily pick attributes like introduction page, formatting, and background from templates and samples.

File formats Supports an array of file types for opening and saving as, like PowerPoint.

HTML/WebCast export You can export Draw and Impress slides to HTML, with or without frames. The exported presentations also can be run automatically for use in kiosk-type environments, or created for use in a webcast.

Special effects Animated objects and text, sound, and slide transitions.

Text formatting Full Writer text entry and formatting, as well as FontWork, a program for advanced text formatting and manipulation effects.

Customized presentations You can save several different versions of a presentation within the same file, without deleting or rearranging slides. In addition, you can attach speaker's notes to each slide, and create handouts by printing several condensed slides on one page.

Insert other documents as OLE objects, insert graphics You can insert other documents such as spreadsheets and graphs as OLE objects, which means you can still edit them once they're inserted. You can include any graphics by inserting graphics or using Draw's graphics tools, all of which are available in Impress.

The Impress Work Area

Impress has five different master views; we've chosen the Drawing view, shown in Figure 25-1, because that's where you'll typically do most of your work. (For more information, see *Using Master Views* on page 659.)

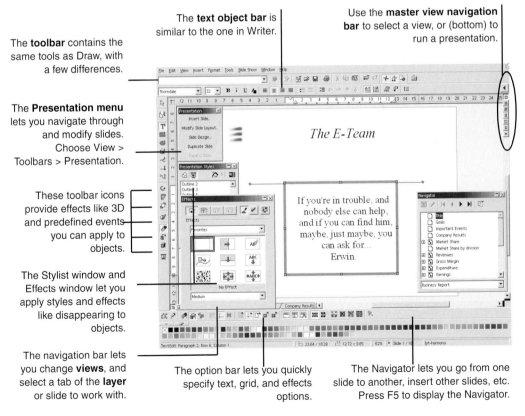

The **text object bar** is similar to the one in Writer.

Use the **master view navigation bar** to select a view, or (bottom) to run a presentation.

The **toolbar** contains the same tools as Draw, with a few differences.

The **Presentation menu** lets you navigate through and modify slides. Choose View > Toolbars > Presentation.

These toolbar icons provide effects like 3D and predefined events you can apply to objects.

The Stylist window and Effects window let you apply styles and effects like disappearing to objects.

The navigation bar lets you change **views**, and select a tab of the **layer** or slide to work with.

The option bar lets you quickly specify text, grid, and effects options.

The Navigator lets you go from one slide to another, insert other slides, etc. Press F5 to display the Navigator.

Figure 25-1 Impress work area

Help With Impress

In addition to the Help topics mentioned in *Getting Help* on page 98, see *Good Online Information Sources* on page 42.

Guided Tour of Impress

Completing all three sections will give you an idea of how the program works.

Creating a Presentation

1   Choose File > AutoPilot > Presentation.

2   Select the From template option. (It might take a while to be available.) Select the Introducing a New Product template from the list.

3   Be sure the Preview option is selected.

4   Click Next.

5   Make a selection in the Slide Design list. These are the backgrounds for the presentation.

6   Click Next.

7   In the Effect list, select Cross-Fade from Left.

8   In the Presentation type selection area, select Automatic and enter 5 seconds as the duration of each page.

9   Click Next.

10 Enter company and presentation information:

   • Name of your company: Six-Fingered Man Home Construction

   • Presentation subject: Fireswamp Summer Homes

   • Further ideas to be presented: Flame-spurt barbecues with each home

11 Click Next.

12 Select the Customer Wishes slide. Click the green arrow to deselect it and remove it from the presentation.

13 Select the Create summary option.

14 Click Create.

15 The presentation will be displayed. In the navigation bar immediately below the work area, click the far left arrow, circled at right.

16 Click the tab for the first slide (Title).

17 Choose File > Save to save the presentation.

18   In the Save window, be sure the Automatic filename extension option is selected. Then enter a name without an extension (no period and nothing after it).

19   For the format, select Impress 6.0 presentation. Note the other formats that are listed, including MS PowerPoint presentation and template. Click Save.

Modifying the Presentation

1   Press F5 and use the Navigator to locate the Next Steps of Action slide. Close the Navigator if it gets in your way.

2   Enter the following text:

- Stabilize quicksand sauerkraut storage
- Domesticate remaining ROUSes
- Flavor flame-spurt barbecues with mesquite

3   Select the second and third bulleted items and indent them. (Click the Demote icon on the object bar above the work area.)

4   Change the bullet style of all three bulleted items (choose Format > Numbering/Bullets).

5   Change the font of bulleted items in the slide (use the Font and Size lists in the object bar, or choose Format > Character).

6   Change the font of all slide titles throughout the presentation. (Choose View > Background > Drawing.) Make the titles red and a little smaller. Switch back to regular view (choose View > Slide).

7   Click through a few of the slides to verify that the slide format was changed everywhere.

8   Right-click on any slide tab and choose Insert Slide. Name the slide and select a slide design, then click OK.

9   Change the layout of the Strengths and Advantages slide from one column to two (choose Format > Modify Layout).

10   Change the background for this slide.

 a.   Choose View > Toolbars > Presentation.

 b.   In the Presentation Menu, click Slide Design.

 c.   Click Load.

 d.   In the Categories list, select Presentation Layouts.

 e.   Select the World background from the Templates list.

 f.   Click More.

 g.   Select the Preview option.

h. Click OK.

i. Be sure the new background is selected in the Slide Design window, then select the Exchange background page option and click OK. (The new background will be used for the entire presentation, replacing the current background.)

11 Set up an interaction so that clicking on the title takes you to Next Steps of Action slide.

12 Choose View > Preview to display the Preview window.

13 Click in the main area of the slide, where the subpoints are. Click the Effects icon (above the Interaction icon in the illustration at right).

14 In the Effects window, click the Text Effects icon and select a category and effect. Click the green arrow to apply the effect.

15 In the master view navigation bar at the right side of the work area, click the Slide view icon. Drag one of the slides to a different position in the presentation.

16 Use the object bar at the top of the work area to switch the slide's transition to automatic and set it to be displayed for 20 seconds (0:00:20).

17 Hide the slide (right-click the slide and choose Show/Hide Slide).

18 Click the Handouts view icon.

19 Choose View > Toolbars > Presentation if the Presentation menu isn't showing, then click Modify Slide Layout.) Select the layout that prints two slides per page, then click OK to close the Modify Slide window.

20 Drag the slides to reposition one above the other, rather than side by side.

21 Choose Insert > Fields > Page Numbers and position it in the lower right corner. (If you have trouble getting a dragging pointer, rather than a text cursor, click in the text until the text frame appears and drag that, or draw a rectangle around it to select it and hold down Shift while using the arrows to position it.)

22 Use the drawing tools to add a blue horizontal line between the first and second rows.

23 Choose Format > Page and click the Page tab; the orientation is shown as landscape. Select Portrait and click OK, then observe the changes on the presentation. Repeat the previous steps to change the orientation back to landscape.

24 Save your changes.

Producing the Presentation

1   Start the presentation. Click the Start Slide Show icon in the toolbar at the right side of the work area.

2   Let the presentation run, to see how it looks and how the slide transitional effects work that you selected.

3   Press Esc to stop the presentation.

Creating a New Presentation

You can create a new presentation in a number of different ways:

*   Just choosing File > New and clicking Create.
*   Using AutoPilot, the Impress wizard (simplest, if you're just starting out)
*   Using a template, without AutoPilot
*   Using a Writer document
*   From scratch

Note – To open a PowerPoint presentation in Impress, see *Opening Existing Presentations* on page 652.

The Quickest Way

1   Choose File > New > Presentation.

2   If the AutoPilot window appears, click Create.

3   In the Slide Design window that appears next, select the second from the left and click OK.

Using AutoPilot to Create a Presentation

You can use AutoPilot to base a presentation on a template, a presentation layout (predefined background and other elements) or an existing presentation. For all, you can then modify the background, transition type, individual pages you want to use, summary information, and other elements.

Use this method if you don't have an existing template that is defined as you need it to be. If you just want to base a presentation on an existing template or presentation and not make many changes, it's much quicker to choose File > New > From Template. Refer to

Basing a Presentation on a Template or Background (Without Using AutoPilot) on page 645.

1   Choose File > AutoPilot > Presentation.

2   In the first window (Figure 25-2), select the Empty presentation or From template option. (Select From template to use either a template or a presentation.) It takes a few seconds for all options to be available.

Note – If the From template option never becomes available and you're in a multi-user environment, you don't have the right permissions to access the templates folder on the server. Contact your system administrator.

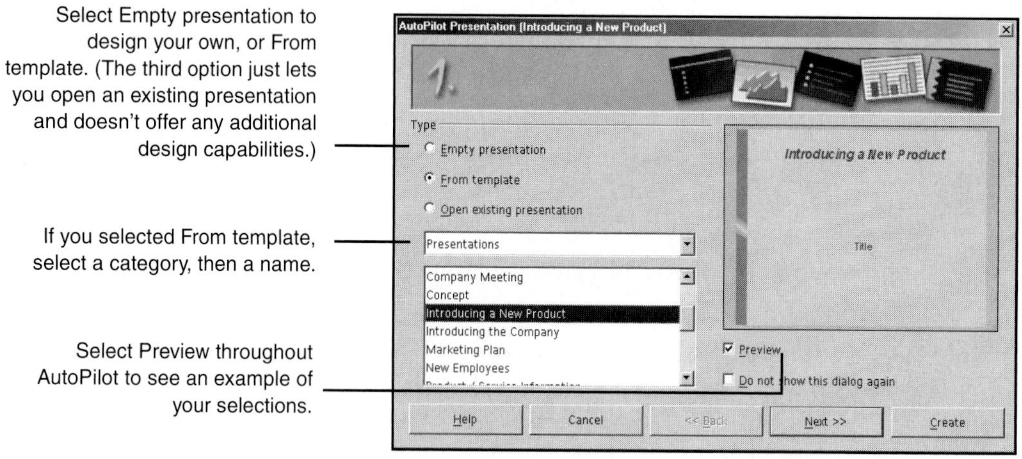

Select Empty presentation to design your own, or From template. (The third option just lets you open an existing presentation and doesn't offer any additional design capabilities.)

If you selected From template, select a category, then a name.

Select Preview throughout AutoPilot to see an example of your selections.

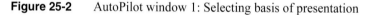

Figure 25-2   AutoPilot window 1: Selecting basis of presentation

3   If you selected From template, select a template category and template or presentation. Select Preview to see an example.

4   In the second window (Figure 25-3), select a design for the background of your presentation and a presentation medium and click Next.

Your selection here is displayed in the background of all slides in your presentation, though you can make slide-specific changes later. It also affects font style and color of the slide foregrounds.

Backgrounds are discussed further in *Presentation Backgrounds* on page 705.

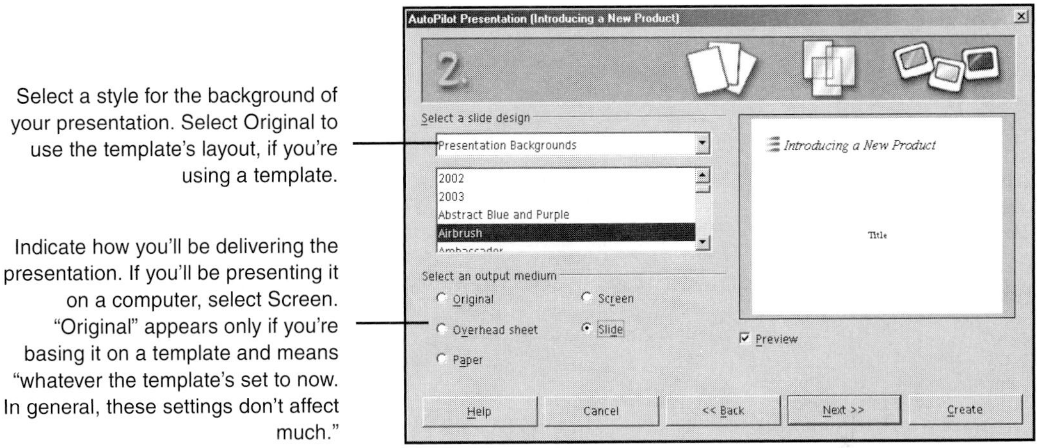

Select a style for the background of your presentation. Select Original to use the template's layout, if you're using a template.

Indicate how you'll be delivering the presentation. If you'll be presenting it on a computer, select Screen. "Original" appears only if you're basing it on a template and means "whatever the template's set to now. In general, these settings don't affect much."

Figure 25-3   AutoPilot window 2: Selecting the background and presentation style

5   The options in the third window (Figure 25-4) relate only to presentations you'll run onscreen, not to presentations you'll just be printing on acetate. Select the transition type you want.

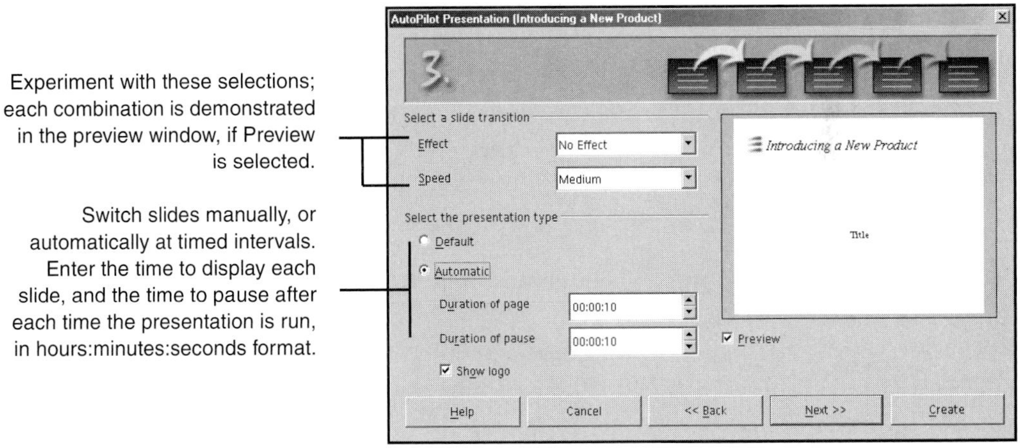

Experiment with these selections; each combination is demonstrated in the preview window, if Preview is selected.

Switch slides manually, or automatically at timed intervals. Enter the time to display each slide, and the time to pause after each time the presentation is run, in hours:minutes:seconds format.

Figure 25-4   AutoPilot window 3: Selecting transition effects

Be sure Preview is selected, if you want to see an example. Each time you change your selections in the Transit or type selection area, the transition will be demonstrated in the preview window.

6   In the Presentation type selection area of the same window, choose whether the presenter will manually change from one slide to another, or if the slide will automatically be shown for a set time.

To prevent the StarOffice logo from being displayed, select Automatic. Deselect the Show logo option. Then if you want to switch back to manual transitions, select the Default option.

7   If you didn't select a template in the first window, skip to step 10.

8   In the fourth window (Figure 25-5), enter descriptive information about the presentation. AutoPilot uses this information in the title page (shown in Figure 25-6).

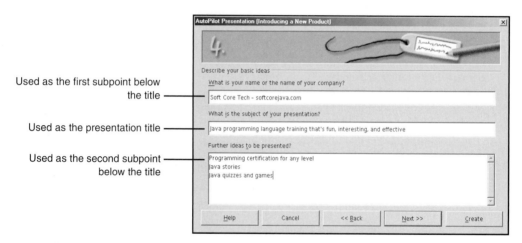

Figure 25-5   AutoPilot window 4: Entering title page information

9   Each template comes with defined slides (referred to in this window as pages). The window in Figure 25-6 lets you select the ones you want to use.

You can add or delete slides later, as well, from templates or existing presentations.

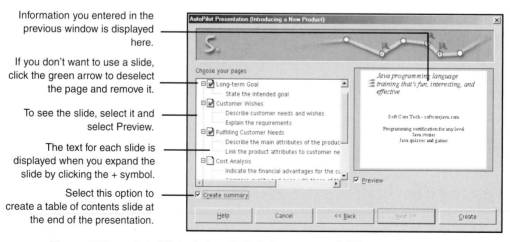

Figure 25-6   AutoPilot window 5: Deleting unwanted slides

10   Click Create to create the presentation.

11   If you didn't select a template or a background, you'll be prompted to choose a slide design in the Modify Layout window. Select a design (select one with bullets shown, if you'll be using bulleted text) and choose OK.

12   Choose File > Save to save the presentation.

In the Save window, save it as a file rather than leaving it as a template. Select StarImpress 6.0 or another presentation format. (If you want to use it as a template in the future, see *Creating and Modifying Templates* on page 654.)

Basing a Presentation on a Template or Background (Without Using AutoPilot)

A template typically has multiple slides with "canned text" you can add to; a presentation layout only has background design.

To bring consistency and clarity to Impress's inconsistent terminology, keep in mind that the items labeled as presentation layouts are really just backgrounds. (A *slide layout* is something else; see *Using the Right Slide Layout* on page 691.)

Use this procedure if you have a template or background that has most of the features you need. Use *Using AutoPilot to Create a Presentation* on page 641 if you want to make considerable changes to the template for your presentation.

1   Choose File > New > Templates and Documents.

2   In the New window, select Presentations, Presentation Backgrounds, or Education. You can also select Standard, which lists all the templates you've created yourself and saved in your user/template folder.

Note – Additional categories will appear if you've added paths using the instructions in *Adding Places to Look for Impress Files* on page 653.

---

3   After selecting a category, select a template from the Templates list (Figure 25-7).

Click More if you want to see more information about each. Select the Preview option to see an example of each selection.

4   Click OK. The selection will be displayed in Impress.

5   Choose File > Save to save the presentation.

In the Save window, be sure to select Impress 6.0 or another presentation format as the file type, instead of the default template format.

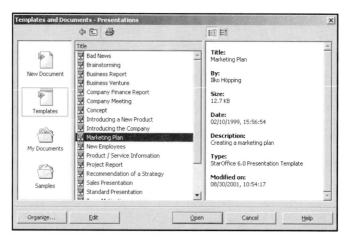

Figure 25-7   Creating a new presentation from a template or presentation layout (a background)

Basing a Presentation on a Writer Document

You can generate an outline, or all the content of a presentation, by using a Writer document as the source. This can be useful if you've already written a report or training manual, for instance, and want to give a presentation of similar material, especially if it's a long document. This creates an extremely simple presentation with no background.

There are two ways to generate the presentation from a Writer document; the navigation is shown in Figure 25-8.

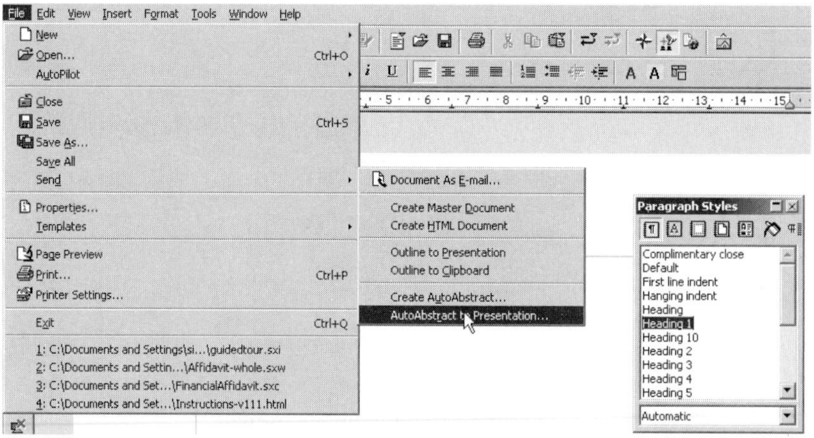

Figure 25-8   The options for sending a Writer document with the right heading styles to an Impress presentation

- Sending an outline to a presentation (in the Writer document, choose File > Send > Outline to Presentation)

- Sending an autoabstract to a presentation (File > Send > AutoAbstract to Presentation)

Note – You must have at least one Heading1 or other numbered heading style in the Writer document for these options to appear in the File menu.

Both approaches get the job done, but using the Send Outline feature is simpler. Review the Before You Begin information, next, then use either of the subsequent procedures to generate the presentation.

Before You Begin

The document you base the presentation outline on **must** be a Writer document, either originally, or another type of document opened in Writer. It also must use the Writer heading styles: Heading 1, Heading 2, and so on. It's all right if you've modified the style attributes, or created new ones with those names, but the styles must have those names, and must be used as the heading styles in the source document.

Don't use bullets in a document you base a presentation on. They end up in the presentation as shown in Figure 25-9.

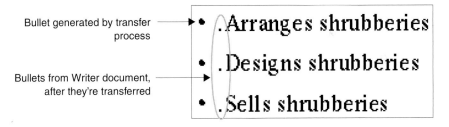

Figure 25-9   Effect of transfer on Writer bullets

Creating a Presentation Using the Send Outline to Presentation Feature

Figure 25-10 shows an example of a Writer document, with styles applied appropriately for transfer via this method, and the styles and formatting the document is converted to in Impress.

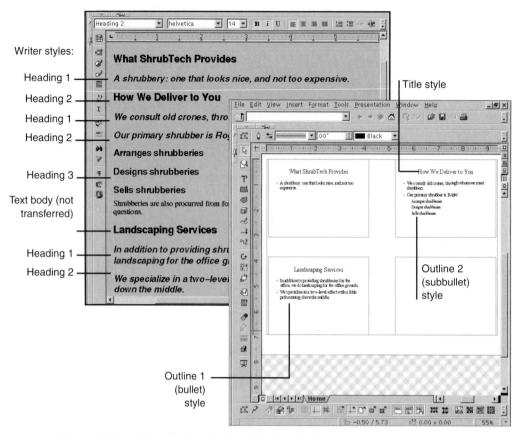

Figure 25-10   Transferring via Send Outline to Presentation

Table 25-1 shows which Writer styles are read by the conversion process and which styles they are converted to in Impress.

Table 25-1   Writer-to-Impress style conversion: Send Outline to Presentation

Writer	Impress
Heading 1	Title (slide title)
	Each slide title has its own slide.
Heading 2	Outline 1 (first bullet)
Heading 3	Outline 2 (indented bullet)
Heading 4	Outline 3 (indented bullet)
Others	Not converted

Follow these steps to prepare and convert the Writer document to a presentation.

1   If the source document isn't in Writer, import it or paste it into a Writer document.

2   Apply styles in Writer.

    If all three heading styles aren't listed in the styles dropdown list, select the text you want to apply one of the missing headings to. Choose Format > Stylist and double-click the style you need.

3   Choose File > Send > Outline to Presentation.

4   The presentation will appear in Impress in outline view.

Creating a Presentation Using the Send AutoAbstract to Presentation Feature

This feature is a little more complicated and non-intuitive than sending an outline to a presentation. Figure 25-11 on page 650 shows an example of the same original Writer document, with styles applied appropriately for transfer via this method, and the styles and formatting the document is converted to in Impress. Table 25-2 expands on the details.

Table 25-2   Writer-to-Impress style conversion: Send AutoAbstract to Presentation

Writer	Impress	Comments
Any Heading style: Heading 1, 2, etc.	Title (slide title) Each slide title has its own slide.	You can limit the levels of headings that are converted; for the Outline levels to convert option (see Figure 25-12 on page 650), enter 2 if you don't want any Heading 3s to have their own slide. However, any text assigned a heading style that you exclude will not be converted at all. For example, if you specify outline levels to convert as 2, no Heading 3 text will be converted at all, to a title *or* an outline. You can convert down to Heading 5; Heading 6 and below can't be converted to a slide title.
Any non-heading style, but not any heading style that you didn't choose to convert with the Outline levels to convert option. (If you converted only down to Heading 3, then Heading 4 and below will be ignored.)	Outline1 (first bullet) Each paragraph becomes a bullet.	Up to five paragraphs below each heading that's converted to Title style can be converted. You can convert fewer if you want. Here's the tricky, non-intuitive part. Assume that the following list is part of your Writer document. You specify only one outline level to convert, so that only Heading 1s are converted to slide titles. You also choose to convert five subpoints in the conversion window. Therefore, you'd assume that the text body text below will be converted: Heading 1 text Heading 2 text text body text However, in reality you'll end up with only one slide, with the Heading 1 text as the title. Not only is the Heading 2 text ignored, but any text following a non-converted heading style is ignored.

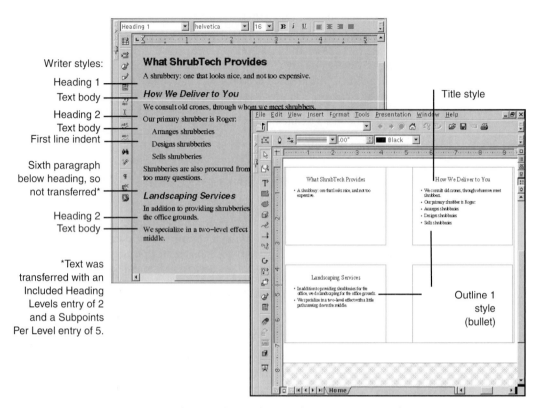

Writer styles:

Heading 1

Text body

Heading 2

Text body

First line indent

Sixth paragraph
below heading, so
not transferred*

Heading 2

Text body

*Text was
transferred with an
Included Heading
Levels entry of 2
and a Subpoints
Per Level entry of 5.

Title style

Outline 1
style
(bullet)

Figure 25-11   Transferring via Send AutoAbstract to Presentation

Follow these steps to prepare and convert the Writer document to a presentation. An
example is shown in Figure 25-12.

Enter the number of heading
levels to make into slide
headings. If you want all text
that has the style Heading 1 or
Heading 2 made into slide
headings, for instance, enter 2.

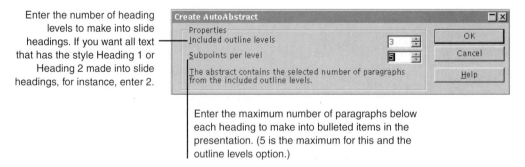

Enter the maximum number of paragraphs below
each heading to make into bulleted items in the
presentation. (5 is the maximum for this and the
outline levels option.)

Figure 25-12   Conversion options for Send AutoAbstract to Presentation

1   If the source document isn't in Writer, import it or paste it into a Writer document.

2 Apply styles. Any text having any Heading style will have the Title style in the presentation and have its own slide.

If Heading styles aren't available in the style dropdown list, select the text you want to apply one of the missing headings to. Choose Format > Stylist and double-click the style you need.

3 Choose File > Send > AutoAbstract to Presentation.

4 In the dialog box (Figure 25-12), enter the transfer options.

Note – Any text in heading styles below the number in the Included outline levels field will be completely ignored by the conversion, and prevent any non-heading text below them from being converted. We recommend that you always convert 5 levels of heading styles.

---

5 The presentation will appear in Impress in outline view.

Checking What Template Your Document Is Based On

If your document is acting weird and you want to make sure you created it based on the right template, choose File > Properties and click the General tab. The template used by the document is displayed at the bottom of the window, as shown in Figure 25-13.

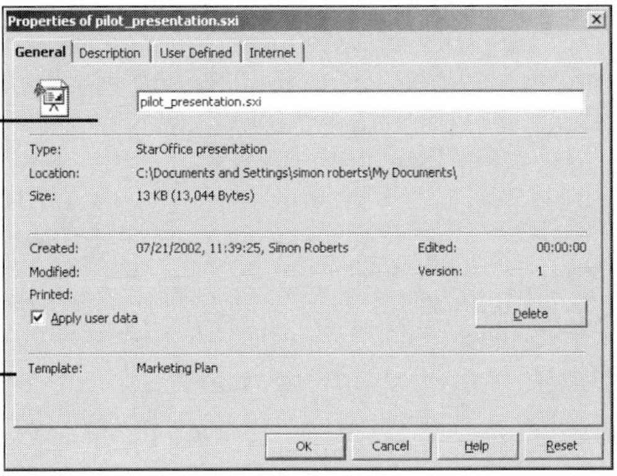

The file name is displayed here. (The file title, displayed in the title bar, is displayed under the Description tab.)

The name (not filename) of the template the document was based on, if any, is displayed here.

Figure 25-13 Viewing the template a document was based on

Creating a New Empty Presentation

If you really want to, you can do all the work of formatting and organizing the presentation yourself. This will create an empty presentation with one slide.

1 Choose File > New > Presentation.

If AutoPilot starts, selecting the Do not show this dialog again option, and clicking Cancel, won't make it go away. Refer to *Turning Off Automatic AutoPilot* on page 653.

2   Choose Format > Modify Layout and select the type of slide structure you want. (For more information, see *Selecting a Slide Layout for a New or Existing Slide* on page 679.)

Entering a Presentation Title

Your presentation is probably still named "Untitled," or the name of the document you based on it. Impress displays this name in the Impress title bar, in the navigation bar at the bottom of the program work area, and in template and presentation layout (background) selection windows.

To change the name:

1   Choose File > Properties.

2   Click the Description tab (Figure 25-14) and enter a different title.

File name is displayed at the top of the properties window and in the General tab. The document title, displayed in the program title bar and task bar, is displayed here.

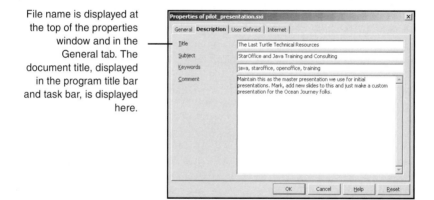

Figure 25-14   Changing the presentation title

Opening Existing Presentations

You can open Impress files as well as those in formats by other vendors, such as PowerPoint.

Not only can you open a Powerpoint file in Impress, but you can save it again as a PowerPoint file. However, both opening and saving take much longer than if you convert the file to Impress.

If you're prompted to select a Filter when opening files, select the type of file. If the file doesn't open correctly, try selecting Draw instead of Impress.

Opening a Presentation File

Choose File > Open and navigate to the file you want, then click Open. If you don't see it, be sure All is selected in the File type list.

Note – If you're opening a file that wasn't created in Impress, such as a PowerPoint presentation, save it in Impress first. A lot of the features won't be available until you do.

Opening a Draw File as a Presentation

Choose File > Open and navigate to the file you want. In the File type list, select Impress and click Open.

You also can select the file in Beamer and choose Open With, then select StarImpress.

Setting Up Impress to Make Creating and Opening Presentations Easier

Completing these procedures will make life simpler when you start using Impress.

Turning Off Automatic AutoPilot

AutoPilot is a powerful "wizard" tool that lets you define many of the features of a new presentation. However, it appears with somewhat annoying and surprising frequency (under File > New, primarily). You can always get to AutoPilot by choosing File > AutoPilot, so you'll probably find it more convenient to keep it from coming up when you choose File > New.

1   Choose Tools > Options > Presentation > General.

2   Deselect the Start with AutoPilot option.

Adding Places to Look for Impress Files

AutoPilot has a window that lists the templates and presentations you can base your new presentation on. However, it's pretty exclusive—it only looks in a few locations.

Note – If you're in a multi-user system, the template folders are typically on the server, not among your own local files.

If you're on a multi-user system and have created your own templates in a different folder, for instance, you won't be able to see them in AutoPilot. Follow these steps to add the locations where you store Impress templates, presentation backgrounds, and presentations.

1   Choose Tools > Options > *program* > Paths.

2   In the list of paths, select Templates.

3   Click Edit.

4   In the Select Paths window, click Add.

5   Navigate to a folder where you store Impress templates, such as your program work folder (`office/user/work`) and click Select. Add any other folders.

6   Click OK in the Select Paths and Paths windows.

The folders you added will show up in AutoPilot with the name Templates.

Creating and Modifying Templates

Having the templates and backgrounds you need makes creating presentations much quicker and more efficient. If you find yourself making the same changes repeatedly to your presentations, it's a good idea to create templates with the elements you need already in them.

Note – By default, when you base a new document on a template, the program lets you pick templates from only a couple different folders, including the `presnt` folder in `share/template/language/`. If you've added folders using the instructions in *Adding Places to Look for Impress Files* on page 653, you'll be able to pick from those, as well. However, to be on the safe side, the procedures in this section tell you to put your templates in only those folders where the program looks by default.

Presentation Templates

Follow the appropriate procedure to create, modify, or name a template.

Creating a Presentation Template

If you want to create your own template to base other presentations on, follow these steps.

1   Select or create the presentation to base the template on.

2   Make any necessary changes; remove any text you don't want in the template.

> **Note –** You can't delete slide layout elements, such as the text frame for the header. The message "This function cannot be completed with the selected objects" will be displayed, or only the text will be deleted. Refer to *Selecting a Slide Layout for a New or Existing Slide* on page 679 to remove elements by applying a blank slide layout, or changing it to one that meets your needs more closely.

3   Choose File > Save as. Save it as an Impress template to the `share/template/` `language/presnt` folder, or in your `user/template` folder.

The template will be listed with the other Impress templates in AutoPilot and other template-related windows.

Modifying a Presentation Template

If you want to change one of the templates provided by Impress, or that you've created yourself, follow these steps. (If you're changing the template, it's a good idea to save the template under a new name, because you won't be able to get the original back except by reinstalling.)

1   Open a template file, typically in the `share/template/language/presnt` folder, or in your `user/template` folder.

2   Make the changes you want to the slides, background, transitions, and other elements.

3   Choose Save as to save it under a new name in the `presnt` folder. Be sure that StarImpress Template is the file type.

Naming a Presentation Template

You can give it a name like the other templates ("Annual Report" and so on) the same way you name presentations.

1   Choose File > Properties and click the Description tab.

2   Enter a name and click OK.

If the template doesn't have a name, the file name will appear in template lists instead.

Background Templates

Follow the appropriate procedure to manage templates for use as backgrounds in your presentations. These templates contain only the background elements; no individual slides are included.

> **Note –** Remember that backgrounds are referred to inconsistently by a variety of names in Impress, including *presentation layouts*.

Creating a Background Template

If you want to create your own background to base other presentations on, follow these steps.

1 Choose File > New > Presentation to open a new, blank presentation.

2 Switch to Background view (see *Using Foreground/Background Views* on page 663).

3 Create the background.

4 Choose File > Save as. Save it as an Impress template to the `share/template/`
`language/layout` folder, or in your `user/template` folder.

It will be listed with the other Impress backgrounds in AutoPilot and other windows.

Modifying a Background Template

If you want to change one of the backgrounds provided by Impress, or that you've created yourself, follow these steps. (It's a good idea to save the background under a new name, because you won't be able to get the original back except by reinstalling.)

1 Open a background file from the `share/template/language/layout` folder, or in your `user/template` folder.

2 Switch to Background view.

3 Make the changes you want.

4 Choose Save as to save it under a new name. Be sure that StarImpress Template is the file type.

Naming a Background Template

You can give it a name like the other backgrounds ("Blue Border," "Sun," and so on) the same way you name presentations and templates.

1 Choose File > Properties and click the Description tab.

2 Enter a name and click OK.

If the background template doesn't have a name, the file name will appear in background lists instead.

Using Master Views, Foreground/ Background Views, and Layers

Review this overview section before you continue to the next chapter, so that you know how to get to the part of your presentation that you need, and view it the way you want to.

You can think of Impress as three-dimensional in its display and editing capabilities. It has three different systems to show different aspects of your presentation: master views, foreground/background views, and layers. It's a good idea to get to know them now, because it can make finding your way through a presentation and getting to the parts you need to edit a lot less frustrating.

Orientation to Each View or Mode

Overview of drawing, outline, slide, notes, and handouts master views
Show different parts of your presentation, such as only the handouts, or only the slide, as well as different displays: one slide at a time or all at once. The Master views are Drawing, Outline, Slide, Notes, and Handout and are always accessible at the right side of the presentation work area at the top. Figure 25-18 shows a more extensive example; you can learn how to use them in *Using Master Views* on page 659.

Overview of foreground/background views, in icons at the bottom of the work area These let you work with the main content of your presentation (content such as charts and text, in Slide view) or the background (page design, in Background view) of your presentation. See Figure 25-15. Figure 25-18 shows a more extensive example; you can learn how to use them in *Using Foreground/Background Views* on page 663.

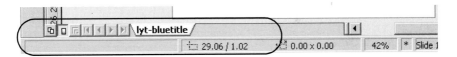

Click the far left icon to see the slide normally.

Click the center icon, shown active, and confusingly titled Master View which has nothing to do with the other Master Views, to see all the backgrounds in your presentation. In this illustration, only one background, titled lyt-bluetitle, is in the presentation.

Figure 25-15   Background view (accessed by clicking the middle icon, Master View)

Overview of layers: extra dimensions for slide foreground or background Layers are something you can do anytime, whether you're seeing the foreground of your slide or the background. However, you can only do it when you're in the normal Drawing master view; there's not much point in having layers when you're just viewing an outline of the presentation in Outline master view, for instance.

Layers are similar to the illustrations in anatomy books, with each layer belonging to a different system: the skeletal system, the digestive system, and so on. Layers let you separate items in one slide into separate groups.

- Layers in the foreground – So, you're in your presentation with normal drawing view, you've got a diagram of the three distinct parts of an airplane engine, and you want to be able to present them separately so the audience can view each system separately, then on top of each other. Or you're doing a Six Sigma Process Diagram, guaranteed to make your company fabulous and efficient, and there's a lot of separate but overlapping processes. Get ready to use layers.

See Figure 25-16. Layout, Controls, and Dimension Lines are three default layers.

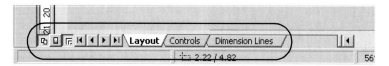

Figure 25-16   The default layers for a slide

* Layers in the background – There's less necessity to use layers in the background, but you can. Just get into background mode, then click the Layers icon too. If you're in background mode (the 2nd icon is clicked) and then layer mode (the 3rd icon is clicked), you just see the slide "Background objects".

  If you're in background mode but not layer mode, you'll see the names of the backgrounds you're using. It's a bit confusing so expect your head to whirl a bit before you've used it much. See Figure 25-16.

The 2nd and 3rd icons are recessed and "background objects," the default layer for backgrounds, is shown. This is layer mode for the background view.

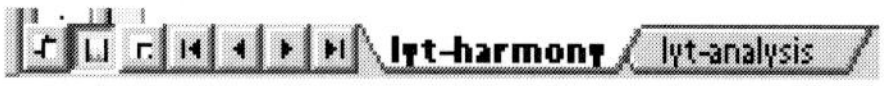

The 2nd icon only is recessed and names of backgrounds are displayed. This isn't layer view; it's just the names of your backgrounds that you've loaded for use in the presentation.

Figure 25-17   Recognizing when you're seeing layers in background view, and just seeing the names of your backgrounds, in background view.

Figure 25-18 shows a more extensive example; you can learn how to use them in *Using Layers* on page 664.

Figure 25-18 shows aspects of master views, foreground/background views, and layers.

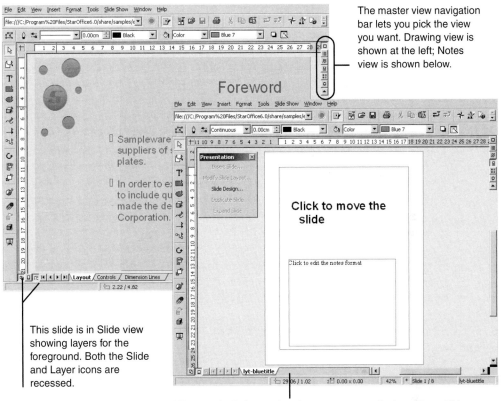

The master view navigation bar lets you pick the view you want. Drawing view is shown at the left; Notes view is shown below.

This slide is in Slide view showing layers for the foreground. Both the Slide and Layer icons are recessed.

When you're in Layer view, layer names are displayed here. This illustration isn't in layer mode, so names of backgrounds are displayed. Layer mode isn't available in Notes view.

Figure 25-18   Master views, foreground/background views, and layers

Using Master Views

Displaying all the elements of a presentation—slides, notes, structure, and so on—would be visually dizzying and logistically difficult. Impress has divided the ways you can look at your presentation into five **master views**: Drawing, Outline, Slide, Notes, and Handout.

Changing From One View to Another

To get to a particular view, use the view bar at the right side of the work area.

Note that the bottom icon, Start slide show, doesn't take you to a different view. It's easy to click this icon by accident. It starts

Drawing view

Outline view

Slide view

Notes view

Handout view

Start slide show

the presentation, giving you a blank screen at first that is somewhat alarming if you don't expect it. To stop the presentation, just press Esc.

Drawing View

You'll spend most of your time in the Drawing view, adding text and graphics. You have the same capabilities here as in Draw, with additional text and effects features.

See Figure 25-18 on page 659 and Figure 25-1 on page 637 for examples of the Drawing view.

Outline View

This view shows the outline of your presentation (Figure 25-19). You can expand and contract heading levels to view only top-level headings, all text, and everything in between, and reorganize the presentation.

Choose whether to show only top-level headings or all levels (subpoints).

Show the text as it's formatted in Drawing view, or in plain text.

Show text in black and white, or as it's colored in Drawing view.

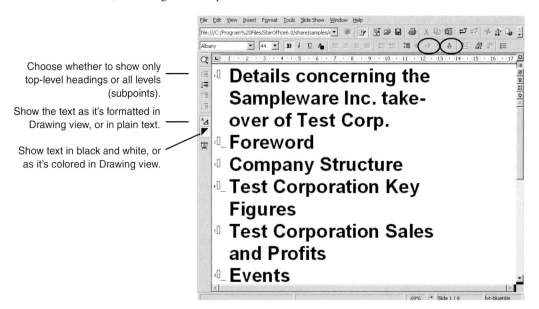

Figure 25-19   Outline view

Slide View

Use the Slide view (Figure 25-20) to get a bird's eye view of your presentation, to rearrange, add, and delete slides, and to specify how each slide changes to the next.

The features on the toolbar are probably still unfamiliar to you at this point; the terms are presented here so that you can start getting oriented, and get to know the work area. All features, such as rehearsing timings and setting up transition types, are covered throughout the Impress chapters.

> **Note –** Choose View > Toolbar > Presentation to display the Presentation menu, which shows the selected effects.

Select the effect you want when the selected slide is displayed during presentation. —

Choose how fast the effect should run. —

Run the presentation onscreen (press Esc to stop). —

Select the transition type and, if Automatic, enter the amount of time to display the slide. —

Clicking Rehearse Timings will run the presentation, with a timer which displays the time each slide has been displayed. —

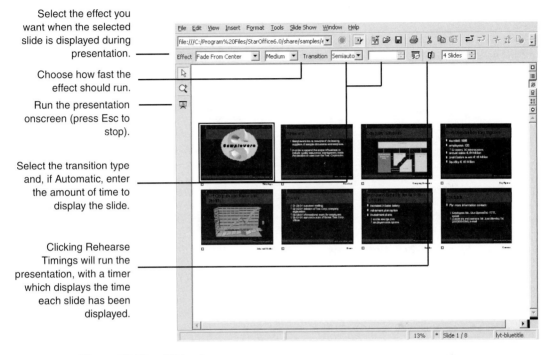

Figure 25-20   Slide view

Notes View

Add speaker notes in this view (Figure 25-21), below the slide area. When you print, you can choose to print with or without the notes. (See *Setting Printing Options* on page 747.)

You can use Draw tools to edit in this view.

Check the font size for your notes before you begin; the default may be larger than you want.

You can use the icons in the toolbar in the slide and the notes area, in Slide or in Background view (slide only).

Move from slide to slide the same way you do in Drawing view.

Slide and Background view are available in Notes view.

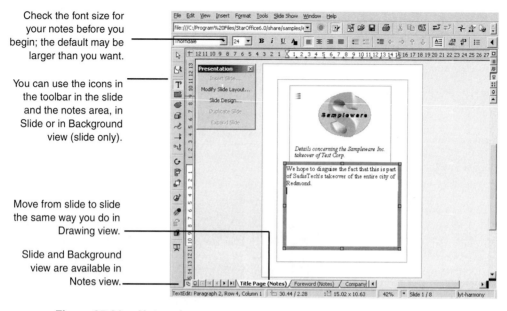

Figure 25-21   Notes view

Handout View

Create audience materials out of the slides using this view (Figure 25-22).

You can use the icons in the toolbar to add to the handouts, but not to edit the slides.

You can use only Background view in Handout view, so any change you make appears on all pages of the handouts.

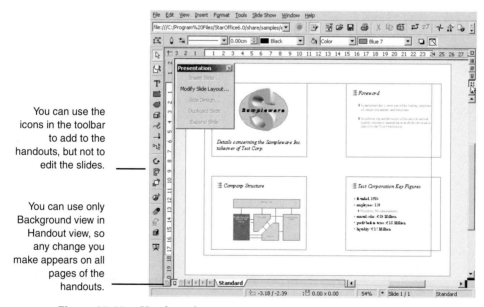

Figure 25-22   Handout view

This view lets you specify the number of slides per page. What you see in the work area is what will be on each page of handouts given to people attending the presentation. You have access to Draw tools here, as well.

You can drag and resize the slides manually. To set the number of slides per handout page, choose Format > Modify Layout. (The maximum per page is six.)

Using Foreground/Background Views

Impress has three additional views that let you see the foreground or background of a slide, as well as layers within each: Slide view, Background view, and Layer view.

- Slide view displays the normal content of a slide.
- Background view displays the elements that are in the background of every slide in the presentation. Use this view to make changes to show up in all slides.
- Layer view lets you see the different layers within a slide foreground, or within a background.

They're available in only two of the master views.

- In Drawing view, you can access all three.
- In Notes view, you can access Slide and Background.

Slide View: The Foreground

In Slide view, you have all the Draw tools and can do the standard editing for developing the presentation. You'll spend much of your time in Drawing view and Slide view.

The changes you make apply only to the current slide, even if you're changing items that belong to a design component used throughout the presentation.

Background View: The Background

This view lets you make changes to the background and related items. The page style (the background design) that you selected in AutoPilot or added yourself is shown in this view.

Layer Mode

You can divide the contents of the slide foreground or background into an unlimited number of *layers*. Layer mode is an enhancement to the other two views.

- Layers in the foreground – See Figure 25-16. Layout, Controls, and Dimension Lines are three default layers.

Figure 25-23   The default layers for a slide

- Layers in the background – See Figure 25-16.

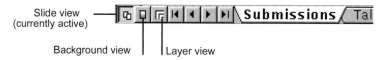

The 2nd and 3rd icons are recessed and "background objects," the default layer for backgrounds, is shown. This is layer mode for the background view.

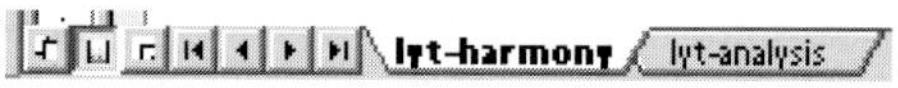

The 2nd icon only is recessed and names of backgrounds are displayed. This isn't layer view; it's just the names of your backgrounds that you've loaded for use in the presentation.

Figure 25-24   Recognizing when you're seeing layers in background view, and just seeing the names of your backgrounds, in background view.

Changing Between Foreground and Background View, and Getting Into and Out of Layer Mode for Each

Choose View from the menu bar, then choose Slide, Background (Drawing, Title, Notes, or Handout), or Layer.

When you're in Drawing, Notes, or Handouts view, you also can use the icons in the navigation bar at the bottom of the work area (Figure 25-25).

Slide view (currently active) ——

Background view

Layer view

Figure 25-25   Navigating between foreground (slide) and background, and layers for each

Using Layers

When you're in Layer mode, you can use layers to separate parts of a slide so that each group can be edited and viewed by itself.

Impress comes with default layers:

- Slide view: Layout (the default), Controls, and Dimension lines

• Background view: Background objects

For example, layers let you draw a car engine diagram with a different subsystem in each layer, or draw a new interdepartmental process with the parts for each department in a different layer. Figure 25-29 on page 666 shows how layers look alone and together.

Layer Quick Facts

You can't delete or rename the default layers, but you can hide them or prevent them from being printed (see *Controlling Whether a Layer Is Printable or Editable (Locked)* on page 667). The default layers are provided with all slides; however any layer you add is specific to the slide you're in when you add it.

You can use layers only when you're in the Drawing master view. Every layer is included in all slides in the presentation; there are no slide-specific layers.

Layers are displayed from left to right and front to back: that is, the layer whose tab is displayed on the left side of the navigation bar is the top layer, and so on. Objects in the top layer will block the view of objects in the same position in subsequent layers.

Creating a Layer

This will add a layer to the right of the Dimension Lines layer—*not* to the right of the layer tab you select. You can't control where they are created. If you create two new layers, Layer4 and Layer5, Figure 25-26 is the result.

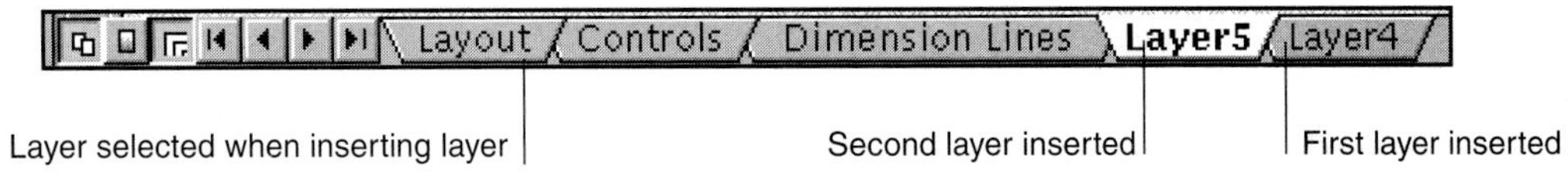

| 品 □ 匠 |◄ ◄ ► ►| \ Layout / Controls / Dimension Lines \ **Layer5** / Layer4 /

Layer selected when inserting layer | Second layer inserted | First layer inserted

Figure 25-26 Order in which layers are inserted

1 Be sure you're in Drawing or Notes view, and Layer view.

2 Click the blank area to the right of the last layer, or right-click a layer tab and choose Insert.

3 Enter the name and other options in the Insert Layer window (Figure 25-27).

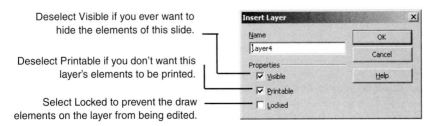

Deselect Visible if you ever want to hide the elements of this slide.

Deselect Printable if you don't want this layer's elements to be printed.

Select Locked to prevent the draw elements on the layer from being edited.

Figure 25-27 Creating a new layer

4   The layer will be created for all slides in the presentation.

Changing Layers

Be sure you're in Layer view. (See *Using Foreground/Background Views* on page 663.) Then click the tab for the layer you want, in the navigation bar at the bottom of the work area (Figure 25-28 on page 666).

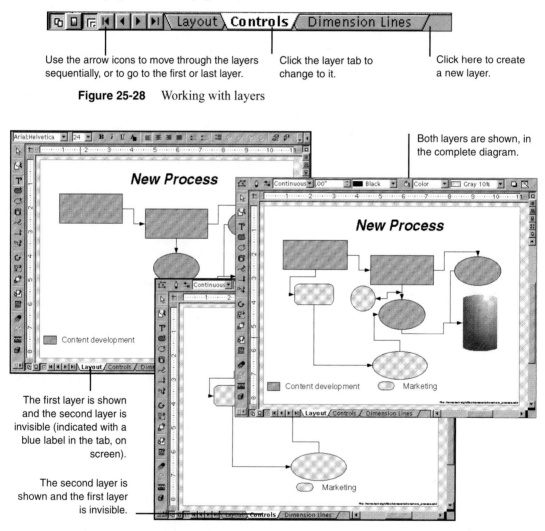

Use the arrow icons to move through the layers sequentially, or to go to the first or last layer.

Click the layer tab to change to it.

Click here to create a new layer.

Figure 25-28   Working with layers

Both layers are shown, in the complete diagram.

The first layer is shown and the second layer is invisible (indicated with a blue label in the tab, on screen).

The second layer is shown and the first layer is invisible.

Figure 25-29   Layered diagram

Controlling Which Layer Is on Top

There isn't a way to explicitly reorder the layers; however, there are a few workarounds:

- Make a layer invisible (see *Hiding One or More Layers*)
- Move objects from one layer to another (see *Moving Objects Among Layers*)
- Delete and re-create layers

The default layer Controls is always on top. As for the other layers, the order in which you draw the objects controls what's on top: the first is on the bottom and last on the top, regardless of the layer.

Changing the arrangements of the objects using the Arrange > Send to back and similar features doesn't change the relationship of objects in different layers, though it does change object relationships within a layer.

Controlling Whether a Layer Is Printable or Editable (Locked)

To protect elements of a layer from being changed, or to keep them from being printed, you can lock the layer.

1   Enter layer view by clicking the Layer icon in the lower left corner.

2   In the navigation bar, right-click the tab of the layer you want to lock.

3   Choose Modify.

4   In the Modify Layer window (it has the same options as the Insert Layer window in Figure 25-27), select Printable, Locked, or both.

5   You'll need to select Printable again when you're ready to print it; selecting the Hidden pages option in the print options window doesn't make it print (see Figure 28-17 on page 747).

Hiding One or More Layers

The layer view in Impress is a little unintuitive. If you have three layers and you click the tab of any of them, you still see all the objects in all layers. You can even edit one layer's objects when you've clicked the tab of another layer. To show only the objects of one layer, or of two, you have to hide the layers that you don't want to see.

1   Right-click the layer tab in the navigation bar.

2   Choose Modify.

3   Deselect Visible.

Note – Invisible layers' names always appear in blue.

Renaming a Layer

1   Right-click the layer tab and choose Rename.

2   Type the new name on the tab.

Deleting a Layer and All Objects in It

This deletes the layer and all objects in it, so move objects out of the layer before beginning if you want to preserve them. Also, remember that the layer will be deleted from all slides in the presentation.

1   Right-click the layer tab.

2   Choose Delete.

3   Click Yes when prompted.

Moving Objects Among Layers

Surprisingly, you can't just cut and paste to move objects from one layer to another; you'll need to drag them instead. You'll need to make sure the tabs of both layers can be displayed simultaneously, so widen the main program window if necessary, or follow the directions in step 3 when you get to it.

1   Navigate to the slide containing the object you want to move.

To copy instead of just moving the object, you need to copy the object in the current slide, then move the copy to the new layer.

2   Switch to Drawing master view, to the view (Slide or Background) that the object is in, and then choose View > Layer.

3   Select the layer that the object is in.

If you can't display the tabs of the current and target layers at once, click on the narrow vertical blank area between the rightmost layer tab and the left scrolling arrow in the navigation bar (Figure 25-30).

Figure 25-30   Increasing display space for layer tabs

The cursor will change to a two-ended arrow. Drag the blank area to the right until there's enough space to display all layer tabs.

4   Be sure that the tab of the layer you want to move the object **to** is showing in the navigation bar.

5   Click on the object, click it again and hold down the mouse, then drag the object a bit. A gray rectangle will appear at the base of the cursor. (Keep holding the mouse button down.)

6   Drag the object to the tab of the layer you want it to be in; the tab will be highlighted when you've succeeded.

7   The object will appear in the same location within the work area in the new layer.

Controlling Workspace Display

You can control several aspects of how your presentations look while you're working with them. Factors such as how large they seem, whether you're using black-and-white or color, can make it easier to develop your work and make it match your needs more closely.

Selecting a Measurement System

To display the top and left rulers, choose Tools > Options > Presentation > View and select the Rulers visible option.

1   Right-click on the ruler at the top or right of the workspace. (If it isn't displayed, choose View > Rulers.)

2   Select a measurement system.

Increasing or Decreasing Display Size (Zooming)

Impress lets you control the size at which your drawing is displayed. If you need to have particularly precise control over how you move objects in the workspace, or want to see an object close-up, you might want to use a high zoom, such as 400%, to view the objects as very large. If you want to see how the object might seem to an audience seeing it from a distance, you can reduce the view to smaller than 100%.

Selecting a Preset Zoom

1   Right-click the zoom field in the status bar below the work area.

2   Select one of the displayed percentages.

Selecting a New Zoom

1   Double-click in the zoom field.

2   Select an existing zoom or enter your own in the Variable field at the bottom of the Zoom window.

3   Click OK.

Using the Zoom Icon

1   Click and hold down the mouse on the Zoom icon in the toolbar, to display the Zoom tearoff menu.

2   Select the type of zoom you want in the Zoom menu.

You can quickly zoom in, out, to 100%, to the previous zoom, and several other options (displayed in tool tips). Each time you click to zoom in or out, the zoom changes by 50% of the current display.

Reducing How Much of a Slide is Displayed

Impress lets you show object outlines when you move them. The default behavior is that, if you have selected several objects to drag across the work area, only a rectangle outlining the group as a whole will be shown. You can make your files appear faster if you reduce what the program needs to draw; you can turn off display of pictures and objects (this includes graphics-based backgrounds) and text.

1   Choose Tools > Options > Presentation > View.

2   Select the Contour of Each Individual Object option, then click OK.

3   Select the options you want (Figure 25-31).

Image placeholders – Only the outline of graphics that you insert, such as graphs, will be shown; a box with intersecting lines inside it will be shown instead.

Contour Mode – Objects you create will not be shown with their area fill (border attributes will still be displayed).

Text Placeholders – A box like the one for picture placeholders will appear instead of text.

Line Contour Only – Select this option to always display lines and contours as fine lines. This display does not depend on the currently used line width.

Contour of Each Individual Object – The program displays the contour line of each individual object when moving this object. This option enables you to see if single objects conflict with other objects in the target position. If unselected, a square contour is displayed that includes all selected objects.

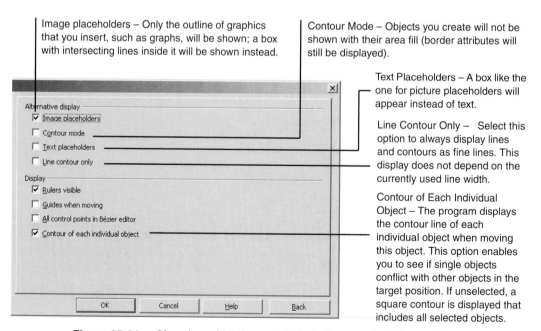

Figure 25-31   Choosing which items to hide in Presentation View window

Note – This doesn't affect printing—if you turn on picture placeholders here, none of your objects or backgrounds will be displayed, but they'll still print normally.

Showing Extended Object Lines to Show Where Object Is Being Moved To

You can display objects with lines coming out of both axes when you move them, to show more clearly where the object will be (Figure 25-32).

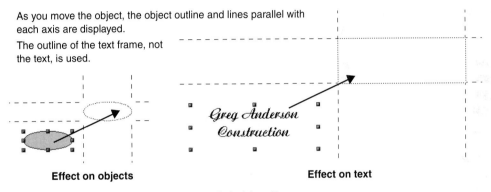

As you move the object, the object outline and lines parallel with each axis are displayed.

The outline of the text frame, not the text, is used.

Effect on objects

Effect on text

Figure 25-32   Displaying extended object lines

To use this feature, choose Tools > Options > Presentation > View, then select the Guides when moving option.

Using the Grid to Draw and Position Objects

This is covered in Draw's *Using the Grid* on page 780. Using the grid lets you "snap" objects you draw and move to the grid lines, so that lines are straight and objects are aligned.

Use the icons on the option bar to control the grid functions (to display it, choose View > Toolbars > Option Bar). Click the Show Grid icon to activate it (Figure 25-33).

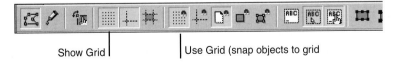

Show Grid | Use Grid (snap objects to grid

Figure 25-33   Grid option icons

Viewing in Grayscale, Color, or Black/White

You can reduce the RAM required to display images by switching to grayscale or black and white, or preview how something will look when printed.

Note – The settings covered in this procedure don't affect printing, but the effects you see are the same you'd get if you printed in grayscale or black and white. To print in grayscale or black and white, see *Printing Without Dark Backgrounds* on page 746.

1   Choose View > Display Quality.

2   Select Color, Grayscale, or Black and White. Figure 25-34 illustrates the effects.

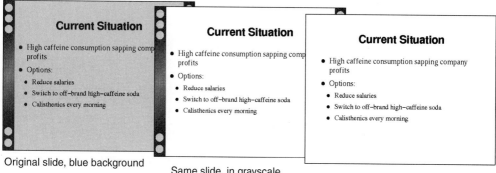

Original slide, blue background   Same slide, in grayscale   Same slide, displayed in black and white

Figure 25-34   Displaying in grayscale or black and white

Developing Presentations

Using the Navigator to Move Among Slides

You can use the Navigator to easily move from one slide to another, among all your open presentations. It's especially useful for editing long documents, for going directly to a certain slide in an extensive presentation, or quickly switch between open documents. The Navigator is a dockable window.

You also can move slides around within and between presentations; see *Inserting Slides Using the Navigator* on page 680 for more information.

1   If you're editing, rather than running the presentation, move to Drawing view.

2   Choose File > Edit > Navigator.

3   To move to a specific slide in the same document, double-click it.

     To move forward or backward in the displayed list of slides, use the arrow icons at the top.

4   To see a list of slides in other presentations or drawings, select it from the list at the bottom of the Navigator (Figure 26-1).

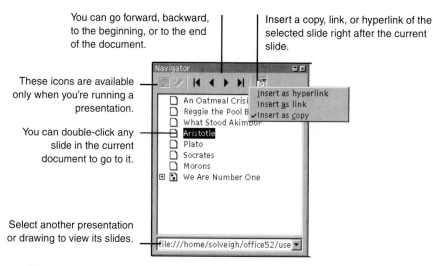

Figure 26-1   Using the Navigator

Organizing Presentations

We assume at this point that you've created a presentation file using the information starting on page 641, and now want to modify the slide order, and insert new ones.

To get your slides and headings in the right order, Impress provides you with several tools. Each one has a different set of capabilities, though there are some overlaps.

- Right-clicking the slide tab in Drawing view
- The Presentation menu, shown in Figure 26-2 (choose View > Toolbars > Presentation, or click the Presentation Box On/Off icon on the right of the object bar)

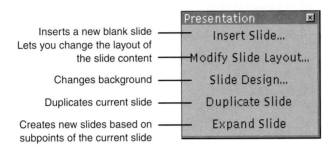

Inserts a new blank slide ——— Insert Slide...
Lets you change the layout of
the slide content ——— Modify Slide Layout...
Changes background ——— Slide Design...
Duplicates current slide ——— Duplicate Slide
Creates new slides based on ——— Expand Slide
subpoints of the current slide

Figure 26-2   Presentation menu

- Outline master view
- Slide master view
- Navigator
- Insert menu (lets you insert a presentation in your current one)

You can also use the summary slide generator to document the slide order once you're done (see *Creating a Summary Slide* on page 684).

Renaming a Slide

In Drawing view, use either method:

- Right-click the slide tab, choose Rename Slide, then type the new name.
- In the Presentation menu, click Modify Slide Layout, then enter a new name in the Modify Slide window.

Deleting a Slide

Use either of the following methods:

- In Drawing view, right-click the slide tab and choose Delete Slide.
- In Slide view, right-click the slide tab and choose Delete Slide.

Rearranging Slides

When you rearrange the order of slides in a presentation you'll be presenting on a computer, you'll need to reassign the transition effects between slides. Refer to *Applying Slide Transition Effects* on page 723 for more information.

Slide View

In Slide view, you can quickly rearrange slide order. If you want to move subpoints from one slide to another, refer to the following section, which describes the process in Outline view. However, moving slides in Slide view is simpler and less error-prone.

Refer to *Using Master Views* on page 659 if you want more information about Slide view.

1   Switch to Slide view.

2   Select the slide you want to move.

3   Drag the slide to where you want the slide to be; a thick black bar will appear where the slide will be positioned when you release the mouse. Figure 26-3 illustrates this.

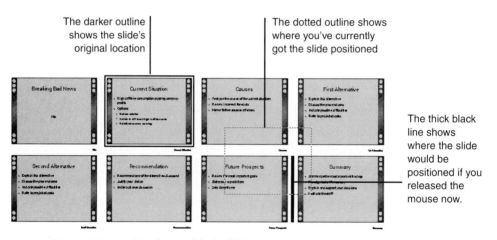

Figure 26-3   Moving a slide in Slide view

Outline View

You can move a part of your presentation to a new location by **dragging** its heading to a different place in the outline, or by using the Move Up and Move Down icons in the **object bar**.

The advantage of using Outline view is, among other factors, that you can view just the text of each heading, as well as viewing or hiding subpoints (the text within each slide).

See *Using Master Views* on page 659 if you want more information about Outline view.

If you're repositioning a slide heading, its subpoints will be moved, as well. (It's possible to insert a heading in the middle of a slide, though, separating heading and bullets—though this might not be what you want.) Graphics remain with the original slide heading.

Dragging

1   Switch to Outline view.

2 Choose to show all text within the presentation, or only level 1 (slide headings), using the icons on the toolbar.

3 Select the slide icon for the a slide heading, or select a subpoint.

The pointer won't change to a positioning pointer; it will still look like an insertion pointer, like one you'd use to type text.

4 Drag the item to its new location.

A thin gray line indicates where the item will be repositioned when you release the mouse (below the line it will appear after).

Note – If you're showing all levels of the presentation, be careful not to accidentally reposition a slide heading in the middle of another slide. You'll get illogical, if amusing, topic mixes.

Using the Object Bar

1 Switch to Outline view.

2 Choose to show all text within the presentation, or only level 1 (slide headings), using the icons on the toolbar.

3 Select the slide heading or subpoint you want to move.

4 Click Move Up or Move Down until the item is in the desired location.

Inserting a New Empty Slide

You can add a slide at a specific spot in your presentation in several ways; we'll cover two here.

When you add a slide, it is added with a specific *layout*. The layout is the structure of the slide: this can include features such as default area for a heading and text, a blank chart with text bullets above it, etc. Depending on how you add the slide, a default will be used, or you can select the one you want.

Note – Impress uses the term "layout" frequently and inconsistently. A layout, or slide layout, is the structure of one slide. A presentation layout (see *Presentation Backgrounds* on page 705) is the background for an entire presentation.

Quickly Adding a Slide

1 Select the slide that you want the new slide to appear immediately after.

2 Click the blank area to the right of the last slide.

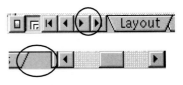

The new slide will be added after the selected slide, and will have the same slide layout and background.

Adding a Slide and Selecting the Layout

1   Move to Drawing view.

2   Select the slide that you want the new slide to appear immediately after.

3   Do one of the following:

- Click the Insert Slide option in the Presentation menu.
- Right-click the tab of the current slide and choose Insert.
- Click the Insert icon on the toolbar and display the Insert tearoff menu, then click the Insert Slide icon.

4   Enter the slide name and select the slide layout you want, and click OK (Figure 26-4 on page 678). The slide will have the same background as the slide right before it.

Note – We strongly recommend that you select the layout in Figure 26-4 that most closely matches the content you're going to add. A lot of default formatting, which makes it easier to add text, comes with the preset layouts. Unless you're just going to import an object and have no text, there isn't much reason to use the completely unformatted layout in the upper left corner.

For instance, if you're a PowerPoint user, you're used to being able to press the Tab key to indent a bulleted item to the next line. This won't happen unless you choose a layout that contains bulleted items.

This name will appear on the slide's tab in the navigation bar.

It's a good idea not to select the unformatted layout if you want text in the slide.

Select the slide layout you want.

Choose whether to include the background (attributes like page color) or background objects (objects like logos).

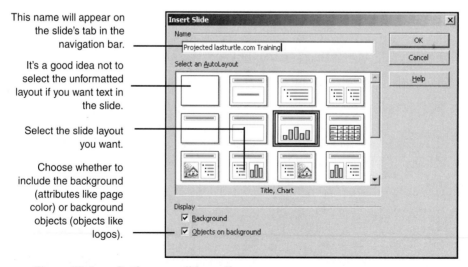

Figure 26-4   Setting new slide attributes

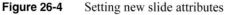

Selecting a Slide Layout for a New or Existing Slide

This is very similar to adding a new slide. Review the precautions at the beginning of *Inserting a New Empty Slide*, then follow these steps.

1   Move to Drawing view.

2   Select the tab of the slide whose layout you want to change.

3   Click the Modify Slide Layout option in the Presentation menu.

4   Select the slide layout you want, then click OK.

Specifying Slide Orientation and Margins

Selecting the slide layout takes care of most of the slide options. However, you can use the Page Setup window to specify other aspects, including slide orientation (portrait or landscape). The options you set here are not slide-specific; they affect the entire file.

For more information on page setup, see Figure 7-37 on page 228.

1   Choose Format > Page.

2   Set page margins and orientation as shown in Figure 26-5, then click OK.

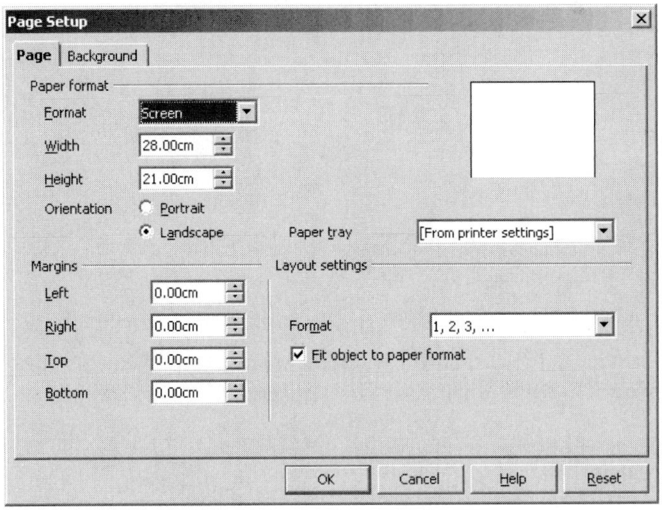

Figure 26-5   Setting slide margins and orientation

3   Slide layouts are designed for portrait orientation, so if necessary, switch to Background view and adjust the text frames of the heading and body to fit the new dimensions.

Inserting Existing Slides from Impress or Draw

Draw and Impress are both based on slides as the basic component of the file, so adding a slide from another presentation or a graphic in an existing Draw file creates a new slide in your presentation. The slides will keep the background and styles from the documents where they are now; they won't get the background and styles of the presentation you insert them in.

Inserting Slides Using the Navigator

You can insert a Draw graphic or a Impress slide from any open presentation or drawing document.

1   Move to Drawing view.

2   Be sure the document you want to copy from (source) and the one you want to copy to (target) are open.

3   Choose Edit > Navigator (Figure 26-6).

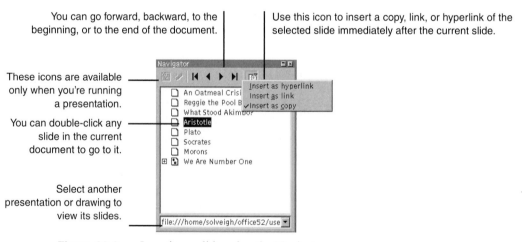

Figure 26-6   Inserting a slide using the Navigator

4   The slides in the current presentation are displayed. Double-click to move to the one you want in front of the slide you'll insert.

5   If you want to copy from another document, select it from the list at the bottom of the Navigator.

6   Select the slide you want to insert.

7   Click the Drag Mode icon and be sure the Insert as copy option is selected.

8   Drag the selected slide to the work area of the current slide.

9   Enter a new name if you're prompted to.

Inserting Slides Using the Insert File Feature

You can insert Draw and Impress files, which will be created as separate slides to the right of the current slide.

For information on inserting HTML and text files into a selected slide, see *Adding Charts, Pictures, and Objects* on page 701.

1   Click the Insert icon on the toolbar at the left of the work area, and display the Insert tearoff menu. Click the Insert File icon.

2   Select the file you want.

3   The file will be listed in the Insert Slides/Objects window (Figure 26-7).

   If the file has more than one slide, select the whole file, or click the + icon and select only the slide or slides you want. Click OK.

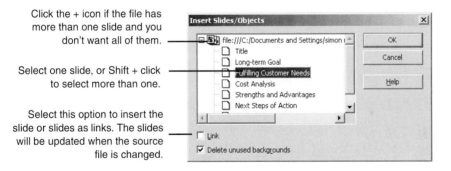

Figure 26-7   Inserting slides from Draw or Impress files

Inserting All the Slides in Another Presentation

1   Move to Drawing view.

2   Move to the slide that's right before where you want the presentation to be inserted.

3   Choose Insert > File.

4   Select the presentation you want, then click OK.

Copying and Duplicating Slides

The goals achieved by copying and duplicating are, of course, the same. Impress provides several ways to do this.

Copying a Slide From Any Presentation in Slide View

You can copy a slide from the current presentation or another one, and paste it into the location you select.

1   Move to Slide view.

2   Select the slide you want to copy.

3   Choose Edit > Copy.

4   Move to the location where you want to paste it.

    The slide will be inserted to the right of the selected slide.

5   Choose Edit > Paste.

Duplicating a Slide in the Same Presentation in Drawing View

The new slide will be added immediately after the duplicated slide, and named "Slide $n+1$." (if you select the fifth slide and duplicate it, the duplicated one will be named "Slide 6").

1   Move to Drawing view.

2   Select the tab of the slide to duplicate.

3   Display the Presentation menu.

4   Click Duplicate Slide.

Promoting and Demoting Subpoints

Promoting subpoints (the bulleted items in each slide) is similar to the expand function on the Presentation menu, which lets you automatically create a new slide for each subpoint in a slide. Refer to *Expanding: Creating a Slide for Each Subpoint* on page 683 if you'd rather use that feature.

Demoting a slide heading to a subpoint will delete all the items in the slide and any objects. Promote subpoints before you demote the slide heading they're under. Also, note that corresponding graphics are not preserved or moved when you delete a slide.

1   Switch to Outline view.

2   Choose to show all text within the presentation, or only level 1 (slide headings), using the icons on the toolbar.

3   Select the slide heading or subpoint you want to change.

4   Click the Promote or Demote icon until the item is at the desired level.

    If you're demoting a slide heading to a subpoint, click Yes to delete the slide and its contents.

Expanding: Creating a Slide for Each Subpoint

You can generate new slides based on the topics, or *subpoints*, in an existing one. This is useful if you find you're trying to cover too much in one slide. For instance, you might have a slide titled "Tourist Destinations of North Dakota" with five bulleted subpoints, then realize that this is far too big a topic to cover in one slide. Expanding the Tourist Destinations slide would delete it and create five new slides, one for each subpoint.

When you expand a slide, the expanded slide is deleted, and one new slide is created for every paragraph you've applied Outline 1 style to. Outline 1 is a presentation style, listed in the Stylist (Format > Stylist) and defined in the Style Catalog (Format > Styles > Catalog). The slides must contain two or more Outline 1 elements to activate the Expand option.

If you want to keep the main slide and expand it into multiple slides, duplicate it first. Also, note that graphics in the expanded slide are not preserved or moved with the subpoints.

1   Move to Drawing view, Outline view, or Slide view.

2   Select the slide to expand.

3   Duplicate it, if you don't want to delete it.

4   Click Expand Slide.

5   Click Yes to delete the expanded slide, when prompted.

The new slides will appear after (to the right of) where the expanded slide was.

Showing and Hiding Slides

You can temporarily hide a slide, without deleting it.

Note – If you often need to hide and show slides to customize presentations for different audiences, refer to *Creating Custom Presentations* on page 725.

---

1   Move to Slide view.

2   Right-click the slide and choose Show/Hide Slide.

    You also can click the Show/Hide icon on the object bar.

3   A hidden slide is indicated by a shadow behind its name
    (Figure 26-8).

Figure 26-8   Hidden slide

Showing and Hiding Subpoints

You can hide all bulleted items, or subpoints, at or below a particular level, using outline view. The subpoints will always be printed; there's no way to control printing hidden subpoints.

1   Click the Outline icon to go to outline view, or choose View > Master View > Outline View. Outline view is shown in Figure 26-9 on page 685.

2   To hide all subpoints, click the First Level icon on the left side of the window.

3   To hide specified levels of subpoints, put your cursor at the lowest hierarchical level you want **displayed**. Click the Hide Subpoints icon. There must be bullet points below the selected level, or the Hide Subpoints icon won't be active.

Creating a Summary Slide

A summary slide functions as a table of contents of your slide titles. It's inserted at the end of your presentation.

You can't update a summary slide if you rearrange slides; you can only delete the existing one and create a new one.

1   Move to Drawing view.

2   Select the tab of the first slide in your presentation that you want included in the summary slide.

3   Choose Insert > Summary Slide.

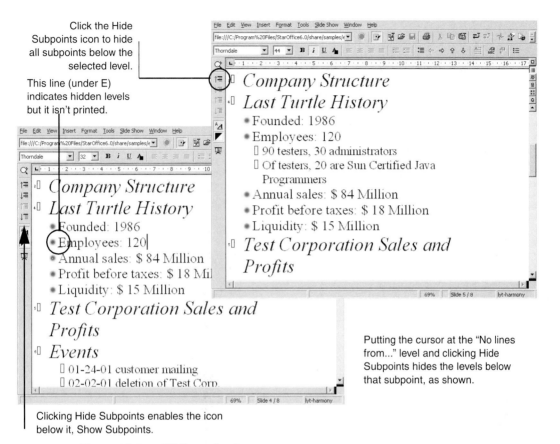

Click the Hide Subpoints icon to hide all subpoints below the selected level.

This line (under E) indicates hidden levels but it isn't printed.

Putting the cursor at the "No lines from..." level and clicking Hide Subpoints hides the levels below that subpoint, as shown.

Clicking Hide Subpoints enables the icon below it, Show Subpoints.

Figure 26-9   Hiding subpoints

Adding Text

Be sure you're in Drawing view, in the correct view (Slide or Background), and the correct layer, if you're using layers. (You can use text in Handout and Notes views, as well, but not to add to the slide contents.)

You'll need to set text editing options, then add a text frame if necessary, and finally the text itself.

Text Editing Options

To know how the text tools will work, you need to set your text editing options first. Use the text icons in the object bar below the work area to set text options. An option is on when it's dimmed and looks indented.

In our experience working with Impress and Draw, we concluded that it's most convenient to choose only the Double-click Text to Edit option.

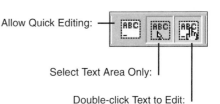

Allow Quick Editing:

Select Text Area Only:

Double-click Text to Edit:

Allow Quick Editing Choose this option if you want to be able to just click in text once and start adding to it or editing it. This option can be a little annoying—it makes it difficult to click on text in order to select the text frame. We recommend that you choose Double-click Text to Edit instead.

Select Text Area Only This option means that you can't click on the text in order to select the whole text frame, and move it, delete it or perform other actions. In order to select the text frame, you need to get into text edit mode first by clicking or double-clicking text. We recommend that you not use it, unless you don't think you'll be frequently selecting text frames.

Double-click Text to Edit This option lets you quickly, but not accidentally, get into text edit mode for any text you double-click. We recommend using this option.

Adding a Standard Preset Text Frame to Your Slide

To add an Impress preset text frame to a blank slide, see *Selecting a Slide Layout for a New or Existing Slide* on page 679. This is the best way to create the structure within which you'll add text.

Using the Text Icons to Create Text Frames

You can create two types of text frames— the area defining where and how text is positioned in your presentation, as well as callout text frames, which include a line extending from the text box to an object.

To activate vertical text, choose Tools > Options > Language Settings > Languages. Under Asian Languages, select Enabled.

Use the tools available from the Text icon in the toolbar at the left side of the work area to create text.

Text Text frame size and text are independent, but you can adapt the text frame to the size of the text.

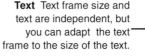

Fit Text to Frame The opposite of the Text icon—text is adapted to fit the height of the text frame. Text does not wrap.

Callouts Creates leader line and box for callout text

You also can double-click any object, such as a rectangle you've drawn, and type inside it.

Don't Make Your Own Text Frames for Presentations

We recommend that, for the main text of your presentations, you choose a slide layout that has a text frame in it already instead of using a blank slide layout and adding your own text frames using the text tool. Using a slide layout with text frames in it is the fastest, easiest, least frustrating way to make a professional-looking presentation, for the following reasons:

- The slide layouts provide a lot of preset formatting that takes a lot of time to re-create on your own.

- Formatting, especially involving tabs, that you add in your own text frames sometimes just up and disappears.

- You can see the text frames of the preset slide layouts when they're not selected and when there's no text in them, which is not possible with the text frames you make with the text icons.

- You can't use the Presentation styles to apply style formatting with text in text-tool frames. You can only use the Character and other formatting windows, which takes longer because you can only apply a few characteristics at a time.

If you don't like the formatting for text in the preset slide layouts, you can change it much more easily than you can the text in your own text frames. See *Creating and Modifying Styles* on page 699.

Horizontal or Vertical Text Icon: Drawing a Text Frame With a Specific Size

This tool is best if you want to control how the text wraps: if you want to write a paragraph that is exactly four inches wide, for instance. Use this tool for most of the text in your presentation.

1   Click the icon.

2   Draw the text frame in the work area.

> **Note –** This is important: if you don't define a width for the text by drawing the text frame and you just start typing, the text won't wrap.

3   Type the text you want.

4   Click the Arrow icon when you're done, or you'll keep accidentally creating more text frames each time you click in the work area.

To set text frame options, see *Setting Text and Text Frame Options* on page 689.

Horizontal or Vertical Fit Text to Size Icon: Sizing the Text to the Frame

This tool is best for short pieces of text, or if you want to quickly but roughly set the size of the text in the frame. The text will be approximately the same height as the frame you draw. (That's **approximately**; the font shrinks somewhat when you deselect the text frame.) In addition, the text won't wrap; it will begin in the center of the text frame and, as you type, extend to the right and left, potentially completely out of the work area. (We generally found this frame annoying.)

1   Click the icon.

2   If you just click in the work area and start typing, the text will have the default font attributes shown in the object bar.

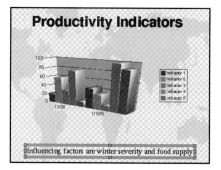

If you draw a text frame, the text will be as large as necessary to fit the text from top to bottom. If you resize the text frame later, the text will be adjusted to fit the new size.

To set text frame options, see *Setting Text and Text Frame Options* on page 689.

Horizontal or Vertical Callouts Icon

This tool draws a line and text frame.

1   Click the icon.

2   Click the mouse where you want the callout line to begin, and drag it to where you want the text to be.

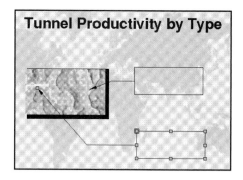

3   Resize the text frame.

4   To enter text, double-click in the frame and start typing.

By default, the text frame will grow as you type; the text won't wrap. To make the text wrap, right-click the text frame and choose Text, then deselect the Fit width to text option in the Text window.

5   Apply line and fill attributes to the callout line and box.

To set additional text frame options, see *Setting Text and Text Frame Options*.

Setting Text and Text Frame Options

Use these options for text in any text frame, including the ones provided in slide layouts, and the text frames. The options also apply to objects you've typed text in by double-clicking in the object.

1 Switch to Drawing view.

2 Select a text frame or object.

3 Choose Format > Text to display the Text window (Figure 26-10). If Text is dimmed, right-click the frame and choose Text.

4 Make the appropriate changes to the text frame or object.

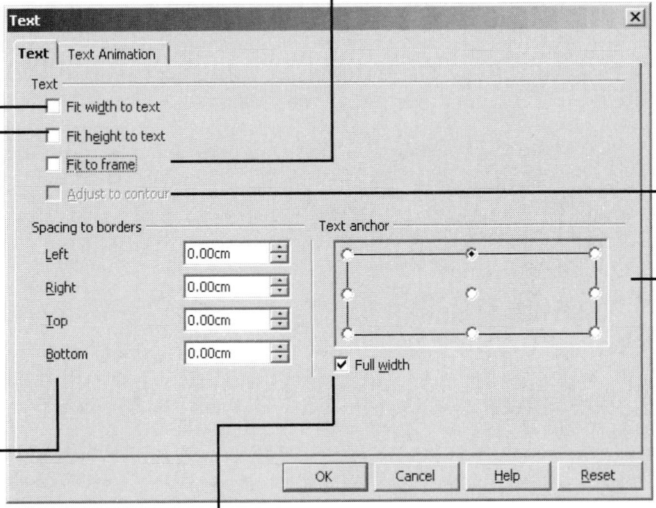
Shrinks or expands the right and left borders of the text frame to fit the widest line of text in the text frame. The frame will continue to adapt as you change text width; text will never wrap.
Shrinks or expands the upper and lower borders of the text frame to fit the largest (highest) text currently in the text frame. The frame will continue to adapt as you change text size.
Enter the distance you want the text from each edge of the text frame. Use negative values if you want the text to go outside the text frame.
This option switches the text frame behavior between that of one drawn with the Text icon, and one drawn using Fit Text to Frame.
This option relates to text that's contoured with FontWork. Selecting the option makes the text disappear, leaving only a contoured line.
Text
Text
Text Animation
Text
Fit width to text
Fit height to text
Fit to frame
Adjust to contour
Spacing to borders
Left
0.00cm
Right
0.00cm
Top
0.00cm
Bottom
0.00cm
Text anchor
Full width
OK
Cancel
Help
Reset
Select this option to display text over the entire width of the draw object. The text will be scaled to fill the whole width; the text height will also adjust proportionally to the modified width.
Indicate where in the frame the text should be anchored. The location selected in the window shown means the first text you typed will be centered, at the top of the frame.

Figure 26-10 Options controlling text in objects and in text frames

Adding Your Text Content to a Presentation

The most important part, of course, is getting what you want to say into the slide. Again, Impress offers a variety of ways to do this.

Typing

Click or double-click in the text frame, depending on the setup options you chose, and add your presentation's contents.

Inserting a File

See *Inserting Text and HTML Files* on page 702.

Pasting

Don't overlook simply pasting in text from other documents. Unless it's from another presentation file, pasting in generally works better than importing or inserting a file. Position the cursor in the text frame before pasting. If you don't position the cursor in a text frame before pasting, a new Text icon type text frame is created for the pasted text.

Writing Text Inside an Object

Double-click in the document and start typing. The text will expand out of the box, so keep an eye on font size. Or right-click and choose Text, then select Fit to Frame to make the text size and width match the size of the object.

Moving the box around once it's got text inside can be a little tricky; the program thinks it's text and just wants to sit there happily typing away. Just move the mouse until the text pointer turns to a crosshairs, as shown at right, and you'll be able to move it around easily.

Getting Into Text Editing Mode

Even with the correct options selected, getting into text editing mode in Impress can be a little tricky. We've found a couple tricks that help:

*   Be sure your text editing options are set up correctly (see page 685).
*   Click in another text frame, such as the title frame, then click back in the subpoint frame.
*   Be sure to click in an area of the text frame where there's text.
*   Just keep clicking in it—you'll get in eventually (not a clever workaround, but one we found did work consistently, if slowly).

To format your text, refer to *Formatting Text* on page 691. That section contains a few key tips that will keep your frustration level down.

Formatting Text

You have the combined capabilities of Draw, Writer, and a few extras that are only in Impress.

Note – Some features, like the features in *Applying Standard Text Formatting* on page 694, need to be applied to the text itself; others, like the formatting covered in *Setting Text and Text Frame Options* on page 689, need to be applied to the text frame. Be sure to select the appropriate item before you start formatting.

It's a good idea to have the Preview window (choose View > Preview; see figure at right) displayed when you're doing any slide editing. It's particularly useful for seeing effects and animation, which you can't see in a static slide.

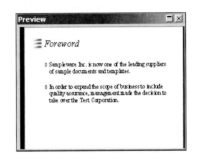

Using the Right Slide Layout

While you can choose a completely unformatted layout for a slide, then use the Text tool to create a text frame for it, that's the hard way. A lot of automatic formatting that will make your life easier is included in the preset layouts (see *Selecting a Slide Layout for a New or Existing Slide* on page 679). If you don't like how the Outline 1 and other styles look, you can change them using procedures in this section.

Using Columns

You can divide your slide into two or more columns using the Modify Layout window described in *Selecting a Slide Layout for a New or Existing Slide*, or by simply manually resizing and copying the text frames.

1   Select the text frame and shrink it to slightly less than half the width of the text area. (For more columns, make the text frame smaller.)

2   Apply any formatting to it; styles, character formats, etc.

3   Copy it and paste it.

4   Position it to the right of the original.

5   Align the text frames using the Alignment tearoff menu, or select the text frames, right-click them, and choose an alignment option. (See *Aligning Objects* on page 775.)

Using the Object Bar for General Formatting

The object bar for text (choose View > Toolbars > Object Bar; see Figure 26-11) lets you quickly apply features like bullets, alignment, and basic text formatting. Tool tips describe each function; most are also available in the other text-related window.

Bold, italicized, underlined, or colored font

Increase or decrease spacing

Indent further, or indent less

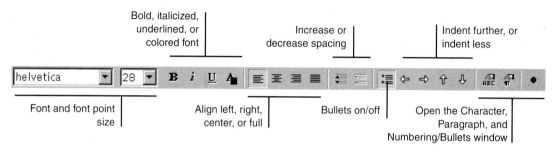

Font and font point size

Align left, right, center, or full

Bullets on/off

Open the Character, Paragraph, and Numbering/Bullets window

Figure 26-11   Quick formatting using the object bar for text

The default text values for any text that you enter is shown in the object bar. To change these values, first be sure no text is selected in the work area. Then choose Format > Character and make the appropriate selections.

Working With Spacing and Indents

Impress has good automatic-indenting features; you can use several approaches, including just pressing Tab or using the indent/promote icons.

Text Frame Adjustments

Resize or move the text frame so the farthest-left text starts where you want it.

Justifying Text

Use the alignment icons to left-justify, center, right-justify, or fully justify your text.

Indenting Text to Make Subbullets

You can press the Tab key to indent text, or use the Promote and Demote icons on the object bar. These are the most convenient methods for quickly indenting or "outdenting" any text. When you press Tab or use the Promote and Demote icons, the styles are automatically changed (one demotion changes Outline1 to Outline2, and so on). See Figure 26-12.

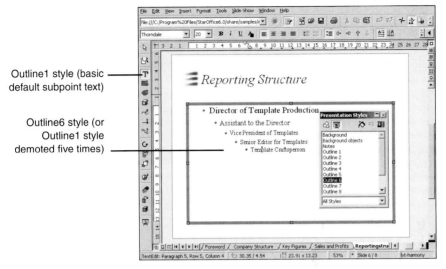

Outline1 style (basic default subpoint text)

Outline6 style (or Outline1 style demoted five times)

Figure 26-12   Indenting subpoints

The Paragraph Window

This window (choose Format > Paragraph; see Figure 26-13) lets you set up spacing, indents, and tabs. Use this window in Drawing, Handout, or Notes view. See *Using the Paragraph Format Window* on page 208 for more information.

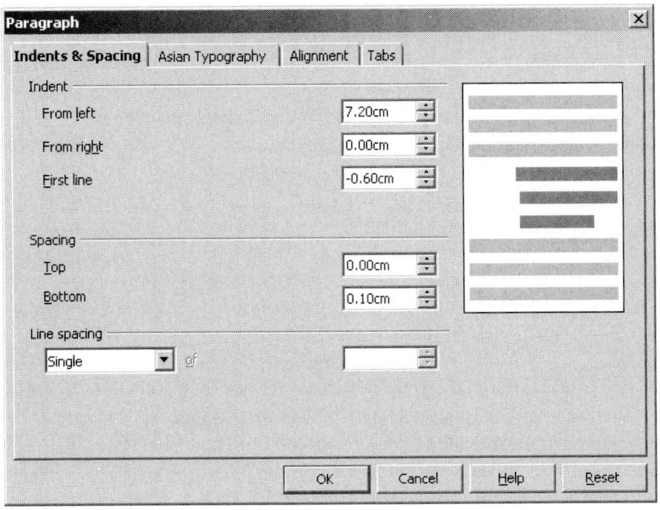

Figure 26-13   Options controlling indent, alignment and tabs

Applying Standard Text Formatting

The Character window (choose Format > Character; see Figure 26-14) lets you apply standard text formatting attributes like font and point size. Use this window in Drawing, Handout, or Notes view. See *Using the Character Formatting Window* on page 200 for more information.

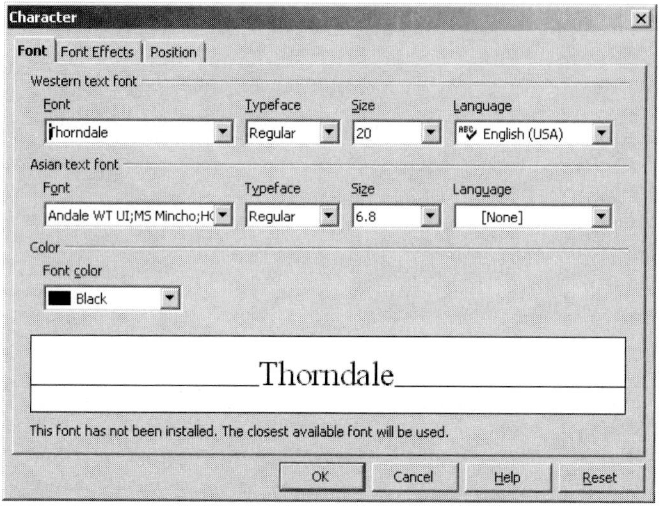

Figure 26-14   Options controlling text formatting

Using Numbering and Bullets

You can quickly control these features on the object bar, or use the numbering and bullets formatting window.

Note – If you've got a dark background, be sure that your bullets are light-colored, or they'll be difficult or impossible to see. Choose Format > Number/Bullets and click the Customize tab to select light-colored bullet graphics from the gallery, or from a file you've created yourself.

Turning Numbering and Bullets On and Off

You can turn this feature on or off for the text that's currently selected using the Bullets on/off icon in the object bar.

If that doesn't work, you'll need to change the slide design to one that contains bullets, to add them, or doesn't contain bullets, to turn them off. Choose Format > Modify Layout and select a layout with the right contents. (For more information, see *Selecting a Slide Layout for a New or Existing Slide* on page 679.)

Full Formatting Capabilities

The Numbering/Bullets window lets you choose what symbols or numbers appear next to paragraphs, and where they're positioned. Bullets and numbering are paragraph-specific; that is, each line in a list can have a different bullet or number style.

Use this window (Figure 26-15) in Drawing, Handout, Outline, or Notes view. Refer to *Using Basic Numbering, Bullets, and Outlining* on page 215 for more information.

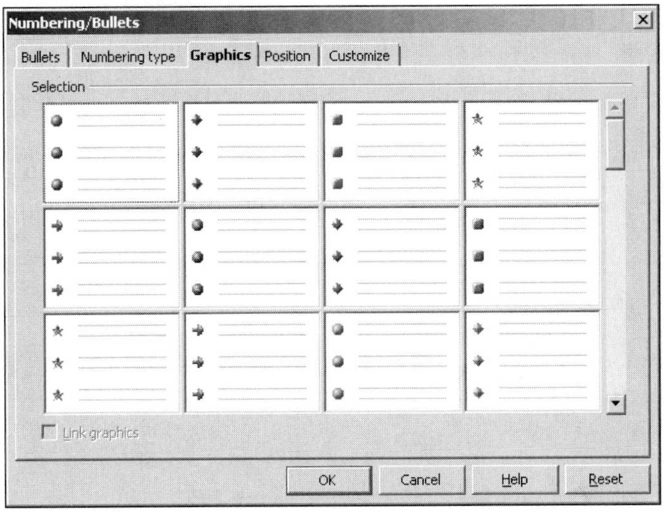

Figure 26-15   Options controlling bullet and numbering type and spacing

Using Styles

Most of your presentations will contain formatting that's already automatically applied through the slide layout or AutoPilot features, and each piece of text has a specific style assigned to it.

Impress is very rigid about what styles it wants in a slide. You can't create new text-formatting styles, or add new styles through the Stylist. The only way you can make other styles available to a slide is to change the slide layout, or to modify existing styles.

Text Effects

As in Draw, you can play with the text to create interesting effects. See the information in Draw, in *Making Exact and Modified Copies* on page 815, *Distorting and Curving Text and Objects With the Effects Tools* on page 817, and *Distorting and Curving Text Using FontWork* on page 818. FontWork (at right) is an add-on program for special font effects.

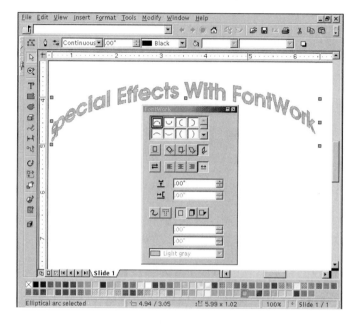

Creating Organizational Charts

One of the most dynamic and exciting things you'll be asked to add to a presentation is the new org chart. See Figure 26-16 for an example of a small one created in Impress.

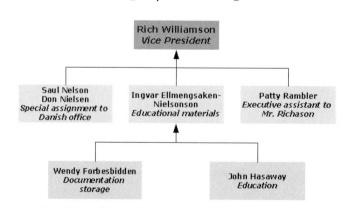

Figure 26-16 Example organizational chart

There's nothing particularly complicated about doing it, but here are some tips to make it easier.

The lines to connect names Use the connector tools. These tools keep their ends attached to whatever boxes you attached them to in the first place. So if by some wild chance there's a reorg in your division, and Patty from Figure 26-16 was going to get promoted to division head, all you'd have to do is move her box around and change her arrow so she's now in charge of the whole group and reports to the CEO. See Figure 26-17.

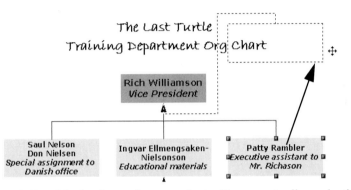

Figure 26-17   Moving boxes from org chart with connector lines adapting to move

Click on the main toolbar at the left as shown to find the connector tools. See *Drawing a Connector* on page 796.

Easily combining names and boxes Type inside boxes. Just double-click inside the rectangle or anything else you've drawn and start typing. Right-click on the border of the box and choose Text, and mark Fit to Frame, to make the text stay inside the box. See *Writing Text Inside an Object* on page 690.

Using just names, without boxes If you want a plain org chart that doesn't have boxes around the names, you can still use the connector lines. Just connect the connector lines to the text frame instead of a box. Right-click the frame and choose Text, then enter the separation you want between the text frame and the text itself, so you can keep the connector line from being right up against the side of the text. See Figure 26-18.

Connect the line to a point on the text frame	Line connects to text frame, next to text contents	Text frame has 1-cm border on left side so connector line is farther from text

Figure 26-18   Connecting connector line to text frame and adding margin between text frame and text contents

Fancier effects for the boxes names appear in Want fancy effects for the top brass? Use a shadow for his or her box. Get fancier with shadows, transparency (to show the power behind the thrown) and other fills by choosing Format > Area.

Make 3D objects, then type in them, using the 3D tools. Apply effects by right-clicking in the shape and choosing Effects.

Positioning the names and boxes To align and distribute the names in the org chart, select three or more objects to distribute, or select two or more objects to align, and right-click to select Align or Distribute. See *Aligning Objects* on page 775 and *Distributing Objects Evenly* on page 775. For more specific positioning, see *Positioning Objects* on page 776.

Actually, everything in the main heading *Positioning and Resizing Objects* on page 774, *Rotating and Flipping Objects* on page 782, and *Setting Drawing Scale and Unit of Measurement* on page 785 is going to be useful.

Modifying Presentation Default Fonts

You can use Background view to easily change text elements that appear throughout your presentation, like the font and font size of the heading in each slide, in Drawing and Notes master views. (You also can use styles to modify defaults; see *Using Text and Object Styles* on page 699.) See Figure 26-19.

1   Choose View > Background, then select Drawing, Notes, or Handout (or switch to Drawing, Notes, or Handout master view, then click the Background view icon).

2   Placeholder text for the styles used in the presentation will appear. Make the changes you want, then switch out of Background view to add content to your presentation.

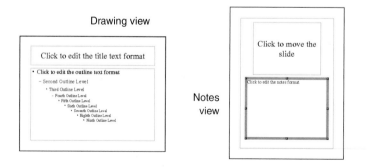

Figure 26-19   Changing default fonts for Drawing and Notes master views

Using Text and Object Styles

Styles let you save a particular set of attributes, such as font, spacing, and bullets; and, for drawing objects, area fill, color, line ends (round, arrow), and so on. It's a good idea to use styles if you need to use an object frequently that's formatted in a particular way, such as a line with an arrow that you've defined yourself, or text formatting for headings.

There are two types of styles in Impress: presentation styles, for text, and graphics styles, for objects.

For an extended explanation of how to import styles, and the ways you can save time using styles, refer to *Power Formatting With Styles* on page 241.

Modifying the default formats for headings and other elements is covered in *Modifying Presentation Default Fonts* on page 698.

Available Styles

The styles available for use, and to be modified, depend upon the slide layout. This is determined by one of the following:

- The layout you selected in the Modify Slide window (choose Format > Modify Layout)
- The template or background you based the presentation on

Applying Styles

Select the object or text, then use either of the following methods to apply the style.

- Display the Stylist (choose Format > Stylist), select the style category you want, and double-click the style.
- Choose Formats > Style > Catalog, select the style category you want, and double-click the style.

Creating and Modifying Styles

Note – For more information, see *Power Formatting With Styles* on page 241. This is in a Writer chapter; however, the principles are the same throughout the program. It tells you not only how to make the styles but to get a style from one document or template to another.

Impress doesn't allow you to create new *presentation* styles, but you can modify the numerous existing ones. You can create new *graphics* styles, or to modify either type of style.

1   Choose Format > Styles > Catalog.

2   Select Presentation Styles and click Modify or select Graphics Styles and click New or Modify.

Presentation styles are primarily for things like bullets and numbering, and you can see the corresponding feature coverage in Impress or Writer chapters.

Graphics styles are for things like fills, line styles, etc., and you can see the correspondent feature coverage in Draw and Impress chapters.

3   Make the settings you want and click OK to save the changes and close the window.

4   Apply the styles using the Stylist. Choose Format > Stylist. Select the item or text to apply the style to, then select Graphics or Presentation styles and double-click the style in the window.

Use Figure 26-20 for guidance.

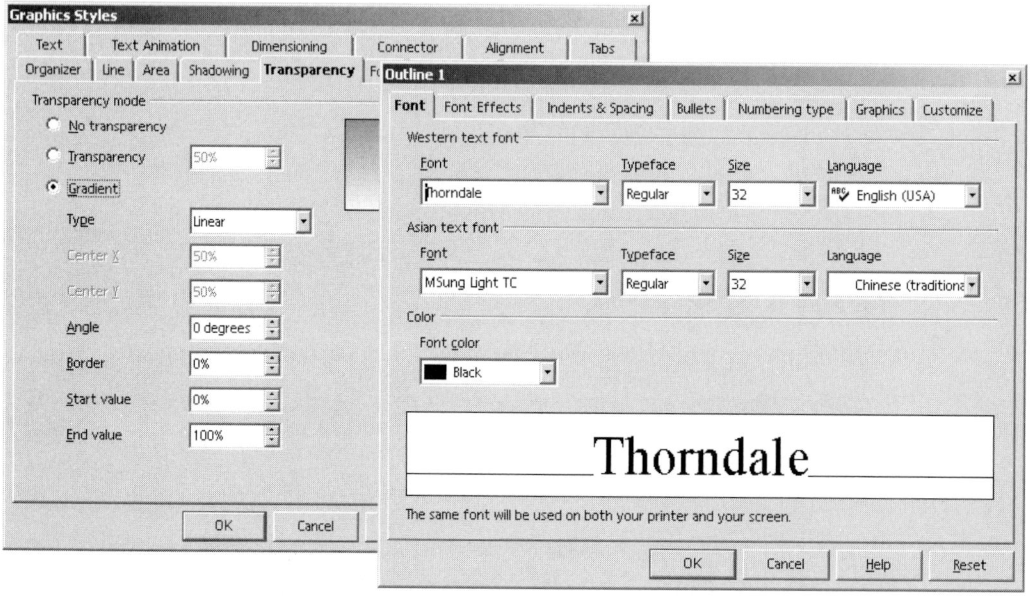

Figure 26-20   The style windows for creating graphics and presentation styles

Making Styles Reusable in Other Documents

Unless you jump through a couple hoops, any styles you create or modify will be available only in the document where you made them. To make them available in other documents:

- Create the styles in a document that you then save as an Impress template.

- Then base new documents on that template by choosing File > New > From template.

You can also import styles from other documents following the instructions in *Loading Individual Styles* on page 259.

Changing the Font Styles for All New Presentations

You can change the styles for a particular presentation, but if you want all new presentations to have a particular set of styles, you need to create a template. (See *Creating and Modifying Templates* on page 654.) Then base new presentations on that template. (See *Basing a Presentation on a Template or Background (Without Using AutoPilot)* on page 645 and *Using AutoPilot to Create a Presentation* on page 641). To affect other StarImpress documents, you need to modify the template.

Adding Charts, Pictures, and Objects

The Insert icon lets you access a variety of features. There isn't much that you can't include in a slide. Most of these capabilities are documented in other parts of this book; references are included on this page.

Figure 26-21 shows the Insert tearoff menu.

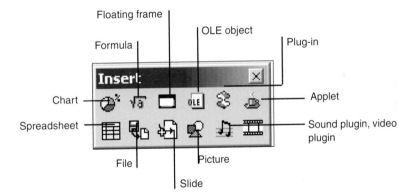

Figure 26-21   Items you can add to presentations

Inserting Other Objects and Files

These features are covered in *Adding Objects and Links to Documents* on page 265.

You can insert pretty much any kind of file, whether Impress or other types, in any document.

The most flexible way to insert files is to use the OLE object icon in Figure 26-21 or to choose Insert > Object > OLE Object. ("OLE object" is an unnecessarily techy way of putting it—OLE is the technology that lets you edit the file once you've inserted it in another file. For example, you can insert an "OLE object," a Draw file, in a Writer file, and edit the drawing right in Writer.

Think Hard Before Linking to Inserted Objects

When you insert an object, you'll frequently be prompted to choose whether to just link to where the object currently is, or not. ("Not" is to embed the object in the file, increasing the file size). An example is shown in Figure 26-23).

Select Link if you want to insert only a link to the file, which is automatically updated if changes are made to the original file. It also helps reduce presentation file size. (Changing the location of the inserted file will break the link.)

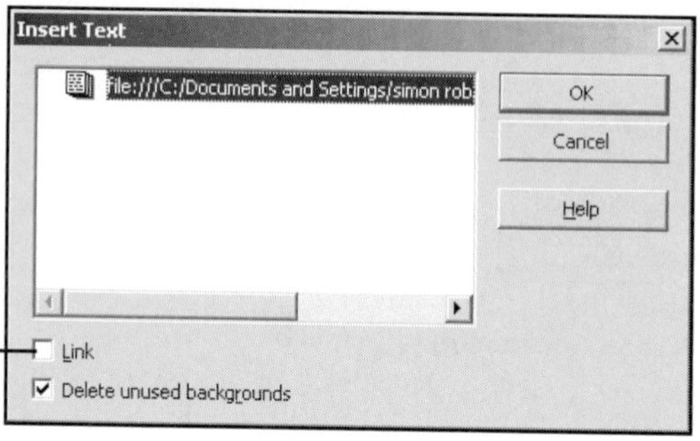

Figure 26-22   Inserting an ASCII or HTML text file

We strongly recommend that you *not* link inserted objects if there's ever a possibility you'll pass the file around as is, without printing to PDF. Just insert it and take the hit of the increased file size. While it reduces file size, it will cause Armageddon-like chaos if you pass the file around to other people in your organization. You'll forget at least once to include a ZIP or JAR of the images or objects, the people receiving them will forget at least once to do one small thing to get the images in the right location, etc.

Inserting Applets and Plug-ins

These features are covered in *Adding Applets and Plugins* on page 489.

Inserting Text and HTML Files

You can insert HTML and text (ASCII, not Writer) files into the current slide. The contents are inserted in a Text icon text frame; if your slide layout contains a preset text frame, it will be ignored and a Text icon text frame will appear over it, with the contents of the imported file.

Formatting for HTML files is retained as are URLs, which remain functional. Importing an HTML file containing URLs can be a very useful technique in some presentations.

When you click a link while you're editing a presentation, the Impress file closes and Web opens the file the URL linked to.

For text files, you might want to paste the contents into a preset Impress text frame, instead of importing.

1   Click the Insert icon on the toolbar at the left of the work area, and display the Insert tearoff menu. Click the Insert File icon on that menu.

2   Select the file you want.

3   The file will be listed in the Insert Text window (Figure 26-23). Select Link if appropriate, then click OK.

Select Link if you want to insert only a link to the file, which is automatically updated if changes are made to the original file. It also helps reduce presentation file size. (Changing the location of the inserted file will break the link.)

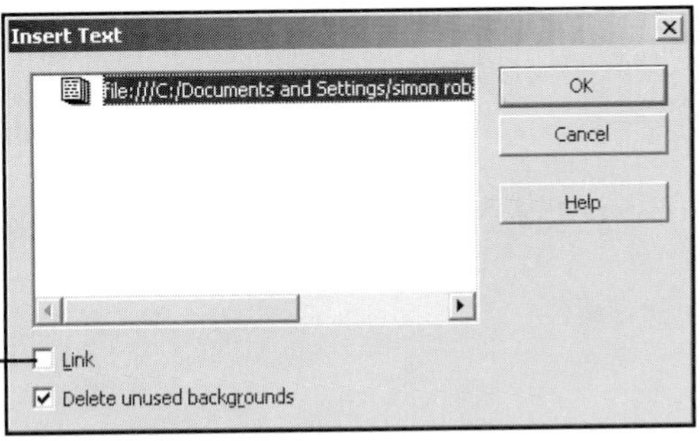

Figure 26-23   Inserting an ASCII or HTML text file

Note – If you select Link and the file is on a Web page or other location you don't own, you could be left hanging during a presentation if the Web server goes down, or the file becomes otherwise unavailable. See *Think Hard Before Linking to Inserted Objects* on page 702.

Inserting Pictures (Images and Drawings)

You can add empty graphics frames or existing graphics files.

Inserting an Existing Graphics File

You can insert any raster file, such as a GIF or JPG, into the current slide.

1   Click the Insert icon on the toolbar and display the Insert tearoff menu, then click the Graphics icon.

You also can choose Insert > Graphics.

2   Select the file you want, then click Open.

Inserting a Drawing Into the Current Slide

To add a new drawing or existing drawing to the slide, use the Insert OLE object feature.

Note – To insert a drawing as a new separate slide, see *Inserting Existing Slides from Impress or Draw* on page 680.

1 Move to Drawing view.

2 Choose Insert > Object > OLE object.

3 In the Insert OLE Object window, select Create new or Create from file (Figure 26-24).

   • If you select Create new, select a file type and click OK. A new empty Draw frame will appear in the slide.

   • If you select Create from file, click Search and select the file, then click OK.

The contents of this file will be inserted in the current slide. (If you insert a draw file with multiple slides, only the first slide will be inserted.)

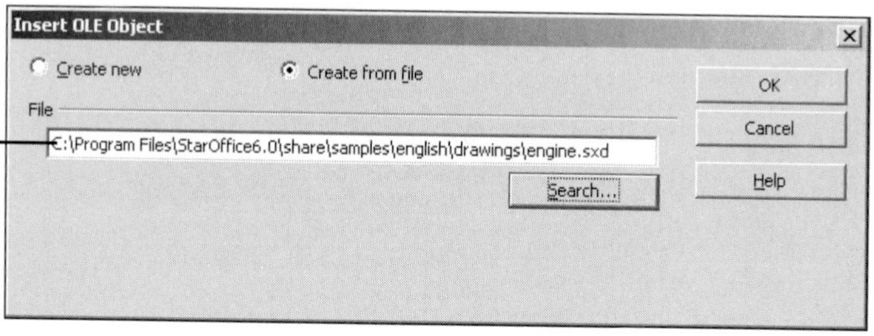

Figure 26-24   Inserting a Draw graphic in the current slide

Inserting Spreadsheets and Other Objects on page 483 illustrates inserting an OLE spreadsheet.

Inserting Page, Date, Time, and Filename Fields

Choose Insert > Field to add a page, date, time, or filename field. Add the field in Slide view if you want it on only one slide, or in Background view if you want it on all slides.

If you're going to be creating handouts with several slides on each page, you can add page numbers to each handout page. See *Creating Slide Handouts* on page 729.

Inserting Buttons, and Other Controls

Figure 26-25 shows form options.

Fields and buttons such as drop-down lists and radio buttons

Controls such as buttons you can attach images and events to

Fields for specific types of information like time, date, and currency

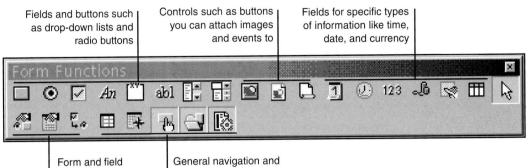

Form and field properties controls

General navigation and mode controls

Figure 26-25   Forms and form components

The Form Functions bar lets you insert buttons, drop-down lists, etc., and attach them to data or events. For example, you could create a button that would open a particular file whenever you clicked on it.

It's beyond the scope of this book to cover them in detail, but some aspects of these features are covered in Chapter 36, *Creating and Using Forms, Controls, and Events*, on page 925.

Presentation Backgrounds

This section covers how to create and modify what's behind the content of your presentation: the colors, logos, or other elements that are repeated on each page.

Before you begin working with backgrounds, be sure that none of the placeholder options in the Presentation Options window are selected. (Choose Tools > Options > Presentation > Contents.)

Creating your own background templates is covered in *Creating and Modifying Templates* on page 654.

Modifying the default formats for headings and other elements is covered in *Modifying Presentation Default Fonts* on page 698.

Note – Graphics in backgrounds generally don't work well when transferred to HTML. Even light-colored ones are sometimes converted to a much darker color. If you need to have an HTML version of the presentation created using the Export to HTML feature, don't use a background with any graphics.

Understanding Backgrounds

Backgrounds are relatively simple, but some of the terminology and the interface raised a couple of issues we wanted to clarify.

Terminology

Impress refers to the background elements of your presentation using many terms: the page layout, presentation layout, slide design, slide layout, and so on. We use *background* for consistency and clarity.

Number of Backgrounds Allowed

When you create a new presentation using AutoPilot, the "page layout," which is the background that you selected, applies to the entire presentation. When you make changes to the presentation in Background view, those changes apply to the whole presentation, as well. However, the Slide Design option in the Presentation menu lets you change backgrounds on a slide-by-slide basis.

Backgrounds and Orientation

Before you begin, be sure the current orientation of your slides is appropriate for the background graphic (if there is a graphic in the background you'll be using). The graphic will be automatically reproportioned to fit the slide orientation, so if you're using portrait orientation and load a landscape-oriented background like World, the world map that appears in the background will be "squished" and lengthened to fit the portrait orientation. You can go into background view and reshape the graphic, but it's still kind of a pain. Likewise, make sure any backgrounds you create are proportioned correctly for portrait orientation, since that's the most common for slide presentations.

Background Images and File Size

If you use raster images as backgrounds (.GIF files and so on, like those you can create in Image), the file sizes of any PostScript files you create will be much larger than if you use vector graphics (like those you can create in Draw).

Backgrounds and Printing Issues

In general, it's a good idea not to use gradient fills, gradient text or complex backgrounds in Star Office presentations as this drastically affects disk space, printing, or download time. You can do a colored background easily that doesn't take much disk space by choosing Format > Page and in the Page tab, selecting a color.

Changing or Adding Backgrounds for a Slide or Presentation

This option lets you select a background from Impress's predefined list, and from any backgrounds you may have created. You can apply the background to one slide, or to the entire presentation.

1   Move to Drawing view or Notes view.

2   Display the Presentation menu. (Choose View > Toolbars > Presentation, or click the Presentation Box On/Off icon on the right side of the object bar.)

3   Select the slide you want to change the background for.

4   Click Slide Design to display the Slide Design window.

5   If the design you want isn't displayed in the Slide Design window, click Load to display the Load Slide Design window (Figure 26-26).

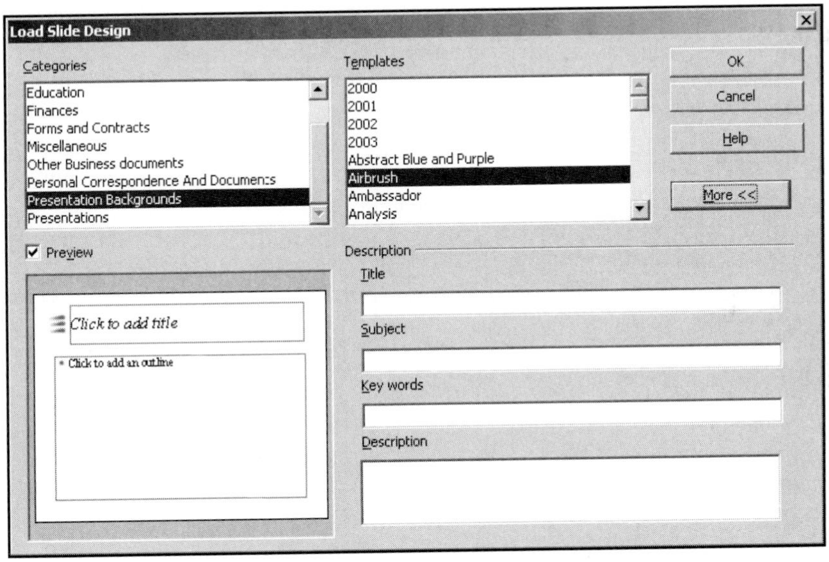

Figure 26-26   Selecting a new background design

6   Select any category that contains a presentation, presentation layout, or presentation template. Presentation Layouts contains backgrounds only.

7   Select a layout and click OK.

8   Select the new background you just loaded.

Note – If you don't select the new background, it won't be saved in the Slide Design window. Impress doesn't allow you to load a new background without applying it.

9   Select the appropriate options in the Slide Design window (Figure 26-27); click OK.

Select the background you want to use.

If this is deselected, the selected background is applied to the current slide; select it to apply the new design to the whole presentation.

Selecting this removes any backgrounds from the above list that are unused, or will be unused based on your other selections in this window.

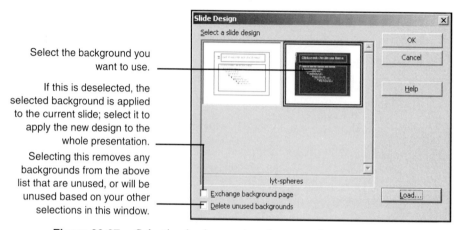

Figure 26-27   Selecting background exchange options

Note – If you select both options, all backgrounds but the selected one will be removed from this window and from your presentation.

Adding a Color, Bitmap, Hatch, or Gradient to a Background

Note – To use one of these items to fill text, see *Formatting Text With Bitmaps, Gradients, and Hatches* on page 773.

Before you begin, be sure that none of the placeholder options in the Presentation Options window are selected. (Choose Tools > Options > Presentation > View.)

If you've already got a background Any changes you make using this method are incorporated into the current background. You can rearrange the current elements of the background so that they're in front of or behind what you've added. (Right-click the element and choose Arrange and the option you want.)

Replacing the current background with another background All changes you make using these steps become part of the background you make them in. If you choose another background according to *Changing or Adding Backgrounds for a Slide or Presentation* on page 707, all your changes will be overridden. They won't be incorporated into the new background.

Caution Backgrounds are all made differently, some with actual graphics and some using the very gradient, color, hatch, and bitmap features you're modifying. If you're not careful to note how the background is made, you may get results you don't want, and will be unable to change it back. Luckily, the changes are applied only to the presentation and not to the background template itself. If you get results you don't want, you can reload the background. Apply a different background to the affected slides, then reapply the original background you were modifying. (See *Changing or Adding Backgrounds for a Slide or Presentation* on page 707.)

In addition, crosshatches and gradients can reduce readability. Plain colors (choose Format > Page and click the Page tab, then select a color) and simple graphics with **small** storage sizes are the best backgrounds.

Follow these steps to add to the background.

1   Switch to Drawing view.

2   Either switch to Background view and select the background you want to modify, or in Slide view, select a slide with the background you want to modify.

3   Save the presentation. The Undo function works inconsistently with page formatting.

4   If you're using more than one background, click the tab of the background you want to modify.

5   Choose Format > Page.

6   Click the Background tab (Figure 26-28).

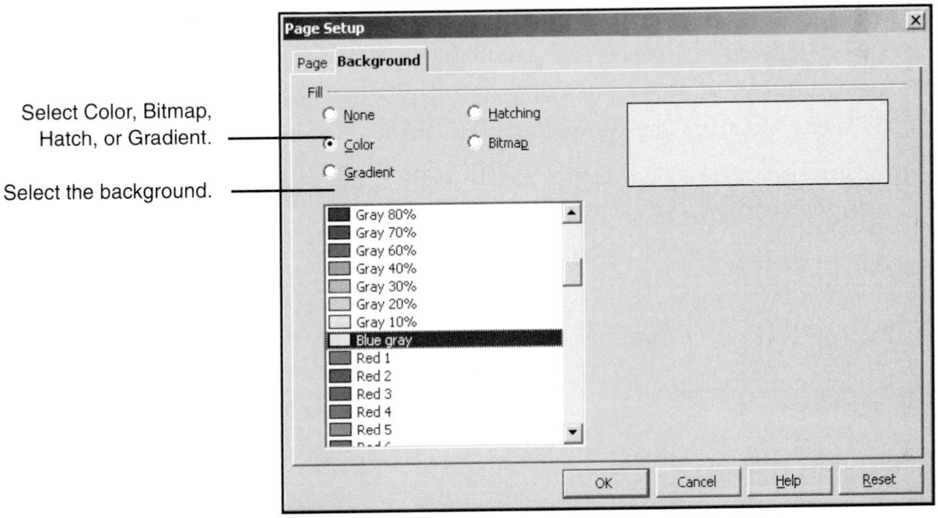

Figure 26-28   Selecting options for a background

7   Select options you want.

For more information on bitmaps, hatches, and gradients, refer to *Applying Attributes Using the Area Window* on page 764, and *Creating and Categorizing Fills and Lines* on page 793.

Adding Objects and Text

If you want to draw, type, or paste things into the background, just switch to Background view and add the elements you want.

Any changes you make using this method are incorporated into the current background, if you have one.

Arranging Objects in a Background

Some objects may appear in front of objects you want seen, or vice versa. Switch to Background view (choose View > Background > Drawing). Right-click on an object and choose Arrange and the option you want. This option is available for all objects, in backgrounds or slide foregrounds. See *Bringing Objects to Front or Back (Arranging)* on page 778.

Creating and Modifying Background Templates

See *Background Templates* on page 655.

Applying a Blank Background

You can make the background blank two different ways: by simply deleting all elements of the background, or by applying a white color to the page.

You can print a dark background as white (and light text in black) by selecting the Black and White option or Grayscale in the Print window (Figure 28-16 on page 746).

You can also create a blank background to apply when you need it. See *Creating a Background Template* on page 656.

You can always apply the background again, by clicking the Slide Design option in the Presentation menu.

To delete background elements:

1   Switch to Background view.

2   If there are two or more backgrounds, select the tab of the one to delete.

3   Delete all components of the background.

4   If color is still displayed, choose Format > Page and click the Background tab. Select the Invisible option.

To temporarily remove a background (this works for most backgrounds, though not all):

1   You can be in either Background or Slide view.

2   Choose Format > Page and click the Background tab.

3   Select Color and select White or another neutral color.

4   If background elements still show, switch to Background view. Select them all and move them to the back. (Right-click and choose Arrange > Send to Back.)

Headers and Footers

Headers and footers, where you can put information like date, time, title, and so on, aren't included in any of the preset slide designs. However, you can add them relatively easily.

Adding a Header or Footer to a Current Document

1   Go to Background view. Click the Layer icon to display the name or names of the background or backgrounds in the presentation.

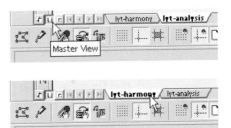

   - To put the header or footer in **only one of your backgrounds**, stop now. Click on the name of the background that you want to add the header or footer to; in the illustration at right, the **lyt-harmony** background is selected so all headers and footers you add now will show up only in slides where that background is used.

   - To put the header or footer **everywhere in your presentation**, period, click on the third icon, Layer, so that the tab Background Objects appears as shown at right.

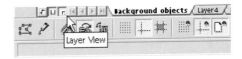

2   Use the Text icon to draw a text box below the slide.

3   Choose Insert > Fields and select the type of information you want to insert, or type additional information.

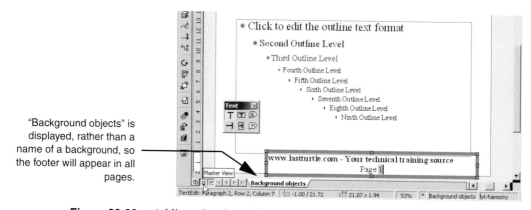

"Background objects" is displayed, rather than a name of a background, so the footer will appear in all pages.

Figure 26-29   Adding a header or footer to a presentation

4   Format the text appropriately.

5   Add any other graphic elements or other text.

6   Switch back to Slide view. Choose Format > Page and click the Page tab. Make sure that any margins you've set don't cut off the header or footer text.

Adding a Header or Footer to a Template

You can include a header or footer by default by repeating the previous procedure on a template, then using that template for future presentations.

Adding a Header or Footer to Handouts

Follow the instructions in *Adding Notes and Creating Handouts* on page 728 to use Impress's Handouts master view. You can add headers and footers there using a text box, as well.

Advanced Presentation Tools

Adding Movement, Sound, and Special Effects to Objects and Text in Slides

Impress has a wide variety of object and text effects you can apply to individual elements of your presentation. This include standard effects, such as moving each line of text in from the left when the slide is shown, and unusual effects such as moving an object along a specific line. The effects are run starting when the slide is displayed.

This procedure covers general use of the Effects window; subsequent procedures cover more specialized uses, and combining the effects with other features.

Note – You can create impressive effects by combining Draw's 3D graphics and Impress's special effects. See *Working With Text* on page 770.

Note – To allow effects to run while you're editing a presentation (not running the presentation), use the Allow Effects icon on the Option bar below the work area. To show the Option bar, choose View > Toolbars > Option Bar.

1   Switch to Drawing view and click the Effects icon on the toolbar. (If you can't find the Effects icon, your window is too small. Lengthen it, or look for the tiny black right-pointing arrow at the bottom of the toolbar and click it; the rest of the toolbar will be displayed.)

2   Choose View > Preview; the Preview window demonstrates each effect you'll select.

3   In the slide, select the object or text in the slide you want to apply the effects to. (If you don't select an object, some icons won't be enabled.)

4   In the Effects window, click the Effects icon (object and text effects) or Text Effects icon.

5   Make the appropriate object or text effect selections; see Figure 27-1 on page 715.

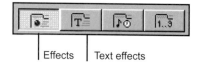

Effects | Text effects

6   Click the green arrow in the upper right corner to apply the effect; it will be run in the Preview window. Make any necessary changes.

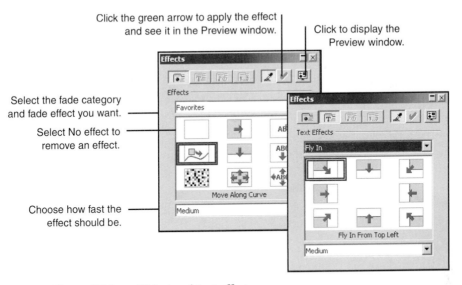

Click the green arrow to apply the effect
and see it in the Preview window.

Click to display the
Preview window.

Select the fade category
and fade effect you want.

Select No effect to
remove an effect.

Choose how fast the
effect should be.

Figure 27-1   Object and text effects

Note – By default, a sound accompanies each effect. Be sure to have the Preview window showing so you're aware of the sounds. If your computer doesn't have sound, that doesn't mean the computer where you do the presentation won't, so be sure to test before you present. To remove a sound, click the Extras icon at the top of the Effects window, then click the Sound icon to deactivate the displayed sound.

---

7   Click the Extras icon and make the appropriate selections (Figure 27-2 on page 716). These will be applied to the currently selected effect. You must have already applied an effect by clicking the green arrow, for the Extras icon to be active.

8   Click the green arrow in the upper right corner to apply the sound.

If the arrow isn't enabled or sound doesn't run, be sure you've got an object selected, that the Sound icon is selected as shown in Figure 27-2, that the Preview window is displayed, and that your computer's sound volume is turned up high enough.

Select a background color
for the item during the effect.
(This may not be available,
depending on the effect you
chose in the other two
windows.)

Click the green arrow to
apply the effect and see
it in the Preview window.

Click Preview to show
the Preview window,
where effects are shown.

To select a color for the item
to turn at the end of the
effect, be sure Object
Invisible is inactive, and click
Fade Object With Color.
Select a color from the list.

Click the Browse icon to
find a sound, or select
one from the list. The file
formats you can select
are listed in the Open
window.

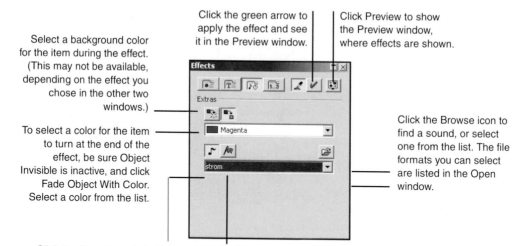

Click the Sound icon to include
audio when the effect runs.

Click the Play in Full icon to hear the entire sound. If you don't select it,
the sound will be played only for the duration of the associated effect.

Figure 27-2   Additional options for a text or object effect

9   Click the Order icon (Figure 27-3). All effects are listed in the order in which they'll
be run. Drag them to a different spot to change the order.

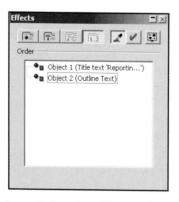

Figure 27-3   Viewing and changing effects order

10   Click the Presentation icon, if you want to run the presentation. Click the
mouse or press the space bar to move from one slide to another; press Escape
to end it.

Making Objects or Text Move Along a Path

You can use the Along a Curve effect in the Effects window to make an object move along any line you draw. Just draw the appropriate path using the Curve tool, and edit it using the Bezier editing tools.

1 Switch to Drawing view.

2 In the slide, draw insert type or paste the item that you want to move and any other objects in the image. For instance, in Figure 27-4 from www.javaranch.com, if you wanted the fly to fly up around the moose and land on his head, you would insert the fly graphic and the moose graphic at the appropriate distances from each other.

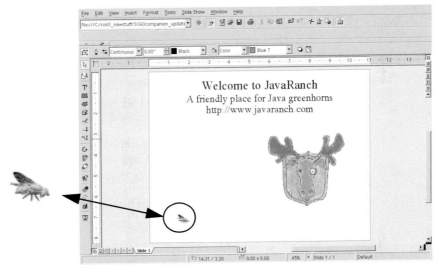

Figure 27-4   Creating the objects in the slide that you want to move

3 Click the Curves icon in the main toolbar at the left and draw the line you want to object to follow.

4 If you need to adjust the line, select it and click the appropriate Bezier curve icons in the upper left portion of the toolbar. The line, being adjusted, is shown in Figure 27-5.

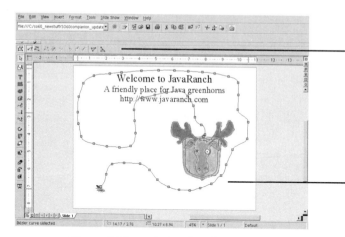

Use the Bezier icons to adjust the line, if necessary. They show up when you select the line. If they don't show up, you probably used the wrong icon to draw the line.

Line was drawn starting at the fly and ending at the top of the moosehead. The fly will follow that line when the effect is completed.

Figure 27-5   Animation for www.javaranch.com

5   Click the Effects icon on the toolbar.

If you can't find the Effects icon, your window is too small. Lengthen it, or look for the tiny black right-pointing arrow at the bottom of the toolbar and click it; the rest of the toolbar will be displayed.

6   Choose View > Preview; the Preview window demonstrates each effect you'll select.

7   Select the object that you want to move, and the line you drew.

8   In the Effects window, click the Effects icon (object and text effects).

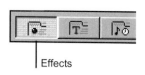

If the object you want moved along the line is text, just click the Effects icon, not Text Effects. Text effects acts on each separate paragraph; Effects acts on whatever you select as one unit, regardless of whether it's text, a curve, polygon, bitmap, etc.

9   Select the Along a Curve effect and the speed; use Figure 27-6 as a reference.

10 Click the green arrow in the upper right corner to apply the effect; it will be run in the Preview window. Make any necessary changes.

11 Click the Extras icon and make the appropriate selections (Figure 27-2). These will be applied to the currently selected effect. For instance, you might want to select a buzzing noise for the javaranch.com example of a fly buzzing up and around the moosehead.

12 Click the green arrow in the upper right corner to apply the sound.

If the arrow isn't enabled or sound doesn't run, be sure you've got an object selected, that the Sound icon is selected as shown in Figure 27-2, that the Preview window is displayed, and that your computer's sound volume is turned up high enough.

Click the green arrow to apply the effect and see it in the Preview window.

Click to display the Preview window.

Select the fade category and fade effect you want.

Select No effect to remove an effect.

Select the Along a Curve effect.

Choose how fast the effect should be.

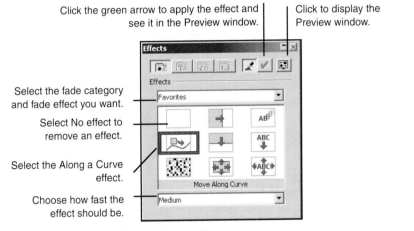

Figure 27-6   Object and text effects

Select a background color for the item during the effect. (This may not be available, depending on the effect you chose in the other two windows.)

To select a color for the item to turn at the end of the effect, be sure Object Invisible is inactive, and click Fade Object With Color. Select a color from the list.

Click the green arrow to apply the effect and see it in the Preview window.

Click Preview to show the Preview window, where effects are shown.

Click the Browse icon to find a sound, or select one from the list. The file formats you can select are listed in the Open window.

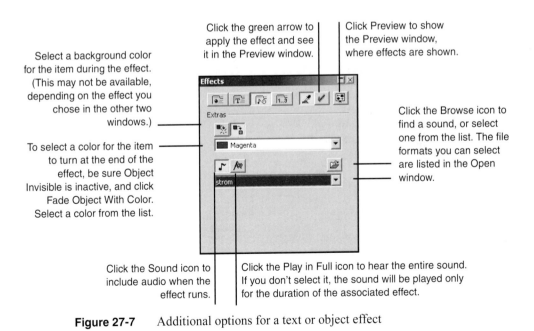

Click the Sound icon to include audio when the effect runs.

Click the Play in Full icon to hear the entire sound. If you don't select it, the sound will be played only for the duration of the associated effect.

Figure 27-7   Additional options for a text or object effect

13 Click the Order icon to see the objects in the order the effects will run. Drag the objects to change the order, if you want.

14 Click the Presentation icon, if you want to run the presentation. Click the mouse or press the space bar to move from one slide to another; press Escape to end it.

Making Effects Run on Two or More Objects Simultaneously

Generally, if you select two or more objects, the effect will be applied to each object, but sequentially, not simultaneously. To make the object effects run at the same time, group the objects to apply the effects to two or more objects simultaneously (select them and right-click, then choose Group.

How Effects Are Applied to Text

Text effects are applied to all text in the text frame, sequentially paragraph by paragraph. For instance, if you click somewhere in the **second** subpoint in a text frame that has three subpoints and apply an effect, the effect will be sequentially applied to all three subpoints, to the **first** subpoint first.

Interaction Effects: Run Macros and More

Impress lets you apply a variety of abilities to any object in a presentation. When you click on the drawing, chart, or other item, you can go to the next or previous slide, a specific slide in another presentation, a Web page, and so on. You can apply the capabilities to any object in the document—a rectangle you've drawn or a graphic you've imported—but not to text. (The program will let you apply the feature, but nothing will happen when you try it out.)

Some of the things you can do include these ideas:

- You can add buttons that help you navigate the presentation, such as first, last, and next, and add sounds to them.

- If your presentation discusses applications, you can create an object (button, rectangle, etc.) that you can click on to start each application.

- And of course it's fun to click on something, like a VP in an org chart, and have that object disappear, perhaps accompanied by a sound.

The features while you're editing the presentation; you don't need to run the presentation to see them work. The mouse pointer changes to a pointing hand when ready.

However, you need to specify that you're allowing interactivity to run. Use the Allow Interaction icon on the Option bar below the work area.

1   Switch to Drawing view.

2   Move to the slide you want to add the interactive object to.

3   Select or add the object; it can be a drawing object, a chart, or any other object, including the controls in the Form tearoff menu.

4   Right-click the object and choose Interaction, or click the Interaction icon in the toolbar.

5   The Interaction window will be displayed (Figure 27-8). Select what you want to happen when the control is clicked.

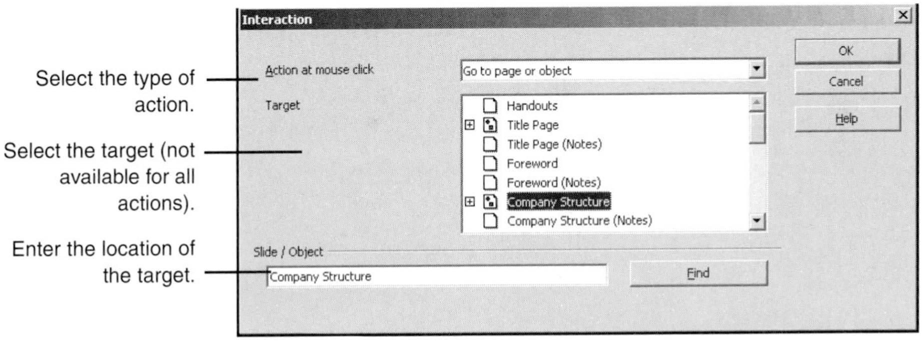

Select the type of action.

Select the target (not available for all actions).

Enter the location of the target.

Figure 27-8   Setting target of an interactive control

Background pages are listed as targets when you select the Go to page or object option. However, choosing to go to one of the background pages takes you to the first slide in the presentation, so it's not a good idea to select a background page.

The Action at mouse click list contains the following options:

•   No action – Use this to remove an existing target.

•   Go to previous slide

•   Go to next slide

•   Go to first slide

•   Go to last slide

•   Go to page or object – Go to one of the pages or objects in the current presentation, in Drawing or Notes view.

•   Go to document – Closes the presentation and opens the document. You can select any document, including Writer documents and graphics.

- Play sound – Plays a sound you select using the Browse button. You can use several sound formats, including files with the extensions .au, .snd, .wav, .voc, .aiff, and .iff.

- Run program.

- Run macro – Runs a macro.

- Exit presentation – Stops running the presentation (doesn't close the file).

Animated GIFs

If you've surfed the Web much, you've seen animated icons flashing information like "New!" or "End Your Elf Dander Problems Today!" with text, graphics, or both.

You can animate any graphic in a GIF format (a raster format that you can create in Image). A series of graphics is used to create the illusion of a moving image.

1   You first need to create the series of images, in Image, Draw, or using existing ones. If you already have the images, skip to the next step.

They don't need to be in GIF format right now; they'll be saved in a GIF file at the end of the process.

You can use a series of images of a cartoon character in different positions, text combined with a blank background to create a flashing effect, or anything else that produces the effect you want.

Note – Use cross-fading to create 10 or 100 different graphics, turning from the first graphic to the second. See *Morphing One Object Into Another Using Cross-Fading* on page 822.

---

2   Paste or import the graphics into a blank slide in Impress. (Choose File > New > Presentation. If AutoPilot starts, close it and choose Tools > Options > Presentation > General and deselect Start with AutoPilots.)

3   If each image is composed of more than one element, such as a sign with a circle and text inside it, be sure to group them. (Select all elements that go together, then right-click and choose Group.)

4   Arrange the images in the order you want them to appear, from *right to left*.

5   Select all images that will be part of the animated GIF.

6   Choose Slide Show > Animation.

7   In the Animation window, select the Bitmap object option.

8 Click the Apply Objects Individually button.

9 The last object (farthest right or down) will be displayed (Figure 27-9) with its corresponding number below it. Enter the appropriate settings for this object: how long it will be displayed and the number of times the series of GIFs will be displayed (make sure this is the same for all graphics).

10 Click the back arrow icon to go to the first bitmap. Repeat the previous step.

11 If necessary, enter 2 in the Image Number field to enter values for the second graphic, and so on.

12 Click Create to create the animated GIF.

13 Copy the GIF into your Web page or presentation if necessary.

14 To save it separately, select it, choose File > Export, and select GIF as the format. Select to save only the selection in the Export window.

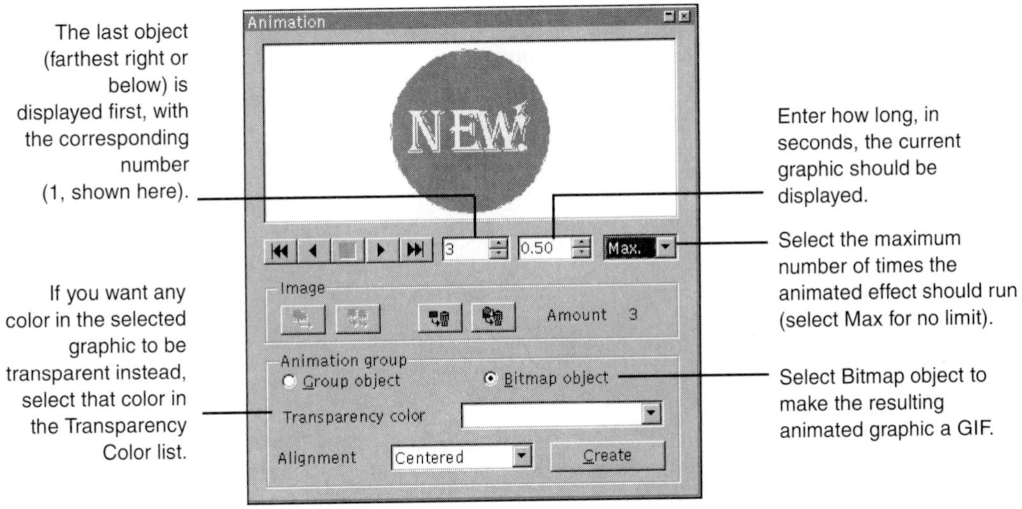

The last object (farthest right or below) is displayed first, with the corresponding number (1, shown here).

Enter how long, in seconds, the current graphic should be displayed.

Select the maximum number of times the animated effect should run (select Max for no limit).

If you want any color in the selected graphic to be transparent instead, select that color in the Transparency Color list.

Select Bitmap object to make the resulting animated graphic a GIF.

Figure 27-9   Creating an animated GIF

Applying Slide Transition Effects

Impress lets you transition from one slide to another with a variety of effects: having the slide appear from the top of bottom, appear Cheshire-cat-like from the middle of the screen, and so on. You also can change from one slide to another manually (by clicking the Space bar or clicking the mouse) or automatically, after a set period of time. These effects, of course, are only available when you run the presentation on a computer.

These effects are in addition to the effects in *Adding Movement, Sound, and Special Effects to Objects and Text in Slides* on page 714; those are applied to individual slide components, whereas these are applied to the entire slide. They take place before the individual effects are run.

1   Switch to Slide view.

2   Select a slide.

3   Open the Preview window (choose View > Preview). The Preview window demonstrates each transition effect you select.

4   Select a slide to apply a transition effect to.

5   Choose Slide Show > Slide Transition. The Slide Transition window will appear.

6   Using the options corresponding to the Effects and Extras icons, select the transition you want, for when you change **to** the selected slide (Figure 27-10 on page 725). Click the green arrow after you apply each effect.

Transition type   There are three transition types: automatic, semiautomatic, and manual. You select the transition type using the Extras icon in the Slide Transition window.

- Automatic – The slide is displayed without any input (like clicking the mouse) and any object or text effects are run as soon as the slide is displayed. The slide is displayed for the specified amount of time.

- Semiautomatic – The slide is displayed only when you click the mouse or press the space bar (when the previous slide is displayed), but any object and text effects are run automatically as soon as the slide is displayed.

- Manual – You must click the mouse or press the space bar to show the slide, then click or press the bar again to run any object or text effects.

Note – The text effects are run one paragraph at a time—even though you only had to select one line of text when selecting the effect to apply the effect to all text within the text frame, the effects are run only one at a time, for the Manual slide transition.

---

7   Click the green arrow to apply the effect.

A small arrow icon appears below the lower left corner of each slide that has an effect assigned to it. You can click it to run the transition (in the work area, not the Preview window).

8   You can click the Presentation icon at the left side of the work area to run it. Press Esc at any time to end the presentation.

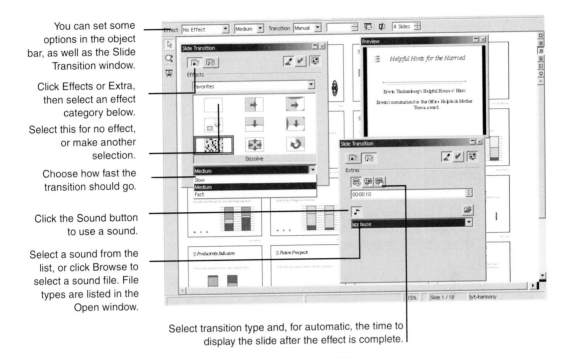

You can set some options in the object bar, as well as the Slide Transition window.

Click Effects or Extra, then select an effect category below.

Select this for no effect, or make another selection.

Choose how fast the transition should go.

Click the Sound button to use a sound.

Select a sound from the list, or click Browse to select a sound file. File types are listed in the Open window.

Select transition type and, for automatic, the time to display the slide after the effect is complete.

Figure 27-10   Applying transition effects to a slide

Creating Custom Presentations

Impress lets you create several different preset customizations of the same presentation. For instance, if you're presenting a new technology, you may want to give similar information to engineers and their managers, but each audience needs a different depth of technical information.

Note – For information about saving several versions of the same document, see *Creating and Controlling Different Document Versions* on page 407.

Creating a Custom Presentation

1   Open the presentation and move to Drawing view.

2   Choose Slide Show > Custom Slide Show.

3   In the Custom Slide Shows window, click New.

4   In the Define Custom Slide Show window (Figure 27-11), enter the appropriate information. Drag the slides up or down to change order.

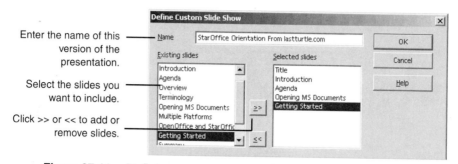

Enter the name of this version of the presentation.

Select the slides you want to include.

Click >> or << to add or remove slides.

Figure 27-11   Defining a custom presentation

Editing or Copying a Custom Presentation

1   Open the presentation.

2   Choose Slide Show > Custom Slide Show.

3   Select a customized version and choose Edit or Copy.

Running a Custom Presentation

1   Choose Slide Show > Custom Slide Show; the Custom Slide Shows window is shown at right.

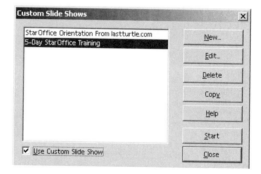

2   Select the slide show to run.

3   Select the Use Custom Slide Show option. If you don't, the entire original presentation will be run.

4   Click Start.

Harmless Pranks

Not that we would endorse *anything* inappropriate in the office, especially not with your boss. But wouldn't it be fun to make an animated Impress presentation, add plenty of sound, and set it up to run in a loop (*Making a Presentation Run in a Loop* on page 733). Then put it in your boss's startup directory, or email it (choose File > Send as Email) labeled something harmless like "Quarterly Report"?

Delivering and Printing Presentations

Adding Notes and Creating Handouts

Once your slides are in good shape, add the speaker's or audience notes, as well as handouts that contain reduced versions of the slides.

Adding Notes

You can use Notes view to add speaker's notes, or to add expanded information based on the slides. You can create training manuals, for instance, by printing student manuals in Notes view with the slides and notes, and giving the instructor the slides to display and discuss during class.

1 Switch to Notes view.

2 Move to the first slide you want to add notes to (Figure 28-1 on page 729).

3 Switch to Background view (choose View > Background > Notes). Click in the notes area and set the correct point size, using the object bar or by choosing Format > Character.

4 Switch back to Slide view.

5 Right-click the zoom field in the status bar below the work area, to zoom in enough to see what you'll be typing.

6 Enter the notes for the speaker. You can use the usual set of editing tools in the toolbar and in the object bar.

7 If you find that you need more room than is available in the notes area, you have a few options:

   • Decrease the font size slightly.

   • Drag the corners of the notes area to resize it.

     Note that the page size is displayed; don't go outside this area. The page size is set using the Page tab of the Page Setup window. If you need to reset margins, choose Format > Page.

   • Split the slide into two or more slides. To add a slide for each subpoint, see *Expanding: Creating a Slide for Each Subpoint* on page 683.

Note – When you print (see *Printing a Presentation* on page 748), be sure to select the Notes option in the Print Options window.

Check the font size for your notes before you begin; the default may be larger than you want.

You can use the icons in the toolbar in the slide and the notes area, in Slide or in Background view (slide area only).

Margins, set using the Page tab of the Page Setup window, are shown; any text outside this area won't be printed.

Move from slide to slide the same way you do in Drawing view.

Slide and Background view are available in Notes view.

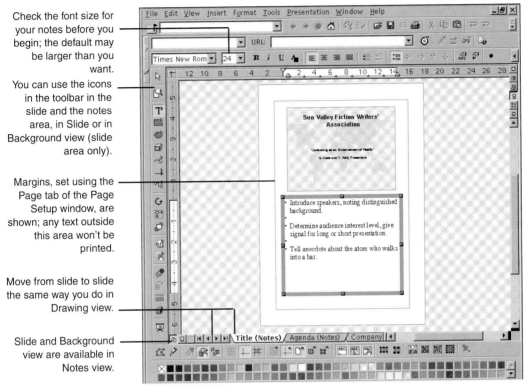

Figure 28-1   Adding speaker's notes

Creating Slide Handouts

If you want to save paper when printing presentations, or provide the audience with reduced-size versions of all your slides, use Handout view.

1   Switch to Handout view, shown in Figure 28-2, by clicking the Handout View icon in the master view navigation bar, or choosing View > Background > Handout.

2   To set the number of slides per handout page, choose Format > Modify Layout and make a selection in the Modify Slide window.

Note – You'll be able to see only the first page of grouped slides. This is normal; the rest of the slides have been arranged correctly and will be printed. Be careful about the changes you make, since all changes will appear on all pages of the handouts.

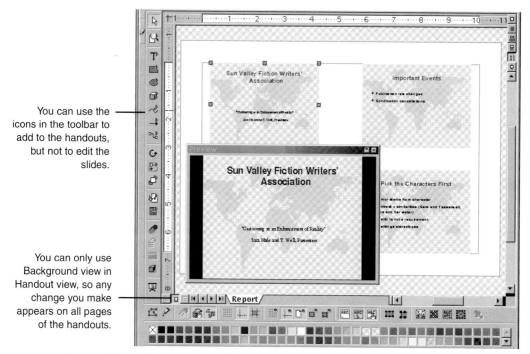

You can use the icons in the toolbar to add to the handouts, but not to edit the slides.

You can only use Background view in Handout view, so any change you make appears on all pages of the handouts.

Figure 28-2 Page setup for handouts

3 The default layout is Landscape (paper is wider than it is high). If you want to print in Portrait view, choose Format > Page and click the Page tab. Select the Portrait option.

4 Manually resize or rearrange the slides, if necessary.

5 Add a title, date fields, or graphics, if you want. You're automatically in Background view when in Handout view, so everything you add will appear on every page as a header, footer, background graphic, or whatever you choose.

- Title and other text – Use the Text tools to add a title at the top of the page, the name of the presenter, or other information.

- Fields – Choose Insert > Field to add a page, date, time, or filename field.

- Graphics – Use the drawing tools to add a logo or other graphic.

Note – When you print (see *Printing a Presentation* on page 748), be sure to select the Handouts option in the Print Options window.

Timing Automatic Presentations

If you want to switch automatically from one slide to another, you can set a specific time for each slide to be displayed. To make it easier for you to figure out how much time each slide should spend onscreen, Impress has a Rehearse Timings feature that displays a counter, and automatically records the time you spend displaying each slide. This lets you rehearse the presentation ahead of time and fine-tune the timing.

You can make adjustments later if necessary.

1   Apply effects, if you want, to individual elements of the slides.

2   Set slide transition effects.

     The type of timing—manual, etc.—can be anything; it will be overridden with Automatic and the time set by this process.

3   Prepare to deliver your presentation; assemble any notes you'll need, etc.

4   Switch to Slide view.

5   Click the Rehearse Timings icon in the object bar.

6   Deliver the information you'll be talking about during this slide, then note the time displayed when you're done.

     The presentation will start running, with the a timer showing how many seconds the slide has been displayed, in the lower left corner of the screen. Note the time when you're done speaking. The time recorded for each slide begins, **not** when the slide is displayed, but when all effects are complete, so take that into account when you note the time.

7   Click the timer to move to the next slide. Repeat the process for each slide.

8   Use the Slide Transition window to adjust the time for each slide, if necessary. (For slides with extensive individual object or text effects, during which you'll be talking, you may want to decrease the time slightly.)

     Note – In general, it's a good idea to err on the generous side when setting timing; you can manually switch to the next slide before the timing is over but you can't delay the transition.

9   Click the Rehearse Presentations icon again, and run the presentation and your delivery again to be sure the timing is correct.

Delivering a Presentation

Now that everything's entered and formatted, it's a relatively simple process to do what you need to present it.

Setting Presentation Preferences

This lets you control how your presentation is run, including how you switch from one slide to another in Manual mode.

1   Choose Presentation > Presentation Settings.

2   Enter the appropriate information in the Slide Show window (Figure 28-3).

If you have interactive elements in your presentation, be sure to select the Mouse pointer visible option.

The Mouse pointer as pen option lets you use the mouse to circle areas onscreen during the presentation. The pointer will change to a pen icon during the presentation, and lets you draw a light green freehand line.

The Change slides manually option overrides, but doesn't delete, automatic settings that you've entered in the Slide object bar or the Slide Transition window.

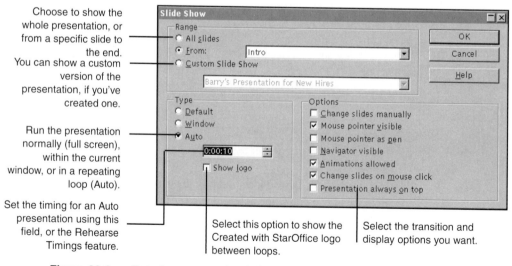

Choose to show the whole presentation, or from a specific slide to the end. You can show a custom version of the presentation, if you've created one.

Run the presentation normally (full screen), within the current window, or in a repeating loop (Auto).

Set the timing for an Auto presentation using this field, or the Rehearse Timings feature.

Select this option to show the Created with StarOffice logo between loops.

Select the transition and display options you want.

Figure 28-3   Entering presentation information

Making a Presentation Run in a Loop

Open the Slide Show window by choosing Slide Show > Presentation Settings. In the Type section, select Auto and change the timing to 00:00:00 (no break between presentations).

Starting and Ending Presentations

Click the Presentation icon, displayed in the navigation bar or toolbar of most views, to start a presentation. Press Esc at any time to quit.

You also can press Ctrl+F2, or right-click and choose Slide Show.

Switching From One Slide to Another

Automatic If your slide show is automatic, just wait for the slide show to run according to its preset times. You can click the mouse or press the spacebar to switch to the next slide at any time. (Be sure the Change slides manually option is deselected in the Slide Show window.)

Manual To run a manual presentation, switch slides according to the options you chose in the Slide Show window. You can click the mouse or press the spacebar, Enter key, page down key, or right arrow key to move forward. To move back, right-click the mouse or use the page up or left arrow key.

Press the Home key to go back to the first slide; press End to go to the last slide.

Using the Navigator to Run Presentations

For particularly lengthy presentations, it's convenient to have the Navigator, which lets you go directly to the slide you want, rather than simply going from one to the next sequentially.

Choose Presentation > Presentation Settings and select the Navigator visible option. Use the navigation arrows to get to the slide you want, or double-click a slide.

Note – If you don't start the presentation with the Navigator, you can open it by pressing F5.

You can resize the Navigator if it gets in your way but is still useful enough to you to keep open.

The selections you make in the Navigator don't override automatic settings, which can interfere with using the Navigator. Be sure to select the Change slides manually option in the Slide Show window. Also, slide transitions cause the Navigator to disappear and reappear; you may not want to use the Navigator with slide transitions.

You also can activate the Mouse pointer as pen option with the Navigator; just click the Pointer icon at the top of the Navigator, if it's not already active.

Running and Editing a Presentation Simultaneously

Impress's Live mode lets you run and edit at the same time. For example, if you're teaching the latest StarOffice course to a group of instructors and they keep interrupting you to ask for changes, this is a good solution.

Note – Select the Change slides manually option in the Slide Show window when using Live mode, to make sure you have enough time to make the changes in each slide.

To enter Live mode, run the presentation with the Navigator. When it's displayed, click the Live Mode icon.

Changing Presentation File Format

You can save the presentation in one of a number of other text or presentation formats, and export any slide to HTML or a raster graphics format.

Saving the Presentation in Another Presentation Format

These formats are all variations on PowerPoint, Impress, Draw, and templates for Impress and Draw.

1   Choose File > Save as.

2   The file formats you can use are listed in the Save as window. Select a format and enter a name.

3   Click Save.

Note – You can open a number of other presentations, including PowerPoint presentations, by simply choosing File > Open.

Converting a Slide to a Raster Graphic

You can export any slide to create a raster graphics version of it (GIF, JPG, EPS, TIF, etc.). The TIF and EPS formats are especially useful if you need to make professional-quality graphics.

1 Move to Drawing view.

2 Move to the slide to export.

3 Choose File > Export.

4 Enter a name and choose the file you want.

5 Click Save.

6 Enter options, if prompted to. (For more information, see *Exporting to Other Raster Formats* on page 842.)

Creating an HTML Version of Your Presentation

You can change your presentation to a Web-enabled HTML format using the Export feature.

Before you begin, check the current settings for export to HTML.

For information about adding Web features, see *Creating Web Pages* on page 445.

You have two types of output formats:

*   Standard HTML pages, with frames or without

*   Automatic or Webcast (for use in kiosk-type environments, or for WebCasting)

The options are sufficiently different that we've created a different procedure for each category.

Before You Begin

Backgrounds We suggest that before you start conversion, you save the presentation under a different name and change the background to a plain, light color without graphics. When setting the background, you may want to just select the Invisible option or select White in the Page Setup window, because the conversion process doesn't usually do a good job of matching the color. Refer to *Presentation Backgrounds* on page 705 for more information.

Slide transitions and sound The Automatic and Webcast formats have options that allow you to either retain the slide-transition effects in the original presentation, or specify them in the export wizard. If you have slide transitions or sound and export to HTML or HTML with Frames, you might be prompted to download a plugin, to get the same functionality. (This varies depending on your operating system, browser, and what plugins you have now.)

Exporting to Standard HTML

Follow these steps to convert a presentation to HTML.

1 Create a folder to hold the HTML and graphics files for the exported presentation.

2 Open the presentation.

3 Choose File > Export.

4 Enter the file name and, in the File type list, select Web Page.

Note – In a multi-user environment, the default location in the Export window is a location on the server. Be sure to change the location if this isn't where you want the exported presentation.

---

5 In the first HTML Export window (Figure 28-4), select New design or select an existing one.

Even if you select an existing design, you can see the following windows where you can modify any of the settings in a current design. If you don't want to make any modifications, click Create now.

If you select an existing design (one you created when exporting previously), you can modify it as much as you want, and save or discard the changes later.

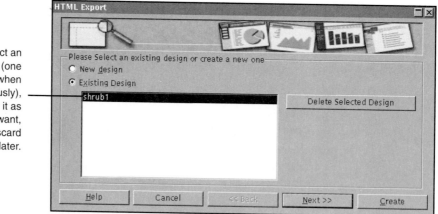

Figure 28-4   Selecting a design or starting a new one

6 In the second window (Figure 28-5), select the type of presentation.

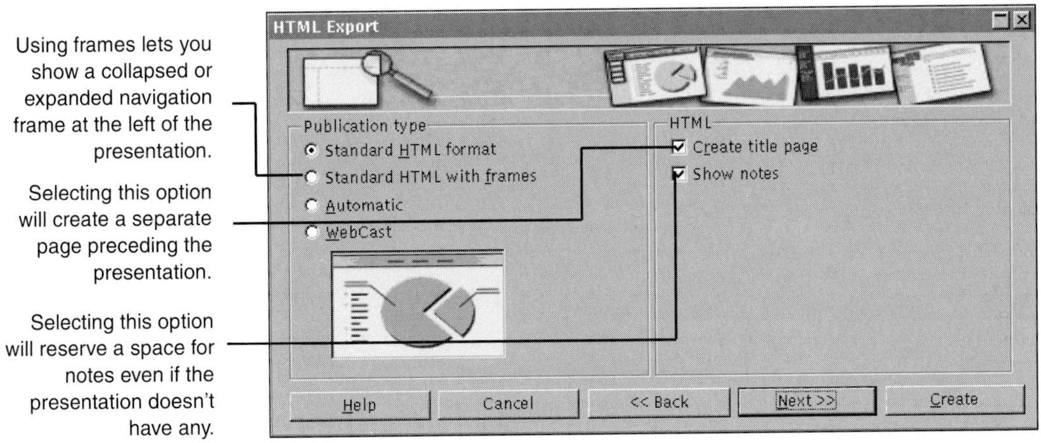

Using frames lets you show a collapsed or expanded navigation frame at the left of the presentation.

Selecting this option will create a separate page preceding the presentation.

Selecting this option will reserve a space for notes even if the presentation doesn't have any.

Figure 28-5   Entering design and image options

If you select the Browser frames, you can still browse a non-frames, text-only version (text instead of navigation buttons) by clicking the text-only button or navigation option at the top of each HTML page.

7   The next window (Figure 28-6) lets you select the graphics type and resolution, and decide whether to export any sound files associated with effects in the presentation.

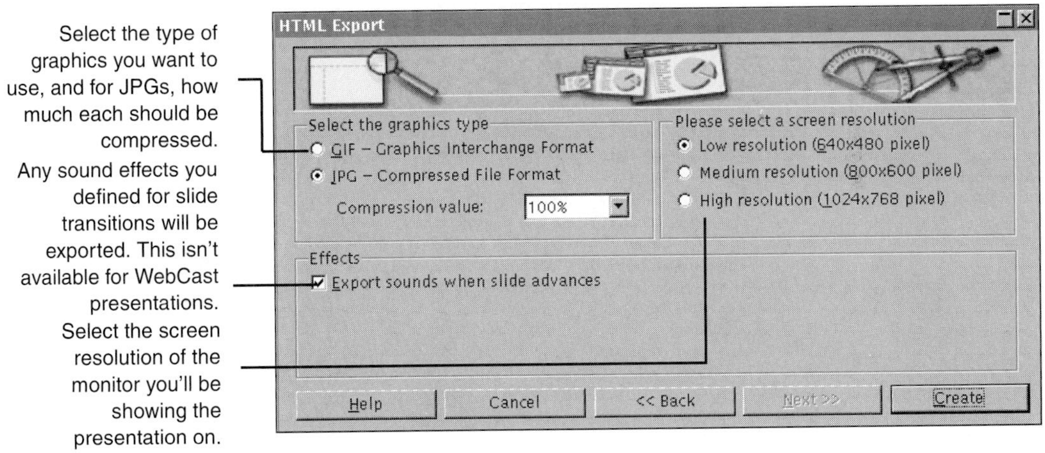

Select the type of graphics you want to use, and for JPGs, how much each should be compressed.

Any sound effects you defined for slide transitions will be exported. This isn't available for WebCast presentations.

Select the screen resolution of the monitor you'll be showing the presentation on.

Figure 28-6   Selecting graphics, screen resolution, and sound-export options

8   In the next window (Figure 28-7), enter information about the presentation.

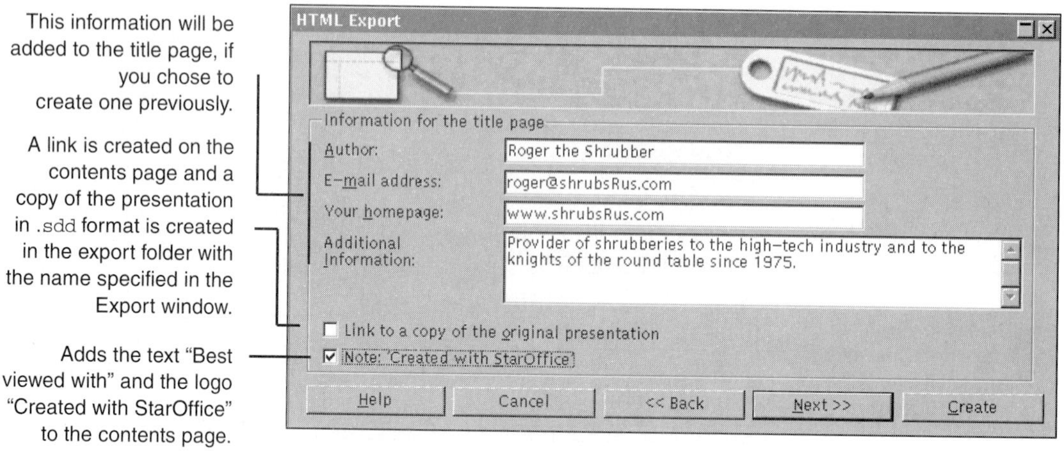

This information will be added to the title page, if you chose to create one previously.

A link is created on the contents page and a copy of the presentation in .sdd format is created in the export folder with the name specified in the Export window.

Adds the text "Best viewed with" and the logo "Created with StarOffice" to the contents page.

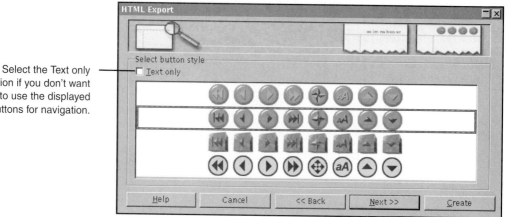

Figure 28-7   Entering author information

Don't select the Link to a copy of the original presentation option unless you want it for informational purposes. Clicking the link just displays garbage characters.

9   In the next window (Figure 28-8), select the type of buttons to use for navigation, or choose text only (the hot-linked words Forward and so on will be used). They will be added at the top of the presentation.

Select the Text only option if you don't want to use the displayed buttons for navigation.

Figure 28-8   Selecting navigation method

10   In the next window, select color options.

Note that the background you choose in Figure 28-9 is used in the background of the HTML pages, behind and in addition to any background or backgrounds used in the presentation you're converting. See Figure 28-10 for an example.

Clicking any of these buttons will open the Color window. Color translation is inexact, at best.

This will not replace the background of your presentation—it serves only as the background in the HTML page.

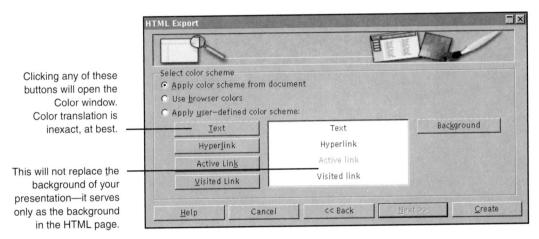

Figure 28-9   Selecting a color scheme

When you click any of the buttons, the Color window will appear.

The color that you get when you look at the HTML version may be only loosely related to the color you choose here. Light green here might end up as light yellow in HTML. Be prepared to tinker a little with the color, or to just choose white.

11 Click Create; to save the design, enter a name and choose Save.

12 To run the HTML version, double-click the appropriate file. If you created a content page, double-click the *x*.htm file, where *x* is the name you entered in the Export window.

If you didn't create a content page:

- For a frames version, double-click the `siframes.htm` file.

- If you didn't convert to frames, double-click the `text0.htm` file.

A converted presentation is shown in Figure 28-10.

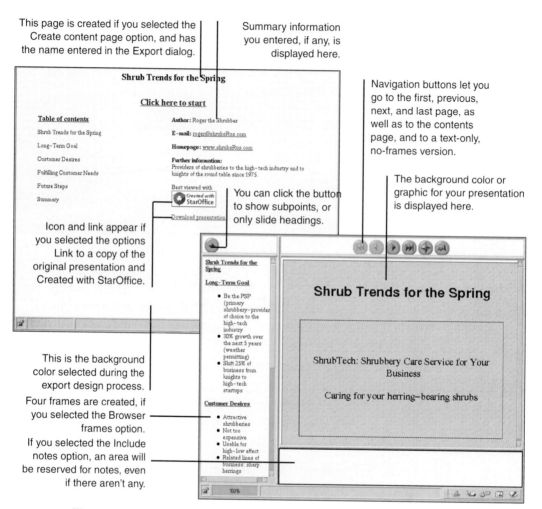

Figure 28-10 Converted HTML presentation

Exporting to an Automatic or WebCast Presentation

An automatic presentation runs in a continuous loop; it's convenient in kiosk-type environments. In a WebCast Export, automatic scripts are generated with Perl or ASP support. This enables the speaker (for example, a speaker in a telephone conference using a slide show in the Internet) to switch to other slides using the audience's Web browser.

Note – The WebCast needs an HTTP server offering Perl or ASP for scripting, such as Microsoft Internet Information Server, or Apache. Therefore, the exporting option depends on the server used. In addition, you need solid knowledge of the server and ASP or Perl so that you can keep on working with the WebCast exported files. The online help included with the program provides additional information about using the exported Web-Cast presentation.

1   Create a folder to hold the files for your exported presentation.

2   Open the presentation.

3   Choose File > Export.

4   Enter the file name and, in the File type list, select HTML (see Figure 28-11).

Note – In a multi-user environment, the default location in the Export window is a location on the server. Be sure to change the location if this isn't where you want the exported presentation.

This name, with an .htm extension, will be the name for your contents page, if you create one.

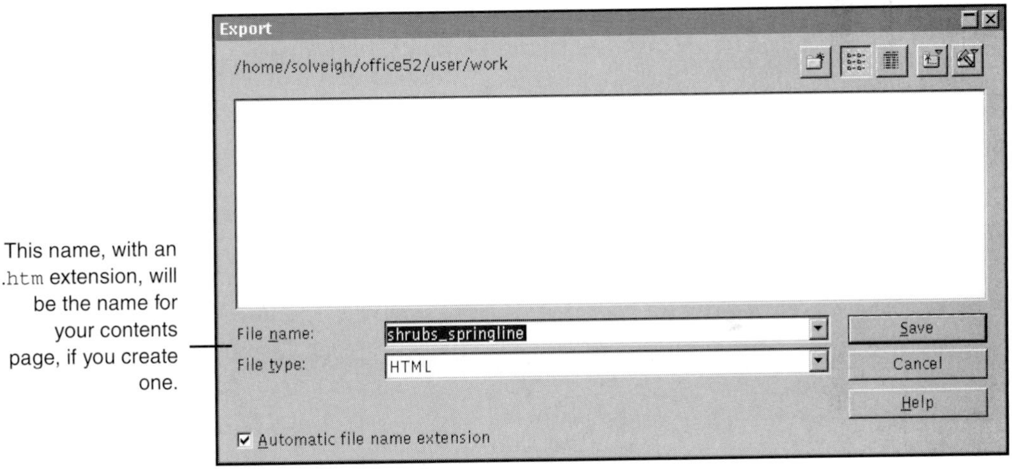

Figure 28-11   Entering the exported presentation name

5   In the first HTML Export window (Figure 28-12), select New design or select an existing one.

If you select an existing design, you can modify it as much as you want, and save or discard the changes.

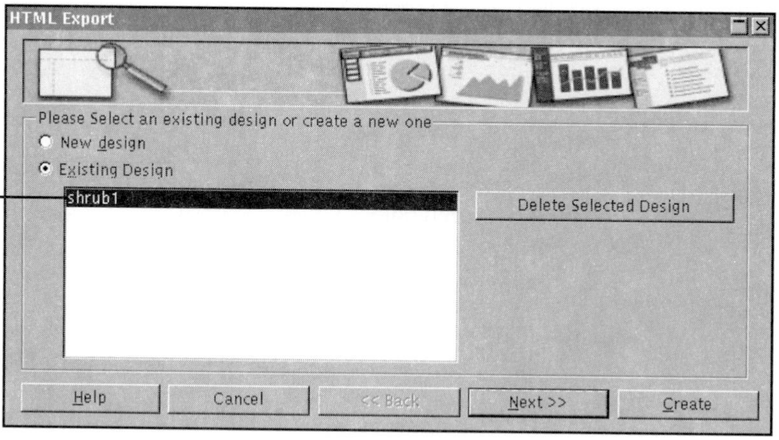

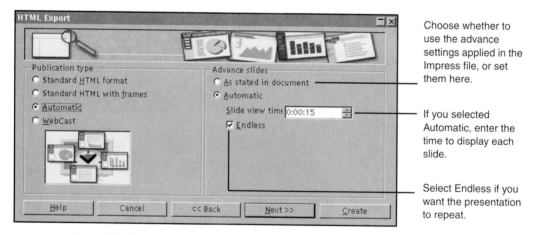

Figure 28-12 Selecting a design or starting a new one

Even if you select an existing design, you can see the following windows where you can modify any of the settings in a current design. If you don't want to make any modifications, click Create now.

6 In the second window, select the type of presentation, Automatic or WebCast. Enter the corresponding options, in the window shown in Figure 28-13 or Figure 28-14, then click Next.

Choose whether to use the advance settings applied in the Impress file, or set them here.

If you selected Automatic, enter the time to display each slide.

Select Endless if you want the presentation to repeat.

Figure 28-13 Entering Automatic options

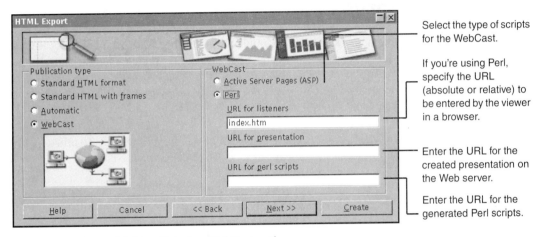

Figure 28-14   Entering WebCast options

7   The next window (Figure 28-15) lets you select the graphics type and resolution, and decide whether to export any sound files associated with effects in the presentation.

Figure 28-15   Selecting graphics, screen resolution, and sound-export options

8   Click Create.

9   To open the presentation, locate the *filename*.htm file in the folder you exported the presentation to.

Printing in Impress

Printing presentations is a little more complex than printing other documents, because there might be notes, handouts, and other components that you might not want printed every time. If you just choose File > Print > OK, you'll get *everything*, including an outline. See *Setting Printing Options* and *Printing a Presentation* to make sure you're printing what you want.

Note – See *Printer Setup and Printing* on page 59 for more information. To print to a file, refer to *Considerations for Printing to PostScript or PDF* on page 81.

Finding Printing Procedures

Most of the procedures you need are in Chapter 4, *Printer Setup and Printing*, on page 59. In particular, see:

*   *Creating UNIX Printers* on page 60
*   *Standard Printing* on page 79
*   *Setting Up Printing to PDF* on page 72
*   *Printing to PostScript and PDF* on page 81
*   *Printing Brochures* on page 90
*   *Printing From the Command Line* on page 83
*   *Specifying Portrait or Landscape Orientation* on page 86
*   *Specifying Print Settings for Bitmaps, Transparency, and Color/Grayscale* on page 89
*   And in the Mail Merge chapter, *Printing* on page 399

The rest of the procedures here cover Impress-specific printing or procedures that aren't worth sending you to the other side of the book for.

Note – The paper size you select is important; if you're having printing problems, check the paper size. If you're in the United States, for example, make sure you select Letter or Legal in the Printer Properties window. (Choose File > Print, select a printer, and click Properties. In the Paper tab, select the right paper size from the Paper size list.)

Printing More Than One Slide on a Page

Use either of the following methods; the handouts feature gives you more control.

*   Use the handouts feature (see *Creating Slide Handouts* on page 729) and select only Handouts in the Contents section of this window.

- You can also tile the slides so that each appears as many times as it can fit on one piece of paper. Be sure that your page size is smaller than the page size of the paper you'll print on, or it'll only fit once and no tiling will occur. Also be sure to match up your page orientation and printer orientation or you'll get unexpected results.

See also *Fitting Multiple Pages Onto One Sheet* on page 88 for information on documents throughout the program.

Cramming a Slide Onto a Page

Sometimes you just need to squish or expand a drawing to get the printed output right. If the slide is too big, you'll generally be notified when you print, and you can choose the Fit to Size option at that point. To be prepared ahead of time, however, you can mark the Fit to Size option using either of the following navigations:

Page Format Window

1 Choose Format > Page and click the Page tab.

2 Select Fit to size and click OK.

Note – If you want to print an image in landscape that's too long to fit the short way onto the landscape page, choose Format > Page. In the Page tab, select Landscape and select Fit to size, then click OK. If Fit to size isn't selected when you mark Landscape, it won't work to apply it after the fact.

Print Options Window

1 Choose File > Print and click the Options button.

2 Select the Fit to page option and click OK.

3 Click OK to print.

You also can refer to *Fitting Multiple Pages Onto One Sheet* on page 88 to see how it's done across the program.

Stretching a Small Slide to Fill a Page

There's a Fill entire page option in the Page Format window, but it doesn't have any effect. You can use the Scale field in the Paper tab of the Printer Properties window (File > Printer Setup, or File > Print > Properties.) (This works intermittently, but with enough consistency to be worth trying.)

Your best bet is to just manually enlarge the elements of the slide; increase font size, etc. Group the graphical elements of the slide, if there are more than one. Then see *Resizing Objects* on page 778.

Printing a Slide Several Times on One Page

You can tile the slide so that it appears as many times as it can fit on one piece of paper. Just choose Tools > Options > Presentation > Print and select Tile.

If you have more than one slide, each slide will be tiled several times on each piece of paper; you won't see all the slides tiled one after another.

Be sure that your page size is smaller than the page size of the paper you'll print on, or it'll only fit once and no tiling will occur. Also be sure to match up your page orientation and printer orientation or you'll get unexpected results.

Printing Without Dark Backgrounds

Figure 28-16 illustrates the effects of printing in grayscale or black and white.

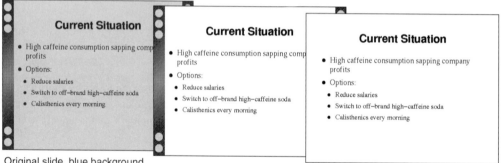

Original slide, blue background

Same slide, in grayscale

Same slide, displayed in black and white

Figure 28-16   Printing in grayscale or black and white

The original slide has a light blue center with bars at the side that fade from light to dark blue. The heading is dark blue and the text is black. If you have a presentation with a heavy dark background that you want to print without bringing your toner cartridge to its knees, you have a couple options:

- The simplest approach is to select either Grayscale or Black-and-White in the print options window (Figure 28-17 on page 747).

- Remove the background (see *Applying a Blank Background* on page 710).

Backgrounds and File Size Issues

If you find that printing the presentation takes longer than it would to transcribe it onto paper by hand, check what's in the background. (See *Presentation Backgrounds* on page 705.) In general, it's a good idea not to use gradient fills, gradient text, or complex backgrounds in presentations because this drastically affects disk space, printing, or download time. You can do a colored background easily that doesn't take much disk space by choosing Format > Page and in the Page tab, selecting a color.

Specifying Landscape or Portrait Orientation

To specify whether the presentation should be portrait or landscape, choose Format > Page and select the Page tab. (This affects all slides in the document, if there is more than one.)

You *can* also set orientation in the Printer Options window. (Choose File > Printer Setup, click Properties and select the Paper tab.) However, all testing indicates that the setting in the Printer Setup window is completely irrelevant; sometimes it changes to reflect what you've set in the Page Setup window, but if you make any changes there, it doesn't affect printing. See also *Specifying Portrait or Landscape Orientation* on page 86 for more information on the ways you can set orientation throughout the program.

Setting Printing Options

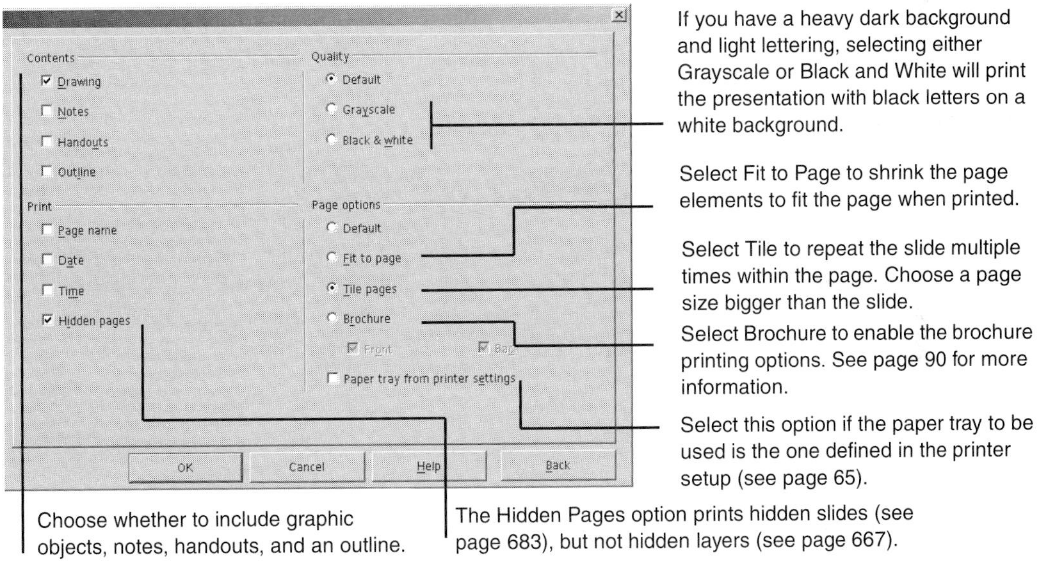
Contents
Drawing
Notes
Handouts
Outline
Print
Page name
Date
Time
Hidden pages
Quality
Default
Grayscale
Black & white
Page options
Default
Fit to page
Tile pages
Brochure
Front
Back
Paper tray from printer settings
OK
Cancel
Help
Back
If you have a heavy dark background and light lettering, selecting either Grayscale or Black and White will print the presentation with black letters on a white background.
Select Fit to Page to shrink the page elements to fit the page when printed.
Select Tile to repeat the slide multiple times within the page. Choose a page size bigger than the slide.
Select Brochure to enable the brochure printing options. See page 90 for more information.
Select this option if the paper tray to be used is the one defined in the printer setup (see page 65).
Choose whether to include graphic objects, notes, handouts, and an outline.
The Hidden Pages option prints hidden slides (see page 683), but not hidden layers (see page 667).

Figure 28-17 Selecting printing options in Impress printing options window

1. Choose Tools > Options > Presentation > Print (Figure 28-17). (You can also choose File > Print and click the Options button.) Using the first approach applies the options you select to all subsequent documents; using the second approach applies the options only to the document you print next.

2   Select what you want to print. Be sure that you select only what you want to print, in the Contents area. If you want to print handouts for your audience, select only Handouts, not Drawing, as well.

Single print jobs and duplex printers Be careful of the Create Single Print Jobs option in the Form Letter or Print Options window, for any application, when you print to a duplex printer. If this option is selected, each new print job will begin on a new page even if you are using a duplex printer. If this field is not checked then the first page of the second copy might be printed on the reverse side of the last page of the first copy, especially if there is an odd page number.

Printing a Presentation

1   Check printing options to choose what parts of the presentation to print (see *Setting Printing Options*).

In particular, be sure to select only Drawing if you just want a regular printout; only Handouts if you want handouts but not the regular presentation, etc.

2   Choose File > Print.

3   Select a printer, or select the Print to file option and enter a file name. To print to a PostScript file, enter a name with a .ps extension.

4   Select what to print: All (the entire document), Pages (a range of pages), or Selection (the currently selected text or objects). Use dashes to form ranges, and use commas or semicolons to separate pages or ranges (1, 3, 4, 6-10).

The page range refers to slides, not pages. If you're printing handouts, keep in mind that entering a range of 1-4 will print only 4 slides, which is only one or two pages.

Note – The program often defaults to Selection, rather than All, as the range of pages to print. Check this each time you print.

---

5   Enter the number of copies and choose whether to collate. Click OK.

Note – If all slides or layers aren't printing, check whether the layers are printable (see page 667) and whether the slides are hidden (page 683). You can choose whether to print hidden slides, using print options (Figure 28-17 on page 747) but you need to go back to the layer tab in the presentation to switch it back to being printable.

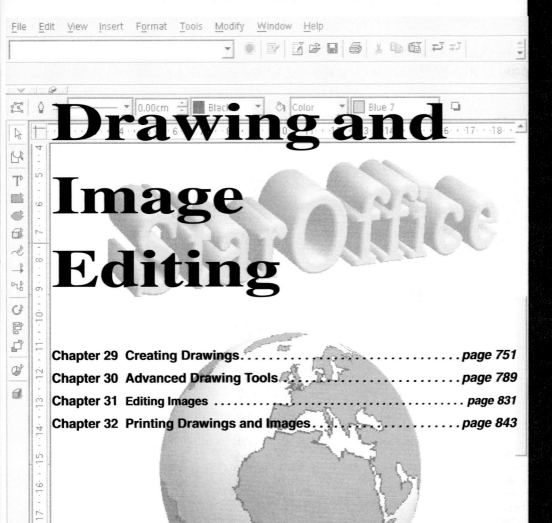

Drawing and Image Editing

Part 6

Creating Drawings

Quick Start

This section contains the following information to help you get started quickly:

- A checklist for quickly making Draw graphics
- Feature overview
- How to create a new Draw file
- A tutorial

See *Setup and Tips* on page 97 for general tips that can make working with Draw easier.

Note – Many features are available throughout the program, but we don't cover them in every program's section. Check the index, or refer to *Setup and Tips* on page 97 or *Writer* on page 165 if you can't find the information you need in the chapters for Draw.

We think Draw is the best, easiest drawing program you've never used. It's a great (and great-priced) compromise between the low end of Paint and the high end of Illustrator or PhotoShop. It's easy to learn, plus it's got very cool effects.

This chapter covers the basics: making a rectangle, setting up the grid, all the stuff you have to do for basic drawing. The next chapter, *Advanced Drawing Tools* on page 789, covers the fun stuff: 3D, distorting shapes, and a lot more.

Quick Start Checklist

If it's 2:45 and you need a drawing for a meeting at 3:00, try these sections:

- Creating or opening a new file – *Creating and Opening Draw Files* on page 758
- Adding shapes – *Creating and Formatting Basic Objects* on page 762
- Adding and formatting text – *Working With Text* on page 770

Creating a New Drawing

To create a new file, choose File > New > Drawing.

Help With Draw and Image Editing

In addition to the Help topics mentioned in *Getting Help* on page 98, see *Good Online Information Sources* on page 42.

The Draw Work Area

The Draw work area is shown in Figure 29-1 on page 753.

The toolbar down the left side of the work area lets you create 2D and 3D shapes, lines, and insert objects like charts. It also includes tools like arranging and skewing objects.

Click the Line and Arrow Style icons to control how lines appear.

Use the icons on the toolbar to create objects, align and arrange them, insert objects, and so on.

To see all the options for an icon, click it, then click the submenu that appears to "tear" it off, as shown.

The option bar offers you precision text, line and object positioning.

The color bar lets you select the color for an object; the same colors are available in the object bar.

To change the measurement system right-click the ruler and select one.

The object bar controls item attributes.

When you use the Text tool, the object bar displays text formatting icons.

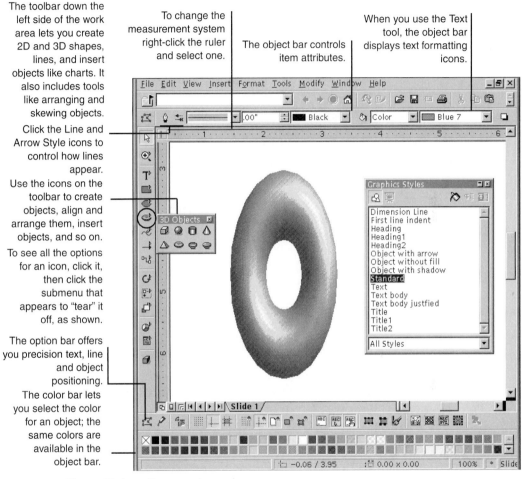

Figure 29-1   Draw work area

The Draw Work Area for Images

The Draw work area with the image-editing toolbars displayed is shown in Figure 29-2 on page 754.

The toolbar allows you to do various modifications like adjusting the red green blue, make it black and white, and flip.

The near left icon produces the Filter tearoff menu.

Choose Tools > Eyedropper to bring up the Eyedropper, which lets you replace any color in an image with any other color.

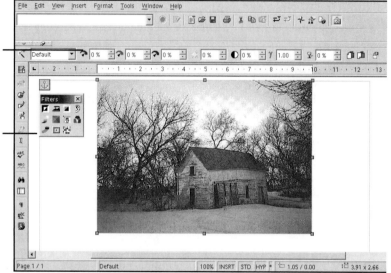

Figure 29-2   Image work area

Drawing and Image-Editing Features

Draw allow you to create and edit both types of images: those based on lines and shapes, or *vector images*, and those based on individual pixels, or *raster images*.

Note – If you're not familiar with the terms *vector* and *raster*, make a note of them at this point; they'll be used in this chapter and the next to differentiate the types of images you can create with each program.

Draw's features include, but aren't limited to, the following.

Extensive object creation and formatting Includes 2D and 3D images, lines, text, and formatting features for each.

Multi-application availability Draw's features are available when you use Writer, Calc, and Impress.

Full Writer text formatting Most of Writer's text features are available in Draw. You can use the existing styles (preset groups of attributes) with objects, lines, and text, or create and modify styles.

FontWork The FontWork program is included, which lets you apply an extraordinary array of font effects, including distorting and curving.

Insert files, OLE objects, graphics You can insert a variety of other files, as well as insert OLE objects such as spreadsheets and graphs.

File formats In addition to supporting an array of files for opening and saving as, you can export Draw and Impress slides to HTML. You can also export to EPS and SVG (scalable vector graphics), an XML-based graphics format.

Basic object creation Includes standard polygon shapes; lets you specify color and fill.

Special effects You can apply image effects such as charcoal sketch and pop art.

Color You can control color aspects such as saturation and brightness, as well as converting to grayscale and black-and-white. You also can *sample* (change specific colors in an image) use the Eyedropper tool.

Guided Tour of Draw: Vector and Raster Graphics

This should take you around ten minutes to complete, and will quickly give you an idea of how the program works.

1 Choose File > New > Drawing.

2 In the option bar below the work area (choose View > Toolbars > Option Bar if it's not displayed), double-click the zoom field that displays a percentage, like 48%. In the Zoom window, select Variable and enter 95%.

3 Click the Rectangle icon on the toolbar at the left side of the work area. Hold down the mouse until the Rectangles tearoff menu appears. Release the mouse, then click again on the top of the menu to "tear it off" (display the menu separately). Move the menu to the right an inch or two.

4 Click the filled square icon in the tearoff menu and draw a square.

5 Change the color of the border using the fields in the object bar above the ruler (the toolbar showing selections like colors and measurements). Hint: The border must have width. If the object bar isn't displayed, choose View > Toolbars > Object Bar.

6 Fill the area with a gradient, also using the object bar. (Select Gradient from the list that displays the word Color, shown at right.)

7 Right-click on the ruler and change the measurement system to centimeters.

8 Select the square and choose Edit > Duplicate. Make one copy of the square, five centimeters to the *left*.

9   Right-click one of the squares and choose Position and Size. Increase the size, and rotate the square 47 degrees around the lower left corner.

10 Choose Format > Stylist.

11 Select one of the squares and apply the Object without fill style. (Hint: double-click the style.)

12 Click the Connector icon in the toolbar.

13 Connect the left side of the left square with the right side of the right square.

14 Convert one of the squares to a 3D rotation object (right-click and choose Convert).

15 Click the Text icon and in the work area, type `What is the airspeed of a laden swallow?` Click outside the text.

16 Note that the text frame around the text keeps enlarging to accommodate the text. To make the text wrap at a certain point, click in the text again, right-click on the text frame, then choose Format > Text. In the Text tab, deselect the Fit width to text option.

17 Double-click the text again, move the cursor to the end of the line and type the following line: `African or European Swallow?` Note that the text now wraps.

18 Click the Text icon again. Draw a text frame approximately two inches wide by one inch high. In it, type `It's not a question of where he grips it! It's a simple question of weight ratios!` When you draw a text frame, the text frame stays at the original horizontal measurement, but lengthens to accommodate additional lines.

19 Select the text you just typed, right-click on it, and choose Format > Character. Make the text 12-point blue Conga.

20 Use the fields on the object bar (above the ruler) to change the text to 23-point red Bembo. (Hint: Select "Conga" and type "Bembo" over it, then press Return.)

21 Right-click the text frame (the rectangle around it—not the text itself) and choose FontWork. Curve the text using any of the icons, then close the window.

22 Double-click in the square that you didn't convert and type `Explain again how sheeps' bladders may be employed to prevent earthquakes.`

23 If the text isn't readable due to the rotation of the object, right-click it and choose Position and Size again, and rotate it so that the text is legible.

24 Right-click the square and choose Text. In the Text tab, select the Fit to Size option.

25 The text is a little too small to read now. Right-click the square again and unmark Fit to size. Select Adjust to contour instead.

26 Move the 3D square so that it overlaps part of the other square. If it's behind the other square, right-click and choose Arrange > Bring to front.

27 Click the Curve icon to display the Curves tearoff
menu.

28 Draw a filled polygon. (Double-click to stop drawing.)

29 Click the Edit Points icon on the left side of the object
bar and select one of the object handles; drag the handle to skew the polygon.

30 Click the Edit Points icon again and select an object handle; see what
happens now when you drag a handle.

31 Create a new drawing and draw a rounded rectangle that touches all four margins on
the page.

32 Choose Format > Page and click the Page tab. Select Landscape rather than Portrait
and click OK.

33 The drawing shows the new margins, within which the image will be printed.

34 Choose Format > Page again and in the Page tab select Fit to size. Click OK. Note
that the rectangle still doesn't fit within the margins.

35 Create another new drawing with a rounded rectangle that touches all four margins.
This time, choose Format > Page and in the Page tab, select Landscape and Fit to size
at the same time. Click OK.

36 Note that this time the shape fits within the margins of the landscape page setup.

37 Choose File > Print and print the drawing to a printer.

38 Choose File > Export and save the drawing as a GIF file. Leave both options marked
in the GIF Options window and click OK.

39 Open a new text document. Choose Tools > Gallery. If Gallery is already marked,
locate the small arrow at the left side of the work area and click it.

40 Open the Pictures section and drag apples.jpg into your work area.

41 Choose File > Export and save it as a TIFF (.tif).

42 Open the TIFF file, note that it opens in Draw.

43 Select the image. Choose Colors > Modify Color Depth > 16 Colors. Note the change.

44 Choose Tools > Eyedropper. Click the check mark, then click on a color in the apple.
Select a different color, or Transparency, to change it to. Change the color; if it
doesn't change, increase the percentage.

45 Click the Color Bar icon and increase the red in the image.

46 Click the Filter icon in the upper left corner and click the bar that appears to tear off
the filter menu. Click the Aging filter.

Creating and Opening Draw Files

Creating a new file is simple; you can open only certain file formats in Draw.

Creating a New Draw File

Choose File > New > Drawing to open a new blank file.

Note – Periodically, Draw gives you bad default margins for a new file. For example, you might end up with the top margin 25 inches below the top of the page (which doesn't leave much room for your drawing). You can't tell just by looking at the work area, so choose Format > Page and in the Page tab, set the orientation and margins correctly.

In addition, check the paper size and select the appropriate size—this depends on the country where you're located, of course. It's a good idea to stay away from User, however, and United States users should typically select Letter.

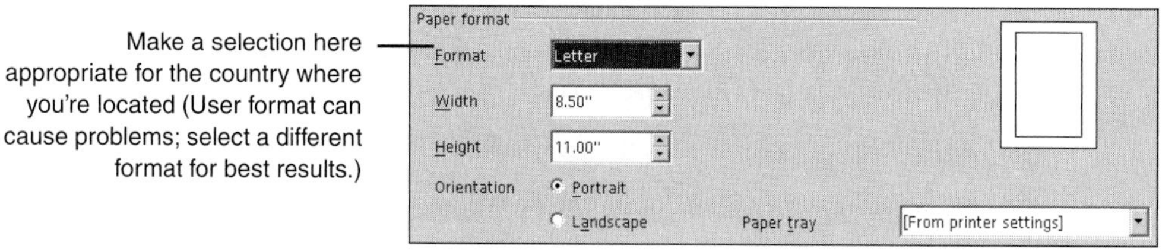

Make a selection here appropriate for the country where you're located (User format can cause problems; select a different format for best results.)

Figure 29-3   Selecting the right paper format

To base a drawing on a template, choose File > New > From template and select the appropriate StarDraw Template file.

Opening a File

Choose File > Open. Any raster (like Paint) or Vector (like Illustrator) image will be opened by default in Draw.

Opening a Draw or Vector Art File

To open an existing Draw file, choose File > Open and select the file, then click Open.

Opening an Impress File as a Draw File

Choose File > Open and select the file. In the File type list, select StarDraw and click Open.

Page Setup

> **Note –** You can create the effect of a multi-page document in Draw using multiple slides; you also can have multiple layers within the same slide. See *Inserting a New Empty Slide* on page 677 and *Using Layers* on page 664 for more information.

Basic Page Setup

You can control the background color and orientation of each slide.

*   To control the background of a Draw document, choose Format > Page, then click the Background tab.
*   To specify whether a document is portrait or landscape orientation, choose Format > Page, then click the Page tab. (This affects all slides in the document, if there is more than one.)

    When you change orientation, the margins often get kerflummoxed and the top margin ends up, for example, 25 inches down from the top. Be sure to check the margins before you click OK (you'll get a warning anyway if the margins are out of range). In addition, check to make sure the paper format is correct; stay away from User, since it can cause a variety of problems.

Page setup is similar to that of Impress. See Figure 7-37 on page 228 and *Specifying Portrait or Landscape Orientation* on page 86 for more information on these Page Setup options.

Inserting Page, Date, Time, and Filename Fields

Choose Insert > Field to add a page, date, time, or filename field. Add the field in Slide mode if you want it on only one slide, or in background mode if you want it on all slides. See also header and footer information in *Creating Slide Handouts* on page 729.

Templates and Styles

Creating a Template

To use a drawing as the basis of subsequent drawings, just choose File > Save as and select the StarDraw template file format. Save it in your `office60/user/template` folder, or in one of the folders within `share/template/language/`. Only files in these locations are available when you choose File > New > From Template, unless you've added locations according to *Adding Places to Look for Impress Files* on page 653.

The section on Writer contains comprehensive information on styles and templates; see *Using Templates* on page 256.

If your document is acting weird and you want to make sure you created it based on the right template, choose File > Properties and click the General tab. The template used by the document is displayed at the bottom of the window.

Creating Sets of Attributes Using Styles

Styles let you save a particular set of attributes, such as font, color, line ends (round, arrow), for text and for objects. It's a good idea to use styles if you need to use an object frequently that's formatted in a particular way, such as a line with an arrow that you've defined yourself, or text formatting for headings.

For an extended explanation of the ways you can save time using styles, refer to *Power Formatting With Styles* on page 241.

Applying Styles

Select the object, then use either of the following methods to apply the style.

*   Display the Stylist (choose Format > Stylist), and double-click the style.
*   Choose Formats > Styles > Catalog, and double-click the style.

Creating and Modifying Styles

Once you modify an existing style, you cannot reset it back to the original settings, though you can modify it again if you remember the original values. You may want to create new styles, rather than changing existing ones.

1   Choose Format > Styles > Catalog to display the Style Catalog (Figure 29-4).

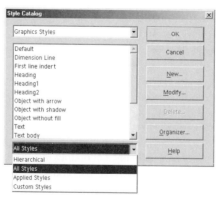

Figure 29-4   Style list

2   Select Graphics Styles from the list at the top; you'll use Presentation Styles in Impress.

If you want to narrow down the styles displayed, make a selection from the bottom list.

- Applied Styles – Displays all styles of the selected style type applied in the current document.

- Custom Styles – Displays all user-defined styles of the current style type.

- Hierarchical – Displays all styles of the current style type in hierarchical structure, similar to the directory structure of your hard drive. To view a sublevel in the hierarchy, click the plus sign next to the respective style name.

3   Select a style that you'll base a new style on, or that you want to modify.

4   Create a new style by clicking Create, or modify an existing one by selecting a style and clicking Modify.

5   The Graphics Styles window appears (Figure 29-5). Make the appropriate entries in each tab, then click OK. Information on the entries for the tabs are covered throughout this chapter.

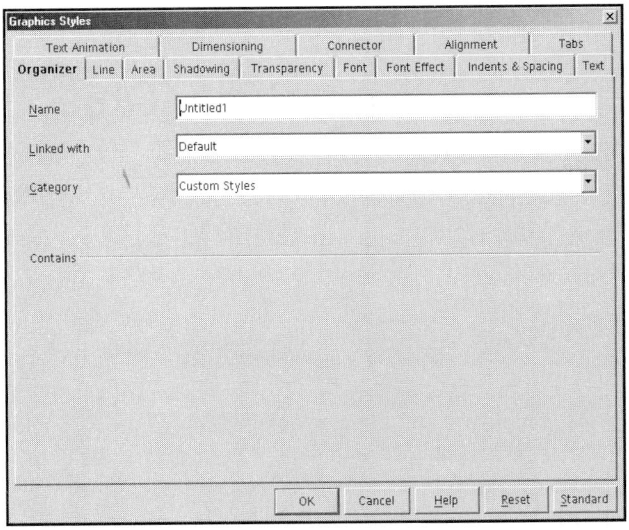

Figure 29-5   Defining new object styles

Making Styles Reusable in Other Documents

Unless you jump through a couple hoops, any styles you create or modify will be available only in the document where you made them. To make them available in other documents:

- Create the styles in a document that you then save as a Draw template.

• Then base new documents on that template by choosing File > New > From template.

You can also import styles from other documents following the instructions in *Loading Individual Styles* on page 259.

Graphics and Color Setup

For options that control memory, color defaults, graphics defaults, and printing, see:

• *Using and Setting Up Graphics and Colors* on page 117
• *Changing the Default Color for New Objects or Creating a New Color* on page 123
• *Specifying Print Settings for Bitmaps, Transparency, and Color/Grayscale* on page 89

Adding Clip Art From the Gallery

To use the Gallery of clip art or add to it, in Draw or any application, see *Using and Setting Up Graphics and Colors* on page 117.

Creating and Formatting Basic Objects

Creating a basic object, such as a square or ellipse, is easy. Use the rectangle or ellipse icon in the toolbar on the left side of the work area.

Toolbar navigation note The green arrows on each icon in the toolbar indicate that you can click on the icon, then click on the menu that appears, and "tear it off"—the menu will remain in the work area. For example, the Rectangle icon has a tearoff menu containing eight shapes.

The icons on the toolbar won't always look the same, however. The last shape that you chose is the shape displayed in the toolbar. The first time you open Draw, the icon looks like this: But if you then draw an empty rounded-corner square, the next time you look for the rectangle icon on the toolbar, the icon will look like this:

Note – You can click an icon and use the tool once (for instance, to draw one rectangle) and then you need to click an icon again. Or you can double-click an icon and use the tool as many times as you want. Just double-click again in the work area when you're done using the tool.

Drawing a Square, Rectangle, Circle, or Ellipse

1   Click the Rectangle or Ellipse icon on the toolbar and choose the shape you want to draw.

2   From the tearoff menu, select the object you want.

3   Draw the object in the work area.

Rounding the Corners of an Existing Rectangle or Square

1   Select the object in the work area.

2   Click the Edit Points icon on the left end of the option bar.

3   The drawing handles will change, and one corner's handles will increase in size.

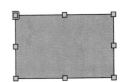

Move the mouse pointer over the larger handle; when the mouse icon changes to a hand, drag the handle to round the corner; all corners will be rounded identically.

Drawing an Arc or Filled Segment

You can draw an arc or a filled segment with the ellipse.

1   Click the Ellipse icon on the toolbar and choose the shape you want to draw.

2   Draw a circle or ellipse.

3   The radius of the shape will appear, and the mouse icon will change to a crosshairs. Click at the point where you want the pie-shaped cutout of the circle to begin.

4   The line will be set, and another moveable radius will appear. Click where you want the other side of the pie-shaped cutout.

The object will appear. You can use the large handles to change the size of the empty area.

Quickly Applying Object Attributes

Note – To select attributes that will be applied to *successive* objects instead of a *current* object, first be sure no objects are selected, then follow the steps in this procedure.

1   Select the object you're working with.

2   Select border options, apply color to the area or border, or select a fill type such as a hatch or bitmap, using the options illustrated in Figure 29-6.

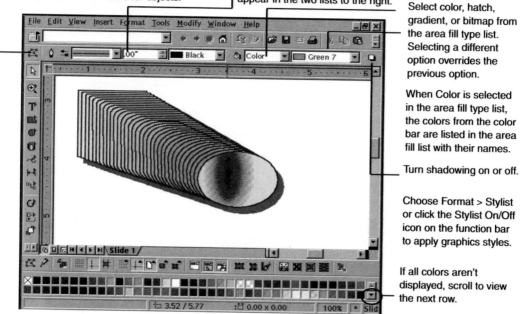

If the object bar doesn't appear when you select a curve, click the Edit Points icon to deselect it. Green handles are standard for objects.

Choose whether to have a border in the line type list. If you choose Continuous or a pattern, width and color options appear in the two lists to the right.

Select color, hatch, gradient, or bitmap from the area fill type list. Selecting a different option overrides the previous option.

When Color is selected in the area fill type list, the colors from the color bar are listed in the area fill list with their names.

Turn shadowing on or off.

Choose Format > Stylist or click the Stylist On/Off icon on the function bar to apply graphics styles.

If all colors aren't displayed, scroll to view the next row.

Figure 29-6   Applying object attributes using the work area

Applying Attributes Using the Area Window

1   To open the Area window, choose Format > Area or click the area icon in the object bar

2   Using each tab, select options shown in the following illustrations (Figure 29-7 through Figure 29-13), then click OK.

Note – Your computer or printer might not be able to handle gradients. If your system grinds to a halt and never actually prints anything, or if you end up with only 1 or 2 color changes instead of the number you entered in the Automatic field, gradients have proved too much for your system. You can also try the Reduce Gradients option: choose Tools > Options > *program* > Print.

If you select None, the object will have no fill, and will be see-through so that an object in back of it will be visible.

Select the color to apply to the object.

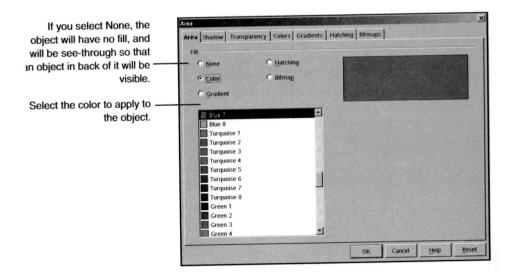

Figure 29-7   Selecting a color

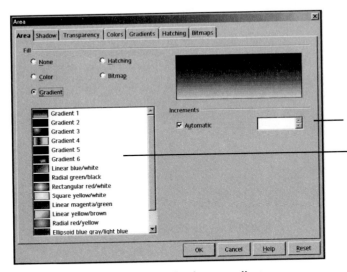

Select Automatic, or enter the number of changes in tone that should appear in the gradient. A higher number will achieve a finer-grained effect; the maximum is 256. (We recommend you enter 256 for a good effect.)

Select a gradient from the list.

Figure 29-8   Selecting a gradient

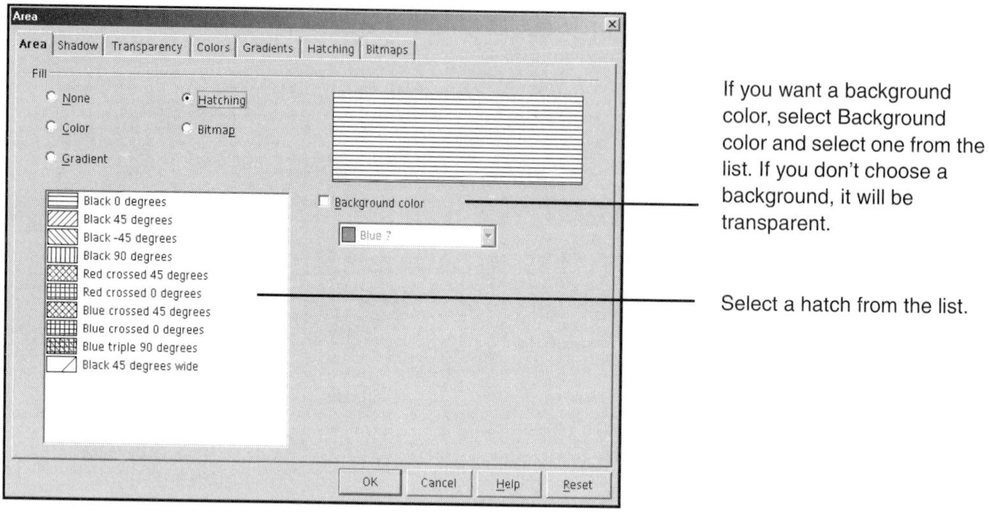

Area
Area | Shadow | Transparency | Colors | Gradients | Hatching | Bitmaps
Fill
None
Color
Gradient
Hatching
Bitmap
Black 0 degrees
Black 45 degrees
Black -45 degrees
Black 90 degrees
Red crossed 45 degrees
Red crossed 0 degrees
Blue crossed 45 degrees
Blue crossed 0 degrees
Blue triple 90 degrees
Black 45 degrees wide
Background color
Blue 7
OK
Cancel
Help
Reset
If you want a background color, select Background color and select one from the list. If you don't choose a background, it will be transparent.
Select a hatch from the list.

Figure 29-9 Selecting a hatch

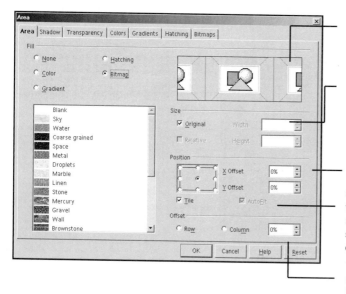

Area
Area | Shadow | Transparency | Colors | Gradients | Hatching | Bitmaps
Fill
None
Color
Gradient
Hatching
Bitmap
Blank
Sky
Water
Coarse grained
Space
Metal
Droplets
Marble
Linen
Stone
Mercury
Gravel
Wall
Brownstone
Size
Original
Relative
Width
Height
Position
X Offset
Y Offset
0%
0%
Tile
AutoFit
Offset
Row
Column
0%
OK
Cancel
Help
Reset
This area previews the effects of your selections.
Select Original to show the bitmap at its original size. Deselect Original and enter measurements for the bitmap in the Width and Height fields. Or select Relative and enter percentages of the bitmap's size in the Width and Height fields.
Use these options to change the point at which the bitmap starts being tiled. The percentage is of the bitmap, not the object you're applying the bitmap fill to.
Select Tile to repeat the bitmap throughout the object area and make the rest of the window options available, or select Autofit to display the bitmap just once, adjusting it to the size of the object.
These options control where, from the center of the object you're applying the bitmap to, the bitmap starts being tiled. See Figure 29-11 for an illustration.

Figure 29-10 Selecting a bitmap and bitmap options

Note – Unmark both Tile and AutoFit to see the bitmap as it is stored on your system, without any effects.

Figure 29-11 illustrates the effects of offset.

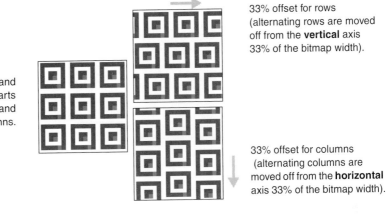

33% offset for rows (alternating rows are moved off from the **vertical** axis 33% of the bitmap width).

0% offset for row and column; bitmap tiling starts at the **center** for rows and columns.

33% offset for columns (alternating columns are moved off from the **horizontal** axis 33% of the bitmap width).

Figure 29-11   Offset for columns and rows

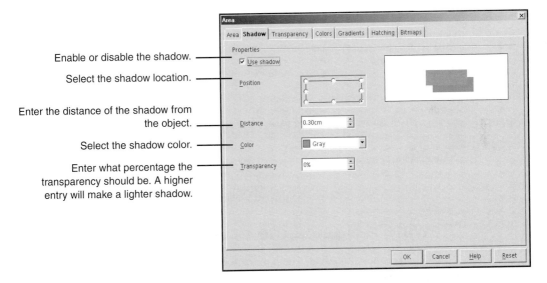

Enable or disable the shadow.

Select the shadow location.

Enter the distance of the shadow from the object.

Select the shadow color.

Enter what percentage the transparency should be. A higher entry will make a lighter shadow.

Figure 29-12   Selecting a shadow

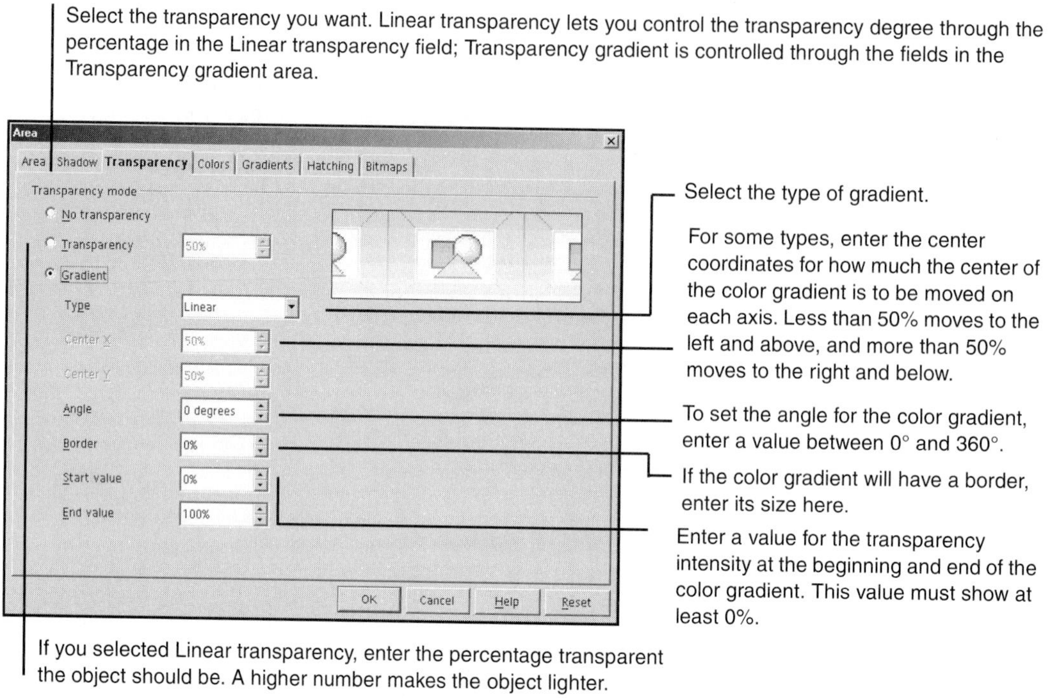

Select the transparency you want. Linear transparency lets you control the transparency degree through the percentage in the Linear transparency field; Transparency gradient is controlled through the fields in the Transparency gradient area.
Area
Area
Shadow
Transparency
Colors
Gradients
Hatching
Bitmaps
Transparency mode
No transparency
Transparency
50%
Gradient
Type
Linear
Center X
50%
Center Y
50%
Angle
0 degrees
Border
0%
Start value
0%
End value
100%
OK
Cancel
Help
Reset
Select the type of gradient.
For some types, enter the center coordinates for how much the center of the color gradient is to be moved on each axis. Less than 50% moves to the left and above, and more than 50% moves to the right and below.
To set the angle for the color gradient, enter a value between 0° and 360°.
If the color gradient will have a border, enter its size here.
Enter a value for the transparency intensity at the beginning and end of the color gradient. This value must show at least 0%.
If you selected Linear transparency, enter the percentage transparent the object should be. A higher number makes the object lighter.

Figure 29-13 Selecting a transparency

Creating and Formatting Lines

Draw provides you with several types of lines: simple lines, connectors that you can use in diagrams and flowcharts, dimension indicator lines, and Bezier curves. You also can apply a variety of attributes, including types of ends, color, width, and so on.

Drawing a Basic Line or Arrow

Lines

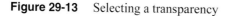

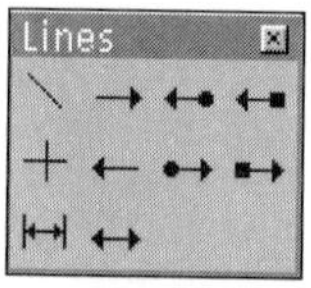

1 Click the Lines and Arrows icon in the toolbar and in the tearoff menu, select the type of line or arrow you want.

2 Draw the line. Use the handles to adjust the line if necessary.

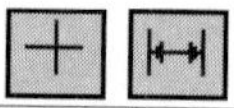

Note – The crosshairs icon allows you to draw a line that is exactly horizontal, perpendicular, or at a 45-degree angle.

Occasionally you'll draw a line that looks fine onscreen but prints with a slight crook in it. You can correct it either of the following ways:

- Select the line, click and hold down the mouse on the end you want to adjust, then press Shift and adjust it. This snaps the line to a vertical or horizontal orientation.

- Zoom in to 400% or higher and adjust it (see *Increasing or Decreasing Display Size (Zooming)* on page 669).

- Snap to the grid or snap points (see *Snapping Objects to a Grid* on page 781).

Quickly Changing Line Attributes

Use the object bar at the top of the work area, shown in Figure 29-14.

Figure 29-14   Line attribute fields

1   Select a Line end type for each end of the line.

2   Select the Line type: Invisible, Continuous, or one of the listed patterns.

3   Select a Line width. The measurement is calibrated in the current measuring system.

4   Select a Line color.

Note – To remove the arrow from a line you drew, click on the line end type icon in Figure 29-14, and select a plain line for each end.

Changing Attributes Using the Line Window

Once you've drawn a line, you can apply a variety of characteristics to it like color, arrows, width, and pattern.

It also lets you set and modify line styles and line style lists, a way of categorizing those styles.

1   Open the Line window using either method:

- Right-click and choose Line.

- Click the Line icon on the left side of the object bar.

2   The Line window will be displayed (Figure 29-15).

Selecting Center positions the center of the arrow or other line end over the end of the line, extending the actual line length.

Select the type of line, color, and width.

If you enter a width greater than zero, you can enter how transparent the line should be.

Select this option to make both ends the same (the displayed selections in the Style fields may not reflect this).

Select a line ending type and width for each end of the line.

Figure 29-15   Applying line attributes

3   Modify any of the displayed options.

4   Click Reset to change the settings back to the originals, click Cancel to close the window without applying changes, or click OK to apply the changes you've made.

Working With Text

Draw has extensive text formatting capabilities; you have the same character formatting options as in Impress and Writer.

Text Tools

Use the tools available from the Text icon in the toolbar at the left side of the work area to create text.

To create text, just click on any of the text icons, draw a text frame in the work area, and type the text. (If you don't type something before you click elsewhere, the frame will disappear and you'll have to start over.) Text entry and

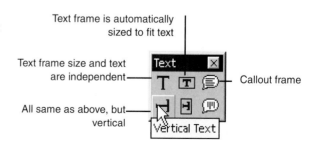

Text frame is automatically sized to fit text

Text frame size and text are independent

Callout frame

All same as above, but vertical

Vertical Text

text formatting features are the same in Impress; refer to *Adding Text* on page 685 and *Formatting Text* on page 691 for more information.

Note – For advanced text effects, see *Distorting and Curving Text and Objects With the Effects Tools* on page 817, and *Distorting and Curving Text Using FontWork* on page 818.

Writing Inside an Object

Double-click any object and start typing when you see the cursor appear inside the object. You can't do this to 3D objects until you've converted them to polygons, bitmaps, etc.

To control whether the text expands beyond the object or stays within it, right click the border of the object and choose Text. Select Fit to Frame to scrunch the text within the object; leave it deselected for normal formatting.

Writing Sideways (Using the Vertical Text Tool)

Note – To enable the vertical text, choose Tools > Options > Language Settings > Language and select the Enable option for Asian Languages.

Then just click on the Text tool on the main toolbar and select the vertical text tool. Click in the document and start typing away.

Vertical text is great for backgrounds (see the background coverage for Impress), and you can create some cool effects by applying FontWork (Format > FontWork).

Creating Vertical Text Inside an Object

1   Draw the object. Determine what proportions you want the object to have once it's rotated 90 degrees and change the shape. For instance, if the object is a rectangle that you want to be 2 inches across by 1 inch high, you'll need to draw it 1 inch wide by 2 inches high.

2   Double-click in the object and type the text normally in an object as described in the following procedure.

3   Click the Rotate icon and rotate the object 90 degrees. You can also right-click the object and choose Position and Size, and make the changes in that window.

Formatting Text Using the Object Bar

When you type or select text, the object bar icons (Figure 29-16) change to tools you can use with text. Tooltips describe the function of each icon.

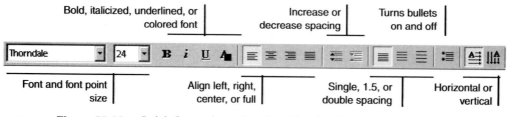

Figure 29-16   Quick formatting using the object bar for text

Note – To see more icons on the object bar or remove them, right-click in a blank spot and choose Visible Buttons. Select the items you want to add to or remove from the object bar.

The default text values for any text that you enter is shown in the object bar. To change these values, first be sure no text is selected in the work area. Then choose Format > Character and make the appropriate selections.

Applying Standard Text Formatting Using the Character Window

The Character window (choose Format > Character as shown at right) lets you apply standard text formatting attributes like font and point size. Use this window in Drawing, Handout, or Notes view. See *Using the Character Formatting Window* on page 200 for more information.

Formatting Text With Bitmaps, Gradients, and Hatches

Not only can you apply preexisting or your own colors to text, you can convert them to verctor objects and then fill them with bitmaps, gradients, or hatches (all of which you can create yourself, as well).

Note – To create bitmaps, gradients, and hatches, see *Creating and Modifying Gradients, Hatches, and Bitmaps* on page 804. For extra effects once you've converted text to vector objects, see *Distorting and Curving Text and Objects With the Effects Tools* on page 817.

1 Type the text, then select the text frame.

2 Right-click and choose Convert, then convert the text to a Polygon, Curve, Contour, or 3D (not 3D rotation object). Selecting Contour preserves the ability to set a color for the outline of each letter using the Line Color dropdown list on the object bar.

3 Select the converted text.

4 Choose the type of fill you want, then the actual fill, from the dropdown lists on the object bar (or from the Character window by choosing Format > Character).

5 The selected fill will appear in the text.

The text, since you converted it, is no longer editable as standard text.

However, you can resize it, widen it, and lengthen it, just as you would any other object, by dragging or using the Resize window.

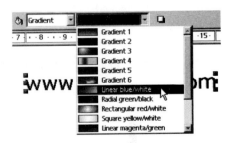

Embossing, Engraving, Outlining, or Shadowing Text

Select the text and choose Format > Character. In the Font Effects tab, under Relief, select Embossed or Engraved. To apply a shadow or outline, select None, then select Outline or Shadow.

Creating an Instant Text Background

You can do this two ways:

- Draw the background, such as a rectangle or even 3D object, then double-click in it and start typing.

- Type the text, then choose Format > Area and apply a color, bitmap, shading, gradient, etc. You can get even cooler effects by making the text 3D first.

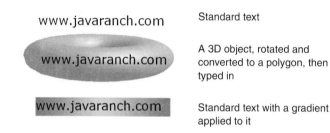

www.javaranch.com   Standard text

A 3D object, rotated and converted to a polygon, then typed in

Standard text with a gradient applied to it

Figure 29-17   Applying a gradient to existing text

Positioning and Resizing Objects

Draw provides a variety of tools that let you position, align, resize, and group objects with precision. Snap/grid features are illustrated in Figure 29-18.

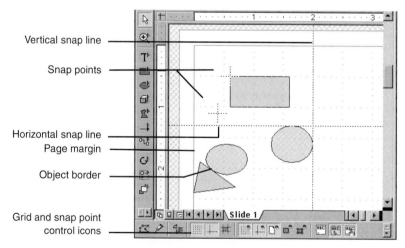

Vertical snap line

Snap points

Horizontal snap line

Page margin

Object border

Grid and snap point control icons

Figure 29-18   Snap/grid object positioning features

Aligning Objects

You can align all objects to uniform lines using the grid or snap points, or align one group at a time.

1   Select the objects.

2   Do either of the following:

- Right-click the objects and choose Alignment.

- Click the Alignment icon on the toolbar to display the Alignment tearoff menu.

3   Select the type of alignment you want.

Distributing Objects Evenly

You can position objects evenly, horizontally or vertically, using the Distribute window. The selected objects will be distributed so that the object's borders (or their center) maintain the same distance from each other.

The objects that are located on the outsides (the first and fifth of five objects, for example), vertical or horizontal, will be considered as borders. That means that they won't be moved when the distribution takes place. The inner objects will be moved to evenly space the objects.

1   Select **three or more objects** to distribute.

2   Right-click on them and choose Distribution. (If Distribution doesn't appear as an option, you haven't selected three or more objects.)

3   Select the option you want in the Distribution window (Figure 29-19) and click OK. (If you're distributing copies of the same object, it doesn't matter which option you select as long as it's within the correct category, Horizontal or Vertical.)

The horizontal distance between the objects' left edges, center, left and right edges, or right edges, will be the same.

The vertical distance between the objects' top, center, top and bottom, or bottom, will be the same.

Figure 29-19   Distributing objects evenly within a drawing

Figure 29-20 shows how each of the four Horizontal options works when you're distributing objects with different shapes. The grid is shown so you can see the contrast in positioning more easily.

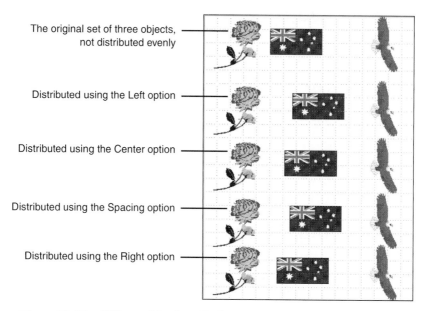

The original set of three objects, not distributed evenly

Distributed using the Left option

Distributed using the Center option

Distributed using the Spacing option

Distributed using the Right option

Figure 29-20   Effects of the four Horizontal distribution options

Positioning Objects

Use the arrow keys, or the Position and Size window. The following procedures include more detail on both approaches.

Moving Objects a Small Amount

To move an object a very small distance in one direction, select the object, then hold down the Shift key. Press the up, down, left, or right arrow key on your keyboard to move the object.

Protecting Objects From Being Moved With the Mouse or Arrow Keys

Use the steps in *Positioning Objects Using the Position and Size Window.* Select the object, then mark the Protect option.

Positioning Objects Using the Position and Size Window

1   Select an object or objects.

2   Choose Format > Position and Size, or right-click the object and choose Position and Size.

3   Choose the Position tab, shown in Figure 29-21.

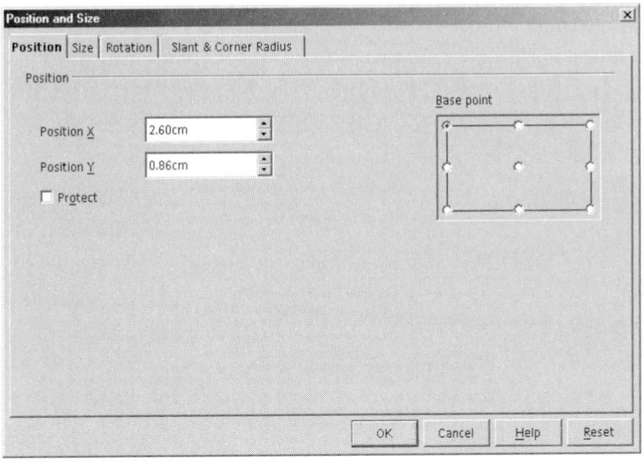

Position and Size

Position | Size | Rotation | Slant & Corner Radius

Position

Position X   `2.60cm`

Position Y   `0.86cm`

☐ Protect

Base point

OK   Cancel   Help   Reset

Figure 29-21   Position and Size window

4   Select the base point from which the change will be based.

If you've selected two or more objects, the base point will be for the collective size, not the size of one of the objects.

5   Enter the new X and Y axes for the object.

6   Select Protect if you don't want to be able to reposition the object with the mouse.

7   Click OK to position the object.

Showing Extended Object Lines When Moving Objects

You can display objects with lines coming out of both axes when you move them, to show more clearly where the object will be (see Figure 29-22).

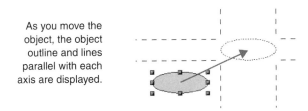

As you move the object, the object outline and lines parallel with each axis are displayed.

Figure 29-22   Displaying extended object lines

To use this feature, choose Tools > Options > Drawing > Layout, then select the Guides when moving option.

Bringing Objects to Front or Back (Arranging)

To determine what objects appear in front of others in your work, you can use Draw's arranging features. The features let you put an object on top or bottom, as well as move it up or down one layer at a time.

1   Select an object.

2   Right-click the object and choose Arrange, or use the Arrange icon in the toolbar at the left side of the work area.

3   Select the appropriate option.

Bring to Front Puts the object on the top layer.

Bring Forward Brings the object one layer forward; it will still be behind an object that you've brought to the front, unless it was only one layer behind, previously.

Send Backward Sends the object one layer back.

Send to Back Puts the object on the bottom layer.

In Front of Object Puts the object immediately in front of the object you select next.

Behind Object Puts the object immediately behind the object you select next.

Resizing Objects

You can do most resizing quickly with your mouse; for more precise resizing, use the Position and Size window.

Using the Mouse

You can resize Bezier curves as well as other shapes, using the mouse.

1   Select an object or objects.

2   Be sure that the green object handles are displayed; if blue object handles are displayed, click the Edit Points icon on the left side of the object bar.

3   To resize proportionately, hold down the Shift key and drag a handle on the object.

    To resize disproportionately, don't hold down the Shift key.

Using the Position and Size Window

1   Select an object or objects.

2   Choose Format > Position and Size, or right-click the object and choose Position and Size.

3   Choose the Size tab.

4   Enter the new height and width of the object. To be sure the object is redrawn proportionately, select the Match option.

If you've selected two or more objects, the new size will be for the collective size.

5   Select the base point from which the change will be based.

If you've selected two or more objects, the base point will be for the collective size.

6   Select Protect if you don't want to be able to resize the object with the mouse.

7   Click OK to resize.

Grouping Objects

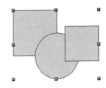

To more easily move objects that belong together, you can group them. Once grouped, you can manipulate the objects as one so that they are easier to move and apply attributes to. If you group three objects of different colors, for instance, you can simply select the group and apply one color to all of them in one step.

1   Select two or more objects.

2   Choose Format > Group, or right-click the objects and choose Group.

3   To ungroup them, make the same selections but choose Ungroup.

Editing Object Groups

1   Right-click the group and choose Edit Group.

2   Make your changes. When you're done, choose Exit Group.

Setting Up the Grid

You can use the grid to help you visually position objects, or "snap" objects to the grid to automatically position objects.

Setting up the Grid

1   Choose Tools > Options > Drawing > Grid.

2   Enter the grid dimensions and whether the standard and snap grids should be synchronized (Figure 29-23 on page 780). Note that Snap to grid and Visible grid are also controllable using the icons on the option bar in the work area.

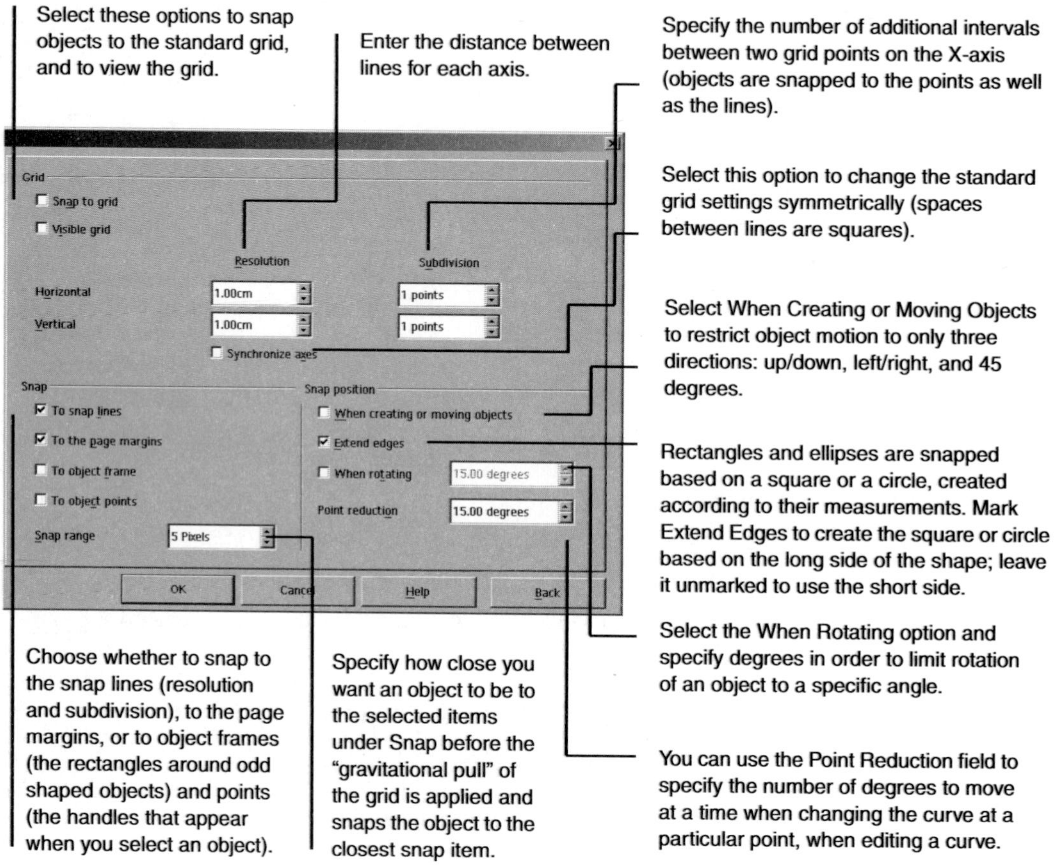
Select these options to snap objects to the standard grid, and to view the grid.
Enter the distance between lines for each axis.
Specify the number of additional intervals between two grid points on the X-axis (objects are snapped to the points as well as the lines).
Select this option to change the standard grid settings symmetrically (spaces between lines are squares).
Select When Creating or Moving Objects to restrict object motion to only three directions: up/down, left/right, and 45 degrees.
Rectangles and ellipses are snapped based on a square or a circle, created according to their measurements. Mark Extend Edges to create the square or circle based on the long side of the shape; leave it unmarked to use the short side.
Select the When Rotating option and specify degrees in order to limit rotation of an object to a specific angle.
You can use the Point Reduction field to specify the number of degrees to move at a time when changing the curve at a particular point, when editing a curve.
Choose whether to snap to the snap lines (resolution and subdivision), to the page margins, or to object frames (the rectangles around odd shaped objects) and points (the handles that appear when you select an object).
Specify how close you want an object to be to the selected items under Snap before the "gravitational pull" of the grid is applied and snaps the object to the closest snap item.
Grid
Snap to grid
Visible grid
Resolution
Subdivision
Horizontal
1.00cm
1 points
Vertical
1.00cm
1 points
Synchronize axes
Snap
To snap lines
To the page margins
To object frame
To object points
Snap range
5 Pixels
Snap position
When creating or moving objects
Extend edges
When rotating
15.00 degrees
Point reduction
15.00 degrees
OK
Cancel
Help
Back

Figure 29-23 Setting grid dimensions

Using the Grid

Once you've specified the dimensions and other options for the grid, you can show it and snap to it.

Use the icons on the option bar, to control the grid functions shown in Figure 29-24. To display it, choose View > Toolbars > Option Bar.

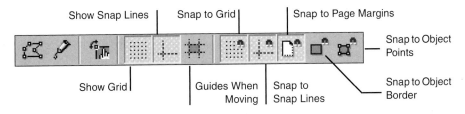

Figure 29-24   Grid option icons

Displaying the Standard Grid

Click the Show Grid icon in the option bar (see Figure 29-24).

Note – If you click Show Grid and nothing seems to appear, have a closer look. The grid points are probably so far apart that the dots marking the lines and points are too light and intermittent to notice at first.

Snapping Objects to a Grid

You can make sure all objects you move or create are automatically aligned on the grid. This also helps you draw straight lines more easily. Just click the Use Grid icon in the option bar of the work area to activate that option.

Note – If you're set up to snap to the grid or other items but don't want to snap a particular object, hold down the Ctrl key while you create or move the object.

Creating and Using Snap Points and Lines

In addition to the snap capabilities of the grid, you can set up specific snap points and lines in the work area to use as guidelines for creating and moving objects. How close you need to move an object to the point or line before it snaps is determined in the snap grid setup window (Figure 29-23).

1   Choose Insert > Insert Snap Point/Line.

2   Select an X and Y axis position, if it's a point; otherwise select only an X axis or a Y axis, as shown in Figure 29-25.

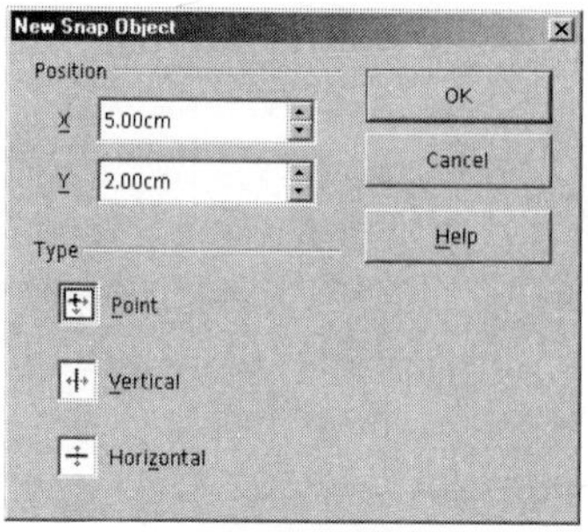

Figure 29-25   Entering information for a new snap point or line.

3   Select the type: the point of intersection of two lines, a horizontal line, or a vertical line.

4   Click OK to close the window and save changes; the point will appear in the drawing area as shown at right.

If the point doesn't appear, click the Show Snap Lines icon in the option bar at the bottom of the work area.

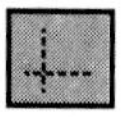

Use the Snap to Snap Lines icon in the same option bar to activate snapping objects to the points.

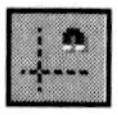

Note – If you're also snapping items to the snap grid, the snap grid takes precedence.

To remove a snap point or line, just right-click on it and choose Delete.

Snapping to the Page Margin and Objects

You can align objects to the page margin and to object borders or *points*. Page margins and object borders are relatively straight-forward; objects you draw or move are snapped to the nearest object's borders, or to the page margin, if you move the object close enough. When you snap to object points, you won't be able to draw or select anything that isn't an object point; your mouse will be drawn to the nearest point of the nearest object. This might be useful in some circumstances; however, we primarily found it annoying.

To snap to any of the three options, just click the appropriate icon (see Figure 29-24 on page 781).

Rotating and Flipping Objects

For advanced object manipulation, and to create modified rotated copies of objects, see *Making Exact and Modified Copies* on page 815, *Distorting and Curving Text and Objects*

With the Effects Tools on page 817, and *Morphing One Object Into Another Using Cross-Fading* on page 822.

Flipping Objects

If you're drawing an image that is the same (a mirror image) on the right and left, you can cut your work in half by creating and copying one side, then flipping the copy. A drawing of a face, some computers, or the front view of a ship could all be done this way.

1   Select an object or objects.

2   Click the Effects icon in the toolbar on the left side of the work area, and select the Flip icon.

3   The flip axis will appear; move it to the right or left, or rotate it to make it horizontal.

4   Right-click and choose Flip > Vertical or Flip > Horizontal.

Rotating Objects Manually

1   Select an object or objects.

2   Click the Effects icon in the toolbar on the left side of the work area, and select the Rotate icon.

3   The rotate icon will appear in the center of the object; reposition it if you want to rotate around a different point, as shown in Figure 29-26.

Red handles appear when the object is ready to rotate.

To rotate around a point other than the center, move the center icon to a different point in the drawing, within the object or outside it.

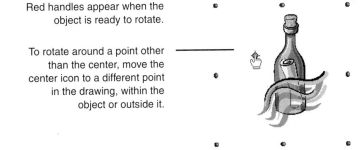

Figure 29-26   Putting an object in rotate mode and moving the rotation point

4   Click one of the corner handles and rotate the object. As shown in Figure 29-26, a dotted frame will show the rotation that you will get, as you rotate, when you release them mouse button.

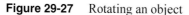

Frame shows how object is being rotated.

Figure 29-27   Rotating an object

Rotating Objects Using the Position and Size Window

1   Select an object or objects.

2   Choose Format > Position and Size, or right-click the object and choose Position and Size, then choose the Rotation tab. The window is shown in Figure 29-28.

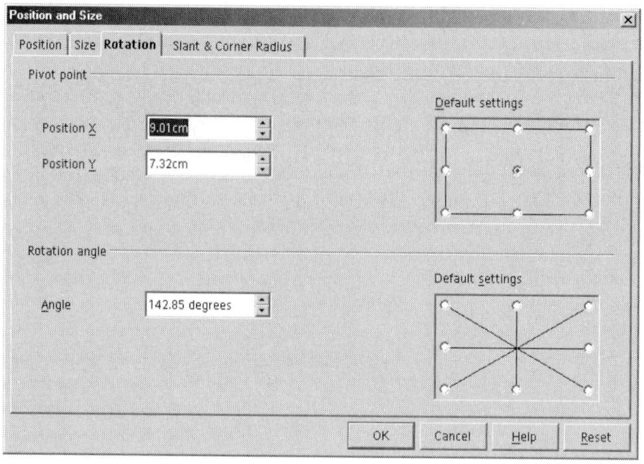

Figure 29-28   Rotating using the Position and Size window

3   Select a rotation point.

4   Enter a rotation angle.

5   Click OK to rotate the object.

Setting Drawing Scale and Unit of Measurement

You can set the *scale* of drawings. This is particularly useful for architectural drawings. In a 1 to 10 scale in centimeters, for instance, every centimeter you draw on-screen will print as 10 centimeters. You can set the scale, anywhere from 1:1 to 1:100, and 2:1 to 100:1.

Selecting a Scale

1   Choose Tools > Options > Drawing > General; the window is shown in Figure 29-29. Be sure the correct measurement system is selected in the Unit of Measurement field.

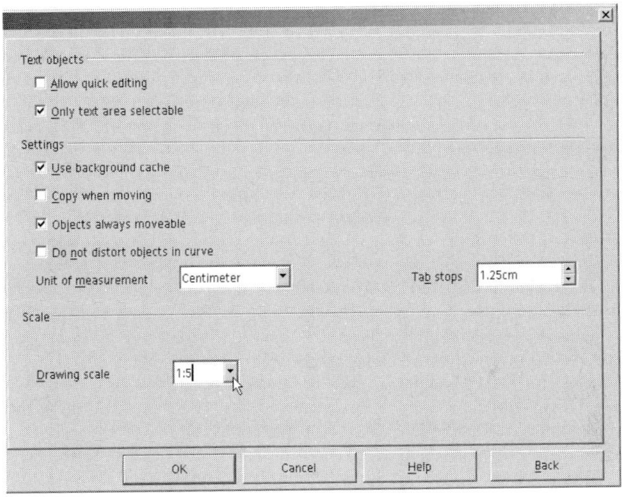

Figure 29-29   Selecting a scale and unit of measurement

2   From the Scale list in the same window, select the scale you want.

3   Click OK.

Selecting a Unit of Measurement

1   Right-click on the ruler at the top or right of the workspace. (If it isn't displayed, choose View > Rulers.) You can also choose Tools > Options > Drawing > General.

2   Select a unit of measurement.

Exporting Drawings to Other Formats

Now that you've made a great drawing, you need to get it into a format that you can put in a Web page, scale up for a poster or down for a bumper sticker, or just put in your document. You'll also need to consider what steps to take to make it scale well.

Exporting to Other Raster or Vector File Formats

Note – If you have problems printing transparent graphics, see *Specifying Print Settings for Bitmaps, Transparency, and Color/Grayscale* on page 89.

1   If you want to only export part of the drawing, select the item or items.

2   Choose File > Export.

3   Navigate to the correct folder and enter a file name.

4   Select the Automatic file name extension option if you want Draw to fill it in automatically. Select Selection if you only want to export what's selected in the drawing.

5   Select a file format, and enter options when prompted to do so; information is provided in Table 29-1.

Note – The HTML export option starts the HTML export feature described in *Creating an HTML Version of Your Presentation* on page 735.

6   Click Save.

Table 29-1   Graphics file formats

Format	Options
BMP	Bitmap. Bitmaps usually have very large file sizes.
	Color resolution Select the color depth. Some depths allow you to use RLE Encoding, a lossless compression scheme for bitmaps.
	Mode Select Original to leave the size unchanged; select Resolution to change the dots per inch of the image; select Size to change the size of the image.
EMF	Enhanced metafile.
	Mode Choose the original size or a modified size.
	Size If you want the exported version to be a different size, enter that size here.

Table 29-1   Graphics file formats

Format	Options
EPS	Encapsulated PostScript. Vector format, excellent for scaling.
	Preview You might want to select both if you're not sure how well you'll be able to print it. Some printers can't handle the actual EPS so print the preview mode. For each you select, a preview graphic in the specified format will be exported along with the actual PostScript file. TIFF preview provides a TIFF raster graphic. If you mark EPSI, a monochrome preview graphic in the EPSI format will be exported together with its PostScript file. This format contains only printable characters of the 7-bit ASCII code.
	Version Select the PostScript level you want to use. For Level 1, compression is not available. Select Level 1 if your PostScript printer doesn't have Level 1 capabilities. Select Level 1 if your output device supports colored bitmaps, palette graphics and compressed graphics.
	Color format Select color or gray scale.
	Compression If you want the data exported in compressed format, select the LZW Encoding option.
	Text settings Select whether text is exported with or without the information on the contour form of each individual character.
GIF	Graphics interchange format. Supports 256 colors; better for high-contrast images.
	Mode Select Interlaced if you want the image to be displayed in a series of passes by browsers.
	Drawing objects Select Save transparent to make the background transparent. Only the objects will then be visible in the GIF image. Use the Eyedropper if you want to later set a color for the transparent value.
JPG	Joint photographic experiments group. Best choice for photographs and other scanned images; supports up to 16.7 million colors. Use this format if low file size is important; it may sacrifice image quality. Recommended for Web use.
	Quality Enter a number below 100 if you want to reduce the file size; doing so also reduces some of the detail in the image
	Color resolution Select Grayscale or True Colors.
MET	OS/2 metafile.
	Mode Choose the original size or a modified size.
	Size If you want the exported version to be a different size, enter that size here.
PBM	Portable bitmap, originally developed to use with email.
	File format Select Binary or Text format. Text results in a file size approximately 8 times bigger than binary.
PCT	Mac Pict.
	Mode Choose the original size or a modified size.
	Size If you want the exported version to be a different size, enter that size here.

Table 29-1   Graphics file formats

Format	Options
PGM	Portable grayscale map, originally developed to use with email. **File format** Select Binary or Text format. Text results in a file size approximately 4 times bigger than binary.
PNG	Portable network graphic. Handles 24-bit color and better. Recommended for Web use (not supported by all browsers). Lets you save up to 16 million colors without compression. **Mode** Enter the compression. 9 is the highest quality. Numbers below 9 may result in loss of quality. **Interlaced** Select Interlaced if you want the image to be displayed in a series of passes by browsers.
PPM	Portable pixel map, originally developed to use with e-mail. **File format** Select Binary or Text format. Text results in a file size approximately 4 times bigger than binary.
RAS	Sun raster file. No save options.
SVG	Scalable vector graphics. Vector format excellent for scaling; stored in an XML format. Readable by Illustrator 9. No save options.
SVM	StarView metafile. **Mode** Enter the compression. 9 is the highest quality. Numbers below 9 may result in loss of quality. **Interlaced** Select Interlaced if you want the image to be displayed in a series of passes by browsers.
TIF	Tagged image file format. Very high quality and file size. No save options.
WMF	Windows metafile. **Mode** Enter the compression. 9 is the highest quality. Numbers below 9 may result in loss of quality. **Interlaced** Select Interlaced if you want the image to be displayed in a series of passes by browsers.
XPM	Supports up to 256 colors, and can be used in C programs. No save options.

Making Images Scale Well

When you increase or decrease the size of a raster object, the new size usually doesn't look that good. Vector objects based on lines are better for resizing. Use Bezier curves or lines when possible; see page 799 in particular. Also, export graphics to SVG or EPS, both of which scale well, rather than to GIF or JPG. Or convert objects to curves or polygons where possible. Right-click an object and choose Convert, then the type to convert to.

Advanced Drawing Tools

About Draw's Advanced Features

We think Draw is the best drawing program you've never used. It's a great (and great-priced) compromise between the low end of Paint and the high end of Illustrator or PhotoShop. It's easy to learn, plus it's got very cool effects.

The previous chapter covered the basics: making a rectangle, setting up the grid, all the stuff you have to do for basic drawing. This chapter covers the fun stuff: 3D, distorting shapes, and a lot more.

Creating Your Own Lines and Arrows

Tired of the options you get with the program? Make your own.

Creating and Modifying Lines

You can modify the preset types of lines and arrows that are displayed in the Line tab of the Line window, and elsewhere in the program. You can also create your own lines.

1   Choose Format > Line, or right-click a line object and choose Line.

2   Click the Line Styles tab.

3   If you're modifying an existing style, select it.

Note – If the style you want to modify isn't displayed in the Line window, click the Load Styles icon and select the list where it is stored. See *Creating and Categorizing Fills and Lines* on page 793 for more information.

---

4   Define the style appropriately, as shown in Figure 30-1.

Select a line style if you're modifying an existing style.

If you're creating a new style, design the style and click Add. To modify a style, select it from Line Style, make modifications to design, then click Modify.

Choose whether to alternate dashes and dots, use only dashes, etc.

Enter the number of dots and dashes. They will be alternated in the line.

Enter the length of each dash and dot. Enter the space between dashes, and between dots.

Select Fit to line width if you want to enter values in the Length and Spacing fields as a percentage of the value in the Width field in the Line tab of this window.

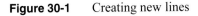

Figure 30-1   Creating new lines

5   Click Add for a new style or Modify for an existing style; enter a name and click OK.

6   Click OK to close the window and save changes.

Creating Arrows and Other Line Endings

If you have a particular type of arrow or other line ending you want to use, it's easy to create it.

Note – This works only for real vector drawings, not bitmaps or bitmaps converted to polygons.

1   Draw the line ending you want or bring it into a Draw document by inserting or pasting. It can be anything as long as it's a vector. The spiral at righ was drawn with the freeform line tool.

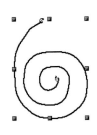

2   Rotate the object 90 degrees if you care which way is up. For no apparent reason, the object will be turned into a line ending flopped 90 degrees from its original position. For instance, if you've got a standard arrow that's wider than it is high, turn it 90 degrees so that it's pointing up and down.

3 Select the object. You must select it first, or you won't have the Add button available in the Line window.

4 Right-click the object, choose Line, and in the Line window select the Arrow Styles tab, shown in Figure 30-2.

5 Click Add and enter a new name for the line ending.

6 The new line ending will appear in the window.

Click Add and enter a name for the line ending; the item you selected will appear at both ends of the displayed line.

This list shows the existing arrow styles.

New line ending is displayed. Note that this object was positioned vertically in the Draw window and turned 90 degrees when created as a line ending.
Also note that it's not as detailed as the original drawing.

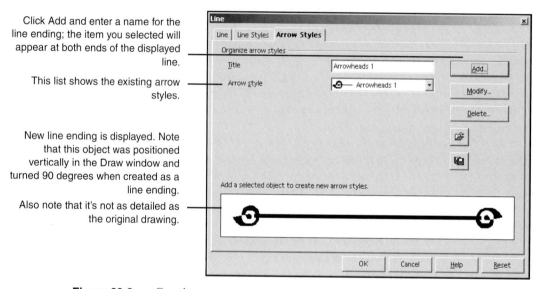

Figure 30-2 Creating new arrows

7 Click OK to close the window and save changes.

8 Apply the arrowhead to lines. You'll need to select the right size in the Line tab of the Line window, as usual; the default size is .12 inch. Figure 30-3 shows the example arrowhead applied to various lines.

Figure 30-3 New arrowhead applied to straight, diagonal, and curved line

Creating and Categorizing Fills and Lines

You can group the sets of line styles and arrow styles into *style lists*. Many program attributes, including lines, colors, and gradients, are stored in these groups, and only one is displayed in the workspace and in the Line window at a time (Figure 30-4). This is convenient if you have several different styles of attributes for different projects and want to keep them separate, so that you don't need to scroll through a long list, looking for the one you need.

Line and arrow lists are stored in the `config` folder with the file extension .sod and .soe, respectively.

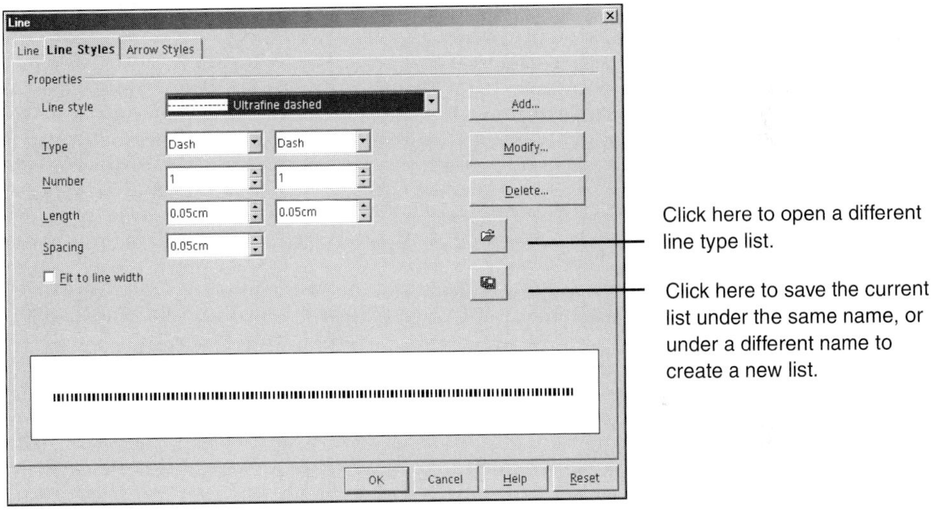

Click here to open a different line type list.

Click here to save the current list under the same name, or under a different name to create a new list.

Figure 30-4   Style list management icons

Selecting a Different List

In the Styles tab, click the Load Styles icon and select the .sod or .soe file you want.

Saving Changes to a List

If you've added or modified a style, click the Save Styles icon to save it in the current list.

Creating Technical Drawings With Dimension Lines and Connectors

Draw provides two useful tools for flowcharts, architectural drawings, and other drawings that are very technical or precise. The tools are the dimension line and the connector.

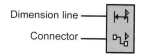

Dimension line ———
Connector ———

Drawing a Dimension Line

1 Click the Lines and Arrows icon and select the dimension tool.

2 Draw the dimension line next to the object whose measurement you want to display (Figure 30-5).

The actual length or width of the object will be displayed, using the measuring system currently selected for the ruler. Modify the drawn line with the handles; you can change the angle or length.

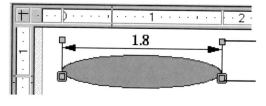

Use the small handles to adjust the length of the guides.

Use the large handles to control the angle of the line.

Figure 30-5 Adjusting a dimension line

Modifying a Dimension Line

The Dimensioning window allows you precise control over the position, distance, and text position of the line.

To draw the dimension line perfectly straight, be sure the grid is on.

1 Open the Dimensioning window (Figure 30-6 on page 795) by right-clicking a dimension line and choosing Dimensions, or choose Format > Dimensions.

2 Make the appropriate changes and click OK.

Figure 30-7 shows where the guides, overhangs, and lines are.

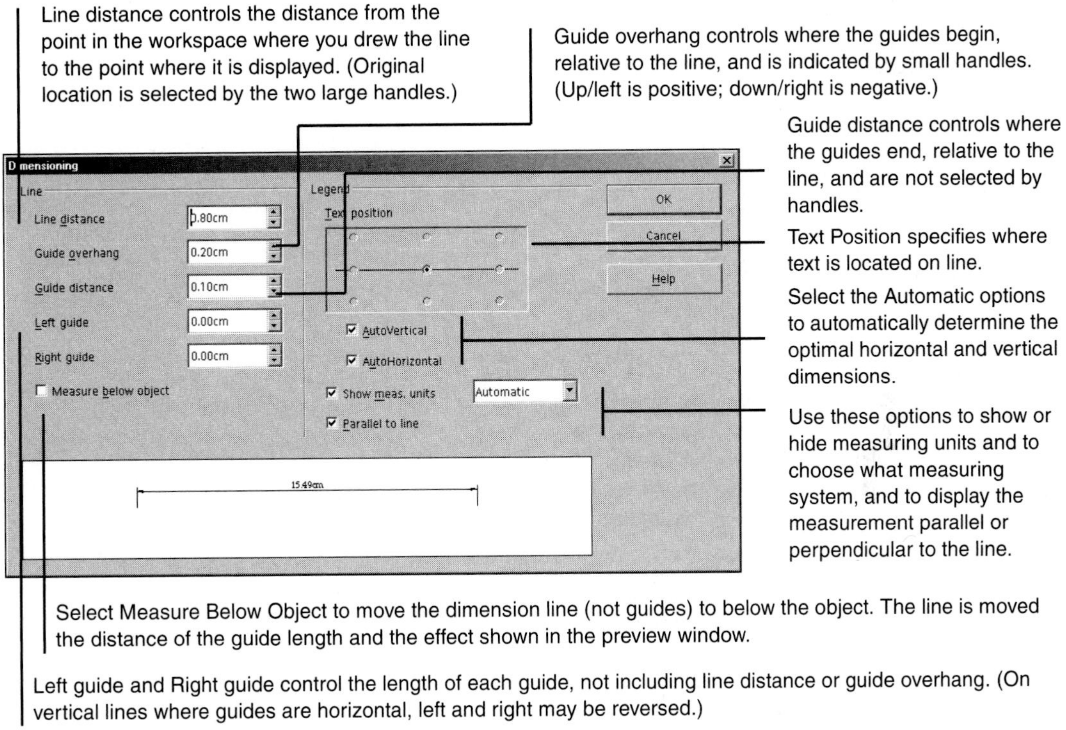

Line distance controls the distance from the point in the workspace where you drew the line to the point where it is displayed. (Original location is selected by the two large handles.)
Guide overhang controls where the guides begin, relative to the line, and is indicated by small handles. (Up/left is positive; down/right is negative.)
Guide distance controls where the guides end, relative to the line, and are not selected by handles.
Text Position specifies where text is located on line.
Select the Automatic options to automatically determine the optimal horizontal and vertical dimensions.
Use these options to show or hide measuring units and to choose what measuring system, and to display the measurement parallel or perpendicular to the line.
Select Measure Below Object to move the dimension line (not guides) to below the object. The line is moved the distance of the guide length and the effect shown in the preview window.
Left guide and Right guide control the length of each guide, not including line distance or guide overhang. (On vertical lines where guides are horizontal, left and right may be reversed.)
Dimensioning
Line
Line distance
Guide overhang
Guide distance
Left guide
Right guide
Measure below object
Legend
Text position
AutoVertical
AutoHorizontal
Show meas. units
Automatic
Parallel to line
OK
Cancel
Help
0.80cm
0.20cm
0.10cm
0.00cm
0.00cm
15.49cm

Figure 30-6 Changing dimension line attributes

Left guide length
Guide overhand
1.9
Line distance
1.7

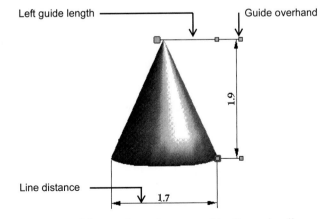

Figure 30-7 Lines and overhangs used in dimension lines

Setting the Scale

Note – You can set many of the options controlling workplace display by choosing Tools > Options > Drawing.

Dimension lines reflect the scale you set. In a 1 to 10 scale in centimeters, for instance, every centimeter you draw on-screen will print as 10 centimeters. You can set the scale, anywhere from 1:1 to 1:100, and 2:1 to 100:1.

1   Choose Tools > Options > Drawing > Layout and be sure the correct measurement system is selected in the Meas. units field.

2   In the options navigation tree on the left, select Zoom.

3   From the Scale list, select the scale you want.

4   Click OK.

Drawing a Connector

Connectors are excellent tools for creating precise diagrams. The connectors automatically attach precisely to the edge of the object you specify, which saves time you would otherwise spend at an 800% zoom, for example, trying to position an ordinary line correctly.

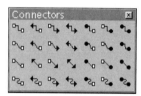

1   Determine the two objects you want to connect.

2   Click the Connector icon and select the type of connector you want to draw.

Tools in the second and third rows with diagonal lines always take the shortest path from one object to another, and only connect the closest connector points.

3   Move the mouse pointer over the first object; its connection points will appear.

4   Click and hold down the mouse on the connection point that you want to connect the line to.

5   Drag the mouse to the second object; its connection points will appear.

6   Position the connector line endpoint on the correct connection point and release the mouse (Figure 30-8). If you move or resize either object, the connector will move with the object.

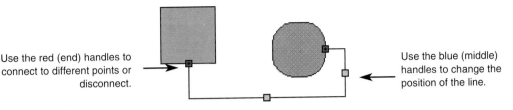

Use the red (end) handles to connect to different points or disconnect.

Use the blue (middle) handles to change the position of the line.

Figure 30-8   Adjusting or connecting connector lines

Only connector tools in the first and fourth rows of the tearoff menu draw lines that, as shown, have multiple directions.

Modifying a Connector

The Connector window allows you precise control over the position, distance, and text position of the line.

1   Open the Connector window (Figure 30-9) by right-clicking a connector and choosing Connector, or choose Format > Connector.

2   Make the appropriate changes; applying changes to a multi-directional connector line is shown. See Figure 30-10 for demonstrations of the terminology.

Controls the type of connector, also displayed in the Connector tearoff menu.

Controls the offset from the original location (left/up is negative, right/down is positive) for each line segment.

These fields control the length of the first and last horizontal and vertical lines (some measurements may not be displayed as entered if overridden by other line measurements).

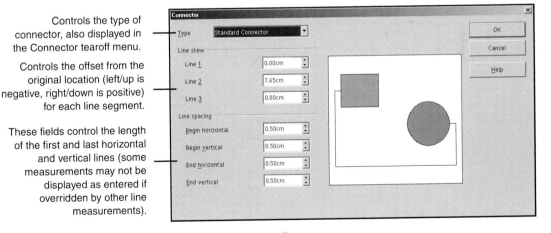

Figure 30-9   Changing connector attributes

Figure 30-10 illustrates the terminology.

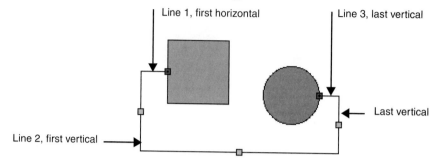

Figure 30-10 illustrates the terminology.

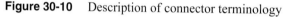

Figure 30-10   Description of connector terminology

Adding Connector Points

You have probably noticed that all objects have predefined connector points. You can specify additional "glue points" so you can have precise control over exactly where the lines connect. You can add them on the border or inside the object.

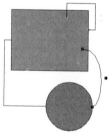

1   Select the object.

2   Choose View > Toolbars and be sure there is a check mark next to Object Bar (displayed at the top of the work area) and Option Bar (displayed at the bottom of the work area).

3   At the bottom of the work area in the Option Bar, click the Edit Glue Points icon. When you click it, it will appear recessed.

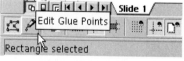

4   Look at the Object Bar at the top of the window; the Edit Glue Points icons are displayed, which you can use to add and modify glue points on any object in the work area.

5   Click the Insert Glue Point icon at the far left and click anywhere to add a glue point. Select the new or existing glue points and use the other icons to modify point attributes.

Connecting Lines to Text Frames

If you want to connect text with lines, for instance in a plain org chart that doesn't have boxes around the names, you can still use the connector lines.

1   Connect the connector lines to the text frame.

2   Right-click the frame and choose Text.

3   In the window that appears, enter the separation you want between the text frame and the text itself, so you can keep the connector line from being right up against the side of the text.

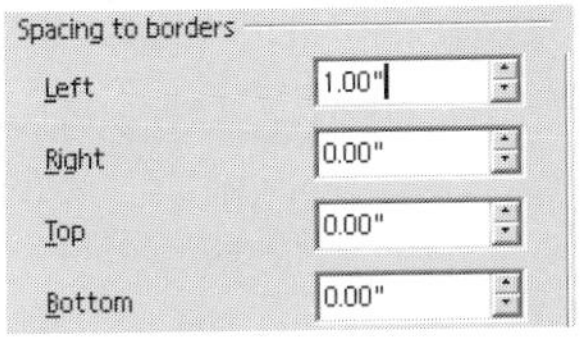

See Figure 30-11 for an example.

Bill Richason   **Bill Richason**   **Bill Richason**

1. Connect the line to a point on the text frame

2. Line connects to text frame, next to text contents

3. Text frame has 1-cm border on left side so connector line is farther

Figure 30-11   Connecting connector line to text frame and adding margin between text frame and text contents

Controlling Arrowheads Quickly

You can switch the ends on a connector line on the toolbar, as shown at right. Just select the line, then click on the Arrows icon the toolbar and select the end you want, for the beginning or end of the line.

Working With Bezier Curves

Bezier curves, lines defined by a series of points, allow you a great deal of control over the shapes you create. Draw provides curved, polygon, and freeform tools.

Creating a Bezier Curve

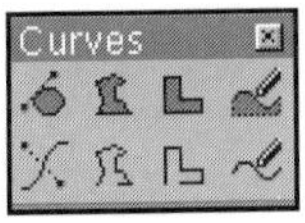

1   Click the Line icon and select the kind of line you want to draw.

2   Draw the line in the workspace.

Click and drag the mouse to the first point where you want to change directions. From then on just move the mouse to the next point where you change directions, and double-click to stop drawing.

Editing a Bezier Curve

Use the object bar (Figure 30-12) to edit a Bezier curve.

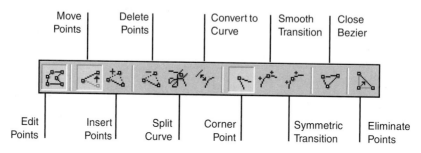

Figure 30-12 Edit Points icons on the object bar

Note – If you want all of the points on a curve to be selected if you only select one, you can set that up in Draw options. Choose Tools > Options > Drawing > Layout. Select the All handles in Bezier editor option, then click OK.

---

1   Select the object.

2   Be sure that the Edit Points icon is clicked, that the Bezier icons are active in the object bar, and that blue handles, rather than green handles, are displayed when you select the object.

Some icons are available only when you select a point.

Click the Edit Points icon if the handles are green. Green handles let you move the object and resize the object proportionately, the same way you would resize a polygon.

3   A number of handles are shown on the curve, one for each point. Select a point to apply changes to; it will turn dark green.

4   Make the appropriate edits, using the editing icons. An example of possible edits is shown in Figure 30-13.

Edit Points Lets you edit a curve.

Move Points Must be active to let you drag a point to a different location.

Insert Points Adds points to the curve. Note: This lets you add points until you click it again to turn it off.

Note – Be sure the Eliminate Points icon is inactive while you're inserting points, or you'll be adding a point and eliminating it a microsecond later.

Delete Points Removes the selected point. The shape will change, connecting the two points on either side.

Split Curve Disconnects the curve at the selected point; incomplete curves can't have fill, so the fill will be removed.

Convert To Curve Changes straight points to curved points, and back. Set Corner Point, Smooth, and Symmetric are applicable only to curved points (when To Curve is active).

Corner Point Lets a point have two separate control handles rather than the usual one.

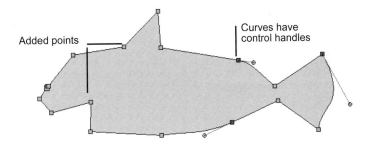

Figure 30-13   Editing Bezier curves

Smooth Transition Reshapes a curve so that both handles of the corner point are aligned parallel, and can only be moved simultaneously. The curves on either side of the point can be different.

Symmetric Transition Converts a corner point or smooth point to a symmetrical point. Both handles of the corner point are aligned parallel and also have the same length. These can only be moved simultaneously. The degree of curvature is in both directions the same.

Close Bezier Closes an open curve. The two points connected are not necessarily the end ones. A line is closed always by combining the last point with the first point (indicated by an enlarged square).

Eliminate Points Deletes the selected (dark green) point.

Modifying and Creating Colors

You can change any of the colors that are displayed in the color bar, or in any of the color lists. This section covers how to create or modify an *individual color* or a *color palette*.

For program-wide color setup, creating new colors for use in all documents and specifying the default color, see *Changing the Default Color for New Objects or Creating a New Color* on page 123.

> **Note –** There's no revert feature to change back modified colors, so we suggest that you create new ones when possible, rather than modifying.

Both color models are included in Draw: RGB and CMYK.

Adding or Modifying an Individual Color

1   Open the Area window, use other of the following methods:

- Click the Area icon in the object bar.
- Right-click an object and choose Area.

2   Click the Color tab.

3   Click the Load Color List icon in the color window to switch palettes, if necessary. That is how you can switch to another palette, such as CMYK; selecting CMYK or RGB from the Color sample list will change only the fields that you can use to adjust an individual color.

4   To change or create a color by changing only the RGB or CMYK values, use the following steps, in the Area window only (Figure 30-14):

- Select a color in the Table area.
- Change the CMYK or RGB values in the fields below the color sample list.
- To add the changes as a new color, click Add and enter a new name. To change the color, just click Modify.

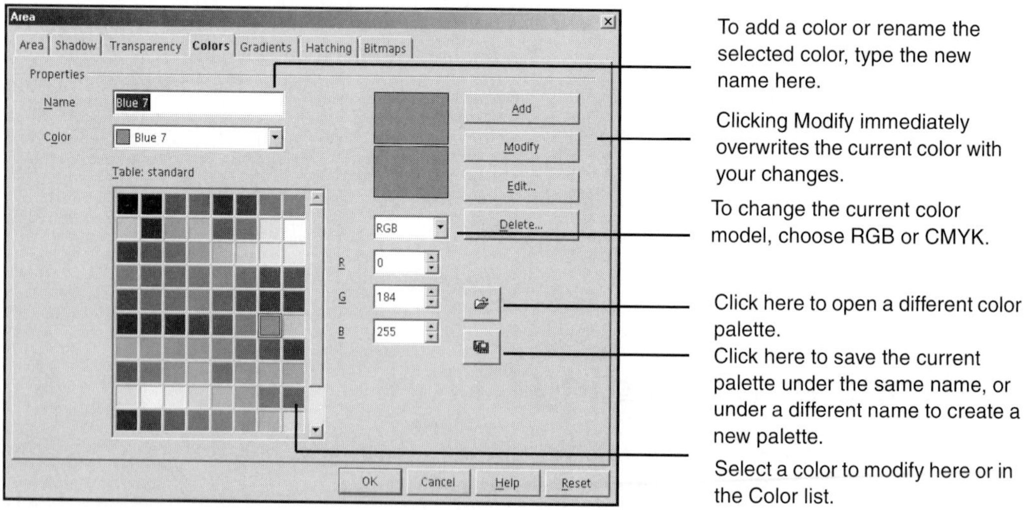

To add a color or rename the selected color, type the new name here.

Clicking Modify immediately overwrites the current color with your changes.

To change the current color model, choose RGB or CMYK.

Click here to open a different color palette.

Click here to save the current palette under the same name, or under a different name to create a new palette.

Select a color to modify here or in the Color list.

Figure 30-14   Color tab of Area window

5 To change or create a color and modify the hue, saturation, and brightness as well as the RGB or CMYK values, use these steps and the Color window (Figure 30-15):

- To create a new color, click Add and enter a new name, then click Edit.
- To modify a color, click Edit.

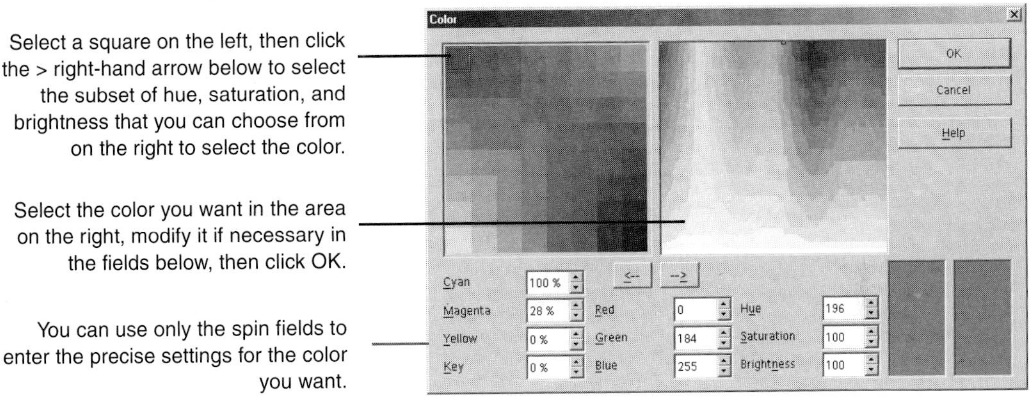

Select a square on the left, then click the > right-hand arrow below to select the subset of hue, saturation, and brightness that you can choose from on the right to select the color.

Select the color you want in the area on the right, modify it if necessary in the fields below, then click OK.

You can use only the spin fields to enter the precise settings for the color you want.

Figure 30-15 Creating or modifying a color in the Color window

Changing Color Palettes

A color palette is a collection of colors displayed in the color bar, or listed in a color list. The file name for the standard color palette is `standard.soc`, and stored in the `user/config` folder.

There are five palettes: `standard.soc`, `web.soc`, `html.soc`, `cmyk.soc`, and `palette.soc`. To change to a different color palette:

1 Choose Format > Area and click the Color tab.

2 Click the Load Color List icon and select any file with a `.soc` extension.

Changes and additions to individual colors are palette-specific; changing in one palette doesn't change the same color in another palette.

Changing Color Models

The color model is what the available colors in the color bar, color lists, and color definition windows are based on. There are two standards: RGB (red-green-blue, the model used by your monitor) and CYMK (cyan-magenta-yellow-black, the model used by commercial printers). RGB is the default. CMYK looks distinctly different, with more pastel colors.

If you'll be printing high-quality color copies of the presentation, you should probably switch color models from RGB to CYMK.

To change the color model before you begin applying colors:

1 Open the Area window, use either of the following methods:

- Click the Area icon in the object bar.
- Right-click an object and choose Area.

2 In the Area window, click the Colors tab.

3 Click Open.

4 Select CMYK or RGB from the Color sample list. This changes the fields below it that you can use to adjust a particular color.

5 To select a different color list and change the colors that appear in the Table area, click the Load Color List icon. In the `user/config` folder, select a file such as `cmyk.soc` file.

Adding or Modifying a Color Palette

1 Open the Area window (choose Format > Area or click the Area icon).

2 Change the palette, if necessary, by clicking the Load Color List icon.

3 Make changes to colors in the palette.

4 Click the Save Color List icon.

5 Add or modify the palette:

- To modify, save the color palette with the current name.
- To add a palette, save it with a different name.

Creating and Modifying Gradients, Hatches, and Bitmaps

> **Note –** To use one of these items to fill text, see *Formatting Text With Bitmaps, Gradients, and Hatches* on page 773.

You can change or add to what the program provides for object area fills.

As with colors and lines, you can add or modify *individual fills*, and you can add or modify *lists of fills*. These lists also are stored in the `config` folder, with the file extension names `.sog`, `.soh`, and `.soe` for gradients, hatches, and bitmaps, respectively.

Gradients

1   Open the Area window by choosing Format > Area.

2   Click the Gradient tab (Figure 30-16).

3   Use the Load Gradients List icon to load the appropriate gradient set, if necessary.

4   Create a new gradient or modify an existing one:

- To create a new gradient, click the Add button and enter a new name; click OK.

- To modify a gradient, select a gradient and click the Modify button, leave the existing name in the field, and click OK.

If you want to save your changes in a different list, click the Save Gradients List icon and save the list under a new name.

Select the gradient type.

Enter the horizontal distance from the left border, and the vertical distance from the top border of the object to the color center. The distance is specified relative to the entire width and height of the object.

Enter a rotation angle for the Linear, Axial, Ellipsoid, Square, and Rectangle gradient types.

Define the border thickness. The measure is specified in relation to the whole area.

Select the beginning and ending colors, and their intensity.

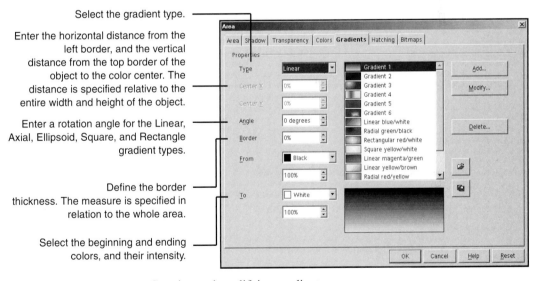

Figure 30-16   Creating and modifying gradients

Hatches

1   Open the Area window (choose Format > Area).

2   Click the Hatching tab (Figure 30-17).

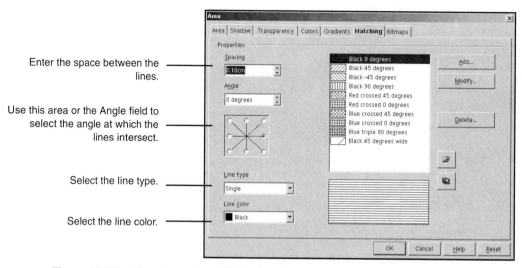

Enter the space between the lines.

Use this area or the Angle field to select the angle at which the lines intersect.

Select the line type.

Select the line color.

Figure 30-17 Creating and modifying hatches

3 Use the Load Hatches List icon to load the appropriate hatch list, if necessary.

4 Create a new hatch or modify an existing one:

- To create a new hatch, click the Add button and enter a new name, then click OK.

- To modify a hatch, select a hatch and click the Modify button, leave the existing name in the field, and click OK.

Keep in mind that when the hatch is applied, you can choose a background color for it, or leave the background blank.

If you want to save your changes in a different list, click the Save Hatch List icon and save the list under a new name.

Bitmaps

You can fill an area with a graphical design of your choosing. You can create one in the Bitmaps tab, import one, modify one, or use existing ones provided with the program.

Note – Some formats, such as .WMF, lose some colors when imported.

---

1 Open the Area window (choose Format > Area).

2 Click the Bitmaps tab (Figure 30-18).

3 Use the Load Bitmaps List icon to load the appropriate bitmaps list, if necessary.

4 Select the source of the bitmap.

- To **draw a new bitmap**, select foreground and background colors and click in the bitmap field to design it.

- To **import a new bitmap**, click Import and select any graphics file, then enter a name and click OK. To add a specific bitmap from the Gallery, select the item in the Gallery and note the location. Then just browse to that location and select the file to import as a bitmap.

- To **modify a bitmap** that you created using the pixel editor (not an existing or imported bitmap), select the appropriate bitmap, click the Modify button, leave the existing name in the field, and click OK.

Note – The bitmaps you create with the pixel editor are going to be a little rough. You'll generally get better results by using Image or Draw to create a raster file, then importing it by clicking Import.

To create a bitmap in this window, select Blank as the type, then select a foreground and background color, then click on each pixel where you want the foreground.

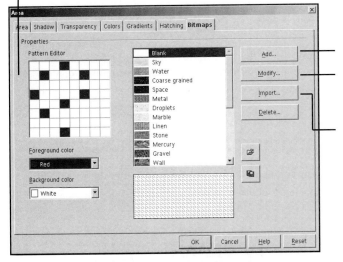

Click Add to add a newly created pattern from the Pattern Editor window.

Click Modify if you've changed the pattern in the Pattern Editor area for an existing bitmap.

To use an existing graphic, click Import to select a file. You can use any raster format, such as GIF, BMP, or JPG.

Figure 30-18   Creating and modifying bitmaps

Creating Three-Dimensional Objects

Draw lets you create impressive three-dimensional, *3D*, effects. You can create a new 3D object or convert a 2D object to 3D, as well as control the appearance of shading and other effects. Use the 3D icon in the toolbar on the left side of the workspace.

Note – You can get particularly interesting-looking 3D objects by converting 2D polygons, using the Effects icon. See *Making Other Cool 3D Shapes By Converting Any Object to 3D* on page 826 for more information.

Creating a 3D Object

1   Click on the 3D Objects icon and select an object to draw.

The possible objects are cube, sphere, cylinders, cones, pyramids, toruses (donuts), shells, and half-spheres.

2   Draw the object in the work area.

You can show the contour lines in a 3D object by selecting Continuous in the Lines list in the object bar. Selecting Invisible shows the object without contour lines. Borders don't apply to 3D objects. Objects in this section are shown both with (in the next procedure) and without contour lines (in the previous step).

Resizing and Changing Proportions

Just grab any of the green handles and drag the handle to increase or decrease size, or change the shape. Some of the shapes have predefined proportions that you can't override while drawing, but you can change after you've released the mouse from the original drawing action.

Rotating and Changing Angles of 3D Objects

When the object is drawn or converted to 3D, it's not always terribly dramatic looking, and is often rather flat-looking. You can use the rotate handles, though, to twist the object around in 3D and jazz it up. An example is shown in Figure 30-19.

As drawn   After rotating

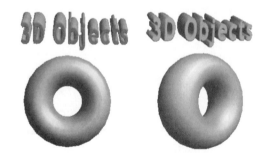

Figure 30-19   Example or rotated 3D objects

1   Select the item, then pause and click it again (not double-clicking). Red handles will appear instead of the standard green ones.

    If you want to rotate text you've converted to 3D, be careful. If you just get one letter selected, deselect it, then click outside the text and regroup it. Repeat the steps in step 1 without double-clicking; pause between selections.

2   Move the mouse over a handle; the rotation icon will appear.

3   Use the appropriate handle to rotate the object, as indicated in Figure 30-20.

      Effect of using the corner rotation handles

      Effect of using the side rotation handles

      Effect of using the top and bottom rotation handles

Figure 30-20   Rotating 3D objects

Merging 3D Objects

You can create the effect of one object intersecting with another using the merging feature.

1   Draw two 3D objects.

2   Select the object you want to appear in front and press Ctrl+X to "cut" the object.

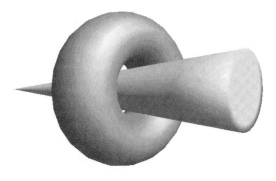

3   Select the object you want to appear in back and press F3.

4   Press Ctrl+V; this pastes the front object onto the back object. Move either object around to position it (the pasted object might not appear at first; move the back object around and it will appear).

Applying 3D Attributes to 3D Objects

Draw provides an almost bewildering array of attributes that you can apply to 3D objects, shown in Figure 30-21.

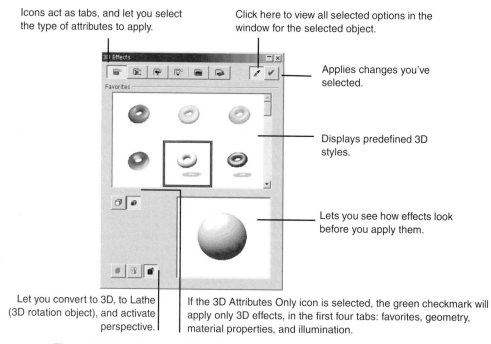

Icons act as tabs, and let you select the type of attributes to apply.

Click here to view all selected options in the window for the selected object.

Applies changes you've selected.

Displays predefined 3D styles.

Lets you see how effects look before you apply them.

Let you convert to 3D, to Lathe (3D rotation object), and activate perspective.

If the 3D Attributes Only icon is selected, the green checkmark will apply only 3D effects, in the first four tabs: favorites, geometry, material properties, and illumination.

Figure 30-21   Applying 3D effects

This includes lighting and shading features, rounded or straight edges, colors, and many other features. You can apply these features to 2D objects if you convert them to 3D first; this includes Bezier curves and text.

It's beyond the scope of this book to tell you how to create the best 3D objects. You'll need to experiment with each of the features to see which ones achieve the specific effects you need for your projects. However, the following procedures do tell you how to apply each type of feature, and show some examples.

1   Draw or select a 3D object.

2   Choose Format > 3D Effects, or click the 3D Controller icon in the toolbar, to open the 3D Effects window.

3   Select any of the effects, then specify which effects you want to apply by clicking the 3D Attributes Only icon (left) or the Assign All Attributes icon to apply only 3D effects: favorites, geometry, material properties, and illumination.

4   Click the green checkmark in the upper right corner to apply changes.

Favorites – Applying a Predefined 3D Style The Favorites icon and corresponding options is selected by default when you open the 3D Effects window. Twelve predefined combinations of effects, or favorites, are available, combining selections from all categories in the 3D Effects window. Select any one to view in the Preview window how it would affect your object.

Geometry – Modifying Angle, Depth and Other Features

These allow you to change a variety of features, including the number of segments. The horizontal and vertical are typically the same; the following illustration shows a normal cone, then the same cone with the settings of 2 horizontal and 14 vertical.

Standard   2H, 14V

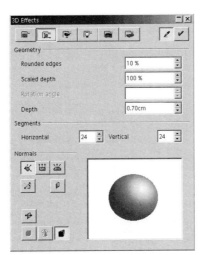

Figure 30-22   Geometry options for 3D objects

Shading Properties – Controlling Shading and Focal Properties This section lets you control shade mode, as well as shadow, camera distance, and focal length. The following illustration shows the different modes.

Gouraud (default)   Phong   Flat

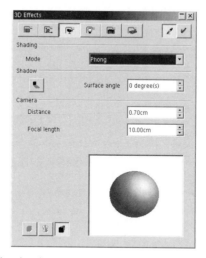

Figure 30-23   Illumination options for 3D objects

Illumination The Illumination section lets you set
options for the light source. You can select a color
for the light source, as well as a color for the
ambient light.

You can modify the colors for each light source and
ambient light setting by clicking the tricolored icon
by each list to open the Colors window, which
allows you to set color values, hue, saturation, and
brightness. However, the changes are permanent
and cannot be reset to the originals. You may want
to leave the defaults as they are and create new
settings.

As you can see in the illustration, the differences
are sometimes slight.

To change or add a color listed in any color list,
refer to *Modifying and Creating Colors* on page 801.

Light source: Light gray

Ambient light: Ambient light:
Yellow 1   Yellow 8

Ambient light: Light gray

Light source: Light source:
Magenta 1   Magenta 8

Figure 30-24   Illumination options for 3D objects

Textures You can use the options available through the Textures tab **only** if the object has a gradient, hatch, or bitmap applied to it, using the Areas window. (Select the object and right-click, then choose Areas.) You can modify a number of attributes, including changing an object to black-and-white and back, without losing the color.

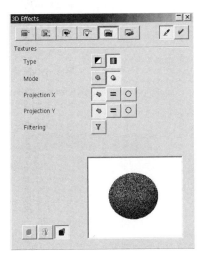

Figure 30-25   Textures options for 3D objects

Material – Choosing a Finish and Color This tab lets you specify color for a set of finish favorites such as gold or plastic: object color, illumination color, specular color, and specular intensity. As in the Illumination tab, you can modify the colors, hue, saturation, and brightness for each selection in each list, using the tricolored icon.

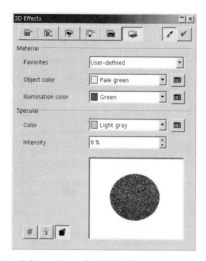

Figure 30-26   Materials options for 3D objects

Adding Other Files or Objects to Drawings

You can insert nearly anything into a file: a new or existing spreadsheet, a chart, a new GIF, whatever. Most of these capabilities are part of other parts of the program, however. This section lists the features you have available, and where to find the information.

The Insert icon lets you access the Insert tearoff menu (Figure 30-27), where many of the insert functions are located.

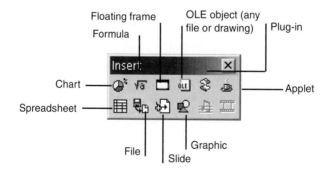

Figure 30-27   Items you can add to drawings

Inserting Other Objects and Files

These features are covered in *Adding Objects and Links to Documents* on page 265.

You can insert pretty much any kind of file in any StarOffice or OpenOffice.org document.

The most flexible way to insert files is to use the OLE object icon in Figure 30-27 or to choose Insert > Object > OLE Object. ("OLE object" is an unnecessarily techy way of putting it—OLE is the technology that lets you edit the file once you've inserted it in another file. For example, you can insert an "OLE object," a Draw file, in a Writer file, and edit the drawing right in Writer.

Inserting Text and HTML Files

You can insert HTML, and text (ASCII, not Writer) files into a drawing. See *Inserting Text and HTML Files* on page 702 in *Developing Presentations*.

Inserting Images

You can add empty graphics frames or existing graphics files. See *Inserting Pictures (Images and Drawings)* on page 703 in *Developing Presentations*.

Inserting Forms, Buttons, and Other Controls

Figure 30-28 shows form options.

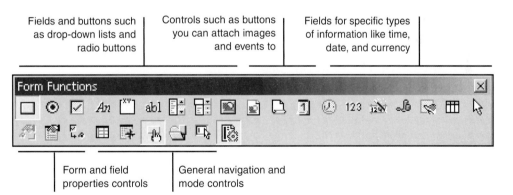

Figure 30-28   Forms and form components

Making Exact and Modified Copies

Draw provides multiple tools to copy and duplicate objects; some allow you to do so quickly, while others provide you precise control over size and positioning.

Copying Objects

1   Select an object using the arrow-shaped Select icon (active by default) and choose Edit > Copy.

2   Move to the drawing where you want the copy, if necessary, and choose Edit > Paste.

Note – The object may appear on top of the original; if so, move it to the side.

Duplicating Objects

You can duplicate quickly, or with more options.

Quickly Making One Copy

1   Select the object.

2   Choose Edit > Duplicate.

3   In the Duplicate window, choose OK.

Advanced Duplicating

You can control the number of copies, the location to which they are moved, rotation, size change, and color change. For example, the original on the left in Figure 30-29 was rotated, enlarged, and changed in color through five copies.

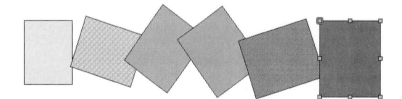

Figure 30-29   Advanced duplicating capabilities

1   Select the object.

2   Choose Edit > Duplicate to open the Duplicate window.

3   Make the appropriate changes (Figure 30-30), then click OK to duplicate.

Enter the number of copies to make.

Enter how far from the upper left corner of the object each successive copy should be.

Enter how much to rotate each successive copy.

Enter how much larger each successive copy should be (not how much bigger the last copy should be).

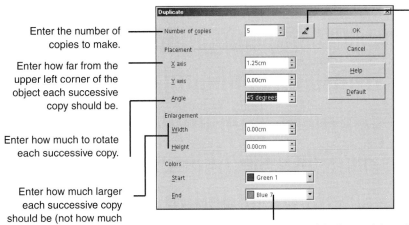

Click the Values from Selection icon to enter the current object's size and color in the X axis, Y axis, and Start fields.

Enter a color to change the original to, and the color for the last copy. Intervening copies will be gradually changed from the start to the end color.

Figure 30-30   Advanced duplicating

Distorting and Curving Text and Objects With the Effects Tools

You can use the Set in circle, Set to circle, and Distort icons on the Effects tearoff menu to achieve extremely interesting effects with objects or text. Figure 30-31 and Figure 30-32 illustrate effects on text and objects.

Original

Set in circle

Slanted

Distorted

Figure 30-31   Distorted and curved text

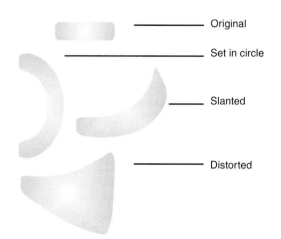

Figure 30-32 Distorted and curved text

1 Select an object or objects.

2 Click the Effects icon in the toolbar on the left side of the work area, and click either of the Set in Circle icons, or the Distort icon.

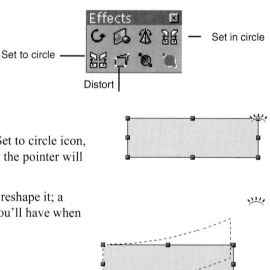

3 Choose Yes when prompted to change the object to a curve.

4 If you selected a Set in circle or Set to circle icon, position the mouse over a corner; the pointer will change to a crown shape.

5 Click on the object and drag it to reshape it; a dotted line will show the effect you'll have when you release the mouse button.

Distorting and Curving Text Using FontWork

See also *Formatting Text With Bitmaps, Gradients, and Hatches* on page 773.

Choose Format > FontWork. FontWork is an add-on program that lets you apply extensive formatting to text, shown in Figure 30-33. Select text and choose Format > FontWork to use it.

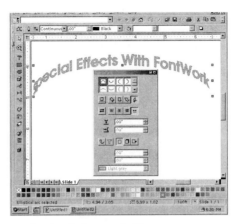

Figure 30-33   FontWork window and effects

Curving Text to a Preset Curve

FontWork has several preset curves you can use to curve text; you can also apply shadows and control alignment.

1   Type or paste the text you want into a drawing.

2   Deselect the text, then click again on the text frame so that green handles appear. Drag the text frame so that the text fills it entirely.

www.lastturtle.com

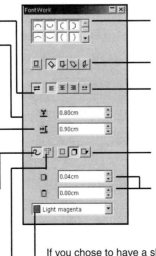

Click this icon to flip the text upside down.
In the Distance field, enter the distance between the text and the curve line, if any.

In the Indent field, if you selected to left align or right align the text, enter the distance between the end of the text and the corresponding end of the curve or object.

Click the Contour icon here to show or hide a line next to the text (for the first two rows of curve icons at the top of the window) or a filled circle (for the final row of icons).

Click the T icon to outline the text.

Click any of these icons to curve the text vertically or horizontally, or in circles (scroll down to see those icons.

Click one of these icons to align the text at any of the angles displayed.

Click an alignment icon to align the text at left, center, right, or stretch/scrunch the text exactly the length of the curve.

Click the shadow icons to turn off shadow; to make a shadow appear a specified distance from the text; or a specified angle from the text.

Enter the distance or degrees for the shadow in these fields.

If you chose to have a shadow, select the shadow color here.

Figure 30-34   Formatting curve on a preset curve and additional options

3   Choose Format > FontWork. In the FontWork window, make the appropriate
     selections, as shown in Figure 30-34.

4   Adjust the shape of the curve by dragging the
     green handles, and format the text if necessary.

     The text size will vary as you change the curve;
     you can't prevent that.

Curving Text Along Any Curve

You can make text follow any curve, not just the ones predefined in FontWork. Just
follow the steps in the next procedure, *Aligning Text to a Curve or Object* on page 820,
and click the Contour icon shown in Figure 30-34 to make the line invisible.

Aligning Text to a Curve or Object

Draw has the power of advanced drawing programs such as Illustrator to align text with
any Bezier curve, or object such as a rectangle, that you choose. The effect works with any
object, but is most effective with polygons, lines, and curves, shown in Figure 30-35.

Figure 30-35   Aligning text to a curve or object

1   Draw a curve using the Bezier curve tools, or draw a polygon using the rectangle or
     oval tools. A curve is shown in Figure 30-36.

Figure 30-36   Creating a curve to align text to, and the Curves tearoff menu

2   Deselect the curve, then select it again and double-click on the curve. When the
     cursor appears, type or paste the text you want to align to the curve. Deselect the text,
     then select the whole object so that green handles appear as shown in Figure 30-37.

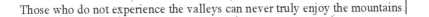

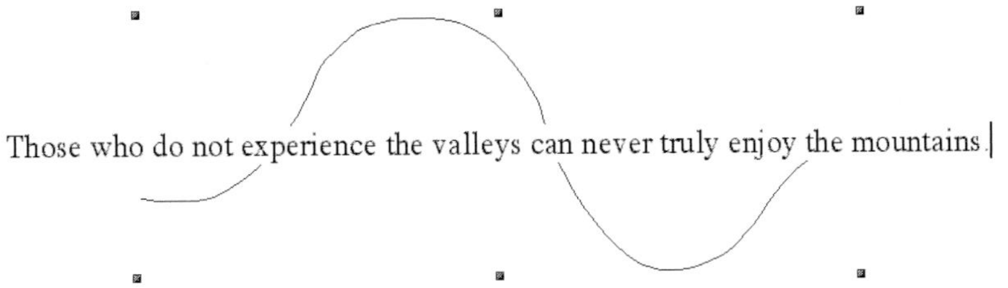

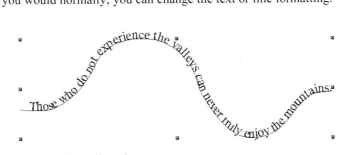

Figure 30-37   Typing or pasting text into an object you will align the text to

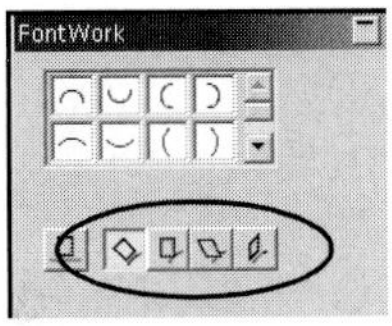

3   Choose Format > FontWork. In the FontWork window, click any of the four circled icons to align the text to the curve.

4   Make any additional selections in the window; refer to Figure 30-34 on page 819.

5   The text appears aligned to the curve or object, as shown in Figure 30-38. Format it as you would normally; you can change the text or line formatting.

Figure 30-38   Text aligned to a curve

Converting Text to 3D and Applying Formatting

You can convert text to 3D (Figure 30-39) by right-clicking the **text frame** (not the text itself) and choosing Convert > Convert to 3D.

www.javaranch.com   Plain text

Text after conversion to 3D (not 3D
Rotation Object)

Text after rotating and applying yellow/
green gradient

Text after applying 3D effect from 3D
controller window

Figure 30-39   Text before and after 3D conversion

Choosing 3D Rotation Object will result in a cool effect, but it won't be legible. Be sure to select 3D.

Figure 30-40   Text after conversion to 3D Rotation Object

Morphing One Object Into Another Using Cross-Fading

Cross-fading incrementally changes one shape into another, as shown in Figure 30-41.

1   Select two objects. (The one created second will appear in full in the resultant cross-fade. In Figure 30-41, the top objects were created second.)

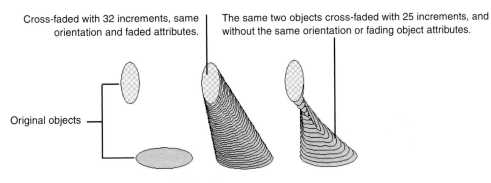

Cross-faded with 32 increments, same orientation and faded attributes.
The same two objects cross-faded with 25 increments, and without the same orientation or fading object attributes.
Original objects

Figure 30-41 Cross-faded objects

2 Choose Edit > Cross-fading.

3 Make the appropriate changes and click OK (Figure 30-42).

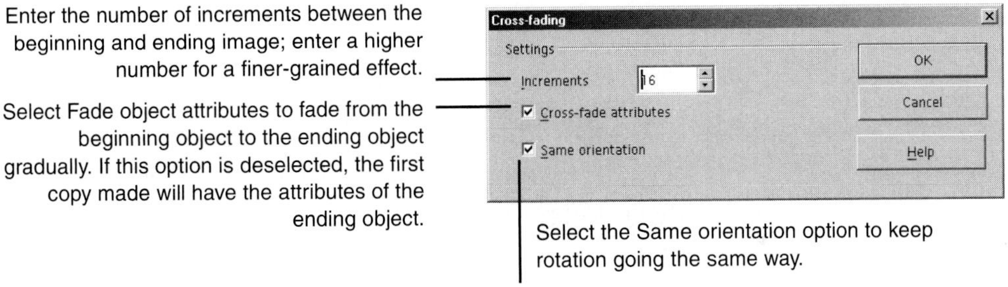

Enter the number of increments between the beginning and ending image; enter a higher number for a finer-grained effect.
Select Fade object attributes to fade from the beginning object to the ending object gradually. If this option is deselected, the first copy made will have the attributes of the ending object.
Cross-fading
Settings
Increments
16
Cross-fade attributes
Same orientation
OK
Cancel
Help
Select the Same orientation option to keep rotation going the same way.

Figure 30-42 Cross-fading objects

Converting Objects to Different Types

You can do some effects, like using the Eyedropper, only to bitmaps. So how do you apply that to a polygon? Just convert it. You can apply gradients and bitmaps to text, but only if they're converted to bitmaps or 3D.

To convert, just right-click on any graphic in Draw, choose Convert, and you'll see what you can convert it to. Table 30-1 summarizes those options.

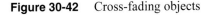

Metafile is a format specific to Microsoft Windows. Unless you've got a good reason, choose bitmap instead, since some of the features for editing rasters in Draw don't work with bitmaps.

Table 30-1   File format conversion

Image to convert	Conversion option	Comments
Polygon (square, oval, etc.)	Curve, contour, 3D, 3D rotation object, bitmap, metafile	
Curve	Polygon, contour, 3D, 3D rotation object, bitmap, metafile	
Contour	Curve, 3D, 3D rotation object, bitmap, metafile	A contour is a group of polygons that make up the object.
Line	Curve, contour, 3D, 3D rotation object, bitmap, metafile	
Bitmap	Polygon, contour, 3D, 3D rotation object, metafile	See *Converting a Raster Object (Image) to a Draw Polygon Object* on page 827.
Metafile	Polygon, contour, 3D, 3D rotation object, bitmap	Conversion to 3D or 3D rotation object loses all color. Only black and white are used in the result.
3D object	Bitmap, metafile	
3D rotation object	Bitmap, metafile	

Converting a Draw Object to Another Draw (Vector) Type

1   Select a curve, line, polygon, or metafile (such as a GIF image you've pasted in from Image).

Some types can't be converted; for instance, 3D object or 3D rotation objects can't be converted to any other shape. In addition, curves drawn with the Polygon curve tools are already considered polygons for this purpose, so they can't be converted to polygons.

2   Right-click it and select Convert.

3   Select one of the listed object types.

You can now edit the object based on its new type; if you converted a

polygon to a curve, for instance, you can edit points using the curve icons on the object bar.

Notes on the different types of conversions follow.

Lines to curves Converting a line to a curve lets you bend it and offers all standard Bezier curve editing features, such as the control handle (shown in Figure 30-43).

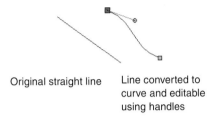

Original straight line   Line converted to
curve and editable
using handles

Figure 30-43   Converting a line to a curve

Polygons to 3D You can convert any object to a 3D object or 3D rotation object; polygons and curves result in the most interesting effects (see Figure 30-44).

Original 2D object
Converted to 3D
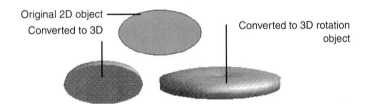
Converted to 3D rotation
object

Figure 30-44   Converting a polygon to 3D

Curves to 3D Rotation You can achieve surprising effects by converting Bezier curves to 3D rotation objects (see Figure 30-45).

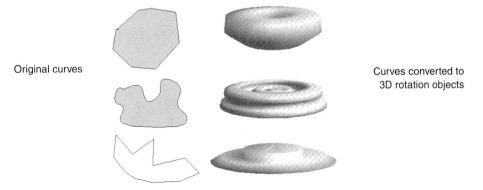

Original curves

Curves converted to
3D rotation objects

Figure 30-45   Converting a curve to a 3D rotation object

Curves to polygons Converting a curve to a polygon is possible, but doesn't result in many useful changes. Many more points are added, dragging a point results in a pointed shape rather than a curve, and the control handle is no longer available. Figure 30-46 shows two curves converted to polygons.

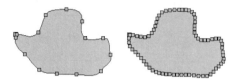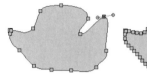

Filled curve   Filled curve, converted to   Filled curve, dragging a   Filled curve, converted to
                polygon   point to a different   polygon, dragging a point
                                              location   to a different location

Figure 30-46   Converting a curve to a polygon

Making Other Cool 3D Shapes By Converting Any Object to 3D

The previous procedure tells you how to convert an object to 3D with relatively interesting results. However, the 3D conversion icon on the Effects tearoff menu gives you much more flexibility. Figure 30-47 shows the contrast.

Original object   3D rotation object   3D rotation object using Effects menu

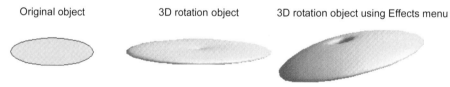

Figure 30-47   Converting to 3D using the Effects tearoff menu

1   Select an object that is a polygon, or convert a raster to a polygon. (You can get some pretty interesting effects applying this to a scanned photo.)

2   Click the Effects icon to display the Effects tearoff menu, then click the In 3D Rotation Object icon.

3   A line will appear to the left of the object. Drag the end to the left or right (in Figure 30-47, the top end of the line was dragged to the left a few degrees).

4   Click in the empty shape to the left of the object; the conversion will take place.

Converting a Raster Object (Image) to a Draw Polygon Object

You can convert raster objects to Draw objects such as polygons and 3D objects.

For all formats but polygons, simply right-click on the object and choose Convert and the type of object you want.

If you're converting a bitmap (not a raster) to a polygon, the window in Figure 30-48 will appear. Choose the appropriate options and click OK.

Note – If you convert a curved bitmap, such as the oval shown in Figure 30-48, then apply a different fill such as another color or pattern, the shape will change to a square or rectangle and you'll lose the original shape.

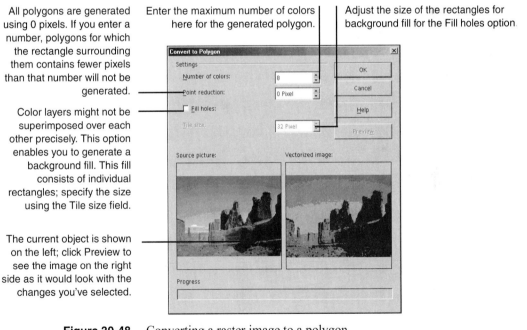

All polygons are generated using 0 pixels. If you enter a number, polygons for which the rectangle surrounding them contains fewer pixels than that number will not be generated.

Enter the maximum number of colors here for the generated polygon.

Adjust the size of the rectangles for background fill for the Fill holes option.

Color layers might not be superimposed over each other precisely. This option enables you to generate a background fill. This fill consists of individual rectangles; specify the size using the Tile size field.

The current object is shown on the left; click Preview to see the image on the right side as it would look with the changes you've selected.

Figure 30-48   Converting a raster image to a polygon

Converting a Draw Object to an Image

You can convert a Draw object (a vector graphic) to a raster type (Image object), so that it's composed of pixels rather than lines. This is useful if you want to sample—change all occurrences of a color in an image to another color. See *Changing Selected Colors in Images Using the Eyedropper* on page 833, as well as Chapter 31, *Editing Images*, on page 831.

Converting by Right-Clicking

You can convert most Draw objects to a bitmap or metafile. Simply right-click on an object or objects and choose Convert > *type*.

Using the Modify Menu

1   Select an object.

2   Choose Modify > Convert, then select the object type. See *Converting Objects to Different Types* on page 823 for information about each type.

Combining Shapes and Creating Lines From Objects

The effects in Figure 30-49 through Figure 30-50 show the effects you can combine, typically only to vector graphics like polygons and Bezier curves.

- Connection – Turning two or more objects into connected unfilled lines, which you can manipulate as you would Bezier curves

- Combining – Two or more objects are turned into lines, preserving the fill color of one, which you can manipulate as you would Bezier curves

- Shapes features – Merge, Subtract, and Intersect

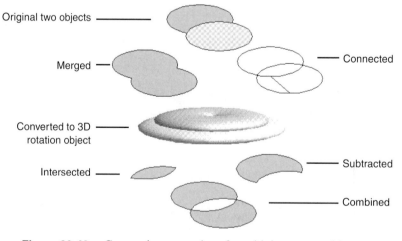

Figure 30-49   Conversion examples of combining vector objects

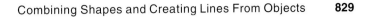

Original objects ———

Merged ———

Connected ———

Intersected ———

Subtracted ———

Combined. Entire
object is colored
using the currently
selected color in the
object bar, not the
color of the polygon.

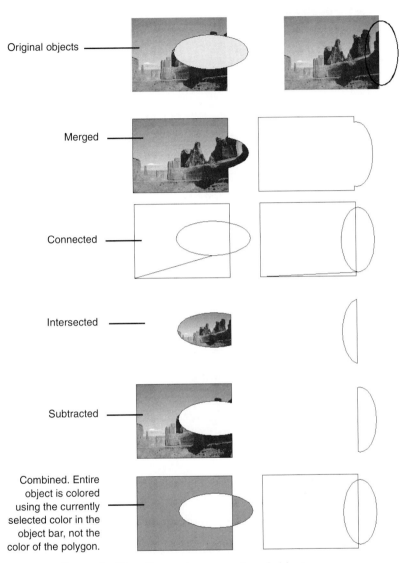

Figure 30-50   Conversion examples of objects

Connecting Objects as a Bezier Curve

1   Select two or more objects.

2   Right-click and choose Connect.

3   The objects will be turned into unfilled lines (Figure 30-51), which you can
manipulate as you would Bezier curves.

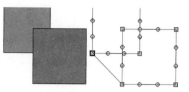

Figure 30-51   Connecting objects

4   Click the Edit Points icon to stop editing; it will become a normal object.

5   Right-click the object and choose Break to turn the object into individual lines.

Note – To return the objects to normal, right-click and select Split, then click Edit Points.

Combining Objects as a Bezier Curve

1   Select two or more objects.

2   Right-click and choose Combine.

3   The objects will be turned into lines, preserving the fill (Figure 30-52), which you can manipulate as you would Bezier curves.

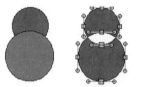

Original objects   Combined object

Figure 30-52   Combining objects

4   Click the Edit Points icon to stop editing; it will become a normal object.

5   Right-click the object and choose Break to turn the object into a individual lines.

Note – To return the objects to normal, right-click and select Split, then click Edit Points.

Merging, Subtracting, and Intersecting

See Figure 30-49 on page 828 for illustrations of these effects.

1   Select two or more objects.

2   Right-click and choose Shape, then Merge, Subtract, or Intersect.

Editing Images

Changing Colors, Contrast, and Intensity

The *graphics object bar* (Figure 31-1) is only available when you select a raster object. It allows you to change color saturation, etc. If it isn't displayed, choose View > Toolbars > Object Bar.

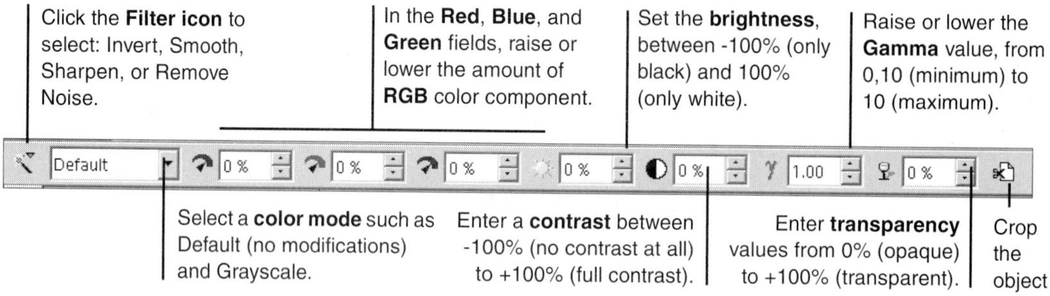

Click the **Filter icon** to select: Invert, Smooth, Sharpen, or Remove Noise.

In the **Red**, **Blue**, and **Green** fields, raise or lower the amount of **RGB** color component.

Set the **brightness**, between -100% (only black) and 100% (only white).

Raise or lower the **Gamma** value, from 0,10 (minimum) to 10 (maximum).

Select a **color mode** such as Default (no modifications) and Grayscale.

Enter a **contrast** between -100% (no contrast at all) to +100% (full contrast).

Enter **transparency** values from 0% (opaque) to +100% (transparent).

Crop the object

Figure 31-1   Graphics object bar – available when raster object is selected

Note – The gamma value is a measurement unit used for contrasting gray tones.

Editing RGB Color Values

You can increase or decrease the red, green, or blue in an image just by entering different numbers or clicking the arrows, in the image toolbar.

To make the toolbar appear, click on the image. Make the adjustments you want by entering a number or clicking the up and down arrows.

Changing Color Resolution

You can reduce the number of colors in a bitmap to optimize it for Web use, for instance. Examples are shown in Figure 31-2.

Original full-color photo   4-bit color palette   1-bit dithering

Figure 31-2   Examples of different color resolutions

To change the resolution, right-click the object and select the appropriate color resolution, as shown in Figure 31-3. You can change the resolution of only one object at a time; if you select two or more objects, the Color Resolution item won't appear.

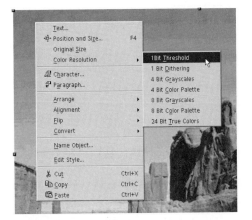

Figure 31-3   Changing color resolution

Changing Selected Colors in Images Using the Eyedropper

One of the most powerful features of Image is the eyedropper. You can use the eyedropper tool to *sample*—change a color to a different color everywhere it appears in your image.

You may get unexpected results; one of the colors you select to be changed might show up in your graphic where you don't expect it. Carefully check the results you get, and be prepared to use the Undo feature.

1   Choose Tools > Eyedropper, to display the Eyedropper window (Figure 31-4).

If you want to simply replace a transparent value with a color, select the Transparency option and select a color. You can replace colors or transparency, but not both.

2   In the Eyedropper window, click the eyedropper icon in the upper left corner.

3   Move the mouse to the first color in the drawing area that you want to replace. You can see the color you're over in the color field in the Eyedropper window. When you see the color you want in that field, click the mouse.

Note – If the mouse pointer turns to the "Ghostbusters" symbol, just click in the Eyedropper window and it'll return to normal.

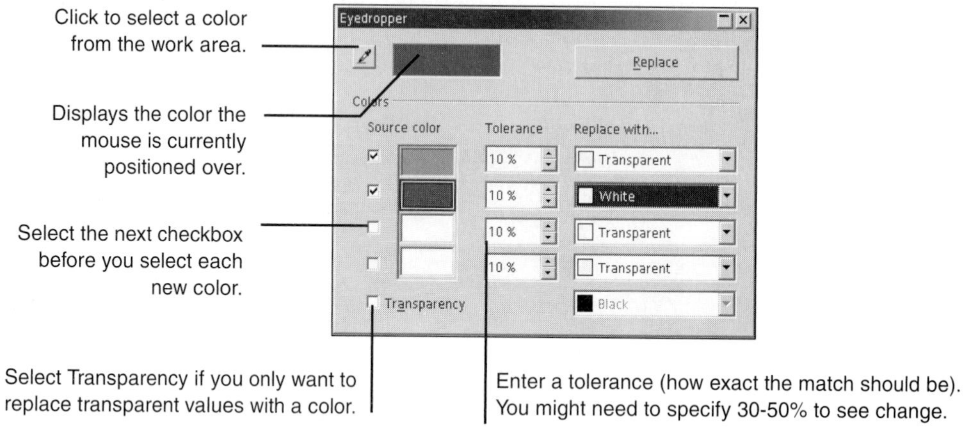

Click to select a color
from the work area.

Displays the color the
mouse is currently
positioned over.

Select the next checkbox
before you select each
new color.

Select Transparency if you only want to
replace transparent values with a color.

Enter a tolerance (how exact the match should be).
You might need to specify 30-50% to see change.

Figure 31-4   Using the Eyedropper

4   Enter the tolerance—how exact the color match should be. Start with the default, 10%, but you'll probably need to increase it to 30% or 50%.

5   In the Replace with list, select the color to change to.

6   To select other colors to change, select the checkbox next to the second of the four color fields. Repeat steps 2–5.

7   Click Replace. If nothing happens, increase the tolerance and click Replace again.

Editing Contrast and Transparency

The image editing toolbar also lets you change the following values:

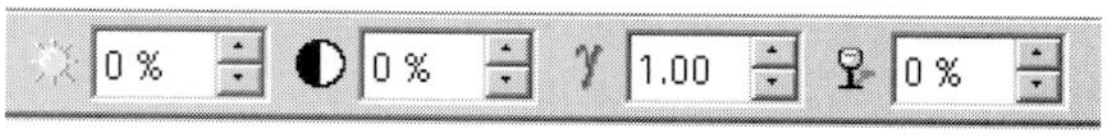

- Brightness – Values between 100% (only black) and 100% (only white).

- Contrast – Values between -100% (no contrast at all) to +100% (full contrast).

- Gamma – Values from .01 (minimum) to 10 (maximum).

- Transparency – Values from 0 to 100%.

To make the toolbar appear, click on the image. Make the adjustments you want by entering a number or clicking the up and down arrows.

Deleting and Cropping an Image

While the image editing software is primarily limited to colors and filters, you can still do some work through cropping and deleting, with a rectangle or with any shape you create.

Cropping Using the Crop Window and a Rectangle Shape

In 5.2, you could just draw a rectangle and click Crop. Now, the standard approach is to bring up the Crop window and type in the distance of the change to make. This is one of the few features that's more annoying in 6.0. However, we've figured out another way to not only crop with the mouse instead of the keyboard, but to crop with any shape you want. See *Cropping an Image in Any Shape* on page 835.

1 Select the image.

2 Click the Crop icon at the far right of the graphics object bar.

3 The Crop window appears; enter the distance down, up, left, and right to bring the border in. The preview shows the effect, as shown in Figure 31-5.When you're satisfied, click OK.

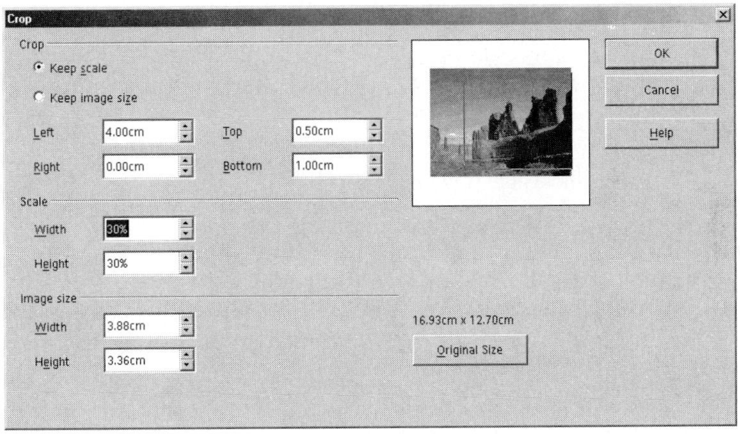

Figure 31-5   Cropping an image in the Crop window

Cropping an Image in Any Shape

1 Select the image to crop.

2 Use the curve, rectangle, or ellipse tool to create any unfilled completed (no ends) shape (you might think of it as your "crop circle").

3 Move it to the location on the image and resize it if necessary to define the size and shape of the picture you want to be left with, as shown in Figure 31-6.

Image to crop

The object you draw to define the
shape and contents of what will
be left after you crop, or "crop
circle.

Figure 31-6   Defining the area of the picture you want

4   Select both objects, then right-click on the objects and choose Shapes > Intersect. The
outside of the image will be removed, leaving the area inside the shape you drew. This
is shown in Figure 31-7.

Figure 31-7   The cropped image, using the Intersect feature

Deleting Part of an Image

As with the previous procedure, just draw the area that you want to remove then select the
new object and the graphic, right-click, and choose Shapes > Subtract as in Figure 31-8.

Figure 31-8   Deleting parts of images

Applying Effects to Modify Graphics' Appearance

The Filter menu let you change how the image appears, using filters such as charcoal sketch and mosaic, and helps you improve the appearance of an image through defining, smoothing, and cleaning up the image.

Creating a Grayscale or Watermark Image

Color modes also let you apply effects: black-and-white, grayscale, and watermark.

1   Select a bitmap or metafile; the image toolbar will appear.

2   From the list at the left displaying Default, select the mode you want.

3   Figure 31-9 shows examples of each.

Grayscale

Watermark

Black and white

Figure 31-9   Graphics object bar color modes

Applying Filters

1   Select a bitmap. If you want to apply a filter to a non-bitmap, right-click the object and choose Convert > Bitmap.

2   Click the Effects icon on the toolbar to open the Filter tearoff menu.

3   Select a filter from the examples shown in Figure 31-10 through Figure 31-19. If filters aren't available, you didn't install them.

Charcoal sketch Outlines images in black and hides all other colors.

Figure 31-10 Charcoal filter

Mosaic and Tile Mosaic groups pixels into rectangles of the same color. In the Mosaic window, enter the width and height of the pixel, and the definition (contrast between adjacent pixels). Like Mosaic, Tile groups pixels to produce a choppier, more "bitmapped" effect. In the Tile window, enter the size of the pixel group to use.

Figure 31-11 Mosaic and Tile filters

Relief Converts image to a relief, which has an effect like a carving or embossed paper.

Figure 31-12   Relief filter

Poster Reduces number of colors. In the Posterize window, enter how many colors to use.

Figure 31-13   Poster filter

Popart Reduces and changes colors.

Figure 31-14   Popart filter

Aging Changes colors partially to grays and brown, to achieve the effect of an old photograph. In the Aging window, enter the percentage to age.

Figure 31-15   Aging filter

Solarization Achieves the effect of a negative. In the Solarization window, enter the percentage controlling how much of the image will be effected. A low percentage will affect most of the image; a high percentage will affect very little of it. Select Invert to invert the pixel color, as well.

50% solarization, inverted

50% solarization

Figure 31-16   Solarization filter, with and without inversion

Definition Increases the contrast between pixels. In the definition window, select Low, Medium, or High.

High definition

Low definition

Figure 31-17 Definition filter

Smooth Decreases the contrast between pixels.

Figure 31-18 Smooth filter

Remove noise Removes extraneous pixels.

Figure 31-19 Remove noise filter

Note – You might not like the results you get by removing noise, depending on the pixels Image considers to be extraneous.

Exporting to Other Raster Formats

See *Exporting Drawings to Other Formats* on page 786.

Printing Drawings and Images

Finding Printing Procedures

Most of the procedures you need are in Chapter 4, *Printer Setup and Printing*, on page 59. In particular, see:

- *Creating UNIX Printers* on page 60
- *Standard Printing* on page 79
- *Setting Up Printing to PDF* on page 72
- *Printing to PostScript and PDF* on page 81
- *Printing Brochures* on page 90
- *Printing From the Command Line* on page 83
- *Specifying Portrait or Landscape Orientation* on page 86
- *Specifying Print Settings for Bitmaps, Transparency, and Color/Grayscale* on page 89
- And in the Mail Merge chapter, *Printing* on page 399

The rest of the procedures here cover Impress-specific printing or procedures that aren't worth sending you to the other side of the book for.

Fitting the Content to the Page

Sometimes the fit isn't quite right; here's how to deal with some of the issues.

Printing More Than One Slide on a Page

For printing purposes, each slide you add to the drawing is considered a page. Save your drawing file as a presentation and use the handouts feature in Impress.

See also *Fitting Multiple Pages Onto One Sheet* on page 88 for information on documents throughout the program.

Page Setup

Choose Format > Page and make sure the page is set up correctly. See *Page Setup* on page 759 for more information.

Cramming a Slide Onto a Page

Sometimes you just need to squish a drawing to get the printed output right. If the slide is too big, you'll generally be notified when you print, and you can choose the Fit to Size option at that point. To be prepared ahead of time, however, you can mark the Fit to Size option using either of the following navigations:

Page Format Window

1 Choose Format > Page and click the Page tab.

2 Select Fit to size and click OK.

Note – If you want to print an image in landscape that's too long to fit the short way onto the landscape page, choose Format > Page. In the Page tab, select Landscape and select Fit to size, then click OK. If Fit to size isn't selected when you mark Landscape, it won't work to apply it after the fact.

Print Options Window

1 Choose File > Print and click the Options button.

2 Select the Fit to page option and click OK.

3 Click OK to print.

You also can refer to *Fitting Multiple Pages Onto One Sheet* on page 88 to see how it's done across the program.

Stretching a Small Drawing to Fill a Page

There's a Fill entire page option in the Page Format window, but it doesn't have any effect. Use the Scale field in the Paper tab of the Printer Properties window (File > Printer Setup, or File > Print > Properties). This works intermittently, but with enough consistency to be worth trying.

Your best bet is to just manually enlarge the drawing, if you want it to fill more of a page than it is now. Group the elements of the drawing, if there are more than one, then resize the group.

Printing the Same Drawing Several Times on One Page

You can tile the drawing so that it appears as many times as it can fit on one piece of paper. Just choose Tools > Options > Drawing > Print and select Tile.

If you have more than one slide, each slide will be tiled several times on each piece of paper; you won't see all the slides tiled one after another.

Be sure that your page size is smaller than the page size of the paper you'll print on, or it'll only fit once and no tiling will occur. Also be sure to match up your page orientation and printer orientation or you'll get unexpected results.

Printing Options Setup

Use the Draw printing setup window (choose Tools > Options > Drawing > Print) to set up printing options. See Figure 32-1. You can also choose File > Print, then click Options.

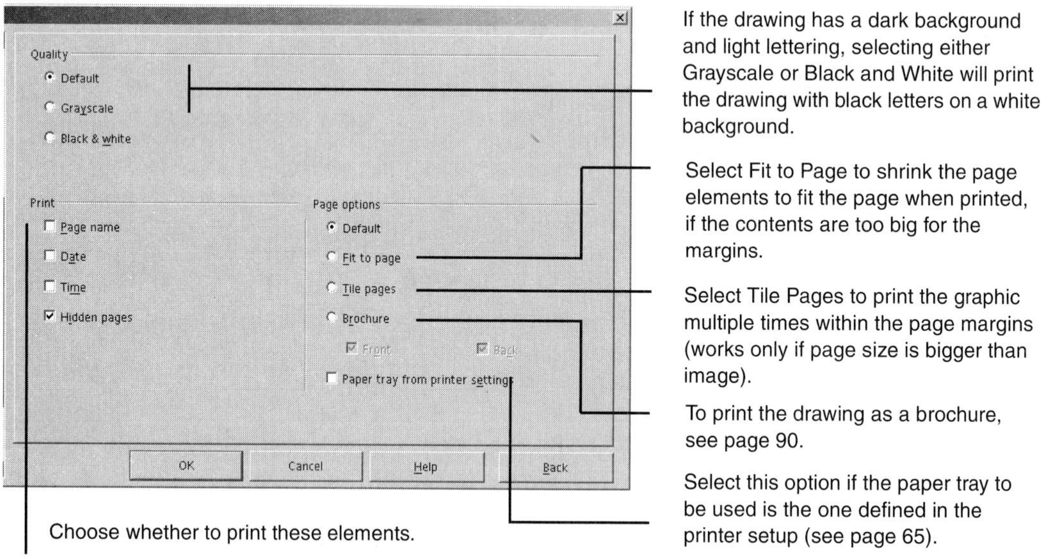
Quality
Default
Grayscale
Black & white
Print
Page name
Date
Time
Hidden pages
Page options
Default
Fit to page
Tile pages
Brochure
Front
Back
Paper tray from printer settings
OK
Cancel
Help
Back
If the drawing has a dark background and light lettering, selecting either Grayscale or Black and White will print the drawing with black letters on a white background.
Select Fit to Page to shrink the page elements to fit the page when printed, if the contents are too big for the margins.
Select Tile Pages to print the graphic multiple times within the page margins (works only if page size is bigger than image).
To print the drawing as a brochure, see page 90.
Select this option if the paper tray to be used is the one defined in the printer setup (see page 65).
Choose whether to print these elements.

Figure 32-1 Printing options for Drawings

Selecting Options in Print Warning Dialog

The following dialog appears if your margins don't match printer settings.

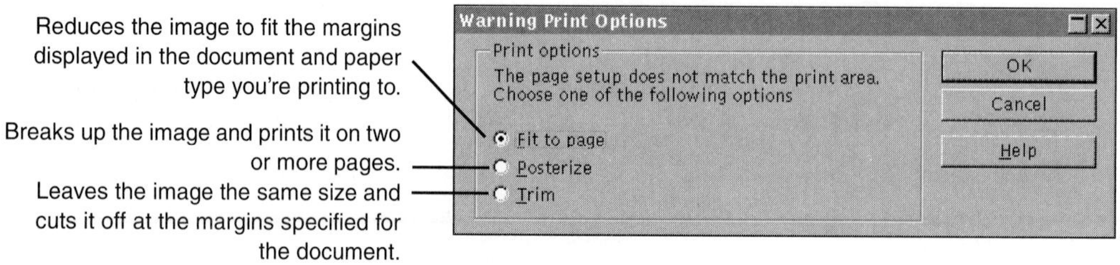
Reduces the image to fit the margins displayed in the document and paper type you're printing to.
Breaks up the image and prints it on two or more pages.
Leaves the image the same size and cuts it off at the margins specified for the document.
Warning Print Options
Print options
The page setup does not match the print area. Choose one of the following options
Fit to page
Posterize
Trim
OK
Cancel
Help

Figure 32-2 Print Options warning window

If you set up the notification described in *Managing Print Warnings* on page 96, or if a slide won't fit the page setup options you've specified, the window in Figure 32-2 will appear when necessary:

Note – If you select Fit to page, the warning window won't appear again for this document.

Printing a Drawing

You can print the whole document, selected slides, or selected objects within a slide to a printer or file. For more information about printing to files, refer to *Considerations for Printing to PostScript or PDF* on page 81.

Follow these steps if you want to specify particular options, or use the Print File Directly icon on the Draw toolbar, which uses the options and printer last selected.

1   To print selected objects within a document, select them now.

2   Choose File > Print.

3   Select a printer, or select the Print to file option and enter a file name. To print to a PostScript file, enter a name with a .ps extension.

4   Click Options and select the appropriate print options (see Figure 32-1). Click OK.

5   Select what to print: All (the entire document), Range (a range of slides), or Selection (the currently selected text or graphics). Use dashes to form ranges, and use commas or semicolons to separate pages or ranges (1, 3, 4, 6-10).

6   Enter the number of copies and, if it's two or more, choose whether to collate.

7   Click Print.

Note – If you have problems printing, check to be sure the margins and orientation are set correctly. (Choose Format > Page and select the Page tab; see Figure 32-3.) You might be printing within margins that aren't actually on the page. In addition, make sure you've selected the right paper format, such as Letter. Sometimes it helps to just restart.

Make a selection here appropriate for the country where you're located. (User format can cause problems; select a different format for best results.)

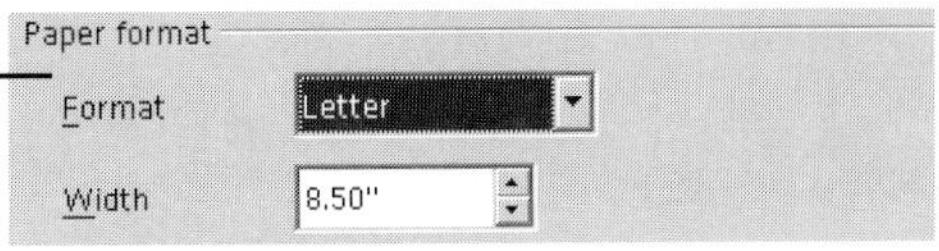

Paper format

Format   Letter

Width   8.50"

Figure 32-3   Setting paper size

Stored Data Fields, Data Sources, and Forms

Overview of Database Connection Features

StarOffice, OpenOffice.org, and Databases

This chapter is just a small orientation to the whole section of stored data and what to do with it. Because of the disparity in how the stored data can be used, and where we hope you'll expect to find the instructions in this book, we've created this central clearing house sort of chapter to get you started.

In the beginning, Sun bought StarOffice and gave it out or sold it with StarBase, as well as Adabas D a relational database, and provided a means of creating databases, and sadly it was Bad. The interface was confusing, and mere mortals threw up their hands in horror and very sensibly used spreadsheets to store their data instead of databases.

But now there's a new data source setup interface, and no more StarBase which for most of us is probably just as well, and it's a whole lot easier and simpler to get stored data out of wherever it's stored and into where you need it, formatted the way you want.

Setting up data sources is a lot easier now OK, if you're dealing with Oracle you have to have the right URLs, drivers, etc. But the part that's in StarOffice and OpenOffice.org is so easy. Take a look at the tutorial if you don't believe us. See *Tutorial: Creating a Data Source* on page 871.

Set up data sources based on text files, spreadsheets, or address books Set up an absolutely plain text file or your address book as the basis for a mail merge. See *Creating a Data Source Based on Text Files* on page 881.

The Databases You Can Connect To

What can you connect to? It all depends on what connection methods, such as JDBC or ADO, your database can talk to. The things you can do include:

*   Connecting to your Oracle databases using ODBC or JDBC. See *Connecting to an Oracle or Other Database Using ODBC* on page 886 and *Connecting to an Oracle, MySQL, or Other Database Using JDBC* on page 892. We recommend JDBC. Also, note that as with anything involving Oracle it won't be a trivial walk in the park, but it works. Note also that StarOffice can't write to Oracle; this is a known problem, so check the www.sun.com/staroffice site for any updates.

*   Connecting to MySQL databases using JDBC.

*   Connecting to Access databases using ADO.

You can migrate 5.2 databases. See *Migrating a StarOffice 5.2 Database and Creating a Data Source* on page 905.

There's other stored data that we've grouped in this part, too. See the next page.

All the Ways You Can Create Stored Data and Bring It Into Documents

StarOffice and OpenOffice.org have a bunch of features relating to predefined, stored information, and how you get it out. However, it's used differently depending on the type of information, and gets all used together sometimes. For instance, the mail merge templates use just about everything, so something simple like predefined name and address get sucked into something more complicated like data sources.

So to clarify what the features are and just where it all is, here's Table 33-1.

Table 33-1   Topics related to stored data and using it

Tasks you want to do	Where you do it	Where to go in this book
Setting up predefined bits of data like signatures, business card information, etc.	AutoText icon in main toolbar	*Creating AutoText Entries* on page 864
Using those predefined bits of data	AutoText icon in main toolbar	*Inserting AutoText Entries in Your Document* on page 868
Setting up predefined bits of data like page numbers, conditional fields, etc.	Insert > Fields > Other, or double-click a field to edit it or create a new one	*Editing Fields* on page 863
Using those bits of data	Insert > Fields > Other	*Inserting Fields* on page 857
Setting up databases/data sources	Tools > Data Sources	Chapter 35, *Creating and Modifying Data Sources*, on page 869.
Taking predefined bits of data and/or fields from data sources, and doing mail merges	File > AutoPilot > Letter or other selections View > Data Source	Chapter 10, *Mail Merges, Business Cards, and More*, on page 351
Creating a form for viewing data source information, containing fields, buttons, etc., using the AutoPilot	File > AutoPilot > Form	*Forms, What Are They Good For?* on page 926
Creating your own form for viewing data source information	Form Functions icon on the main toolbar	*Basics for Creating a Form on Your Own* on page 936
Making fields in forms run a macro when you complete a task in a form.	Form Functions icon on the main toolbar, right-click and choose Control or Form	*Macro and Events Basics* on page 951
Bring a data source into a spreadsheet using the Data Pilot	Data > Data Pilot	*Simple Procedures for Bringing Data Sources Into Spreadsheets* on page 519

Help With Data Sources

In addition to the Help topics mentioned in *Getting Help* on page 98, see *Good Online Information Sources* on page 42.

Setting Up Stored Data in Fields and AutoText

Creating and Using Fields

Fields are bits of information, such as page numbers, dates, document headings, cross-references, index markers, database fields, and a host of other information that Writer generates or that you can insert. You can insert them quickly from the Insert menu, but they're all accessible and editable from the Fields window: choose Insert > Fields > Other.

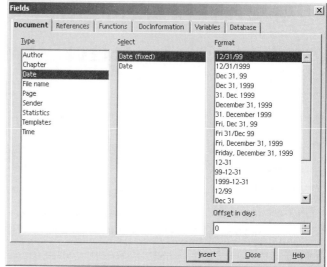

For example, you can insert a field into a document that shows the date that the document was last modified, or you can insert page numbering to show the current page number along with the total page count, as shown in Figure 34-1.

Much of the business card information is defined in headers, as well as a lot of what you see in templates. You can also define conditional fields that print a different value based on whether a condition is true.

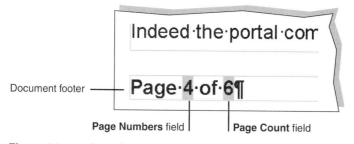

Document footer ——— **Page·4·of·6¶**

Page Numbers field   **Page Count** field

Figure 34-1   Inserting page numbering and page count fields

Inserting Fields

1   Click in the exact spot in the document where you want to
    insert a field.

2   In the toolbar, click and hold down the Insert Fields tool,
    and choose the field you want to insert. (You can also
    choose Insert > Fields.)

    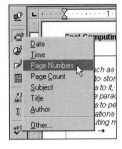

    If you don't see the field you want, choose Other, and select
    the field you want to use in the Fields window. For
    definitions of the fields in this window, see Table 34-1 on
    page 858.

Changing the Date Format for the Date Field

When you choose Insert > Fields > Date, it's always inserted in MM/DD/YY format. We
don't know how to change this default format, but you can do either of the following:

*   You can change the format each time by double-clicking the field and selecting a
    different format in the Edit Fields window.

*   Select the inserted date field after you've correctly formatted it, then select it and
    create a new AutoText entry. See *Creating and Inserting AutoText* on page 864.

Turning Off the Gray Background

Any time you insert a field or any other element that's generated by Writer, it is displayed
with a nonprinting gray background by default. If you don't want to see the gray
background on-screen, choose View > Field Shadings.

However, we recommend leaving field shading on, because it helps you distinguish
between what you enter as text and what is generated by Writer.

Advanced Field Definition and Use With the "Other" Fields

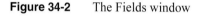

Each tab in the Fields window has a Type list. When you select a field type, related options display in the right area of the window.

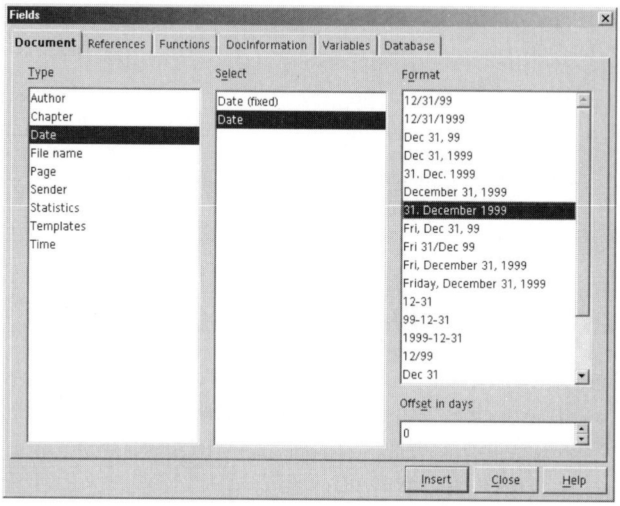

In this example, you can select a fixed or current date, then select the format for the date as you want it to display in the document.

Figure 34-2   The Fields window

When you click and hold on the Insert Fields tool in the toolbar, then choose Other (or choose Insert > Fields > Other), the Fields window is displayed (Figure 34-2) to let you select another type of field.

You can leave the Fields window open, and switch back and forth between it and your document. Table 34-1 describes the fields available in the Fields window.

Table 34-1   Descriptions of "Other" fields

Field	Description
Document tab	
About Document fields	These fields are for inserting values primarily stored in the windows accessible through File > Properties and Tools > Options > *program* > User data.
Sender	The author of the document, as identified in Tools > Options > *program* > User Data. Select the Fixed content option if you don't want the name of the author to change when someone else opens the document.
Chapter	Think of this as "chapter-level heading" instead. Use this to display the current document heading in the header or footer (called running heads). In the Level field, set the level of heading you want to display. Levels map directly to chapter numbering styles. See *Outline Numbering* on page 308.

Table 34-1   Descriptions of "Other" fields

Field	Description
Date	Inserts the current date, based on the computer's date setting. Select Date (fixed) if you want the date to remain what it was when you inserted it. Select Date if you want the date to update each time the document is opened. Select the formatting under the far right Format column.
Document Template	Inserts basic information about the template the document is based on, from File > Properties.
File Name	Lets you insert the name of the file in different ways. Select the Fixed content box if you want to display the original file name if it's later changed.
Page	Inserts a page number. Select the As Page Style format to use the default numbering format set up in the current page style. Otherwise, select the numbering style you want to use.
Sender	Inserts select information about the person sending the document, as defined in Tools > Options > General > User Data.
Statistics	Gives you the count of the number of different elements in the document: words, characters, pages, graphics, etc., from File > Properties.
Time	Inserts the time, based on the computer's clock. Select Time (fixed) if you want the time to remain what it was when you inserted it (further testing needs to be done to see if this makes time stand still). Select Time if you want the time to update each time the document is opened. You can enter a positive or negative offset number to adjust the inserted time relative to the current time. You can also select Additional Formats in the Format list and define your own time format.
References tab	
About Reference fields	This is where you insert the references or referenced fields into the active document. References are referenced fields within the same document or within sub-documents of a master document.
	The advantage of entering a cross-reference as a field is that you do not have to adjust the references manually every time you change the document. Just update the fields with F9 and the references in the document are updated too.
Set Reference	Use this for cross-referencing. In Writer, you don't cross-reference existing content. You must put (set) a reference in the spot you want to cross-reference. Click where you want to reference, enter the name of the reference point (usually the name of a heading, figure, or table you want to cross-reference), and click Insert. The reference names you've entered display in the Selection list, where you can cross-reference them using Insert Reference (next).
	In an HTML document, reference fields entered this way will be ignored. For the target in HTML documents, you have to insert a reference field.

Table 34-1   Descriptions of "Other" fields

Field	Description
Insert Reference	When you want to cross-reference something (either in the current document or in another file that's part of a master document), select Insert Reference, select the item you want to cross-reference (in the Selection list), select the format for the cross-reference, and click Insert. (For more information, see *Cross-Referencing* on page 324.) You can also use above/below, which inserts the words *above* or *below* if the reference occurs before or after the insertion point. For example, "See Water Ballet for Dogs above." But for heaven's sake, if you use above/below, make sure the reference is physically on the same page as the cross-reference. If it's not, you may have your poor readers looking randomly up at the sky or down at the floor trying to find the reference.
Bookmarks	You can also cross-reference bookmarks you've inserted using Insert > Bookmark. When you insert bookmarks in an HTML document, Writer creates an <A NAME=*bookmarkname*> reference for internal page jumps. However, bookmarks in a Writer document are not converted to <A NAME=> references if you convert the document to HTML.
Functions tab	
About function fields	Function fields execute a certain function which can be tied to a condition, depending on the field type. You can define fields that execute a certain macro when clicked with the mouse or fields that hide a text passage depending on a certain condition. For graphics, tables, frames and other objects, you can define placeholders in order to insert the objects into the document when needed.
Conditional Text	Insert text depending on a condition. Under Condition, enter x eq 1, for example, where x is a field in the document. Under Then, enter text that is inserted if x=1. Under Else, enter text that is inserted otherwise. X can be determined with the field types "Set variable" or with an input field for a new variable.
Input Field	Inserting form fields for text input. You can add a remark. When you click the Insert button, the dialog Input Field appears, where you can enter and edit the desired text.
Execute Macro	Insert a text field that automatically executes an assigned macro following a double-click. You can choose the desired macro with the Macro button. After choosing the macro, you can enter the necessary remarks in the text field Remark.
Placeholder	Insert a placeholder in the document. You determine the placeholder type under Format. Enter the description in the Text field Placeholder. If you click the placeholder in the document, you can insert the object that is represented by the placeholder.

Table 34-1   Descriptions of "Other" fields

Field	Description
Hidden Text	Insert text that is hidden if a condition is met. In order to hide such text on screen, deselect the option Hidden Text under Tools > Options > Text document > Contents.
Hidden Paragraph	Hide a paragraph if the condition entered under Condition is true. These fields can be used, for example, to suppress empty paragraphs during printing. To hide such paragraphs on screen, deactivate the menu command View > Hidden Paragraphs or the option Hidden Paragraphs under Tools > Options > Text document > Contents.
	The conditions for "Hidden Text" and "Hidden Paragraph" can now be formulated in a similar manner. In earlier document formats, up until StarWriter 4.0, the reversed logic was valid for "Hidden text". When saving and loading older formats, the logic for "Hidden text" is therefore automatically reversed.
Combine Characters (only when Asian fonts are supported)	Combine 1 to 6 characters that are treated as one normal character after they have been successfully combined.
DocInformation tab	
About DocInformation	These fields let you insert information stored in the window accessed through File > Properties. The Document tab lets you access other fields from that same window.
Created	Lets you insert the name of the author who created the document, and the time and date the document was created. Select the Fixed content option to keep this information from changing when other people open and change the document.
Description	Inserts the document description, taken from the Comment field of the document properties (File > Properties, Description tab).
Document Number	Inserts the number of times the document has been saved.
Editing Time	Inserts information about time spent editing the document.
Info	Inserts the information from the selected Info field, taken from the Info fields of the document properties (File > Properties, User Defined tab).
Keywords	Inserts the keywords assigned to the document, taken from the Keywords field of the document properties (File > Properties, Description tab).
Modified	Inserts the name of the author who last modified the document, or the time and date the document was last modified.
Most Recent Print	Inserts the name of the author who last printed the document, or the time and date the document was last printed.

Table 34-1   Descriptions of "Other" fields

Field	Description
Subject	Inserts the subject of the document, taken from the Subject field of the document properties (File > Properties, Description tab).
Title	Inserts the title of the document, taken from the Title field of the document properties (File > Properties, Description tab).
Variables tab	
About Variables fields	With variable fields, you can control the content of your document dynamically. For example, you can change the counting of the page variables or define numberings as variables in order to enable automatic updating. You can define variables individually or select them from preset variable types.
Set Variable	Lets you create and insert a variable in a document that can be used as a trigger for conditions. For example, you can create a variable to trigger certain sections of the document to be hidden if the variable is a certain value.
Show Variable	Inserts the value of a selected variable in the document.
DDE Field	Lets you insert a Dynamic Data Exchange (DDE) link to another document.
Insert Formula	Lets you enter a formula and insert the results in the document.
Input Field	Lets you select a predefined variable and turn it into a hyperlink that brings up a window to let you change its value.
Number Range	Lets you insert a number, as well as incorporate the chapter number (set up in Tools > Outline Numbering), for a drawing, graphic, illustration, table, or for text in general.
Set Page Variable	For use with the Show Page Variable. Lets you set a marker in the document from which to begin page counting. Be sure to select "on". You can also enter an offset, positive or negative, with relation to the marker. An offset of -1 would be as if the marker were inserted 1 page earlier. See the next description for how you might use this.
Show Page Variable	Inserts the number of pages from the Set Page Variable marker to where this variable is inserted. One way to use this would be to set a marker (using Set Page Variable) in a document at the beginning of a topic, and at the end of the topic (say it's five pages later), type, "The past <#> pages described the three major factors to overcome in order to successfully build a summer home in a fire swamp", where <#> is the inserted Show Page Variable.

Table 34-1   Descriptions of "Other" fields

Field	Description
User Field	Lets you create a variable that will be the same wherever you insert it and change universally when you change it in one place. For example, say you want to insert the text "Microsoft" throughout a document. If you know the value of that variable is going to change, like from "Microsoft" to "Monopoly", a user field lets you change it in one place and it updates everywhere. To help automate the changing of its value, select the first instance of a user variable in the document, and insert an Input field so that all you have to do to change the value of the field is click on it and make the change in the window that appears.
Database tab	
Any Record	Lets you set a condition on database records to determine which records are used in a mail merge. Click the Help button in this window for more details. TRUE is the default condition, which means all selected records will be included.
Database Name	Inserts into the document the name of the database selected in the Database selection area.
Form letter field	Lets you insert database fields in a document to set up a mail merge.
Next record	Inserts a Next record marker between mail merge groupings in a document to print consecutive records on the same page. The records you want to include must be selected in the data source viewer window.
Record number	Inserts in the document the number of the record that's selected in the data source viewer window.

Editing Fields

You can't edit a field by typing in it. You have to either replace it with another field or double-click it to open the Edit Fields window and redefine the field. Refer to Table 34-1 for help on types of fields.

User-Definable Number Formatting for Cells and Fields

When you select Additional Formats in the far right Format column in the Fields Window, the Number Formatting window appears. To learn how to create your own numbering formats, see *Number Formatting in Cells* on page 280.

Condition Syntax

See the online help for extensive conditional syntax information.

Note – See also conditions used in sections, in *Hiding a Section With or Without a Condition* on page 417.

Creating and Inserting AutoText

If there's a set of boilerplate text you use frequently that you don't want to retype every time you use it, such as an email signature, trademarked term, or company letterhead heading, create

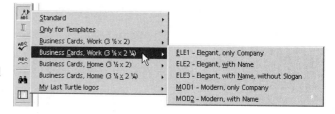

an AutoText entry for it in Writer. This is also used when you create business cards from the templates or use other business correspondence templates. When you do this, you can insert it quickly—either with a keyboard shortcut or by selecting it from a list of AutoText items.

AutoText entries can be formatted and can include graphics, tables, and fields.

Creating AutoText Entries

1   In a Writer document, create the text you want to turn into AutoText. Apply formatting and include graphics if desired.

2   Select the text and elements you want to include.

3   Click the AutoText tool in the main toolbar to display the AutoText window.

4   Type a Name and Shortcut for the new AutoText.

5   Select the category (below the Name field) in which you want to store the new AutoText (see Figure 34-3).

Categories are simply containers for organizing AutoText items. If you want to create your own categories for storing AutoText items, see *Adding New AutoText Categories* on page 866.

6   Click and hold down the AutoText button, and select New, as shown at right.

7   The new AutoText name is displayed in its category. Click the + symbol to the left of the category you added it to, to see the name.

8   Click Close, or click Insert if you want to add it to your document. This is a good idea, just to test the AutoText. Also click on the AutoText icon in the main toolbar and see that the new item shows up, in the category you added it to.

Enter new AutoText Name.

Writer suggests a keyboard shortcut; accept the default or enter your own.

AutoText categories. To add one, see *Adding New AutoText Categories* on page 866.

Select these boxes if you want to keep the path to the AutoText folder relative rather than hard-coded; for example, if you plan on moving program folders to different places on a network server.

Click Path to create a new location for storing AutoText. See *Adding New Locations to Store AutoText* on page 866.

Figure 34-3   The AutoText window

The Path button If you want to use other paths than the default AutoText path, you must add the new paths either by clicking the Path button in the AutoText dialog or by modifying the AutoText option by choosing Tools > Options > *program* > Paths. See *Adding New Locations to Store AutoText* on page 866.

The entries AutoCorrect, AutoText, Basic, Templates and Gallery in that Paths window may indicate more than one path. In a network environment, for example, the {netinstall} directory contains several files. They are accessible to all users, but cannot normally be changed, since users have read-only access. For that reason, AutoText modules defined by the users themselves are automatically placed in the directory below {userinstall}, to which he also has write-access.

Editing Existing AutoText Items

1 With Writer active, click the AutoText tool in the toolbar.

2 Select the name of the AutoText you want to edit.

3 Click the AutoText button and select Edit. The AutoText window closes and the AutoText opens in a new Writer document.

4 Make edits to the AutoText in Writer.

5 Select the edited AutoText.

6 Click the AutoText tool in the toolbar.

7 In the AutoText window, select the name of the AutoText you edited.

8 Click the AutoText button and select Replace.

9 Click Close.

Adding New Locations to Store AutoText

If you want to store AutoText in a location other than the default locations, you need to explicitly add it using this procedure.

1 With Writer active, click the AutoText tool in the toolbar.

2 In the AutoText window (see Figure 34-5), click the Path button.

3 The Path window will appear (see Figure 34-5). Enter the new location and click OK.

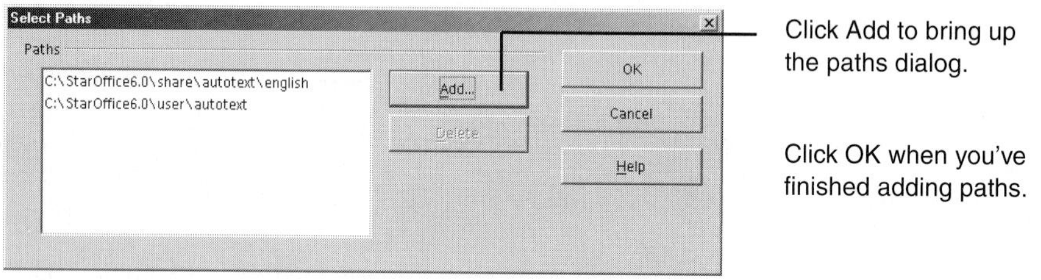
Select Paths
Paths
C:\StarOffice6.0\share\autotext\english
C:\StarOffice6.0\user\autotext
Add...
Delete
OK
Cancel
Help
Click Add to bring up the paths dialog.
Click OK when you've finished adding paths.

Figure 34-4 Adding a new AutoText location

Adding New AutoText Categories

The AutoText categories are simply storage containers for organizing AutoText. Writer comes with three predefined categories: signature, standard, and template. You can add your own categories for storing AutoText you create.

You might want to add a new location for the AutoText category before you begin; you can't add it on the fly. If you do, see *Adding New Locations to Store AutoText* on page 866.

1   With Writer active, click the AutoText tool in the toolbar.

2   In the AutoText window (see Figure 34-5), click the Categories button.

3   In the Categories window, type the name of the category you want to add.

4   Click New.

5   Click OK.

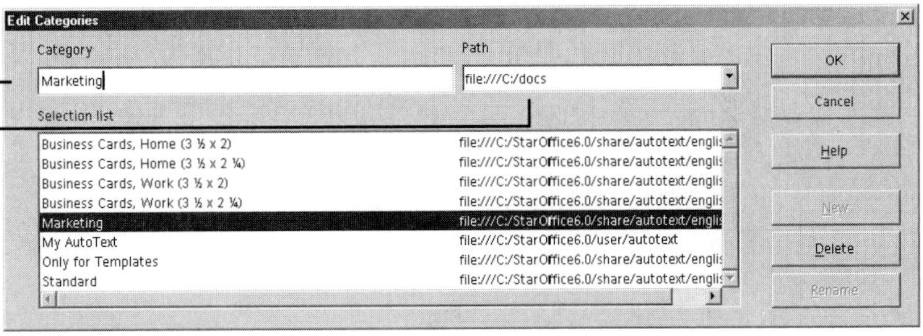

Type the name of
the new category
and click New. ────

Path where the
category will be
stored. If the path
you want isn't
here, see *Adding
New Locations to
Store AutoText* on
page 866.

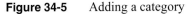

Figure 34-5   Adding a category

Moving AutoText to Different Categories

To move AutoText items from one category to another, drag the AutoText item you want to move into the new category, as shown in Figure 34-6.

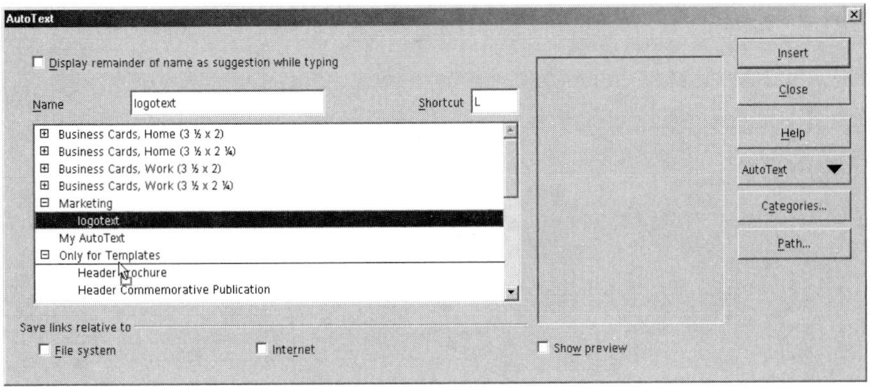

Figure 34-6   Dragging AutoText into another category

Inserting AutoText Entries in Your Document

See the previous procedures for information on creating, editing, and organizing AutoText.

1 In your open document, click where you want to insert the AutoText.

2 Click and hold the AutoText tool in the toolbar, choose the category of the AutoText, and select the AutoText name, as shown in Figure 34-7.

If you know the shortcut for the AutoText you want to insert, you can also type it (for example, "SL") and press the F3 key.

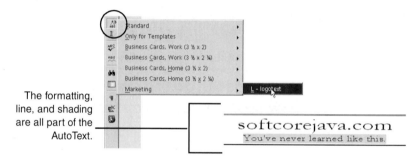

The formatting, line, and shading are all part of the AutoText.

Figure 34-7 AutoText inserted from the toolbar

Note – To use and edit the information in the Fields window, see *Creating and Using Fields* on page 856.

Creating and Modifying Data Sources

What to Do in This Chapter

1   Are you new to data sources? Go through the first section, *Understanding Data Sources and Completing a Tutorial* on page 870.

2   Then make sure all your data is ready to have a data source set up for it. See *Preparing to Create Data Sources* on page 874.

3   Then you'll be ready to actually create the data sources. See *Creating Data Sources* on page 880.

4   After that you're on your own. Your options include:

   • *Creating and Modifying Tables* on page 909

   • *Bringing New Data Into a New or Existing Table* on page 916

   • *Creating Queries* on page 917

   • *Sorting and Filtering Information in the Data Source Viewer* on page 920

   • *Exporting Data Sources to Another Format* on page 922

Understanding Data Sources and Completing a Tutorial

This isn't so much a quick start as an orientation session; if you're a little wobbly on databases, take a few minutes to read this and you'll be ready to go.

If you're a little leary of databases but feel like you should get to know them, don't worry. You can get a whole lot of cool features out of very little work . It can be extremely simple to get the information in your data source (generic term for database or other source of stored data) into documents. So just repeat to yourself, Who's Afraid of the Data Source? and use the explanations and tutorial in this section to get comfortable; soon you'll be a data source power user.

What's a Database? Or a Data Source?

A data source is anything you've got stored data in, more or less. See Figure 35-1.

Note – From now on, we'll just use the term "data source" generically to refer to your data, whether it's a spreadsheet, a database, or whatever.

3) You use a StarOffice or OpenOffice.org document to view the data. The spreadsheet or text document connects to the data source, and the data source knows how to get to the data.

2) You set up the **data source** definition in StarOffice or OpenOffice.org by just telling the program where the data is, how to get at it, etc. The information you provide varies depending on where the data is. The data source is just the middleman, more or less.

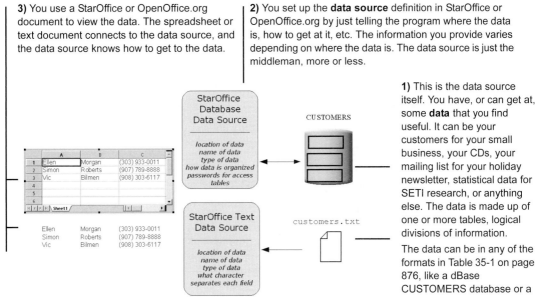

1) This is the data source itself. You have, or can get at, some **data** that you find useful. It can be your customers for your small business, your CDs, your mailing list for your holiday newsletter, statistical data for SETI research, or anything else. The data is made up of one or more tables, logical divisions of information.

The data can be in any of the formats in Table 35-1 on page 876, like a dBase CUSTOMERS database or a plain customers.txt file. You can have several files in the same data source.

For data sources that connect to databases, you can change data in a data source viewing window. However, you can't do that with data sources based on text files or spreadsheets—you need to open and change the documents themselves.

Figure 35-1   What a data source is: StarOffice example shown

Tutorial: Creating a Data Source

Walk through this tutorial to get comfortable with data sources. You'll complete steps for the three items referenced in Figure 35-1: creating the data itself, setting up the data source so the program can get at the data, and pulling the data into a standard document.

1   Create a new plain text file using Notepad.

2   Type the following exactly. Where you see *TAB*, press the TAB key; where you see *RETURN*, press the RETURN or ENTER key.

```
Firstname TAB Lastname TAB Phone RETURN
Ellen TAB Martin TAB (303) 926-0998 RETURN
Michael TAB Flanders TAB (907) 296-4499 RETURN
Donald TAB Swann TAB (908) 555-2121 RETURN
```

3   Save the file and call it `names1.txt`. Save it in your `office/user` directory.

4   Go to that directory and make a copy of the file; call it `names2.txt`.

5   Open names2.txt and change the name Ellen to Mary; change the name Michael to Simon; and change the name Donald to Victor. This is just to make the data different enough so you can tell instantly which table you're using.

Note – Be sure not to delete any of the tabs or carriage returns.

---

6   Save the file and close it and make sure that names1.txt and names2.txt are both still in your office/user directory.

7   Start StarOffice or OpenOffice.org if it's not started already.

8   Choose Tools > Data Sources. Click New Data Source and enter data; see Figure 35-2.

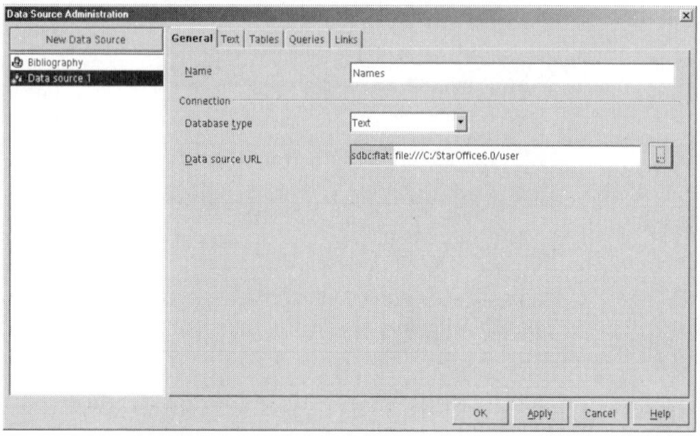

Figure 35-2   Creating a text file data source

9   Click the Text tab and enter the information shown in Figure 35-2.

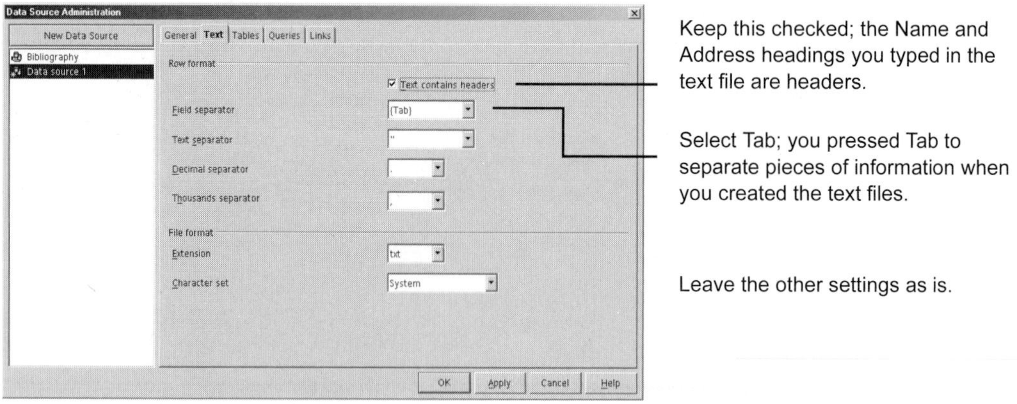

Keep this checked; the Name and Address headings you typed in the text file are headers.

Select Tab; you pressed Tab to separate pieces of information when you created the text files.

Leave the other settings as is.

Figure 35-3   Specifying what your text files are like

10 Click the Tables tab and you'll see the window shown in Figure 35-2.

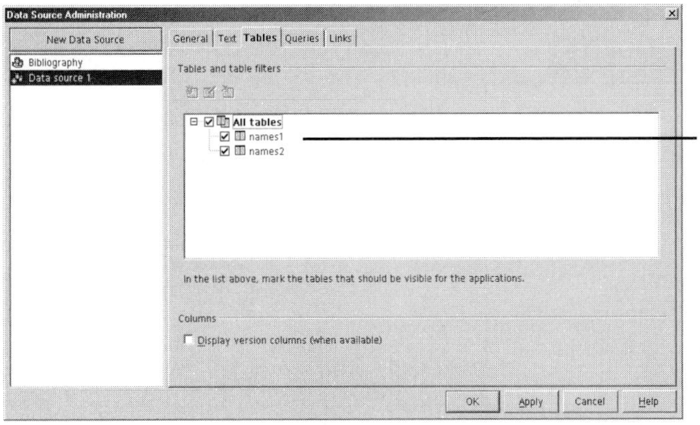

The names of the files you created, without the .txt extensions, are the table names.

Figure 35-4   Specifying what your text files are like

11 Click OK to save changes and close the window.

12 Open a new spreadsheet (File > New > Spreadsheet).

13 Choose View > Data Sources. The window should now look like Figure 35-5. If you can't see the top of the spreadsheet, click the circled stickpin icon in Figure 35-5.

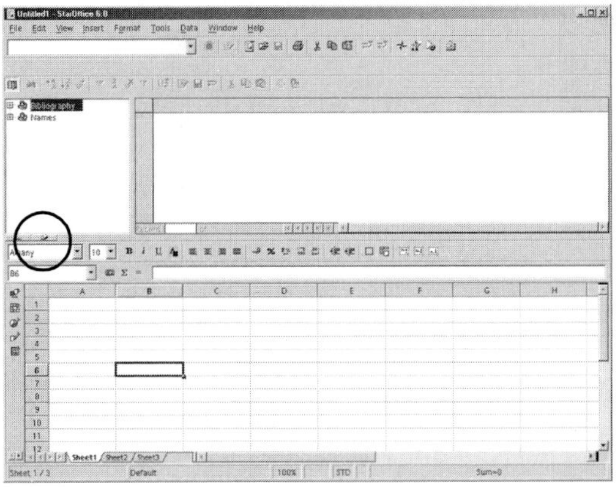

Figure 35-5   Specifying what your text files are like

14 Click the plus sign to expand your Names data source, the Tables category, and the names1.txt table. Select that table and wait a few seconds; the information in the data source table will be displayed as shown in Figure 35-5. (If it isn't displayed, double-click names1.txt.)

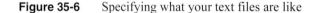

Figure 35-6   Specifying what your text files are like

15 Click the upper left corner of the displayed data, and drag the data into the spreadsheet below, as shown in Figure 35-7.

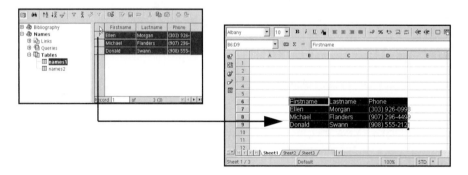

Figure 35-7   Specifying what your text files are like

You're done—you've created data in a text file form, created a data source to access that data, and brought the data into a spreadsheet. While creating a data source from a database, and creating mail merges rather than just bringing in the data, are slightly more challenging, the same principles apply. You should have a sense of how the process works now, as well as understanding that data source setup is pretty slick.

Preparing to Create Data Sources

If you completed the tutorial, or if you were already all over the database thing, here's where you start creating the data sources.

Note – StarOffice cannot edit Oracle databases. This is a known problem, so check the `sun.com/staroffice` site periodically to see if they've come up with a patch.

Understand the Kinds of Data You Can Connect to Using a Data Source

General Notes

Read the following before you begin.

Do a Dry Run

If this is the first data source you set up, you might want to consider doing a practice run, just connecting to a dBase database. (Create a basic spreadsheet of data, save it as dBase). Make sure it's working correctly by editing the data (*Editing Data Using the Data Source Viewer* on page 917) using data entry forms (*Using Forms for Data Entry* on page 959), or doing a mailing (*Creating Mail Merge Letters and Faxes With Data Sources Using AutoPilots* on page 380). In addition, use a test application to make sure that your database is running and accessible from the computer you're using.

Platform Notes

It's a good idea to use JDBC rather than ODBC on Linux and Solaris.

If you're on Windows, you should have an ODBC driver already, in the MDAC package. You can also go on microsoft.com and look for it in `http://www.microsoft.com/data/mdac21info/manifest_intro.htm`.

Database Notes: What Connection Types to Use for What Databases

Use ODBC or JDBC if you want to connect to databases like Oracle.

If you're connecting to an Access database, we recommend that you connect via ADO. See *Connecting to an Access or Other Database Using ADO* on page 896. If you have problems doing that, export the databases to `.dbf`, dBase.

If you're working with Oracle or any similarly robust and complex database, do it hand in hand with your Oracle administrator (and not the intern—get the head person). Get some pizza and Mountain Dew, and sit down to do this together. You'll need to have installed the Oracle Database Client software, and created a new service name. Your Oracle system administrator can tell you how to get the software and create the service name; with enough pizza, he or she might just take care of it. Just make sure you get the exact service name, however; you'll need it to set up your ODBC data source here in StarOffice or OpenOffice.org.

Data Source Types

You can create different types of data sources, as simple as a text file or two, or as complex as connecting to any database that supports JDBC or ODBC connectivity.

Figure 35-8 shows the data source type dropdown list in the data source setup window; Table 35-1 provides more information about each.

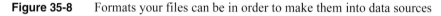

Figure 35-8   Formats your files can be in order to make them into data sources

Many of the technologies involved (such as Oracle, DB2, ADO, ODBC, and JDBC) require specialized knowledge to use. If all you want to do is create a simple database, use dBase.

Table 35-1 gives you a basic overview of the types of data sources you can create, and it provides important factors to consider for creating each type.

Table 35-1   Types of data sources you can create

Database Type	Description
dBase	dBase is perhaps the most useful type of database and the easiest to use for single, non-relational databases. Calc can open and save to dBase files, and you can save a file as a dBase database. This means, for example, that you can open a delimited text file in Calc (possibly created from something like an external address book) and convert it to a dBase file, or easily convert a dBase database to a spreadsheet file. **The dBase tables must have the .dbf extension in lower case.**
ADO	Lets you connect to a data source using a Microsoft ActiveX Data Objects (ADO) interface. Password protection for ADO connections is supported. To use ADO, you must have Microsoft Access 2000 or the ISGData Control for ADO (available from www.microsoft.com/data) installed on your system. If you have problems, export the databases to .dbf, dBase.

Table 35-1   Types of data sources you can create

Database Type	Description
Adabas D	Adabas is not available with OpenOffice.org. **OpenOffice.org** This is a slightly restricted version; the restrictions are listed at *Limitations* on page 36. Adabas D is for more serious database work than what is provided by the dBase type. You can set up relations between tables as well as the following fairly intensely techy options: you can specify data buffer size and data increment, view database statistics such as database size and memory usage, connect to backup files, and the database connection is shut down automatically when you close StarOffice. Adabas also supports password protection. To use Adabas on a standalone system, you must install the Adabas server separately. The Adabas installation program launches automatically when you're done installing StarOffice. By default, data sources are stored in the adabas/sql folder off your system's root directory. For more information, see the copious Adabas information in the online help.
ODBC	Use this type or JDBC to connect to any database, such as Oracle or Access, that is not listed as a specific database type. The 32bit ODBC functions required here can be installed on your system at any time with the help of the setup program supplied with your database. You can then update the properties via the Control Panel. Password protection for ODBC database connections is supported. A table must have a *clear index*, if you want to edit or add records through StarOffice or OpenOffice.org. Your system must have the right ODBC drivers installed to create an ODBC connection; obtain them from the database manufacturer. Only the ODBC 3 standard is supported.
JDBC	Use this type or ODBC to connect to any database, such as Oracle or Access, that is not listed as a specific database type. JDBC is platform independent, while ODBC drivers are platform dependent. A JDBC driver must be installed on your system to use JDBC. A Sun Microsystems JDBC driver is provided in StarOffice by default, and is displayed in the JDBC Driver Class field of the JDBC tab. You must enter the driver classes in the java.ini file or by choosing Tools > Options > *program* > Security and entering the classes in the Class path field. This is covered in *Connecting to an Oracle, MySQL, or Other Database Using JDBC* on page 892. Password protection for JDBC database connections is supported.
Address book	You can select an address book in Outlook Express (a.k.a. Windows address book), Outlook, LDAP, or Mozilla (Netscape) formats. Note that Mozilla must be version 6.0 or later.

Table 35-1　　Types of data sources you can create

Database Type	Description
Text	Lets you open a delimited text file as a database. (Delimited just means a space, tab, or something separates every field.) Text data sources are mostly read-only. The only way to modify or enter data in them is in the text file itself using a text editor or Calc. In text format databases, data is stored as unformatted ASCII files. Every data record has its own row. The data fields are divided by separators such as tabs or commas, and text in the data fields is typically in quotation marks. Text database connections are read-only in StarOffice and OpenOffice.org. You must edit the text source directly to change the data. If you want to convert the text database to one you can edit in the data source viewer in StarOffice or OpenOffice.org, open the file in Calc (selecting the file type Text CSV) and save it as a dBase file.
Spreadsheet	Lets you open a StarOffice, OpenOffice.org, or Microsoft spreadsheet as a data source. Spreadsheet data sources are read-only. The only way to modify or enter data in them is in the file itself.

Prepare Files and Databases For Use as Data Sources

Before you begin, think about what data you want to be able to get into forms, mail merges, and other documents. Is it in:

- A StarBase database?
- A text document?
- A spreadsheet?
- An Oracle database?

Your data source can be any of the formats listed in Figure 35-8 and Table 35-1.

Got drivers?　Make sure you've got the drivers you need to connect to Oracle, Access, or anything else driver-oriented. You'll also probably want a database administrator.

If your file is plain text　If you've got a plain text file, just make sure that the fields (i.e., first names, last names, email addresses or January sales, February sales) are separated by a semicolon (;), comma (,), colon (:), tab, space, or another character, which you can enter when you're setting up the data source.

If your file is Word, WordPerfect, etc.　If the text file is something more complicated than just plain text, export it to plain text before you start. If you get a choice, export it as tab-delimited or something-delimited; it'll make things simpler and potentially avoid unexpected results when you create the data source.

If your address book format isn't supported If your address book isn't one of the supported formats (Netscape/Mozilla address books need to be version 6.x), export the address book to a character-delimited text file.

If your file is a non-StarOffice or OpenOffice.org spreadsheet It's safest to convert it to Calc (just open it in Calc and save it in Calc format).

If the database is from StarOffice 5.2 If the source is an old format from StarOffice 5.2, see *Migrating a StarOffice 5.2 Database and Creating a Data Source* on page 905.

If you want to make an editable database from a text file or spreadsheet If you want to be able to edit the data through forms or other means, save the file as a dBase file. (First, get a text file into spreadsheet format using the instructions in See *Importing a Text File or Spreadsheet* on page 517.)

If the source is a database Make sure it's accessible through one of the formats in Figure 35-8 and Table 35-1. If it isn't, follow these steps:

- From the application that you use to work with the external database, save the database as a delimited text file.

- Open the delimited text file in Calc. See *Importing a Text File or Spreadsheet* on page 517.

- Save the spreadsheet and use the Spreadsheet data type when setting up the data source. Or save the spreadsheet as a dBase file by choosing File > Save As and setting the file type to dBase.

Note – If you want to be able to edit the data from a form or similar viewing/input format, save it as dBase.

If you want your data source divided up Sometimes you might just have one data source with all the data together. If you're just keeping your mailing list in one data source and you only send a letter once a month to everyone on that list, you don't need to go any further. However, what if you realize after a while that you only want to send your holiday newsletter to friends and family, your daily "I'm still unemployed, is anyone hiring?" letters to professional acquaintances, and your triweekly amusing short stories to the other members of the Fertile, Minnesota Writers' Club?

Then it's time for tables or queries.

Tables are just subdivisions of the data source.

- When you create a data source based on text files, everything in the directory you specify becomes a table. So if you set up the Contacts data source and point it at your bulging `C:\mycontacts` directory, you get three tables: `holiday`, `jobsearch`, and `stories`.

- When you create a data source based on a spreadsheet, every sheet in the spreadsheet is a table.

• For all the other databases, it depends on the database structure you set up.

So now, consider whether you'll need to structure your text files, spreadsheets, or other data differently, for the tables you might need, and subdivide and organize your data sources as necessary.

Queries are subsections of your data too, but they're created differently. You create a query for a particular table. "Give me the phone numbers of all the people in the hiring table of the Contacts data source who live in Colorado and whose emails end in @enron.com" would be a good query. Assuming that you have fields in your hiring table for phone numbers, state, and emails. And assuming that you're not bothering to ask them for a job.

You can create queries at any time; don't worry about it right now, just know you can do it. See *Exporting Data Sources to Another Format* on page 922.

Creating Data Sources

If you completed the tutorial, or if you were already all over the database thing and skipped to this procedure, here's where you start creating the data sources.

Note – For extra tips, see `http://dba.openoffice.org/FAQ`.

UNIX Database Access With ODBC and MySQL

Are you on UNIX but you haven't decided for sure what to do? Consider unixODBC and MySQL. An excellent document from containing instructions for doing so is at `http://openoffice.homelinux.org/index.php?s=38`

Database information for ODBC and UNIX can be found at `http://unixodbc.org`. See `http://www.unixodbc.org/doc/OOoMySQL.pdf` in particular.

Creating a Data Source Based on Text Files

Follow this procedure to define the data source for a plain text file or files.

1   Create one directory containing only the text file or files that you want in the data source. You will be able to specify only the directory, not the full path to the file. Each text file will be a table in the data source.

2   Choose Tools > Data Sources. The Data Source window will appear.

3   Click New Data Source. Enter new information as shown in Figure 35-9.

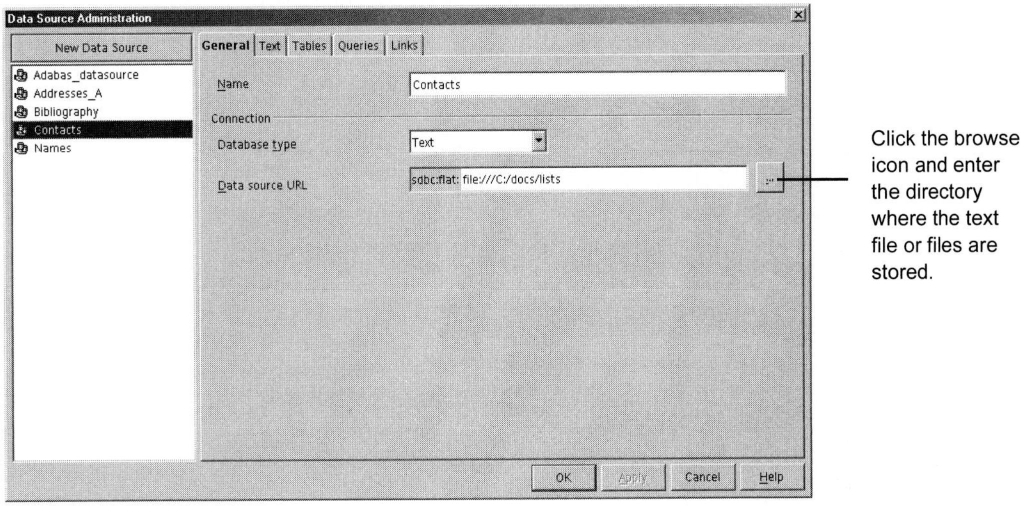

Click the browse icon and enter the directory where the text file or files are stored.

Figure 35-9   Entering the name and connection type

4   Click Text. Enter new information as shown in Figure 35-10.

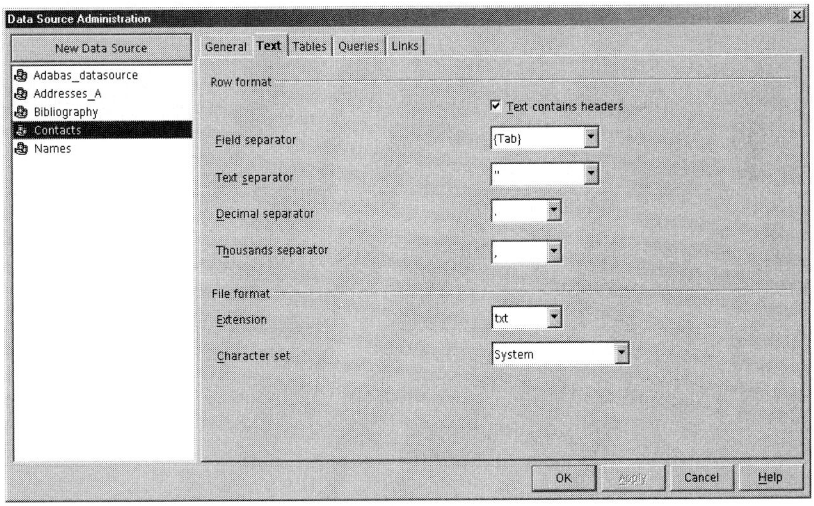

Figure 35-10   Selecting the tables to include in the data source

5   Click the Queries tab; the window is shown in Figure 35-11. For more information on queries, see *Creating Queries* on page 917.

- Click the SQL icon to enter new SQL queries, if you want, for the data source. In the query you can specify only one table, and it must be one of the tables that was displayed and selected in the Tables tab.

Example: `Select firstname, lastname from sales where state = 'CO'`

- Click the New Query Design icon to create queries using a GUI tool where you don't need to know SQL.

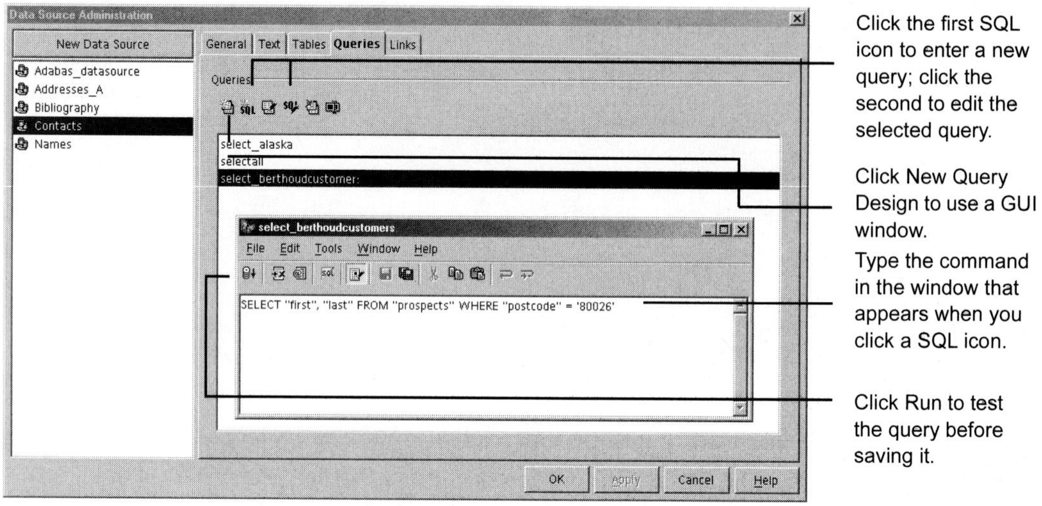

Click the first SQL icon to enter a new query; click the second to edit the selected query.

Click New Query Design to use a GUI window.

Type the command in the window that appears when you click a SQL icon.

Click Run to test the query before saving it.

Figure 35-11   Creating or selecting queries for the data source

6   Click the Links tab; the window is shown in Figure 35-12. Click the New Link icon if you want to link to other files. This is primarily used for linking to forms that display this data source's data. See Chapter 36, *Creating and Using Forms, Controls, and Events*, on page 925.

7   Click OK. The data source is now ready to use in mail merges, forms, spreadsheets, and other Writer documents.

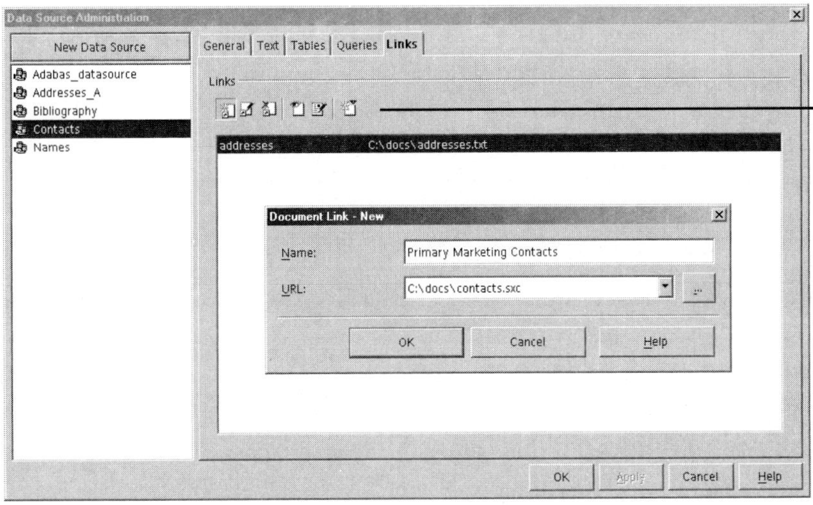

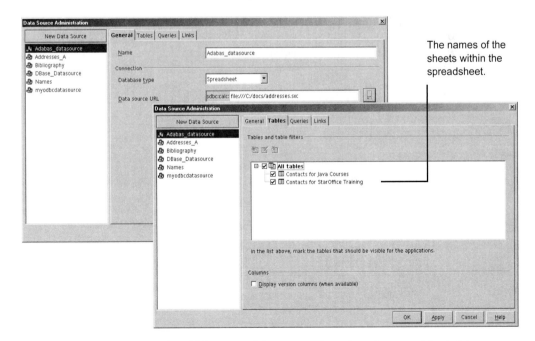

From left to right, icons that affect the link to the document:

- Add a link
- Edit the link
- Delete the link
- Continuing, the icons that let you edit the linked document itself
- Open the document for the selected link
- Edit the document
- Create a new document to use for a link

Figure 35-12   Creating and selecting links to other files

Creating a Data Source for a Spreadsheet

1   Choose Tools > Data Sources. The Data Source window will appear.

The names of the sheets within the spreadsheet.

Figure 35-13   Specifying spreadsheet-specific options for spreadsheet data sources

2 Follow the steps for *Creating a Data Source Based on Text Files* on page 881, with the following differences:

- In the first window, select Spreadsheet as the type. Then select the actual spreadsheet that you want as the data type rather than the directory where it is; each sheet will be a separate table. This is shown in Figure 35-13.

- There is no Text tab.

Connecting to a dBase Database

dBase isn't a standard database. dBase is based on the contents of a directory, like data sources that you create based on .txt files. So each .dbf file in the directory you point to is a table in your data source.

dBase databases are easy to create—take a spreadsheet, save it as dBase, and you've got yourself a database. Editable, too, through forms or just straight in the data source viewer. Performance isn't all that it could be, of course, but for personal or small business use, you could do a lot worse.

1 Choose Tools > Data Sources. The Data Source window will appear.

2 Click the General tab if it isn't already displayed.

3 Click New Data Source.

4 Name the data source.

5 Select dBase as the type.

6 Click the browse icon for the Database URL field and specify the directory where the dBase file or files are. The window is shown in Figure 35-14.

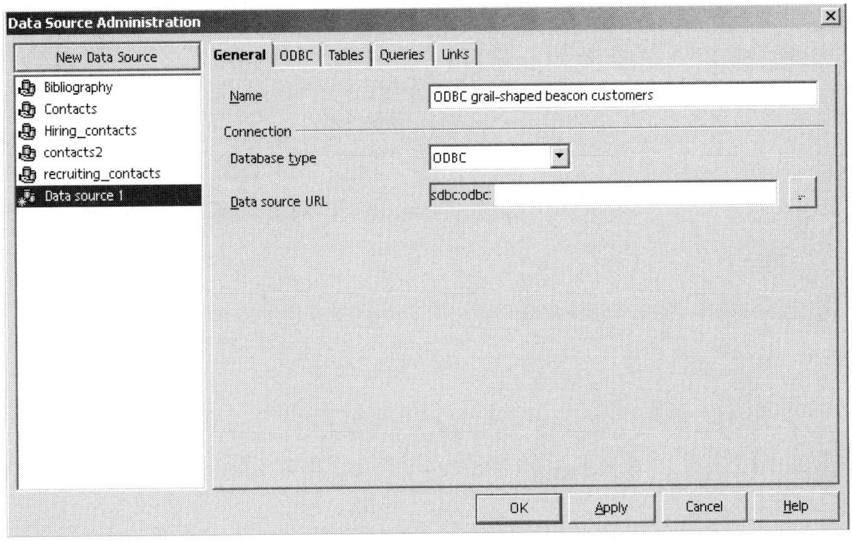

Figure 35-14   Naming the data source and specifying the database URL

7   Click the dBase tab. The window is shown in Figure 35-15.

8   Click the Queries tab and create queries if you want. For more information on queries, see *Creating Queries* on page 917.

- Click the SQL icon to enter new SQL queries, if you want, for the data source. In the query you can specify only one table, and it must be one of the tables that was displayed and selected in the Tables tab.

  Example: `Select firstname, lastname from sales where state = 'CO'`

- Click the New Query Design icon to create queries using a GUI tool where you don't need to know SQL.

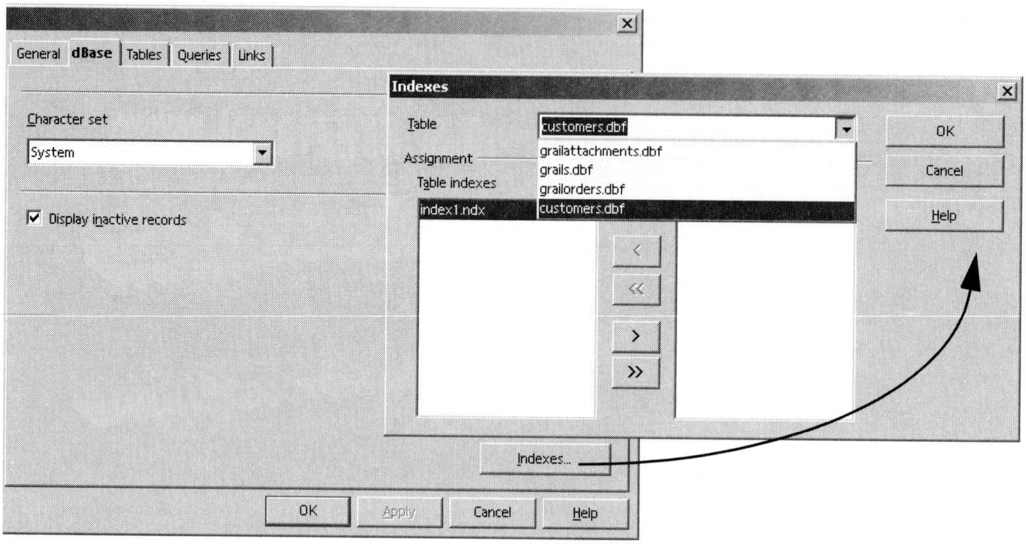

Figure 35-15   Specifying character set and index options

9   Click the Links tab. Connect any file that you want to be able to get at from the database in the future; if you have a form you'll use to view this data, you might want to link it here.

10   Click OK to close the window and save changes.

Connecting to an Oracle or Other Database Using ODBC

Note – StarOffice cannot edit Oracle databases. This is a known problem, so check the sun.com/staroffice site periodically to see if they've come up with a patch.

Before You Begin

Do a Dry Run

If this is the first data source you set up, you might want to consider doing a practice run, just connecting to a dBase database. (Create a basic spreadsheet of data, save it as dBase). Make sure it's working correctly by editing the data (*Editing Data Using the Data Source Viewer* on page 917) using data entry forms (*Using Forms for Data Entry* on page 959), or doing a mailing (*Creating Mail Merge Letters and Faxes With Data Sources Using AutoPilots* on page 380). In addition, use a test application to make sure that your database is running and accessible from the computer you're using.

Platform Notes

It's a good idea to use JDBC rather than ODBC on Linux and Solaris.

If you're on Windows, you should have an ODBC driver already, in the MDAC package. You can also go on microsoft.com and look for it in `http://www.microsoft.com/data/mdac21info/manifest_intro.htm`.

For Linux-specific tips for setting up MySQL with ODBC, see `http://openoffice.homelinux.org/index.php?s=38`

Database Notes

Use ODBC or JDBC if you want to connect to databases like Oracle.

If you're connecting to an Access database, we recommend that you connect via ADO instead. See *Connecting to an Access or Other Database Using ADO* on page 896.

If you're working with Oracle or any similarly robust and complex database, do it hand in hand with your Oracle administrator (and not the intern—get the head person). Get some pizza and Mountain Dew, and sit down to do this together. You'll need to have installed the Oracle Database Client software, and created a new service name. Your Oracle system administrator can tell you how to get the software and create the service name; with enough pizza, he or she might just take care of it. Just make sure you get the exact service name, however; you'll need it to set up your ODBC data source here in the program.

Creating the Data Source

See also *Setting up Connection Pooling* on page 908.

1   Choose Tools > Data Sources. The Data Source window will appear.

2   Click the General tab if it isn't already displayed.

3   Click New Data Source.

4   Name the data source; this can be anything, as long as it's something that will make you and other users think, "Oh, that's that ODBC database with the customer list for our grail-shaped beacons." (Or whatever's in the database.) The window is shown in Figure 35-16.

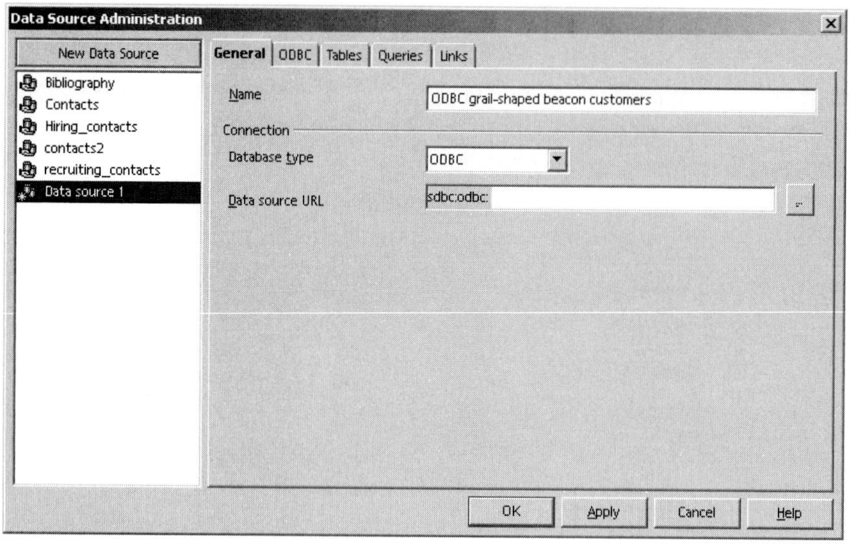

Figure 35-16   Naming the data source

5   Select ODBC from the Database Type list.

6   Click the browse icon by the URL field; the window in Figure 35-17 appears.

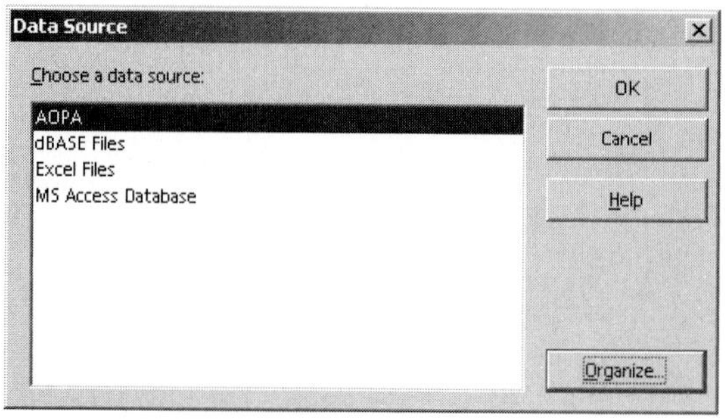

Figure 35-17   Data Source window

7   Click the Organize button to set up the ODBC data source. The ODBC Data Source
Administration window will appear, shown in Figure 35-18.

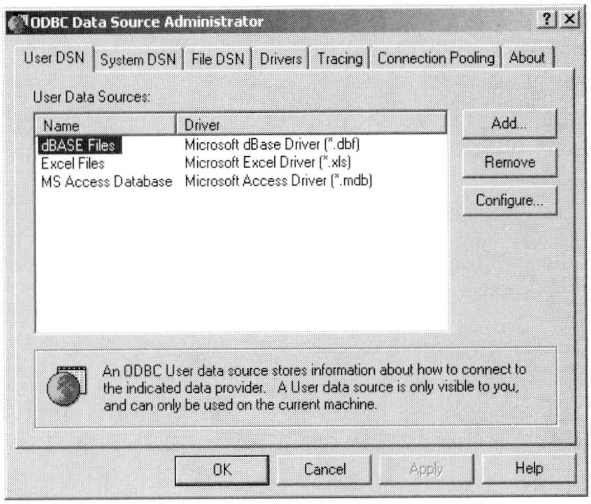

Figure 35-18   ODBC data source administration

8   Click the Add button. The Create New Data Source window will appear, shown in Figure 35-19. Select the ODBC driver to use and click Finish.

If a message states that the client software was not installed, you need to install the client software mentioned at the beginning of this procedure.

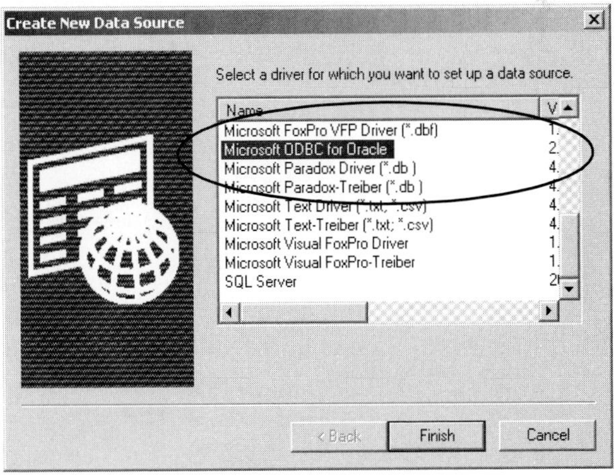

Figure 35-19   Selecting an ODBC driver

9   The Driver Setup window for the driver you selected will appear. Make the appropriate entries as outlined in the following information, then click OK.

Oracle setup

- Data Source Name – Enter the name of the Oracle data source.

- Service Name – Enter the same service name you specified when setting up the database. Your database administrator should be able to give you this.

- User ID – Ask your database administrator for a valid user ID to use to access the database.

- Other options – Consult your database administrator and database documentation for information on the appropriate selections.

Setup for other database types

See Figure 35-20 for what some of the windows looks like; consult your database administrator and database documentation for more information.

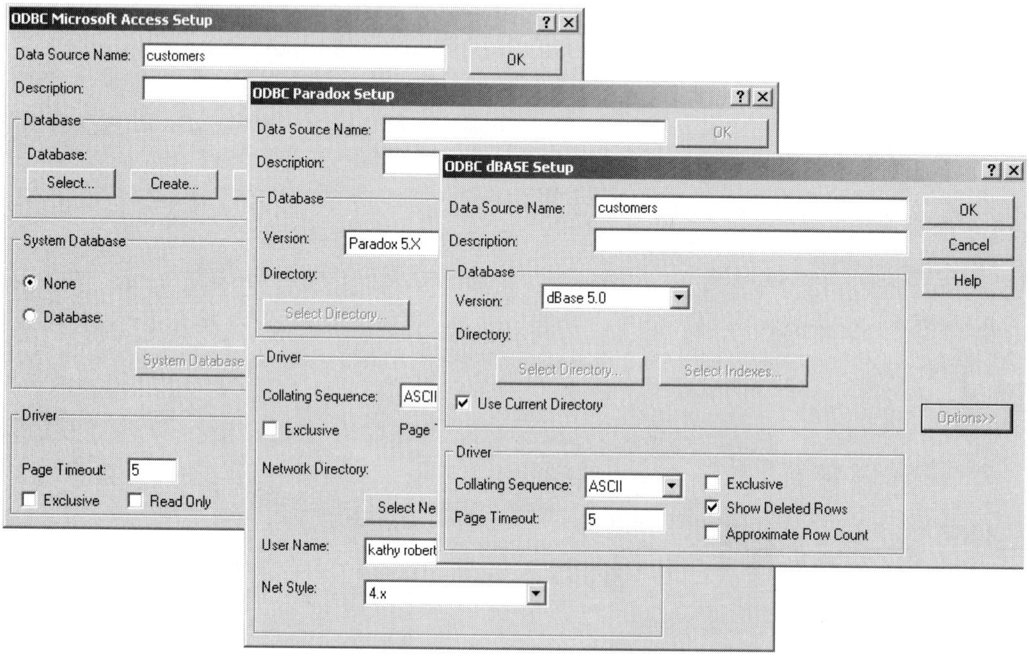

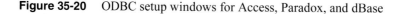

Figure 35-20   ODBC setup windows for Access, Paradox, and dBase

10   The Data Source window will appear, with the new data source connection added. Select it if necessary and click OK.

11   In the Data Source Administration window, click the ODBC tab. Enter the user ID you just specified and whether a password is required. Specify any driver settings that your database administrator wants. The window is shown in Figure 35-21.

If you select this option, the current data source of the Catalog is used. This might be necessary if, for example, the ODBC data source is a database server. You might run into problems when using the Catalog if, for instance, a dBase driver is used. In that case, keep this option unmarked.

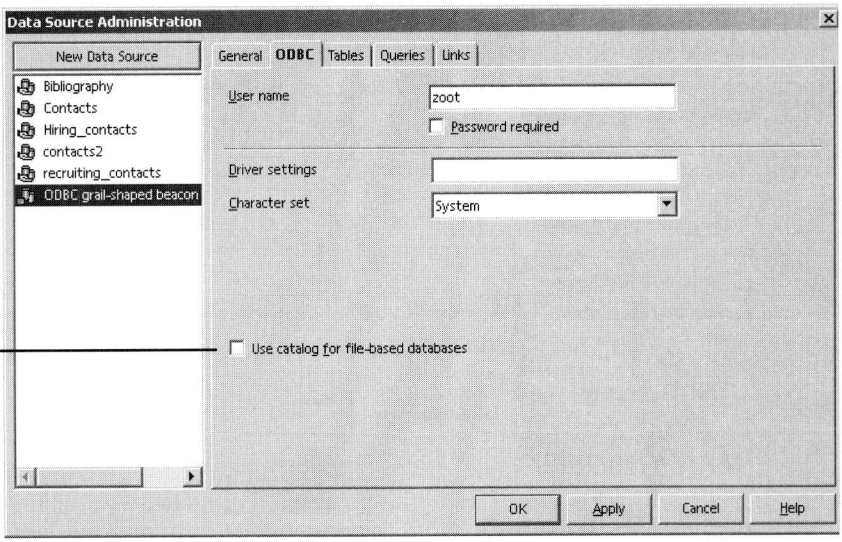

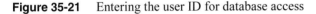

Figure 35-21 Entering the user ID for database access

12 Click the Tables tab and unmark any tables that shouldn't be accessible to users; the system tables, for instance.

13 Add any queries or links as outlined in Figure 35-11 on page 883 and Figure 35-12 on page 883.

14 Click OK to save the data source. If errors occur, consult the following.

- If a message appears stating that a connection to the data source could not be established, check the user name, service name, and talk to your database administrator. Also use another tool, on the current computer, to verify whether the database is accessible.

- If that or other errors occur, check the TNSNAMES.ORA file. Make sure that it exists, that it's in the right location, and that it doesn't have any syntax errors. This is where you provide your database administrator with dessert and some free movie coupons.

- Go back and select the Password Required checkbox, if it isn't marked, and try again.

Tracing and connection pooling The Data Source Administrator window contains additional configuration tabs. Open the Data Source window and select the ODBC data source, then click the browse icon by the URL field. Next, click the Organizer tab, then click the Tracing and Connection Pooling tabs, shown in Figure 35-22 and Figure 35-23. Consult your database administrator for what entries to add to these windows.

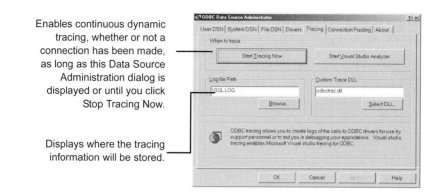

Enables continuous dynamic tracing, whether or not a connection has been made, as long as this Data Source Administration dialog is displayed or until you click Stop Tracing Now.

Displays where the tracing information will be stored.

Figure 35-22   Setting tracing options for an ODBC data source

Enables performance monitoring for the selected connection.

Lists each installed ODBC driver with its connection pooling timeout option.

Specifies in seconds the amount of time to wait before retrying.

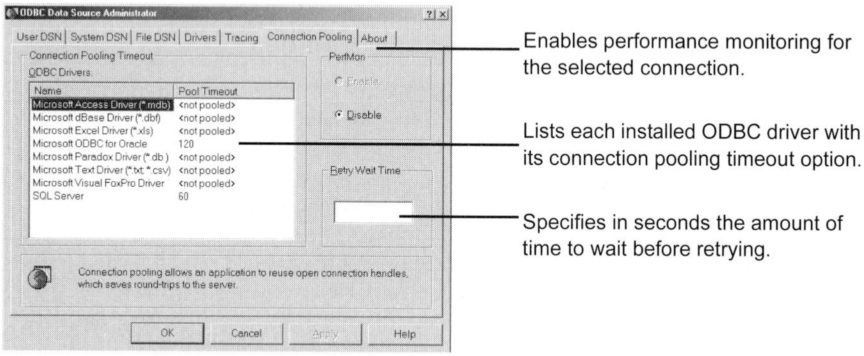

Figure 35-23   Setting connection pooling options for an ODBC data source

Connecting to an Oracle, MySQL, or Other Database Using JDBC

Note – StarOffice cannot edit Oracle databases. This is a known problem, so check the `sun.com/staroffice` site periodically to see if they've come up with a patch.

Before You Begin

Do a Dry Run

If this is the first data source you set up, you might want to consider doing a practice run, just connecting to a dBase database. (Create a basic spreadsheet of data, save it as dBase). Make sure it's working correctly by editing the data (*Editing Data Using the Data Source Viewer* on page 917) using data entry forms (*Using Forms for Data Entry* on page 959), or doing a mailing (*Creating Mail Merge Letters and Faxes With Data Sources Using AutoPilots* on page 380). In addition, use a test application to make sure that your database is running and accessible from the computer you're using.

Platform Notes

We recommend ODBC for use on Windows, and JDBC for use on Linux and Solaris.

Database Notes

Use ODBC or JDBC if you want to connect to databases like Oracle.

If you're using MySQL, we recommend the `m.m.mysql-2.0.4-bin.jar` driver archive, available from www.mysql.org.

Before you begin, enter the JDBC driver classes in the java.ini file, or choose Tools > Options > *program* > Security and enter the classes in the Classpath field. The window is shown in Figure 35-24.

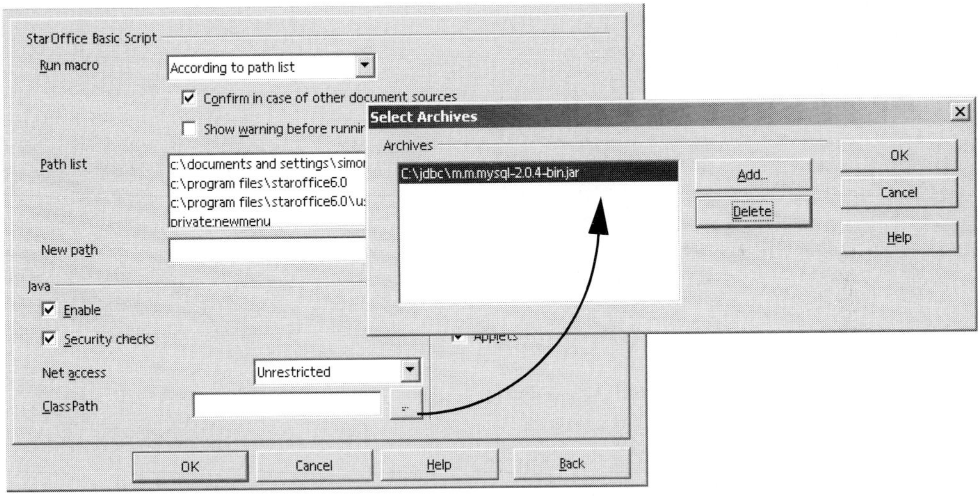

Figure 35-24   Adding drivers to the classpath

If you're working with Oracle or any similarly robust and complex database, do it hand in hand with your Oracle administrator (and not the intern—get the head person). Get some pizza and Mountain Dew, and sit down to do this together. You'll need to have installed the Oracle Database Client software, and created a new service name. Your Oracle system administrator can tell you how to get the software and create the service name; with enough pizza, he or she might just take care of it. Just make sure you get the exact service name, however; you'll need it to set up your data source here in the office suite.

Creating the Data Source

1   Choose Tools > Data Sources. The Data Source window will appear.

2   Click the General tab if it isn't already displayed.

3   Click New Data Source.

4   Name the data source; this can be anything, as long as it's something that will make you and other users think, "Oh, that's that JDBC database with the product information about our grail-shaped beacons." (Or whatever's in the database.) The window is shown in Figure 35-25.

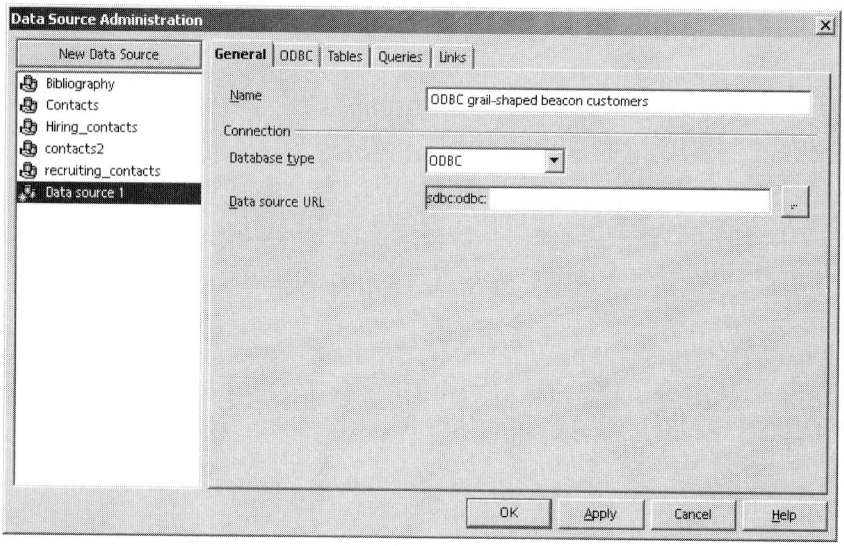

Figure 35-25   Naming the data source

5   Select JDBC from the Database Type list.

6   Enter the URL to the database in the Data source URL field. An Oracle example is shown in Figure 35-26 and a MySQL example is shown in Figure 35-27; additional information follows both.

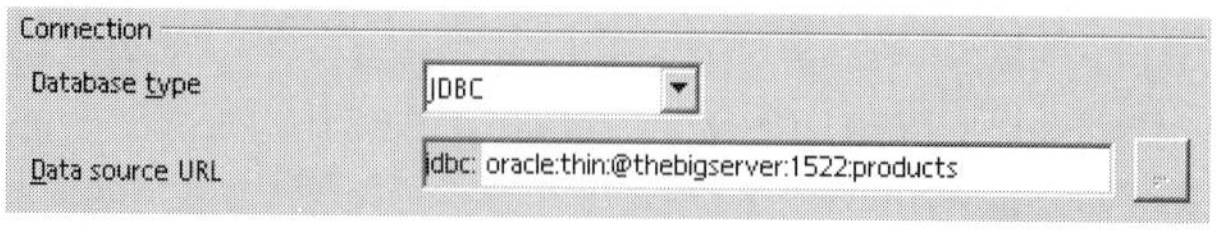

Figure 35-26   Specifying the URL to an Oracle database

URLs for Oracle databases The format of the URL is as follows:

```
oracle:thin:@hostname:port:databasename
```

Hostname – The machine the database is on.

Port – The port the Oracle database listens on, on that machine.

Database name – Just the name of the Oracle database.

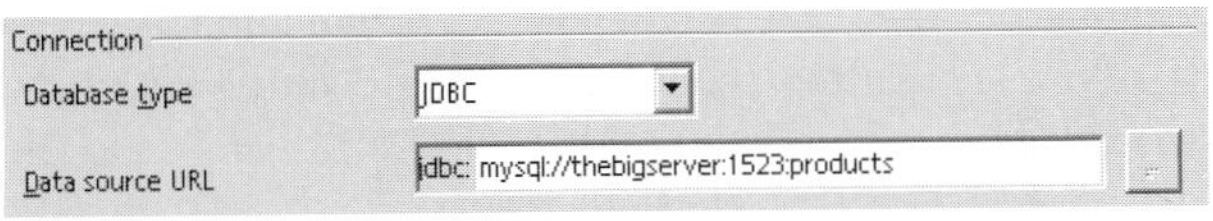

Figure 35-27   Specifying the URL to a MySQL database

URLs for MySQL databases The format of the URL is as follows:

- URL – `mysql://hostname:port/databasename`
- Hostname – The machine the database is on.
- Port – The port the database listens on, on that machine. The MySQL default is 3306.
- Database name – Just the name of the Oracle database.

7   Click the JDBC tab and specify the driver class. For Oracle 8.x, for instance, the class is `oracle.jdbc.driver.OracleDriver`. For MySQL, it's `org.gjt.mm.mysql.Driver`. The window is shown in Figure 35-28.

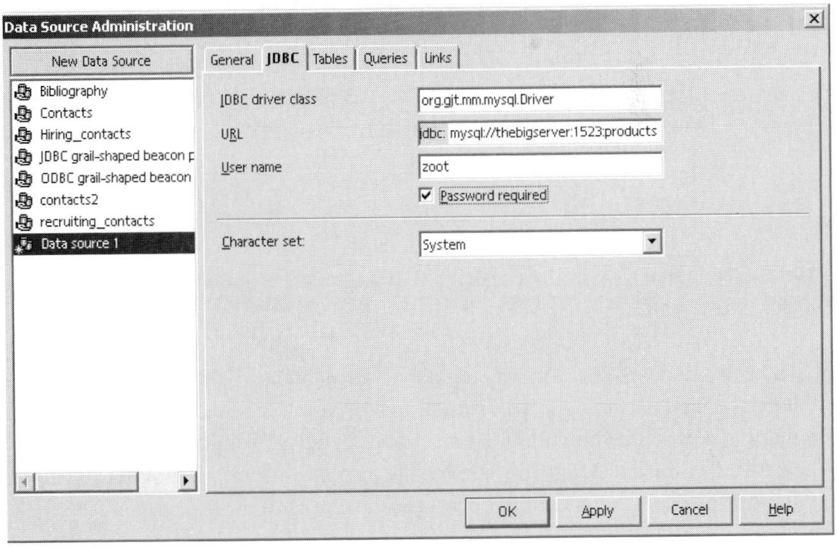

Figure 35-28   Specifying the driver class

8   Click the Tables tab and if prompted enter a password. Deselect any tables that should not be available to users.

9   Add any queries or links as outlined in Figure 35-11 on page 883 and Figure 35-12 on page 883.

10 Click OK to save the data source. If errors occur, consult the following.

- If a message appears stating that a connection to the data source could not be established, check the user name, URL, and talk to your database administrator. Also use another tool, on the current computer, to verify whether the database is accessible.

- Check whether the JDBC driver archive is in the classpath and check the driver classname you entered under the JDBC tab.

- Get the latest version of your driver.

- Remove write access for the user to the database. StarOffice can't write to Oracle databases.

- Go back and select the Password Required checkbox, if it isn't marked, and try again.

Connecting to an Access or Other Database Using ADO

Note – UNIX users might want to consider unixODBC and MySQL instead of Access. An excellent document from containing instructions for doing so is at `http://openoffice.homelinux.org/index.php?s=38`

Database information for ODBC and UNIX can be found at `http://unixodbc.org`. See `http://www.unixodbc.org/doc/OOoMySQL.pdf` in particular.

Before You Begin

Note – You need to install Access 2000 or an update from `www.microsoft.com/data` in order to use ADO.

ADO is a Windows-specific way to connect to a database, often used to connect to Access databases. You use an interface, similar to a driver, to connect to a database; the database vendor can provide you with it. Contact your database vendor or see www.able-consulting.com. The Microsoft home page also has information on ADO and Access. If you have problems connecting, export the databases to .dbf, dBase.

You'll need Microsoft's Data Access Components (MDAC) to use ADO. Windows 2000 and XP have MDAC built in; for other versions, go to microsoft.com/data and find the MDAC manifest.

Creating the Data Source

1   Choose Tools > Data Sources. The Data Source window will appear.

2   Click the General tab if it isn't already displayed.

3   Click New Data Source.

4   Name the data source.

5   Select ADO as the database type.

6   Enter the URL to the database. The window is shown in Figure 35-29 with an
     example of a URL to an Access database; additional information about URL syntax
     follows.

Microsoft Access URL syntax

```
PROVIDER=Microsoft.Jet.OLEDB.4.0;DATA SOURCE=access_mdb_file.mdb
```

where the *access_mdb_file.mdb* is the full path and filename of the .mdb file.

Microsoft SQL Server URL syntax

```
PROVIDER=sqloledb;DATA SOURCE=servername;INITIAL CATALOG=catalogname
```

where the *servername* is the host name of the computer where SQL Server is
installed, and *catalogname* is the initial catalog of the database. This is the database
that's run on the server.

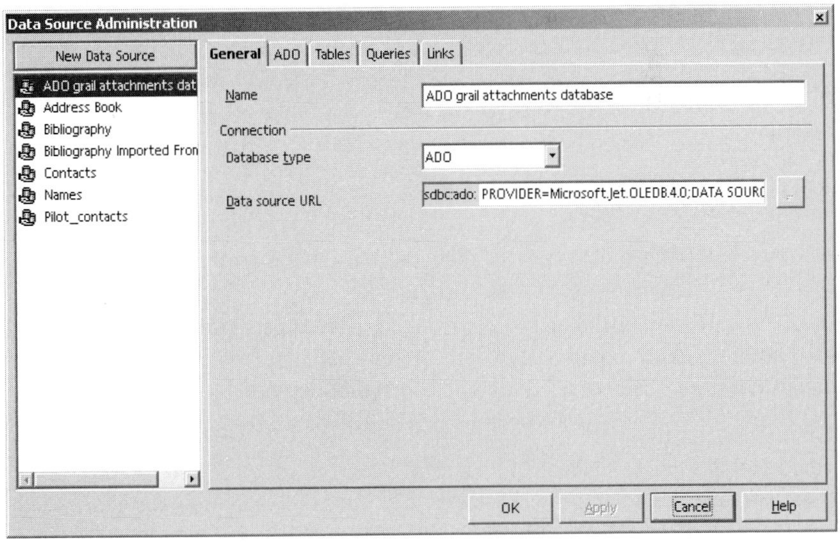

Figure 35-29   URL to an Access database, accessible through ADO

7   Click the ADO tab. Specify the user ID to use to access the database, and select
     Password Required if appropriate. The window is shown in Figure 35-30.

8   Click the Tables tab and unmark any tables users shouldn't have access to.

9   Set up queries if you want.

- Click the SQL icon to enter new SQL queries, if you want, for the data source. In the query you can specify only one table, and it must be one of the tables that was displayed and selected in the Tables tab.

- Click the New Query Design icon to create queries using a GUI tool where you don't need to know SQL. For more information see *Creating Queries* on page 917.

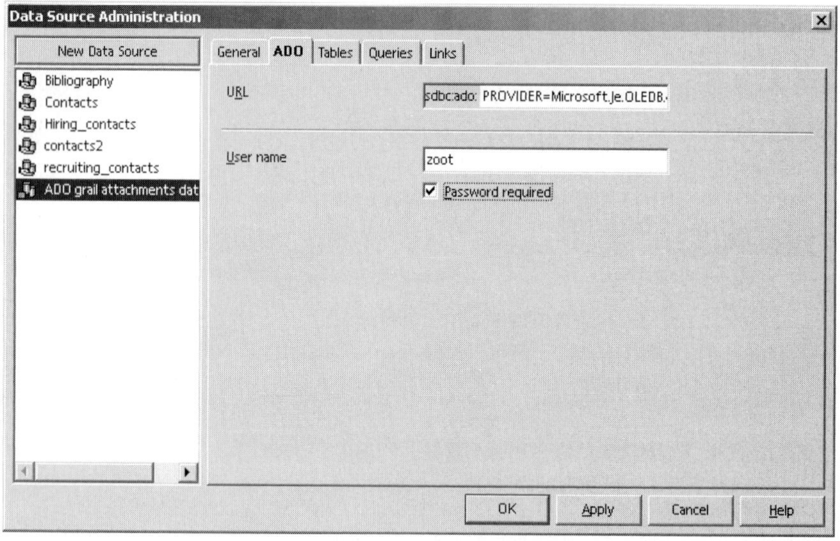

Figure 35-30   Specifying a user for access to a database through ADO

10   Click OK to save the data source and close the window.

- If you get errors, check that you're using the right names for the database, server, username, password, and so on.

- Ping the server and server computer to make sure they're running, and test accessing the database fro another computer.

Creating an Adabas Database and Data Source Connecting to It

Adabas is not included with OpenOffice.org.

OpenOffice.org

Before You Begin

If this is the first data source you set up, you might want to consider doing a practice run, just connecting to a dBase database. (Create a basic spreadsheet of data, save it as dBase). Make sure it's working correctly by editing the data (*Editing Data Using the Data Source Viewer* on page 917) using data entry forms (*Using Forms for Data Entry* on page 959), or doing a mailing (*Creating Mail Merge Letters and Faxes With Data Sources Using AutoPilots* on page 380). In addition, use a test application to make sure that your database is running and accessible from the computer you're using.

Installation

To install Adabas, do so when prompted at the end of the standard StarOffice installation, or start the Adabas installation by locating the setup file, `adabas` or `adabas.exe`, within the `operatingsystem`/`adabas` directory on your CD or the downloaded installation directory.

See *Installing Adabas for Use With StarOffice* on page 36.

Limitations

Adabas is a database from Software AG provided with StarOffice. It isn't the standard version; there's a five-user limit as well as a hundred-user limit. Contact Software AG or `www.adabas.com` if you want more.

Adabas directory names can have a maximum of 40 characters and a minimum of 10 characters. If you do the math, that means you're got only 15-30 left over for the Adabas directory name. Keep the DBROOT directory as short as you possibly can.

The name of the Adabas database you create is limited to a quaintly old-fashioned 8 characters.

Creating a New Adabas Database

1   Choose Tools > Data Sources.

2   Click New Data Source.

3   Enter a name for the StarOffice data source to connect to the database. The data source name can be anything; it's the database name that has the limit of eight characters.

4   Select Adabas as the data source type.

5   If you've already created the database, enter the URL in the Database URL field in the form `servername:databasename`.

6   In the Data Source Administration window's General tab, select Adabas from the Database Type list. The completed window is shown in Figure 35-32. Click Apply.

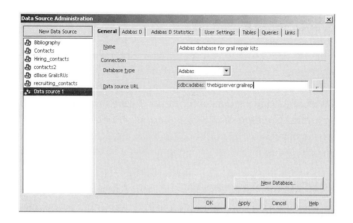

Figure 35-31   Making initial entries for a new data source connection to an Adabas database

7   Click New Database to create the database and enter the necessary information in the window shown in Figure 35-32 and the subsequent notes.

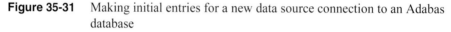

Figure 35-32   Creating a new Adabas database

More on the three file names you specified:

- SYSDEVSPACE – This file links the logical data pages of the database and where they actually are on your disk, Guard this file with your life, or at least a very good backup system; if you lose this file, you lose the database. The file will vary in size between 2 and 800 MB.

- TRANSACTIONLOG – Adabas use this file to store the transaction log. Make it the same size as database.

- DATADEVSPACE – This file stores the actual data, and it has to be the same size as the database. Default size is 20 MB.

As you've probably concluded by now, the directory where you're putting all this needs to be able to get at least 2.5 times the amount of space taken up by the database. Preferably more.

8 Click OK to create the database.

9 Click the Tables tab. Hide the system-y tables that users won't be interested in by deselecting each; the window is shown in Figure 35-33.

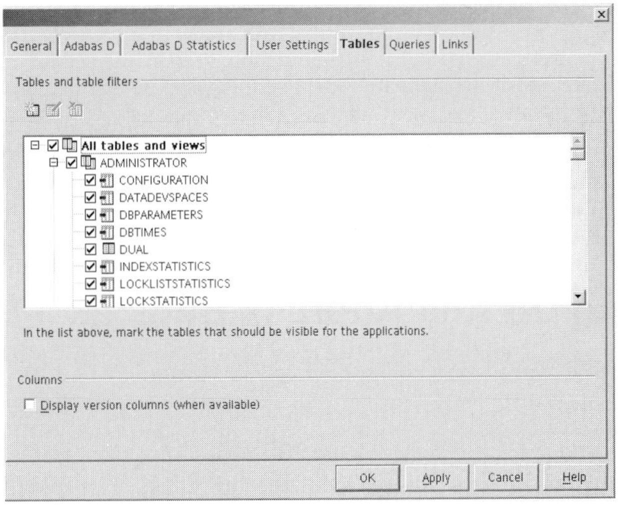

Figure 35-33 Selecting tables to use in the data source

10 Click the Users tab to define a standard user for access to the database.

11 Click the Settings tab shown in Figure 35-34 and specify access privileges; click OK.

12 Click the Queries and Links tabs, and enter any SQL queries for the data source, and specify any files you want to link to the data source. The Link capability is primarily used for linking to forms that display this data source's data. See Chapter 36, *Creating and Using Forms, Controls, and Events*, on page 925.

13 Click OK to save changes to the data source and close the window.

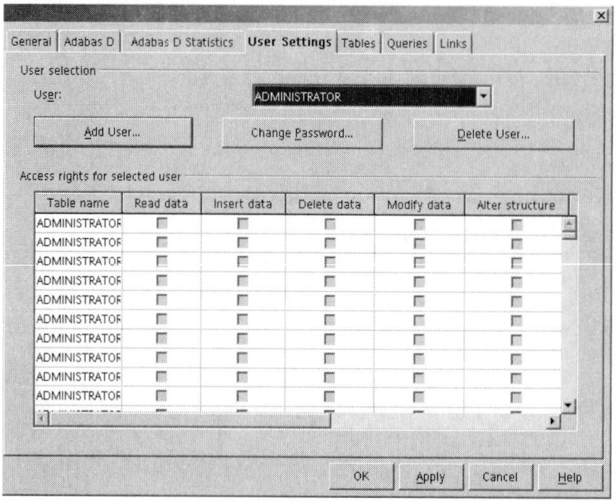

Figure 35-34 Setting access privileges for a new Adabas database

Note – Watch out for the standard Adabas tools. They create databases by default with 50 users. Only 5 users, of course, can be used in the StarOffice-issued version, so this creates overcrowding problems, which leads to anger, which leads to hate, which leads to the dark side. And doesn't do your data sources any good, either. To change this, start the main configuration tool called xcontrol to change the kernel parameter MAXUSERTASKS to 3.

Setting Up Any Address Book as a Data Source

If you have several address books, complete this procedure once for each, and just name the data sources differently.

1 If the Address AutoPilot in Figure 35-35 hasn't appeared just through your starting the program, in StarOffice or OpenOffice.org choose File > AutoPilot > Address Data Source. You can also get at these windows by choose Tools > Data Source, click New Data Source, and selecting Address Book as the data source type.

2 Select your address book type. The windows that you see will depend on your choice here.

Mozilla/Netscape, Windows, Outlook If you've got a compliant address book, just select that type and click Next. After a few minutes, you'll get the "that's all folks" message and you're done.

LDAP After you select LDAP and click Next, you might be prompted to enter additional information. Click the Settings button and enter the appropriate settings in the window shown in Figure 35-36.

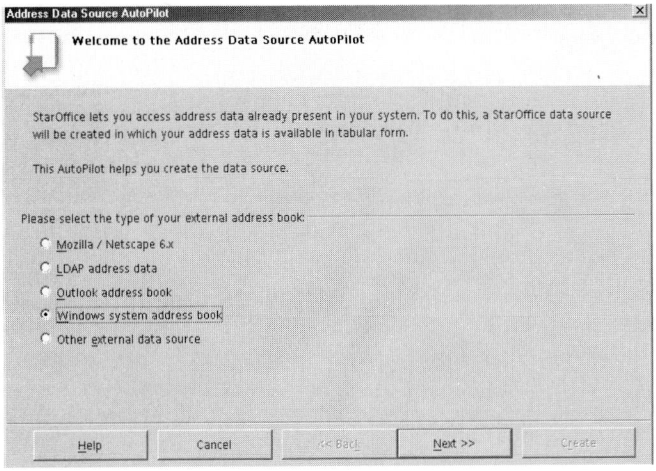

Figure 35-35   The first window for creating a data source from your address book.

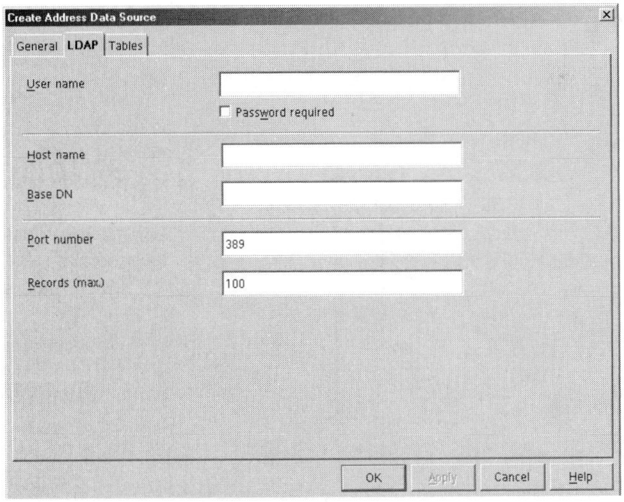

Figure 35-36   Entering LDAP information

Other (such as another address book exported to tab-delimited text) You definitely need to enter more information for this type. Click Next and you'll be prompted to enter more information. Click Settings and enter information in the windows shown in Figure 35-38 and Figure 35-37.

3 After the message"That's all the information we needed, thanks" just click Next. The window in Figure 35-39 will appear; name the new data source. You're done.

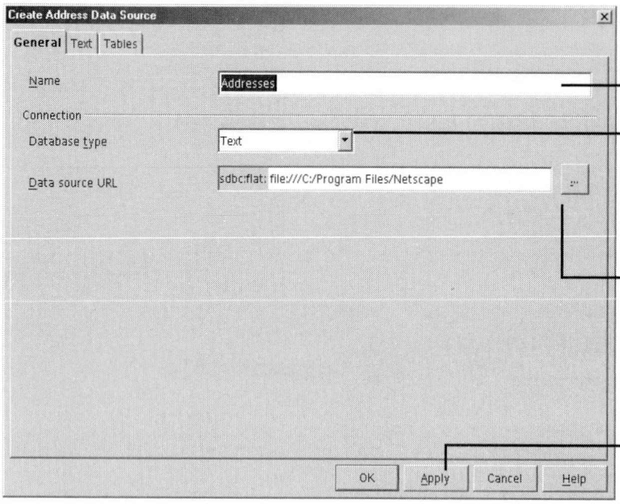

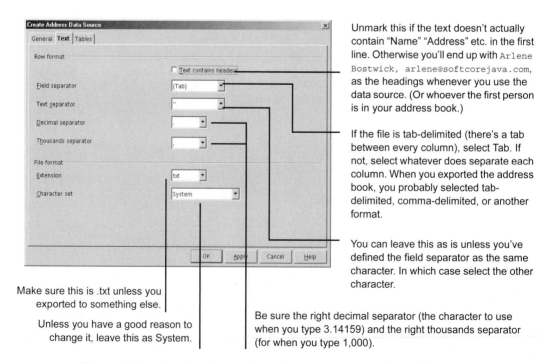

Enter a name, then select text as the database type and browse to the folder containing the exported file. It doesn't let you specify the file in the browse window but it works fine anyway.

When you select Text in the Database Type list, the URL changes so it ends in flat.

Click the browse button and enter the **directory** where your address file is. It doesn't let you specify the filename, so once you've specified the directory, just type the filename.

Click Apply, then click the Text tab.

Figure 35-37   Entering additional information about the data format

Unmark this if the text doesn't actually contain "Name" "Address" etc. in the first line. Otherwise you'll end up with Arlene Bostwick, arlene@softcorejava.com, as the headings whenever you use the data source. (Or whoever the first person is in your address book.)

If the file is tab-delimited (there's a tab between every column), select Tab. If not, select whatever does separate each column. When you exported the address book, you probably selected tab-delimited, comma-delimited, or another format.

You can leave this as is unless you've defined the field separator as the same character. In which case select the other character.

Make sure this is .txt unless you exported to something else.

Unless you have a good reason to change it, leave this as System.

Be sure the right decimal separator (the character to use when you type 3.14159) and the right thousands separator (for when you type 1,000).

Figure 35-38   Entering the location of the exported text address file

Field separator This separator delimits the single data fields from each other.. You can choose among a semicolon (;), comma (,), colon (:), tab, space, or another character, which you can enter in the respective combo box.

4   The window in Figure 35-39 appears; name the data source and you're done.

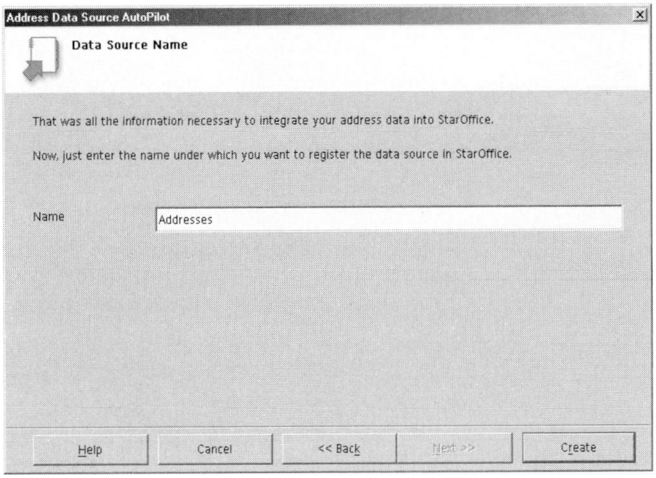

Figure 35-39   Naming the data source

To use the data source you set up, open any document and choose Tools > Data Sources. More specifically, use it when you choose File > AutoPilot > *document_type*, or whenever you do a mail merge. For more information, see Chapter 10, *Mail Merges, Business Cards, and More*, on page 351.

Migrating a StarOffice 5.2 Database and Creating a Data Source

The StarOffice 5.2 database format isn't supported now, but you can migrate it to a usable format and create a data source so you can connect to it. The AutoPilot creates a new dBase file based on the old database.

Note – The windows that appear in the AutoPilot vary depending on how the old database was set up. For that reason, and because they're self explanatory, we don't display all the windows. Follow the AutoPilot through and use the directions onscreen.

1   Choose File > AutoPilot > StarOffice 5.2 Database Import. The window in Figure 35-40 will appear.

Specify the full path to the .sdb
StarBase database file. ———

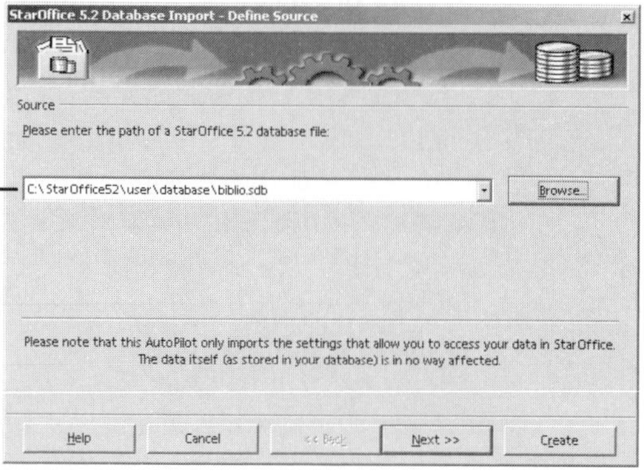

Figure 35-40   Specifying the database to convert

2   Click Next; the window in Figure 35-41 will appear. The windows that you get after
this will depend on whether there are any queries or forms attached to the database.
We'll ignore those for the most part; the AutoPilot is self explanatory.

Select the queries and form documents, if you want to convert them. Click Next and
enter information as prompted.

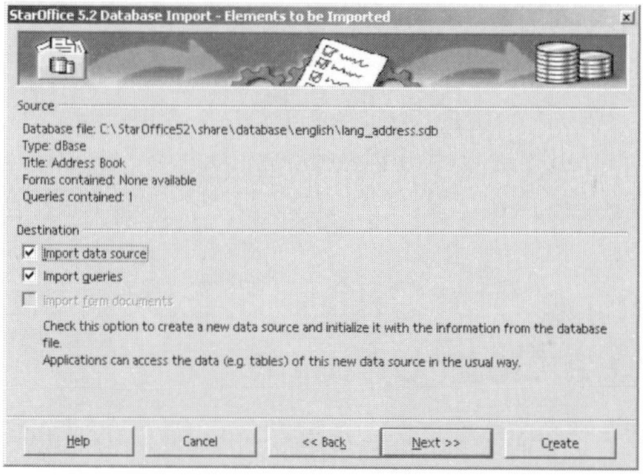

Figure 35-41   Selecting the items to convert

3   After you've specified how you want to convert forms and queries, the window in
Figure 35-42 *might* appear. You can accept the default directory. This window is a
little weird; it just wants a little reassurance that yes, that's the database you specified
before, and sure, go ahead and put that .dbf extension at the end.

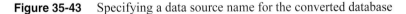

The **$** appears by default in the new path field; **remove it.**

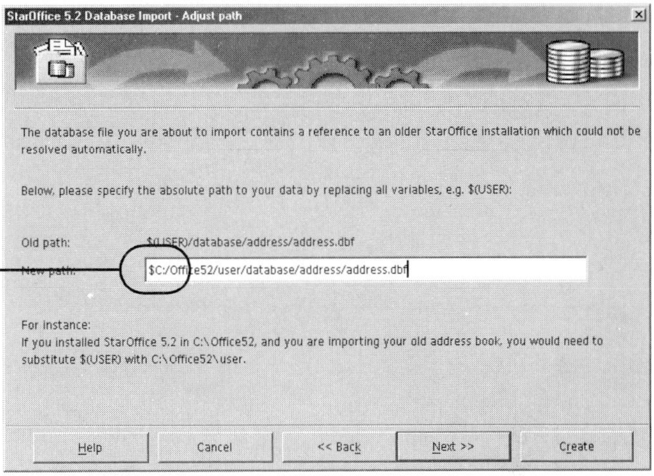

Figure 35-42   Specifying the absolute directory of the old database (doesn't always appear)

4   Click Next; the window in Figure 35-43 will appear. Type the name for the new 6.0 data source that you want to see in data source lists.

Type the name for the new data source.

Keep this selected to bring up the Data Source Administration window to verify that everything was set up correctly.

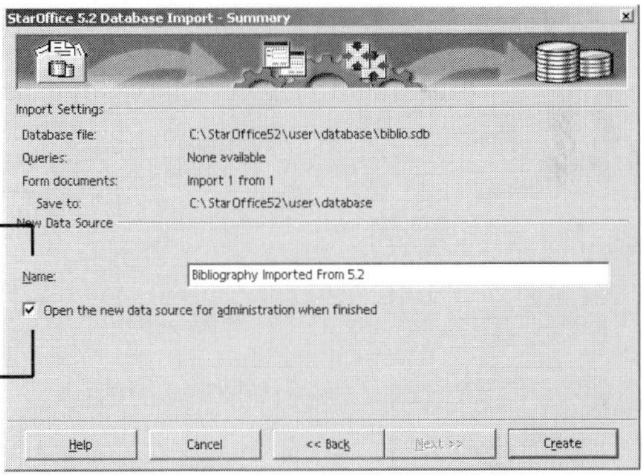

Figure 35-43   Specifying a data source name for the converted database

5   Click Create; the window in Figure 35-44 will appear. Click each tab to make sure the data source was created correctly and the database was converted correctly.

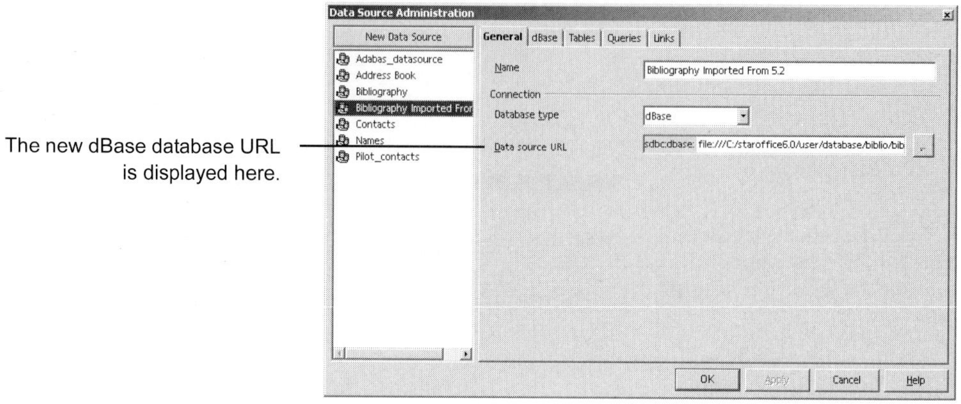

The new dBase database URL is displayed here.

Figure 35-44 Verifying the new data source and converted database

Setting up Connection Pooling

Creating a connection to a data source is a fair bit of work for your computer and programs, so this lets you manage the connections: keep them around for a while in case another process needs them, but then delete them if no one wants them. It brings to mind rather sad memories of junior high dances.

For all types of sources, choose Tools > Options > Data Sources > Connections and see if you want to modify the settings for any of the drivers, or deactivate connection pooling period. The window shown in Figure 35-45.

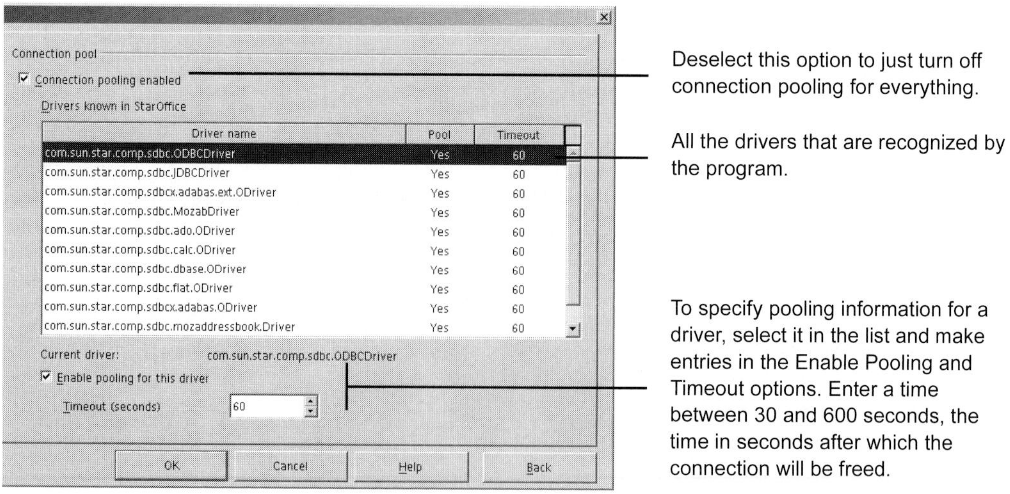

Deselect this option to just turn off connection pooling for everything.

All the drivers that are recognized by the program.

To specify pooling information for a driver, select it in the list and make entries in the Enable Pooling and Timeout options. Enter a time between 30 and 600 seconds, the time in seconds after which the connection will be freed.

Figure 35-45 Data source settings

Creating and Modifying Tables

Every data source has one or more tables. It's just a way of dividing and organizing data.

About Tables

Sometimes you might just have one data source with all the data together. If you're just keeping your mailing list in one data source and you only send a letter once a month to everyone on that list, you don't need to go any further.

However, what if you realize after a while that you only want to send your holiday newsletter to friends and family, and your daily "I'm still unemployed, is anyone hiring?" letters to professional acquaintances, and your triweekly amusing short stories to the other members of the Fertile, Minnesota Writers' Club?

Then it's time for tables or queries.

About tables When you do anything with a data source, you have to pick the table or query to use; if you didn't make any tables, your data source is automatically given a table that just contains everything in the data source. You can only use one table or query; you can't select both the `jobsearch` table and the `stories` table from the `peopleIsendlettersto` data source.

You can use tables or queries Queries and tables are interchangeable for the purposes of using their data in documents.

Tables Tables are just subdivisions of the data source.

- When you create a data source based on text files, everything in the directory you specify becomes a table. So if you set up the Contacts data source and point it at your bulging `C:\mycontacts` directory where the separate lists of people you send letters to are, you get three tables: `holiday`, `jobsearch`, and `stories`.

- When you create a data source based on a spreadsheet, every sheet in the spreadsheet is a table.

- For all the other databases, it depends on the database structure you set up.

So now, consider whether you'll need to structure your text files, spreadsheets, or other data differently, for the tables you might need, and subdivide and organize your data sources as necessary.

Queries Queries are subsections of your data too, but they're created differently. You create a query for a particular table.

- "Give me the phone numbers of all the people in the hiring table of the Contacts data source who live in Colorado and whose emails end in `@enron.com`" would be a good query. Assuming that you have fields in your hiring table for phone numbers, state, and emails. And assuming that you're not bothering to ask them for a job.

- You set up queries either using SQL to write it out, or using the Query window.

To create queries, see *Creating Queries* on page 917.

Creating New Tables for Spreadsheet and Text File Data Sources

You can add tables to text file and spreadsheet data sources just by creating more files or sheets.

Then open the data source definition window again for the data source and be sure in the Table tab that every table is selected that you want available for use.

Creating New Tables and Fields for Any Data Source Except Text Files and Spreadsheets

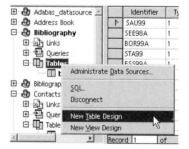

1   Choose View > Data Sources.

2   Select the data source you want to add a table to and expand it so the Tables category shows.

3   Right-click on Tables and choose New Table Design, as shown at right.

4   The Table Design window will appear. This is where you design the table as well as each field.

In the following examples starting with Figure 35-46, the example of the existing StarOffice bibliography data source is used. A new table is added to it to track information about promoting books of authors in the bibliography.

5   The Table Design window shown in Figure 35-46 is fairly intuitive. Briefly, just enter the names of the fields you want in the table (there's a limit on the number of characters in the field name), select the type of data, and add comments if you want. In the lower area, specify the field length, the default value if any, and format if any. For some fields like decimals, you'll have more options.

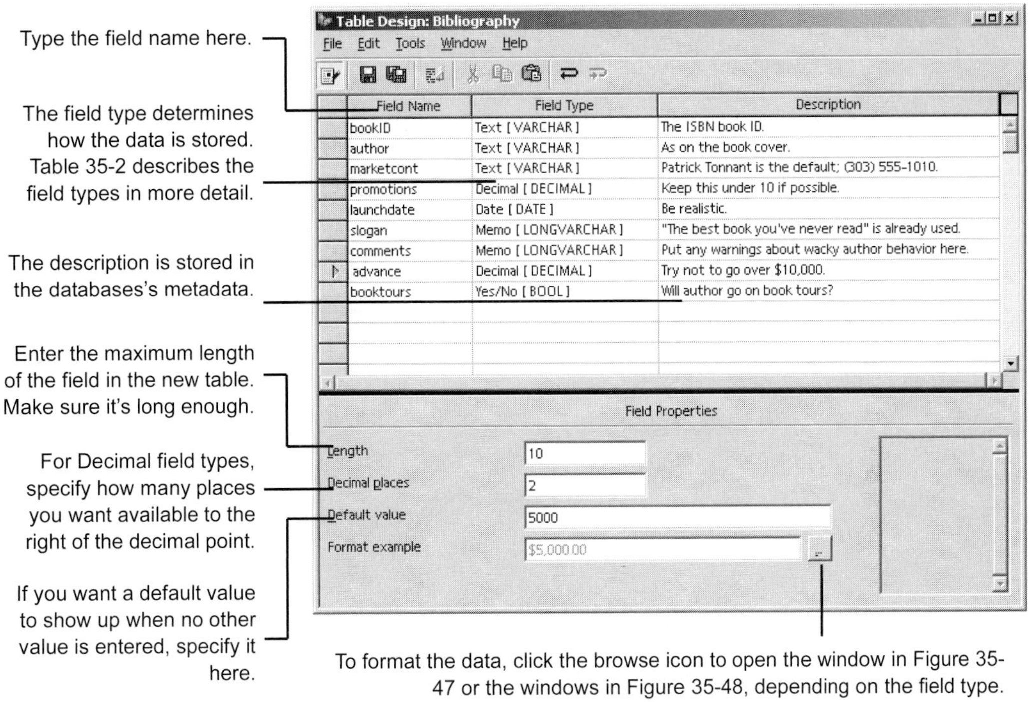

Type the field name here.

The field type determines
how the data is stored.
Table 35-2 describes the
field types in more detail.

The description is stored in
the databases's metadata.

Enter the maximum length
of the field in the new table.
Make sure it's long enough.

For Decimal field types,
specify how many places
you want available to the
right of the decimal point.

If you want a default value
to show up when no other
value is entered, specify it
here.

To format the data, click the browse icon to open the window in Figure 35-
47 or the windows in Figure 35-48, depending on the field type.

Figure 35-46   A new table for bibliography

Table 35-2 describes the field types you can select.

Table 35-2   Field types

Field type	Length limit	Description
Yes/No (BOOL)	1	Stores a value of 0 (no) or 1 (yes).
Memo (LONG VARCHAR)	65,535	Use this for long text fields like comments.
Text (fix) (CHAR)	254	Use this for shorter text fields. The entire 254 characters are stored regardless of whether you've put data in them.
Decimal (DECIMAL)	20	Use this for whole or partial numbers; anything you'll need to express a decimal value for. You can specify the number of figures to the right of the decimal points, such as two for storing dollars. The numbers to the right of the decimal point are included in the total of 20 you're allowed. Format it by clicking the browse icon and selecting the format in the windows in Figure 35-48.

Table 35-2   Field types

Field type	Length limit	Description
Text (VARCHAR)	254	Use this for any text field like a name, book title, etc.
Date (DATE)	N/A	Format the date by clicking the browse icon and selecting the format in the window in Figure 35-47.

6   Use the windows in Figure 35-47 and Figure 35-48 for guidance in creating the fields.

Figure 35-47 shows the Field Format window where you can specify how each date field is formatted. Open it by clicking the browse icon next to the Format field in the Table Design window.

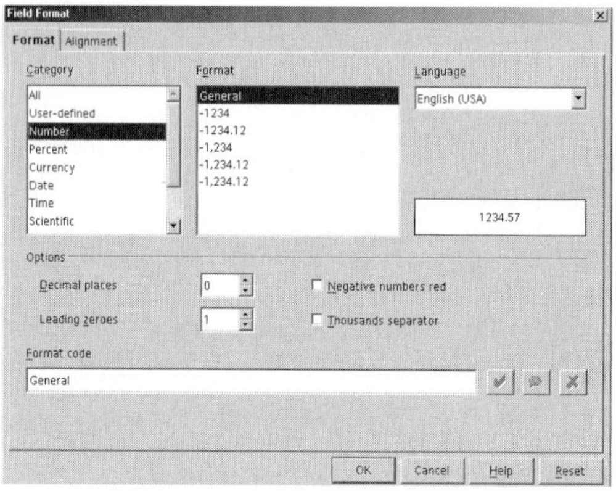

Figure 35-47   Formatting the new field (dates)

Figure 35-48 shows the Field Format window where you can specify how each non-date field is formatted. Open it by clicking the browse icon next to the Format field in the Table Design window.

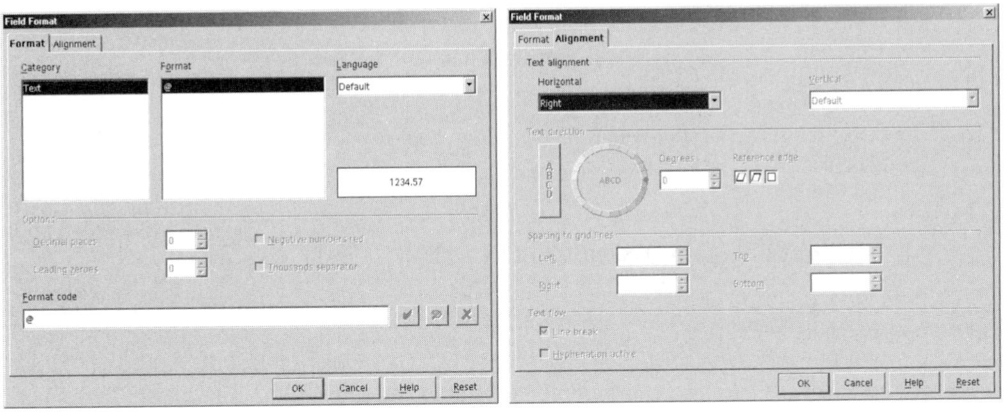

Figure 35-48   Formatting the new field (other styles)

7   You'll need a key for the table. Click the Index Design icon on the object bar and make the appropriate entries in the Index Design window.

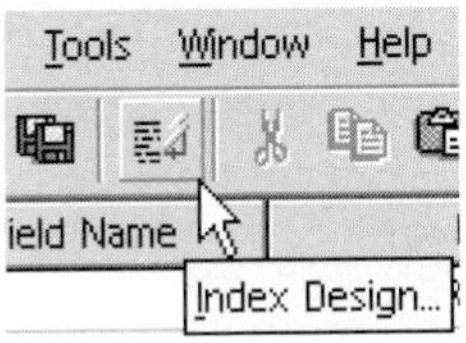

Figure 35-49 shows the Index Design window. Set up the index field or fields, then click OK.

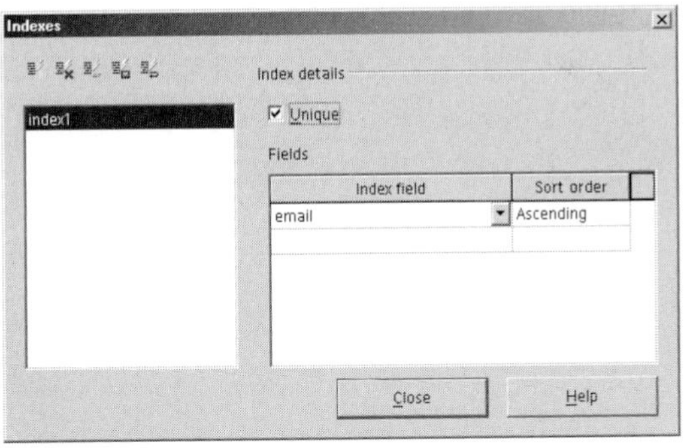

Figure 35-49   Index design field

8   Click the Save icon when you're done and name the table in the window that appears.

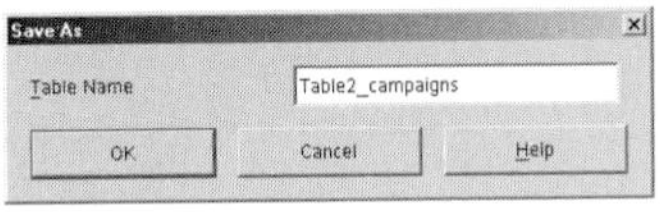

Renaming

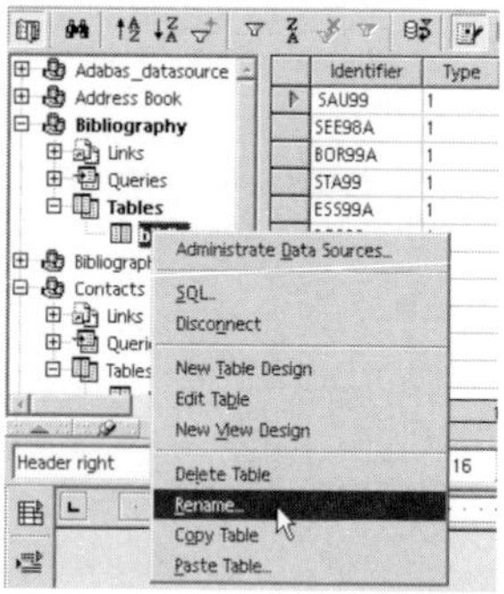

Just right-click on a table and choose Rename, then type the new name.

Be sure not to violate the naming requirements of your database.

Copying Tables to Another Data Source

You can copy tables between data sources of the same type. Just right-click on the table and choose Copy Table, then go to the other data source, right-click on the Tables heading of that data source, and choose Paste Table.

In the Copy Table windows that appear, shown in Figure 35-50, select the appropriate options. Click Next to select the fields to include, then click Next again to specify the field options for each field. Click Create to finish pasting the table.

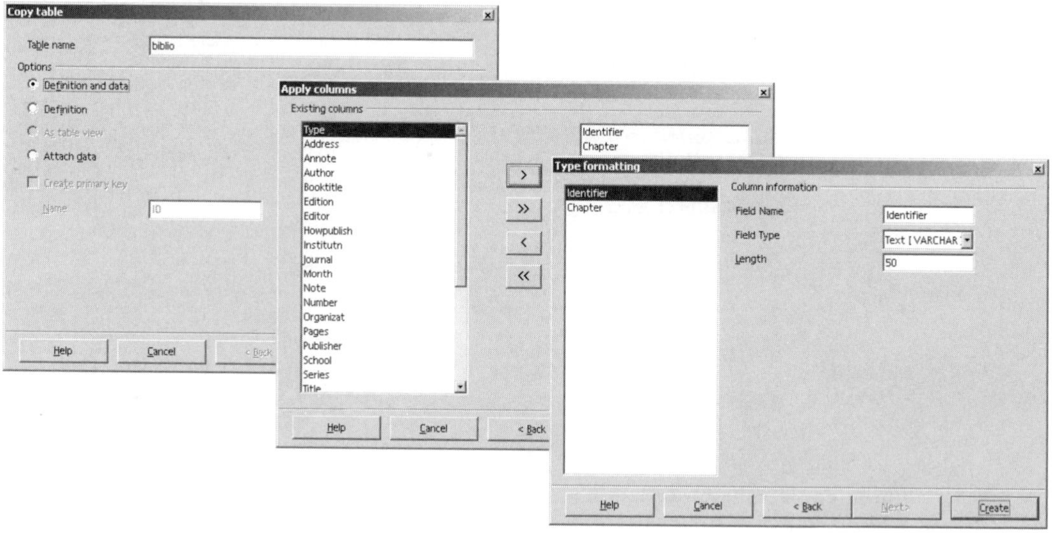

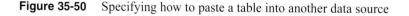

Figure 35-50   Specifying how to paste a table into another data source

Modifying a Table or Field

1   Choose View > Data Sources.

2   Select the data source you want to add a table to and expand it so the Tables category shows.

3   Right-click on Tables and choose New Table Design, as shown at right.

4   In the table design window, make the necessary changes. Refer to *Creating New Tables and Fields for Any Data Source Except Text Files and Spreadsheets* on page 910 for more information.

5   Then click the Save icon on the object bar to save changes.

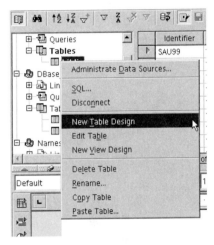

Using the Execute SQL Statement Window

In the data source viewer window, right click on any table and choose SQL. The Execute SQL Statement will appear.

This window lets you use SQL for data source administration. The command entered does not lead to the display of filtered database content. It's only for commands like Grant, Create Table, Drop Table, and so on. The data source must support these SQL commands—dBase, for example, cannot execute all the commands mentioned here for SQL. The status window indicates if the command has been successfully executed.

To use SQL in a query, right-click on the Query option below the data source, and choose the New SQL Command option.

Bringing New Data Into a New or Existing Table

So you've got a new table or field—great. Now what? To get data into it, you have a number of options.

Use Your Database Tools

If your database has tools that let you easily and quickly import data into a new table, use them. Consult your database's documentation for more information.

Use the Form

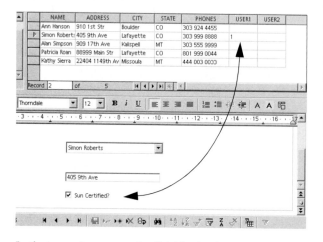

You might have just created the new field to store information from a new field in a data entry form. For instance, if you've recently decided whether you want to track whether your customers are Sun Certified Java Programmers. You'll need a field on the form to record that, and a field in your table to store the 1 for yes or the 0 for no.

In that case, just set up the field in the form to store data in your new field. (Right-click the field, choose Control, select the Data tab, and select the field.) For more information, see *Basics for Creating a Form on Your Own* on page 936.

Then use the form to go through each record and make the appropriate entry in the field.

If you simply created an entire new field and the quickest way you can think of is to just enter it through the form, then go ahead and do that. See *Adding a Record* on page 959.

Editing Data Using the Data Source Viewer

This applies to all data sources except text files, spreadsheets, and address books, and of course if your JDBC connection or database setup doesn't allow it, you won't be able to use it either.

However, for basic data sources like dBase, just choose View > Data Source and type the data you want in each field.

Entering a Longer Value Than the Field Wants to Accept

When you create a data source, the maximum field length is defined as the longest field in any record. For instance, your maximum field length for last names might be 13 letters, because of Alan van Luxembourg. However, when Ruth Robinson gets remarried and changes her name to Ruth Robinson Boughten-Wise, you're not going to have room in the Last Name field for "Robinson Boughten-Wise".

How do we solve this? Easy, just edit the table definition and increase the maximum field size. See *Modifying a Table or Field* on page 915 for more information.

Creating Queries

Note – Once you create a query, you can use it for mail merges the same way you do a database table.

Queries help you focus in on specific information in your database. For example, in a huge database with lots of fields, you can create a query that shows just first names and email addresses; or you can create a query that just shows mailing label information.

Or let's say you're going to drum up business for your Java certification seminars, so you want to call all the people in your list of contacts in a 20 mile radius who aren't Java certified. Figure 35-51 shows the table that will be the basis for examples in this section.

NAME	ADDRESS	CITY	STATE	PHONES	USER1	USER
Marilyn Haugl	1660 45th Avenue	Lafayette	CO	303 999 8888	0	
Alan Simpsonc	909 17th Ave	Kalispell	MT	303 555 4444	1	
Simon Roberts	10580 Madison Av	Boulder	CO	303 555 1212	1	
Kathy Sierra	113 1st A	Missoula	MT	444 003 0033	1	
Floyd Jones	3340 Golden Rd	Golden	CO	303 888 9900	0	
Bert Bates	10580 W 105th Av	Golden	CO	907 789 0071	1	
Alexis Smith	11 Lyndon Str	Boulder	CO	303 990 1212	0	

Record 7   of   9

Figure 35-51   Data source viewer window, showing data to run a query on

You can write the query in straight SQL, or use the Query Definition window. You can edit a query created by the Query Definition window in the SQL editing window, and vice versa.

Writing or Editing a SQL Query

1   Open the SQL query composition/editing window.

- In the data source viewer, right-click on Query and choose New SQL Command.

  Note that if you are attempting to edit an existing query, this will open the query editing window with the graphical interface, not the SQL writing window.

- You can also go into the Data Source administration window and select the data source, then select the Query tab. Click the Enter SQL Command icon.

2   Type the SQL command. For full SQL syntax consult your SQL documentation. The online help also contains examples and additional information.

An example is shown in Figure 35-52. The code says, give me the contents of the NAME field and the PHONES field in the `contacts_marketing` table, but only for the people who have O stored in their USER1 field (the field where whether they're Java certified is stored) and who live in Boulder or Golden. And list the results in ascending order by the contents of the NAME field.

The program converts query window queries to SQL, and sometimes in the process lists the table name twice. You can leave it as is or delete one of them; it doesn't seem to matter.

Figure 35-52   Writing or editing a query in SQL

3   Save the query by clicking the Save icon and enter a name for the query.

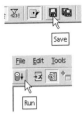

4   Run the query by clicking the Run icon.

5   The results will appear in the query window, shown in Figure 35-52.

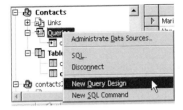

Figure 35-53   Results of the query, run in the SQL query composition window

Using the Query Definition Window

1   Choose View > Data Source to open the data source viewer. Then open the query definition window by right-clicking on the Queries option and selecting New Query Design.

2   Use the query design window in Figure 35-54 to compose the query. The online help contains examples and additional information.

Note – Right-click in the area on the left below the Or options and select Distinct Values, if you want to only get one record back when data appears multiple times. For example, to record all the last names in your address database in a query but the name "Sierra" occurs several times, you can choose the Unique Values command to specify in the query that the name "Sierra" will occur only once. In SQL this command corresponds to DISTINCT keyword.

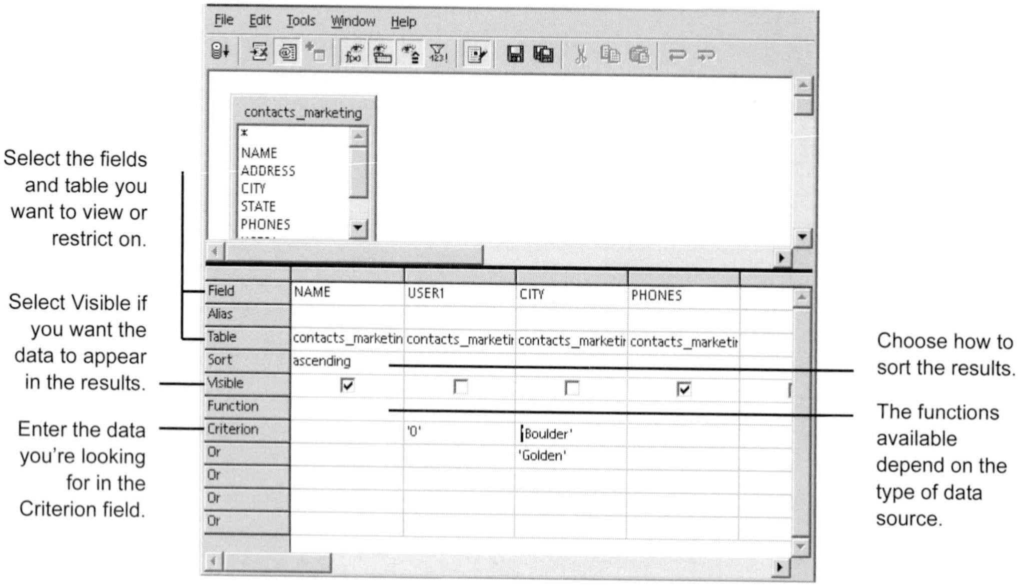

Select the fields and table you want to view or restrict on.

Select Visible if you want the data to appear in the results.

Enter the data you're looking for in the Criterion field.

Choose how to sort the results.

The functions available depend on the type of data source.

Figure 35-54   Selecting what you want to see in the query

3   Save the query by clicking the Save icon and enter a name for the query.

4   Run the query by clicking the Run icon at right.

5   The results will appear in the query design window, as shown in Figure 35-55.

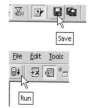

Figure 35-55   Results of the query, run in the query design window

Sorting and Filtering Information in the Data Source Viewer

You've got additional, quicker options for restricting information, in the window you get by choosing View > Data Sources.

Sorting

You've got two ways to approach sorting; the quick sort ascending or descending icons and a little more control with the sort window.

Quick Sort

Open the data source viewer by choosing View > Data Source.

Click in the field you want to sort by, then click the Sort Ascending or Sort Descending icon in the object bar above the data source.

Using the Sort Window

1   Click the Sort icon in the object bar above the data source.

2   In the Sort Order window in Figure 35-56, make your selections and click OK.

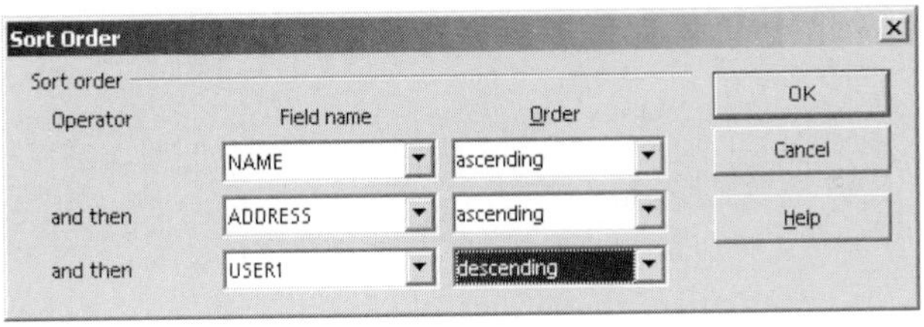

Figure 35-56   Sort Order window

Filtering

You've got two ways to approach filtering; the quick AutoFilter and a little more control with the default filter.

AutoFilter

The AutoFilter lets you see only the records with the currently selected data in a particular field. For instance, if you want to see only the people who live in Boulder, select the CITY field for someone from Boulder and click the AutoFilter icon. This is illustrated in Figure 35-57.

1   Open the data source viewer by choosing View > Data Source.

2   Click in the field that has the information you want to match.

3   Click the AutoFilter icon.

NAME	ADDRESS	CITY	STATE	PHONES	USER1
Simon Robe AutoFilter adison Av		Boulder	CO	303 555 1212	1
Alexis Smith	11 Lyndon Str	Boulder	CO	303 990 1212	0
Marian Ward	900 2nd Wilderne	Boulder	CO	303 926 4455	0

Figure 35-57   Using AutoFilter

4   To remove the filter, click the Apply Filter icon. It will appear
lighter and recessed when the filter is applied; when you click it in
that state the filter will be taken off and the icon will be the same
shade as the other icons again.

Default Filter

1   Open the data source viewer by choosing View > Data Source.

2   Click the Default Filter icon. Make your selections in the Filter window in Figure 35-
55 and click OK.

Filter

Criteria

Operator	Field name	Condition	Value	
	CITY	=	Boulder	OK
AND	USER1	=	0	Cancel
AND	- none -			Help

Figure 35-58   Using the default filter window

3   To remove the filter, click the Apply Filter icon. It will appear
lighter and recessed when the filter is applied; when you click it in
that state the filter will be taken off and the icon will be the same
shade as the other icons again.

Exporting Data Sources to Another Format

Use this procedure if you need to convert a data source you're using in StarOffice or
OpenOffice.org to a database in another application. This assumes that the other
application can import delimited text files.

Basic Exporting

1 Move a database table into a Calc spreadsheet. See *Using the Data Pilot to Make a Spreadsheet With Automatic Totals* on page 520.

2 Save the spreadsheet as a delimited text file. *Importing a Text File or Spreadsheet* on page 517.

   If the other application can import dBase files, you can also save the spreadsheet as a dBase file.

Converting to Writer, RTF, and HTML Tables

To convert a database table to a table in a Writer, HTML, or RTF (Rich Text Format) document, open the document in StarOffice, hold down the Shift key, and drag a table from the Explorer window into a document.

If you want more control over which database fields are added to the table, drag the database table into the document without holding down the Shift key. In the Insert Database Columns window, select the fields you want to include.

Editing Data in Data Sources Using the Data Source Viewer

This applies to all data sources except text files, spreadsheets, and address books.

Bring up the data source viewer as shown in Figure 35-59 and start typing. Again, as with renaming, if this would upset your database administrator, it's probably not a good idea.

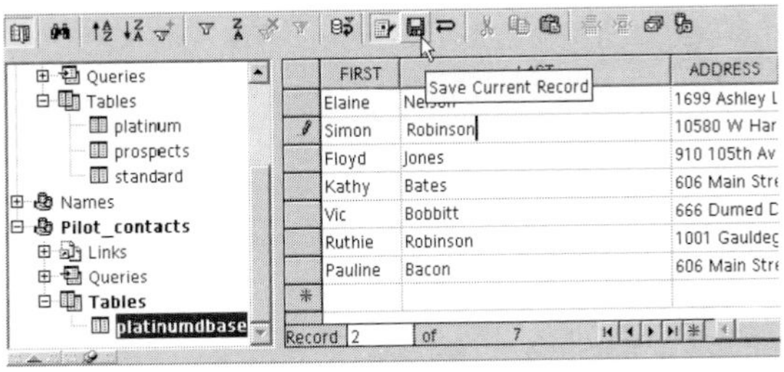

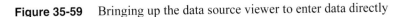

Figure 35-59 Bringing up the data source viewer to enter data directly

The process after this is similar to using a form. For details, see *Using Forms for Data Entry* on page 959.

Creating and Using Forms, Controls, and Events

Forms, What Are They Good For?

Quick terminology note In the following procedures, we'll use the term *control*. A control is an object on a form that connects with some field in a table or query, allowing you to enter data for that field through the form. Examples of controls are text boxes, drop-down lists, and check boxes. By default, the forms you create with AutoPilot will contain mostly labels and text boxes. The labels tell you the name of the field, and the text boxes let you enter data in the field.

Introduction to Forms

Forms let you create a graphical environment for working with your data sources. You can create forms that show all fields in a data source, or you can create forms that show only specific fields. For example, you could create a form that lets you view and modify only name and email address information for your contacts, or use a query to create a form for only certain records.

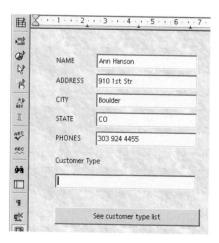

You can create a form for a query. Since a query is only a part of a table, a form for a query really just supports the table. Creating a form for a query lets you work on smaller groupings of fields.

Using Forms to View Data

Note – For more information, see *Using Forms to View Data* on page 954.

Once your form is put together, via the AutoPilot or your own efforts, your users can run through the form in a number of ways. See Figure 36-1.

*   Just clicking through the records in order, using the icons at the bottom of any form, AutoPilot-created or from scratch.

*   Using the sort icons, also available, to see data in a particular order

*   Using the search feature

*   Using filters to narrow down the data to, for instance, everyone in the customer database who's complained bitterly about the Enterprise JavaBeans course.

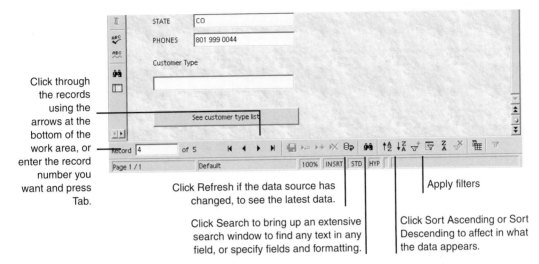

Click through the records using the arrows at the bottom of the work area, or enter the record number you want and press Tab.

Click Refresh if the data source has changed, to see the latest data.

Click Search to bring up an extensive search window to find any text in any field, or specify fields and formatting.

Apply filters

Click Sort Ascending or Sort Descending to affect in what the data appears.

Figure 36-1   Example of how to find data in a form

Using Forms for Data Entry (Writin', Insertin', and Deletin')

If your data source is up to it and if you think it's a good decision for your security situation, then you can very easily use forms for data entry.

- Change existing data
- Delete existing records
- Add new records

Note – StarOffice cannot edit Oracle databases. This is a known problem, so check the sun.com/staroffice site periodically to see if they've come up with a patch.

First note It helps if you have the following skills too, but that's just for adding more powerful processing:

- Do anything with SQL (are you the MacGyver of SQL?)
- Learn to write macros

Second note This depends on your database, of course. Is your security set up so people can just edit it from forms? That might not always be wise. Likewise, data sources based on text files and spreadsheets aren't editable. Though you can save either form as .DBF and then you've got an editable data source.

Third note The form setup and how it interacts with data sources is weird once in a while. It's not wildly inconsistent but it does help if you kill an occasional chicken.

That said, Figure 36-2 shows how you'd add a record to a data source, as well as the tools to use for deleting. (Except, as noted, with AutoPilot forms which are rigidly read-only.)

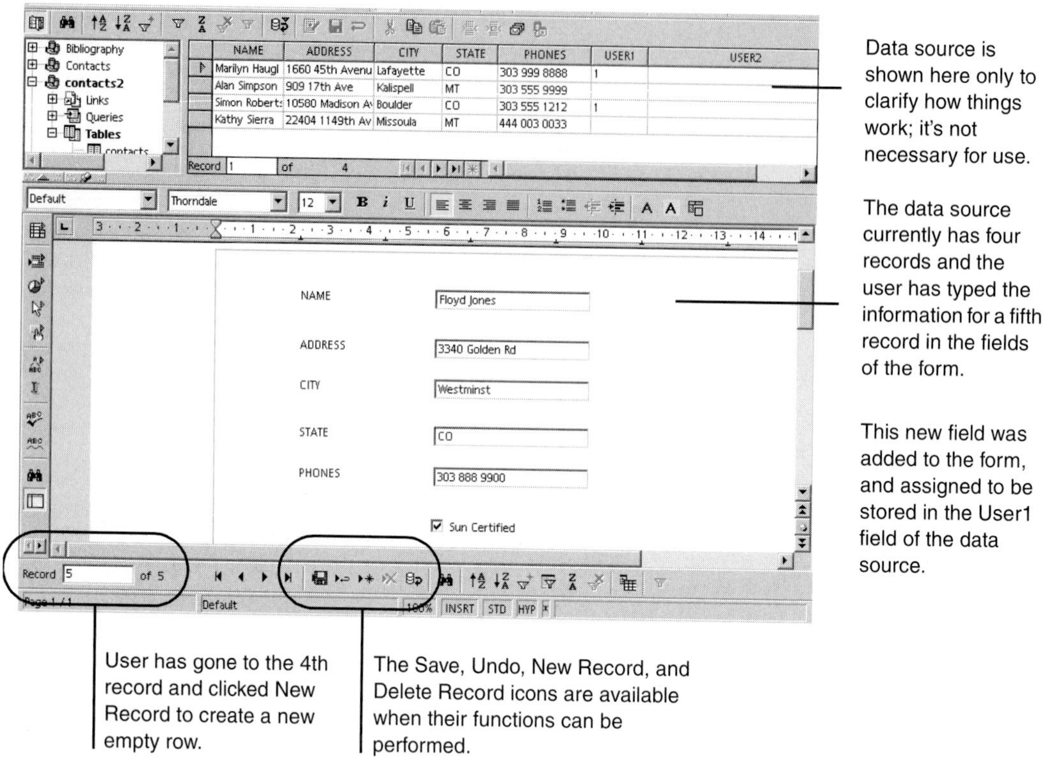

Data source is shown here only to clarify how things work; it's not necessary for use.

The data source currently has four records and the user has typed the information for a fifth record in the fields of the form.

This new field was added to the form, and assigned to be stored in the User1 field of the data source.

NAME	ADDRESS	CITY	STATE	PHONES	USER1	USER2
Marilyn Haugl	1660 45th Avenu	Lafayette	CO	303 999 8888	1	
Alan Simpson	909 17th Ave	Kalispell	MT	303 555 9999		
Simon Robert:	10580 Madison A	Boulder	CO	303 555 1212	1	
Kathy Sierra	22404 1149th Av	Missoula	MT	444 003 0033		

Record 1 of 4

Default   Thorndale   12   **B** *i* U

NAME   Floyd Jones

ADDRESS   3340 Golden Rd

CITY   Westminst

STATE   CO

PHONES   303 888 9900

☑ Sun Certified

Record 5 of 5

User has gone to the 4th record and clicked New Record to create a new empty row.

The Save, Undo, New Record, and Delete Record icons are available when their functions can be performed.

Figure 36-2   Go to the end of the table and type the data

With the new empty row available, type the data, then click Save Record.

In the data source viewer window, you can click Refresh to make the change show up.

Figure 36-4 shows the resulting change to the data source.

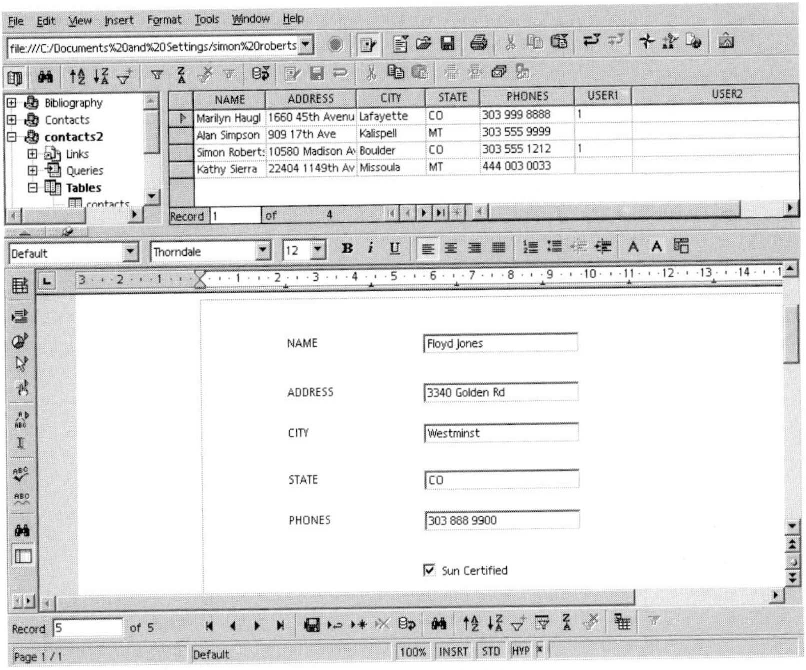

Figure 36-3   See the results in the data source

Making a Basic Data Entry Form

For instance, if you want to create a basic form where you can read and edit a dBase data source full of your business contacts, you could do that easily. Make a new HTML or Writer document, get the Forms tearoff menu up, drag the fields onto the form (more on that later), and you're good to go. The change to any field is made as soon as the focus leaves the field. An example is shown in Figure 36-4.

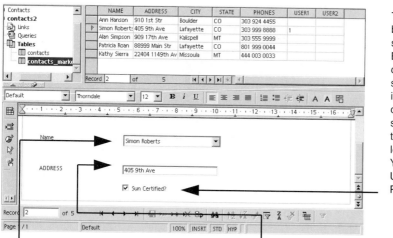

The Sun Certified check box was created from scratch using the Check Box control icon. Then after creation, it was set up to store data that users add to it in the User1 field in the contacts_marketing data source. As you can see in the data source viewer at left, a 1, corresponding to Yes, is now stored in the User1 field for Simon Roberts.

Name field was created by adding a combo box field and specifying that it displays the Name field from the contacts_marketing data source.

Address field was simply added by using the Add Field control and dragging it from the popup Fields window into the form. This field also is stored in the data source.

Figure 36-4   A simple data editing form for a dBase database

The Kinds of Controls (Labels, Buttons, Fields, Etc.) You Can Have in a Form

You can also add text and graphics to a form, making it a more pleasant and user-friendly tool for working with your data.

To see all the controls available, click and hold down the Form icon on the toolbar, as shown in Figure 36-5. Hold the mouse pointer over each one to see the name; not all controls are available all the time.

Fields and buttons such as dropdown lists and radio buttons.

Controls such as buttons you can attach images and events to.

Fields for specific types of information like time, date, and currency.

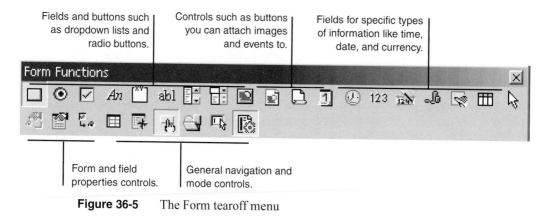

Form and field properties controls.

General navigation and mode controls.

Figure 36-5   The Form tearoff menu

Figure 36-6 shows examples of some of the fields.

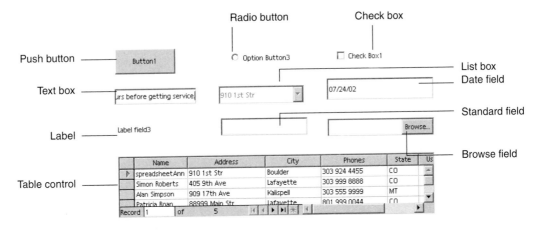

Figure 36-6   Form controls

Getting in Deeper With SQL, Macros, and Events

To add records or do any processing, you need to take a deep breath and do some SQL, macros, or both. Right click any control and choose Form or Control, and take a look at the options on the Data and Events tabs.

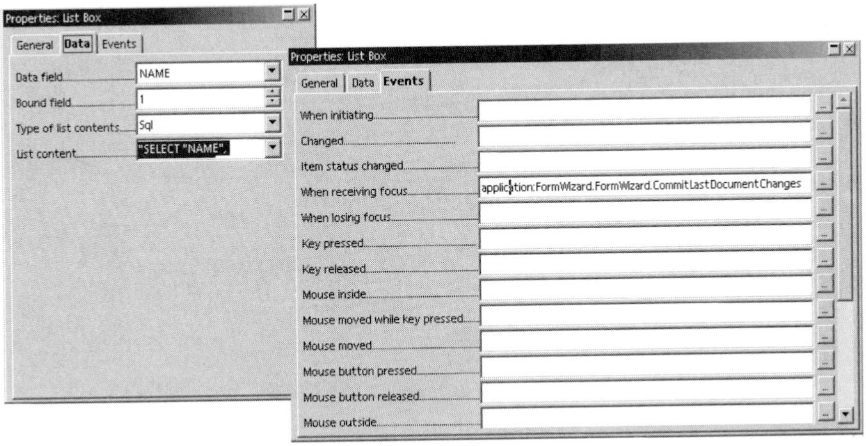

Figure 36-7   Adding macros and SQL to a control

You can associate SQL programming with the data, and macros with events. Events (shown at right) are things that users do like clicking, going from one field to another, etc.

So you can do macro X when a user completes event Y, liking running the OpenFile macro when the Click Button event happens.

There are a bunch of existing macros (see Figure 36-8), and the help provides a description of each one. You can get the whole macro API from www.openoffice.org. See also *Macro Basics* on page 965.

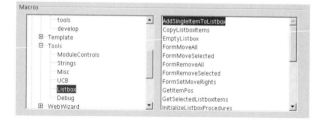

Since going into how to use a couple new programming languages isn't something our editor is going to allow us time for, you won't find extensive guidance on how to create great data entry forms in this book. However, we do cover how to add controls to forms, and the Help has a lot of great information on macros. In addition, you're likely to get a lot of help from the great resources and mailing lists at www.openoffice.org.

Creating a Form Using AutoPilot

AutoPilot forms let you design and create documents for viewing your data source data, any way you want. The generated form is kind of like the data source viewer that you get when you choose View > Data Source, in that both allow you to sort, filter, etc. However, the form is a separate document that you can distribute to everyone in your organization, and you can add features to it using events and macros.

Note – AutoPilot forms are read-only by default.

The AutoPilot makes the design and creation really easy, and finding the data you want is even easier. An example is shown in Figure 36-8.

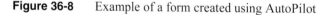

Figure 36-8   Example of a form created using AutoPilot

The AutoPilot is the simplest way to create a form. After you create a basic form with AutoPilot you can modify it in Form Design.

1   Choose File > AutoPilot > Form. The program will process for a while.

2   The window shown in Figure 36-9 will appear. Select the data source and table you want to use.

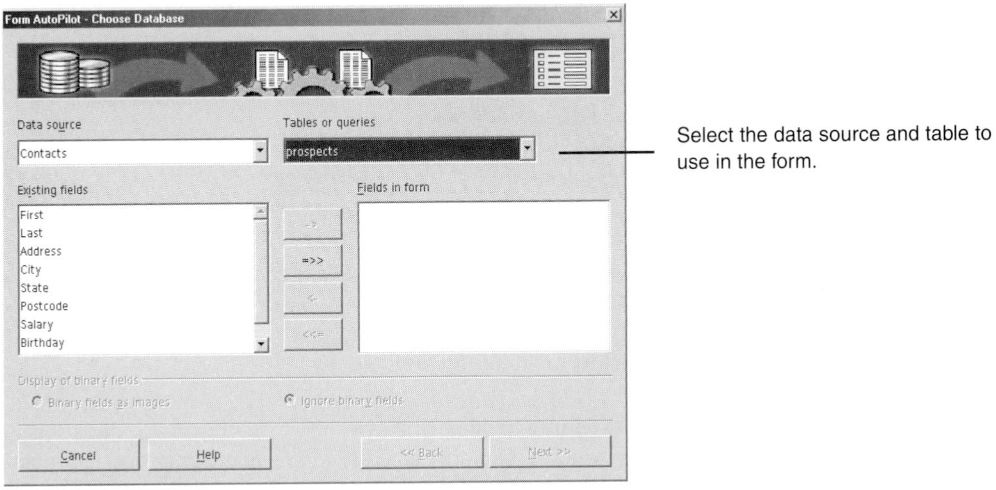

Select the data source and table to use in the form.

Figure 36-9   The first form AutoPilot window

3   Use the arrows between the two lists to add the fields you want; see Figure 36-10.

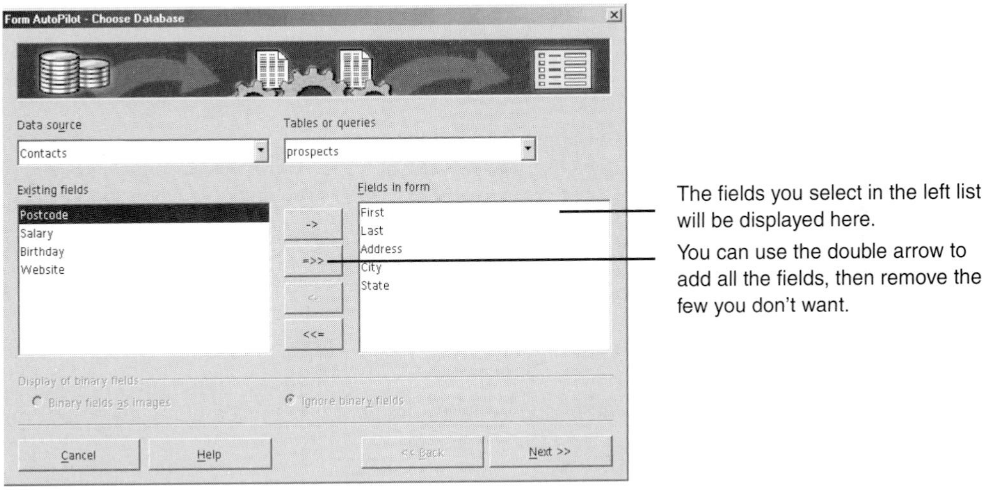

The fields you select in the left list will be displayed here.

You can use the double arrow to add all the fields, then remove the few you don't want.

Figure 36-10   The first form AutoPilot window

4 Click Next and select layout options in the window shown in Figure 36-11.

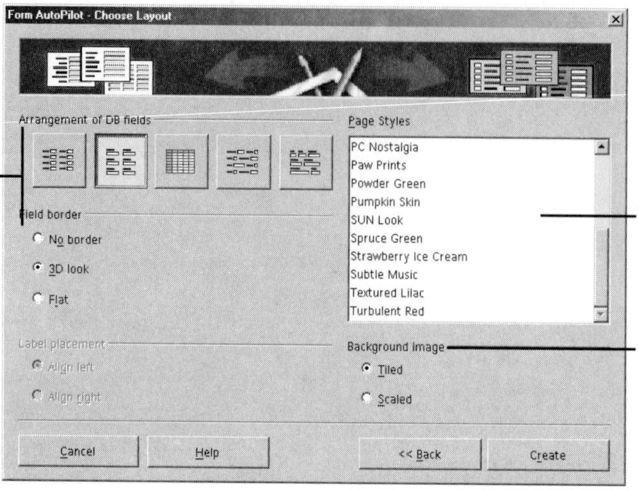
Form AutoPilot - Choose Layout
Arrangement of DB fields
Field border
No border
3D look
Flat
Label placement
Align left
Align right
Page Styles
PC Nostalgia
Paw Prints
Powder Green
Pumpkin Skin
SUN Look
Spruce Green
Strawberry Ice Cream
Subtle Music
Textured Lilac
Turbulent Red
Background image
Tiled
Scaled
Cancel
Help
<< Back
Create
Specify how you want the fields displayed, and how the field borders should look.
Select a different color scheme, if you want. We love the name "Turbulent Red" but it's a little Strong after you look at it for a while.
You can change from Tiled to Scaled for the background image used in the style you selected in the Page Styles list.

Figure 36-11 The first form AutoPilot window

5 Click Create. You'll be prompted to save it as a "TextDokument;" (the translation isn't complete everywhere). Don't change the file format. Enter the right name and location for the form file; see Figure 36-12.

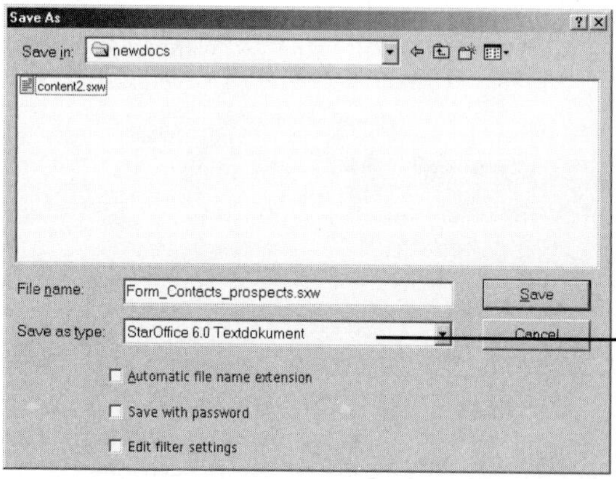
Save As
Save in: newdocs
content2.sxw
File name: Form_Contacts_prospects.sxw
Save as type: StarOffice 6.0 Textdokument
Save
Cancel
Automatic file name extension
Save with password
Edit filter settings
Leave this file format as is and just enter the file name and location.

Figure 36-12 The first form AutoPilot window

6 The form will appear, as shown in Figure 36-12. It's just a fancy version of a Writer document; it has the `.sxw` file extension.

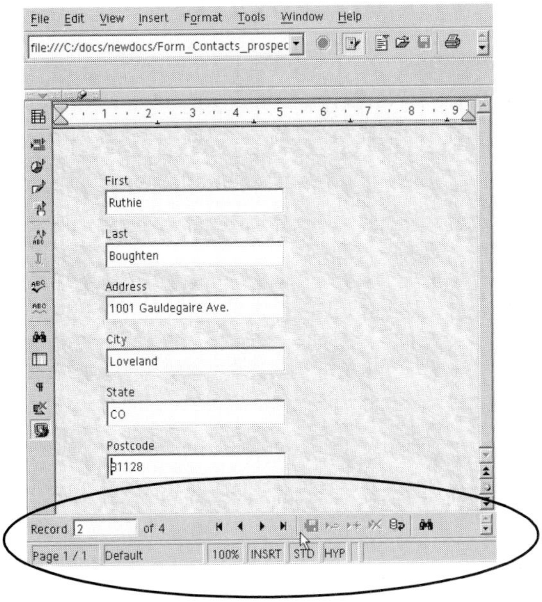

Figure 36-13   The first form AutoPilot window

The icons and fields at the bottom let you scroll through, refresh, and search for data.

Use the search and navigation icons to find the data you want; for more information see *Using Forms to View Data* on page 954 and *Sorting* on page 955.

You can use Form Design mode to add, remove, and rearrange fields, and add other elements such as text and graphics. To modify the form, see *Form Modification Basics* on page 937.

Table controls If you selected the default format, the middle format in Figure 36-11, a table control is created in the resulting form, grouping the fields and display area. You can create one yourself, without going through the AutoPilot, by clicking the Table Control icon on the Form Functions tearoff menu and drawing the area of the control in your document. See Figure 36-14.

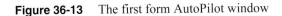

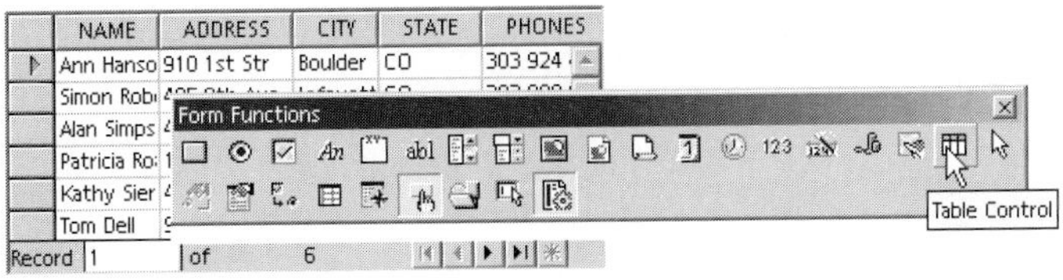

Figure 36-14   Table control and Table Control icon

Basics for Creating a Form on Your Own

The AutoPilot does a few things for you that you'll need to know how to do yourself. If you want your form to allow data entry, you'll need to create your own form.

Once you start creating your own forms, you're potentially into programming land, security land, data evaluation land, etc. So we don't provide all the answers, but we do point out the basics that you'll need to do.

Specify Where the Form's Data Comes From

Bring up the Form tearoff menu and click the Form Properties icon.

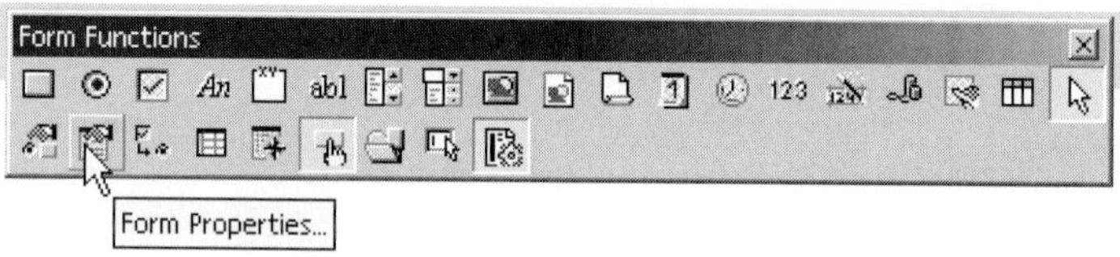

If the icon isn't active, click any of the other control icons, like Check Box, and draw a check box in the document. Then the program will recognize that you're probably building a form and need the Form Properties control.

In the Data tab, specify the data source, if that's how you're using the form, and the table or query within the data source. See Figure 36-15.

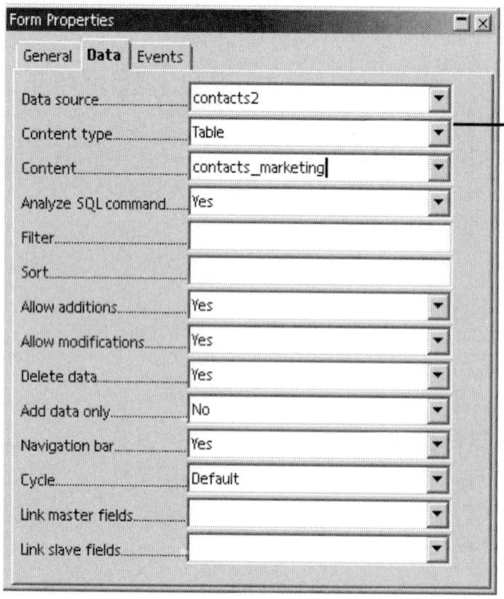

Specify whether you're using a Table, Query, or SQL command to get data out of the data source and into the form. You can set up each in Chapter 35, *Creating and Modifying Data Sources*, on page 869.

Figure 36-15 Specifying the form's data source

Change any other settings necessary; see the online help for more information.

Set Up Form-Level Processing

You can specify macros to run when form events occur. With the form properties window still open, click the Events tab, shown in Figure 36-16. Add an existing macro or one of your own to any of the events. For more information on macros, see the appendix.

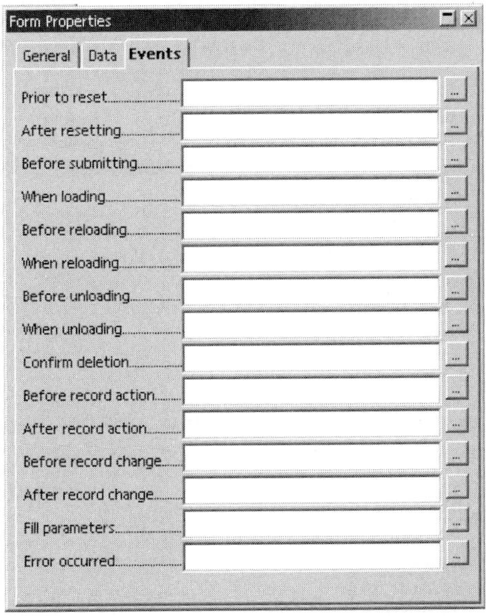

Figure 36-16   Form-level events you can assign macros to

Add Controls and Formatting

Now you get to the fun part, adding the fields and buttons, plus any graphics, headings, page formatting, or other elements unrelated to the functionality.

To do this, find the instructions you need in the sections in the rest of this chapter. We haven't covered all the fields, since many of them are simple to add, or are similar to the ones we do cover.

Form Modification Basics

After you've created a form with AutoPilot, you can rearrange, add, remove, and change the look of fields. You can also add text, graphics, and other elements to the form to make it more user friendly and attractive.

Switching From Edit Mode to Design Mode

You can toggle between two modes: one in which you can edit the control (design mode), and one in which the control performs whatever actions you've assigned to it. The controls function only when design mode is off; you can edit the control only in design mode.

To switch, use the Design Mode On/Off icon on the Form Functions tearoff menu or on the form functions object bar.

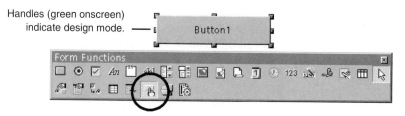

Handles (green onscreen) indicate design mode.

Figure 36-17   Design mode on/off icon

If you distribute the file for use, keep in mind that others will open the file in design mode, by default. To use the controls, they'll need to switch off design mode with the icon in Figure 36-17, or switch off editing for the entire document using the Edit File icon in the function bar, shown at the right.

Basic Form Modification

1   In the form you want to modify, bring up the form functions tearoff menu. Locate the Form Functions icon in the main toolbar at the left, and click the icon as shown below. Then click the Form Design button to get into editable design mode.

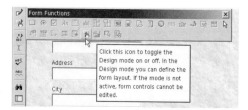

Click this icon to toggle the Design mode on or off. In the Design mode you can define the form layout. If the mode is not active, form controls cannot be edited.

The fields in the form are now selectable objects that you can move and modify.

2   Arrange and add elements, such as text and graphics, using the toolbar and object bar, as shown in Figure 36-18.

3   When you're finished, click the Save Document icon on the function bar to save the modifications.

4   To begin using the form, click the Edit File icon on the function bar.

In the example in Figure 36-18, an animated GIF and an explanatory paragraph were added to the form. To make this happen, all the controls were grouped and anchored to the first paragraph, and wrapping for the grouped object was set to None. The animated GIF was inserted and anchored above the first paragraph. The ruler was added to the workspace (View > Ruler), and the second paragraph, containing the text beneath the EMAIL field, was indented to fit under the entry box for the field.

To change the properties of the fields, select a field, right-click, and choose Group > Ungroup. This separates a field's label from the actual control where data is entered. Then select the field or label you want to modify, right-click, and choose the appropriate option. The Control option lets you change the look and behavior of the control.

In Form Design, you have the same set of tools available as you do when working with an HTML or Writer document.

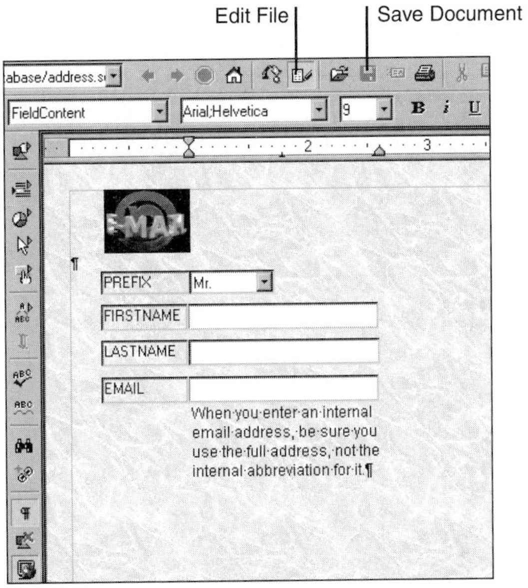

Figure 36-18   Modifying and enhancing a form using Form Design

---

Note – If you need help lining up elements on a form, use a grid. To do this, choose Tools > Options > Text Document > Grid, select the Visible Grid and/or Snap to Grid options, and change the grid Resolution (size of squares) and Subdivision (number of dots between intersections) to set the grid the way you want it.

Changing a Field's Label

By default, a field on a form uses the name of the data source field it's connected to. You can change the name of the label to make it more readable, especially if the name of the field in the data source is cryptic.

1   In the form you want to modify, click
     the Form Design button to get into
     editable design mode.

2   Select the label of the field you want to
     change.

     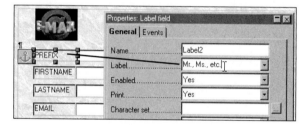

     If you can't select the label separately,
     right-click the selected field and choose Group > Ungroup.

3   Right-click the selected label and choose Control.

4   In the Properties window, change the Label field, as shown in Figure 36-19.

5   Close the Properties window.

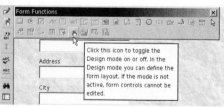

Figure 36-19   Changing a field's label

Setting the Tab Order in Forms

Most people who do data entry don't like to take their hands off the keyboard. To move
from field to field, they like to use the Tab key, which means the order in which the cursor
jumps from field to field is important. This procedure shows you how to change the order
in which the cursor jumps from field to field when you press the Tab key.

1   In the form you want to
     modify, click the Form
     Design button to get into
     editable design mode. Any
     example is shown in the
     illustration at right.

2   On the toolbar, click and
     hold down the Form icon, then click the Tab Order icon.

3   In the Tab Order window, rearrange the order of the fields in the list, or click the
     Automatic Sort button to have the program set the order automatically.

4   Close the Tab Order window, and click the Save Document icon on the function bar.

Adding and Replacing Controls

Note – There are many controls you can add to a form, as well as hundreds of other modifications you can make to them. We don't cover them all, either the controls or the possibilities for programming, evaluating data, etc. Use the examples provided here to get started, then use the online help, or consult a mailing list at www.openoffice.org.

Adding Data Entry Fields to a Form

After you create a form with AutoPilot, you may want to add data source fields not originally included when you created the form. Here's how.

1   In the form you want to modify, click the Form Design button to get into editable design mode.

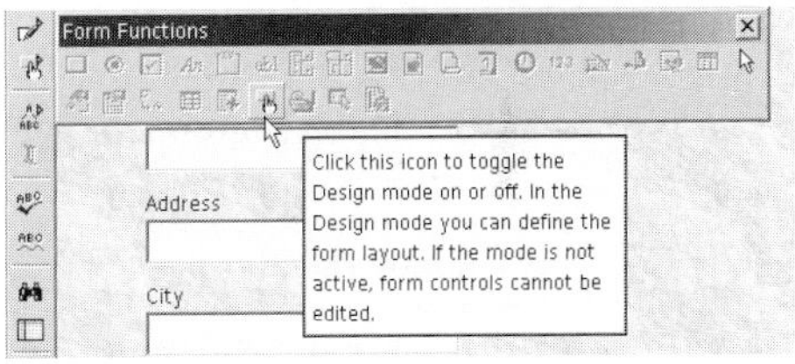

2   In the Form tearoff menu, click the Add Field icon circled in Figure 36-20.

3   The Add Field window will appear, with the current data source displayed in the window. Drag the field you want to the form. (If you're working with a new document without an assigned data source, you'll be prompted to specify one.)

From the list of fields, drag the name of the field you want onto the form. The program creates the appropriate control based on the field type.

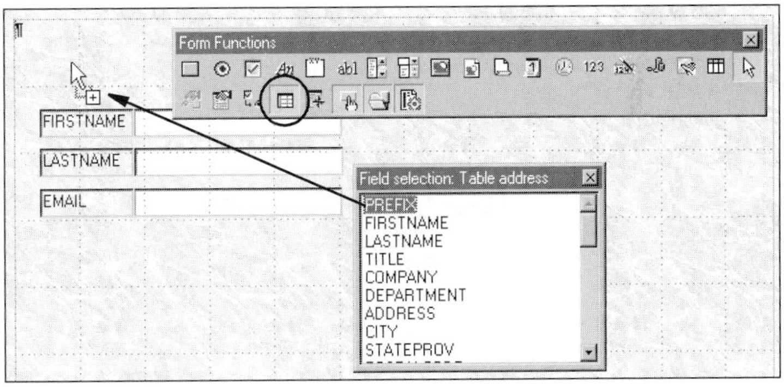

Figure 36-20   Adding a field to a form

The program knows which type of control to create based on the type of field you're adding.

4   Position and modify the control as necessary. See the text following this procedure for more information.

5   When you're finished, click the Save Document icon on the function bar.After you add a field, its label may not be lined up the way you want it. To move the label,

select the control, right-click it, and choose Group > Ungroup. Then select the label, which is now a separate object from the control, and move it to where you want it.

The label or control may not have the background you want. For example, if the other fields in the form are 3D, the new field may not be. To change that, select the new field or its label, right-click, choose Control, and change the Border or Background Color properties.

You can also change the controls used in a form. For example, you can convert a text box to a drop-down list of predefined values, letting you enter data by choosing rather than typing. See *Creating a Pick List of Values*, next.

Adding a Button

Add a push button to a form, then connect a macro to it, connect SQL to it, just open a file with it, or another task. You have a lot of options.

1   Click the Button icon on the Form tearoff menu.

2   Draw the button.

3   Right-click the button and choose Control. In the General tab in Figure 36-21, enter the label and other information you want for the button.

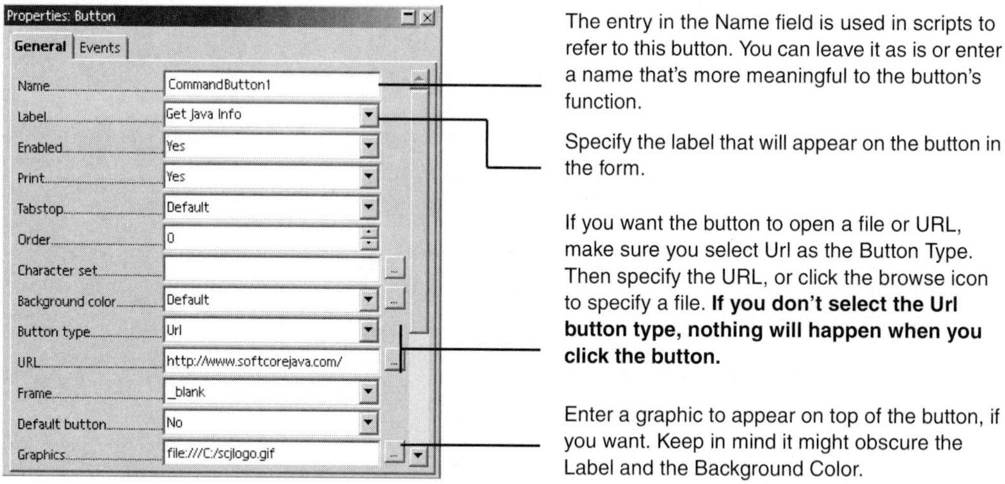

The entry in the Name field is used in scripts to refer to this button. You can leave it as is or enter a name that's more meaningful to the button's function.

Specify the label that will appear on the button in the form.

If you want the button to open a file or URL, make sure you select Url as the Button Type. Then specify the URL, or click the browse icon to specify a file. **If you don't select the Url button type, nothing will happen when you click the button.**

Enter a graphic to appear on top of the button, if you want. Keep in mind it might obscure the Label and the Background Color.

Figure 36-21   Specifying display and action options for a button that opens a URL

4   If you want to attach a macro to the button so that a macro runs when an event occurs, click the Events tab as well, as shown in Figure 36-22, and specify a macro. Attaching macros is covered in more detail in *Macro and Events Basics* on page 951.

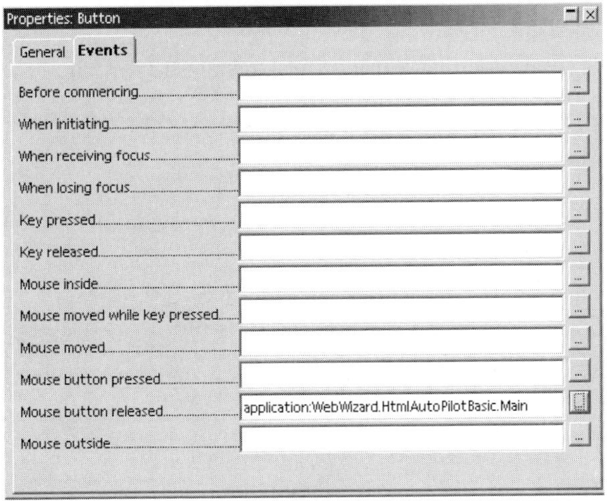

Figure 36-22   Attaching a macro to a button event

Creating a Pick List of Values

One of the most useful changes you can make to a form is converting a text box control to a list box control. When you have a known set of values and data entry must remain consistent (that is, typos aren't allowed), a control that lets you select from a list rather than manually typing data is essential. This procedure shows you how to make that conversion.

Note – How the data gets in and out of your data source—or doesn't—is up to you to determine, based on your data source and users' needs. See *Getting in Deeper With SQL, Macros, and Events* on page 931.

---

1   Ungroup the control from its label by selecting the control, right-clicking, and choosing Group > Ungroup.

2   Right-click the text box control, choose Replace With, and choose List Box.

3   Right-click the control again, and choose Control.

4   In the Properties window, select the General tab, and click the List Entries field.

5   In the List Entries, enter the list of items you want in the pick list, as shown in Figure 36-23.

   • Type the first value

   • Press Shift + Enter

   • Type the second value, and so on

6   In the same window, select Yes in the list labeled Dropdown.

7   Select the Data tab, and in the List Content field, create the same list you did in the General tab (in the List Entries field), using Shift + Enter again.

8   Make sure the Type of List Contents field is set to Valuelist.

9   Close the Properties window, and click the Save Document icon on the function bar.

10 To test the new field, click the Edit File icon on the function bar, which gets you out of edit mode and lets you use the form.

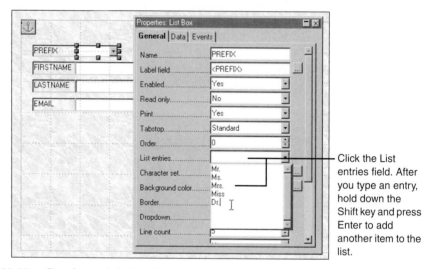

Figure 36-23   Creating a pick list of values for a field

Adding a Check Box

A check box was added to the form in Figure 36-4 on page 930 which wasn't in the original database. You have the option to store the data entered in that check box in the database in an available field or to store it just for use in the form.

1   Click the Check Box icon on the Form tearoff menu.

2   Draw the check box.

3   Right-click the check box and select Form. Enter the appropriate values as shown in Figure 36-26.

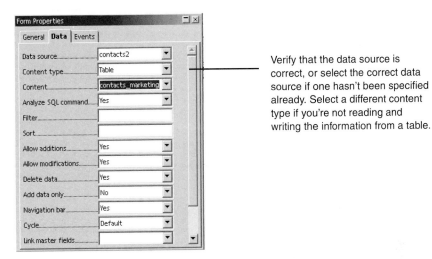

Figure 36-24 Specifying form values for a check box

4 Close the Form properties window. Right-click the check box and select Control. Enter the appropriate values as shown in Figure 36-25.

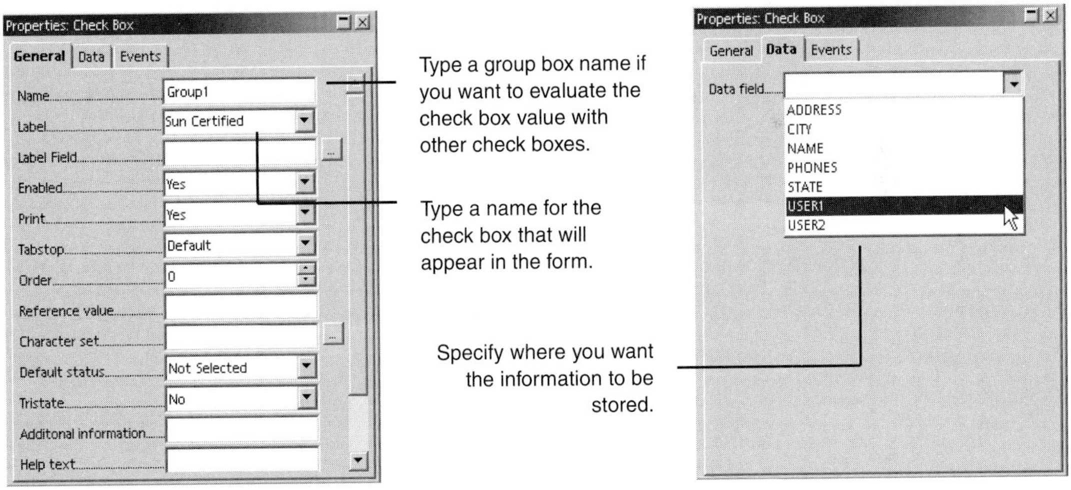

Type a group box name if you want to evaluate the check box value with other check boxes.

Type a name for the check box that will appear in the form.

Specify where you want the information to be stored.

Figure 36-25 Specifying control values for a check box

Adding a Group Box

Use a group box to group check boxes or radio buttons for processing as a unit. In the Name field of the control's Properties window, enter the same group box name for every check box or radio button in order to group them.

1   Click the Group Box
    icon on the Form tearoff
    menu.

2   The fields window
    appears where you're prompted to specify the data for the control. Type the values
    you want and click Next; see Figure 36-26.

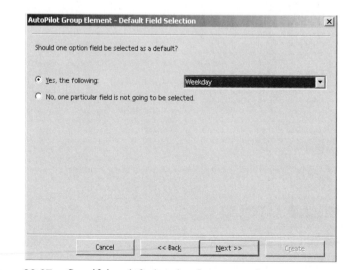

Figure 36-26   Specifying values for a group box

3   Select the default value you want and click Next; see Figure 36-27.

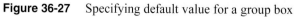

Figure 36-27   Specifying default value for a group box

4   The next window lets you specify which existing field in your specified data source should be used to store the data from the new control. Select an appropriate field and click Next, or select No if you don't want the data stored and just want to use it in the form. See Figure 36-28.

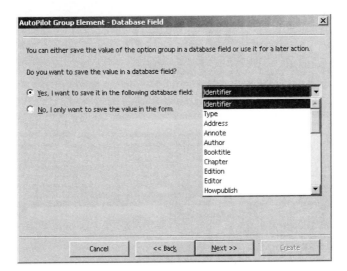

Figure 36-28   Specifying where the control's data will be stored

5   Specify the label for the control you want to appear in the form, and click Create. See Figure 36-29.

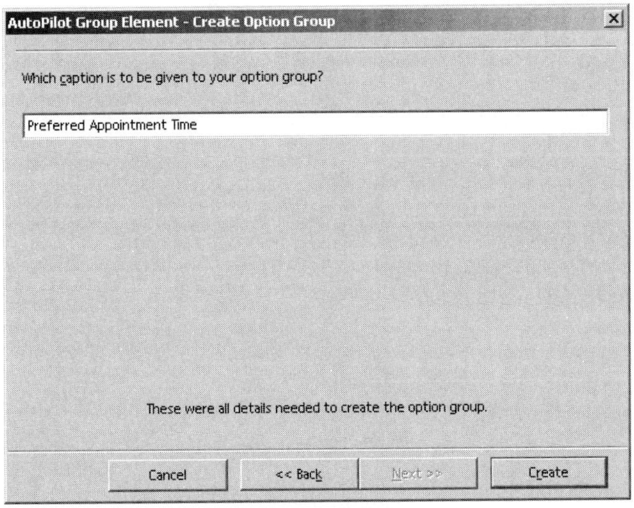

Figure 36-29   Specifying values for a group box

The control will appear in the form.

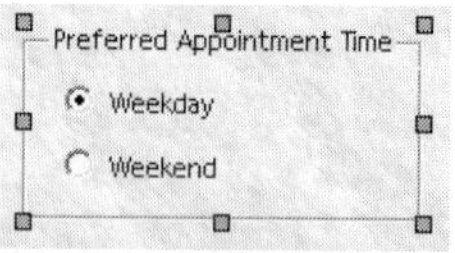

Adding a List Box

1   Click the List
    Box icon on
    the Form
    tearoff menu.

2   If you haven't specified a data source for the document, you'll be prompted to do so
    in the first window. Select a data source and click Next. See Figure 36-30.

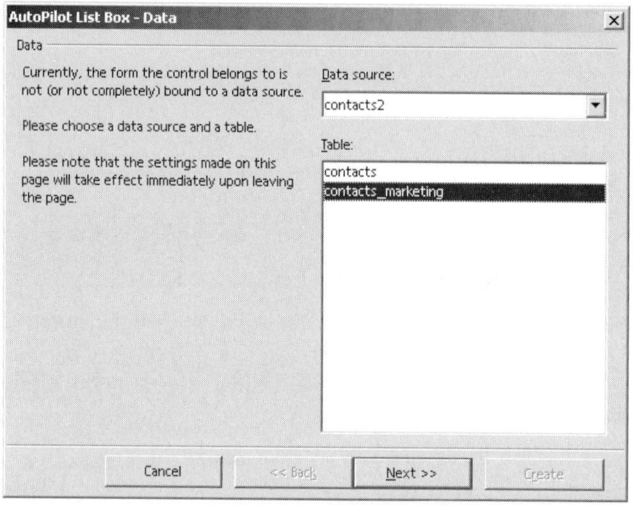

Figure 36-30   Selecting a data source for the list box

3   Select the table to use and click Next. See Figure 36-31. Select the same table as in
    Figure 36-30. We have no idea why you're allowed to select a table again, because if
    it's not exactly the same as the table in Figure 36-30, no data shows up in your list
    box once you've created it.

4   The next two windows prompt you to enter the field that's the source of data for the
    field...and then will prompt you to specify two more fields. Review the following
    information, then go to the next step and make your selections.

    •   Figure 36-33 shows where the data goes afterwards. You can right-click the list
        box after you've created it and choose Control, then click the Data tab and fiddle
        with it as you like. Consult the help for more information.

    •   However, mostly you should just select the same field every time you're asked,
        and not worry about anything else.

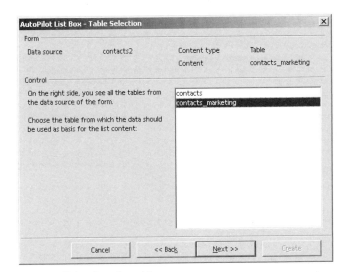

Figure 36-31   Selecting the table to use

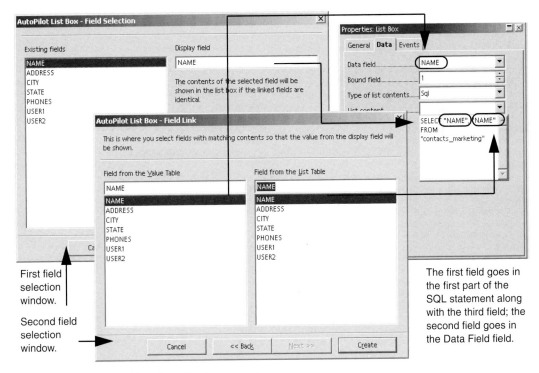

First field selection window.

Second field selection window.

The first field goes in the first part of the SQL statement along with the third field; the second field goes in the Data Field field.

Figure 36-32   How list boxes work

5   Select the field to display and click Next. See Figure 36-33.

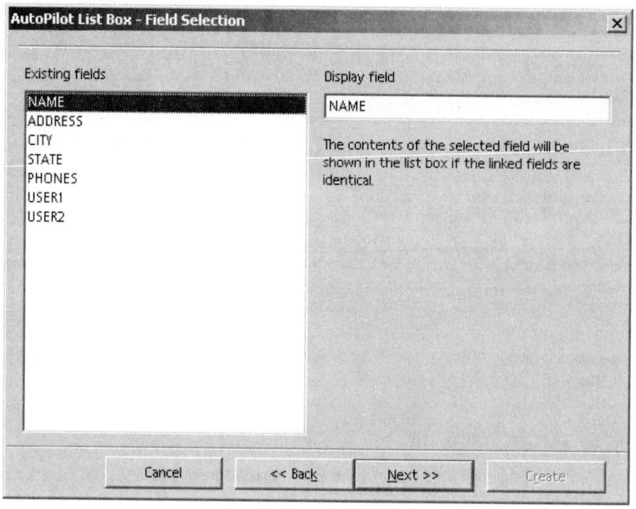

Figure 36-33 Selecting the field to display

6 Unless you're a power user and have a good reason next to, your selections in
Figure 36-34 for Field From Value Table and Field From List Table should be the
same field you've already selected. Click Create.

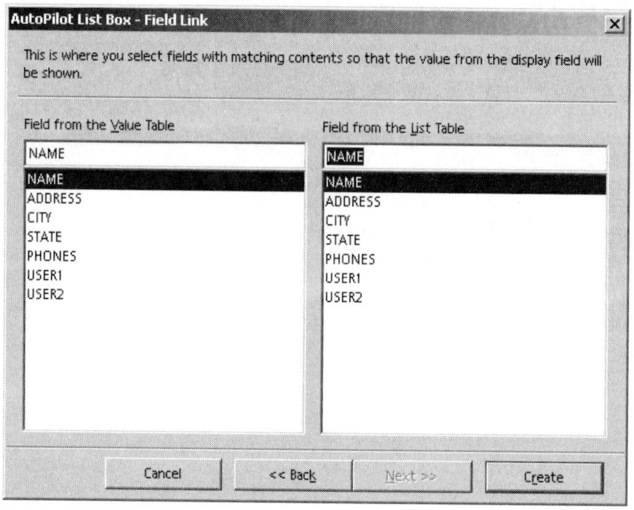

Figure 36-34 Select the same fields again

7 The control will appear.

Sautter, Karlheinz

Here you indicate via which fields, tables of values and list tables are linked.

The value table is the table of the current form where the list field is inserted. The list table is the table whose data should be shown in the list field. Both tables must be linked over a mutual data field. These links are to be entered on this page of the AutoPilot. The field names must not necessarily be the same (this depends upon how the field names are defined in both tables), but both fields must have the same field type.

Macro and Events Basics

Right-click a control and choose Form or Control, and you'll get the properties window in Figure 36-35. The window shows the events that a control or form can have; you can attach a macro to each one, to control what happens when that event occurs.

Enter the internal name for the control.

Enter the name, if any, you want displayed on the control.

Choose how the control will function within the tab sequence.

Enter the control's position in the tab sequence.

Select Yes to make the focus go to this control by default.

Specify a graphic, if you want one to appear on the control.

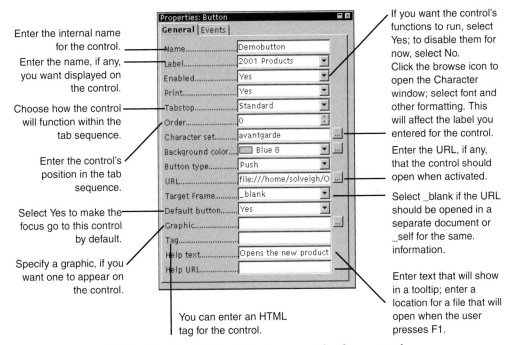

If you want the control's functions to run, select Yes; to disable them for now, select No.
Click the browse icon to open the Character window; select font and other formatting. This will affect the label you entered for the control.

Enter the URL, if any, that the control should open when activated.

Select _blank if the URL should be opened in a separate document or _self for the same. information.

You can enter an HTML tag for the control.

Enter text that will show in a tooltip; enter a location for a file that will open when the user presses F1.

Figure 36-35   Entering URL and display properties for a control

Overview of Events

In addition to just specifying a URL for the control, you can specify macros, either existing ones or your own macros, to be executed when certain *events* happen. Events are actions like clicking the mouse, releasing the mouse, moving the focus (pressing Tab), and typing.

Table 36-1 lists the events and what each means. All events are not available for each control.

Table 36-1 Control events

Event	Description
Before update	This event takes place before the content of the control field is updated from a linked data base.
After update	This event takes place, after the content of a control field was updated from attached data.
Item status changed	This event takes place if the status of the control field is changed. This event takes place if you select a new entry in a list or a combo box or with a check box or option field if the condition of the control field changes.
Text modified	This event takes place if you enter or modify text in an input field.
Before commencing (also called Action started)	This event takes place if an action is executed by clicking the control field. Initiating an action is not the same as executing an action. If you click a Submit button, it initiates the "send" action but the send process will start when the "Action performed" event occurs. With "Action started" you have the possibility to choose. If the linked method sends back FALSE, "Action performed" will not be executed.
When initiating (also called Action performed)	This event takes place if an action actually starts executing. If, for example, you have a Submit button type in your form, the send process executes the action. The "When executing" event corresponds to the start of the send process. This field is only available if you have inserted normal buttons. It isn't available with graphic buttons.
Focus gained	This event takes place if a control field receives the focus (if it is selected or gets the focus because a user tabs to it). The focus is the thin dotted line visible around the selected item in a window.
Focus lost	This event takes place if a control field loses the focus (if you tab to another field, for example).
Key typed	This event takes place if the user presses any key. For example, this event can be related with a macro input verification.
Key released	This event takes place when the user releases the pressed key.
Mouse inside	This event takes place if the user presses any key. For example, this event can be related with a macro input verification.
Mouse dragged while key pressed	This event takes place if the mouse is dragged while a key is pressed.
Mouse movement	This event takes place if the mouse is moved.
Mouse pressed	This event takes place if any mouse button is pressed.
Mouse released	This event takes place if a pressed mouse button is released.

Table 36-1   Control events

Event	Description
Mouse outside	This event takes place when the mouse is outside the control field.
Before resetting	This event occurs before a formula is reset. The linked macro can, for example, prevent this action by returning "FALSE". A formula is reset if one of the following conditions is met: • The user presses an (HTML) button that is defined as a reset button • A new and empty record is created in a formula that is linked to a data source. In the last record, for example, the Next Record button may be pressed.
After resetting	This event occurs after a formula has been reset.
Modified	This event takes place, when the control loses the focus and the contents of the control were changed since it lost the focus.

Adding a Macro to an Event

Follow these steps to assign macros to events. Use Figure 36-36 for guidance.

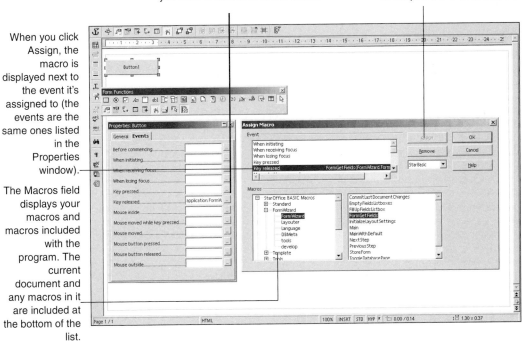

Click the browse icon next to the event you want to associate with a macro.

Click Assign to assign a macro or script to the selected event.

When you click Assign, the macro is displayed next to the event it's assigned to (the events are the same ones listed in the Properties window).

The Macros field displays your macros and macros included with the program. The current document and any macros in it are included at the bottom of the list.

Figure 36-36   Assigning a macro to a control's events

1   Right-click the control and choose Control.

2   Click the Events tab (Figure 36-36).

3   Select an event to assign a macro to.

4   Enter the appropriate information, then close the window.

Using Forms to View Data

Figure 36-37 gives a brief description of the environment for working with forms.

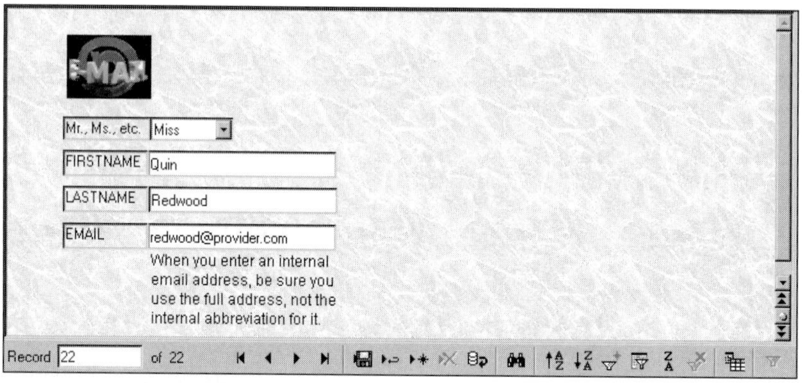

When you're using a form, there is a set of tools at the bottom of it to let you navigate between records, create and delete records, find records, and sort and filter records.

Figure 36-37   Using a form

Just Using the Form to Find Your Way Through the Data

First, make sure you're not in design mode. See *Switching From Edit Mode to Design Mode* on page 938.

Click the navigation arrows at the bottom of the work area to go to the beginning, end, previous, or next record. Or type a record number in the Record field to go directly to that record.

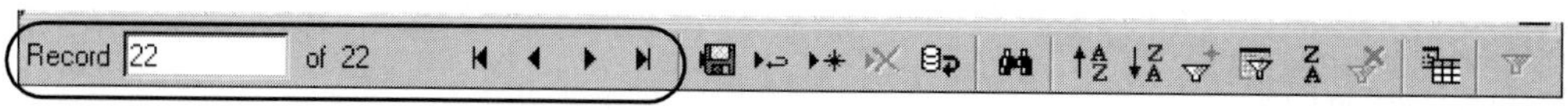

Searching for Specific Records

Searching for data in a data source works on the same principle as searching for a word in a text document: you tell the search tool what you want to find, and the tool locates the next item matching the search criteria. To search for a data record in a form, follow these steps.

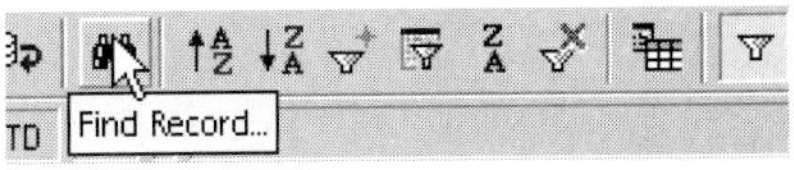

1   Click the Find Record icon (binoculars).

2   In the Data Record Search window, set the search options. Use Figure 36-38 for guidance.

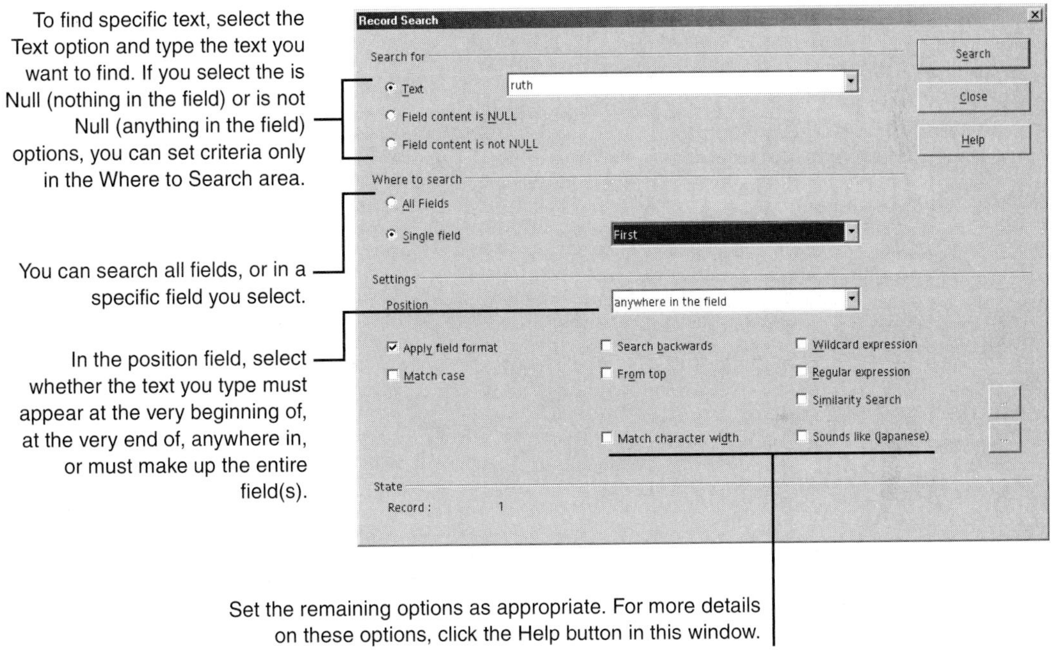

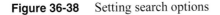

To find specific text, select the Text option and type the text you want to find. If you select the is Null (nothing in the field) or is not Null (anything in the field) options, you can set criteria only in the Where to Search area.

You can search all fields, or in a specific field you select.

In the position field, select whether the text you type must appear at the very beginning of, at the very end of, anywhere in, or must make up the entire field(s).

Set the remaining options as appropriate. For more details on these options, click the Help button in this window.

Figure 36-38   Setting search options

3   Click the Search button. From whichever record the cursor is in, the next record meeting the search criteria is found.

Sorting

With a form open in data entry mode, select the field you want to sort, and click the Sort Ascending or Sort Descending icon, as shown in Figure 36-39.

Mr., Ms., etc.
Miss
FIRSTNAME
Quin
LASTNAME
Redwood
EMAIL
redwood@provider.com
When you enter an internal email address, be sure you use the full address, not the internal abbreviation for it.
Record 6
of 22

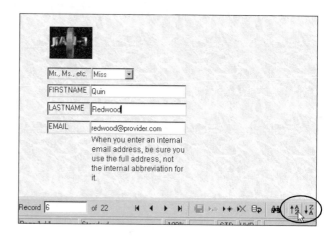

In a form, click in the field you want to sort on, then click the Ascending or Descending icon.

Figure 36-39 Sorting on a single field

Filtering Data

Note – The online help has extensive information about additional functions and features to use in filters.

You've got two ways to approach filtering; the quick AutoFilter and a little more control with the form-based filter.

AutoFilter

The AutoFilter lets you see only the records with the currently selected data in a particular field. For instance, if you want to see only the people who live in Boulder, select the CITY field for someone from Boulder and click the AutoFilter icon. This is illustrated in Figure 36-40.

1 Open the data source viewer by choosing View > Data Source.

2 Click in the field that has the information you want to match.

3 Click the AutoFilter icon.

NAME
ADDRESS
CITY
STATE
PHONES
USER1
Simon Robe
AutoFilter
adison A
Boulder
CO
303 555 1212
1
Alexis Smith
11 Lyndon Str
Boulder
CO
303 990 1212
0
Marian Ward
900 2nd Wilderne
Boulder
CO
303 926 4455
0

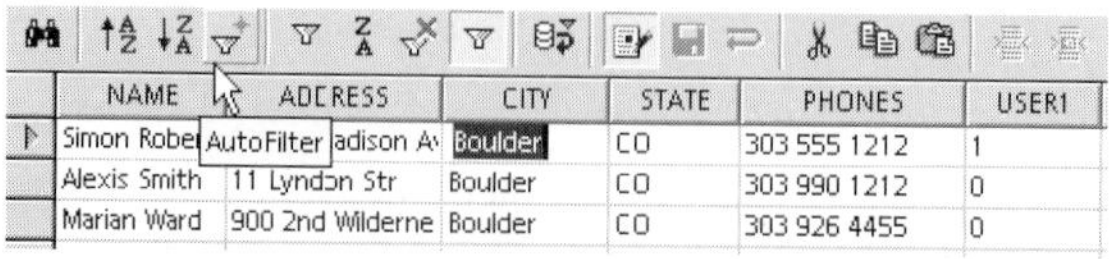

Figure 36-40 Using AutoFilter

4   To remove the filter, click the Apply Filter icon. It will
appear lighter and recessed when the filter is applied;
when you click it in that state the filter will be taken off
and the icon will be the same shade as the other icons
again.

Form-Based Filters

This filter lets you type what you want into the form, with some help from the form filter
navigation window.

1   Click the Form-Based Filter icon in the toolbar.

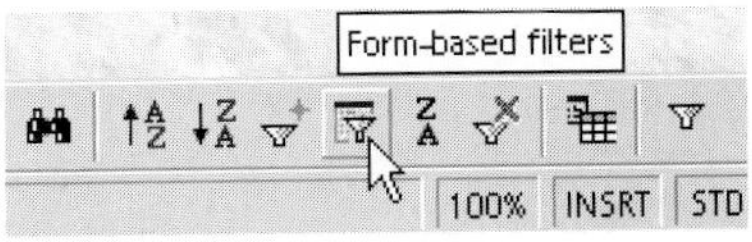

2   The main form toolbar will disappear and three
new buttons or icons will appear at the left
bottom corner of the work area. Click the Filter
Navigator to see the Filter Navigator window in Figure 36-41.

3   In the appropriate fields, type the values you want to restrict the filter on.

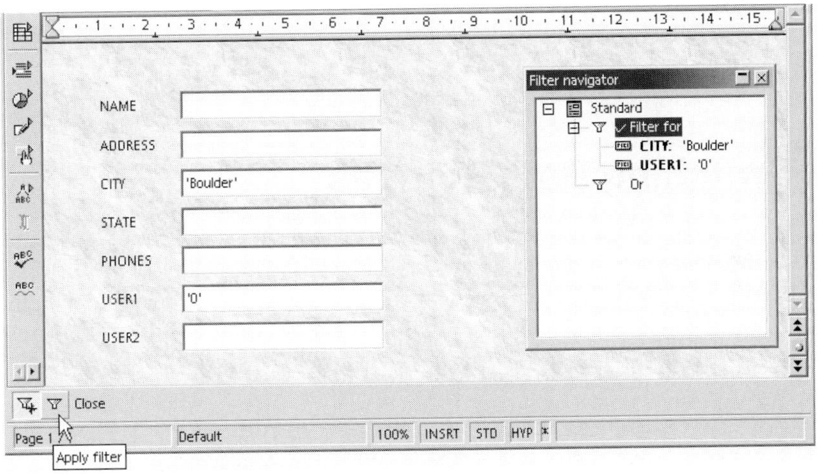

Figure 36-41   Entering the criteria for the filter

4   Click the Apply Filter icon; only the records meeting the criteria you specified will be
displayed in the form, as shown in Figure 36-42.

Figure 36-42   The results of a form-based filter

5   To remove the filter, click the Apply Filter icon at the
      far right side of the bottom toolbar. It will appear lighter
      and recessed when the filter is applied; when you click it
      in that state the filter will be taken off and the icon will
      be the same shade as the other icons again.

Switching Data Sources

If you've got a few different data sources that you use in the form, or if you just want to
see whether your current customer data form will work with the new mailing list you
bought, choose Edit > Exchange Data Source. Select a new data source in the window
shown in Figure 36-43.

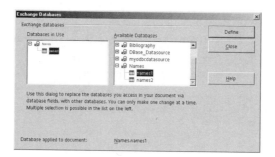

Figure 36-43   Using a different data source

Using Forms for Data Entry

If your data source is up to it and if you think it's a good decision for your security situation, then you can very easily use forms for data entry.

First note It helps if you have the following skills too, but that's just for adding more powerful processing:

- Do anything with SQL (are you the MacGyver of SQL?)
- Learn to write macros

Second note This depends on your database, of course. Is your security set up so people can just edit it from forms? That might not always be wise. Likewise, data sources based on text files and spreadsheets aren't editable. Though you can save either form as .DBF and then you've got an editable data source.

Third note The form setup and how it interacts with data sources is weird once in a while. It's not wildly inconsistent but it does help if you kill an occasional chicken.

Adding a Record

1   Open the form you want to use.

   You might be able to get at it by choosing View > Data Sources and opening the Links section for the data source you're working with. If you or the person who set up the data source was thinking ahead, there'll be a linked data entry form for that data source.

2   Go to the end of the data source. Do so by using the Last Record icon in the toolbar at the bottom of the work area, or by typing the number of the last record in the Record field. Technically, you don't have to go to the last record, but the new record is created at the end of the table anyway.

3   Click the New Record icon at the bottom of the form.

4   Type the new data in the appropriate fields in the form, as shown in Figure 36-2.

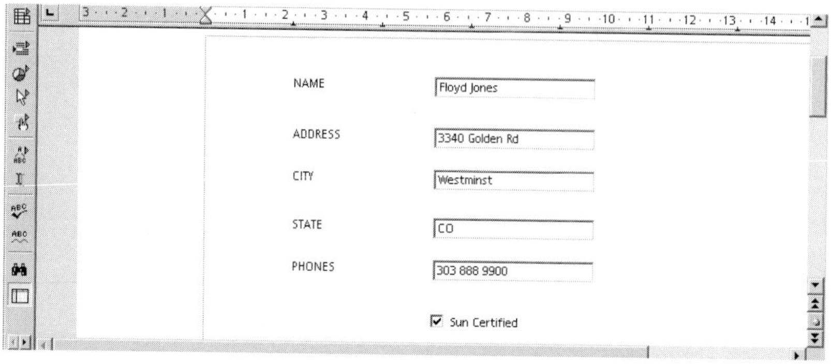

Figure 36-44   Go to the end of the table and type the data

5   Click the Save Record icon at the bottom of the form.

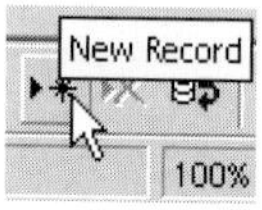

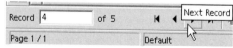

If you're looking at the data source viewer window (View > Data Sources), you can click Refresh above the data source fields to make the change show up.

Deleting a Record

1   Open the form.

2   Navigate to the record you want to delete by using the navigation arrows at the bottom of the work area, or by typing the record number in the Record field. You can also search for it; see *Searching for Specific Records* on page 955.

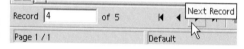

3   Click the Delete Record icon.

Changing a Record

1   Open the form.

2   Navigate to the record you want to delete by using the navigation arrows at the bottom of the work area, or by typing the record number in the Record field. You can also search for it; see *Searching for Specific Records* on page 955.

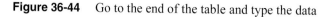

3   Before you type anything new: the
    changes take place as you type them.

    NAME   Alan Simpson

    Type the new data in the fields; for
    instance, to change an address, just
    type the new address over the old address in the address field.

    ADDRESS   909 17th Ave

4   Just to be sure, click the Save Record icon at
    the bottom of the form.

    Save Record

    Default   100%

Trying to Enter Data in a Field That Doesn't Want It

Having problems entering additional text in a field that seems to be fine for all the other records? Odds are it's just a table design issue: maximum field length. How to solve this? Easy, just edit the table definition and increase the maximum field size. See *Creating New Tables and Fields for Any Data Source Except Text Files and Spreadsheets* on page 910 for more information.

Appendix: Macros

What's in This Appendix

By and large, this book is for Mortal Users—nonprogrammers. And this book is also finite. So we have not provided extensive coverage of writing macros.

However, this appendix does give you a start in the right direction. What you get is:

- Pointers on where to get more information, in the next section.
- A brief introduction to macros.
- An introduction to the macro writing environment and some troubleshooting and tips.

Finding Macros and Macro Information

The folks in OpenOffice.org do a great job of providing macros. See the following, which is by no means all inclusive:

- The basic resource is the programmers' tutorial at `http://api.openoffice.org/basic/man/tutorial/tutorial.pdf`. This is for Star Office 5.2, but still applicable.
- You can get the whole API (the grammar—how to write macros) from `www.openoffice.org`. Sign up for developer and user mailing lists on `www.openoffice.org`. Specifically, see:
  - The specific API, which you might not find entirely useful: `http://api.openoffice.org/common/ref/com/sun/star/module-ix.html`
  - `http://api.openoffice.org`
  - `http://framework.openoffice.org`
  - `http://api.openoffice.org/documentation_guide.html`
  - There are more detailed manuals aimed at Java programmers:
    - `http://www.openoffice.org/files/22/115/Text.pdf`
    - `http://www.openoffice.org/files/22/115/Spreadsheet.pdf`
- Andrew Brown's Useful Macros site is at `http://www.darwinwars.com/lunatic/bugs/oo_macros.html`.
- Help and how tos can be found at `http://home.nikocity.de/sysentw/FAQ/SO-FAQ_English_Version/Answers/answers_9.html`.
- You can find a growing collection of macros and templates at `www.ooextras.org`.
- Go to the mailing list page `http://www.openoffice.org/mail_list.html` and search the users and developers mailing list archives for "macro" and other keywords. If you can't find what you want, sign up for the list you want (probably users, possibly developers) and ask your question.

In addition, check out the help. There's an example macro for every function.

Macro Basics

Macros are little programs written in a language specific to StarOffice and OpenOffice.org. Macros can do things like open a file when you do a particular task, process data, or take your grandmother's credit cards and buy $3000 worth of cat toys. Pretty much whatever you want.

You can hook them up to events, things like clicking the mouse button or putting the pointer in a field, as well as just run'em.

There are a bunch of existing macros (see Figure 36-45), as well, and the help provides a description of each one.

Figure 36-45   Existing macros you can use

You can also write your own in the macro composition window. Here's one in Figure 36-46 that when filled in will export a single drawing page from a loaded Draw or Impress document to a `wmf`, from the great folks on the OpenOffice.org mailing lists.

```
XDrawPage thePage = ...;
  String Url = ...;

  Object xPorterService =
  xMSF.createInstance("com.sun.star.drawing.GraphicExporterFilter");
  XExporter xPorter = (XExporter)
  UnoRuntime.queryInterface(XExporter.class, xPorterService);
  XFilter xFilter = (XFilter) UnoRuntime.queryInterface(XFilter.class,
  xPorterService);
  XComponent xComp = (XComponent)
  UnoRuntime.queryInterface(XComponent.class,thePage);
  xPorter.setSourceDocument(xComp);
  PropertyValue propertyvalues[] = new PropertyValue[2];
  propertyvalues[0] = new PropertyValue();
  propertyvalues[0].Name = "FilterName";
  propertyvalues[0].Value = "WMF";
  propertyvalues[1] = new PropertyValue();
  propertyvalues[1].Name = "URL";
  propertyvalues[1].Value = Url;
```

```
xFilter.filter(propertyvalues);
```

Figure 36-46   Macro that exports a drawing from Draw or Impress to .wmf, from the
OpenOffice.org archives

Migrating Macros

By and large, no 5.1 or previous macros are converted or supported in StarOffice 6.0 or
OpenOffice.org 1.0. Macros from StarOffice 5.2 macros should work and require only
limited changes.

The new XML file format requires a new Dialog editor with a completely different format.
This makes it impossible to use the old Dialog from StarOffice 4.0 and 5.x in StarOffice
6.0 software. You have to re-create all Dialogs from the scratch.

VBA macros cannot be converted automatically into StarBasic.

Macros in a Microsoft Office document cannot be run in StarOffice or OpenOffice.org.
You *can* view the original Microsoft VBA macro source after opening the Microsoft
document (choose Tools > Macros after opening the document), but the macros will be
commented out.

Guided Tour

This should take about ten minutes, and will give you an idea of how the program works.

1   Choose Tools > Macro.

2   Click Organizer.

3   In the Macro Organizer window, click the Libraries tab.

4   Click the New button and name the new library GuidedTour. Click OK.

5   Click the Modules tab.

6   Look in the Module list; the GuidedTour library and the default module Module1 are
displayed in alphabetical order within the module list.

7   Click the New Module button. Name the new module GuidedModule and click OK.
(A module is a way of grouping macros; a library in turn groups modules.)

8   Click the Close button of the Macro Organizer window.

9   In the main Macro window, locate the GuidedTour library. Select the GuidedModule
module you created.

10   Click New.

11   The Basic editing environment is displayed.

12   Press F1 to bring up macro help. Click the Index tab and select the help for the subtraction operator, –. The corresponding help will come up in the right panel.

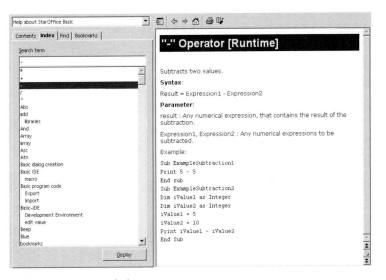

Figure 36-47   Macro help

13   Copy and paste the example macro into the macro writing window. Delete the Main macro will doing so.

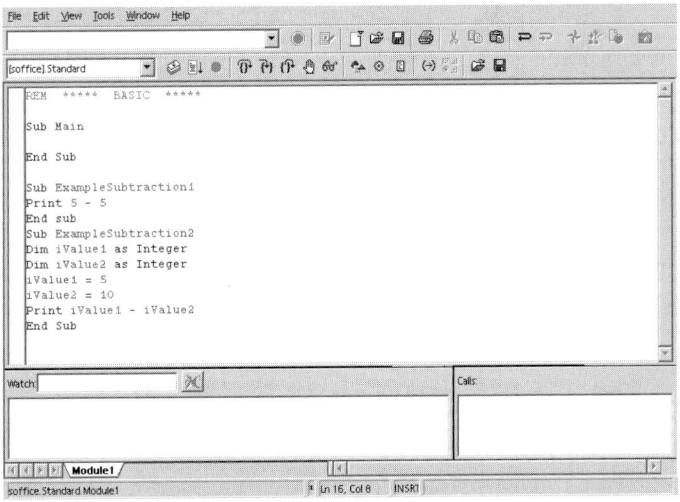

Figure 36-48   Pasting example macro from help into macro editing window

14 Click the Run icon in the macro object bar at the top of the work area.

15 Click it for each line of the macro. Respond as appropriate to the dialog boxes that appear. Note messages that appear in the bottom area of the window.

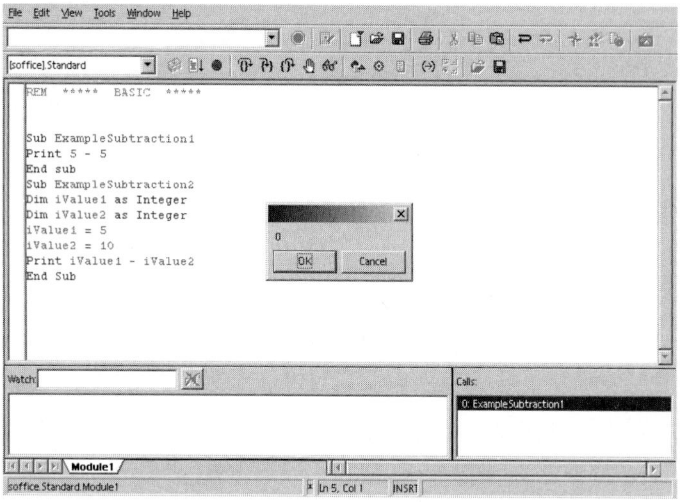

Figure 36-49   Running the macro step by step

16 Delete subtraction example 1 by deleting the first three lines, Sub through End Sub.

17 Change the remaining macro by adding another value and changing the final print line as shown:

```
iValue3 = 7

Print iValue1 - iValue2 + (iValue1 * iValue3)

End Sub
```

18 Save the macro (choose File > Save).

19 Run the macro again.

The Basic Macro Editing Window

Figure 36-50 on page 969 shows the IDE, or independent development environment, where you can edit macros and access macro features. (Choose Tools > Macro, select a macro, click Edit.)

To switch from one library to another, select a library from the list at the left side of the macro toolbar.

To switch to a different module in the IDE, click the tab of the module you want, at the bottom of the work area.

To see a different macro, scroll up and down with the appropriate module.

Click **Object Catalog** to open the Objects window, which lets you reorganize macros and insert references to them in other macros.

Click **Macros** to open the Macro window; click **Modules** to manage modules and libraries.

Click **Save Source As** to save the macro in a specific file.

The current **library** is shown here.

Commands are in green, values are in, red, comments are in gray, and standard StarOffice Basic commands are in blue.

Click **Run** to run the first macro in the module.

Click **Stop** to stop the currently running macro.

Click **Single Step** to run the macro one step at a time.

Click **Breakpoint** to insert a point in the macro at which you can run the macro one step at a time.

The **current modules** are displayed here.

The **library and module** are displayed here.

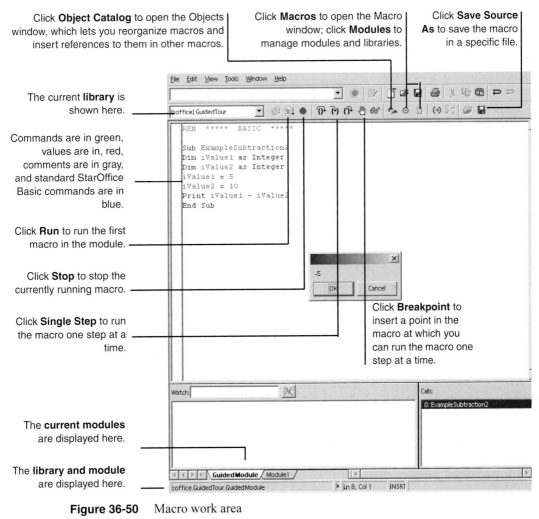

Figure 36-50   Macro work area

Macro Setup Options

See *Specifying StarBasic Macro Options* on page 151.

Choose Tools > Options > Browser > HTML and select the StarBasic option. You must select this option *before* you create any script that you want to saved in an HTML document.

Basic scripts have to be in the header of the HTML document. After you add the macro to the document, it will appear in the source text of the HTML document (in the header) with the following syntax (a "Hello World" example macro is used):

```
<HEAD>
(any additional content)
<SCRIPT LANGUAGE="STARBASIC">
<!--
' $LIBRARY: library_name
' $MODULE: module_name
Sub test
msgbox "Hello World"
End Sub
// -->
</SCRIPT>
</HEAD>
```

Organizing Your Macros

If you just want to leap in and record a few macros, go ahead and just store them in the default location (Standard); you won't need this information. However, if you'll be using more than a few, it's a good idea to read this section and organize your macros according to their function.

How Macros Are Organized

The interface isn't set up very well for quick, easy macro recording. Macros are categorized in a pathname-like structure: one or more macros are stored in a module, within a library, within a file.

If you've used other macro programs, it might seem odd and unnecessarily complicated that you need to store macros in a library/module/macro tree structure, instead of just recording the macro file and storing it anywhere.

You can store your recorded macros in modules in the Standard library, or you can create your own new libraries. You can't add your macros to any of the other libraries listed, such as CreateReport (though you can add any macros in any libraries to your documents).

Figure 36-51 shows the Macros window (choose Tools > Macro). This shows how macros that you just store within the Standard library are organized.

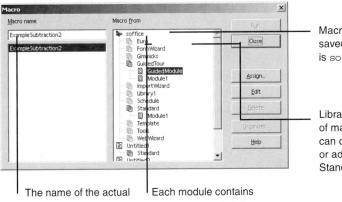

Macro file – Macros are saved in a file; the default is `soffice.sbl`.

Libraries group modules of macros together. You can create new libraries or add to the default, Standard.

The name of the actual macro.   Each module contains one or more macros.

Figure 36-51   How macros are organized in the Macros window

Organization Recommendations

Take note of the following limitations.

More than one macro in a module   When you use the Step and Run icons in the macro toolbar to run the macro one step at a time, only the first macro in the module is run, which may not be the one you want.

Size limit   There is a limit of 64k on the amount of code allowed in one module.

Getting at a macro to add it to a document   Most of the macro-insertion features let you insert a macro from the Standard and other libraries, and from the document you're currently in, but not any other documents you've created. Keep this in mind when you're deciding where to put macros.

Based on this, you can make your life as simple as possible by following these tips:

- If you're creating macros that a lot of people will want to use, or that you plan to run from a different document, create one or more libraries for your macros (*Creating a New Library* on page 971). Don't just assign them to one of your own documents.

- Create a new module for each macro you write (*Creating a New Module* on page 972).

Creating a New Library

1   Click the Modules icon on the macro toolbar.

2   In the Macro Organizer window, click the Libraries tab.

3   Click the New button to display the Macro Organizer window (Figure 36-52).

4   Enter the name in the New Library dialog.

You can select the Attach file option to create the new library as a separate file in `office/basic`. If you don't do so, it will be stored in the `soffice.sbl` file. In addition, macros stored as a separate file will not be loaded automatically after starting the program, but instead must be activated manually (in the Macros window by clicking Run) or by another macro.

This isn't your only chance to save the library as a separate file; you can edit the macro, then click the Save Source As icon on the macro object bar.

5   Click OK.

6   A default module named Module1 was created and listed below the new library at the bottom of the Module/Dialog list. Click the Modules tab and select the new library. Highlight the name and rename it, based on the task that the macro you'll store in it will perform.

Note – The other libraries contain macros you can associate with events in hyperlinks and documents. See *Adding Applets and Plugins* on page 489.

Ignore all libraries listed except the Standard library, and the ones you've created.

If a file name isn't listed next to the library, it's stored in the `soffice.sbl` file.

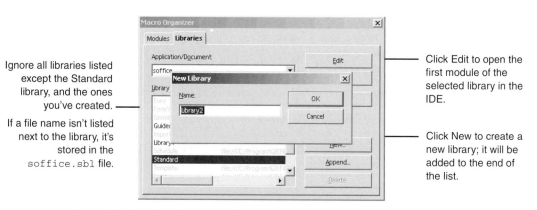

Click Edit to open the first module of the selected library in the IDE.

Click New to create a new library; it will be added to the end of the list.

Figure 36-52   Creating a new library in the macro organizer

Creating a New Module

You can do so through the Organizer, or by opening a current library in the IDE.

Using the Organizer

1   Click the Modules icon on the macro toolbar.

2   In the Macro Organizer window (Figure 36-53), click the Modules tab.

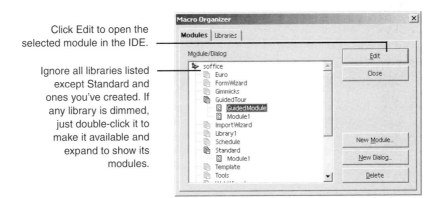

Click Edit to open the selected module in the IDE.

Ignore all libraries listed except Standard and ones you've created. If any library is dimmed, just double-click it to make it available and expand to show its modules.

Figure 36-53   Creating new modules using the Organizer

3   Select the library to add it to.

You can add only to Standard and to libraries you've created. If the library name is dimmed, double-click it.

4   Click the New Module button.

5   Enter the name, be sure BASIC is selected, and click OK.

Using the IDE

1   Click the Macros icon on the macro toolbar.

2   Select a module within the library you want to add to and click Edit.

3   Right-click on a tab of an existing module and choose Insert > BASIC Module.

Managing Macros, Modules, and Libraries

Use this information to move modules or macros around, rename, delete, and perform other similar tasks.

Moving a Module to a Different Library Using the Organizer

You can drag a module from one library to another in the organizer.

1   Click the Modules icon on the macro toolbar.

2   In the Organizer window, click the Modules tab.

3   Select the module you want to move.

Drag it to the new library; a line indicates where the module will be moved to when you release the mouse button.

4   Select the module and click Edit, then choose File > Save.

Moving Macros and Modules Using the IDE

You also can simply cut and paste macros from one module to another, in the same library or a different library.

1   Click the Macros icon on the macro toolbar.

2   Select a module and click Edit.

3   Select the macro or macros to move, then cut and paste them to a new module or library.

   • To select a module in the same library, click the right tab below the work area.

   • To select a new library, select it from the list in the work area upper right corner.

4   Choose File > Save to save the changes.

Renaming a Module

1   Click the Macros icon on the macro toolbar.

2   Select the module and click Edit.

3   Right-click on a tab of an existing module and choose Rename. Type the new name on the tab.

Hiding a Module

You can temporarily remove the module without deleting it.

1   Click the Macros icon on the macro toolbar.

2   Select the module and click Edit.

3   Right-click on a tab of an existing module and choose Hide.

Deleting Macros

To delete one or two macros, it's quickest to use the Macros window.

1   Click the Macros icon on the macro toolbar, then select the module and click Edit.

2   Select the correct category, library, and module, then select the macro and click Delete.

If you want to delete a lot of macros from a module, it's quickest to go to the IDE and delete the text of the macros, or delete the entire module.

1   Click the Macros icon on the macro toolbar, then select the module and click Edit.

2   In the IDE text window, delete the text of each macro. Remember that the beginning and ending of each macro is selected by the following:

```
Sub macroname
End Sub
```

Deleting Modules

Either of the following methods is quick; they just provide alternate navigation.

Use this method if you're sure you want to delete it.

1   Click the Modules icon on the macro toolbar.

2   Click the Modules tab if it's not active.

3   Select a module and click Delete.

Use this method if you want to look at the module before you delete it.

1   Click the Macros icon on the macro toolbar, then select the module and click Edit.

2   Right-click the tab of the module and choose Delete.

Running Macros

Running the macro, of course, is where you see whether the recording process translates into something useful.

Note – Don't be surprised if it doesn't run correctly the first time. If there are errors, see *Opening and Editing Macros* on page 978. You can also insert *breakpoints* during macros, which stop the process at certain points. These are useful because you can examine the results of a particular step, then continue playing the macro, or play it one step at a time. See *Using Breakpoints to Stop Macros at a Specified Point* on page 978.

Use any of the following procedures to run the macro.

Assigning a Shortcut Key to a Macro

If you'll be running the macro several times and it's not connected to a button or other element yet, it's a good idea to set up a shortcut to it, using the Configuration window. (For more information about setting up shortcut keys, see *Assigning Shortcut Keys to Menu Items* on page 106.)

1   Switch to the application you want to run the macro in.

2   Choose Tools > Configuration.

3   The Keyboard tab should be in front; if not, click it.

4   Select the StarOffice option (see Figure 36-54) unless you need the key only in Writer.

5   In the lower left corner in the Category list, scroll down until you see StarOffice BASIC Macros a little over halfway down. (The earlier list item, BASIC, lets you assign shortcut keys to functions like Add Breakpoint.)

6   Select StarOffice BASIC and, if it's not expanded to show libraries and modules, click the + icon next to it to expand it.

7   Expand the macro library, such as Standard, and select a module and macro.

8   The Keyboard lists all the preset combinations that you can use to start the macro, as shown in Figure 36-54. Select the one you want for the selected macro.

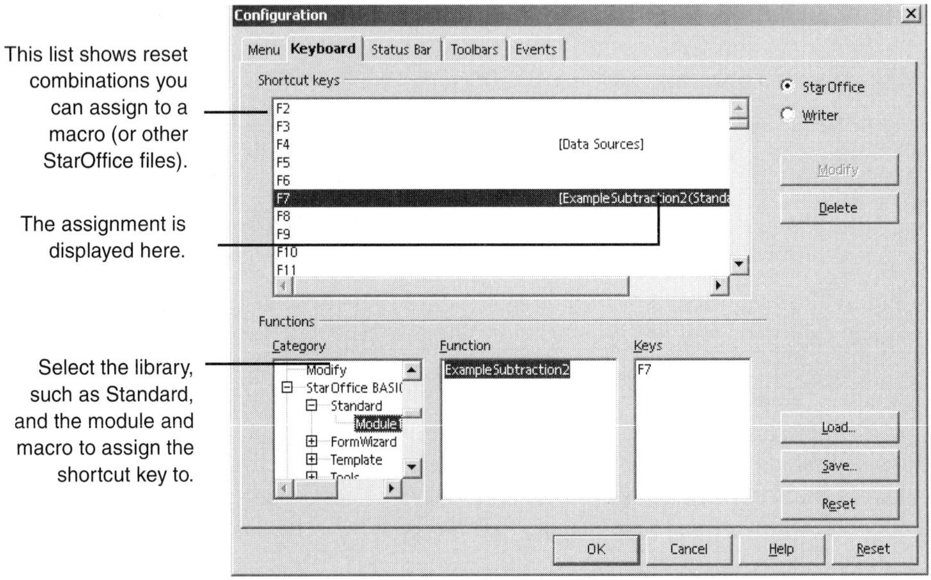

This list shows reset combinations you can assign to a macro (or other StarOffice files).

The assignment is displayed here.

Select the library, such as Standard, and the module and macro to assign the shortcut key to.

Figure 36-54   Setting up a shortcut key to run a macro

9   Select Modify to associate the shortcut key with the macro.

10   Click OK.

Running a Macro From Start to Finish

You can run a macro in the IDE or in the application where the macro will run, if the necessary conditions to start the macro are available. For instance, if the first step to run the macro is making a selection from the File menu, you can run the macro from anywhere. If the first step is in a Writer document, it must be open and be the active document.

You can quickly run a macro using any of the following methods.

Running the First Macro in a Module

This works only if a macro is open in the IDE window (the icon will be dimmed if no macros are open). It will run only the first macro in the current module; only one module and library can be open at a time.

1   Open a macro in the IDE window.

2   Click the Run icon in the macro toolbar.

Running a Selected Macro

1   Click the Macros icon on the macro toolbar.

2   In the Macro window, select the library, module, and macro to run, and click Run.

Running a Macro One Step at a Time

Unfortunately, there is no debugging program for macros. However, you can run the script one step at a time to see what happens at each step.

1   Be sure the macro is the first one in the module, if there is more than one.

Cut and paste it to move it to the top, or create a new module (right-click the current module tab and choose Insert > BASIC Module) and paste the macro into the new module.

2   In the IDE or in the application where the macro will run, click the Single Step icon on the macro toolbar.

3   The macro will run one step at a time; click the icon again to go to each new line. Click the Step Back icon to repeat the previous step.

If an error occurs, the IDE will be displayed with an error message and an arrow pointing to the line.

4   Click the Stop icon to stop before the macro has run completely.

Using Breakpoints to Stop Macros at a Specified Point

You can add a breakpoint that stops the macro on the line you select. You can then run the macro manually step by step using the Single Step icons (see *Running a Macro One Step at a Time*).

Note – When you insert the breakpoint, the program checks the entire macro for errors; you can't insert one if there are any problems anywhere in the code. You might need to comment out problem lines before you can add the breakpoint.

---

1   Open the macro in the IDE.

2   Position the cursor on the line where you want to switch from automatic to manual.

3   Click the Breakpoint icon in the macro toolbar.

4   A red circle will appear to the left of the line.

```
Selection.Insert( "Miracle Max" )
```

To remove the breakpoint, just click the Breakpoint icon again.

Opening and Editing Macros

You'll probably need to tweak at least half the macros you have or use, to fix them or to make them do something extra. In addition, if others are going to use and perhaps troubleshoot your macros, it's a good idea to add comments describing what some of the lines do.

Note – You'll be relentlessly prompted for a password if you try to edit the existing macros. You just can't. Which is probably just as well. You can add them, unedited, to documents using the procedures covered in *Adding a Macro to a Document* on page 979.

Adding Comments

To add descriptions about what lines do in the macro, just press Enter to add a new line, and begin the line with a single quote or the letters REM in all uppercase.

```
'This line starts an animated GIF showing two
'right-handed men fencing.
Documents.Open( "file:///home/magentaf/gifs/inigo.gif")
```

Comments are shown in light gray text.

Troubleshooting Tips

When an error occurs when you're running a macro, an error message will appear and Basic will point to the line containing the error.

Pinpointing problems If you're having problems, always use the Single Step feature to run the macro one step at a time (see *Running a Macro One Step at a Time* on page 977). If the error occurs late in the macro, add a breakpoint.

Comment out lines that are creating problems. If it's optional, add a single quote mark in front of it to "comment it out". The text will turn gray and the macro will run without that line. You can use this technique to pin down the source of errors.

Macros that create new files For macros that create new files, you might need to edit some of the macros. The following lines are generated when you create a new Writer file, for example:

```
Documents.Open( "file:///home/magentaf/Office/config/new/_05_text.url", "", "",
    "", 0, "file:///home/magentaf/Office/config/new/" )
    [Untitled1:1].Activate()
```

If you already had an untitled document open, though, the line will be recorded as **Untitled1**:1 instead and you'll get an error when you run the file. The program likes all the untitled files it opens to be titled **Untitled1**. Change this line if you encounter errors.

You can't edit the file name so that it's named "Annual Report" or whatever you're going to save the document as; the program will complain and give you an error.

Note – Web has a feature that lets you create hyperlinks that open new files. You might want to use it instead, if appropriate for your project. See *Linking to a New Empty File* on page 480.

Adding a Macro to a Document

Perhaps the most useful thing you can do with macros is add them to other documents, such as Web pages or presentations. Web is full of features that let you set up hyperlinks to macros, Basic scripts, and JavaScript. Even simple macros such as opening a new file and typing a few lines of text, or deleting lines or objects in the current or another document, or can be effective and useful within documents such as presentations and Web pages.

Table 36-2 summarizes the ways you can add macros to documents, and where to find that information.

Table 36-2   Adding macros to each type of document

Feature	Where to go to find the information
Interaction	*Interaction Effects: Run Macros and More* on page 720
Form functions	Chapter 36, *Creating and Using Forms, Controls, and Events*, on page 925
Hyperlinks	*Using Macros, Scripts, and Events* on page 491
Shortcut keys	*Assigning a Shortcut Key to a Macro* on page 975

Note – Most of the macro-insertion features let you insert a macro from the Standard and other libraries, and from the document you're currently in, but not from any other documents you've created. If you're having trouble finding the macro you want, it's probably in a separate document. You'll need to cut and paste it into a module in the Standard library, a new library, or create a module for it in your current document.

Index

Symbols

30, 156
! 564
###
   in spreadsheet cells 533
   turned into underline 133
$ (absolute cell reference marker) 572
) 565
) in formulas 565
= ^ * / + - =
   564

Numerics

0 values, hiding 545
1/2 to .5, changing 534
1/2, 1/4, 3/4 128
1st, 2nd, 3rd, 4th 127
3D
   3D effects window 810
   attributes, applying
     changes 811
   changing angles and
     rotating 808
   charts, rotating 600
   conversion options 824
   conversion using Effects
     tearoff menu 826
   conversion, example 828
   converting polygons to 825
   converting text to 821
   cool effects 809
   display 121
   display options 121
   formatting 3D objects 810

   geometry, modifying 811
   objects, creating 808
   objects, merging 809
   rotation object, converting
     curves to 825
3D Controller icon
   can't find 714, 718
45-degree lines, drawing 768

A

absolute
   cell references 572
   cell references, applying 513
   paths 475
   URLs 141
accents
   inserting 188
**Accept or Reject Changes
window**
   Calc 623
   Writer 425
accepting
   document changes (Calc) 623
   document changes
     (Writer) 425
Access
   ADO data source 896
   database connection
     overview 852
   syntax with ADO 897
Acrobat
   See also PDF
   UNIX PDF setup 72
Action at mouse click field
   interaction 721
Action performed event

   defined 952
Action started event
   defined 952
**Active Server Pages WebCast
options** 743
ActiveX Data Objects 876
Adabas
   creating database and data
     source 899
   creating database and
     passwords 900
   documentation 57
   in 6.0 12, 56
   installing 36
   limitations 36, 899
   not in OpenOffice.org 10
   overview 877
ADD (Writer task bar) 185
adding
   (+) in formulas 564
   AutoText categories 182, 866
   cells automatically 568
   cells quickly 567
   dictionaries for spell
     check 192
   floating frames (Calc) 602
   floating frames (Writer) 234
   notes to documents (Calc) 624
   notes to documents
     (Writer) 428
   sheets to a spreadsheet 525
   text boxes (Writer) 233
**Additional Settings for UNIX
Printers option** 66
address books
   creating data source from,
     overview 878
   creating data sources 902
   migrating 50

E

informIT

YOUR GUIDE TO IT REFERENCE

Articles

Keep your edge with thousands of free articles, in-depth features, interviews, and IT reference recommendations – all written by experts you know and trust.

Online Books

Answers in an instant from **InformIT Online Book's** 600+ fully searchable on line books. Sign up now and get your first 14 days **free**.

POWERED BY

Catalog

Review online sample chapters, author biographies and customer rankings and choose exactly the right book from a selection of over 5,000 titles.